the BERKELEY

CRITICAL ACCLAIM FOR THE BERKELEY GUIDES

"Planet-wise instruction for [the] cash conscious . . . for the price, the time of your life." —*Details*

"[The Berkeley Guides are] brimming with useful information for the low-budget traveler—material delivered in a fresh, funny, and often irreverent way." —*The Philadelphia Inquirer*

"The [Berkeley Guides] are deservedly popular because of their extensive coverage, entertaining style of writing, and heavy emphasis on budget travel . . . If you are looking for tips on hostels, vegetarian food, and hitchhiking, there are no books finer." —*San Diego Union-Tribune*

"[The Berkeley Guides] offer straight dirt on everything from hostels to look for and beaches to avoid to museums least likely to attract your parents . . . they're fresher than Harvard's Let's Go series." —*Seventeen*

"The [Berkeley Guides] give a rare glimpse into the real cultures of Europe, Canada, Mexico, and the United States . . . with in-depth historical backgrounds on each place and a creative, often poetical style of prose." —*Eugene Weekly*

"The new On the Loose guides are more comprehensive, informative and witty than Let's Go." —*Glamour*

"The Berkeley Guides have more and better maps, and on average, the nuts and bolts descriptions of such things as hotels and restaurants tend to be more illuminating than the often terse and sometimes vague entries in the 'Let's Go' guides." —*San José Mercury News*

"The well-organized guides list can't miss sights, offbeat attractions and cheap thrills, such as festivals and walks. And they're fun to read." —*New York Newsday*

"Reading (these guides) is a lot like listening to a first-hand report from a friend...They're also just plain fun to read." —*Greensboro News & Record*

"Written for the young and young at heart...you'll find this thick, fact-filled guide makes entertaining reading." —*St. Louis Dispatch*

"...bright articulate guidebooks. The irreverent yet straightforward prose is easy to read and offers a sense of the adventures awaiting travelers off the beaten path." —*Portland Oregonian*

♻ THE BERKELEY GUIDES are printed using soy-based ink on 100% recycled paper, including 50% post-consumer fiber and 100% de-inked newspapers, magazines and catalogs. What's the use of traveling if there's nothing left to see?

THE BERKELEY GUIDES
California 1996
Central America (2nd Edition)
Eastern Europe (3rd Edition)
Europe 1996
France 1996
Germany & Austria 1996
Great Britain & Ireland 1996
Italy 1996
London 1996
Mexico 1996
Pacific Northwest & Alaska
  (2nd Edition)
Paris 1996
San Francisco 1996

the BERKELEY guides

mexico '96

On the Loose
On the Cheap
Off the Beaten
Path

WRITTEN BY BERKELEY STUDENTS IN COOPERATION WITH
THE ASSOCIATED STUDENTS OF THE UNIVERSITY OF CALIFORNIA

COPYRIGHT © 1995 BY FODOR'S TRAVEL PUBLICATIONS, INC.

The Berkeley Guides is a registered trademark of Fodor's Travel Publications, Inc.

All rights reserved under International and Pan-American Copyright Conventions. Published in the United States by Fodor's Travel Publications, Inc., a subsidiary of Random House, Inc., New York, and simultaneously in Canada by Random House of Canada Limited, Toronto. Distributed by Random House, Inc., New York.

No maps, illustrations, or other portions of this book may be reproduced in any form without written permission from the publisher.

ISBN 0-679-02987-7

THE BERKELEY GUIDE TO MEXICO

Editors: Beth Cardier, David Henschel
Managing Editors: Nicole Harb, Kristina Malsberger, Sharron S. Wood
Executive Editor: Scott McNeely
Creative Director: Fabrizio LaRocca
Cartographer: David Lindroth; Eureka Cartography
Text Design: Tigist Getachew
Cover Design: Fabrizio La Rocca
Cover Art: Poul Lange (3-Dart), © Robert Frerck/Tony Stone (photo in frame), Paul D'Innocenzo (still life)

SPECIAL SALES

The Berkeley Guides and all Fodor's Travel Publications are available at special discounts for bulk purchases for sales promotions or premiums. Special editions, including personalized covers, excerpts of existing guides, and corporate imprints, can be created in large quantities for special needs. For more information, contact your local bookseller or write to Special Markets, Fodor's Travel Publications, 201 E. 50th Street, New York, NY 10022. Inquiries from Canada should be directed to your local Canadian bookseller or sent to Random House of Canada, Ltd., Marketing Department, 1265 Aerowood Drive, Mississauga, Ontario L4W 1B9. Inquiries from the United Kingdom should be sent to Fodor's Travel Publications, 20 Vauxhall Bridge Road, London, England SW1V 2SA.

MANUFACTURED IN THE UNITED STATES OF AMERICA

10 9 8 7 6 5 4 3 2 1

Contents

WHAT THE BERKELEY GUIDES ARE ALL ABOUT viii
THANKS TO YOU ix
BERKELEY BIOS x
MAP OF MEXICO xii–xiii
INTRODUCTION xv

1 BASICS 1
Planning Your Trip 1
When to Go 1
Government Tourist Offices 3
Budget Travel Organizations 4
Student ID Cards 4
Passports, Visas, and Tourist Cards 5
Getting the Best Airfares 7
Money 9
Getting Money From Home 11
What to Pack 12
Staying Healthy 14
Resources for Women 19
Resources for People of Color 20
Resources for Gays and Lesbians 20
Resources for the Disabled 20
Working in Mexico 21
Studying in Mexico 22
Volunteer Programs 22
Coming and Going 22
Customs and Duties 22
By Air 24
By Car 25
By Bus 26
Staying in Mexico 26
Getting Around 26
Phones 28
Mail 29
Business Hours 29
Where to Sleep 29
Food 30
Language 30
Crime and Punishment 31
Further Reading 31

2 MEXICO CITY AND ENVIRONS 33
Basics 34
Map of Mexico City 36–37
Map of Mexico City Metro 44
Map of Mexico City Bus Routes 46–47
Where to Sleep 48
Map of Mexico City Lodging 50–51
Food 55
Worth Seeing 59
Map of the Zócalo and Alameda Central 60
Map of Chapultepec and Zona Rosa 66
Map of San Ángel and Coyoacán 69
Shopping 73
After Dark 75
Outdoor Activities 79
Near Mexico City 80
Map of Teotihuacán 81

3 BAJA CALIFORNIA 85
Map of Baja California Norte 86
Baja California Norte 87
Tijuana 87
Map of Tijuana 89
Mexicali 95
Ensenada 97
Map of Ensenada 98
San Felipe 102
San Quintín 104
Baja California Sur 105
Guerrero Negro 105
Map of Baja California Sur 106
San Ignacio 108
Santa Rosalía 110
Mulegé 111
Loreto 113
La Paz 116
Map of La Paz 117
Los Cabos 120
Map of Los Cabos 121
Map of San José del Cabo 122
Map of Cabo San Lucas 124

v

4 SONORA AND LOS MOCHIS 127
Map of Sonora 128
Nogales 129
Hermosillo 132
Guaymas 136
Los Mochis 140

5 NORTH CENTRAL MEXICO AND THE COPPER CANYON 145
Ciudad Juárez 146
Map of Chihuahua and Durango 147
Nuevo Casas Grandes and Paquimé 150
Chihuahua 152
Map of Chihuahua city 153
Creel and The Copper Canyon 156
Map of The Copper Canyon 157
Durango 163

6 NORTHEASTERN MEXICO 167
Matamoros 167
Map of Northeastern Mexico 168
Reynosa 171
Nuevo Laredo 174
Monterrey 177
Map of Monterrey 179
Saltillo 183
Tampico 186

7 EL BAJIO 189
San Luis Potosí 190
Map of El Bajío 191
Querétaro 197
Map of Querétaro 199
San Miguel de Allende 206
Map of San Miguel de Allende 207
Guanajuato 212
Map of Guanajuato 214

8 THE HEARTLAND 221
Zacatecas 221
Aguascalientes 227
Guadalajara 230
Map of Guadalajara 231
Map of Tlaquepaque 241
Uruapan 246
Pátzcuaro 251
Map of Pátzcuaro 252
Morelia 257
Map of Morelia 258

9 THE PACIFIC COAST 265
Map of The Pacific Coast 266
Mazatlán 267
Map of Mazatlán 268
San Blas 274
Tepic 278
Puerto Vallarta 281
Map of Puerto Vallarta 282
Bahía de Navidad 288
Manzanillo 292
Map of Manzanillo 293
Colima 298
Ixtapa/Zihuatanejo 303
Map of Zihuatanejo 304
Acapulco 308
Map of Acapulco 310–311

10 CENTRAL CITIES 319
Cuernavaca 319
Map of Central Cities 320
Map of Cuernavaca 322
Tlaxcala 332
Map of Tlaxcala 333
Puebla 340
Taxco 353
Map of Taxco 354
Chilpancingo 358

11 VERACRUZ 361
Map of East Central Mexico 362
Veracruz 362
Map of Veracruz city 363
Los Tuxtlas 369
Jalapa 374
Papantla de Olarte 378
Tuxpán 382

12 OAXACA 385
Map of Oaxaca 386
Oaxaca de Juárez 386
Map of Oaxaca de Juárez 388
Map of Monte Albán 395
Oaxaca Coast 398
The Isthmus of Tehuantepec 408

13 CHIAPAS AND TABASCO 411
Tuxtla Gutiérrez 412
Map of Chiapas and Tabasco 413
San Cristóbal de las Casas 420
Map of San Cristóbal de las Casas 421
Ocosingo and Toniná Ruins 429
Palenque 431
Map of Palenque Ruins 436
Comitán and Lagos de Montebello 439
Tapachula 444
Villahermosa 448

14 THE YUCATÁN PENINSULA 457
Map of the Yucatán Peninsula 458–459
Campeche 460
The Puuc Region 467
Map of Uxmal 470
Mérida 474
Map of Mérida 475
Chichén Itzá 487
Map of Chichén Itzá 488
Valladolid 492
Cancún 495
Map of Cancún 496
Isla Mujeres 501
Map of Isla Mujeres 502
Playa del Carmen 507
Cozumel 511
Map of Cozumel 512
Tulum 518
Map of Tulum 519
Map of Cobá 524
Chetumal 524

SPANISH GLOSSARY 529

INDEX 534

What the Berkeley Guides Are All About

Four years ago, a motley bunch of U.C. Berkeley students launched a new series of guidebooks—*The Berkeley Guides.* Since then, we've been busy writing and editing 13 books to destinations across the globe, from California, Mexico, and Central America to Europe and Eastern Europe. Along the way our writers have weathered bus plunges, rabies, and guerrilla attacks, landed bush planes above the Arctic Circle, gotten lost in the woods (proverbially and literally), and broken bread with all sorts of peculiar characters—from Mafia dons and Hell's Angel bikers to indigenous families deep in the Chiapan jungle.

Coordinating the efforts of 65 U.C. Berkeley writers back at the office is an equally daunting task (have you ever tried to track manuscript from Morocco?). But that's the whole point of *The Berkeley Guides*: to bring you the most up-to-date info on prices, the latest budget-travel trends, the newest restaurants and hostels, where to catch your next train—all written and edited by people who know what cheap travel is all about.

You see, it's one of life's weird truisms that the more cheaply you travel, the more you inevitably experience. If you're looking for five-star meals, air-conditioned tour buses, and reviews of the same old tourist traps, you're holding the wrong guidebook. Instead, *The Berkeley Guides* give you an in-depth look at local culture, detailed coverage of small towns and off-beat sights, bars, and cafés where tourists rarely tread, plus no-nonsense practical info that deals with the real problems of real people (where to get aspirin at 3 AM, where to launder those dirty socks).

Coming from a community as diverse as Berkeley, we also wanted our guides to be useful to everyone, so we tell you if a place is wheelchair accessible, if it provides resources for gay and lesbian travelers, and if it's safe for women traveling solo. Many of us are Californians, which means most of us like trees and mountain trails. It also means we emphasize the outdoors in every *Berkeley Guide* and include lots of info about hiking and tips on protecting the environment. To minimize our impact on the environment, we print our books on recycled paper using soy-based inks.

Most important, these guides are for travelers who want to see more than just the main sights. We find out what local people do for fun, where they go to eat, drink, or just hang out. Most guidebooks lead you down the tourist trail, ignoring important local issues, events, and culture. In *The Berkeley Guides* we give you the information you need to understand what's going on around you, whether it's the latest on the devaluation of the peso or the uprisings in Chiapas.

We've done our best to make sure the information in *The Berkeley Guides* is accurate, but time doesn't stand still: Prices change, places go out of business, currencies get devalued. Call ahead when it's really important, and try not to get too stressed out.

Thanks to You

Putting together a guidebook to Mexico is always an adventure. Our writers pressed on despite crashed buses, sprained ankles, various gastrointestinal disorders, and the innumerable distractions that stood in the way of getting their manuscript back to Berkeley on time. Throughout Mexico our writers relied on helpful souls for their advice and encouragement, and we'd like to thank the following people—as well as the hundreds of others who our writers met in passing on the road. Drop a line—a postcard, a scrawled note on toilet paper, whatever—and we'll try our best to acknowledge your contribution. Our address is 515 Eshleman Hall, University of California, Berkeley, CA 94720.

Ann (Querétaro); Arturo (San Luis Potosí); Juan Bananas (San Blas); The Bretón family (Puebla); Carlos (Acapulco); Centro INAH's Library (Oaxaca); Julio César (Campeche); Chip (Oakland, CA); Tanya Cornish (Creel); Carlos E. Cortés (Uruapan); Euridice Prado Cota (Morelia); Miguel Ángel Delgado (Mérida); Mike Ericquista (Puerto Peñasco); Moisés Escalante (Isla Holbox); Noel González (Creel); "Gypsy Joe" Graham (Santa Rosalía); Jim Hoffmann (California); Julián "el puto tripper de los cojones" Izko (Pamplona, España); Juan (Chilpancingo); Rose, Luis, Adrián, and Daniel Kornhauser (Mexico City); Lenny and Arnold (Jalapa); Susana Mahieux (Guadalajara); Máximo (Mexicaltitlán); Alfredo Ricárdez Miguel (Tehuantepec); Jimena Olvenes Montiel (Mexico City); Lorena Muro (Ensenada); Oscar and Leticia (Reynosa); Pepe and Julia (Mexico City); Gonzalo Pérez Pérez (Tlaxcala); Licenciada María Trinidad Pulido (Comitán); Guillermo Ramírez (Ensenada); Mauricio y Catarina Ranc (Guadalajara); Gregorio (Mulegé); Roberto (Melaque); Salvador (Río Verde); Stuart "el otro puto tripper de los cojones" Seaborn (Pleasanton, CA); Amy Wasserman (La Jolla, CA); and Sergio Zarala (Cancún).

The editors are especially grateful to the following people, who provided advice, information, and moral support: Daniel Billet (Los Angeles, CA), Jorge Gamboa (Mexican Government Tourism Office, Los Angeles, CA), Diane and Lauren Henschel (Manhattan Beach, CA), Martín Rosa Rodríguez (Valle de Bravo), and Jaideep Singh (Berkeley, CA).

We are also indebted to the namy readers who wrote in with feedback and new information: Timothy Abbadusky (St. Louis, MO), Louis W. Adams Jr. (Ft. Lauderdale, FL), Ahab Afifi (San Fernando, CA), Hilde Bettum, Danielle Carroll, Kellie McAlister, and Alice Price-Williams (Glasgow University, Scotland), Corina Corder (Cincinatti, OH), Kevin Day (Coatzacoalcos), Deb Ellis (Minneapolis, MN), Jorge A. Gallardo (Oaxaca), Tianna Langham (Redlands, CA), John McCafferty (Santa Barbara, CA), Teri Mendelsohn (Cambridge, MA), Eric G. Nilsson (Chicago, IL), Tom Noble (Manassas, VA), Steve Reidsma (Anchorage, AL), Wanda Reindorf (Guanajuato), Bruce Thomason (Shepherdsville, KT), Jennifer Walker (San Cristóbal), Marc Wallis (Seattle, WA), Dave West (Silver Spring, MD), Viola Woodward (Enosburg Falls, VT), Jaime Verdugo-Erivez (El Paso, TX), Jolee Zola (Revere, MA), and the "two gringas" who kept us abreast of their wild adventures with a postcard trail.

Berkeley Bios

Behind every restaurant blurb, lodging review, and introduction in this book lurks a student writer. You might recognize the type—perpetually short on time, money, and clean underwear. Six Berkeley students spent the summer traveling around Mexico researching and writing this book. Back in Berkeley two envious editors enjoyed Mexico vicariously at their all-too-stationary computers.

The Writers

After searching various pharmacies in Puerto Vallarta for the perfect no-itch cream to smooth on her 43 mosquito bites, **Anna Gorman** concluded that the water-loving insects *liked* the smell of repellent. Anna returned to the beach anyway, where she twisted her ankle dodging time-share salesmen. When Anna wasn't scrambling around the coastal resorts checking out cheesy bars and run-down hotels, she was able to swim with turtles in a natural spring, sip coconut juice in a small beach hut, and shop in a Huichol arts-and-crafts center. Anna left the beaches, lagoons, and jungles of the Pacific Coast to work on her master's degree in journalism at Columbia University.

During her travels, **Lourdes Haro** was hungry, showerless for days, toilet-paperless, stranded in various Latin American towns, and otherwise down-and-out, but somehow something kept her going. It must have been her intimate fascination with her long-lost country's myth-ridden culture, or maybe even the second-class bus rides to nowhere towns that left her with the sensation that she couldn't be more alive. However, she wasn't too happy after the time her bus crashed attempting to pass on a blind curve, leaving the vehicle teetering on a Chiapan cliffside while its passengers scrambled to jump out of the rear windows. For the time being, Lourdes is back in the Bay Area, contemplating law school or graduate studies.

After three weeks of storming through Mexico City, **Viviana Mahieux** decided to cruise through the rest of her itinerary by telepathy. A few unfortunate mishaps later, she realized that the dense layer of smog coating the capital was clairvoyant-resisting and sabotaged all of her attempts to communicate with the outside world. So she spared her editor a potential heart attack and resumed her trip through the Central Cities and the Heartland. Viviana plans to finish her B.A. in History and Comparative Literature in December 1995, at which time she will spend a few months figuring out how to figure out what to do with herself.

It was not until **Shayna Samuels** pretended to be a married nun in search of a cure for her rare venereal disease that the persistent men of Chihuahua, Sonora, and Baja California finally thought it best to leave her free of unwanted company. With the heavy Spanish accent she picked up during her year in Sevilla and the cowboy hat she picked up in El Fuerte, Shayna biked and hiked her way into the Copper Canyon and snorkeled in the exotic Sea of Cortez. She plans to use her undergraduate degrees in Comparative Literature and Conservation and Resource Studies to look for jobs that pay her to roam the planet.

After getting attacked by a variety of four- and six-legged creatures on her way down to the Yucatán Peninsula, **Lean Sweeney** later ran into worse problems with the two-legged inhabitants of Cancún; they became less of a problem after she started bedding down in the most slime-ridden flea-bag hotels in town. After an extended trek through Tabasco and Mexico City following her itinerary, Lean plans on buying some new underwear and settling down somewhere near Isla Holbox, where she'll earn a living counting flamingo eggs (after she figures out the bus schedule).

Lynette Ubois eagerly accepted the opportunity to escape her doctoral dissertation (entitled "Whoops, There It Is! Onomatopoeia in *Moby Dick*") by covering the Veracruz and El Bajío chapters for the Berkeley Guides. During the rest of her summer, she plans to parlay her childhood acting experience on *The Bionic Woman* into a juicy part on the popular telenovela *La Dueña*.

The Editors

Aussie **Beth Cardier** enthusiastically put aside her usual pastimes (short fiction writing and sleep) to organize 150,000 words for the Guides. In 1996 she plans to finally do some laundry and will spend her spare moments wishing that the Australian and American continents would drift closer together.

David Henschel, after spending his junior year abroad in Madrid, Spain, turned his attention south of the border while finishing up his B.A. in Political Science with a minor in Spanish Language and Literatures. Evidently, spending seven months sleeping, breathing, and living Mexico had some impact on him, for at press time he was preparing to kiss his Castillian accent good-bye and spend the year working at the Mexican Consulate before going to graduate school.

México

United States

OKLAHOMA
ARKANSAS
TENN.
TEXAS
MISS.
ALA.
LOUISIANA

Rio Grande

Gulf of México

★ Guadalupe
○ Monterrey
NUEVO LEON

TAMAULIPAS

★ Ciudad Victoria

San Luis Potosí
SAN LUIS POTOSI

○ Tampico

San Miguel de Allende
QUERÉTARO   VERACRUZ
HIDALGO
México City ★ Pachuca
D.F.
TLAXCALA   ○ Veracruz
★ Tlaxcala   ★ Jalapa
Puebla
Cuernavaca
MORELOS   PUEBLA

SIERRA MADRE DEL SUR

★ Mérida
YUCATAN
Cancún

Campeche ★
QUINTANA ROO
Cozumel

TABASCO   CAMPECHE
○ Villahermosa
★ Chetumal

★ Oaxaca
OAXACA
San Cristóbal de las Casas
★ Tuxtla Gutiérrez
CHIAPAS

BELIZE

Caribbean Sea

GUATEMALA
HONDURAS

xiii

Escape to ancient cities and

journey to  *exotic islands with*

CNN Travel Guide, a wealth of valuable advice.

Host Valerie Voss will take you

to all of your favorite destinations,

 *including those off the beaten path.*

'Tune-in to your passport to the world.

CNN TRAVEL GUIDE
SATURDAY 12:30 PM ET   SUNDAY 4:30 PM ET

Introduction
By Lynette Ubois

Tourism is a major industry in Mexico, and when the package-tour crowd descends, they generally get the Mexico they've paid to see: long stretches of tropical beach, magnificent ruins, and well-kept colonial towns. These pre-arranged visions of Mexico aren't false, but they hardly encompass the incredible range of experiences this diverse country has to offer. Step beyond these simple dreams of Mexico, and you'll encounter a much more complex and intriguing picture. Whether you find yourself camping on a deserted beach in Baja, sampling fried grasshoppers in Oaxaca's thriving markets, or just hanging out with university students at a local *peña* (musical gathering), a trip to Mexico can open up your senses—and your worldview—in ways you've never imagined.

Few countries in the world can rival Mexico's variety, and new visitors will be confronted by widely contrasting landscapes, lifestyles, and beliefs. The spectacular diversity of the land itself is one of the principle pleasures of traveling here. From the high desert plains of the north to the dense rain forests in the south, Mexico's environment and climate are marked by vivid extremes. The brief, wild, summer thunderstorms over the desert, the steady, insect-humming heat of the jungles, the sharp, cool air of mountain towns, and the soft breezes over ocean waters all invite you to savor the natural world. These striking variations in the physical environment mirror economic, social, and cultural contrasts: Corrugated tin shacks line the roads to luxury resorts, indigenous people proudly wearing traditional costumes faithfully attend Catholic Mass, and subsistence farmers plow their fields with yoked oxen while the children of the rich sit inside their luxurious homes and watch MTV. Such contrasts form the unusual textures of daily Mexican life.

Mexico is the largest Spanish-speaking country in the world, and after Brazil, it is the most populous country in Latin America. Despite deep ties to rural, agricultural life, most of the population—about 75%—is now concentrated in urban areas. With a population of 15 million, Mexico City still ranks as the largest city in the country (and 2nd largest in the world), but increasing industrialization along the United States–Mexico border draws huge numbers of Mexican immigrants to the country's border towns each year. As industry grows in the north, it brings the kind of big-city problems endemic to the capital, such as heavy pollution and stark inequities between the haves and the have-nots. *Maquiladoras,* foreign-owned factories set up to take advantage of cheap and available Mexican labor, hold out the promise of steady employment, but most workers are faced with appalling health conditions and little or no job security. Virtually non-existent environmental restrictions on these factories mean that this present day "industrial revolution" has an increasingly detrimental effect on the land as well as the people.

This Dickensian nightmare may seem worlds away from the relaxed beaches or the vibrant indigenous market towns that most travelers experience, but the force uniting every aspect of Mexican life is the country's vulnerable economy. In December 1994, the Mexican government devalued the peso by 50%, sending an already faltering economy into a tailspin. In the perverse logic of the world market, the peso's devaluation makes Mexico even more available to the traveler (foreign currencies are much stronger against the peso) while it makes the Mexicans' own lives that much harder by decreasing the spending power of their now severely undervalued salaries. People on the street will tell you that the devaluation has caused the worst economic depression that they've seen in years, and this crisis comes on the heels of a series of political upheavals.

On January 1, 1994, the North American Free Trade Agreement (NAFTA) went into effect and sparked a surprisingly well-organized uprising in the rural southern state of Chiapas. Calling themselves the Zapatista National Liberation Army (EZLN), these dissenters took up arms, demanding recognition for indigenous rights to land, social services, and open access to democratic government. Nearly 150 people were killed in brief skirmishes before a truce was signed and the Mexican government agreed to serious political talks with the rebels. Three months later, the front runner in the presidential campaign, Luis Donaldo Colosio, was assassinated in Tijuana—as it turned out, by members of his own party, the ruling Partido Revolucionario Institucional (PRI). In August 1994, the PRI's Ernesto Zedillo was elected president in what were considered to be the cleanest national elections yet—though how fair they really were is up for considerable debate. Zedillo's presidency has been marred by economic instability and continued social unrest; the fact that the leading right-wing opposition—Partido Accion Nacional (PAN)—won a significant gubernatorial race in the state of Jalisco early in 1995 has stirred some anticipation of wider-reaching political change.

Mexico's complicated and contentious political landscape is nothing new, and the disparities of today's society have deep historical roots. Even a brief look at Mexico's past reveals a history of complex interdependencies, competing interests, and repeated patterns of loss and survival. Pre-Colombian cultures evolved through a successive series of civilizations, which sometimes coexisted as watchful neighbors, but more often faced each other in war. The process of empire building in Mesoamerica was certainly as bloody as any modern imperialist project, but conquering civilizations did not destroy all traces of their enemies. Instead, a kind of absorption process occurred, so that traditions such as the "Long Count," a calendar that reaches back to August 13, 3114 BC, survived until the arrival of Cortés. The Olmec, probable creators of this calendar, are considered the "mother culture" of Mesoamerica; their practice of human sacrifice was common to most major Mesoamerican civilizations, as was their obsession with the ritual ball game, whose courts are found at the ruined cities of many later civilizations. Centuries after the fall of the Olmecs, several sophisticated cultures emerged concurrently, including the Maya, whose commanding cities spread from northern Chiapas all the way to Honduras; the Zapotec, whose most important center lies in Oaxaca, at Monte Albán; and the builders of Teotihuacán, the great urban center just outside present-day Mexico City. Of these powerful civilizations, the Maya were perhaps the most advanced, developing sophisticated calendars and astronomical charts, as well as a complex writing system that included over 300 glyphs. Sometime in the 10th century, most Mayan cities were abandoned, for reasons still unclear to archaeologists—some say environmental depredation, others point to internal social conflicts, and still others claim war was the cause.

The final dominating culture of pre-Colombian Mexico was, of course, the Aztec, who arrived in the valley of Mexico in the middle of the 12th century and busily went to work building their own city and conquering others. By the time Hernán Cortés and his crew showed up in 1519, the Aztec empire was roughly equivalent in size to modern-day France. The Aztec rulers hadn't made many friends during their rise to power, and Cortés, who was nothing if not politically savvy, built alliances with disgruntled cultures like the Gulf Coast Totonac, who hoped to throw off the yoke of Aztec domination (which included, among other things, mandatory tribute of humans prepared for sacrifice). But the changes that occurred with the fall of the Aztec empire proved that the new order would be far more destructive than anyone could have imagined. Thousands of Mayan books were destroyed, and Aztec temples were pulled down and rebuilt as Catholic churches and Spanish military fortifications. Long-standing social structures were eradicated, as priests and farmers alike became low-class citizens and slaves. Within 20 years the indigenous population, wiped out by battle and new, European diseases, dropped from around 22 million to just 1.5 million.

Although the indigenous people did not bear their fate without resistance, uprisings were scattered, infrequent, and mostly ineffective. Not until significant numbers of disaffected members of a middle class emerged did any widespread, coordinated effort to throw off Spanish rule begin. The fight for Mexican independence not only meant battle with Spain, but it also required wars with other greedy foreign powers intent on gaining some of Mexico's vast wealth. The amount of upheaval these struggles caused can be gauged by Mexico's celebration of *two* independence days: September 16, the day Father Miguel Hidalgo proclaimed independence from Spain in 1810, and May 5, the day invading French forces were defeated at Puebla in 1862. Although Mexico won its war against Spain in 1821, its new national status was threatened by foreign invasions for another 40 years. During these years, Mexico suffered the tremendous loss of half its territory to the land-hungry United States—California, Arizona, New Mexico, and Texas were all turned over to the States in 1848. France had its eye on Mexico as well; its troops arrived in 1861, clearing the way for a new emperor, Maximilian, Archduke of Austria. Even after France's defeat in 1862, French troops did not completely withdraw from the country until 1867, the year Maximilian was executed by firing squad in Querétaro.

By the turn of the 20th century, many of the problems that exist today were established: a few *hacendados* (landowners) and foreign investors owned all of Mexico's wealth; indigenous people had been dispossessed of their land and relocated; and a vast, complicated network of patronage had taken hold of all government processes. At the same time, under the 34-year reign of dictator Porfirio Díaz, Mexico also moved towards modernization: Rail and telegraph lines were greatly expanded and certain public work projects went up, such as the elegant wrought-iron bandstands that still grace the central plazas of many large cities. But these gains were far outweighed by their costs, which included rigged elections, a stifled press, and a deeply impoverished majority. In 1910, these problems spurred the 10-year Mexican Revolution, a series of civil wars fought by competing parties with very different social and political interests. The revolutionary leader Emiliano Zapata, a *campesino* (peasant) from Morelos, emerged as the strongest voice for indigenous rights—his 1911 Plan of Ayala called for immediate restoration of land to the dispossessed. Though he won several significant battles, Zapata was finally outdone by stronger, more moneyed forces in 1919. He agreed to meet his opposition peacefully at a large hacienda near Cuatla, but federal agents assassinated him as he rode through the gate.

Mexico's long and varied past clearly demands the vivid and dramatic scope that its most famous 20th-century art form, the mural, lends it. In the great works of artists such as Diego Rivera, historical figures like Zapata, Hidalgo, and Moctezuma take on heroic form. But in today's politics, heroes are few and public admiration is scarce. For the last six and a half decades, the monolithic PRI party has had a stranglehold on political power, and the party now carries the burden of Mexico's social, political, and economic woes. The PRI's recent efforts to privatize basic services—telephones, water, electricity—leave much of the populous nervous and skeptical about the real beneficiaries of economic reform. The flight of ex-president Carlos Salinas, accompanied by rumors of enormous bank accounts abroad, has only increased cynicism towards the government. Ask a new friend about support for the PRI, and you are likely to hear, "Support? They don't need support—they always win."

You may catch a glimpse of these troubles, in the form of sign-wielding protests in front of a local city hall or in discreet notices at historical sites that decry the low wages of federal museum workers. More striking than these current signs of discontent, though, are the many reminders of cultural survival—and celebration—in the face of on-going adversity. From the Huichol artisan who reveals the spiritual world through elaborate beadwork to the exuberant national confrontation with death marked by Day of the Dead festivities, Mexican people in various walks of life find surprising and creative ways to express hope and the chance for renewal. For travelers who plunge wholeheartedly into the contradictions, problems, and unexpected joys of Mexico, this underlying promise of renewal will become a vivid and unforgettable reality.

STUDENT TRAVEL.

Two ways to spend $1000:

A. 10 CDs, trendy boots, two surfwear T-shirts, wild haircut, navel ring, a new tattoo, party all week, one bottle of aspirin.

B. Air ticket to somewhere exciting, rail pass, backpack, meet people, experience new cultures, learn about the world.

Education is expensive. Spend wisely.

STA Travel: 800-777-0112 • http://www.sta-travel.com

New York: 212-627-3111
Boston: 617-266-6014
Philadelphia: 215-382-2928
Washington DC: 202-887-0912
Chicago: 312-786-9050
San Francisco: 415-391-8407
Los Angeles: 213-934-8722
Seattle: 206-633-5000

STA TRAVEL
We've been there.

BASICS   1

If you've ever traveled with anyone before, you know the two types of people in the world: the planners and the nonplanners. You also know that travel brings out the very worst in both groups: Left to their own devices, the planners will have you goose-stepping from attraction to attraction on a cultural blitzkrieg, while the nonplanners will invariably miss the flight, the bus, and the point. This Basics chapter offers you a middle ground, providing enough information to help plan your trip without saddling you with an itinerary or invasion plan. Keep in mind that companies go out of business, prices inevitably go up, and, hey, we're only too human.

Planning Your Trip

WHEN TO GO

The two traditional vacation times in Mexico are Semana Santa (Holy Week, the week before Easter) and the period from Christmas through New Year's. Carnaval is a week-long festival involving costumes, parades, and a great deal of general revelry that takes place in February, during the week preceding Ash Wednesday. During these holidays, hotels in most beach communities, even small ones, are usually booked well in advance, prices may be jacked up, and armies of towel-toting tourists swarm the beaches. Resorts popular with college students (e.g., any place with a beach) tend to fill up in the summer months, when schools are out. To avoid hordes of foreign and local tourists, heavy rains, and high prices, the best times to go are October, March, April, and early May.

CLIMATE The climate in Mexico, from the wet, tropical Yucatán to the dry, hot northwest, is as varied as the country's landscape. Mountains and desert, sea and jungle—there's little room for generalities. The southern region tends to be hot and humid, the north more temperate. Both must contend with the country's long rainy season, which extends from May until mid-October. The south gets a more generous helping of rain—more than 100 inches a year.

HOLIDAYS On public holidays, expect a spirit of celebration and most businesses (especially offices) to be closed. The following are some of the most important Mexico-wide holidays. Regional festivals are listed in individual chapters.

January 1: The **New Year** is celebrated with mariachi music, midnight church bells, and an early morning *misa de gallo* (rooster mass). Many agricultural and livestock fairs are also held around this date.

January 6: **El Día de los Reyes** (Feast of the Epiphany or Three Kings Day) is a traditional day of gift-giving. This is also the day when the founding of Mérida is celebrated.

February 5: **Día de la Constitución,** or Constitution Day, is a national holiday during which official speeches and ceremonies are conducted nationwide.

March 21: **Natalicio de Benito Juárez** and **Día de la Primavera** celebrates the birthday of Mexico's reformist president Benito Juárez and marks the date of the spring equinox.

May 1: All businesses—even movie theaters—close as **Día del Trabajo** (Labor Day) is celebrated with workers' parades and speeches.

May 5: **Cinco de Mayo** is a national holiday that celebrates the Mexican defeat of the French at the Battle of Puebla.

September 15–16: **Día de la Independencia** (Independence Day) commemorates the speech, or *grito,* by Father Miguel Hidalgo that called for rebellion against the Spanish in 1810.

November 1–2: On the **Día de los Muertos** (Day of the Dead) dead friends, relatives, and ancestors are honored. People visit the graves of the dearly departed and build altars in their homes with offerings of food, flowers, fruits, and sweets.

November 20: The **Aniversario de la Revolución** recalls the Mexican Revolution with parades, speeches, and patriotic events.

December 12: **Día de la Virgen de Guadalupe** (Day of the Virgin of Guadalupe) honors the patron saint of Mexico with religious rites, processions, and pilgrimages.

December 24–25: **Navidad** (Christmas) is celebrated as it is all over the Americas, with dinner and midnight mass on Christmas Eve, followed by mass on Christmas Day.

The Highs and the Lows

Average daily highs and lows stack up as follows:

City	January: High/Low	June: High/Low
Acapulco	88°F/72°F	91°F/77°F
	31°C/22°C	33°C/25°C
Cozumel	82°F/68°F	89°F/75°F
	28°C/20°C	32°C/24°C
Ensenada	64°F/45°F	75°F/61°F
	18°C/7°C	32°C/24°C
Guadalajara	75°F/45°F	79°F/59°F
	24°C/7°C	24°C/15°C
La Paz	72°F/57°F	95°F/75°F
	22°C/14°C	35°C/24°C
Mexico City	70°F/41°F	73°F/52°F
	21°C/5°C	23°C/11°C
Monterrey	68°F/48°F	91°F/72°F
	20°C/9°C	34°C/22°C
Puerto Vallarta	84°F/63°F	95°F/73°F
	29°C/17°C	35°C/23°C

GOVERNMENT TOURIST OFFICES

Aside from offering the usual glossy tourist brochures, state and local tourist offices can answer general questions about travel in their area or refer you to other organizations for more information. Be as specific as possible when writing to request information or you may just end up with a stack of glossy brochures on expensive jungle expeditions. If you can get someone to answer questions over the phone, so much the better—the offices are often staffed by natives.

IN THE UNITED STATES The **Mexican Government Tourism Office** (405 Park Ave., Suite 1402, New York, NY 10022, tel. 212/755-4756, fax 212/753-2874; 10100 Santa Monica Blvd., Los Angeles, CA 90067, tel. 310/203-8191, fax 310/203-8316; 2707 N. Loop West, Suite 450, Houston, TX 77008, tel. 713/880-5153, fax 713/880-1833; 1911 Pennsylvania Ave. NW, Washington, D.C., 20036, tel. 202/728-1750, fax 202/728-1758; 128 Aragon Ave., Coral Gables, FL 33134, tel. 305/443-9160, fax 305/443-1186; 70 East Lake St., Suite 1413, Chicago, IL 60601, tel. 312/606-9252) can answer questions and provide maps and travel information.

IN CANADA The **Mexican Government Tourism Office** (2 Bloor St., West, Suite 1801, Toronto, Ont. M4W3E2, tel. 416/925-0704. fax 416/925-1876; 1 Place Ville Marie, Montreal, Suite 2409, Que. H3B3M9, tel. 514/871-1052, fax 514/871-3825; 999 W. Hastings St., Suite 1617, Vancouver, BC V6C2W2, tel. 604/669-2845, fax 604/669-3498) has travel information and maps.

STA Offices

- **UNITED STATES. CALIFORNIA:** Berkeley (tel. 510/642-3000), Los Angeles (tel. 213/934-8722), San Francisco (tel. 415/391-8407), Santa Monica (tel. 310/394-5126), Westwood (tel. 310/824-1574). **MASSACHUSETTS:** Boston (tel. 617/266-6014), Cambridge (tel. 617/576-4623). **NEW YORK:** Columbia University (tel. 212/854-2224), West Village (tel. 212/627-3111). **PENNSYLVANIA:** Philadelphia (tel. 215/382-2928). **WASHINGTON:** Seattle (tel. 206/633-5000). **WASHINGTON D.C.** (tel. 202/887-0912).

- **INTERNATIONAL. AUSTRALIA:** Adelaide (tel. 08/223-2426), Brisbane (tel. 07/221-9388), Cairns (tel. 070/314199), Darwin (tel. 089/412955), Melbourne (tel. 03/349-2411), Perth (tel. 09/227-7569), Sydney (tel. 02/212-1255). **AUSTRIA:** Graz (tel. 0316/32482), Innsbruck (tel. 0512/588997), Linz (tel. 0732/775893), Salzburg (tel. 0662/883252), Vienna (tel. 0222/401480 or 0222/5050-1280). **DENMARK:** Copenhagen (tel. 031/35-88-44). **FRANCE:** Paris (tel. 01/43-25-00-76). **GERMANY:** Berlin (tel. 030/281-6741), Frankfurt (tel. 069/430191 or 069/703035), Hamburg (tel. 040/442363). **GREECE:** Athens (tel. 01/32-21-267). **ITALY:** Bologna (tel. 051/261802), Florence (tel. 055/289721), Genoa (tel. 010/564366), Milan (tel. 02/5830-4121), Naples (tel. 081/552-7960), Rome (tel. 06/467-9291), Venice (tel. 041/520-5660). **NETHERLANDS:** Amsterdam (tel. 020/626-2557). **NEW ZEALAND:** Auckland (tel. 09/309-9995), Christchurch (tel. 03/379-9098), Wellington (tel. 04/385-0561). **SPAIN:** Barcelona (tel. 03/487-9546), Madrid (tel. 01/541-7372). **SWEDEN:** Göteborg (tel. 031/774-0025). **SWITZERLAND:** Lausanne (tel. 0121/617-58-11), Zurich (tel. 01/297-11-11). **TURKEY:** Istanbul (tel. 01/252-59-21). **UNITED KINGDOM:** London (tel. 0171/937-9962).

IN THE UNITED KINGDOM The **Mexican Government Tourism Office** in London (6061 Trafalgar Sq., London, England WIX 1 PB, tel. 171/734-10-58) supplies maps and travel information.

BUDGET TRAVEL ORGANIZATIONS

Council on International Educational Exchange (Council) is a private, nonprofit organization that administers work, volunteer, academic, and professional programs worldwide. Its travel division, **Council Travel,** is a full-service travel agency specializing in student, youth, and budget travel. They offer discounted airfares, rail passes, accommodations, guidebooks, budget tours, and travel gear. They also issue the ISIC, GO25, and ITIC identity cards (*see* Student ID Cards, *below*), as well as Hostelling International cards. Forty-one Council Travel offices serve the budget traveler in the United States, and there are about a dozen overseas (including ones in Britain, France, and Germany). Council also puts out a variety of publications, including the free *Student Travels* magazine, a gold mine of travel tips (including information on work- and study-abroad opportunities). *205 E. 42nd St., New York, NY 10017, tel. 212/661-1414.*

South American Explorers Club has a great deal of info about Mexico and Central America (notwithstanding the fact that neither of these is in South America). Among other things, membership gets you the quarterly *South American Explorer* magazine, which covers all sorts of off-the-beaten-track activities; access to "Trip Reports" submitted by club members after their travels; and discounts for club maps and brochures. Annual membership is $30. *126 Indian Creek Rd., Ithaca, NY 14850, tel. 607/277-0488.*

STA Travel, the world's largest travel organization catering to students and young people, has over 100 offices worldwide and offers low-price airfares to destinations around the globe, as well as rail passes, car rentals, tours, you name it. STA issues the ISIC and the GO25 youth cards (*see* Student ID Cards, *below*), both of which prove eligibility for student airfares and other travel discounts. Call 800/777-0122 or the nearest STA office for more information.

Travel CUTS is a full-service travel agency that sells discounted airline tickets to Canadian students and issues the ISIC, GO25, ITIC, and HI cards. Their 35 offices are on or near college campuses. Call weekdays 9-5 for information and reservations. *187 College St., Toronto, Ont. M5T 1P7, tel. 416/979-2406.*

STUDENT ID CARDS

Foreign student ID cards are not universally accepted in Mexico; discounts for museum and theater admission usually apply exclusively to students at Mexican universities. Don't leave your student ID at home, though, because discounts are often left to the discretion of the person working the door. While an ID card issued by a home university or college may be sufficient to prove student status for admission discounts, the following cards have the extra feature of providing insurance in case of accident or other catastrophes.

If purchased in the United States, the $18 cost for the popular **International Student Identity Card** (**ISIC**) card also buys you $3,000 in emergency medical coverage; limited hospital coverage; and access to a 24-hour international, toll-free hotline for assistance in medical, legal, and financial emergencies. In the United States, apply to CIEE or STA; in Canada, the ISIC is available for C$15 from **Travel CUTS** (*see* Budget Travel Organizations, *above*). In the United Kingdom, students with valid university IDs can purchase the ISIC at any student union or student-travel company. Applicants must submit a photo as well as proof of current full-time student status, age, and nationality.

The **Go 25: International Youth Travel Card** (**GO25**) is issued to travelers (students and non-students) between the ages of 12 and 25 and provides services and benefits similar to those given by the ISIC card. The $10 card is available from the same organizations that sell the ISIC. When applying, bring a passport-size photo and your passport as proof of your age.

The $19 **International Teacher Identity Card (ITIC),** sponsored by the International Student Travel Confederation, is available to teachers of all grade levels, from kindergarten to graduate school. The services and benefits you get when buying the card are similar to those for the three previous cards. When you buy the card, ask for the *International Teacher Identity Card Handbook*, which has all the details.

PASSPORTS, VISAS, AND TOURIST CARDS

All foreigners traveling for more than 72 hours in Mexico must obtain a tourist card. Although adult U.S. and Canadian citizens technically need only a birth certificate and a photo ID to obtain one, a passport is sure to come in handy in case of a problem. Minors must present a notarized consent form signed by both parents (or single parent) and their passport or birth certificate. Legal permanent residents of the United States must have an alien registration card and a passport or driver's license. Western Europeans, Aussies, and Kiwis must present a passport; citizens of all other countries must obtain a visa at any Mexican consulate.

TOURIST CARDS If you intend to visit border towns only, you can do so without a tourist card (called an F.M.T.) for up to 72 hours. Otherwise you must show proof of citizenship (either an original birth certificate and a photo ID, or a passport) and obtain a tourist card. Driver's licenses, credit cards, and military papers will not suffice. A naturalized citizen must carry at least one of the following documents: naturalization papers, a U.S. passport, or an affidavit of citizenship. F.M.T.s are available at Mexican government border offices at any port of entry, on flights into Mexico, any Mexican Ministry of Tourism or consulate in the United States, and travel agencies. No matter where you get it, when crossing the border you must sign the card in the presence of the Mexican immigration official, who may also ask to see proof of citizenship. Be sure to hold on to your receipt, because you are required to fork it over on departure. If you lose it, expect to visit with the border officials for a while.

Council Travel Offices in the United States

ARIZONA: Tempe (tel. 602/966–3544). **CALIFORNIA:** Berkeley (tel. 510/848–8604), Davis (tel. 916/752–2285), La Jolla (tel. 619/452–0630), Long Beach (tel. 310/598–3338), Los Angeles (tel. 310/208–3551), Palo Alto (tel. 415/325–3888), San Diego (tel. 619/270–6401), San Francisco (tel. 415/421–3473 or 415/566–6222), Santa Barbara (tel. 805/562–8080). **COLORADO:** Boulder (tel. 303/447–8101), Denver (tel. 303/571–0630). **CONNECTICUT:** New Haven (tel. 203/562–5335). **FLORIDA:** Miami (tel. 305/670–9261). **GEORGIA:** Atlanta (tel. 404/377–9997). **ILLINOIS:** Chicago (tel. 312/951-0585), Evanston (tel. 708/475–5070). **INDIANA:** Bloomington (tel. 812/330–1600). **LOUISIANA:** New Orleans (tel. 504/866–1767). **MASSACHUSETTS:** Amherst (tel. 413/256–1261), Boston (tel. 617/266–1926), Cambridge (tel. 617/497–1497 or 617/225–2555). **MICHIGAN:** Ann Arbor (tel. 313/998–0200). **MINNESOTA:** Minneapolis (tel. 612/379–2323). **NEW YORK:** New York (tel. 212/661–1450, 212/666–4177, or 212/254–2525). **NORTH CAROLINA:** Chapel Hill (tel. 919/942–2334). **OHIO:** Columbus (tel. 614/294–8696). **OREGON:** Portland (tel. 503/228–1900). **PENNSYLVANIA:** Philadelphia (tel. 215/382–0343), Pittsburgh (tel. 412/683–1881). **RHODE ISLAND:** Providence (tel. 401/331–5810). **TEXAS:** Austin (tel. 512/472-4931), Dallas (tel. 214/363–9941). **UTAH:** Salt Lake City (tel. 801/582–5840). **WASHINGTON:** Seattle (tel. 206/632–2448 or 206/329–4567). **WASHINGTON, D.C.** (tel. 202/337–6464). For U.S. cities not listed, call tel. 800/2–COUNCIL.

Tourist cards last up to six months, at which time you must go to the local **Delegación de Servicios Migratorios** to apply for a new one. When you hand in the completed application form upon entering Mexico, tell the immigration official you plan to stay for the full six months. If you estimate a shorter period of time and later decide to prolong your stay, you'll have to go through an incredible amount of administrative hassle and line-waiting to get your card extended. Upon leaving Mexico, your card is taken and a new one is issued if and when you return. If you lose your card, you must also go to the Delegación de Servicios Migratorios. To cut through at least a portion of the red tape involved, it is a good idea to make a photocopy of your card and keep it in a separate place to speed up the creaky replacement process. Carry the original with you at all times; it's required by law.

OBTAINING A PASSPORT

➢ **U.S. CITIZENS** • First-time applicants, travelers whose most recent passport was issued more than 12 years ago or before they were 18, travelers whose passports have been lost or stolen, and travelers between the ages of 13 and 17 (a parent must also accompany them) must apply for a passport in person. Other renewals can be taken care of by mail. Apply at one of the 13 U.S. Passport Agency offices a *minimum* of five weeks before your departure. For fastest processing, apply between August and December. If you blow it, you can have a passport issued within five days of departure if you have your plane ticket in hand and pay the additional $30 fee to expedite processing. This method will probably work, but if there's one little glitch in the system, you're out of luck. Local county courthouses, many state and probate courts, and some post offices also accept passport applications. Have the following items ready when you go to get your passport:

- A completed passport application (form DSP-11), available at courthouses, some post offices, and passport agencies.

- Proof of citizenship (certified copy of birth certificate, naturalization papers, or previous passport issued in the past 12 years).

- Proof of identity with your photograph and signature (for example, a valid driver's license, employee ID card, military ID, student ID).

- Two recent, identical, two-square-inch photographs (black-and-white or color head shots).

- A $55 application fee for a 10-year passport, $30 for those under 18 for a five-year passport. First-time applicants are also hit with a $10 surcharge. If you're paying cash, exact change is necessary; checks or money orders should be made out to Passport Services.

Those lucky enough to be able to renew their passports by mail must send a completed Form DSP-82 (available from a Passport Agency); two recent, identical passport photos; their current passport (less than 12 years old); and a check or money order for $55 ($30 if under 18). Send everything to the nearest Passport Agency. Renewals take from three to four weeks. For more information or an application, contact the **Department of State Office of Passport Services** (tel. 202/647–0518) and dial your way through their message maze. Passport applications can be picked up at U.S. post offices, at federal or state courts, and at U.S. Passport Agencies in Boston, Chicago, Honolulu, Houston, Los Angeles, Miami, New Orleans, New York, Philadelphia, San Francisco, Seattle, Stamford, and Washington, DC.

➢ **CANADIAN CITIZENS** • Canadians should send a completed passport application (available at any post office, passport office, and many travel agencies) to the **Bureau of Passports** (Suite 215, West Tower, Guy Favreau Complex, 200 Rene Levesque Boulevard West, Montréal, Qué. H2Z 1X4, tel. 514/283–2152). Include C$35; two recent, identical passport photographs; the signature of a guarantor (a Canadian citizen who has known you for at least two years and is a mayor, practicing lawyer, notary public, judge, magistrate, police officer, signing officer at a bank, medical doctor, or dentist); and proof of Canadian citizenship (original birth certificate or other official document as specified). You can also apply in person at regional passport offices in many locations, including Edmonton, Halifax, Montreal, Toronto, Vancouver, and Winnipeg. Passports have a shelf life of five years and are not renewable. Processing takes about two weeks by mail and five working days for in-person applications.

➢ **U.K. CITIZENS** • Passport applications are available through travel agencies, a main post office, or one of six regional passport offices (in London, Liverpool, Peterborough, Belfast, Glasgow, and Newport). The application must be countersigned by your bank manager or by a solicitor, barrister, doctor, clergyman, or justice of the peace who knows you personally. Send or drop off the completed form; two recent, identical passport photos; and a £25 fee to a regional passport office (address is on the form). Passports are valid for 10 years (five years for those under 16) and take about four weeks to process.

➢ **AUSTRALIAN CITIZENS** • Australians must visit a post office or passport office to complete the passport application process. A 10-year passport for those over 18 costs AUS$77. The under-18 crowd can get a five-year passport for AUS$38. For more information, call toll-free in Australia 008/02–60–22 weekdays during regular business hours.

➢ **NEW ZEALAND CITIZENS** • Passport applications can be found at any post office or consulate. Completed applications must be accompanied by proof of citizenship and two passport-size photos. The fee is NZ$55 for a 10-year passport. Processing takes about three weeks.

LOST PASSPORTS If your passport is lost or stolen while traveling, you should immediately notify the local police and nearest embassy or consulate. A consular officer should be able to wade through some red tape and issue you a new one, or at least get you back into your country of origin without one. The process will be slowed up considerably if you don't have some other forms of identification on you, so you're well advised to carry other forms of ID—a driver's license, a copy of your birth certificate, a student ID—separate from your passport, and tuck a few photocopies of the front page of your passport in your luggage and your traveling companion's pockets.

A U.S. embassy or consulate will only issue a new passport in emergencies. In non-emergency situations, the staff will affirm your affidavit swearing to U.S. citizenship, and this paper will get you back to the United States. The British embassy or consulate requires a police report, any form of identification, and three passport-size photos. They will replace the passport in four working days. Canadian citizens face the same requirements as the Brits, but you must have a guarantor with you. Since most travelers do not know a local guarantor (see Obtaining a Passport, Canadian Citizens, *above,* for requirements), there is also the option of paying an officer of the consulate/embassy to act in that capacity—proving once again that throwing enough money at a problem usually makes it go away. A replacement passport usually takes five working days. New Zealand officials ask for two passport-size photos, while the Australians require three, but both can usually replace a passport in 24 hours.

GETTING THE BEST AIRFARES

While your travel plans are still in the fantasy stage, start studying the travel sections of major Sunday newspapers: Courier companies, charter flights, and fare brokers often list incredibly cheap flights. Travel agents are another obvious resource, as they have access to computer networks that show the lowest fares before they're even advertised. However, budget travelers are the bane of travel agents, whose commission is based on the ticket prices. That said, agencies on or near college campuses—try STA or Council Travel (see Budget Travel Organizations, *above*)—actually cater to this pariah class and can help you find cheap deals.

Flexibility is the key to getting a serious bargain on airfare. If you can play around with your departure date, destination, amount of luggage carried, and return date, you will probably save money. Options include charter flights, flying standby, student discounts, courier flights, and APEX (Advanced Purchase Excursion) and Super APEX fares; read on to help get through this maze. Hot tips when making reservations: If the reservation clerk tells you that the least expensive seats are no longer available on a certain flight, ask to be put on a waiting list. If the airline doesn't keep waiting lists for the lowest fares, call them on subsequent mornings and ask about cancellations and last-minute openings—airlines trying to fill all their seats sometimes add additional cut-rate tickets at the last moment. When setting travel dates, remember that off-season fares can be as much as 50% lower. A useful resource is Michael McColl's ***The Worldwide Guide to Cheap Airfares,*** an in-depth account of how to find cheap tickets and generally beat the system. If you don't find it at your local bookstore, you can mail a check for $14.95 plus $2.50 for shipping and handling to Insider Publications (2124 Kittredge St., 3rd Floor, Berkeley, CA 94703), or call 800/782–6657 and order with a credit card.

APEX TICKETS If you're not a student or the kind of person to spend days scouring newspapers for the lowest fare, APEX (advance purchase excursion) tickets bought directly from the airlines—every airline has them—or from your travel agent are the simplest way to go. If you know exactly when you want to leave and it's not tomorrow (or the next day), ask for the APEX fare when making your reservation—it'll save you a bundle and guarantee you a seat. Regular APEX fares normally apply to tickets bought at least 21 days in advance; you can get Super-APEX fares if you know your travel plans at least one month in advance. Here's the catch: If you cancel or change your plans, you'll pay a penalty, anywhere from $50 to $100, and the cheapest fares limit your stay to 1–3 months.

CONSOLIDATORS AND BUCKET SHOPS Consolidator companies, also known as bucket shops, buy blocks of tickets at wholesale prices from airlines trying to fill flights. Check out any consolidator's reputation with the Better Business Bureau before starting; most are perfectly reliable, but better safe than sorry. If everything works as planned, you'll save 10%–40% on the published APEX fare. There are, however, some drawbacks to consolidator tickets: They're often non-refundable, and the flights to choose from often feature indirect routes, long layovers in connecting cities, and undesirable seating assignments. If your flight is delayed or canceled, you'll also have a tough time switching airlines. As with charter flights, you risk taking a huge loss if you change your travel plans. If possible, pay with a credit card, so that if your ticket never arrives you don't have to pay. Bucket shops generally advertise in newspapers—be sure to check restrictions, refund possibilities, and payment conditions. One last suggestion: Confirm your reservation with the airline both before and after you buy a consolidated ticket. This not only decreases the chance of fraud, but also ensures that you won't be the first to get bumped if the airline overbooks. For more details, contact one of the following consolidators.

Mena Travel (2479 N. Clark St., Chicago, IL 60614, tel. 800/536–6362 or 312/472–5361, fax 312/472–2829) is a consolidator specializing in Latin American destinations. **Travel Time** (1 Halladie Plaza, Suite 406, San Francisco, CA 94102, tel. 800/956–9327 or 415/677–0799, fax 415/391–1856) is a discount travel agency serving Mexico, Hawaii, and Europe. Round-trip air fare to Cancún averages $270.

STANDBY AND THREE-DAY-ADVANCE-PURCHASE FARES Flying standby is almost a thing of the past. The idea is to purchase an open ticket and wait for the next available seat on the next available flight to your chosen destination. However, most airlines have dumped standby policies in favor of three-day-advance-purchase youth fares, which are open only to people under 25 and (as the name states) can only be purchased within three days of departure. Return flights must also be booked no more than three days prior to departure. If you meet the above criteria, expect 10%–50% savings on published APEX fares. If you're desperate to get to Mexico by Wednesday, try **Last Minute Travel Club** (tel. 617/267–9800).

CHARTER FLIGHTS Charter flights have vastly different characteristics, depending on the company you're dealing with. Generally speaking, a charter company either buys a block of tickets on a regularly scheduled commercial flight and sells them at a discount (the prevalent form in the United States) or leases the whole plane and then offers relatively cheap fares to the public (most common in the United Kingdom). Summer charter flights fill up the quickest and should be booked a couple of months in advance. Despite a few potential drawbacks—among them infrequent flights, restrictive return-date requirements, lickety-split payment demands, frequent bankruptcies—charter companies often offer the cheapest tickets around, especially during high season when APEX fares are most expensive. Make sure you find out a company's policy on refunds should a flight be canceled by either yourself or the airline. You can minimize risks by checking the company's reputation with the Better Business Bureau and taking out enough trip-cancellation insurance to cover the operator's potential failure. The list below is far from exhaustive; check newspaper travel sections for more extensive listings. Council Travel and STA (*see* Budget Travel Organizations, *above*) also offer exclusively negotiated discount airfares on scheduled airlines.

SunTrips (SunTrips Building, 2350 Paragon Dr., San Jose, CA 95131, tel. 800/786–8747 or 408/432–1101) is a charter operator specializing in destinations in Europe, the United States, and Mexico. **Wings of the World (WOW)**, which can be reached at 800/U-FLY-WOW, is a charter operator with flights to Mexico City. WOW flies from most major U.S. airports and requires no specified length of stay. They do, however, require at least a seven-day advance purchase for best prices.

STUDENT DISCOUNTS Student discounts on airline tickets are offered through **Council Travel**, the **Educational Travel Center, STA Travel**, and **Travel CUTS** (*see* Budget Travel Organizations, *above*). **Campus Connection** (1100 E. Marlton Pike, Cherry Hill, NJ 08032, tel. 800/428–3235), exclusively for students under 25, searches airline computer networks for the cheapest student fares to worldwide destinations. They don't always have the best price, but because they deal directly with the airlines you won't get stuck with a heavily restricted or fraudulent ticket. Keep in mind that most airlines will often *not* entitle you to frequent-flyer mileage for discounted student, youth, or teacher tickets. For discount tickets based on your status as a student, youth, or teacher, have an ID that proves it when you check in: an International Student Identity Card (ISIC), Youth Identity Card, or International Teacher Identity Card (ITIC).

COURIER FLIGHTS A few restrictions and inconveniences are the price you'll pay for the colossal savings on airfare offered to air couriers—travelers who accompany letters and packages between designated points. The way it works is simple. Courier companies list whatever flights are available for the next week or so. After you book the flight, you sign a contract with the company to act as a courier (some places make you pay a deposit, to be refunded after the successful completion of your assignment). On the day of departure, you arrive at the airport a few hours early, meet someone who hands you a ticket and customs forms, and off you go. After you land, you simply clear customs with the courier luggage, and deliver it to a waiting agent.

The main restrictions are (1) flights can be booked only a week or two in advance, and often only a few days in advance, (2) you are allowed carry-on luggage only, because the courier uses your checked-luggage allowance to transport the time-sensitive shipment, (3) you must return within one or two weeks, sometimes within 30 days, (4) most courier companies only issue tickets to travelers over the age of 18.

Both **Now Voyager** (74 Varick St., Suite 307, New York, NY 10013, tel. 212/431–1616) and **World Courier** (137-42 Guy Brewer Blvd., Jamaica, NY 11434, tel. 718/978–9522, fax 718/276–6932) serve Mexico City. For other courier companies, check newspaper travel sections, the yellow pages of your phone directory, or mail away for a telephone directory that lists companies by the cities to which they fly. One of the better publications is **Air Courier Bulletin** (IAATC, 8 South J St., Box 1349, Lake Worth, FL 33460, tel. 407/582–8320), sent to IAATC members every two months once you pay the $35 annual fee. Another good resource is the newsletter published by **Travel Unlimited** (Box 1058, Allston, MA 02134), which costs $25 for 12 issues. Publications you can find in the bookstores include **Air Courier Bargains** ($14.95), published by The Intrepid Traveler, and *The Courier Air Travel Handbook* ($9.95), published by Thunderbird Press.

MONEY

"Nuevo pesos," or new peso notes come in denominations of 10, 20, 50, and 100 pesos. Old bills also continue to circulate; they're still valid and come with three zeroes attached (i.e., 10,000 = 10; 50,000 = 50). The "no change" dilemma will often confront you: Many shop and restaurant owners don't have change for your purchase even if the note you offer is valued as low as $3.50. In these situations, you'll just have to chill while they run next door to see if anyone else can make change. Enough of these encounters may compel you to request *billetes chicos* (small bills) when you exchange money. All prices in this book are given in U.S. dollars.

HOW MUCH IT WILL COST The past year has been a bad one for the Mexican economy—the peso lost half its value. Devaluation plus steady inflation mean that the dollar (and most other foreign currencies) goes much further right now. At press time the peso was not fluctuating wildly, and prices in this book are based on the exchange rate of 6 pesos to one dollar. Mexico is a bargain for travelers used to Western European and U.S. prices: Lodging, food, and drink are all much cheaper. Prices vary according to the universal rule, however—the more cosmopolitan the city, the more expensive the tortilla. Your travel to and from Mexico will probably be your biggest expense, then lodging and transport.

➤ **WHERE TO SLEEP** • Most travelers bed down in hotels, though camping is usually a safe option. Hotels range from dirt cheap (about $3 per person) to stratospheric. In a typical city, expect to pay $6–$12 for a single, $8–$15 for a double, and a couple of bucks extra for an additional person or air-conditioning. A room with a double bed often costs a dollar or two less than a room with two singles. Mexico's few hostels rarely cost more than $5 a night.

➤ **FOOD** • If you're willing to forgo tourist fare, you'll be able to spend very little money on food without losing too much weight. One sure cost-cutting strategy in more expensive cities, or whenever you are feeling a painful cash crunch, is to buy fresh fruits and vegetables at the local market (every city, town, and village has one). Most markets also have small *fondas* (covered food stands) offering *comidas corridas* (fixed-price lunch specials) for less than $3. *Panaderías* (bakeries) sell cheap breads and pastries. More variety and more risk is involved when you buy from street vendors, who sell tacos, tamales, corn soup, and the like for rock-bottom prices. Even the most hygienic-looking stand can sell you a dysentery sandwich, but following the crowds is usually the best strategy for finding well-prepared food.

➤ **TRANSPORT** • Buses are widely used in Mexico, so fares remain very low. Buses range from antiquated second-class school buses to first-class *especial* coaches with air-conditioning, reclining seats, videos, and meal service. Prices correlate less with the number of hours traveled than with the popularity of the route—heavily traveled routes are served by more classes of service at lower prices than less frequently covered ones. Trains (especially second class) are considerably cheaper than buses, but much slower and often less comfortable. Domestic plane fares will flatten your wallet considerably (*see* Getting Around, *below*).

➤ **ENTERTAINMENT** • Fun may be free, but entertainment costs can be very high in big cities, where getting a foot in the door of an average club means coughing up anywhere from $5 to $30. Drink prices at an average bar are comparable to those north of the border: Beers run $1–$2 at popular watering holes. Movie tickets, at least, are a reasonable $2–$3. In many cities, thanks to government subsidies, entrance to some theater, dance, and musical events is free (these bargains are usually cultural events featuring traditional music or dance). If your cash flow has dwindled to a drip, join the locals for traditional (and free) entertainment—an early evening stroll around the town's *zócalo* (main square).

TRAVELING WITH MONEY Cash never goes out of style, but traveler's checks and a major credit card are usually the safest and most convenient way to pay for goods and services on the road. Depending on the length of your trip, strike a balance among these three forms of currency, and protect yourself by carrying cash in a money belt or "necklace" pouch (available at luggage or camping stores) or front pocket; keeping accurate records of traveler's checks' serial numbers; and recording credit-card numbers and an emergency number for reporting the cards' loss or theft. Carrying at least some cash is wise; most budget establishments will accept cash only, and, outside of urban areas, changing traveler's checks may prove difficult. Bring about $100 (in as many single bills as possible) in cash; changing U.S. dollars will be easier than cashing traveler's checks. Credit cards are rarely accepted by budget establishments in Mexico, but they do come in handy at mid-range hotels and restaurants and Visa and MasterCard can be used to obtain cash advances in banks or at ATM machines (*see* Cash Machines, *below*). An American Express card will allow you to cash personal checks at any American Express office (*see* Obtaining Money from Home, *below*), but AmEx is not hooked up to any Mexican ATMs.

CHANGING MONEY You can turn your cash or traveler's checks into pesos at most banks or go to a private exchange office, called a *casa de cambio*. Most banks only change money on weekdays until 2 (though they stay open until 5), while casas de cambio generally stay open until 6 and often operate on weekends. Bank rates are regulated by the federal government and therefore invariable, while casas de cambio have slightly more variable rates. Some hotels also exchange money, but they usually do it at extortionate rates. It helps to exchange money early in the day, because after the banks are closed, everybody else's rates tend to worsen. You can buy pesos at your local bank before departing, but this is probably only necessary if you're arriving in the middle of the night, when money-exchange booths are likely to be closed.

TRAVELER'S CHECKS Budget establishments in Mexico are extremely unlikely to accept traveler's checks of any sort. They are accepted at most banks, casas de cambio, and some fancy hotels. Most American Express offices claim to change AmEx checks, but they don't always have much cash. Some banks and credit unions will issue checks free to established customers, but most charge a 1%–2% commission fee. Members of the American Automobile Association (AAA) can purchase American Express traveler's checks from the AAA commission-free. Buy the bulk of your traveler's checks in small denominations (a pack of five $20 checks is the smallest); many establishments won't accept large bills. Hold on to your receipts after exchanging your checks; once you're home it's easier to convert foreign currency into dollars if you have the receipts.

Even if you don't have an AmEx gold card, you can still get American Express Traveler's Checks free with an AAA membership. Talk to the cashier at your local AAA office.

➤ **LOST AND STOLEN CHECKS** • Unlike cash, lost or stolen traveler's checks can be replaced or refunded *if* you can produce the purchase agreement and a record of the checks' serial numbers (especially of those you've already cashed). Sign all the checks when you buy them; you'll endorse them a second time to exchange them for cash or make purchases. Common sense dictates that you keep the purchase agreement separate from your checks. Caution-happy travelers will even give a copy of the purchase agreement and checks' serial numbers to someone back home. In a safe place—or several safe places—also record the toll-free or collect telephone number to call in case of an emergency. Most issuers of traveler's checks promise to refund or replace lost or stolen checks in 24 hours, but you can practically see them crossing their fingers behind their backs. If you are traveling in a remote area, expect this process to take longer.

GETTING MONEY FROM HOME

Provided there is money at home to be had, here are some ways to get it:

- If you're an **American Express** cardholder, cash a personal check at an American Express office for up to $1,000 ($5,000 for gold cardholders) every 21 days; you'll be paid in U.S. traveler's checks or, in some instances, in foreign currency.

- An **American Express** *MoneyGram*^{SM} can be a dream come true if you can convince someone back home to go to an American Express MoneyGram agent and fill out the necessary forms. You don't have to be an AmEx cardholder to send or receive a MoneyGram: simply pay up to $1,000 with a credit card or cash (and anything over that in cash) and, as quick as 10 minutes later, it's ready to be picked up. Fees vary according to the amount of money sent but average about 3%–10%. You have to get the transaction reference number from the sender and show ID when picking up the money. MoneyGram has an agreement with Banamex to guarantee the exchange rate—other transfer locations (AmEx offices, casas de cambio) *may* have better rates, but won't guarantee them. Be certain that whoever sends you money spells your name exactly as it appears on your ID—Mexican banks, especially Banamex, are very picky about such details. For locations of American Express MoneyGram agents call 800/926–9400; from overseas call 303/980–3340 collect or contact the nearest AmEx agent.

- **MasterCard** and **Visa** cardholders can get cash advances from many banks, even in small towns, but keep in mind that most banks charge a commission for this handy-dandy service. If you get a four-digit PIN number for your card before you leave home, you can also withdraw cash at many ATM machines (*see* Cash Machines, *below*).

- Have funds sent through **Western Union** (tel. 800/325–6000). Although this has a certain glamorous ring, it's very expensive. If you have a MasterCard or Visa, you can have money sent up to your card's credit limit. If not, have someone take cash, a certified cashier's check, or a healthy MasterCard or Visa to a Western Union office. The money will reach the requested destination in minutes but may not be available for several more hours or days, depending on the whim of the local authorities. Fees range from 4% to 10% depending on the amount sent.

- In dire emergencies (arrest, hospitalization, or worse) there is one more way American citizens can receive money overseas: by setting up a **Department of State Trust Fund**. A friend or family member sends money to the Department of State, which then transfers the money to the U.S. embassy or consulate in the city in which you're stranded. Once this account is established, you can send and receive money through Western Union, bank wire, or mail, all payable to the Department of State. For information, talk to the Department of State's Citizens' Emergency Center (tel. 202/647–5225).

CASH MACHINES Virtually all U.S. banks belong to a network of **ATMs** (Automated Teller Machines), which gobble up bank cards and spit out cash 24 hours a day in cities throughout the world. The networks most commonly found in Mexico are **Cirrus** and **Plus**. Major banks, and their handy ATMs, are plentiful except in the smaller, more remote towns. If your transaction cannot be completed—an annoyingly common occurrence—chances are that the computer lines are busy, and you'll just have to try again later. Another problem is that some Mexican ATMs only accept PINs of four or fewer digits; if your PIN is longer, ask your bank about changing it. The ATMs at Banamex tend to be the most reliable, and give you a generally excellent rate of exchange. That said, remember that your bank back home will charge you a fee for each withdrawal you make in Mexico. Some banks charge a percentage of the withdrawal, while others charge a fixed fee each for transaction. If your bank takes a fixed fee, consider taking out larger chunks of cash to cut down on your number of transactions–and therefore fees. **Visa** and **MasterCard** also work in many Mexican ATMs (*see* Obtaining Money from Home, *above*), but **American Express** does not.

WHAT TO PACK

As little as possible. Besides the usual suspects—clothes, toiletries, camera, a Walkman, and a good book—bring along a day pack or some type of smaller receptacle for stuff; it'll come in handy not only for day excursions but also for those places where you plan to stay for only one or two days. You can usually check cumbersome bags at the bus or train station and just carry the essentials with you while you go looking for lodging.

Backpacks are the most manageable way to lug belongings around, but they instantly brand you a foreign tourist. Also, outside pockets on backpacks are especially vulnerable to pickpockets, so don't store any valuables there. Like new shoes, fully packed luggage should be broken in: If you can't tote your bag all the way around the block at home, it's going to be worse than a ball and chain in Mexico. Leaving some room for gifts and souvenirs is also wise.

The Four Rules of Luggage

- *You must be able to carry it at least a mile in steamy hot weather.*

- *You must be able to fit it into a conventional storage locker or be fully prepared to schlep it with you everywhere.*

- *Keep anything you cherish in the middle of your bag. Pack your heaviest stuff in the middle of a pack and whatever you need quick access to (maps, guidebooks, address book) in an outer pocket. Keep money and travel documents on your body if possible.*

- *Attach a clearly marked, water-resistant luggage tag to your bag or write directly on the luggage with indelible ink. Also put some identifying paper or tag inside.*

By distributing the weight of your luggage across shoulders and hips, backpacks ease the burden of traveling. You can actually choose among three types of packs: external-frame packs (for longer travels or use on groomed trails), internal-frame packs (for longer travels across rougher terrain), and travel packs (hybrid packs that fit under an airline seat and travel well in cities or the back country). Although external frames achieve the best weight distribution and allow airspace between you and your goodies, they're more awkward and less flexible than packs with an internal frame. Since an external frame backpack will run you about $100–$225 (internal frames are about $50 more), be sure to have it fitted correctly when you buy it. Check to see that it is waterproof, or bring an extra waterproof poncho to throw over it in downpours.

BEDDING If you're planning to stay in hotels, you won't need to bring any bedding. Depending on where you're headed and during what time of year, though, you may want to pack a sheet, a light sleeping bag, or a thermal bag for sleeping on the beach or in a hammock. If you have a backpack, consider a sleeping mat that can be rolled tightly and strapped onto the bottom of your pack; these make train- and bus-station floors a tad more comfy. Sleep sheets often come in handy to make up for skimpy (or scary) bedding.

THE SLEEP SHEET DEFINED: *Take a big sheet. Fold it down the middle the long way. Sew one short side and the long, open side. Turn inside out. Get inside. Sleep.*

CLOTHING Smart—and not terribly fashion-conscious—travelers will bring two outfits and learn to wash clothes by hand regularly. Packing light does not mean relying on a pair of cut-off shorts and a tank top to get you through any situation, though. Shorts will make you awfully conspicuous in small Mexican towns, and women wearing them will attract attention they could probably live without. At resorts and most beach areas, however, shorts are fairly common and locals have become accustomed to seeing lots of foreign flesh. In general, though, you may find that Mexicans dress a little more formally than gringos, and Mexican women generally stay more covered than their northern counterparts. At the very least, bring comfortable easy-to-clean clothes. Black hides dirt but also absorbs heat. Artificial fabrics don't breathe and will make you hotter than you'd thought possible, so go with light cotton instead.

For maximum comfort, bring cotton pants (two pairs are about right); these will also dry more quickly than jeans. Bring several T-shirts and one sweatshirt or sweater for cooler nights. Socks and undies don't take up too much room, so throw in a couple extra pairs. In jungle areas, you'll need to wear socks and long pants to prevent bug bites and scratches from possibly toxic plants. You'll probably want a swimsuit even if you're not headed for the beach—you never know when you'll stumble across a swimming hole, river, or public pool. Rain gear is a must if you're traveling during rainy season; hooded plastic ponchos can be purchased at most sporting goods or Army-Navy surplus stores.

Recommended footware: a sturdy pair of walking shoes or hiking boots (broken in before your trip), a spare pair of shoes (preferably sandals), and plastic sandals or thongs to protect feet on shower floors and for camping or beach-hopping. Since many Mexico shoe stores don't carry sizes larger than seven for either men or women, you may be in serious trouble if you have big feet and your shoes give out. Your only option may be to ask a marketplace artisan to customize a pair of leather sandals.

LAUNDRY Lavanderías (laundromats) exist in all parts of Mexico and usually charge about $1–$2 per kilo. Hotel rooms are often the best (and certainly the cheapest) place to do laundry. A bring-your-own laundry service includes: a plastic bottle of liquid detergent or soap (powder doesn't break down as well), about six feet of clothesline (enough to tie to two stable objects), and some plastic clips (bobby pins or paper clips can substitute). Porch railings, shower curtain rods, bathtubs, and faucets can all serve as wet-laundry hangers if you forget the clothesline. All of these things are, of course, available in stores in Mexico, as well.

Dr. Bronner's Magic Soap is safe for both clothes and your bod, and the label is cool reading material on long train rides.

TOILETRIES You can find almost any toiletry you might need in a Mexican pharmacy—probably even the brand you're used to—at a reasonable price. If you do bring your favorite brands of shampoo, soap, and other necessities, put them in small containers to avoid bulk and weight. Use a separate, waterproof bag for containers that seal tightly; the pressure on airplanes can cause lids to pop off and create instant moisturizer slicks inside your luggage. Contact-lens wearers should bring all the paraphernalia they need to conduct chemical warfare on their lenses, though saline solution is available at pharmacies. Finally, bring insect repellent, sunscreen, and lip balm from home. **Avon "Skin So Soft"** body moisturizer is the best bug repellent in the world, even if it's not marketed as such. Check the phone book under AVON and make an appointment with your friendly Avon representative. Another option is **Green Ban's** environmentally sound insect repellent: stinky, but reasonably effective.

CAMERAS AND FILM While traveling, keep film as cool as possible, away from direct sunlight or blazing campfires. On a plane, unprocessed film is safest in your carry-on luggage—ask security to inspect it by hand. (It helps to keep your film in a plastic bag, ready for quick inspection.) The higher the film speed, the more susceptible it is to damage. If your camera is new, or new to you, shoot and develop a few rolls before leaving home to avoid spoiling travel footage with prominent thumb shots. Unless you're an artiste, the smaller and lighter the camera, the better, although consider splurging on a $15 skylight filter to protect your lens and reduce haze in your photos. Also pack some lens tissue and an extra battery for cameras with built-in light meters. For any photo-related questions, call the **Kodak Information Center** (tel. 800/242–2424).

CAMPING GEAR Before packing loads of camping gear, seriously consider how much camping you will actually do versus how much trouble it will be to haul around your tent, sleeping bag, stove, and accoutrements in the heat. Also consider climate in choosing what to bring; camping in dry Baja provides different concerns than camping in the tropical, humid Lacandón jungle.

Down sleeping bags are more expensive but much warmer than synthetic bags, and can be scrunched into a tiny sack, but they're useless when wet. For further protection against cold from the ground, pick up an Ensolite pad or other thin foam pad that can be rolled up and tied to your pack. High-tech sleeping pads like Therma-Rests are a bit expensive, but worth it if you're a serious camper. For camping in damp areas, make sure your tent has edges that can be turned up off the ground to prevent water from seeping in, or bring a plastic tarp along. Also check the tent's windows and front flaps for mosquito-proof netting, and make sure the front flap can be completely zipped shut during rain. The synthetic variety is more water-resistant and shelters against wind. Test the weight of the tent and try to visualize yourself packing it around on your back.

MISCELLANEOUS Stuff you might not think to take but will be damn glad to have: (1) extra day-pack for valuables or short jaunts; (2) a flashlight, good for electricity failures, reading in the dark, and exploring caves; (3) Walkman, entertainment for bus and train rides; (4) a pocket knife for cutting fruit, spreading cheese, removing splinters, and opening bottles; (5) water bottle; (6) sunglasses; (7) several large zip-type plastic bags, useful for wet swim suits, towels, leaky bottles, and rancid socks; (8) travel alarm clock; (9) needle and small spool of thread; (10) batteries; (11) books.

STAYING HEALTHY

For many people, traveling in Mexico means an extended case of the ever-unpopular Montezuma's revenge, a.k.a. *turista* (tourists' disease). You will experience this, in some form, at least once. Symptoms of turista are obvious: diarrhea and stomach ache, sometimes accompanied by fatigue or nausea. If you are severely nauseated or vomiting, have a high, prolonged fever, or there is blood in your stools, see a doctor—you could have food poisoning. Unfamiliar foods and changes in climate and lifestyle can all contribute to diarrhea. Bacteria from contaminated food or drink can cause hepatitis A, typhoid, salmonella, giardiasis, and dysentery. Prevention is your best ally. Avoid street food that looks like it's been sitting out for a while, and don't eat any raw fruits or vegetables that you can't peel without washing them well in a solution of purified water and a little bit of vinegar. As for water, you can hassle with iodine drops

Reality check. Call home.

AT&T USADirect® and World Connect.® The fast, easy way to call most anywhere. Take out AT&T Calling Card or your local calling card.** Lift phone. Dial AT&T Access Number for country you're calling from. Connect to English-speaking operator or voice prompt. Reach the States or over 205 countries. Talk. Say goodbye. Hang up. Resume vacation. Relax with AT&T. That's Your True Choice.℠ AT&T.

Argentina♦ 001-800-200-1111	Guyana†† 165	
Belize♦ 555	Honduras † 123	
Bolivia* 0-800-1112	Mexico◊◊◊ ■ 95-800-462-4240	
Brazil 000-8010	Nicaragua 174	
Chile 1-23-0-0311	Panama ■ 109	
Colombia 980-11-0010	Paraguay (Asuncion City)† 0081-800	
Costa Rica*■ 0-800-0-114-114	Peru†■ 171	
Ecuador* 999-119	Suriname 156	
El Salvador■ 190	Uruguay 00-0410	
Guatemala* 190	Venezuela*■ 80-011-120	

Your True Choice

**You can also call collect or use most U.S. local calling cards. Countries in bold face permit country-to-country calling in addition to calls to the U.S. World Connect® prices consist of USADirect® rates plus an additional charge based on the country you are calling. Collect calling available to the U.S. only.
*Public phones require deposit of coin or phone card. †May not be available from every phone. ††Collect calling only. ♦ Not available from public phones.
◊◊◊When calling from public phones, use phones marked "Ladatel". ■ World Connect calls can only be placed to this country. ©1995 AT&T.

For a free wallet sized card of all AT&T Access Numbers, call: 1-800-241-5555.

All the best trips start with Fodor's.

EXPLORING GUIDES

At last, the color of an art book combined with the usefulness of a complete guide.

"As stylish and attractive as any guide published."
—*The New York Times*

"Worth reading before, during, and after a trip."
—*The Philadelphia Inquirer*

More than 30 destinations available worldwide. $19.95 each.

BERKELEY GUIDES

The budget traveler's handbook

"Berkeley's scribes put the funk back in travel." —*Time*

"Fresh, funny, and funky as well as useful."
—*The Boston Globe*

"Well-organized, clear and very easy to read."
—*America Online*

14 destinations worldwide. Priced between $13.00 - $19.50.
($17.95 - $27.00 Canada)

AFFORDABLES

"All the maps and itinerary ideas of Fodor's established Gold Guides with a bonus—shortcuts to savings."
—*USA Today*

"Travelers with champagne tastes and beer budgets will welcome this series from Fodor's."
—*Hartford Courant*

"It's obvious these Fodor's folk have secrets we civilians don't." —*New York Daily News*

Also available: Florida, Europe, France, London, Paris. Priced between $11.00 - $18.00 ($14.50 - $24.00 Canada).

At bookstores, or call **1-800-533-6478**

The name that means smart travel.™

or expensive purifiers, but the best idea is to stick to bottled water. Don't assume, however, that water or fruit drinks sold in nice restaurants is purified. However, if you spend your whole trip consuming only what appears sterile, you'll miss out. The best strategy is to give your immune system a little time to get used to the new challenges it faces by exercising restraint during the first week or so of your trip.

For up-to-the-minute information about health risks and disease precautions in all parts of the world, you can call the U.S. Centers for Disease Control's 24-hour **International Travelers' Hotline** (tel. 404/332-4559). You can listen to recorded information or receive faxes of current reports. The **Department of State's Citizens Emergency Center** (Bureau of Consular Affairs, Room 4811, N.S., U.S. Dept. of State, Washington, DC 20520, tel. 202/647-5225, modem 202/647-9125 or 202/647-3000) provides written and recorded travel advisories. The "return fax line" offers you several prompts and will return information immediately to your fax number.

BEFORE YOU GO Use your upcoming trip as an excuse to update routine immunizations. These include measles, mumps, rubella, diphtheria, tetanus, pertussis, polio, haemophilus influenza, and hepatitis B. Also consider updating your influenza and pneumococcal vaccines. Immune globulin (IG) is suggested if you are traveling to underdeveloped countries that may have dubious sanitation. Beyond that, the vaccines you should get are determined by your specific destinations and a careful consideration of the vaccines' effectiveness and side effects. Be sure to check with your physician to be sure you get all of the shots you need and are able to take before you go. If your doctor isn't familiar with the risks associated with travel in your destination, you might be better off at a travel clinic (sometimes located in international airports). Ask your doctor to suggest one.

Finally, compared to the risks of malaria and dengue fever, sunburn may not seem very important, but you're much more likely to suffer from a painful sunburn than any exotic disease. Even if you have a dark complexion, bring plenty of powerful sunscreen, and slather it on at every opportunity.

➤ **HEALTH AND ACCIDENT INSURANCE** • Some general health-insurance plans cover health expenses incurred while traveling, so review your existing health policies (or a parent's policy, if you're a dependent) before leaving home. Most university health-insurance plans stop and start with the school year, so don't count on school spirit to pull you through. Canadian travelers should check with their provincial ministry of health to see if their resident health-insurance plan covers them on the road.

Organizations such as STA and Council (*see* Budget Travel Organizations, *above*), as well as some credit-card conglomerates, include health-and-accident coverage with the purchase of an ID or credit card. If you purchase an ISIC card you're automatically insured for $100 a day for in-hospital sickness expenses, up to $3,000 for accident-related medical expenses, and $25,000 for emergency medical evacuation. For details, request a summary of coverage from Council (205 East 42nd St., New York, NY 10017, tel. 212/661-1414). Council Travel and STA also offer short-term insurance coverage designed specifically for the budget traveler. Otherwise, several private companies offer coverage designed to supplement existing traveler health insurance; for more details contact your favorite student travel organization or one of the agencies listed below.

Other reputable organizations worth checking into include **Carefree Travel Insurance** (100 Garden City Plaza, Box 9366, Garden City, NY 11530, tel. 516/294-0220 or 800/323-3149), **International SOS Assistance** (Box 11568, Philadelphia, PA 19116, tel. 215/244-1500 or 800/523-8930), **Travel Guard** (1145 Clark St., Stevens Point, WI 54481, tel. 715/345-0505 or 800/782-5151), and **Wallach & Company** (107 W. Federal St., Box 480, Middleburg, VA 22117, tel. 800/237-6615, fax 703/687-3172).

➤ **MEDICAL ASSISTANCE** • Mexico has socialized medicine, and, happily, travelers can take advantage of this. Nearly every city or town has a **Centro de Salud** (government health center) or **Cruz Roja** (Red Cross) office, where you can receive free emergency medical care.

The surroundings may look less than sanitary, but the visit and any drugs you may need are free. English-speaking doctors are found only in larger cities; a list of them is usually available from your embassy, in local tourist offices, or in the phone book. In smaller places, bring your dictionary—English-speaking doctors are rare. To better inform yourself before you go, or to have an emergency number handy, contact the organizations below.

International Association for Medical Assistance to Travellers (IAMAT) offers free membership (donations are much appreciated) and entitles you to a worldwide directory of qualified English-speaking physicians who are on 24-hour call and who have agreed to a fixed-fee schedule. Also helpful are IAMAT's health pamphlets, such as the frequently updated "World Climate Chart," "World Malaria Risk Chart," and "World Immunization Chart." *United States: 417 Center St., Lewiston, NY 14092, tel. 716/754–4883. Canada: 40 Regal Rd., Guelph, Ont. N1K 1B5, tel. 519/836–0102. Switzerland: 57 Voirets, 1212 Grand-Lancy-Geneva. New Zealand: Box 5049, Christchurch 5.*

British travelers can join **Europ Assistance Worldwide Services** (252 High St., Croyden, Surrey CR0 1NF, tel. 0181/680–1234) to gain access to a 24-hour, 365-day-a-year telephone hotline that can help in a medical emergency. The American branch of this organization is **Travel Assistance International** (1133 15th St. NW, Suite 400, Washington, D.C. 20005, tel. 800/821–2828), which offers emergency evacuation services and 24-hour medical referrals. An individual membership costs $62 for up to 15 days, $164 for 60 days.

Medic Alert offers an internationally recognized identification bracelet and necklace that indicate the bearer's medical condition, drug allergies, or current medication information. It also provides the number of Medic Alert's 24-hour hotline, through which members' medical histories are available. Lifetime membership in the United States is yours for the cost of the ID bracelet or necklace ($35–$75). *Medic Alert Foundation International, Box 1009, Turlock, CA 95381, tel. 800/432–5378; in Canada, tel. 800/668–1507; in southern Australia, tel. 618/274–0422; in western Australia, tel. 619/277–9999; in New Zealand, tel. 644/528–8219; in the U.K., tel. 4471/833–3034.*

Diabetic travelers should contact one of the following organizations for resources and medical referrals: **American Diabetes Association** (1660 Duke St., Alexandria, VA 22314, tel. 703/549–1500 or 800/232–3472), **Canadian Diabetes Association** (15 Toronto St., Suite 1001, Toronto, Ont. M5C 2E3, tel. 416/363–3373), and **International Diabetes Federation** (International Association Centre, Rue Washington 40, B-1050 Brussels, Belgium, tel. 02/647–4414 or fax 032/2649–3269). *The Diabetic Traveler* (1596 Washington Blvd., Stamford, CT 06902, tel. 203/327–5832), published four times a year, lists vacations geared toward diabetics and offers travel and medical advice. Subscriptions are $18.95. An informative article entitled "Management of Diabetes During Intercontinental Travel" and an insulin adjustment card are available for free.

➢ **PRESCRIPTIONS** • Some drugs sold in the States by prescription only are sold over the counter in Mexico. Just to be on the safe side, however, bring as much as you need of any prescription drugs as well as your written prescription (packed separately). Ask your doctor to type the prescription and include the following information: dosage, the generic name, and the manufacturer's name. To avoid problems clearing customs, diabetic travelers carrying syringes should have handy a letter from their physician confirming their need for insulin injections. No matter where you're traveling, most cities have at least one all-night pharmacy, and many that don't actually stay open advertise *servicio nocturno* (night service), meaning that someone sleeps on site and you can ring the doorbell and wake them up at all hours, should need arise.

➢ **FIRST-AID KIT** • For about 97% of your trip, a first aid kit may mean nothing to you but extra bulk. However, in an emergency you'll be glad to have even the most basic medical supplies. Prepackaged kits are available, but you can pack your own from the following list: bandages, waterproof surgical tape and gauze pads, antiseptic, cortisone cream, tweezers, a thermometer in a sturdy case, an antacid such as Alka-Seltzer, something for diarrhea (Pepto-Bismol or Immodium), and, of course, aspirin. If you're prone to motion sickness or are planning to use particularly rough modes of transportation during your travels, take along some Dramamine as well. No matter what your coloring, if you'll be exposed to sunlight for any length of time, pack sunscreen to protect against cancer-causing rays. Women: If prone to yeast infections, you can now buy over-the-counter medication (Monistat or Gynelotrimin) that will save you prolonged grief on the road. However, self-medicating should only be relied on for short-term illnesses; seek professional help if any medical symptoms persist or worsen.

➤ **CONTRACEPTIVES AND SAFE SEX** • AIDS and other STDs (sexually transmitted diseases) do not respect national boundaries, and protection when you travel takes the same forms as it does at home. If you are contemplating an exchange of bodily fluids, latex condoms and/or dental dams are the best forms of protection against STDs. If you're on the pill, be sure to fill your prescription before departure and bring enough to carry you through your trip; you may not be able to get the same dosage or type of pills in Mexico. Birth control in general can even be a touchy subject in this still predominantly Catholic country, and while you can buy it, you're probably better off bringing your own. Pack condoms or diaphragms in a pouch or case where they will not become squashed or damaged. Council Travel (*see* Budget Travel Organizations, *above*) distributes a free "AIDS and International Travel" brochure containing information on safe sex, HIV testing, and hotline numbers.

➤ **WOMEN'S MEDICAL AID** • Most towns have a medical center—and some larger ones have planning centers—at which gynecologists are on staff and most routine examinations can be performed, including pregnancy tests. In bigger cities, medical care is of higher quality, female doctors are more common, and doctors will often send you to a *clínica de analisis* (analysis clinic) for tests, which are generally inexpensive. Although abortions are practiced in private clinics and private hospitals, Mexico is not a safe place to get one. It's important to keep in mind that in addition to the fact that the doctor may not have appropriate or sanitary equipment, you're not insured should complications arise.

DISEASES FROM FOOD AND WATER Contaminated food and drink are the major causes of turista. The best treatment for diarrhea is rehydration plus rest. Plenty of liquid remedies are available at Mexican supermarkets and restaurants, including *té de manzanilla* (chamomile tea), *jugo de manzana* (apple juice), and other noncitrus fruit drinks. Avoid carbonated liquids, coffee, milk, cocoa, and alcohol. In severe cases, doctors will suggest an oral rehydration liquid that you can concoct yourself by mixing purified water with a few pinches of salt and a couple of teaspoons of sugar. If you're hungry, stick to small portions of dry toast, banana, and *caldo de pollo* (chicken broth); avoid greasy, spicy foods. The best cure for diarrhea is to let it pass out of your system, but if you are very uncomfortable or need to travel to your next location, ask a local doctor for prescription drugs or tell a pharmacist you need something for turista. Drugs such as Bactrim and Septra (available in the States) may help shorten the time you suffer. Lomotil or Imodium may decrease the number of trips you make to the toilet; however, if you have a serious infection, these drugs can cause more serious complications. If you maintain a fever over 102°F, if you have persistent vomiting, if you cannot rehydrate, if your stool is bloody, or if your bout lasts longer than a week, seek immediate medical attention.

To avoid this nasty annoyance, be sure to drink only boiled (20 minutes in higher elevations) or chemically disinfected water. Don't even brush your teeth with water that hasn't been treated. You can purchase water disinfectants such as Globaline and Potable-Aqua in the States before you leave. If your boiled water seems flat and tasteless, add a pinch of salt to bring back some taste. It may seem self evident, but do NOT add ice cubes to boiled water.

Also be careful in selecting your foods. Raw foods are often contaminated, so be wary of salads, uncooked produce, milk, and milk products. Meats and shellfish are usually suspect as well. To be on the safe side, peel fruit yourself, don't eat any cooked foods that have been allowed to cool, and avoid raw dishes such as ceviche. Many fish, such as reef fish, red snapper, amberjack, grouper, sea bass, barracuda, and puffer fish, should be avoided at all times due to the high levels of toxins in the areas they inhabit. You may think it safe to consume suspect foods if you see people of the region doing so, but think twice. These folks may have developed immune systems to combat sicknesses you aren't prepared for, or they may live with chronic illness themselves.

Cholera, a distressing intestinal infection, is caused by a bacterium carried in bad water or food. The vaccine is discouraged by U.S. Centers for Disease Control. It's characterized by profuse diarrhea, vomiting, cramping, and dehydration. If you think you may have contracted cholera, seek medical attention right away. Most people recuperate with simple fluid and electrolyte-replacement treatment—rehydration packets called *suero oral* are sold at any pharmacy. Cholera tends only to be a problem in the southern, poorer states—right now it's at epidemic proportions in some areas of Oaxaca, Chiapas, and the Yucatán Peninsula.

Typhoid, a bacterial infection common in Mexico, can be spread through contaminated food and water and through contact with contaminated people. Fever, headaches, exhaustion, loss of appetite, and constipation all indicate an onslaught of typhoid. If you think you have contracted typhoid, seek medical attention right away. Typhoid vaccine is available in oral form, taken over a week, and as a series of injections taken over a month. The vaccine is only about 70%–90% effective, so it is important to drink only bottled, boiled, or treated water and to eat foods that have been cooked thoroughly.

Hepatitis A, a viral infection that attacks the liver, is transmitted through contaminated food and water or between people. It causes exhaustion, fever, loss of appetite, queasiness, dark urine, jaundice, vomiting, light stools, and achiness. It is prevalent in rural areas of Mexico, and there is no specific treatment available. To avoid hepatitis A, be sure to drink only treated water and thoroughly cooked foods (are we getting through to you yet?). It is also a good idea to receive a dose of immune globulin (formerly known as gamma globulin) before traveling. Check with your doctor regarding dosage requirements for the length of your stay. Also, when you are in another country, be aware that what they advertise as immune globulin may not be equal to what you would receive in the United States.

INSECT-BORNE DISEASES Mexico—especially the southern states—is teeming with mosquitoes, flies, fleas, ticks, and lice, all ready to give travelers a mélange of foul diseases. For starters, you should reduce your exposure to mosquitoes by using mosquito netting and wearing clothes that cover most of your body. Beyond that, *bring the strongest insect repellent you can find and use it.* The CDC recommends DEET, and you can also purchase spray repellents and Permethrin, which can be sprayed on clothing and bedding. You'll still get nailed, but why surrender to the critters without a fight?

If all of this sounds a bit too much like chemical warfare to you, there are a few other options. Thanks to modern science, we know mosquitoes don't like the taste of vitamin B. By megadosing (using two to four times the recommended daily allowance) on B-complex vitamins daily for at least a month before your trip, you'll put enough of the stuff in your blood to make you a less delectable dish than your friends. It won't completely solve the problem, but most people who try notice the difference. Be warned, though, that taking large doses of vitamin B (or any other vitamin) can have side effects and may not be good for you in the long run. Your pee will be bright orange, too. Another option is to apply Avon "Skin-So-Soft" Moisturizer, which bugs can't stand. The Marines have been using the stuff for years.

Malaria thrives in many areas of Mexico. According to the CDC, the states with the highest incidence of malaria (in decreasing order) are: Oaxaca, Chiapas, Guerrero, Campeche, and Quintana Roo. Usually resembling a feverish flu at the onset, malaria's symptoms can include chills, aches, and weariness. It can lead to anemia, kidney failure, coma, and death if neglected. If you experience any of these symptoms while traveling or up to a year after exposure, seek medical attention. Unfortunately, the antimalaria drugs available aren't 100% effective. If you are going to a risky area, chloroquine or melfoquine are the recommended deterrents. Both drug regimens begin a week before you enter the malarious zone. Be sure to consult your doctor about side effects before taking either of these treatments.

Yellow fever, a viral disease spread by the bite of evening-feeding mosquitoes, is a very rare problem for tourists these days. It's characterized by headaches, chills, fever, and vomiting, and can develop into jaundice, internal bleeding, and kidney failure. There is no specific drug to treat this disease, so you may want to consider getting a vaccination (although Mexico does not require a yellow fever vaccine certificate before being allowed to enter the country) before you leave—consult your doctor before receiving this one-dose shot.

Dengue Fever is transmitted by the aedes mosquito, which, unlike other mosquitoes, is most active during the day and around dawn and dusk. Dengue usually becomes epidemic during and after rainy seasons. It is most common in urban areas, especially below an elevation of 4,000 feet, but is found in rural areas as well. Since there is no vaccine, the best way to avoid dengue is to protect yourself from mosquito attacks: Wear clothes that do not leave you exposed, sleep under mosquito netting, and slather on that insect repellant. Dengue suddenly manifests itself with flu-like characteristics, a high fever, severe headache, joint and muscle aches, nausea, and vomiting. About three or four days after the fever appears, a rash develops. There is no vaccination for dengue, and treatment is simple rest, fluid intake, and over-the-counter fever-reducing medications. Avoid aspirin. Dengue lasts for up to ten days, and full recovery may take up to a month. There are more intense and rare forms of dengue that are characterized by faintness, shock, and general bleeding. If you develop any of these symptoms during your trip or up to a month after your return, visit your doctor immediately.

OTHER DISEASES In addition to all the diseases and viruses Mexico has to offer, **parasites** abound. They are transmitted through bad food and water, directly through contact with infected water and soil, or by insect bites. Again, be sure to use precautions to avoid insect bites, drink and eat foods you know are safe, and be sure to wear shoes to avoid direct penetration. **Rabies** is also a concern in Mexico for anyone traveling in rural regions or areas with large dog populations. Rabies is a viral infection, contracted by the bite of an infected animal, that attacks the central nervous system. A pre-exposure rabies vaccination series provides adequate initial protection, but, if you are bitten by a potentially rabid animal, you will need additional inoculations. Be safe, not sorry, and don't pet stray dogs, cats, or other mammals.

RESOURCES FOR WOMEN

Foreign commentators (travel guides not least among them) are constantly referring to the chauvinism and sexual aggressiveness of Mexican men. And while this is largely a caricature, it's clear that Mexican *machismo* (probably most accurately translated as sexism) is not completely dismissable as a stereotype. Foreign women traveling alone in Mexico *do* tend to receive plenty of *piropos* (compliments) from total strangers, but there are few places in the world where they don't. Your best resource is common sense, especially where safety is concerned. If you are traveling alone, don't let your gender prevent you from adventuring, but think twice about hitchhiking or camping solo.

ORGANIZATIONS **Pacific Harbor Travel** (519 Seabright Ave., Suite 201, Santa Cruz, CA 95062, tel. 408/427–5000) specializes in independent adventure travel with an emphasis on women's travel. They're one of the better known agencies for women's travel. **Women Welcome Women (WWW)** (Contact F. Alexander, 8/A Chestnut Ave., High Wycombe, Buckinghamshire HP11 1DJ, England) is a nonprofit organization aimed at bringing together women of all nationalities. WWW can get you in touch with women around the globe who are interested in every variety of women's issues. **Woodswomen** (25 W. Diamond Lake Rd., Minneapolis, MN 55419, tel. 612/822–3809 or 800/279–0555, fax 612/822–3814) specializes in adventure travel for women of all ages. This nonprofit organization, which claims to be the largest and most extensive women's travel outfit in the world, organizes safe, educational, and environmental excursions for their members. Yearly membership donations start at $20.

PUBLICATIONS Along with the lesbian-oriented *Women's Traveller* and *Are You Two . . . Together?,* major travel publications for women include *Women Travel: Adventures, Advice, and Experience* ($12.95), published by Prentice Hall and available at bookstores. Over 70 countries receive some sort of coverage in the form of journal entries and short articles. As far as practical travel information goes, it offers few details on prices, phone numbers, and addresses. Thalia Zepatos's *A Journey of One's Own* ($13), available at most bookstores, is fun to read but has little information on Mexico. Still, it's a good resource for general travel info.

RESOURCES FOR PEOPLE OF COLOR

Mexico is both racially diverse and very stratified. While exceptions certainly exist, in general the elite is almost entirely white, the middle class is *mestizo* (of mixed descent), and the substantial Indian population lives for the most part in rural poverty. This said, racism is not likely to be a significant problem for travelers. The worst thing you are likely to encounter is curiosity. Black and Asian people are rare enough in some parts of Mexico that they can receive some undue attention. Absurd questions, such as "Why are you black?" may be unsettling, but it is important to realize that they are generally quite harmless and simply stem from unfamiliarity. Keep in mind that other travelers encounter similar situations irrespective of color.

RESOURCES FOR GAYS AND LESBIANS

Gender roles in Mexico are pretty rigidly defined, especially in rural areas. Openly gay couples are a rare sight, and two people of the same gender sometimes have trouble getting a *cama matrimonial* (double bed) even in places accustomed to receiving a lot of tourists. This could be attributed to the influence of the Catholic Church—Mexico is a devoutly Catholic country, and the Church has historically exerted a powerful influence on both Mexican politics and the mores and attitudes of the Mexican people. However, the same rules that apply all over the world apply in Mexico: Alternative lifestyles (whether they be homosexuality or any other bending of conventional roles) are more easily accepted in metropolitan centers such as Acapulco, Guadalajara, and Mexico City.

ORGANIZATIONS The **International Gay Travel Association (IGTA)** (Box 4974, Key West, FL 33041, tel. 800/448-8550, fax 395/286-6533) is a nonprofit organization that lists travel agents in your area who can provide tips or arrange tours for just about any area in Mexico. The **International Lesbian and Gay Association (ILGA)** (81 Rue Marche au Charbon, 1000 Brussels 1, Belgium, tel. 02/502-24-71) is an excellent source for info about conditions, specific resources, and trouble spots in dozens of countries.

PUBLICATIONS The *Damron Address Book* ($13.95 plus shipping) is an excellent resource focusing on gay male travel in a variety of destinations including Mexico, the United States, Canada, and parts of Central America. The folks at their office can also sell you a copy of *Spartacus* ($29.95), which bills itself as *the* guide for the gay/lesbian traveler, with practical tips and reviews of hotels and agencies in over 160 countries, including info on hotspots in Mexico. *Box 422458, San Francisco, CA 94142, tel. 415/255-0404 or 800/462-6654.*

The guidebook *Places of Interest,* published by Ferrari, includes listings for accommodations and nightlife, as well as general articles about gay/lesbian culture in Mexico and elsewhere. To order, send a check or money order for $19.50. *Box 37887, Phoenix, AZ, 85069, tel. 602/863-2408.*

One of the better gay and lesbian travel newsletters is *Out and About,* with listings of gay-friendly hotels and travel agencies, plus health cautions for travelers with HIV. A 10-issue subscription costs $49; single issues cost about $7. *Tel. 800/929-2268 for subscriptions.*

RESOURCES FOR THE DISABLED

Mexico is poorly equipped for disabled travelers. Most hotels and restaurants have at least a few steps and are not easily accessible. Rooms called "wheelchair accessible" by hotel owners are usually on the ground floor, but the doorways and bathroom may not be maneuverable. There are no special discounts or passes for disabled travelers in Mexico, nor is public transportation, including the Mexico City Metro, wheelchair accessible. Renting or bringing a car or van is your best bet. Roads and sidewalks are often crowded, in poor condition, and without ramps, and people on the street will not usually assist you unless expressly asked.

Whenever possible, reviews in this book will indicate whether establishments are wheelchair accessible. The best choice of accessible lodging is found in resorts like Acapulco and Mazatlán, as well as other tourist-frequented locations. It's a good idea to call ahead to find out what a hotel can offer. Keep in mind, though, that many hotel proprietors don't understand the notion of accessibility. Despite these barriers, disabled Mexicans manage to negotiate places that most travelers outside Mexico would not consider accessible.

ORGANIZATIONS Directions Unlimited (720 N. Bedford Rd., Bedford Hills, NY 10507, tel. 800/533–5343 or 914/241–1700 in NY) organizes individual and group tours for the disabled. **Flying Wheels Travel** (143 W. Bridge St., Box 382, Owatonna, MN 55060, tel. 800/535–6790 or 507/451–5005 in MN) arranges cruises, tours, and vacation travel itineraries. **Mobility International USA (MIUSA)** (Box 10767, Eugene, OR 97440, tel. and TYY 503/343–1284, fax 503/343–6812) is a nonprofit organization that coordinates exchange programs for disabled people around the world. MIUSA also offers information on accommodations and organized study programs for members ($25 annually). Nonmembers may subscribe to the newsletter for $15. **Moss Rehabilitation Hospital's Travel Information Service** (1200 W. Tabor Rd., Philadelphia, PA 19141, tel. 215/456–9900, TYY 215/456–9602) provides information on tourist sights, transportation, accommodations, and accessibility in destinations around the world. You can request information by phone only. The service is free.

PUBLICATIONS Twin Peaks Press specializes in books for the disabled, such as *Travel for the Disabled*, which offers helpful hints as well as a comprehensive list of guidebooks and facilities geared to the disabled. Their *Directory of Travel Agencies for the Disabled* lists more than 350 agencies throughout the world. Each is $19.95 plus $3 ($4.50 for both) shipping and handling. Twin Peaks also offers a "Traveling Nurse's Network," which connects disabled travelers with registered nurses to aid and accompany them on their trip. Travelers fill out an application that Twin Peaks matches to nurses' applications in their files. An application is $10. *Box 129, Vancouver, WA 98666, tel. 360/694–2462 or 800/637–2256 for orders only.*

WORKING IN MEXICO

If you have sea legs and happen to be headed where the wind is blowing, head down to the marina and ask about crew jobs. Waterside resorts are always eager to put gringos into the "career of a lifetime"—time shares. Demand also exists for English teachers and for English-speakers to work in posh hotels. Advertisements for such positions appear in newspaper classified ads, especially the English-language newspapers; also try calling language schools or hotels directly. The legal requirements for work are stringent (*see below*).

LEGAL REQUIREMENTS By law, a foreigner may legally work in Mexico only if contracted in his or her native country before arriving in Mexico. A Brit, for example, would need a work permit sponsored by his or her employer in England; the employer's affiliate in Mexico would process the permit and pave the way for the newcomer in Mexico. The process is very bureaucratic, and the professions with the best chance of success are those that require specific skills, such as engineering.

ORGANIZATIONS The easiest way to arrange work abroad is through Council's **Work Abroad Department** (205 E. 42nd St., New York, NY 10017, tel. 212/661–1414 ext. 1130). The program enables you to work abroad for three to six months. Participants must be U.S. citizens, 18 years or older, and full-time students for the semester preceding their stay overseas. Past participants have worked at all types of jobs, including hotel and restaurant work, office and sales help, and occasionally career-related internships. A good working knowledge of Spanish is required. The cost of the program is $160, which includes legal work permission documents, orientation and program materials, access to job and housing listings, and on-going support services overseas. Council's Work Abroad Program is only open to U.S. students; Canadians should contact **Travel CUTS** (*see Budget Travel Organizations, above*), which has similar programs for Canadian students who want to work abroad for up to six months.

The **YMCA** oversees a variety of international work exchanges in over 25 countries; the most popular is the **International Camp Counselor Program (ICCP)**, which entails teaching English, building houses, hanging out with local kids, you name it. The program rarely lasts longer than a summer, and participants stay at local YMCAs or with families. Don't expect to make much money. Write for a detailed brochure. *71 W. 23rd St., Suite 1904, New York, NY 10010, tel. 212/727–8800.*

PUBLICATIONS Council (*see* Budget Travel Organizations, *above*) publishes two excellent resource books with complete details on work/travel opportunities. The most valuable is **Work, Study, Travel Abroad: The Whole World Handbook** ($13.95), which gives the lowdown on scholarships, grants, fellowships, study-abroad programs, and work exchanges. Also worthwhile is Council's **The High-School Student's Guide to Study, Travel, and Adventure Abroad** ($13.95). Both books can be shipped to you book-rate ($1.50) or first-class ($3).

The U.K.-based Vacation Work Press publishes two first-rate guides to working abroad: **Directory of Overseas Summer Jobs** (£9) and Susan Griffith's **Work Your Way Around the World** (£12). The first lists over 45,000 jobs worldwide; the latter has fewer listings but makes a more interesting read. Look for them at bookstores, or contact the publisher directly. *9 Park East End, Oxford OX1 1HJ, England, tel. 0865/241978.*

STUDYING IN MEXICO

Many Mexican universities are open to foreigners for Spanish-language programs and general enrollment. Language schools are listed in the Basics sections for the cities where they exist, but the most popular (and consequently the most packed with English speakers) places to study are Cuernavaca and San Miguel de Allende, as well as the more cosmopolitan Mexico City and Guadalajara. For more information on options for study in Mexico, contact **The National Registration Center for Study Abroad** (823 N. 2nd St., Milwaukee, WI 53203, tel. 414/278–0631), Council's **College and University Programs Department** (205 E. 42nd St., New York, NY 10017, tel. 212/661–1414), or write or call the **Institute of International Education for Latin America** (Londres 16, Piso 2, Distrito Federal, CP, 06700, México, tel. 5/703–10–67 or 5/211–00–42; or Box 3087, Laredo, TX 78044-3089 in the U.S.).

VOLUNTEER PROGRAMS

ORGANIZATIONS Council's **Voluntary Services Department** (205 E. 42nd St., New York, NY 10017, tel. 212/661–1414, ext. 1139) offers two- to four-week environmental or community service projects in 22 countries around the globe. Participants must be 18 or older and pay a $165 placement fee. Council also publishes **Volunteer! The Comprehensive Guide to Voluntary Service in the U.S. and Abroad** ($12.95, plus $1.50 postage), which describes nearly 200 organizations around the world that offer volunteer positions.

At one time or another everyone considers joining the **Peace Corps** for two years of volunteer service abroad. You don't have to be an expert in your field, but you do need a college degree and a strong sense of commitment. Room and board is provided, along with a small monthly stipend. *1990 K St. NW, Washington, D.C. 20526, tel. 800/424–8580.*

Volunteers for Peace (VFP) sponsors two- to three-week international workcamps in the United States, Europe, Africa, Asia, and Central America for around $150. Send for their *International Workcamp Directory* ($10); it lists over 800 volunteer opportunities. *43 Tiffany Rd., Belmont, VT, 05730, tel. 802/259–2759, fax 802/259–2922.*

PUBLICATIONS Bill McMillon's **Volunteer Vacations** ($12.95) lists hundreds of organizations and volunteer opportunities in the United States and abroad. Look for it in your local bookstore. The Archaeological Institute of America annually publishes **Archaeological Fieldwork Opportunities,** a very detailed listing of field projects around the world. *656 Beacon St., Boston, MA 02215-2010, tel. 617/353–9361, fax 617/353–6550.*

Coming and Going

CUSTOMS AND DUTIES

ARRIVING IN MEXICO When going through customs, looking composed and presentable expedites the process. If you're bringing any foreign-made equipment with you from home, such as cameras or video gear, it's wise to carry the original receipt or register it with customs before leaving the United States (ask for U.S. Customs Form 4457). Otherwise, you may end up paying duty on your return. To avoid problems, don't even think about drugs. Being cited for drug possession is no joke, and embassies and consulates often can't do much to persuade country officials to release accused drug traffickers/users (see Crime and Punishment, below).

If you're arriving in Mexico City, you may be one of the one in 10 people whose luggage is searched. Before passing through customs you'll press a button in front of a small stoplight apparatus. If the resulting light is green, you can pass go; if it's red, officials search your baggage. You will be given a baggage-declaration form to itemize what you're bringing into the country. You're allowed to bring in three liters of spirits or wine for personal use, 400 cigarettes, two boxes of cigars, a reasonable amount of perfume for personal use, one movie camera and one regular camera, eight rolls of film for each, and gift items not to exceed a total of $120. There are no restrictions or limitations on the amount of cash, foreign currencies, checks, or drafts that can be imported or exported by visitors.

When passing through customs, it helps not to have one of the following: a nose ring, an eyebrow ring, long hair, facial hair, Doc Martens and/or a T-shirt reading "Gas, Grass, or Ass—no one rides for free."

RETURNING HOME It's best to have all the souvenirs and gifts you're bringing home in an easily accessible place, just in case officials would like to have a peek.

➢ **U.S. CUSTOMS** • Like most government organizations, the U.S. Customs Service enforces a number of mysterious rules that presumably make sense to some bureaucrat somewhere. You're unlikely to have run-ins with customs as long as you *never* carry any illegal drugs in your luggage. When you return to the United States you have to declare all items you bought abroad, but you won't have to pay duty unless you come home with more than $400 worth of foreign goods, including items bought in duty-free stores. For purchases between $400 and $1,000 you have to pay a 10% duty. You also have to pay tax if you exceed your duty-free allowances: one liter of alcohol or wine (for those 21 and over), 100 non-Cuban cigars or 200 cigarettes, and one bottle of perfume. A free leaflet about customs regulations and illegal souvenirs, "Know Before You Go," is available from the **U.S. Customs Service** (Box 7407, Washington, D.C. 20044, tel. 202/927-6724).

➢ **CANADIAN CUSTOMS** • Exemptions for returning Canadians range from $20 to $500, depending on how long you've been out of the country: for two days out, you're allowed to return with C$200 worth of goods; for one week out, you're allowed C$500 worth. Above these limits, you'll be taxed about 15%. Duty-free limits are: up to 50 cigars, 200 cigarettes, 400 grams of tobacco, and 1.14 liters of liquor—all must be declared in writing upon arrival at customs and must be with you or in your checked baggage. To mail back gifts, label the package: "Unsolicited Gift–Value under C$60." For more scintillating details, call the automated information line of the **Revenue Canada Customs, Excise and Taxation Department** (2265 St. Laurent Blvd. S., Ottawa, Ont., K1G 4K3, tel. 613/993-0534 or 991-3881), where you may request a copy of the Canadian Customs brochure "I Declare/Je Déclare."

➢ **U.K. CUSTOMS** • Travelers age 17 or over who return to the United Kingdom may bring back the following duty-free goods: 200 cigarettes or 100 cigarillos or 50 cigars or 250 grams of tobacco; one liter of alcohol over 22% volume or two liters of alcohol under 22% volume, plus two liters of still table wine; 60 ml of perfume and 250 ml of toilet water; and other goods worth up to £136. If returning from another EU country, you can choose, instead, to bring in the following, provided they were *not* bought in a duty-free shop: 300 cigarettes or 150 cigarillos or 75 cigars or 400 grams of tobacco; 1.5 liters of alcohol over 22% volume or three liters of alcohol under 22% volume, plus five liters of still table wine; 75 grams of perfume and ⅜ liter of toilet water; and other goods worth up to £250. For further information or a copy of "A Guide for Travellers," which details standard customs procedures as well as what you may bring into the United Kingdom from abroad, contact **HM Customs and Excise** (Dorset House, Stamford St., London SE1 9PY, tel. 0171/928-3344).

➢ **AUSTRALIAN CUSTOMS** • Australian travelers 18 and over may bring back, duty free: one liter of alcohol; 250 grams of tobacco products (equivalent to 250 cigarettes or cigars); and other articles worth up to $AUS400. If you're under 18, your duty-free allowance is $AUS200. To avoid paying duty on goods you mail back to Australia, mark the package: "Australian goods returned." For more rules and regulations, request the pamphlet "Customs Information for Travellers" from a local **Collector of Customs** (GPO Box 8, Sydney NSW 2001, tel. 02/226–5997).

➢ **NEW ZEALAND CUSTOMS** • Although greeted with a "*Haere Mai*" ("Welcome to New Zealand"), homeward-bound travelers face a number of restrictions. Travelers over age 17 are allowed, duty-free: 200 cigarettes or 250 grams of tobacco or 50 cigars or a combo of all three up to 250 grams; 4.5 liters of wine or beer and one 1,125-ml. bottle of spirits; and goods with a combined value up to NZ$700. If you want more details, ask for the pamphlet "Customs Guide for Travellers" from a New Zealand consulate.

BY AIR

On your fateful departure day, remember that check-in time for international flights is a long two hours before the scheduled departure. One more news bulletin: Flights lasting more than six hours are smoking flights—so if fumes make you queasy, book short air-hops or ask for seats as far away from the smoking section as possible; if you love to light up, book long and straight.

FROM THE UNITED STATES Airlines serving Mexico with direct flights from major U.S. cities include **Aerocalifornia** (tel. 800/237–6225) from Los Angeles; **Aeroméxico** (tel. 800/237–6639) from Houston, Los Angeles, Miami, New York, and Tucson; **American** (tel. 800/433–7300) from Dallas/Fort Worth, Miami, and Raleigh/Durham; **Continental** (tel. 800/525–0280) from Houston and Newark; **Delta** (tel. 800/345–3400) from Atlanta, Dallas/Fort Worth, Los Angeles, and Orlando; **Mexicana** (tel. 800/531–7921) from Chicago, Denver, Los Angeles, Miami, Newark, San Antonio, San Francisco, and San Jose; **Northwest** (tel. 800/225–2525) from Detroit, Minneapolis, and Tampa; and **United** (tel. 800/241–6522) from Chicago, Dulles/Washington, Los Angeles, and San Francisco.

One of the cheapest ways to get to Mexico from the West Coast of the United States is on a Mexicana Airlines red-eye, appropriately nicknamed *El Tecolote* (The Owl), which flies from San Francisco and Los Angeles to Guadalajara and Mexico City. Other cheap flights depart from southern California and are bound for Tijuana, where travelers grab a domestic flight to their final destination. If you're on your way to Mexico from Europe, it is generally cheapest to fly to a U.S. city first, and then connect to a Mexico-bound flight. When homeward-bound, be prepared to pay a departure tax of $12 (payable in cash only) at the airport.

LUGGAGE You've heard it a million times. Now you'll hear it once again: Pack light. U.S. airlines allow passengers to check two pieces of luggage, neither of which can exceed 62 inches (length + width + height) or weigh more than 70 pounds. If your airline accepts excess baggage, it will probably charge you for it. Foreign-airline policies vary, so call or check with a travel agent before you show up at the airport with one bag too many. If you're traveling with a pack, tie all loose straps to each other or onto the pack itself, as they tend to get caught in luggage conveyer belts. Put valuables like cameras and important documents in the middle of packs, wadded inside clothing, because outside pockets are extremely vulnerable to probing fingers.

Bikes in Flight

Most airlines will ship bikes as luggage, provided they are dismantled and put into a box. Call to see if your airline sells bike boxes (around $10). International travelers can substitute a bike for the second piece of checked luggage at no extra charge; otherwise, it will cost $100 extra. Domestic flights are less gracious and uniformly charge bike-toting travelers a $45 fee.

Anything you'll need during the flight (and valuables to be kept under close surveillance) should be stowed in a carry-on bag. Foreign airlines have different policies but generally allow only one carry-on in tourist class, in addition to a handbag and a bag filled with duty-free goodies. The carry-on bag cannot exceed 45 inches (length + width + height) and must fit under the seat or in the overhead luggage compartment. Call for the airline's current policy. Passengers on U.S. airlines are limited to one carry-on bag, plus coat, camera, and handbag. Carry-on bags must fit under the seat in front of you; maximum dimensions are 9 x 45 x 22 inches. Hanging bags can have a maximum dimension of 4 x 23 x 45 inches; to fit in an overhead bin, bags can have a maximum dimension of 10 x 14 x 36 inches. If your bag is too porky for compartments, be prepared for the humiliation of rejection and last-minute baggage check.

Anything you'll need during the flight (and valuables to be kept under close surveillance) should be stowed in a carry-on bag. Foreign airlines have different policies but generally allow only one carry-on in tourist class, in addition to a handbag and a bag filled with duty-free goodies. The carry-on bag cannot exceed 45 inches (length + width + height) and must fit under the seat or in the overhead luggage compartment. Call for the airline's current policy. Passengers on U.S. airlines are limited to one carry-on bag, plus coat, camera, and handbag. Carry-on bags must fit under the seat in front of you; maximum dimensions are 9 x 45 x 22 inches. Hanging bags can have a maximum dimension of 4 x 23 x 45 inches; to fit in an overhead bin, bags can have a maximum dimension of 10 x 14 x 36 inches. If your bag is too porky for compartments, be prepared for the humiliation of rejection and last-minute baggage check.

BY CAR

Bringing a car into Mexico has become seriously complicated. The owner of the vehicle must provide proof of ownership, state registration, and a valid driver's license issued outside Mexico. The owner must also provide a credit card number (American Express, Visa, Diner's Club, or MasterCard) or a bond as security against selling the car while in Mexico. All documents and credit cards must be in the name of the owner, who must be driving the car. If your permit runs out or you are found without the proper documents, your car can be immediately confiscated. However, these restrictions only apply for bringing a car into mainland Mexico—Baja is trouble-free motoring. The foreign insurance on your car is not valid in Mexico. Mexican insurance is sold by the day near border crossings; rates are approximately $10 per day with liability only, $14 for full coverage. Prices will vary with the value of the car, and rates get cheaper the longer the period of coverage. The border officials do not care if you buy any or not, but a cop farther south (or anyone with whom you are involved in an accident) very well might.

Compared to bus and train ticket prices in Mexico, renting a car there is outrageously expensive unless you share the cost with other travelers.

A VW is probably your best bet for Mexican car travel. (The Beetle was manufactured just outside Puebla and remains the most popular car in Mexico.) Avoid fuel-injection engines if you have a choice: The simpler the car, the better. Parts and knowledgeable mechanics can be extremely hard to find for European cars such as BMWs, Saabs, Volvos, and Citroëns, and high-priced American models. Road conditions in Mexico are variable: Big (and often very expensive) toll roads between most major cities are often in perfect condition, while some areas have only rutted, poorly marked roads and terrible traffic. Two excellent road atlases published in Mexico are Pemex's *Atlas de Carreteras y Ciudades Turísticas* and another put out by Guía Roji. Both of these are widely available in bookstores and at newsstands.

RENTAL CARS If you want to rent in the United States and drive down to Mexico, you'll find rental companies less than obliging. You can rent a car from Avis (tel. 800/331–1084) in Yuma, Arizona, or San Diego, California, and drive it into Mexico, but only in the Baja Peninsula and only for a maximum of 450 miles round-trip. **Dollar** (tel. 800/800–4000) will allow you to drive 150 miles into Mexico from San Diego or from McAllen, Texas, only as far as Monterrey. Finally, **Thrifty** (tel. 800/367–2277) allows you to drive from San Diego into Mexico, but only for 70 kilometers.

If your travel dates are fairly rigid, setting up a car rental through an agency in the United States is a cheaper alternative to renting south of the border. You will save at least $10 per day and will be assured of actually getting a car. Check with agencies to see if they have branches in the Mexican city you desire; **Avis** (tel. 800/331–1212), **Budget** (tel. 800/527–0700), **Dollar** (tel. 800/800–4000), **Hertz** (tel. 800/654– 3001), and **National** (tel. 800/227–3876) all rent cars in Mexico, and their prices are basically the same. Each of these companies requires you to purchase Mexican insurance (usually about $20 per day), and all rental agencies add a 10% tax to the price. An average rate for a Volkswagen Beetle with stick shift, unlimited mileage, and basic insurance coverage is $50–$60 per day. Most agencies rent only to drivers 25 years old or over, but some have lower age requirements in Mexico than in the United States. For example, you need only be 21 years old at Avis and 22 at National (though you do need two major credit cards). Cash or credit cards are usually accepted as payment.

BY BUS

Unless you're on a tour, such as those run by Green Tortoise (*see below*), you can't get a direct bus into Mexico. Rather, you must trundle down to the border, cross, and then change to a Mexican bus on the other side to continue your journey (*see* Getting Around By Bus, *below*). **Greyhound** (tel. 800/231–2222) serves El Paso, Del Rio, Laredo, McAllen, San Antonio, Eagle Pass, and Brownsville, Texas; Nogales, Arizona; and Calexico and San Diego, California. Their sole Mexican destination is Tijuana. Otherwise, Greyhound will get you to, but not across, the border; you'll have to pick up a Mexican bus on the other side.

Amtrak (tel. 800/872–7245) will get you as far as San Diego, El Paso, or San Antonio. The **San Diego Trolley** (tel. 619/231–8549) will take you from the city to the border for $1.75. Once in Tijuana, you can catch a bus to just about anywhere in Mexico. From San Antonio, you'll have to catch another bus to Laredo, on the border. From El Paso or Laredo, you'll be able to walk across the border.

Green Tortoise Adventure Travel (494 Broadway, San Francisco, CA 94133, tel. 415/821–0803 or 800/867–8647 outside CA) is the cheap alternative to humdrum bus travel. From November through April, Green Tortoise buses—equipped with sleeping pads, kitchens, and stereos—offer 14-day trips from the West Coast of the United States to Baja. In November and December, limited space is available for longer trips to Mexico City, Mérida, and Guatemala.

Staying in Mexico

GETTING AROUND

BY BUS Bus travel throughout Mexico is cheap and easy (*see* How Much it Will Cost, *above*). Buses are basically divided into first and second class, but in reality run the gamut from dilapidated school buses with shrines to the Virgin of Guadalupe attached to the grill and blasting *ranchera* music, to luxury liners with on-board movies. Most of the time, however, second-class means a comfortable bus with no air-conditioning that makes a number of stops, while first-class service consists of a similar bus, chilled beyond reason, and a direct ride. The super-deluxe buses are usually designated *plus* or *especial*. These can get pretty pricey, but in general the difference in price between first and second class is minimal.

BY TRAIN Of all the forms of transport in Mexico, trains have the worst reputation: notoriously run-down, slow, late, and a haven for thieves. Depending on the type of train and route, they can arrive absurdly late or leave absurdly early, but they are always slower than buses. There are several classes of service, not all of which are available for any given route. Special first class usually has air-conditioning and functioning bathrooms with water. A limited number of expensive sleeper cars are available on some trains offering special first class. Buying a ticket is also a uniquely frustrating experience, as ticket offices are often closed most of the day, generally until trains actually roll in. Advantages to train travel include great scenery, a certain romantic air, and a leisurely pace.

BY CAR Go where you want to, when you want to, roll the windows down, and pop in your favorite tape as you cruise down the highway. Sounds heavenly, but be ready for anything: Driving in a foreign country is always an adventure, and the quality of Mexican roads varies substantially. Drivers need a current license and registration, as well as a vehicle permit from border officials for cars not registered in Mexico. For the lowdown on permit procedures, *see* Coming and Going By Car, *above*. Roadside emergency service is available in much of the country from the **Green Angels,** a group of radio-dispatched, English-speaking mechanics. If you break down, pull over and pop your hood up; one will come cruising along if you wait long enough and pray hard enough. Service is free.

The maximum speed on most highways is 100 kilometers per hour (120 on some expressways). On smaller roads, however, you'll be lucky to do half that, as many roads, even those connecting major towns, are single-lane routes clogged with smoke-belching trucks. Trucks will often help you out by flashing their turn signals to let you know that it is safe to pass. Driving at night is discouraged, as roads are often poorly marked and, in rural areas, animals wandering onto roadways can be a major hazard. If you have an accident, notify the police immediately; take pictures of all cars involved; and, if possible, collect information from the other driver (provided he or she hasn't driven away). Even if the accident wasn't your fault, the rule in Mexico is "guilty until proven innocent," and the police will not necessarily take your word as gospel if the other driver blames you. Photos will strengthen your case.

You are required to stop and show your personal and vehicle documents at *all* roadside customs checkpoints. You are also required to stop anytime a police officer waves you over, but be cautious: Travelers are the favorite targets of robbers who pose as police officers. Highways 1 and 15 in Sinaloa have become infamous due to the high incidence of this sort of robbery. As for gas, since Pemex is Mexico's state-owned oil monopoly, all the gas you buy will be Pemex. Quality is low, so you may hear some unfamiliar engine knocks. Pemex's unleaded *Magna Sin* gas should be safe for most vehicles requiring unleaded gasoline. Gas prices are also considerably higher than in the States. Fill up when you see a station, since the next one may have a broken pump.

The **Asociación Mexicana Automovilística (AMA),** Mexico's motoring club, provides roadside repairs, fuel and tire service, plus free towing (up to 10 km) in Mexico City, Puebla, and Cuernavaca to any tourist in need. *Orizaba 7, Col. Roma, Distrito Federal, CP 06700, México, tel. 5/511–62–85. Emergency tel. 5/588–70–40 or 5/761–60–22.*

BY MOTORCYCLE Motorcycling conditions in Mexico are not ideal. Roads are not always in the best condition, but there are plenty of long stretches to open up the bike and enjoy watching the land whiz by. Small dirt bikes are good for bouncing around the desert. For best results, though, bring your own bike, because rentals are quite expensive. You should know how to do your own repairs and bring plenty of supplies. As with any vehicle in Mexico, avoid driving at night.

BY PLANE Domestic plane travel is expensive. You'll save travel time, but it will cost about four times as much as a first-class bus. **Mexicana** and **Aeroméxico** are government-subsidized and offer similar fares. (Unfortunately, no discounts are available on any flights.) **Aerocalifornia** (tel. 5/514–6678 in Mexico City) flies between Baja California cities and some places in northwestern Mexico. **Aerolitoral** serves various destinations in northwest Mexico, including Los Mochis and La Paz. **Aeromar** (tel. 5/574–9211 in Mexico City) flies from Mexico City to Guadalajara. **Aerocaribe** and **Aviacsa** operate in southeast Mexico.

BY BIKE Bike travel in Mexico is for the hardy and experienced rider. Some roads have never seen a bicycle, and drivers are not used to bikers. In addition, most Mexican roads lack shoulders and are often pitted. Don't expect to find rental outfits, either; if available, rental bikes will probably be granny-style relics good for short excursions only. Despite these drawbacks, traveling by bike in Mexico can be fun if you plan ahead. Bikes are especially useful for travel to places where there are only dirt roads or tracks, or where public transportation is scant. In the Yucatán, for example, bikes are a primary form of transportation for locals, and bike-repair shops are common even in smaller towns. When planning your trip, consult an up-to-date AAA, Pemex, or Guía Roji map. Be sure to carry plenty of water and everything you might need to repair your bike. Pack extra patch kits as shards of glass often litter the roads. If you can take your bike apart and fold it up, buses will allow you to store it in the cargo space. Bikers in the Copper Canyon can transport their bikes on the trains.

Some adventurous cyclists have organized tours of Baja; write to **The Touring Exchange** (Box 265, Port Townsend, WA, 98368) for details. **Backroads Bicycle Touring** (1516 5th St., Berkeley, CA 94710–1740, tel. 800/245–3874) offers trips around Baja and the Yucatán. If you go on your own and plan on biking only part of the way, Amtrak will transport your bike to the border. They provide the bike box, but require you to disassemble the bike. A good book that explores the coastal route from Canada to Mexico is *Bicycling the Pacific Coast,* by Tom Kirkendall and Vicky Spring (The Mountaineers, 306 2nd Ave. W, Seattle, WA 98119; $12.95).

HITCHING Hitchhikers are a rarity in northern Mexico and in densely populated urban areas. Near resort areas in Baja and rural areas of southern Mexico, hitching is more common and probably safer. Reports of robberies and violence come from all parts of the country, though, so keep your belongings and your wits close by, and don't hitch alone if you can possibly avoid it. Offer gas money and be somewhat flexible, but never accept a ride if you are unsure about the driver. Always be aware of your location and options. Don't hesitate to tell a driver to stop if you feel at all unsafe, and try not to sit in between people, so you're free to bolt if necessary.

PHONES

Like some other public services in the country, Mexican phones are a crap shoot. Your experiences will vary with the phone, the place, the time, and perhaps the alignment of the heavens that particular day. Many different options for making phone calls exist, but none are completely reliable everywhere. Simply put: Calling out of Mexico can be a challenging, frustrating, and expensive experience.

The country code for Mexico is **52**. The city code for Mexico City is 5. Dial 02 for the domestic operator in Mexico; 09 for the international operator (who should speak English or be able to find someone who does); 04 for local information; and 01 for long-distance information. You can dial long-distance calls directly: to the United States, dial 95 + area code + number; direct to the rest of the world, dial 98 + country code + city code + number; direct to other parts of Mexico, dial 91 + number. Long-distance carriers in the United States often have direct numbers that you can dial to access an operator to place a collect or calling-card call. Ask your carrier if they have an access number *before* departure. **AT&T**'s is 95 + 800/462–4240; **Sprint**'s is 95 + 800/877–8000.

CALLING WITHIN MEXICO Public phones are found all over most Mexican cities. Not so common is a pay phone that works. Calling within cities is pretty cheap, but long-distance calls can add up fast. For local or long-distance calls, another possibility is to find a *caseta de larga distancia,* a telephone service usually operated out of a store such as a *papelería* (stationery store), pharmacy, restaurant, or other small business; look for the phone symbol on the door. Most casetas charge you even to make a collect call, so it's better to call collect (*al cobrar*) from a pay phone, if possible.

In some areas, pay phones also accept pre-paid cards, called **Ladatel** cards, sold in 10-, 30-, or 50-peso denominations (approximately $1.75, $5, or $8.25) at newsstands or pharmacies. To use a Ladatel card, simply insert it in the slot of a silver **Multitarjetas** phone, dial 95 (for calls to the States), and the area code and number you're trying to reach. Credit is deleted from the card as you use it, and your balance is displayed on a small screen on the phone so you can keep tabs on how much you've got left.

INTERNATIONAL CALLS For an international collect or calling-card call, dial the long-distance operator (09), wait as long as 30 minutes for the bilingual long-distance operator to pick up the line, and give him or her the number you want to call and your name or card number, as appropriate. You can also use a Latadel card (*see above*) to make an international call. Casetas de larga distancia may cost more to use than pay phones, but you have a better chance of immediate success. To make the call, write down the number you'd like to call, and the person on duty will give you a rate and dial for you. Rates seem to vary widely, so shop around. Sometimes you can make collect calls (*al cobrar* or. *cobrada*) from casetas, and sometimes you cannot, depending on the individual operator and possibly your degree of visible desperation. Casetas will generally charge 50¢–$1.50 to place a collect call, and some charge by the minute on collect calls, as well.

MAIL

All cities and most towns have an *oficina de correos* (post office) that sells stamps and has *Lista de Correos* (poste restante) service (*see* Receiving Mail, *below*). Some post offices also offer telegram, fax, and express mail services.

SENDING MAIL HOME Mail to points beyond Mexico takes anywhere from one to six weeks to arrive, depending on your luck and the size of the city from which you mail the missive. If you're in a hurry, you can send a letter registered mail, which takes about five to seven days, or by Mexpost, the fastest (about two days) and most expensive method. Mailing a package involves buying the necessary paper, tape, box, and string, then visiting the post office and the customs office. Go to the post office first for instructions, as the procedure varies from city to city. Do not attempt to pack up and wrap the goods yourself; the post office worker will rip everything apart to inspect the contents and charge you to rewrap it Mexican-style. They will also charge you duty tax. The whole process can take up to an hour, so be patient.

RECEIVING MAIL You can receive fan mail in Mexico via Lista de Correos, which is basically general delivery service. Mail is held up to 10 days, then returned to sender if you don't show up with a picture ID and fetch it. For the Lista de Correos address in any given town, look under the heading "Mail" for that town.

BUSINESS HOURS

Business hours vary from city to city, but most businesses, including banks, open around 9 AM. Everything but restaurants closes between 2 PM and 4 PM for the lunchtime siesta, then reopens until 6, 7, or 8. Banks that offer money-exchange service almost always stop doing so at noon or 1 PM, regardless of when the bank itself closes. Most businesses are closed on Sunday, or open only in the morning; the same goes for holidays.

WHERE TO SLEEP

Mexico offers nearly every type of hotel imaginable, from spotless, sterile rooms, to cozy, colonial houses, to cubicles with bare concrete floors and saggy beds. In general the more you pay for a room, the better quality you'll receive, though this—like everything in Mexico—is variable. Check-out time at most hotels is 1 PM, and you can usually leave your valuables behind the desk while you roam about during the day. Some places will watch your backpack for several days, usually at no charge. Hotel/motel chains are not in the budget range, and what most people understand as bed-and-breakfasts are very rare in Mexico, though some budget places will include breakfast in the price of a room. The hotels featured in this book are generally the cheapest we could find, moderately priced ones with character, or more upscale places with budget deals. The price categories in this book typically refer to the cost of the least expensive double room available plus tax.

Mexico also has a network of about 16 youth hostels, called *villas juveniles*. No sort of membership card is necessary to stay in the hostels—you can leave that HI card you used in Europe at home. Though they usually cost less than $5 a night, they can be a major hassle to get to.

CAMPING A host of camping opportunities exist in Mexico, but don't expect the typical U.S.-style campground. Mexico's campgrounds are usually nothing more than trailer parks with running water, cooking areas, and room to pitch tents; sites can cost $1–$8. To enjoy more rustic surroundings, you can set up camp off the road or on the beach in relative safety, and save loads of money. Do not camp, however, at archaeological sites or in marijuana-growing areas. For more detailed camping information and humorous camping anecdotes, look to *The People's Guide to Camping in Mexico* by Carl Franz.

ROUGHING IT Along Mexico's coasts, you can usually sleep on the beach for free; just ask a local to make sure it's permissible. Nine times out of 10 it will be just fine. Hammocks are another alternative; lots of beach communities have hammock hooks between trees or inside palapa huts where you can string a hammock for free or for a nominal fee. Within cities, it's hard to find a place to rough it without being picked up by police. Public parks are rare. You could always dance the night away at a disco, though, or hit the all-night cantina. Some bus stations are open 24 hours, though you may be the sole bench occupant.

LODGING ALTERNATIVES Formed in the aftermath of World War II, **Servas** is a membership organization dedicated to promoting peace and understanding around the globe that enables you to arrange two-night stays with host families. Becoming a member makes you eligible for their host list directory for any country you desire. Servas has 204 hosts scattered throughout Mexico, though some regions have only one or two per state. Servas is not for tourists or weekend travelers; peace-minded individuals who want more than a free bed can write or call for an application and an interview. You can arrange a stay with a Servas host or host family in advance or just try your luck when you reach the country. Membership is $55 per year, and a deposit of $25 is required for up to five host lists. *United States: 11 John St., Suite 407, New York, NY 10038, tel. 212/267–0252. Canada: 229 Hilcrest Ave., Willowdale, Ont. M2N 3P3, tel. 416/221–6434. U.K.: 4 Southfield Rd., Burley-In-Warfedle, Ilkley, West Yorks, LS29 7PA. Australia: 1 Moonyah Ct., Cooma, NSW, 2630, tel. 645–25981. New Zealand: 24 Rahiri Rd., Mt. Eden, Auckland, 4., tel. 9/630–6279.*

FOOD

The first thing many people hear when they tell people they're going to Mexico is "Don't drink the water." However, if you're too cautious, you'll miss out on one of the most enjoyable experiences of any trip: trying all the good stuff there is to eat. Start off slowly, giving your system time to adjust, and follow crowds of locals to find the best (and probably safest) food in town.

Mexican restaurant dining can be a disconcerting experience at first. When you sit down, a waiter brings you a menu, then returns after about 30 seconds to take your order. He or she expects you to be ready; if you need more time, you'll have to ask for it and you might get a look of surprise. This speediness is balanced by the length of time it takes to actually receive your food—sometimes decades. Choosing a dish gets even more complicated when you try to order and find out that maybe 5% of the items on the menu are actually available, as in this following traveler's experience: "Good morning! I'd like the mixed fruit plate, please, but could I have it without papaya?" "Of course. No papaya." "Uh, excuse me, but this plate has only papaya." "Oh, yes, sir, it's the only kind of fruit we have right now."

Mexicans like meat and eat it for breakfast, lunch, and dinner. Vegetarian restaurants are difficult to find, but with the abundance of beans, tortillas, fresh fruit, vegetables, and nuts, herbivores should do just fine. Be aware lard is often used in the preparation of tortillas. The price categories used in this book are loosely based on the assumption that you are going to chow down a main course, a drink, and maybe a cup of coffee. Antacids are extra. For more info about health risks from food, *see* Staying Healthy, *above*.

Standard practice in Mexico is to tip 10% or a bit higher at sit-down restaurants and bars—there's no need to tip at food stands. Tip taxi drivers if they offer suggestions and don't rip you off (be sure to fix the price first). Tip if you're too lazy to carry your bags yourself and someone helps you out.

LANGUAGE

Although Spanish is the official language of Mexico, different Mayan tongues are also spoken as a first language in a few places, especially in the south, and variants of Nahuatl, the Aztec language, are also common. Knowing even a little Spanish, though, makes your trip more enjoyable, and Mexicans generally appreciate the fact that you're trying. Upper-class Mexicans commonly speak English and/or one or two other European languages, but in general, English is not commonly spoken or understood. See the glossary at the back of the book for some useful phrases.

About 32% of all adults in the southern state of Chiapas do not speak Spanish.

CRIME AND PUNISHMENT

The moment you step onto Mexican soil, you're subject to the legal theory that you're guilty until proven innocent. The government is cracking down hard on drug trafficking, and police are quick to prosecute anyone found in possession. Of all foreign drug prosecutions in the world, those filed in Mexico account for over 20%. Travelers with as little as a third of an ounce of marijuana have been arrested and thrown in jail. Legally, the government can keep you in one of its miserable cells for up to seven years, and since you are not protected by the laws of your native land after you cross the Mexican border, your embassy can do little for you. The situation can be grim, to say the least.

Apart from drugs, police rarely hassle travelers unless they are excessively loud, drunk, or involved in a brawl, in which case the police can keep you overnight in jail and take your money, as well as fine you. Remember, no one will be on your side, so be careful. If you do get into a scrape with the law, you can call the **Citizens' Emergency Center** (tel. 202/647–5225) in the United States, weekdays 8:15 AM–10 PM, Saturday 9 AM–3 PM. After hours and on Sundays, call the emergency duty officer (tel. 202/634–3600). In Mexico you can also call the **Procuraduría de Protección al Turista** (Attorney General for the Protection of Tourists), where English is spoken. The 24-hour hotline in Mexico City is 5/250–01–51, or dial the operator for assistance.

PROTECTING YOUR VALUABLES Money belts may be dorky and bulky, but it's better to be embarrassed than broke. You'd be wise to carry all cash, traveler's checks, credit cards, and your passport in an inaccessible place: A front or inner pocket or a bag or pouch that fits underneath your clothes, or even in your shoes. Neck pouches and money belts are sold in luggage or camping-supply stores. Waist packs (smallish zippered nylon bags that are strapped around your waist or hips) are safe if your keep the pack part in front of your body, safer still if your shirt or sweater hangs over the pack.

When is it safe to take your valuables off your body? Hostels and even hotel rooms are not necessarily safe; don't leave anything valuable out in the open. When sleeping or leaving your room, keep what you cherish on your body or at least inside your sleep sheet (if you're in it). And it may go without saying, but *never* leave your pack unguarded or with a total stranger in train or bus stations or any other public place, not even if you're only planning to be gone for a minute—it's not worth the risk. If you're carrying a smaller bag with a strap (or a camera), sling it crosswise over your body and try to keep your arm down over the bag in front of you. Back pockets are fine for maps, but don't keep a wallet back there; you might get the wrong kind of admiring attention. The best way to avoid theft is to leave expensive jewelry and cameras at home. When packing, ask yourself if you can go on living if a given item is lost or stolen. If not, put that item right back where it belongs—safe at home. The U.S. Printing Office publishes a particularly useful pamphlet called "Safe Trip Abroad" ($1). Send a check and a S.A.S.E. to: Superintendent of Documents, U.S. Printing Office, Washington, DC 20402. You can also phone the office at 202/512–1800.

FURTHER READING

PRE-COLUMBIAN, COLONIAL, AND MODERN MEXICO Good general reference works include: Roderic A. Camp's *Politics in Mexico* (Oxford University Press, 1993); David Carrasco's *Montezuma's Mexico* (University Press of Colorado, 1992); Jorge G. Castañeda and Robert A. Pastor's *Limits to Friendship: The United States and Mexico* (Vintage Books, 1988); Michael D. Coe's *In the Land of the Olmec* (University of Texas Press, 1980); Hernán Cortés's *Letters From Mexico* (Yale University Press, 1986); John M. Hart's *Revolutionary Mexico* (University of California Press, 1987); Bartólome de Las Casas's *The Devastation of the Indies* (Johns Hopkins University Press, 1992); Michael C. Meyer and William L. Sherman's *The Course of Mexican History* (Oxford University Press, 1991); and Mary Miller and Karl Taube's *The Gods and Symbols of Ancient Mexico and the Maya* (Thames and Hudson, 1993). If you prefer to read about the ancient Mexican civilizations in their own words, a few texts remain and have been translated. *The Destruction of the Jaguar: Poems from the Books of Chilam*

Balam, translated by Christopher Sawyer Lucanno and available from City Lights Books and *Popol Vuh* (Touchstone Press,1986) are both based on ancient Maya codices. A translation of the Aztec *Codex Chimalpopoca* is also available from the University of Arizona Press.

MODERN LITERATURE IN TRANSLATION Mexican literature is obviously a vast and varied field, but the following works are highly recommended: Carlos Fuentes's *Where the Air is Clear* (Noonday Press, 1960), *Aura* (Deutsch, 1990), and *The Old Gringo* (Farrar, Straus, and Giroux, 1985); Octavio Paz's *The Labyrinth of Solitude* (Fondo de Cultura Económica, 1959) and *A Tree Within* (New Directions, 1988); Juan Rulfo's *The Burning Plain, and Other Stories* (University of Texas Press, 1990) and *Pedro Páramo* (Grove Weidenfeld, 1990); and Alan Trueblood's *A Sor Juana Anthology* (Harvard University Press, 1988).

What Did You Call Me?

Travelers who consider themselves well educated in the Spanish language often find themselves befuddled when trying to interpret Mexican slang. For example, if someone tells you, "No me mames," don't take it literally (Don't suck on me). You're actually being asked to lay off. The use of the words for mother and father often have nothing to do with the family. If something "no tiene madre" (has no mother) it's absolutely the coolest. "Que padre" (literally, how father) is equivalent to "how cool." "Pinche" (damn) is a word you will hear in every other sentence. "Pendejo" roughly translates as "ass" or "idiot." Other handy expressions include "híjole," an exclamation meaning anything from "wow" to "shit" to "uh-oh"; "andale," which means "hurry up," "really," or "go for it"; and "güero" or "güera." meaning, basically, "white boy" (or girl). For more banal expressions, see the glossary at the back of the book.

MEXICO CITY AND ENVIRONS

2

By Viviana Mahieux

The first thing to strike you about Mexico City is the sheer number of people. It's simply mind-boggling to grasp that so many people could possibly exist. To comprehend how these multitudes can actually share a city is an even greater challenge. Take the Metro, for example. At rush hour, it's packed so tightly that you won't be able to move an inch, and the concept of personal space ceases to exist. Upon exiting the station, you're engulfed by the swarming *tianguis* (open-air market). After squeezing your way through the crowd, you reach your bus only to realize that forty other people are planning to board and you have to stand at the end of the line. This odyssey, experienced by milions of *chilangos* (a slightly nastly label for Mexico City residents) on a daily basis, defines the city's personality. Although you'd think the dominant moods of such a harried group would be confusion and frustration, spend time talking to local residents, hanging out in the city's bustling cafés, or just watching families gather in the Zócalo at dusk, and you'll realize this isn't the case. Sure, multitudes can mean chaos; but they can also create contrast, movement, and vitality.

Within the country, Mexico City is known as México D.F., or just "D.F." (Distrito Federal). Unofficial nicknames include "Chilangolandia" (a fusion of "chilango" and "Disneylandia") and "DFectuoso," a pun on the defects of D.F. life.

This capital of several consecutive civilizations has been located in the Valley of Mexico since about 1325, when the Aztecs, or Mexicas, founded the city of Tenochtitlán. Although the Spanish conquistador Cortés briefly toyed with the idea of moving the capital out of the valley, he ultimately adopted an "If it ain't broke, don't fix it" attitude. While the valley itself has always enjoyed a relatively temperate climate, the almost uninterrupted range of volcanic mountains that surrounds it is one of the main reasons the city is usually blanketed by a thick, brown layer of smog. Moreover, the soft soil upon which the city is built (the site was a lake, but has been gradually filled in by successive civilizations) has caused many of the city's buildings to sink several inches per year. But despite all its serious problems, the oldest capital in the Americas has always remained the ultimate seat of Mexican political power. During times of violent upheaval, the crucial question—from independence fighter Padre Hidalgo to the revolutionaries Villa and Zapata—has always been, "Did they hold the capital?"

And who holds the capital today? Mexico City is a complex blend of cultures and classes. Expatriates, political exiles, immigrants, and visitors from around the world mix with Mexicans from every state in the country. Rural migrants pour into the city daily, looking for work and a better standard of living, draining resources and labor from the countryside. These *campesinos* (peasants) usually end up in slums, each family member working as he or she can, selling chewing gum or shining shoes on street corners and in the Metro. Residents call them *paracaidistas* (parachuters), because they come out of nowhere and seize any scrap of land available, from abandoned lots to the meager strips of land beside railroad tracks. Such poverty is well-hidden from the delicate eyes of those who occupy the more posh districts of town, such as Polanco, Lomas, and Coyoacán. Any meeting between the two classes reveals an unsettling and somewhat depressing contrast: Poor children peddle roses and put on street shows late at night for the crowds of trendy *fresas* (spoiled rich kids) who clubhop in their bright red Jettas.

> *Fair-skinned and/or blond women receive plenty of attention from D.F. men, usually in the form of catcalls, though sometimes as up close and personal as an ass-pinch. These unwelcome advances seldom lead to anything more serious, but follow standard precautions and watch your butt.*

Yes, Mexico City is a mixed bag; it has a bit of everything, not all good and not all evil. So how do you answer those kids in the Zócalo who want to know if you like their home? Even if you find the city overwhelming, it does grow on you, and it can even become an addiction. Aficionados of Mexico City even feel the same inexplicable and irrational passion that many feel for their first loves. You may be reluctant to embrace this unwieldy city of staggering pollution and obvious overcrowding, but if you come with your arms open and your preconceptions in check, you'll find warmth, friendship, and genuine hospitality.

Basics

AMERICAN EXPRESS This main branch replaces and sells traveler's checks, cashes cardholders' personal checks, and provides travel services. Avoid changing money here since the rates are poor. They'll hold cardholders' mail at the following address: Paseo de la Reforma 234, esq. Havre, Col. Juárez, México, D.F., CP 06600, México. Tel. 5/514–06–29 or 5/207–72–82. Open weekdays 9–6, Sat. 9–1. From Metro Insurgentes, take Génova north to Reforma, turn right and go 2 blocks. Hotel Nikko office: Campos Eliseos 204, tel. 5/282–21–47; Metro: Auditorio. Hotel Camino Real office: Mariano Escobedo 700, Col. Anzures, tel. 5/203–11–48; Metro: Chapultepec.

BOOKSTORES In a city with more than 30,000 English-speaking expatriates, you'll have very little trouble locating English-language publications. *The Mexico City News* contains summaries of national and international news, entertainment, classifieds, and, most important, horoscopes and Ann Landers. *The Mexico City Daily Bulletin* is full of ads and handy sections like "Bible Digest" and "The World of Science." Published Tuesday–Sunday, it's available free at many hotels and at tourist offices. Look beyond the propaganda for helpful suggestions about hotels, restaurants, and places to shop, and cut out the great city map to carry around with you. For a consistently good selection of newspapers and magazines in English, or the latest Danielle Steele for those long hours at the bus station, try the ubiquitous **Sanborns**.

> *Wander around Mexico City for a day, and you can't help noticing a Sanborns. This restaurant/retail chain is rumored to have connections to Carlos Salinas de Gortari—many people believe that the former president is the real owner and that the chain was part of his many commercial ventures.*

The American Bookstore offers a large selection of books and magazines in English, as well as the *Guía Roji* and the *Guía Pronto*, two good maps of Mexico City. Madero 25, tel. 5/512–03–06. 4½ blocks west of Zócalo. Open Mon.–Sat. 9:30–7.

The **Benjamin Franklin Library**, in the U.S. Embassy, is meant to nurture understanding between the two nations. Even mutual understanding has its limits, however: Only Mexico City residents can check out books. The library has a good reference section, numerous novels, and U.S. periodicals and magazines. On the second floor, the English Language Program's office lists institutions looking for English teachers. Londres 16, tel. 5/211–00–42. Open Mon. and Fri. 3–7:30, Tues.–Thurs. 10–3.

Casa Libros, a used book store run by the American Benevolent Society, is way out in the boondocks, but since new books in English are prohibitively expensive everywhere else, stock up while you're here. The store also has smaller selections of books in Portuguese, Spanish, Italian, and German. *Monte Athos 355, Col. Lomas de Chapultepec, tel. 5/546–51–23. Off Reforma beyond Chapultepec Park. Open Mon.–Sat. 10–5.*

Gandhi, a coffeeshop/bookstore in San Ángel, has a book selection worthy of acclaim. Most of the titles here are in Spanish, supplemented by gorgeous art books and a handful of English titles. For those who make a hobby of spotting famous literati, Mario Vargas Llosa has been known to browse here among the UNAM students perusing the shelves. The store's other branch, called **El Parnaso**, is in Coyoacán, on the corner of Carrillo Puerto and Jardín Centenario. *M. A. de Quevedo 134, tel. 5/662–06–00 or 5/661–09–11. ½ block west of Metro M. A. de Quevedo. Open weekdays 9 AM–11 PM, weekends 10–10.*

CASAS DE CAMBIO All banks offer the same government-set *tipo de cambio* (exchange rate), but they often change money only until noon or 1:30. Banks do have ATM machines (called *cajas permanentes*) that spit out cash in pesos, but if you need to change money, they usually require you to run a lengthy bureaucratic obstacle course of signatures and receipts before the financial alchemists will turn your foreign currency into pesos. **Banamex** is the most accessible bank, with branches on practically every block in the downtown area.

If time is more important than filthy lucre, however, you'll find several **casas de cambio** throughout the city with longer hours but poorer exchange rates. That said, the best rates can usually be found in the Zona Rosa. **Casa de Cambio Consultoria Internacional** (Río Tíber 110, tel. 5/207–99–20) is open weekdays 8 AM–8:35 PM and Saturdays 8–2. You can also try **Casa de Cambio Ameres** (Ameres 40, tel. 5/207–05–97), open weekdays 8:30 AM–5:30 PM and Saturdays 8:30–2.

DISCOUNT TRAVEL AGENCIES **Agencia de Viajes Tony Pérez** does a lot of business with the U.S. Embassy across the street and knows about the latest airline promotions. *Río Volga 1, at Río Danubio, tel. 5/533–11–48 or 5/533–11–49. Near Ángel de la Independencia monument, across from Zona Rosa. Open weekdays 8:30–6:30, Sat. 9–1.*

Turismo Mirey wins the prize for most honest travel agency in the D.F. They go out of their way to find you the best deals and offer great day trips from Mexico City. For $30 a person, you can visit the pyramids of Teotihuacán, transportation and tour included. *Londres 44, in the Zona Rosa, tel. 5/514–57–93 or 5/514–47–72. Open weekdays 9:30–6:30, Sat. 11–2.*

If you're interested in attending religious services of just about any denomination, call the British consulate; they'll be glad to set you on the right(eous) path.

EMBASSIES **Australia.** *Jaime Balmes 11, 10th floor, Plaza Polanco, Torre B, tel. 5/395–99–88 for information or 5/404–20–46 for emergencies. Metro: Polanco. Open weekdays 9–1.*

Canada. The embassy also has a lending library. *Schiller 529, at Tres Picos, Col. Polanco, tel. 5/254–32–88, fax 5/545–17–69. Metro: Polanco. Embassy and library open weekdays 9–12:30. Office and library closed Canadian and Mexican holidays.*

New Zealand. *Homero 229, 8th floor, Col. Polanco, tel. 5/250–59–99 for information, 5/445–27–48 or 5/250–16–89 for emergencies. Metro: Polanco. Open Mon.–Thurs. 8:30–2 and 3:30–5:30, Fri. 8:30–2; closed Mexican holidays.*

United Kingdom. *Lerma 71, Col. Cuauhtémoc, tel. 5/207–24–49 or 5/207–20–89. Metro: Insurgentes. Open weekdays 8:30–3:30; weekdays 9–2 for visas and registration; closed some Mexican and all British holidays.*

United States. *Paseo de la Reforma 305, Col. Cuauhtémoc, near Ángel de la Independencia monument, tel. 5/211–00–42, fax 5/511–99–80. Metro: Insurgentes. Open weekdays 8:30–5; closed Mexican and U.S. holidays.*

EMERGENCIES You can call the **fire department** (tel. 5/768–37–00), the **Cruz Roja** (Red Cross, tel. 5/557–57–57) directly, or ring the **Tourist Security Patrol** (tel. 5/250–82–21 or 5/250–01–23) 24 hours a day.

The **Procuraduría General de Justicia** (Public Prosecutor) offers emergency assistance to tourists in Mexico City. Police, lawyers, and a doctor staff the two offices 24 hours a day. If you

Mexico City

Mexico City

lose your passport or are a victim of a more serious crime, you can make a report in English, and the staff will translate it into Spanish for you. *Zona Rosa: Florencia 20, tel. 5/625–70–20 or 5/625–87–61; Metro: Insurgentes. Centro: Argentina, at San Ildefonso, tel. 5/625–87–62; Metro: Zócalo.*

LAUNDRY **Lavandería Edison** is the laundromat closest to the hotels in the Metro Revolución area, though once you get a look at their prices, you'll realize your clothes aren't so dirty after all. Doing your own dirty work costs $1.75 wash and $1.75 dry; letting someone else handle it (1-hour service) costs $6. *Edison 91, near Monumento de la Revolución, no phone. From Metro Revolución, walk toward the monument on Buenavista and turn right on Edison. Open weekdays 10–7, Sat. 10–6.*

Lavandería San Pablo is close to the downtown area. Three kilos of dirty duds cost $2 if you do them yourself, $6 if you leave them to be washed (same-day service). *Las Cruces 56, btw San Pablo and Regina, tel. 5/522–67–23. Open Mon.–Sat. 9–7, Sun. 9–1.*

LUGGAGE STORAGE If your hotel won't take your bags, the airport, train station, and all four bus stations have luggage storage (*see* Coming and Going, *below*). If you'll be gone more than a few days, use the service at the airport or at TAPO (the eastern bus station), where you can keep the key to your locker.

MAIL The **Dirección General de Correos** (main post office), in a neo-Renaissance building across from Bellas Artes, sells stamps at the ESTAMPILLAS windows and distributes mail at the LISTA Y POSTE RESTANTE window. Mail sent to you at the following address will be held for up to 10 days: Lista de Correos, Administración 1, Palacio Postal, México, D.F., CP 06002, México. Smaller branches can be found at the Central Poniente and Central Sur bus stations, and the UNAM campus next to the main library. *Main branch: Lázaro Cárdenas, at Tacuba, tel. 5/521–73–94. 1 block from the Alameda Central. Open weekdays 8–6, Sat. 8–4, Sun. 8–1.*

For fax service, money orders, and telegrams, **Telecom** is just down the street from the post office. *Tacuba 8, next to Museo Nacional de Arte, tel. 5/512–21–95 or 5/512–59–98. Open weekdays 9–7, Sat. 9–1.*

MEDICAL AID Two private hospitals with English-speaking staff are the **Hospital Español** (Ejército Nacional 613, Col. Polanco, tel. 5/203–37–35) and the **American British Cowdray Hospital (ABC)** (Sur 138, at Observatorio, tel. 5/230–80–00). To reach the latter from Metro Tacubaya, take pesero CUAJIMALTA or NAVIDAD to Colonia Las Américas.

If you need free or inexpensive medical care, the following hospitals also have some English-speaking staff: **Hospital General Balbuena (DDF)** (Cecilio Robelo y Sur 103, Col. Jardín Balbuena, tel. 5/764–03–39; Metro: Moctezuma) and **Hospital Santa Fé** (San Luis Potosí 43, tel. 5/574–10–11; Metro: Chilpancingo).

For late-night pharmaceuticals, **Sanborns** (open daily 7:30 AM–11 PM) is your best bet. The pharmacy chain **El Fénix** also has several stores throughout the city, including one at Madero 39 (tel. 5/521–98–02), open Monday–Saturday 8–9, Sunday 10–7. For 24-hour service try **Vyb** (San Jerónimo 630, in Comercial San Jerónimo, near Periférico Sur, tel. 5/595–59–83 or 5/595–59–98). Each of the bus stations also has a 24-hour pharmacy.

PHONES

➤ **LOCAL CALLS** • Local calls can be made from either the blue or gray Ladatel phones (20¢) or at any orange public phone (these also have a coin slot, but most have been free since the 1985 earthquake). The real challenge in Mexico City isn't finding a phone per se; it's finding a phone that works. Working phones are identified by the long line of folks waiting to use them; if you don't feel like spending quality queue time with the masses, you'll find that many establishments will let you use their phone for a bit more money, depending on how benevolent they are. For local directory assistance, dial an operator at 04.

➤ **LONG-DISTANCE CALLS** • By far the easiest way to make a long-distance call is with a prepaid card on a Ladatel Multitarjetas public phone, thereby eliminating the hassle of making change. You can buy Ladatel phone cards at any newsstand, lottery booth, or Sanborns (*see* Food, *below*) in 10-, 30-, or 50-nuevo peso denominations. To use an AT&T calling card, dial 95/800–462–4240 without depositing money to get an AT&T USA-Direct operator. For a Sprint operator, dial 95/800–877–8000.

A more expensive option is going to a *caseta de larga distancia* (long-distance telephone office), generally marked with a large, blue sign. You can find them in all bus stations, the airport and the train station; some (airport, Central Poniente, Tasqueña) are open 24 hours. In each case, you place the call and pay when you're done.

SCHOOLS UNAM (Universidad Nacional Autónoma de México) makes it very easy for visitors to take classes on its campus through the Centro de Enseñanza para Extranjeros (School for Foreign Students). They offer intensive and regular semester courses in Spanish, Chicano studies, art, history, and literature to anyone with a high school degree, and tuition is only about $450 per semester. Most classes are in Spanish, a few in English. Being registered here also gives you access to the university's facilities, such as gyms, swimming pools, libraries, and the campus medical center. *Mailing address: CEPE, Aptdo. Postal 70-391, C.U. Delegación Coyoacán, México, D.F., CP 04510, México. Tel. 5/622–24–70, fax 5/616–26–72.*

VISITOR INFORMATION Tourist offices in both the international and domestic terminals of the **airport** and in the **TAPO** (*see* Coming and Going, by bus, *below*) offer help with directions and hotel reservations. The **Asociación Méxicana de Hoteles y Moteles** (tel. 5/203–04–66) also has offices at the airport, and will make reservations for you. They're located next to the baggage claims at the domestic and international terminals, before the immigration booths. Once you cross immigration, you can't reenter.

The **Dirección General de Turismo** is centrally located in the Zona Rosa. During peak tourist season (July and August), the office has tons of maps and information on shopping centers, museums and galleries, the Metro, and other cities and regions in the country, but there are plenty of resources available year-round. The staff is helpful but not as bilingual as one would hope, and their information tends to be a bit outdated. *Amberes 54, at Londres, tel. 5/525–93–80 or 5/525–93–82. Open weekdays 9–9, weekends 9–7.*

Another good source of information is the **Secretaría de Turismo** (SECTUR), whose competent and friendly English-speaking staff distributes brochures and maps, assists in trip planning, and makes hotel reservations anywhere in Mexico. SECTUR's 24-hour complaint and emergency phone number is 5/250–01–23. They also have a 24-hour, multilingual tourist information number (5/250–01–51) and two toll-free numbers: in Mexico: Dial 91–800–9–03–92; from the U.S., dial 800/482–9832. *Presidente Mazarik 172, Col. Polanco, tel. 5/250–85–55 and 5/255–22–95. For information, tel. 5/255–32–12 ext. 191; for reservations, tel. 5/250–62–30. From Metro Polanco, walk south on Horacio and 2 blocks west on Hegel. Open weekdays 8 AM–9 PM and Sat. 10–3.*

COMING AND GOING

BY BUS Each of Mexico City's four main bus terminals is located at a different cardinal point of the city. The terminals generally service the corresponding section of the country, but there are exceptions, so don't be surprised to find southbound buses at the northern station. If you're traveling during Christmas, Easter, or during the peak tourist months of July and August, buy your tickets well in advance and be prepared for a mob scene. Tickets for most buses go on sale about three weeks before the departure date. It's best to check your baggage about half an hour before departure and board 20 minutes in advance. Find out the departure point for your bus and stick close by; the boarding announcements are virtually unintelligible, even to Spanish-speakers. Each of the stations has luggage storage (about 30¢ per hour), casas de cambio, a post office, caseta de larga distancia, pharmacy, and Ladatel phones.

If you plan to cross the U.S.–Mexico border by bus, you can purchase connecting tickets for U.S.-bound buses at **Greyhound** (Paseo de la Reforma 27, tel. 5/535–42–00 or 5/535–26–18). Another option is **Estrella Blanca** (Terminal Central del Norte, tel. 5/729–07–25), which lets you purchase Greyhound tickets for trips across the Texas and New Mexico borders.

➤ **TERMINAL CENTRAL DE AUTOBUSES DEL NORTE** • The northern terminal (Av. de los 100 Metros 4907, tel. 5/587–59–67 or 5/587–59–73) is a massive semicircular building across the street from Metro Autobuses del Norte. The bus station is huge and intimidating, but if you want to go anywhere north of Mexico City, you'll have to come here. Companies serving this station include: **Tres Estrellas de Oro** (tel. 5/729–07–62), with service to Guadalajara ($31), Hermosillo ($64), Mazatlán ($35), Puerto Vallarta ($32), Querétaro ($6), and Tijuana ($68), among other destinations; **Flecha Amarilla** (tel. 5/567–80–33), with buses leaving for Aguascalientes ($13), Guadalajara ($18), Morelia ($9) and San Miguel de Allende ($7); **Omnibuses de México** (tel. 5/567–67–56) with service to Chihuahua ($45), Durango ($28), and Guanajuato ($12); **Autobuses del Oriente (ADO)** (tel. 5/587–66–88) with buses to Jalapa ($10), Oaxaca ($16), Puebla ($5), and Veracruz ($14); and **Estrella Blanca** (tel. 5/729–07–25), which goes to Nuevo Laredo ($72) and Monterrey ($60). Prices listed here are generally the lowest one-way fares available; all long-distance buses have a TV, air-conditioning, and cushy seats.

Autobuses del Norte is the biggest and best-equipped station in the city. It has a **casa de cambio** (open weekdays 8–8 and weekends 9–4), Banamex ATM, a 24-hour **caseta de larga distancia,** and **luggage lockers** ($1.50–$2.50 for 24 hours). A small booth marked HOTELES ASOCIADOS (tel. 5/587–85–51; open weekdays 2–9) offers free help with hotel reservations.

There are no budget hotels near the terminal, but you can easily reach the centro by public transportation. A regulated taxi to a hotel in the centro will cost you about $4; buy a ticket at the taxi booth next to the Banamex ATM. Collective taxis are about half that price, but you may have to wait for half an hour and tip whoever found the cab for you. For a pesero, go down into the Metro, cross under the street: The RUTA 1 BELLAS ARTES pesero runs to the Bellas Artes/Alameda Central area and the RUTA 88 METRO REVOLUCION goes to the hotels near Metro Revolución. If you're dying for that first Metro ride, jump on line 5 toward Pantitlán, change at Metro La Raza to line 3 towards Universidad (inconvenient if you have a lot of luggage, since the "Tunnel of Science" connecting the two lines is a thousand miles long), and get off at Metro Juárez or Metro Hidalgo, where there are many budget hotels.

➤ **TERMINAL CENTRAL DEL SUR/TASQUEÑA** • Tasqueña (Tasqueña 1320, tel. 5/544–21–01), as this station is usually called, is easily reached from the Metro station of the same name on line 2. This southern terminal is almost always a madhouse, with huge lines of people carrying armfuls of packages. Service from Tasqueña runs mostly to the south and southwest of Mexico. **Estrella de Oro** (tel. 5/549–85–20) services Acapulco ($25, express; $15 with stops) and Ixtapa/Zihuatahejo ($35 express; $20 with stops). **Autopulman de Morelos** (tel. 5/581–74–49 or 5/581–13–11) goes to Cuernavaca ($3), Cuautla ($3), and Tepostlán ($2.50). **Cristóbal Colón** (tel. 5/544–24–14), which offers wheelchair access to its buses, serves Oaxaca ($15), Huatulco ($24), Puebla ($4), and Puerto Escondido ($27). Tasqueña lacks a casa de cambio or ATM, but has a **caseta de larga distancia,** open daily 24 hours, that accepts both Visa and MasterCard. The caseta also has a fax, photocopying machine, and doubles as a travel agency offering cheap packages to the beach. There is also a **pharmacy** and **luggage storage** (opposite door 3; $1.50–$2.50 per day) both open 24 hours.

The Metro is by far the cheapest transport from Tasqueña to the budget hotels in the centro, but taxis provide a more comfortable alternative. The ticket system mandates a rate of about $5 to the downtown area and $6 to the airport; purchase tickets at the taxi booth in front of door 3. You can also go out to the street and attempt to bargain with the drivers, although if the meter works, your fare is not negotiable.

➤ **TERMINAL AUTOBUSES DE PASAJEROS DE ORIENTE (TAPO)** • TAPO (Zaragoza 200, tel. 5/762–59–77) is in a working-class area just east of the city center and is easily reached from the adjacent San Lázaro Metro station (line 1). Buses depart this large, clean, dome-shaped terminal for eastern destinations, although you can also catch a south-bound bus from here. **ADO** (tel. 5/542–71–92 or 5/542–71–98) serves Cancún ($48), Jalapa ($11), Oaxaca ($17), and Veracruz ($16). **Cristóbal Colón** (tel. 5/542–72–83) serves Oaxaca de Juárez ($15), San Cristobal de las Casas ($34), and Tuxtla Gutierrez ($32). **Luggage storage** ($2.50 for 24 hours), a **caseta de larga distancia** (open daily 8 AM–11PM), a Banamex **ATM**, and the friendly bilingual staff at the **tourist information desk** (near the Metro exit; open daily 9–9) make this one of the more pleasant if not comical terminals to be stranded in. The boarding announcements at TAPO are audible but not necessarily intelligible if you've fallen prey to the music videos, played here on large monitors.

There are several ways to reach the cheap hotels in the centro: The RUTA 22 ZOCALO/BELLAS ARTES pesero or the ALAMEDA bus will pick you up right in front of the terminal; or take the Metro toward Observatorio and get off at Balderas, change to line 3, head toward Indios Verdes, and get off at Juárez. You can also take a taxi for $2.50 to the downtown area, $3.50 to the airport.

➤ **TERMINAL CENTRAL PONIENTE** • If hell were a bus station, this would be it. The terminal (cnr of Sur 122 and Río Tacubaya) is huge and dark, and the roof leaks. Of course it's not all bad—there's 24-hour **luggage storage** in room E ($1 for 24 hours), a 24-hour **caseta de larga distancia** from which you can call your loved ones and share your misery, and a **post office** (open weekdays 8 AM–7 PM). From here, **Flecha Amarilla** (tel. 5/271–27–24 or 5/271–24–65), hidden under the green sign of SERVICIOS COORDINADOS, serves Morelia ($8) and Pátzcuaro ($10). **Tres Estrellas de Oro** (tel. 5/271–05–78) serves Tijuana ($68), Mazatlán ($35), and Guadalajara ($20). **Enlaces Tenestres Nacionales (ETN)** (tel. 5/271–03–05), which goes to Morelia ($16), Uruapan ($20) and Guadalajara ($27), has its own, closed-off waiting room—although it appears highly uncomfortable, it's the safest place in the station to crash for the night.

Transportation to the station from downtown is easiest by Metro: Take line 1 to Observatorio and follow the SALIDA TERMINAL DE AUTOBUSES FORANEOS signs. To reach the centro from the station, take line 1 to Pino Suárez, switch to line 2, and get off at Zócalo. Otherwise, get a regulated taxi ticket to the downtown area (about $5) in the station.

BY TRAIN The train is slow, and it's not fun. Any illusions you may have had about dashing through the countryside by night (thereby saving money on hotels) should be quickly forgotten. Of course you can't ignore the fact that second-class train tickets are 60% (first-class 20%) cheaper than bus prices. **Estación Central Buenavista** is in a rather run-down area of the city—not the best place to lug your suitcase around late at night, but the floor is clean enough to sit on or, if need be, sleep on. At least it's a snap to get to; both the Guerrero and Revolución Metro stops are within 6 or 7 blocks of the station. Peseros and buses that stop outside of the Metro stations can take you right to the train station entrance. Even taking a taxi is surprisingly inexpensive—a ride from the Alameda Central/Bellas Artes area will only cost you about $2. It's about $1 to the closest budget hotel area, or you can simply walk south on Insurgentes Sur to just below Metro Revolución. To reach hotels south of the Alameda by minibus, take a RUTA 99 ALAMEDA/BELLAS ARTES pesero from Metro Revolución; to reach lodging near the Zócalo, take RUTA 99 TACUBA.

The friendly folks at the **information booth** (left of the ticket window, tel. 5/547–65–93 or 5/547–10–84) field queries (in Spanish) about rail travel daily 6:30 AM–9:30 PM. For help in English, stop by the **Oficina Comercial de Pasajeros** (next to caseta de larga distancia, tel. 5/547–86–55; open weekdays 10–3 and 5:30–8). **Luggage storage** (down ramp across from second-class ticket booth) costs $1 a bag for 24 hours, but they're only open 6:30 AM–9:30 PM. Come any later and you'll be dismayed to find that your bag is locked up, and the guy who can unlock the door has gone to visit his mother-in-law in Michoacán. There is no ATM near the station, but you can go to **Banamex** or **Bancomer** near Metro Revolución on Buenavista. The **caseta de larga distancia** is open Monday–Saturday 8 AM–9:30 PM and Sunday 9–9. If you need to stock up before a long trip, the nearby **supermarket** (Insurgentes, behind the big Suburbia store) is open Monday–Saturday 8 AM–10:30 PM and Sunday 8 AM–10 PM.

First-class and sleeper-car tickets can be purchased with cash or credit card from any one of the BOLETOS windows. Yes, they're usually almost twice as expensive as second-class tickets, but at least you're guaranteed a seat and won't run the risk of having to stand for 36 hours. Likewise, if you're going on a long trip, the sleeper cars (available only on some routes) are indispensable and well worth the money. The truly organized traveler can purchase a first-class ticket (in person only) up to one month in advance of the departure date; the chronically indecisive can get a full refund for tickets canceled at least 24 hours prior to departure. Trains are packed during the summer and Christmas season, so make reservations in advance if possible.

Second-class tickets (same-day cash purchases only) are sold from a line of windows hidden in the back of the building: Go down the ramp at either side of the main building to find the second-class *taquillas* (ticket counters) open from 6 AM until the last train leaves. Seats are not reserved, so it's best to arrive at least 1 to 4 hours before departure; the earlier you get here, the better your chance of getting a seat. You can get refunds for second-class tickets up to 3 hours before departure.

The first-class **Tren División del Norte** leaves daily at 8 PM for Ciudad Juárez (36 hrs, $35), stopping along the way in Querétaro, Aguascalientes, Zacatecas, and Chihuahua, among many other cities. **Tren Tapatío** leaves daily at 8:30 PM for Guadalajara; first-class fare is $11, and $30 will get you a sleeping berth. **Tren Regiomontano** departs at 6 PM for Monterrey (14 hrs; 1st class $15, sleeping berth $45), stopping in San Luis Potosí and Saltillo. To Oaxaca, take **Tren Oaxaqueño** (14 hrs, $10 1st class), which leaves daily at 7 PM and stops in Puebla and Tehuacán. The **Tren Jarocho** departs daily for Veracruz at 9:15 PM (11 hrs; $8.50 first class, $22 sleeping berth). The second-class **Tren 51** leaves daily at 7:45 AM for Veracruz (12 hrs, $4.50).

BY PLANE The **Aeropuerto Internacional de la Ciudad de México** is big but manageable and always buzzing with activity. The uncomfortable plastic chairs in the lounges are difficult to nest in, but you can spend a night slumped in one of them without being hassled, since flights come and go at all hours. Most major carriers, including Mexicana, American, Delta, Air France, and Iberia, operate from this airport, which connects Mexico with just about every destination in the world.

At the airport, **Bancomer** (open daily 6 AM–10 PM) and **Banamex** (open daily 6 AM–8 PM) have the same exchange rates, and the latter has a 24-hour ATM that accepts Cirrus and Plus cards. **Storage lockers** ($3 for 24 hours) in both the domestic and the international terminals are always open; the lockers are located in terminal E, right across from customs, and in terminal A, behind the stairs to the restaurants. There are two **tourist information offices** (tel. 5/762–67–63 or 5/762–67–73; open daily 9–9), one in domestic terminal A and the other in international terminal F. Their friendly and well-informed staff makes hotel reservations, provides directions and maps, and dispenses advice. The office of the **Asociación Mexicana de Hoteles y Moteles** (*see* Visitor Information, *above*), which can recommend accommodations for every budget, also has offices in terminals A and F, and purports to be open 24 hours a day. The **Caseta Pública** in terminal F is open 24 hours. You can call long distance and send faxes, but you cannot make collect calls. The airport also has a **pharmacy,** open daily 7 AM–10 PM.

➤ **AIRPORT TRANSIT** • The only realistic airport transportation for budget travelers is the **Metro.** It's a cheap but fairly time-consuming (1 hour to the centro) way to travel and probably not the safest after dark especially since you'll have to make at least one line change to get to or from downtown. From the international exit, turn left, and walk for about a kilometer—think twice about doing it with a heavy suitcase. The station, Terminal Aérea, is on line 5. Just remember that the Metro does not run past 12:30 AM. If you have a late flight, your only option is to take a taxi, or crash at the airport until 6 AM, when the metro starts running again. **Taxi** service to and from the airport abounds, and drivers aggressively woo tourists at every available opportunity. Service from the airport, however, is regulated, and you must purchase a ticket at the office in the far end of the domestic terminal or at the international terminal next to the baggage claim, where prices are set according to destination and number of passengers. Rates for downtown-bound taxis run from about $3 for one or two people to $12 for three or four passengers. Taxis not officially designated to work the airport offer somewhat lower fares; you'll find them lurking near the fringes of the airport, especially near the Metro Terminal Aérea. If you have an early flight or just plain want to make it there on time, designated airport taxis (tel. 5/571–93–44 or 5/571–92–97) will pick you up anywhere in the D.F. and drive you to the airport for a small fortune (about $15 from the Alameda), but you must call a day in advance.

BY CAR The main highways approaching Mexico City are 85 from the north, 136 and 150 from the east, 95 from the south, and 15 from the west. A quick count of the roadkill and the memorial crosses on the sides of the roads will help you understand why many Mexicans keep religious figurines on their dashboards or hanging from their rearview mirrors—no doubt you'll want to set up a similar shrine of your own.

GETTING AROUND

Mexico City's size serves to confuse and intimidate. The streets are not all neatly set out in a grid, and their names can change as often as five times as they pass through some of the 350 *colonias* (neighborhoods). You can orient yourself in the downtown area by using the two major arteries, Paseo de la Reforma and Avenida Insurgentes, as guides. Insurgentes runs north–south, intersecting Reforma in the busy downtown area and continuing south through the trendy Zona Rosa. Reforma passes through Chapultepec Park in the southwest of the city and continues north through the downtown, almost touching the Alameda Central. Here Reforma intersects another important street, Avenida Juárez. West of Reforma, Juárez ends in the Plaza de la República and the Monumento a la Revolución; east of Reforma, Juárez runs from the Alameda Central to the Zócalo, becoming Avenida Madero as it runs through the *centro histórico* (historic center) of the D.F.

An intricate web of public transportation connects the neighborhoods of this overwhelming city. While most points of interest are accessible on foot from centrally located Metro stops, exploring the entire city may require a mind-boggling combination of Metros, buses, taxis, and peseros.

An *abono de transporte* (transport pass; about $2) is good for 15 days of unlimited travel both on buses and the Metro. It goes on sale twice a month, about three days before the first and then three days before the middle of the month, at Metro and lottery ticket booths. It's a worthwhile investment if you plan to explore the city on public transportation or if you're staying at least two weeks.

BY METRO The Metro is by far the fastest and cheapest way to explore Mexico City, and is simple to use: Each of the nine lines is color coded, and stations are named for major sights nearby. Route maps are posted throughout every station, and free *Red del Metro* maps are available at the information booths of the principal stations. To avoid accumulating a pocketful of change every time you buy a ticket (10¢), you can buy 10 at a time; they don't expire. Transfers don't cost extra, but make sure not to follow the crowds out of the station; once you pass through the *salida* (exit), you'll need a new ticket to reenter.

Large backpacks or luggage are technically not allowed on the Metro, though it's unlikely anyone will stop you. Because of crowds, however, it's actually difficult to fit into the Metro with a large bag during peak hours, when the trains become a claustrophic nightmare. When it's crowded, get close to the door well before your stop—the rush of incoming passengers gives you little time to exit. During rush hours (7–10 and 5–9), the first car on lines 1, 2, and 3 is reserved for women and children, and guards posted at the gates strictly enforce the rule. Lines 1, 2, and 3 run weekdays 5 AM–12:30 AM and lines 4–9 run weekdays 6 AM–12:30 AM. All lines run Saturday 6 AM–1:30 AM and Sunday 7 AM–12:30 AM.

Physical harassment on the Metro or a crowded bus is fairly common. To avoid being grabbed by a stranger, try to stand with your back to a wall or to a friend. If hands start to stray, attract the attention of other passengers. Men are less likely to be hassled, so a woman with her back to a male friend is the safest bet for both parties.

BY BUS Every day, hundreds of thousands of passengers ride Mexico City's buses. Although the system serves the entire city (destinations are marked on the windshields), two routes are particularly useful and run all night long: **Ruta 55**, the principal route between the Zócalo and Chapultepec Park, along the Paseo de la Reforma, Juárez, and Madero; and **Ruta 17**, the route connecting Metro Indios Verdes to *Ciudad Universitaria* (University City, or UNAM), passing along Insurgentes through San Ángel. While service is generally reliable and always cheap (about 10¢), the lumbering vehicles absolutely crawl during rush hours (7 AM–10 AM and 5 PM–9 PM). Buses are often extremely crowded during these peak hours, so keep an eye on your pockets, bags, and the people around you; thieves thrive in the close atmosphere and often work in teams. Be particularly wary in heavily touristed areas like the Zona Rosa.

BY PESERO Throughout the D.F., *peseros,* which include *combis* (old VW vans) and *micros* (a slightly larger version of the combi), squeeze through impossible spaces, turn left from the far right lane, go from full throttle to a dead stop in seconds, and manage to deliver people alive to thousands of street corners all over the city. Peseros cover general zones marked by a number, preceded by the words RUTA NO. painted on the side of the minibus. Individual routes within the zones vary, though, so it's a good idea to ignore the ruta numbers and concentrate on reading the destination posted in the window. Corners with stoplights and bus stops are the easiest places to catch peseros, but they generally stop wherever you hail them. Designated stops along Insurgentes and Reforma, however, are indicated by a white and green sign. The fare is based upon how far you go: about 15¢ for up to 5 kilometers, 25¢ for 5–12 kilometers, and 35¢ for 12 kilometers or more. For more information or to file a complaint, call 5/605–66–67 or 5/605–59–22.

The word "pesero" dates from the good old days when a ride actually cost one peso.

BY TAXI Taxis are easy to come by all over the D.F., especially in the downtown area, and are available when the sign on the dash says LIBRE. The big American sedans parked outside most major hotels (and all around the Zona Rosa) are tourist taxis whose English-speaking drivers will gladly take you on shopping tours or off to see the sites. Of course, at the end of your leisurely drive through the city they'll also charge you a small fortune. Stick to the "real" taxis—usually VW Bugs and small sedans. Certified drivers prominently display a government license with a photo and all their stats. If the meter works, the driver will tell you, and the standard, nonnegotiable rate will be used. However, if the meter is "broken," you'll have a chance to bargain for your ride before you get in. Not only do you avoid being overcharged by taking the metered green VW Bugs, but they're also more environmentally sound, using only unleaded gasoline. After 10 PM, the fare goes up by about one-third and drivers tend to be reluctant to venture very far out of the city. Also beware of crossing the line between the D.F. and the *Estado de México.* Although there is no visible difference between these two areas, taxi drivers automatically double their rates once they cross the border. Tipping is necessary only when the driver helps you with your bags, drives in a non-life-threatening manner, or otherwise goes out of his way to make your journey somewhat pleasurable.

Radio-dispatched *sitio* taxis will fetch you wherever you are. If you have an early flight or bus departure, you can call the night before and request a driver at a specific time, although finding a cab downtown isn't a problem at any hour. It's best to call and remind them half an hour before they're supposed to arrive. Several companies are listed in the phone book under *Sitios de Automóviles,* or try **Taxi-Radio** (tel. 5/566–00–77 or 5/566–72–66), with free wake-up call service; or **Servicios Taxi-Mex** (tel. 5/538–49–66 or 5/538–99–37) for airport service only.

BY CAR Only the very brave or very foolish attempt to drive in the D.F. Parking is nearly impossible to find, roads are confusing, traffic is hellish, and most other drivers are *totalmente locos.* To add to the confusion, all cars are prohibited from driving one to two days a week, depending on the pollution level. The days are determined either by a colored sticker on the car or the last digit of the vehicle's license plate number. To figure out which days apply to you, call one of the rental agencies or check with a traffic cop. If you are driving, get a good street map like the *Guía Roji* or the *Guía Pronto* and try to drive like a chilango—fearlessly and with death as your backseat driver.

To rent a car you must have a credit card and a driver's license and be willing to shell out some moolah. (The most affordable rental goes for about $45 a day, mileage and insurance included.) Though the minimum age requirement differs from company to company (Hertz will rent to 21-year-olds, but most companies have a minimum age requirement of 25), one thing remains constant: All companies charge a 15% government tax. Rental company offices at the airport are open 24 hours, and there are a slew of branches in the Zona Rosa. Major companies include **Avis** (tel. 5/588–88–88 or toll free 91–800–70–777), **Budget** (tel. 5/566–68–00), **Dollar** (tel. 5/207–38–38), **Hertz** (tel. 5/592–60–82 or toll-free 91–800–70–016), and **National** (tel. 5/525–75–43 or toll free 91–800–90–186).

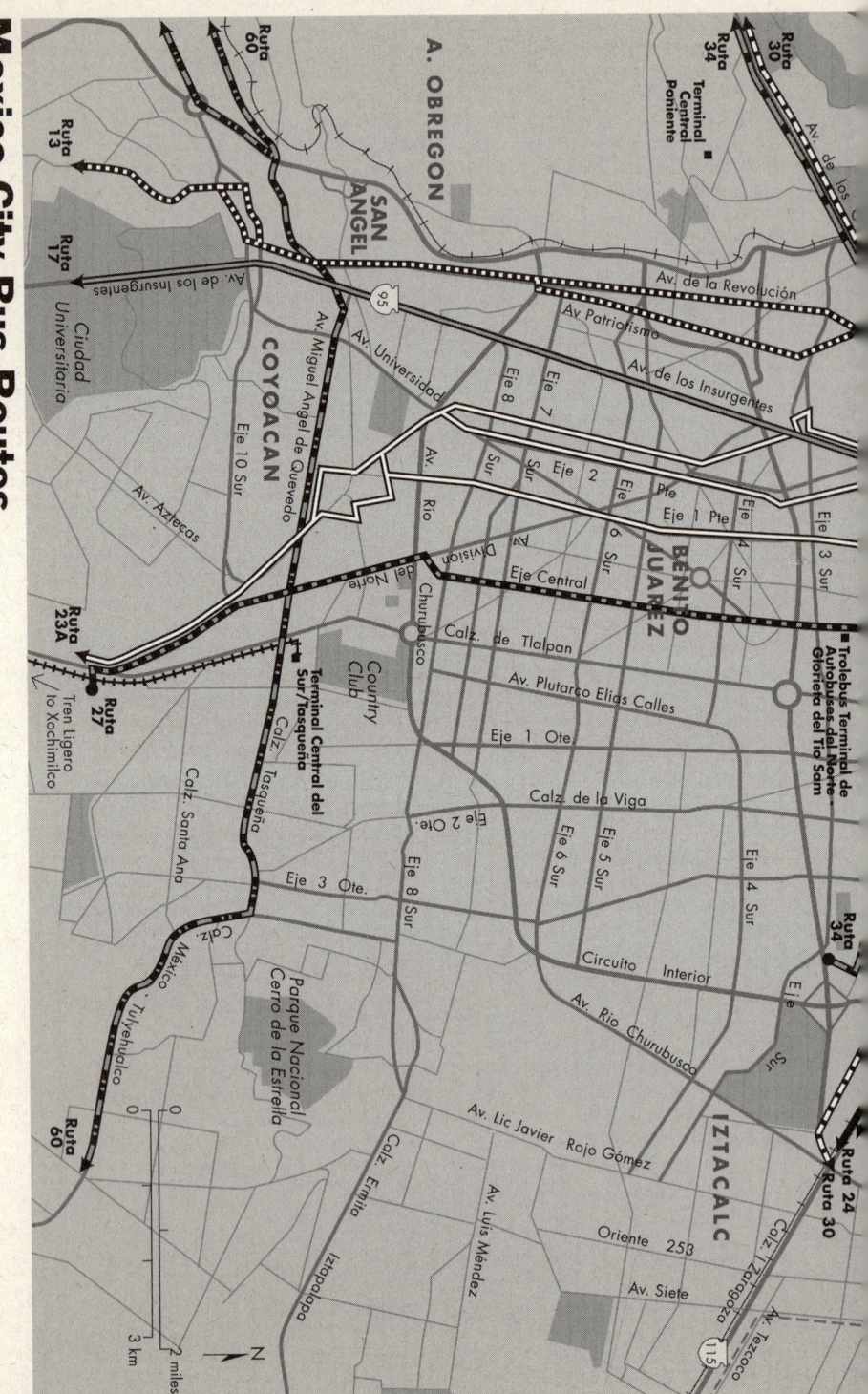

Where to Sleep

Cheap hotels in Mexico City inevitably share one characteristic: that faint but ever-present Ajax aroma. Other than that, the only thing they have in common is their price. The budget hotel areas listed here are conveniently clustered around Metro stops Pino Suárez, Zócalo, Bellas Artes, and Revolución. Reservations are *always* a good idea, especially during Semana Santa (Holy Week) and the summer months. If you don't make reservations, arrive as early in the morning as possible to stake your claim. Checkout is usually 2 PM, and tax is included in the government-controlled price.

NEAR THE ZOCALO

The huge colonial buildings in the area near the Zócalo have been divided over time to create a densely populated commercial and residential area that also houses dozens of budget hotels. The busy downtown area is also a heavily traveled part of the tourist trail: Step out your hotel door and you're in the center of everything. At night, however, all the bustle gives way to virtual stillness, so be cautious about wandering the deserted streets, especially alone.

➤ **UNDER $10** • **Hotel Cuba.** This hotel is grim and needs work, but it's just about the best deal in town: Singles cost $6.50, doubles $7.50 for one bed, $8 for two beds. The bathrooms are surprisingly clean (if you ignore the peeling wallpaper), but don't waste your time waiting for hot water. Phones and TVs have been added in an attempt to upgrade the hotel's status, and the roomy elevator makes this one of the very few cheap hotels in Mexico City that is relatively wheelchair accessible (there are two steps at the entryway). *República de Cuba 69, tel. 5/518–12–80. From Metro Allende, make a left on República de Chile, walk 1 block to República de Cuba, and turn left. 36 rooms, all with bath. Garage, luggage storage.*

Hotel Principal. The management of this nunnery-turned-hotel has done wonders to liven up the place—plants and natural light make it look like a giant greenhouse. Clean and comfortable rooms run $6 for a single without bath, $7 for a double. If you'd rather have a bathroom (soap and towels included) all to yourself, you'll pay a mere $11 for a single, $12.50 for a double. *Bolívar 29, btw 16 de Septiembre and Madero, tel. 5/521–13–33 or 5/521–20–32. From Metro Allende, walk 1 block west on Tacuba to Bolívar, turn left and walk 3 blocks. 100 rooms, 60 with bath. Luggage storage, meal service. Wheelchair access.*

Hotel Zamora. The recently renovated entry hall will give you hope, but that will vanish after a few steps—after all, this is a *budget* hotel. If you have a bathroom, don't bother looking for the toilet seat—it's gone. The señora who runs the place is easily rubbed the wrong way, but smile insistently, and she'll mellow out. Rooms are pretty clean and incredibly cheap. Singles are $5, $6.50 with bath; doubles $8, $10 with bath. *5 de Mayo 50, tel. 5/512–82–45. From Metro Allende, walk on Tacuba to Isabel la Católica, and turn right on 5 de Mayo. 36 rooms, 20 with bath.*

➤ **UNDER $15** • **Hotel Habana.** The Habana is in a grungy area, down the street from a porn theater, but it's nicely maintained and quiet. Most of the guests who pass through the cool marble entryway are Mexicans traveling on business; there are also some families and a few European students. The rooms are huge, with beds and TVs to match their size. Singles are $9, doubles $11.50. *República de Cuba 77, btw Palma and Chile, tel. 5/518–15–89 or 5/518–15–90. From Metro Allende, walk 2 blocks north on República de Chile to República de Cuba, then right. 51 rooms, all with bath. Luggage storage. Reservations advised.*

Hotel Juárez. Tucked away from bustling 5 de Mayo, this budget hotel is hard to find but worth the effort. The cool, trickling fountain in the Moorish-style lobby sets the tone, although the dim corridors make you wonder how much the management is trying to save on electricity. The paneled rooms, with TV, phone, and even piped-in Muzak, are a great deal at $11 for a single, $12.50 for a double with one bed, and $14 for two beds. *Cerrada de 5 de Mayo 17, btw Isabel la Católica and Palma, tel. 5/512–69–29 or 5/518–47–18. From Metro Allende, walk 1 block south to 5 de Mayo; hotel is on side street. 38 rooms, all with bath. Luggage storage. Reservations advised.*

Hotel San Antonio. This quiet hotel on a dead-end alley usually has vacancies even in the afternoon. Persevere until you find it (it's only a block from the Zócalo) and you'll be rewarded with goodies like a TV, phone, soap, and towels. The small, bright rooms, priced $9–$10 for a single, $11.50 for a double, and $15 for four people in a double, have green bedspreads and impeccably clean bathrooms with water that takes a while to get hot. Avoid the noisy rooms on the ground floor. *Cerrada de 5 de Mayo 29, tel. 5/512–99–06. From the Zócalo, walk west on 5 de Mayo to Cerrada de 5 de Mayo. 44 rooms, 40 with bath. Wheelchair access.*

Hotel Washington. There's always someone hanging out in the lobby of Hotel Washington—probably because the rooms are so damn small. Less claustrophobic but noisier are the rooms with French doors that open onto tiny balconies overlooking the street. On the plus side, there's hot water. Singles cost $11.50, doubles $13.50–$15. *5 de Mayo 54, tel. 5/512–35–02 or 5/521–11–43. From Metro Allende, walk south on Tacuba to Isabel la Católica, right on 5 de Mayo. 47 rooms, all with bath. Luggage storage. Wheelchair access. MC, V.*

➤ **UNDER $20** • **Hotel Isabel.** The economy rooms in this large, comfortable hotel see hordes of European backpackers. The giant, carpeted rooms aren't that cheap and are almost always stuffy in the summer, and cold in the winter. But after the two-for-one happy hour at the bar, who cares? Rooms that look out onto Isabel la Católica tend to be noisy. Try to get a room on the fourth floor, which has an outdoor patio facing away from the street. Singles or doubles with a clean communal bathroom cost $9. Singles with private bath run $11, doubles $18. *Isabel la Católica 63, tel. 5/518–12–13. 4 blocks north of Metro Isabel la Católica. 76 rooms, 64 with bath. MC, V.*

➤ **UNDER $25** • **Hotel Canadá.** This hotel tries to make you feel important from the moment you walk in. A uniformed bellboy greets you at the door, the reception staff is always on its best behavior, and the rooms, although small, possess all the amenities needed to pamper yourself. Singles go for $18, doubles $23, and triples $28. *5 de Mayo 47, tel. 5/518–21–06. From Metro Allende, take Tacuba east, right on Isabel la Católica, and right on 5 de Mayo. 84 rooms, all with bath. Laundry, safety vaults, travel agency. Wheelchair access. MC, V.*

➤ **UNDER $35** • **Hotel Catedral.** If you're feeling used and abused by the smog and traffic, spend a night or two in this very comfortable hotel. Rooms are decorated in soothing pastels, and the beds and mirrors are tastefully trimmed in oak. Singles cost $23.50, doubles $31.50, and all rooms have TVs, phones, and huge closets. For a real splurge, get the junior suite with a Jacuzzi for $36. The large, clean bathrooms have huge showers and rivers of hot water. *Donceles 95, tel. 5/518–52–32. From Zócalo, north on República de Brasil 3 blocks, right on Donceles. 116 rooms, all with bath. Bar, garage, laundry, luggage storage, restaurant, safe-deposit box. Reservations advised. AE, MC, V.*

Hotel Gillow. A short walk from the Zócalo, this luxury hotel has huge rooms and all the accoutrements: restaurants, room service, TVs, and phones. Bathrooms have a tub and wood-trimmed mirror. Singles cost $21.50, doubles $27.50. *Isabel la Católica 17, btw Madero and 5 de Mayo, tel. 5/518–14–40. From Zócalo, walk west on 5 de Mayo, left on Isabel la Católica. 103 rooms, all with bath. Laundry, luggage storage (for nonguests also), travel agency. AE, MC, V.*

Excuse Me, But Do You Have the Time?

If you find yourself on Calle Uruguay (just southwest of the Zócalo), look for number 90. It was the home of Count Juan Manuel Solórzano, an eccentric gentleman with the most disquieting of habits: After dark, he walked in front of his house and asked passersby for the time. If they knew (and were naive enough to tell him), Don Juan killed them on the spot. Legend has it that just before he committed his bloody deeds, he would heartily congratulate them for knowing—with exactitude—the hour of their death.

Mexico City Lodging

Casa de los Amigos, 1
Hotel Calvin, 12
Hotel Canadá, 25
Hotel Carlton, 10
Hotel Catedral, 28
Hotel Cuba, 18
Hotel del Valle, 14
Hotel Edison, 3
Hotel Fleming, 13
Hotel Frimont, 11
Hotel Gillow, 24
Hotel Habana, 19
Hotel Ibiza, 7
Hotel Isabel, 20
Hotel Juárez, 21
Hotel Latino, 30
Hotel Marlowe, 15
Hotel Monte Carlo, 27
Hotel Oxford, 8
Hotel Parador Washington, 5
Hotel Paraíso, 9
Hotel Pennsylvania, 6
Hotel Principal, 17
Hotel Roble, 29
Hotel San Antonio, 26
Hotel San Miguel, 31
Hotel Texas, 2
Hotel Toledo, 16
Hotel Washington, 23
Hotel Zamora, 22
Casa González, 4

SOUTH OF THE ALAMEDA CENTRAL

The area just south of the Alameda Central is packed with hotels, cheap *taquería* chains, and stores selling all sorts of odds and ends. Most hotels are just a short walk from the Palacio de Bellas Artes and the Museo Mural de Diego Rivera. The small *barrio chino* (Chinatown) on Dolores is also nearby. Although the area is fairly safe and a bit more lively at night than the neighborhoods around the Zócalo, take normal precautions when out late.

➤ **UNDER $15** • **Hotel Calvin.** This hotel is right across from the Metropolitano movie theater and it's bright sign, making it a cinch to find at night. The peach-colored rooms ($8.50 singles, $11.50 doubles) come equipped with TV and phone; for one with a Jacuzzi, you'll shell out $16.50. Try to get a room facing away from the Metropolitano sign, especially if you plan on turning in early. The large bathrooms are shedding paint and some are missing toilet seats, but they're clean and have warm water. *Azueta 33, tel. 5/521–79–52. From Metro Juárez, walk 1 block east on Independencia to Azueta. 29 rooms, all with bath. Laundry, luggage storage. Reservations advised. MC, V.*

Hotel del Valle. Don't be put off by the nondescript lobby or rooms. The location and price (singles $10, doubles $10–$11) are good, and the bathrooms are as clean as they come. Plus, each room comes equipped with phone and TV. The reliable but somewhat dilapidated elevator makes this hotel relatively wheelchair accessible (one step at front door). *Independencia 35, tel. 5/521–80–67. From Metro Juárez, walk 1 block north to Independencia, then right 4 blocks. 48 rooms, all with bath. Laundry, luggage storage. Reservations advised. AE, MC, V.*

Hotel Toledo. The lobby is cozy and welcoming despite the *telenovelas* (soap operas) flickering on the TV. A mint-green stairway winds up to rooms with polished wood floors, wood furniture, TVs, and comfy wool bedspreads. The bathrooms are small but clean and have reliable hot water. The hotel's character along with its decent prices (singles $9, doubles $10–$12; $16.50 for three people) make it one of the best budget places to stay in Mexico City. *López 22, tel. 5/521–32–49 or 5/518–56–31. From Metro Bellas Artes, east on Hidalgo to Cárdenas (Eje Central), right to Independencia, and left on López. 35 rooms, all with bath. Laundry, luggage storage. Reservations advised.*

➤ **UNDER $30** • **Hotel Fleming.** Don't let the vinyl in the '50s-style lobby fool you—this is a posh hotel. Spacious rooms with plenty of mirrors and matching pastel curtains and comforters have TVs, phones, and other extras. Singles are $23, doubles $28.50. For 10 bucks more you can get a room with a Jacuzzi. *Revillagigedo 35, tel. 5/510–45–30. From Metro Juárez, go 2 blocks east on Juárez, right on Revillagigedo. 75 rooms, all with bath. Garage, laundry, luggage storage, restaurant. Reserve at least 2 days in advance. AE, MC, V.*

Hotel Marlowe. The beautiful, fully carpeted rooms here have large desks, TVs, and touch-tone telephones, while the impeccable bathrooms have so much hot water their full-length mirrors become steamy enough to write notes to the next occupant. Switches on the headboard of each bed control the TV and lights—if you're bored or broke, sit in bed and flip the switches for that *Saturday Night Fever* effect. Singles cost $25, doubles $27–$28.50. *Independencia 17, btw López and Dolores, tel. 5/521–95–40. 5 blocks east of Metro Juárez. 106 rooms, all with bath. Bar, garage, laundry, luggage storage, restaurant. Wheelchair access. MC, V.*

NEAR METRO REVOLUCION

The budget hotels in the Metro Revolución area are all clustered within a block of each other, as if they couldn't bear a meter's separation. A possible explanation is that, like most hotels in Mexico City, they're run by Spanish expatriates. Despite the peaceful atmosphere on the tree-lined streets, it's only a five-minute Metro ride to the hustle and bustle of the city center. The area is also bordered by major thoroughfares—Insurgentes Norte, Puente de Alvarado, and Reforma—that provide easy access to all points in the city.

➤ **UNDER $15** • **Casa de los Amigos.** This Quaker house doesn't cater to the party-till-you-puke tourist variety; rather, the friendly, English-speaking staff welcomes travelers who are dedicated to promoting peace and justice. You don't have to pass a test to stay here, but you must abide by some of the Casa's rules: No alcohol or drugs are allowed, and you must step out on the patio to satisfy your nicotine urges. In return you'll get the lowdown on volunteer opportunities and Spanish language classes in Mexico and Guatemala, as well as use of their library. Guests have kitchen privileges, and the Casa serves huge, healthy breakfasts ($1.50) from 8 to 9:30 AM, the perfect time to socialize with other young international travelers. Single-sex dorm beds are $5, and singles and doubles with private bath are $7.50 and $11, respectively. An apartment with kitchen and bathroom for one person costs $13, $15 for two, $17.50 for three, or $20 for four. Fax them in advance of your arrival to ensure there's space. *Ignacio Mariscal 132, Col. Revolución, tel. 5/705–06–46 or 5/705–05–21, fax 5/705–07–71. From Metro Revolución, walk south on Ponciano Amiaga and turn right on Mariscal; it's across from the Gran Hotel Texas. 24 dorm beds, 3 singles and 3 doubles without bath, 2 doubles with bath, 1 apartment. Laundry, luggage storage (20¢ a day).*

➤ **UNDER $15** • **Hotel Carlton.** Across the street from a tree-filled plaza, this hotel doesn't live up to its ritzy name (although the staff sure seems to think so), but the rooms and bathrooms are spacious and clean. Hot water is readily available. The management fumigates the place once a month—the odor is unpleasant, but at least you can rest assured that nothing will slither, crawl, or otherwise find its way into your bed. Singles cost $10, doubles $12. *Ignacio Mariscal 32-B, tel. 5/566–29–11 or 5/566–29–14. From Metro Revolución, walk east on Puente de Alvarado to Ramos Arizpe and right 1 block. 41 rooms, all with bath. Laundry, luggage storage, restaurant. Reservations advised.*

Hotel Ibiza. Okay, so this recently remodeled hotel looks like an outdoor bathroom struggling to be elegant with its pink and gray marble, but it's new, clean, and has an elevator. Of course, you get all the amenities that accompany modernity: a phone, TV, hot water, and piped-in music. Singles are $8, doubles $12. *Ponciano Amiaga 22, tel. 5/566–81–55. 1 block south of Metro Revolución. 33 rooms, all with bath. Limited luggage storage. Wheelchair access.*

Hotel Oxford. With wood-paneled walls and gray marble floors, the hotel's entrance hall tries valiantly to live up to its British namesake. The rooms are huge, clean, and win the prize for clashing patterns; ask for one overlooking the plaza. Singles are $8.50–$10, doubles $13.50, triples $16.50, and quadruples $18.50. If you need a stiff drink, the bar next door offers room service from noon to midnight. *Ignacio Mariscal 67, tel. 5/566–05–00. From Metro Revolución, take Ponciano Arriaga to Ignacio Mariscal. 45 rooms, all with bath. Luggage storage, safe-deposit boxes.*

Hotel Paraíso. If comfortable but run-down rooms done up in pastel colors are your idea of paradise, then this is the place for you. The rooms are large, the bathrooms clean, and the price is right: $7.50–$8 for a single, $10 for a double, $12 for a triple, and $14 for a quad. *Ignacio Mariscal 99, tel. 5/566–80–77. From Metro Revolución, go 1 block east on Puente de Alvarado, 2 blocks south on Ponciano Arriaga, left on Ignacio Mariscal. 45 rooms, all with bath. Laundry, luggage storage. Wheelchair access.*

Hotel Pennsylvania. The newly renovated "king-size" rooms (singles $10, doubles $12) are done in light peach and baby blue, while the older, cheaper, and mustier rooms (singles $7, doubles $8.50) tend to have a more motley decor. Showering should be considered a lesson in patience: The hot water will come, eventually. *Ignacio Mariscal 101, tel. 5/703–13–84. From Metro Revolución, walk 1 block east on Puente de Alvarado, right on Ponciano Arriaga, left on Ignacio Mariscal. 90 rooms, all with bath. Wheelchair access.*

➤ **UNDER $20** • **Gran Hotel Texas.** Yet another hotel with an American name and a Spanish owner. The well-kept rooms include a phone, cable TV, and purified drinking water. Singles are $16.50, doubles $18.50. *Ignacio Mariscal 129, btw Ponciano Amiaga and J. M. Iglesias, tel. and fax 5/705–57–82. 60 rooms with bath. Garage, laundry, luggage storage.*

Hotel Edison. The attractive outdoor courtyard with lush plants is an oasis of tranquility in this otherwise noisy little hotel. The large rooms come with a TV and phone and cost $15 (singles), $18 (doubles), $21.50 (triples), and $25 (quads). Clean, tiled bathrooms flow hot water plentifully. *Edison 106, tel. 5/566–09–33 or 5/566–09–34. From Metro Revolución, walk south on Ponciano Amiaga and turn right on Edison. 45 rooms, all with bath. Garage.*

Hotel Frimont. If you're one of those people who coordinate their socks and underwear, this place is for you; everything is done in a tasteful light brown and sky blue. Spacious rooms come with their own TV and touch-tone phone, and almost-scalding water steams out of the shower. Should you find yourself low on pesos, the friendly staff offers currency exchange. There are also Ladatel phones in the lobby. Many business travelers take advantage of the reasonable prices: singles $14.50, doubles $15–$18. *Jesús Terán 35, tel. 5/705–41–69. From Metro Revolución, walk east on Puente de Alvarado, right on Jesús Terán. 85 rooms, all with bath. Garage, laundry, luggage storage, restaurant, travel agency. Reservations advised. MC, V.*

NEAR METRO PINO SUAREZ

The hotels here appeal to traveling salespeople and tourists willing to stay a bit out of the way. There isn't much to see in these few blocks south of the Zócalo, but the hotels are cheap, you're likely to find vacancies year-round, and getting to the major sights is a breeze, thanks to the Metro. During the day the streets are crowded with shoppers looking for bargains on everything from clothing to cashews. At night, however, it's obscenely quiet—great for sleeping, but a bit scary if you're out alone.

➤ **UNDER $15** • **Hotel Latino.** This modern, pastel-decor hotel has its advantages: TVs, cleanliness, great water pressure, and incredibly quiet rooms (perhaps because they have no windows). On the downside, you may have to wade through hordes of people waiting for the bus right in front of the hotel's only entrance. Singles and doubles are $10. *Netzahualcóyotl 201, tel. 5/522–36–47. Catercorner to Metro Pino Suárez. 40 rooms, all with bath. Luggage storage (free), room service. Reservations advised.*

Hotel Monte Carlo. This beautiful, quiet hotel is by far the nicest in its price range. A large, marble staircase rises from the lobby to the black-and-white-tiled second floor. The huge rooms, complete with kitschy decorations and French doors, are spotless, and the bathrooms have hot water. Rooms without baths have sinks, and all rooms have phones. Singles are $8.50 ($12.50 with bath), doubles $9 ($16 with bath). *República de Uruguay 69, tel. 5/518–14–18 or 5/521–25–59. From Metro Pino Suárez. walk south on Pino Suárez, left on República de Uruguay. 60 rooms, 36 with bath. Garage, luggage storage (free), money exchange. Reservations advised. Wheelchair access (1 step).*

Hotel San Miguel. The only thing you might remember about this place a week later is its bright cotton-candy-pink exterior. Interior rooms share a view of large, steel hot-water tanks, but then again, the water in the bathrooms *is* hot. Singles are $8.50, doubles $13.50. *José María Izazaga 146, at Av. Pino Suárez, tel. 5/522–86–20 or 5/522–86–21. Across from Metro Pino Suárez. 40 rooms, all with bath. Luggage storage.*

➤ **UNDER $20** • **Hotel Roble.** While the pastel walls of this hotel contrast painfully with the crimson carpet, the rooms are small, tidy, and comfortable. The water in the clean bathrooms gets hot if you give it time. Singles are $11.50, doubles $14–$15.50. The restaurant next door serves a filling breakfast for about $3. *República de Uruguay 109, tel. 5/522–78–30 or 5/522–80–83. From Metro Pino Suárez, walk south on Pino Suárez and turn left on República de Uruguay. 61 rooms, all with bath. Luggage storage, restaurant. MC, V.*

ZONA ROSA

Hotels in the Zona Rosa are as posh and expensive as the bars and restaurants that surround them. Still, you can find comfortable and affordable lodging in the residential areas bordering the tourist zone. Insurgentes and Paseo de la Reforma run right through the area, and the greenery of Parque Chapultepec is easily accessible.

➤ **UNDER $20** • **Hotel Parador Washington.** This sprawling pink building on a tree-lined plaza boasts Sevillian architecture, large airy rooms, and one of the friendliest staffs around. The manager is always willing to give you free Spanish lessons, and will tell you all about his experiences with the KGB. Singles are $13, doubles $15. *Dinamarca 42, at Londres, tel. 5/703–08–93. From Metro Insurgentes, go 4 blocks east on Chapultepec, and left on Dinamarca. 40 rooms, all with bath. Laundry, luggage storage, restaurant.*

➢ **UNDER $30** • **Casa González.** This guesthouse is so secluded that you may feel as if you've accidentally stumbled into a 19th-century home. You'll never feel like an intruder, however, since the tastefully decorated living room looks as if it has been anticipating your arrival. The cozy, old-fashioned rooms are immaculate, graced with wood furniture, and the spotless bathrooms, complete with tubs, are lined with traditional *azulejos* (tiles). Singles cost $20–$23, doubles $27. Señor González, who speaks fluent English, cooks delicious, relatively inexpensive meals to order (breakfast $4.25, dinner $10), so let him know if you'll be coming home to eat. *Río Sena 69, tel. 5/514–33–02. From Metro Insurgentes, take Génova across Reforma and Río Lerma. 20 rooms, all with bath. Luggage storage (free).*

ROUGHING IT

If you're a thrill seeker or incredibly poor, there are always the bus stations. Yes, you can crash at any one of these for the night, but who knows if your stuff will be with you when you awake; stash your valuables in a luggage locker. If you have a late flight or layover (or no money), you can always try sleeping on the extremely uncooperative plastic chairs in the airport lounges. In case of utmost desperation, try the benches of the Alameda, temporary havens for many of Mexico City's homeless, but, as always, be aware of your surroundings. For a close-up experience in Mexican political activism, join the occasional hunger strikers on the Zócalo, who camp out under roughly constructed tents.

Food

You can spend plenty of pesos eating your way through Mexico City, which has a wide range of restaurants, from inexpensive to refined. All over the city, but particularly in the Zona Rosa, you can find just about anything to suit your tastes—from snazzy sushi bars to the ubiquitous Taco Bell.

It's possible to eat for very little money, but only if you're not scared by the myth that eating at tiny mom-and-pop operations or at street stands will send you running for the bathroom. The food at these places is usually cooked to order, so you can tell if it has been sitting out too long or hasn't been cooked well enough. If there's a crowd of local folk at a certain place, you can bet the food there is good. Another budget survival tactic is the *comida corrida* (pre-prepared lunch special), usually beans and rice with meat, plus coffee and sometimes soup or salad, usually for under $4. Try the restaurants along Isabel La Católica in the downtown area: They usually post their daily comida corrida conspicuously. If you don't mind standing, *puestecitos* (food stands) can almost always be found surrounding Metro stations, selling everything from *tacos de cabeza* (head meat tacos) to *tamarindo* (tamarind) candy. Cheap fruits and vegetables as well as taco stands can also be found at the markets (*see* Shopping, *below*), and for those with delicate tummies or sudden, uncontrollable hankerings for a hamburger, there is always **Sanborns** or **Vips**, chain restaurants serving a hybrid of American and Mexican cuisines.

SOME HEALTHY STREET EATS:

- *Alegrías: large cookies made with amaranth (a whitish grain) and honey*
- *Cocktel de frutas: sliced mangos, papayas, watermelon, or jicama, with salt, lemon, and chile*
- *Licuados: milk blended with such fruits as banana, mamey, or papaya*

ZOCALO/BELLAS ARTES

Plenty of restaurants crowd the center of the city, from humble *fondas* (food stands) to elegant tourist-oriented places. Satisfy your sweet tooth at **Dulcería Celaya** (5 de Mayo 39), still located in the same beautiful 19th-century building in which it was founded in 1874. *Churro* (an elongated, sugar-coated donut) fans crowd into the 24-hour **Churrería El Moro** (Lázaro Cárdenas 42, tel. 5/512–08–26). **La Michoacana,** an ice cream and *agua fresca* (juice drink) chain, has branches sprinkled over the city. Forgo the usual vanilla ice cream and go for more adventurous flavors such as guanabana, mamey, or alfalfa.

➢ **UNDER $5** • **Café El Popular.** This restaurant lives up to its name: At breakfast or lunch you'll probably have to wait for a seat. Try the ever-popular *huevos rancheros* (fried eggs on a corn tortilla with spicy *ranchero* sauce) for $1.50, or the tamales (80¢). The waitresses (who aren't exactly famous for their speed) tempt you with pastries while you wait for your food, but try to restrain yourself—they keep tabs and charge for every morsel eaten. *5 de Mayo 52, 1 block west of the Zócalo, tel. 5/518–60–81. Open 24 hrs.*

Café Cinco de Mayo. Come here to slurp delicious soup and soak in the lunch-counter atmosphere, complete with twirling stools. A full Mexican food menu is also featured, but the soups are the real draw; among the best are lentil ($1.50) and cream of mushroom ($1.75). *5 de Mayo 57, tel. 5/510–19–95. 1 block west of Zócalo. Open daily 7 AM–11 PM. Wheelchair access.*

Super Soya. Everything in this bright little health food store and vegetarian restaurant is orange: the floor, counters, and even the waitresses' uniforms. At lunchtime you'll have to fight for a seat to enjoy your soyburger ($1) or veggie taco (40¢). A large fruit salad with yogurt is $2. If you crave ice cream, don't miss the fragrant, homemade waffle cones. *Tacuba 40, at Motolinia, no phone. Near Metro Allende. Open daily 9–9.*

El Vegetariano. You'll have to hunt carefully to find this hotbed of vegetarianism—it's up a long, narrow stairway squeezed between two jewelry shops. Look for the doormat in the entryway. From 1 to 7 they serve a filling veggie *menú del día* (daily special) that includes fruit or vegetable salad, hot or cold soup, two main dishes, dessert, and *agua fresca* for only $3.50. À la carte dishes, such as mushrooms in *salsa verde* (green sauce), are $2. With any luck, you'll catch the occasional piano player, who will liven up your meal with an off-tune version of *The Lone Ranger* theme. *Madero 56, tel. 5/521–68–80. 1 block west of the Zócalo. Open Mon.–Sat. 8–7.*

➢ **UNDER $10** • **Café de Tacuba.** Founded in 1912, this expensive but lovely chandelier-lit restaurant is perfect for a splurge. If you can keep from laughing at the ridiculously huge bows stuck to the waitresses' heads, you'll enjoy the traditional spinach-topped *enchiladas tacuba* ($6) and the filling *pozole* (corn soup; $4.50). Lighter dishes, such as garlic soup, cost less than $2. The café usually gets pretty crowded for lunch and dinner, especially Thursday–Sunday between 6 and 10, when there's live music. *Tacuba 28, near Metro Allende, tel. 5/512–84–82. Open daily 8 AM–11:30 PM. Wheelchair access. AE, MC, V.*

La Ópera. Once a popular cantina, this restaurant/bar boasts a colorful history. Porfirio Díaz and his decadent crowd drank here, and Pancho Villa once stormed in and shot holes in the ceiling. Today the old fashioned, carved wood booths and gilded, ornate ceiling (complete with bullet holes) make this an elegant escape from the hectic rhythm of the Zócalo. Enjoy the delicious paella for $7 or the varying *menú del día* for $5.50. If you're feeling adventurous, ask for the *Pancho Villa* cocktail—tequila served in a hollowed cucumber, accompanied by *sangrita* (tomato juice) in a fresh tomato ($2.50–$3.50, depending on the tequila you select). *5 de Mayo 10, at Filomeno Mata, tel. 5/512–89–59. 5 blocks from the Zócalo. Open Mon.–Sat. 1 PM–midnight, Sun. 1–6. Wheelchair access. AE, MC, V.*

Sanborns. The baroque building that houses this Sanborns branch, better known as *La Casa de los Azulejos* (The House of Tiles), has a topsy-turvy history. Originally the residence of aristocrats, it became the elite Mexico City Jockey Club, and, during the revolutionary turmoil, served as the headquarters for anarchist groups. Today it looks more like a museum than a restaurant. *Enchiladas suizas* (enchiladas in cheese sauce) cost about $3.50, as does a burger with fries. *Madero 4, tel. 5/518–66–76. From Metro Bellas Artes, walk south on Lázaro Cárdenas, left on Madero. Open daily 7:30 AM–11 PM.*

ZONA ROSA

The Zona Rosa brims with restaurants, bars, and nightspots—most of them beyond a budget traveler's means. Some streets are closed to vehicular traffic, and pedestrians leisurely stroll past street performers and beggars. Copenhague, a tiny block-long street just south of Paseo de la Reforma, has a great variety of restaurants and boutiques, but this area tends to be pricey. If your purse is as empty as your belly, there are cheaper joints on Chapultepec near Amberes, right outside Metro Insurgentes. To eat away from the tourist zone, cross Reforma and continue beyond the U.S. Embassy to Río Lerma (or any other street whose name begins with Río), where you'll find small restaurants offering cheap but tasty comidas corridas.

➢ **UNDER $5** • **El Gallito Taquería.** This taquería serves a variety of hot, delicious snacks sure to satisfy most late-night cravings. The restaurant fills up by 3 AM, when the clubs in the Zona are closed but no one's ready to go home. A filling order of *tacos poblanos con queso* (tacos prepared with pork and cheese) is $4. Vegetarians also have it made here: Meatless tacos will cost you about $2.50. *Liverpool 115, tel. 5/511–14–36. ½ block north of Génova. Open Mon.–Thurs. 10 AM–5 AM, Fri. and Sat. 10 AM–6 AM, Sun. noon–2 AM.*

El Huarache Azteca. Though slightly grimy and yellowed with age, this small, nondescript restaurant lures hungry locals on their lunch break, causing the occasional wait. In the morning, typical Mexican breakfasts—eggs and rice, *huaraches* (long, stuffed tortillas), and juice—are served for $1.50. The *comida corrida* ($2.50) will fill you up. *Chapultepec 317, at Amberes, tel. 5/525–13–04. Open Mon.–Sat. 7:30–7:30. Wheelchair access.*

Kobá-Ich. This small, clean restaurant seems to attract a largely foreign clientele, perhaps because of the posted sign claiming to provide "All the flavor of Yucatán at your table." One taste of the *pollo pibil* (chicken baked in banana leaves; $5)—so tender it falls off the bone—and you'll be hooked. For the more adventurous, there are *tacos de cazón* (baby shark tacos; $2.50). *Londres 136-A, btw Génova and Amberes, tel. 5/208–57–91. From Metro Insurgentes, take Génova to Londres and turn left. Open Mon.–Sat. 8 AM–10 PM.*

Restaurant Parri. This bright, airy restaurant all done up in red and white is the place to go for chicken. The *parri tampiqueña* (a quarter of a flame-broiled chicken, an enchilada, guacamole, and refried beans; $4.50) is especially good. *Hamburgo 154, at Génova, tel. 5/207–07–57. Open Mon.–Thurs. 8 AM–1 AM, Fri. and Sat. 8 AM–3 AM. Wheelchair access.*

➢ **UNDER $10** • **Fonda El Refugio.** The gleaming white walls, impeccably shined copper pots, and small wooden tables in this elegant little restaurant contrast with the colorful blue lining on the wall and the bright pink chimney. The clientele consists mostly of expatriates and tourists. The *sopa de hongos* (mushroom soup; $2.75) and the *pescado a la veracruzana* (red snapper cooked with tomatoes, onions, capers, peppers, and herbs; $9) both go well with the $3 powerhouse margaritas. *Liverpool 166, at Génova, tel. 5/207–27–32. Open Mon.–Sat. 1–1.*

➢ **UNDER $15** • **Bellinghausen.** Don't let the German name deceive you—this posh restaurant in the center of the Zona Rosa specializes in Mexican food. The wood-paneled interior and the outdoor garden create a cozy, upscale atmosphere, which explains why the place is popular among Mexico City's businessmen. The food is delicious and well worth the splurge. Try fried *huachinango* (fish) for $10, or the *filete chemita* (beef) for $11. Especially good is *chiles en nogada* (stuffed chiles topped with cream), a Puebla specialty available only in September. *Londres 95, at Niza, tel. 5/207–49–78. Open daily 1–10:30. Wheelchair access. MC, V.*

COYOACAN

Although people come to Coyoacán from all over the D.F., the area manages to retain the atmosphere of a small neighborhood, where cozy family establishments and tiny taquerías cluster around plazas. About 1½ blocks south of the plazas on Carrillo Puerto is a particularly inviting collection of fondas and taquerías. Or walk 4 blocks north on Allende to the Mercado, where you can fill yourself up on fresh fruit and veggies or delicious chicken, shrimp, or beef tostadas for about $2.

➢ **UNDER $5** • **Merendero "Las Lupitas."** On a narrow, cobblestone street just off sleepy Plaza Santa Catarina, this restaurant is about as picturesque as it gets. The dining area is suffused with natural light, earth-tone tiles cover the floor, and sturdy wooden beams support the ceiling. The food has a *norteño* (northern Mexican) influence, so they use flour rather than corn tortillas. The lightly fried cheese or meat *empanadas* (turnovers) are practically greaseless and cost less than $3, and a filling comida corrida goes for $5. Saturdays are especially busy, and you can expect a short wait for dinner on weekends. *Jardín de Santa Catarina 4, at Francisco*

Sosa, tel. 5/554–33–53. From Jardín Centenario, walk west on Francisco Sosa for a few blocks. Open daily 7–midnight.

Taco Inn. As the name suggests, this *taquería* is clean, colorful, and gringo-pandering. The food, however, is as authentic as it gets. Try the delicious beef tacos with cilantro and onions for $1, or the ignominiously named *gringas* (pork and cheese sandwiched between two flour tortillas) for $1.50. *Presidente Carranza 106, at Carrillo Puerto, tel. 5/554–02–88 or 5/554–06–73. From Jardín Centenario, turn left on Carrillo Puerto. Open Mon.–Thurs. 2 PM–1 AM, Fri. and Sat. 2 PM–3 AM. AE, MC, V.*

El Tarro de Coyoacán. This joint is the perfect place to relax and cool down from the daily heat. The combination of their *tortas de chorizo* ($4) and a few large beers ($2) may numb you to the blaring disco music. *Camillo Puerto 9, around cnr from Jardín Centenario, tel. 5/554–47–58. Open daily 7 AM–2 AM. MC, V.*

➤ **UNDER $10** • **Fonda El Morral.** Founded in 1967, this bright, Spanish-style fonda has beautiful wrought-iron windows and blue-and-white-tiled doorways. The comida corrida here is a reasonable $3.50, while a generous and sizzling *carne tampiqueña* (grilled meat) goes for $6. *Allende 2, tel. 5/554–02–98. From Metro Coyoacán, take pesero VILLA COAPA to Jardín Centenario. Open daily 8 AM–9 PM.*

SAN ANGEL

Most visitors avoid the busy Avenidas Insurgentes and Revolución and head up to the quiet cobblestoned streets of Plaza San Jacinto to relax and enjoy the serenity of this small, colonial neighborhood. There's a good selection of restaurants along Madero, but even cheaper fare can be found on the side streets near the Pemex station at the base of the Plaza del Carmen. The intersection of Quevedo and Universidad (near Metro M. A. de Quevedo) is another great place to find small, hectic restaurants or *puestecitos* (food stands), where you'll find fast, cheap food.

La Casona del Elefante. Next to the Bazar Sábado (*see* Shopping, *below*), the entry to this sophisticated and relatively inexpensive Indian restaurant is hidden behind a group of tall potted plants. The reward for your little scavenger hunt is delicious food served by frenzied waiters in glittery Indian vests. A tray of spicy salsas arrives at your table before you know what to order, although service slows considerably after that. All of the meat curries ($6) are recommended, and the curried vegetables make a good meal for about $4. *Plaza San Jacinto 9, tel. 5/616–16–01 or 5/616–22–08. From Metro M. A. de Quevedo, west on Quevedo, left on La Paz; when it forks, take Madero to Plaza San Jacinto. Open Mon.–Thurs. 1–11, Fri. and Sat. 1–midnight, Sun. 1–6.*

Fechoria. This Argentine restaurant has a huge upstairs window through which you look down upon sweaty pedestrians—if only they knew you were relaxing in front of a plate of ricotta ravioli ($5) and a cool glass of wine ($1.50). Expect a youthful, hungry crowd on weekends. *La Paz 58-A, tel. 5/550–18–34. From Metro M.A. de Quevedo, walk west on Quevedo to La Paz. Open Mon.–Thurs. 1–11, Fri. and Sat. 1–midnight, Sun 1–7. AE, MC, V.*

Parrilla El Tecolote. This taquería stands out for its incredibly inexpensive food. The waiters are in a constant, frantic rush, and by 1 or 2 PM the place is packed. Keep cool in the dark interior with a bowl of *sopa de verduras con pollo* (vegetable soup with chicken) for $1, or the filling comida corrida ($1.50). The innocuous-looking light-green salsa will have you begging for a glass of water. *M. A. de Quevedo 75, no phone. 1½ blocks from Metro M. A. de Quevedo.*

CAFES

½ Luna Café. This tiny café on the western tip of the Zona Rosa is the perfect place to escape from the hectic pace of the surrounding area. Its small wooden tables are perfect for writing letters, and strong cappuccino in only $1. *Florencia 36, btw Lonches and Hamburgo, tel. 5/511–27–77. Metro: Insurgentes. Open weekdays 8 AM–9 PM, Sat. 10–6.*

Café Gandhi. If you packed a beret, whip it out for a visit to this well-known gallery/bookstore/coffeehouse. Strong cappuccino can be ordered with Kahlua or Amaretto ($2) for an added kick. Service is about as slow as the chess players who pass entire afternoons brooding over moves while their cigarettes burn low. Nonsmokers can rejoice, however; the enlightened management provides a tiny no-smoking section. *M. A. de Quevedo 128, Coyoacán, tel. 5/550–25–24 or 5/548–98–87. Near Metro M. A. de Quevedo. Open weekdays 9:30 AM–11 PM, weekends 10:30–10.*

El Parnaso Café. Bliss is sitting comfortably beneath the shady awnings of this popular café/bookstore in the eastern corner of Coyoacán's Jardín Centenario. Although it gets crowded on weekends, it's quite acceptable to share a table. The waiters are always on the run, so they don't pay much attention to you—but once you get your coffee (about $1), the afternoon is yours. *Carillo Puerto 2, tel. 5/554–22–25. From Metro M. A. de Quevedo, take pesero VILLA COAPA to Jardín Centenario. Open daily 9 AM–10 PM. Wheelchair access.*

UNAM Café. Stop by if you happen to find yourself south of the UNAM campus or waiting for a show in the Centro Cultural Universitario. Huge windows afford a great view of theatergoers meandering past the fountain just outside. Professors and intellectuals discuss ideas over strong cups of coffee (less than $1). *Centro Cultural Universitario, UNAM. From Insurgentes, take TLALPAN-JOYA bus and get off at 3rd pedestrian overpass on campus. From Metro Universidad, take a pesero to Centro Cultural Universitario.*

La Vienet Café. After a visit to the Kahlo museum, be sure to stop by this little café for some of the sweetest desserts around. Its balcony and beautiful wrought-iron chairs almost make you forget that the best of Barry Manilow is playing in the background. A bite of the delicious mocha cake ($1.50) may anesthetize you to "Copacabana." *Viena, at Abasolo, tel. 5/554–45–23. 2 blocks north and 1 block east of Frida Kahlo museum. Open Tues.–Sun. 8–8.*

Worth Seeing

Although you could live in Mexico City for years and still never see all there is to see, the worthwhile attractions are clustered in separate districts, making the mammoth Distrito Federal easier to manage. Keep in mind that each area has a distinct personality that goes beyond the tourist attractions; you'll understand life in Mexico City better hanging out than by storming through the sights on automatic pilot. If you decide to do the **Zócalo** and rush blindly from museum to museum, you'll miss the center's character. In the **Alameda Central** you may have to wade through hordes of hurried businessmen on breaks, aggressive street vendors, and spaced-out tourists, while in the calmer southern parts of **Coyoacán** and **San Ángel** you'll encounter a more leisurely lifestyle, conducive to students browsing in bookstores and people chatting in cafés and plazas. Nearby, the **Ciudad Universitaria** is the place to mingle with college students. **Parque Chapultepec** provides a green escape from the cars and the crowds—climb up **Cerro Chapulín**, and gaze at the hectic city life from a distance.

The ambience of the **Zona Rosa** seems to agree with upper-class chilangos, kids hanging out after class, hurdy-gurdy men playing music for pesos and, of course, tons of tourists. The district was designed for pedestrians: Wide brick paths weave between statues and well-pruned shrubs. Clean-cut business types take their lunch breaks here, and students wander the streets, ice cream in hand, to ogle the glitzy shops. At night, cars with deafening techno-pop pouring from their open windows crawl along the avenues while disco and barhoppers dressed in black try their best to look cool as they mingle outside the doorways of the popular clubs.

ALAMEDA CENTRAL

The Alameda Central was the site of a *tianguis* (open-air market) in Aztec times and of the burning of heretics during the Inquisition. By the mid-19th century it had become a park where the rich strolled under the trees, while the poor (who were kept out) looked on. Now everybody meanders through the park, lounging during lunch hour, playing chess, sleeping on the grass,

Zócalo and the Alameda Central

Casa de los Azulejos, **10**
La Catedral Metropolitana, **13**
Monumento a Benito Juárez, **3**
Museo de Artes e Industrias Populares, **4**
Museo de la Caricatura, **11**
Museo Franz Mayer, **5**
Museo Mural de Diego Rivera, **2**
Museo Nacional de Arte, **8**
Museo Nacional de la Revolución, **1**
Palacio de Bellas Artes, **7**
Palacio Nacional, **14**
Plaza de Tres Culturas, **6**
Templo Mayor, **12**
Torre Latinoamericana, **9**

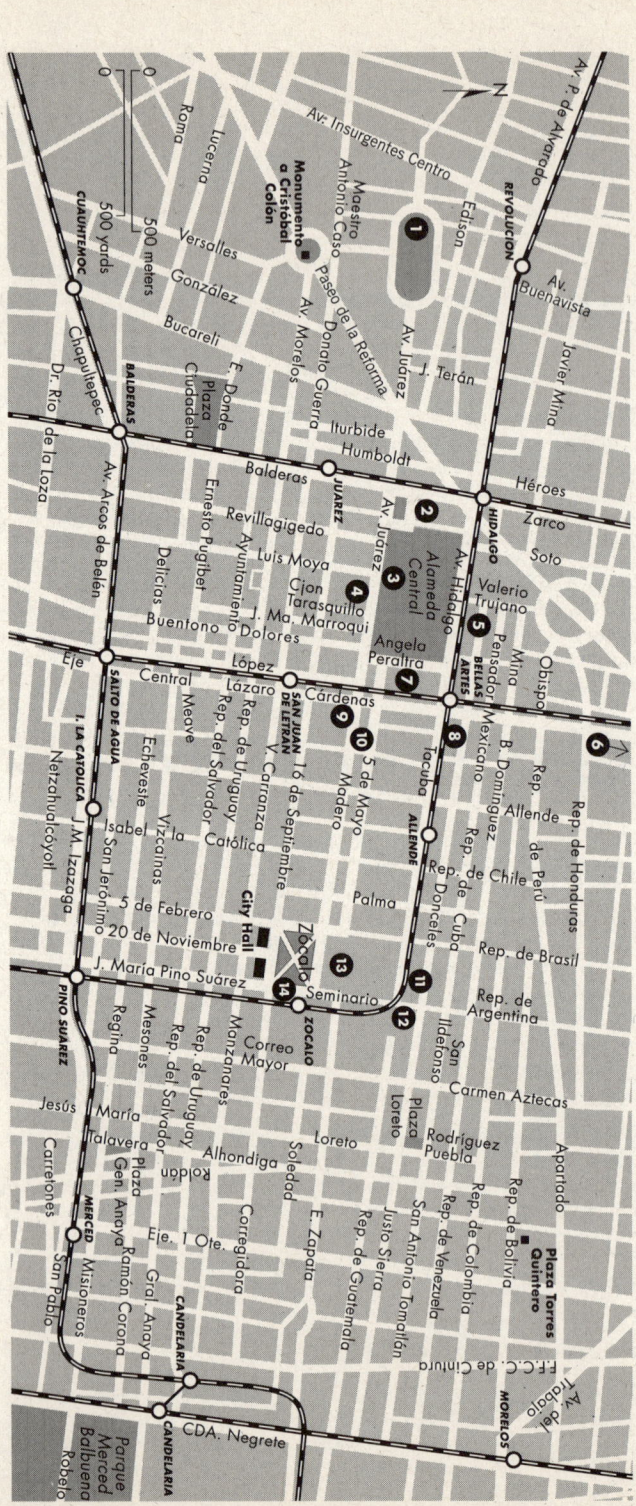

or smooching on the benches. The white marble semicircle on the south side of the park (bordering Avenida Juárez) is the **Monumento a Benito Juárez** (opposite Metro Bellas Artes), commemorating the hero of the Reform period. On the eastern edge of the park, the **Casa de Los Azulejos** (Madero 4, behind Bellas Artes) peeks out from behind the Palacio de Bellas Artes. Although somewhat dulled by a thin layer of urban grime, the beautiful tiles covering the Casa are a quintessential example of ornaments in Colonial architecture.

MUSEO DE ARTES E INDUSTRIAS POPULARES The bright, Pepto-pink walls of this one-room museum make it feel more like a *mercado de artesanía* (crafts market) than a museum. Children's toys, ceremonial masks, traditional regional dresses, and weaving from all over Mexico are displayed behind glass. The principal appeal of this museum is that it's free: The exhibits, although interesting, aren't presented very well. An unintended architectural exhibit is on view through the windows: You can see the massive structural damage sustained by the surrounding buildings in the 1985 quake. *Juárez 44, tel. 5/518–30–58. Metro Bellas Artes or Metro Hidalgo. Walk behind the museum store down alleyway García Lorca and through doorway labeled EDIFICIO F. Admission free. Museum open weekdays 10–3; gift shop open weekdays 10–6.*

MUSEO FRANZ MAYER The building housing the Franz Mayer Museum is worth a visit in itself. Originally built in the 16th century, and alternately used as a hospital, an orphanage, and a convent, the exterior of the museum is in perfect condition. It has a large inside courtyard with a refreshing fountain. In 1980 the building was turned over to the Franz Mayer Cultural Trust. The musuem displays an impressive collection of Mexican ceramics, furniture, and paintings, amassed by Franz Mayer (a.k.a. Don Pancho), a German-born farmer who lived in Mexico nearly his entire life. *Hidalgo, in front of Metro Bellas Artes, tel. 5/518–22–65. Admission: $1.25, 40¢ students. Open Tues.–Sun. 10–5. Guided tours Tues.–Fri. 10:30, 11:30, 12:30, 1:30, Sat. 10:30, 11:30, and 12:30.*

The Hospital de Jesús on Pino Suárez (the entrance is down the alleyway next to Gigo's Pizza) stands on the site where the Aztec Emperor Montezuma II stood face to face for the first time with Hernán Cortés. The hospital itself, the oldest in the Americas, was founded by Cortés in 1524.

MUSEO MURAL DE DIEGO RIVERA Diego Rivera's mural *Sueño de una Tarde Dominical en la Alameda Central* (Dream of a Sunday Afternoon in the Alameda Central) is showcased in its own museum. Despite its apparently uncontroversial subject matter, the work initially caused a stir because Rivera captioned it "Dios no existe" (God doesn't exist). After several incidents of vandalism, Rivera painted over the offending words with "Conferencia de Letrán, año de 1836," a reference to a speech given by the mid-19th century radical congressman Ignacio Ramírez, in which he declared God to be "nonexistent." The museum also hosts intriguing temporary modern art and photography exhibits. *Plaza Solidaridad, tel. 5/510–23–29 or 5/512–07–54. In far western cnr of Alameda Central. From Metro Balderas, cross street to Plaza Solidarida. From Metro Juárez, north on Balderas to plaza. Admission: $1, free students. Open Tues.–Sun. 10–6.*

MUSEO NACIONAL DE ARTE This imposing stone building, once home to the Palacio de Communicación (Communications Palace), now houses an impressive collection of artwork on two floors, each open on alternate days of the week. The 20th-century exhibits on the first floor include some of the more famous works in post-revolutionary *indigenismo* (indigenous style). Indigenismo painters, including Rivera, Orozco, and Siquieros, glorified rural life, the *indígena* (indigenous person), and the *campesino* (peasant), finding in these figures a new understanding of *lo mexicano* (Mexicanness) and a basis for a "national" style. Nineteenth-century works like those of José María Velasco (famous for his innovative landscapes) are on the second floor. *Tacuba 8, tel. 5/521–74–61. Metro: Bellas Artes or Allende. Admission: $1.50, free Sun. Open Tues.–Sun. 10–5:30.*

MUSEO NACIONAL DE LA REVOLUCION Just a few blocks from the Alameda, the **Monumento a la Revolución,** which houses this museum in its basement, is well worth the detour. Newspapers, films, and dioramas carefully document more than half a century of Mexican history, from the presidency of Benito Juárez to the signing of the constitution in 1917. *Plaza de* la República, tel. 5/546–21–15. From Alameda Central, walk west on Juárez. From Metro Revolución, follow Ponciano Arriaga to plaza. Admission free. Open Tues.–Sat. 9–5, Sun. 9–3.

PALACIO DE BELLAS ARTES Construction of the neoclassical Palace of Fine Arts began in 1904 under President Porfirio Díaz. It was scheduled for completion in 1910, the centennial of Mexican independence, but neither Díaz nor Italian architect Adamo Boari took the area's porous subsoil into account (the building is still sinking today). Technical difficulties coupled with the upheaval of the Mexican Revolution delayed completion of the building until July 1932. By then architectural fads had changed, and the building was given an art deco interior by architect Federico Mariscal, who combined geometric shapes, straight lines, and traditional Mexican forms.

Today breathtaking murals by Rivera and Siqueiros grace the walls, and a chandelier portraying the two volcanoes to the south of the Distrito Federal, designed by Gerardo Murillo (a.k.a Dr. Atl) and assembled by Tiffany's of New York City, hangs in the main amphitheater. The **Ballet Folklórico**, the **Compañía Nacional de Danza** (National Ballet), and the **Orquesta Sinfónica Nacional** (National Symphony Orchestra) perform here. Tickets for performances (*see* After Dark, *below*) can be purchased at counters (open Mon.–Sat. 11–7 and Sun. 9–7) on the first floor of the palace, next to the main entrance.

The top floor of the palace houses the **Museo Nacional de Arquitectura** (National Architecture Museum), whose permanent collection includes the plans for the future construction of Bellas Artes and murals by Diego Rivera, Siqueiros, Orozco, and Tamayo. For guided tours, call 5/510–13–88 in advance. *Lázaro Cárdenas, at Juárez, across from Alameda Central, tel. 5/512–36–33. Metro: Bellas Artes. Admission: $1.75, temporary exhibits free. Museum open Tues.–Sun. 10–6. Wheelchair access.*

PLAZA DE LAS TRES CULTURAS/TLATELOLCO At the center of the Tlatelolco District, this plaza is best known for the events that took place here the evening of October 2, 1968. The preceding week had been one of political protest and riots, including the army occupation of the National University and at least one student's death. Discontent focused on President Díaz Ordaz's anti-activist laws criminalizing "social dissolution," the use of a paramilitary riot squad (*grenaderos*) against students, and the huge expenses incurred by Mexico's preparations for hosting the 1968 summer Olympics. On the evening of October 2, about 5,000 people gathered on the Plaza de las Tres Culturas in a peaceful demonstration to decry the government's failure to meet student demands. They were met by army and police units in tanks and armored cars. The government claims to this day that snipers in surrounding apartment buildings then opened fire, which police returned. Others claim that the army shot first. At any rate, few today doubt that the death toll was well into the hundreds.

The plaza is named for its symbols of the three main cultures of Mexico—indigenous, Spanish, and mestizo—and is home to the ruins of a pre-Hispanic ceremonial center. The **Iglesia de Santiago Tlatelolco** (1609), amidst a huge complex of apartment buildings around the plaza, is representative of the colonial period, and houses the baptismal font of Juan Diego, the

The Man Without a Face

Despite Diego Rivera's outspoken opposition to capitalism, in 1933 John D. Rockefeller commissioned him to paint a mural, called "Man at the Crossing of the Ways," for the RCA Building in New York City. Rockefeller was nervous about the first sketches that Rivera showed him. His uneasiness quickly turned to anger when, much to his multimillionaire surprise, the faceless man helping a group of workers in the sketches was transformed into Lenin in the mural. Although the tycoon ordered the mural's destruction, Rivera soon found a home for a reproduction of his masterpiece in the Palacio de Bellas Artes (see above).

Indian convert to whom the Virgin of Guadalupe appeared in 1531. Mestizo culture is represented on the plaza by the ultramodern Ministry of Foreign Affairs. *From Metro Tlatelolco, east on Manuel González, right on Lázaro Cárdenas.*

TORRE LATINOAMERICANA This 41-story tower springs up amid the downtown colonial buildings. The view from the *mirador* (observation deck) will leave you breathless, especially if you decide to forgo the elevator. If the line of voyeurs waiting to use the telescopes is too long, head to the fantastic **Sea World Aquarium** (the highest aquarium in the world) on the 38th floor. *Lázaro Cárdenas, 3 blocks from Metro Bellas Artes. Open daily 10 AM–11 PM. Tower admission: $2.50. Aquarium admission: an additional $1.50.*

ZOCALO

The spot presently occupied by Mexico City's Zócalo was at the center of the Aztec capital of Tenochtitlán. Sadly, hardly anything from this majestic era remains: Arrogant and anxious to secure a hold on the New World, the Spanish built directly on top of Aztec structures. Beginning in the 16th century, ornate churches and convents, fancy mansions, and other stately edifices were constructed around the plaza, sometimes incorporating the volcanic stone pilfered from Aztec buildings. Toward the end of the 19th century, the upper classes began moving out of the crowded downtown, leaving their mansions to be partitioned and occupied by the working class and the poor. Today the Zócalo, bordered by some of the most beautiful buildings of the colonial era, is a constant buzz of activity. Men in search of employment line up by the cathedral gate and busloads of school children on field trips periodically mob the plaza. The Zócalo is also the city's forum for political activity. Most protest marches end here, and many anti-PRI groups distribute flyers or sell newsletters on the plaza. This is also the place to stock up on Carlos Salinas de Gortari puppets or Subcomandante Marcos T-shirts.

LA CATEDRAL METROPOLITANA This enormous cathedral on the north side of the Zócalo was built between 1573 and 1813. The first large altar in the center of the cathedral, the **Altar de Perdón,** is a copy of the original that burned in a 1967 fire. Smaller chapels line both sides of the cathedral. All are beautiful, but a few deserve special attention. The first chapel on the left contains a display with sculpted flowers, each with four petals—an example of the indigenous influence on the church's architecture. The four petals represent the Aztec view of the universe, each petal symbolizing one of the four principal gods. Toward the back of the church is the third chapel (also on the left), containing **El Señor del Cacoa,** an image of Christ fashioned from corn paste, human nails, and hair. The paintings in the seventh chapel are dedicated to Felipe de Jesús, a martyred saint, and illustrate the story of his journey to Mexico from the Philippines. Apparently his ship was blown off course and wrecked in Japan, where he was condemned to death by the emperor. Legend has it that before his execution he predicted that the city in which he died (Nagasaki) would go up in flames.

For more information on the history and architecture of the cathedral, ask at the information booth for a guide named Martín Castellanos. For $10 this artist-turned-tour-guide will tell you everything there is to know about La Catedral—or any other place in Mexico City for that mat-

The Pedestal

The Zócalo—officially called the Plaza de la Constitución—is the largest plaza in the Western Hemisphere. The word "Zócalo" actually means "pedestal." In the 19th century there were plans to build a monument to Mexican Independence in Mexico City's main plaza. For whatever reason, the monument was never built, and all that remains of those designs is the name for the base of the monument—the "pedestal"—that never came into being. The misnomer stuck and is now the term applied to the main plazas of most Mexican cities.

ter. Other, unofficial guides are available for $3.50, but they pale in comparison. *Zócalo, across from Palacio Nacional.*

MUSEO DE LA CARICATURA Formerly the Colegio de Cristo (College of Christ), this beautiful building now houses the Latin American Cartoon Museum. The drawings run the gamut from sophisticated political commentary and satire to simple jokes that don't demand any knowledge of Spanish. During restoration of the building after the 1985 earthquake, pre-Columbian artifacts, including the sculpted head of a serpent, were unearthed here. The serpent's head was left as it was found and can still be seen at the back of the museum. Upstairs is the **Salón de la Plástica Mexicana,** with a small collection of 20th-century art. **La Catrina,** the tiny café in the courtyard, is the perfect place to take a breather. *Donceles 99, tel. 5/789-14-08 or 5/795-11-87. 2 blocks north of Zócalo, btw Brasil and Argentina. From Metro Allende, east on Tacuba, left on Brasil and right on Donceles. Admission: $1, 50¢ students. Open weekdays 10-6, weekends 10-5.*

PALACIO NACIONAL The National Palace was built under the direction of Hernán Cortés, on the site where Moctezuma's Grand Palace once stood. In fact, the *tezontle* (volcanic rock) now in the facade was taken from the Grand Palace and incorporated into the Spanish design. It was in the courtyard of this impressive edifice that Cortés entertained guests with Mexico's first bullfights. A starving, angry mob tore the palace down in 1692, but it was reconstructed the following year. Today the bell rung by Padre Hidalgo to proclaim Mexico's independence in 1810 hangs on the central facade; inside you'll find the offices of the president, the Federal Treasury, and the National Archive.

The second story of the Palace's main courtyard is covered with more than 1,200 square feet of murals that took Diego Rivera and his assistants more than 16 years to paint (1929-45). The series, called *Epic of the Mexican People in Their Struggle for Freedom and Independence,* portrays two millennia of Mexican history. The hero of the pre-Hispanic panels is the plumed serpent god of wind, Quetzalcoatl, whose prophesied return supposedly facilitated Cortés's conquest. Also prominent are a man offering a human arm for sale; Spanish soldiers arriving in the not-so-New World; Spanish priests; bell-ringing Hidalgo and reform-writing Juárez; revolutionaries Zapata and Pancho Villa; and even Karl Marx, smiling amid scenes of class struggle. The remaining murals in the corridor, painted from 1945 to 1951, show the capital city of Tenochtitlán and the vibrant market of Tlatelolco before the Spanish Conquest. Today a visit to the Palacio speaks volumes about the country's political uneasiness: Heavily armed guards flank the door and patrol the interior. To get in, you have to leave an ID at the door. *East side of Zócalo, tel. 5/512-20-60. Admission free. Open daily 9-5.*

TEMPLO MAYOR The Templo Mayor (Great Temple) was the political and spiritual center of the Aztec empire. For more than 400 years it remained buried beneath the Zócalo until, in February 1978, electric-company workers struck a small section of stone that turned out to be a portion of an eight-ton carving of Coyolxauhqui, goddess of the moon.

The temple itself was a massive structure, improved and enlarged on at least five separate occasions. Each renovation was a symbolic affirmation of the reigning Aztec's supremacy in the conquered Valley of Mexico. While most temples are typically dedicated to one major deity, the Templo Mayor was dedicated to both Huitzilopochtli (hummingbird god of the sun) and Tlaloc (god of rain and lightning). The Aztecs sacrificed as many as 10,000 persons every year (most of them either human victims from conquered tribes or rival warriors captured in ritual "flower wars") in an effort to appease the gods and scare the bejesus out of any tribes who dared defy Aztec hegemony. According to Aztec religion, without this sort of divine nourishment the sun god would refuse to move across the sky and Tlaloc would withhold the water for the crops.

Artifacts found during the excavation of the Templo Mayor are displayed in the **Museo del Templo Mayor.** Included in the exhibit are ceramic warriors, stone knives, skulls of sacrificial victims, the massive stone disk of the moon goddess, and a miniature model of Tenochtitlán. Free tours are available in English and Spanish, but you have to reserve two weeks in advance. Certified tourist office guides are available at the door and charge about $10 for a group tour. *On Zócalo, at Seminario and República de Guatemala, tel. 5/542-06-06 or 5/542-47-84, fax 5/542-17-17. Admission: $2.75, free Sun. Open Tues.-Sun. 9-5.*

BOSQUE DE CHAPULTEPEC

Known simply as "Chapultepec," this park is a haven from all things urban for families, joggers, cyclists, and young lovers. Unfortunately, all these people usually want to escape city life together, and the park tends to be quite crowded on weekends. Guarding the entrance to the park is the **Monumento a los Niños Héroes,** in honor of six young military cadets who died defending *la patria* (the fatherland) during the U.S. invasion in 1847, which cost Mexico almost half its national territory, including what are now the states of Texas, California, Arizona, New Mexico, and Nevada. Outdoor diversions are also plentiful: Tuesday–Sunday you can boat on the unsettlingly bright green lake for $1.50 an hour (up to five people), or traipse around the zoo for free. On any day of the week you can see how long that taco you had for lunch stays down on one of the many rides in **La Feria** amusement park (admission $3). Chapultepec also harbors many of Mexico's most significant monuments and museums, including the world-famous Museo Nacional de Antropología (*see below*). Both Metro Chapultepec and Metro Auditorio are located inside the park, and buses and peseros to the park run west from the centro down Paseo de la Reforma.

CASTILLO DE CHAPULTEPEC Chapultepec Castle sits perched atop the *Cerro Chapulín* (Grasshopper Hill), overlooking the entire Valley of Mexico. The oldest part of the castle still standing dates to 1785, when Viceroy Bernardo de Galvez built the first fort here. In 1841 the castle was converted into a military academy. Shortly after, at the end of the bloody battle for Mexico City during the U.S. invasion, a young cadet named Juan Escutia (one of the six honored by the Monumento a los Niños Héroes), realizing the battle was lost, climbed to the top of the northern tower, wrapped himself in the Mexican flag, and jumped to his glorious death. A tomb at the foot of the hill marks the place where he landed. Almost 20 years later, Emperor Maximilian, installed by the French, remodeled the castle and moved in. Chapultepec Castle would remain the official residence of the head of state until 1944, when President Lázaro Cárdenas moved to Los Pinos, the current presidential residence, and gave the castle to the Mexican people as the **Museo Nacional de Historia** (National History Museum). It now houses exhibits on social, economic, cultural, and political history, complemented by murals by José Clemente Orozco and Diego Rivera. The eternally lazy can take a train from Niños Héroes to the top of the hill for 60¢. *Uphill, beyond Monumento a Los Niños Héroes, tel. 5/553–62–46, 5/553–63–96 or 5/553–62–02. Admission: $2.50; free Sun. and students. Open Tues.–Sun. 9–5; ticket sales stop at 4 PM.*

MUSEO DE ARTE MODERNO Amid the greenery of Chapultepec Park, this museum is dedicated to modern painting, photography, and sculpture. The permanent collection includes work by Frida Kahlo, Dr. Atl (Gerardo Murillo), Rufino Tamayo, and Diego Rivera. The annex to the main building houses temporary exhibits of contemporary Mexican and international painting, lithography, sculpture, and photography. The surrounding gardens are sprinkled with off-the-wall sculptures. *South side of Reforma, at Gandhi, tel. 5/553–62–11 or 5/211–87–29 Admission: $2.50; free Sun. and students. Open Tues.–Sun. 10–5:30.*

MUSEO NACIONAL DE ANTROPOLOGIA Mexico's complex anthropological heritage demands a museum as grand as this one. It is by far the best in the country, with perhaps the finest archaeological collection in the world; each room displays artifacts from a different geographic region and/or culture. Pace yourself—if you try to cover it all at once, you'll end up hating the place. Make sure to check out stelae from Tula, a town north of Mexico City, with bas-reliefs carvings that indicate a heavy Maya influence. The museum also houses the original *Piedra del Sol*, the famous Aztec calendar. Guided tours in Spanish, English, and French are available Tuesday–Saturday at 9:30 AM and 5:30 PM. The museum's **Auditorio Jaime Torres Bodet** shows ethnographic films in Spanish daily at 6 PM. *Paseo de la Reforma, at Gandhi, tel. 5/553–62–66 or 5/553–63–86. Admission: $2.50, free Sun. Open Tues.–Sat. 9–7, Sun. 10–6. Wheelchair access.*

MUSEO TAMAYO DE ARTE CONTEMPORANEO INTERNACIONAL Finding this museum hidden within the dense foliage of Chapultepec Park requires the skill of a 16th-century navigator. Don't give up—it's worth the search. In 1981, Mexican artist Rufino Tamayo and his wife, Olga, donated their personal collection of painting and sculpture to the people, establishing this sleek, granite museum. It contains paintings by Pablo Picasso, René Magritte, Joan

Chapultepec and Zona Rosa

Castillo de Chapultepec, **5**
Monumento a los Niños Héroes, **7**
Museo de Arte Moderno, **6**
Museo Nacional de Antropología, **3**
Museo Tamayo, **4**
Plaza de Tres Culturas/Tlatelolco, **8**
Sala de Arte Publico Siqueiros, **1**
Zoológico, **2**

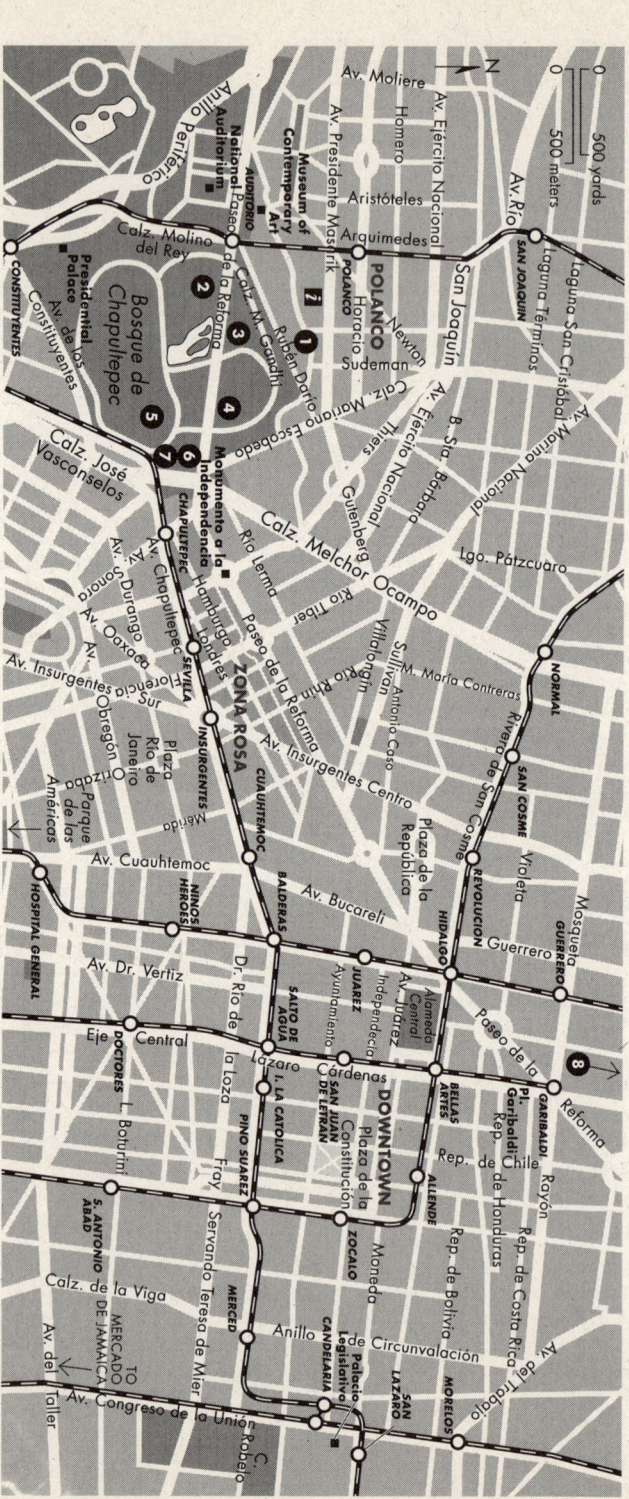

Miró, and quite a few of Tamayo's own works. Check out the aquatic sculptures at the front of the museum, which were once immersed for months at a time in the Atlantic Ocean to become oxidized. *Reforma, at Gandhi, tel. 5/286–58–89. Walk around Museo de Arte Moderno to Reforma. Admission: $2.50; free Sun. and students. Open Tues.–Sun. 10–6.*

SALA DE ARTE PUBLICO SIQUEIROS Just before his death muralist David Alfaro Siqueiros (a supporter of Stalin who had been involved in an unsuccessful attempt to assassinate Trotsky) bequeathed his home and studio to the people of Mexico. The interior walls of his workshop are covered with murals, and the house is cluttered with paintings, photographs, and some of the sketches he made for his most famous works, such as *New Democracy,* currently on display in the Palacio de Bellas Artes (*see above*). *Tres Picos 29, btw Schiller and Hegel, Col. Polanco, tel. 5/531–33–94 or 5/545–59–52. From Metro Auditorio, north on Arquimedes, right on Rubén Darío, left on Hegel, and right on Tres Picos. Admission: $1, free students. Open Tues.–Sun. 10–6.*

ZOOLOGICO DE CHAPULTEPEC In its recent remodeling campaign, the zoo forsook cages and fences in an attempt to preserve wildlife in a setting similar to its natural habitat. You'll see coyotes trotting in the desert and huge hippos half-submerged in a swamp. The only inconvenience of this natural setting is that it's easy for the animals to camouflage themselves, and you may find yourself in front of a sign that says LIONS, wondering where the lions are. A glimpse of the panda bears, however, is well worth the trip: This is the zoo in which the panda has best survived in captivity. *Reforma, next to the lake, tel. 5/553–62–63, 5/553–6229, or 5/256–41–04. First entrance to park from Metro Auditorio. Admission free. Open Tues.–Sun. 9–5.*

SAN ANGEL

The past 50 years have seen this *pueblito* (village) develop into an exclusive suburb for Mexico City's rich. The sprawl of the city, however, impinges upon San Ángel's tranquility: Avenidas Insurgentes and Revolución transect the suburb, bringing traffic, noise, and a lively nightlife. Still, this neighborhood has its share of quiet, cobblestoned streets and colonial architecture, with homes hidden behind high walls.

In the center of San Ángel is the **Plaza San Jacinto,** where artists peddle their wares on lazy Saturday afternoons. It's now a lively spot, but it was the end of the line for about 50 Irish soldiers in 1847. They came to fight in the Mexican–American War on the American side, but later deserted and joined the Catholic Mexicans. Needless to say, the American soldiers who later caught them were none too pleased. Before executing them, they branded the Irish soldiers' foreheads with the letter *D* for deserter.

On weekends, the plaza fills up with gawking tourists and wandering *fresas* (upper-class preppies) who migrate over to the **Bazar del Sábado** (open 10–8) to buy fashionable handicrafts from vendors that accept credit cards. Despite the commercialism, the market has retained its charm and is well worth the visit. West of Insurgentes, the **Monumento a Obregón,** in honor of the general of the Mexican Revolution, dominates the corner of La Paz and Insurgentes.

CONVENTO E IGLESIA DEL CARMEN This mazelike cloister, with its tiled domes and fountains, has been converted into a museum displaying religious artifacts and rotating art exhibits. Those interested in undertaking should check out the mummified corpses on display; those fascinated by alternative bed accoutrements should see the pillow made of wood in the bedroom on the top floor. For an added kick, relax on the tomb-like benches in the back garden, and ignore the passing cars on Insurgentes. *Revolución, at La Paz, tel. 5/548–28–38, 5/548–53–12, or 5/548–75–77. From Metro M. A. de Quevedo, walk west on Quevedo, left on La Paz, and left again on Revolución. Admission: $2.50, free Sun. Open Tues.–Sun. 10–5.*

MUSEO CARILLO GIL Álvaro Carrillo Gil, a doctor and pharmaceuticals producer, set up this spacious museum to house his art collection, which features works by Diego Rivera, Wolfgang Paalen, David Alfaro Siqueiros, Gunther Gerzso, and José Clemente Orozco. Dr. Gil liked slapping paint on the canvas as well, and some of his own creations hang on the gleaming white walls. The museum also hosts rotating exhibits by

Diego Rivera once said: "Art is like ham. It nourishes people."

contemporary Mexican artists. *Revolución 1608, at Desierto de los Leones, tel. 5/550–39–83 or 5/550–62–89. From Metro M.A. de Quevedo, walk west to Revolución and turn right. Admission: $1, 50¢ students; free Sun. Open Tues.–Sun. 10–6. Wheelchair access.*

MUSEO ESTUDIO DIEGO RIVERA Paints are still on the shelves, and his denim jacket and shoes sit on a wicker chair, waiting: The museum that once was home to Diego Rivera appears as if the muralist could return at any moment to continue work or share some tequila with his cronies Leon Trotsky, Lázaro Cárdenas, or John Dos Passos. A huge pair of sandals, left next to his bed, makes it obvious why no other artist has been able to follow in his footsteps. Juan O'Gorman, a famous architect and close friend of Rivera's, designed the house in the spirit of functionalism, with large wrought-iron doors, windows framed in industrial steel, and exposed plumbing and electrical wiring. *Diego Rivera 2, at Altavista, tel. 5/616–09–96 or 5/550–11–89. Take pesero* RUTA 43 ALTAVISTA *from cnr of Revolución and La Paz (in front of Pemex station), or walk 15 min along Altavista. Admission: $1.50, free Sun. Open Tues.–Sun. 10–6.*

COYOACAN

Coyoacán was a rural village until the '40s, when wealthy chilangos began moving out here to escape the urban madness of Mexico City. Now it's just half an hour by Metro from the center of town and has evolved into one of the many suburbs engulfed by the D.F.'s sprawl. Centuries-old homes, narrow cobblestoned streets, an abundance of bohemian markets and restaurants, and proximity to the Universidad Nacional Autónoma de México (*see below*) attract an affluent and academic elite. Although Coyoacán and San Ángel are often paired together, Coyoacán attracts a more artsy, politically conscious group.

On weekends there are concerts and handicraft vendors in the **Jardín Centenario** between Puerto Carillo and Tres Cruces. Next door, families wander around **Plaza Hidalgo,** enjoying the karate demonstrations or exercise classes going on outside. The red building on the plaza's north side is the **Palacio de Cortés,** once the conquistador's home and now Coyoacán's administrative center. In the back portion of the palace are the offices of the **Foro Cultural Coyoacanense** (tel. 5/658–48–91), whose friendly staff provides loads of information (ask them to tell you about Cortés's secret tunnel) as well as the scoop on free concerts.

The **Casa de la Cultura Jesús Reyes Hëroes** (Francisco Sosa 202, tel. 5/658–55–19 or 5/658–52–71) publishes an indispensable monthly calendar of cultural activities in Coyoacán. If you can get a group of 10 or so people together, call 5/658–55–02 for a guided walking tour of the neighborhood's main attractions. The tour is free and begins at 10 AM, weekends only. The group leaves from the kiosk in Plaza Hidalgo and wanders through some of the most beautiful sections of Coyoacán—including the **Casa de la Malinche,** the house Cortés built for his Aztec translator and lover; the **Plaza de la Concepción;** the beautiful, tree-filled **Viveros de Coyoacán;** and even part of the UNAM campus. If you can't get a group together, try crashing one—they usually don't mind an extra pair of feet. Just get there early, bring a comfy pair of walking shoes, and blend in. *From Metro Coyoacán, take pesero* PLAZA VILLA COAPA.

MUSEO CASA DE LEON TROTSKY This lime green house was the home of one of the most important figures of the Russian Revolution, and it's history reads like a soap opera. In 1937, after being exiled from the Soviet Union, Leon Trotsky was granted asylum in Mexico by President Lázaro Cárdenas at the urging of muralist Diego Rivera, whom Trotsky had met in Paris. Upon their arrival, Trotsky and his wife moved to this anonymous and forbidding fortress (whose turrets were manned by armed guards). The first attempt to assassinate Trotsky (involving Siqueiros, a Mexican muralist and Stalinist) left bullet holes that are still visible in Trotsky's bedroom. Unfortunately for Leon, the second attempt was successful. The study where Trotsky was fatally stabbed remains untouched: On the desk lies an article he was going over when Ramón Mercader, his secretary's boyfriend, stabbed him with an ice pick on August 29, 1940. The house also contains less morbid memorabilia, from a tin of Colgate tooth powder to cases of books in English, Spanish, and Russian. The guards wandering throughout the grounds are knowledgeable and willing to answer questions, though not all speak English. If you manage to communicate with them, they'll tell you, among other things, how Trotsky's teeth left a permanent scar on Mercader's hand; how he clung to life for 26 hours; what his last

San Ángel and Coyoacán

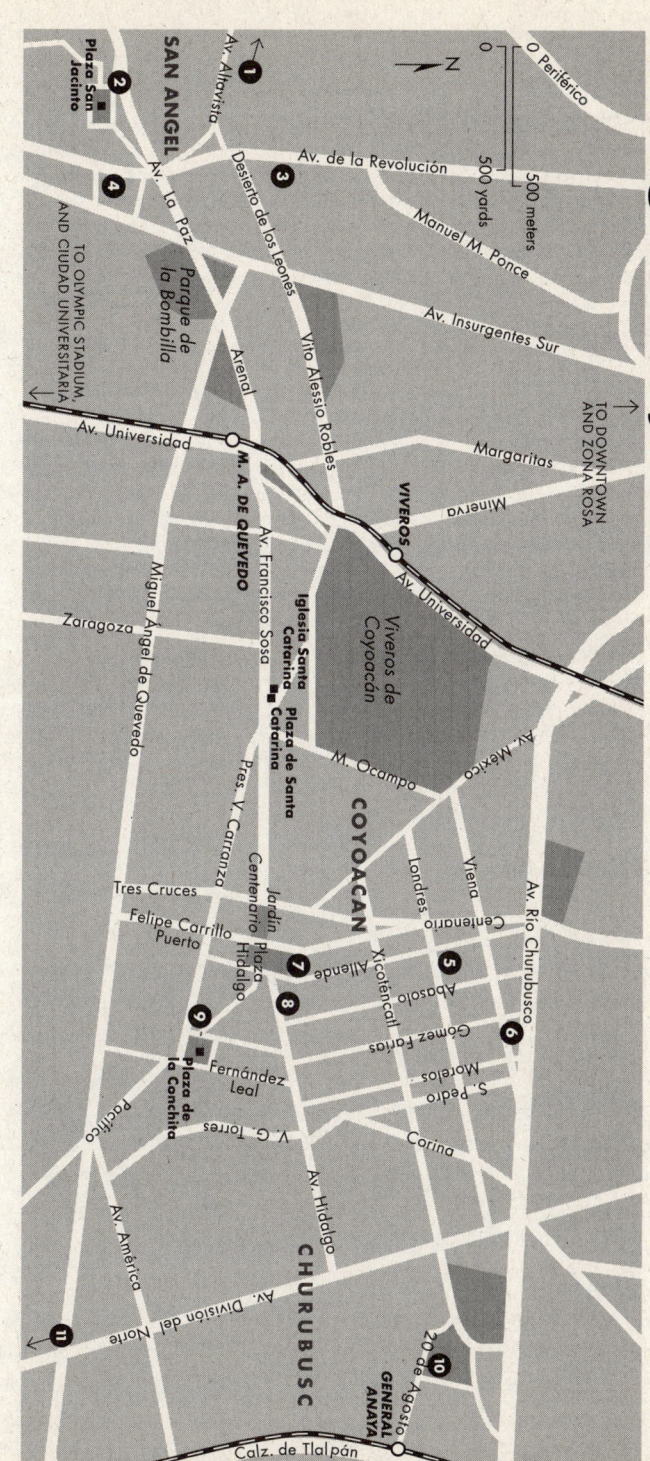

Bazar Sábado, **2**
Casa de la Malinche, **9**
Convento e Iglesia del Carmen, **4**
Museo Carrillo Gil, **3**
Museo Casa de Leon Trotsky, **6**
Museo de Culturas Populares, **8**
Museo de Frida Kahlo, **5**
Museo del Anahuacalli, **11**
Museo Estudio Diego Rivera, **1**
Museo Nacional de las Intervenciones, **10**
Palacio de Cortés, **7**

words were; and where his ashes are interred in the garden. *Río Churubusco 410, btw Gómez Farías and Morelos, tel. 5/658–87–32. From Plaza Hidalgo, walk north on Allende about 6 blocks, then right. Admission: $2, $1 students. Open Tues.–Sun. 10–6.*

MUSEO DE CULTURAS POPULARES Rotating exhibits of folk art from Mexico and elsewhere are beautifully displayed here, accompanied by plentiful information (in Spanish). More than just a museum, this solid colonial building has become a center for community activities, hosting art and dance workshops. The monthly newsletter *El Canario de Coyoacán* is distributed here, and has info on music and dance shows in Coyoacán. *Hidalgo 289, btw Allende and Abasolo, tel. 5/658–12–65. From Metro Coyoacán, take pesero* PLAZA VILLA COAPA *to Jardín Centenario and walk a few blocks along Hidalgo. Admission free. Open Tues.–Sat. 9:30–6, Sun. 9:30–5.*

MUSEO DE FRIDA KAHLO This blue house in Coyoacán is where painter Frida Kahlo (*see box, below*) was born, grew up, and lived briefly with husband Diego Rivera until she died in 1954. Now a museum, the building is filled with colorful and sad remnants of Kahlo's life: self-portraits; illustrated journals; love notes; pictures of Mao Tse-Tung, Lenin, and Stalin; clunky clay jewelry; and the beautifully embroidered traditional skirts Kahlo favored. Life-size papier-mâché statues and other folk art collected by Kahlo and Rivera adorn the house and lush garden. As a result of childhood polio and a bus accident when she was a teenager, Kahlo spent much of her life in pain, enduring more than 30 difficult operations. Her decorated body cast and her startling paintings convey both her intense emotional and physical suffering, as well as her pride in and passion for Mexican culture. *Londres 247, at Allende, tel. 5/554–59–99. From Metro Coyoacán, take pesero* PLAZA VILLA COAPA *to the plaza, and walk 5 blocks north on Allende. Admission: $1.50, $1 students. Open Tues.–Sun. 10–6.*

MUSEO DEL ANAHUACALLI What *do* you do with all those pre-Columbian artifacts you've collected over the years? If you're Diego Rivera, you design your own museum. The huge black building that houses Rivera's collection was constructed in the 1960s from dark volcanic rock. Even if you're tired of archaeological treasures, visit the building just because it's so strange, like an aboveground tomb that promises (and delivers) echoing footfalls amid eerie silence. The third floor displays sketches for some of Rivera's murals, including *Man at the Crossroads,*

Frida

Frida Kahlo, probably the most famous Mexican woman artist ever, was born and died in La Casa Azul in Coyoacán. Her image now adorns T-shirts and postcards all over the world, and she has become something of a feminist icon both in Mexico and abroad. Her paintings are as colorful and flamboyant as was their main subject—Frida herself. Born to a Hungarian Jewish father and a Mexican mother in 1907 (though she often claimed that her birth date was 1910, the year the Revolution began), she was almost killed in a bus accident when she was a teenager, which left her in almost constant pain for the rest of her life. She depicted that suffering in her paintings, which often represent her bleeding, cracked open, or torn apart and sewn back together. Other themes are political (she was a Communist and a revolutionary who, in spite of her devotion to Stalin, became involved with Leon Trotsky when he lived in Mexico), or concern aspects of her personal life, such as her stormy marriage to Diego Rivera. Her frank, unapologetic portrayal of her own pain, physical and emotional, illustrates her public refusal to be a "typical" Mexican woman, a sufrida (long-suffering woman) who bears her sorrow in silence. Her last painting, completed eight days before she died, shows juicy melons, cut open and waiting to be eaten. It is titled *Viva la Vida* (Live Life).

now in the Palacio de Bellas Artes (*see* box, The Man Without a Face, *above*). *Calle del Museo 150, tel. 5/677–29–84 or 5/677–28–73. From Metro Tasqueña, take trolley to Xotepingo stop; exit to right at the* CALLE DEL MUSEO *sign, backtrack to intersection, and turn left. Admission free. Open Tues.–Sun. 10–6.*

MUSEO NACIONAL DE LAS INTERVENCIONES This museum is housed in the beautifully maintained Ex-Convento de Churubusco, the site of a ferocious battle during the Mexican-American War. On display are guns, flags, pictures, documents, maps, and other artifacts chronicling interventions by foreign countries, in particular France and the United States. *20 de Agosto, at General Anaya, tel. 5/604–06–09. From Metro General Anaya; exit to 20 de Agosto and walk 4 blocks. Admission: $2; free students and Sun. Open Tues.–Sun. 9–6.*

UNIVERSIDAD NACIONAL AUTONOMA DE MEXICO (UNAM)

The National Autonomous University of Mexico, one of the oldest universities in the Americas, rests upon a lava bed in a residential district in the southern part of the city. Originally made up of various *facultades* (schools) scattered throughout the city, the UNAM was consolidated into one huge campus in the 1950s and now has more than 100,000 students. The campus is generally known as the *Ciudad Universitaria* (University City), or simply C.U., a name well deserved considering you have to take a bus just to cross campus.

A generation or two ago, a degree from the UNAM was a ticket into political circles and positions of power, but these days the political and business elite tend to come from private institutions. The UNAM is confronted by the same severe economic problems that plague most public universities: Professors skip classes when low incomes force them to take additional jobs, and overenrollment puts pressure on an already populous campus. Despite all its problems, however, the university retains its well-deserved reputation for academic excellence and continues to attract students from around the world. Students choose a major early, and then take the same classes with the same students. By graduation, they are often a tightly knit group.

Today the campus is a center of political activity. In sympathy with the Zapatista movement in Chiapas, students have staged several marches and hunger strikes in protest of the government. Many believe that while the government pretends to tolerate UNAM's high level of political activity, it does so only to identify its opposition. Students have clashed with the state before—most famously and violently in 1968, when government tanks occupied the UNAM. The confrontation culminated with the massacre at Tlatelolco in early October that same year (*see* Plaza de las Tres Cultures/Tlatelolco, *above*).

The university's architects wanted the campus to incorporate the best of traditional and modern design and still harmonize with the natural landscape of cactus and black volcanic rock. They succeeded with the huge volcano-shaped **Estadio Olímpico** (Olympic Stadium). The stadium was the site of the 1968 Olympics, and continues to host university sporting events, including home games of UNAM's soccer team, Los Pumas. The outer ramps of the stadium are decorated with yet another Diego Rivera mural, this one titled *La Universidad, la familia mexicana, la paz y la juventud deportista* (University, Mexican Family, Peace, and Athletic Youth). Murals by Carlos Mérida, David Alfaro Siqueiros, and Juan O'Gorman can be found just about everywhere on the campus, from the **Torre de la Rectoría** (Tower of the Rectory) on the northwest side of campus to the **Vestíbulo de la Sala Nezahualcóyotl** in the south.

The **Espacio Escultórico** (Sculpture Space), an ecological reserve at the southern end of the campus, is home to numerous sculptures by Mexican artists. The reserve is easily accessible via a long, winding, lava path, and is popular for climbing, picnics, or cutting class on a sunny afternoon. Just down the street, behind the **Biblioteca Nacional** (National Library; open weekdays 9–7) is another long, winding sculpture, *Las Serpientes del Pedregal*, which slithers around the library. The campus is full of free perks for broke student look-alikes, and there are often free concerts or lectures in the evenings. Check the flyers posted around campus for more

UNAM tuition costs less than a bottle of Peñafiel, and about as much as a pack of gum (about 1¢ or 200 old pesos a year). Any attempts to raise it are met with angry protests by students.

info, or pick up a free copy of *Gazeta UNAM*. Transportation on campus is free, so exploring is easy if you can figure out the intricate web of peseros needed to cross the campus. Take TLAL-PAN JOYA *pesero south on Insurgentes to 3rd pedestrian overpass on campus, cross street, and head north past Biblioteca Nacional. Or from Metro Universidad exit through Salida E, and take pesero* ZONA CULTURAL *to Espacio Escultórico.*

LA VILLA DE GUADALUPE

La Villa, with two basilicas dedicated to the Virgin of Guadalupe, is the most revered Christian site in Mexico. To this day, millions flock to the site where the Virgin Mary is said to have appeared to Juan Diego, an indigenous convert to Christianity, in 1531. Unlike the fair Mary of the Roman Catholic tradition, the Virgin of Guadalupe had a brown complexion and spoke Nahuatl, Diego's native tongue. The Virgin instructed Diego to gather a bunch of roses—an impossible task in winter—as a testament of the truthfulness of his vision. When Diego told his story to a priest, the father scoffed, calling him a heretic and claiming that the story was pure fantasy. Yet when Juan Diego opened his cloak, out fell the roses the Virgin had told him to gather, leaving an image of the Virgin imprinted on the inside of the cloak.

The museum in the **Antigua Basílica** (the original basilica, dating to 1536) contains exhibits of European and Mexican colonial art. In the hulking, gray mass that is the **Basílica Nueva,** you can glide past Juan Diego's cloak on a moving sidewalk. The new basilica was built in 1976 to accommodate increasing numbers of pilgrims on the Virgin's feast day, December 12 (*see* Festivals, *below*). The tile-covered **Capilla del Pocito** houses a well of (rumor has it) miracle water. *Calzada de Guadalupe, btw Juan de Zumárraga and Hidalgo, near Metro La Villa. Basílica admission: 20¢. Open Tues.–Sun. 10–6.*

CHEAP THRILLS

In colonial times, when literacy rates were low, scribes would sit in the plazas and read or write letters for a nominal fee. Today the tradition continues (although in a slightly modernized form) on the **Plaza Santo Domingo.** Modern-day scribes can be found in the local plaza with their typewriters, transcribing everything from term papers to love letters. In a row across from the typists are the printers, who churn out everything from business cards to wedding invitations. Both printers and typists work the plaza daily from about 9 to 6. *3 blocks north of Zócalo on Monte de Piedad, which becomes República de Brasil.*

The following museums are free any day of the week with a valid student ID:
- *Museo Mural de Diego Rivera*
- *Museo de Arte Moderno*
- *Museo Tamayo*
- *Museo Nacional de Historia*

Whether you're desperate to replenish your dwindling travel funds, or just woke up feeling really lucky, you can always give the **Lotería Nacional** (National Lottery) a whirl. For 50¢–$1 (depending on the game) you can close your eyes, cross your fingers, and wait for the winning numbers to be announced on Channel 13 or posted on lottery booths around town. Just walk to any lottery ticket booth in Mexico City, hand the ticket seller four pesos, and proudly announce, "Quiero ser millonario/a." Rhythmic drummers and Aztec dancers grace the Zócalo daily, from about 10 to 5. Passively observe or join in if you have no shame and think you can follow the deceivingly simple-looking steps. On weekend evenings Coyoacán's Plaza Hidalgo and Jardín Centenario also see plenty of activity. These usually peaceful areas become packed with families and young couples milling around, listening to street performers and musicians. You can usually find anything from modern dance to clowns to traditional South American music. Grab a bag of warm *churros* and a hot chocolate from the vendors lining the street, and take advantage of the free culture.

FESTIVALS

Easter (late March/early April): Like everywhere else in Mexico, Semana Santa (Holy Week) is the cause for celebrations and religious processions throughout the city. In Iztapalapa, in the southeastern part of the city (Metro: Iztapalapa), devotees reenact the Stations of the Cross, complete with a dramatization of the crucifixion. If you're into mutilation or S&M, this is the place to go: The reenactments are often bloody. On a lighter note, on **Sábado de Gloria** (the Saturday before Easter Sunday), people often run around throwing water at each other. Although this act originally had religious significance, any such meaning is often lost amid the *relajo* (chaos).

September 15 and 16, Independence celebrations: Weeks ahead of time, the city is festooned in the national colors: red, green, and white. The celebrations commence on the evening of the 15th, when the president steps onto the balcony at the Palacio Nacional to read Hidalgo's *grito*, the call for independence that provoked 10 years of struggle against the Spanish. The Zócalo is so packed with people that you could faint and still not hit the ground; confetti lies inches thick throughout the centro; and fireworks explode all night long.

October 2, Anniversary of the Massacre at Tlatelolco: People gather in the black-draped Plaza de las Tres Culturas in the early afternoon, and at about 5 PM begin marching through the city streets to the Zócalo. Because the commemoration is not supported by the government—it was responsible for hundreds of deaths here in the 1968 massacre (*see* Plaza de las Tres Culturas/Tlatelolco, *above*)—the marchers' path is periodically blocked by the feared *grenaderos* (riot police). But, as the Mexicans say, "Perro que ladra no muerde" ("A dog that barks won't bite"), and the police usually only detain the crowd for about half an hour before allowing the marchers to continue. The event brings together relatives of the victims, students of all ages, workers, and opposition sympathizers who carry banners and sing bawdy songs mocking the government.

December 12, Feast Day of the Virgin of Guadalupe: The celebration of the patron saint of Mexico fills the beautifully decorated city with processions and dances. On this day the area around the Basílica de Guadalupe is probably the most exciting and most crowded place in Mexico. (*See* La Villa de Guadalupe, *above*.)

December 25, Christmas Day: For *Navidades* (Christmas), the entire city is draped with lights, especially spectacular on the Zócalo. Don't miss the *posadas*, traditional Christmas parties with piñatas and plays, which start about two weeks before Christmas, or the *pastorelas*, religious comedies which reenact Mexican holiday traditions.

Shopping

Everything can be purchased in Mexico City, from a Gucci bag to the silverwork and *artesanía* (crafts) for which the country is famous. Those heading out to the wilderness can also stock up on socks, deodorant, or a new pair of shoes, and all sorts of camping gear is available at **Deportes Martí** (Venustiano Carranza 19, Col. Centro, tel. 5/585-02-99). If you're shopping for clothing, boutiques in both the **Zona Rosa** and **Polanco** sell international fashions at high prices. For cheaper clothing, try the area around Metro Pino Suárez, just south of the Zócalo, where you can get a decent pair of fake Levi's for about $10. If for some reason you must go to a mall, take the TLALPAN-JOYA pesero south on Insurgentes to **Perisur**, home to Sears, Guess, and other embarrassing U.S. exports. Another good mall (if such a thing exists) is **Pabellón Polanco** (Vázquez de Mella and Ejército Nacional). From Metro Polanco, walk north on Arquímedes to Ejército National, cross the street, hail a pesero to the periférico, and ask to be let off at Pabellón Polanco. A good, if somewhat overstimulating, source for just about anything is the department store/restaurant chain **Sanborns** (*see* Food, *above*).

MARKETS AND ARTESANIA Handicrafts are generally more expensive in Mexico City than elsewhere in the country. Stalls with all sorts of goodies are set up on the Zócalo, just west of the cathedral, during the height of tourist season (July and August). Even more expensive wares are sold year-round in the Zona Rosa on Génova, near Reforma.

La Ciudadela. Tucked away through a doorless iron entryway, this market consists of wall-to-wall handicraft stores. Mounds of beautiful silver jewelry from Taxco, bags and jackets from Chiapas, and even those "My parents went to Mexico City . . ." T-shirts (available in English and *español*) can be found if you look hard enough. The merchants are tourist-wise—many accept credit cards, but bargaining is still expected. *Balderas, at Plaza La Ciudadela. 5 blocks south of Metro Juárez, or 1 long block north of Metro Balderas. Open daily 10–7.*

Fonart. High-quality, government-approved folk art is available in any one of the several Fonart (National Fund for the Promotion of Arts and Crafts) outlets in the city. The pieces come from all over Mexico, so you can get just about anything here, though it will probably cost you at least twice as much as it would in that remote highland village. *Juárez 89, tel. 5/521–01–71. Other locations: Londres 136, Zona Rosa, tel. 5/525–20–26; Patriotismo 691, Metro Mixcoac, tel. 5/563–40–60; Carranza 115, Coyoacán, tel. 5/254–62–70. All stores open Mon.–Sat. 10–7.*

La Lagunilla. Once known as the Thieves' Market, La Lugunilla consists of three main markets: The **Mercado de Ropa** (Eje 1 Norte, btw Allende and Chile) sells shimmery dresses à la *Saturday Night Fever*, while the **Mercado de Comestibles** (Eje 1 Norte, at Comonfort) sells fruit and vegetables. The **Mercado de Artesanía** overflows with furniture, coins, tacky paintings of the Last Supper, and a smattering of nice antiques. This market is at its liveliest on Sunday, when curio stalls are set up outside the main building. *Allende, btw República de Honduras and Ecuador, east of Reforma. Metro: Garibaldi. Open daily 9–7.*

Mercado de Jamaica. The odors of meat, onions, and tacos waft through the corridors of this market where bananas, pineapples, papayas, and mangos sit in enormous heaps. But the market is mainly known for the rows of stalls with huge bunches of roses, carnations, lilies, and birds of paradise. *Morelos (Eje 3 Sur), at H. Congreso. Metro: Jamaica. Open daily 8–6.*

Mercado San Juan. Officially the Mercado de Curiosidades Centro Artesanal, this conglomeration of tiny shops in a pink-and-white concrete building feels more like a shopping mall than a craft market. However, good-quality artesanía, blankets, hammocks, silver, and mounds of tourist trinkets can be found here. Don't expect too much leeway in the prices—anything short of throwing yourself on the market floor and weeping uncontrollably will probably not move the gringo-wise vendors. *Ayuntamiento, at Dolores, 4 blocks south of Metro Juárez and Alameda Central. Open Mon.–Sat. 9–7, Sun. 9–4.*

La Merced and **Sonora** are separate markets connected by a small side street, Cabaña. Edible goods are sold in the huge warehouse of La Merced, pervaded by the sweet smell of fresh fruits and vegetables. Also inside is the **Mercado de Dulces** (candy market) with more sweets than you've ever seen in your life. Outside you can buy just about any useful item: umbrellas, pots, pans, clothes, and even some toiletries. Sonora, just across the way, promises to cure what ails you. Herbal potions guarantee effectiveness against everything from evil spirits to impotence. At the very back, tropical birds, goats, puppies, and other sad caged animals are also for sale: some for pets, and some as food, no doubt. *Mercado de La Merced: Circunvalación, at San Pablo. Metro: Merced. Mercado Sonora: 2 blocks south of La Merced on Fray Servando Teresa de Mier. Both open daily 8 AM–7 PM.*

Tepito. Anything in the way of consumer goods can be purchased in this semidisreputable market, raided almost daily by police in search of illegal merchandise. The selection is overwhelming—you can find everything from electronics to athletic shoes. But much like a mall full

---

In June, Your Name is Pedro

For Mexican Catholics, your Saint's Day is a day on which you receive gifts and the well-wishing of friends and family. Every day of the year is a Saint's Day: For example, if your name were Pedro, you would celebrate on the Día de San Pedro (June 29). Even if your name is Moonbeam, you can celebrate the Saint's Day/anniversary festivals held at markets throughout the city, with free food, drink, song, and dance. Ask at the markets about dates.

of crazed grandmothers on the last day of Macy's white sale, it's crowded and rough, so leave your valuables at home and bring a *cuate* (buddy) to watch your back. *Eje 1 Nte, at Aztecas. From Metro Guerrero, take pesero* TEPITO. *Open daily 8–6, except after police raids.*

Tianguis El Chopo. This punk-style swap meet is a change of pace from the fruits and trinkets of most of the city's markets—you'll find fliers, info on bands, T-shirts, and underground magazines. You may even come away sporting a new tattoo. This is also the place for info on raves—ask a vendor or check out the flyers. *Sol, near train station. Metro: La Raza. Open Sat. 10–4.*

Having marital problems? Vendors at Mercado Sonora claim the answer lies in controlling your spouse. For one peso, buy a little sachet of magic with titles such as "Sígueme y obedéceme" (Follow and obey me) and "Yo domino a mi mujer" (I dominate my woman).

After Dark

El reventón (the party) starts late and keeps going until the early hours of the morning; even after the clubs close at 3 AM, people grab a taco and beer and wait until the more respectable hour of 4 to mosey off to bed. The most lively areas at night are the Zona Rosa and Insurgentes Sur in Colonia Juárez. Clubs are the places to be, whether they play disco or *música tropical,* a mix of salsa, merengue, and cumbia. Dance club covers are usually quite high, but women often get in free or at a reduced price. Movies and cafés provide a cheaper alternative. *Tiempo Libre* ($1 at most newsstands) lists places to go and things to see, from tango bars to discos to plays.

For cruising, by car or on foot, and watching the scene, the **Zona Rosa** is always happening. A variety of people—snazzy clubgoers in black evening wear, "cool" teenagers in ripped jeans, and camera-toting tourists—come here to see and be seen. The local **Vips** and **Sanborns** (*see* Food, *above*) are central to hanging out in the '90s. At night these chain restaurants fill up with people having a cup of coffee and a cigarette before heading off to a movie or dance club.

A favorite nightspot with locals and tourists alike, **Plaza Garibaldi** (Eje Central and República de Perú) heats up with competing mariachi bands in full regalia, who sing of lost love and cheatin' women. Couples come to be serenaded, and foreigners come to experience "traditional" Mexico. Buying a song can be a bit pricey, but it's simple enough to walk around and listen in on other people's favorite mariachi tunes. Otherwise, you can always escape to one of the cantinas or dance clubs (many of which charge no cover) that line the square.

The **theater** scene in Mexico City offers a wide variety of performances, from musicals to works by Mexican and international playwrights—David Mamet in Spanish is an interesting linguistic experience. Check listings in *Tiempo Libre.*

BARS **Bar Mata.** High up on the fourth floor of a colonial building in the centro, this bar is one of the hottest spots around for the under-30 crowd. This is not a loud, smoke-filled grind factory; the music is low enough to carry on a conversation, and the atmosphere is conducive to mingling and flirting. The place to be is the open-air roof, where you can sip your beer ($1.50) and look out on the view of the Alameda. There's no cover or drink minimum. The place gets packed after about 10:30. *Filomeno Mata 11, at 5 de Mayo, tel. 5/518–02–37. Metro: Bellas Artes. Open Tues.–Sun. 8 PM–2 AM.*

Bar Milan. This bar is among the most unpretentious around. The crowd is young, the music low, and it's by far the best place to just stop by and have a beer ($2). *Milán 18, tel. 5/592–00–31. Metro: Cuauhtémoc. No cover. Open Tues.–Sun. 8 PM–2 AM.*

La Casa del Inquisidor. This huge, two-story bar is decorated like an inquisitor's home: Start off by having a drink in his garden, and by the end of the evening you may end up partying in his closet. This is a hard place to leave, especially if you go for one of the bar's adventuresome drinks, such as *medias de seda* (silk stockings), *semen de burro* (donkey semen) or *orgasmo* (Do you really need a translation?). There's no cover charge, and drinks go for $2–$4. *Durango 181,*

The five best tequilas, according to a bartender at La Guadalupana:
- *Herradura Blanco, Reposado*
- *Sauza, Generaciones*
- *Sauza, Conmemorativo*
- *Cuervo, 1800*
- *Sauza, Hornitos*

2 blocks from Metro Insurgentes, tel. 5/511–673-15. Open Tues.–Sun. 8 PM–2:30 AM. Wheelchair access. AE, MC, V.

La Guadalupana. This Coyoacán, cantina dating from 1932, is heavy on atmosphere and local color and is always packed with regulars. Sit at the cloth-draped tables or stand at the bar while you deliberate on which of the eight available tequilas to order. The crowd is overwhelmingly male, so unaccompanied women will be the target of quite a bit of friendly attention (and possibly free drinks). If you're harassed, however, the waiters will politely remove the offender from your area and, if necessary, from the establishment. Higuera 14, tel. 5/554–65–53. From Metro Coyoacán, take pesero VILLA COAPA to Plaza Hidalgo. Open Mon.–Sat. noon–midnight, Sun. noon–6 PM.

CINEMAS Most U.S. movies show in Mexico within a few months of their release, so finding a film in English is easy. They're listed in *Tiempo Libre* (*see above*) by title and theater. The films are sometimes in poor condition, full of scratches and squiggly lines, and the volume tends to be low, since most of the audience depends on the subtitles, but for $2 (half-price on Wednesdays) it's not so bad. Paseo de la Reforma in the Zona Rosa has quite a few big screens showing recent American and European films; look for **Diana** (Reforma 423, near Metro Insurgentes, tel. 5/511–32–36), **Latino I** (Reforma 296, near Metro Insurgentes, tel. 5/525–87–57), **París** (Reforma 92, near Metro Hidalgo, tel. 5/535–32–71), and **Paseo** (Reforma 35, tel. 5/546–58–43). For artsier films (and an artsier crowd), check out the government-run **Cineteca** (México-Coyoacán 389, near Metro Coyoacán, tel. 5/688–32–72).

"You haven't been to Mexico if you haven't been to Plaza Garibaldi at night." — Alberto, a native chilango.

DANCE The **Ballet Folklórico de México,** which performs in the Palacio de Bellas Artes (*see* Worth Seeing, *above*), is world-renowned for its stunning presentations of Mexican regional folk dances, spectacles that are popular among locals and tourists alike. Performances are Wednesday evenings at 8:30 and Sunday mornings at 9:30. You can buy tickets ($15–$21) on the first floor of the Palacio (Mon.–Sat. 11–7, Sun. 9–7) or try Ticketmaster (tel. 5/325–9000). Tickets for other concerts and plays held here (listed in *Tiempo Libre*) are sold Monday–Saturday 11–3 and 5–7, Sunday 10:30–7.

GAY CLUBS **Bota's Bar.** One of the most happening gay bars in the D.F., Bota's has enough mirrored walls and bright neon lights to snap you out of the deepest funk. The transvestite shows (Thurs.–Sat.) and frequent striptease competitions are *the* perfect opportunity to make your presence felt in Mexico City. The $5 cover includes two drinks. The gay bar is upstairs from the other nongay and unhip Bota's. *Niza 45, tel. 5/514–46–00. Metro: Insurgentes. Open Thurs.–Sun. 9 PM–4 AM.*

Butterfly. This techno club looks more like a bus terminal than a disco. With five bars, two snack shacks, about 50 tables, and a huge dance floor that's packed to capacity, it's by far the largest gay club in town. The two transvestite shows (11 PM and 1 AM) are rumored to be the best around. It's rather tricky to find since there is no sign, but it's a block and a half from Metro San Juan de Letrán. Cover is $5 and includes a drink. *Izazaga 9, tel. 5/761–18–61. Open daily 9:30 PM–2:30 AM.*

Spartacus. Dim lights, throbbing techno-pop, and a drag show (every night around 10) make this place especially popular with gay men. Cover is $2. *Cuauhtémoc 8, Ciudad Neza, tel. 5/558–49–59 or 5/792–44–70. Metro: Cuauhtémoc. Open Fri. and Sat. 8 PM–6 AM.*

El Taller. There's no sign, only a small, inconspicuous door that marks the entrance to this popular gay bar in the Zona Rosa. Stairs lead down to a dark, grooving disco of *men only* (women are not allowed). Outside, a low profile is maintained so as not to upset the city fathers. The $3 cover includes one drink; Monday there's no cover. *Florencia 37, Zona Rosa, tel. 5/533–49–70. 1½ blocks from Ángel de la Independencia monument. Metro: Insurgentes. Open daily 9:30 PM–3:30 AM.*

El Vaquero. You'll have to search a bit for this inconspicuous bar; it's squeezed between a laundromat and a bookstore in a small commercial center. The music here is mostly Latin, and if you like to *cumbia*, this is the place to do it. The management is extremely concerned with keeping things hush-hush, so it may be difficult to get anyone on the phone. The cover is $4. *Insurgentes Sur 1231, 3 blocks from Rockotitlán, tel. 5/598–25–95. Take pesero* SAN ANGEL *south on Insurgentes. Open Thurs.–Sat. 9* PM*–2* AM.

MUSIC AND DANCING Mexico City's music scene has something for everyone—if you're a night person, that is. The *Rock en Español* (Rock in Spanish) movement is gaining strength, and new bands abound, playing everything from mainstream pop to obscure punk.

➢ **JAZZ** • **La Mansión.** This classy restaurant is a laid-back place to listen to jazz. Also to its credit are great margaritas ($2.50) and the non-existent cover. Live music, played Wednesday–Saturday, starts at 8. *Taine 322, Polanco, tel. 5/545–43–08. Metro: Polanco. Open Wed.–Sun. 1–11.*

New Orleans. This restaurant/bar boasts (and delivers) the best jazz bands in Mexico City. But beware—you'll be expected to order something, and the $4 cover charge will be slyly added to your bill before you leave. *Revolución 1980, San Ángel, tel. 5/550–19–08. Metro: M. A. de Quevedo. Open Tues.–Sat. 8:30–2.*

➢ **ROCK, RAP, AND ALTERNATIVE MUSIC** • **El Antro.** The name translates directly as The Joint (the type you go to, not the type you smoke), and offers just what the name suggests: an obscure place to enjoy music that's as alternative as it gets in Mexico City. Cover is $5, and drinks are reasonably cheap (about $1.50). *Carretera México–Xochimilco 14, in front of La Luna, tel. 5/655–10–84 or 5/655–12–73. Open Thurs.–Sat. 8:30–2. Wheelchair access.*

El Hijo del Cuervo. Young, hip students pack into this cool art deco bar for an interesting mix of rock and *canto nuevo* (synonymous with canción nueva), and the occasional theater show. Check *Tiempo Libre* under "bares con variedad" or "teatro bar" for schedules. Cover varies (up to $5) depending on the show. *Jardín Centenario 17, Coyoacán, tel. 5/658–53–06. From Metro Coyoacán, take pesero* VILLA COAPA *to jardín. Open daily 1* PM*–midnight. Wheelchair access.*

Rockotitlán. After jamming nonstop for more than nine years, this bar deserves a medal for longevity. Come listen to Mexico's best rock, alternative, and funk bands in an unpretentious setting that manages to look simultaneously like a garage and an outdoor terrace. Check Tiempo Libre to find out who's playing. Cover ranges from $5 to $15, depending on the band. Women usually pay less. *Insurgentes Sur 953, Col. Nápoles, tel. 5/687–78–93. Take pesero* SAN ANGEL *south on Insurgentes; it's on the 3rd floor of a small commercial building on a traffic circle. Open daily 10* PM*–2* AM*. Wheelchair access.*

To find out about Mexico City's underground scene, ask patrons at El Antro or Rockotitlán. You can also check La Lagunilla market for flyers.

Rockstock. This place is considered by many to be *the* club in Mexico City—get here before 10:30 PM or you'll have to wait to get in. Cover is $12 for men, free for women. Or make goo-goo eyes at the young bouncers who pick and choose among the mass of black-swathed bodies jamming the entryway. The crowd is young, not too dressed up, and there to party. *Reforma 260, Zona Rosa, tel. 5/533–09–06. From Metro Insurgentes, take Génova north to Reforma and turn right. Open Thurs.–Sat. 9* PM*–3* AM.

➢ **MUSICA TROPICAL** • **Bar León.** The live music at this swanky club lures the cool and goofy alike. Patrons are a mix of students, foreigners from the hotel upstairs, and regulars who effortlessly avoid wildly gyrating duos practicing the basic steps. Cover is $5, with a one-drink minimum. *República de Brasil 5, Col. Centro, just north of cathedral, tel. 5/510–29–79. Metro: Allende. Open Wed.–Sat. 9* PM*–3* AM.

Mocamboo. Ask a group of young Mexicanos where you should go to dance salsa and merengue and they'll say the Mocamboo "es padre!" (is cool). Three different orchestras play hour-long sets to a filled-to-capacity dance floor. It's so packed here you don't need to know how to dance salsa to look like a pro—just get in the middle, smile, and let the people around you do all the work. Cover ranges from $5–$10 depending on the band, the day of the week, and your chromosomes. *Puebla 191, Col. Roma, tel. 5/533–64–64. From Metro Insurgentes, west to Chapultepec, right on Puebla. Open Mon.–Sat. 9 PM–4 AM.*

Salón Q. This huge salsa club is one of the more popular places to come and shake your booty. The crowd is young, the music loud, and the drinks are expensive but strong. Cover is about $9. *Reforma 169, Col. Guerrero, tel. 5/529–34–95. Metro: Insurgentes. Open Fri. and Sat. 9 PM–4 AM.*

➣ **DANCE HALLS** • *Salones de baile* (dance halls) are the essence of working-class popular culture in Mexico City. The dance-hall craze, which began in the late 1920s, reached a peak during World War II, when live bands played mambo, swing, fox-trot, and the ever-popular *danzón* to crowds of eager young dancers. The youth of today prefer the downtown discos, and salones are slowly fading away. The two dance halls listed below attract a crowd of 20- to 80-year-olds whose common denominator is their love of dancing and dressing up.

Salón Colonia. Opened in 1922, Colonia is Mexico City's original dance hall and a favorite with the older crowd. The atmosphere is low-key, and the folks on the dance floor are friendly—it's the perfect place to practice your moves. Cover is $3 for men, $1.50 for women. *Manuel M. Flores 33, Col. Obrera, tel. 5/578–06–19. 3½ blocks east of Metro San Antonio. Open Mon., Wed., and Sun. 6 PM–11 PM.*

Salón Los Ángeles. This place attracts a younger crowd that moves to the sounds of salsa instead of the slower *danzón*. The 1930s decor looks as if it came right from an old Mexican movie, with a soda fountain and a huge, open dance floor. The Los Ángeles attracts internationally known musicians about once a month. Cover for those groups is $5, but otherwise they charge $2 for men and $1 for women. *Lerdo 206, near Flores Magon, Col. Guerrero, tel. 5/597–51–81. Metro: Insurgentes. Open Wed., Fri., and Sun. 6 PM–11 PM.*

➣ **PEÑAS** • *Peñas* (musical gatherings) appeared in the mid-'60s, when leftists gathered to sing songs of revolution, using the music of rural Latin America then ignored by commercial radio. When dictatorships throughout the Americas imposed *apagones culturales* (cultural blackouts), artists were forced into exile, prompting thousands of Chileans, Uruguayans, Brazilians, among others, to make their way to Mexico City, bringing *nueva canción*, the folk music that is still an important element of peña atmosphere. Although these days peñas are less ardently revolutionary, with a feel somewhere between a café and a bar, they function as cultural centers where people relax, listen to music or poetry, or just spend time with friends.

El Condor Pasa. This classic peña with a comfortable, low-key atmosphere is a great place to hear live Latin American folk music. The cover is only about $2, and drinks are all well under $2.50. *Rafael Checa 1, Col. San Ángel, tel. 5/548–20–50. Take pesero SAN ANGEL to the end of the line, walk back 1 block on Insurgentes, and turn left on small road btw Mercado de Discos and Mama's Pizza. Open Tues.–Sat. 7 PM–1 AM.*

If you just want a little agua, ask for "Un Monterrey en las rocas" (A Monterrey on the rocks), or water with ice. The expression springs from the people of Monterrey's ignominious reputation as the stingiest in the country.

Hostería El Trobador. Walk into this restaurant/bar, and you'll think you walked into an old ranch house from the northern territories of Cohahuila—a great atmosphere if you don't mind a dead antelope staring you down from the wall. El Trobador offers live Latin American folk music, nueva canción, and sappy romantic music six days a week with no cover charge or drink minimum. *Presidente Carranza 82, at 5 de Febrero, Col. Coyoacán, tel. 5/554–72–47. From Metro Coyoacán, take pesero VILLA COAPA to the Jardín; the peña is 3 blocks away. Open Mon.–Sat. 11 AM–5 PM (restaurant) and 7 PM–1 AM (peña).*

Mesón de la Guitarra. One look at the decked-out crowd at this fancy peña and it becomes obvious that this place is for having a good time, not planning revolutions. Under the same management, **Peña Gallos** (Revolución 736, near Metro Mixcoac, tel. 5/563–09–63) is larger, but identical in every other respect. Cover is $4 in both peñas, although women get in free on

Thursdays, and everyone gets in free after midnight on Fridays and Saturdays. Reservations are a good idea if you plan to arrive after 9:30. *Félix Cuevas 332, tel. 5/559–15–35 or 5/559–24–35. Take a bus down Insurgentes Sur to Félix Cuevas, ask to be let off at the Liverpool department store, and walk east 5 blocks. Open Thurs.–Sat. 7 PM–2 AM.*

Outdoor Activities

Outdoor activities for the budget traveler are scarce in this sprawling metropolis. If you're dying for some activity, however, jogging is an option. **Chapultepec** is a good area for a run, but if you want more variety, jog in a residential area like **Lomas de Chapultepec,** with its manageable hills and larger-than-life mansions to keep you entertained. To get here from Chapultepec, take a KM 15.5 POR PALMAS westbound on Paseo de la Reforma. To return, hop on any bus or pesero labeled M. AUDITORIO, M. CHAPULTEPEC, or ZOCALO.

SOCCER Mexican *fútbol* (soccer) is the passion of the country, and matches practically paralyze the entire city. The professional season lasts from September to May or June, and most games take place in the gigantic **Estadio Azteca,** in the southern part of the city. From Metro Tasqueña, catch a *tren ligero* (a sort of trolley) or *trolebus* (electric bus) straight to the stadium. One of the most popular teams that plays in Azteca is América, a powerhouse with lots of fans and rivals. Tickets for the games (sold at the taquillas outside) cost between $8 and $15; you can buy them the day of the game, but try to arrive at least an hour before kickoff. The Pumas of UNAM play in the stadium at the Ciudad Universitaria (*see* UNAM in Worth Seeing, *above*).

Good places for pickup soccer games:
- *Parque Estadio, near Metro Hospital General*
- *General Parque Les Venadas, near Metro División del Norte*
- *Parque Pilares, Col. del Valle*

HORSE RACES AND RODEOS You can risk what little money you have at the **Hipódromo de las Américas.** The entrance fee to the track is 15¢, and once you're inside, you only need 20¢ to gamble. The horses run Tuesday, Thursday, and Friday 5:30 PM–10:30 PM and weekends 2:45–8. *Industria Militar, tel. 5/557–41–00. From Metro Polanco, walk 2 blocks north to Av. Ejército Nacional to catch pesero* DEFENSA NACIONAL.

Charreadas (rodeos) are held Sunday at noon in two locations in the D.F.: **Lienzo Charro de la Villa** (Metro: Indios Verdes) and **Lienzo del Charro** (Constituyentes 500; take any pesero from Metro Chapultepec). A show usually costs about $1. Check in the newspaper *Ovaciones* for any announcements regarding propective rodeos or call 5/277-87-06 or 5/277-87-10, weekdays 9–5.

BULLFIGHTING Brought to Mexico by Hernán Cortés, the tradition of bullfighting continues today. Although the very best matadors perform in the fall, an off-season *corrida* (bullfight) with a novice matador is still worth a trip to the arena, especially if you've never seen a corrida before. **Plaza México** is the largest bullfighting arena in the world, and corridas are held Sundays at 4 PM. Ticket prices range from 75¢ to $8, with seats on the sunny side (*sol*) tending to be cheaper and rowdier than the seats on the shady side (*sombra*). The ticket window is open Thursday, Friday, and Saturday 9:30–1 and 3:30–7, and on Sunday (corrida day) from 9:30 until the third bull dies. Get there about an hour before the corrida. *Augusto Rodín 241, Ciudad de los Deportes, tel. 5/563–39–59. Take pesero* INSURGENTES SUR/SAN ANGEL *south on Insurgentes Sur.*

JAI ALAI The skill and coordination required to play *frontón* (jai alai), a lightning-fast Basque handball game (the fist-sized balls have been clocked at more than 110 mph), draws crowds of spectators. Of course, they aren't so awestruck they forget to place bets, which—at about a dollar a match—are as innocuous as they come. You can check out the action at **Frontón México** (NW cnr of Plaza de la República) Monday–Thursday and Saturday from 6 PM to 1 AM. Women's matches are played at **Frontón Metropolitano** (Bahía de Todos los Santos 190) Monday–Saturday 4–10.

Near Mexico City

XOCHIMILCO

More than 700 years ago the Valley of Mexico was almost entirely underwater. This shortage of terra firma prompted the Xochimilcos to build a series of *chinampas* (floating islands of mud, reeds, and grasses) and anchor them to the lakebed with long poles. As the natural grasses and reeds on the islands began to grow, their roots extended into the water, becoming permanently affixed to the lakebed. As more and more of these floating islands took root, the lake was slowly transformed into a maze of canals. Even now, after six centuries of conquest, colonialism, and change, Xochimilco, 21 kilometers south of Mexico City's Zócalo, remains a testament to this ingenious innovation.

Xochimilco, with its central plaza and market, feels like a small village rather than a group of drifting islands. The gardens are a favorite picnic spot for middle-class families, but visitors are rare during the week. Sunday is the busiest day, when you'll be squashed by boats on all sides. Enterprising boat owners pick out tourists and try to persuade them to commit to their *lancha* (flat-bottom boat) before they've even seen the water. Although the government sets prices, you can usually negotiate. A ride in a more touristy *chalupa* (small canoe) lasts around 2 hours and costs around $5 for two or more people. You can bring your own lunch, or buy warm tamales from the smaller lanchas that circulate on the lake.

COMING AND GOING The easiest way to reach Xochimilco is to take the Metro to Tasqueña, hop on the tren ligero, and get off at the last station. From here, walk south on Cuauhtémoc to José María Morelos, make a left and you'll be in the town center. The trip from Tasqueña to Xochimilco takes less than 1 hour.

TEOTIHUACAN

By the 12th century, when the Aztecs migrated to the Valley of Mexico, Teotihuacán had already been abandoned for more than 500 years. Awestruck by the massive stone temples jutting high above the lush, green valley floor, the Aztecs named the mysterious ruins "Place of the Gods."

More than a millennium has passed since the Teotihuacanos inhabited the beautiful stone city, and information about the ancient civilization remains scant. Archaeologists have managed only to divide the history of the site into four distinct stages. What was to become the greatest city of Mesoamerica began in a rather humble way, consisting of a few farming villages in the center of the Valle de Teotihuacán around 900 BC. Gradually the villages grew into larger settlements, increasing their wealth through mining and trading obsidian with neighboring settlements. By around 100 BC, Teotihuacán was a prosperous, urban society controlled by an ecclesiastic oligarchy.

The powerful union of religious and political authorities made it possible to mobilize a labor force capable of building two massive pyramids: the **Pirámide del Sol** (Pyramid of the Sun) and the **Pirámide de la Luna** (Pyramid of the Moon). By around 300 AD, archaeologists believe, Teotihuacán had reached the apogee of its power; its empire spread outward from the valley across Mesoamerica. The Teotihuacanos' expansionist thirst was temporarily quenched, and they turned their attentions to beautifying their capital city. It is from this period that the most impressive artwork dates. Around 650 AD, the city began to wane, although no one is quite sure why. Buildings eroded and the city was slowly abandoned. Eventually, Teotihuacán was pillaged by outsiders, forcing the remaining residents to migrate elsewhere, leaving the once-great city to be enveloped by the surrounding vegetation.

Cleared of foliage, the ruins have been groomed for easy tourist access. After you enter the archaeological zone and cross the main thoroughfare, **Avenida de los Muertos** (Avenue of the Dead), you come to the **Ciudadela** (Citadel), a huge square with apartment complexes and temples. The detail and workmanship of the artwork here have led archaeologists to speculate that

Teotihuacán

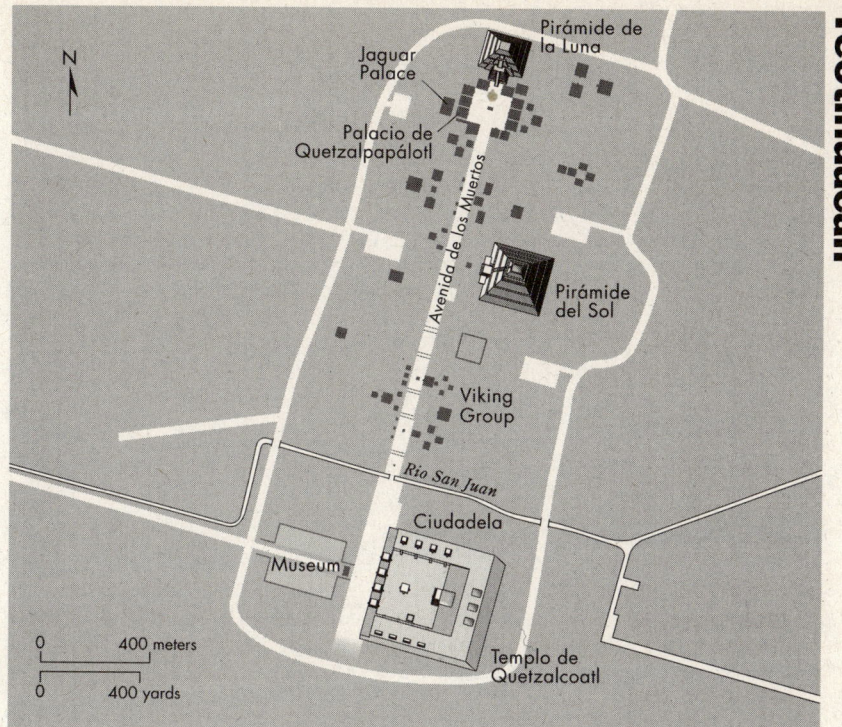

they were once the living quarters of ruling priests. At the far end of the citadel is the **Templo de Quetzalcoatl,** made up of two pyramids; the one on top is a reconstruction of the older pyramid below. The facade of the older one bears bas-reliefs of the plumed serpent Quetzalcoatl (with a lion's mane around his head) and the square-faced rain god Tlaloc. For a better view of the sculptures, go around to the walkway between the two buildings. Halfway down the Avenue of the Dead is the enormous, unmistakable **Pirámide del Sol**; rising more than 65 meters high, it's the third-largest pyramid in the world. The view of lush green mountains and white fluffy clouds, after 248 steps, is breathtaking, and so is the climb. Discovered in 1962, the **Palacio de Quetzalpapálotl** was probably the home of a powerful Teotihuacano, and is now almost fully reconstructed. Some of the butterflies carved into the columns still have their original beady obsidian eyes, which gaze, as they have for centuries, over the beautiful open plazas of the city. Just west of the palace is the **Jaguar Palace,** with reconditioned red-and-green murals showing jaguars dressed in feathers and performing various human activities. These same brilliant reds and greens, as well as blacks and yellows, once covered much of the city. A thorough tour of the ruins would take an entire day, but you can see a lot, if not every pyramid, in 3 or 4 hours. Admission: about $2.50. Open daily 8–5.

COMING AND GOING Autobuses Teotihuacán (tel. 5/587–05–01) departs from the far north end of the Autobuses del Norte terminal in Mexico City about every 20 minutes 6 AM–3 PM. The bus (1 hr, $1.25) drops you off at the main entrance, Puerta 1. The last bus back to Mexico City leaves Teotihuacán at 6 PM.

FOOD Just outside Puerta 1, a series of fondas sell comida corrida for about $2, in addition to the usual tacos and tortas.

If you're prone to sunburn, bring a hat and sunscreen to Teotihuacán. The hot sun beams down on the valley, and there isn't any smog to filter it. However, even during summer a chilly wind blows, so wear layers. A water bottle is also a good idea, because the climbing is hard work, especially at this altitude.

Although no food or drink is officially permitted in the archaeological zone (except in the overpriced restaurant inside the complex), no one searches bags at the entrance, and the garbage cans on the site are filled with food wrappers and drink bottles. It's doubtful anyone will complain if you pull out some bread and cheese, as long as you take your trash with you.

TULA

The small city of Tula, known in ancient times as Tollán, is a favorite retreat for day-trippers. If you stay overnight, you'll escape the frenzy of Mexico City but not the air pollution, which is still present 70 or so kilometers north of the D.F. Tula's main attraction is the archaeological site displaying remnants of the Toltec civilization's capital city, complete with ball courts, pyramids, and a palace. Ancient Tula, thought to have been occupied from 900 AD to 1150 AD, was inhabited by as many as 40,000 people at its height. The reigning symbols of the site are the *atlantes*—imposing, 4-meter-high warriors, some of which were used as roof supports. Hundreds of these once brightly painted statues and reliefs are dedicated to Quetzalcoatl, the plumed serpent god. The site itself is on the outskirts of town, some 3 kilometers from the bus station and best reached by taxi (about $2). Alternately, you can catch a TEPETITLAN or ACTOPAN pesero. These leave from Tula's zócalo and zoom by the ruins, so make sure you tell the driver you'd like to be tossed out near "Las Pirámides." *Admission: $2, free Sun. Open Tues.–Sun. 9:30–4:30.*

COMING AND GOING Autotransportes **Valle de Mezquital** departs Mexico City from the Autobuses del Norte terminal (sala 8) for Tula (1½ hrs, $2.50) every 30 minutes from 5 AM to 10:30 PM.

WHERE TO SLEEP Directly east of the bus station is **Motel Lizbeth** (Ocampo 200, tel. 773/2–00–45), a clean, modern, and expensive outfit; singles are $21, doubles $23. Downtown opposite the cathedral is **Hotel Cuellar** (5 de Mayo 23, tel. 773/2–04–42), a smaller hotel with singles for $9, doubles $11.

VALLE DE BRAVO

Valle de Bravo's popularity with upper-class *chilangos* has given it a split personality. During the week, the village sees little activity as locals go about their business. From Friday to Sunday, however, Valle becomes crowded with weekenders who come to hike, waterski, windsurf, and hanglide. Although these activities have given Valle de Bravo the image of a posh resort town, it's filled with plenty of thrills for the budget traveler. The village's red tile roofs and impeccable stone-paved streets are wonderfully maintained, and the designation of the nearby hills and **Lago Avándaro** (Lake Avándaro) as ecological reserves has kept the area clean and unpolluted.

BASICS **Centro de Cambio Valle** (Benito Juárez 103, at Porfirio Díaz, tel. 726/2–40–05) exchanges money daily 9–3. The **post office** (Joaquín Pagaza 200, tel. 726/2–03–73) is open weekdays 9–4 and Saturday 9–1. Ladatel phones abound, and the **caseta de larga distancia y fax** (Plaza de la Independencia 6, tel. 726/2–09–00) is open 7 AM–9 PM. The main plaza is lined with pharmacies, including **Farmacia y Perfumería Naty** (Miguel Hidalgo 100, tel. 2–01–62), open 8–3 and 4–9.

COMING AND GOING **México–Zinacantepec** buses depart Mexico City's Central Poniente for Valle de Bravo (3 hrs, $4.50) every 20 minutes 5 AM–7:30 PM. The last bus from Valle de Bravo back to Mexico City leaves at 7 PM from the Central Camionera (cnr 16 de Septiembre and Zaragoza).

WHERE TO SLEEP Despite the abundance of luxury hotels in Valle, there are a few good budget places, including **Hotel Mary** (Jardín Central, facing the plaza, tel. 726/2–29–67), with singles for $12.50 and doubles for $16. **Posada María Isabel** (Vergel 104, tel. 726/2–30–36) has a well-kept patio-garden and medium-size rooms for $11.50 (singles) and $13 (doubles). When the weather is good, your best option is to camp. Go down to the piers (from the plaza, walk down Joaquín Pagaza and turn right on Calle de la Cruz) and take a collectivo boat ride ($2.50) across the lake to the free campgrounds.

FOOD Many of Valle's restaurants are only open on weekends and are well above the budget traveler's range. There are a few exceptions: **El Bocaito** (Vergel 202, tel. 726/2-01-33; open Fri.–Sun. 1–1) serves incredible homemade pizzas for about $4. **La Cueva del León** (Plaza de la Independencia 2, tel. 726/2-40-62; open Wed.–Mon. 11–11) has colorful tables overlooking the plaza. Try their grilled trout (fresh from Lake Avándaro) for about $4. Try **Restaurant Alma Edith** (5 de Febrero, at Villegra, tel. 726/2-40-49) for generous comidas corridas ($4). You can also sample tacos at the main market (cnr of Hidalgo and Independencia).

OUTDOOR ACTIVITIES Although it's best to come on the weekend to thoroughly enjoy Valle's water sports, there's still plenty to do during the week. If you're rarin' to waterski, you can rent a *lancha rápida* (motorboat) for $34 per half day (equipment included; up to five people), or just take a leisurely boat ride for $2.50. To explore the village, rent a bike ($2.50 an hr) from the shop on 17 de Septiembre 200 (open daily 9–8).

When it comes to hiking, the courageous attack the steep **Cerro de la Peña**, a half-hour walk northwest of town. You won't need rock-climbing equipment, just a lot of stamina to reach the cross on the top of the hill, where you'll be rewarded with a stunning view of the lake and the town. The less active take a collective taxi from the center (50¢) to the nearby town of **Avándaro** and walk the 3-kilometer **Velo de Novia** trail, which borders a small cascade and follows the stream into the surrounding hills. If this still sounds like too much exertion, rent a horse for about $6 an hour and let it do all the work.

BAJA CALIFORNIA   3
By Shayna Samuels

The image of a tall, spiny saguaro cactus framed against the cool blue of the Pacific typifies the rugged landscape of Baja. Throw in bustling, northern cities and southern resorts—both renowned for wild nightlife—and sedate, out-of-the-way towns and you'll have an idea of the range of the peninsula's diversity. This variety attracts very different types of travelers, including those who do nothing except fry their skin by day and their brain cells by night, and sports enthusiasts who come for the windsurfing, fishing, and scuba diving.

Only in recent years, with the influx of people from all over the country, has Baja become genuinely integrated into mainstream Mexican culture and consciousness. Before then, the peninsula was largely considered frontier territory. Although Hernán Cortés officially "discovered" Baja while looking for Amazon queens and pearls, Jesuit missionaries in the late 17th century were the first Europeans to settle the peninsula successfully. From their original outpost in Loreto, the Spaniards extended the Spanish frontier into what is now northern California. With Mexico's independence and the demise of the missions however, Baja withered, leaving a few scattered ranches and mining towns, that stood untouched until tourism briefly boomed in the 1930s. It wasn't until the early 1970s, with the completion of the Trans-Peninsular Highway (Highway 1), that Baja's isolation finally eroded and the region became a popular destination.

Baja's economic boom means that prices are often higher here than in other parts of Mexico.

Today, Baja California Norte (Northern Baja California) is characterized by border towns where tourists (primarily American college students) come to get drunk and party, and beach towns, filled with similarly-minded tourists who leave the city to frolick on the sand. Baja California Sur (Southern Baja California) is much more mellow. This region is less developed, and tourism here centers around a different kind of beach-related activities: sailing, fishing, and whale-watching. Or, if a four-wheel drive makes itself available, you can venture to the isolated Sierra la Giganta mountains. At the southernmost tip of the peninsula is Los Cabos, a region famous for white sandy beaches and the vivid hue of its waters. Cabo San Lucas, is the major resort town here, where self-indulgence reigns supreme and fishing ranks a close second. San José del Cabo, just to the east, is a quieter city. Although these two towns are rapidly being built up, there are still miles of infrequently visited coastline along the Pacific and between San José del Cabo and La Paz. Without a private vehicle, however, these isolated regions are nearly inaccessible without risking a sore thumb. La Paz, the state's capital, is more of a transportation hub than a vacation getaway, but nearby reefs and coral forests offer excellent underwater fun.

Baja California Norte

Baja California Norte is a favorite with tourists, thousands of whom cross the border into Tijuana in search of exotica; most just end up buying trinkets and partying until they drop. Farther south, the beach towns of Rosarito, Ensenada, and San Felipe attract similar weekend crowds seeking daytime fun and nighttime parties. Because of the region's tawdry reputation, people interested in an authentic "Mexican" experience often skip Tijuana and its environs altogether. The perversities of tourism taken to extremes aside, northern Baja is intriguing, if you're willing to wander off the tourist track and explore: The region is very diverse, partly because of the migrants who come from all over Mexico to look for work in the region's growing economy.

Tijuana

Sprawling along what is reputed to be the most heavily crossed border in the world, Tijuana largely attracts tourists with a single objective: to party. Popular wisdom among foreigners and other Mexicans contends that Tijuana is more an amalgamation of Mexican and gringo cultures than a "real" Mexican city, and a lawless den of hedonism at that. In certain respects, these impressions are accurate, and those shy of crowds of foreigners, made-for-export *artesanía* (crafts), dollar beers, and eyebrow-raising sex shows may want to avoid this city altogether. The main drag, Avenida Revolución, is by day a magnet for the middle-age, trinket-buying crowd; by night, it attracts partyers (mostly under 21) who drink, dance, and pass out. Just one block west of Revolución, however, is Tijuana's principal commercial street, Avenida Constitución, which is lined with pharmacies, hardware stores, and clothing shops. Constitución's buzzing pace, microphone-wielding salesmen, and strolling families with fathers and sons in cowboy hats could be part of any city in northern Mexico.

BASICS

AMERICAN EXPRESS The AmEx office is in the **Viajes Carrousel** travel agency. Whether or not you're a cardholder, you can change up to $100 or have your mail held here. *Sánchez Taboada, at Clemente Orozco, tel. 66/34–36–60. Open weekdays 9–6, Sat. 9:30–1. Mailing address: Blvd. Sánchez Taboada y Clemente Orozco, Edificio Husa, Zona Río, Tijuana, Baja California Norte, CP 22320, México.*

AUTO PARTS/SERVICE Serviautos and Servipartes (Revolución 216, at Coahuila, tel. 66/85–97–22) can help you out Monday–Saturday 8:30–7:30. The **Green Angels** (tel. 66/23–77–35), a government service, offers free assistance to drivers with car trouble. Call them and they'll come to you.

CASAS DE CAMBIO American dollars are accepted in Tijuana, Mexicali, Ensenada, and Rosarito, but you'll get a poor exchange rate. Moneychangers abound in Tijuana's tourist district, but only deal in cash. For changing pesos to dollars, you'll find the best rates at moneychangers on San Ysidro Boulevard in San Ysidro, just before you cross the border. To purchase

---

Beware the Convenient Telephone

Capitol Network Systems Inc. (CNSI), a Texas-based company, has plastered northern Mexico with white, smiling signs reading TO CALL THE U.S.A. COLLECT OR WITH A CREDIT CARD: SIMPLY DIAL 0. Things aren't as happy as they seem: This writer was charged $19 for the first minute and $3 for each additional minute to call Los Angeles. It's worth it to give the cash to the Mexican economy and dial direct via a caseta de larga distancia, or to call collect through a Mexican operator by dialing 09.

or change traveler's checks, try the AmEx office (*see above*) or **Banamex** (La Juventud, just across pedestrian bridge, tel. 66/83–52–48). The latter is open for exchange weekdays 9–5. ATMs accepting Visa and MasterCard can be found at most banks. Try **Bancomer** on Constitución and Calle 5a; **Bital** on Revolución and Calle 2a; or **Serfín** on Constitución and Calle 6a.

CONSULATES Canada. Citizens of Australia can also find help at the Canadian consulate. *Germán Gedovius 5–202, Zona Río, tel. 66/84–04–61. Open weekdays 9–1.*

United Kingdom. *Salinas 1500, tel. 66/81–73–23. Open weekdays 9–2 and 4–6.*

United States. In an after-hours emergency, call the San Diego office at 619/585–2000 and an agent in Tijuana will be contacted. *Tapachula 96, Col. Hipódromo, tel. 66/81–74–00. Open weekdays 8–4:30.*

CROSSING THE BORDER U.S. and Canadian citizens don't need tourist cards to travel as far south as Ensenada (including San Felipe), or farther down the mainland to Mazatlán; when entering or leaving Baja by land, a driver's license or birth certificate is sufficient identification. For travel south of Ensenada, tourist cards are available from the Oficina de Migración (immigration office, tel. 65/52–69–93; open 24 hrs) just across the border, under the bridge that passes over the freeway. It's a good idea to bring your passport if you plan to travel elsewhere in the country, especially southern Mexico. For more information on visas and tourist cards, *see* Chapter 1, Basics.

EMERGENCIES In Tijuana, contact the **police** at 134 ; the **fire** department at 136; the **Cruz Roja** (for an ambulance) at 132.

LAUNDRY Tijuana's laundromats are inconvenient, and you're probably better off rinsing your undies in the hotel sink. If you're desperate, however, try **Limpiaduría Lavandería,** where washing and drying your own clothes costs $2 (soap is an extra 50¢), and giving the honor to someone else costs $3. *Centro Comercial Plaza Río, Suite 25-A.B.C.D., Zona Río, tel. 66/84–02–26. Open daily 7 AM–11 PM.*

MAIL It's cheaper and faster to send international mail from the United States than from Mexico. If that's impractical, Tijuana's **post office** is on Avenida Negrete and Calle 11a. They'll hold mail for you at the following address for up to 10 days: Lista de Correos, Avenida Negrete y Calle 11a, Tijuana, Baja California Norte, CP 22000, México. **Telecomm** next door will let you send telegrams, faxes, and telexes. *Post office tel. 66/84–79–50. Open weekdays 8–5, Sat. 9:30 AM–1 PM. Telecomm open weekdays 8–8, weekends 8–1.*

MEDICAL AID Many San Diegans go to Tijuana for dental work, which can cost up to two-thirds less than in the States, and dentists line the streets off Revolución. Dr. Manuel R. Laza at the **Centro Médico España** (Calle 2a No. 1844, near Constitución, tel. 66/85–24–50) speaks English and is available Monday–Saturday 8:30–8; Sundays until 2 PM. Plenty of 24-hour pharmacies lie along Constitución, including **Farmacia Regis** (tel. 66/85–13–49; 24 hrs), at the corner of Calle 5a.

PHONES Collect calls are easy to place from Tijuana's pay phones, but it's more expensive to make international calls from Mexico than from the United States. If you want to call from a *caseta de larga distancia* (long-distance telephone office) go to **Copias Rubi**, where calls to the States are discounted 50% weekdays after 8 PM, all day on Saturdays, and Sundays until 5 PM. *Calle 7a No. 1906, near Constitución, tel. 66/85–03–11. Open daily 9 AM–10 PM.*

VISITOR INFORMATION Tijuana has a number of tourist offices. The most centrally located is run by **CANACO** (Revolución, at Calle 1a, tel. 66/88–16–85; open daily 9–7), the Tijuana Chamber of Commerce. It has an English-speaking staff, decent maps, and a public phone and rest room. Just across the San Ysidro border into Mexico (it's in the building on your left just after the taxi stand) is the **Tourism and Convention Bureau** (tel. 66/83–13-11 or 66/83–14–05; open Wed.–Mon. 9–7), which also sells auto insurance. Another less busy bureau (tel. 66/83–14–05; open daily 9–7) is across the street, in the small, white building shared with Smokin' Joes liquor.

COMING AND GOING

BY BUS Tijuana has two bus stations, the **Central Camionera,** which is served by major mainland companies, and the **Central Viejo,** for buses to Tecate. **Greyhound/Trailways** (tel. 66/21-29-48) buses to the United States depart from both stations, as well as from the station on the San Ysidro side of the border (799-E San Ysidro Blvd., tel. 619/428-1194). They leave every hour 5 AM–6 PM for San Diego (50 min, $4) and Los Angeles (3½ hrs, $13), and you can change in Los Angeles to continue on to San Francisco (12–13 hrs, $62) or Seattle (34 hrs, $106). There are large, expensive lockers in San Ysidro's Greyhound bus station, but it's better to lug your gear next door to **UPS** (open Mon.–Sat. 9–6, Sun. 10–2), which only charges $1 for 24 hours.

Three bus companies share the **Central Camionera** (tel. 66/26-17-01) on the eastern edge of Tijuana, far from the budget hotel area and most tourist activities. **Transportes Norte de Sonora** operates buses throughout the country, including frequent first- and second-class services to Guadalajara (36 hrs; $56.50 1st class, $49 2nd class) and Mexico City (48 hrs; $68 1st class, $59 2nd class). **Transportes Pacífico** (tel. 66/21-26-06) also has express buses down the mainland coast to Guadalajara and Mexico City. **Autotransportes de Baja California** (tel. 66/21-23-04) serves Baja with hourly first- and second-class buses 6 AM–8 PM to Mexicali (3 hrs, $7–$8), San Felipe (6 hrs, $12–$15), and Ensenada (1½ hrs, $4–$5). La Paz (22 hrs, $39.50) is served only by first-class buses, with departures at 8 AM, noon, 6 PM, and 9 PM.

A taxi will take you down Revolución to the Central Camionera for $7–$10, but your best option is to catch a brown-and-white colectivo (15 min, $1) marked CENTRAL CAMIONERA from the stop on Madero, between Calles 2a and 3a. To get from the bus station to the budget-hotel/tourist area, find a bus marked CENTRO. The station offers luggage storage (open daily 6:30 AM–10:30 PM) for 65¢ an hour. You can also place long distance calls (cash only) here from the 24-hour **Sendetel** (tel. 66/21-23-04) booth. Money exchange is available daily 6 AM-10 PM.

Buses to Tecate (1½ hrs, $1.50) leave from the **Central Viejo** (Madero, at Calle 1a, tel. 66/88-07-52) 5:30 AM-9 PM. The station is within walking distance of both the border and the budget-hotel area. To reach the station from the border, cross over the Río Tijuana pedestrian bridge and continue straight on Calle 1a. To reach the budget-hotel area from the bus station, continue on Calle 1a to Coahuila.

BY TROLLEY The wheelchair-accessible **San Diego Trolley** (tel. 619/231-8549) runs from the America Plaza Transfer Station (C St., btw Kettner and India) in downtown San Diego to San Ysidro and stops right at the border. Trolleys make the 45-minute trip about every 15 minutes 5 AM-12:15 AM, except on Saturday night, when hourly service continues from midnight until 5 AM Sunday. Many trolley stations along the line provide free parking, which can save you $7 in parking expenses at San Ysidro. Be sure to park in a guarded and lighted parking lot.

BY CAR There are two border crossings in Tijuana. The San Ysidro-Tijuana crossing is the busiest; on weekends and holidays, the wait to enter the United States by car can be two hours. Lines are shorter at the less central Otay Mesa border (near Tijuana airport, 10 minutes east of San Diego), but it's only open 6 AM-10 PM. For more details about the legal and financial formalities involved with taking a car into Mexico, *see* Chapter 1, Basics.

BY PLANE Domestic plane fares in Mexico are no bargain, but they're usually substantially cheaper than international flights into Mexico. If you're in Southern California, you're better off crossing into Tijuana and buying your ticket there. When you leave Mexico, don't forget the $12 departure tax payable only in pesos (except in Los Cabos, where you can pay in U.S. dollars). The airport is on the eastern edge of the city by the Otay Mesa border crossing. From the San Ysidro border or downtown, a taxi ride costs $7-$10. The city bus marked AEROPUERTO makes the trip to the airport in 30-40 minutes. Catch it at the traffic circle near the border.

The **Aerocalifornia** office (Plazería Commercial Center, across from Cultural Center, tel. 66/84-20-07 or 800/258-3311 in the U.S.) is open weekdays 8-7. They serve Los Angeles and Phoenix in the United States, and also fly daily to La Paz, and four times per day to Mexico City. **Aeroméxico** (Revolución, at Calle 8a, tel. 66/85-44-01 or 800/237-6639 in the U.S.) and **Mexicana** (Paseo de los Héroes 112, tel. 66/82-41-83 or 800/531-7921 in the U.S.) both offer flights throughout Mexico at comparable prices.

GETTING AROUND

Tijuana, unlike most Mexican cities, lacks a definite center; there's no principal church or square by which to orient yourself. Avenidas Revolución and Constitución are the heart of nightlife, and are the most "central" aspect of town. Bars, dance clubs, street vendors, and the jai alai arena are all located in this area, which is best explored on foot. Avenidas run north-south; calles, east-west. Address numbers were just changed in 1993 (for the third time in recent history), so many buildings have two, or even three numbers; the ones written in blue are current. To reach the bullring or racetrack on Boulevard Agua Caliente, take a minibus from the stop on Madero between Calles 2a and 4a, since both sites are far from the center.

BY BUS Buses marked 5 or 10 CENTRO go down Agua Caliente, but peseros are faster and come more frequently (both cost less than $1). The peseros on the Agua Caliente route are red-and-black station wagons; catch them on Calle 2a near Avenida Revolución. Tan-and-white station wagons go to the Glorieta Cuauhtémoc and the shopping centers along the Río Tijuana; catch them on Calle 3a. Buses to the airport and the bus station stop at the traffic circle across from the border crossing and on Calle 4a at Niños Héroes. The easiest way to reach the border from downtown is to catch a **Mexi-Coach** bus ($1), which leaves Revolución (btw Calles 6 and 7) every half hour 9-9.

BY TAXI Cabs don't have meters, so be sure to negotiate the fare before entering. A trip between the border and downtown should cost about $3, while a ride from the border or city center to the Central Camionera or airport should run $7-$10.

WHERE TO SLEEP

The really cheap hotels are northwest of Revolución, and around Coahuila. They're only a little darker, dingier, and noisier than those on or around Revolución, which cost $5–$10 more. Women, however, may find the attention they get in the red-light district bothersome and should think twice before staying here. All the hotels listed below have hot water 24 hours a day.

➤ **UNDER $15** • **Hotel y Baños Enva.** The small, dark rooms of this hotel face a newly painted courtyard, and though a bit worn, each has a fairly clean private bathroom. Men who don't like the look of their shower can go next door to the baths and use the sauna, whirlpool, and steam baths for $3, but women are unwelcome at the facilities. Singles cost $9, doubles $12.50. *Artículo 123 (Calle 1a) No. 1918, near Constitución, tel. 66/85–22–41. 38 rooms, all with bath. Luggage storage.*

➤ **UNDER $20** • **Hotel Catalina.** Clean, quiet, and comfortable, this is the best in the heart of the tourist area. Singles cost $10 and doubles cost $15 (one bed) and $19 (two beds). Some rooms have TVs and all have phones that let you make free local or collect international calls. Reservations are recommended on weekends. *Calle 5a, at Madero, tel. 66/85–97–48. 38 rooms, all with bath. Luggage storage. Reservations by mail: P.O. Box 3544, San Ysidro, CA 92073, U.S.A.*

Hotel París. Although semi-expensive (singles $20, doubles $25) and a little noisy on weekends, this five-story hotel is centrally located. Here, you're guaranteed a safe, spotless room with air-conditioning, TV, and your own phone. *Calle 5, btw Revolución and Constitución, tel. 66/85–30–23. 40 rooms, all with bath.*

Tijuana's budget hotels fill up quickly on weekends, so make reservations or come early on Friday to stake out your room.

Hotel San Nicolás. This quiet, safe hotel has a liveable lobby with couches, a TV, and local phones; singles here are $14, doubles $19. You can enjoy a picnic on the tables in the rear lot, or take advantage of the secure parking area. The front desk also changes money, and long-distance collect calls can be made around the clock. Best of all, **Hotel Económico** next door (where sad, dark cubicles run $10 for a single, $14 for a double) has a decent restaurant. *Madero 538, btw Calles 1a and 2a, tel. 66/88–04–18. 28 rooms, all with bath.*

HOSTELS **Villa Juvenil.** If by some odd chance you're in Tijuana to sleep and not to party, make the 10-minute drive from downtown to this hostel, where $5 ($4 students) will get you a bunk bed in a five-person room. The passable bathrooms are co-ed and there are no shower curtains (can you hear the cheesy porno music yet?) To check in, you must get here by 7 PM, when the office closes. *Airport Hwy and Via Oriente, Zona Río, tel. 66/34–30–89. Take colectivo marked EL POSTAL from Calle 3a and Revolución, and ask driver to stop at CREA, the adjoining sports facility. Curfew 10 PM.*

ROUGHING IT Camping is free on the beaches outside Tijuana, but the destitutes and drunkards make it unsafe. The beaches are also dirty and far from downtown, and foot traffic headed north may interrupt your rest. People heading out on early buses have been known to sleep at the Central Camionera station, which has luggage storage and is well lit.

FOOD

Because people move here from all over Mexico, Tijuana is a great place to sample the diversity of Mexican cuisine. Food stalls at the **mercado municipal** (Niños Héroes, btw Calles 1a and

2a), serve dishes from Jalisco, Guanajuato, Michoacán, Guaymas, and other areas for $3–$5. There's also a good selection of inexpensive eateries along Calle 2a, between Revolución and Constitución, which cater primarily to a working-class clientele. Prices on Revolución tend to be higher than on surrounding streets, and more expensive restaurants are along Agua Caliente.

Café Pekín. This family-style Chinese restaurant is popular with locals and serves terrific $3–$5 lunch combos (an egg roll, almond veggies, two super-hot chiles, and either a huge pile of fried rice or pineapple chicken). Huge dinners also cost $3–$5, and you can get food to go. *Constitución 1435, at Calle 7a, tel. 66/85–24–30. Open daily 11 AM–midnight.*

Restaurant Los Norteños. Tables outside this small restaurant are great for watching the action on Plaza Revolución. Breakfast costs less than $2. If you've hit taco overload, try the meat or veggie sandwiches ($2–$3). *Constitución 530, near Calle 2a, tel. 66/85–68–55. Open 24 hrs.*

Tortas Ricardo's. Looking somewhat like a 50's diner, this 24-hour restaurant has an extensive menu and serves breakfasts ($1–$3) at any hour. It also has salads ($2–$3), traditional Mexican food ($2–$3), and fish or meat dishes ($4–$6). *Cnr of Calle 7a and Madero, tel. 66/85–40–31. Open 24 hrs.*

La Vuelta. This fabulous place doubles as an all-hours nightclub, which features live mariachi music (Monday–Saturday 8 PM; Sunday 6:30 PM). The grilled meats ($7–$10) and *antojitos* (appetizers) are delicious. If you can't afford that, nurse a $2 beer or the two-for-one margaritas (available weekdays 7 AM–10 PM), and plunge into the free chips, salsa, and atmosphere. *Revolución, at Calle 11a, tel. 66/85–72–09. At curve where Revolución changes to Agua Caliente. Open 24 hrs.*

AFTER DARK

Finding something to do at night is not a problem here. Barkers along Revolución (btw Calles 1a and 2a) lure young, minimally clad revelers into neon-lit dance halls with offers of free tequila. If you feel like getting smashed and grooving to the latest American hits, the following places fit the bill. Happily, none charges a cover, so you can scope out each club until you find your niche or become too drunk to care. Typically, a margarita costs $3–$4, and beer is $2.50. **Tilly's Fifth Avenue** (Calle 5a No. 901, at Revolución, tel. 66/85–72–45) and **People's** (Calle 2a, at Revolución, tel. 66/85–45–72) are both open Monday–Thursday 11 AM–2 AM and Friday–Sunday until dawn. Saturday nights are the most popular—so popular that they may charge men a $3–$5 cover on holiday weekends. **Red Square** (Revolución, near Calle 6a, tel. 66/88–27–82) features a red spiral staircase leading up to the roof. Here you can sip (or pound) margaritas from noon until 3 AM, while watching the commotion below.

If you're tired of dancing with the under-dressed and underage, try to keep up with the locals at the restaurant/nightclub **La Vuelta** (*see* Food, *above*). On Friday, Saturday, and Sunday nights, **Disco Salsa** (Revolución 751, btw Calles 1a and 2a) plays salsa and merengue, while **La Loa** (Revolución, at Calle 2a) is the place to hear bands. **El Ranchero** (Plaza Santa Cecilia 769, tel. 66/85–28–00) is a no-games gay bar, frequented by both tourists and locals. Women are welcome but are a striking minority. El Ranchero is open Sunday–Thursday 10 PM–5 AM, Friday and Saturday 10 PM–8 AM.

CLUBS **La Estrella.** Packed with locals, this is the place to dance to cumbia and an occasional salsa tune. Hard-working Tijuanenses come here to let loose, and women without men in tow should be prepared to dance a lot. The $2 cover (for men only) includes a free Tecate, but those without an attitude may want to skip this club—La Estrella occasionally gets rough. *Calle 6a, tel. 66/88–13–49. Just east of Revolución under star sign. Open daily 10 AM–3 AM.*

Mike's Disco. If you're looking for a way into the gay scene in Tijuana, this is a good place to start. The main draw at this alternative nightclub is the shows where men dress up like famous Mexican actresses and sing torch songs (every night, midnight and 3 AM). The cover on Friday and Saturday nights is $4—regardless of gender, refreshingly. You can pick up the newspaper *Frontera Gay* to get an idea of what else is going on around town. *Revolución 1220, near Calle 6a, tel. 66/85–35–34. Open weekdays (except Wed.) 9 PM–3 AM, weekends until 7 AM.*

Most of the dancing in small bars and clubs on Coahuila is done by strippers. Women walking through the area may feel uncomfortable and should be cautious at night in this neighborhood.

SPECTATOR SPORTS

JAI ALAI This Basque game, known as *frontón* in Spanish, is played at **El Palacio Frontón** (Revolución, near Calle 7a, tel. 66/38–43–07), a dramatic Moorish-style palace. Something like racquetball, the game is played with a curved, wicker basket, three walls, and a balsa-wood, goatskin-wrapped ball moving at about 160 mph. Almost as fun as watching jai alai is betting on it. Next door, you can wager on football, baseball, and horse races. For game times call 66/85–25–24 or 66/38–43–08.

There's elegant seating at El Palacio Frontón, where you can order cocktails as you watch the game; if you dare, try the clamáto (clam sauce, tomato juice, and vodka; $2).

DOG RACES Yet another opportunity to lose your money awaits at the greyhound races at **Caliente Race Track.** Races are usually held at 8 PM, and there are matinees on weekends. A few km east of town, where Agua Caliente becomes Díaz Ordaz, tel. 66/81–78–11. Take bus marked BLVD AGUA CALIENTE *from Calle 2a (10 min, 40¢).*

BULLFIGHTING Tijuana has two bullrings, **El Toreo de Tijuana,** the downtown bullring on Agua Caliente, and the preferred, beachside **Plaza de Toros Monumental,** the second-largest bullring in the world, known as the "Bullring by the Sea." Fights take place May–late September on Sundays at 4 PM. Tickets start at $7 (for seats in the sun), and $10 (for seats in the shade). The bloodthirsty can purchase $50 seats that will put them close enough to get splattered. Buy tickets at the caseta on Revolución (btw Calles 3a and 4a, tel. 66/85–22–10), open weekends 10 AM–7 PM, or at the ring (Highway 1D, by the ocean); get there early to guarantee yourself a ticket. The easiest way to reach the Plaza is to take a Mexi-Coach bus (½ hr, $2) at 3:30 PM from Revolución (btw Calles 6a and 7a). Or take a blue-and-white bus marked PLAYAS from Calle 3a and Niños Héroes (40¢).

NEAR TIJUANA

ROSARITO About 45 kilometers from the border, Rosarito is one big, expensive beach party. This is the first popular beach south of Tijuana—not because it's so great, but because it's easy to get to—and you'll know you've reached a tourist trap when a fish taco costs nearly $1. Drunk American college students are abundant here, especially on weekends or during summer months, and most can be found in **Papas and Beer on the Beach** (Coronado, at Eucalipto 400, tel. 661/2–04–44), a popular outside bar, volleyball court, and dance club. The cover charge is $3–$10 (depending on how busy it is), and a margarita costs $4.50. The best time to show up in Rosarito is May 14, when parades, traditional dances, and the crowning of an annually selected queen celebrate the founding of Rosarito.

Around 20 minutes south of Rosarito by car, **Puerto Nuevo** consists of a cluster of restaurants, each trying to sell you the lobster for which the town is famous. The town has become so popular, however, that restaurants now charge $15 for a plate of crustaceans. Forget the food, and come to Puerto Nuevo for the surfing—it has better waves and fewer swimmers than Rosarito.

➤ **BASICS** • You can take medical problems to English-speaking Dr. Luis Gutiérrez Martínez (Benito Juárez 854, across from Rosarito Beach Hotel, tel. 661/2–28–47). His office is open daily 10–2 and 4–7:30. Conveniently, he shares an office with **GTE,** where you can make collect and credit-card calls with no connection fees. Phones are available daily 8 AM–8:30 PM, and on Sundays, there's a 50% discount on calls within Mexico. The **tourist office** (Benito Juárez 100, next to police station, tel. 661/2–02–00) has a friendly, English-speaking staff that give out maps of Baja Monday–Saturday 9–7, Sunday 10–6.

➤ **COMING AND GOING** • Buses don't serve Rosarito; *colectivos* (communal taxis) do. To reach downtown Tijuana from Rosarito (1 hr, 50¢), catch a yellow-and-white colectivo from half a block north of the Rosarito Beach Hotel—these run 24 hours a day. To reach Puerto Nuevo (15 min, 60¢), take the white taxi with burgundy and blue stripes that runs from the Brisas del Mar Hotel (Benito Juárez 22), daily 5 AM–11 PM. To reach Ensenada (1 hr, $2), take this same taxi to *las casetas* (toll booths) on the way out of town, then flag down a bus traveling from Tijuana to Ensenada. Buses marked ENSENADA pass by every half hour 7 AM–10 PM.

➤ **WHERE TO SLEEP** • The popularity of Rosarito beach, especially on weekends and holidays, makes it hard to find a cheap place to crash. Large, expensive, American-owned hotels and resorts have taken over, but **Villa Nueva** (Benito Juárez 97, no phone) still provides dingy rooms for about $20 (single or double), and the owner speaks some English. Another option is to rent a tiny cabin, one block from the beach (cnr of Sánchez Taboada and Cárdenas, tel. 661/2–09–76). Walk two blocks towards the beach from the red CALIMAX sign on Benito Juárez; cabins are $10 for up to two people. Camping on the beach is the cheapest option, but is not recommended for people traveling alone.

TECATE If you want a break from the hectic pace of Tijuana, head one hour east by bus to Tecate. Set on the outskirts of the Sierra de Juárez, this small, elevated rural town happens to lie right on the United States–Mexico border. No city sits across from Tecate on the American side, and the Mexican government has not developed the town for tourism, which accounts for its slow pace. There's not much to do in Tecate, but if you plan a couple of days in advance, you can take a free tour of the huge **Tecate Brewing Company** (Guerra 70, tel. 665/4–20–11 ext. 180 *or* 182). The brewery is open 8–noon and 1–5, and tours are given at varying times, depending on their production schedule. For samples stop by the new beer garden, **Jardín de Cerveza** (Hidalgo, tel. 665/4–20–11, ext. 123; open Tues.–Sat. 10–5, Sun. 10–4). People from surrounding ranches and northern Baja descend upon the town July 8–25 for a traditional *fiesta ranchera* (country fair), including food, crafts, music, and dancing.

➤ **BASICS** • Change cash and traveler's checks at **Bancomer** (Juárez, at Presidente Cárdenas, tel. 665/4–19–14) weekdays 9 AM–1:30 PM; it also has an ATM that accepts Plus and Cirrus cards. There's a **Computel** phone office in the bus station on Juárez that's open daily 7 AM–10 PM, but you can't make collect or credit card calls here. For **medical aid,** English-speaking Dr. Nestor López Arellano (Presidente E. Calles 56, tel. 665/4–07–39) is available weekdays 8–8, Saturday 8–6. **Farmacia del Parque** (Benito Juárez 270, tel. 665/4–54–12) is open daily 8 AM–11 PM. The **tourist office** (tel. 665/4–10–95) on the zócalo is open weekdays 8–7, weekends 10–3.

➤ **COMING AND GOING** • From either of Tijuana's two bus stations, buses to Tecate ($2) leave every half hour 5:30 AM–9 PM. From Tecate, seven buses go to Ensenada (2 hrs, $3) 8 AM–10 PM daily. Buses also leave for Mexicali ($5) every hour 7 AM–10 PM. Tecate's **bus station** (tel. 665/4–23–43) is on Benito Juárez, toward the east side of town. As you leave the station, turn left on Juárez and walk one block to the zócalo.

➤ **WHERE TO SLEEP AND EAT** • The cheapest lodging in Tecate is at the skanky **Hotel México** (Juárez 230, near bus station, tel. 665/4–15–04). If saggy beds, a little street noise, and a few drunk hangers about don't bother you, you can get a single for $5 or a double for $7 with unpleasant, shared bathroom facilities. Call first, however, as it's sometimes closed. Singles and doubles with private bath are $10. **Motel Paraíso** (Alderete 83, at Juárez, tel. 665/4–17–16) has comfortable, clean rooms, each with a fan and private bath; singles cost $10, doubles $13. To get here, walk about five blocks west of the zócalo on Juárez. The rooms are basically the same at **Hotel Tecate** (SW cnr of zócalo, at Libertad and Presidente Cárdenas, tel. 665/4–11–16). You pay a bit extra for the convenient location; singles and doubles with private bath are $14 without TV, $17 with TV.

To eat well and hang with the locals, try **Jardín Tecate** (south side of zócalo, tel. 665/4–34–53), which serves a menu including chef salads ($2.50), onion soup ($2), and garlic fish ($3) from 7 AM to 10 PM daily. **Restaurant Íntimo** (Juárez 181, tel. 665/4–48–19) has picnic tables in the front garden and is a nice place for breakfast (omelets and hotcakes cost $2). They also serve *pescado veracruzano* (red snapper cooked in tomatoes, onions, capers, peppers, and herbs; $4) and a *comida corrida* (pre-prepared lunch special; $2.50).

Mexicali

Huge, poor, and urban, Mexicali is easily stereotyped in familiar border-town terms. It's similar in character to Tijuana, but because of its relative isolation (160 kilometers east of Tijuana), awful summer heat, and the absence of tourist diversions, Mexicali is much less frequently visited. The city is aggressively trying to shed its tawdry image and recruit more respectable tourists/shoppers, as the downtown shopping center and the new Centro Cívico-Comercial (commercial and civic center) attest. But the fact that Mexicali is the capital of Baja California Norte (Northern Baja) and an important agricultural and industrial center doesn't carry much weight with vacationers. Most tourists spend only as much time here as is necessary to fill the gas tank, but immigrants from rural Mexico flock here seeking work in the *maquiladoras* (foreign-owned factories in duty-free zones), set up near the border.

Mexicali's most distinct feature is its large Chinese population, made up mostly of descendants of immigrants brought to Mexico to build the Imperial Canal to the north in 1902. The city has numerous Chinese restaurants and shops, an annual Chinese food fair in June, and even a small Chinese-language newspaper.

For more cultural diversions, Mexicali's free **Museo Regional de la Universidad de Baja California** (Reforma, at Calle L, tel. 65/54–19–77) includes exhibits on human evolution, geological photography, paleontology, and the colonial history of Baja California. If you're in Mexicali during the beginning of October, check out the city's biggest bash, the 15-day **Fiesta del Sol** (Sun Festival), which features live music, drinking and dancing, cockfights, and cultural exhibits. It's held at the **Parque Vicente Guerrero** on López Mateos. At least one Sunday a month between October and May, Mexicali's **Plaza de Toros Calafia** plays host to some of the best matadors and bulls in all of Mexico; the cheapest tickets, available at the Centro Cívico (Calafia, at Avenida de los Héroes, no phone), cost about $10.

BASICS

AUTO PARTS/SERVICE Oasa sells auto parts and repairs cars. *López Mateos 850, tel. 65/52–82–15. Open Mon.–Sat. 8–6, Sun. 9–2.*

CASAS DE CAMBIO Casas de cambio are easy to find near the border crossing and are generally open Monday–Saturday 9–6, but most will only change cash. Banks here change traveler's checks and give cash advances on Visa and MasterCard. **Bancomer** (Madero, 1 block from border, tel. 65/54–26–00) changes money weekdays 9–1 and has an ATM.

CROSSING THE BORDER U.S. and Canadian citizens do not need tourist cards if they are either traveling from the border to Ensenada (including San Felipe), or down the mainland coast to Mazatlán; when entering or leaving Baja by land, a driver's license or birth certificate will generally suffice as ID. For travel south of Ensenada or Mazatlán, *see* Crossing the Border, Tijuana, *above*. For more information on visas and tourist cards, as well as the formalities involved in bringing a car into Mexico, *see* Chapter 1, Basics.

EMERGENCIES Dial 134 from any phone for the **police,** 136 for the **fire department,** or 132 for an **ambulance.**

MAIL The post office is a few blocks from the border, but it's cheaper and quicker to send international mail from the United States. They'll hold mail sent to you at the following address for up to 10 days: Lista de Correos 3, Mexicali, Baja California Norte, CP 21101, México. Madero 491, tel. 65/52-25-08. Open weekdays 8-6, Sat. 9-1.

MEDICAL AID Benavides pharmacy (Reforma, at José Azueta, tel. 65/52-29-18) has a helpful staff, and is open daily 8 AM-10 PM. For an English-speaking doctor, Dr. Juan David Molina Velasco provides 24-hour emergency service. *Madero 420, Suite 102, tel. 65/52-65-60 or, for after-hrs emergencies, 65/65-32-67. Open weekdays 10-3 and 5-8, Sat. 10-3; shorter hrs during summer.*

PHONES You can make long-distance calls from the caseta at Madero 412 (tel. 65/52-66-72) or another one across from Hotel 16 de Septiembre at Altamirano 380 (tel. 65/52-21-97). Both close around 7:30 PM, and all calls must be paid in advance, which means no collect calls.

VISITOR INFORMATION The tourist office, opposite a statue of General Vicente Guerrero astride a rearing horse, has a cornucopia of maps, pamphlets, and newspapers in English. English-speaking employees are available except 2 PM-4 PM, when they're out to lunch. *López Mateos, at Compresora, about 2 km from border, tel. 65/57-23-76. Open weekdays 9-5.*

COMING AND GOING

BY BUS The **Central Camionera** (tel. 65/57-24-20) is in the Centro Cívico-Comercial on Independencia. Four companies operate from this station and share the same phone number. The counters to your right as you enter the station sell first-class tickets, those on the left sell second-class. **Tres Estrellas de Oro** offers first-class service to Baja and major cities on the mainland, with departures to destinations such as Guadalajara ($63, 32 hrs) and Mazatlán ($42, 24 hrs) every half-hour around the clock, and hourly departures for Mexico City (42 hrs, $70). **Autotransportes del Pacífico** buses also travel to the Pacific coast, Guadalajara, and Mexico City for about the same price. **Transportes Norte de Sonora** serves the western mainland all the way to Mexico City. **Autotransportes de Baja California** has both first- and second-class service throughout Baja. Hourly buses from Mexicali leave for Tijuana (2½ hrs; $7 1st class, $5.50 2nd class) and Ensenada (4 hrs, $9 1st class only). Second-class buses depart for San Felipe (2½ hrs, $5.50) at 8 AM, noon, and 3 PM. First-class buses (2½ hrs, $7) leave at 8 PM and 10:50 PM. The station also has a **Computel** office open 24 hours a day for long-distance calls. Use a public phone to call collect.

BY TRAIN The train station is at the south end of Ulises Irigoyen, north of the intersection with López Mateos. To get here, catch a bus marked FERROCARRIL (40¢). One first-class and one second-class train departs daily for Guadalajara, with connections to Mexico City. Both trains stop at all major cities on the way (the second-class train makes many more stops); and you can transfer at Los Mochis for the Copper Canyon train. The first-class train takes about 36 hours to Guadalajara and costs $35 for a comfortable reserved seat (make reservations in advance). The second-class train to Guadalajara takes about two days and costs only $19. Second-class seats are not reserved, however, so arrive about four hours early. For more information, contact **Ferrocarril Sonora-Baja California** (tel. 65/57-23-86).

GETTING AROUND

Mexicali has two downtown areas on opposite sides of town. The first, **La Frontera** (the border), a.k.a. *el mero centro* (the very center), is characterized by cheap hotels, taco stands, Chinese restaurants, and loads of street vendors. The **Centro Cívico** (civic center) is home to government offices, the city hospital, the Calafia bullfighting arena, and the bus and train stations. Both areas are easily explored on foot, but to get from one to the other take a city bus (40¢) down Boulevard López Mateos, the city's main thoroughfare. Buses to other parts of the city congregate near the border on the west side of Reforma or on Altamirano, near Madero. To reach the budget hotels in La Frontera from the bus terminal, cross the pedestrian bridge, continue a half block down López Mateos, and hail a bus marked CENTRO. Conveniently, their last stop is on Altamirano, near Hotel 16 de Septiembre and Hotel Altamirano. Taxis are not worth the expense ($5–$8) unless you have a carload or it's late at night. From the bus station, cab prices are pre-set, so don't bother bargaining.

WHERE TO SLEEP

The cheapest hotels are in the Frontera area, and are accessible on foot from any of the local bus stops on Reforma or Altamirano. Most hotels on Reforma are seedy and unsanitary, but cheap. Accommodations near the Centro Cívico are nicer but difficult to find and more expensive. At **Hotel 16 de Septiembre** (Altamirano 353, tel. 65/52–60–70) the bathrooms, rather than the rooms themselves, make for a pleasant stay; the spacious, tiled shower stalls are among the cleanest in Mexicali and compensate for the dungeon-like windowless rooms. A single is $5, $8 with private bath and air-conditioning; doubles $5 and $10. **Hotel Altamirano** (Altamirano 378, tel. 65/52–83–94) has small rooms and a fairly sanitary communal bath, but singles are only $4.50, doubles $5. Air-conditioning and carpeting in each room make **Hotel Plaza** (Madero 366, 1 block from border, tel. 65/52–97–59) reasonably comfortable. A single costs $11, a double $15—more if you want a TV and phone.

FOOD

The border area abounds with cheap places to eat, primarily taco stands and Chinese restaurants. At **Restaurant Buendía** (Altamirano 263, tel. 65/52–69–25), the Mexican-Chinese decor is complemented by the Mexican-Chinese menu. Heaping portions of chow mein or wonton go for $3.50, and Mexican dishes cost $2–$4. **El Nuevo Ken Seng** (Reforma 264, tel. 65/53–46–71) is a dingy downtown restaurant that serves some of the best Chinese food in Mexico ($2–$4). Open 6–6, it's a hangout for cabbies and drunks; women may not want to linger here after dark. **Nevería Blanca Nieves** (Reforma 503, tel. 65/52–94–85; open daily 7 AM–9:30 PM), done in turquoise vinyl, is crowded with old Happys, Dopeys, and Sneezys downing malts ($1.50) and sundaes ($2) at the soda fountain. They've got a great breakfast menu ($2–$3) and salads and sandwiches for $2–$4.

Ensenada

Since the completion of the toll road between Tijuana and Ensenada in 1973, Ensenada has blossomed into one of Baja's most popular resorts. Cruise ships call regularly in the port here, and passengers tired of shuffleboard head for the fine beaches nearby. Surfers catch waves both north and south of the city, and sport fishers pursue yellowtail and marlin. By night, Ensenada offers a miniaturized version of Tijuana-style nightlife, attracting crowds of hell-raising U.S. college students and Mexicans. But, with a population of about 200,000, Ensenada is considerably smaller than Tijuana, and its pace is less frenetic.

The missionaries who colonized much of Baja skipped Ensenada on their trek north because it lacked fresh water. The city's first major growth period came in the 1870s after gold was discovered, in Real de Castillo, to the east. Following the discovery, Ensenada became the major supply center, seaport, and, for a while, even the capital of northern Baja. It also enjoyed a brief fling with the Hollywood jet set, serving as a playground for the Southern California elite during Prohibition. With the repeal of Prohibition and the Mexican government's decision to make gambling illegal, tourism in Ensenada dried up. More recently, the loosening of restrictions on foreign ownership of beachside property has spurred a dramatic increase in the number of visitors here. Today, the hills surrounding Ensenada are terraced with tar-paper shacks, home to the city's most recent migrants, who have come to look for work in northern Baja's booming construction industry.

BASICS

➢ **CASAS DE CAMBIO** • Dollars are accepted—and expected—everywhere in Ensenada. **Banco Mexicano** and **Serfín** (both on Ruíz, at Calle 3a) change cash and traveler's checks weekdays 9–1:30 and give cash advances on Visa and MasterCard; Serfín has an ATM. Change cash

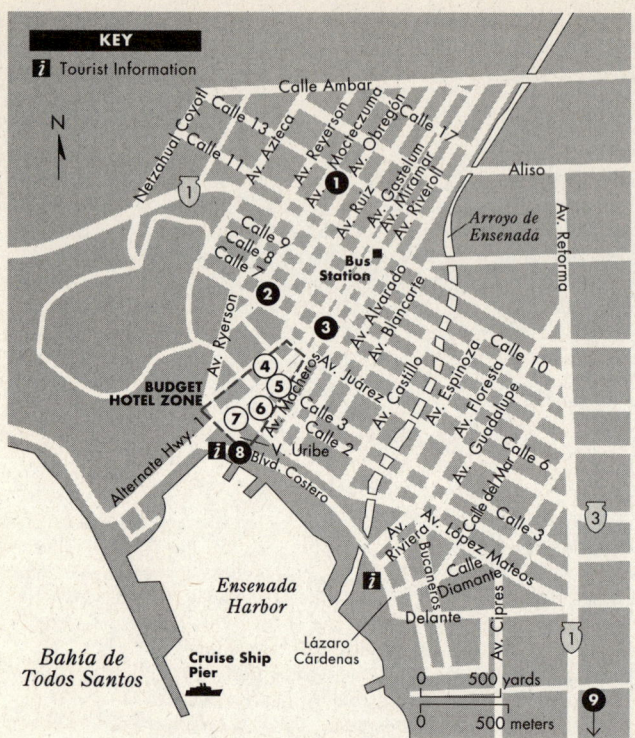

and traveler's checks at **Cambio de Cheques** (López Mateos 1001-1, at Blancarte, tel. 617/8–14–59), open Sunday–Friday 9–7, Saturday 9:30–3:30. They'll also allow you to make long-distance calls, including international credit card and collect calls, for a 50¢ charge.

➤ **EMERGENCIES** • Dial 134 from any phone for the **police**; 136 for the **fire** department; or 132 for the **Cruz Roja** (ambulance).

➤ **LAUNDRY** • **El Lavadero** has automatic washers ($1 per load) and dryers (25¢ for 10 min). If you prefer to leave the dirty work to someone else, same-day service is available ($1 extra per load). Obregón 664, btw Calles 6a and 7a, tel. 617/8–27–37. Open Mon.–Sat. 7:30 AM–8 PM.

➤ **MAIL** • The post office, near Hotel Riviera del Pacífico, will hold mail sent to you at the following address for up to 10 days: Lista de Correos, Administración 1, Avenida López Mateos, Ensenada, Baja California Norte, CP 22800, México. López Mateos, at Floresta, tel. 617/6–10–88. Open weekdays 8–7, Sat. 9–1.

➤ **MEDICAL AID** • For an English-speaking doctor, contact Dr. Antonio Orosco Soto (Riveroll 679, btw Calles 6a and 7a, tel. 617/4–03–90), who has office hours daily 10–1 and 5–8. For 24-hour emergency service, call Dr. Orosco at home (tel. 617/6–42–29). You can pick up whatever he prescribes for you at **Farmacia Regia**. Calle 28-B, at Miramar, tel. 617/4–05–57. Open Mon.–Sat. 8 AM–10 PM, Sun. 8 AM–9 PM.

➤ **PHONES** • You can make collect calls from public phones along López Mateos or at the Cambio de Cheques (see above).

➤ **VISITOR INFORMATION** • The **tourist information booth** at the north end of the waterfront has a friendly, English-speaking staff, but they don't know much about out-of-the-way places. Costero, at Gastelum, tel. 617/8–24–11. Open weekdays 9–7, Sat. 10–4, Sun. 10–3.

Baja's **State Secretary of Tourism,** farther south, has fewer pamphlets about local merchants but a more knowledgable staff and better general info about Baja. *Centro de Gobierno, Costero 1477, at Las Rocas, tel. 617/2–30–22 ext. 3181 or 3182. Open weekdays 9–7, Sat. 10–3, Sun. 10–2.*

COMING AND GOING **Transportes Norte de Sonora (TNS)** and **Autotransportes de Baja California (ABC)** serve Ensenada's bus terminal (Riveroll, at Calle 10a, tel. 617/8–66–80). TNS has first-class departures for Guadalajara (36 hrs, $50) at 3 PM, 8:30 PM, and midnight, and leaves for Mexico City (48 hrs, $59) at 11:30 AM and 4:30 PM. Ensenada is a major stop on bus routes up and down Baja, and ABC has frequent first- and second-class buses bound for San Quintín (3 hrs, $5), La Paz (18–20 hrs, $36), and towns in between. Buses depart 5:30 AM–8 PM for Mexicali (3 hrs, $13); at 8 AM and 6 PM for San Felipe (3½ hrs, $8); and hourly for Tijuana (2 hrs, $3.50–$4.50). The station has 24-hour luggage storage (50¢ for 5 hrs) and a caseta de larga distancia for cash calls only (open daily 7:30 AM–10 PM). To reach the budget-hotel area from the bus station, turn right as you leave the station and walk eight blocks. It's a seedy part of town, so be careful walking alone at night. Colectivos also run to the center of town for 50¢.

GETTING AROUND Except for the beaches, which lie 10 kilometers south of town and beyond, Ensenada is easy to cover on foot. The main tourist drag, Avenida López Mateos (a.k.a. Calle 1a), runs more or less parallel to Boulevard Costero and the waterfront. **Riviera del Pacífico,** an elegant old hotel along López Mateos, serves as a good landmark. To reach the **Estero** or **El Faro** beaches, flag down a yellow-and-white CHAPULTEPEC van from anywhere along the waterfront on Boulevard Costero. The buses stop within 3 kilometers of the beach. You can also take a red-and-white CHAPULTEPEC bus from the van depot (Calle 6a, at Ruíz) or from Avenida Juárez. Get off at the ESTERO beach sign, and walk the 2–3 kilometers to the beach. To reach **La Bufadora** (*see* Near Ensenada, *below*) take the yellow-and-white MANEADERO van all the way to Maneadero and change to a blue van ($1) for the remaining 16 miles. Vans and buses run daily 6 AM–10 PM.

WHERE TO SLEEP Ensenada has plenty of cheap rooms, but the low price is often the only thing they have going for them. The budget-hotel area is between Calles 2a and 3a, and on Avenidas Miramar and Gastelum. Miramar is a run-down street lined with bars, so if you arrive after dark, try Gastelum first. The inexpensive hotels are mostly occupied by fishermen and their families, and backpackers may get strange looks. Rooms are usually clean but worn, and communal and private bathrooms are often in need of a good scrubbing. If you're determined to sleep cheap and everything else is full, try **Hotel Río** (Miramar 231, tel. 617/8–37–33), which has 52 rooms, 10 of which are clean and reserved for tourists. These cost $7 for one or two people.

➤ **UNDER $10** • **Hotel El Pacífico No. 1.** El Pacífico is a popular stop for European cyclists on their way up or down the peninsula. Basic singles and doubles are the same price— $4.50 without bath and $7 with. The private baths are surprisingly clean, and the communal ones are nothing you can't deal with, but the thin walls make for a potentially noisy evening. If you ask nicely, the owners may let you use the kitchen facilities. *Gastelum 235, btw Calles 2a and 3a, no phone. 30 rooms, 12 with bath. Luggage storage.*

Motel Perla del Pacífico. To compensate for the seedy location, they run a tight ship here, with no alcohol or visitors in the clean but dark rooms. Even the communal baths are up to *Good Housekeeping* standards, making the $6 singles and doubles with shared bath a great deal. A single or double with bath costs $10. Prices rise $2–$5 during holiday weekends and other busy times of the year. *Miramar 229, tel. 617/8–30–51. 72 rooms, 41 with bath. Luggage storage, parking.*

➤ **UNDER $30** • **Motel 49.** The lingering aroma of disinfectant acts as a constant reminder of how clean the large, modern rooms in this hotel are. Singles and doubles both cost $25; some have TVs. *Miramar 6, btw Costero and López Mateos, tel. 617/4–03–08. 29 rooms, all with bath. Luggage storage, parking. Wheelchair access.*

Motel Caribe. Right in the center of the tourist strip, this motel has large, newly carpeted rooms and big windows and beds without the big price tag you'd expect. The bathrooms are a sight for sore eyes, and rooms toward the back get less street noise. Reservations are always recommended but only essential on holiday weekends. Singles cost $20, doubles $27.50, but it's 10% less during the week. *López Mateos 627 and 628, near Miramar, tel. 617/8–34–31. 40 rooms, all with bath. Luggage storage, parking.*

➤ **CAMPING** • **El Faro Beach** has a nice stretch of white sand for camping if you don't mind being 10 kilometers from town. Facilities include toilets and showers. A site for a car with two people costs $7, motorcycles $2, and only 50¢ for people without a vehicle. Campsites with no showers or RV hook-ups at **La Bufadora** cost $5 for a carload of two, and $2 for each additional person. You can also camp for free on any undeveloped beach between Ensenada and La Bufadora, but watch out for trucks and motorcycles in the dunes. For directions to the beaches, *see* Getting Around, *above.*

FOOD Ensenada's specialty is fish tacos. You can find the best and cheapest at the many seafood stalls surrounding the **fish market** or in the pink **Plaza de Mariscos** (Costero, at Virgilio Uribe). Besides the mouth-watering tacos, piled high with cilantro, salsa, guacamole, onions, and tomatoes, you can also buy fresh seafood cocktails and *mariscos* (shellfish) prepared in a variety of ways. Cheap restaurants serving Mexican food that will fill your stomach without dazzling your palate can be found between Calles 2a and 3a and between Miramar and Gastelum. **Gigante** is a supermarket open 7 AM–10 PM daily (Gastelum 672, at López Mateos, tel. 617/8–26–44), and they accept traveler's checks, Visa, or MasterCard.

El Charro. For a break from seafood, El Charro serves excellent spit-roasted chicken, dished up with tortillas and condiments, and complimented by wine from the Bodega de Santo Tomás (*see* Worth Seeing, *below*). A log cabin complete with fireplace and dark, smoky atmosphere, this place is right in the heart of the tourist area. Half a roasted chicken costs $8. *López Mateos 475, near Gastelum, tel. 617/8–38–81. Open daily 11:30 AM–2 AM.*

La Embotelladora Vieja. Splurge and experience culinary bliss in what used to be a wine-aging room. You can dine among wooden casks and choose from a list of 37 Baja California wines. Start with the cream of garlic soup ($3) and continue with the *mantarraya* (manta ray) in sauvignon blanc and green pepper sauce ($11), finishing in grand style with chocolate crepes flambé ($5). *Miramar, at Calle 7a, tel. 617/4–08–07. Open Mon.–Sat. noon–11.*

Mariscos de Bahía de Ensenada. It's recommended by locals as the best place for fresh and inexpensive seafood (they catch their own). It's also great for a long, sit-down meal. The tortilla-maker in the window attracts some tourists, but Mexicans often outnumber foreigners. Anything that's not seafood is expensive, but shrimp ($5), squid ($4.50), and fresh fish ($4) are good deals. *Riveroll 109, at López Mateos, tel. 617/8–10–15. Open daily 10–10. MC, V.*

CAFES **Café Café.** Dive into a dose of San Francisco at the hippest place in town, decorated with recycled furniture and the work of local artists. Come to play a game of backgammon, drink a cup of coffee flavored with molasses, or simply pick up flyers on events in Ensenada. *López Mateos, near Gastelum, tel. 617/8–35–44. Open Mon.–Thurs. 5 PM–10 PM, Fri. whenever the owners wake up until 1:30 AM, Sat. 9 AM–1:30 AM, Sun. 9 AM–10 PM.*

Pueblo Café and Deli. Locals and tourists come here to enjoy the eclectic music, wine, beer bar, and California cuisine. It's a great place for breakfast, when omelets are $3 and french toast and eggs are $3.50. Vegetarians will be delighted by their salads—try the Oriental ($4). *Ruíz 96, btw Calle 1a and Virgilio Uribe, tel. 617/8–80–55. Open daily 8 AM–midnight.*

WORTH SEEING The waterfront (Boulevard Costero) and the tourist drag (López Mateos) serve as the town's focal points. Avenida Juárez, about six blocks inland, is the main commercial street where locals gather. The **fish market** at the north end of Boulevard Costero displays the richness of northern Baja's coastal waters: tuna, shrimp, squid, marlin, and snapper. Come early in the morning to see fishermen preparing for the day's work, or in the late afternoon when the *pangas* (fishing boats) bring in the latest catch.

The remnants of Ensenada's "frontier" past are still visible in the older neighborhood in the northwest part of the city, especially along Avenida Reyerson. **Parque Revolución** (btw Calles 6a and 7a and Obregón and Moctezuma) is the place to park yourself on a bench in the shade and watch old men chat. For a glimpse behind the scenes at Baja's oldest commercial winery, visit the **Bodegas de Santo Tomás** (Miramar 666, btw Calles 6a and 7a, tel. 617/8-25-09) a legacy of the Dominican fathers of the Santo Tomás mission. Although the grapes are grown 50 kilometers south of the city, wine production was moved to this large warehouse in the middle of Ensenada in 1934. Half-hour bilingual guided tours of the warehouse end with rewarding wine tasting. Admission is $2, and tours are given daily at 11 AM, 1 PM, and 3 PM. A statue of **La Diosa Tara**, an East Asian goddess painted in vivid colors, sits peacefully on a hill watching over the city. Visiting her will not only bring you knowledge and compassion, but a great view of Ensenada.

AFTER DARK Ensenada's nightlife centers around López Mateos, especially near the corner of Ruíz. Take your pick from a number of dark, neon-lit nightclubs that feature loud American music and crowds of college students from southern California. At the all-American club **Viva Tequila** (López Mateos, at Riveroll, tel. 617/4-04-47), people head to the second floor on weekends to mingle beneath the stars until 2 AM. Beers are a reasonable $1.50, margaritas are $1, and *antojitos* (appetizers) are served Monday–Thursday 10 AM–6 PM. The ever-popular **Papas and Beer** (López Mateos, at Ruíz, tel. 617/4-01-45) provides plenty of beer ($2.50), booze, and boogie 10 AM–3 AM daily. Locals head to the southern end of López Mateos to dance in Latin-style discos like **Hussong's Cantina** (Ruíz 113, at López Mateos, tel. 617/8-32-10), a historic establishment that retains its character despite its popularity with tourists. For an alternative to drinking and dancing, visit one of the **billiard halls** along Calle 2a, between Gastelum and Miramar. Go by day if you actually want to play billiards (each joint has a few pool tables), or by night to take in the scene. Women are rare in these places after dark, however. **Coyote Club** (Costero 1000, near Diamante) is the only gay bar in Ensenada.

OUTDOOR ACTIVITIES

➤ **BEACHES** • For cleanish sand and moderate waves, the best beaches are 10 kilometers south of town: **Mona Lisa**, **El Faro**, and **Estero**. Rent a horse (right on the beach; $8–$10 an hr) and gallop down an empty stretch of sand, or plow through the empty dunes in a four-wheel drive or ATV (*see below*). For directions to the beaches *see* Getting Around, *above*.

➤ **WATER SPORTS** • Ensenada is an angler's town. Most sportfishing outfitters are located next to the fish market, just off Boulevard Costero, including **Gordo's Sport Fishing** (open 24 hrs), where they'll take you out to sea for $35 per day. If you prefer fish as swimming companions rather than entrées, try snorkeling or scuba-diving at **El Faro** and **Estero** beaches, or off the **Banda Peninsula**. Here you can see surfperch, rockfish, barracuda, dolphins and sharks, most of which do not eat people. In Maneadero, the area immediately south of Ensenada, well-used masks, snorkels, and fins are easy to come by ($6 a day). Scuba equipment is available at Estero Beach, and you can dive at La Bufadora (*see below*).

The best surfing is north of Ensenada, but the waves crash on a rocky shore, which may prove dangerous for beginners. The waves aren't as vicious near El Faro and Estero beaches—a few places here rent old, trashed boards, and prices fluctuate with demand, so smile your darnedest. **Sam's Beach Toy Rentals** (Estero beach) rents boards for $10 a day. They also rent boogie boards ($5 a day) and sea kayaks ($20 a day). Sam's is 1½ kilometers from Highway 1 at the Estero Beach turnoff.

➤ **THREE-WHEELIN'** • For those who would rather tear up some Baja landscape, the dunes south of Ensenada are prime terrain for off-road vehicles. Around El Faro Beach, Estero Beach, and Maneadero, you can rent ATVs for about $20; Sam's Toy Rentals (*see above*) has a sizable collection.

NEAR ENSENADA

LA BUFADORA Although the surrounding coastal cliffs are spectacular in their own right, the main attraction here is the dramatic blowhole, La Bufadora, which sprays water and foam as high as 55 meters into the air. Local legend has it that the geyser's real source is a whale that ventured beneath the rocks as a calf and grew too big to escape. The blowhole is at **Punta Banda**, 45 minutes south of Ensenada, and is easy to reach via public transport (*see* Coming and Going, in Ensenada, *above*). If you're feeling particularly adventurous (and rich), **Dale's La**

Bufadora Dive (Calle 10 No. 320, just off main road at La Bufadora, tel. 617/3–20–92) rents complete scuba equipment ($25) and offers boat dives into the depths of La Bufadora for $20 per person ($50 minimum). Dives begin at 9 AM and noon. You can also rent snorkel equipment for $15. Dale's is open weekdays 8–3, weekends 8–6.

Dale also rents out a house by the day or week that can sleep up to 15 people for $10 per person per night. Call him at 617/3–20–92 for inquiries about reservations or more info. Campsites without water or hook-ups at **Rancho La Bufadora** (Calle 10 No. 305, right across from Dale's, tel. 617/8–17–72) cost $5 per night for a carload of two; each additional person is $1.50 extra. Otherwise, you can camp at nearby **La Jolla Beach Camp** (Carretera La Bufadora Km. 12.5, tel. 617/3–20–05), which has showers and a minimart ($6 for 2 people).

SIERRA DE JUÁREZ The craggy mountain range of the Sierra de Juárez and the Sierra San Pedro Mártir runs down the spine of northern Baja. The Sierra de Juárez begins south of the U.S. border and extends south to meet the Sierra San Pedro Mártir where Highway 3 cuts across the peninsula. The Sierra de Juárez range is home to the **Parque Nacional Constitución de 1857,** a great place for some quiet camping. The park is on a plateau covered with ponderosa pines, and surrounds Laguna Hanson, a clear, cold mountain lake. Hiking trails are rare or unmarked, so you'll need a compass and topographical maps. There are few formal campsites, but finding a spot shouldn't be a problem except during *Semana Santa* (Holy Week—the week preceeding Easter), when the park fills up. No buses serve the dirt roads that access the park, so take your own vehicle or hitchhike. The best way to get here is from Highway 3: An hour east of Ensenada, the road forks at a point called Negros. Here, a dirt road continues for 48 kilometers to the southwestern entrance of the park, near Laguna Hanson. This can really be rustic, so be prepared; bring extra water, enough gas, and a spare tire.

Even fewer people visit the rugged, granite terrain of the **Parque Nacional Sierra San Pedro Mártir,** where Baja's highest point, **Piacacho del Diablo** (Devil's Peak) soars to 3,500 meters. Inside the park, you can hike along small mountain paths through *piñon* (nut pine) and oak trees, as well as the rare San Pedro Mártir cypress. The mountains are also home to mountain goats and puma. Rock climbers will find a number of challenging rocks, including the Class 3 ascent up Devil's Peak. Bring plenty of water, food, a repair kit, and enough gas for the round trip; supplies are scarce in these parts. Three routes penetrate these mountains, but you'll need a car that can take a beating. The easiest route to the park, but not to Devil's Peak, is the 24-kilometer dirt road off Highway 3 at San Matías. This leads to Mike's Sky Ranch at the northwestern base of the park. Otherwise, a dirt road 16 kilometers south of Colonet along Highway 1 heads 80 kilometers east through San Telmo to Devil's Peak. To reach the eastern base of the park from San Felipe, take the dirt road that runs to Rancho Santa Clara, near Laguna Diablo. For more information on the trails in this park, get a copy of *The Baja Adventure Book* by Walt Peterson (The Wilderness Press, 1992).

San Felipe

Those who love fishing, sailing, and off-roading flock to San Felipe, on the northern coast of the Sea of Cortez. Although the surrounding desert and extremely hot summers prevented any permanent settlement until the 1920s, this small beach town is not undiscovered. With the completion of Highway 5 from Mexicali in 1951, fishermen flocked to San Felipe and were soon followed by other sport-lovers. Sailors from all over Mexico and the United States blow through in April and October to compete in Hobie Cat races, and college students from the States trek down for Spring Break (late March to early April) to test the limits of inebriation. If you don't mind the heat, averaging 37°C (100°F) in the summer, you can have the town to yourself in July and August.

BASICS

➢ **CASAS DE CAMBIO** • **Prestaciones de Servicios Mitla** (cnr of Mar de Cortez and Chetumal, tel. 657/7–11–32) will change traveler's checks and cash daily 9–9. You can also use your Visa (but not your ATM card) at the ATM at **Bancomer** (Mar de Cortez 165, tel. 657/7–10–51) from 8:30 to 2 PM on weekdays.

➤ **MEDICAL AID** • Dr. Ubaldo Espinoza Ángel (Mar de Cortez 238, tel. 657/7-11-43) speaks English and is available for drop-ins daily 5 PM-8 PM. For emergencies, call Dr. Gerardo Olvera Duran at his office (Mar de Cortez 238, tel. 657/7-11-43) or 24-hours daily at his home (tel. 657/7-15-84). Buy your drugs at **Farmacia San Ángel Inn.** Chetumal, near Mar de Cortez, tel. 657/7-10-43. Open weekdays 9-9, weekends 9 AM-10 PM.

➤ **PHONES AND MAIL** • The **post office** (Mar Blanco 187, tel. 657/7-13-30) is open weekdays 8-3 and Saturday 9-1. From Mar de Cortez, walk five blocks away from the beach along Chetumal and turn left at Mar Blanco. **Farmacia San Ángel Inn** (*see above*) charges only $1 for international collect and credit-card calls, and you can also make regular long-distance calls.

➤ **VISITOR INFORMATION** • The semi-English-speaking staff can tell you anything you want to know about San Felipe, but not much on the rest of Baja. Mar de Cortez 300, at Manzanillo, tel. 657/7-11-55. Open weekdays 8-7, Sat. 9-3, Sun. 10-1.

COMING AND GOING

➤ **BY BUS** • **Autotransportes de Baja California (ABC)** buses leave San Felipe's terminal (Mar Caribe, btw Manzanillo and the Pemex gas station, tel. 657/7-15-16) daily at 8 AM and 6 PM for Ensenada (3½ hrs, $7), and at 6 AM and 7:30 PM for Tijuana (5 hrs, $12.50). Buses leave for Mexicali five times daily (2½ hrs, $7.50). None venture onto the dirt roads south of San Felipe, however, so your best bet is to rent an ATV.

➤ **HITCHING** • The odds of finding somebody headed east from Ensenada (Hwy. 3) or south from Mexicali (Hwy. 5) are good, since San Felipe is one of a small number of destinations along either route. Look for a chauffeur at gas stations on the outskirts of town.

WHERE TO SLEEP
Hotels are expensive, so camping is your best option. There are plenty of RV trailerparks along Mar de Cortez, including **Playa Laura RV** (Mar de Cortez No. 333, tel. 657/7-11-28), which rents tents or trailers for two people ($15), and spaces for cars ($11) or pedestrian campers ($5); the managers will usually watch your bags. However, pitching a tent along the beach north of the trailer parks won't cost anything, and toilets (35¢) and showers ($1) are nearby. If you're lucky you'll find an empty room at José's house (Manzanillo 244, no phone), with clean, air-conditioned singles for $17 and doubles for $25 (both include use of the kitchen and a big front porch). He'll even pay for your taxi from the bus station. If you robbed a bank in Arizona, **Chapala Motel** (Mar de Cortez 142, tel. 657/7-12-40) is one of the nicer hotels downtown, although this doesn't necessarily mean it's worth $40 for a single or double on weekends ($30 weekdays). However, some rooms have kitchenettes and wheelchair access, and Visa and MasterCard are accepted, so at least you won't feel the cost until you get home.

FOOD
It's no surprise that the meal of choice in this fishing town is seafood. Fish and shrimp tacos, ceviche, and clams are served from picnic tables along the *malecón* (boardwalk) for 65¢-$5. At **Restaurant y Mariscos Puerto Padre** (Mar de Cortez 316, tel. 657/7-13-35; open daily 7 AM-10 PM) you can order breakfast ($2), or a seafood entrée ($6). If the sun gets too hot, the air-conditioned **Los Gemelos** (Mar de Cortez 136, near Chetumal, tel. 657/7-10-63) serves seafood and Mexican dishes ($4) daily 6 AM-11 PM.

OUTDOOR ACTIVITIES
The sandy desert that borders San Felipe to the west and the dunes and dirt roads to the south are inviting landscapes for motorcyclists and ATV riders. Rent a vehicle at **Bahía ATV** (malecón 122, no phone) for $10 an hour, or haggle for a full-day deal. Riding on the beach is illegal, so unless you're willing to risk the $100 fine, don't try it. The calm surf and strong winds of the Sea of Cortez are perfect for windsurfing; launch your sailboard at any beach south of **Punta Estrella**. These can be rented from Charters Mar de Cortez (*see below*) for $20 an hour. The wide beach in town is also good for catching rays, playing Frisbee, and swimming.

➤ **FISHING** • Locals and their generations-old fishing boats head out to sea from San Felipe. If you're broke, try to finagle tackle and a boat ride with a local in exchange for beer. Otherwise, **Tommy Sport Fishing** (Costero 176, no phone) organizes sport-fishing tours—the catch often includes white sea bass, corvina, dorado, yellowtail, and other sea creatures. Trips require at least four people (five maximum), and cost $25 per person.

➤ **SAILING** • About 10 kilometers from town, **Charters Mar de Cortez** (El Dorado Travel Center, on airport road, tel. 657/7-17-78 or 657/7-12-77) rents Hobie Cats ($25 an hr), kayaks ($15 an hr), paddle boats ($15 an hr) and sail boards ($20 an hr). They run two-hour cruises with unlimited beverages for $30 per person, and full-day cruises for $60 per person. Sailing lessons are available for $75-$100, and custom cruises are $50-$100 per person per day.

San Quintín

The twin towns of San Quintín and Lázaro Cárdenas parallel Highway 1 for several kilometers, their ugly cinderblock stores and restaurants doing nothing to attract tourists. Separated by a bridge and 3 kilometers of highway, both towns lie humble and windblown, although Lázaro Cárdenas has more markets and restaurants to choose from. However, those not immediately scared away will find empty beaches and an abundance of sole and white sea bass in the Bahía del San Quintín, a few kilometers away. Huge chocolate clams (named for the brown coloring on their edges) can be found along the bay's best beach, **Playa Santa María** (near Hotel La Pinta and Motel Cielito Lindo), and are free if you dig them yourself; fresh fish and crab can be bought cheaply from local fishermen. San Quintín's beautiful volcanic peninsula juts out to the south, protecting the bay from the windy Pacific Ocean.

BASICS In Lázaro Cárdenas, **Banco Internacional** (Ignacio L. Alcérraga, north side of park, tel. 616/5-21-25) doesn't have an ATM, but will change cash or traveler's check weekdays 8-5. At the south end of San Quintín, **Lavamática M.A.C.** (Hwy 1, tel. 616/5-25-83; open Sun.-Fri. 8 AM-9 PM) has automatic washers and dryers ($1 each). Pay an extra 50¢ and you can lounge on the beach while the staff does it for you. Near the bus station in Lázaro Cárdenas, **Farmacia San Carlos** (Carretera Transpeninsular, tel. 616/5-25-29; open daily 8:30-8:30) offers local and long-distance collect ($1) or cash telephone service, as well as medicine. In Lázaro Cárdenas, the **post office** (Carretera Transpeninsular, no phone) is open weekdays 8-5, Saturday 8-noon. They'll hold mail sent to you at the following address for up to 10 days: Lista de Correos, Valle de San Quintín, Baja California Norte, CP 22930, México.

COMING AND GOING Both San Quintín and Lázaro Cárdenas are major stopping points along Highway 1. To reach the peninsula, get off in San Quintín; for the beaches south of town, get off in Lázaro Cárdenas. Buses stop in San Quintín and at the **Autotransportes de Baja California (ABC)** bus station (Carretera Transpeninsular, tel. 616/5-30-51) at the southern end of Lázaro Cárdenas. From here, three buses a day head south toward La Paz (19 hrs, $31) at 1 PM, 5 PM, and 11 PM stopping in Guerrero Negro (7 hrs, $11). Five buses go north to Tijuana (5 hrs, $9) at 6 AM, 7 AM, 9 AM, 5 PM, and 7 PM, and four buses destined for Mexicali (7 hrs, $12.50) leave at 7 AM, 10 AM, 1 PM, and 4 PM, stopping in Ensenada (3½ hrs, $5). They'll store your luggage for free at the station, but there's nothing formal or secure about the setup. **Autotransportes Aragón**, a smaller station farther north, has more frequent buses to Ensenada and Tijuana.

GETTING AROUND San Quintín is 5 kilometers from the shoreline at the beginning of the peninsula. To travel between San Quintín and Lázaro Cárdenas, or to reach Playa Santa María, catch a blue-and-white or green-and-yellow microbus from anywhere along the highway. Microbuses run every 15 minutes 6-6, and will let you off 5 kilometers from either Hotel La Pinta or Motel Cielito Lindo—both close to the beach. If you're driving look for the HOTEL LA PURITA sign along the highway. You can hitch a ride with local fishermen, but it'll be hard to distinguish between you and the catch of the day when you get off.

WHERE TO SLEEP As there's nothing of interest in San Quintín or Lázaro Cárdenas, and as they're both a few miles from the beach, staying in town is a dismal prospect. Your best bet for lodging in this area is to camp for free along the stretch of open, isolated coast (there's little protection from the wind, however). **Playa Santa María** is the easiest to reach—pitch your tent around Hotel La Pinta. If you're not prepared to camp, **Motel Chávez** (Hwy. 1, at south end of San Quintín, tel. 616/5-20-05) is the best deal in town. Spotless rooms for $12.50 (singles) and $29 (for up to four people) are reasonable by northern Baja standards. **Motel Romo** (Hwy. 1, tel. 616/5-23-96) is close to the bus station and has nice rooms with spotless baths for $9.50 a single and $12 a double, and they accept MasterCard and Visa. Their popular restaurant is open daily 7 AM–11 PM.

FOOD San Quintín specializes in clams, and white shells litter the area around the roadside food stands that sell the tasty, tight-lipped critters. **Palapa El Paraíso** (300 meters north of Pemex in San Quintín, no phone) offers shady outdoor seating where you can enjoy delicious, huge steamed clams for $2 a plate or a $3 clam cocktail. Lázaro Cárdenas has several cheap restaurants. Near the bus station, fill up on fish tacos with cilantro, guacamole, tomatoes, and onions at the unmarked white shack (open 7 AM–8 PM) next to Hamburguesas Doña Magui. **Viejo San Quintín** (east side of highway, Lázaro Cárdenas, no phone; open daily 8 AM–9 PM) has a long menu, which includes omelets ($3), and T-bone steaks ($4.50).

Baja California Sur

Southern Baja is a land for escapists. Tourism here centers around camping, fishing, swimming, exploring the miles of lonely beaches, and whale-watching (January–March). Highway 1 runs through a number of small towns, which, except for the French mining town of Santa Rosalía, bear the imprint of the Spanish missionaries who founded them as outposts of "civilization"; adobe missions built with Indian labor still survive. Dirt roads criss-cross the Sierra (the mountainous interior), connecting isolated hamlets, ranches, abandoned missions, and small fishing villages.

Guerrero Negro

The only sign of civilization on the nine-hour drive between San Quintín and San Ignacio besides Highway 1 is the wind-chilled town of Guerrero Negro. Located on the dividing line between northern and southern Baja, Guerrero Negro greets visitors with a giant, metallic eagle adorned with birds nests, which marks the exact middle of Baja California. Cacti and coyote fill the desert on one side of Guerrero Negro and on the other, across the San José estuary, near-white sand dunes rest like an unstraightened tablecloth.

This dramatic landscape gives way to the waters of the Pacific, seasonal home to thousands of grey whales who migrate from the Bering Sea to Baja. They come to birth their calves in the warm, calm waters of Scammon's Lagoon (27 kilometers south of town). This lagoon, also known as **Laguna Ojo de Liebre** (Hare's Eye Lagoon), is within the bounds of **Parque Natural de Ballena Gris** (Gray Whale Natural Park), established to protect the whales from poachers. Bring binoculars to better admire the spouts of water shooting high into the air and the huge 4-meter-wide flukes thundering against the water. Farther south, in **Laguna de San Ignacio,** you can hire a boat from local fishermen to get a spectacularly close view—the whales sometimes swim so close to the boat that you can touch their barnacle-encrusted backs. During the first two weekends of February the town honors these giants at the **Festival de Las Ballenas** (the Festival of the Whales), which features regional food, dances, and the selection of a local queen. Aside from the brief deluge of whale-watching tourists, Guerrero Negro lives off the world's largest solar-evaporated mine. If evaporative salt-production techniques don't turn you on, there's no reason to stop in this town outside whale-watching season.

No public transportation goes to the lagoon. If you want to hitchhike, look around the western part of town in the morning for tourists who can give you a ride back (you don't want to get stuck at the lagoon). You can also join an organized tour in town, although reservations are recommended, especially during January and February. **Cabañas Don Miguelito** (*see* Where to Sleep, *below*) runs day-long trips ($35 per person, including lunch) to the lagoon and to the hunting-oriented cave paintings ($60 per person) of La Sierra de San Francisco (*see* Near San Ignacio, *below*). Tours operate April–June and October–November. **Agencia de Viajes Mario's** (Emiliano Zapata, tel. 115/7-10-88) also organizes whale-watching trips and two-day tours to the cave paintings ($35 per person), both only available when the whales are around.

Baja California Sur

BASICS

➤ **AUTO PARTS/SERVICE** • Boulevard Zapata is loaded with specialty mechanics. The staff at **Autopartes Sandy** speak English. *Zapata, tel. 115/7-00-51. Open Mon.-Sat. 8-8, Sun. 8-1.*

➤ **CASAS DE CAMBIO** • **Banamex** only changes cash, but has an ATM that accepts Cirrus, Plus, MasterCard, and Visa. *Av. Baja California, just past saltworks, tel. 115/7-05-55. Open weekdays 8:30-1.*

➤ **EMERGENCIES** • The 24-hour phone line is 115/7-16-15 for the **police**; 115/7-05-05 for the **fire department**; and 115/7-11-44 for an **ambulance**.

➤ **MEDICAL AID** • If the **Clínica Hospital** is no longer under renovation, it's open 24 hours daily and offers a variety of services, including dental and pediatric. **Farmacia San Martín** not only has everything you need for scrapes and bruises, but a long-distance telephone service as well. *Zapata, tel. 115/7-09-11. Open Mon.-Sat. 8 AM-10 PM, Sun. 9-4.*

➤ **PHONES AND MAIL** • There are no phones on the street, but you can make long distance cash or credit card calls at Farmacia San Martín (*see above*). The **post office** (open weekdays 8-3) is in the old section of Guerrero Negro, in a round building on an unnamed street. To reach it, walk past the square and turn left at the Lion's Club and elementary school. They'll hold mail sent to you at the following address for up to 10 days: Lista de Correos, Guerrero Negro, Baja California Sur, CP 23940, México.

COMING AND GOING Autotransportes de Baja California (**ABC**) and **Águila** both serve the **Terminal de Autobuses** (near highway on motel strip, tel. 115/7-06-11). Six northbound buses pass through Guerrero Negro between 2:30 AM and 10 PM daily, stopping in San Quintín (7 hrs, $12), Ensenada (10 hrs, $17), and Tijuana (12 hrs, $19). Seven buses head south daily between 4 AM and 11 PM, stopping in San Ignacio (2 hrs, $5), Santa Rosalía (3 hrs, $6.50), Mulegé (4 hrs, $7.50), Loreto (6 hrs, $12), and La Paz (10-12 hrs, $20.50).

GETTING AROUND Guerrero Negro is divided into two very different halves: the old section around the square, and the new commercial and tourist strip on Zapata near the highway. A yellow mini-bus travels between them every half hour, but it's only a 20- to 30-minute walk. Taxis are another option, as is jumping in the back of some kind soul's truck. Dirt roads lead from town to Scammon's Lagoon and Bahía de Tortugas, and you'll need your own transportation to reach either (unless you're with a tour). The latter has an airstrip, and chartered planes (tel. 115/7-00-56) fly there from Guerrero Negro (½ hr, $15) daily at 10 AM—but it's another $15 to get back again a few hours later. Try scamming a ride with the mailman, who leaves the post office between 7 and 8 AM.

WHERE TO SLEEP Although the hotels near the bus station in Guerrero Negro look cheap, only some are within the budget traveler's reach. All fill up December–March, so call ahead for reservations. In the new part of town, the more reasonable joints include **Hotel San José** (across from bus terminal, tel. 115/7-15-20), **Motel Las Ballenas** (behind El Morro, tel. 115/7-01-16), and **Motel Brisa Salina** (Zapata, tel. 115/7-13-25). All of their clean singles ($12) and doubles ($14) have color TV's, but, Motel Brisa Salina, with its well-kept courtyard, has the most charm of the three. On the right as you exit the bus station, look for **Malarrimo** (tel. 115/7-02-50 or 115/7-00-20), which has beautiful, clean, quiet rooms in modern bungalows for $22 (singles) and $25 (doubles). Malarrimo is run by the same management as **Cabañas Don Miguelito,** an RV park that charges $10 per space for two people (additional persons $3 each). If the above hotels will break your budget, try **Motel Gámez** (Zapata, tel. 115/7-03-70), on the other side of town. The sheets and curtains droop forlornly, but singles are $6, doubles $8.

FOOD If you're passing through Guerrero Negro, you don't have to wander far from the bus terminal to eat well. Next door, **Cocina Económica Lety** (open daily 7 AM–10 PM) is recommended by locals and has great Mexican dishes ($3–$5). Around the first bend in Zapata there are a string of cheap eateries. **Café Alejandra** (just past the first Pemex station; open daily

7 AM–10 PM), sells $3 eggs and plain ol' $2 burgers. In the evenings, hot dog vendors hit the streets, selling dogs smothered in beans and chile for $1.

NEAR GUERRERO NEGRO

THE LONELY COAST About 35 kilometers southeast of Guerrero Negro is the hot, dry **Vizcaíno Desert**, which juts out into the Pacific Ocean. Although arid, it's no barren wasteland: A few several-hundred-year-old plants, such as *tillandsia recurvata* (ball moss) and *datillo* (a.k.a. *yucca valida*, resembling the Joshua tree) manage to live in this harsh environment. Due to deep wells, Ejido Vizcaíno, a small spice-farming community, also thrives in the midst of the desert, as do crops such as tomatoes, onions, oranges, and grapes. At the peninsula's northern edge is a junk collector's dream come true: **Playa Malarrimo**, otherwise known as Scavenger's Beach. This shore lies perpendicular to the currents moving down Baja's Pacific coast, and acts as a junkyard for ocean debris.

Everything—from huge whale bones to bottles stuffed with rescue notes—eventually drifts ashore at Playa Malarrimo.

The southern side of the peninsula, from **Bahía de Tortugas** to **Punta Abreojos**, is an empty stretch of coastline. From January to mid-March, you can see whales calving in **Laguna Ojo de Liebre**, and sea turtles laying eggs in the small Bahía de Tortugas. See Guerrero Negro for information on tours.

San Ignacio

The verdant town of San Ignacio rests over an underground stream that brings the desert to life with birds, insects, flowers, and fruit trees. Date palms, introduced by Jesuit missionaries, dominate the landscape. This is a good departure point for whale-watching in **Laguna de San Ignacio** or exploring pre-Colonial cave paintings in the **Sierra de San Francisco** and the **Sierra de Santa Marta**. If you arrive from northern Baja, San Ignacio is the first town you'll encounter laid out in traditional Mexican fashion, with a zócalo at the center of everything. Life for San Ignacio's residents revolves around this tree-shaded square and the adjacent Misión San Ignacio de Loyola. Jesuits began constructing the mission's four-foot-thick walls out of volcanic rock in 1716, but it wasn't completed until the Dominicans took over and finished the job in 1786. A particularly beautiful mass is held Sundays at 11 AM. Next door, the **Museo Local de San Ignacio** (admission free; open weekdays 8–8, Sat. 8–6) has displays (in Spanish) on the cave paintings, including photographs and a small replica in the back.

Many of the buildings around the square, shaded by Indian laurel trees, are more than a century old, their adobe walls sometimes peeking through new layers of plaster and paint. Fall is the time to pick dates and grapes and make homemade wine, another legacy of the missionaries. Sample the local wine, goat cheese, and *cajeta* (a sweet made from goat's milk) from ranches in the surrounding Sierra. Residents of San Ignacio used to live off the land, but the town is now primarily a supply center, and several residents have migrated to the coast to earn their living fishing. Many return by July 27, though, to get their fill of mariachi music and tecate at San Ignacio's five-day fiesta. For information about the town and the surrounding area, ask Jorge Fischer at his grocery store/tourist information center on the plaza (tel. 115/4–01–50).

COMING AND GOING The bus station consists of two shaded benches on the highway, 3 kilometers outside town. The one next to the Pemex station is the stop for buses going north; cross the street for southbound buses. Seven buses go south to La Paz (6 hrs, $16) every day between 6 AM and 1 AM. Buses headed north to Tijuana (14 hrs, $75) and Ensenada (12 hrs, $13) pass through town five times a day. Staff at the store next to the Pemex station can tell you about changes in schedule, but you buy a ticket on the bus. The Pemex station is also an easy place to hitch a ride. The only way to ride from the bus stop into town is by taxi ($2), but the walk is pleasant, if sweaty. To return to the station, find the taxi that hovers around the plaza day and night.

WHERE TO SLEEP San Ignacio may be restful, but unless you're prepared to camp, it's not a cheap place to spend the night. Running water is sporadic, so check the sink before you sign in. **Motel Posada** (Carranza, tel. 115/4–03–13) offers clean rooms with the most reliable water supply in town (singles $17, doubles $20). To get here, follow the curving road that runs along the front of the mission. If you prefer to stay in a local home, **Lonchería Chalita** (Hidalgo 9, west side of zócalo, tel. 115/4–00–18) has two small, stuffy rooms ($9 singles or doubles). Although there's a private entrance, the friendly family encourages you to walk through their kitchen and backyard gardens. They also serve the best meals in town. The small, family-owned cottages of **Pablo Cordán Vega**, a.k.a. Lupita's (Hidalgo, tel. 115/4–00–66) have front porches, but often lack water ($9 singles or doubles). Ask at the neighboring **Abarrotes Jordán** (tel. 115/4–03–17) if nobody's around.

➤ **CAMPING** • San Ignacio has several campgrounds, and they're all fairly cheap. The best is **Las Candelarias**, a few hundred meters down the dirt road (alongside Trailer Park El Padrino). Here you can camp for $2 in a well-maintained grove of date palms, but the bathrooms are simple outhouses without showers. The best swimming hole around is also here, which is free whether or not you're a guest. **Trailer Park El Padrino** (1½ kilometers south of Hwy. 1, near Hotel La Pinta, tel. 115/4–00–89) provides campgrounds, toilets, and showers ($7 per car), and their on-site restaurant serves cold beer and margaritas. Other campgrounds have back-breakingly hard ground or are infested with insects. Camping is free just past Hotel La Pinta, but the persistent braying of a burro is a hefty price to pay for a free night.

FOOD There are only a few restaurants in town, the best of which is **Lonchería Chalita** (Hidalgo 9, west side of zócalo, tel. 115/4–00–18), where the elderly owners have turned their living room into a restaurant. The comida corrida costs $3, while the Mexican à la carte menu is $2–$4. **Rene's Restaurant/Bar** (Hidalgo 39, no phone) has a thatched-roof, a variety of breakfasts (including french toast; $2), and two evening dinners of fish ($5) or shrimp ($7).

NEAR SAN IGNACIO

Gray whales stop in **Laguna de San Ignacio** January–March as they migrate from Alaska to Baja. The lagoon is two hours southwest of San Ignacio, 74 kilometers along rough dirt roads, so you'll need to drive a sturdy car, hitch (and expect to be stranded for a while), or hire a guide (*see below*). Once there, hire a local fisherman to take you out in his boat (about $20).

To reach the **cave paintings** in Sierra de San Francisco and Sierra de Santa Marta from San Ignacio, you'll need to make a mule-back trek through Baja's high desert mountains. The trip is spectacular in its own right, and the caves are one of Baja's most incredible experiences. The now-faded paintings depict giant men, fish, deer, and hunting scenes. When the missions in the area declined, many indigenous Baja Californians fled to the Sierra de San Francisco, where their descendants remain today, living off their gardens, goats, and, more recently, fees from guiding visitors to the caves. To get to the trail head on your own, you'll need to drive or hitch. Finding a guide at the caves is no problem, however—they foist themselves on visitors.

Boojum Trees

Straight out of a Dr. Seuss book, this oddly shaped species has been described most accurately as an upside-down carrot. Outliving seven human generations and growing up to 27 meters tall, boojum trees tower over their neighbors: datalillos, elephant trees, and giant cardon cacti. Boojums are endemic to a small region in Baja California, ranging from El Rosarío in the north to Las Tres Vírgenes near San Ignacio in the south, and can be best seen from Highway 1 at Cataviña. A small colony also exists in the Sonoran desert. The boojum's common name, cirio, originated when Spanish missionaries noticed a resemblance between the slender candles used in church services (cirios) and the hanging yellow flowers of the tree.

Entrance to the caves, including guide, is $10; mules to get you from cave to cave cost another $10 per day.

If you don't have your own transportation and don't want to hitch, a last resort is Oscar Fisher of San Ignacio's Motel Posada (see Where to Sleep, above), or his brother, Jorge Fisher, who can be found at his grocery store/tourist information center (see San Ignacio, above). Both take up to six people on $120 day-long trips to the caves (price includes guide and transportation: car and mule). Oscar also runs tours to the Laguna San Ignacio ($45 per person), a two-hour drive and two-hour boat ride. Jorge will do it for $20–$120 per person, depending on the number of people and type of boat.

Santa Rosalía

Traveling south down Highway 1, Santa Rosalía is the first town on the Sea of Cortez. Founded by El Boleo, a French copper-mining company in the mid-1800s, Santa Rosalía looks unlike any other town in Mexico: French-style buildings constructed with imported European wood have long, sloping roofs hanging over small, fenced porches. Santa Rosalía was laid out in a regimented fashion, with rows of identical houses corresponding to various ranks within the company, and the old residences of French mining officials sit high above the canyon where the town lies. Some locals have blond hair or East Indian features, testament to the varied ancestry of the town's original workers, which included native Californian, French, East Indian, and Chinese people.

Santa Rosalía is home to the Iglesia Santa Bárbara, a prefabricated iron church designed by Alexandre Gustave Eiffel (of Tower fame) and imported from Europe by the mining company that founded the town.

When the mining company left in the early 1950s, Santa Rosalía's economy hit a slump and never recovered. Today, most residents make their living from the sea or by working in plaster mines on nearby Isla de San Marcos. Santa Rosalía is one of Baja's poorer towns, with an unkempt central square and houses in need of repainting. There are also no good beaches in Santa Rosalía proper; explorers must go 3 kilometers north of town to rocky **Playa Santa María** for surf and chocolate-clam digging. Unsociable beach-goers can travel a little further to the more isolated shoreline near the fishing village of **Punta Chivato**.

BASICS Autopartes Plaza (Constitución, tel. 115/2-01-67; open daily 8 AM–9 PM) has a helpful, English-speaking staff and almost any part you could need. You can change cash and traveler's checks weekdays 8:30–1 at **Bancomer** (tel. 115/2-02-65) and **Banamex** (tel. 115/2-09-84), both on Obregón, at Altamirano. They also give cash advances on Visa and MasterCard. The one pay phone on the plaza only accepts local calls, and nobody will let you make a collect call anywhere in town. The **post office** (Constitución, btw Calle 2 and Altamirano, tel. 115/2-03-44) is open weekdays 8–3, Saturday 8–noon. They'll hold mail sent to the following address for 10 days: Lista de Correos, Avenida Constitución, Santa Rosalía, Baja California Sur, CP 23920, México.

The numbers for **police** are 115/2-02-90 and 115/2-05-05; the **fire department** can be reached at 115/2-01-88, and the number for the **Red Cross** is 115/2-06-40. For less urgent medical attention, **Farmacia Central** (Obregón, at Plaza, tel. 115/2-20-70, fax 115/2-22-70) sells drugs, and English-speaking Dr. Eduardo Antonio Chang Tam can help with general medical problems. The pharmacy, open Monday–Saturday 8 AM–10 PM, Sundays 9–1 and 7–10, also has fax service and a caseta de larga distancia, but calls must be cash only.

COMING AND GOING

➢ **BY BUS** • Autobuses de Baja California (ABC) (tel. 115/2-01-50) buses run from the terminal south of town on Highway 1, a quick taxi ride ($1.50) or 10-minute walk from downtown. Seven buses head south daily between 8 AM and 2 AM, stopping in Mulegé (1 hr, $1.50), Loreto (3 hrs, $5), and La Paz (8 hrs, $18). Five buses a day go north to Tijuana (14 hrs, $24), stopping in Guerrero Negro ($6.50, 3 hrs) and Mexicali ($30, 16 hrs). To reach the beach at

Punta Chivato, hop on any southbound bus and ask the driver to let you off. You can also try to catch a ride at the Pemex station on Highway 1 before the bus terminal.

➤ **BY FERRY** • **Sematur,** off Highway 1, offers bi-weekly ferry service from Santa Rosalía to Guaymas in the state of Sonora. Ferries to Guaymas (7 hrs) leave Wednesday and Sunday at 8 AM; seats costs $10, and a bed in a four-person cabin costs $41. To bring a car to the mainland, get a car permit from the **Delegación de Servicios Migratorios** offices next to the ferry office (for more information, see Chapter 1). The office opens sporadically; the best time to catch them is around 3 PM on Tuesdays and Fridays, when the ferry arrives from Guaymas. Pier south of town, tel. 115/2-00-13 or 115/2-00-14.

WHERE TO SLEEP The huge front porch of the 110-year-old **Hotel Francés** (Jean Mitchel Cousteau, tel. 115/2-20-52) is an excellent place to sip a margarita ($2), while enjoying fresh seafood ($7–$10) and a view of the sea. The wood-furnished rooms with showers and bathtubs cost $14 for a single and $17 for a double, and include use of the pool. A cheaper option is the clean and centrally located **Hotel Olvera** (Plaza 14, tel. 115/2-00-57). A single room with a TV costs $8, doubles are $10 ($11 with air-conditioning). The closest place to camp is **RV Park San Lucas Cove,** on the beach 14 kilometers south of Santa Rosalía, off Highway 1. They charge $6 a night per vehicle, and have new flush toilets and a hot shower.

FOOD Santa Rosalía has a few decent restaurants but the stands selling fresh fish tacos during the day and beef tacos or quesadillas at night are the way to eat well. Be sure to get your midnight snacks before 10 PM, however, as nothing stays open later. For a sit-down meal, **Steak House Don Ramón** (Constitución, at Plaza, no phone; open Mon.–Sat. 8:30 AM–10 PM) serves breakfasts of chimichangas ($2) or cheese omelets ($2.50), and an excellent filet mignon ($5) later in the day. Be sure to stop by **Panadería El Boleo** (Revolución, at Calle 4a), a bakery founded by the French mining company to supply the town with baguettes. Thirty years later, their French bread and pastries are still delicious. If you're up before 8 AM, peek through the side doors and watch the bakers loading dough into brick wood-burning ovens.

CHEAP THRILLS Other than poking around the rusty locomotives and copper-works (officially closed to the public) near the harbor breakwater, there's not much to do here but read in the shade, sweat in the sun, or fish. If the latter sounds fun, talk to English-speaking Ángel Jesús Rodríguez (tel. 115/2-00-11) who works at the **Santa Rosalía Marina** (on the water where Americans anchor their yachts) Monday–Saturday 8–3. His friends take tourist groups on fishing trips ($60 for a 5-hour trip).

Mulegé

The Santa Rosalía River courses through Mulegé, watering the small forest of date palms and creating a seaside desert oasis, just 18 kilometers north of the spectacular beaches of **Bahía de Concepción.** Here the calm, warm waters, in a wide spectrum of blues, contrast sharply with the surrounding semi-desert landscape. Mulegé's own rocky beach lies at the mouth of the river, 2 kilometers east of town along the main road, and although the beach is not as white-sand spectacular as those farther south, it's a pleasant walk and okay for swimming; best of all, camping here is free. Mulegé is a popular take-off point for the Cochimi Indian cave paintings in Trinidad, San Boritas, and Piedras Pintas, and for whale-watching expeditions to Magdalena Bay. For information on tours, see Visitor Information, below.

Once a place of simple beauty, Mulegé is growing to resemble an American suburb, and *palapas* (thatched-roof huts) for rent now crowd the beaches. Although everything from T-shirt and curio shops to recently paved roads caters to the town's tourist industry, Mulegé hasn't completely lost its small-town charm, and still harbors remnants of its traditional past. One such relic is the **Misión Santa Rosalía de Mulegé,** built in 1766 and reconstructed in the early 1970s, which overlooks the town and a sea of date palms. The free **Museo Mulegé** (open daily 9–1) is housed in a building that served as a prison from 1906 to 1975, and now features artifacts from the original mission, old mining lamps from Santa Rosalía, and arrowheads that were dug up in the area. Not surprisingly, you won't find a wild nightlife here, but many restaurants offer live music on weekends, and if you're struck by the sudden urge to swim, the sea is always open late.

BASICS

➤ **AUTO PARTS/SERVICE** • **Refaccionaria Mulegé** sells parts and can recommend a mechanic to suit your needs. *Gral. Martínez, near Zaragoza, tel. 115/3–00–41. Open Mon.–Sat. 8–1 and 3–7.*

➤ **CASAS DE CAMBIO** • **Servicio de Cambio** (Moctezuma 7, no phone) changes cash or travelers checks Monday–Saturday 9–1 and 3–7, but since they're the only casa de cambio in Mulegé, the rates are terrible. You're better off bringing pesos from another city, or using U.S. dollars, which are accepted by most establishments.

➤ **LAUNDRY** • **Lavamática Claudia** has self-service washers ($1.50) and dryers (50¢). *Moctezuma, tel. 115/3–00–57. Open Mon.–Sat. 8–6.*

➤ **MAIL AND PHONES** • The drugstore **Mini-Super Padillo** (tel. 115/3–01–90) on Zaragoza and General Martínez, has long-distance telephone service, daily 8 AM–9 PM. The **post office** (Gral. Martínez, across from Pemex, tel. 115/3–02–05) is open weekdays 8–3. They'll hold mail sent to you at the following address for 10 days: Lista de Correos, Fte. Jardín Corona, Col. Centro, Mulegé, Baja California Sur, CP 23900, México.

➤ **MEDICAL AID** • The staff at the **Farmacia** can offer advice in broken English about minor medical problems. *Madero, on the plaza, tel. 115/3–00–42. Open daily 8–1 and 3–10.*

➤ **VISITOR INFORMATION** • The tourist office is run by Javier, the owner of **Hotel and Restaurant Las Casitas** (Madero 50, tel. 115/3–00–19). He can provide you with information on kayaking tours, fishing expeditions, and trips to see the Cochimi Indian cave paintings. You can also try finding Kerry Otterstrom at the restaurant **El Candil** (cnr of Zaragoza and Madero, fax. 115/3–01–90) daily between 4 and 6 PM. Kerry offers tours to the Cochimi Indian cave paintings (thought to be over 14,000 years old), and will share his knowledge of legends and local flora and fauna.

COMING AND GOING

Mulegé is small and easy to navigate. If you don't have a car, it's a 30-minute walk or a five-minute bus ride to Mulegé's beach. The better beaches of Bahía de Concepción are too far away to reach on foot, but it's easy to hitchhike. You can also catch a southbound bus from town to the beach; flag down one heading north to return to Mulegé.

At the entrance to town (the "Y") is a shaded bench that functions as the bus station. Seven northbound buses pass through with stops in Santa Rosalía (1 hr, $1.50) and Tijuana (15 hrs, $26). Eight buses per day go south to Loreto (2 hrs, $3.50) and La Paz (7 hrs, $12). Ask a taxi driver when the buses are expected to pass, but be prepared to wait because schedules are rarely kept. Buy your tickets a day before traveling to guarantee yourself a seat.

WHERE TO SLEEP

Most beds for rent in Mulegé start at $15, but three guest houses offer cheaper, simpler rooms. At **Casa de Huéspedes Manuelita's** (Moctezuma, tel. 115/3–01–75) the facilities are spartan, but the private baths are fairly clean, and you pay only $4.50 for a single; $6 for a double. At **Casa de Huéspedes Canett** (Francisco, at Madero, tel. 115/3–02–72), singles with rickety beds and acceptable baths are $3, doubles $5. **Hotel Suites Rosita** (Madero 2, no phone) is a deal if you're traveling with friends. The huge apartment-style rooms come complete with kitchenette, living room, two separate bedrooms, and air-conditioning, and cost $21 for up to five people.

➤ **CAMPING** • Camping is free on Mulegé's beach (the southern end is less rocky), 3 kilometers east of town, but it's not as safe or as peaceful as the beaches farther south. **Orchard RV Park Resort** (south side of river, tel. 115/3–03–00), a half-kilometer walk from town, is the closest and most deluxe campground, with clean, white-tiled bathrooms, a volleyball court, bonfire pit, and shady fruit trees. The owner can also be persuaded to show you his favorite clam-digging spots at Bahía de Concepción. One person in a tent costs $6, two people in a tent is $7, and space for an RV costs $15. Farther up the road is **Villa María Isabel** (tel. 115/3–

02–21), a smaller RV park with laundry service, a pool, and a delicious bakery (bakery open Oct.–June). Tent camping costs $4 per person with use of all on-site facilities.

FOOD Restaurants in Mulegé are not cheap, but worth the extra money. The most inexpensive ones are near the bus stop on Highway 1: Join the crowds waiting for great guacamole around **Taquería Doney's** (Moctezuma, near bus station; closed Wed.). **La Cabaña** (Moctezuma, across from bus station, no phone) serves an egg-and-tortilla breakfast for $2, as well as Mexican lunch and dinner plates for $2.50–$4. On Fridays from October to June, head for **Las Casitas** (Madero 50, tel. 115/3–00–19) for the mariachi buffet ($5). Mexican and seafood dishes of all kinds are served for $6–$10, and they've got a salad ($2.50) for vegetarians. The restaurant is open daily 7 AM–10 PM, except on the weekends when they open up the place as a disco (open 7 PM–2 AM). If you get a sudden craving for chocolate-chip cookies, try the bakery at Villa María Isabel (*see* Camping, *above*).

OUTDOOR ACTIVITIES Baja Tropicales at Hotel Las Casitas (Madero 50, tel. 115/3–00–19) rents kayaks ($25–$35 per day) so you can paddle along the river among the date palms. Tours of Bahía de Concepción with a knowledgeable, English-speaking guide can also be arranged for $39, which includes a lunch of clams that you collect yourself.

The warm, plankton-rich waters here usually offer good visibility and teem with colorful aquatic life. The best diving spots are off the Santa Inez islands and are accessible only by boat. **Mulegé Divers** offers snorkeling trips for $20 ($25 with gear; $10 for gear only) and scuba-diving forays, which run $30–$50 per person, depending on how much equipment you rent. Gral. Martínez, tel. 115/3–00–59. Open Mon.–Sat. 9–1 and 3–6.

NEAR MULEGE

BAHIA DE CONCEPCION The most beautiful bays in Baja lie along Highway 1, south of Mulegé. The highway runs along 40 curvy kilometers of coastline, where hidden coves open onto white-sand beaches and electric-blue water—excellent for snorkeling, scuba-diving, kayaking, swimming, and windsurfing. The first beach you'll hit heading south is **Playa Punta Arena** (20 km from Mulegé on Highway 1), popular among sailboarders. **Playa Santispac,** 24 kilometers south of Mulegé, can turn into RV-camper hell overnight, but for the most part, it's a mellow stretch of sand with good facilities. Local entrepreneurs provide tourists with palapas ($5 per night), showers ($1), and fairly inexpensive restaurants. Sign up with **Baja Tropicales** (next to Playa Posada Concepción, fax 115/3–01–90) for a $39 kayaking excursion, complete with a guide knowledgeable about the birds, fish, and shells of the area. Snorkeling gear is an affordable $5. A few kilometers to the south, the beautiful beaches of **Playa Escondida, Playa Los Cocos, Bahía Los Burros,** and **El Coyote** remain unexploited, and have more modest facilities (i.e., pit toilets and scattered palapas). **Playa Requeson,** 14 kilometers south of El Coyote, surrounds a bay so shallow that you can walk across the sand bar to a small volcanic island. To reach any of these places, catch a southbound bus from Mulegé and ask the driver to drop you off on the highway in front of any of the beaches.

Loreto

Life in Loreto revolves around fishing and not much else. For many years, this town was only accessible to the wealthy or adventurous who flew in on private planes or arrived by yacht. Today it plays host to fishermen from all over, who cast for dolphin fish, marlin, and sailfish. The beaches in Loreto are small and grungy—it's more fun to go out in a *panga* (a small metal boat) than to swim. Just south of Loreto, a 38-kilometer stretch of coastline around **Nopoló** and **Puerto Escondido** has been elected as a luxury beach resort area by Fonatur, the tourist-development arm of the Mexican government. Development began in 1982, but enthusiasm and funds drifted elsewhere before Escondido was completely adulterated. Now a rocky shore, complete with yachts, a parking lot where you can car-camp for free, and man-made canals surrounds a hotel frozen in mid-construction. The beaches of Nopoló are nicer than those in

Loreto, but no budget lodgings exist there. A more popular diversion is the reefs around **Isla del Carmen, Isla Coronada,** and **Isla Danzante,** which offer good diving and snorkeling.

Loreto is the oldest permanent settlement in the Californias. Founded in 1697, this was the "heart and brains" of the chain of Jesuit, Dominican, and Franciscan missions that colonized Baja and California Alta (present-day California). The **Misión de Nuestra Señora de Loreto,** built in the late 1600s in the shape of a Greek cross, was the first of Baja's missions and is still the town's social and religious center. Beautifully restored in the early 1970s, the chapel is impressive for its masonry, wood ceiling beams, and gilded altar bearing the figure of the **Virgen de Loreto**—famous throughout Baja for her miraculous powers. Every September 8, the statue is paraded down from her mountain shrine to Loreto, where a fiesta with music, dancing, eating, and drinking, is held in her honor. Next to the church is the **Museo de las Misiones** (admission $1.50; open weekdays 9–5, weekends until 4), which features relics from missions throughout Mexico.

Stingrays are known to lurk in the sand off Loreto's beaches; as you walk though the water, shuffle your feet in the sand to scare them off. Their bites hurt like hell for 3–5 hours and should be cleaned thoroughly with boiling water to prevent infection.

BASICS

➢ **CASAS DE CAMBIO** • **Bancomer** changes cash and traveler's checks weekdays 8:30–1. *Salvatierra, at Madero, tel. 113/5–00–14.*

➢ **LAUNDRY** • Full-service laundry (no self-service) is $2 a load at **Lavandería El Remojón** (Salvatierra 79, no phone). They're supposed to be open Monday–Saturday 8–8, Sunday 8–2, but if no one's around, they're probably across the street at the artesanía/junk-shop/unhelpful-tourist-information tent that they also run.

➢ **MEDICAL AID** • Dr. Miguel Moreno Abaroa speaks English and can be found at the **Centro de Salud** (Salvatierra 79, near Hotel Salvatierra, tel. 113/5–00–39; open 24 hrs). **Farmacia de la California** has basic medical supplies and a knowledgeable staff. *Salvatierra 66, tel. 113/5–03–41. Open daily 8 AM–10 PM.*

➢ **PHONES AND MAIL** • Loreto's only pay phone is in **Supermercado El Pescador** (NE end of Salvatierra, tel. 113/5–00–60; open daily 7 AM–10 PM). For long-distance calls, **Caseta Soledad** charges a $2 connection fee for collect calls, or $1.50 per minute to call the U.S. direct. The **post office** (Deportiva, tel. 113/5–06–47; open weekdays 8–3, Sat. 9–1) is located off the west end of Salvatierra, near the Cruz Roja building. They'll hold mail sent to you at the following address for 10 days: Lista de Correos, Loreto, Baja California Sur, CP 23880, México.

COMING AND GOING

➢ **BY BUS** • The bus station (tel. 113/5–07–67), served by **Autotransportes de Baja California (ABC)** and **Águila,** is at the beginning of Salvatierra and Paseo Tamará, a 10-minute walk east of the town center. Five buses a day travel south to Ciudad Constitución (2 hrs, $3.50) and La Paz (5 hrs, $8.50) between 8 AM and midnight. Northbound buses to Tijuana (18 hrs, $32) leave at 3 PM and 9 PM; two others going to Santa Rosalía (3 hrs, $5) leave at 2 PM and 5 PM. Morning buses heading in either direction are often very crowded, but after a stop or two, there's more room.

➢ **BY PLANE** • **Aerocalifornia** has one flight per day at 9:35 AM (except on Tuesdays, when it leaves at 7 PM) from Loreto's airport (Carretera Transpeninsular Km. 112, 3 km south of town, tel. 113/5–05–55) to Los Angeles ($159 one-way). Catch connecting flights in La Paz to San Diego, Phoenix, and other cities on the Baja Peninsula and the mainland. Yellow-and-white vans irregularly shuttle people from (and only *from*) the airport to Loreto ($3)—the alternative is a $5 taxi ride. Taking a taxi (or hitching) is the only way to reach the airport from town.

WHERE TO SLEEP

Most hotels in Loreto are geared toward anglers who have a larger lodging allowance than the average budget traveler. If you can forgo the facilities, camp for free on Loreto's beaches. Those north of town are more private, but if you're feeling nervous, ask the guys at the army post (Calle de la Playa, near Carrillo) if you can pitch your tent on the beach across from them. The guards should protect you from any unwanted guests (at least, those not in uniform). Camping at **Loremar** (Zaragoza and Green, 1 km south of town) or **El Moro RV Park** (closer to the center, on Rosendo Robles) is also cheap; Loremar is nicer, though, and offers camping for three people, toilets, and showers for $10.

Although **Hotel Salvatierra** (Salvatierra 125, tel. 113/5-00-21) is not the cheapest hotel in town or the closest to the water, its rooms are clean and air-conditioned, and the singles ($11) and doubles ($15) have great bathrooms. It's only a five- or 10-minute walk to the town plaza from here, and the bus station is almost next door. **Hotel San Martín** (Juárez 4, at Davis, tel. 113/5-04-42), long considered the best backpacker hangout of the area, caters to young travelers from all over the world. Singles and doubles with fans are $8 and $12 (respectively), but the hotel is likely to be closed during the off-season (July and August).

FOOD The cheapest restaurants in Loreto are on Hidalgo, at the fork in Salvatierra. Of these, **Restaurant Acapulco** (open daily 7 AM–8:30 PM) takes the cake with its enormous comidas corridas ($2) and friendly clientele. **Café Olé** (Madero, near zócalo, tel. 113/3-04-96; open daily 7 AM–10 PM) serves oatmeal and fruit salad ($2) for breakfast with banana splits ($2.50) for dessert at sunny outdoor tables. For seafood, follow the fisherfolk to **Embarcadero** (Calle de la Playa, up from Hotel La Misión, tel. 113/5-01-65). Steamed clams are $4, and a fish dinner is $5 (slightly cheaper if you bring your own fish). They're open Thursday–Tuesday 6 AM–9 PM.

OUTDOOR ACTIVITIES Prices for fishing trips vary, so shop around: Ask the fishermen coming into the marina in the afternoon, or befriend a tourist with a private boat. **Alfredo's Sport Fishing** (Calle de la Playa, tel. 113/5-01-32) offers excursions costing a hefty $100 for two people (negotiable during the low season; boat and fishing licenses included), plus $8 per rod. Alfredo's also rents cars for $56 per day or 25¢ per kilometer.

Islas del Carmen, Coronada, and **Danzante** are the best places for scuba divers to see dorado, yellowtail, sailfish, roosterfish, and even sea lions. Snorkeling is also popular in the shallow water surrounding Nopoló and Puerto Escondido. **Deportes Blazer** (Hidalgo 23, tel. 113/5-09-11; open Mon.–Sat. 9–1 and 3–7) rents scuba equipment for $27 and snorkeling gear for $7. You can also just rent tanks ($7). Guided underwater tours aren't offered, but the staff have good advice for those doing it on their own. **Hotel Oasis** (Calle del la Playa, tel. 113/5-01-12) also arranges fishing tours ($110 for up to 3 people plus $8 for gear) year round, as well as kayak and horseback-riding excursions (prices vary). Whale-watching trips go to Magdalena Bay ($115 per person) December–March. From the United States, contact Trudi Angell at **Sea Kayak Adventures in Baja** (707/942-4450) for more information.

NEAR LORETO

SAN JAVIER The one-street village of San Javier is in the mountains, 32 kilometers southwest of Loreto. The main reason to make the trek here is to see the beautiful **Misión de San Javier,** a well-preserved mission built in Moorish style, with domes and exquisitely detailed stone carvings. The town and surrounding ranches are more modest—most people here grow their own food and herd goats. Their houses consist of large palapas with a small adobe building for cooking and storing belongings. Days in this mountain desert are hot and the sunlight is punishing, but the evenings are quiet and beautiful. The road from Loreto to San Javier is rough, and while taxis do make the trip for a large sum ($50), it's best driven in a high clearance car or jeep. You can camp for free in San Javier near the dam, or rent a room from Doña Elena; ask around. Bring your own bottled water, as it is not sold up here. If you're in the area December 1–3, don't miss the big Saint's Day celebration, which resounds with music, dancing, drinking, and horse races.

La Paz

Although beautiful desert beaches are only 15 minutes away by bus, La Paz is not a beach town. Rather, this capital of southern Baja is a sophisticated city with a university and a good museum. Tourists do come here, but the new airport outside Los Cabos is causing many to bypass La Paz altogether. Mainland-bound travelers are most likely to pass through on their way to pick up the ferry to Mazatlán or Los Mochis. Those who do, miss out: The ocean surrounding La Paz contains spectacular rocky reefs, a black coral forest, and an enormous variety of marine life. Visitors here also enjoy excellent scuba diving, snorkeling, and kayaking.

As the first large city south of Ensenada, La Paz, with over–air-conditioned stores and greasy international food, may come as a shock to those who have already adapted to the dusty backroads of Baja.

La Paz was founded by Hernán Cortés in 1535 during his search for pearls (pearl diving continued until the 1940s) and was developed by Jesuit missionaries. The center of social life has now shifted from the mission and zócalo to the malecón, which is lined with restaurants and bars. On weekend evenings, after older residents have finished their promenade along the water, the malecón transforms into a hangout spot for local youth.

BASICS

AMERICAN EXPRESS The travel agency **Turismo La Paz** provides AmEx services, including cashing personal checks for cardholders and holding letters (not packages) for two weeks. *Esquerro 1679, La Paz, Baja California Sur, CP 23000, México, tel. 112/2–76–76 or 112/2–83–00. Behind Hotel Perla. Open weekdays 9–2 and 4–6, Sat. 9–2.*

CASAS DE CAMBIO **Banco Mexicano** (Arreola, at Esquerro) has shorter lines than AmEx (across the street) and changes cash and traveler's checks weekdays 9–noon. However AmEx has a 24-hour ATM that accepts Visa, MasterCard, Cirrus, and Plus.

EMERGENCIES You can dial 06 from any phone in La Paz to reach the **police, fire** department, or an **ambulance**.

MAIL The post office is one block from the main plaza. They'll hold mail sent to you at the following address for 10 days: Lista de Correos, Centro La Paz, Baja California Sur, CP 23000, México. *Revolución, at Constitución, tel. 112/2–03–88. Open weekdays 8–7, Sat. 9–1.*

MEDICAL AID For serious medical attention, the **Centro de Salud** on the corner of Altamirano and 5 de Mayo is open weekdays 8–8. For less urgent problems, the **Farmacia Baja California** (Madero, on plaza, tel. 112/2–02–40) is open Monday–Saturday 7 AM–11 PM, Sundays 8 AM–10 PM.

PHONES There's a **Computel** caseta in the bus terminal (open daily 7 AM–9:30 PM), and many businesses along the malecón have phones you can use to make collect and credit-card calls. The bookstore at Arreola 25-A, at Obregón has long-distance phones ($1.50 a minute to the U.S.) and is a good place for a private conversation. *Open weekdays 10–3:30 and 5–9:30, Sat. 10–9:30, Sun. 9–5.*

VISITOR INFORMATION The staff at the tourist office are knowledgeable and speak English, but be prepared to ask lots of questions, because they don't offer information voluntarily (they also may not be open when they are supposed to be). Pick up maps and southern Baja's free English papers here. *Obregón, at 16 de Septiembre, tel. 112/2–59–39. Open weekdays 8–8.*

COMING AND GOING

BY BUS The main bus station (Jalisco, at Héroes de la Independencia, tel. 112/2–64–76 or 112/2–42–70) has **Autobuses de Baja California (ABC)** and **Águila** buses and is a 30-minute walk or a $2.50 taxi ride from downtown. Downtown city buses marked IMSS will also let you off three blocks from the terminal. To get downtown from the terminal, take any city bus

La Paz

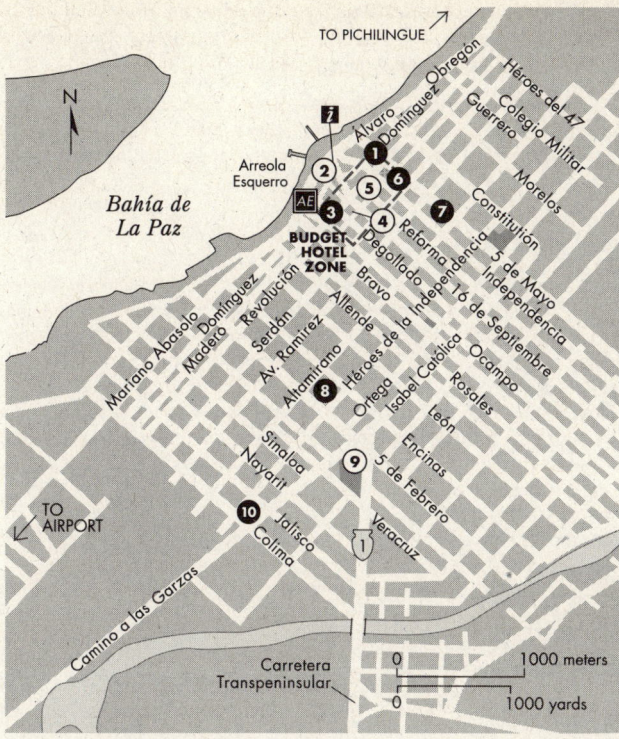

Sights ●
Biblioteca de las Californias, **1**
Bus Station, **10**
Cathedral, **6**
Mercado Municipal, **3**
Museo de Antropología, **7**
Teatro de La Cuidad (City Theater), **8**

Lodging ○
Hotel Yeneka, **5**
Pensión California, **4**
Suites Misión, **2**
Villa Juvenil (Youth Hostel), **9**

and get off at the municipal market (Revolución, at Degollado). Buses for Tijuana (22 hrs, $39.50) and destinations en route depart La Paz four times daily. Eight buses depart daily for Cabo San Lucas and San José del Cabo ($4.50). The Pacific route through Todo Santos (1 hr, $2) takes 2½ hours to Los Cabos—an hour less than the route via Los Barriles (2 hrs, $3). Águila buses also depart from the more convenient **Terminal Malecón** (Obregón, near tourist office, tel. 112/2-78-98) with more frequent service to Cabo San Lucas at the same price. Eight buses depart daily for Los Cabos (via Todos Santos), and seven run via Los Barriles. The bus to the beaches and the ferry terminal in Pichilingue (10 per day, 20 min, $1) also leave from Terminal Malecón. On weekends most buses will go as far as El Tecolote, but otherwise not beyond Pichilingue. The last bus back to La Paz departs Pichilingue at 6 PM.

BY FERRY Sematur offers passenger and vehicle service from Pichilingue to Topolobampo (near Los Mochis) and Mazatlán, but buying tickets is a hassle if you don't plan ahead. Boats for Topolobampo depart Pichilingue Monday–Saturday at 11 AM, arriving at 7 PM that evening. On Tuesdays however, the ship carries "dangerous cargo" and—get this—women are forbidden on board. The ride costs $10 for a seat, and $20 for a bed (only available Wednesdays and Thursdays). The boat to Mazatlán (18 hrs) leaves daily at 3 PM; it costs $15 for a seat and $30 for a bunk (not available Wednesdays). Ferry tickets can be purchased one day ahead of time from the **Sematur office** (5 de Mayo, at Guillermo Prieto, tel. 112/5-38-33), which is open weekdays 8–1 and 4–6, and weekends 8–1, but if you want to leave on a day when beds are available it's easier to buy tickets in advance from **Agencia de Viajes Yurimar** (5 de Mayo, near Domínguez, tel. 112/2-86-00; open weekdays 9–7, Sat. 9–2). To reach the Sematur ferry station, go to Pichilingue, a half-hour south of La Paz (see *Coming and Going By Bus*, *above*). Arrive at the station an hour before departure.

If you want to take a vehicle to the mainland, get a car permit from the **Oficina de Banjercito** (next to ferry station; open weekdays 8–1) in Pichilingue. Bring your passport, drivers license, and registration or ownership papers. With permit in hand, go to the Sematur office (*see above*) to reserve a place. Price varies according to the size of the vehicle, but an average car costs about $100. Try to arrive at the ferry terminal four hours prior to departure.

BY PLANE From La Paz, **Aerocalifornia** (tel. 112/5-10-23) and **Aeroméxico** (tel. 112/2-00-91) service Mazatlán ($68 one-way), Mexico City ($142 one-way), and Los Angeles ($270 round-trip). Taxis are the only transportation from town to the airport (8 kilometers)—a monopoly that is reflected in the price ($7).

GETTING AROUND

The downtown area doesn't follow the rest of the city's grid pattern, but most sights in La Paz are here, within easy walking distance of each other. Get your bearings from the cathedral and market (both on Revolución), which mark the limits of the downtown area. Obregón (the boardwalk, or *malecón*) runs along the water and is also a major reference point. To reach the main bus station, youth hostel, or cultural center, catch a bus at the municipal market on Revolución at Degollado. The Pichilingue beach and Sematur ferry terminal are south of La Paz, and are easily reached by bus (½ hr) from Terminal Malecón (*see* Coming and Going By Bus, *above*). From the ferry terminal, walk south for five minutes to Pichilingue beach. To reach any of the three beaches south of Pichilingue (Puerto Balandra, El Tecolote, and Playa el Coyote), take the bus to Pichilingue, then hitch or catch a cab ($3). On the weekends, buses from Terminal Malecón run as far as Playa el Tecolote.

WHERE TO SLEEP

La Paz boasts a number of inexpensive lodgings with tons of character, especially in the downtown area. If you're traveling with several people, **Suites Misión** (Obregón 220, near Arreola, tel. 112/2-00-14) offers small, $25 suites that have a living room, kitchen, balcony with a sea view, and a bedroom with two double beds; reservations are necessary. The office is open 9-2 and 4-7:30; if it's closed, try **Curios Mary** (next door, tel. 112/2-08-15), the owner's jewelry and picture-frame store. Camping in La Paz isn't worth it, considering the number of decent hotels in the city center for the same price. Campsites are abundant 2 kilometers southwest of town, and cost about $10 for two people with an automobile. Cheaper rates may be offered to walk-in tent campers.

A few hotel owners in La Paz, banking on the appreciation of budget travelers for anything idiosyncratic, creatively use novelties in their decorating schemes. Pensión California uses whalebones as an attraction, and Hotel Yeneka has a chained spider monkey living on the roof.

Hotel Yeneka. There are cheaper places around, but not with rooms this large and well furnished. The lobby resembles an artfully tended junkyard, with a rusty Model-A and other discarded machinery. Singles cost $10, doubles $13, and all have clean bathrooms. Long-term stays can be arranged at a better price. Madero 1520, btw 16 de Septiembre and Independencia, tel. 112/5-46-88. 20 rooms, all with bath. Laundry ($2.50), luggage storage. Wheelchair access.

Pensión California. This classic budget traveler's abode offers nothing but a mattress on a cement bed, a ceiling fan, buzzing fluorescent lights, and a primitive bathroom. You can use the communal stove and laundry, although unattended bras have been known to disappear. Singles cost $6.50, doubles $9. Degollado 209, ½ block from market, tel. 112/2-28-96. 25 rooms, all with bath. Luggage storage. Wheelchair access.

HOSTELS **Villa Juvenil (CREA).** In a sports complex outside the center of town, this hostel offers standard bunks in excessively air-conditioned single-sex dorms for $3.50. The communal baths are well kept and there's a laundromat and grocery store nearby, but this place is rather inconvenient from downtown. Tell the staff if you'll be staggering in after 11 PM so they can leave the gate open. *5 de Febrero, at Carretera al Sur (Hwy. 1S), tel. 112/2-46-15. From bus station, down Jalisco and left on Camino a las Garzas; or take bus marked CREA or 5 DE FEBRERO. 70 beds. Reception open 7 AM-11 PM. Luggage storage, no alcohol.*

FOOD

The nicest places to eat in La Paz overlook the water. Apart from sidewalk vendors, however, eateries along the malecón are usually pricey. **El Camarón Feliz** (Obregón, at Bravo, tel. 112/2-90-11; open daily noon-11) is a reasonably priced restaurant on the malecón, serving fish ($5), stuffed crab au gratin ($5), and shrimp ($11). The thrifty should stick with Mexican dishes or come for happy hour (daily 4-6) when all national drinks are two for one. Cheaper eats lie downtown, especially in the **market** (Revolución, at Degollado) where *loncherías* (snack bars) serve comidas corridas for $3. As you enter, the cooks yell out their offerings to draw your attention; try **Conchería Colonial** (inside the market) for a $3 seafood feast.

El Quinto Sol. La Paz's vegetarian restaurant and health-food store sells granola, wheat germ, vitamins, and other healthy items. Mexican dishes ($3-$5) are made with tofu or wheat gluten as a substitute for meat. For breakfast, try a bowl of yogurt, fresh fruit, and granola ($2.50). *Belisario Domínguez 12, at Independencia, tel. 112/2-16-92. 1 block from plaza. Open Mon.-Sat. 8 AM-9:30 PM.*

El Intimo (Esquerro 60; open Mon.-Sat. 7 PM-3 AM), one of La Paz's most popular bars, features live music every Monday, Friday, and Saturday night. While you're here, try a shot of Damiana ($1.50), a sweet liquor from a local desert plant that's thought to be an aphrodisiac.

Restaurant de Mariscos Mar de Cortez. If you don't mind eating in an out-of-the-way restaurant decorated with dead turtles and blowfish, try the tasty $4 marlin or $6 shrimp. *5 de Febrero, at Guillermo Prieto, tel. 112/2-29-08. From market, 5 DE FEBRERO or CREA bus; exit at stone church with 2 towers. Open daily 9-9.*

WORTH SEEING

If you've been combing the beaches for weeks, La Paz is the place to stock up on culture. The modern **Teatro de la Cuidad** (Navarro, at Gómez Farías, tel. 112/5-03-76) presents folkloric dance, music, and theater performances. Buy tickets weekdays 10-1 and 4-8 in front of the theater. **Biblioteca de las Californias** (across from cathedral, in old Municipal Palace; open daily 8-3) is a unique library with an extensive collection of material on Baja in both English and Spanish. The small **Museo de Antropología** (5 de Mayo, at Altamirano; open weekdays 8-6, Sat. 9-2) provides information on the history and people of the peninsula, and the docent speaks English. A donation is requested, so leave a few pesos to be polite.

OUTDOOR ACTIVITIES

The beaches in town are small and lousy for sunbathing; the farther from La Paz, the better. Northwest of town lie **Playas Hamacas** and **Comitán**, and in the opposite direction are gorgeous sands and free camping opportunities at **Playas Palmira, El Coromuel, Caimancito, Punta Colorada, Tesoro,** and **Pichilingue.** The last is just a five-minute walk from the ferry terminal. To reach the others, take a bus toward Pichilingue and ask the driver to let you off. The best beaches, **Balandra, El Tecolote,** and **El Coyote** lie beyond Pichilingue and can be reached by bus (weekends only), by cab ($10), or by thumb. El Tecolote is popular, with a restaurant, bar, and rest rooms. Puerto Balandra, a beautiful cove with white sandy beaches, was once a pirate's refuge.

The waters around La Paz also offer prime scuba diving. The most popular sites are around **Espíritu Santo** island, where clear waters give excellent visibility almost year-round. For $96 per person, **Viajes Palmira** (Obregón, btw Rosales and Allende, tel. 112/2-40-30 or 112/5-72-78) offers a two-tank dive including equipment, guides, lunch, and a boat ride. They also run snorkeling trips to the same island for $40. Full-day fishing trips including rods, licenses, a boat, and a guide are also available ($170 for two people), and whale-watching trips are $90 per person in season (Jan.-Mar.). **Baja Diving Service** (Obregón, near 16 Septiembre, tel. 112/2-18-26, fax 112/2-86-44) offers an all-day scuba tour ($77), a one-tank night excursion ($45), and snorkeling ($40). They also rent kayaks ($30-$45) and mountain bikes ($16 per day or $2.50 per hr), and sell fishing tackle and rods. If you're not keen on a package deal, rent scuba equipment for $15. About 30 minutes southwest of town, calm water is protected by rocky reefs, which make the area perfect for kayaking. Ask at **Hotel Yeneka** (*see* Where to Sleep, *above*) for mountain bike ($8 per day), horse ($42 per day) and boat ($42 per person per day) rentals.

Los Cabos
San José del Cabo, Cabo San Lucas, and the stretch of beach between them make up the peninsula's primary tourist destination. In 1982 the Mexican government decided to propel Los Cabos into tourist consciousness, and began a promotional blitz. Their plans largely succeeded, especially in Cabo San Lucas, which now has far too many resorts. San José del Cabo has managed to avoid becoming hotel hell, and retains a certain modicum of charm and local identity. Even if you are normally turned off by places that receive this kind of hoopla, the beauty of Los Cabos justifies the attention. If that fails, you can retreat back up the peninsula to the quiet town of Todos Santos or hang out with windsurfers in Los Barriles or Buenavista. People come to this region in droves to enjoy kilometers of white beaches and warm, turquoise waters that swell into good surfing waves. A few gorgeous, isolated, and unspoiled spots still remain here—but you'd better hurry.

San José del Cabo

Until recently, San José del Cabo dominated the tip of the peninsula. Jesuits founded the town in the 1700s, taking advantage of an underground stream that surfaces nearby to create a large natural estuary. The mission, zócalo, and other buildings erected during that period give San José del Cabo a sense of history—it feels more like a real Mexican town than a tourist trap. About 46 kilometers northeast of San José del Cabo, Cabo Pulmo has the peninsula's only coral reef, and hundreds of brightly colored fish are visible in the clear water offshore. **Pepe's Dive Center** offers dive tours daily at 10 AM—ask at Casa de Huéspedes Señor Mañana (*see below*).

BASICS The best rates (and longest lines) for traveler's checks are at **Bancomer** (Zaragoza, at Morelos, tel. 114/2–00–40) on weekdays 8:30–1:30. Rates at the exchange booth (tel. 114/2–00–40) farther up Zaragoza are not as good, but they're open Monday–Saturday 8 AM–9 PM and Sundays until 5. Almost all the restaurants, hotels, and shops accept Visa, MasterCard, and AmEx, as well as traveler's checks. **Casitas y Casitas** (cnr of Obregón and Hidalgo, tel. 114/2–24–64) has long-distance telephone service 8 AM–9 PM daily and charges 40¢ to make a collect call. Don't use the more up-scale telephone office down the street near Zaragoza unless you want to pay twice as much for direct calls. The **post office** (Mijares, at Margarita Maza de Juárez, tel. 114/2–09–11) will hold mail sent to you at the following address for 10 days: Lista de Correos, Blvd. Mijares, San José del Cabo, Baja California Sur, CP 23400, México. You can pick up and send mail weekdays 8–7, Saturday 9–1.

The phone number for the **police** is 114/2–03–61 or 114/2–30–61; for the **Cruz Roja** (ambulance), it's 114/2–03–16. **Lavandería VERA** (González, east of bus station; open Mon.–Sat. 8–8) sells suds and has self-serve washers for $1.50; dryers are $2. Next to the zócalo, the **tourist office** (Zaragoza, at Mijares, tel. 114/2–04–46), is open weekdays 9–3, and carries mostly resort brochures. The staff's English isn't great, but they're eager to help.

COMING AND GOING The bus station (tel. 114/2–11–00) is on González, near Highway 1, on the southwest edge of town. From here, it's a 30-minute walk or $1.50 cab ride east down González and north up Mijares to the town center. Fourteen buses leave daily for La Paz (3 hrs, $5), half via Los Barriles (1 hr, $2) and half via Todos Santos (1½ hrs, $3.50). Ten buses head to Cabo San Lucas (30 min, $1) and one bus leaves daily at 4 PM for Tijuana (26 hrs, $43); for more frequent departures to other destinations, transfer in La Paz.

➤ **BY PLANE** • The **Aeropuerto Internacional Los Cabos** is served by **Aerocalifornia** (tel. 114/3–08–48), **Mexicana** (tel. 114/2–27–22), **Alaska** (tel. 114/2–10–15), and **United** (tel. 95/800–00–30–07 or 114/2–28–81). Vans charging $10–$20 shuttle people between the

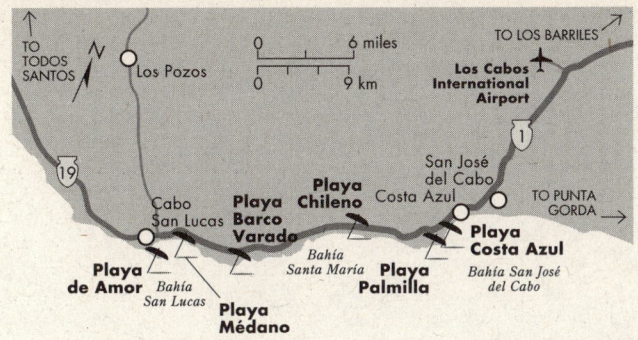

Los Cabos

airport and Los Cabos, but they don't go in the other direction—try to get a free ride from one of the time-share sellers. A bus heading towards La Paz will drop you on the highway near the airport (15 min, $1), but you'll have to walk 1½ kilometers from there, unless a taxi (15 min, $6) is waiting (a definite possibility).

WHERE TO SLEEP If you've got camping gear, use it here—hotels are expensive and beautiful beach sites are plentiful along the coast. Otherwise, rest your head on a freshly washed Star Wars pillowcase and eat in the small restaurant at **Hotel Consuelo** (Morelos, above Cerro de la Cruz, tel. 114/2–06–43). It's the cheapest place in town ($6 a single and $8 a double), and is only a 10-minute walk from the center. Clean, well-ventilated **Hotel Ceci** (Zaragoza 22, near church, no phone) is right in the center of the tourist zone; singles or doubles are $10 with a fan, $13 with air-conditioning. At **Casa de Huéspedes Señor Mañana** (Obregón 1, 1 block from central plaza, tel. 114/2–04–62), watch for falling mangos and guavas as you hang your hammock under a palapa for $5 (watch out for mosquitoes as well). Groovy jungle rooms start at $15 for both singles and doubles, and most rooms have private baths. With reservations you will also be picked up at the airport at no cost. Monthly rates are $230 for a single, $250 a double, and the common cooking and dining facilities include dibs on whatever's ripe on the premises. Super-clean **Hotel Colli** (Hidalgo, near Zaragoza, tel. 114/2–07–25) offers quiet, secure singles for $12.50, and doubles for $15. Rooms cost $17 and $20 with air-conditioning and all rooms have a private bathroom, but prices rise during tourist season.

➢ **CAMPING** • You can pitch your tent anywhere along the beach near town (though it's best to avoid the big hotels or the mosquito-ridden estuary) as long as you set up camp late, don't build a fire, and leave in the morning. A few kilometers down the road toward Cabo San Lucas you can set up at a more permanent surfer camp next to the **Costa Azul Hotel**. Two trailer parks, **Brisas del Mar** and **Montanes de Palmillas,** outside town on the highway toward Cabo San Lucas, charge $15 for two people in a tent. It's expensive, but both have showers, flush toilets, a pool, laundry, and a restaurant.

Secret Surfing Spots

Surfers will find treasures around Los Cabos that don't appear on maps: Nine Palms is the spot for long boarders, Punto Perfecto has Hawaii-size waves, and La Bocana is a walk-in freshwater estuary that features giant tubes, created when heavy rains open up the river mouth. Once you're in the vicinity, ask anybody with long hair and a tan to point you in the right direction.

San José del Cabo

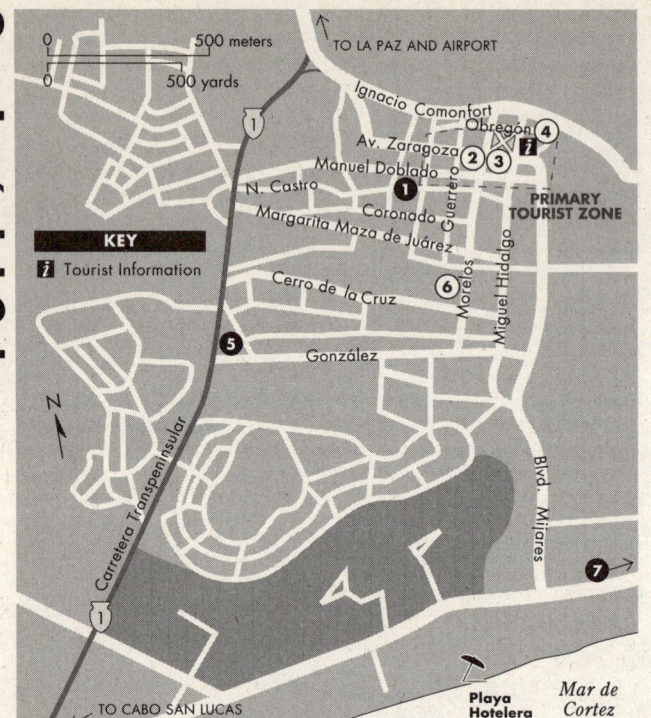

Sights ●
Bus station, 5
Estuary, 7
Mercado Municipal, 1

Lodging ○
Casa de Huéspedes, 4
Hotel Ceci, 2
Hotel Colli, 3
Hotel Consuelo, 6

FOOD   Food stalls at the **mercado municipal** (Castro, at Vicente Ibarra) serve seasonal fare and $2.50 comidas corridas—get here early, though, because food runs out by 4 PM. For a cup of coffee (and a chance to practice your English), **El Café Fiesta** (Mijares 14, at Zaragoza, tel. 114/2-28-08; open daily 7 AM-10 PM) has endless refills and a patio to watch passers-by from. Their extensive vegetarian menu ranges from lentil soup ($2) to veggie tamales ($3.50). **Café Rosy** (Zaragoza, at Green, no phone) is a more traditional Mexican restaurant with more traditional Mexican prices. Burrito and taco plates ($1-$3) are served weekdays 9 AM-10 PM. For something different, try the $4 combination dinner at **Restaurant-Bar Cantón** (Zaragoza, tel. 114/2-04-03), which includes eggrolls, rice, and an entrée (vegetarian dishes available).

AFTER DARK   For real disco action, head to Cabo San Lucas. If you can't get motivated, the **Eclipse** (Mijares, near Coronado; open Thursday-Sunday) is the local downtown disco. Beers are $1 during happy hour (6 PM-10 PM), but this doesn't make up for the blaring TVs, obnoxious karaoke, and the louses who pay the $5 weekend cover (no charge Thurs.) to hang out here and bother women. **Bones** is a disco (Mijares, next to Hotel Presidente, tel. 114/2-02-11) specializing in noisy explosions and fancy lightworks Tuesday-Sunday 9 PM-3 AM. Cover is $3.50 except Wednesdays, when women get in free; drinks cost $1.50-$5.

OUTDOOR ACTIVITIES   The water in front of most of San José's beach hotels has strong currents and swimming can be dangerous, so both residents and tourists head to Hotel Palmilla's **Playa Palmilla,** 7 kilometers west of town. Surfboards ($15 a day), boogie boards ($8 a day), snorkel gear ($8 a day), fish tackle ($10 a day), and bicycles ($11 a day) are available from **Killer Hook Surfshop** (Hidalgo, near Zaragoza, tel. 114/2-24-30; open Mon.-Sat. 8-8). The owner, Rafael, can fill you in on the best surf spots, as well as answer general questions about the surrounding beaches. For other choice local surf spots, see box, *above*. If you'd rather swim in a pool, try sneaking into a hotel. (Forget the uptight Hotel Presidente, where all guests are required to wear a bracelet for identification.)

Cabo San Lucas

Cabo San Lucas was originally a small fishing village, where a few hardy or rich sportfishermen boated or flew in to go after huge marlin and sailfish. Over the past decade, however, spectacular growth has turned Cabo into a tourist nightmare. The small town is congested, claustrophobic, and expensive, although one compensation for this over-development is the availability of all sorts of watersports equipment (for a small mound of cash). The beaches, happily, are still free of charge. On the street, English is the lingua franca, U.S. dollars are expected, and the major hotels water the desert green. Stray a few blocks north of the tourist track to the dirt roads and taco stands, however, and you'll discover Cabo as it existed before the landscape architects arrived.

BASICS Moneychangers line Lázaro Cárdenas between Hidalgo and Matamoros, but U.S. dollars are preferred in most places, and credit cards and traveler's checks are widely accepted. If you do need pesos, **Bancomer** (Cárdenas, btw Hidalgo and Guerrero, tel. 114/3-19-50) is open for money exchange weekdays 8:30–noon, and **Union Bank** across the street has an ATM that accepts Cirrus, Visa, and MasterCard. The Cabo San Lucas **post office** (Lázaro Cárdenas, at 16 de Septiembre, tel. 114/3-00-48), open weekdays 9-6, Saturdays 9-1, will hold mail sent to you at the following address for 10 days: Lista de Correos, Av. Lázaro Cárdenas, Cabo San Lucas, Baja California Sur, CP 23410, México. Public phones are common downtown, but you can place calls from most resort hotels in the area. For cash calls, the **Casa de Larga Distancia** (Lázaro Cárdenas, at San Lucas, tel. 114/3-00-80) is your best bet, but they charge a $1 connection fee if you call collect. There's no extra charge for local calls at the phones next to the elevators in **Plaza Las Glorias**—just dial 0 first.

The phone number for the **police** is 114/3-00-57; for the **Cruz Roja** (ambulance service), it's 114/3-33-00. **Farmacia Sinaloa** (Madero, near Marina, tel. 114/66-4-17; open daily 9-2 and 3-9:30) has an English-speaking employee who can recommend a good hangover regimen or refer you to a doctor. **Libros** (Plaza Bonita, on Marina, tel. 114/3-31-71), open daily 9-9, has an adequate supply of best-sellers in English, as well as a selection of magazines and newspapers in both English and Spanish. The local **lavandería** (San Lucas, btw 5 de Mayo and Constitución, tel. 114/3-20-25; closed Sun.) charges $2 to wash and dry your own clothes or $3.50 to do it for you. There are several booths around town that claim to be tourist information centers, but they generally can't offer more than a map and a smile. For thorough advice in English, seek the people behind the information desk at **Hotel Plaza Las Glorias**.

COMING AND GOING The **bus station** (Zaragoza, at 16 de Septiembre, tel. 114/3-04-00), two blocks from downtown and 10 blocks from the hostel, is served by the **Autobuses de Baja California (ABC)** and **Águila** bus lines. Frequent buses leave daily for La Paz (3 hrs, $4), San José del Cabo (½ hr, $1), and Todos Santos (1 hr, $2). For other destinations, travel to La Paz and transfer.

➤ **BY PLANE** • There is one airport for both Cabos (see San José del Cabo, above). The cheapest way to reach the airport from Cabo San Lucas is on a bus headed to La Paz via San José del Cabo, which will drop you off near the airport on Highway 1 (1 hr, $6). If there are no taxis waiting to drive you the remaining kilometer, the walk is easy. You can take a shuttle to Cabo San Lucas from the airport for $20, or you can take a cheaper shuttle to San José and then take the bus to Cabo San Lucas (see above).

WHERE TO SLEEP Lodging here is generally expensive, with your cheapest options being the youth hostel (see below) and camping on the beach. Campers should head out of town towards Migriño or Playa los Cerritos on the Pacific, or to Cabo Pulmo on the sea side, as you're likely to be hassled if you try to sleep in front of the big hotels.

Hotel Dos Mares. This place is relatively clean and quiet, given its central location. Singles and doubles are $25, whether or not they have air-conditioning or a kitchen. The algae-green pool is available to guests willing to brave it. Weekly and monthly rentals ($150–$630) are also available. Zapata, near marina, tel. 114/3-03-30. 42 rooms, all with bath. Luggage storage.

Cabo S. Lucas

Hotel Mar de Cortez. One glance at the tropical courtyard and inviting swimming pool convinces most budget travelers they couldn't possibly afford to stay here, but they may be wrong. A basic, well-maintained room with one bed and air-conditioning costs $35 for one person and $40 for two. A third person costs $4.50 extra. *Lázaro Cárdenas 11, at Guerrero, tel. 114/3-00-32. 72 rooms, all with bath. Luggage storage. Wheelchair access.*

Siesta Suites Hotel. If you are planning to stay for a few days and can split the cost with someone, this place is the way to go. Each of the fairly new and spanking-clean suites has a private kitchen. Doubles run $45 ($55 with air-conditioning) and are big enough to squeeze in several additional bodies (for $10 per person). The weekly rate is $275 ($330 with a/c). *Zapata, next to Hotel Dos Mares, tel. 114/3-27-73. 12 rooms, all with bath. Luggage storage.*

➤ **HOSTELS • Villas Juveniles (CREA).** The youth hostel is the cheapest place to stay in Cabo San Lucas, though you may have to ask them to turn on the water and electricity for you. The inconvenient walk from the center of town (or the $2 taxi ride) is compensated for by the lack of curfew or check-in time and the prices: A night in a single-sex dorm costs $5, a private room with your own bath costs $7 ($5 per person if you share it with the mate of your choice). Bring your own toilet paper. *Av. de la Juventud, 3 blocks east of Morelos, tel. 114/3-01-48. From downtown, walk 15 min up Morelos. 176 beds. Luggage storage, no alcohol.*

➤ **CAMPING •** Hotel owners don't like you to crash on the beaches near town, so head for those a few kilometers away—they're gorgeous, secluded, and the way to go if you've got gear and are not traveling alone. For something more organized, **Club Cabo** (tel. 114/3-33-48) charges $5 for two people in a tent, $12 in an RV, and $40 for a little house. **Vagabundos** (tel. 114/3-02-90) charges $16 for two people regardless of whether they're in a 50-foot Winnebago or a four-foot tent. Both sites are 3–4 kilometers east on Highway 1.

FOOD Surprisingly, Cabo San Lucas has several decently priced restaurants, mostly on or north of Niños Héroes. Along Morelos (near Lázaro Cárdenas) you'll find a number of authentic Mexican restaurants frequented by the locals. **Café Cabo** (Morelos, near Lázaro Cárdenas, no phone) has a cheery staff and serves big breakfasts for $3, as well as sandwiches ($2), hamburgers ($2.50), and fajitas ($3.50) in the afternoon. For neo-hippie California culture or cuisine, **Mama's Royal Café** (cnr of Hidalgo and Zapata, tel. 114/3-42-90) delivers on both scores. Omelets, salads, and sandwiches here all cost $5. **Mariscos Mocambo** (Morelos, at 20 de Noviembre, tel. 114/3-21-22; open daily 9–9) is the undisputed favorite among locals, who spend their afternoons over red snapper (sold by weight), crab in garlic sauce ($6), or seafood soup ($5). The fresh-squeezed king-size lemonade ($1) is also good. At **Hippy Rick's Fish 'N Chips** (Plaza de los Mariachis, on Blvd. Marina, no phone; open daily 7 AM–midnight), Rick himself will serve you a big plate of crispy, English-style fish and fries for $5. For a mango shake add another $3.

AFTER DARK Cabo San Lucas is *the* center for nightlife in southern Baja. The crowd drinks $1 margaritas at **Río Grill** until 9 PM, then makes its way to the **Giggling Marlin** (tel. 114/3-

11–82). The last stop is at **El Squid Roe** (tel. 114/3–11–69) where the sufficiently inebriated dance themselves silly to pop hits of the '80s; food and beer are served, but tequila shots are more popular. All these bars are on Boulevard Marina (the main drag), which turns into Lázaro Cárdenas, and none charges a cover. Just off the main drag lies the infamous **Cabo Wabo** (Guerrero, near Lázaro Cárdenas, tel. 114/3–11–88), owned by members of Van Halen. Well-known acts often play here on weekends, and any fool who's got $15 burning a hole in his pocket (and that's just the cover) can come here to look for aging rock stars.

OUTDOOR ACTIVITIES Cabo San Lucas's waters are ideal for any water sport—you can rent everything from waterbikes to catamarans, Windsurfers to wave runners. Try **Plaza Las Glorias Beach Club** for these toys. Travelers with tight budgets may want to rent more economical equipment, such as snorkel gear ($10 a day), surfboards ($15–$20 a day), or boogie boards ($5 a day) at **Cabo Sports Center** (Madero, near Guerrero, tel. 114/3–07–32; open daily 9–9). For the very daring, **Baja Bungee** sends people attached to a big rubber band off a 27-meter tower ($35 per jump); contact Alex Darquea at Siesta Suites (tel. 114/3–27–73). You can get a $10 discount on your jump if you buy it with a $30 parasail at **The Activity Center** (by Las Palmas Restaurant on Medano Beach, tel. 114/3–30–93), which serves as a ticket outlet for all of Cabo San Lucas' water sports and activities.

Los Arcos and **Lover's Beach** sit at the tip of the rocky peninsula, south of town. Here the Pacific Ocean and the Sea of Cortez meet, the waves sculpting formations and tunnels in the offshore rocks. Many locals will try to lure you onto their boats for trips to Lover's Beach, but the 30-minute hike is easy and offers spectacular views. Another option is to take a $6 ride in the glass-bottom boat that leaves periodically from behind **Plaza Las Glorias Beach Club,** daily 9:30–2. Currents in the water here send a cascade of sand spiraling to a depth of about 30 meters. You can view the top of the sand waterfall with snorkeling equipment, but to get the full effect, and to enjoy the diversity of the marine life here, scuba diving is the way to go. **Cabo Acuadeportes** (a.k.a. Water Sports Center at Hotel Plaza Las Glorias, Hotel Pueblo Bonito, or Chileno Beach, tel. 114/3–01–17) arranges trips to the sand waterfall, Pelican Rock, Los Arcos, and Cabo Pulmo (Baja's only coral reef). If you're a certified diver, this isn't a place you want to miss, and if you aren't certified, it's a great place to start. Trips cost $80 for certified divers (if you don't have your PADI card with you, they can call to get your number). Diving certification courses cost $400, and resort courses are $90 with equipment. **Dive Adventures** (Plaza Bonita, tel. 114/3–26–30) and **Cabo Diving Services** (Marina, across from Plaza Las Glorias, tel. 114/3–01–50) both have similar prices and trips to the same sites. It's a matter of deciding where you'd like to dive and then calling to see who's going there on the day you want to go.

NEAR LOS CABOS

TODOS SANTOS Good (but sometimes dangerous) surf, free camping, and the absence of obtrusive hotels make Todos Santos the perfect place to retire at 20. Founded by Jesuit missionaries in 1734, and subsequently abandoned due to resistance from the local Pericú people, Todos Santos was finally permanently settled by sugar-planting mestizos in the 19th century. When the sugarcane industry collapsed, the newly unemployed began growing chiles and raising cattle for beef. Today Todos Santos remains a small town that revolves slowly about its shady zócalo. Despite the slow pace, adventurous visitors will find kayaking, sailing, sailboarding, and cruises easily accessible.

➤ **BASICS** • **Bancomer** (Juárez, at Obregón, tel. 114/5–03–90) exchanges cash and traveler's checks weekdays 8:30–2:30. The **post office** (Colegio Militar, near Marqués de León) is open weekdays 8–1 and 3–5. For a small connection fee ($1), you can make collect and credit-card calls at the *caseta* (phone office) in **Pilar's O.G. Fish Tacos** (Colegio Militar, tel. 114/5–01–46), which also serves as the **bus station**. The caseta is open daily 7–6:30, but believe us, DO NOT stop here for lunch. **Farmacia Todos Santos** on Juárez is open daily 7 AM–10 PM, but you can knock at the door at any hour for emergency help. Otherwise, the **Centro de Salud** (Juárez, btw Zaragoza and Degollado, tel. 114/5–00–95) is open 24 hours and Dr. Zapata speaks English. **El Tecolote** English bookstore (Juárez) doubles as a tourist information source and the hub of the resident gringos' social network. They can tell you where the best beaches are, as well as trade used books (two for one) from 9:30 to 5 daily. Next door is **The Message Center** (open Mon.–Sat. 8–5), where you can make direct international calls, call collect, use a calling card, receive phone messages (at 114/5–00–03), send a fax, or receive one (at 114/5–02–88).

➤ **COMING AND GOING** • Buses depart Pilar's (*see above*) for Cabo San Lucas (1 hr, $2) every couple of hours 8 AM–9 PM; those continuing on to San José del Cabo leave four times daily (1½ hrs, $2.50). Frequent buses also leave for La Paz (1 hr, $2). You can store a few bags for free at Pilar's.

➤ **WHERE TO SLEEP** • There's a sandy stretch of beach that's good for camping 2 kilometers south of town. You can also camp at an RV park at **Playa San Pedrito,** 6 kilometers to the south, or on an empty beach at **Playa Las Palmas,** a few kilometers further. Buses headed for Cabo San Lucas will drop you off along the highway, but it's still a two- to three-kilometer walk; although easy, hitching is not recommended for lone travelers. If you want a room try the clean and affordable **Hotel Miramar** (Mutualismo, at Pedrajo, tel. 114/5–03–41). This tranquil retreat at the town's edge is wheelchair-accessible and has parking, a laundromat next door, and a swimming pool; single rooms are $8, doubles $12.50. Clean, centrally located, and pool-blessed is **Motel Guluarte** (cnr of Juárez and Morelos, no phone); singles are $10 (doubles $13), and rooms upstairs have shared balconies with rocking chairs.

➤ **FOOD** • **Caffé Todos Santos** (cnr of Centenario and Topete, no phone; open Tues.–Sun. 7 AM–8 PM) has all-you-can-eat blueberry or banana pancakes ($4), bagels and cream cheese ($1.50) and real coffee for breakfast. Later in the day they serve sandwiches and salads. **Restaurant Las Fuentes** (Delgado, at Colegio Militar, no phone) has patio tables and a varied menu—most meals cost $3–$6. **Lonchería Karla** (Colegio Militar, opposite park, no phone) has $2.50 plates of tacos, tamales, and other antojitos.

SONORA AND LOS MOCHIS   4

By Shayna Samuels

Sonora has always resisted visitors. The indigenous people of this region—the Yaqui, Seri, Guarijio, Mayo, and Papago—adapted to the region's sweltering deserts, but were as fierce as the harsh soils they walked upon. When European settlers arrived, they were opposed by blistering summers and long battles with native tribes. Although the indigenous people were occasionally successful in rebelling, their traditions and rituals were eventually smothered by damned rivers and chemical fertilizers, as Sonora grew wealthy on agriculture. It is now the second richest state in the Republic, and its proximity to Arizona has given rise to a number of *maquiladoras* (foreign-owned factories), where U.S. companies continue to benefit from the cheap price of Mexican labor. It's no wonder Sonorans ask tourists in an ambiguous tone if they are from "*el otro lado*" ("the other side").

Travelers without reptilian blood may be tempted to bypass the northwest corner of Mexico—during summer months the 40°C (100°F) heat plus humidity can be almost unbearable. There are some visitor-friendly areas here, however. Nogales caters to day-tripping souvenir seekers with colorful markets full of woven blankets, wrought-iron furniture, and handmade crafts from all over the country. The almost-unspoiled beaches of San Carlos, Bahía Kino, and Puerto Peñasco are the best spots to cool off with a swim, and the sleepy, colonial town of Alamos recalls its days as a prosperous mining town, with narrow cobblestone streets and elegantly restored haciendas. Hermosillo has museums, parks, and an unique ecology center to keep you entertained, and south of this state capital, mountains give way to the sandy ochres and yellows of the Sonoran desert. Although it's not particularly pretty, you'll also more than likely visit Los Mochis. The city is a transportation hub and is an essential stop if you plan to take a ferry to Baja or the train through the Copper Canyon (*see* Chapter 5).

The Sonoran Yaqui people are famous for their perpetual resistance to outside domination. Porfirio Díaz set the army against them in the 1890s when they objected to his selling their land to private investors, and thousands of prisoners were sent to work building railroads in southern Mexico. Even so, the Yaqui were not fully "subdued" (that is, they kept killing settlers) until the late 1920s.

Nogales

The unimpressive town of Nogales, Mexico, crowds against the border across from Nogales, Arizona. Like Tijuana to the west (but on a much smaller scale), this city is famous for its shopping and attracts hordes of Arizonans bargaining for tacky knickknacks. This is the place to find that stuffed armadillo that's been eluding you back home. Blue glass from Guadalajara, silver from Zacatecas, and burnished pottery from Oaxaca are available throughout the city, although you'll find them at lower prices farther south. Nogales also has a decent bullfighting arena, which is the hot spot during **Cinco de Mayo.** This festival, including bullfights, cockfights, horse races, and *artesanía* (crafts) exhibitions, celebrates Mexico's defeat of the French in the battle of Puebla and lasts from the end of April until May 5.

Nogales ("walnut trees" in English) serves as a major export depot for Sonora's rich agricultural produce but, like many of its border cousins, has also been affected by important economic changes over the past decade. Foreign (mostly U.S.) companies take advantage of cheap Mexican labor by setting up an increasing number of industrial parks and *maquiladoras* in special duty-free zones. Poor workers' *colonias* (neighborhoods) overlook the town, their shacks and small houses sloping perilously on the hillsides.

BASICS

CASAS DE CAMBIO Banks on the U.S. side don't change dollars into pesos, but **Bank of America** (tel. 520/287–6553), about one block into the States, has an ATM and is open weekdays 9–6, Saturdays 9–2. On the Mexican side, you'll find several money-exchange offices along Campillo, one block from the border. Or try **Casa de Cambio Gaby** (Morelos 18, near Ochoa, tel. 631/2–19–09), open Monday–Saturday 8–6. **Bancomer** (López Mateos, 5 blocks south of border crossing, tel. 631/2–10–48) has an ATM that accepts Visa cards.

CROSSING THE BORDER Both the U.S. and Mexican customs offices at Nogales are open 24 hours a day. Americans and Canadians planning to stay in Mexico longer than 72 hours or going south of the border towns need tourist cards. Present proof of citizenship at the **Mexican Government Tourist Office** or at the **Mexican Government Border Office** in Nogales (tel. 631/2–17–55; open 24 hours). It's immediately to the right when you cross the border. Bringing a car is a little trickier (*see* Coming and Going, *below*).

EMERGENCIES Bilingual operators staff the emergency telephone service (tel. 91/525–001–23 or 91/525–001–51) 24 hours a day. There are also direct numbers for the **police** (tel. 631/6–15–64 or 631/2–17–67) and **fire** and **ambulance** service (tel. 631/4–07–69).

MAIL The *oficina de correos* (post office) will hold mail sent to you at the following address for up to 10 days: Lista de Correos, Benito Juárez y Calle Campillo, Nogales, Sonora, CP 84000, México. Benito Juárez, at Campillo, tel. 631/2–12–47. 2 blocks from border crossing. Open weekdays 8–7, Sat. 8–noon.

MEDICAL AID Several reputable, English-speaking medical offices are found in the first few blocks of Obregón. Try **Roberto Belches Vásquez, MD** (tel. 631/2–37–21) and **Rene Romo De Vivar, DDS** (Obregón 263, tel. 631/2–05–00). For less urgent medical attention, **Farmacia San Xavier** (Campillo 73, 2 blocks from border crossing, tel. 631/2–55–03) is open 24 hours and the staff speaks English.

PHONES Working (yes, working!) Ladatel pay phones can be found along major streets, and there is a *caseta de larga distancia* (long-distance phone office) in the bus terminal. **Nabila** (tel. 631/2–01–42; open daily 8–6), a small bric-a-brac shop a few blocks down Obregón on the left-hand side charges $1.50 to make a collect call, $1.50 per minute to dial direct.

VISITOR INFORMATION The English-speaking tourist office, on the right just across the border, hands out a bite-size city map. Fortunately, Nogales is easy to navigate. *López Mateos, at Internacional, tel. 631/2–06–66. Open daily 8–6.*

COMING AND GOING

Almost everything you could need or want to see is near the border crossing area and easily accessible on foot. Local buses run to other parts of town from López Mateos. Taxis will charge you roughly $1 per kilometer, but be sure to set a price before getting in.

BY CAR If you're driving less than 21 kilometers across the border, no special rules apply; bringing a car further into Mexico is not complicated if you're properly prepared. At a 21-kilometer mark south of the border $10 will be charged to your credit card. If you don't have one, a cash deposit equal to the value of your vehicle ($500–$20,000) will be accepted; you'll get it back (plus interest) upon leaving the country. You must also purchase Mexican auto insurance ($8) from the **Puerta de Mexico Edificio Banderas** (government border office; tel. 800/446-8277; open Mon.–Sat. 7 AM–10 PM, Sun. 7–1), just over the border in Nogales. Bring 1) registration under your name, 2) your driver's license, and 3) your passport, plus a photocopy of each. U.S. rental cars are not permitted past the 21-kilometer mark, but everyone else is allowed a permit for up to 6 months.

BY BUS There is a new bus station in Nogales, but it's 6 kilometers from the center of town on Highway 15—you can get here on one of the local CENTRAL CAMIONERA buses (40¢) that run along López Mateos. Three bus companies use the station: **Transportes Norte de Sonora** (tel. 631/3-17-00) and **Tres Estrellas de Oro** (tel. 631/3-02-33) serve Baja as well as mainland Mexico; **Transportes del Pacífico** (tel. 631/3-16-06) serves the western mainland. Four daily buses go to Mexico City (1½ days; $73 1st class, $63 2nd class). Tres Estrellas and Transportes Norte de Sonora each have an evening departure for Mexicali (9 hrs; $17.50 1st class, $16 2nd class). You can also take any bus headed south to Santa Ana ($3.50 1st class, $3 2nd class) and transfer there to a Mexicali-bound bus. Buses also leave Nogales for Tijuana (12 hrs; $24 1st class, $20 2nd class), Hermosillo (5 hrs; $9 1st class, $7 2nd class), Guaymas (7 hrs; $12 1st class, $11 2nd class), Los Mochis (12 hrs; $11 1st class, $23 2nd class), Mazatlán (17 hrs; $38 1st class, $33 2nd class), and Guadalajara (31 hrs; $53 1st class, $46 2nd class). The terminal has phones, luggage storage (50¢ per bag per hr), and a money-exchange booth.

On the Arizona side of the border, **Grey Line** (tel. 520/287-5628; open 7 AM–9 PM daily) has frequent, direct service to Tucson (1½ hrs, $6.50) and scheduled connections throughout the States and will let you cram your luggage in a locker for $1. Collective taxi/vans go directly to the airport in Tucson from here for $11 per person.

BY TRAIN The train station (tel. 631/3-02-05 or 631/3-10-91) is across from the bus station, 6 kilometers outside town (off Highway 15), and can be reached via any local bus marked CENTRAL CAMIONERA or FERROCARRIL (40¢) or by taxi ($5 from the center). Daily first- and second-class rail service runs to Benjamin Hill ($4 1st class, $3 2nd class), Hermosillo ($5 1st class, $3 2nd class), Sufragio (transfer point for the Copper Canyon; $14 1st class, $10 2nd class), Mazatlán ($21 1st class, $15 2nd class), and Guadalajara ($32 1st class, $25 2nd class). For Mexico City, change trains in Guadalajara; for Mexicali, change in Benjamin Hill. The second-class train leaves at 7 AM; the first-class train at 4:30 PM. The main difference is the lack of temperature control in second class. Tickets can be purchased at the station; be sure to arrive at least 30 minutes prior to departure.

WHERE TO SLEEP

If you're going further into Mexico, you might be better off avoiding Nogales's overpriced hotels, and taking an overnight bus straight out of town. If you do decide to stay, the wheelchair-accessible **Hotel Yolanda** (Morelos, on a walkway just off Campillo, no phone), is the cheapest in town. The decent rooms with private bathrooms and hot water are worth the price ($8.50 singles, $14 doubles), if you can tolerate the saggy beds and lack of ventilation. **Hotel Orizaba** (Juárez 29, near Campillo, tel. 631/2-58-55) has similar conditions and prices ($10 singles, $12.50 doubles), except they give you a fan instead of your own bathroom. The communal baths get nasty when the place is full, but they do have hot water. **Hotel Pasaje** (Obregón 75, near Campillo, tel. 631/2-00-18), though relatively expensive, is the best deal in town. The small, clean rooms ($20 singles, $25 doubles) are cozy and have private baths, hot water, and air-conditioning; some even have TVs.

FOOD

There are no supermarkets in the downtown area, and the Nogales restaurant scene is pricey unless you get off of the main boulevard. Taquerías and push-cart vendors, found on almost every corner, are an inexpensive alternative at $2–$3 a meal, and cheap eateries can also be found along Ochoa. Of these, the 24-hour **Restaurant Café Río Sonora** (Ochoa, near Hidalgo, tel. 631/2-03-89) serves the best and cheapest multicourse *comida corrida* (pre-prepared lunch special; $2). **Café Olga** (Juárez, at Campillo, tel. 631/2-16-41) is a popular breakfast spot where hot cakes and eggs are just $3. **La Fábula** (López Mateos, near Vásquez, tel. 631/2-20-48), near the local bus terminal in the center of town, serves up good Chicago-style pizza ($6 for a small, $9 for a large) daily noon–11 PM.

AFTER DARK

Except for weekends, when Arizonans cross the border to whoop it up Mexican style, Nogales's night life is pretty mellow. **Harlow's Discotheque** (Elías 21, no phone; cover $5) has all the latest in lasers, lights, and hip-hop music. On Fridays and Saturdays, locals head to **Monaro** (Colonia La Loma; cover $3.50) to drink and dance to cumbia and salsa. About 1 kilometer down Obregón is **Mr. Don** (Obregón 1036, tel. 631/3-19-07; open Fri. and Sat. 9 PM–3 AM), a huge disco that plays everything from salsa to rap. On Fridays there's no cover, and on Saturdays it's $8—but you can drink all you want for that price. The popular **Epidaurus** (Privada Becerril and Corinto, just off Obregón, tel. 631/3-26-13; cover $9) attracts hordes of locals and tourists looking to boogey on the weekends. The bar is open Tuesday–Sunday 5 PM–1 AM, and the disco is open Friday and Saturday 5 PM–3 AM.

Near Nogales

PUERTO PEÑASCO

Founded as a fishing village in 1927, this relatively undeveloped tourist trap (known by most as "Rocky Point") sits on the lonely northern coast of the Sea of Cortez. The town is surrounded by the **Desierto de Altar,** where the temperature often soars to more than 37°C (100°F) in summer. The best time of year to visit the area is late spring, when temperatures are milder and the cholla, saguaro, organ pipe, and barrel cacti bloom into red, yellow, and white flowers. Vacationing Arizo-

Jesuit Father Eusebio Kino, who established a number of missions in northwestern Mexico in the late 17th century, reportedly drew a parallel between the Desierto de Altar and his vision of Hell.

Pick Your Poison

Like tequila, mezcal comes from the fermented heart of the maguey plant (a large succulent), except tequila comes from only one species of maguey. Mezcal is a mixture, and comes in several different classes. The cheapest is pechuga or minero and isn't as smooth as mezcal de cordon or mezcal de punto, both of which consist of only the first and finest drops to fall from the distillery. All mezcal is clear, but will take on a distinct color and flavor if stored in wood. The infamous "worm" (a beetle larva that lives in the maguey) also imparts its own distinctive flavor. On special occasions, look for pechuga especial, distilled with apples, oranges, and chicken for an extra flavorful brew.

nans in search of the sea congregate on the southern side of town, armed with their RVs, dune buggies, and Jet Skis. Besides heading to the beach, there is little to do or see here, except on June 1st, when Nogales celebrates **Navy Day** with mariachi music, parades, and beauty pageants. In mid-June, there's also an annual fishing tournament where you can eat enough seafood to just about grow fins yourself. Although you probably can't afford the lobster at **La Casa del Captán** (tel. 638/3–56–98), you can still drive up to the hill where the restaurant is perched (above Malecón), and witness the fiery sunset ease the city into another clear, starry night. About 48 kilometers away, on the road to Sonoita is the volcanic **El Pinacate**, famous for enormous craters that resemble the surface of the moon.

COMING AND GOING To reach Puerto Peñasco from Nogales, take a **Tres Estrellas de Oro** bus to Carborca (4 hrs, $9) and transfer to a Puerto Peñasco-bound bus (2 hrs, $2). Trains also run from Puerto Peñasco to Mexicali (4 hrs, $4.50), Caborca (2 hrs, $2), Hermosillo (6 hrs, $4), and Ciudad Obregón (9 hrs, $6).

WHERE TO SLEEP AND EAT Unfortunately the rich have a monopoly over most beachfront hotels, but **Motel Davis** (Emiliano Zapata 100, near Calle 13, tel. 638/3–43–14) offers well-maintained air-conditioned singles and doubles for $10–$15. If you're broke, try camping on peaceful **Playa Sandy** for $3. **Restaurant Los Arcos** (Eusebio Kino, at Tamaulipas, tel. 638/3–35–97) has a breakfast special for $2 and is open daily 7:30 AM–10 PM. You can also head for one of the many seafood stands near the end of Boulevard Kino. **Manny's Beach Club** (Playa Miramar, tel. 638/3–36–05) has a raging happy hour every night from 5–7 PM, when beers are $1 and Jimmy Buffett's "Margaritaville" is played over and over for the amusement of drunk gringos.

Hermosillo

This prosperous capital city of **Sonora** boasts a state university and a population of almost a half million. You might expect such a place to be dynamic and exciting, but it's actually big, hot, dirty, crime ridden, and exhausting. If you're stuck here, at least you can still see traces of colonial history in residential architecture or in grand public buildings such as the **Catedral de la Asunción** and the **Palacio de Gobierno**, on the central Plaza Zaragoza. You can also take a two-hour stroll around the **Centro Ecológico de Sonora** (southern outskirts of town, off Hwy. 15, tel. 62/13–35–37) to see flora and fauna from the local desert. At the eastern base of **Cerro de la Campana** (Bell Hill), the free **Museo de Sonora** (tel. 62/12–13–62) holds a fine collection of pre-Columbian artifacts and is open Wednesday–Saturday 10–5, Sundays 9–4. Nearby, the **Capilla del Carmen** (Chapel of Carmen) occasionally holds a "mariachi mass"—a loud, colorful trumpet-and guitar-accompanied Sunday mass that's worth getting out of bed to attend (*see box* Liberation Theology, in Chapter 10). Other special events include **La Fiesta de la Vendimia** (the grape harvest celebration) in mid-July and Yaqui Indian dances, held during **Semana Santa** (Holy Week, the week before Easter). Most visitors, however, prefer to head south to beach resorts such as the Bahía Kino towns and, farther south, Mazatlán.

BASICS

AMERICAN EXPRESS The AmEx office in **Hermex Travel** sells traveler's checks, insurance, and plane tickets, and cashes personal checks for card holders. *Rosales, at Monterrey. Open weekdays 9–1 and 3–6, Sat. 9–noon. Mailing address: Edif. Lupita, Hermosillo, Sonora, CP 83000, México.*

CASAS DE CAMBIO A number of banks line Rosales (in the downtown area) and Eusebio Kino, in the northwest corner of town. **Bancomer** (Sonora, at Matamoros, tel. 62/12–13–62) changes traveler's checks weekdays 9–1 and has a *caja permanente* (ATM) that takes Visa cards. More ATMs can be found downtown, on Serdán between Juárez and Jesús García.

CONSULATES United States. The consulate has an answering machine that is checked hourly when the consulate is not open. *Monterrey 142, behind Hotel Calinda, tel. 62/17–25–42. Open weekdays 8–4:30.*

EMERGENCIES Dial 08 for emergencies, or call the **police** (tel. 62/13–40–46); **fire** (tel. 62/12–01–97); or **ambulance** (tel. 62/4–07–69).

LAUNDRY Lavandería Automática de Hermosillo charges $1.50 to wash and $1.50 to dry. *Cnr of Sonora and Yáñez, tel. 62/7–55–01. Open Mon.–Sat. 8–8, Sun. 8–1.*

MAIL The post office downtown will hold mail sent to you at the following address for 10 days: Lista de Correos, Blvd. Rosales, Hermosillo, Sonora, CP 83000, México. You can send or receive telegrams and faxes at the office next door. *Post office: Serdán, at Rosales, tel. 62/12–00–11. Open weekdays 8–7, Sat. 8–noon.*

MEDICAL AID Clínica del Noroeste (L.D. Colosio and Juárez, tel. 62/12–18–90) has 24-hour emergency service and some English-speaking doctors. Nonemergencies are handled weekdays 8–8, Saturdays 8–1. You'll also be happy to know that, if the need arises, there's a 24-hour funeral home right around the corner. For simpler problems, **Farmacia Margarita** (Morelia 93, at Guerrero, tel. 62/13–15–90) is open 24 hours.

PHONES There are pay phones along the streets, but finding one that works could take you all day. It's quicker to head to **Hotel Monte Carlo** (*see* Where to Sleep, *below*), which has working ones. Long-distance calls and faxes can be placed at **Farmacia Margarita** (*see above*).

VISITOR INFORMATION The **Secretaría al Fomento de Turismo** (Secretary of Tourism), in the Centro del Gobierno Edifico Estatal, usually has someone on hand who speaks English, but anyone here can load you down with brochures and maps. *Blvd. Paseo Canal and Comonfort, 3rd floor, tel. 62/17–00–76. Open weekdays 8–4 and 5–9, Sat. 10–1.*

COMING AND GOING

BY BUS Three main bus companies serve Hermosillo's **Central Camionera** (Transversal 400): **Transportes Norte de Sonora** (tel. 62/13–24–16), **Transportes del Pacífico** (tel. 62/17–05–80), and **Tres Estrellas de Oro** (tel. 62/13–24–16). To reach the Central Camionera from downtown, take any bus marked CIRCUITO NORTE, PERIFERICO or TRANSVERSAL (40¢). Taxis charge $5 from the station to downtown, but you can pay less (about $3) if you walk away from the station and flag one down. Buses run north to Tijuana (12 hrs, $22), stopping in Nogales (3½ hrs, $7) and Mexicali (10 hrs, $17); and south to Mexico City (31 hrs, $54), stopping in Guaymas (2 hrs, $3.50), Los Mochis (7 hrs, $12.50), Mazatlán (12 hrs, $26), and Guadalajara (26 hrs, $39). Luggage storage and money exchange are available at the terminal.

BY TRAIN The train station (tel. 62/15–35–77 or 62/10–34–57) is 3 kilometers north of town, just off Highway 15. First-class trains leave for Mexicali (10 hrs, $22) and Nogales (4 hrs, $8) daily at 5 PM. Second-class service to these same destinations leaves at 1 AM, takes somewhat longer, and costs about one-third of the price of first-class. First-class trains for Guadalajara (22 hrs, $55) leave daily at 8 PM. Second-class trains to Guadalajara (at least 27 hrs, $17) leave daily at noon. If you're Mexico City bound, you'll need to change trains in Guadalajara. Buses marked EST. FERR. will take you from the market in central Hermosillo to the station; a cab from the center is $4.

BY PLANE Aeroméxico (tel. 62/16–82–59) and **Mexicana** (tel. 62/17–11–03) serve Hermosillo with several daily flights from Tucson and Dallas in the United States, as well as from Mexico. The airport lies 10 kilometers from town on the road to Bahía Kino and Nuevo Kino. Taxis ($8–$12) are the best way to reach the airport, but you can also catch a bus on Boulevard Luis Encinas (40¢).

GETTING AROUND

With several hills to orient you, it's difficult to get lost in Hermosillo. The most prominent hill downtown is **Cerro de la Campana.** Highway 15 runs through Hermosillo and on to Nogales to the north. Boulevard Transversal transects the city northwest–southeast. Local buses are cheap (40¢) and dependable, if not always fast. Taxis charge roughly $1 per kilometer, but it may cost two or three times as much at night or from the bus station.

WHERE TO SLEEP

The government shut down most of the flophouses along Sonora and Juárez due to rampant drugs and prostitution, thus limiting options for budget travelers. Spared from the sweep was **Casa de Huéspedes Hotel Carmelita** (Sonora, btw Revolución and Gonzáles, tel. 62/13–13–96), where a decrepit room with a bath costs $8.50 and singles and doubles without a bath are $6.50. Women (and even some men) may get hassled in this area after dark.

Hotel Monte Carlo. Ignore the drunks hanging around outside and the stuffed deer heads hanging in the lobby, because inside this older hotel you'll find clean private bathrooms and good air-conditioning. Singles are $15, doubles $16, quads $20. *Juárez, at Sonora, opposite Plaza Juárez, tel. 62/12–08–53. 28 rooms, all with bath.*

Hotel San Andrés. Hermosillo may not be the place for a big splurge, but the travel-weary can head here for security and relative opulence. The big rooms have TVs, phones, heat, and air-conditioning. The hotel also has a restaurant, bar, and shaded outdoor patio. Singles cost $22, doubles $27. *Oaxaca 14, near Plaza Juárez, tel. 62/17–30–99. 83 rooms, all with bath.*

Hotel Washington. The Washington offers old but clean rooms, all with warm water in their bathrooms. On the down side, the plumbing is leaky, mornings can be noisy thanks to the local bus depot out front, and the air-conditioning is weak. Singles cost $10, doubles $11 (1 bed), $12.50 (2 beds). *Noriega 68, at Matamoros, tel. 62/13–11–83. 28 rooms, all with bath.*

FOOD

The downtown area is loaded with cheap taquerías and street vendors selling everything from fruit to hot dogs. Here, you can go to dinner with $5 in your pocket and come back with a full belly and some change. Fresh, cheap fruits and vegetables are sold at the **mercado municipal** (Matamoros, at Roberto Elías Calles). For basic, fast, and cheap Mexican food downtown, **Cenaduría Yáñez** (Yáñez Sur 7, tel. 62/14–18–72; open daily noon–midnight) serves up spicy tacos or *burritos de machaca* (chopped-beef burritos) for $1.50. **Café Lydia** (Sonora, at González, no phone) opens bright and early for decent breakfasts ($2).

Café Monte Carlo. The baseball paraphernalia covering the walls adds ambiance to this eclectic place. Try a tongue omelet ($2) with pineapple juice ($1) for breakfast. The extensive dinner menu includes chicken in green sauce ($3), or liver and onions ($2.50). *Juárez, at Sonora, tel. 62/12–22–59. Open Mon.–Sat. 7 AM–10 PM.*

La Huerta. This restaurant is a bit out of the way, but worth the trip for delicious seafood at reasonable prices. The *pescado a la veracruzana* (red snapper cooked in tomatoes, onions, capers, peppers, and herbs; $7) is a welcome relief from tacos and beans. *San Luis Potosí 109, tel. 62/14–82–88. From Plaza Zaragoza, take the MORELOS, KINO, or HUERTA bus to San Luis Potosí (50¢). Open daily noon–7 PM.*

Jung. The wholesome fare at this vegetarian restaurant includes salads, sandwiches, and entrées, all fashioned from fresh fruits and vegetables and whole-wheat breads ($2–$5). *Niños Héroes 75, near Matamoros, tel. 62/13–28–82.*

CHEAP THRILLS

Hermosillo is short on diversions, but on a nice afternoon try the **Parque Madero** (Jesús García, btw P. Elías and Norwalk), not far from the Cerro de la Campana. The jungle gyms, long slides, merry-go-rounds, and swings here send the local kiddies wild—you might as well play too. On hot days, watch out for children who jump into the fountain, emerge dripping and jubilant, and embrace anyone not quick enough to get out of the way.

AFTER DARK

Downtown Hermosillo (especially the area surrounding Plaza Juárez) is filled with men looking for trouble at night. For diehards, there's **Blocky'O** (Rodríguez, at Juárez, tel. 62/15–18–88), a huge disco with frequent bar specials. A little farther south, just off Rodríguez, you'll find **Nova Olimpia** (Frontera, at C. L. de Soria, tel. 62/17-30-13), where the music alternates nightly between cumbia, salsa, and disco. Both clubs charge a $5 cover for men, and $3 for women. A few blocks farther south, **Marco 'n' Charlie's** (Blvd. Rodríguez 78, tel. 62/15-30-61; open Mon.-Sat. 1 PM-2 AM) doesn't charge a cover, and is a popular bar and grill for young, middle-class locals.

Near Hermosillo

BAHIA KINO

The two towns of Kino Viejo and Kino Nuevo share the Bahía Kino on the Sea of Cortez, and both are blessed with pristine beaches, warm, clear waters, and a population of manta rays and pelicans. Although both towns are easily explored from Hermosillo (about 120 kilometers away), they couldn't be more different. The poor, sleepy fishing village of **Kino Viejo** was established in the 1700s by the Jesuit priest Eusebio Kino as a mission for Seri Indians; today it consists of a few stores, restaurants, and fishermen's houses strung along a dusty road. The charm of this town is in its friendly atmosphere (sometimes a little too friendly for women traveling alone), cheap, fresh seafood, and colorful sunsets. **Kino Nuevo** is a haven for American retirees, who have created a secluded, sanitized version of the States behind a fenced-in, faux-villa facade. The small **Museo de los Seris** in Kino Nuevo serves up historical and cultural information on the indigenous Seris, who you may see selling the ironwood sculptures for which they are known. Local hustlers may try to persuade you to visit the Isla del Tiburón (Shark Island), home to Seri Indians until they were forcibly resettled in the '50s. The island is now a fragile wildlife refuge for tortoises, rams, coyotes, and birds; please don't visit.

Summer is the best time to visit the Kinos: The resident Americans stay indoors to avoid the blistering heat, and the sea is the perfect temperature for swimming.

COMING AND GOING Ten buses run from Hermosillo to the Kinos (2 hrs, $3) 5:40 AM-5:30 PM. Buses depart from the old **Transportes Norte de Sonora** station (Sonora, btw Revolución and González), not the Central Camionera. These buses pass through both Kinos every 1-2 hours, but walking and hitching between towns is easy. To return to Hermosillo, catch the bus on the main road in either Kino between 6 AM and 5:30 PM.

WHERE TO SLEEP Kino Nuevo has the only hotels, the cheapest of which is **Hotel Saro** (midway down the road in Kino Nuevo, tel. 624/2-00-07), where clean singles are $25, doubles $30, and you can pay by MasterCard or Visa. In the off-season various RV parks in the Kinos rent tent spaces for $5-$10, which includes use of their bathroom and shower facilities. In Kino Nuevo, try **Trailer Park Kino Bay** (tel. 624/2-02-16) at the end of the road, or **Islandia Marina** (tel. 624/2-00-81) on the water near Puerto Peñasco and Guerrero. The latter has beach bungalows with kitchen facilities ($22 for 4) right on the water. You can also string up a hammock or plop your tent under one of the many *palapas* (thatched huts) along the 18-kilometer beach in Kino Nuevo for free. Camping here is generally safe, but you need to watch your stuff. Avoid camping on the beach in Kino Viejo; there's a lot of foot traffic here at night.

FOOD Kino Viejo has a few good restaurants, and a number of fish and taco stands. In Kino Nuevo, you can enjoy a shrimp cocktail ($4) or ceviche ($5) overlooking the sea at **La Palapa** (mid-way down the road, tel. 624/2-02-10; open daily 8 AM-10 PM). For finer dining, wander a little farther down the road to **El Pargo Rojo** (tel. 624/2-02-05; open daily noon-10), which serves New York steak ($7.50) and tasty piña coladas ($2.50). As with every place in Kino Nuevo, they accept credit cards. **Restaurant Dorita** (open daily 7-7), just opposite the police station/post office/Red Cross building on the main drag, serves good, cheap lunches (about $5) amid bustling families.

OUTDOOR ACTIVITIES Water sports in the bay are too inviting to pass up, but unfortunately there's no place to rent equipment. If you have your own, pick any spot and dive in; if you don't, your best bet is to make friends with a family who will loan you theirs. Better yet, head to the water in Kino Viejo in the early morning when the fishermen push their *pangas* (fishing boats) off the sand, and see if you can go along (you'll probably be expected to help with the nets).

LA PINTADA

The archaeological site at La Pintada, sixty kilometers south of Hermosillo off Highway 15, was once a refuge for Pima, Yaqui, and Seri Indians fleeing the Spanish. The area is now filled with vibrantly colored rock paintings, many of which depict hunting rituals. Catch a bus toward Guaymas and ask the driver to let you off at La Pintada, or join a research group from Hermosillo's university during the school year. Contact the tourist office in Hermosillo for more information.

Guaymas

The port city of Guaymas provides a welcome respite from the sweltering heat inland. Although there's not much to see here (Guaymas seems more concerned with commerce and fishing than tourism), you can wander along the docks, watch the fishing boats, or check out the people. An extensive shrimp and sardine-fishing fleet operates from these docks, and seafood processing is one of the main local industries (check out the town's **Monumento al Pescador,** an enormous statue of a fisherman battling a huge fish). The town's **Plaza de San Fernando** (in front of the Parroquia de San Fernando) is a good place to sit back, enjoy a *refresco* (soda), and watch the kids run around in the midday sun. Another reason to visit is strictly practical: There is twice-weekly ferry service from Guaymas to Santa Rosalía, on the Baja Peninsula.

Locals head to the uninspiring Playa Miramar in summer, but the best beaches by far are in nearby San Carlos.

BASICS

AUTO PARTS/SERVICE Auto Partes Ibarra, S.A. sells parts and can recommend mechanics in broken English. *Serdán 251, tel. 622/2–01–36 or 622/2–31–36. Open Mon.–Sat. 8–noon and 2–6.*

CASAS DE CAMBIO There are a number of banks along Avenida Serdán. **Bancomer** (Serdán, at Calle 18) changes cash and traveler's checks weekdays 8:30 AM–12:30 PM, and their 24-hour ATM accepts Visa. The **Banamex** ATM (Serdán, at Calle 20) accepts Plus and Cirrus. **Servicios del Pacífico** (Serdán 223, btw Calles 16 and 17, tel. 622/2–75–33) has better hours (Mon.–Sat. 8–7) but charges 1.5%–2% commission.

EMERGENCIES Police (tel. 622/4–01–04); fire (tel. 622/2–00–10); ambulance (tel. 622/4–08–76).

LAUNDRY Guaymas Superlava has automatic washers for $1.50 and $4, and dryers for $2.50. They will also do up to 3 kilos for you ($5). *García López 884, 1½ km west of bus station, tel. 622/2–54–00. Open Mon.–Sat. 8–7.*

MAIL The post office will hold mail sent to you at the following address for up to 10 days: Lista de Correos, Av. 10, Guaymas, Sonora, CP 85400, México. *Av. 10, at Calle 20. tel. 622/2–07–57. Open weekdays 8–7, Sat. 8–noon.*

MEDICAL AID Farmacia Sonora Centro (Serdán, at Calle 18, tel. 622/2–30–44) is open 24 hours. Unfortunately nobody here speaks English. For more urgent medical attention, there are several doctor's offices in the plaza on Serdán between Calles 18 and 19. **Dr. David Robles Rendón** is a general practitioner, but does not speak English. *Serdán, at Calle 17, tel. 622/2–83–13 or 622/2–16–69. Open weekdays 8–1 and 5–8, Sat. 8–1.*

PHONES The public phones along the streets often don't work. You can make local, long-distance, and international calls from the caseta at **Farmacia Eco San Alberto,** which charges 20¢ to call collect. *Calle 19, 1 block south of Serdán, tel. 622/4–20–44. Open daily 8 AM–9 PM.*

COMING AND GOING

In Guaymas, Highway 15 becomes García López. Avenida Serdán runs from García López on the east side of town, is central to everything but the beaches, and is served by rickety but well-marked local buses. Buses marked PLAYA MIRAMAR and SAN CARLOS (65¢) make the 15-minute trip out to Playas Miramar and San Carlos, respectively. Both stop in front of the Comex building on Serdán, near Calle 16.

BY BUS Buses here are more convenient than trains since they run more frequently and the station is centrally located. Three bus lines, **Transportes Norte de Sonora** (tel. 622/2–12–71), **Transportes del Pacífico** (tel. 622/2–30–19), and **Tres Estrellas de Oro** (tel. 622/2–12–71), operate from terminals on Rodríguez near Calle 13, two blocks south of Serdán. Buses depart hourly, heading south to Mexico City (29 hrs, $61), with stops in Los Mochis (5 hrs, $11), Mazatlán (10 hrs, $26), and Guadalajara (24 hrs, $41); and north to Tijuana (17 hrs, $29), stopping in Hermosillo (1½ hrs, $4), Nogales (5 hrs, $12), and Mexicali (15 hrs, $23). Transportes del Pacífico leaves frequently for Navojoa (3 hrs, $6), the transfer point for Alamos.

BY TRAIN The train station (tel. 622/3–10–65) is 10 kilometers south of Guaymas in a town called Empalme. To get here, take a red-and-white TNS (Transportes Norte de Sonora) bus (50¢) marked EMPALME from any bus stop on Serdán or from the Transportes Norte de Sonora station; a taxi costs $5. If you're coming from the south, buses stop in Empalme on the way to Guaymas, but either way, the bus stop is 1 kilometer from the station. Northbound trains run to Mexicali (12 hrs, $15 1st class; 15 hrs, $8 2nd class), Nogales (6 hrs, $7.50 1st class; 8 hrs, $4.50 2nd class), and Hermosillo (1½ hrs, $3 1st class; 2 hrs, $1.50 2nd class). Southbound trains depart for Guadalajara (the transfer point for Mexico City; 24 hrs, $24 1st class; 26 hrs, $13.50 2nd class).

BY PLANE **Aeroméxico,** which serves most of Mexico, flies into the Guaymas airport, 13 kilometers north of town. One-way fares to La Paz are about $120; to Mexico City, about $135. Buses to the airport (marked SAN JOSE) stop in front of Comex on Serdán (near Calle 16) every half hour (25 min, 50¢). A taxi to the airport should cost no more than $4. You can buy tickets at the **airport office.** *Office: Serdán, at Calle 16, tel. 622/2–01–23. Open weekdays 8–1 and 2–4:30, Sat. 8–1.*

BY FERRY The **Sematur ferry terminal** (tel. 622/2–23–24) is at the east end of town, just off Serdán. Ferries to Santa Rosalía, on the Baja coast, run on Tuesday and Friday at 8 AM ($10, $26 tourist class). You can put a car on the ferry as well, but it's expensive—they charge by size, and the smallest car costs $80. You can buy tickets at the ferry terminal Mondays and Thursdays 8–3 or the morning of departure 6 AM–7:30 AM.

WHERE TO SLEEP

There are plenty of clean, quiet, reasonably priced hotels on and near Serdán. **Casa de Huéspedes Lupita** (Calle 15 No. 125, tel. 622/2–84–09) is only a few blocks from Serdán and the bus terminals. Singles with bath are $7, doubles $9. Without bath the prices drop to $5 and $7 (respectively) and you might as well save your dough—the communal baths are pleasant, and the lukewarm water doesn't get any warmer in the pricier rooms. Although the area around **Motel del Puerto** (Yañez 92, off Abelordo L. Rodríguez, tel. 622/4–34–08 or 622/2–24–91) is seedy at night, its basic, clean rooms have fresh sheets, curtains, clean bathrooms, hot water, and air-conditioning. Singles are $11, doubles $15, and the lobby even has a long-distance telephone. For a slightly higher price, the same level of cleanliness and comfort can be found at **Hotel Santa Rita** (Serdán, at Calle 9, tel. 622/4–14–64 or 622/2–81–00), a short walk from the center of town. Small rooms with TV and air-conditioning are available for $15

137

(singles) and $18 (doubles). They take traveler's checks, AmEx, and Visa, and have some wheelchair-accessible rooms.

FOOD

Serdán is lined with reasonably priced restaurants, bars, *loncherías* (snack bars), and taquerías serving fresh local seafood and typical Mexican dishes. Buy fresh fruits and veggies at the **mercado municipal**, in a long building one block south of Serdán, near the intersection with Yáñez. If you prefer to splurge, **Del Mar** (Calle 17, at Serdán, tel. 622/4–02–25) serves high-quality cuts of beef and excellent fresh seafood dishes such as shrimp flambé ($7) and lobster burritos ($6) in a cool, dark refuge from the sun. For a traditional Mexican breakfast, **Restaurant Las Cazuelas** (Av. 12, at Calle 15, tel. 622/2–65–96) serves eggs, rice, and beans ($2.50) and a tasty comida corrida ($3). They're open Tuesday–Saturday 8 AM–9 PM, and Sundays until 3 PM. **Restaurant Todos Comen** (Serdán, at Calle 15, tel. 622/2–11–00; open daily 7 AM–midnight) has a selection of breakfast dishes, most under $3. Later on, they serve fish fillet ($3) and *bistec ranchero* (steak cooked with chiles, tomatoes, and onions; $5).

Near Guaymas

SAN CARLOS

The desert escapes into the azure waves of the Sea of Cortéz at San Carlos, where Mt. Teta Kawi dominates the shoreline. More and more diving enthusiasts from the United States call this town home, and you'll find them putting on the golf courses and schmoozing at nearby Club Med. If you have the cash, it's easy to participate in a number of watersports here, including sailing, kayaking, jet skiing, and—for a slower pace—fishing. San Carlos hosts an international fishing tournament in July and a multilevel sailing competition called Cristóbal Colón (Christopher Columbus) around October 12.

COMING AND GOING Buses marked SAN CARLOS leave from Serdán in Guaymas every half-hour, starting at 6 AM (30 min, $1), and the last bus returns to Guaymas from San Carlos at 9 PM. Taxis and cars provide the only means of transportation to the less populated beaches of **Frenchie's Cove, Lalo Cove** (both about 7 kilometers from the center of town), **Catch 22** beach (8 kilometers), and **Las Mangas** (16 kilometers, $7 by taxi).

WHERE TO SLEEP Unless you've got a tent, you'll want to make San Carlos a day trip. The cheapest hotels are **Hotel Fiesta** (at entrance to town, 1½ km down main road, tel. 622/6–02–29) and **Motel Crestón** (tel. 622/6–00–20), but both charge more than $30 for double rooms. Both have a pool, long-distance phone service, and accept Visa and MasterCard, but Hotel Fiesta has a private beach and a restaurant. For $7 a night you can camp at **Teta Kawi Trailer Park** (behind Best Western, tel. 622/6–02–20), just outside town toward Guaymas, or next door at **Totonaka Trailor Park** and take advantage of the swimming pools and nearby laundry ($1.50). Beach camping is legal but watch your stuff—there can be a lot of foot traffic at night. The best places to camp are **Playa San Francisco** (just before entrance to town), **Lalo Cove**, and **Catch 22** (in front of Howard Johnson's).

FOOD Food stands along the main street are the cheapest way to fill your belly. However, if you want to have a real sit-down meal, try **Rosa Cantina** (tel. 622/6–10–00) on the main drag, which has a long list of breakfast items ($3), a salad bar ($2.50), and pork chops ($5.50). The **San Carlos Grill** (at turnoff to the marina, tel. 622/6–05–09) specializes in Lingo Gringo (beef fillet, $5) accompanied by a frosty margarita ($1.50).

OUTDOOR ACTIVITIES You can rent anything on the main beach, from windsurfing equipment ($20 an hr), to Jet Skis ($55 an hr), to banana boat rides where you're pulled behind a boat on a rubber float ($5.50 an hr). Diving is also big in San Carlos: **El Mar Diving Center** (263 Creston, tel. 622/6–04–04), **Gary's** (near El Mar on the main road), and **Cortés Explorations** (near the marina, tel. 622/6–08–08) all rent quality gear and organize trips. A two-tank dive to sites off nearby islands goes for $60 (add another $30 if you need equipment) and resort courses are $70. Gary's also organizes fishing trips.

CIUDAD OBREGON

Ciudad Obregón, 130 kilometers southeast of Guaymas, is surrounded by fields of corn, cotton, and shrubbery that magically spill over with daisies, roses, orchids, sunflowers, gardenias, and gladiolas in the spring. There isn't much else to see or do in Obregón, but if you want to be able to boast to those back home that you spent the night in the garbanzo capital of the world, or if you just have to get off that damn bus for a day, this isn't the worst place to end up. There's a movie theater ($2) down the street from the bus station, and **Biblioteca Pública Museo de los Yaquis** (Allende, at 5 de Febrero, tel. 641/14–31–55; open weekdays 8–6) holds an extensive collection of Yaqui crafts.

COMING AND GOING Obregón is on Highway 15, and most buses headed north and south make a stop here. The **bus station** (tel. 641/2–12–71) is in the southeast corner of town, near the junction of Rodolfo Elías Calles and California. Daily trains depart from the **train station** in the sketchy neighborhood near Sufragio and Guerrero, about two kilometers northeast of the bus station.

WHERE TO SLEEP If you must spend the night, **Casa de Huéspedes Nayarit** (5 de Febrero 771, at Rodolfo Elías Calles, tel. 641/6–75–59) is clean and air-conditioned. Singles cost $10, doubles $14. The friendly family who runs **Restaurant Lonchería Ruíz** (in front of bus station) will set you up in a run-down but comfortable, air-conditioned single for $7; doubles cost $9. If worse comes to worst, **Casa de Huéspedes Bien Estar** (California 511, near Zaragoza, no phone) can put you up in one of its 11 cells (all with access to a grimy communal bath lacking privacy and hot water) for $5 (doubles or singles).

FOOD Taquerías and other fast-food stands crowd the streets, especially near the bus terminal. In front of the bus station, **Restaurant Lonchería Ruíz** (no phone; open 24 hours) serves a flavorful plate of *pollo asado* (grilled chicken; $2). The modern **Santa Anita** (cnr of 6 de Abril and Tobasco, 4 blocks NE of bus station, no phone), open daily 7–midnight, serves a large-portioned daily special plus dessert and a drink for $3. **Merendero La Reja** (Nuevo León 532 Sur, at Niños Héroes, tel. 641/13–46–01) specializes in *cabrito* (kid; $8).

ALAMOS

This small city, 53 kilometers east of Navojoa, is one of the oldest in northern Mexico. Once the land of the indigenous Guarijio people, Alamos was converted into a silver mining town by European businessmen seeking their fortune. It may be a bit complicated to reach, but once you get here, the narrow cobblestone streets, horseback ranchers in cowboy hats, and secluded haciendas with elegant inner courtyards may charm you into staying longer than you had planned.

Entertainment in Alamos comes in the form of exploring the crumbling adobe buildings. The **Iglesia de la Purísima Concepción** has a towering three-tier bell tower and impressive architecture, while the beautiful **Hotel Mansión de la Condesa Magdalena** (Obregón, tel. 642/8–02–21) is worth peeking into even though you probably can't afford to stay. **Plaza de las Armas** is a beautiful park that livens with kids, couples, and people-watchers as soon as the sun dips below the horizon. At the north end of the plaza, the **Museo Costumbrista de Sonora** (admission: 50¢) also merits a visit for its displays on Sonora's history. It's open Wednesday–Sunday 9–1 and 3–6. During summer months, *brincadores*, or Mexican jumping beans (actually, butterfly larva) can be seen hopping around **Parque Chalatón**. From the plaza, walk south down Juárez, make a right on Mina (which turns into Chihuahua), and go left on Chalatón.

BASICS You can change cash or traveler's checks 8:30–1 at the **Bancomer** (tel. 642/8–03–25) at the south end of Plaza de las Armas, but there are no ATMs anywhere in the city. The **post office** is next to the police station on Madero. There are no public phones on the streets here, but Polo's Restaurant (tel. 642/8–00–01), at the far end of Zaragoza, has a small caseta that charges $1.50 for collect and credit-card calls. The **tourist office** (tel. 642/8–04–50) below Hotel Los Portales, is open weekdays 9–2 and 4–7, Saturday 9–2. You can rent bicycles ($1 an hr) on Plaza de las Armas, next to Bancomer, 8–1 and 3–6, but it will be a bumpy ride along the cobblestone streets.

COMING AND GOING Alamos is only accessible by car or a local bus from the town of Navojoa. After the **Transportes del Pacífico** bus from Guaymas lets you off at the corner of Revolución and Guerrero in Navojoa, walk 10 minutes down Guerrero (toward the town center) to a small terminal at the corner of Rincón. Buses leave here for Alamos (1 hr, $1) every 40 minutes 6:30 AM–midnight. From Alamos, hourly buses (last bus 6:30 PM) make the return trip to Navojoa from the station on Morelos, at Plaza Alameda.

WHERE TO SLEEP Rooms in Alamos are not cheap. The short walk to **Motel Somar** (Madero 110, tel. 642/8–01–95) from the center of town is more than compensated for by the reasonable prices ($14 singles, $16 doubles), comfortable, wheelchair-accessible rooms with fans, and fairly clean, private bathrooms. If you know you'll be staying here, ask the bus driver to drop you off when you see the MOTEL SOMAR sign on your left as you enter town. Next door, **Dolisa Motel** (Madero 72, tel. 642/8–01–31) has singles ($15) and doubles ($17) with TV, air-conditioning, and possibly a fridge (depending on the room). **Hotel Casa de los Tesoros** (Obregón 10, behind cathedral, tel. 642/8–00–10), a former convent, has also been beautifully restored, and has air-conditioning, fireplaces, an inner courtyard with a pool, and a restaurant serving Mexican and Puerto Rican food. Singles are $42, doubles $50, and it's wheelchair accessible.

➤ **CAMPING** • The **Dolisa Motel** (see Where to Sleep, above) has a big, dirt lot where you can pitch a tent ($4.50 for 2 people) or park an RV ($10). There are also a few RV parks where $10 will get you a tent site for two with showers and a swimming pool; try **Trailer Park Acosta Ranch** (tel. 642/8–02–46), just over a kilometer from town near the cemetery, and **Los Alamos Trailer Park** (tel. 642/8–03–32), at the entrance of town on the highway.

FOOD The vendors clustered around Plaza Alameda serve tacos and such for about $1. The **mercado municipal** (east end of plaza) has inexpensive meats, cheeses, and locally grown fruits and vegetables, but you can eat almost as cheaply at some local restaurants. **Taquería Blanquita** (Antonio Rosales, next to market) is packed with locals from 6 AM until 11 PM. Long, get-to-know-your-neighbor tables are generously stocked with chile and guacamole to dress the $2 comida corrida. The air-conditioned **Restaurant Bar María Bonita** (Rosales 36, tel. 642/8–04–92) overlooks a garden and serves terrific, reasonably priced food. Breakfasts are $3, plates of tostadas or enchiladas are $4, and fish or shrimp with rice, beans, and salad is $7. **Las Palmeras** (Plaza de las Armas, tel. 642/8–00–65; open daily 7 AM–10 PM) has outdoor patio seating with a view of the church, $3 vegetable salads, and real coffee.

Los Mochis

Just over the **Sonora-Sinaloa border** on Highway 15, the agricultural boomtown of Los Mochis is surrounded by farmland. The city was founded in 1893 by Benjamin Johnston, who managed to buy huge quantities of land during Porfirio Díaz's massive land grab (just before the turn of the century). During this time almost one fifth of the entire Republic was turned over to Díaz's friends and foreign investors. Díaz developed sugar production in this area, and brought the Chihuahua al Pacífico railroad across the Sierra Madre Occidental mountains to Los Mochis. Today, most tourists pass through only to catch that train for the famous Copper Canyon ride, or to board a Baja-bound ferry. Aside from this, Los Mochis and its environs boast few points of local interest, apart from the town's lively Sunday morning market, or the remains of Johnston's opulent estate, with its pleasant botanical garden.

BASICS

AMERICAN EXPRESS The AmEx representative in **Viajes Krystal** changes traveler's checks and provides cardholder services (mail service, advances on AmEx cards, and personal check cashing). The travel agency (open Mon.–Sat. 8:30–6:30, Sun. 10–1) also sells plane, bus, and train tickets (1st class only). *Alvaro Obregón 471-A Pte., Los Mochis, Sinaloa, CP 81200, México. Tel. 681/2-20-84 or 681/2-41-39. Open weekdays 8:30-1 and 3-6:30, Sat. 8:30-2.*

BOOKSTORES Librería Los Mochis has a wide selection of literature in Spanish, as well as a few English newspapers and magazines. *Madero 402, at Leyva, tel. 681/5-72-42. Open daily 8 AM-10 PM.*

CASAS DE CAMBIO A number of banks and several casas de cambio line Calle Leyva downtown. **Servicio de Cambio** (Leyva 271 Sur, near Juárez, tel. 681/2-56-66) changes cash and traveler's checks weekdays 8 AM-7:30 PM, and Saturdays until 7 PM. If you get going early, you can get much better rates at **Bancomer** (Leyva, at Juárez, tel. 681/5-80-01): The exchange window is open until 1 PM, but try to be in line by noon.

EMERGENCIES You can reach the **police, fire department,** or **ambulance** service by dialing 06 from any public phone.

LAUNDRY The self-serve **Lavarama** is around the corner from the bus terminals. Automatic washers cost $1.50, dryers $2, soap 50¢, and they'll do it all for you for another 50¢ per load. *Juárez 225, tel. 681/2-81-20. Open daily 8-7.*

MAIL The post office will hold mail sent to you at the following address for up to 10 days: Lista de Correos, Los Mochis, Sinaloa, CP 81281, México. *226 Ordóñez Pte., tel. 681/2-08-23. Open weekdays 8-6:30, Sat. 9-1.*

MEDICAL AID **Farmacia San Jorge** (Flores and Independencia, tel. 681/5-74-74) is open 24 hours. For more urgent medical attention, the 24-hour **Centro Médico de Los Mochis** has some English-speaking doctors. *Rosendo G. Castro, btw Allende and Guillermo Prieto, tel. 681/2-74-26 or 681/2-01-98.*

PHONES Most of the public phones on the streets seem to be just for show, and the ones that work are surrounded by noisy traffic. At the quiet **Fax Tel** (Leyva, btw Hidalgo and Obregón, tel. and fax 681/8-10-20), you can make local or long-distance cash calls and use the fax machine 8 AM-10 PM daily.

VISITOR INFORMATION The small tourist office in the **Unidad Administrativo** building is intimidatingly disguised as a private office, behind dark, reflective windows. Don't be deterred: The English-speaking staff is happy to help you. *Allende, at Cuauhtémoc, tel. 681/2-66-40. Open weekdays 8-3 and 4-7.*

COMING AND GOING

BY BUS Unless you're heading straight to Chihuahua via the Copper Canyon, traveling by bus is the easiest way to leave Los Mochis. The **Tres Estrellas de Oro** (tel. 681/2-17-57) terminal is on Juárez, at Degollado. The **Transportes Norte de Sonora** (tel. 8-49-67) and **Transportes del Pacífico** (tel. 681/2-03-41) terminals are a few blocks north of downtown, side-by-side on José María Morelos between Leyva and Zaragoza. All three stations are open 24 hours, but none have luggage storage. The busier terminals on Morelos offer first- and second-class service to Mazatlán (6 hrs, $10-$12), Guadalajara (11 hrs, $22-$27), Mexico City (24 hrs, $32-$44), Nogales (10 hrs, $15-$20), Mexicali (22 hrs, $23-$30), Tijuana (24 hrs, $25-$32), and Navojoa (3 hrs, $4-$5).

BY TRAIN The railroad station (tel. 681/2-93-85), 2 kilometers from downtown on the southeastern outskirts of town, is the southwestern terminus of the famous **Chihuahua al Pacífico** iron rooster that winds its way through the Copper Canyon region (*see* Chapter 5). If you only take one train ride in Mexico, this should be it. Two trains depart from Los Mochis in the morning, arriving in Chihuahua (13 hrs; $24 1st class, $7 2nd class) some 12 hours later: the first-class *Vista,* departing at 6 AM with stops in the Copper Canyon towns of Bahuichivo (6½ hrs, $10), Divisadero (7½ hrs, $11), and Creel (9½ hrs, $13); and the second-class *Mixto* (also called *pollero* or *burro*), departing at 7 AM and costing about $3, $4, and $5 for the same stops. The amount of time the Mixto train will take to arrive in any given destination is anybody's guess, but you can be sure it won't be fast.

Buy tickets a day in advance if you can; travel agencies and most hotels sell tickets for the Vista train, but Mixto tickets are available only at the train station. Although buses marked COL. FERR. go to the train station, they don't operate in the early morning and are therefore useless to most travelers, since this is precisely when the trains leave. Instead, look for taxis ($5) in front of Hotel Santa Rita on Leyva and Hidalgo. Travelers heading north toward Mexicali ($24 1st class, $8 2nd class) or south to Guadalajara ($25 1st class, $7 2nd class) need to depart from the Sufragio station on the **Ferrocarril del Pacífico** line (tel. 681/4-01-28). To reach Sufragio, take a bus headed for El Fuerte (50 min).

BY FERRY You can buy tickets for a Sematur ferry to La Paz (on the Baja Peninsula) at **Viajes Paotam** (Serapio Rendón 517 Pte., tel. 681/5-19-14) in Los Mochis; open Monday-Saturday 8-1 and 3-7, Sunday 9-1. Second class (a hard seat) is $10, tourist class (a cushy seat) $20, a cabin $30. Be sure to buy tickets at least 24 hours in advance if you're determined to leave on a specific day. Second-class ferries leave weekdays, those with tourist class and cabins only Wednesdays and Thursdays. Ferries leave from the dock in Topolobampo, 25 kilometers west of Los Mochis, at around 10 AM, and the trip takes about nine hours. Buses marked TOPOLOBAMPO (60¢) leave from the corner of Cuauhtémoc and Prieto every 15 minutes 6 AM-8 PM, stopping along Boulevard Rosendo G. Castro on the way out of town. They also leave from the Alianza de Transportes de Norte Sinaloa on Calle Zaragoza.

BY PLANE The Los Mochis airport, 20 kilometers south of town, is served primarily by **Aerocalifornia** (tel. 681/5-21-30 or 681/5-22-50) and **Aeroméxico** (tel. 681/5-25-70), which provide limited service to major Mexican cities such as Guadalajara ($130) and Mazatlán ($75), and to Tucson ($160) or Los Angeles ($150). Depending on the season, students can receive a discount of up to 25%, so it's worth mentioning. Take a taxi to the airport ($12) or else take the TOPOLABAMPO bus to the main crossroads (look for the sign that says AIRPORT 5 KILOMETERS) and either walk the five kilometers to the airport or hitch a ride.

GETTING AROUND

Los Mochis is easily navigated, and everything but the train station, airport, and ferry terminal is accessible on foot. Calles Allende, Guillermo Prieto, Zaragoza, and Leyva run parallel to each other, with hotels, drugstores, restaurants, and just about anything else you could need clustered between Boulevard Castro and Avenida Madero. People congregate at **Plaza Fiesta Las Palmas** and the nearby **Parque Sinaloa**, at the corner of Avenida Obregón and Boulevard Antonio Rosales. City buses are easily hailed all around town, and many originate at the **mercado**, at Guillermo Prieto and Cuauhtémoc (20¢).

WHERE TO SLEEP

Most budget accommodations in the downtown area need a good scrubbing but are fairly comfortable and centrally located. Above Bar Apache 7, **Hotel Los Arcos** (Allende 534 Sur, btw Castro and Obregón, tel. 681/2-32-53) features lousy air-conditioning and a grimy communal bathroom with hot water. The tiny rooms need painting, but the management is always cheery and the price is right; singles are $5, doubles $7. The interior of **Hotel del Parque** (Obregón 600, tel. 681/2-02-60) is better than the exterior would lead you to believe, but not by much. This wheelchair-accessible hotel, close to the refreshingly vegetated Plazuela del 27 de Septiembre, offers basic rooms with fans for $10 (singles) and $12 (doubles), but there's no hot water in the bathrooms. **Hotel del Valle** (Guillermo Prieto, at Independencia, tel. 681/2-01-05) is fairly modern, and those with cash-flow problems will be happy to find that Visa and MasterCard are accepted here. The shabby but comfortable rooms have fans and bathrooms with hot water. Singles start at $10, doubles at $12 (with TV and phone, $13 and $15 respectively). The colonial-style **Hotel Montecarlo** (Ángel Flores 322 Sur, at Independencia, tel. 681/2-18-18) is tucked between a restaurant and a noisy bar in the downtown area, not far from the cathedral. Rooms on the second story have small balconies, and all rooms have air-conditioning, TV, a phone, and clean bathrooms with hot water. Singles are $13, doubles $19 ($21 with wheelchair access).

CAMPING Los Mochis Trailer Park (1 km west of Hwy. 15, tel. 681/2-68-17) charges $10 for two people and is almost 2 kilometers out of town. In addition to the communal bath facilities, there are coin-op laundry machines and a recreation room.

FOOD

The downtown area teems with fish, taco, and fruit stands. The **mercado municipal** (Guillermo Prieto, at Cuauhtémoc Pte.) has excellent fresh vegetables and fruits, a huge fish and meat market, and several decent *comedores* (sit-down food stands). **Restaurant Chic's** (Plaza Fiesta, Rosales, at Obregón, tel. 681/5-47-09), a few blocks west of downtown, seems characterless, but once the families start strolling in after mass, it's a good place to people-watch. Try the $4 breakfast of tamales, *chorizo* (spicy sausage), and beans, or the fresh fruit plate ($3). Chic's is open daily 6:30 AM–midnight. **El Taquito** (Leyva, btw Hidalgo and Independencia, tel. 681/2-81-19) not only looks like Denny's and tastes like Denny's, but it's open 24 hours for late-night binges, just like Denny's. Mushroom omelets and French toast (both $3) are served for breakfast, and hamburgers and fries are on the menu for lunch ($3). **El Farallón** (Obregón, at Ángel Flores, tel. 681/2-14-28), specializing in fresh, spicy seafood, is a favorite of Los Mochis businessmen. Dishes such as calamari ($10) and ceviche ($5) come with tortillas and beans. **Jugos Chapala** (Independencia 366; open 7 AM–11 PM) has fresh carrot, strawberry, and papaya juices (to name a few) for $1–$2. For a drink with more kick, try the bar at **Hotel Santa Anita** (Leyva, btw Obregón and Hidalgo, tel. 681/8-70-46), open daily 11 AM–2 AM.

> Minors, women, and uniformed men aren't allowed in most cantinas in Los Mochis. If you qualify for entrance, you'll see men letting loose their repressions, fighting, hugging, caressing, crying, and, finally, stumbling home wrapped in each other's arms.

CHEAP THRILLS

If you happen to be here on Sunday around 11 AM, be sure to visit the *tianguis* (open-air market), in the downtown shopping area (on Leyva, just across Rendon), where all kinds of supermarket-style junk is sold. The city's locals flock here once church services are over, and the shops and stalls are packed with hagglers. Come early, though—everything closes down by 2 PM.

The **Parque Ecológico de Sinaloa** occupies the grounds of sugar baron and town founder Benjamin Johnston's former estate. This park is home to trees imported from around the world, such as towering palms from Cuba and fuzzy cypress from Arizona. Near the entrance, a giant tree bears Indian carvings of an eagle, bear, snake, deer, and other animals, including Mr. Johnston himself. There's also a children's playground right in front of the gardens, where, if you're lucky, you can join an impromptu soccer game. *On Rosales, behind Woolworth shopping center, no phone. Open daily 8–7.*

The free **Museo Regional del Valle del Fuerte** has photographs, artifacts, and notes (in Spanish) illustrating the history of northern Mexico. *Calle Obregón, just east of Rosales, no phone. Open daily 10–1 and 4–7.*

Near Los Mochis

Buses headed for the towns of Topolobampo and El Fuerte depart Los Mochis from the **Alianza de Transportes de Norte Sinaloa** station on Zaragoza between Cuauhtémoc and Ordóñez, just west of the post office. Buses to Topolobampo (40 min, 60¢) leave about every half hour 7 AM–8 PM. If you're heading for La Paz, don't get off at the first bus station in Topolobampo— the bus will continue on to the ferry dock, or you could take a taxi for less than $2. Buses to El Fuerte (1½ hrs, $2.50) depart a little less often, 7 AM–6 PM.

TOPOLOBAMPO

About 25 kilometers west of Los Mochis is the town of Topolobampo, founded at the end of the 19th century by a bunch of Americans looking to set up a socialist utopia. This dream was soon squashed when the colonists began fighting amongst themselves and Los Mochis sugar baron Benjamin Johnston managed to scoop up the water rights to the area and evict everybody. Today, the harbor town is largely dependent on shrimping and industry, and sea lions frolic in the deep bay, using Isla El Farallón, just off the coast, as a breeding ground. You are most likely to come here only to get on or off the ferry, but if you do stay a day or two you can take advantage of the spectacular natural surroundings of this less-than-spectacular town.

Although the harbor itself lacks swimming or sunning beaches, shell collectors will have a ball here. Boat rides to the five islands in the bay near Topolobampo can be arranged through Teodolfo Cital at the **Sociedad Cooperativa de Servicios Turísticos,** which looks like a vacant, unfinished house (next to the customs building, on the water). They'll take groups of eight people to the virgin beach at **Playa Copas** ($25 a person), the duck sanctuary at **Isla Santuario** ($25 a person), **Isla Santa María** ($50 a person), or **Isla El Farallón,** where the sea lions play in clear water ($117 a person, including fishing equipment). They also take shorter fishing trips around the bay for $17 an hour. Bargaining is always an option. Lodging in Topolobampo is scarce and expensive, and camping is unsafe. If you're stuck, you can get a $12 dorm bed at **Pensión Paotám** (at the ferry dock), or pay $17 for a single, $33 for a double.

EL FUERTE

The desert town of El Fuerte was originally founded in 1564 as a gateway to the northern Indian territories of Sonora, Arizona, and California. It was not easily won land for the Spanish, however, and they spent the next 50 years fending off the fierce Tehueco, Sinaloa, and Zuaque Indians. In 1610 a fort was built here, and the following three centuries saw the area around El Fuerte grow into one of the most important commercial and agricultural centers in northeastern Mexico.

Today this small colonial city, 75 kilometers east of Los Mochis, attracts fishermen to nearby **Lake Hidalgo** (11 kilometers north), **Lake Domínguez** (19 kilometers west), and the **Fuerte River** (a 10-minute walk west from the plaza), all known for their largemouth bass. If you didn't bring your fishing gear, you can swim in the lakes or the river, or enjoy the town's few attractions, including **La Iglesia del Sagrado Corazón de Jesús** (church of the Sacred Heart of Jesus), built in 1854; the **Palacio Municipal**; and **La Casa de la Cultura** (admission free, open 10–7 daily), all of which surround the shaded Plaza de Armas at Degollado and Rosales. Perhaps the best reason to visit El Fuerte is to splurge on a room at **Posada Hidalgo** (Hidalgo, just off plaza, tel. 681/5–70–46), a former colonial mansion. At $40 for two people, it has exotic gardens, outdoor patios, and a swimming pool. The staff is also more than willing to provide you with information on the city's attractions, whether or not you're a guest. Stop at **Restaurant Supremo** (cnr of Rosales and Constitución) for fresh bass ($5) and a ham and egg breakfast ($3).

NORTH CENTRAL MEXICO AND THE COPPER CANYON

5

By Shayna Samuels with Viviana Mahieux

The north central states of Chihuahua and Durango are characterized by their vast deserts, which circle the magnificent Sierra Madre Occidental mountain range. Regal cactus and run-down *ranchitos* (small farms) freckle the landscape, and when farmers aren't working the tomato, green pepper, and corn fields, they can be heard gossiping behind the closed doors of local bars. Two founding fathers of contemporary Mexico, Miguel Hidalgo and Pancho Villa, called this region home, and today north central Mexico remains at the forefront of popular dissent—Chihuahua being a longstanding bastion of support for the PAN (Mexico's leading opposition party). A five-year drought currently plagues the region, however, and small farmers now fight financial hardship as their livelihoods wither with dying crops and animals.

The highlights of this region begin to reveal themselves after you pass the overpopulated, drug-infested border town of Ciudad Juárez. Many tourists are attracted to the enigmatic pre-Columbian ruins of Paquimé and the lively, historic city of Chihuahua, although most visit the state of Chihuahua (which means "dry, sandy place" in the Tarahumara language) for its natural beauty. The Sierra Madre Occidental comprises five large canyons, through which thread massive waterfalls, rivers, and hot springs. The most famous being the Copper Canyon, in the Sierra Tarahumara. The 670-kilometer-long Chihuahua al Pacífico railway weaves through the canyons, conveniently stopping at popular jumping-off points for hiking and camping in the canyon such as Creel, Divisadero, and Bahuichivo. These mountains have been inhabited for centuries by the indigenous Tarahumara people. While some have been displaced due to the mining and lumber industries, 50,000 still uphold traditional culture on their original lands. The train also passes through the village of Cuauhtémoc, sometimes called the "granary of the state," where a group of German Mennonites have lived since 1921. Known for their austere lifestyle and efficient agricultural techniques, they generally remain culturally isolated from the rest of Mexico.

The dusty landscape around the capital city of the state of Durango is what many people picture when they think of Mexico—probably because it's been used as the setting for a number of Hollywood westerns. The city of Durango itself is a pleasant surprise for most travelers: Once you get past the urban sprawl at the outskirts, you'll find a friendly colonial city with pretty streets perfect for aimless wandering.

Ciudad Juárez

If you find yourself in Ciudad Juárez, leave fast. Only hang around if: (1) you are in need of an inexpensive root canal; (2) you are planning on getting married at least 25 times and want the perfect dress for each occasion; or (3) you are wanted by the law on both sides of the border and want to be able to hop jurisdictions easily. Yes, Ciudad Juárez exhibits the worst aspects of both Mexico and the United States: U.S. companies set up plants here to capitalize on cheap Mexican labor, and a majority of Juárez's population currently works in *maquiladoras* (foreign-owned factories in duty-free zones). Many Mexicans are injured or killed as they try to cross the border illegally; intense heat and cold in the workers' settlements not served by public utilities claim more lives; and toxic dumping, often by U.S. companies unwilling to pay hazardous-waste disposal fees in the States, exacts an additional health toll.

If you are stranded in Ciudad Juárez, consider it a sociological exercise, and try not to get too depressed. Make the best of it by admiring the city's turn-of-the-century architecture on Calle Panamá, or stock up on colorful trinkets at the Plaza de las Américas, Juárez's best attempt at a tourist trap. The city's more dubious offerings include a sleazy bar scene and a flourishing sex trade. However, you lucked out if you're passing through during the last two weeks of June: The **Feria Juárez** will be in full swing, featuring amusement-park rides and arts-and-crafts displays in the Parque del Chamizal on Colegio Militar. Another special event is the **Festival de la Raza**, celebrated during the first week of May with dancing, films, theater, and music, all culminating in a big **Cinco de Mayo** bash and a parade along Avenida Juárez.

BASICS

AMERICAN EXPRESS The AmEx representatives at **Sun Travel**, across the border in El Paso, can help with lost or stolen checks, insurance, and transportation arrangements. The office also sells traveler's checks, offers MoneyGram service, and holds mail for cardholders. The AmEx office in Juárez only offers travel services. *3100 North Mesa, Suite B, El Paso, Texas 79902, U.S.A, tel. 915/532–8900. Open weekdays 7:30–5:30. In Juárez: Av. Lincoln 1320, Local (suite) 175, tel. 16/29–27–40.*

CASAS DE CAMBIO Many money-exchange places line Avenida Juárez near the bridge. After business hours, try **Banamex's** *cajas permanentes* (ATMs), on the corner of Avenidas Juárez and 16 de Septiembre.

CONSULATES United Kingdom. *Fresno 185, tel. 16/18–73–51.*

United States. *López Mateos Nte. 924, tel. 16/13–40–50.*

CROSSING THE BORDER When entering Mexico, pick up a tourist card in El Paso at the immigration office (open 24 hours) near the Stanton Street Bridge, or at the **Mexican Consulate** (E. San Antonio St., tel. 915/533–3644; open weekdays 9–1). If you travel further than 32 kilometers from the border, you may be asked to show the card at checkpoints. Bringing a car into Mexico is complicated but possible (*see* Coming and Going, *below*). For more information, *see* Passports, Visas, and Tourist Cards in Chapter 1, or call the customs office at the border (tel. 16/16–08–25).

EMERGENCIES For emergency assistance (including **ambulance** service) call the **police** (tel. 16/15–15–98) in Ciudad Juárez, or dial 911 from any phone on the U.S. side of the border.

LAUNDRY Lavasolas. *5 de Mayo and Tlaxcala, tel. 16/12–54–61.*

MAIL The slightly chaotic and inconspicuous **post office** is located downstairs on Francisco Villa, at Calle De la Peña (just south of Av. 16 de Septiembre). It's open weekdays 9–7, Saturday 9–5, Sunday 9–noon.

MEDICAL AID Hospital General (Paseo Triunfo de la República 2401, tel. 16/13–15–71) offers emergency care but no English-speaking operators. **Farmacia Iris** (16 de Septiembre, at Corona, tel. 16/12–81–90) is small but is open Monday–Saturday until midnight.

PHONES Public phones here are dependable for cash, credit (Visa, MasterCard, and calling cards), and even collect calls. For Mexican long distance, dial 02; to call El Paso, dial 95; for other international calls, dial 09 or your long-distance carrier's access number.

VISITOR INFORMATION The **El Paso Tourism Office** (1 Civic Center Plaza, tel. 800/351–6024; open weekdays 8–5) provides information for travelers crossing into Mexico, as does the **El Paso Chamber of Commerce** (10 Civic Center Plaza, tel. 915/534–0512; open weekdays 8–5). Ciudad Juárez's **tourist office** is on the ground floor of the Palacio Municipal, just west of the Stanton Street Bridge. The friendly staff speaks English. *Villa, at malecón, tel. 16/15–23–01. Open weekdays 8–6, Sat. 9–1.*

COMING AND GOING

BY BUS The bus terminal (tel. 16/10–64–14) is way out of Juárez, at the junction of Highways 2 and 45. The monstrous building has two long-distance telephone offices, a money-changing booth, cafeterias, and 24-hour luggage storage (30¢ per hr). **Estrella Blanca** (tel. 16/29–22–29) has hourly service to Chihuahua (4½ hrs, $10), Nuevo Casas Grandes (4 hrs, $7), Mazatlán (21 hrs, $45), and Durango (14 hrs, $40). Four buses also depart daily to Mexico City (26 hrs, $49). **Transportes Chihuahuenses** (tel. 16/29–22–29) and **Tres Estrellas de Oro** serve the same routes, and **Turistar, Omnibus,** and **Futura** charge a few dollars more for *especial* first class (with air-conditioning, bathrooms, and onboard movies). **Greyhound** bus tickets can also be purchased here for trips to Los Angeles ($35), Albuquerque ($36), and Denver ($69), as well as other U.S. destinations. To reach the bus station from downtown, take a bus marked CENTRAL CAMIONERA and ask the bus driver where to get off; allow at least an hour. A taxi is faster and should cost $7 to downtown.

BY TRAIN The train station (Juan Gabriel, tel. 16/12–31–88) is 12 long blocks down the tracks from the Stanton Street Bridge. Two trains daily leave Ciudad Juárez headed south to Mexico City ($35 1st class, $20 2nd class) with stops in Chihuahua ($7 1st class, $4 2nd class), Zacatecas ($23 1st class, $13 2nd class), and Aguascalientes ($25 1st class, $14 2nd class). The second-class train leaves at 7 AM, and tickets go on sale at 6 AM. Tickets for the 10 PM first-class departure can be purchased in advance Monday–Saturday 9 AM–noon. They usually sell out, so plan ahead. If you're looking for a taxi from the station, it's better to walk a block or two toward downtown and hail one there, where prices are less likely to be inflated.

BY CAR You can bring a car into Mexico for a period of up to 90 days. To cross the border with your car, present the title (in your name) and a current driver's license. You also have to provide a guarantee (like your credit-card number) that you'll bring the car back across once your permit expires (if you don't you'll be charged a fine). Those without a credit card will have to buy a bond from one of the bond sellers close to the border. Customs officials don't care if you buy Mexican insurance or not, but a policeman farther south (or the 'other party' in case of an accident) might. Insurance is available from a number of companies near the border.

BY PLANE The airport is far from the center of town, just off Highway 45. **Aeroméxico** (tel. 16/13–80–89 or 800/237–6639 from the U.S.) is the main carrier, with daily flights to Chihuahua ($105 one-way), Mexico City ($105 one-way), and Mazatlán ($106 one-way). A taxi from downtown to the terminal costs $10, but it's cheaper to grab a CENTRAL CAMIONERA bus, get off at the bus station, and take a taxi the rest of the way.

GETTING AROUND

Juárez is spread out, and transport terminals are all far from each other. Fortunately, budget accommodations and restaurants cluster along Avenida Juárez between the Stanton Street Bridge and Avenida 16 de Septiembre. The downtown area is also fairly easy to navigate on foot. Unfortunately, finding local buses that travel to outlying points can be confusing, due to the number of one-way streets. Buses generally arrive and depart from Avenidas Lerdo and Vicente Guerrero, south of Avenida 16 de Septiembre. They run until midnight and tickets

(20¢) can be purchased from the driver. Bus 34 goes from the town square in El Paso (within walking distance of the border) to the El Paso airport. Taxis are plentiful, though not cheap—settle on a price before you get in, and don't hesitate to negotiate. Fares should run $1–$2 a kilometer. The local yellow pages also list several car rental options, including **Hertz** (Paseo Triunfo de la República, tel. 16/13–80–60), with cars for about $30 per day.

WHERE TO SLEEP

Most tourists stay in El Paso rather than Juárez, so lodging options are limited. The real cheapies are run-down and often charge by the hour, but there are several reasonable places on or near Avenida Juárez. Plan on arriving in Juárez's bus terminal during the day, however, because this area is not safe after dark. If you do, your best bet is to stay put: The station is brightly lit and sleeping here is probably safer than lugging your bags down a dark street. If you simply must reach a hotel before morning, call 16/12–00–17 for a taxi.

The small, wheelchair-accessible **Hotel Génova** (Moctezuma 569 Nte., off Colón and Lerdo, tel. 16/15–01–43) is off the beaten path, but at least you won't be kept awake by noise from the downtown discos. The friendly staff will turn on the air-conditioning in your room at no extra charge, and patience will bring hot water to your shower. Singles are $5.50, doubles $7, all with bath. The hot and noisy **Bombín Café Bary Hotel** (Colón, at Manuel Doblado, tel. 16/14–23–20) has plenty of Formica, Naugahyde, and chrome furniture. The rooms (singles $6, doubles $11.50) are decent though, and each has a private bathroom with hot water. The four-story **Hotel Juárez** (Lerdo 143 Nte., off 16 de Septiembre, tel. 16/15–02–98) is straight down from the Stanton Street Bridge on Lerdo. The rooms are a bit larger than average, and all have bathrooms in need of a scrubbing. Singles are $7.60, doubles $8.80. On the east side of Juárez, **Hotel Morán** (Juárez 264 Nte., tel. 16/15–08–12) is a favorite with families. The small but comfortable rooms feature pink bedspreads and baths with cranky plumbing. Singles and doubles are $15, with cable in every room.

HOSTELS **Gardner Hotel/Youth Hostel.** This hostel in El Paso is clean and the staff are friendly. It's also conveniently situated near the Mexican Consulate, the Greyhound bus station, and the border. You don't have to be an AYH or HI member to stay here, but prices are cheaper if you are. A dorm bed with a shared bath and communal kitchen privileges costs $12.50 ($15.50 nonmembers). Single rooms, with TV, phones, and shared or private baths are also available ($22.50 with shared bath). *311 E. Franklin St., El Paso, tel. 915/532–3661. No curfew. Laundry ($2 per load), luggage storage, sheets ($2). MC, V.*

FOOD

Restaurants and taco stands line Avenida Juárez, and the lively **mercado municipal** on Avenida 16 de Septiembre offers fresh fruit, vegetables, and cheeses. If you're a recent arrival to Mexico, be kind to your stomach: Wait a few days before diving mouth-first into every facet of the local menu. **Antojitos La Herradura** (A. González 184, tel. 16/12–09–32) serves a $5 *comida corrida* (pre-prepared lunch special) to satisfy even the hungriest traveler. For late-night cravings, **El Coyote Inválido** (Juárez 615, at Colón, tel. 16/14–27–27; open daily 7 AM–4 AM) is basic and economical. The $5 comida corrida and the *pollo en mole* (chicken in chile and chocolate sauce; $4.50) are the most popular dishes. Juárez's most tradition-steeped eatery, **Restaurant La Sevillana** (González 140 Pte., tel. 16/12–05–58; open daily 8–6), behind the old bullring, has been churning out the same dishes for 40 years. Try the pancakes and coffee ($3), or the *picadillo con chile verde* (shredded beef with green chile sauce; $5). **S-Mart**, an American-style supermarket, can be found at the entrance of Plaza de las Américas (Lincoln and 16 de Septiembre), Juárez's gringo shopping mall.

WORTH SEEING

Most of the city's main attractions are downtown, within walking distance of Avenida Juárez. Getting to the sights farther out will take planning, but if you're stuck here anyhow, it's worth

The Mexican Revolution officially ended in Ciudad Juárez with the signing of the Tratado de Ciudad Juárez (Juárez Treaty), which provided for the stepping down of Porfirio Díaz and his administration.

the extra hours to visit them. Bullfights occur on Sundays at the **Plaza de Toros Monumental** (Paseo Triunfo de la República and López Mateos) from April to August; the best time to catch a *charreada* (rodeo) is from April to October at the **López Mateos Charro** (Av. del Charro). For a dose of history, try the 19th-century customs building, **Antigua Aduana** (16 de Septiembre and Juárez, tel. 16/12–47–07; open Tues.–Sun. 10–6). The building now houses the **Museo de Historia** (admission free), a small collection including Madero's 1910 Mercedes Benz and Benito Juárez's carriage. For a look at indigenous artifacts and contemporary local art, take a bus marked 8A or PRONAF from Avenida 16 de Septiembre or Ignacio Mejía to the free **Museo de Arte y Historia** (tel. 16/16–74–13; open Tues.–Sun. 11–7).

AFTER DARK

Every storefront on Avenida Juárez not open during the day magically transforms into a disco or bar after dark, as teenagers from both sides of the border throw themselves into mass alcohol consumption. Since you won't get a wink of sleep amidst the train whistles and rock bands, you might as well paint on your acid-washed jeans and join the debauchery. Most places charge a $3–$8 cover, but if you come before 10 PM or on a slow night, you can often get in free. If you're a woman traveling alone, stay on your toes—the streets can be dangerous at night. Heavy-metal fans will like **Spanky's** (Juárez 887; open Thurs.–Sun. 8 PM–4 AM), where beer is served in *yardas* (literally, yards). **Alive** is a popular dance spot half a block from the Stanton Street Bridge, where the latest hip-hop is played in a cave-like den. To avoid this scene and enjoy a well-crafted mixed drink, head to the **Kentucky Club** (Juárez 629, tel. 16/14–99–90), a haven of Naugahyde couches and decades-old sports memorabilia. For slightly tamer bars and discos, try those across the street from Plaza de las Américas (Lincoln and 16 de Septiembre), or on Avenida Lincoln. You can also listen to strolling musicians at the **Plaza del Mariachi,** farther south on the east side of Avenida Juárez.

Nuevo Casas Grandes and Paquimé

The Paquimé ruins dissolve further into the soil with each passing "tiempo de aire," or windy season—visit while you still can.

Some 260 kilometers southwest of Ciudad Juárez lie the twin towns of Nuevo Casas Grandes and Casas Grandes. The true attraction of this area lies a short walk (and centuries) away—the elaborate maze-like ruins of Paquimé. Located near the aspen-lined Casas Grandes River, this site was inhabited by Pima, Concho, and Tolima peoples between AD 700 and 1500, and served as a center for trade with the Pueblo civilizations of the southwest United States. The ever-brown peaks of the Sierra Madre Occidental still surround these ruins, with their unique mixture of architectural styles: T-shaped doors (similar to those of Pueblo dwellings) coexist with Mesoamerican masonry techniques. Paquimé was a sophisticated settlement, whose residents raised fowl and manufactured jewelry. Today, you can still see evidence of this sophistication, from the recently restored heat-shielding walls to the intricate indoor plumbing systems. Although an on-site museum is being constructed, Paquimé's artifacts are now on display at the Museo Nacional de Antropología in Mexico City (*see* Worth Seeing, in Chapter 2). Admission to the ruins is about $1.50 (except Sundays when it's free), but if the caretaker's not there, you can just cruise on in. The ruins are open daily 10–5. All of the establishments listed below are in Nuevo Casas Grandes.

BASICS

CASAS DE CAMBIO Several banks and money-exchange places can be found at 5 de Mayo and Constitución. Both **Serfín** (open weekdays 9–1:30) and **Inverlat** (open weekdays 9–noon) change cash and traveler's checks and have ATMs that accept Visa, MasterCard, Cirrus, and Plus. **Cambios California** has better hours but changes cash only. *Constitución 207, tel. 169/4–32–32. Open weekdays 9–2 and 3:30–7, Sat. 9–2 and 3:30–6.*

MEDICAL AID The English-speaking **Dr. Amaro Prieto Saldovar** works in association with **Farmacia de la Clínica.** *5 de Mayo 404, tel. 169/4–07–70. Open daily 9 AM–11 PM.*

PHONES AND MAIL The full-service **post office** (16 de Septiembre, 1 block east of Obregón, tel. 169/4–20–16) is open weekdays 8–6, and Saturdays 8–1. You can find public phones in **Cambios California** (*see above*) and in **Denni's** and **Dino's** (*see* Where to Sleep and Eat, *below*). **Teléfono Larga Distancia** has a *caseta de larga distancia* (long-distance phone office) that allows collect and credit-card calls. *Obregón, near 5 de Mayo, across from Estrella Blanca bus terminal, tel. 169/4–12–71. Open Mon.–Sat. 9 AM–10 PM.*

COMING AND GOING

Most visitors use Nuevo Casas Grandes, a two-horse town 8 kilometers from Casas Grandes and the ruins, as a stopover between Juárez and Chihuahua, and visit Paquimé as a day excursion.

BY BUS Nuevo Casas Grandes has two terminals—**Omnibus** and **Estrella Blanca**—adjacent to one another on Obregón, at 5 de Mayo. Both have 10 buses daily to Juárez (4 hrs, $7) and at least seven buses to Chihuahua (5½ hrs, $9). Only Omnibus has air-conditioning, TV, and bathrooms. Neither station has luggage storage. To reach Casas Grandes and Paquimé from Nuevo Casas Grandes, grab an orange bus marked either COL JUAREZ or CASAS GRANDES (30¢) on Constitución and 16 de Septiembre. After a 15-minute ride you will be deposited at the zócalo in Casas Grandes. A 10-minute walk down Constitución past the park will take you to the ruins. The last bus returns to Nuevos Casas Grandes at 8:30 PM.

WHERE TO SLEEP AND EAT

Unfortunately, the few hotels in Nuevos Casas Grandes are rather expensive. Your best hope is the comfortable and friendly **Hotel Juárez** (Obregón 110, next to Estrella Blanca, tel. 169/4–02–33), where clean singles are $6, doubles $8 (plus a 15% discount if you flash a copy of this book). There's also a room that will hold up to five people for $17. **Motel Piñón** (Juárez 605, tel. 169/4–01–66) has a swimming pool and is everybody's favorite. Be sure to check out their private mini-museum of *ollas* (clay pots) from Paquimé. Singles are $18, doubles $20, and they accept Visa and MasterCard, as does the wheelchair-accessible **Hotel Paquimé** (Juárez 401, tel. 169/4–13–20). In the newly renovated part, singles are $18 and doubles $21, whereas in the old part, singles are $15 and doubles are $16. All include air-conditioning, TV, and a phone. You're just as well off at the **Hotel California** (Constitución 209, tel. 169/4–11–10), which bears a remarkable resemblance to the Holiday Inn, and has air-conditioned singles ($15) and doubles ($19).

Cheap food is scarce in Casas Grandes, so shoestring travelers will want to eat their fill in Nuevo Casas Grandes, where plenty of taquerías and restaurants can be found near the bus station or along Juárez. For a good sit-down meal try **Denni's** (Juárez 412, at Urueta, tel. 169/4–10–75), which bears no relation to the cheesy U.S. chain. A juicy T-bone steak is $7. **Dinno's Pizza** (Constitución and Minerva, tel. 169/4–02–40) makes a decent pie starting at about $5. **Nevería Chuchy** (Constitución 202, tel. 169/4–07–09) is a fun soda fountain with sandwiches ($1), burgers ($1.50), and ice-cream cones ($1); all the kids in town wind up here at some point during the day. Although you won't find a raging night life in Nuevo Casas, **El Bandido** (Juárez and Del Prado, tel. 169/4–03–29; open daily 1 PM–1 AM) fills up on weekends with locals who still enjoy shakin' it to the hits of the '80s.

Chihuahua

The city of Chihuahua, capital of Chihuahua state, lies on a high hilly plain some 375 kilometers south of Ciudad Juárez. Agriculture and lumber are the primary money makers here, so you won't get the feeling that you are a big, walking peso, as you may in its much poorer and more tourism-dependent neighbor to the north.

Chihuahua has long played a leading role in Mexican history: Founded in 1709, it witnessed the execution of Independence leaders Padre Miguel Hidalgo and Ignacio Allende. In 1847 it fell to U.S. forces, and was occupied by Pancho Villa's army during the Mexican Revolution. The days of invading hordes are long over, however, and the primary reason travelers visit today is the Copper Canyon train that stops here. There's no reason to hurry to leave, however—a day or two can happily be spent exploring the city's cathedral and historical museums. While touring the city, it's impossible not to recognize the indigenous Tarahumara people begging for money, most notably the women, wearing multi-layered, brightly colored blouses, skirts, and head coverings. You may also see an occasional Mennonite in somber dress. These generally reclusive people live in the community of Cuauhtémoc, a short train ride from Chihuahua, and are best known for their famous Mennonite or Chihuahua cheese.

Special events here include the **Feria de Santa Rita** (held the last two weeks of May), when Chihuahuenses pay homage to their patron saint with food, music, and regional crafts at the fairgrounds on the Carretera al Aeropuerto. Catch a rodeo during the state fair, **ExpoGan**, which is held at the Unión Ganadera (just outside town) in the second week of October. People come from all over the state on the eve of September 15 to celebrate **Mexican Independence** with a fireworks display at the Palacio del Gobierno. Holidays are also marked by bullfights, which are held at the **Plaza de Toros** (Lisboa, at Reforma).

BASICS

AMERICAN EXPRESS The AmEx representative in the **Rojo y Casavantes** travel agency sells traveler's checks, replaces lost or stolen checks and AmEx cards, and offers MoneyGram service, but doesn't exchange traveler's checks or cash personal checks. Cardholders can, however, have their mail held here. *Guerrero 1207, Chihuahua, Chihuahua, CP 31000, México, tel. 14/15-58-58. Open weekdays 9-6, Sat. 9-noon.*

CASAS DE CAMBIO Most banks change money weekdays 9:30-noon, but several on Avenida Independencia have ATMs. **Serfín's** ATM (Independencia, at Juárez) accepts Visa, MasterCard, Cirrus, and Plus. The best rates for cash (and the shortest lines) are at **Centro de Cambio Rachasa** (Independencia 401, at Victoria, tel. 14/15-14-14; open Mon.-Sat. 9-9). They change traveler's checks and cash, but charge a 2% commission. The best hours (and good rates) can be found at **Grupo Rachasa** (Niños Héroes 800, at Ocampo, tel. 14/15-36-62), open daily 9-9.

EMERGENCIES As in the United States, you can dial 911 from any phone here for emergency assistance.

MAIL The post office is in the Palacio Federal, just opposite the old Palacio del Gobierno. They offer all the usual services and will hold mail sent to you at the following address for up to 10 days: Lista de Correos, Admon. 1, Chihuahua, Chihuahua, CP 31000, México. *Libertad, btw Carranza and Guerrero, tel. 14/15-14-17. Open weekdays 8-7, Sat. 9-1.*

MEDICAL AID **Clínica del Parque** (Calle de la Llave, at Calle 12a, tel. 14/15-74-11) offers 24-hour emergency service and has some English-speaking doctors. For a dentist, try **Central Médico Dental** (Niños Héroes 606, tel. 14/16-18-80), open Monday-Saturday 9-1 and 4-8. About three blocks from the Palacio del Gobierno is the 24-hour **Farmacia Mendoza** (Aldama 1901, tel. 14/16-44-14). Though not technically open, many pharmacies advertise *servicio nocturno* (night service); ring their buzzer at any hour of the night and wake somebody if necessary.

PHONES You'll find Ladatel public phones on the main square. For cash calls, the Central Camionera (*see* Coming and Going, *below*) has a caseta de larga distancia, but it doesn't allow

Chihuahua City

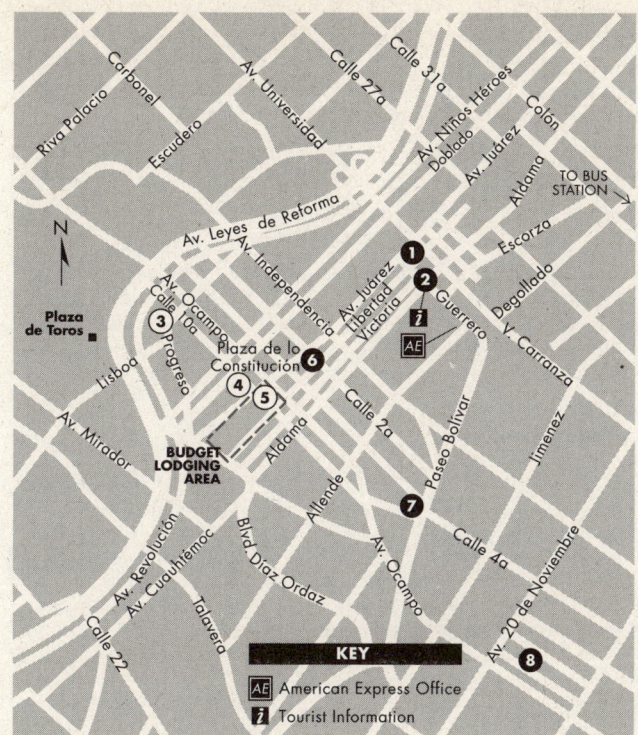

Sights ●
Catedral Metropolitana de Chihuahua, **6**
Palacio del Gobierno, **2**
Palacio Federal, **1**
Museo de la Revolución Mexicana, **8**
Quinta Gameros, **7**

Lodgings ○
Hotel Carmen **5**
Hotel del Cobre **3**
Posada Aida **4**

collect or credit-card calls. Downtown, the staff of the **Servicio de Larga Distancia** (Independencia 608, near Morelos, tel. 14/10-24-00) may be persuaded to place a collect or credit-card call for a small fee (and a big smile).

VISITOR INFORMATION The state tourism office is in the Palacio de Gobierno. There's usually someone on duty who speaks English, and maps and brochures are plentiful. *Calle 11a, at Libertad, tel. 14/10-10-77. Open Mon.-Sat. 9-7, Sun. 9-2.*

COMING AND GOING

BY BUS Chihuahua is a main hub for bus transportation, and the companies serving its **Central Camionera** run routes all over Mexico. The modern terminal contains a phone office, 24-hour luggage storage (50¢ per hour), and a 24-hour cafeteria. Frequent first-class service is available to Creel (4½ hrs, $9), Ciudad Juárez (4½ hrs, $12), Mexico City (22 hrs, $46), Guadalajara (18 hrs, $38), Monterrey (12 hrs, $24.50), and Nuevo Casas Grandes (3 hrs, $9). To get here from downtown, take a city bus marked CENTRAL CAMIONERA from the corner of Ocampo and Juárez. If you arrive in town at night, your only choice is to take a taxi from the station to downtown: Don't let the driver charge you more than $5.

BY TRAIN If you're on your way to Creel, the ride on the **Chihuahua al Pacífico** (Méndez, at Calle 24a, tel. 14/20-70-47), the famous Copper Canyon train, is much more scenic than traveling by bus. Two trains run daily to Los Mochis ($24 1st class, $7 2nd class) stopping in Creel ($11 1st class, $3 2nd class), Divisadero ($13 1st class, $4 2nd class), Bahuichivo ($14.50 1st class, $4 2nd class), and Sufragio ($22 1st class, $6 2nd class). Leaving at 7 AM, the first-class *Vista* train passes through Creel around noon and arrives in Los Mochis about 9 PM. The second-class *Mixto* train leaves Chihuahua at 8 AM and arrives in Los Mochis anytime between midnight and 5 AM. As a rule, second-class trains always lollygag and arrive late, but all in all they aren't that bad. The windows open (they don't on first-class trains) and the crowd includes food vendors, musicians, and other colorful characters. To be certain of a first-class seat, you have to shell out extra dough to buy your ticket in advance from **Mexico by Train** (tel. 800/321–1699 in the U.S.). However, this is only really necessary during Semana Santa, the first week in July (when schools get out), and from late September to mid-November. To reach the terminal, take a bus marked COL. ROSALIA or STA. ROSA down Ocampo.

The station for the **Juárez–Chihuahua–México** route (tel. 14/10–5–14) is at the north entrance to town, just off Avenida Tecnológico. From here you can catch notoriously slow second-class trains to Ciudad Juárez ($4) and Mexico City ($13, 30 hrs). To get here, hop on a COLON bus from downtown.

BY PLANE The international airport is 14 kilometers out of town. Any bus marked COL. AEROPUERTO will get you here for about 35¢; a taxi will cost $6. **Aeroméxico** (tel. 19/800–90–999), **SAM** (tel. 14/16–28–28), and **Taesa** (tel. 91/800–90–463) all serve Chihuahua's airport with flights to U.S. cities like El Paso ($89 one-way) and Dallas ($249 one-way), as well as Mazatlán ($139 one-way) and Mexico City ($137 one-way).

GETTING AROUND

The downtown area, roughly 10 blocks by 3, contains virtually all the town's points of interest, including the **Plaza de la Constitución** (Chihuahua's zócalo) and the cathedral, as well as budget rooms and eateries. Odd-numbered streets lie north of Independencia, the core of the downtown area, and even-numbered streets are to the south. Buses for points all around the city leave from the corner of Ocampo and Juárez until about 8 PM. Tickets are 20¢ and can be bought from the driver. Taxis (usually consisting of a sorry-looking Subaru with a helpful driver) are relatively cheap, and, unless you're headed to the airport or have just stepped out of an expensive hotel, you can get practically anywhere for a few dollars.

WHERE TO SLEEP

Chihuahua's hotels are clustered together southwest of the Plaza de la Constitución, and most are well maintained and clean. Those listed here are the best of the cheapies, and all have hot water and air-conditioning. Keep in mind though that water is rationed in Chihuahua, and its availability is often limited in the evenings. Although the rooms are small, **Hotel Carmen** (Juárez, at Calle 10a, tel. 14/15–70–96) is centrally located, clean, and comfortable, and each of its rooms is equipped with a spotless bathroom. Be sure to check out the closed-circuit TV that monitors, strangely enough, the nearby Hotel Roma's lobby. Who do you think the people at the Roma are watching? Singles are $6, doubles $7. Close to downtown, **Posada Aida** (Calle 10a 105, btw Juárez and Doblado, tel. 14/15–38–30) is the best deal in Chihuahua. The sheets are fresh, the bathrooms clean, the staff friendly, and the pleasant Spanish-style courtyard is a good place to unwind if you're prepared to chat—the owner loves company. You'll pay $4 for a single and $5 for a double, all with private bath. Although the clean and comfy rooms at **Hotel del Cobre** (Calle 10a, at Progreso, tel. 14/15–17–58) fill fast, they're not necessarily worth the extra money. Singles are $12, doubles $16, all with bath. There's a cafeteria and pharmacy here too.

FOOD

Seafood stalls and hot-dog stands sprout from almost every corner in downtown Chihuahua, and fresh fruits, vegetables, meats, and cheeses are always available at the **mercado popular** (just north of Calle 4a, btw Niños Héroes and Juárez). The excellent **Restaurant Los Olivos** (Calle de la Llave 202, btw Calles 2a and 4a, tel. 14/10–01–61) serves organic fruits and vegetables, soy-based entrées, and egg dishes in a smoke-free environment polluted only by New Age Muzak. Whole-wheat pancakes are about $2 and a fruit plate smothered with yogurt, granola, and honey is $2.50. Los Olivos is open Sunday–Friday, noon–5. Late-night noshers sit in chrome and beige-vinyl booths in the wheelchair-accessible **Café Merino** (Ocampo, at Juárez, tel. 14/10–29–44; open daily 8 AM–midnight), downing standard diner grub: eggs, sausage, toast, pancakes . . . you get the idea. Breakfast with coffee and juice costs about $4, and the

$1.50 hamburgers and $5 *enchiladas de pollo en mole* (enchiladas with chicken in a chile and chocolate sauce) are also popular lunch items. At **Dinno's Pizza** (Doblado 301, at Calle 3a, tel. 14/16–57–07), eager-to-please waiters serve a decent pie fairly quickly. Ambience consists of scattered pictures of Italy and an occasional sports program on the overhead TV. Dinno's special jumbo pizza costs about $7; a plain medium costs $4. This wheelchair-accessible restaurant is open daily 8:30 AM–midnight.

WORTH SEEING

In addition to the shaded plazas and cobblestone streets, there's a good deal of culture and history to be absorbed here, much of it free. The town's main church, the baroque **Catedral Metropolitana de Chihuahua,** is on the **Plaza de la Constitución,** also called the Plaza de Armas. The cathedral is dedicated to St. Francis of Assisi, and its exterior is adorned with statues of Francis and the 12 Apostles. Inside, the **Museo de Arte Sacro** (Museum of Sacred Art, tel. 14/10–38–77) houses a collection of 18th-century religious art. Admission to the museum is 50¢, and it's open weekdays 10–2 and 4–6.

The **Palacio del Gobierno** and the **Palacio Federal** face each other on Juárez, between Guerrero and Carranza. The Palacio Federal contains the tower in which Padre Miguel Hidalgo was held prisoner before being executed. Although visitors can no longer climb the tower, the entrance has been turned into a small museum called **Calabozo de Hidalgo** (tel. 14/15–15–26 ext. 1056), or Hidalgo's cell, containing Hidalgo's Bible, crucifix, and pistol. Efrén García Díaz, the museum's caretaker, will share relevant history for the admission price of 20¢, Tuesday–Sunday 9–8. The Palacio del Gobierno (now home to the state tourism office) is where Hidalgo was actually executed; a plaque on the inner courtyard wall marks the spot. The Palacio del Gobierno also houses murals by Aarón Piña Mora, depicting historic events from the 16th century up to the Mexican Revolution.

MUSEO DE LA REVOLUCION MEXICANA Quinta Luz, as the former home of legendary Francisco "Pancho" Villa is sometimes called, is Chihuahua's biggest attraction. One of his many wives, Luz Corral, gave personal tours of the building until her death. The mansion was built by Pancho himself and is now dedicated to telling the history of the Mexican Revolution through photographs, treaties, maps, and artifacts—including weapons and the 1922 Dodge Villa he was driving when he was assassinated. See if you can count the bullet holes. Most Chihuahuenses are familiar with the museum; don't hesitate to ask for directions. *Calle 10a No. 3014, about 1½ km from downtown, tel. 14/16–29–68. Take bus marked* COL. DALES *or* OCAMPO. *Admission: $1. Open daily 9–1 and 3–7.*

QUINTA GAMEROS This turn-of-the-century manor was built in French Nouveau style by one Manuel Gameros to impress his fiancée, who nevertheless turned her affection to another. It is now home to a museum displaying the mansion's original furniture, gilt-framed paintings, and ornate chandeliers, as well as the works of local art students, an exhibit on the ruins at Paquimé, and several rotating exhibits. Look for the reclining, headless nude on the outside upper reaches of the building, as well as the Little Red Riding Hood motif in the child's room, complete with a snarling wolf on the headboard of the bed. *Paseo Bolívar 401, at Calle 4a, tel. 14/16–66–84. Admission: $1. Open Tues.–Sun. 10–2 and 4–7.*

AFTER DARK

Chihuahua is not a big party town, and movies are one of the more popular evening diversions. **Sala 2001** (Guerrero, at Escorza, tel. 14/16–50–00) and **Cinema Revolución** (Josué Neri Santos 700, just west of Palacio Federal, tel. 14/10–49–00) both show Hollywood films with Spanish subtitles and the occasional Latin American or Spanish flick for about $2. The disco **Robin Hood** (Cuauhtémoc 2207) charges $3 at the door and is the only dance place around where gay couples are tolerated: Public displays of affection remain an exclusively heterosexual privilege in these parts. As the disco is quite a walk south of downtown, you're better off taking a taxi. **Hobbet** (Reforma 103, tel. 14/14–31–52) is a piano bar similar to those found in the nicer hotels in town, but the drink prices and upscale dress code are prohibitive.

Creel and the Copper Canyon

With majestic 3600-meter-high peaks, and dramatic gorges dropping over a kilometer into raging waters, the region known as the Copper Canyon (Las Barrancas del Cobre) makes humble anyone subject to her beauty. In the late spring and early summer, protruding brown rocks absorb the sun's intense heat, while the Apache pines and Chihuahua ash hold their breath until the first gray clouds appear. By September, after the heavy rains, the canyons are thick with the green layers of vegetation that provide food for the polecats, skunks, and salamanders that roam the region.

A treasure for nature lovers, the five canyons and four main rivers in this area offer plenty of opportunities for hiking, mountain biking, and horseback riding. Guides are almost always recommended, not only because trails are rough and not clearly marked, but because of the illegal marijuana fields, which are extremely dangerous to stumble upon. Creel, about halfway between Chihuahua and Los Mochis, is the most convenient take-off point for camping and hiking trips, and has become a favorite among backpackers. The most popular times to visit are September and October, when the waterfalls are at their best, or during the week-long festival for Semana Santa (Holy Week—the week preceding Easter).

Las Barrancas only became accessible to the public in 1961, with the completion of the Chihuahua al Pacífico railroad. It took nearly 100 years to complete and boasts some 87 tunnels and 37 bridges. Long before Las Barrancas was discovered by miners and tourists, however, the area was home to indigenous Tarahumara people. Although their culture was strongly influenced by the Jesuit missionaries during the 17th and 18th centuries, the 50,000 Tarahumara that remain tenaciously maintain one of the most traditional indigenous cultures in North America. They continue to live in and around the canyons, farming and weaving pine-needle baskets, the majority of which are sold to tourists.

GETTING AROUND

BY BUS Trains are the primary mode of transportation through the canyons, but you can shorten the train ride in either direction by taking an **Estrella Blanca** bus. Eight daily buses run between Creel and Chihuahua (4 hrs direct, 5 hrs indirect; $8). If you attempt this, board at either Chihuahua or Creel; boarding at intermediate points may leave you standing, due to lack of seats, for many leg-numbing hours.

BY TRAIN Two trains run daily between Chihuahua and Los Mochis in each direction: the first-class *Vista* and the second-class *Mixto*. Both stop in most small towns in between, including Cuauhtémoc, Creel, Divisadero, and Bahuichivo. The Vista is faster and more comfortable, with climate control and bathrooms, but at $24 for the journey, it's almost four times the price of the second-class ride. The first-class train is popular during the summer and fall, so try to book ahead if you're traveling then. Bring toilet paper and, for the mountainous areas, warm clothing; in first class you'll probably even need a sweater in the lowlands, as the air-conditioning is over-enthusiastically used. Tickets for the *Mixto* are only available the morning of departure, so be prepared to fight tooth and nail for both tickets and seats during Semana Santa and September and October. For specific information on prices and departures, *see* Coming and Going, in Chihuahua, *above;* Creel, *below;* and Los Mochis in Chapter 7. Starting your trip in Los Mochis is recommended, especially since the *Mixto* leaving from Chihuahua will probably pass the Barrancas in the dark. If you're heading out of Chihuahua, the best view is on the right until you pass Creel and on your left from Creel to Los Mochis.

The second-class train has an unpredictable schedule and no reserved seating, but it provides the best opportunity to meet local campesinos (peasants) and their poultry.

BY CAR There is no place to rent a car between Chihuahua and Los Mochis, but it is possible to drive from Chihuahua to Divisadero along Highway 16. Since the road stops just after Divisadero, however, the train is the only way to reach Los Mochis. If you do end up driving, the

The Copper Canyon

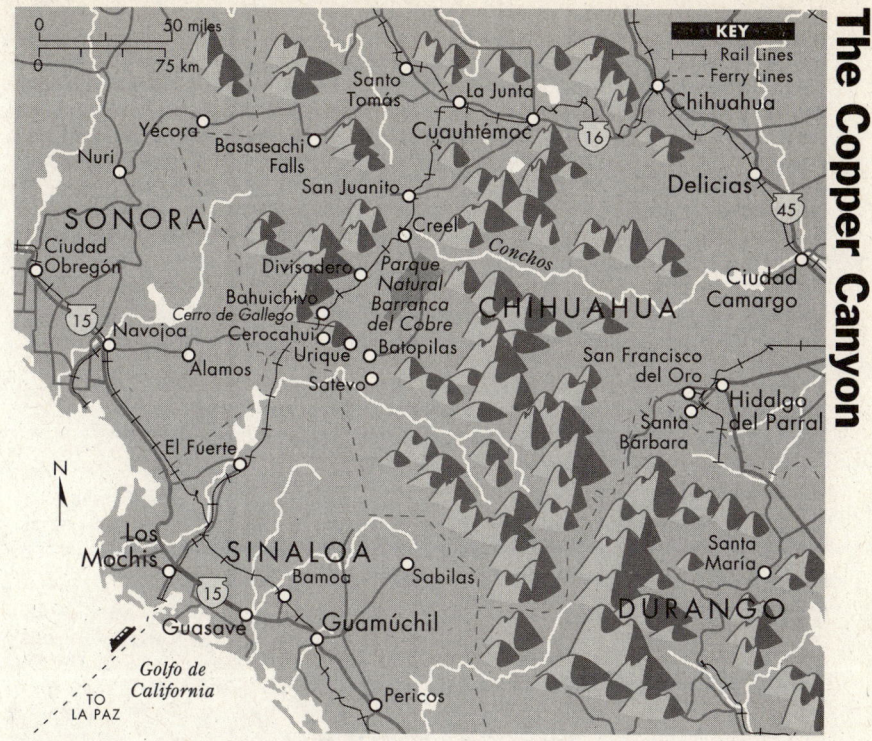

roads around the canyons (off the main highway) are rough and unmarked; taking the bus or hitchhiking with someone who knows the area is probably the safest way to go.

HITCHING Barring walking for days, hitchhiking is the only way to reach some points off the rail line. In rural areas it's fairly safe and common, but traveling in groups is always best. Some days you'll wait so long you can feel yourself getting older, especially on Sundays, when nobody's off to work. Trucks may charge a few dollars, depending on the length of the journey.

HIKING Extreme temperatures, lack of resupply points, and a wide range of altitudes make hiking in the Copper Canyon a challenge. However, if you know where you're going and have the proper equipment, overnight trips are undoubtedly the best way to see the canyons. Pick up hiking supplies in Los Mochis or Chihuahua. In Chihuahua, **Sears** (Libertad 106, tel. 14/16–52–72) is the most convenient place to purchase camping or hiking gear, and it's open Monday–Saturday 10–8, Sunday 11–7. Rather unhelpful topographical maps are available in Creel, as is the best book on the region, *Mexico's Copper Canyon Country,* by M. John Fayhee. Within the canyons, the best jumping-off points for hikes are Creel, Divisadero, and Bahuichivo, and it's easy to find a guide in these places. Use your head, though—holdups have been reported by tourists. Get someone moderately trustworthy (i.e. a hotel owner, rather than the guy hanging out on the corner) to refer you to a reputable guide.

Creel

Set in a shallow valley high in the Sierra Madre (about halfway between Los Mochis and Chihuahua), the growing town of Creel is rapidly becoming a favorite stop on the Chihuahua al Pacífico line for travelers who want to explore the Barrancas without too much hassle. The friendly, knowledgeable locals are accustomed to tourists, and may recommend you visit the one small local crafts museum, **Casa de Las Artesanías** (cnr of Villa and Zapata, tel. 145/6–

00–80; admission: 50¢), open Monday–Saturday, 9–1 and 3–7, Sundays 9–1. The best way to enjoy the surrounding area, with its stunning green pine trees and drought-ridden mountain peaks, is on bike, horse, or foot. Popular destinations include **Cusárare**, a waterfall 22 kilometers away; **Lake Arareco**, 7 kilometers south of Creel; and **San Ignacio**, 4 kilometers south, past the town cemetery and a few Tarahumara caves. San Ignacio is a modest mission built in 1744, where masses are still held each Sunday at noon in the Tarahumara language. Even if you don't join a group tour from one of the hotels, it's a good idea to ask around for tips on trails. You can also hitch or organize a ride outside town to the nearby attractions of **Batopilas** and **Basaseachic Falls.**

BASICS

CASAS DE CAMBIO Serfín (tel. 145/6–00–60), just east of the tracks, changes money weekdays 9 –1:30, and charges a "flexible" (you shouldn't have to pay more than 2%) commission on traveler's checks.

LAUNDRY Lavandería Santa María belongs to the resort-like Pension Creel. One load costs $1.50 to wash and dry. Pay an additional 20¢ and someone will do the dirty work for you. López Mateos 61, tel. 145/6–00–71. Open weekdays 9–2 and 3–6, Sat. 9–2.

MEDICAL AID There are a few English-speaking doctors at **La Clínica Santa Teresita** (Parroquia, behind Margarita's, tel. 145/6–01–05), which offers a variety of services, including dental and emergency care. For pharmaceuticals and advice about minor medical problems, look for **Farmacia Rodríguez** (López Mateos 43, tel. 145/6–00–52; open Mon.–Sat. 9–1 and 3–7).

PHONES AND MAIL Papelería de Todo (López Mateos 30, tel. 145/6–01–22), open Monday–Saturday 9–8 and Sunday 9–5, has a caseta de larga distancia and charges less than $1

The Footrunners

The name "Tarahumara" is a Spanish rendition of the natives' original word for themselves—Rarámuri, or "footrunners." More than 15,000 years ago, these people arrived from Asia, making their home in a 32,000-square-kilometer stretch (now known as the Sierra Tarahumara) of the Sierra Madre Occidental. Since that time, indigenous settlements have remained largely untouched by modern civilization, despite numerous attempts by outsiders to convert them to Christianity, or enslave them as laborers in precious-metal mines. Although the Tarahumara resisted Jesuit influence by hiding in the mountains, or by organizing violent rebellions, many aspects of Christianity have become part of their traditional religious ceremonies and rituals. The Virgin of Guadalupe fiesta (December 12) and Semana Santa (Holy Week) are both celebrated with elaborate costumes and dancing, and the sun is honored as the symbol of God, or Onorúame, who is both the father and mother of the people.

Today, many Tarahumara are visible begging in Chihuahua or selling crafts to tourists in small mountain towns such as Creel or Divisadero, while suffering from malnutrition or tuberculosis. Those who remain deep in the canyons are also threatened by the expanding lumber and tourist industries. When traveling in the Copper Canyon, remember to be respectful of the land and its residents. Although entering the inhabited cliffside caves and photographing the colorfully clothed women may seem appealing, it is important to ask for permission first, and comply if the request is denied.

for collect calls. It also has a pay phone and a fax machine. The **post office** (Enrique Creel 4, tel. 145/6–02–58; open weekdays 9–4) is in the Presidencia Municipal, south of the zócalo. They'll hold mail sent to you at the following address for up to 10 days: Lista de Correos, Presidencia Municipal, Creel, Chihuahua, CP 33200, México.

VISITOR INFORMATION The **Complejo Turístico Arareco** (tel. 145/6–01–26; open Mon.–Sat. 9–6) on López Mateos has a rough map of the area and provides information on tours. They arrange rowboat rentals for Lake Arareco (up to 6 people; $4 an hr) and rent bicycles ($1 an hr). Information in English is available at **Artesanías Misión** (tel. 145/6–00–97; open Mon.–Sat. 9:30–1 and 5–8, Sun. 9:30–1), next to Serfín.

COMING AND GOING

BY BUS The **Estrella Blanca** terminal (tel. 145/6–00–73) is directly across the tracks from the train station. Eight buses depart Creel every 1½ hours between 7 AM and 5:30 PM for Chihuahua (4 hrs, $8), stopping at most of the towns along the way. Tickets for Batopilas (7 hrs, $7) can be bought at the no-name craft store across from Restaurant Lupita (*see* Food, *below*) on López Mateos.

BY TRAIN The train tracks run along the west edge of town, and the station is very close to food and lodging. First-class trains to Chihuahua leave Creel at about 3:15 PM, second-class at 5:30 PM. First- and second-class trains heading to Los Mochis leave Creel at about 12:30 PM and 2 PM, respectively. The first-class trains are rarely late; the second-class trains show up when they feel like it, so be prepared to wait. You can buy tickets on the train.

WHERE TO SLEEP

As soon as you step off the train you will be assailed by a horde of children beckoning you to **Margarita's** (Mateos 11, tel. 145/6–00–45). Make the kids happy and jump on the hotel's courtesy shuttle, as you will inevitably end up there anyhow. The owner, Margarita, provides whatever type of accommodation you can afford, from a $2 mattress on the floor, to a $4 bunk or a $14 double room with private bath. Although the toilets are occasionally out of order, communal meals (breakfast and dinner) are included in the price. She has also recently opened another place with more upscale rooms so be careful not to let the driver take you there. Margarita's is very well known—summer finds it packed with groups of oh-so-cosmopolitan international travelers, and when there's demand, the staff leads guided tours (about $5) to Cusárare Falls, Recohuata Hot Springs, and the Copper Canyon at Divisadero. If you prefer to avoid the highly social scene at Margarita's, **Casa Valenzuela** (López Mateos 68, tel. 145/6–01–04) is ususally semi-vacant, and the proprietor will accommodate your needs and budget. The communal bathroom is tiny and fairly clean, but the ceiling sags. Well, okay, the beds sag, too. Singles are $8.50, doubles $17, and five of the 13 rooms have baths. **Although New Pensión Creel** (López Mateos 61, tel. 145/6–00–71) is 1 kilometer out of town, it's worth the trek for the clean and cozy two- to four-person rooms ($7.50 per person, including breakfast). The B&B has a spacious patio, kitchen, common area, and laundry, and tours of the canyon can be arranged with the staff. To get here, walk south down López Matos and turn left after Calle La Terminal. Look for the tin roof with PENSION CREEL in red letters.

CAMPING There is an official campground next to **Lake Arareco** that costs $2 per night. The entrance is at the small white house, on the way to the lake. The only thing to prevent you from camping anywhere else for free is lack of a flat spot and the occasional scorpion.

FOOD

Café El Manzano, just off the train tracks, is a favorite of rail crews. Large portions of tasty Mexican food cost about $2, and the service is fast and friendly. **Mi Café** (López Mateos 21) has only one table and feels more like a home than a restaurant. Chicken tosadas and *ceviche* (fish pickled in lime juice) both cost $1, and are served daily 9–9:30. Open even later (a daring 10 PM) is **Restaurant Lupita,** also on López Mateos. Morning hotcakes are just $1.50. Later, try *bistec ranchero* (steak cooked with tomatoes and onions) or fish fillet, both $3. You can purchase fresh fruits and vegetables from the grocery stores along López Mateos. Not surprisingly, the most popular bar in town also belongs to Margarita. Looking somewhat like a remodeled kitchen, **Margaritás Plaza Mexicana** (Chapultepec, off López Mateos, tel. 145/6–02–45) is the place to go for a $1 evening beer.

OUTDOOR ACTIVITIES

Creel is a convenient base from which to explore the natural beauty of the canyons and the rivers that tumble through them. While river-rafting is strictly for those adventurers who bring their own equipment (including rain), you can rent horses and mountain bikes in Creel, or take off on hikes that last between one hour and several days. Remember to take it easy for a while and let your body get used to changes in altitude. Guided tours are available to almost anyplace in the area. Try Complejo Turístico Arareco (*see* Visitor Information, *above*), join a group from Margarita's, or arrange your own tour by asking around at the main plaza; many residents own trucks, are quite knowledgeable, and will take you anywhere if the price is right.

HIKING Topographical maps and guidebooks are available at **Artesanías Misión** (*see* Visitor Information, *above*), but most of what you'll find is pretty useless. You're better off with a live guide—ask at Margarita's or the adjacent **Expediciones Umárike**. Creel is the base for long treks to Basaseachic Falls and Batopilas (*see* Near Creel, *below*), but those with less time or less ambition may prefer to meander over to the statue of Jesus in the hills 15 minutes west of town, where you'll find a nice picnic spot. For another easy hike (this one along clearly marked trails), head to the nearby **Valle de las Monjas** (Valley of the Monks), so named for the rocks said to resemble a huddle of monks (1½-hour walk). Also close by is the **Valle de los Hongos** (Valley of the Mushrooms), where a few rock formations resemble—surprise—overgrown mushrooms (half-hour each way). While most of the Tarahumara caves in the area are abandoned, **Cueva Sebastián**, a few kilometers south of Creel at San Ignacio, is still inhabited and accessible by foot. The Tarahumara do not welcome visitors inside their homes, but there are tours available that have been given permission to enter the caves. To reach any of these places, ask directions from anyone in Creel.

NEAR CREEL

BASASEACHIC FALLS A four-hour drive northwest from Creel are the magnificent Basaseachic Falls, which plunge 250 meters into a pool below. This area is most magnificent after the rainy season (July–August). Tours can be arranged in Creel for groups of four or more (the ones from Margarita's are $15 a person), or you can hitch from the town of **La Junta**, on the Pacífico rail line. If you do hitch, plan to stay overnight in the park—good (free) camping spots abound. Hiking trails are a dime a dozen, and there's an excellent swimming hole at the waterfall's edge. Bring your own supplies because there are no shops at all.

BATOPILAS About 140 kilometers south of Creel, in the heart of the canyon region, is the small mining town of Batopilas. Located beside the river of the same name, this untouristed town is hard to reach, but provides great access to the canyons. The tiny town of **Satevo**, which has a spooky abandoned mission worth exploring, is an easy 4-kilometer hike south; about 6 kilometers north is **La Bufa**, a forgotten gold mine. Both of these trails are marked, but a guide is recommended. The cheapest bus to Batopilas departs Creel at 7 AM on Tuesdays, Thursdays, and Saturdays (7 hrs, $7); a smaller but faster bus (4 hrs, $11) runs every Monday, Wednesday, and Friday at 11 AM. Both leave from an unnamed craft store across from Restaurant Lupita (*see* Food in Creel, *above*) on López Mateos. The return bus departs Batopilas at 4 AM (yes, AM) on Mondays, Wednesdays, and Fridays, and the trip takes eight hours. The road has been called the best and worst in North America: The scenery is magnificent, but the switchbacks are stomach-wrenching. Batopilas is also accessible by trail from both Urique and Cerocahui, off the Bahuichivo rail stop (*see below*).

> *When the Batopilas mines were in full operation, they produced chunks of silver as big as basketballs—the profits of which would be used, in part, to throw lavish high-society parties in the town's grand haciendas.*

➤ **WHERE TO SLEEP AND EAT** • Bring all necessary camping supplies with you (including food) to avoid Batopilas's steep prices. You can swim and camp by the river, but it's not advised in the summer months when the creepy-crawlies are out in legion. Deforestation upstream has also made dangerous flash floods frequent, so exercise caution near the river. A few small eateries here will provide the calories to keep you going, and rooms are available for about $10 per person at **Posada Carmen** and **Hotel Batopilas,** and occasionally at the Tarahumara artesanía shop for a little less.

Divisadero

Only from Divisadero can you see the three canyons—Tararecua, Urique, and Copper—merge, their never-ending peaks woven together by rivers. The Chihuahua al Pacífico train stops here for 15 minutes so tourists can snap pictures, buy baskets, and gawk over the canyon rim. If you want to stop and hike, you can catch a later train for a small surcharge. If you want to stay, you're better off hiking away from town and camping (ask permission before pitching a tent on someone's land), or renting a room from a local family (up to $10 a night): All hotel rooms within walking distance begin at $86. Food and craft stands—selling cheap burritos and ridiculously priced Tarahumara crafts—provide info on either option. Even if you're not one of the privileged guests at **Hotel Divisadero Barrancas,** you can rent bikes here ($4.50 per hour), or tag along with a tour into the canyons (minimum of $6). You can also hire a guide yourself for overnight trips down to the **Río Urique.** Less formidable is the 2-kilometer hike from the north side of the hotel to an abandoned Tarahumara cliff dwelling.

Bahuichivo

Brick and mud houses and few wandering chickens are about all you'll see along the windy dirt roads of this *muy tranquilo* (very mellow) small town. Bahuichivo hugs the railroad tracks 260 kilometers north of Los Mochis, and is a good departure point for exploring Cerocahui and Urique, or for hiking down into the canyon's hot belly. If you're foraging for food, head to **La Amistad,** 100 meters uphill from the train station. Decorated with red-and-white checkered tablecloths, dried scorpions in picture frames, and a broken armoire displaying Japanese Coke bottles, this place serves whatever local fare is available for about $2. Aside from a few small markets, there is no place in town to buy supplies for a long hike or camping trip. For overnight stays, **Hotel el Camino Real** (mid-hill on your right, no phone) has decent rooms for $4.50 (singles) and $7 (doubles). For $3.50 per person, simple, clean rooms can also be found at **Hotel Viajero** (tel. 158/2-06-04). Neither of these hotels has electricity or private bathrooms, but the kerosene effect is sort of romantic. For medical help, see the reputable Dr. Leyva—his office is labeled FARMACIA ADRIANA and is near the store Abarrotes Gabby.

Since Bahuichivo is a stop on the Chihuahua al Pacífico railway, it's the best place from which to set out for Cerocahui and Urique. To reach Urique from Bahuichivo (3 hrs, $5), hop on the white van marked TRANSPORTES CAÑON URIQUE, which comes to meet the first-class train at about 3:30 PM. The van will sometimes wait for the second-class train, and will then leave at 6 PM. The van passes through Cerocahui ($2) on it's way to Urique. It's also easy to hitch between Cerocahui and Bahuichivo.

Cerocahui

At 1½ kilometers above sea level, Cerocahuis's twisting, no-name streets are nestled deep in one of the Sierra Madre's gorges. This isolated village offers perhaps the most spectacular stargazing in Mexico; when the electricity goes out after 10 PM, you're left standing amidst oak and pine trees under a pantheon of stars. If you're fortunate enough to be here during Semana Santa, be sure to catch the *matachines* (Tarahumara dances) at the old **Jesuit mission.** Founded in 1680 and restored in 1940, the mission still operates a boarding school for Tarahumara children. Services are held in the school's *iglesia* (church) weekday nights at 7:30

(if the padre is in town) and Sundays at 8 AM and noon. On June 24, locals douse each other with water in homage to John the Baptist.

From July to April, water is also abundant in the nearby waterfalls (a 2-kilometer hike from town), or you can explore the abandoned **Sangre de Cristo** gold mines (3 kilometers from town). Each reasonably marked hike is short, and can be done on horseback or by foot. From here, you can also set out on a two- to three-day trek/horseback ride to Batopilas (*see* Near Creel, *above*), but you'll need a guide. Information is available in broken English from the knowledgeable Eduardo Muñoz, at the small artesanía shop on the way out of town (towards the waterfall). He'll gladly lead hikes to anywhere (including Batopilas) for a negotiable price. He or someone at Hotel Misión (off the central plaza) can also get you a horse to rent ($4 an hour).

Overlooking Cerocahui, Cerro de Gallego (Gallego Hill) was named at the end of the 19th century after Father Gallego, a padre from Urique who was found dead, still wearing his priestly garb, in a nearby cave.

BASICS In 1995, the town's first **telephones** rang amongst the hills. Long-distance calls can be made from the building behind the new blue TELEFONIA RURAL sign, at the end of the road heading north from the plaza. It's open Monday–Saturday 9–1:30 and 3–6. Right next door is the town *clínica* (hospital), open daily 9–2 and 4–7. The easiest way to reach Cerocahui is to hop on a van ($2) marked TRANSPORTES CAÑON URIQUE from Bahuichivo (*see* Bahuichivo, *above*) or to hitch a ride.

WHERE TO SLEEP AND EAT Rooms with private baths and hot water are available at **El Rarámuri** for $7 (singles) and $10 (doubles). It's the white house on the way out of town towards the waterfall. A woman known as **Fea** (meaning ugly, but said with endearment) has a house on the plaza in front of the church, with a few crude rooms ($5 a person) and a communal bath that sometimes works. **Monse Chávez** also rents shabby rooms in her home for $2 a bed, if you don't mind the outdoor latrine. Follow the main road from the plaza until you reach the yellow house on your left (or ask around for Monse). To camp, pick a spot and ask permission from the landowner—it shouldn't be a problem, although they may charge a small fee. The only restaurant in town is diagonally across from the plaza, and it's more a living room than anything else. The menu changes daily, but meals are always less than $5. Otherwise a woman named Raquel Morriz, who lives next to El Rarámuri, will serve you a meal in her kitchen for about $3. A scarce supply of snacks are available at the markets around town.

Paraíso del Oso

Named for the Yogi Bear-shaped rock that towers overhead, Paraíso del Oso (Paradise of the Bear) is a comfortable hacienda-style hotel situated 3 kilometers north of Cerocahui. Rooms here cover the whole price spectrum, from $6 rooms with bunk beds to $117 luxury pads. You can also pitch a tent for $6, but bring your own food—meals can be expensive. Even if you're not a hotel guest, bilingual staff members with knowledge of the region's natural history take morning groups into the canyon for a small fee. Spectacular hikes are led up streams and over mesas to a cave filled with crosses, each commemorating an Indian that died, probably during a cholera epidemic introduced by Pancho Villa's troops. A van displaying the hotel logo meets the daily first-class train in Bahuichivo to pick up guests, so approach it if you're interested. For reservations (a good idea in September and October), write to Doug (Diego) Rhodes, P.O. Box 31089, El Paso, TX 79931, U.S.A. Messages in Spanish can be left for Diego at tel. 158/6–06–19.

Urique

Thirty-eight kilometers southeast of Cerocahui, the village of Urique features the gushing **Río Urique**, and fantastic views of the surrounding canyon. You can take day hikes along the river, or walk down the dirt road at the edge of town to explore **Chiflón**, an abandoned mine near the foot of a 1-meter-wide, 110-meter-long hanging footbridge. Although belly flops off the bridge *are not* advised, this is a great spot for a swim as long as the water isn't raging from heavy rains. It's also a good idea to avoid Urique in early summer, as the river will be nearly dry and temperatures reach 37° C (100°F).

COMING AND GOING Vans leave Urique in time to meet the first-class train in Bahuichivo and return to Urique sometime after 7 PM (3 hrs, $5). The more expensive way to get here is to arrange a ride through the Hotel Misión in Cerocahui ($16 a person), but someone on the street may be talked into to driving you here for a smaller fee and a smile.

WHERE TO SLEEP AND EAT Urique boasts three hotels, but your best bet is **Hotel Cañón Urique**, on the main drag beneath the huge ceiba tree. Singles with private bath are $6, doubles are $10, and the rooms in the rear buffer the cries of farm animals. If you've brought camping equipment, ask for Tom and Keith's house (a couple of friendly expatriates from the States). They've got a great camping area under the mesquite trees by the river (watch out for small, biting chiggers during the rainy season), and a $1 donation is requested for use of the squat toilet and fresh water. The best eats in town are found at **Restaurant Plaza,** down the street from Hotel Cañón Urique. About $3 will get you the meal of the day between 6 AM and 11 PM. Travelers have complained about the town's other main restaurant, the **Zulema,** so don't risk it.

Durango

Resting in the Valle del Guadiana, the modern, industrialized city of Durango offers a hilly downtown area that retains some superb colonial architecture. If the dusty downtown landscape and exceptionally clear light you see on the bus ride into town strike a familiar chord, you're not crazy. You probably *have* seen the place before, as the area has been used in a number of Hollywood productions, including *Big Jake,* starring John Wayne. Proud of its contributions to the film industry, the tourism office often organizes weekend trips to two "western" towns used as film sets. Of these, **Villa del Oeste** (Village of the West) is the only one still used for moviemaking. Another set is known as **Chupaderos,** and although it's been forgotten by film, it has become a refuge for destitute people, who live in the sets.

Every July, Durango wraps two weeks of **Feria Nacional** around two significant dates: July 4, the day of the Virgen del Refugio; and July 22, the anniversary of Durango's 1563 founding by Francisco de Ibarra. The festival has taken on national status, and people come from all around to bet on cockfights, bid on cows, and enjoy the music, food, and rides.

BASICS

AMERICAN EXPRESS AmEx services are provided by friendly, English-speaking representatives in the travel agency **Touris Viajes,** a few long blocks west of the Plaza de Armas. You can buy or change traveler's checks here and have lost or stolen traveler's checks or AmEx cards replaced. Cardholders can also have their mail held or cash a personal check here. *20 de Noviembre 810 Ote., tel. 18/17–00–83, fax 18/17–01–43. Take orange bus from stop marked* NARANJA *on cnr of Victoria and 20 de Noviembre. Open weekdays 9–7, Sat. 10–5.*

CASAS DE CAMBIO Serfín (20 de Noviembre 400 Ote., tel. 18/1–15–03) only changes traveler's checks weekdays 9–1:30. **Mundinero,** next door to the AmEx office, changes both cash and traveler's check and has decent hours; unfortunately, the rates here are lousy. *20 de Noviembre 806 Ote., tel. 18/18–86–24. Open weekdays 9:30–2 and 4–6:30, Sat. 10–2.*

EMERGENCIES In case of trouble, call the **police** (cnr Prolongación Felipe Pescador and Independencia, tel. 18/17–54–06). For an ambulance, call the **Cruz Roja** (cnr 5 de Febrero and Trabajo, tel. 18/17–34–44).

LAUNDRY The friendly guys at **Lavandería Automática Ale** will wash, dry, fold, and even deliver your clothes ($3). *Lázaro Cárdenas 232 Nte., tel. 18/17-22-20. Take orange bus from stop marked* NARANJA *on cnr of Victoria and 20 de Noviembre. Open Mon.–Sat. 9-7.*

MAIL The full-service post office will hold mail sent to you at the following address for up to 10 days: Lista de Correos, Administración No. 1, 20 de Noviembre 500-B Ote., Durango, Durango, CP 34001, México. *20 de Noviembre, btw Cuauhtémoc and Roncal, tel. 18/11-41-05. Open weekdays 8-7, Sat. 9-noon.*

MEDICAL AID Two 24-hour clinics are: **Hospital San Jorge** (Libertad 249, tel. 18/17-22-10) and **Hospital de La Paz** (5 de Febrero 903, tel. 18/18-95-41). **Farmacia el Fénix** (20 de Noviembre, at Victoria, tel. 18/11-40-41) has a knowledgeable staff and carries a lot of U.S. brands, but closes daily at 9:30 PM. For 24-hour service, go to **Farmacia del Ahorro** (20 de Noviembre 100 Ote., no phone).

PHONES Several casetas de larga distancia line 5 de Febrero. For some reason, most resent being asked to place collect calls, so you might have to plug your ears and scream into the public phones on the street corners or in the Plaza de Armas. If you need to call collect, walk the three blocks to the caseta at Bruno Martínez 206 Sur (tel. 18/13-30-01; open daily 8 AM-9:30 PM). They charge 50¢ for a collect call.

VISITOR INFORMATION The staff of the state tourism office is multilingual, friendly, and thoroughly helpful. Stop by for the great city maps and informative pamphlets (in English) about Durango. *Hidalgo 408 Sur, tel. 18/11-21-39. West of plaza on 20 de Noviembre, left on Hidalgo. Open weekdays 8:30-3 and 6-8, weekends 10-1.*

COMING AND GOING

BY BUS The **Central Camionera** is 4 kilometers east of the town center, but regular city buses and cheap taxis (about $3 to the central plaza) make it accessible. The station is served by a number of national lines, including **Omnibus de México** (tel. 18/18-33-61) and **Transportes del Norte** (tel. 18/18-33-04), which shares a phone with **Estrella Blanca, Futura,** and **Transportes Chihuahuenses.** First-class buses run daily to points all over Mexico, including Chihuahua city (9 hrs, $19), Ciudad Juárez (12 hrs, $30), Mazatlán (7 hrs, $10), Mexico City (12 hrs, $28), Monterrey (9 hrs, $24), and Saltillo (7½ hrs, $17). A small pharmacy and long-distance telephone service are available at the station.

BY TRAIN Durango's train station (tel. 18/11-22-94) is right below the Cerro del Mercado, off Avenida Felipe Pescador, about nine blocks north of the plaza. A first-class train to Mexico City (15 hrs, $18) departs at 6 AM. Another leaves for Ciudad Juárez (11 hrs, $18) at 7 AM, with a stop in Chihuahua (8 hrs, $12). Other destinations include Monterrey (11 hrs, $7), Saltillo (9 hrs, $11), and Zacatecas (16 hrs, $5). The ticket office is only open 5 AM-noon. To get here, take the bus marked FERR.

GETTING AROUND

The main thoroughfare, **20 de Noviembre,** runs east–west. Victoria, Constitución, and Juárez are the main streets that intersect 20 de Noviembre, in the heart of the downtown area. Parallel to 20 de Noviembre are Pino Suárez and 5 de Febrero on the south side, Negrete and Aquiles Serdán on the north side. The main square, called the **Plaza de Armas,** is off 20 de Noviembre, between Juárez and Constitutión. Addresses contain cardinal directions—Nte. for north, Sur for south, Ote. for east, and Pte. for west—which indicate where they are in relation to the plaza. City buses congregate near the plaza, and taxis charge 40¢ a kilometer.

WHERE TO SLEEP

There are a few decent, central places, but budget hotels in Durango tend to be bottom-of-the-barrel. Around festival time (the first two weeks in July) make reservations, or expect to stay far from downtown, pay a lot, and get little. The cheapest place downtown is the scruffy, none-too-clean **Hotel Gallo** (5 de Febrero 117, tel. 18/11-52-90), where singles are $6, doubles $7.

Hotel María del Pilar. The best of the cheapies. Rooms are drab and have peeling paint, but they're clean and relatively comfy, with phones and spotless bathrooms with plenty of hot water. Singles $9, doubles $10. *Pino Suárez 410 Pte., tel. 18/11–54–71. From Plaza, walk south on Juárez, left on Pino Suárez. Wheelchair access.*

Hotel Posada Durán. Everybody's favorite, this colonial hotel next to the cathedral has large wooden doors, a bar, and a courtyard with a fountain. The impeccable rooms have wood floors, and some have big glass doors that open onto balconies; singles are $12.50, doubles $15. The spotless bathrooms have plenty of scalding water. *20 de Noviembre 506 Pte., at Juárez, tel. 18/11–24–12. 15 rooms, all with bath. Reservations advised. MC, V.*

Hotel Reyes. It smells like disinfectant, but it's clean and has an amiable staff. Singles are $9, doubles $10.50, and each room has a good (if tiny) bathroom. *20 de Noviembre 220 Ote., near León de la Peña, tel. 18/13–02–03. Look for huge Soriana supermarket across the street.*

Posada San Jorge. A good bet for your money, this downtown hotel has a covered inner courtyard filled with green, leafy life. Both singles and doubles (both $7) have telephones and clean bathrooms (with hot water). *Constitución 102 Sur, tel. 18/13–32–57. From Plaza, walk 1½ blocks on Constitutión, past cathedral. 25 rooms, all with bath. MC, V.*

FOOD

There are almost no outstanding budget eateries downtown: A few small places serve almost identical comidas corridas, but aside from the bountiful hot-dog stands, not many distinguish themselves. The **mercado** on 20 de Noviembre, right near Hotel Reyes (*see above*), is a good place to get fresh fruits and vegetables; *fondas* (covered food stands) toward the back serve standard meals for about $1.50.

The state of Durango is famous for its huge desert scorpions, but have no fear—the only scorpion you'll probably encounter is a caramel one, sold at candy and souvenir shops.

La Casa de la Monja. Despite the name (the nun's house), this colonial building has a rustic elegance. Enjoy the $7 specialty *puntas de filete a la monja* (nun style beef—whoa) or the $3.50 *comida del día* (daily menu, including soup, main dish, and dessert) beside the interior garden and fountain. *Negrete Pte. 308, cnr of Madero, tel. 18/11–71–62. Open daily 8 AM–11 PM. Wheelchair access.*

La Posta. This chic little place serves $4.50 *machaca durangueña* (Durango-style shredded beef) and $2.50 *plato surtido* (enchiladas, tosadas and burritos). Although the menu may not be terribly varied, the dessert menu is a chocoholic's dream come true. *Negrete 1005, cnr of Independencia, tel. 18/25–15–00. Open Tues.–Sun. 1 PM–11 PM. Wheelchair access.*

Restaurant Vegetariano Samadhi. The tiny vegetarian joint sells delicious whole wheat *pan dulce* (sweet rolls) for 50¢. Add an order of yogurt with fruit and honey ($1), and you have the perfect breakfast. Comidas corridas ($2.50) are a filling lunch option. *Negrete 403 Pte., no phone. Open daily 8 AM–10 PM.*

Sloan's. This small restaurant/bar is almost always full of young people and music, as well as a bizarre clutter of plane propellers, drum sets, and other random junk. Both roast beef and Italian-style spaghetti cost $5; a monster-size piña colada is $2.50. Don't miss the happy hour 6 PM–8 PM. *Negrete 1003 Pte., tel. 18/12–21–99. Open daily 6 PM–midnight. Wheelchair access.*

WORTH SEEING

Fortunately, most of Durango's interesting sights are well within walking distance of the main **Plaza de Armas**; the huge, baroque **Catedral Basílica Menor**, Durango's main church, faces the plaza. The best of the outlying sights is the **Parque Guadiana** (on Carretera Durango–Mazatlán). Fourteen long blocks from the main plaza, this park is a favorite spot for sports-minded locals. Miles of dirt paths makes it ideal for runners and bicyclists alike, and the huge public swimming pool is a great place to beat the afternoon heat. Free aerobics classes are held daily at 7 AM in the little clearing behind the pool. Just across the highway is the **Zoológico Sahuatoba** (tel. 18/12-44-57), where you can gawk at the lions, panthers, hippos, and snakes free of charge.

CASA DE LOS CONDES DE SUCHIL Once an aristocratic residence, this churrigueresque (ultra-baroque) palace is now inhabited by pricey shops. Come to browse or to admire the arched courtyard and well-preserved masonry and stone carvings. *5 de Febrero, at Madero. Open daily 10–8.*

MUSEO REGIONAL DE DURANGO Built in the second half of the 19th century by architect Stanislaus Slonecky, the Regional Museum of Durango was originally a residence. Today, the two-story building houses fossilized remains dating to the Paleozoic era. A mummified set of child-size human remains is also on display; its discovery in nearby El Mezquital has led some archaeologists to believe that a colony of pygmies once lived in Durango. The museum also houses paintings, textiles, and sculptures. *Victoria 100 Sur, tel. 18/12-53-11. Admission: $1. Open weekdays 10–3.*

PALACIO DE GOBIERNO This impressive 18th-century baroque palace houses the offices of state officials, including that of the governor of Durango state. The reason to visit, however, is the impressive murals on the top floor, which depict Durango's indigenous population's struggle for survival (a continuing battle for many in the southernmost portion of the state). On the ground floor, you'll find an unfinished mural abandoned by painter Manuel Guerrero Lourdes in 1936. The state of Durango never got around to paying the master his salary. In protest, he refused to finish the painting. *5 de Febrero, at Zaragoza. From Plaza, head 4 blocks west. Admission free. Open daily 7 AM–8 PM.*

AFTER DARK

Nightlife isn't exactly hip-hoppin' in Durango, but things liven up on weekends. Hang out with local youth at **Aquellos Tiempos** (5 de Febrero, at Zarco; no cover), the place to be on Fridays and Saturdays. Also worth checking out is the *ranchera* (country) and disco music at **Cyclons** (Blvd. Domingo Arrieta Sur; $3 cover). **Buchagas Pool and Snack Bar** (20 de Noviembre 310 Ote., tel. 18/12-40-64) is a respectable place to play eight ball (tables are $4 per hour) and down a few pricey beers. They stay open into the wee hours, but do not admit patrons after 10 PM.

NORTHEASTERN MEXICO   6

By Lean Sweeney

Just across the border from the dry, abandoned ranches of southern Texas, Mexico's increasingly industrial northeast region stretches southward, a vast reminder of the country's dependence on foreign industry and weekend tourism to bolster its unstable economy. In December 1994, one year after NAFTA was put into effect, foreign investors pulled out of Mexico, leaving border towns like Nuevo Laredo, Matamoros, and Reynosa glutted with disillusioned job-seekers from all over the country. Stricter immigration policies have further exacerbated the situation; an increased influx of American tourists is jarringly contrasted by the cutthroat policies encountered at the border-town exits.

Despite suffering a repeated pattern of economic boom and bust, northeasterners somehow manage to strike a balance between modern materialism and the preservation of age-old cultural traditions. In border towns like Reynosa, vendors from all over Mexico sell their handmade crafts in open markets; you'll find fresh red crab and baby shrimp sold by the kilo in port towns like Tampico. In Saltillo, the slow-paced capital of Coahuila State and the original residence of revolutionary leader-turned-governor Venustiano Carranza, serape-makers still produce the magnificently colored vests and blankets of their Tlaxcalan ancestors. Just 230 kilometers south of the U.S. border is Mexico's third largest city, Monterrey, home to a number of excellent museums and one of Latin America's finest universities.

Although the northeastern landscape tends to be mostly dry, the coastal towns of Matamoros and Tampico are surprisingly plush and verdant—home to extensive stretches of beach that provide refreshing relief from the heat of the city. If you're a serious nature lover, the Parque Nacional Cumbres de Monterrey, an hour from Monterrey, offers dozens of hiking, spelunking, and camping opportunities.

Matamoros

Matamoros is the easternmost border crossing between the United States and Mexico. The city hugs the Río Bravo (or Rio Grande, as it's known in the States) 38 kilometers west of the Gulf Coast and is connected to Brownsville, Texas, by a 100-meter bridge. Most of the city's inhabitants are employed in the ever-present *maquiladoras* (foreign-owned factories in duty-free zones), and the devaluation of the peso over the past year has also left many jobless and desperate. Still, some relics of Matamoros's preindustrial history still stand, and a few small galleries and theaters offer affordable glimpses of work by local and regional artists.

Northeastern Mexico

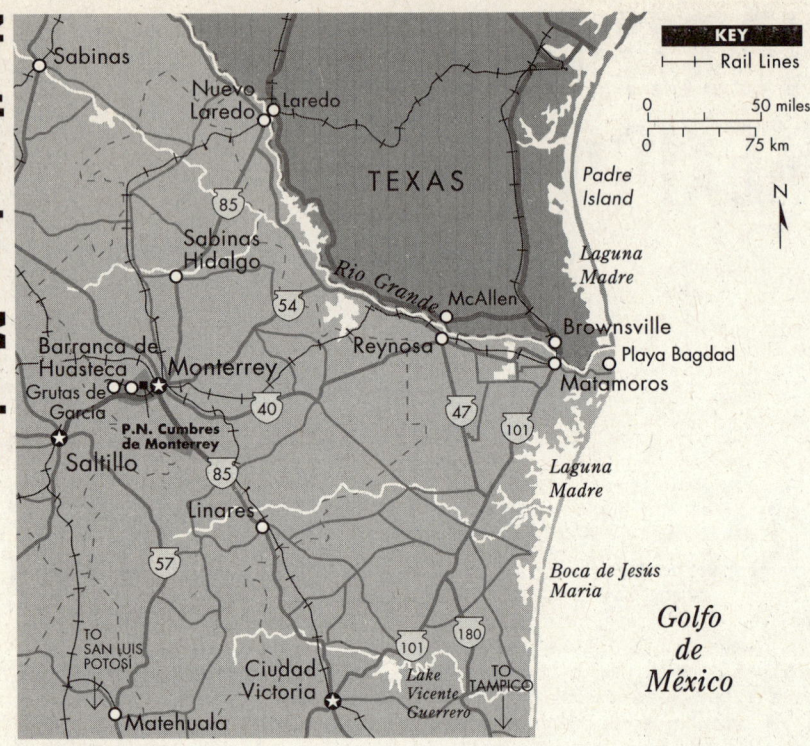

BASICS

AMERICAN EXPRESS Viajes Axial grudgingly admits it's affiliated with American Express and doesn't change money. They only replace lost American Express cards and hold members' mail. *Morelos 94–107, Centro, CP 87300, Matamoros, Tamaulipas, México, tel. 88/13–69–69. Open weekdays 8–6, Sat. 9–1.*

CASAS DE CAMBIO Banamex changes cash and traveler's checks weekdays 9–5. They also have an ATM that accepts Plus, Cirrus, MasterCard, Visa, and, surprisingly, American Express. *Calle 7, at Morelos, tel. 88/13–60–35.*

CONSULATES The **American Consulate** is a madhouse. To avoid standing in line, show the guard your passport. *Calle 1 No. 2002, at Azaleas, tel. 88/12–44–02.* Take the yellow PRIMERA POPULAR/PUENTE pesera (minibus) from the bus station or from the Tours-Transport office (see Visitor Information, below). *Open weekdays 8–10 and 1–4.*

CROSSING THE BORDER If you're only staying in Matamoros a couple of days, simply show the scowling border guard your passport or any other picture ID. If you plan to travel more than 22 kilometers into Mexico, get a tourist card (see Chapter 1, Basics) at the crossing.

EMERGENCIES In an emergency, call the **police** (Luis Caballero at R. F. García, tel. 88/17–22–05) or the **fire** department (tel. 88/12–00–03). For an ambulance, call the **Cruz Roja** (Luis Caballero at Durango, tel. 88/12–00–44). Free emergency care is available at the **Centro de Salud** (Cnr of Calle 6 and Querétaro, tel. 88/17–49–30 or 88/17–19–16).

MEDICAL AID For minor medical emergencies, the well-stocked **Benavides** pharmacy is the most convenient to downtown. *Guerrero, at Calle 10, tel. 88/16–69–58. Open daily 8 AM–9 PM.*

PHONES AND MAIL The main **post office** (Calle 6 No. 214) will hold your mail at the following address for up to 10 days: Lista de Correos, Matamoros, Tamaulipas, CP 87300, México. There's also a branch at the Matamoros bus depot open daily 9–noon and 3–8. For faster delivery, mail your letters from the Brownsville post office (1001 E. Elizabeth St., at Calle 10, tel. 210/546–9462).

You can make collect and credit-card international calls from the shiny aluminum Ladatel **pay phones** (not the orange ones) in Plaza Hidalgo, Plaza Allende, and the bus and train stations.

VISITOR INFORMATION A few blocks from the international bridge is the small white **Tours-Transport** building (Tamaulipas and Álvaro Obregón, tel. 88/12–21–18), where friendly older men make a group effort to answer your questions. It's open daily 8–6. The **Brownsville Chamber of Commerce** has excellent street maps of Brownsville and Matamoros. *1600 E. Elizabeth St., Brownsville, tel. 210/542–4341. 1 block from international bridge. Open daily 9–5.*

COMING AND GOING

BY BUS The **Central de Autobuses** (Calle 1, at Canales) is 25 blocks south of the international bridge. To get here, flag down a CENTRAL pesera at the international bridge or in Plaza Hidalgo. First-class **ADO** (tel. 88/12–01–81) serves Veracruz twice daily (16 hrs, $36). **Omnibus de México** (tel. 88/13–27–68) has first- and second-class service to most major cities. Second-class is cheaper but generally takes an hour longer and lacks air-conditioning, and, in some cases, bathrooms. Several daily buses make the trip to Monterrey (5 hrs, $9 1st class), Reynosa (2 hrs; $3 1st class, $2 2nd class), and Nuevo Laredo (3 per day, 6 hrs, $9 1st class). Inside the terminal you'll find a post office, plenty of Ladatel phones, an air-conditioned, 24-hour cafeteria, and luggage lockers ($3 per day).

BY TRAIN El **Tamaulipeco**, offering both first- and second-class service, crawls from Matamoros to Monterrey via Reynosa in 6 hours. There's one daily departure at 9:20 AM, and tickets ($6 1st class, $4 2nd class) are sold 8–9 AM only, so get there early. *Hidalgo, btw Calles 9 and 10, tel. 88/16–67–06.*

BY PLANE Aeroméxico (tel. 88/12–24–60) offers one flight daily to Mexico City; cost at press time was $115 one-way. Matamoros's airport is 17 kilometers south of town, toward Ciudad Victoria. The frequent blue AEROPUERTO pesera from Plaza Allende (Independencia, at Calle 10) drops you off a kilometer from the airport. A taxi costs about $5.

GETTING AROUND

For a city of its size, Matamoros is easily navigable. All north–south streets are numbered, and their cross streets form a neat grid. The city center is bordered by **Plaza Hidalgo** to the south and the **Mercado Juárez** to the north. The **puente internacional** (international bridge) and the **puente viejo** (old bridge) are both 8 blocks north of downtown Matamoros, and the former connects Matamoros and Brownsville. Walking is the easiest and fastest way to cross the border (50¢ each way); drivers pay $2. Peseras run about every 20 minutes to the bridge, bus station, and American Consulate.

WHERE TO SLEEP

Rooms in Matamoros are expensive by Mexican standards, but they're half the price of those in Brownsville. Budget hotels, virtually indistinguishable from one another, are clustered on and near Calle Abasolo. **Hotel Majestic** (Abasolo 89, btw Calles 8 and 9, tel. 88/13–36–80) is for those willing to put up with cockroaches in exchange for bargain-basement prices (doubles $8; $9 with TV). Keep in mind that Matamoros isn't the safest city in Mexico, and the cheaper hotels tend to attract a sketchier clientele.

Casa de Huéspedes Margarita. The cheap, fan-only rooms can get pretty sticky (pay the extra dollar for air-conditioning), but roaches are as scarce as the hot water is plentiful. Sparsely-furnished bedrooms (singles $6, doubles $8) open onto a cheery pool-blue patio. *Calle 4, btw Abasolo and Matamoros, tel. 88/13–72–78.*

Hotel Alameda. At $8 for a single and $10 for a double, this is one of the best deals around. The immaculate rooms are deliciously cool and the snack options in the lobby rival those of any American movie theater. For all this, you'll gladly put up with the pervasive smell of air freshener. *Victoria 91, btw Calles 10 and 11, tel. 88/16–77–90.*

ROUGHING IT Matamoros can be a risky place to rough it, but desperate travelers have been known to try the bustling and uncomfortable bus station. If you have a sleeping bag, you can camp for free on the beach at Playa Bagdad (*see Near Matamoros, below*).

FOOD

Head to the Mercado Juárez for tacos, *tortas* (sandwiches), and other cheap eats. The heat may be unbearable, but if you're on a tight budget, remember the direct correlation between air-conditioning and high prices. The smell of freshly ground coffee wafts from **Los Panchos Café y Pan,** a large, spartan breakfast joint across from the public bathrooms on Plaza Allende.

Café El Económico. The huge serve-yourself buffet makes this place a mecca for starving travelers. It's only 25¢ for a soda and $1.75–$3 for a helping of *gorditas* (fried dough balls you can fill with vegetables, beans, or meat). Die-hard *telenovela* (soap opera) fans can watch the boob tube while eating. *Calle 10 No. 157, btw González and Abasolo, tel. 88/12–14–58. Wheelchair access.*

La Canasta. If Howard Johnson's decided to go Mexican, this is what it would look like. Local kids crowd around the orange formica tables gobbling down the famous double burger with cheese ($2). The $1 burritos and 50¢ tacos with cheese are as cheap as they come. *Abasolo, btw Calle 7 and 8, tel. 88/12–29–00. Open daily 9–7. Wheelchair access.*

Las Dos Repúblicas. This strange half-restaurant, half-store has air-conditioning and tables suitable for Munchkins. But at $4 an entrée, the flautas (six fried, meat-filled tortillas with beans, chips, guacamole, and sour cream) or quesadillas (six tortillas with white Chihuahua cheese and hot sauce) are a great deal. Wash it all down with an 18-ounce margarita, which may be a whopping 6 bucks, but you won't be needing another. *Calle 9, at Matamoros, tel. 88/16–68–94. Open daily 9–8. Wheelchair access.*

The northeast isn't famous for its food and drink, but caffeine addicts will get a serious buzz from café de olla, a blend of coffee, chocolate, and cinnamon brewed slowly in a clay pot.

Pin-Pon Papas. The guy behind the counter is as goofy as the restaurant's name, but he serves a mean baked potato ($1) topped with cauliflower, broccoli, and *chayote* (a green squash-like vegetable). Seats are scarce here, and the cramped service counter serves as gossip central. *Calle 5, btw Bravo and Bustamante, tel. 88/13–53–42. Open Tues.–Sun. 11–9:30.*

WORTH SEEING

As evidenced by swarms of U.S. tourists, Matamoros's main draw is its excellent shopping. Loudly colored serapes, bullwhips, and mounds of silver jewelry are sold at **Mercado Juárez** (Matamoros, at Calle 10) and at Matamoros's old market, **Pasaje Juárez** (Calle 8, across from Hotel Roma). Stop in at the **Gift Sohp** (no, folks, that's not a typo) on Pasaje Juárez, where leather rifle cases hang menacingly from the serape-covered walls, and silver-and-turquoise belt buckles are the size of small tortillas. The city's last remaining art gallery is housed in the slightly yellowing but nonetheless regal **Teatro Reforma** (Calle 6, at Abasolo, tel. 88/12–51–20), where a surprising number of local artists exhibit their work. Admission to the gallery is free; it's open Tuesday–Saturday 8–4. The Teatro also hosts regional and local dance and theater. Nearby **Calle Abasolo** is closed to traffic, making it an ideal spot to grab a seat and watch the river of pedestrians ebb and flow through the shops.

Air-conditioning adds to the appeal of the small stone fortress of the **Casa Mata,** established in 1845 to defend the city against an anticipated U.S. invasion. It wasn't completed in time, however, and U.S. troops under Zachary Taylor were able to capture Matamoros easily in 1846. The fortress is now a museum housing photos and artifacts, mainly from the Mexican Revolution. *Guatemala and Santos Degollado. Admission free. Open Tues.–Sat. 9:30–5:30 and Sun. 9:30–3:30.*

CHEAP THRILLS

When the energy-sapping heat becomes too much, head for the swimming pool at the **Centro Deportivo Eduardo Chávez** (Guatemala, near Laura Villar, tel. 88/16–28–37), across from Casa Mata (*see* Worth Seeing, *above*). This clean 50-meter pool is filled with madly splashing local kids by midday, so get your laps done early. There are dressing rooms and showers, but you must bring your own towel. The pool is open late March to mid-September, daily 8–noon and 2–6; admission is $2, $1 students. Just north of the city is the bustling and brightly tiled **Instituto de Bellas Artes** (Calle 8, btw Iturbide and Hidalgo, tel. 89/13–51–94), where artists of all ages come to take classes in everything from sculpture and photography to Mexican folk dancing. Unobtrusive visitors can watch dancers practice the beautiful *huapango* (a rhythmic folkdance) weekdays 4–8. On Sundays, avid soccer players ignore the midday heat and flock to the patchy field behind the old **Museo de Maíz** (cnr of Calle 5 and Constitución) for a serious pickup game.

AFTER DARK

Like other border towns, Matamoros attracts throngs of tourists for a night of unbridled indulgence. Middle-aged bachelors and bachelorettes hang out at **Los Canos** (Álvaro Obregón 83, tel. 88/12–50–85), where you can dance to country music on an elevated dance floor without anyone laughing at you. The club is open daily 10 AM–2 AM, with live music Thursday–Sunday, 9–midnight. A mellower crowd frequents **La Tequila** (Álvaro Obregón 42, tel. 88/16–75–22), the best spot if you really want to dance (as opposed to standing around and gawking). The club is open until 2 or 3 AM, with a $3 cover Friday and Saturday ($2 Thursday and Sunday). To escape the tourist scene, walk toward the old bridge to **El Hobie** (Constitución 496, no phone). The owner may be gruff but he's eager to serve you powerful concoctions like "Kiss on the Butt" (piña colada and sex on the beach combined; $2) or "Saddam Hussein" (a staggering mixture of clear liquors and lime; $2).

Near Matamoros

PLAYA BAGDAD During the U.S. Civil War, Playa Bagdad was the Confederacy's only open harbor. Freighters skirting the Union naval blockade unloaded their war supplies here and loaded up with Confederate cotton destined for Europe. Today, *palapas* (palm-covered huts) run the length of the shore, and dozens of restaurants offer fresh seafood at reasonable prices. Showers and bathrooms are free, but drivers pay $8 to park. Camping is perfectly free and legal, but be careful—the beach is deserted at night and far from civilization. To get here from Matamoros, take a blue pesera marked PLAYA (1 hr, $1.50) from Independencia and Calle 11. The last pesera back to town leaves at 7 PM. If you want the beach all to yourself, come on a weekday afternoon, when the place is vacant.

Reynosa

Because of Mexico's plummeting economy, Reynosa has become a destination for opportunity-seeking Mexicans and Americans hoping to take advantage of favorable exchange rates. Although Reynosa is a convenient starting point if you're bound for Mexico City, Monterrey, or El Bajío, its still a border town of limited charm. Nonetheless, the city is not without its long-held traditions; agricultural goods are brought in weekly from as far as San Luis Potosí, Veracruz, and Sinaloa to be sold at Reynosa's spectacular open-air market along with regional crops like okra, wheat, and corn. The market (Colón, btw Hidalgo and Blvd. Morelos) stretches for 2 blocks and on a typical day the smells of fruit, sweat, leather, and tamales intertwine as they waft through the crowded streets. At night, tourists from nearby McAllen, Texas, stop shopping and flock to the Zona Rosa for the raucous nightlife.

BASICS

AMERICAN EXPRESS Erika Viajes, 8 blocks from the plaza, provides limited American Express services: They won't cash personal checks, but they do replace lost traveler's checks, hold cardmembers' mail, and sell traveler's checks. *Ávila Camacho 1325, at Lázaro Cárdenas, tel. 89/22–60–16. Open weekdays 9–6, Sat. 9–1.*

CASAS DE CAMBIO You'll pass several casas de cambio on Zaragoza heading downtown from the international border, most of which don't cash traveler's checks but offer excellent rates for American dollars. If you've only got traveler's checks, pray the manager is on duty at **Casa de Cambio Sogo**—he has to approve the transaction. *Juárez 610 Nte., no phone. Open weekdays 9–6, Sat. 9–2.*

CROSSING THE BORDER You can stay in Reynosa up to 72 hours without getting a tourist card, but if you plan to stay longer or venture more than 22 kilometers into Mexico, get one at the border crossing (*see* Passports, Visas, and Tourist Cards in Chapter 1).

EMERGENCIES You can call the **police** (Morelos, at Argentina, tel. 89/22–00–08); **fire** department (tel. 89/24–39–99); or **Cruz Roja** (tel. 89/22–13–14) for an **ambulance**.

MEDICAL AID **Farmacia López** is open 24 hours. *Aldama 101, at Hidalgo, tel. 88/22–84–84 or 88/22–96–67.*

PHONES AND MAIL The only public phone within 2 blocks of the bus station is at **7-Eleven**, across the street from the east side of the station. There's a cluster of **pay phones** in the plaza, where you'll also find a *caseta de larga distancia* (long-distance booth) and public fax office (Hidalgo 990, tel. 89/22–85–93) that's open daily 8 AM–10 PM. The main **post office** (Cnr of Díaz and Colón, near the train station) is open weekdays 8–8 and Saturday 9–1. They'll hold your mail at the following address for up to 10 days: Lista de Correos, Reynosa, Tamaulipas, CP 88620, México.

VISITOR INFORMATION Reynosa doesn't have an official tourist office, but Sr. Jorge Treviño, head of the city's commercial and tourism development office, is eager to supply transport information, historical facts about the city, a free map, and a grand tour of his tiny office. He's available Monday–Saturday 8 AM–10 PM. *Morelos 320, 2 blocks west of Plaza Hidalgo, tel. 89/22–10–71 or 89/22–24–36.*

COMING AND GOING

A bridge over the Río Bravo connects Reynosa and McAllen, Texas. Reynosa is small; its downtown area, laid out in a grid, can be crossed in less than 15 minutes. **Hidalgo** is the principal north–south axis, and **Morelos** the main east–west axis. Minibuses (25¢) run from the bridge to the plaza, the train station, and the bus depot.

BY BUS The **Central Camionera** (Colon 1001, tel. 89/22–84–08) is behind the Gigante supermarket, 5 blocks south and 10 blocks east of the main plaza. To get here, catch a C. CAMIONERA/OBRERO microbus from the bridge or the center of town. There have been a few thefts in and around the station, so be extra careful, especially at night. The station and its caseta de larga distancia are open 24 hours; luggage storage is available 6 AM–9 PM (25¢ per hour, $1 per day). There's frequent service to Matamoros (2 hrs, $3) and Río Bravo (½ hr, $1). First-class buses also leave for Monterrey (3 per day, 3 hrs, $7). First-class **Omnibus de México** (tel. 89/22–33–07) sends buses west to Chihuahua (15 hrs, $37) and south to Mexico City (13 hrs, $40). **Transportes del Norte** (tel. 89/22–04–92) goes daily to Guadalajara (18 hrs, $40) and Mexico City (15 hrs, $33). **Autobuses del Oriente (ADO)** (tel. 89/22–87–13) has first-class buses to Tampico (3 per day, 6½ hrs, $14), Tuxpan (3 per day, 10 hrs, $20), and Veracruz City (daily, 16 hrs, $36).

BY TRAIN The train station (tel. 89/22–00–85) is south of the town plaza, at the end of Hidalgo. The special first-class **El Tamaulipeco** departs at 11:25 AM daily for Monterrey (4½ hrs, $9). The train to Matamoros leaves at 2:40 PM (2½ hrs, $3). Tickets are sold from 10:30 AM until they're gone or until Margarita, the cashier, gets tired of sitting around. The C. CAMIONERA/OBRERO and COLON microbuses run from the bridge and bus depot down Calle Colón, where you can get off at Hidalgo and walk south a short block to the tracks.

WHERE TO SLEEP

Hotels in the Zona Rosa and around the central plaza cater to businesspeople and vacationers, and are priced accordingly. For a budget room, head toward the train station; the cheapest rooms are found just north of the tracks.

Hotel Avenida. The seductively frosty air-conditioning makes this immaculate little hotel a hard one to turn down; at $10 a room (singles and doubles) it's an affordable luxury. A grassy, partially shaded patio borders spotless rooms with clean carpets and TVs. *Zaragoza 885 Ote., tel. 89/22–05–92. 26 rooms, all with bath. Luggage storage. Wheelchair access.*

Hotel Estación. The "Station," just across the tracks from the train depot and a few blocks south of downtown, couldn't be more convenient. If you're tired enough, you won't even hear the roar of passing trains. Rooms are small but relatively clean, and rickety air-conditioners manage to keep the rooms cool. Singles and doubles go for $7 ($8 with air-conditioning). Avoid the cheaper rooms with only a fan; they're incredibly stuffy and usually lack hot water. *Hidalgo 305, tel. 89/22–73–02. 40 rooms, all with bath. Luggage storage.*

Hotel Nuevo León. If you've ever wanted to spend the night in a colonial ranch house, here's your chance. Dark wood stairs lead to low-ceilinged rooms complete with squeaky narrow dressers and miniature double beds. Singles are $7, doubles $9. *P. Díaz 580, tel. 89/22–13–10. 28 rooms, all with bath.*

FOOD

Cheap taco stands and carts selling *elote* (grilled corn on the cob) can be found on almost every corner, and the piles of fruit at the open market provide some of the freshest and cheapest snacks around. For sit-down meals, cruise the **peatonal** (pedestrian-only street), which leads to the more elegant eateries around the main plaza.

The mirror-lined **Café París** (Hidalgo 815, tel. 89/22–55–35) is always full, so you may have to loom in the doorway until someone vacates one of the paisley-cushioned booths. The delicious *comida corrida* (pre-prepared lunch special), served between noon and 2, is a steal at $2; a filling breakfast omelet is $3. In the evening, the bar is a good place to hang out, with two-for-one white Russians ($2.50) and potent margaritas. **La Fogata** (Matamoros 750, tel. 89/12–47–72), an elegant, air-conditioned restaurant/piano bar, is the place for a splurge. *Cabrito* (grilled baby goat) is $8, and beers are just $1. Vegetarians won't find much here beside the *queso flameado* (cheese broiled in a smoky oven) for $4. Enjoy the live music daily 2–6 and 7–midnight.

CHEAP THRILLS

On the weekend, maquiladora workers escape the relentless Reynosa heat and head out to **Bocatoma,** where the Río Bravo separates Reynosa from Mission, Texas. Plenty of serious water-seekers can be found splashing around the tree-lined shore at the southeast edge of the river. You can also join one of the haphazard kickball games in the center of the park, or just kick back and take in the cool breeze. The river can get pretty trashed by the end of the day, so come early. To get to "the Boca," take Bus 22 or a MAGNIPARK bus from the corner of Porfirio Díaz and Colón. After the 25-minute ride, you'll be let off a 20-minute walk from the park's entrance. Walk north for about five minutes to the SEYMOUR sign on the right-hand side of the road, turn left and take the center dirt road toward the BIENVENIDOS sign all the way to the park.

AFTER DARK

At night, Reynosa gets overwhelming rowdy and seedy. Fortunately, most of the serious drug trafficking, prostitution, and violence is relegated to the city's *Zona Roja* (red-light district), located a good 10 blocks west of the city center. A little easier to swallow is the Zona Rosa, a five-block section of streets bordering the international bridge that becomes flooded with 18-year-olds blasting techno from their cars. If you really want to boogie, head to **El Rodeo** (Allende 890, just south of the bridge, tel. 89/22–95–33), where the gaping mouth of an enormous plaster bull serves as the entrance. The large circular dance floor is suitable for any number of spastic moves. **Fiesta Mexicana** (Ocampo 1140, at Allende, tel. 89/22–01–11) has a mellower atmosphere and an older crowd. The house band plays everything from *baladas* (ballads) to salsa, Friday–Sunday 8 PM–3 AM. Friday and Sunday there's no cover, and Saturday it's only $4, including one free drink.

Nuevo Laredo

Of all the eastern border towns, Nuevo Laredo, just over the international bridge from Laredo, Texas, gets the largest onslaught of American souvenir-seekers. Shopping is the primary pursuit here, and you'll find a warren of stalls and shops concentrated on Avenida Guerrero in a seven-block stretch that extends from the international bridge to the main plaza. In addition to the standard border-town schlock, Nuevo Laredo's shops stock a good selection of high-quality handicrafts imported from all over Mexico, available at somewhat inflated prices. Wander a few blocks off the main drag in any direction for better prices and smaller crowds. There's also a large crafts market on the east side of Guerrero, just north of the plaza.

Nuevo Laredo's vibrant commercialism takes the form of overflowing stalls, street vendors parading meter-high stacks of straw hats, and little kids standing against shaded walls with photos of the latest lucha libre (wrestling) heroes.

Nuevo Laredo was founded after the Treaty of Guadalupe Hidalgo in 1848, which ended the Mexican-American War. The treaty established the Río Bravo (or Rio Grande) as the border between the two countries, and forced Mexico to give up a substantial amount of territory. Many of Laredo's Mexican residents, suddenly finding themselves living in the United States, crossed the river and founded Nuevo Laredo on what had been the outskirts of town. Today, Nuevo Laredo's economy depends largely on gringos who head south for a few days of drunken revelry, returning home with suitcases full of souvenirs, a bottle of tequila, and a mean hangover.

BASICS

AMERICAN EXPRESS You can replace lost AmEx traveler's checks, change traveler's checks, cash personal checks, receive mail, and buy traveler's checks at **Lozano Viajes Internacionales**. *Paseo Reforma 3311, Col. Jardín, Nuevo Laredo, Tamaulipas, CP 88260, tel. 87/15–44–55. Open weekdays 9–5:30.*

CASAS DE CAMBIO Change cash at one of several **casas de cambio** on Guerrero, just below the international bridge. To change traveler's checks, try **Lozano Viajes Internacionales** (*see above*) or **Divisas Terminal** (open Mon.–Sat. 6 AM–10 PM, Sun. 6 AM–8 PM) in the bus station. **Banamex** (Guerrero, btw Canales and Madero, tel. 87/12–30–01) has an ATM that accepts Cirrus, Plus, Visa, and MasterCard.

CROSSING THE BORDER Although it's unlikely anyone will stop you from sauntering past the customs guards and making your way into Mexico unmolested, it's best to have a passport or other photo ID. If you plan on traveling farther south (22 kilometers or more) or staying in Mexico longer than 72 hours, cross the parking lot west of the international bridge and ask the immigration office for a tourist card (*see* Passports, Visas, and Tourist Cards, Chapter 1).

EMERGENCIES In an emergency, dial 06. You can also call the **police** (tel. 87/12–21–46); **fire** department (87/12–21–24); or **Cruz Roja** (tel. 87/12–09–49) for an **ambulance**.

MEDICAL AID The **Cruz Roja** (Independencia 1619, at San Antonio, tel. 87/12-09-49) offers emergency and routine medical care. There are a number of well-stocked **Benavides** pharmacies throughout town. Try the one on Guerrero (at Padre Mier, tel. 87/12-21-60) open daily 8 AM–10 PM. For 24-hour service, head next door to **Farmacia Calderón** (Guerrero 704, tel. 87/12-55-63).

PHONES AND MAIL It's quickest and cheapest to drop foreign mail at the U.S. post office, about 6 blocks north of the border. The main **post office** (Reynosa, at Dr. Mier, tel. 87/12-20-90), behind the Palacio Municipal, is open weekdays 8–7 and Saturday 9–1. They'll hold your mail at the following address for up to 10 days: Lista de Correos, Nuevo Laredo, Tamaulipas, CP 88000, México. In the same building is a telegram and fax service (both sending only) open weekdays 9–7, weekends 9–noon.

Ladatel pay **phones** can be found on Plaza Hidalgo, but it's cheaper to place international calls from the States; pay phones are across the international bridge, just past U.S. customs.

VISITOR INFORMATION The **tourist office** is housed in a large dusty booth on the west sidewalk of the international bridge. An official secretary is available from 8 to 2, but from 2 to 8 a more helpful social service occupies the office; they'll help you dig up tourist pamphlets, and often supply free maps of Nuevo Laredo and other border towns. *Puente Internacional, tel. 87/12-01-04.*

COMING AND GOING

BY BUS The **Terminal Central Maclovio Herrera** (J. R. Romo 3800) is a 25-minute bus ride south of the bridge. Take a 50¢ PUENTE/CENTRAL or CAMIONERA/CARRETERA bus from the corner of Juárez and Victoria or from Galeano on the east side of the square. The 10-minute taxi ride costs $2. **Transportes Frontera** (tel. 87/14-08-29) runs nonstop buses every 3 hours to Mexico City (15 hrs, $32 1st class; 15 hrs, $29 2nd class). Buses also leave hourly for Saltillo (4 hrs, $9 1st class; 5 hrs, $8 2nd class), San Luis Potosí (12 hrs, $21, 1st class only), and Monterrey (3 hrs, $8, 1st class only). First-class **Omnibus de México** (tel. 87/14-06-17) serves nearby cities as well as Zacatecas (8 hrs, $21) and Guadalajara (14 hrs, $31). A caseta de larga distancia is open 24 hours a day, and the casa de cambio (open weekdays 6 AM–10 PM, Sun. 6 AM–8 PM) changes traveler's checks. Luggage storage is available Monday–Saturday 7 AM–10 PM, Sunday 7–5.

BY TRAIN The **train station** is on López de Lara, at Gutiérrez, about a dozen short blocks west of the main plaza. It's a 15-minute walk from the border to the station; otherwise, take an ARTEGA GONZALEZ bus from Juárez and Victoria. The first-class train to Mexico City (25 hrs, $22) leaves daily at 6:55 PM, with stops in Monterrey (3½ hrs, $5), Saltillo (7½ hrs, $7), San Luis Potosí (15½ hrs, $21), San Miguel de Allende (18½ hrs, $24), and Querétaro (19½ hrs, $18), among others. For trips to Mexico City, San Luis Potosí, San Miguel de Allende, and Querétaro, first-class includes air-conditioning. All tickets go on sale daily at 5:30 PM.

BY PLANE **Mexicana** (tel. 87/12-22-11) flies to Guadalajara and Mexico City. Cost at press time for a one-way ticket to either city was $94. The airport is 15 kilometers south of town, and there's no public transportation here. A taxi costs about $3. Hitchhiking is a possibility, but for the most part you'll be ignored.

GETTING AROUND

Nuevo Laredo is split down the middle by **Avenida Guerrero,** which runs north–south from the **international bridge** to **Avenida Reforma** (which connects up with the highway to Monterrey). The city's two main squares, **Plaza Juárez** and **Plaza Hidalgo,** are also located on Guerrero, at the edges of the six-block area that makes up the central market. Buses marked PUENTE/CENTRAL and CAMIONERA/CARRETERA (50¢) run down Guerrero to the bus station; green-and-white 1B buses run from Plaza Hidalgo east to the train station.

WHERE TO SLEEP

Hotels tend to be either too expensive or dreadfully run-down; your best bet for something in between is the area around Avenida Guerrero, between the bridge and central square. The streets stay lit until 9 or 10 PM, and Guerrero is almost always busy. Nevertheless, be careful of the many thieves who target tourists.

Los Dos Laredos. Hidden among the casas de cambio near the bridge, this hotel is surprisingly clean and friendly. The throb of nearby discos can be heard late into the night, but you can't beat the $6 singles and $8 doubles. Rooms are for the most part sunny and spacious, and fluffy towels make up for the wimpy water pressure. On weekends, check in before 6 PM, as this place tends to fill up. *Matamoros 108, at 15 de Junio, tel. 87/12–24–19. 23 rooms, all with bath.*

Hotel La Finca. Large, comfy rooms with air-conditioning and color TVs are standard here. Expect soft, clean towels in the bathrooms, and hot water day and night. Singles are $12, doubles $13. *Reynosa 811, tel. 87/12–04–70. 25 rooms, all with bath. Luggage storage.*

Hotel Romanos. This is by far the cleanest, most reliable hotel in town. Pearly-white bed covers and spotless bathrooms are complemented by blissfully cool air-conditioning and plenty of hot water. Singles and doubles are only $8, $11.50 with color TV. *Dr. Mier 2402, tel. 87/12–23–91. 15 rooms, all with bath. Luggage storage. Wheelchair access.*

FOOD

The dining scene here includes everything from cheap taco stands and fast-food joints to overpriced eateries that cater to touring Texans. For moderately priced restaurants, explore the side streets south of the main plaza.

Cafetería Modelo. After a long day of shopping (or a long night at the discos), come here for the huge all-day breakfasts and a mellow atmosphere. Try the huevos rancheros with orange juice ($2.50) or fill up on an order of tamales (4 pieces of chicken coated in cornmeal; $2), served with beans and coffee. *Dr. Mier, at Ocampo, tel. 87/12–15–66. Open daily 7 AM–3 AM. Wheelchair access.*

El Principal. While the bare walls and fluorescent lighting create a hospital-like ambiance, the meal-sized *botanas* (appetizers) are a real bargain. Try the *queso flameado* (cheese broiled in a smoky oven; 50¢) accompanied by a stack of piping hot tortillas. *624 Guerrero, tel. 87/12–13–01. Open daily 8 AM–11:30 PM.*

Restaurant Hotel Reforma. This 24-hour restaurant at one of the classier hotels in town isn't much to look at, but it's always packed at lunchtime with hotel guests and local families. They come for one of the best comidas corridas around—including salad, soup, dessert, and your choice of chicken or breaded beef, all for $4. *Guerrero 806, tel. 87/12–34–88.*

AFTER DARK

Nuevo Laredo's nighttime activities are every bit as frenzied as its daytime shopping. The most touristy and expensive discos are located on the south end of Guerrero, but local crowds head 1 block south of 15 de Mayo at **OK Tequila** (Victoria, at Matamoros, tel. 87/12–07–76), which plays everything from '70s hits to salsa and nueva canción. On Saturday nights, a $15 cover enables you to invent an unlimited amount of alcoholic stews at the open bar; Thursday and Friday nights, cover is only $1 for women, $2 for men. Solitary night owls should seek out **Pepper's Haus** (Cnr of Perú and Ocampo, no phone). This drive-through cocktail and *botana* (appetizer) joint is packed early at night, but empties out when the discos open, making it the perfect place to sit under the trees and sip a cool beer ($1). If you really want to savor the outdoors, grab a popsicle and take a spin in a horse-drawn cart ($3 an hour).

Monterrey

In this metropolis of four million people, decadence and absolute poverty coexist side by side, a jarring reminder that Monterrey is the country's unchallenged industrial giant. In juxtaposition to the city's grand buildings and luxurious suburbs is the ring of squalid huts and smoke-belching factories known as the *cinturón de miseria* (belt of misery). Pollution is a serious problem here, and unless you confine yourself to Monterrey's sprawling but manageable center, it's likely you'll end up with a serious case of the urban-industrial blues.

After founding Monterrey in the late 1500s, the Spanish encouraged settlement in the region by granting vast tracts of land to a handful of families. The success of these sheep ranchers quickly created a small, wealthy elite, who, following the construction of a railroad in the 1880s, decided to invest in industry. The powerful Garza Sada family refined the art of mass-produced beer, and religiously reinvested the profits. They established glass factories and cardboard mills, and even produced their own barrels and delivery wagons. To ensure proper training for the future leaders of this vast industrial empire, the Garza Sadas founded the **Instituto Tecnológico de Monterrey,** now considered one of the best universities in Latin America.

Life in Monterrey, also known as "the Pittsburgh of Mexico," is hectic, and staying here can be quite expensive. Even so, those who take the time to wander the busy streets will encounter the region's best museums, good examples of colonial and modern civic architecture, and a spectacular central plaza that gives great views of the Sierra Madre, which form a semicircle around the southern edge of town. These pine-forested mountains are home to the **Parque Nacional Cumbres de Monterrey** (Summits of Monterrey National Park), known for several beautiful caves and waterfalls, as well as **La Silla** (The Chair), a saddle-shaped rock formation that is the symbol of Monterrey.

BASICS

AMERICAN EXPRESS The new AmEx office appears disorganized, but the staff is patient and friendly. They cash personal checks, replace lost or stolen traveler's checks, and hold card members' mail indefinitely at: Avenida San Pedro 215 Nte, Colonia de Valle, San Pedro Garza García, Nuevo León. *214 Pino Suárez, at Isaac Garza, tel. 8/318–33–85. Open weekdays 9–6, Sat. 9–noon. From the Zona Rosa, take* RUTA *39 bus north on Pino Suárez and get off at Isaac Garza.*

BOOKSTORES The **American Bookstore** (Garza Sada 2404a, near the Pemex station, tel. 8/387–08–38) has a great selection of English books.

CASAS DE CAMBIO **Base Internacional** (Pino Suárez Nte. 1217, tel. 8/372–86–22), just north of Avenida Colón and the Cuauhtémoc metro stop, changes traveler's checks weekdays 9–6, Saturday 9–1. **Casa de Cambio Euromex** (Juárez, at Padre Mier, tel. 8/318–17–73; open weekdays 9–6) only changes cash. **Banamex** (Pino Suárez 933 Nte.) has an ATM that accepts Cirrus, Plus, MasterCard, and Visa.

CONSULATES **United States.** This office will replace birth certificates and lost passports, provide tax information and a notary public, and will help in emergency situations. *Constitución Pte. 411, tel. 8/345–21–20. Open weekdays 8–2.*

EMERGENCIES In an emergency, contact the **police** (Venustiano Carranza 215 Nte, tel. 8/370–00–48) or the **fire** department (tel. 8/342–00–53). For an **ambulance,** call the **Cruz Roja** (tel. 8/342–12–12).

LAUNDRY At **Lavandería Automática Express,** you can get 3 kilos of clothes washed for about $4. *Garza Sada 3022, no phone. Open Mon.–Sat. 9:30–8:30.*

MEDICAL AID For nonemergency consultations, try the **Cruz Roja clinic** (Alfonso Reyes, Col. del Prado, tel. 8/342–12–12), near the Plaza de Toros. **Benavides** pharmacy (Morales 499, tel. 8/345–02–57) is open daily 7 AM–10 PM. For 24-hour service, try **Farmacia Medix** (Pino Suárez 510 Sur, tel. 8/342–90–02).

PHONES AND MAIL The main **post office** is in the basement of the Palacio Federal building, at the north end of the Macroplaza. They'll hold your mail at the following address for up to 10 days: Lista de Correos, Administración 1, Monterrey, Nuevo León, CP 64000, México. *Washington, at Zaragoza, tel. 8/342–40–03. Open weekdays 8–7, Sat. 9–1.*

Phone calls from casetas are unjustifiably expensive here, so it's best to use one of the many **Latadel** phones scattered throughout the city. You can buy Latadel phone cards in 20-, 30-, or 50-peso units at most large supermarkets or drugstores (look for the Latadel sign in the store window); try **El Niagara** (Morelos 359 Ote., Zona Rosa, tel. 8/342–40–23), open daily 9:30–8.

VISITOR INFORMATION **Infotour** (Zaragoza, at Matamoros, tel. 8/345–08–70), under the Macroplaza, stocks great brochures and maps, and has a friendly English-speaking staff. It's open daily 10–5. For information about special expositions or fairs, call **Expo Guadalupe** at 8/340–07–07.

COMING AND GOING

BY BUS The huge **Central de Autobuses** is an impressive transport hub serving virtually the entire country. Frequent buses leave for the border towns of Nuevo Laredo (2 ½ hrs, $8 1st class), Reynosa (3½ hrs, $7 1st class), and Matamoros (3 hrs, $9 1st class). Numerous first-class buses also head to Tampico (8 hrs, $16), Saltillo (1½ hrs, $3) and Mexico City (13 hrs, $30). Major first-class bus lines include **Omnibus de México** (tel. 8/374–07–16), which serves Chihuahua (12 hrs, $25) and Juárez (18 hrs, $38); **Transportes del Norte** (tel. 8/318–37–45), which, in conjunction with **Greyhound**, goes to San Antonio (7 hrs, $25), Dallas (12 hrs, $46), and Houston (10 hrs, $40). For other destinations, try **Transportes Zua Zua** (tel. 8/374–04–20) or **Tres Estrellas de Oro** (tel. 83/74–24–10). The terminal has a post office, 24-hour pharmacy, luggage lockers ($3 a day), Ladatel phones, and a medical center. Well-policed departure gates and plenty of traffic make this place perfectly safe to hang out in, but sleeping might be a little uncomfortable.

The bus terminal is on Colón, near Cuauhtémoc in the northwestern part of the city. The easiest way to get here is to take the Line 1 metro to the Central stop. From downtown, catch the RUTA 39 bus, which runs from the Macroplaza north along Juárez, to the bus station. From the bus station to downtown, catch the RUTA 45 bus at Bernardo Reyes and Colón or a RUTA 206 PERIFERICO bus on Suárez.

BY TRAIN Three trains pass through Monterrey's station (tel. 8/375–46–04) daily. The first-class **El Regiomontano,** with seats and sleeping berths, runs from Monterrey to Saltillo (2 hrs, $2) and San Luis Potosí (10 hrs, $8). The 14-hour trip to Mexico City costs $18 ($45 for a sleeping berth), and the train leaves at 7:50 PM. The first-class **El Tamaulipeco** travels to Matamoros via Reynosa (6½ hrs, $6). The Mexico City–Monterrey–Nuevo Laredo train is also first-class only. The trip from Monterrey to Mexico City ($18) is 17 hours long, with stops in Saltillo (3 hrs, $13), San Luis Potosí (10 hrs, $8), and Querétaro. The trip to Nuevo Laredo (5 hrs, $5) is direct. Tickets for all trains are sold the day of departure only at the TAQUILLA window, 8:30–12:30 and 4–8.

The train depot is 6 blocks northwest of the bus station and the Central metro stop. To reach downtown, cross Venustiano Carranza in front of the train station, head east 2 blocks on Calzada Victoria to Bernardo Reyes, and take a RUTA 39 or RUTA 45 bus. For the bus station, get off at Colón; otherwise, both buses will let you off at the Macroplaza. The other option is to hoof it to the bus station and catch a bus there (*see above*).

BY PLANE The **Aeropuerto Internacional Mariano Escobedo** (tel. 8/345–44–32), equipped with luggage storage ($4) and a money exchange booth, is 6 kilometers northeast of downtown. The only way to get here is by taxi, which will cost about $10. **Aeroméxico** (tel. 8/344–77–30) and **Mexicana** (tel. 8/344–77–10) serve most domestic destinations. At press time, the flight to Mexico City on Mexicana cost $56. **American Airlines** (tel. 8/340–30–31) had five flights a day to Dallas ($105 one-way).

Monterrey

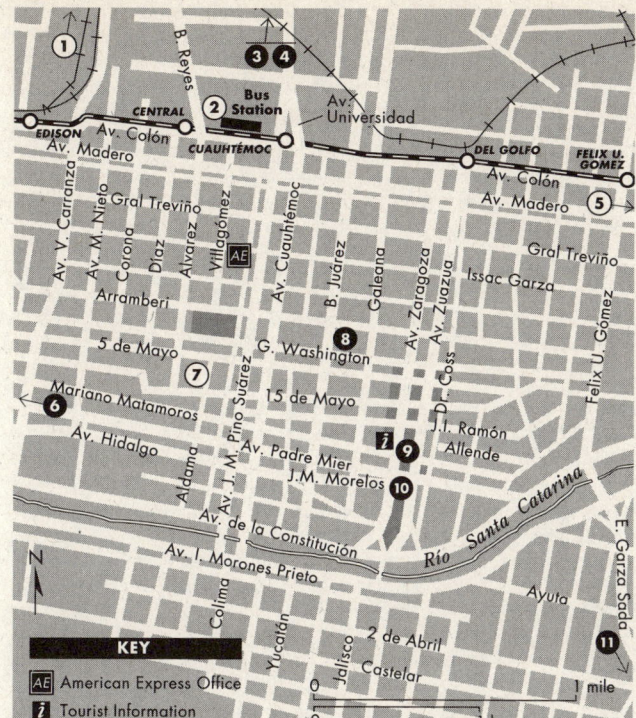

Sights ●
Cervecería Cuauhtémoc, 3
El Obispado, 6
Instituto Tecnológico de Monterrey, 11
Macroplaza, 9
Mercado Juárez, 8
Museo de Arte Contemporáneo (MARCO), 10
Parque de los Niños Héroes, 4

Lodging ○
Hotel Estación, 1
Hotel Posada de los Reyes, 7
Hotel Victoria, 2
Villa Deportiva Juvenil, 5

GETTING AROUND

Monterrey is a sprawling monstrosity, and very few places are within walking distance of one another. Luckily, the extensive public transit system makes it easy to get around. Downtown, also called the **Zona Rosa,** is the city's luxury hotel and shopping area, bordered on the east by the **Macroplaza** and on the west by **Avenida Juárez.** The intersection of Juárez and Arramberi marks the official center of town, and addresses to the west of this intersection are followed by "Poniente" or "Pte."; to the east, by "Oriente" or "Ote."; to the north, by "Norte" or "Nte."; and to the south, by "Sur." Street numbers become larger the farther you move from the intersection.

BY METRO The new Monterrey Metro is a modern and efficient system that runs across the city along elevated tracks. There are two lines: Line 1 runs east–west from Exposición to the city's westernmost perimeter, and Line 2 runs north–south from the Cuauhtémoc Brewery to the Macroplaza. Purchase tickets from station vending machines in units of one, two, three, or eight rides; each ride costs less than 50¢. The metro runs daily 4:45 AM–11:45 PM.

BY BUS Monterrey's loud, rickety, smoke-belching buses go everywhere. The buses on each route are color-coded, and the names of major stops are often painted across the windshield—sometimes they're even legible. There are a few fixed bus stops, marked by blue PARADA signs, but buses will stop anywhere; just wave madly at any corner along a route. Most buses run until midnight, except the 24-hour RUTA 1 bus.

WHERE TO SLEEP

Monterrey's relative wealth, combined with a steady flow of business travelers, keeps hotel prices high, though there are some shoestring fleabags clustered by the obnoxiously loud bus station.

Hotel Estación. The hotel's stern management keeps things clean and quiet and charges $10 (single or double) for spartan rooms with fans. The bathrooms are small but decent, and the hot water flows readily. The primary draw, however, is the hotel's proximity to the train station. Rooms fill fast, so come early. *Victoria 1450, tel. 8/375-07-55. From train station, cross Nieto and turn right. 25 rooms, all with bath. Luggage storage. Wheelchair access.*

Hotel Posada de Los Reyes. Conveniently located 2 blocks from Pino Suárez in the Zona Rosa, this hotel serves a surprisingly familial clientele. Wall-to-wall carpeting covers rooms big enough to dance in, and vigorous air-conditioning seems to keep the cockroaches at bay. Singles and doubles are $14. *Aldama 446 Sur, tel. 8/43-18-80. 23 rooms, all with bath.*

Hotel Victoria. Although this hotel's proximity to the bus station is convenient, the exhaust-filled air has made for a slightly yellowed interior. Still, the rooms (singles $11, doubles $13) are spacious and well-kept, and the water here is sizzling—just wait patiently for its grudging arrival. *Bernardo Reyes 1205 Nte., tel. 8/375-69-19. 1 block NW of bus depot. 75 rooms, all with bath. Luggage storage.*

HOSTELS **Villa Deportiva Juvenil.** This enormous gym-like dormitory sits above a small school on the eastern side of the city. It's easily accessible by metro, and the central patio is a beautiful place to breathe in some fresh air and look at the stars. Singles cost $5, or you can share a quad for $2 apiece. Free camping on the grassy outdoor patio is also an option, though giggling throngs of curious schoolchildren appear in the morning. If you need to call here, do so before 6 PM. *Madero 418 Ote, at Parque Fundidor, tel. 8/355-73-80. Take metro Line 1 (direction: Exposición) to Y Griega; walk 1 block west, turn left on Preciliano Elizondo, and head south one block. Or take* RUTA *72 bus from Macroplaza to cnr of Preciliano Elizondo and Colón. 350 beds. No curfew. Luggage storage, showers.*

FOOD

Food stands in the major markets offer the best meal deals in town—grilled meats and rice-and-beans platters are less than $2. Come early, as popular dishes usually run out by 2 or 3 PM. The fast-food chain **El Pollo Loco** (open daily 10 AM–11 PM) has several branches that serve large chicken combination plates for $4. Most of Monterrey's moderately priced restaurants can be found in the Zona Rosa.

➢ **UNDER $5** • **Café Sevilla.** For that late-night snack, this somewhat grungy 24-hour coffee shop serves taco plates, burgers, tasty enchiladas ($2), and surprisingly good coffee ($1). It's a favorite with bus drivers—always an encouraging sign. *Colón, at Villagran, no phone. Just west of bus depot.*

Los Girasoles. Vegetarians will revel in this haven of meatless delights. The comida corrida ($3) changes daily, but always features vegetable combinations like hot broccoli, spinach, and potato soup and vegetarian "pescado" (grilled filet of potato and shredded cheese). If you're not up for the full 5-course menu, 3 items cost $2. Still, you may want to stick around for one of the fruit, yogurt, and granola desserts. *961 Ocampo, at Cuauhtémoc, tel. 8/343-70-00. Open daily 11-7:30.*

Las Monjitas. If you can stop laughing at the waitresses' nun outfits long enough to eat, you'll enjoy the tasty food at this taquería chain. Try the house specialty: bite-size pieces of steak sautéed with peppers, onions, mushrooms, sausage, and bacon, served with a huge platter of tortillas for about $3. Live xylophone music accompanies the meal. *Morelos 240 Ote., at Galeana, tel. 8/342-85-67. Open daily 8 AM–10:30 PM.*

Restaurant El Palmito. If you're on your way to the "Tec" (Instituto Tecnológico), make sure to stop here for some of the best tacos in town. Three carne asada tacos and a Coke are just $3. Vegetarians won't find much here, but the baked potatoes are big, buttery affairs ($1). The place gets packed around 9 PM, when service can be slow. *2 de Abril 2902, 3 blocks from Garza Sada, tel. 8/359-96-50. Open daily 12:30-midnight.*

Torta 'n Go. Despite the cheesy name, this is the place to go for great *tortas calientes* (warm sandwiches). Delicious steak sandwiches with cheese, onion, tomato, chile, and avocado cost

$2, and breakfasts are about $1. *Padre Mier 402 Ote., at Carranza, tel. 8/340-17-72. Open Mon.-Sat. 9 AM-10 PM, Sun. 1-10.*

WORTH SEEING

Architecturally distinguished buildings—some colonial, some modern—make a walk around town interesting in itself, but there are also a number of museums worth visiting. The many parks and plazas are great for relaxing, but if you just want to check out the scene, head to the Zona Rosa.

CERVECERIA CUAUHTEMOC Named after the famous Aztec ruler, the **Cuauhtémoc Brewery** is the heart of an industrial empire producing a number of brands of beer. Brewery tours are offered Tuesday–Friday at 11, noon, and 3. One of the complex's older buildings has been converted into a collection of hodgepodge museums, but the unlimited beer in the tree-lined **beer garden** (open Tues.–Sun. 11–4:45) is the biggest draw and definitely makes the trip worthwhile. Two huge copper brewing tanks descend from the ceiling of the **Museo de Monterrey,** housed within the walls of the original brewery. The museum also exhibits a collection of etchings, lithographs, and oil paintings. The **Salón de la Fama** (Hall of Fame) just south of the present brewery, provides a dizzying array of memorabilia from Mexico's baseball legends. The adjacent **Museo Deportivo** (sports museum) contains exhibits on Mexican boxing, bullfighting, and American college football. *Universidad 2202, about 10 blocks north of bus station. Take RUTA 1 bus to Cuauhtémoc at Anaya; cross the street and head south ½ block. Admission free. Open Tues.–Fri. 9:30–5:30, weekends 10:30–6:30.*

For frosty mugs of beer, head to the beer garden at Cuauhtémoc Brewery, where the drinks are free.

INSTITUTO TECNOLOGICO DE MONTERREY One of the top business and technical schools in Latin America, the institute was founded by Monterrey's industrial elite to train future managers and engineers. The school's modern, geometric campus, built around a central patio, is a great place to hang out and meet locals and exchange students. The Tec, as it is known, lies in the far southeast corner of Monterrey; from downtown, take a RUTA 1 bus from Pino Suárez and get off under the overpass at the university's entrance.

MACROPLAZA At the heart of Monterrey is one of the world's largest public squares. Extending over 40 acres, the plaza begins on Washington, runs past the Palacio del Gobierno (city hall), and ends at the Santa Catarina riverbank. The southernmost boundary is marked by a beautiful Rufino Tamayo sculpture entitled *Homage to the Sun.* The sound of gushing fountains and the pleasant aromas in the square's gardens offer a needed respite from the deafening roar of Monterrey's traffic. Stop in at **Infotour** (*see* Visitor Information, *above*) for a detailed guide to this central plaza.

MUSEO DE ARTE CONTEMPORANEO (MARCO) A huge black sculpture of a bird by artist Juan Soriano welcomes you into the air-conditioned halls of this architecturally daring art center. The museum contains 14 exhibit halls and features a posh little café where weekly poetry readings are held. The museum also offers bus trips to other artistically significant parts of the city. *Zuazua, at Ocampo, tel. 8/342-48-20. Admission: $2, $1 students; free Wed. Open Tues. and Thurs.–Sat. 11–7, Wed. and Sun. 11–9.*

Luck of All Sorts

Every year thousands of hopeful fortune-seekers buy tickets for the SORTEO-TEC, a national lottery promoted by Monterrey's Instituto Tecnológico. The grand prize is a dream house designed, engineered, and constructed by university-chosen experts, complete with money for furnishings and upkeep—a sum large enough to guarantee the winner a cockroach-free future for years to come.

EL OBISPADO Droves of couples start climbing the long winding road to this tiny baptistry in the late afternoon, giving themselves plenty of time to catch their breath before watching the sunset from one of the city's highest points. Constructed in 1788, the baptistry served as a fort during the Mexican-American War and the French Intervention. Today, it houses a number of artifacts, including 300-year-old branding irons and serapes from as early as the late 1600s. *Far west end of Padre Mier, tel. 8/346–04–04. From Macroplaza,* RUTA *4 pesera to foot of Calle El Gollado; walk 15 min. up the hill. Admission: $2. Open Tues.–Sun. 10–5.*

PARQUE DE LOS NINOS HEROES This extensive stretch of green encompasses meandering paths, lovely gardens, and a small man-made lake where people rent rowboats. Several excellent museums and a guano-filled aviary also provide interesting stopping points within the park. Auto enthusiasts will be thoroughly impressed by the **Museo del Automóvil** (Car Museum), where some of the earliest models are on display. At the **Museo de la Fauna** (Fauna Museum), a pantheon of stuffed wildlife inhabits the dimly lit rooms, including a 6-foot-tall polar bear and ivory-tusked elephant head. In the **Museo de la Pinacoteca,** an exhibit of beautiful bronze and wood sculptures is surrounded by a collection of paintings by artists from the state of Nuevo León (*see box below*). The 50¢ park admission includes everything but rowboat rental and a $1 donation for animal care at the Fauna Museum. Make sure to get a map at the office to the north of the main entrance. *From Pino Suárez, catch a* RUTA *17 bus and get off across the street from park entrance. To return to town, take the same bus north. Park open daily 10–6.*

AFTER DARK

Nightlife in Monterrey is varied and lively but spread out across the city. **Kaos** (Garza Sada, at Revolución) is a dark, split-level club playing modern Mexican and American dance music. The cover is $4, drinks are $2; take a RUTA 1 bus to the main entrance of the university ("the Tec"), then transfer to a SATELITE bus. All this transferring can be pretty difficult after 1 AM; a cab to most of the budget hotels is about $5. Popular mariachi, salsa, and rock bands play at **El Mesón de Gallo** (Padre Mier 943 Pte, tel. 8/342–12–87), a candlelit colonial home turned nightclub, located just east of the Macroplaza. The cover is $3. West of the Zona Rosa, **Koko Loco** (Pino Suárez, at Padre Mier) is the most convenient place for techno addicts to get their nightly fix. The club is open Thursday–Saturday 9:30 PM–2 AM, and the cover is $3. Around the corner at **Pachanga** (Pino Suárez 849 Sur, tel. 8/340–45–23), you can do the cumbía Fridays 7 PM–2 AM (no cover). On Saturday, women get in for $1 (men $2); Sunday everyone pays $2. If you're willing to splurge for some serious people-watching and one of the best cabaret shows around, head to **Antonio's Le Club** (Constitución 1471, at Carranza, no phone) where the $8.50 cover is well worth it. The show starts at 10:30, but if you get there early you can head to the bar next door for drinks and zebra-skin decor. To reach Antonio's, take a RUTA 126 or RUTA 130 bus to Carranza on Constitutión, and walk west 1 block. To get back into town before midnight, take the CENTRO bus from Hidalgo, 1 block north of Carranza. After midnight, your best bet is a $2 taxi ride back into town. Antonio's is open Monday–Saturday 7:30 PM–2 AM.

Skip That Trip to the Louvre

In the Museo de la Pinacoteca in the Parque de los Niños Héroes is a collection of artwork created almost exclusively by artists from Nuevo León. The first painting on the right side is El Nacionalista, by Carlos Saenz. Stand to the left of the painting and notice how the subject's body—his feet, shoulders, and even his eyes—seem to be oriented to your left. Then slowly move to your right, noting how the fixed stare of the poncho-clad gentleman shifts magically as you move. This technique, mastered by Saenz, is the same that Leonardo da Vinci used for his smirking Mona Lisa.

Near Monterrey

LA CASCADA COLA DE CABALLO

An hour northwest of Monterrey, in the Sierra Madre mountains just off Highway 85, is the **Parque Nacional Cumbres de Monterrey**. One of the highlights of a trip here is a view of **La Cascada Cola de Caballo** (Horse Tail Falls), a dramatic waterfall that tumbles down from the pine-forested heights. The waterfall is about 1 kilometer from the park entrance, up a cobblestone road. You can rent a docile horse from the local kids who hang out by the ticket booth for about $3, or hop on a horse-drawn carriage for $2.50; entrance to the falls (open daily 8–7) will set you back $2.

COMING AND GOING Horse Tail Falls lies 6 kilometers up a winding road from the small town of **El Cercado**. From Monterrey's central bus station, **Autobuses Amarillos** buses leave every 15 minutes between 4:30 AM and 11:45 PM, and the 45-minute ride costs $2. From the stop in El Cercado, walk 2 blocks to the town plaza and take a pesero (blue or orange van) to the foot of the falls; the fare ($1 partway, $5 to the entrance) is higher on weekends. The last pesero heads back to the plaza at 7:15 PM sharp, and it's a long, mosquito-ridden walk back to town.

From the pool at the foot of the falls, you can follow one of two short hiking paths that lead upstream and cross small wooden bridges laid haphazardly over the gurgling water.

CAMPING You can pitch your tent upstream from the falls, 1 kilometer up the road from the turquoise entrance gate. The best sites are located on the north bank of the stream, where the ground is flat and the area more private. There are toilets and sinks with nonpotable water near the entrance to the falls. Use of the grounds and facilities is free.

GRUTAS DE GARCIA

The awe-inspiring subterranean caverns of García have, sadly, been transformed into an overdone tourist attraction, the sort of place where stalagmites carry names such as Christmas Tree and the Hand of Death. But don't run screaming, because the impressive natural beauty of the caves overshadows the thick crowds and glittering signs. For $6 you can ride a tram to the cave entrance; it leaves every 10 minutes from 10 AM to 4 PM and often fills up. The more rugged alternative is to make the steep, 20-minute hike up the gorgeous mountain path from Villa de García (bring some water). You may also want to bring a picnic, though there is a small restaurant here. A one-hour guided tour of the caves is included in the entrance fee.

COMING AND GOING The Grutas de García are just outside Villa de García. From Monterrey, catch one of the frequent MONTERREY–VILLA DE GARCIA buses (1 hr, $2) from the corner of Colón and B. Reyes, opposite the Hotel Victoria (*see* Where to Sleep, *above*). To return to Monterrey, take the MONTERREY–VILLA DE GARCIA bus, which leaves every 15 minutes from the opposite side of the drop-off point. Monterrey's **Infotour** office (*see* Visitor Information, *above*) organizes its own cave tours in English and Spanish on Thursdays and Saturdays at 1:30 PM.

Saltillo

Set 1,600 meters up in the mountains, the capital of Coahuila state is a great place to take a deep breath and relax after the pollution and bustle of Monterrey, an hour to the southwest. Saltillo's industrial complexes, including Chrysler and GM plants, are relegated to the suburbs, leaving the downtown plazas and parks clean and tranquil.

Saltillo grew up around the **Plaza de Armas**, bordered by the elegant **Palacio de Gobierno** (Government Palace) and the **Catedral de Santiago**, with an elaborately carved stone facade that's considered one of the finest in Mexico. For a great view of the city, walk from the cathedral south along Hidalgo to the Plaza de México. If you're in town mid-July through early August, head to the fairgrounds to watch the entire town celebrate the **Feria Anual** (Annual Fair), with games, dancing, regional foods, roller coasters, crafts, and bloody *palenques* (cockfights).

You'll always find colorful handicrafts and cheap, filling meals at the **Mercado Juárez,** Saltillo's vibrant marketplace.

BASICS

CASAS DE CAMBIO Serfín (tel. 84/14-90-97), on the corner of Allende and Lerdo de Tejada, changes cash and traveler's checks weekdays 9:30-1. For 24-hour instant cash gratification, use the ATM at **Banamex** (Allende, at Ocampo, tel. 84/14-49-17), which accepts Cirrus, Plus, MasterCard, and Visa.

EMERGENCIES You can reach the **police** round the clock at 84/16-21-83. For medical emergencies, call the **Cruz Roja** (84/14-33-33 ext. 25). For other emergencies call the police radio patrol (84/14-16-16), the fire station (84/15-41-22), or Mexico's emergency operator (06).

PHONES AND MAIL At the main **post office** (Victoria 453, btw Acuña and Padre Flores, tel. 84/14-90-97), they'll hold your mail at the following address for up to 10 days: Lista de Correos, Saltillo, Coahuila, CP 25001, México. The office is open weekdays 7-7, Saturdays 9-1. There's a small cluster of Ladatel **phones** in Plaza Acuña near the Mercado Juárez and a few more sprinkled in Plaza San Francisco (Juárez, behind the cathedral). Otherwise, you can make international calls (though no collect calls) from Café Victoria (*see* Food, *below*) for $3 a minute.

VISITOR INFORMATION Saltillo's tourist office is located in the majestic but irritatingly hard-to-reach **Torre de Saltillo.** The office can supply you with a decent map for free, but that's about it. *Periférico Echeverría 1560, 5th floor, tel. 84/15-17-14. From Aldama at Hidalgo, take Combi 9 north, get off at Gigante Supermarket on Periférico Echeverría, and walk 3 blocks east. Open Mon.-Sat. 9-5.*

COMING AND GOING

BY BUS Saltillo's **Central de Autobuses** is about 2 kilometers southwest of the centro. Most smaller second-class lines provide service to obscure destinations, but the major **Transportes Frontera** (tel. 84/17-00-76) goes to Monterrey (every ½ hr, 2 hrs, $3), Ciudad Juárez (18 hrs, $29) and Mexico City (12 hrs, $30). Six first-class lines, among them the ubiquitous **Omnibus de México** (tel. 84/17-03-15) and **Transportes del Norte** (tel. 84/17-09-02), have frequent service to Guadalajara (10 hrs, $25), Mazatlán (16 hrs, $30), Ciudad Juárez (15 hrs, $34), and Matamoros (5 hrs, $9). **Greyhound** tickets to destinations in the United States and Canada via Texas are sold by Transportes del Norte. The station has a 24-hour long-distance/fax office and Ladatel phones that accept credit cards and coins. Luggage storage is available 6 AM–9 PM (25¢ per hr); to reach the station from downtown, catch the RUTA 9 bus on Aldaman and Hidalgo.

BY TRAIN The **Estación de Ferrocarril** is a large, impressive building a few blocks southwest of Parque Zaragoza on Emilio Carranza. Three trains a day connect Saltillo to eight other cities in the republic. The first-class **Regiomontano** heads south to San Luis Potosí (6 hrs; $12 1st class, $28 sleeper car), and Mexico City (12 hrs; $33 1st class, $60 sleeper car) and north to Monterrey (3 hrs; $20 sleeper car only). The first-class **México–Monterrey–Nuevo Laredo** train heads south to

Stop and Smell the Roses

If you want to escape the city and simply exist for an afternoon, head out to the tranquil village of Arteaga, 20 kilometers east of Saltillo on the San Luis Potosí–Mexico City highway. You can daydream by the quiet stream that meanders through town, or search out the waterfall on the outskirts for an afternoon picnic. From Saltillo, second-class buses marked ARTEAGA *make the one-hour trek for less than $1.*

Mexico City (16 hrs, $21) and north to Nuevo Laredo (16 hrs, $8), stopping in Monterrey (3 hrs, $3). The **Coahuilense** runs to Piedras Negras ($6 2nd class, $10 reserved seat).

WHERE TO SLEEP AND EAT

Saltillo was overlooked when it came to supplying the budget travelers of the world with a comfy place to spend the night. The cheap hotels that do exist are in the city center, near Plaza Acuña. The **Hotel Bristol** (Aldama 405 Pte., tel. 84/12–91–20) is by far the best option, with mosquito-free rooms and clean bathrooms. Singles are $7, doubles $8. Even cheaper is **Hotel Ávila** (Padre Flores 211, tel. 84/12–59–16). Rooms are spacious and the water pressure is strong enough to wash your hair and clothes, but you may have to contend with a steady stream of fleas or ants sharing the hotel facilities.

Saltillo doesn't offer fabulous cuisine, but you can grab a taco or slurp down some homemade soup at the *fondas* (covered food stands) in the Mercado Juárez in Plaza Acuña. Locals pack into **Taquería El Pastor** (Aldama 340 Pte., tel. 84/12–21–12) to wolf down corn tortillas filled with carne asada and *carne al pastor* (marinated pork). The taquería is open Sunday–Thursday 8 AM–midnight, Friday and Saturday 8 AM–1 AM. The unofficial house specialty at **Café Victoria** (Padre Flores 221, tel. 84/14–98–00; open daily 7 AM–11 PM) is the *palomas con aguacate* (flour tortillas filled with shredded beef and avocado; $3.50). A good comida corrida is available daily 11:30–4.

WORTH SEEING

Saltillo's winding streets may be colonial and quaint, but they're also confusing. Fortunately, most sights are within walking distance of the **Plaza de Armas** (Hidalgo and Juárez), where the graceful **Catedral** shines in the strong Saltillo sun. Opposite the cathedral is the **Palacio del Gobierno,** a squat rose-colored building that houses government offices and beautiful murals illustrating the political history of Coahuila, painted by Spanish artist Salvador Almaraz y Tarazona.

CULTURAL CENTERS/GALLERIES Saltillo is home to an abundance of artists who show their work in spaces throughout the city. There are a few larger, more established museums and galleries, such as the free **Centro Cultural Universitario,** where you'll find arrowheads, stone figures, and a hoop from a pre-Columbian ball court. Frequented by university students, this is also an excellent place to find out about free concerts, theater, and poetry readings, many of which happen in the centro or in the Jardín del Arte, across the street. For special event information, call 84/10–25–42. *Aldama, at G. Cepeda, tel. 84/12–68–57. Open Tues.-Sun. 10–7. Wheelchair access.*

Also free is the **Centro de Arte Contemporáneo,** which houses everything from paintings to sculpture. *Behind the cathedral, tel. 84/10–09–32. Open weekdays 10–1 and 4–7, Sat. 10–1.*

Finally, the pleasantly cool **Instituto Coahuilense de Cultura** exhibits sculpture, *artesanía* (crafts), painting, woodwork, and photography by artists from the state of Coahuila. *Juárez, at Hidalgo, tel. 84/14–22–45. Open Tues.-Sun. 9–7.*

EL SERAPE DE SALTILLO A small, rusting yellow sign swinging rythmically in the afternoon breeze is the only marker for this fabulous serape factory-cum-store. Everything from silver earrings and chocolate beaters to teacups and cured tree bark is for sale in the tiny store, but the real draw is watching nimble-fingered craftspeople make the serapes. The store is open Monday–Saturday 9–1 and 3–7, but the serape makers only work during the week. *Hidalgo 305 Sur, no phone.*

AFTER DARK

Saltillo doesn't have a lot to offer anyone over 15 years of age, and the streets are pretty empty by 11 PM. University students desperate to let off a little steam head to **Sahara** (Blvd. Fundidores, kilómetro 3.5, tel. 84/30–25–25), a hopping techno disco also frequented by tourists from nearby expensive hotels. Cover on Fridays is a whopping $4, but all other nights are free (except Sundays, when it's closed). To get here, take the ZARAGOZA bus from Padre Treviño and Xicotencatl. An eclectic variety of music and $1 beers attract a more diverse crowd to **El Zaguán** (Ocampo 338, tel. 84/14–76–67; open daily noon–1 AM), where small wooden tables and candlelight augment the overdone colonial atmosphere. Real penny-pinchers can grab a 50¢ *yuki* (snow cone) from one of the vendors on **Plaza Acuña** and head to the patio behind **Palacio del Gobierno** to watch the blossoming adolescents overcome the embarrassment of their first romantic encounters.

OUTDOOR ACTIVITIES

Fishing in the man-made lake at **Ciudad Deportiva** (Sports City) is permitted every Sunday, and the tennis and basketball courts here are open to the public. To get here, take the ZAPALINOME bus from Perez Treviño and Xicotencatl to Ciudad Deportiva. For a pleasant change of scene, take a leisurely stroll through the town of **Arteaga**, a half-hour ride from Saltillo on the ARTEAGA bus from Perez Treviño and Xicotencatl. If you're set on hitting the hills, continue 20 minutes farther on the same bus to **Bella Unión** and a dusty parking lot. From here you can climb up two separate plateaus and take in the relentless, mountainous landscape while the hot desert air blows in your hair. Dip your feet in the river before heading back to the parking lot to catch the bus to Saltillo.

Tampico

Lush mango trees and endless white sand beaches make Tampico one of the more enjoyable places to visit in the northeast. Originally serving as a refuge for Huastecan tribes escaping the mosquito-ridden basin of the nearby Río Panuco, Tampico is now a bustling port town with a large open market and a traffic-filled central plaza (Plaza de la Libertad). Although the humid, salty air has taken a toll on the city's older buildings, some well-preserved structures still line the plaza and the sand-dusted streets; during the month-long **Feria de Abril** (April Fair), celebrating the anniversary of the Mexican Republic, the plaza is home to live concerts, theater, and historical presentations. If you're interested in indigenous culture, a short bus ride outside the city will take you to the **Pirámide de las Flores**, a partially excavated Huastecan pyramid dating from the 12th century. Still, Tampico's main draw is its glistening shoreline. Bordered by the Gulf of Mexico to the east, the Río Panuco to the south, and the Río Tamesi lagoons to the west, Tampico offers an array of aquatic activities and the chance to laze the day away in the tropical heat.

BASICS

AMERICAN EXPRESS The AmEx office is in **Viajes Pozos**, a travel agency about 10 minutes from downtown. The staff begrudgingly cashes personal checks, holds client mail, and sells and replaces traveler's checks. *Zapote 206, Colonia Águila, Tampico, Tamaulipas, CP 89220, tel. 12/13–72–00 or 12/17–14–76. Open weekdays 9–2 and 4–6, Sat. 10–1.*

CASAS DE CAMBIO Central **Divisa** (Benito Juárez 215 Sur, tel. 13/12–90–00) has long hours and decent rates. They change both cash and traveler's checks weekdays 9–6, Saturdays 9–1. **Banamex** (Madero, at Aduana) has an ATM that accepts MasterCard and Banamex cards only.

EMERGENCIES Dial 12/12–10–32 for the **police**; 12/12–12–22 for the **fire department**; or 12/12–13–33 for the **Cruz Roja** or an **ambulance**.

MEDICAL AID **Benavides** is a large, well-equipped pharmacy right off the Plaza de Armas. *Olmos, at Carranza, tel. 12/19–25–28. Open Mon.–Sat. 8 AM–11 PM, Sun. 8 AM–10 PM.*

PHONES AND MAIL The **post office** (Madero 309, 3 blocks from Plaza de Armas, tel. 12/12–19–27) will hold mail sent to the following address for up to 10 days: Lista de Correos, Tampico, Tamaulipas, CP 89000, México. Right outside the post office are shiny new Ladatel **phones**, but they're almost always in use. More can be found on the Plaza de Armas. Purchase Ladatel cards at Refresquería La Victoria (*see* Food, *below*).

VISITOR INFORMATION The **tourist office** does little more than hand you a map or two and send you on your merry way. Look for a small, dark stairway squeezed next to a *refresquería* (drink stand). Carranza, at Olmos, above Benavides pharmacy, tel. 12/12–26–78. Open weekdays 9–7.

COMING AND GOING

BY BUS Tampico's **Central de Autobuses** has both first- and second-class terminals divided by a small verdant courtyard, making comparing ticket prices a breeze. **ADO** (tel. 12/13–43–39) and **Transportes Futura/Transportes del Norte** (tel. 12/13–46–55) are major first-class carriers with service to Matamoros (7 hrs, $15) and Mexico City (10 hrs, $15). Second-class lines include **Transportes Frontera** (tel. 12/13–42–35), **Blancos** (tel. 12/13–42–35), and **Oriente Golfo** (tel. 12/13–46–02). Destinations include Monterrey (8 hrs, $14), Reynosa (7 hrs, $14), and Mexico City (9 hrs, $16). Each terminal is equipped with Ladatel phones and casetas de large distancia. Lockers in the first-class terminal swallow your gear for $4 a day. To get downtown, catch a *micro* (minibus) marked CENTRAL CAMIONERA PERIMETRAL in front of the station; to reach the terminal, take the same micro from the corner of Madero and Colón.

BY TRAIN Once a bustling doorway to the northeast, the **Estación de Ferrocarriles de Tampico** has been all but forgotten. Three lonely trains a day still lumber to San Luis Potosí (10 hrs, $5), Ciudad Victoria (4 hrs, $3), and Monterrey (10 hrs, $4.50). Tickets are sold only 6–8 AM. Aduana and Héroes de Nacozari, tel. 12/12–19–83.

BY PLANE The **Aeropuerto Francisco Javier Mina** (Universidad 700, tel. 12/28–21–95) is a small airport in the northwest corner of town. **Mexicana** (tel. 12/13–97–59), **Aeroméxico** (tel. 12/17–08–02), and **Aerolitoral** (tel. 12/28–08–57) serve both domestic and international destinations. Flights to Mexico City are $47 with reservations made 3 days in advance. To get downtown, catch an AVIACION POR BULEVAR micro to Carranza and walk 4 blocks to the Plaza de Armas.

WHERE TO SLEEP

Rooms here tend to be mediocre and extremely overpriced. There are a few hotels with more reasonable rates a few blocks from the Plaza de Armas, but the neighborhood tends to be unsafe and poorly lit late at night. The aging but clean **Hotel Imperial** (López de Lara, at Carranza, tel. 12/14–13–63) is the cheapest budget hotel near the plaza. Dingy carpeting in every room provides a dusty-attic ambiance, and the air-conditioners—standard in every room—shudder and wheeze so hard you almost feel sorry for them. Singles and doubles, all with phones and TVs, cost $11; MasterCard and Visa are accepted. Downtown, you'll find the **Hotel Posada Don Francisco** (Díaz Mirón 710, tel. 12/19–25–34), one of your cleaner budget options. *Económico* rooms, cooled with fans, are spacious, clean, and a real bargain at $8 for a single or double with phone, TV, and plenty of hot water.

Hotels along the beach tend to be pricey and a tad run-down. The bright red-and-white **Hotel Orinoco** (NW of beach entrance, off Blvd. Casero, no phone) tends to fill up fast, so get here early in the day to stake your claim. Rooms are carpeted, and cooled by a noisy but relatively effective floor fan. Singles and doubles are $15, and six people can crash here for less than $5 each. If the great outdoors calls you, pitch a tent for free on **Playa Miramar,** where bathrooms and showers cost less than a taco in the nearby hotels and eateries.

FOOD

Like almost everything else in Tampico, food is overpriced. It's possible to eat cheaply, but only if you're not paranoid that eating at street stands will send you running for the bathroom. The food at the **mercado** on Juárez is cheap, cooked to order, and delicious. Try the *milanesa* (thinly sliced, breaded beef) with tortillas, beans, rice, salad, and a soft drink for $3. Most people come to the **Restaurant y Cafetería Emir** (Olmos 207, tel. 12/12–03–64; open daily 6 AM–midnight) for the delicious $3 *filete de sol,* two deceivingly fish-like slabs of shrimp held together by a fine layer of egg and salted bread crumbs. Factor in the beans, home fries, salad, and fresh bread that are included, and it's clear why almost no one finishes the dish. **Restaurante/Refresquería Élite** (Díaz Mirón 211 Ote., tel. 12/12–03–64) is also a good place for local fish dishes, as well as the $1 piping hot *sopa xochitl,* a chicken soup with an exotic combination of tomato, avocado, onion, and cilantro.

OUTDOOR ACTIVITIES

Ten kilometers of white sand and blue-green waters make **Playa Miramar** a popular stretch of the Gulf of Mexico. The beach is divided into four sections; going from north to south you'll hit **Playa Darío, Playa Tampico, Playa Bañario,** and finally **Playa Escollera.** Beautiful views of the extensive shoreline can be had from the high-cliffed entrance to Playa Escollera, at the southeast end of the city. Bring a picnic and hang out at the pleasantly cool, grassy spots just west of the cliff's edge. The best place for swimming and lounging is Playa Tampico. You'll have to bring your own towels, but showers are only 25¢ a pop at any of the hotels along the beach, and you can rent beach chairs for $3 at the small straw huts near the beach entrance. When the scorching sun settles below the waves, shoot some hoops at the basketball court behind Hotel Orinoco (*see* Where To Sleep, *above*). To reach any of the beaches, catch a PLAYA micro from in front of Hotel Mundo on Díaz Mirón. Micros run about every five minutes during the day, and every 20 minutes after 7:30 PM; the last bus from the beach leaves around 11 PM.

If you're tired of sand in unmentionable places, the two Olympic-size pools at Tampico's newly remodeled sports center, **Unidad Deportiva Tampico** (Blvd. López Mateos) provide an excellent alternative to the beach. It's open Monday–Saturday 9–6 and it costs $3 to get in. To get here, take the MADERO micro from the plaza, and tell the driver to drop you off at the *alberca* (pool).

AFTER DARK

Avenida Universidad, the long winding street that borders the university, is the best place to start the evening. Most clubs luring the student population don't have a cover before 11 PM, and beers run about $2.50. To shake your booty to techno, head to **Eclipse** (Universidad 2004, tel. 12/13–14–95). The cover is $3 on Fridays, $4 on Saturdays, and it's open daily 9 PM–3 AM. The cheesy ranch-style facade of **Restaurante/Bar Santa Fe 1900** (Cnr of Universidad and Francita) may be daunting, but it's surprisingly cozy inside and near the live music (7 PM–closing) is free. If you want to stay in the city center, try **El Globito** (north side of Plaza de Armas, no phone). The delicious smoothies and milk shakes ($1.50) are pretty expensive, but they're enormous. El Globito is open 24 hours a day and stays happening late into the night.

EL BAJÍO   7
By Lynette Ubois

For those interested in colonial history and baroque architecture, the Bajío offers a pleasant change from Mexico's popular beaches. Encompassing the states of Querétaro, Guanajuato, and San Luis Potosí, the region is a spectacular mix of fertile valleys, dry hills sprinkled with strange cacti and other succulents, town centers with tranquil plazas, and busy industrial zones. Staunch traditionalism and progressive ideals coexist here in a strange harmony, and the result is a region rich in folklore and legends, as well as innovative cultural and artistic activity.

The wide, fertile plains of this region are ringed by high mountain peaks, and the vast tablelands of the Bajío (which means lowland) are themselves 1,675–2,135 meters above sea level. Rich in both agricultural and mineral resources, the Bajío has long been exploited for its abundant natural wealth. Archaeologists believe that even before the Spanish arrived, the region had nearly 750 active mines, which were probably worked by slave labor. Silver lust lured the Spanish here, and they eventually found incredibly lucrative veins throughout the region. During the 17th and 18th centuries, Guanajuato alone was responsible for 30%–40% of the world's silver production. In addition to mineral wealth, the Spanish also "discovered" the richness of the volcanic soil. Grand *encomiendas* (plantations) were established, where farmers grew a variety of Old World and New World crops, especially corn, but also including wheat, squash, grapes, and pears. Franciscan friars also colonized the region; by 1740, Father Junipero Serra, who later established the mission system along the California coast, had overseen the construction of five baroque churches in the remote highlands of Querétaro.

By the early 19th century, the newly wealthy conquerors had established an exploitative economic system in the Bajío; untold numbers of indigenous laborers died building opulent churches and enormous mansions for those of Spanish descent. It is therefore not surprising that the battle for Mexican independence began in Querétaro and the small town of Dolores Hidalgo, where important leaders of the War of Independence—including Ignacio Allende, Miguel Hidalgo, and Doña Josefa Ortiz—began their revolutionary exploits. Towns throughout the Bajío are fiercely proud of these leaders' accomplishments, which earned the region the nickname "The Cradle of Independence."

Today, international agricultural and automotive companies have large factories here, but fortunately for the traveler, the region is not an industrial wasteland—many colonial cities have been preserved as national landmarks. As a result, the Bajío has a vibrant sense of history, made visible in the well-maintained baroque churches, narrow cobblestoned streets, and excellent museums of its major cities. Both Querétaro and Guanajuato are thriving cultural centers, with large active populations of artists, musicians, and students. San Miguel de Allende, well-known for its expatriate American population, is so laid-back that you may want to stay a few years. For the more vigorous visitor, San Luis Potosí offers access to waterfalls, caves, and *balnearios* (swimming areas).

San Luis Potosí

Without the colonial-era plazas and churches in the center of town, San Luis Potosí might seem as sterile as a big U.S. Midwestern town. Broom-wielding shopkeepers keep the sidewalks immaculate, and the town's skyscrapers and occasional Burger King might remind you more of Ohio than Mexico. But in spite of recent development, San Luis has managed to retain much of its Mexican character: Men in cowboy hats saunter the streets, old women haggle over the price of meat in the crowded markets, and clowns and musicians play to evening crowds in the plazas. Many fine examples of baroque and neoclassical architecture serve as elegant reminders of the city's heyday as a colonial capital, whose domain once encompassed most of northern Mexico, Texas, and Louisiana.

Silver was discovered in the nearby hills of San Pedro in the 16th century, and "Minas del Potosí" was added to the city's name in the hope that the mines here would yield wealth equal to that found in Potosí, Bolivia. But the silver was soon depleted, and other minerals and a burgeoning dairy industry are now the basis of the city's economy. Today the mines in the San Pedro hills still function, but they are fundamentally tourist attractions. San Luis Potosí also has its share of high culture, with abundant theatrical performances, concerts, and conferences—the majority of which are free.

Though there's plenty to see and do in San Luis, perhaps the best reason to visit is the area beyond the capital city. **Santa María del Río,** a town specializing in the production of *rebozos* (silk shawls), is only a short day trip away, and campers or adventurers can head to the caves and waterfalls of **Río Verde** and **Ciudad Valles.** The **Querétaro Missions** and the gardens and mansion of **Xilitla** are interesting for anyone with the slightest interest in architecture. The ghost mining town of **Real de Catorce** is also worth a visit—take the train for the full 19th-century effect.

BASICS

AMERICAN EXPRESS The AmEx office in the **Agencia de Grandes Viajes** offers the usual services for cardholders. They deliver MoneyGrams, exchange traveler's checks, and replace lost checks for cardmembers and noncardmembers alike. They will hold mail for you for up to ten days if it's sent to you at this address: *Carranza 1077, San Luis Potosí, San Luis Potosí, CP 78250, México; tel. 48/17–60–04, fax 48/11–11–66. Walk 10 blocks west of Plaza de Armas. Open weekdays 9–2 and 4–6, Sat. 10–1.*

AUTO PARTS/SERVICE Refaccionaria y Rectificaciones Miguel sells and installs most auto parts and makes house calls at no extra charge. *Damián Carmona 1565, tel. 48/14–31–77. In front of Jardín de Santiago. Open Mon.–Sat. 9–2 and 4–7.*

BOOKSTORES Librería Cristal (Carranza 765, tel. 48/12–80–15) has a large and varied selection of books in Spanish. **Librería Española** (Othón 170, tel. 48/12–57–81) and **Librería Universitaria** (Álvaro Obregón, tel. 48/12–67–49) are both smaller than Cristal, but they sometimes stock books in English. All are open Monday–Saturday 9–2 and 4–7.

CASAS DE CAMBIO Banks on the Plaza de Armas are open weekdays 9–5. **Banamex** (Obregón 355, tel. 48/12–16–56) changes currency and cashes traveler's checks weekdays 9–noon and also has a 24-hour ATM. Near the Alameda, **El Amigo** (Manuel José Othón 455, tel. 48/14–79–95) has good rates and long hours: weekdays 9–8, Saturday 9–6.

EMERGENCIES The number for the **police** department is 48/12–25–82; for an **ambulance** call 48/15–33–32.

LAUNDRY Lavanderías Automáticas Superwash will wash 3 kilos of dirty clothes for $2, or you can wash and dry them yourself for 75¢ per load. On weekdays, pick-up and delivery ser-

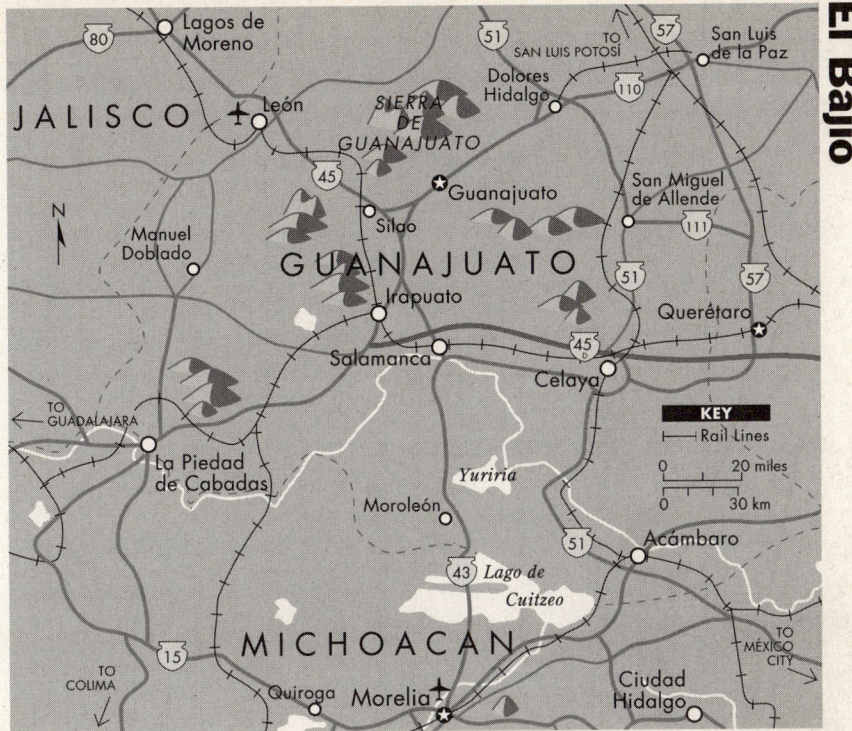

vice is free, so you only have to haul your clothes to the front door. If you arrange for early morning pick-up, your clothes should be back by the evening. *Carranza 1093, tel. 48/13-93-22. Walk 10 blocks west of Plaza de Armas. Open Mon.-Sat. 8-8, Sun. 9-2.*

MAIL The **post office** offers all the usual services and will hold mail sent to you at the following address for up to 10 days: Lista de Correos, Morelos 235, San Luis Potosí, San Luis Potosí, CP 78000, México. *Morelos 235, tel. 48/12-27-40. Walk 2 blocks north and 1 block east of Plaza de Armas. Open weekdays 8-7, Sat. 9-1.*

MEDICAL AID The **Beneficiencia Española** (Carranza 1090, tel. 48/11-56-96) and the **Cruz Roja** (Juárez 540, tel. 48/15-33-32) provide 24-hour medical service. **Farmacia La Perla** (Escobedo, at Los Bravo, tel. 48/12-59-22) is open 24 hours a day.

PHONES **Computel,** right across from the tourist office, has high-tech long-distance service and charges about $2 for a 10-minute international collect call. You can also make cash calls here. *Carranza 360, tel. 48/12-01-13. Walk 3 blocks west of the Plaza de Armas.*

SCHOOLS The **Centro de Idiomas** (Zaragoza 410, tel. 48/12-49-55), associated with the Universidad Autónoma de San Luis Potosí, offers 2½-month Spanish classes for about $65. Contact the director, Lic. María Luisa Sánchez Almazán, for registration information.

VISITOR INFORMATION The **Centro de Turismo** has a well-informed staff that will weigh you down with maps and brochures. They can even provide guided tours of the city's historical center for $3. Many of the employees speak English. *Carranza 325, tel. 48/12-30-68. Walk 3 blocks west of Plaza de Armas. Open weekdays 8-8, Sat. 9-1 and 4-8.*

COMING AND GOING

BY BUS The **Central Camionera** lies a few kilometers east of the central plaza. To get downtown from the terminal, turn left as you leave, walk two blocks to Avenida de las Torres, and catch the ALAMEDA bus across from the Hotel Central. Luggage storage is available at the station 7 AM–9 PM daily. **Flecha Amarilla** (tel. 48/18-29-23) has frequent service to Mexico City (6 hrs, $11) and Guanajuato (4 hrs, $6). **Estrella Blanca** (tel. 48/18-29-63) serves Aguascalientes (3 hrs, $6) and Zacatecas (3 hrs, $5). **Omnibuses de Oriente** (tel. 48/18-29-41) travels to Guadalajara (6 hrs, $10) and Ciudad Victoria (5 hrs, $8.50) every hour, 24 hours daily, as well as to intra-state destinations such as Río Verde (2 hrs, $4). **Omnibus de México** (tel. 48/18-29-51) has three buses a day to Tampico (7 hrs, $11).

BY TRAIN Buses to Mexico City (8 hrs; $9 1st class, $5 2nd class) depart daily at 10 PM. Second-class trains leave for Aguascalientes (4 hrs, $2.50) at noon and for Real de Catorce (3 hrs, $2.50) and Nuevo Laredo ($7.50, 12 hrs) at 5:30 PM. The ticket office is open daily 7:15 AM–6 PM. Tickets go on sale 45 minutes before departure, but get in line at least 1½ hours before departure. There's a market nearby where you can stock up on food for the long journey. Buses run east from the station to the Central Camionera and the youth hostel; ask the driver to drop you off at your destination. *Othón, at 20 de Noviembre, tel. 48/12-21-23. Located just north of the Alameda.*

GETTING AROUND

Most attractions are within walking distance of the **Plaza de Armas**, also known as **Jardín Hidalgo**, which defines the center of town. There are four main streets stemming from the Plaza de Armas. Carranza runs west–east, changing into Los Bravo as it passes just north of the Plaza de Armas. Madero runs east–west and becomes Othón as it passes just south of the Plaza. The streets that form the east and west borders of the Plaza are Hidalgo/Zaragoza and Allende/5 de Mayo, respectively. East on Othón from the Plaza is the **Alameda** (near the cheap food, hotels, and train station); for shopping walk north, to Hidalgo. On the plaza, the cathedral's two bright blue neon crosses form a shining nighttime reference point. City buses, which are rarely necessary, run 6 AM–11 PM and cost about 40¢.

WHERE TO SLEEP

The cheapest place to crash is the youth hostel, which is near the bus station. Don't stay here unless you're looking for a quick place to rest before catching the next bus out, though—the area is sleazy and far removed from the action. The areas around the Plaza de Armas and the Alameda offer reasonably priced rooms and more convenience. Tourists with nearly empty pockets can squeeze into one of the tiny, cramped, not-so-clean rooms at **Hotel Ma Elena** (Jiménez 243, ½ block west of the train station, tel. 48/12-47-52), where singles and doubles without baths are $3.50, $4.50 with (scary) baths.

➢ **UNDER $10** • **Hotel Alameda.** This is the cheapest place to stay without having to sacrifice too many comforts—rooms are small and dark but fairly clean, and the management is friendly enough. If you plan to use your bed for sleeping, the nonstop cumbia tunes from the bar next door may make it difficult. Singles are $5, doubles $6. *La Perla 3, tel. 48/18-65-58. Just off Othón, behind Pemex. 13 rooms, all with bath. Luggage storage. Wheelchair access.*

Hotel Jardín Potosí. Sunny hallways welcome you to spacious rooms (singles $9, doubles $10) with well-scrubbed bathrooms. Not all the rooms are as sunny as the courtyard, so ask to see a couple before you decide. The restaurant on the first floor is cheap and clean. *Los Bravo 530, tel. 48/12-31-52. From the Alameda, 1 block north on 20 de Noviembre and left on Los Bravo. 57 rooms, all with bath. Wheelchair access.*

➢ **UNDER $15** • **Hotel Anáhuac.** The sunny rooms here are immaculate, and there's a good, cheap restaurant right next door. Since it's one block farther from the Alameda than the other budget hotels, it's a bit quieter at night. Singles are $12.50, doubles are $14. *Xochitl 140, tel. 48/12-65-04. From the Alameda, go 1 block north on 20 de Noviembre, left on Los Bravo, and right on Xochitl. 45 rooms, all with bath. Wheelchair access. MC, V.*

Hotel Plaza. Although this hotel is well past its prime, its central location and balconies overlooking the plaza make it worthwhile. Large, carpeted rooms hint at the hotel's former glory, and the staff is extremely friendly and accommodating. Most rooms have bathrooms with hot water that takes a few minutes to kick in. Singles cost $9, doubles are $11, and rooms with balconies and space for 2–5 people cost $15. *Jardín Hidalgo 22, on Plaza de Armas, tel. 48/12–46–31. 27 rooms, 25 with bath.*

HOSTELS **Villa Juvenil San Luis Potosí/CREA.** This state-run hostel packs 'em in eight to a single-sex room, but at $2 a pop, who can complain? There are baseball and soccer fields and over a dozen basketball courts at your disposal here, but the pool is off-limits. Lack of publicity means that the place is never full; lack of locker keys means you have to check your bags when not in your room. Bring your own towel, soap, and toilet paper. *Diagonal Sur, tel. 48/18–16–17. Walk 1 block from bus station; it's opposite traffic circle on Diagonal Sur. 72 beds.*

FOOD

San Luis Potosí has a number of regional specialties, including *enchiladas potosinas* (small, fan-shaped enchiladas with cheese and red sauce) and *zahacuil* (Huastecan pork tamales). The food may be creative, but the ambiance at most restaurants is not—the popular ones resemble diners, complete with vinyl booths and fake plants. Food stands on the plazas are few, but several hole-in-the-wall spots along Carranza and Othón offer cheap, standard Mexican fare. Start the day at **Panificadora La Noria** (Carranza 333, tel. 48/12–56–92), which sells pastries and fresh breads beginning at 6:30 AM.

El Bocolito. This place benefits a cooperative for indigenous students, and its humble decor gives it a down-home feel. Unique specialties include *sarape* (sautéed onions, peppers, ham, sausage, and cheese; $3.50), and *bocolitos* (thick tortilla-style bread stuffed with cheese, cilantro, and refried beans; $2.50). *Guerrero 2, at Aldama, tel. 48/12–76–94. Open Mon.–Sat. 8:30 AM–10:30 PM; Sun. noon–10:30.*

Café Pacífico. The atmosphere at this 24-hour café is sterile, but the place is cheap and convenient. Enchiladas, *chilaquiles* (tortilla strips doused with salsa and sour cream), or *enchiladas potosinas* are available for less than $5. Breakfasts cost $2–$3. *Constitución 200, 4 blocks east of Plaza de Armas, tel. 48/12–54–14.*

La Corriente. This restaurant pleases with stone- and tile-decorated walls and lots of greenery. Try a Northern Mexican specialty such as *chamorro pibil* (pork in sweet mole sauce wrapped in banana leaf) for $4.50, or a mixed plate of eight different dishes for $3. Breakfast is served 8 AM–11:30 AM, comida corrida and the buffet are served 1–7, and *antojitos* (appetizers) and cocktails are served after 7 PM. *Carranza 700, 6½ blocks west of Plaza de Armas, tel. 48/12–93–04. Open Mon.–Sat. 8 AM–midnight, Sun. 8–6.*

Tropicana. This semi-vegetarian restaurant with counter seating is a hidden treasure. Huge fresh fruit drinks ($1–$3) with goofy names like "Tú y Yo" (You and I) and "Sensual" are made with everything from strawberries and papaya to alfalfa and egg. Quesadillas with avocado are $1. Yogurt with honey and granola is 75¢, as is ginseng tea with honey. The *comida corrida* (pre-prepared lunch special) is just $1.50. *Othón 355-B, tel. 48/12–81–69. On NE cnr of Plaza del Carmen. Open Mon.–Sat. 9 AM–10 PM, Sun. 3:30–9:30.*

WORTH SEEING

All of the sights below are within easy walking distance of the Plaza de Armas. Sunday is the best sight-seeing day—museums and churches are open, and the numerous plazas often have free daytime theater and puppet shows or early evening concerts. Vendors sell food and regional handicrafts, and the streets are filled with families and couples out for a Sunday stroll. For a schedule of most free events, pick up the monthly publication *Guiarte* from the tourist office. Upcoming classical music concerts, plays, and literary events are also announced on the billboard outside the **Casa de Artesanías** (Plaza de San Francisco, tel. 48/12–75–21), a government-run store that has a good selection of crafts from all over Mexico, but no bargain prices.

CENTRO DE DIFUSION CULTURAL This free three-story museum displays the work of local artists in periodic exhibitions. The center also has a theater that shows free performances—ask at the tourist office for a schedule. *Universidad, at Negrete, tel. 48/12-43-33. South side of Alameda. Open Tues.-Sat. 10-2 and 5-8, Sun. 10-2 and 6-8.*

MUSEO NACIONAL DE LA MASCARA This museum holds a collection of more than 1,000 ceremonial and decorative masks from all over Mexico. The written explanations in Spanish describe in detail the history and significance of the Mesoamerican masks and the festivals in which they are used. Not to be missed are the eerie exhibits of devil masks or the impressive *gigantes* (giants) of San Luis—eight huge puppets (about 10 feet high) used in the festival of Corpus Christi. These represent royal couples from the four parts of the world known to Columbus—Asia, Africa, the Americas, and Europe. *Villerías 200, tel. 48/12-30-25. Walk 2 blocks east of Plaza de Armas on Othón, then right 2 blocks on Escobedo. Admission free. Open Tues.-Fri. 10-2 and 4-6, Sat. and Sun. 10-2.*

MUSEO REGIONAL POTOSINO This museum, housed in a former Franciscan Monastery, has one of the largest collections of artifacts from San Luis Potosí's Huasteca region, including a reproduction of a famous statue said to represent the young Quetzalcoatl, *adolescente huasteco*. The lower floor also has a small mineral exhibit and an interesting series of early 20th-century photographs of the streets of San Luis, alongside current photographs of the same areas. Upstairs is the monastery's chamber of the Virgin, now restored, as well as a few 19th-century religious paintings. *Galeana 450, behind Templo de San Francisco. Admission free. Open Tues.-Fri. 10-1 and 3-6, Sat. 10-noon, Sun. 10-1.*

CHURCHES San Luis Potosí is divided into seven barrios, and the center of each neighborhood's social activities is its church. Among the most notable is the **Catedral** (Othón 105) in the Plaza de Armas. Built in 1670, the cathedral's baroque facade features Italian marble statues of the 12 Apostles. Although some baroque paintings still remain, the interior has been remodeled with neoclassical altars and, the hippest addition, a 1950s neon blue cross. Another major church is the **Templo de San Francisco** (Universidad 180), in the plaza of the same name, which has a pink limestone baroque facade. It was built in 1686 to honor St. Francis of Assisi, and several paintings and stone carvings in the church depict scenes from his life. The strange artwork in the church—including a chandelier shaped like a boat and a toy truck in the hands of a statue of Sebastián de Aparicio—also symbolizes Francisco's evangelical travels. Construction began in 1749 on the **Templo del Carmen** (Villerías 105), on the plaza of the same name. The temple represents a mixture of styles, with a churrigueresque (ultra-baroque) facade and neoclassical structures in back. The interior contains an astonishing amount of gold leaf, most notably on the gold-covered altar of the Virgin's Chapel. Mass times are posted in church entryways, but you can drop in on any of them from about 8 AM to 9 PM.

CHEAP THRILLS

The **Parque Tangamanga**, an expanse of lakes, trees, sports fields, and gardens a few kilometers southwest of the Plaza de Armas, is the best place to escape the smog and traffic of San Luis Potosí. But nature is hardly the only thing you'll find in the park; it also houses museums, a planetarium, and the huge, open-air **Teatro de la Ciudad**. The free **Museo de Arte Popular** (Parque Tangamanga, tel. 48/12-15-85) displays regional handicrafts and a selection of pre-Columbian artifacts. The museum is open Monday 10-3, Tuesday-Saturday 10-1:45 and 4-5:45, Sunday 10-2:45. The many cultural events held in the park and at the theater are publicized in *Guiarte*, available at the tourist office. To get here, catch the PERIMETRAL or RUTA 32 bus from Constitución near the Alameda; the bus driver will drop you at Avenida Nacho, near the park's main entrance. To get back to town, walk four long blocks to Diagonal Sur and catch the bus heading back to the Alameda. Several kilometers west of the Plaza de Armas is the **Casa de la Cultura** (Carranza 1815, tel. 48/13-22-47), which hosts more cultural events and art exhibits, as well as free films in styles ranging from documentary to avant-garde. The taxi ride here costs $1.50. Call ahead to find out what's happening, or check the listings in *Guiarte*.

> *"Chichimeca"—the generic name for the nomadic bands who inhabited the northern Bajío—means "lineage of the dog." Actually this was a compliment; many Aztec dynasties claimed this heritage.*

FESTIVALS

San Luis Potosí is one of the oldest cities in northeastern Mexico, with a rich tradition of religious festivals and fairs. Mid-January brings pilgrims to the shrine of **San Sebastián** in the barrio of the same name. In May, the 10-day **Festival de las Artes** brings music, theater, and dance—much of it free to the public. In July, contemporary dance troupes come to town for the **Festival de la Danza**. On August 25th, the city celebrates its patron saint, **San Luis Rey**, with a parade and fiesta. The second half of August is also the time of the **Feria Nacional Potosina** (National Fair).

AFTER DARK

Nightlife in San Luis Potosí is dead Sunday through Wednesday and explosive Thursday through Saturday. One of the more popular bars in town is **Puff!** (Carranza 1145, tel. 48/13-65-53); there's no cover charge for the discotheque (opens at 11 PM). In case you're wondering where they still play Lionel Richie tunes, sit at the bar in the early evening and you'll see that you've come to the right place. The newly remodeled **Tennis Company** (Carranza 423, tel. 48/14-70-34) charges a $5 cover and attracts a young crowd with disco and pop music. **Oasis,** in the Hotel María Dolores (Carretera a México, Km. 417, tel. 48/22-18-82; cover $8.50), is one of the most popular out-of-the-way clubs for rich kids (those with cars) looking for love. The gay scene in San Luis is pretty lively, at least by Mexican standards. Meeting areas include the arches at the Plaza de Armas in the early evening and in the plaza itself later on. **Cherry's Grill** (Universidad, btw 5 de Mayo and Zaragoza) is a popular, if somewhat divey, gay bar. **Chey's** (on Julián de los Reyes) is a gay disco that is open on weekends. It's best reached by taxi as it's quite a distance from the central plaza.

Mariachi bands practice in the evenings on the Jardín Escontría on Los Bravo, turning the otherwise unattractive plaza into a romantic spot for an early evening stroll.

Near San Luis Potosí

SANTA MARIA DEL RIO This small, unassuming town is famous for handcrafted cotton and silk *rebozos* (shawls). These are made with techniques that originated in Asia, were passed on to Spain during the Moorish invasion, and were then brought to Mexico with the conquistadores. See how the patterned shawls are woven today in the **Escuela del Rebozo** (tel. 485/3-00-62). To reach Santa María, take the **Autobuses Potosinos** line from San Luis Potosí; buses (1 hr, $1.50) leave every half hour between 6 AM and 11:45 PM.

REAL DE CATORCE Perched among the high, desolate peaks of the northern *altiplano* (highlands), Real de Catorce is a dusty ghost-town straight out of a B-grade western. Established in 1778 as a mining town, its glory days were in the 19th century. In the early 20th century, when the price of silver dropped, so did the population: from 144,000 to 2,700. Today, the town's residents number less than 1,000, making exploration of the abandoned mines, baroque churches, and stone amphitheaters (once used for bull- and cockfights) a somewhat lonely experience—although recent tourist popularity has caused some souvenir shops to sprout up. Huichol Indians from Nayarit and Jalisco visit Real de Catorce every autumn to harvest peyote (used for religious rites) in the nearby hills. **Estrella Blanca** offers one direct bus per day ($7), which leaves San Luis at 3:30 PM. There is also hourly service to Matehuala (2½ hrs, $5), where minibuses wait to take travelers into Real de Catorce.

RIO VERDE Surrounded by acres of orange trees and fields of corn and chiles, the little town of Río Verde lives up to its name—even the zócalo is awash in green. In the lush countryside around the town, you'll find ample opportunities for swimming, camping, and spelunking. The largest and most developed swimming area lies about 14 kilometers from town at **Laguna de la Media Luna.** This sparkling clear lake is popular with scuba divers and snorkelers for its varied aquatic plants and underwater fossilized trees. You can camp here for $1, and there are a few little restaurants that rent inner tubes. To rent scuba gear, make arrangements at the restaurant/bar/disco/store **La Cabaña** (Carretera San Luis-Río Verde, Km. 127.5, tel. 487/2-06-25). Less developed, but popular with locals, are the double swimming holes, **Los Anteojitos** (little eyeglasses). You can usually camp in the thick grass here for free, but a caretaker may appear and charge you a dollar or two. A desert-like beauty surrounds the ponds of **El Charco Azul** and, farther afield, the fishing at **San Sebastian** is rumored to be the best in the area. Both are very rustic, but camping is free and, according to locals, safe. About 30 kilometers from town, spelunkers can explore the caves at **Las Grutas de Catedral** and **Las Grutas de Ángel**, where rock formations look vaguely like angels, altars, and pipe organs. The caves can be reached by a three-kilometer trail that leads out of the small community of Los Alamitos, where you can hire guides to take you in.

You'll have to make friends with someone who owns a car, or else hire a taxi to get to these areas—buses don't run on these backcountry dirt roads. Most journeys should cost $6–$10. Friendly *taxista* Salvador Hernández Castro is willing to drive just about anywhere; ask for him around the bus station, or call him at home (tel. 487/2-23-07). Get a map of the area from the **Cámara Nacional de Comercio, Servicios, y Turismo Río Verde** (Jardín de San Antonio "F", tel. 487/2-08-02), which is open weekdays 9:30-2 and 4:30-7, Saturdays 9:30-noon.

➢ **COMING AND GOING** • **Omnibuses de Oriente** (tel. 48/18-29-41) runs buses hourly from San Luis Potosí to Río Verde (2 hrs, $4). From Río Verde, **Omnibuses de Oriente** (tel. 487/2-01-12) and **Sistema** (tel. 487/2-12-88) make hourly runs to Ciudad Valles (2 hrs, $4).

➢ **WHERE TO SLEEP AND EAT** • **Hotel Morelos** (Morelos 216, no phone) is the best deal in town; it's clean, close to the plaza, and cheap—singles and doubles without bath are $3.50; the one room with a bath is $7. To get here from the bus station, go left on the San Luis Potosí-Río Verde highway, and then right on Morelos. The older and grander **Hotel Plaza** (Constitucion "F," right on the zócalo, tel. 487/2-01-00) has a large courtyard and spacious, tiled rooms. Singles are $14, doubles $16. Food in Río Verde is hearty, if uninspired. Try the busy **Restaurant Rivera** (tel. 487/2-01-03; open 24 hrs.), right on the zócalo, where you'll spend less than $4 on generous portions of tacos, enchiladas, and other *antojitos*.

CIUDAD VALLES

The only reason to come to Ciudad Valles is to arrange excursions into the vast, untouristed countryside beyond the city limits—a region full of untouched rivers, waterfalls, and caves. The city itself has little to offer, unless you enjoy long city blocks choked by cinderblock buildings and speeding cars. The Valles **tourist office** (Carranza 53 Sur, tel. 138/2-01-44) gives out free maps on the rare occasions when they're in stock. Groups of four or more can arrange excursions with Ana Maria Musa at **Antani Viajes**, in the lobby of the **Hotel Don Antonio** (Blvd. México-Laredo 15, tel. 138/1-19-16). She speaks some English and understands budget travel, so she won't push you to take on some expensive deal. The main bus line in Ciudad Valles is **Vencedor** (tel. 138/2-37-55); buses run hourly to Río Verde (2 hrs, $4), San Luis Potosí (5½ hrs, $7) and Tampico (2½ hrs, $4).

➢ **WHERE TO SLEEP AND EAT** • Hotels are not particularly cheap, but try **Hotel Boulevard** (Blvd. México-Laredo 19, tel. 138/2-01-28), on the main road. It has clean rooms with fans at $7 for singles, $8 for doubles. Otherwise you can camp right in the city for $6, on the extensive grounds of **Hotel Valles** (Blvd. México-Laredo 36 Nte., tel. 138/2-00-50). They allow access to showers, bathrooms, and their large, inviting, blue-tile pool. (If you want to splurge on a room, singles are $32, doubles $36.) Dining options are pretty undistinguished here; lots of cheap food stands line Juárez near Boulevard México-Laredo. The restaurant at **Hotel Piña** (Juárez 210, tel. 138/2-01-83), serves decent plates of spaghetti ($1–$2) and large cheesy pizzas ($4), and also sells maps of the region (50¢).

➢ **OUTDOOR ACTIVITIES** • The dense tropical rainforest around Ciudad Valles is ripe for exploration by the adventurous. There's little tourist infrastructure here, so be prepared to hike, haggle with *taxistas*, and hire the occasional guide to get you to where you want to go. **Las Cascadas de Micos**, a series of cascades and swimming holes, lies about 18 kilometers north of Highway 70, just east of Valles. A round-trip taxi ride costs about $12; there's also a no-frills campsite here. Farther east, mid-way to Río Verde, is **La Cascada Tamasopo**, where a confluence of mountain rivers and streams form several high falls that crash into swimmable pools. Tamasopo also has campgrounds. Just 2 kilometers away are more pools at **El Trampolín**, which also boasts a natural limestone bridge. One **Vencedor** bus (tel. 138/2–32–81) leaves the central station at Ciudad Valles for Tamasopo (2 hrs, $2) at 2:30 AM daily. Alternately, you can take one of the more frequent local Vencedor buses to Río Verde (1½ hrs, $2); get off at the Tamasopo *crucero* (intersection), and walk the 8 kilometers north to the falls.

More spectacular is the 11-meter-high **Cascada de Tamul**, the highest waterfall in the region. It's also more remote, and locals discourage camping in the wilderness here. Ask the Vencedor driver to drop you at the *crucero* at El Sauz, on Highway 70, then hire a taxi or hitch south down the dirt road to the small town of Tanchachín. Here you can hire a boat to go upriver to the falls. **Puente de Dios**, off the road to Xilitla (*see below*) is another spot where the river Tampaón has carved a natural rock bridge. To get here, take a Vencedor bus to Santiaguillo; from here hitch or hire a taxi to Tantizohuiche, where you can hire a guide. If you're tired of splashing around, head to the **So-tano de las Golondrinas** (near the town of Aquismón, on the road to Xilitla), a 375-meter shaft in the earth, with a 70-meter neck and a 250-meter bottom. It's home to hundreds of swallows, who swoosh out of the ground at sunrise. Vencedor buses run regularly to Aquismón (40 min, $1), where you can arrange transport to the *So-tano* (literally, basement).

QUERETARO MISSIONS Nestled among the rugged hills of the Sierra Gorda is a series of five small missions, constructed in the mid-18th century under the evangelizing gaze of Father Junipero Serra. The elaborate facade of each church is carved in a baroque style, and displays both indigenous and Catholic iconography: Life-size saints do battle with demons and dragons, while flowers and grapes bloom peacefully beside them. The largest of the five mission-towns, **Jalpan** has the most places to stay, and is a good base for daytrips to the other missions. The fancy **Mesón de Fray Junipero Serro** (Carretera Río Verde, tel. 429/6–01–64) charges $17.50 for a single or a double. The more modest **Camino Viejo** (tel. 429/6–01–85) charges $11 for a single or double. Jalpan also has a new museum, the **Museo Historico de la Sierra Gorda** (admission: $1; open Mon.–Sat. 10–3, Sun. 9–1). At **Conca**, the next largest town, ask for directions to the thermal springs, near the hotel Mesón de San Nícolas. The other three Querétaro missions, **Lahda**, **Tancogol**, and **Tilaco**, are very small and remote; it may be best to plan a day trip from Jalpan.

➤ **COMING AND GOING** • The fastest and most direct way to reach the Querétaro missions, is by bus from Río Verde or Ciudad Valles. From Río Verde, **Omnibuses de Oriente** (tel. 487/2–01–12) runs buses hourly through Conca to Jalpan (2 hrs, $3). **Vencedor** (tel. 138/2–37–55) also runs this route hourly from Ciudad Valles (3½ hrs, $4).

XILITLA Located on the slopes of the Sierra Gorda, Xilitla overlooks the deep green gorges cut by the Tahculín River. An Augustine church and convent were built here early in the Spanish Conquest (about 1557); their thick walls were designed to ward off Huastec attacks. About 3 kilometers outside town, the ruins of a mansion/castle lie moldering in the jungle. Built by Sir Edward James, an illegitimate son of King Edward VII of England, the house and gardens were designed to mimic the surrounding vegetation in a style James claimed "integrated architecture into nature." Take a look at the giant concrete mushrooms and blue metal snakes to see if he succeeded. Just outside the garden walls, you'll find **Las Pozas**, a series of waterfalls that plunge into several inviting pools. One kilometer back toward town, on the other side of the highway, enormous saltpeter stalactites can be found in the **Cueva de Salitre**. From Río Verde, one **Sistema** bus (tel. 487/2–12–88) leaves at 6:45 PM for Xilitla (5 hrs, $6). **Vencedor** (tel. 138/2–37–55) buses also run hourly from Ciudad Valles to Xilitla (1½ hrs, $2).

Querétaro

Downtown Querétaro is a great example of the juxtaposition of past and present so common in Mexican cities: Centuries-old colonial buildings now house electronic appliance and women's lingerie shops, and fast-food joints adjoin national monuments. The heart of Querétaro is an exquisite stretch of tree-shaded cobblestone streets lined with colonial mansions and punctuated by quiet plazas and well-kept gardens. Always an important center for the surrounding agricultural and cattle-raising country, this bustling state capital now has a population of more than one million people—but is still worlds away from the pollution and chaos of Mexico City, which is just a 3-hour bus trip away. Women can walk alone at night on well-lit streets with a sense of security, and the universities attract young students and bohemian types, who can be seen playing chess in cafés. And, like other university cities, Querétaro has an active central square and a rocking nightlife.

Some of the most important events in Mexican history took place in Querétaro; you'll see historic landmarks on almost every city block. The struggle for independence received a push here from Querétaro resident Doña Josefa Ortiz, who sent word to conspirators Miguel Hidalgo and Ignacio Allende that their plans for rebellion had been discovered. Hidalgo acted immediately, sounding the cry for independence in the nearby town of Dolores (now Dolores Hidalgo). Ortiz, also known as La Corregidora, was later executed for her subversive activities; her heroism is commemorated in the **Plaza de la Corregidora** and **La Tumba de Doña Josefa**. The **Convento de la Santa Cruz** was the site of Emperor Maximilian's imprisonment before his execution on the **Cerro de las Campanas** (Hill of the Church Bells), just north of town. The signing of the 1917 constitution and the formation of the PRI, Mexico's ruling party, both took place in Querétaro. Querétaro was also the site of a sadder day in Mexican history, the signing of the Treaty of Guadalupe Hidalgo, under which Mexico ceded Texas, New Mexico, and the California territories to the United States.

BASICS

AMERICAN EXPRESS Turismo Beverly is a travel agency that provides all American Express services. *Tecnológico 118, Local 1, Querétaro, Querétaro, CP 76030, México, tel. 42/16–12–60. From Alameda, take any bus on Constituyentes east to Tecnológico and walk south 1½ blocks. Open weekdays 9–2 and 4–7, Sat. 9–1.*

AUTO PARTS/SERVICE Several auto parts stores and mechanics are located on Zaragoza between Ignacio Pérez and Montes. **Refaccionaría Capricornio** (Calzada Zaragoza 69-A, tel. 42/15–05–09; open daily 9–7) sells auto parts and can recommend a mechanic.

BOOKSTORES Unidad Cultural del Centro (16 de Septiembre 1, tel. 42/12–01–39) sells newspapers and tons of books (in Spanish) on Mexican history, literature, art, and film; it's open daily 9–8:30. **Fonart** (Angela Peralta 20, btw Corregidora and Pasteur, tel. 42/12–26–48), the government-sponsored *artesenía* (crafts) store, has a shelf or two devoted to English-language books; oddly, most are about the Internet. The store and its adjacent café are open Monday–Saturday 10–2 and 5–9.

CASAS DE CAMBIO Both **Banamex** (16 de Septiembre 1, tel. 42/12–01–39) and **Bancrecer** (Juárez 15, tel. 42/12–06–77) cash traveler's checks and exchange currency weekdays 9–1:30 and give cash advances on Visa or MasterCard at the ATMs that are open 24 hours. Better rates can sometimes be found at **Cambio La Pasada** (Allende 2, no phone), which is open Monday–Saturday 9–6.

EMERGENCIES Police 42/12–02–06; **ambulance** 42/13–28–04.

LAUNDRY Laundromats are scarce near the center of town, so you'll have to schlep your clothes six blocks south of downtown to Avenida Zaragoza. **Lavandería Automática La Cascada**, in the big shopping center on Constituyentes, charges about $2.50 for a three-kilo self-service load or $4 for full service. *In Comercial Mexicana, tel. 42/16–56–96. Open daily 9–8.*

MAIL The **post office** will hold mail addressed to you for up to 10 days if it's sent to the following address: Lista de Correos, Administración 1, Arteaga 7, Querétaro, Querétaro, CP 76000, México. They also provide all the usual services. *From Jardín Zenéa, walk 2 blocks south on Juárez, turn right on Arteaga. Open weekdays 8–7, Sat. 9–1.*

MEDICAL AID Grupo Médico Zaragoza (Zaragoza 39, tel. 42/16–76–38) is a large, centrally located medical center that provides most medical services 24 hours a day. **Farmacia Querétaro** (Constituyentes 17, at Ignacio de las Casas, tel. 42/12–44–23) is also open 24 hours.

PHONES You'll find Ladatel pay phones on the Jardín Zenéa and the Plaza de la Independencia. The **caseta de larga distancia** (long-distance telephone office) charges $2.50 for collect calls. *5 de Mayo 33, 1 block west of Jardín Zenéa. Open Mon.–Sat. 9:30–2 and 4:30–9.*

Querétaro

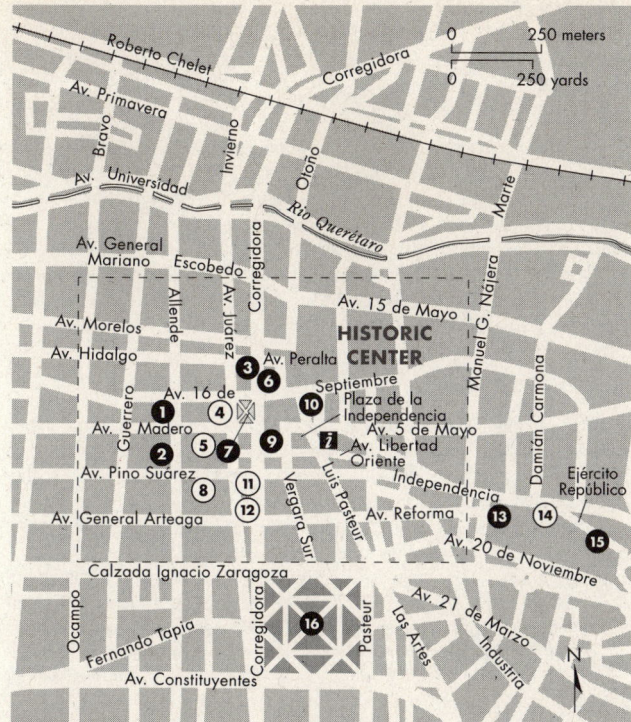

Sights ●
Alameda, **16**
Calzada de los Arcos, **15**
Convento de la Santa Cruz, **13**
Jardín Zenéa (zócalo), **7**
Museo de Arte de Querétaro, **2**
Museo Regional, **9**
Palacio del Gobierno Federal, **10**
Plaza de la Corregidora, **6**
Teatro de la República, **3**
Templo de Santa Clara, **1**

Lodging ○
Hotel Hidalgo, **5**
Hotel Plaza, **4**
Hotel San Francisco, **12**
Posada Academia, **8**
Posada Colonial, **11**
Villa Juvenil (CREA), **14**

SCHOOLS The **Universidad Autónoma de Querétaro** has four-to-six week summer and winter courses in beginning, intermediate, and advanced Spanish. Courses cover all aspects of the language, including grammar, pronunciation, and conversation. For more information, write to: Escuela de Idiomas, Centro Universitario, Cerro de las Campanas, Querétaro, Querétaro, CP 76000, México. *In Centro Universitario, Hidalgo, tel. 42/16–74–66. From Jardín Zenéa,* RUTA R *bus to the university.*

VISITOR INFORMATION The enthusiastic staff at the **Centro de Información Turística** (Luis Pasteur, at Andador Libertad, tel. 42/14–56–23) will gladly give out maps, brochures, and tips about the city. The office is open weekdays 9–2 and 5–8. For more detailed information, go to the **Secretaría de Turismo**. Ask for Luis Alejandro Bustamante—he understands budget travel and won't try to coax you into an expensive hotel. *Constituyentes 102 Ote., tel. 42/13–84–83. Open weekdays 9–2 and 5–8.*

COMING AND GOING

BY BUS Querétaro has just opened a fancy new bus station about 6 kilometers south of the *zócalo* (main square). The station has two separate buildings, one for mostly first class service (Sala A) and another for second class (Sala B); at press time, a third *sala* was under construction. Each building has restaurants, phones, waiting areas, and luggage storage. Taxis wait at either side; rather than negotiating your fare, you need to buy a taxi ticket from the kiosk near the exit. It costs about $1.50 to get to the zócalo, or you can take an *urbano* (local city bus) for about 50¢. Walk to the end of Sala B (and past any adjacent construction), and take the RUTA 8 minibus to the center.

Major bus lines leave from each sala. **Omnibus de México** (tel. 42/12–08–13) has service to Aguascalientes (4 hrs, $11) and leaves from Sala A. **Estrella Blanca** (tel. 42/29–02–02) departs from Sala B and goes to Zacatecas (5 hrs, $13), San Luis Potosí (3 hrs, $7), and Mexico City (3 hrs, $7). **Herradura de Plata** (42/29–02–45) runs buses to San Miguel de Allende from Sala B every 40 minutes (1 hr, $2). **Flecha Amarilla** (tel. 42/11–40–01) has five second-class buses a day to Guanajuato (2½ hrs, $4). They leave from Sala B. Locals say sarcastically that Flecha Amarilla's motto should be BETTER DEAD THAN LATE. They do offer the only service to some destinations, so you may not have much choice.

BY TRAIN The small, well-kept train station is 3 kilometers north of the historic center. Taxis between the station and the center cost about $2 each way, but you can catch the RUTA 8 minibus from the station to the Jardín Zenéa (the central plaza). At press time, only second-class trains were running. Trains to Mexico City ($3) leave twice a day, at 4 AM and 4 PM. The train for Ciudad Juárez ($17), on the U.S. border, departs daily at 2 PM. There is also a train to Guadalajara ($4), which leaves at 12:30 AM. No one in a responsible position is willing to hazard a guess as to how long these trips take, which may be an indication of the reliability of the service. *Héroes de la Nacozari, tel. 42/12–17–03. Ticket sales daily 9–11 and noon–5.*

GETTING AROUND

Most of the sights are within walking distance of the Jardín Zenéa (the central plaza), also known as the Jardín Obregón. Not surprisingly, most of the budget hotels are here as well. The two main north–south drags near Jardín Zenéa—Juárez to the west and Corregidora to the east—stem from the Alameda. The Jardín is bordered on the north by 16 de Septiembre, and Madero borders it on the south. Many of the city's streets are closed to cars—these are called *andadores* (walking streets). The cheapest way to get away from the historic center is to catch one of the abundant white minibuses. These travel within the city of Querétaro only, cost about 60¢, and run from 7 AM to 10 PM. The destination of each bus is painted on the front windshield, and you can flag them down on busy streets and intersections (as in all Mexican cities). Generally, buses on Corregidora are headed north and only those on Juárez go south.

WHERE TO SLEEP

If you have the money, stay in a moderately priced place. Querétaro's bargain hotels are near the noisy Jardín Zenéa, so you can expect a fair amount of late-night racket. The more expensive hotels near the old bus station aren't much better, and the cheapest hotels are only semi-clean and usually attract couples looking for a place to consummate their newfound affection. During December, hotels are booked solid for the Exposición Ganadera (a sort of county fair); to play it safe, you may want to reserve a month or so in advance.

➤ **UNDER $10** • **Hotel Hidalgo.** Huge wooden doors open onto this hotel's sunny courtyard. Rooms have TVs and clean bathrooms, and some have balconies overlooking the cobblestone street. The friendly proprietors speak English, but they aren't around very often. Singles cost $8.50, doubles $10. *Madero Pte. 11, 1 block west of Jardín Zenéa, tel. 42/12–00–81. 40 rooms, all with bath. Luggage storage. Wheelchair access.*

Hotel San Francisco. On the bustling Avenida Corregidora, this dark and spartan hotel attracts mostly Mexican families and businessmen. Rooms are clean—if the overpowering smell of disinfectant is any indication—and there's always hot water. Rooms are $8.50 for a single, $10 for a double. *Corregidora 114, tel. 42/12–08–58. 58 rooms, all with bath. Luggage storage. Reservations advised. Wheelchair access.*

Posada Academia. Rooms are dark but relatively clean, and include TVs and hot water all day long. The old woman who runs the place is cheerful and chatty, and she casts a blind eye to all the sex going on in the hotel. Singles are $5, doubles $7. *Pino Suárez 3, 1 block south of Jardín Zenéa, no phone. 18 rooms, all with bath.*

Posada Colonial. The lobby is inviting, but the extremely small rooms aren't clean. They are very cheap, though: A single with shared bath is $3 ($6 with private bath). Doubles are $5 with shared bath, $8 with a private one. For $1, you can have a breakfast of eggs, bread, and juice brought to your room. Many of the guests probably don't notice the decor; once again, love (or, at least, lust) is in the air here. *Juárez 19, 3 blocks south of Jardín Zenéa, tel. 42/12–02–39. 16 rooms, 8 with bath.*

➤ **UNDER $15** • **Hotel Plaza.** This is your best option in this price range. Singles are $11, doubles $13.50. Rooms are clean and bright and have TVs and phones. It's right on the central square, so ask for a room away from the street, as the traffic is noisy at night. *Juárez 23, on west side of Jardín Zenéa, tel. 42/12-11-38. 29 rooms, all with bath. MC, V.*

HOSTELS **Villa Juvenil (CREA).** If you don't mind the 15-minute walk to the center of town, or the busloads of high school students traipsing in at all hours of the night, this is a good place to stay. It's clean and cheerful, and dorm beds go for $1.50 per person. There's also a place for hanging hand-washed clothes. Sometimes the hostel is filled with student groups, so call ahead if you don't want to take your chances. *Ejército Republicano, tel. 42/23-11-20. From Jardín Zenéa, go south 2 blocks on Corregidora, left on Independencia, right at fork to Ejército Republicano, and continue to crest of hill by the church. Luggage storage.*

FOOD

There are so many good, cheap things to eat in Querétaro that it's hard to know where to begin. By eating at food stands on the street, you can spend less than $5 on breakfast, lunch, *and* dinner (yes, all three combined). In the morning, vendors work the Jardín Zenéa and Avenidas Constituyentes and Zaragoza around the Alameda, selling 30¢ tamales and *atole* (a sweet corn-based drink, similar to hot chocolate). At lunchtime, you can buy fresh fruit cups doused with lime and chiles (75¢) and tacos (25¢). Around 6 PM-7 PM, the stands along the pedestrian streets in the center sell grilled corn on the cob (25¢) and seafood tostadas (75¢). Take a good look at the fish before you buy, as it may not be as fresh as the vendors will have you believe. Food stands are generally your best bet; most cheaper restaurants are mediocre, and expensive restaurants cater shamelessly to tourists.

Sola? Solita?

When they reveal that they are traveling alone, tourists, especially female ones, often encounter incredulous responses from Mexicans. The double request for confirmation— "Sola? Solita?" ("Alone? All by your little self?"), asked by everyone from the grandma at the hotel desk to the university student sitting in a café—may momentarily give you cause for concern. You needn't worry, it's a cultural difference. Most Mexicans react this way not only because they are concerned about your safety, but also because of the close familial bonds that exist in their own culture. Mexican youth travel with family and friends, and, as one female university student explained, "My parents would worry if I traveled by myself."

The influence of family is strong, especially since most people live with their parents until they get married. Bragging about your studio apartment back home usually results not in envy but pity: For many Mexicans, living and traveling alone implies that your family doesn't care much for you. The extended family is a source of economic and emotional support, and any relative, no matter how distant, is welcome to show up looking for a meal, a job, or a place to stay. Typical outings, whether a month-long vacation at the beach or a Sunday afternoon in the park, almost always involve the entire family. The bonus of all this group activity is that the solo traveler is rarely at a loss for company: Many Mexicans are perfectly willing to expand the family temporarily to include a lone gringo for the day.

➤ **UNDER $5** • **Café del Fondo.** Since its recent move, this popular café may have lost some of its architectural charm but none of its devoted bohemian following. The entranceway displays posters for current concerts and art exhibitions, and artsy types lounge in the simple white-washed rooms, dawdling for hours over $2 *cafés exóticos* (cinnamon- or alcohol-spiked coffees). Cheap, filling breakfast ($1–$1.50) and lunch ($2) specials are also available. *Pino Suárez 9, tel. 42/12-09-05. Open daily 7:30 AM–10 PM. Wheelchair access.*

Comedor Vegetariano Natura. The decor is decidedly *Brady Bunch* rec room, complete with wood paneling and wall-sized forest posters, but the food is good. Try the mushroom and cheese soy burgers ($1.25), soy enchiladas ($2), or a fruit and yogurt shake. If you're suffering from a gastrointestinal disorder, the restaurant also sells natural remedies, including horsehair tea for dysentery. *Vergara 7, tel. 42/04-12-22. From Jardín Zenéa, walk 2 blocks east on 5 de Mayo, then right on Vergara. Open Mon.–Sat. 8 AM–9 PM.*

La Mariposa. This popular café/ice-cream parlor has been around for more than 50 years, and its original peacock-blue decor is kept lovingly clean. Delicious milkshakes are $1 and light lunches cost about $2.50. Check out the tempting sweets at the back counter. *Peralta 7, tel. 42/12-11-66. Walk 2 blocks north of Jardín Zenéa. Open daily 8 AM–9:30 PM.*

Restaurant Punto y Coma. This place is filled with students at midday, so conversation is pretty easy to come by. Your choice from the *menú del día* (daily special) will cost $2 or $3 and includes soup, tortillas, rice, an entrée, and dessert. Meat lovers should try the *hígado encebollado* (liver in onions), when it's available; vegetarians will appreciate the terrific lentil soup. Tortillas are made fresh in the front of the restaurant. *16 de Septiembre 27, 1 block east of Jardín Zenéa, tel. 42/14-16-66. Open daily 8–6.*

➤ **UNDER $10** • **Café Tulipe.** Mexican and international students frequent this pleasant café and restaurant at night. Solo diners can amuse themselves by checking out the art prints on the wall and the prominently displayed dessert cart. Try the *crema conde* ($2), a soup made of black beans, cream, oregano, and *epazote* (an herb particular to Mexico). Other dishes include chicken in orange sauce ($5) and fondue for two ($8). Service is friendly and unobtrusive. *Calzada de los Arcos 3, tel. 42/13-63-91. Walk 1½ blocks west of base of Ejército Republicano. Open Sun.–Wed. 8 AM–10 PM, Thurs.–Sat. 8 AM–11 PM.*

WORTH SEEING

Though Querétaro is large and ever-expanding, most sights are in the compact historical center, within walking distance of the Jardín Zenéa. **Parque Cerro de las Campanas** is on the northwest end of the city, while the **Convento de la Santa Cruz** is 1 kilometer east of downtown. The **tourist office** (Luis Pasteur 4, at Libertad, tel. 42/12-13-92, or 42/12-14-12) offers extensive and informative walking tours of the city, conducted in Spanish or (if you pre-arrange) English. Tours begin daily at 10:30 AM, and last for 2½–3 hours. They are a good way to get a sense of the city's history and cost just $1.50 (plus any museum entrance fees).

CONVENTO DE LA SANTA CRUZ This still-functioning 16th-century convent is home to about 40 monks who serenely go about their business while tourists traipse through the building. Guides will take you on a 15-minute tour in Spanish or English and always ask for a small tip for their services. Original furnishings and paintings are on display in several rooms, including the cell where Emperor Maximilian awaited his execution. The branches of the famous **Árbol de las Espinas** (Thorn Tree), in one of the convent's many patios, are filled with cross-shaped thorns. According to legend, the tree grows where a friar named Margil de Jesús buried his cane. Nearby is the city's emblem, **Calzada de los Arcos,** Querétaro's huge, pink, 18th-century stone aqueduct. Though the Calzada no longer carries water, it is one of the largest aqueducts ever constructed in the Americas. *From Jardín Zenéa, go 1 block south on Corregidora, then left on Independencia about 6 blocks. Small donation requested. Open Mon.–Sat. 9–2 and 4–6, Sun. 9–4:30. Wheelchair access.*

MUSEO DE ARTE DE QUERETARO This 18th-century building, once an Augustine monastery, was recently renovated and now houses a varied art collection. Most works date from the 16th, 17th, and 18th centuries, but several rooms on the ground floor are devoted to temporary exhibits of the works of contemporary Mexican artists and photographers, as well as shows by students from the University of Querétaro. *Allende 14, near Pino Suárez, tel. 42/12–35–23. Admission: $1.50; free with student ID and all day Tues. Open Tues.–Sun. 11–7. Wheelchair access.*

MUSEO REGIONAL This regional museum is in an ornate building, once a Franciscan convent, that dates from the 17th century. The collection includes pre-Columbian artifacts from Querétaro state and an interesting display of items of historical import, including early copies of the first Mexican constitution and the coffin used to bring Emperor Maximilian's body to its final resting place. *Corregidora 3, SE cnr of Jardín Zenéa, tel. 42/12–20–31. Admission free. Open Tues.–Sun. 10:30–4:30. Wheelchair access.*

PALACIO DEL GOBIERNO FEDERAL Also called the Palacio Municipal or the Casa de la Corregidora, this enormous, neo-classical 18th-century building was once the home of Querétaro's mayor-magistrate (El Corregidor) and his wife, Doña Josefa Ortiz de Domínguez (La Corregidora). A large room over the main entrance is now used as the governor's conference room; it is also the place where Doña Josefa was held under house arrest during the first rumblings of the War for Independence. As the story goes, she managed to whisper a message through the key hole, warning Father Hidalgo that their plot to declare independence from Spain had been discovered. A few days later, he gave his famous call for liberty in the nearby town of Dolores Hidalgo, and the "Grito de Dolores" became the spark needed to ignite public support for independence. Today, with its arched walkways and gracious courtyards, the palacio brightens the bureaucratic lives of municipal administrators, whose offices are housed here. The guards will let you wander the building; if you want the full tour, ask if Isadora Salvala is around. At night, the fountain in the plaza is lit up. *5 de Mayo, at Pasteur, tel. 42/12–91–00. Open weekdays 8 AM–9 PM, Sat. 9–2. Wheelchair access.*

PARQUE CERRO DE LAS CAMPANAS This quiet park was established on the site where Emperor Maximilian and the royalist generals Tomás Mejía and Miguel Miramón were executed. A chapel is dedicated to them, as is a small museum, complete with a brief video in English and Spanish about the events leading up to the execution. The 20-meter-tall monument to Benito Juárez on the grounds is also worth a look—not that you could miss it. *Gómez Farías, tel. 42/15–20–75. From center, west on Morelos 9 blocks. Admission free. Park open daily 6–6. Museum open Tues.–Sun. 10–2 and 3:30–6.*

PLAZA DE LA CORREGIDORA This pleasant square is named after the heroine of the Independence movement, Doña Josefa (*see* Palacio del Gobierno Federal, *above*), whose statue graces the plaza. The **Árbol de la Amistad** (Friendship Tree), planted here in 1977 in a mixture of soils from around the world, symbolizes Querétaro's hospitality. Surrounding the square are several outdoor cafés and restaurants. *Corregidora, 1 block north of Jardín Zenéa.*

TEATRO DE LA REPUBLICA This imposing neoclassical building was the site of some of the most important events in Mexican history, including the sentencing of Emperor Maximilian to death in 1867 and the drafting of the new constitution in 1917. Although you probably won't witness anything nearly so momentous, you could catch one of the theater's occasional plays or concerts. Check at the box office to find out what's going on. *Angela Peralta 22, 1 block north of Jardín Zenéa. Hours to view building: weekdays 10–2 and 5–8, Sat. 9–noon. Wheelchair access.*

TEMPLO DE SANTA CLARA This 17th-century church sits in the tree-filled Jardín Madero. Exquisite baroque artwork and several gilded altar pieces grace the church's interior. Next to the church stands the **Fuente de Neptuno** (Neptune's Fountain), designed by renowned architect and Bajío native Eduardo Tresguerra. The fountain originally belonged to the monks of San Antonio, who sold it (along with part of their land) during tight economic times. *On Madero, at Allende, about 2 blocks west of Jardín Zenéa. Wheelchair access.*

CHEAP THRILLS

The huge, resplendent **Parque Alameda** (at Zaragoza and Corregidora; open daily 6 AM–8 PM) is the best place in town to rest your aching feet. It is also rumored to be a favorite cruising place for gay men. The nearby **El Molino** bakery (Juárez, at Zaragoza) sells sweet treats you can eat or feed to the ducks in the pond while lounging on the lush grass. This tranquillity is only slightly disturbed by the **open-air market** (*tianguis*) outside the park, where you can pick up a new belt or the latest Gloria Trevi tape. If you are tough enough to hang with mariachi bands (lone women might want to think twice about this), you can head up to the corner of Universidad and Invierno (4 blocks north of Jardín Zenéa, on Juaréz), where musicians hang out, pitch coins, and strum their instruments while they wait to get hired.

FESTIVALS

Querétaro hosts a full-scale *pamplonada* (running of the bulls) on July 26, as part of its **Fiestas de Santa Ana**—a celebration of one of the two patron saints of the city. During the first two weeks of December, the city holds the **Exposición Gonadera**, a huge agricultural fair that includes more bullfighting and rodeos, along with carnival rides, music, and a lot of food. The usual big holidays (Holy Week, Day of the Dead, Independence Day) are also celebrated here with style. The night before Easter Sunday, folks around town burn Judas in effigy.

AFTER DARK

At night, Querétaro's historical center is taken over by a nocturnal animal—the lounge lizard. By 9:30 almost every café and restaurant around **Plaza Corregidora** boasts a singer with synthesizer accompaniment; the soulful crooning echoes across the plaza until the wee hours of the morning. Club-hoppers usually head for the bars and discos lining Boulevard Bernardo Quintana on the east side of town. Things begin to rock just before midnight and continue until everyone decides they're done, or until dawn—whichever comes first. For a quieter evening, head for Café Tulipe or Café del Fondo (*see* Food, *above*), both of which serve coffee and dessert until 10 PM. "High-culture" is also active, with plays, music, dance concerts, and art-film screenings happening in various theaters around the city. The tourist office gives out monthly calendars of such events, or you can check the posters at the Museo Regional and in various cafés in the town center.

BARS Students with money to burn hang out at **J.B.J. O'Brien's** (Bernardo Quintana 13, tel. 42/13-01-48), which has pool tables and karaoke, and is next to a popular disco of the same name. A similar crowd is attracted to the bar/restaurant chain **Freeday** (Constituyentes 119 Ote., tel. 42/23-32-12), and **Carlos 'N Charlie's** (Bernardo Quintana 160, tel. 42/13-90-36), which both feature live music Thursday through Saturday nights. They also offer free appetizers and drinks—but not until you're too drunk to need any more.

CINEMAS **Cinema Premier 70** (Corregidora, at Independencia, tel. 42/14-05-10) shows American and Mexican movies for about $1.50; movies from the United States are usually not dubbed in Spanish, but ask. The Museo Regional (*see* Worth Seeing, *above*) has regular film festivals featuring avant-garde and international films; check the entryway billboard for details.

CLUBS The enormous excess of glitter and lights called **Qiu** (Monte Sinai 103, tel. 42/13-03-61) is a disco that plays mostly pop, and charges a $6 cover. On weekends, the disco inside the Hotel Santa Maria, **La Iguana** (Universidad, no phone), attracts the largest gay crowd in town. You'll have to take a taxi to either one of these discos; the drivers know where they are, and will charge you about $2-$3 to get you there from Jardín Zenéa. For those searching for an alternative to the disco scene, **Quadros** (5 de Mayo 16, tel. 42/12-04-45) comes as a welcome change of pace. Housed in a former mansion just three blocks from the Jardín Zenéa, this new nightclub has three rooms whose walls showcase the work of local painters and photographers. Jazz and folk concerts and occasional poetry readings attract students and artists—when it gets late, they push away the tables and dance in the courtyard.

Near Querétaro

SAN JUAN DEL RIO

Some 54 kilometers southeast of Querétaro, the town of San Juan del Río boasts wide tile-work sidewalks, shady central streets, and well-maintained colonial churches. A particularly interesting church is the **Parroquia de Santo Domingo,** built in the 17th century; its most striking feature is the statue over the main altar of Christ with African features. The **Museo de la Santa Cruz** (2 de Abril, no phone; open weekdays 9:30–2 and 4–6, weekends 10:30–4) houses local pre-Columbian artifacts. San Juan del Río is a pleasant place to purchase the handwoven items, such as baskets and blankets, that Querétaro state is famous for—check out the local artesanía (crafts) shops. Stands along the portales (porches) on Avenida Juárez also sell artesanía. The state of Querétaro is also famous for its nearby opal mines; visit **La Guadalupana** (16 de Septiembre 16, tel. 467/2-09-13), where gemstones are cut and polished on site.

Some of the best fighting bulls come from the Bajío—if a bull is a real champion, his sperm is frozen and saved to produce powerful future generations.

In mid-June, usually beginning around the 15th, the town hosts an enormous festival in honor of its patron saint, San Juan Bautista. Events happen all over town during the week-long festival: Bullfights, cockfights, bicycle races, and beauty contests ("Mister y Miss" San Juan) are mixed in with plays, concerts, and dance performances. Find the friendly **tourist office** (Juárez 30, at Oriente, tel. 467/2-08-84) for details. If you plan to stay, the small, very basic **Hotel Posada** (Guadalupe Victoria 7, tel. 467/2-01-23) has a cheery riot of greenery in its courtyard. Singles and doubles are $8 with a bath, and $7 without. From the tourist office, take a left on Ignacio Allende and another left on Guadalupe Victoria. A big step up in luxury, but not in price, is **Hotel Layseca** (Juárez 9, tel. 467/20-01-10), which has large rooms clustered around a gracious courtyard. Singles cost $11 and doubles are $13.50.

COMING AND GOING Clase Premier buses depart for San Juan del Río (30 min, $1) every 10 minutes from Sala A in Querétaro's Central de Autobuses; when you arrive at San Juan's bus terminal, just head out the front door and catch a bus marked CENTRO. The principal intersection for the downtown area is at Juárez and Hidalgo.

SAN JOAQUIN

About three hours northwest of Querétaro, in the high mountainous region called the Sierra Gorda, lies the tiny town of San Joaquín. Apart from the visitors who stop here on their way to the nearby ruins of **Toluquilla** and **Ranas,** this quiet rural settlement is the type of place where the bickering of backyard roosters and hens drowns out the noise from infrequent passing trucks. The zócalo looks more like a wide sidewalk, but the many freshly painted houses give an air of prosperity. There's even a "luxury" hotel here: **Hotel Mesón de San Joaquín** (Guadalupe Victoria 4, tel. 467/12-53-15), which has slightly upscale versions of the basic cinderblock special (singles $11, doubles $12). The manager, Mario Torres Camacho, is happy to answer questions about the town. If you'd rather camp, do it for free at **Campo Alegro,** a small stretch of pine forest at the top of a hill overlooking the town. To reach the camp, walk up Guadalupe Victoria from either the Flecha Amarilla or Flecha Azul bus stop (if you're facing town, it's the street to your far left). Once you reach the central church, follow the blue signs with pictures of pine trees on them. Alternatively, you may be able to stay with a family ($5 is a polite amount to offer for their trouble); ask around at the Flecha Amarilla bus-stop. If you're hungry, stop at one of the loncherias (lunch counters) near the church, or **Café Fonda** (Insurgentes, at Flecha Amarilla bus stop, no phone) for drinks and yogurt. There is also a restaurant in the Hotel Mesón, which has a bar and provides pretty much the only after dark entertainment in town.

Both **Flecha Azul** and **Flecha Amarilla** run buses between Querétaro and San Joaquín (3 hrs, $2.50); the last Flecha Azul bus leaves San Joaquín at 3:30 PM, and Flecha Amarilla's final bus is rumored to leave at 4:20.

RUINS

➤ **RANAS** • Strategically located on a high slope, these modest ruins are thought to have served simultaneous functions—as a ceremonial center, trading post, and defensive structure. Built between the 7th and 8th centuries, this small city is divided into two parts. The ceremonial center, made up of several pyramids, covers the top of a steep hill. On the flatlands below are a provincial-sized ball court and the remains of what may have been military structures.

From ceramic shards found here, archeologists believe that the original inhabitants had extensive contact with the larger cities of El Tajín, on the Gulf Coast, and Teotihuacán (near Mexico City). The city was abandoned after the 11th century, and taken over by the Chichimeca people sometime in the 16th century. Ranas won't overwhelm you with architectural splendor (its buildings resemble huge party-hats), but it will allow you to experience ruins as ruins—not as a touristy reconstructed version of Mexico's indigenous past. To get here, walk straight up Calle Insurgento from the Flecha Amarilla bus stop and follow the signs at the top of the hill. The ruins are about 3 kilometers from town. You can also hitch rides from the *colectivo* pick-up trucks that pass by the Flecha Amarilla stop. Admission $1.25, 50¢ with student ID. Open daily 9–5.

➤ **TOLUQUILLA** • Smaller and slightly more remote than Ranas (*see above*), Toluquilla is similar in its history and architectural style. The ruins here include two ball courts that stretch in succession along the crest of the mountain top and other remaining walls and foundations that are thought to have been military fortifications. As at Ranas, the term "lowly workers" is literally true—those who cultivated the fields and worked in the mines probably lived below the city. Although the ruins themselves aren't much, the elevation—even higher than at Ranas—provides a glorious view of the Sierra Gorda's blue peaks. It's a tempting campsite, but the guards are not impressed with the idea, and will give you a scary talk about the snakes that live among the ancient structures. To get here, your best bet is to take a *colectivo* pick-up from the Flecha Amarilla station—just tell the driver you want to get off at Toluquilla. Walking will take a good 2½ hours; walk back out of town along the main road, turn left at the blue sign with the picture of a pyramid on it, and follow the skinny highway. Admission free. Open daily 10–4.

San Miguel de Allende

The modest *pueblo* (town) of San Miguel de Allende, in Guanajuato state, seduces newcomers within a matter of days, and it's difficult to explain why. Ask any non-native resident why artists, troubadours, and tourists are drawn to this city and the expatriate is usually at a loss for words. Other towns in Mexico, they will assure you, are more picturesque, have better nightlife, and exhibit a more liberal attitude. The attraction, it seems, lies in the open, honest friendliness of the young artist community, the ease with which you become familiar with the entire town, and the creature comforts (complete with cobblestone streets and wrought-iron street lamps) provided by the relative affluence here. This is a place where people set down roots, whether to study Spanish at one of the language schools; to paint, sculpt, or dance at the Bellas Artes; or simply to live their version of the good life.

The gringo population of San Miguel is one of the largest in Mexico, a fact that causes many travelers to ignore the town in search of more "authenticity." This is unfortunate, as not all the expatriates are boorish tourists, disrespectful of Mexican culture. Many play crucial roles in San Miguel society, whether by helping maintain the historical integrity of the town or doing social service work. Moreover, the Mexican residents still have a strong hold on local custom, demonstrated during the many *días de fiesta*. If you find yourself partying the night away with the locals, however, keep this in mind: The town is more than 1½ kilometers above sea level, and until your body gets used to the altitude, heavy drinking will result in a killer hangover.

San Miguel was declared a national monument by the Mexican government in 1926, rendering it next to impossible to make any modern architectural or planning changes to the town; you can thank the well-meaning government every time you trip over an uneven cobblestone.

The town was named after the Spanish friar Juan de San Miguel, who chose to establish a mission on the site because of its proximity to spring waters. In 1810, native son Ignacio Allende was a big player in the independence movement, plotting rebellion against Spanish rule—in his honor, the name of the town was changed to San Miguel de Allende in 1826. In spite of the colonial architecture and ambiance, you won't be happy here if you really want to avoid gringolandia. The presence of the gringos has had one unpleasant side effect—prices here are higher than in nearby towns,

San Miguel de Allende

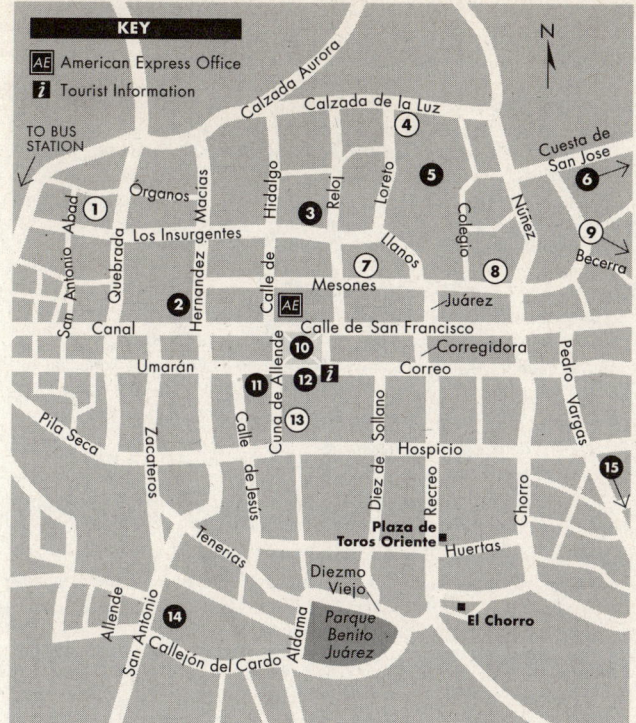

Sights ●
Bellas Artes, **2**
Biblioteca Pública, **3**
El Mirador, **15**
Instituto Allende, **14**
Jardín Botánica, **6**
Mercado Ignacio Ramírez, **5**
Museo Histórico, **11**
Parroquia de San Miguel Arcángel, **12**
Plaza Principal (El Jardín), **10**

Lodging ○
Casa de Huéspedes, **7**
Hostal Internacional, **1**
Hotel La Huerta, **9**
Hotel Parador de San Sebastián, **8**
Hotel Quinta Loreto, **4**
Posada de Allende, **13**

though budget travelers can still get by. In spite of these drawbacks, if you give San Miguel de Allende a chance, your stay of just a few days may stretch into a few weeks or more.

BASICS

AMERICAN EXPRESS The AmEx representative, **Viajes Vertiz,** holds mail for cardholders. They won't cash traveler's checks, but emergency check cashing is available. Hidalgo 1, ½ block north of Plaza Principal, tel. 415/2–18–56. Open weekdays 9–2 and 4–6:30, Sat. 10–2. Mailing address: Hidalgo 1, Aptdo. Postal 486, San Miguel de Allende, Guanajuato, CP 37700, México.

BOOKSTORES El Colibrí, in business for 35 years, has an extensive selection of English-language paperbacks and magazines, as well as art supplies. Diez de Sollano 30, 1 block east of Plaza Principal, tel. 465/2–07–51. Open weekdays 10–2 and 4–7.

CASAS DE CAMBIO Although the Plaza Principal is surrounded by several banks, **Casa de Cambio Deal** (Correo 15, no phone; open weekdays 9–6, Sat. 9–1:45) is your best bet because it doesn't charge a commission and is open longer. **Banamex** (cnr of Canal and Hidalgo) also changes cash and traveler's checks and has an ATM.

CONSULATES In case you hadn't noticed that San Miguel de Allende is practically a U.S. colony, there's even an American consulate in this small pueblo. Macías 72, tel. 465/2–23–57 or 465/2–00–68 for emergencies. Open Mon. and Wed. 9–1 and 4–7, Tues. and Thurs. 4–7, or by appointment.

EMERGENCIES Police 465/2–00–22; ambulance 465/2–16–16.

LAUNDRY Lava Mágico has some English-speaking staff who will wash, dry, and fold a load of clothes for $3. No self-service facilities are available, but if you drop off your clothes before noon, you'll get them back the same day. Pila Seca 5, tel. 415/2–08–99. Open daily 8–8.

MAIL The full-service **post office** will hold mail for up to 10 days if it's sent to you at the following address: Lista de Correos, Correo 18, San Miguel de Allende, Guanajuato, CP 37700, México. *Correo 18, tel. 415/2-00-89. Walk 2 blocks east of Plaza Principal. Open weekdays 8-7, Sat. 9-1.*

MEDICAL AID You'll have no trouble finding a pharmacy in San Miguel, but Chelo at **Botica Agundis** (Canal 26, tel. 415/2-11-98) speaks English and is particularly helpful. The sign says they're open Monday–Saturday 10–10, but Chelo says she's there daily until midnight. For more urgent medical assistance, **Hospital Unión Médica** provides 24-hour medical treatment and can refer you to an English-speaking physician. *San Francisco 50, tel. 415/2-22-33. Walk 4 blocks east of Plaza Principal.*

PHONES The pay phones in San Miguel are in sad shape. You can make long-distance calls daily, 7 AM–11 PM, in the **Central de Autobuses** (*see* Coming and Going, *below*). In the center of town, **Caseta de Pepe** (Sollano 4, tel. 415/2-60-61; open daily 8 AM–9:30 PM) charges about $1.50 per minute for international calls, but nothing to place a collect call. **La Conexión** has phone, fax, and mail service, and the staff is good about offering advice to lost newcomers. *Aldama 1, tel. and fax 415/2-16-87. Open weekdays 8-8, Sat. 8-3, Sun. 10-2.*

SCHOOLS Although people from all over the world descend upon San Miguel for the language and fine arts classes, they often end up speaking more English than Spanish. By studying during the school year instead of the summer, you'll avoid a few of those English-language conversations. You can also take classes in traditional jewelry making, pottery, and sculpture offered by local artisans, as well as lessons in traditional dance and folklore. Schools tend to offer courses in continuous four-week sessions, but most are very willing to structure private lessons according to individual need. If you don't want to commit to an entire course, Spanish classes are also offered at the Hostal Internacional (*see* Where to Sleep, *below*).

Academia Hispano Americano (Mesones 4, tel. 415/2-03-49) offers Spanish and literature classes, from beginning to advanced levels. Scholarships and homestays are also available. **Bellas Artes/Centro Cultural El Nigromante** (Macías 75, tel. 415/2-02-89) is a fine arts school offering classes in dance, art, and music. The director, Carmen Masip de Hawkins, can provide specific information on courses and prices. **Centro Mexicano de Lengua y Cultura de San Miguel** (Orizaba 15, tel. 415/2-07-63) offers individual or group instruction in Spanish, English, French, or Italian, from basic to advanced levels. **Instituto Allende** (Ancha de San Antonio 20, tel. 465/2-01-90) is an internationally recognized fine arts school, but it is rumored to be resting on its laurels. Some say the high population of hobbyists detracts from the needs of its more dedicated students.

VISITOR INFORMATION Pick up a copy of the local English-language newspaper, *Atención San Miguel* (50¢), for listings of events, religious services, literary discussion groups, and rental housing. Further information can be found on bulletin boards at cafés, hotels, and Bellas Artes (*see* Worth Seeing, *below*). You can also visit the **tourist office** (south side of Plaza Principal, tel. 415/2-17-47); some of the staff members speak English, and they'll load you down with maps, brochures, and hotel listings. They also have information on Spanish and art classes; open weekdays 10-2:45 and 5-7, Saturday 10-1.

On Tuesdays, locals set up La Plazita, a market that stretches for four blocks. Pirated cassette tapes, spangly hair baubles, and nylon underwear share space with pastries and fresh fruit. To get here from the Plaza Principal, go three blocks west on Canal and turn right on San Antonio Abad.

COMING AND GOING

BY BUS San Miguel de Allende's **Central de Autobuses** is about 10 minutes from the center of town. To get to town, hop on any local bus marked CENTRO. The main bus lines here are **Flecha Amarilla** (tel. 415/2-00-84) and **Autotransportes Herradura de Plata** (tel. 415/2-07-05). Frequent buses leave for Mexico City (3½ hrs, $8), Querétaro (1 hr, $2), Guanajuato (1½ hrs, $3.50), Dolores Hidalgo (45 min, $1.50), and San Luis Potosí (6 hrs, $5). The bus station has long-distance telephone service (open 7 AM–11 PM) and luggage storage (open 7 AM–10 PM).

BY TRAIN Trains are generally slower than buses. They leave at 1 PM for Mexico City ($6 1st class, $3 2nd class) and Querétaro ($1.50 1st class, 75¢ 2nd class); the train to Monterrey departs at 2:30 PM ($12 1st class, $7 2nd class). The bus marked CENTRO will take you from the train station to the center of town (Plaza Principal). *Calzada de la Estación, tel. 415/2–00–07. Open for ticket sales Mon.–Sat. 10–3, Sun. noon–3.*

GETTING AROUND

San Miguel is a small town, and most attractions are easily accessible on foot. Though picturesque, the cobblestone streets are impossibly lumpy and at times very steep—wheelchairs would have great difficulty here. The central **Plaza Principal** is surrounded by a neat grid of streets, around which all street names change. **Canal,** which borders the plaza on its northern edge, turns into **San Francisco** to the east of the plaza; on the plaza's south side, **Umarán** goes to the west and **Correo** to the east. The only buses you're likely to need are those that run up and down Canal to the bus and train stations; buses run from about 7 AM to 10 PM, and cost around 40¢. Taxi fares from the center to the stations are $2.

WHERE TO SLEEP

Most hotels are near the Plaza Principal, and rooms range from the impossibly expensive to reasonable. Your best bet, however, is the **Hostal Internacional** (*see below*). If you're planning an extended stay, check the bulletin boards in stores and restaurants around town for rental lists. You can also check with **A-1 Real Estate** (Cuna de Allende 11, tel. 415/2–16–30), which lists apartments for rent from $200 to more than $1,000 per month. Discounts for prepayment and long-term stays are often available. Homestays are another option (*see* Schools, *above*). The prices listed here apply in the low season. During high season (Oct.–Jan.), hotel prices are jacked up by as much as 100%.

➢ **UNDER $10** • **Hotel La Huerta.** Cheap rooms and peace and quiet make up for the 10-minute walk you'll have to make from the Plaza Principal. The rooms are clean and airy and open onto communal sitting rooms. Singles are $6.50, doubles $8. *Cerrada de Becerra, tel. 465/2–08–81. From Plaza Principal, 1 block north on Reloj, right on Mesones 5 blocks, right on Atascadero. 15 rooms, all with bath.*

➢ **UNDER $15** • **Casa de Huéspedes.** The tiled, plant-filled courtyard lends some exoticism to this tiny, friendly guest house. Rooms are large and well-lit, with balconies opening onto the street. The staff is amiable, and there's hot water 24 hours a day. Singles cost $8; doubles are $13. *Mesones 27, 2½ blocks from Plaza Principal, tel. 465/2–13–78. 6 rooms, all with bath.*

Hotel Parador de San Sebastián. Every room is clean and has antique oak furnishings—some even have a small kitchen, complete with utensils. Don't expect to take a hot shower in the afternoon, though; hot water is only available 8 AM–noon and 8 PM–midnight. Singles are $11, doubles $15. *Mesones 7, tel. 465/2–07–07. From Plaza Principal, walk 1½ blocks east. 24 rooms, all with bath.*

➢ **UNDER $25** • **Quinta Loreto.** Spacious, clean rooms with patios, a large garden, and free use of the pool and tennis court make the Quinta Loreto worth the extra bucks. Singles are $15, and doubles cost $21. Rooms upstairs have better views, but are hotter than those downstairs. Most guests are foreign tourists. *Loreto 15, tel. 465/2–00–42. From Plaza Principal, 2 blocks up Reloj, right on Insurgentes 1 block, left on Loreto. 38 rooms, all with bath. AE, MC, V.*

HOSTELS **Hostal Internacional.** This hostel gives you so much for your money, there's no reason not to stay here if there's room. For $4–$5 (it's cheaper with a hostel card), you sleep in single-sex dorm rooms and wake up to a free breakfast (there's also coffee and tea all day long). For another $1.50 per day, you can use the kitchen facilities. Rooms and bathrooms are cleaner than those in some hotels, and the friendly manager gets rave reviews from his guests. He also pays a local teacher to give Spanish classes (Mon.–Thurs. 4:30 PM–6:30 PM); you can join in for about $1.50. Most private rooms cost $12; two private rooms are available for $8–$10. *Órganos 34, tel. 465/2–06–74. From Plaza Principal, 1 block west on Canal, right on Macías 3 blocks, left on Órganos 3 blocks. Laundry.*

FOOD

One result of the influx of foreigners in San Miguel is the presence of an extraordinary number of restaurants that cater to a wide range of tastes and budgets. Wandering around the downtown area, you'll find just about anything you want, from standard tacos and *tortas* (sandwiches) to Lebanese or Italian food. You can get cheap and tasty baked goods at **Panadería La Espiga** (Insurgentes 9, tel. 415/2–15–80). The Mercado Ignacio Ramírez (Av. Colegio, tel. 415/2–28–44) has *comedores* (sit-down food stands), where you can watch the town's culinary masters prepare tacos, tostadas, gorditas, and more. Prices are very reasonable and the food stands are generally open until dusk.

➤ **UNDER $5** • **Las Palomas.** Tacos, tostadas, and quesadillas with chicken mole, *nopales* (grilled cactus), or spicy pork fillings are super-cheap here—three tacos and a drink come to less than $2. The seating is arranged around the small kitchen so you can watch your food being prepared. *Mesones 60, btw Hidalgo and Macías, no phone. Open daily 9–9.*

La Piñata. This unassuming corner diner serves up mountains of cheap food. Scrambled-egg breakfasts, including fresh-squeezed juice and toast, are $1.50; tostadas and quesadillas cost less than $1. Try the sugarcane, grapefruit, or carrot juice for $1. *Jesús 1, 1 block west of Plaza Principal, no phone. Open Wed.–Mon. 9–9, Tues. 9–2. Wheelchair access.*

El Ten-ten Pie. This restaurant serves up tacos and burritos (some of them vegetarian) in a relaxing space filled with works by local artisans. The manager guarantees the meat for the 50¢ tacos is fresh, and the vegetables are washed in purified water. Try the excellent flan ($2). You can also while away the hours playing chess or backgammon. *Cuna de Allende 21, no phone. Open daily noon–midnight. Wheelchair access.*

➤ **UNDER $10** • **Mama Mía.** Although some sort of Mexican plate is always available, this restaurant serves primarily Italian food. The open-air patio is filled with hanging plants, friendly people, and live Andean music every night around 8 PM. It's a great place to eat and sip red wine. Small pizzas with tons of cheese are $7; other pasta dishes cost $6–$9. Breakfasts are cheaper at $1.50–$3. *Umarán 8, ½ block west of Plaza Principal, tel. 415/2–20–63. Open Sun.–Thurs. 8 AM–midnight, Fri. and Sat. 8 AM–1 AM.*

Mesón de San José. This restaurant is inside an interior courtyard overhung with branches and flowers, and every meal comes with fresh whole wheat bread. If that isn't enough, Mesón de San José also serves a delicacy usually reserved for holiday meals: *chiles en nogada* (chiles stuffed with beef and covered in a walnut sauce and pomegranate seeds; $7).The *quesadilla gourmet* ($5), a flour tortilla stuffed with spinach, mushrooms, and cheese, will fill you up—if the free bread hasn't already done so. *Mesones 38, 3 blocks from Plaza Principal, tel. 415/2–38–48. Open daily 8 AM–10 PM.*

CAFES Cafés in San Miguel de Allende are mostly gringo hangouts where tourists and expats drink cappuccino. **El Buen Café** (Jesús 23, tel. 415/2-58-07) hosts nightly book discussions and poetry readings and has live music Friday and Saturday evenings from 6 PM to 8 PM. Coffee is about $1, and sandwiches and crepes cost under $5. If you want to escape gringos, try a bar or cantina, identifiable by western-style swinging doors (*see* After Dark, *below*).

WORTH SEEING

BELLAS ARTES/CENTRO CULTURAL EL NIGROMANTE Built in 1765, this former convent now houses a school of fine arts. A peaceful central courtyard and fountain are surrounded by two floors of art workshops and music rooms. Murals by muralist David Siqueiros (contemporary of Diego Rivera) adorn the interior walls, and a small gallery on the first floor exhibits work by local artists. The café serves light lunches for less than $5. *Macías 75, 1½ blocks west of Plaza Principal, tel. 415/2–02–89. Admission free. Open Mon.–Sat. 9–8, Sun. 10–3.*

BIBLIOTECA PUBLICA San Miguel's public library has a great collection of books in both Spanish and English and is a great place to find out what's going on in town. A bulletin board in the foyer announces upcoming events, and the town's English-language newspaper, *Atención San Miguel,* is sold at the front desk. English-language books are also sold, as well as current Mexican newspapers and magazines. You can also buy a book in English on San Miguel de Allende's history, but they'll let you take a peek at it for free. On Tuesdays and Thursdays, people meet in the library's sun-filled courtyard from 5 PM to 7 PM for a free, informal English–Spanish exchange. To borrow books, you must plunk down a refundable $30 deposit and supply two passport pictures. *Insurgentes 25, tel. 415/2–02–93. Open weekdays 10–2 and 4–7, Sat. 10–2.*

INSTITUTO ALLENDE Once the country mansion of the Count and Countess de la Canal, this impressive 18th-century building now houses a school of the arts, languages, and social studies. Visitors from around the world study in the lush gardens overflowing with bougainvillea, rose bushes, and ivy. There is also a small gallery with rotating art exhibits. *Ancha San Antonio 20, tel. 415/2–01–90. Office open weekdays 9–1 and 3–5.*

Travelers are advised not to go through the hills at the end of Calzada de La Luz in order to reach the Jardín Botánico. Stick to the sidewalks, as several muggings have occurred in these hills, known as the Cerros de las Tres Cruces.

JARDIN BOTANICO EL CHARCO DEL INGENIO One of the best-kept secrets of San Miguel, this 47-hectare area is located in and around a canyon that offers hours of hiking and climbing opportunities. The view of the city from here is excellent. The garden itself features cacti and other succulents, along with other flora typical of the region. You'll also find the ruins of a colonial mill. *Diez de Sollano 21, tel. 415/2–29–90. Take Cuesta de San José to Montitlán, go left, and follow road until it becomes unpaved; take right-hand path up hill. Admission: $1. Open daily until dusk.*

MERCADO IGNACIO RAMIREZ This enormous open-air market takes place daily and extends over several city blocks. Be prepared for sensory overload: Squealing pigs and squawking chickens drown out blaring pop music, while the neon colors of cheap clothing compete with the glowing tones of tomatoes and melons. *Behind Plaza Cívica. From Plaza Principal, 1 block north on Reloj and right on Mesones.*

MUSEO HISTORICO DE SAN MIGUEL DE ALLENDE This former mansion is the birthplace of Ignacio Allende. It's now a museum that exhibits Allende's clothing and personal effects, as well as pre-Columbian artifacts from Guanajuato state. The placards and posters will tell you more than you ever wanted to know about the history of San Miguel. *Cuna de Allende 1, SW cnr of Plaza Principal, tel. 415/2–44–65. Admission free. Open Tues.–Sun. 9–4.*

PARROQUIA DE SAN MIGUEL ARCANGEL Not only is this church worth seeing, but you'd have to be blind *not* to see it. In the 18th century, the parish priest commissioned a stone carver, Cerefino Gutiérrez, to replace the original two-towered facade. Gutiérrez was an indigenous local with no formal training, and so he drew his plans in the sand every day with a stick. The pseudo-Gothic exterior contrasts sharply with the *mudéjar* (Moorish-influenced) interior. *South side of Plaza Principal. Open 7 AM–10 PM.*

CHEAP THRILLS

The wrought-iron benches on the Plaza Principal, also known as **El Jardín** (the garden), are the best place to sit and get a feel for the town. The plaza is also the favorite Sunday-night cruising spot for local youth. **El Mirador** (the lookout), up a steep hill and away from the center of town, is a popular place to view the sunset. Ask a local to set you in the right direction. The **Parque Juárez** is particularly beautiful, teeming with plants, flowers, and birds. The walk here from the center of town is a pretty one: Facing the church on the zócalo, walk down Diez de Sollano—the street that runs along its left side. After three short blocks, you'll walk right into the park's front gate. Turn left on Calle Tenerías (which passes in front of the park) and walk two blocks to reach **El Chorro,** a series of underground springs enclosed by a colonial building. Peer inside what looks like an old mansion to see the wells that once supplied the town with water. Today, these natural springs function as a "public laundry," where locals gather during the day to wash clothes and occasionally each other.

FESTIVALS

The birth of the town's namesake, Ignacio Allende, is celebrated January 21 with a military parade. A procession featuring people wearing comical costume takes place around June 12 when the **Fiesta de San Antonio de Padua** commemorates one of the town's patron saints. September 16 is the **Día de la Independencia,** celebrated with a marathon race and a reenactment of Father Hidalgo's "Grito de Dolores" (which signaled the beginning of the Mexican Revolution). The third Saturday in September is **Sanmiguelada,** marked by a wild *corrida de toros* (running of the bulls); on the 29th of that month a feast is held in honor of **San Miguel Arcángel,** the town's patron saint. The day is celebrated with a parade of *xóchiles* (huge decorations of flowers, plants, and corn) and *concheros* (shell dancers). With all of these events happening in September, be sure to make hotel reservations first.

AFTER DARK

San Miguel's bars and discos will not disappoint those wanting to party; most rock on until about 6 AM. Despite the large gay and lesbian population, due to state *prostitution* laws, there can be no actual gay bars—try to figure out that twisted bit of logic. **La Cucaracha** (Zacateros 22, no phone) is one of the few cantinas that officially allows women to enter, but lone females should only go if they're in the mood to hang out with a bunch of drunken middle-aged men. **Villa Jacaranda Cine Bar** (Aldama 53, tel. 415/2–10–15) is a happening club that shows movies in English for about $5 (this price includes one drink). If you don't feel like bar hopping, you can always hang out in the Plaza Principal, where the whole town comes to see and be seen. **Cinema Gemelos** (Plaza Real de Conde, tel. 415/2–64–08) shows first-run Hollywood movies and has a two-for-one night on Wednesdays.

Bar Coco. This small bar is a great find for those who want to spend the evening with real live Mexicans. Food is served until midnight, there's a two-for-one happy hour between 6 PM and 8 PM, and patrons are treated to live music beginning at 9:30 PM. *Macías 85, at Umarán, tel. 415/2–26–43. Open Tues.–Sun. until the crowd goes home.*

Laberinto's. This club plays a mix of Latin and American dance music and is always crowded with locals on weekends. Cover charge is $2.50, except on Thursdays and Sundays, when it's free. *Ancha de San Antonio 7, tel. 415/2–03–62. Open Tues.–Sun. 10 PM–3 AM.*

Pancho y Lefty's. Nightly rock music attracts a lively crowd of Mexicans and some gringos. Unfortunately, the talented bands play only covers, but it's still the most popular place for partying until 1 AM. *Mesones 99, tel. 415/2–19–58. Open nightly 8–1:30.*

El Ring. One of the most popular nightspots in town, El Ring is a discotheque circa 1978, complete with flashing laser lights and pulsating music. There's no cover charge for couples, so singles in the know avoid the $5 charge by entering into instant relationships at the door. *Hidalgo 25. 1 block from Plaza Principal. Open Tues.–Sun. 9 PM–3 AM.*

Guanajuato

If you visit only one city in the Bajío, make sure it's Guanajuato. By the time of the Spanish conquest, this high valley had long been inhabited by indigenous people, but these days the city is defined by the beautiful architecture that is the product of the colonial era's silver-driven prosperity. Guanajuato was also the scene of the first major military confrontation between rebel forces and royalist troops on September 28, 1810; monuments to the city's revolutionary heroes are everywhere. Today, internationally recognized musicians, artists, and dancers blend with throngs of university students to lend the place a playful vitality. The city's winding streets and subterranean roadways are so confusing that you could easily lose yourself here, but you probably won't be in any hurry to leave.

In addition to the city's historical importance, Guanajuato is distinguished by a number of unusual points of interest, including the **Museo de las Momias,** a bizarre museum exhibiting well-preserved human corpses, and the home in which artist Diego Rivera was born. If you're in town in mid-October, don't miss the **Festival Internacional Cervantino,** when artists, musicians, and dance troupes from around the world come to honor *Don Quixote* author Miguel de Cervantes. The city is overrun during the festival, so make hotel reservations well in advance if you plan to attend.

BASICS

AUTO PARTS/SERVICE Refacciones Sánchez has parts for most cars. Walter speaks both English and Spanish and will gladly recommend a mechanic. *Paseo de la Presa 28-E, tel. 473/2-00-28. Open weekdays 9:30–3 and 4:30–8, Sat. 9–4.*

BOOKSTORES Though there are no English-language bookstores in Guanajuato, the chain store **Librería de Cristal** has a great selection of literature, textbooks, and music in Spanish. *Plaza Agora del Baratillo 4, on NW side of Jardín de la Unión, tel. 473/2–24–48. Open Mon.–Sat. 10–9, Sun. noon–8.*

CASAS DE CAMBIO Banamex (Plaza de los Ángeles, tel. 473/2–08–00) cashes traveler's checks and does currency exchange from 9 to 2 on weekdays. Its ATM accepts Visa, Cirrus, Plus, and MasterCard.

EMERGENCIES The phone number of the **police** station is 473/2–02–66; the **Cruz Roja** (ambulance service) is 473/2–04–87.

LAUNDRY Lavandería del Centro will wash, dry, and fold 4 kilos of laundry for $4 a load. *Sopeña 26, tel. 473/2–06–80. Near Museo Iconográfico del Quijote, west on Juárez from Jardín de la Unión. Open Mon.–Sat. 9–8.*

MAIL The city's post office is near the University of Guanajuato. They will hold mail for up to 10 days that's sent to you at the following address: Lista de Correos, Guanajuato, Guanajuato, CP 36000, México. *Ayuntamiento 25, tel. 473/2–03–85. Open weekdays 8–8, Sat. 9–1.*

MEDICAL AID The **Hospital Regional de Guanajuato** (Carretera Guanajuato Cilao, tel. 473/2–08–59) has 24-hour medical service and a few English-speaking doctors. **Farmacia Santa Fe** (Plaza de la Paz 52, tel. 473/2–01–70) gives discounts on prescriptions.

PHONES Ladatel phones can be found all along Juárez and on the northeast side of the Jardín de la Unión. International collect calls at **Caseta Selene Miscelanea** (Juárez 110, open Mon.–Sat. 10 AM–11 PM) cost $2.

SCHOOLS The **University of Guanajuato** has an exchange program with several American universities, but you don't have to be affiliated with any of them to take Spanish-language and literature classes at their **Centro de Idiomas.** Programs are in semester units and run from July to December and January to June. Six-week summer sessions are also available. Courses cost about $250. Homestays with local families can be arranged. *Lascurain de Retana 5, tel. 473/2–72–53. For registration information, write to Lic. Patricia Begne, Directora del Centro de Idiomas, Universidad de Guanajuato, Lascurain de Retana 5, Guanajuato, Guanajuato, CP 36000, México.*

VISITOR INFORMATION The staff at the **tourist information office** (Plaza de la Paz 14, near the basilica, tel. 473/2–00–86) is happy to answer questions and hand you a free map. The office is open weekdays 8:30–8:30, weekends 10–2.

COMING AND GOING

BY BUS The **Central de Autobuses** (Carretera Guanajuato Cilao, Km. 8, tel. 473/2–71–45) is served by four main lines: **Omnibus de México** (tel. 473/3–13–56), **Flecha Amarilla** (tel. 473/3–13–33), **Estrella Blanca** (tel. 473/2–75–63), and **Primera Plus** (tel. 473/3–13–33). Buses to Mexico City (4½ hrs, $10) leave seven times daily. Buses also leave frequently for

Guanajuato

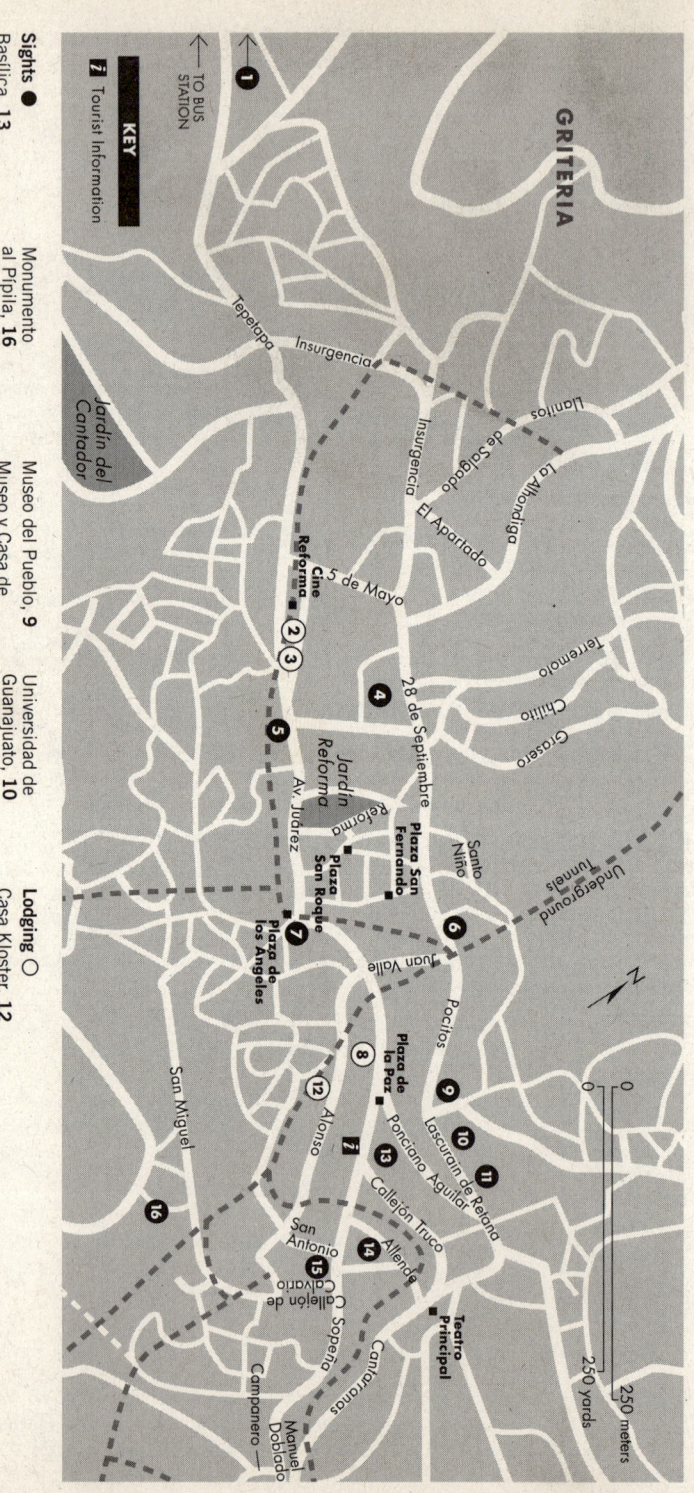

Sights ●
Basílica, **13**
Callejón del Beso, **7**
Jardín de la Unión, **14**
Mercado Hidalgo, **5**
Monumento al Pípila, **16**
Museo de la Alhóndiga de Granaditas, **4**
Museo de las Momias, **1**
Museo del Pueblo, **9**
Museo y Casa de Diego Rivera, **6**
Teatro Juárez, **15**
Templo de la Compañía, **11**
Universidad de Guanajuato, **10**

Lodging ○
Casa Kloster, **12**
Posada de la Condesa, **8**
Posada del Carmen, **3**
Posada Juárez, **2**

León (1 hr, $1.50), San Miguel de Allende (1½ hrs, $2.50), Dolores Hidalgo (1½ hrs, $1.25), and San Luis Potosí (5 hrs, $6). From mid-morning to mid-afternoon, buses leave for Querétaro (3 hrs, $5.50), Guadalajara (5 hrs, $8), and Morelia (4 hrs, $5). Luggage storage is available 7 AM–9:30 PM.

GETTING AROUND

Whoever planned—or rather, didn't plan—this city was playing a mischievous joke on the uptight proponents of the simple grid system. You're gonna get lost. For those who wish to impose order amid the chaos, the most important street to remember is **Avenida Juárez**, the main thoroughfare. As you head east, Juárez turns into **Sopeña** near the main plaza, the **Jardín de la Unión**. Most directions to Guanajuato's sites use the Jardín as a reference point. The bus station is more than 6 kilometers west of the city, so take a city bus marked CENTRO (or a taxi; $1.50) on Avenida Juárez to the center of town. For an inexpensive hotel, get off at the busy Jardín Reforma bus stop, near the Cine Reforma. City buses run 6 AM–10 PM.

WHERE TO SLEEP

Most budget hotels are located along Avenida Juárez between the train station and the Cine Reforma. Conveniently, this area is also near many of the city's attractions and much of the action. As you continue east along Juárez toward the Jardín de la Unión, accommodations become more attractive and more expensive. The Casa Kloster (*see below*) is among the few cheap hotels in this area. If you're planning to come in mid-October, you must make reservations 4–6 months in advance, due to the Cervantes Festival. When hotels are packed, the tourist office will provide information on families who will house travelers for low prices.

Casa Kloster. If you can live with a few house rules, this wholesome hotel is wonderful. Run by the hospitable Pérez family, it has clean rooms, spotless communal bathrooms, and an interior courtyard filled with plants and chirping birds. Couples must be discreet (what Grandma doesn't know won't hurt her), and you must be quiet at night. Nevertheless, this place is always full of backpack-toting gringos, so be sure to call ahead. Rooms are $10 per person. *Alonso 32, tel. 473/2–00–88. 18 rooms, none with bath.*

Posada de la Condesa. This posada is much cheaper than most of its neighbors in this area. Rooms are cramped but clean, and all have private baths with 'round-the-clock hot water. Singles and doubles go for about $6. *Plaza de la Paz 60, tel. 473/2–14–62. From Jardín de la Unión, west on Juárez. 22 rooms, all with bath.*

Posada del Carmen. Run by a friendly, professional staff, this clean and cheerful place even does laundry, at just $1.50 per kilo. Off-season prices are $8 for a single, $10 for a double; prices go up during the Cervantes festival. *Juárez 111-A, tel. 473/2–93–30. 17 rooms, all with bath. Laundry. Wheelchair access.*

Posada Juárez. This is the best of the budget hotels near the Cine Reforma. The management is slightly distracted by all the activity on the street, but rooms are clean and smell good, and some even have TVs. Ask for a sunny room on the second floor. Singles are $8, doubles $10. Prices rise $5–$10 during the Cervantes festival. *Juárez 117, tel. 473/2–25–29. 43 rooms, all with bath.*

FOOD

Restaurants are clustered on Avenida Juárez and the surrounding streets. A number of cheap food stands can also be found at **Mercado Hidalgo**, in the ornate former train station (on Juárez between Cine Reforma and the Jardín Reforma). For a strange sweet treat, try *momias*—a hard, mummy-shaped sugarcane candy that is sold both at the **Museo de las Momias** (*see below*) and stores around town. Close to the Jardín de la Unión is the **Pastelería de la Paz** (Plaza de la Paz 53, tel. 473/2–18–69), which sells scrumptious baked treats as early as 6:30 AM.

➤ **UNDER $5** • **La Pasadita Lonchería.** This post-party hot spot doesn't even open until 8 PM. You can satiate your late-night cravings with typical Mexican dishes for a few dollars while you get the scoop on the evening's action. *Cantarranas 70, no phone. From north end of Jardín de la Unión, right on Allende and right on Cantarranas. Open until dawn.*

El Pingüis. Tucked in the northeast corner of the Jardín de la Unión, this cheap eatery is always full. A breakfast of *huevos a la mexicana* (eggs scrambled with peppers, tomato, and onion), served with beans, bread, and a cup of coffee is $2. Lunch items include enchiladas ($2), steak ($2.50), and sandwiches ($1–$2). Inside, bulletin boards are crowded with information on upcoming concerts, art exhibits, and apartments for rent. The name of the restaurant isn't posted—look for the brown-and-white awnings marked RESTAURANT and CAFETERIA. *Jardín de la Unión, tel. 473/2-14-14. Open daily 8:30 AM–9:30 PM.*

For an evening snack, head for the stand at the southwest corner of the Jardín de la Unión. The proprietor, Daniel, whips up a delicious cup of boiled corn with cream, cheese, and chili powder for $1. **Restaurant Vegetariano.** The owners may not have put much imagination into naming the restaurant, but the inspired food more than makes up for it. The menú del día includes salad, vegetable, rice, soup, and an entrée for $2.50. A $2 breakfast is also available, and a huge pot of herbal tea is included with every meal. *Callejón de Calixto 22, tel. 473/2-20-62. Upstairs from Plaza de los Ángeles. Open daily 8–6.*

Tasca de los Santos. This candlelit restaurant near the basilica has tasty Spanish food and attentive waiters. Recommended are the *pollo al vino blanco* (chicken in white wine; $5) and the $3 *tapas* (Spanish appetizers). *Plaza de la Paz 28, off Juárez, tel. 473/2-23-20.*

➤ **UNDER $10** • **Restaurant El Agora del Baratillo.** This restaurant near the Jardín de la Unión offers patio dining complete with wrought-iron tables covered with checkered tablecloths. The *comida corrida* ($8) is more expensive than any entrée on the menu, but that's because it also includes a glass of wine. Breakfast *chilaquiles* (a mass of tortillas and eggs with spicy salsa) also come with fruit, yogurt, and coffee—all for about $2.50. *Jardín de la Unión 4, tel. 473/2-33-00. Just past Hotel Posada San José. Open daily 8 AM–9 PM. Kitchen closes at 5:30 PM.*

WORTH SEEING

Getting lost in Guanajuato is, strangely enough, one of the more enjoyable things to do in the city. Most sights are near the center of town and are easy to see in a few days on foot. The maze of twisting *callejones* (alleyways) lead to unknown destinations, and you may stumble across colonial architecture and museums along the way. All museums are closed on Mondays and have limited hours on Sundays.

BASILICA The baroque facade of the **Basílica Colegiata de Nuestra Señora de Guanajuato** is painted a buttery yellow and resembles one of the pastries sold at the nearby Pastelería de la Paz (*see* Food, *above*). Constructed in 1693, the basilica is illuminated by sparkling crystal chandeliers, and houses a bejeweled wooden statue of the Virgin, said to be the oldest existing Christian statue in Mexico. *Plaza de la Paz, near Juárez. Open daily 8–8.*

EL CALLEJÓN DEL BESO For a few coins, the young men lingering around the "Alley of the Kiss" will tell you the legend associated with this spot. If you don't understand Spanish, just nod your head. You're probably hearing a version of the following: A young woman named Doña Carmen, the only child of a violent father, fell in love with a man named Don Luis. When her father found out about the courtship, he threatened to marry her off to a rich, old Spaniard. Not knowing what to do, Doña Carmen sought the help of her friend Doña Brígida, who, together with Don Luis, devised a plan. The alleyway that separated Doña Carmen's house from the one across the way was so narrow that the houses almost touched, so Don Luis arranged to buy the neighboring house for a steep price. One starry night, as Doña Carmen went out onto her balcony, she was pleasantly surprised by the nearness of her lover. The enraged voice of Doña Carmen's father surprised them, however, and the father proceeded to plunge a dagger into his daughter's heart. Don Luis was only able to lean over and leave a kiss on her lifeless hand. Then, distraught with grief, he took his own life. Current tradition holds that, if you kiss your loved one on the third step up to the balcony on which Don Luis died, you'll enjoy seven years of good luck. Lone females need not fear, however—one of the men standing by will

THE HEARTLAND 8
By Viviana Mahieux

The area encompassing the states of Michoacán, Jalisco, Zacatecas, and Aguascalientes is not easily definable. From the dry hills of Zacatecas to the rich green of Michoacán, the climate is as variable as the characters of this region's cities. One thing you can be sure of: The Heartland is not the place to find picture-perfect beaches, enigmatic ruins, or mobs of camera-toting tourists. Instead, expect cities with cobblestone streets, stately colonial buildings, a fair share of traffic, and a progressive, youthful population.

In pre-Columbian Mexico, the Heartland was inhabited by numerous peoples, including the Otomís, Chichimecas, and Purépechas. The Purépechas (Tarascos, in Spanish), who left evidence of advanced metalworking techniques, came to dominate the other groups, forming a vast empire in the 14th century. When the Spanish discovered silver in Zacatecas and in the Bajío, the Heartland was profoundly affected, and every effort was made to supply the mines with labor, often at the expense of Indian lives. Later, independence leader José María Morelos was born, and his native city was renamed in his honor by the newly formed republic.

The Heartland's historical significance and architectural splendor aren't its only attractions; its cities tend to be exuberant, with many university students, well-known artists, and remnants of indigenous culture. In Pátzcuaro and Uruapan, you can hike to waterfalls, lakes, and volcanoes, or get a close look at the village life of the Purépecha people, who still speak their native tongue. You can head north to Zacatecas to admire the works of painter Francisco Goitia and the extensive art collection of Pedro Coronel, as well as to indulge in cultural events and local mezcal. Finally Guadalajara, Mexico's second-largest city, offers a cosmopolitan alternative to the capital while retaining an unusual degree of small-town flavor, not to mention plenty of opportunities to enjoy mariachi music, dancing, and tequila.

Zacatecas

Perched in hilly country at about 2,700 meters, Zacatecas has chaotic *adoquín* (cobblestone) streets, beautiful colonial buildings, a history built on silver mines, and a big university. The art museums are fantastic, and the streets are alive weekend nights. Despite all these attractions, relatively few foreign tourists visit the city.

Although indigenous people knew of the mineral riches of the area long before the conquistadors arrived, it was not until the Spanish forced the mining of local hills that the city of Zacatecas was founded. Legend says that a silver trinket given to one Spaniard brought on the mining fever. The first operations began in the mid-16th century, and by 1728 local mines were producing one-fifth of the country's silver. The silver barons' extravagant mansions bear witness to the prosperity of old Zacatecas.

Silver mining tapered off during the fight for independence and declined even further during the Revolution, as political control of the area was hotly contested. Benito Juárez and his troops fought a decisive battle against local insurgents here in 1871, and Zacatecas was again the site of fighting in 1914, when Pancho Villa and his ragtag army routed 12,000 Huerta loyalists.

The buildings in the historic center of Zacatecas are made of a sandstone called cantera rosa, giving it a Miami Beach-pink brightness.

Amid the mining and fighting, Zacatecas remained a haven for intellectuals and artists, among them renowned artists Francisco Goitia and Pedro Coronel, whose namesake museums are world famous. Other Zacatecan cultural treasures have remained relatively untouched, including perhaps the finest example of colonial baroque architecture in all of Mexico, the **Catedral Basílica Menor**; a colonial **aqueduct**; and churches and haciendas. Though currently home to a population of almost one million, Zacatecas maintains a small town, traditional attitude in many ways: don't expect to do much here between 2 and 5 in the afternoon, when all the downtown businesses shut down for lunch. Straw hats and cowboy boots are almost mandatory gear for men of all ages, and women tend to disappear from the streets after 9 PM unless accompanied. However, the presence of the state university here guarantees the existence of open-minded students, who can be found in cafés and plazas around the city. The local economy is now largely dairy-based, giving the city a funny mix of students and farmers with a lot of art thrown in. The drawbacks to Zacatecas are minor: The high altitude requires a period of adjustment, and the city can be chilly, even in summer.

BASICS

AMERICAN EXPRESS **Viajes Mazzocco,** the AmEx representative, offers the usual services for cardholders, including emergency check-cashing and mail holding. *Enlace 115, Colonia Sierra de Alicia, Zacatecas, Zacatecas, CP 98001, México, tel. 492/2–08–59. From cathedral, take Hidalgo (becomes Ortega), right on Enrique Estrada just before aqueduct, left on Enlace after Museo Goitia. Open weekdays 9–7, Sat. 9–noon.*

CASAS DE CAMBIO **Banamex** (Hidalgo 132, tel. 492/2–58–02) changes traveler's checks and cash weekdays 9–noon and has an ATM that accepts Cirrus, Plus, Visa, and MasterCard. **Casa de Cambio PRODIRA** (Independencia 94, tel. 492/4–02–82; open weekdays 9–6, Sat. 9–3) changes cash on Saturday.

EMERGENCIES In an emergency, call the **police** (tel. 492/2–01–06) or the **Cruz Roja** (tel. 492/2–30–05). For medical or legal help call the toll-free tourist line (tel. 91/800–9–03–92).

LAUNDRY **Lavandería Aquazac** will wash and dry your clothes for $1 a kilo. Bring your clothes in before noon to get them back the same day. *López Velarde 609, tel. 492/4–01–82. Across from Hotel Colón. Open weekdays 9–2 and 4–6:30, Sat. 9–2.*

MAIL The post office will hold mail sent to you at the following address for up to 10 days: Lista de Correos, Zacatecas, Zacatecas, CP 98001, México. *Allende 111, tel. 492/2–01–96. Open weekdays 8–7, Sat. 9–1.*

MEDICAL AID **Farmacia Issstezac** (Dr. Hierro 512, tel. 492/2-88-89) is open round the clock. **Clínica Hospital Santa Elena** is open 24 hours and has English-speaking doctors. *Guerrero 143, tel. 492/2–68–61. From cathedral, SW on Hidalgo, left on Allende, right on Guerrero.*

Clínica Dental Zacatecas gives free dental exams. *Salazar 338, tel. 492/2–68–03. From pedestrian bridge on López Mateos, ½ block west to Salazar. Open weekdays 9:30–2 and 4–8, Sat. 9:30–2.*

PHONES For collect calls, use the Ladatel phones near the cathedral. You can also make international calls from the caseta de larga distancia (Callejón de Cuevas 103) in the centro. They're open weekdays 9–9, Saturday 9–2 and 4–8.

VISITOR INFORMATION The **Módulo de Información de Turismo** (Hidalgo 93, no phone; open Mon.–Sat. 9–8, Sun 9–5) is as professional as can be. The English-speaking staff has plenty of brochures, a great street map, and even computers to give you all the information you might (or might not) need. For tourist information over the phone, call 492/4–05–52.

COMING AND GOING

BY BUS The **Central Camionera** (Terrenos de la Isabélica 1) is on the western edge of town, and the RUTA 8 bus runs to and from downtown until about 9:30 PM. A taxi ride to the downtown area costs about $1.50. **Estrella Blanca** (tel. 492/2–06–84) travels to Aguascalientes (2½ hrs, $3.50); Durango ($5 hrs, $9); Guadalajara (6 hrs, $11); Mexico City (8 hrs, $16); and San Luis Potosí (3½ hrs, $4.50) almost every hour. **Omnibus de México** (tel. 492/2–54–95) serves the above destinations and has one bus per day to Guanajuato (6 hrs, $9), leaving at 5:30 AM. Luggage storage is available ($1 per day) 7 AM–10 PM.

BY TRAIN The train station (tel. 492/2–02–95) is just off González Ortega, south of downtown. Buses marked FERR stop near the terminal, but a taxi ride costs only about $1 from downtown. Two daily southbound trains leave at about 4:55 AM (2nd class; buy tickets on the train) and 8:15 PM (1st class; buy tickets from 7 PM until the train leaves) for Aguascalientes (3 hrs; $2 1st class, 85¢ 2nd class), León (7 hrs; $4 1st class, $2 2nd class), and Mexico City (13 hrs; 1st class only, $8). A northbound, first-class train to Chihuahua (16 hrs, $11) and Ciudad Juárez (22 hrs, $15) leaves at 9:55 AM; tickets are sold 8–10 AM.

GETTING AROUND

Although everything you could want to see is in or near downtown, it's easy to get lost here. The pattern of the streets is dictated by topography. There are many side streets, *callejones* (alleyways), and winding thoroughfares. The main street running northeast–southwest is Avenida Hidalgo, which intersects Avenida Juárez. The **Catedral Basílica Menor**, at the heart of town, is a convenient, easily visible landmark.

WHERE TO SLEEP

The hotel strip, López Mateos, just south of the center, has plenty of places to stay in all price categories. The five-minute walk to downtown is pretty entertaining—watch out for speeding buses and candy vendors who take up most of the narrow sidewalk space. To reach the center from López Mateos, walk west to Arroyo de la Plata. Turn right and walk north as the street becomes Tacuba. You could also rough it on the safe but uncomfortable seats in the bus station.

➤ **UNDER $10** • **Hotel Conde de Villareal.** Because this hole-in-the-wall hotel is closer to town, they charge more than what the rooms are worth. Nevertheless, it's still budget-friendly, if you don't mind green paint, the pervasive smell of mildew, and keeping company with the mostly single men who stay here. Singles are $5, doubles $6–$7. *Zamora 303, tel. 492/2–12–00. From pedestrian bridge on López Mateos, go ½ block west and right on Salazar until it becomes Zamora. 28 rooms, all with bath.*

Hotel Río Grande. Rooms in this three-story hotel overlook either a central courtyard or the city. Medium-size rooms are immaculate, with tiled floors, big comfy beds, and 24-hour hot water. The place is popular with backpackers and traveling families, all attracted by the great rates: Singles cost about $5, doubles $7–$8.50. If you get a room overlooking the city, don't walk around the terrace in your underwear unless you want to give the binocular-wielding mechanics across the street a thrill. *Calzada de la Paz 513, tel. 492/2–53–49. From pedestrian bridge on Mateos, walk right on Calzada de la Paz; a HOTEL sign directs you up the hill. 64 rooms, all with bath.*

➤ **UNDER $15** • **Hotel Colón.** This clean and comfy hotel has more frills than many budget places. Rooms are carpeted and have TVs and phones, although the location right on López Mateos means the traffic noise might disturb your pleasant dreams. Families on vacation make up most of the guests. Singles are $10.50, doubles $12.50. *López Mateos 105, tel. 492/2–*

89–25 or 492/2–04–64. East on López Mateos, 5 blocks past pedestrian bridge. 37 rooms, all with bath. Wheelchair access. MC, V.

Hotel Gami. This newly built, three-story hotel is about the same distance south of downtown as the Hotel Colón. It's a great place to meet traveling students, and the management makes special deals with student groups. The large rooms have new red carpeting, a TV, and small, clean bathrooms. Singles are $10, doubles $11.50. *López Mateos 309, tel. 492/2–80–05. About 3 blocks east of pedestrian bridge. 60 rooms, all with bath. Laundry. MC, V.*

➢ **UNDER $25** • **Posada de los Condes.** Smack dab in the center of town, this hotel has very large, spotless rooms, some with balconies and French windows. Singles are $17, doubles $20. *Juárez 107, tel. 492/2–10–93. From López Mateos, left on Salazar just before pedestrian bridge, right on Zamora, left on Juárez. 57 rooms, all with bath. Luggage storage. Reservations advised. Wheelchair access.*

FOOD

Zacatecan restaurants cater to a wide variety of tastes, offering everything from Greek to Italian to Chinese cuisine. Tons of small restaurants also serve *menudo* (tripe soup) and tacos made with every meat imaginable. Regional specialties are primarily in the dessert family; among these are *queso de tuna* (a hard, dark-brown candy made from the *tuna*, or prickly pear, available primarily July and August), *dulce de leche* (a candy made from milk that's so sweet it hurts your teeth), and *capirotada* (a sort of bread pudding with raisins and cinnamon), available around Easter.

➢ **UNDER $5** • **Restaurant Camino Real.** This nondescript little eatery has all the ingredients for a good meal—it's clean, cheap, has good food, and efficient, smiling service from the hermaphrodite waitress (waiter?). A filling comida corrida goes for $2, and their generous breakfast is $2. *López Mateos 420, ½ block past pedestrian bridge, no phone. Open daily 8 AM–midnight.*

Taquería y Rosticería La Única. The walk past roasting chickens and meat to the clean, wood-paneled dining area here will make you hungry for the meal to come. A big plate of roasted chicken with refried beans, salad, homemade potato chips, tortillas, and all the salsa and *rajas* (chile strips) you want is a steal at $1.50. Tacos are about 20¢ each and come in all types, from carne asada to *sesos* (brains) and *lengua* (tongue). *Aldama 245, tel. 492/2–57–75. From cathedral, SW on Hidalgo, left on Juárez to Aldama (also known as Zamora). Open daily 7 AM–1 AM. Wheelchair access.*

➢ **UNDER $10** • **La Cantera Musical.** This fun, brightly decorated place is popular with local families and tourists. Excellent *ranchera* music and a mini-reproduction of the *teleférico* (tram) strung across the ceiling are amusing. The biggest seller is the *asado de Boda Jerezano* (pork with chiles, orange, and laurel, served with rice) for $4.50, but other Mexican fare is available for less; try the *platillo ranchero*, a selection of appetizers such as quesadillas, *chicharrón* (pork rind) and guacamole ($5) for two people. *Tacuba 16, tel. 492/2–88–28. Underneath Mercado González Ortega. Open daily 8 AM–11 PM.*

El Dragón de Oro. Come here for something other than the same old tacos. If you're lucky, the stereo will be playing old American country and jazz to accompany your Chinese dinner. The *pollo almendrado* (almond chicken) is about $5, while the *sopa fu chuc* (a tofu and noodle soup in a miso-like broth) and wonton soup are perfect light choices for $2.50. Vegetarians will rejoice in the overflowing plate of chop suey for $5, which could easily fill two. *González Ortega, at Rayón, tel. 492/4–09–90. From cathedral, SW on Hidalgo (which becomes Ortega), 2 blocks past aqueduct. Open daily 2–10.*

WORTH SEEING

There's no way to see all of Zacatecas in one day; think about exploring one cluster of sights each day. Suggested areas for exploration include all points southwest (the aqueduct, Enrique Estrada park, and Goitia museum); hilltop sights (the Mina el Edén, Cerro de la

Bufa, and teleférico); and the center of town (the two Coronel museums, the cathedral, and the Palacio del Gobierno). The museums are excellent. Check the weekly cultural paper *Tips* for a listing of upcoming shows, concerts, and exhibits—it's available free at the tourist office and around town.

ACUEDUCTO DEL CUBO This colonial aqueduct, constructed entirely of magnificent rose-color sandstone formed into 39 high arches, is a strange and beautiful sight in the middle of the city. Just behind the aqueduct is the old **Plaza de Toros,** which has been refashioned into an incredible luxury hotel—it's worth a look inside, but run if anyone asks if you need a room. **Across the street is Parque Enrique Estrada** (not to be confused with the hunk from CHiPs), a gorgeous, lush park with fountains, a waterfall, and romantic couples. *From cathedral, SW on Hidalgo (which becomes Ortega) for about 6 blocks.*

CATEDRAL BASILICA MENOR This cathedral, on the corner of Hidalgo and Aguascalientes, is without a doubt the most imposing structure in Zacatecas, and one of the finest examples of Mexican baroque architecture in the country, at least on the outside. The cathedral was built between 1612 and 1752, but the more recently refurbished interior is as powerful in its neoclassical simplicity as the exterior is in its complexity. Just down the street is the state-operated theater, the **Teatro Calderón** (Hidalgo 501, tel. 492/2–86–20). Built in the late 19th century, the theater has beautiful stained-glass windows and is the venue for national and international ballets, operas, and plays. Check *Tips* for shows. Tickets run $2–$15, and the box office is open daily 4 PM–8 PM. Students congregate on the steps outside the theater.

CERRO DE LA BUFA Thought by the thirsty Spaniards to resemble a *bufa* (wineskin), this mountain offers a magnificent view of Zacatecas and the surrounding countryside. You can hike a strenuous half-hour or take the teleférico to the top and explore the **Museo de la Toma de Zacatecas,** a museum dedicated to Pancho Villa's 1914 victory here, with photographs, diagrams, a cannon, and some weapons. Admission is about $1 (students half that), and the museum is open Tuesday–Sunday 10–5. Beside the museum is an 18th-century chapel honoring the patroness of Zacatecas, called **La Capilla de la Virgen del Patrocinio.** Just in back of the chapel is the **Mausoleo a los Hombres Ilustres de Zacatecas.** Both are free and open daily 9–6. *SW on Hidalgo to Callejón Luis Moya, right to Calle de la Mantequilla, then left and up, up, and up, across road to path.*

MINA EL EDEN A healthy 20-minute walk straight up Juárez past the huge red IMSS Hospital takes you to another of Zacatecas's star attractions. The tour of this mine is conducted in Spanish and begins with a ride on a miniature train into the middle level of the mine. In the mid-1500s, when the mine was at its peak, an average of eight slaves, responsible for carrying heavy loads through the wet darkness, died here each day. Conditions changed somewhat after independence and again with the Revolution, but mining continued (without electricity) until 1964, when incorrectly placed explosives caused the lower levels to flood. Ironically, the mine is now home to a disco (*see* After Dark, *below*). Bring a sweater for the tour, as it gets pretty chilly down here. *Mina el Edén, tel. 492/2–30–02. From cathedral, SW on Hidalgo 4 blocks, right on Juárez (becomes Torreón), and turn right after hospital. Admission: $2.50. Open daily 11–7:30.*

MUSEO FRANCISCO GOITIA The French-style mansion was built in 1948 for the governor, but now houses works by the Zacatecan artist Francisco Goitia, a 20th-century painter most famous for his *Tata Jesucristo.* One hundred years of Zacatecan art, including works by other modern artists, are represented here. The grounds are beautiful, overflowing with well-tended flower beds and fountains. *Enrique Estrada 102, tel. 492/12–02–11. From cathedral, walk 6 blocks on Hidalgo and turn right on Miguel M. Ponce; the museum is just past the park. Admission: $1.50. Open Tues.–Sun. 10–1 and 5–8.*

MUSEO PEDRO CORONEL Two blocks northeast of the cathedral is a museum dedicated to Zacatecas's favorite son, artist Pedro Coronel. Coronel was also a prolific collector (in fact, a much better collector than artist), and the works on display here are world-famous. You'll find works by Goya, Miró, Cocteau, Kandinsky, Motherwell, Picasso, Chagall, and Dalí; ancient Greek pottery and statues; Indian, Chinese, Tibetan, and Japanese art; and a large collection of African and Latin American masks. *Plaza de Santo Domingo, tel. 492/2–80–21. From* cathedral, walk up steps next to visitor info. Admission: $1.50, 75¢ students. Open Mon.–Wed., Fri., Sat. 10–2 and 4–7, Sun. 10–5.

MUSEO RAFAEL CORONEL Named for Pedro Coronel's brother, this museum is housed in the former Convento y Templo de San Francisco, and is best known by locals as "Museo de las Máscaras" ("Museum of the Masks"). The grounds are beautiful enough in their own right, while the collection of character masks used in regional festivals is so enormous that you'll have a problem deciding where to look first. Detailed explanations in Spanish give a historical and cultural background for the masks, and a video provides more information. The museum also contains a collection of 19th-century puppets. *Ex-Convento de San Francisco, tel. 492/2–81–16. From cathedral, NE on Hidalgo (which becomes Juan de Tolosa) and left at fountain along Abasolo. Admission: $1.50, 75¢ with student ID. Open Mon.–Tues. 10–2 and 4–7, Thurs.–Sat. 10–2 and 4–7, Sun. 10–5.*

PALACIO DEL GOBIERNO Adjacent to the cathedral is the 1927 state capital building, originally the mansion of a local silver baron. Inside you'll find a brilliant mural of Zacatecas's history by the noted Zacatecan artist Antonio Pintor Rodríguez. The mural was completed in 1970. *Hidalgo 602. Admission free. Open weekdays 8–3:30 and 6–9.*

TELEFERICO This Swiss-made tram offers unparalleled views of Zacatecas. The ride is best combined with the Mina del Edén tour, since at the end of the visit you have the option of taking the elevator to the top of the Cerro del Grillo (Cricket Hill). Otherwise, you'll have to struggle up the exhausting flight of stairs next to the mine entrance, or hike up the Cerro de la Bufa to take a short ride on the tram (10 min each way). *Fare: $1.50 round-trip. Tram runs Tues.–Sun. 10–6, weather permitting.*

AFTER DARK

You'll be at a loss for things to do at night during the week, but Zacatecas picks up on the weekends. Two discos pump out the latest dance mixes and some disco favorites. **El Elefante Blanco** (Paseo Díaz Ordaz 2, tel. 492/2–71–04), near the teleférico station atop Cerro del Grillo, offers great views of nighttime Zacatecas for the steep cover charge of $5. Drinks are $2. **El Melacante** (tel. 492/2–30–02), also known as La Mina, is situated deep in the Mina El Edén. Although you may balk at the $5 cover (more than most miners earned in a year), it's the most popular dance spot. Drinks here also run $1.50–$2. Both discos are open Thursday–Sunday 9:30 PM–3 AM. **La Terraza** (Centro Comercial El Mercado G. Ortega, tel. 492/2–32–70) closes by 9 PM, but beer is cheap (less than $1) and you can dine on the balcony. Another bar popular with the younger crowd is **Reina María 2 English Pub** (Tacuba 208, across from Plazuela Goitia). Highly recommended is the oddly named **Mr. Coyote** (Caretera Panamericana 727, tel. 492/2–08–49) in the Hotel El Convento. For about a $2.50 Fridays and Saturdays, you'll get to hang out with the Zacatecan collegiate crowd, amid loud disco music and pool tables. For movies, try **Biblioteca Mauricio Magdaleno**, across from Plaza Independencia, where a video center shows excellent free Mexican films and dubbed or subtitled foreign films nightly at 5:30. At the entrance is a bulletin board with notices of upcoming local events, or look in *Tips* (see *Worth Seeing, above*) for more info.

For a night of inexpensive fun, hang out in the Plazuela Goitia (on Hidalgo, ½ block before the cathedral) where bands play on weekends. If you're lucky, you'll run into a private fiesta, known as a "callejonada," with music and a donkey with gallons of mezcal on its back.

Aguascalientes

A huge and expanding industrial city, Aguascalientes, capital of the state of the same name, has less colonial charm than other, more popular, Heartland destinations. The occasional colonial building lifts its weary head from the sprawl, but the city is mostly a tangle of modern buildings and neon. Even the *aguas calientes* (thermal waters) that originally attracted colonists to the region are no longer very thrilling or even hot for that matter.

The main reason to stop here today is to visit the art museums displaying works by famous locals Saturnino Herrán, Jesús Contreras, and Enrique Díaz de León. In keeping with the city's artistic legacy, there are at least a dozen art, music, and dance schools that offer a wide variety of classes. These schools, along with the presence of the state university, ensure that you'll see plenty of young, open-minded students, most of whom are extremely friendly and curious about visitors. In fact, Aguascalientes is so devoid of tourists that people bend over backward to help you out

The Spanish dubbed Aguascalientes "ciudad perforada" (perforated city) because of the catacombs and tunnels that indigenous peoples built beneath it before the conquest.

here. The city is famous for its month-long bash commemorating the **Feast of San Marcos** on April 25. The nationally renowned *feria* (fair) attracts Mexican and international artists, musicians, actors, dancers, and poets.

BASICS

AMERICAN EXPRESS You'd better hope you don't get all your money stolen along with your traveler's checks, because you'll need a taxi ($1) to reach **Viajes Chavoya,** the representative for AmEx. They provide all the regular services for cardholders, including cashing traveler's checks and holding mail. *Centro Comercial El Dorado, Local 11, CP 20000, México, tel. 49/13–63–76. Open weekdays 10–2 and 4–7, Sat. 10–1.*

BOOKSTORES **Librería Universal** has books in Spanish on all topics. *Madero 208, tel. 49/15–11–84. Open Mon.–Sat. 9:30–2 and 4–8:30.*

CASAS DE CAMBIO **Banamex** (Plaza de la Patria, at 5 de Mayo, tel. 49/16–65–70) changes currency weekdays 9–1:30 and has an ATM that accepts Cirrus, Plus, Visa, and MasterCard. To change cash on Saturdays, head to **Operadora Internacional** (Juan de Monotoro 120, tel. 49/15–79–79; open Mon.–Sat. 10–2).

EMERGENCIES Call the **police** (49/14–30–43 or 49/14–20–50) or **Cruz Roja** (tel. 49/15–20–55) for ambulance service.

LAUNDRY **Lavamatic** will wash your clothes for $1 a kilo, or you can do it yourself for about $1 per medium load (about 3½ kilos). *Montoro 418-B, 4 blocks east of Plaza de la Patria, tel. 49/16–41–81. Open weekdays 9–2 and 4–8, Sat. 9–8.*

MAIL AND PHONES Ladatel public phones are located on the Plaza de la Patria. Some accept cards and some work with coins. At the large pink post office, they'll hold mail sent to you at the following address for up to 10 days: Lista de Correos, Aguascalientes, Aguascalientes, CP 20000, México. *Hospitalidad 108, tel. 49/15–21–18. From Plaza de la Patria, 1 block east on Madero, 1 block north on Morelos, right on Hospitalidad. Open weekdays 8–7, Sat. 9–1.*

MEDICAL AID The **Hospital Hidalgo** (Galeana 161, south of Plaza de la Patria, tel. 49/15–31–42), with some English-speaking doctors, is downtown and open 24 hours. **Farmacia Sánchez** (Madero 215, east of Plaza de la Patria, tel. 49/15–66–10) has 24-hour service.

SCHOOLS Museums as well as dance and music schools around the city offer courses. Check with the **Casa de la Cultura** (*see* Worth Seeing, *below*) or any of the museums for current course listings.

VISITOR INFORMATION The **Dirección General de Turismo** doesn't have much, but they do have a map of the city and are happy to answer questions. Some of the staff speaks English.

South of Plaza de la Patria, next to Palacio del Gobierno, tel. 49/12–35–11 ext. 132. Open weekdays 8:30–3 and 5–7, Sat. 10–1.

COMING AND GOING

BY BUS The **Central Camionera,** open 24 hours, is on the south edge of town, just off Avenida de la Convención. Numerous bus lines have service here, including **Estrella Blanca** (tel. 49/78–20–54), which goes to Guadalajara (3 hrs, $5), Mexico City (6½ hrs, $11), and Zacatecas (2½ hrs, $3.50), as well as other destinations. If you don't want to stop in every town on your way from point A to point B, **Omnibus de México** (tel. 49/78–27–70) offers quicker first-class service to all of the above destinations for a few dollars more. The bus station has a high-tech long-distance phone service and luggage storage. Taxis to downtown should cost $1.50, or you can take one of the many buses lined up near the front entrance. Lines 9 and 13 go to the center.

BY TRAIN The train station (tel. 49/15–21–51) is on the eastern edge of town, some 5 kilometers from downtown. First-class trains depart daily to Ciudad Juárez (24 hrs, $15) at 7:20 PM, with stops in Zacatecas and Chihuahua, and to Mexico City (11 hrs, $8) at 10:55 PM, stopping in Querétaro.

GETTING AROUND

Everything you'll want is within walking distance of the **Plaza de la Patria** (the main square). At first, the downtown area seems confusing because the streets fan out from the plaza, but it's not that tough if you keep in mind that the streets change names at the plaza. Heading south, Juárez and 5 de Mayo change into Colón and José María Chávez, respectively, after passing the plaza. Madero, one of the two main drags to the east, becomes Carranza after the plaza. The other main street, Montoro, ends at the plaza. López Mateos, where many bars and nightclubs are, runs east–west about two blocks south of the plaza.

WHERE TO SLEEP

Downtown is the place for budget travelers to be. What the hotels listed below lack in sophistication, they make up in convenience by putting you right in the middle of things.

Hotel Imperial. Black wrought-iron staircases, an inner courtyard, and clean, large rooms, some with balconies, are what this older hotel has to offer. The management is so eager to please that they'll even offer discounts if you stay for more than one day. Singles are $12, doubles $13.50. *5 de Mayo 106, north side of plaza, tel. 49/15–16–50. 65 rooms, all with bath. Laundry, luggage storage. MC, V.*

Hotel Rosales. This hotel might have been the inspiration for an M.C. Escher painting: An endless succession of halls leads to a number of inner courtyards, dizzying tile patterns adorn the floor, and spiral staircases lead to single rooms at odd levels. The woman who manages the place, despite her sweetness, seems to have been affected by the strange surroundings as well. Singles are $8.50, doubles $10. *Victoria 104, tel. 49/15–21–65. ½ block north of Plaza de la Patria. 40 rooms, all with bath. Luggage storage. Wheelchair access.*

Hotel Señorial. Rooms here have less character than those at Hotel Rosales, but they're also less worn and quieter. The management is extremely accommodating. Singles are $10, doubles $13.50. *Colón 104, SE cnr of Plaza de la Patria, tel. 49/15–16–30. 32 rooms, all with bath. Reservations advised in high season. Wheelchair access.*

FOOD

➢ **UNDER $5** • **Jugos Acapulco.** This hamburger joint is a popular student hangout. The afternoon comida corrida is $2.50, while a hamburger with fries costs $1.25. Try the delicious all-natural *cerveza de raíz* (root beer) for $1. *Allende 106, tel. 49/18–15–20. 1 block north of Plaza de la Patria. Open daily 7 AM–9 PM. Wheelchair access.*

Lonchería Max. If you have the late-night munchies, this taquería holds vampire hours: 8 PM–4 AM or so. Max himself reads minds and will usually have another taco prepared for you just when it's time. Though only a sandwich-and-taco joint, the place is packed on the weekends with drunks, families, and nighthawks. Tacos are 30¢ apiece, and sandwiches $1. *331 Madero, 3 blocks east of Plaza de la Patria, no phone. Wheelchair access.*

➤ **UNDER $10** • **Fonda la Oaxaqueña.** This tiny, colorful no-nonsense fonda serves only specialties from Oaxaca. Build up your courage and try the crunchy *chapulines* (grasshoppers) for $2. The *mole oaxaqueño* (a darker version of the typical mole) fetches $2.50. *López Mateos Pte. 203, no phone. From plaza, walk south on José María Chavez, turn right on López Mateos and walk 2 blocks. Open Wed.–Mon. noon–1 AM. Wheelchair access.*

Restaurant Mitla. The classiest bargain in town has service not only with a smile, but in dress whites and ties, no less. This restaurant is a favorite with families, legislators, and cabbies alike. Full meals and drinks are on the expensive side. Try the *tampiqueña tradicional* (beef in salsa with tortillas) for $5. You can get cheaper meals and breakfast ($2–$3) here as well. Try the *molletes* (a roll covered with beans and cheese) for $1.25. *Madero 220, tel. 49/16–36–79. East of Plaza de la Patria. Open daily 7 AM–midnight. Wheelchair access.*

Restaurant Vegetariano. Vegetarians swoon over this all-you-can-eat meatless buffet. Dishes change daily, but expect to find tasty selections like tofu in tomato and onion sauce, brown rice and broccoli, salads, and spinach soup. Add a pitcher of the daily beverage (made from anything from oats to parsley) and your total is only $3. *López Velarde 210, no phone. From Plaza de la Patria, 2 blocks east on Madero, left on Hidalgo (which becomes López Velarde); restaurant is behind health food store. Buffet served Mon.–Sat. 1:30–5. Wheelchair access.*

WORTH SEEING

The **Plaza de la Patria** is the heart of downtown and the site of political demonstrations and concerts; it's partially shaded, full of fountains, and a good place just to hang out. Here you'll find the **Exedra,** a monument to King Carlos IV built in 1807 and later capped with the eagle-and-serpent symbol of revolutionary Mexico. You'll also find the **Palacio de Gobierno** (open daily 7 AM–8:30 PM), a fantastic example of colonial architecture with a deep-red hue created from sandstone and *tezontle* stones. Inside, 111 arches open onto two inner courtyards. The real highlight of the building, however, is the massive, colorful, and forceful murals by Chilean painter Osvaldo Barra, detailing the history of Aguascalientes. Barra, whose mentor was none other than Diego Rivera, worked on these murals in 1961–62, 1989, and 1991. About three blocks west of the Plaza is the **Jardín San Marcos,** which overflows with greenery and couples making out in the evening. Adjacent to the Jardín is the huge and often-empty **Plaza San Marcos,** which livens up every year during the fair with casinos, performers, and craft stands.

> *If you're at the Plaza de la Patria at 6 PM, you'll witness the Ceremonía de la Bandera (flag ceremony), when a group of prancing, uncoordinated soldiers march the flag into the Palacio de Gobierno for the night.*

CASA DE LA CULTURA Just behind the cathedral and plaza, the "Casa" is the artistic and social headquarters of Aguascalientes. Built in 1625 as a hacienda for a prominent Spanish family, the building has also been used as a monastery, seminary, and correctional school. Today it hosts rotating art exhibits, films, recitals, and classes of all kinds: dance, music, theater, pottery, and language. Something's always happening here; it should be the first place you look for information about upcoming events. *Carranza 101, tel. 49/15–00–97. West of Plaza de la Patria. Admission to exhibits free. Open weekdays 7–2 and 5–9, weekends 11–8.*

MUSEO DE AGUASCALIENTES Self-taught architect J. Refugio Reyes Rivas undertook the construction of this bright orange building at the turn of the 20th century, creating an edifice in the neoclassical style with a few random details from his other favorite styles thrown in for good measure. Works by the famous local artist Saturnino Herrán are paired with appropriate quotes from Ramón López Velarde, famous local poet and friend of the painter. Other rooms have changing exhibits by contemporary artists. Check the billboard at the entryway for piano concerts held here on Sundays. *Zaragoza 505, tel. 49/15–90–43. Admission: 50¢, 25¢ students; free Sun. Open Tues.–Sun. 11–6. From Plaza de la Patria, walk 3 blocks east on Madero, left on Zaragoza for 3½ blocks.*

Across the street from the museum is the **Templo de San Antonio,** a bizarre structure with some neoclassical elements and a tall, domed bell tower. The interior is an explosion of colorful murals depicting events in the life of Saint Anthony.

MUSEO DE ARTE CONTEMPORANEO This small but exquisite museum concentrates on local as well as nationally recognized artists of the abstract, surreal, and *arte fantástico* movements. *Montoro 222, tel. 49/18–69–01. 1½ blocks east of Plaza de la Patria. Admission: 50¢, students free. Open Tues.–Sun. 10–6.*

MUSEO DE JOSE GUADALUPE POSADA This small museum is dedicated to the artist and journalist whose political caricatures and prints helped stir dissent against Porfirio Díaz during the Revolution. The museum exhibits his art, contains a public library, and offers printing and painting classes. *North side of Jardín del Encino, tel. 49/15–45–56. From Plaza de la Patria, south on José María Chávez, 4 blocks left on Pimentel. Admission: 50¢, 25¢ with student ID. Open Tues.–Sun. 10–6.*

Next door to the museum is the **Parroquia del Encino,** a baroque church with a black statue of Christ as well as huge 19th-century oil paintings depicting the Stations of the Cross. *Open daily 6–1 and 4–9. Mass schedule posted at entryway.*

AFTER DARK

Aguascalientes's hip bars and nightclubs are a $2 taxi ride from the center. For closer-to-home fun, there are a number of working-class joints blaring the latest *quebradita* and *ranchera* music along López Mateos. If you prefer more bourgeois hangouts, the place to be is **The Station** (Carretera al Campestre 129, tel. 49/12–09–91), which is crowded Fridays and Saturdays with the beautiful people and those who want them. There's no cover and beers are $2. **Alcatraz** (Aguascalientes Nte., near Pulgas Pandas sports club) is another good bar with the same people and the same music. For dancing, **El Cabus** (Hotel Las Trojes, Carretera al Campestre, tel. 49/73–00–06) packs in up to 400 people and dominates the music scene, with a $2 cover Thursday and Friday and a $4 cover Saturday. A quieter early evening scene can be found at **Café Parroquia** (Hidalgo, just before López Velarde, no phone), attracting bohemians who spend hours over cappuccino and cigarettes. It's open until 9 PM, and coffee is about $1.

Guadalajara

Despite a population of 5 million, Guadalajara seems like a relatively small city. The anonymity of late-20th-century urban life hasn't made itself felt here: Introduce one Guadalajaran (or *tapatío,* as they call themselves) to another and inevitably they will realize they have a friend or associate in common. People on the street are friendly and accessible, and almost always go out of their way to give you directions or show you around.

Guadalajara is considered the birthplace of several things "typically Mexican": the woeful love songs of the mariachi, the flirtatious jarabe tapatío (known to gringos as the Mexican hat dance), and charreadas (rodeos).

In 1531 conquistador Nuño Beltrán de Guzmán of Guadalajara, Spain, sent one of his strongmen, Juan de Oñate, to establish a city that would connect the coastal territories with the interior. A settlement of Indians—the Caxcanes—rebelled against Spanish rule, and in 1542 killed Pedro de Alvarado, who had been sent to put down the rebellion. During the colonial era, Guadalajara was the capital of the *audiencia* (administrative territory) of Nueva Galicia, which encompassed the western coast of Mexico from Jalisco all the way up through California. The city has often been characterized as politically conservative, mostly because it was here that the PAN (Partido de Acción Nacional), often linked

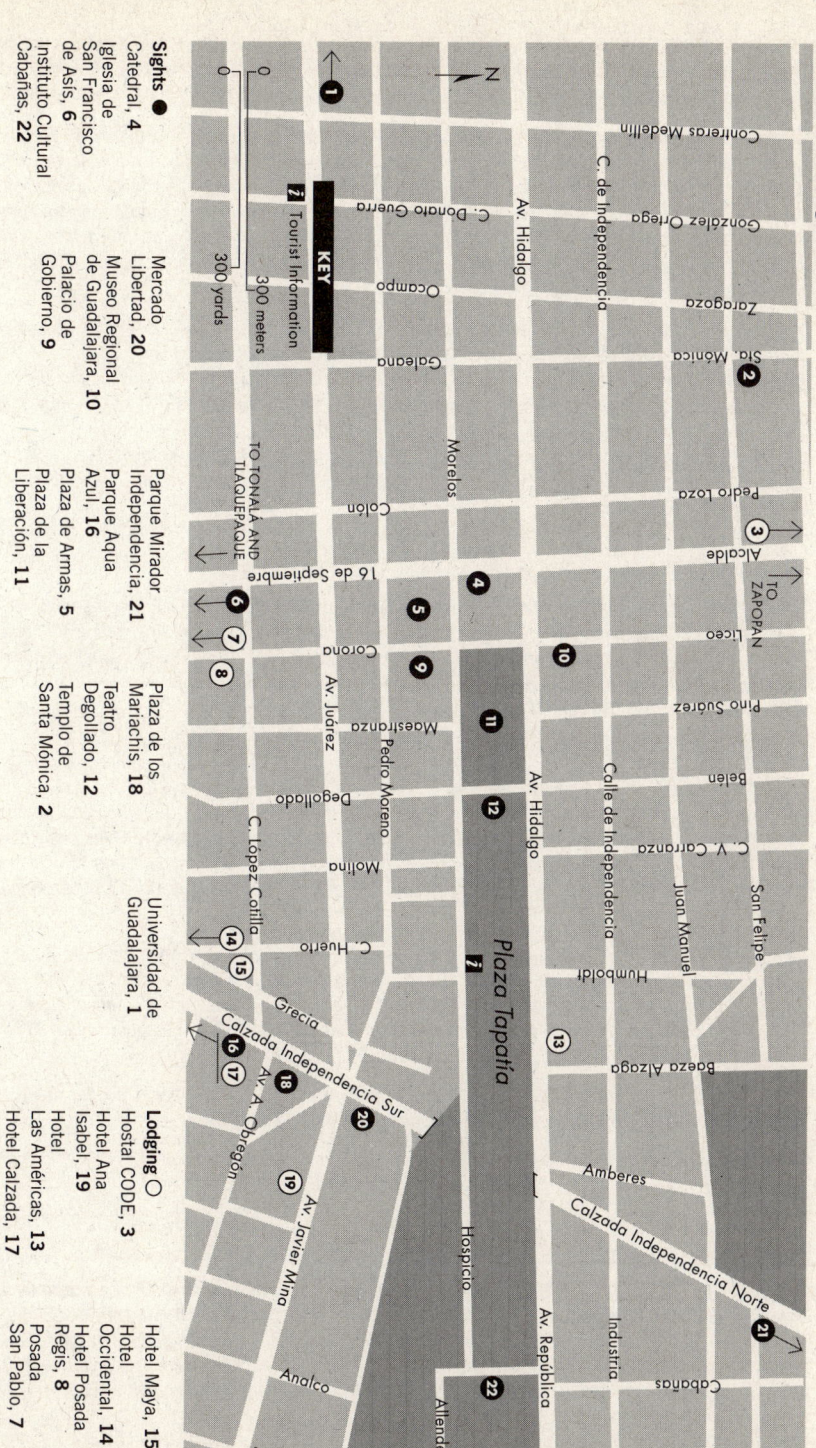

to the Catholic Church, was organized in the early part of the century. The students of the public Universidad de Guadalajara, however, ensure that the city is constantly infused with new blood, and the gay population here is visible and as "out" as is possible in Mexico.

Like any expanding city, Guadalajara is experiencing growing pains that are hard to ignore. Children sleep on the city's sidewalks, and, as in Mexico City, pollution worsens as the city absorbs surrounding suburbs. The newly elected PAN government hasn't done much to confront the problem. In fact, the first law that this traditionally Catholic party put on the table was one prohibiting miniskirts inside government offices—mandatory length was lowered to a few inches below the knee. The law provided for a great deal of laughter, but has all the while failed to cap drug trafficking and corruption.

Nevertheless, there's plenty to see in Guadalajara. Several murals by José Clemente Orozco, a native of Jalisco, are at the Instituto Cultural Cabañas, Universidad de Guadalajara, and the Palacio de Gobierno. Mariachi music fills the Plaza de los Mariachis every night, where people pay to hear their favorite songs played especially for them. In the towns of Tlaquepaque and Tonalá (officially independent of Guadalajara, but geographically surrounded by it), you'll find plenty of local handicrafts. Close to the city is Lake Chapala, a favorite getaway for Guadalajarans and retired Americans, while in the nearby town of Tequila, you can take distillery tours that end with free shots.

BASICS

AMERICAN EXPRESS All of the usual services are provided by this AmEx representative—traveler's-check exchange as well as personal-check cashing and mail holding for cardholders. *Vallarta 2440, Guadalajara, Jalisco, CP 44680, México, tel. 3/615–89–10. West of downtown on Juárez/Vallarta, in Plaza los Arcos; take* PAR VIAL *or Bus 500 from downtown on Juárez. Open weekdays 9–6, Sat. 9–1.*

BOOKSTORES **Librería México** has a huge selection of popular magazines in English and some paperback bestsellers. *Plaza del Sol, tel. 3/821–01–14. Open daily 8:30 AM–9:30 PM.*

El Libro Antiguo, 1½ blocks north of the Plaza de la Liberación, swaps used books and sells English paperbacks, though most of what they carry is 1950s pulp fiction with titles like *Impatient Virgin* and *Lovers and Libertines*. Still, a few cheap treasures can be found amidst the junk, and if you read Spanish, there are plenty of choices. *Pino Suárez 86, Col. Centro, no phone. Open Mon.–Sat. 9–8.*

CASAS DE CAMBIO **Banamex** (Juárez 237, tel. 3/679–32–52) changes traveler's checks and cash weekdays 9–1 and has an ATM that accepts Cirrus and Plus cards. They also give cash advances on MasterCard or Visa. For better hours, try any of the money-changers cluttering López Cotilla between Corona and Maestranza. **Cambio de Divisas** has good rates. *López Cotilla 175, tel. 3/614–65–65. Open Mon.–Sat. 9–5, Sun. 11–2.*

CONSULATES **Canada.** *Hotel Fiesta Americana, Aurelio Aceves 225, Local 30, tel. 3/625–34–34 ext. 3005. Near Glorieta Minerva. Open weekdays 9:30–1:30.*

United Kingdom. *M.A. de Quevedo 601, btw Parra and Acuña, tel. 3/616–06–29. Open weekdays 10–1.*

United States. *Progreso 175, Col. Centro, tel. 3/625–27–00, emergency tel. 3/625–55–53. Open weekdays 8–noon.*

DISCOUNT TRAVEL AGENCIES Faculty and students make up most of the clientele at **Agencia de Viajes Universidad de Guadalajara** (Vallarta 976, in the basement, tel. 3/625–85–52), so the staff knows about the cheapest plane fares and vacation packages. To get here, take the PAR VIAL or Bus 500 from downtown on Juárez. For a totally hassle-free reservation, go to **Mapamundi** (Hidalgo, 2009, tel. 3/616–37–97). The friendly, English-speaking staff is especially up on internatonal travel.

LAUNDRY At **Lavandería Lavarami** you can get about 3½ kilos of your clothes washed, dried, and folded for $3.75. They'll also pick up and deliver if you call them. You can do your own clothes for about $2 a load. *Juárez 1520, tel. 3/657–16–83. Open Mon.–Sat. 9–8, Sun. 10–2.*

MAIL The full-service post office will hold mail sent to you at the following address for up to 10 days: Lista de Correos, Administración de Correo 1, Guadalajara, Jalisco, CP 44100, México. *Independencia, at Carranza, tel. 3/614–74–25. 3 blocks north of Plaza Tapatía. Open weekdays 8–7, Sat. 9–1.*

MEDICAL AID Both **Hospital del Carmen** (Soledad Orozco 203, tel. 3/813–00–42) and **Hospital Regional ISSSTE** (Av. de las Américas, tel. 3/633–02–48 or 3/633–02–52) are open 24 hours. The first has English-speaking doctors; the second is closer to downtown. **Farmacia Guadalajara** has 24-hour service. Call for other locations within the city. *Av. de las Américas 2, near Plaza del Sol, tel. 3/615–85–16.*

PHONES You can make collect or phone-card calls at any working Ladatel phone in the Plaza Tapatía or Plaza de la Liberación. The caseta de larga distancia next to El Libro Antiguo (*see* Bookstores, *above*) charges about 70¢ for a three-minute collect call. You can pay for direct-dialed calls here, as well, but rates are much higher than with a Ladatel card. *Pino Suárez 92, Col. Centro. Open weekdays 10–8, Sat. 10–7.*

SCHOOLS The **University of Guadalajara** has five-week Spanish language courses, as well as classes on Mexican culture, literature, and history for foreign students. For more information call Centro de Estudios Para Extranjeros between 9 and 4 at 3/653–21–50 or 3/653–60–24, or write to Lic. Adriana Ayala Rubio, Guanajuato 1047, Aptdo. Postal 1, Guillón 2130, Guadalajara, Jalisco, CP 44000, México.

The **Casa de la Cultura** offers free weekend classes in Nahuatl (the Aztec language), which are open to beginners; call the Casa for the schedule. You can also study art, theater, folkloric dance, and music here. *Constituyentes, btw Calz. Independencia Sur and 16 de Septiembre, tel. 3/619–36–11. Near Parque Agua Azul. Open Mon.–Sat. 10–9.*

VISITOR INFORMATION The helpful, English-speaking staff at the **Secretaría de Turismo de Jalisco** gives out complete maps of the city and information about upcoming cultural events. There are several tourist-information centers dotting the main plazas, but you'll get the most info at the main office. *Morelos 102, Plaza Tapatía, tel. 3/658–22–22 or 3/614–86–86. Open weekdays 9–8, weekends 9–1.*

COMING AND GOING

BY BUS The **Central Camionera Nueva,** the main bus station, is on the *Carretera libre a Zapotlanejo* (free road to Zapotlanejo) between Tlaquepaque and Tonalá, about half an hour southeast of downtown. Buses arrive here from destinations over 100 kilometers away. The huge, horseshoe-shaped structure is divided into seven terminals, each with its own group of bus lines. Each terminal has Ladatel phones, restaurants, and luggage storage—the storage in Terminal 1 is open 24 hours. The cheapest way to get downtown is on city bus 102 or minibus 644. Bus 275 (50¢) takes you up Avenida 16 de Septiembre to the old bus station. Taxis from the bus station to downtown cost about $3.50; you have to buy your ticket at the terminal booth.

Leaving Guadalajara should be a breeze, as hundreds of buses depart daily. However, the problem lies in deciding which line to take, since they're spread out over seven terminals stretching for almost a kilometer. Running around to all of them is not a wise idea, so call ahead to several lines. If you're not one to plan ahead, go to **Flecha Amarilla** (tel. 3/600–03–99 or 3/600–00–14) in the first terminal for the cheapest fares and slowest buses. Destinations include Morelia (every 2 hrs, 6 hrs, $8) and Mexico City (15 per day, 9 hrs, $18). Other lines include **Autobuses del Occidente** (tel. 3/657–64–60), with buses to Morelia (6 hrs, $12.50), and **Rojo de los Altos** (tel. 3/679–04–55), with service to Ciudad Juárez (24 hrs, $48) and Zacatecas (5½ hrs, $8). **ETN** (tel. 3/657–43–53) is a good but somewhat pricey first-class line with frequent departures to Aguascalientes (3 hrs, $7), Manzanillo (6 hrs, $17), and Mexico City (8 hrs, $27).

The **Antigua Central Camionera,** the old bus station on 5 de Febrero, sends buses to destinations within 100 kilometers of Guadalajara. Luggage storage is available 7 AM–8 PM. **Autotransportes Guadalajara Chapala** (tel. 3/619–56–75) leaves every half-hour 7 AM–8 PM for cities around Lake Chapala. **Rojo de los Altos** (tel. 3/619–23–09) leaves for Tequila and Amatitlán (2 hrs, $1.50) every 20 minutes 6 AM–9 PM. **Autotransportes del Sur de Jalisco** (tel. 3/650–23–99) leaves for Tapalpa (3 hrs, $2.50) every hour 6:45 AM–5:45 PM. To reach the station, take Bus 110 south on 16 de Septiembre.

You can purchase bus tickets for a number of first-class lines from **Global Travel** (Calz. Independencia Nte. 254, under Plaza Tapatía, tel. 3/617–33–30) for no extra charge. They're open weekdays 9–6:30, Saturday 9–4:30.

BY TRAIN The **train station** (tel. 3/650–08–26) is a little south of downtown, about two blocks from Parque Agua Azul (*see* Worth Seeing, *below*). The train to Mexico City leaves daily at 9 PM and takes 11½ hours. Sleepers with two beds cost about $30, but seats are a steal at $11 first-class, $6 second-class. The first-class train to Mexicali (36 hrs, $38) leaves daily at 9:30 AM, with stops in Mazatlán (9 hrs, $11) and Sufragio (16 hrs, $18). Much cheaper and slower is the second-class train to Mexicali (2 days, $21), which leaves daily at noon. All train tickets must be purchased on the day of departure. There is a long-distance telephone office as well as several stores selling food in the station. *Open daily 7 AM–9 PM. Tickets sold weekdays 9–1, Sat. 9 AM–11 PM, and Sun. before the train leaves. Take Bus 62 south on Calz. Independencia or Bus 54 south on 16 de Septiembre.*

BY PLANE Guadalajara's airport (tel. 3/688–51–20) is served by **Aerocalifornia** (tel. 3/826–88–50), **Aeroméxico** (tel. 3/621–74–55), **American** (tel. 3/616–40–90), **Continental** (tel. 3/647–46–05), **Delta** (tel. 3/630–35–30), and **Mexicana** (tel. 3/647–22–22). The cheapest one-way ticket to Mexico City is about $60.

Taxis to the center of town from the airport cost $6.50, but, inexplicably, the ride in the other direction is $8. If you go to the taxi office, you can get a better rate—as low as $5. In either case, you should call a day ahead to reserve a taxi. Airport lockers cost about $1 per day. *Taxi office: Enrique Díaz de León 954, at Francia, tel. 3/612–93–37 or 3/612–93–39. Near Glorieta Pila Moderna.*

GETTING AROUND

Although Guadalajara is the second largest city in Mexico, it's easy to get around if you stick to the historic center. Downtown, things revolve around the huge **Plaza Tapatía** and surrounding streets. The plaza is bordered by Hidalgo to the north, Morelos to the south, Avenida 16 de Septiembre to the west, and Calzada Independencia (not to be confused with Calle Independencia, a smaller street) to the east. Avenida Juárez heads west from downtown into the university area, crossing the wide, jam-packed Federalismo; after that it becomes Vallarta, crossing Chapultepec and Avenida de las Américas, and ends at a rotary called **Glorieta Minerva.** If you plan to enjoy the nightlife, you'll get to know López Mateos, which takes you south of Minerva to the huge shopping mall, **Plaza del Sol,** and the dozens of bars and clubs nearby.

BY SUBWAY Guadalajara's *tren ligero* (light-rail train) is the fastest way to travel long distances. It runs both above and below ground, traveling the length of Federalismo between the Periférico Sur and the Periférico Norte stations, as well as east–west along Juárez and Vallarta from Parque Revolución to Tetlán. It runs 6 AM–11 PM, and the fare is 35¢.

BY BUS Hundreds of buses and minibuses run all over Guadalajara. There is frequent service 5 AM–11 PM and the fare is 25¢. To reach the Plaza del Sol and the all-important nightlife on López Mateos, take Bus 258 from Calzada Independencia heading south. To reach Tlaquepaque, the Central Camionera, or Tonalá from downtown, catch Bus 275 on Avenida 16 de Septiembre heading south; to Zapopan take the same bus running north. For destinations along Calzada Independencia such as Parque Agua Azul and the train station, hop on Bus 62. The PAR VIAL, which runs west on Juárez/Vallarta to the Minerva and east on Hidalgo to downtown, passes the university. Blue **Tur** buses offer air-conditioned comfort and cost 70¢. The 707 runs west on Juárez/Vallarta, while the 706 goes from 16 de Septiembre to Tlaquepaque and Tonalá.

BY TAXI Taxis are the only way to get around late at night. Cabs line up in front of expensive hotels, but these charge higher rates than those you hail on the street. A ride from the bar/club area around the Plaza del Sol to the center of town should cost about $2. As night wears on, taxis jack up their rates by $1 or $2.

WHERE TO SLEEP

Guadalajara has plenty of beds in the $10–$15 range. The nicest inexpensive places to stay are small *posadas* (inns), which are usually family-run; unfortunately, due to a recent drop in tourism, most in the downtown area have closed. A number of budget hotels are scattered throughout the center of town, generally south of the historic center or near the Mercado Libertad. The cheapest joints are along Calzada Independencia and near the old bus station, but these are pretty sleazy. If you plan to stay a while, *casas de huéspedes* (rooming houses) rent rooms by the month for a little more than $100. Ask for a list from the Universidad de Guadalajara's center for foreign students, or at the state tourist office (*see* Visitor Information, *above*). The drawback to nearly all budget hotels in Guadalajara is the noise from street traffic, but you can often avoid it by requesting a room facing away from the street.

DOWNTOWN The best reason to stay downtown is the proximity to sights in the center as well as to the bus lines that will take you elsewhere. The neighborhoods southeast of the Plaza Tapatía have cheap accommodations, but you might not feel safe walking alone here at night. Directly northeast you'll find a similar situation, but as long as you stay within a five-block radius of the plaza, you shouldn't encounter anything too scary.

➤ **UNDER $15** • **Hotel Las Américas.** This hotel's convenient location across from the Plaza Tapatía is about all it has going for it. Admittedly, rooms have TVs and phones, and the area is pretty safe, but this doesn't quite make up for the dim atmosphere. Singles are $10, one-bed doubles are $11, and two-bed rooms are $13.50. *Hidalgo 76, tel. 3/613–96–22. 3 blocks east of Teatro Degollado. 49 rooms, all with bath. Luggage storage. Wheelchair access.*

Hotel Ana Isabel. Despite its somewhat unpleasant location across from the Mercado Libertad, this hotel is a good choice. A long plant-filled hallway leads to peaceful rooms with ceiling fans, large bathrooms, and black-and-white TVs. Singles are $9 ($8 if you stay on the top floor and hike up two flights of steps), doubles $11. You can also get free coffee and huge smiles from the manager all day long. *Javier Mina 164, tel. 3/617–79–20. South side of Mercado Libertad. 42 rooms, all with bath.*

Hotel Maya. There's nothing really outstanding about this hotel, but it's decent and clean, and has phones, walk-in closets, and enormous bathrooms attached to each room. Location—just two blocks away from the Plaza Tapatía and the Mercado Libertad—is a plus. Singles are $19, doubles $11.50. *López Cotilla 39, tel. 3/614–54–54. 55 rooms, all with bath. Luggage storage. Reservations advised Easter week and summer. Wheelchair access.*

Hotel Occidental. The hotel is clean and the staff young, raucous, and friendly—you won't have trouble making friends here, especially if you're female. It's situated in a grungy alley, but the brightly painted halls and rooms are sure to cheer you up once you're inside, if the smell of disinfectant doesn't knock you out first. The *matrimonial* (double) beds were made with a very slim couple in mind. Singles are $10.50, one-bed doubles $13. Some rooms have phones. *Huerto, at Villa Gómez, tel. 3/613–84–06. 3 blocks south of Plaza Tapatía. 51 rooms, all with bath.*

Posada San Pablo. Owner Lili and her family make you feel right at home in the San Pablo's noisy but spacious rooms. A sweeping marble staircase leads up to a courtyard filled with plants and canaries, where you can relax and chat (or try to) with backpackers from all over the world. Hot water is scarce in the evenings. Singles cost $8, doubles $10.50. A few economical rooms without private bath are decent enough for $6.50 (singles) and $8 (doubles).

Madero 218, at Corona, tel. 3/613–33–12. 2 blocks south of Juárez, next to El Quinto Poder record store. 15 rooms, some with bath. Laundry. Reservation advised.

➢ **UNDER $20** • **Hotel Posada Regis.** This place has small, carpeted rooms and a relaxing, if somewhat dilapidated, elegance. It's the place to stay if you are short on cash and need to exercise your plastic; otherwise you'll get a better deal at one of the cheaper places. Singles are $13.50, doubles $19, but the prices go down if you stay a week or longer. *Corona 171, at López Cotilla, tel. 3/613–30–26. 1 block south of Juárez. 18 rooms, all with bath. Laundry, luggage storage, restaurant. MC, V.*

NEAR CALZADA INDEPENDENCIA SUR **Hotel Calzada.** This place is right on the bus line to the train station, but if you're not headed that way you might want to find a hotel closer to the center. McDonald's-style red-and-yellow tiles can't quite brighten the small, dark rooms or detract attention from the hotel's run-down state. The price is persuasive, though: One or two people in one bed costs $5; two beds in a room are $6.50. If you're strapped for cash, the owner will let you stay in a smaller downstairs room for a couple of bucks. *Calz. Independencia Sur 808, at Av. de Paz, tel. 3/614–67–28. A few blocks south of Glorieta Minerva. 74 rooms, all with bath. Luggage storage. Wheelchair access.*

HOSTELS **CODE.** The youth hostel, affiliated with a sports complex, has four dorm rooms, each stuffed with 20 bunk beds. The facility is clean, with private showers and toilet paper (a real luxury). It's set away from downtown noise, but access to the city is still quick and easy. The doors close at 11 AM, so if you miss the curfew, prepare to stay out until 6 AM. Beds (including sheets) cost $2.50. *Prolongación Alcalde 1360, near the glorieta (roundabout), no phone. From downtown, Bus 231 up Alcalde, and get off ½ block after Instituto de la Artesanía Jalisciense. 80 beds, none with bath. Check-in 8–2 and 3–9. Luggage storage (free). Closed Christmas and Easter.*

FOOD

It may sound silly, but Guadalajara is a great place to get Mexican food. It's a big city, but the cuisine isn't as international as you might expect. Tourists—foreigners and Mexicans alike—come here for that "authentic" Mexican experience, so this is a good place to really dig into those tamales *con mucho gusto*. Regional specialties include *tortas ahogadas* (literally "drowned sandwiches," generously bathed in a tomato-based sauce). Also popular is *jericalla*, a rich, sweet custard. You'll find both at the stands in the Mercado Libertad.

DOWNTOWN The center of town does not cater to people searching for a fine dining experience, but you'll find lots of cheap fast food here, particularly tortas. During the afternoon on Moreno (1 block north of Juárez), tons of small shops offer specials such as five tacos or three tostadas for less than a dollar. The **Mercado Libertad** has dozens of food stalls with probably the cheapest meals in town, but one jocose resident ominously called those meals *platillos de cólera* (plates of cholera), so watch your step. For a cheap breakfast, **Croissants Alfredo** (Morelos 229, across from Plaza de la Liberación; open daily 8 AM–9:30 PM) has baked goodies for about 30¢ apiece.

➢ **UNDER $5** • **La Chata.** In business for over half a century, this cheerful restaurant serving traditional food is a great choice if you can spare some money. Though you can get cheaper dishes like *sopes* (fried tortillas topped with beans, salsa, and meat or cheese) for less than $2, you'll probably want to try a specialty such as the *platillo jalisciense* (one-quarter of a chicken, french fries, a sope, one enchilada, and one flauta) for $4. Breakfast here is cheaper than at many places downtown, with egg dishes for $2.50. *Corona 126, tel. 3/613–05–88. 2 blocks south of Plaza Tapatía. Open daily 9 AM–10:30 PM.*

Gorditas Estilo Durango. Students short on cash come here for *gorditas* (thick corn tortillas) stuffed with sausage, cheese, or shredded beef for less than $1 each. The menú del día (soup, refried beans, an entrée, and a drink) is another filling meal at $2. *Moreno 552, at Díaz de León, tel. 3/626–47–23. Open Mon.–Sat. 8–6.*

Krishna Prasadam. The peacock feathers and pictures of Hindu deities on the wall might give the impression that you took a wrong turn somewhere and left Mexico. The delicious comida corrida ($2.50), which includes veggie soup, tofu and peppers in tomato sauce, breaded vegetables, copious amounts of salad and whole-wheat tortillas, fruit, and a yogurt drink, will do nothing to dispel that impression. *Madero 694, at Federalismo, tel. 3/626–18–22. Open Mon.–Sat. 6 AM–8 PM.*

El Mexicano. It doesn't take a genius to guess what type of food this joint serves—and if the smell of grilled meat and tacos doesn't lure you in, the clown-dressed waiter at the door will do the job. Comidas corridas go for $2, and the specialty, *birria de chiva* (goat stew) is mouthwatering at $3. *Morelos 81, tel. 3/658–03–45. 1½ blocks east of Plaza Libertad. Open daily 9 AM–10 PM. Wheelchair access.*

Restaurant Panamerican. This is a good place to grab some food while you're near the Plaza de los Mariachis. Though the place itself lacks atmosphere, the food, especially the chicken mole ($2.50), is excellent. The egg or chicken chilaquiles are the best breakfast deal in town at $1. *Plaza de los Mariachis 47, no phone. Open daily 9 AM–1 AM.*

Restaurant Sandy's. Despite its generic name, this restaurant delivers an out-of-the-ordinary menu. You can get an overflowing platter of chop suey for $4, or a burger with mushrooms for $3.50. The location is an added plus, as you can look down on the shady Plaza de la Rotonda from the terrace. *Cnr of Independencia and Alcalde, upstairs, tel. 3/853–08–91. Open daily 8 AM–10 PM.*

AVENIDA CHAPULTEPEC/AVENIDA AMERICAS

Restaurants get more upscale the farther west you go, as the area between Chapultepec and Américas attests. Nevertheless, many restaurants are accessible to the budget traveler, and the peaceful, residential neighborhood is a welcome break from the topsy-turvy bustle of downtown. To get here, catch a PAR VIAL bus or take a leisurely walk (25 minutes) from downtown. Food ranges from unique regional specialties to fast food.

➢ **UNDER $5** • **Los Itacates.** The Mexican equivalent of the power-lunch meeting place, this restaurant specializes in traditional dishes such as *coachal* (shredded chicken and pork with corn). The house specialty is *pollo itacates* (one-quarter of a chicken with cheese enchiladas, potatoes, and rice). Both dishes are about $3.50. A breakfast buffet is also served for $3. *Chapultepec Nte. 110, tel. 3/625–11–06. A few blocks north of Vallarta. Open Mon.–Sat. 8 AM–11 PM, Sun. 8–7.*

Las Margaritas. A friendly, English-speaking staff and unique vegetarian entrées make this small restaurant a perfect place for lunch *al fresco*. The lentil salad includes cottage cheese, tomato, and onions and is served with bread for $4. The owner is extremely proud of what he claims is his internationally known *cacerola margarita*, a veggie casserole with mushrooms, olives, and soybeans, topped with cheese. Breakfasts are $2–$3, and the comida corrida includes soup, bread, veggies, an entrée, dessert, and coffee for $3. *López Cotilla 1477, at Chapultepec, tel. 3/616–89–06. Open Mon.–Sat. 8 AM–9 PM, Sun. 10–6.*

➢ **UNDER $10** • **Los Otates.** Food here is pricey but delicious, and both indoor and outdoor dining are available. The restaurant is hailed in Guadalajara for its *molcajete* dishes ($3–$7), mixtures of meat or seafood, salsa, and spices served in a large stone bowl with tortillas. Try the *crepas de huitlacoche* (corn fungus-filled crepes). *López Cotilla 1835, tel. 3/615–63–01. Open Mon.–Sat. 8 AM–midnight, Sun. 9–7.*

PLAZA DEL SOL

Plaza del Sol is a massive open-air shopping mall popular with Guadalajara's nouveaux riches. The neon lights, pulsing rock music, and not-so-subliminal messages to shop like crazy will soon have you longing for the taco stands and grittier life of downtown. On the plus side, the food around here is excellent, if a bit expensive.

Dainzú. In the middle of an upper-class residential neighborhood, this small restaurant introduced Oaxacan cuisine to Guadalajara in 1986. The soups ($2) are fantastic; classic Oaxacan entrées such as *tlayuda con tasajo* ($7), a large corn tortilla cooked with black beans and cheese and a huge slab of marinated meat on the side, easily fill two after a serving of soup. *Diamante 2598-A, tel. 3/647–50–86. From Mariano Otero, east past Expo to Av. Faro, then right on Diamante. Open Tues.–Sat. 1–10:30, Sun. 1–8.*

CAFES **El Café.** If you're going to take in a movie at the **Videosala** (see After Dark, below), this place next door offers outdoor tables on a lush patio and a bizarre, quasi-Victorian atmosphere indoors, complete with velvet and huge, costumed dolls. Coffee drinks run $1–$2, and they also have light sandwiches and desserts for $2–$3. Hidalgo 1292, no phone. Open Mon.–Sat. 9 AM–10 PM.

Café La Paloma. La Paloma hops every night of the week with a few bohemian types scattered among the Guadalajaran youth, all smoking and looking cool. Coffee and beers are both $1, and you can fill up on various tacos and tortas for about $2. The house specialty, Santa Perico (Kahlua, Rompope, vodka, and pineapple juice) will jolt you back to life for $2. López Cotilla 1855, tel. 3/630–01–95. 1 block west of Av. de las Américas. Open daily 9 AM–10 PM.

WORTH SEEING

Most of Guadalajara's sights are on or around the Plaza Tapatía, in what is known as the *centro histórico* (historic center). To tour this area, get a map of the center from the tourist office and hoof it. Although Guadalajara's three important suburbs (Tlaquepaque, Tonalá, and Zapopan) are officially separate from the city, they have been engulfed by the metropolis and are easily reached by city bus.

CENTRO HISTORICO The most important church in Guadalajara is the **Catedral.** Completed in 1618 after 57 years of work, Guadalajara's religious centerpiece has undergone numerous modifications over the centuries, culminating in an eclectic combination of baroque, Renaissance, Moorish, and neo-Gothic styles. Its twin yellow spires were added in 1854, after an earthquake destroyed the original towers. The cathedral contains an excellent collection of religious art, relics of Guadalajara's colonial-era wealth and importance. King Fernando VII of Spain gave the city 10 silver-and-gilt altars in gratitude for financial aid during the Napoleonic Wars. Carved from a single piece of balsa, the altar and statue dedicated to Our Lady of the Rose was a gift from King Carlos V in the 16th century. To the right of the main altar are the remains of St. Innocence, brought here from the catacombs in Rome. Over the sacristy is Bartolomé Esteban Murillos's *La Concepción Inmaculada*. The schedule for mass is posted at the entryway. The service is especially beautiful and solemn—don't wander around gawking during the ceremony, as some tourists have been known to do. Hidalgo, at Alcalde. Open daily 7 AM–9 PM.

Those unashamed of being tourists can take a ride on one of the numerous calandrias (horse-drawn carriages) that crowd the center. A 45-minute scenic tour costs $10, but it sure beats walking for a change.

➤ **CHURCHES** • The baroque **Iglesia de San Francisco de Asis** was one of Guadalajara's first churches. Columns with vine-like ornamentation in the entryway lead into the plateresque interior. Note the Santo Niño de Atocha with a homemade sweater and little bears to the right of the main altar. *16 de Septiembre, at Prisciliano Sánchez.*

The **Capilla de Nuestra Señora de Aranzazu** is the only remaining chapel of the five that once surrounded the Iglesia de San Francisco; the others have been demolished. The chapel is unique among Guadalajara's churches because of its three richly detailed wooden churrigueresque (ultra-baroque) altarpieces, considered among the finest in the world. Their physical size and presence overpower the small interior of the church for a fascinating effect. *16 de Septiembre, at Prisciliano Sánchez.*

The **Templo de Santa Mónica** was built in 1773 for the Augustinian nuns who lived next door. The church is considered one of the city's finest examples of baroque architecture, and residents regard it as one of the loveliest churches as well. In the northwest corner of the building is a statue of St. Christopher with mestizo features. *Santa Mónica, at San Felipe.*

➤ **INSTITUTO CULTURAL CABANAS** • Built between 1805 and 1810, this place was an orphanage until 1979. An important example of neoclassical architecture and full of wonderful courtyards, it now houses the city's cultural center, with art exhibits, a small theater/cinema, and a cafeteria. In the late 1930s, José Clemente Orozco painted a series of murals on the ceiling and walls of the building's main chapel, including what is considered his finest work, *The Man of Fire*. Besides the murals, some of Orozco's lithographs and paintings are on display here. Excellent tours are given in both Spanish and English. Guides work on a volunteer basis and should be tipped—$2 is appropriate. *Hospicio 8, east end of Plaza Tapatía, tel. 3/618–81–35. Admission: $1.50, 50¢ students; free Sun. Open Tues.–Sat. 10–6, Sun. 10–3.*

➤ **MERCADO LIBERTAD (SAN JUAN DE DIOS)** • Heavily promoted by the tourism department, this market is just a larger version of markets found all over Mexico. The existing market was built in the 1950s (which explains the architecture), but people have been buying and selling here for more than 400 years. Three stories of jam-packed stalls and shouting vendors are more than sufficient to satisfy the pickiest shopper or cultural anthropologist. There's a large, cheap food area as well. Next to the market is the **Plaza de los Mariachis** (*see* After Dark, *below*). *Javier Mina and Calz. Independencia Sur. Open daily 6 AM–8 PM.*

➤ **MUSEO REGIONAL DE GUADALAJARA** • The displays of pre-Columbian artifacts here are impressive, and the exhibit tracing Jalisco's history is interesting if you read Spanish. There's also a collection of colonial paintings, the most impressive of which is the newly restored *Alegoría del Paraíso de las Monjas Carmelitas*. In this 17th-century painting, a crucified Jesus's spurting blood turns into a field of flowers, plants, and trees at his feet, while a group of Carmelite nuns looks on approvingly. *Liceo 60, north side of Plaza de la Liberación, tel. 3/614–99–57. Admission: $2.50, free Sun. and holidays. Open Tues.–Sun. 9–3:45.*

➤ **PALACIO DE GOBIERNO** • The governor of New Galicia (a colonial administrative region including what is now Jalisco, Nayarit, and southern Sinaloa) had this stately churrigueresque mansion built in 1643. It was here that independence fighter Miguel Hidalgo decreed the abolition of slavery in 1810, and where Benito Juárez was almost assassinated by his enemies in 1858, before Don Guillermo Prieto stopped the would-be killers with the now-famous phrase, "*Los valientes no asesinan*" (The brave do not kill). Today, the main attraction is Orozco's dramatic *Social Struggle* in the stairwell on the right. It features a huge portrait of a white-haired Hidalgo jumping out from the chaos of war, fascism, communism, and ecclesiastical oppression. *Corona, btw Morelos and Pedro Moreno. Admission free. Open daily 9–9.*

Across the street is the **Plaza de Armas**. France donated the wrought-iron kiosk, which is decorated with half-naked women, in 1910. Today, the bright green kiosk is surrounded by eerie contrasts—small children run around feeding flocks of pigeons, while political banners and hunger strikers' tents are pitched in a corner. Municipal bands give free concerts here Thursday and Sunday at 7 PM.

➤ **TEATRO DEGOLLADO** • One of Guadalajara's most cherished possessions is this neoclassical opera house, modeled after Milan's La Scala and opened in 1866. Above the Corinthian columns grandly marking the theater's entrance is a relief depicting Apollo and the nine Muses. The interior was exquisitely restored in 1988, and if you don't attend a performance here, make sure to take a look when it's open to the public. The university's renowned **Ballet Folklórico** performs here every Sunday at 10 AM. Tickets range from $2.50 to $10. For some strange reason, the main gringo attraction at the theater is the postcard stand in the lobby. *Belén, at Hidalgo, box office tel. 3/614–47–73. Box office open daily 10–1 and 4–7. Theater open to public Mon.–Sat. 10–2.*

➤ **UNIVERSIDAD DE GUADALAJARA** • The university's administrative offices are in a beautiful turn-of-the-century building. Two famous Orozco murals are on view at the auditorium, one on the dome and another behind the stage. Across the street, take the elevator to the top floor of the university's main building (a big cement block) for a good view of southeastern Guadalajara. The **Cine Foro** in the basement of the same building puts on movies, plays, and concerts; check the billboard at the box office for upcoming events. One block south of the university is the **Templo Expiatorio** (Madero and Escorza), a pseudo-Gothic cathedral that's just been completed after nearly 100 years of construction. It's so dark and imposing that you almost expect to hear Gregorian chants issuing from the choir. *Vallarta, at Enrique Díaz de León. Take Bus PAR VIAL west on Juárez and ask to be let off on Guadalajara.*

SOUTH OF THE CENTRO HISTORICO Guadalajara's premier getaway is the **Parque Agua Azul**. Nine hectares of eucalyptus, pine, and jacaranda entice you onto shady paths, benches, and grassy spots. There's also a small orchid greenhouse, a butterfly house, and a huge aviary where you can get up close and personal with parrots, peacocks, and other exotic birds. *Calz. Independencia Sur, just south of Niños Héroes. Take Bus 62 south on Independencia and ask to be let off at Niños Héroes. Admission: $1. Open Tues.–Sun. 10–5:30.*

At the northern end of the park is the **Casa de Artesanías de Jalisco**, a fabulous government-run crafts store, laid out like a museum with examples of crafts from various regions in Mexico. Prices here are generally too high for mere mortals, but it's a good place to check out quality items before buying from street vendors. *Calz. Gallo 20, tel. 3/619–46–64. Next to park cafeteria. Open weekdays 10–7, Sat. 10–4, Sun. 11–3.*

The **Teatro Experimental de Jalisco**, next to the park's main entrance, performs everything from Shakespeare to Mexican avant-garde. Check the bulletin board near the park entrance, or take a glance at *Tentaciones* (*see* After Dark, *below*), or call 3/619–37–70 for information.

The **Museo de Arqueología del Occidente** is small, well-organized, and packed with pottery produced by indigenous peoples of western Mexico. *Calz. Independencia Sur, at Calz. Campesino, across from the park. Admission: 20¢. Open Tues.–Sun. 10–2 and 4–7.*

TLAQUEPAQUE Guadalajara's elite made Tlaquepaque a country retreat, but Guadalajara's automobiles and city sprawl later impinged on its rustic appeal. The town's spacious country homes fell into disrepair and continued to deteriorate until the 1960s, when artists converted the buildings into studios. Today, Tlaquepaque's center is a lively and colorful pedestrian zone lined with gallery after gallery of often overpriced handmade crafts and rustic furniture. Browsing is perfectly acceptable, and, as always, the vendors on the street offer a better deal and often a better selection on most items.

The main drag in Tlaquepaque is Independencia, a pedestrian-only street. **Artmex la Rosa de Cristal** (Independencia 232, tel. 3/639–71–80), a glass manufacturer, opens its studio to the public on weekdays 10–2 and Saturdays 10–noon; go for a demonstration of the ancient craft of glassblowing and then browse through the shop. The free **Museo Regional de la Cerámica** (Independencia 237), housed in an old country estate, exhibits the wonderful work of master potters and operates a small gift shop. Independencia ends in the lively **El Parián** plaza (Independencia and Madero). Named after the Chinese section of Manila, the plaza is a great place to grab a beer and refuse the advances of mariachi bands and portrait artists. Several bars are situated on the outer part of the plaza, while the gazebo in the center features local bands on weekends. For maps, information on festivals, or any other queries, head to the **tourist office** (tel. 3/635–05–96) at Sánchez 74, right next to the post office. *To Tlaquepaque, take Bus 275 or 275-A south on 16 de Septiembre; after traveling about ½ hr down Revolución, get off at small traffic circle just after passing under brick arches, and walk NW to Independencia.*

Tonalá was governed by a woman, Cihualpilli Tzapotzintli, when the Spaniards arrived in 1530. She decided to welcome the newcomers peacefully, despite the opposition of her male advisors. So much for women's intuition.

Nearly all of the restaurants here are overpriced, so if you're going to have a sit-down meal, go where it's worth the extra pesos. **Restaurante Sin Nombre** (Madero 80, tel. 3/695–45–20; open daily 8 AM–9 PM) has excellent food, served on a beautiful outdoor patio. The waiter will recite you the menu in English or Spanish as peacocks crow in the background. Soups and salads are around $3, main dishes around $6. Meat lovers can sample a $3 plate of *birria* (roasted goat or pork stew) at **Birriería El Sope** (D. Guerra 142, tel. 3/635–65–38). The restaurant is open daily 9–7.

TONALA This smaller, humbler version of Tlaquepaque is also a famous crafts center. In fact, many of the ceramics and other crafts sold in Tlaquepaque are made here, where prices are cheaper. The simple adobe houses and more down-to-earth feel of the town draw those tired of the tourist track (although

Tlaquepaque

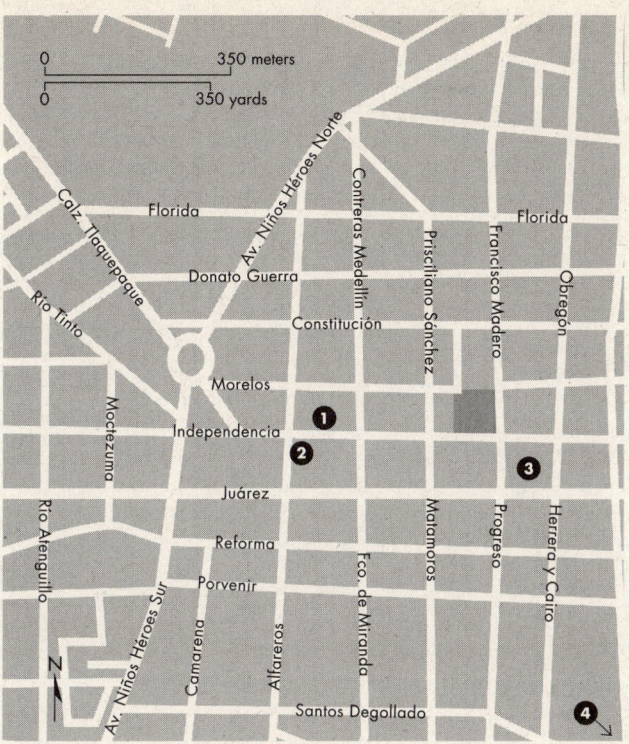

Artmex la Rosa de Cristal, **1**
El Parián, **3**
Museo Regional de la Cerámica, **2**
Tonalá, **4**

plenty of full-on tourists come here as well). The small tourist-information booth right on the Plaza Principal gives out maps and entertaining brochures, and the staff is quite friendly. Every Thursday and Sunday from 8 to 4 there is a *tianguis* (open-air market) whose alfresco vendors sell local wares at discount prices, as well as trinkets from Hong Kong. The free **Museo Nacional de la Cerámica** (Constitución 110, tel. 3/683–04–94; open Tues.–Sun. 9–1 and 4–6) displays pottery from different states and eras and has a workshop and small store. Also worth a visit is the **Santuario del Sagrado Corazón**, with its brightly painted interior and Sacred Heart sculptures. Behind the altar is a striking representation of Jesus Christ rising from the earth amidst huge, gray clouds. Also, don't miss the chance to witness a charreada complete with lassoes and wild-horse taming. **Lienzo Charro González Valle** stages these rodeos every Saturday at 4 PM; tickets are $3. *To reach Tonalá, take Bus 275 or 275-A south on 16 de Septiembre, past Tlaquepaque.*

ZAPOPAN Another victim of Guadalajara's voracious appetite is Zapopan, about 11 kilometers north of Guadalajara's center. Zapopan boasts the **Basílica de Zapopan**, an 18th-century structure that has an ornate baroque facade and a tiled dome, and which is home to the **Virgen de Zapopan**. This 10-inch figurine is said to be one of Mexico's strongest miracle-workers; veneration culminates in a pilgrimage every October 12, when over one million of the faithful honor the figurine's return to the basilica after her annual tour of every church in her diocese. The statuette first achieved fame in 1541, when it is said to have inspired disorganized Spanish troops who were attempting to crush an indigenous uprising. The small **Museo Huichol,** at the east end of the basilica, is run by a priest who proselytizes among the Huichol people (*see box, below*). The museum exhibits colorful examples of clothing, beadwork, and the unique, elaborate renditions of Huichol myths "painted" entirely with yarn. Most items are for sale; proceeds benefit the Huichol people. For more information, Zapopan's **visitor information** center is in the **Casa de Cultura** (Vicente Guerrero 233, tel. 3/633–05–71). *To Zapopan, take Bus 275 north on 16 de Septiembre.*

CHEAP THRILLS

On the northeastern edge of Guadalajara, Calzada Independencia comes to an abrupt end at the **Barranca de Oblatos,** a 630-meter-deep canyon. On weekends, the canyon park lures families with its numerous jungle gyms; others are drawn by spectacular views of the landscape and its vegetation. Especially worthwhile is the **Cola de Caballo** (Horsetail) waterfall near the mirador. *Take* MIRADOR *bus north on Calz. Independencia until it turns left on Volcán Zacapu. Admission: 20¢. Open daily 7–7.*

A full Sunday, and then some, could be spent browsing the rows of stands in **El Baratillo,** Mexico's second-largest outdoor market. Stretching primarily along Javier Mina, it forms a huge maze covering some 30–40 city blocks. Just when you think you've seen it all—the shoelaces, cassettes, vegetables, new and used clothes, a new drill press, live pigs and goats—something else pops up. *Take* PAR VIAL *bus east on Hidalgo until you see market. Open Sun. 8* AM*–4* PM.

Still looking for that long-lost Andy Gibb record? Then head on over to the **Roxy and Roll** record store, where vinyl is alive and well in a variety of used records, from John Denver and Olivia Newton-John to obscure jazz and classical. The records are $2.50–$3. *Mezquitan 126, btw Juan Manuel and Independencia, near Centro Cultural Roxy. Open Mon.–Sat. 10–8.*

If you didn't get enough dancing on Saturday night, head out to the *tardeada* (afternoon dance) held outside the arena after the bullfights in the small town of **Santa María Tequisquiapan.** Cowboy culture appears in all its glory—men in cowboy hats and boots swing their partners to *ranchera* music. Admission is $2 (women can usually get in free), and the fun lasts from about 5 to 10 PM. Check with the tourist office to see if there's a bullfight that Sunday. *Take tren ligero south to Periférico Sur stop and ask someone to point you toward Santa María Tequisquiapan; it's a 10-min walk.*

FESTIVALS

Lake Chapala (*see* Near Guadalajara, *below*) is the place to be for **Carnaval** (late February or early March). The **Fiestas de Junio,** from mid-June to early July, celebrate the artesanía of Tlaquepaque with music, dancing, cockfights, and loads of food and drink.

The **Fiesta de Santiago Apostol** takes place in Tonalá every July 25. The fair lasts all day and culminates in the *Danza de los Tastoanes,* an indigenous dance reenacting the Spanish conquest.

The Struggle of the Huichol

Most Huichol Indians live in northern Jalisco and southern Nayarit, in a 240,000-hectare reservation granted them in 1953. The reservation is only accessible by plane, and often the Huichol will travel for five days to bring their handicrafts to the museum in Zapopan. Although the Catholic Church, specifically the Franciscan order, has made a slight dent in the Huichol's religious beliefs, their primary spiritual leaders are shamans, who have a great deal of political influence in the Huichol community. The people insist on maintaining their traditions, as well as their land, resulting in an ongoing conflict with local landowners. Twenty-two hectares are currently in dispute, and there have been allegations of human rights violations perpetrated by landowners. The government's Human Rights Comission (CEDH) has been investigating the violations since 1993 and has granted some financial and political support to the Huichol, but no resolution has been found. With the PRI governing party facing serious challenges, it's unlikely the Huichol problem will receive much attention in the near future.

The **Fiestas de Octubre** is Guadalajara's month-long commercial and cultural fair. If you're not interested in exhibits demonstrating the richness of Jalisco's agriculture and industry, then pottery demonstrations, cheese and wine tastings, and musical performances—from folk to experimental—should keep you busy. Smack in the middle of the Fiestas de Octubre, on October 12th, Guadalajara celebrates the **Día de la Virgen de Zapopan** (*see* Worth Seeing, *above*), when pilgrims walk the 7 kilometers between Guadalajara's cathedral and Zapopan's basilica.

AFTER DARK

Guadalajara has raging nightlife almost seven nights a week, despite the best efforts of city government. Guadalajara once rivaled Mexico City in good times till daybreak, but now ordinances require all fun to stop at 2 AM. Of course, it doesn't. Plenty of bars keep going until 3, and there are always taco stands open until dawn.

The beauty of nightlife here is its diversity. The old standbys—bars and discos—are clustered around Avenidas Chapultepec and Vallarta, though you'll need plenty of money and connections for the guy at the door to decide you're cool enough to get in. The alternative scene is also alive and well. Raves, complete with ecstasy and other Alice-in-Wonderland digestibles, are currently outlawed, but they continue underground. For information on the alternative scene, check with the guys at **El Quinto Poder** music shop (Madero 210, tel. 3/614–05–42) or at **Centro Cultural Roxy** (*see* Music, *below*). For a calmer evening, check out *Siglo 21*, a daily paper that lists movies, theaters, galleries, music, and dance. The Friday entertainment section, called "Tentaciones," has the most expansive information. The Sunday edition of *El Informador* also has a good listing of upcoming events.

The San Francisco of Mexico, Guadalajara boasts a substantial gay population and has plenty of happening gay and lesbian clubs. Obregón and Calles 50–60 encompass one of the more popular gay districts, although places are scattered throughout the city.

Flanking the cathedral are three quasi-plazas, **Plaza de Armas, Plaza Libertad,** and **Plaza de la Liberación,** that buzz with frolicking people of all ages during the evening, especially on weekends. Caricaturists and marimba players call out to passersby, while mimes, puppet shows, and musicians enthrall small crowds. In the bandstand of the Plaza de Armas, the Jalisco State Band gives free concerts (the sounds of which are piped into the Plaza de la Liberación) Thursday and Sunday at 7 PM.

Next to the Iglesia San Juan de Dios and Mercado Libertad, the **Plaza de los Mariachis** is actually a large alley lined with tables and worked by strolling musicians. Songs cost about $5

The $30,000 Cock

If you're interested in learning more about Mexican culture—and the Mexican psyche—drop by Veterinaria Gallero, a store that specializes in fighting cocks. Those for sale are on display, and if you have about $120, you too could be the proud owner of a (cheap) fighting cock. Mexican cocks fight with various types of weapons attached to their feet, from the inch-long arma de filo (blade) to the shorter navaja corta (razor). Cocks of Asian origin are favored, as are those with shorter spurs. The friendly vet will happily answer your questions about the contests and tell you where to find one. Normal wagers for cockfights are about $30–$50, though they can climb as high as $30,000. Losses like this can be a double bummer, for not only are you suddenly destitute, but your favored cock is a heap of dead feathers. Calz. Independencia Sur 500, tel. 3/658–18–40. Open weekdays 9:30–2 and 4–7, Sat. 9:30–2:30.

apiece, but you hardly need to pay for them or understand the lyrics to enjoy them. Sit at the first set of tables near the entrance, grab a $1 beer, and weep loudly as the music tugs your heartstrings.

BARS **Black Beards.** This bar is a Guadalajara institution. Come to hear live jazz and blues Thursday and Saturday. Other days, the music varies. The $4 cover includes two drinks. *Justo Sierra 2194, no phone. Open Wed. noon–11, Thurs.–Sun. noon–3 AM. Wheelchair access.*

Duran Duran. Okay, so the name is super-cheesy, but it's *the* place to hang out as you make up your mind where to end up for the night. Beer is cheap (less than $1), and the *queso fundido* (tortillas with melted cheese) kills the sharpest of hunger pangs for $2. *Juárez 14, at Huerta, tel. 3/614–60–19. Open daily noon–midnight.*

Subterraneo. Guadalajara's number-one alternative hangout is a long, dim bar with tables on the back patio. Patrons average at least five (visible) piercings. Live rock is the musical offering Fridays, and Saturday is the only day with a cover, when you're required to down $2 worth of drinks. The dark beer is so good it won't feel like much of a sacrifice. *Vallarta 1480, at Chapultepec, no phone. Open Tues.–Sun. 8 PM–1 AM.*

Vantage. Escape the teenyboppers who dominate other bars. The 25–30 set hangs out here, and gays and lesbians will feel comfortable in the mixed crowd. Wednesday nights are free for women—otherwise everyone pays $3. Beers are $1.50, mixed drinks $2. *Lope de Vega 325, tel. 3/616–88–02. Open Wed.–Sat. 9:30 PM–3 AM.*

CINEMAS Dozens of theaters around the city show fairly recent undubbed American and other foreign films. Current listings are in the daily paper *Siglo 21*. The **Cine Foro** at the Universidad de Guadalajara and the cinema at the Instituto Cultural Cabañas are good places for quality movies (*see* Worth Seeing, *above*). Tickets are usually around $1.50.

The University of Guadalajara's **Videosala** (Hidalgo 1296, tel. 36/25–57–23) shows videos of foreign and national art films weekdays for $3. They put out a monthly program guide, available there or at the info booth in the university building on Vallarta. Videosala also has rooms devoted to works made in video, both foreign and domestic, from video art to TV docudramas.

DANCING Guadalajara has its share of big, flashy, and rather expensive discos. Come here to hang out with the city's hip, upper-middle-class youth and dance to the latest disco sounds. Among the "in" and trendy, **Lado B** (Vallarta 2451, tel. 3/616–82–97), with a wacky setting and unwacky music and crowd, competes with **La Marcha** (Vallarta 2648, tel. 3/615–89–99), a baroque-style disco. Both offer all-you-can-drink open bars in exchange for having to shell out $6 if you're female, $12 if you're male. To rub elbows with Guadalajara's Porsche-driving youth, saunter into **El Metro** (Pablo Neruda 3980, near Universidad Autónoma, tel. 3/640–30–57).

Of the *salones* (dance halls) that host live *bandas* playing traditional Mexican music, **Salón Corona** (López Mateos 2380, tel. 3/647–08–82) is one of the best. Women get in free Monday–Thursday. Also renowned is **Copacabana** (López Mateos, no phone), which plays live salsa and merengue; cover is $3. **Casino Veracruz** (Manzano 486, tel. 3/613–44–22) has tropical and salsa music; cover is $2.50.

GAY BARS AND CLUBS The place to be during the week is the coverless **Máscaras** (Maestranzas 238, at P. Sánchez, tel. 3/614–81–03). On weekends, the three main discos heat up: **Mónica's** (Obregón 1713, near Calle 64) is mostly for gay men while **La Malinche** (Obregón 1230, near Calle 50) attracts transvestites and lesbians. **S.O.S.** (Av. de la Paz 1413, at Federalismo) is the hottest club for both gays and lesbians. All three charge a $3.50 cover and feature transvestite shows.

MUSIC The **Centro Cultural Roxy** (Mezquitan 80, at Hidalgo, tel. 3/658–00–53), in a converted art-deco movie theater, is *the* hip urban/underground hangout in Guadalajara. The art gallery Galería Margaritte is in front, while dance, theater, performance art, movies, and live music (everything from rock to reggae) are put on in the gutted theater. Come here to sample Mexico's best (usually) underground bands. Shows are normally Thursday–Sunday, but call beforehand or check *Tentaciones* for more information.

Peña Cuicacalli is Guadalajara's most popular *casa del canto*. The large, dim *peña* (club) attracts a mixed, enthusiastic audience. Music ranges from folk to salsa to *nueva canción* and rock. Cover varies from $2.50 to $5. *Niños Héroes 1988, tel. 3/625–46–90. Intersection of Glorieta Niños Héroes and Chapultepec. Open Tues.–Sun.; hours vary.*

La Peñita Teccizli is a restaurant with nightly live music similar to that found at Cuicacalli, and a friendly, peña ambience predominates. Sundays are free nights; other nights you pay about $2–$5 to hear jazz, Afro-Antillean, blues, and Latin American music. The music usually starts at 9 PM (7 PM on Sundays). The tourist office has monthly performance schedules. Beer is $1.50, wine, $2. *Vallarta 1110, tel. 3/625–58–53. Open daily noon–midnight.*

Near Guadalajara

LAKE CHAPALA

Mexico's largest lake, bordered by green, almost-tropical mountains, is a pleasant place to spend the weekend. Although the lake itself is plagued by severe ecological problems—the water from the Río Lerma is severely polluted, and huge pipelines pump water daily toward Guadalajara—the area offers a number of recreational activities, including the opportunity to take a budget-unfriendly $15 boat ride to Scorpion Island.

The town of Chapala is a popular retirement community, and during the week English is frequently heard in the town's restaurants. On weekends, families from Guadalajara take over the boardwalk, and the air is festive with the sounds of vendors hawking ice cream and fried fish.

In Defense of El Mariachi

Mariachi music has been around since the 16th century, when Mexican bands started playing the son, a type of music from Galicia in northern Spain. At first the bands simply accompanied groups performing popular dances such as the jarabe, but by the 19th century they were gaining popularity and performing without the dancers. It wasn't until the modern age that the insistent trumpets now dominating the mariachi sound were added—commercial radio stations decided that raising the decibel level would make the music more popular.

Mariachi bands today generally consist of two or more guitars, violins, trumpets, and the occasional harp. A guitar thumps in the background while the other instruments hum along at a rip-roaring pace or slow down to jerk tears from listeners. The songs generally concern heartbreak, heavy drinking, and love for the fatherland, and are punctuated by yells and yodels.

Outside Mexico, mariachi music is probably the best known—and least respected—Mexican popular music. The musicians' mournful "ay-ay-ay" and their often-garish costumes lead many foreigners to condemn the genre as tacky. Although high-society Mexican usually describe mariachi as "de pueblo" (lower-class), most of them nevertheless know all the tunes by heart and end up singing along after a few shots of tequila. Sure enough, the music sells, not only in the record stores, but also live, in places like Guadalajara's Plaza de los Mariachis, where listeners shell out up to $5 for a song.

COMING AND GOING Buses leave from the old bus station (*see* Coming and Going, in Guadalajara, *above*) every half-hour 7 AM–8 PM (45 min, $1). Buses to Guadalajara depart every half-hour until 9 PM from the bus station on Madero in Chapala.

WHERE TO SLEEP AND EAT The only cheap place to stay in Chapala is the **Casa de Huéspedes Las Palmitas** (Juárez 531, behind market, tel. 376/5–30–70). Basic rooms in this old converted house cost $5 singles, $7 doubles. A number of fairly decent restaurants hug the lakeshore, and they're not too outrageously priced. **La Playita** (Acapulquito Local 4, tel. 376/5–41–40) serves up big plates of fish and shrimp *al ajo* (with garlic) for $4, but you can get cheaper fare like chiles rellenos for $2. On the boardwalk, vendors sell candy, nuts, and drinks that you can fill up on for even less money. Grab a bag of pistachios ($1 for ¼ kilo), sit on a nearby bench, and watch a slow Sunday afternoon go by.

TEQUILA

As the name suggests, this is the home of Mexico's national drink, tequila. Nearly everyone here works in the *agave* (the cactus from which tequila is made) fields or in one of the town's 10 tequila distilleries. Cuervo, Sauza, and other companies produce their stuff here, and many offer tours in the late morning. **José Cuervo** (24 de Enero 73, 3 blocks from bus station, tel. 374/2–00–11) gives tours Mondays, Tuesdays, and Fridays 11–noon, ending with a free tasting. Groups of more than five people should make an appointment. If you really like tequila, go to the **Herradura** distillery in the nearby town of Amatitán, which makes Mexico's best. You need to make an appointment to take the free tour; call the Herradura office in Guadalajara (3/614–04–00 or 3/614–06–52) and ask to speak to Angélica Cortés.

COMING AND GOING Buses leave from the old bus station (*see* Coming and Going, in Guadalajara, *above*) in Guadalajara every 20 minutes between 6 AM and 9 PM. The trip takes a little less than 2 hours and costs $2.50. If you want to spend the night, Tequila has plenty of cheap places to stay, most catering to migrant workers.

Uruapan

Travelers looking for picturesque towns filled with well-preserved colonial architecure might want to avoid this small highland city. With few exceptions, Uruapan—with blocks of dull modern buildings alongside their run-down colonial ancestors—is difficult to appreciate. The city's true lure is its rich natural setting. The **Parque Nacional Eduardo Ruíz**, just blocks from the center of town, offers a fresh, quiet retreat from city life. Other highlights include an excursion to the **Tzararacua** waterfall and a horseback ride to the inactive (you hope) **Volcán Paricutín**.

Otomí and Chontal people took advantage of the rich vegetation and free-flowing waters for centuries before Spaniards arrived in Uruapan. When Father Juan de San Miguel showed up in 1531, he established a feudal *encomienda* system, reducing the indigenous peoples to serfs upon whose backs agrarian Uruapan grew and prospered. Today it's known for its flower production and for being the world's avocado capital, producing five different varieties of the creamy fruit. Every November, the city trembles with excitement during the week-long **Feria del Aguacate** (Avocado Fair). In fact, Uruapan finds some reason to break out the avocados and *charanda* (a local liquor) almost monthly. Among the biggest events is **Semana Santa** (Holy Week), which includes a parade with people in traditional costumes. On June 30, the **Fiesta de San Pedro** honors the apostle Peter with a parade, band, indigenous dances, and lots of booze. On July 23 the **Fiesta de Santa María de Magdalena** honors the biblical prostitute-turned-saint with processions and performances of traditional dances reenacting battles between Moors and Christians. **El Día de San Francisco** commemorates Uruapan's patron saint October 4 with a dance by Purépecha women.

Even when there's no festival going on, the people of Uruapan are friendly and the occasional visitor is received with open-armed hospitality. Surprisingly, the city has a sizable population of hipster/slacker/artist types, much like those you'd find in San Miguel de Allende, with the requisite alternative attitude, long hair, and recreational drug use.

BASICS

CASAS DE CAMBIO **Banamex** (Morelos, at Cupatitzio, tel. 452/3–92–90) changes traveler's checks and cash 9 AM–noon weekdays and has an ATM that accepts Cirrus and Plus cards. Inside the bank, you can get one of those dangerously tempting cash advances on your Visa or MasterCard. On Saturdays, change money at **Compra y Venta de Dólares.** Cupatitzio 34, tel. 452/4–79–00. 1½ blocks south of Jardín Morelos. Open weekdays 9–2 and 4–7, Sat. 9–2.

EMERGENCIES For emergency assistance or an **ambulance,** call the **police** (tel. 452/4–06–20).

MAIL The full-service post office will hold mail sent to you at the following address for up to 10 days: Lista de Correos, Uruapan, Michoacán, CP 60001, México. *Reforma 13, tel. 452/3–56–30. From Jardín Morelos, walk 3 blocks south on Cupatitzio, left on Reforma. Open weekdays 8–7, Sat. 9–1.*

MEDICAL AID The **Hospital Civil** (La Quinta 6, tel. 452/3–46–60) in front of the Parque Nacional has emergency service and a 24-hour pharmacy. Other pharmacies in town rotate night hours on a monthly basis—ask any one of them to find out who's on duty.

PHONES The caseta de larga distancia at the **Restaurant Las Palmas** (Donato Guerra 2, tel. 452/4–65–45) charges a $1 connection fee for a collect call. **Ladatel** phones are a rare find, but there are some in working order south of the plaza, on the corner of Morelos and Aldama. Ladatel cards can be purchased on Jardín Morelos, in **Kodak Photo 30** (Portal Carrillo 14).

VISITOR INFORMATION The town's tourist office provides cheerful attention, maps, and lots of information on where to go and how to get there. Some staff members speak English. *Ocampo 64, downstairs in Hotel Plaza, tel. 452/3–61–72. Open Mon.–Sat. 9–2 and 4–7, Sun. 9–2.*

COMING AND GOING

BY BUS The **Central de Autobuses de Uruapan** (Carretera a Pátzcuaro Km. 1, tel. 452/3–44–05) is about 3 kilometers northeast of Jardín Morelos. Buses marked CENTRO go to the town center; buses to the terminal from downtown are marked CENTRAL. A taxi from the bus station to the center of town should be about $2. **Flecha Amarilla** (tel. 452/4–39–82), the cheapest line, has buses to Guadalajara (2 per day, 6 hrs, $6), Mexico City (3 per day, 8 hrs, $11), Querétaro (4 per day, 6 hrs, $7), and San Luis Potosí (3 per day, 9 hrs, $10). **ETN** (tel. 452/3–86–08), the cushy line, takes passengers to Guadalajara (6 per day, 4½ hrs, $13), Mexico City (6 per day, 6 hrs, $20), and Morelia (4 per day, 2 hrs, $8). For short distances try **Ruta Paraíso** (tel. 452/4–41–54) or **Autotransportes Galeana** (no phone), both of which have service to Pátzcuaro every 15 minutes. The bus station has a caseta de larga distancia and luggage storage.

BY TRAIN The station is about 11 blocks from the center of town, and easily accessible by the FERR bus or taxi ($1.50). Trains to Mexico City leave at 6:35 AM (2nd class) and 7:15 PM (1st class), making stops in Pátzcuaro and Morelia as well as other cities. The trip all the way to the capital costs $9 first class, $5 second class. A train also leaves for the coastal city of Lázaro Cárdenas (6 hrs; $5 1st class, $3 2nd class) daily at 10 AM. *Paseo Lázaro Cárdenas, at end of Av. Américas, tel. 452/4–09–81. Ticket office open Mon. and Wed.–Sat. 7:30–7:30, Tues. and Sun. 9–12:30 and 4–7:15.*

GETTING AROUND

Although the city is fairly large, three areas are of most interest to the visitor—the bus station, the **Jardín Morelos** (main plaza), and the strip of bars on Paseo Lázaro Cárdenas. Most buses pass the Jardín Morelos, and routes or destinations are written on the windshield. You'll have to take a taxi to sample the nightlife on Lázaro Cárdenas, since buses (20¢) only run 6 AM–9 PM. Taxi fare is about $1.50.

WHERE TO SLEEP

Most of the hotels directly on the Jardín Morelos have seen better days or are out of budget range. Fortunately, there are decent, inexpensive hotels within a short walk of the jardín. Tourism isn't big in Uruapan, so you should never have trouble getting a room, even when the city's festivals are in full swing. Roughing it should be feasible on the Jardín Morelos, but after the cold and rain, you'll be heading staight for a hotel.

Hotel Capri. The paint is peeling in these dark rooms, but they're clean and have adequate bathrooms. The friendly owners go to extreme lengths to make you feel at home. Rooms with one bed are $4; with two they're $5. *Portal Santo Degollado 10, no phone. 28 rooms, all with bath. Luggage storage. Wheelchair access.*

Hotel del Parque. The plain, medium-size rooms here are clean and airy, and couches and a TV in the lobby invite you to hang out with the families who share the place with you. If you don't mind the seven-block walk to the center, you'll appreciate the location in front of the Parque Nacional. Singles are $6, doubles $8. *Independencia, at La Quinta, tel. 452/4-38-45. 14 rooms, all with bath.*

Hotel Mi Solar. If spacious rooms, an indoor patio, and clean bathrooms with hot water do it for you, stay here. The hotel is popular with foreign travelers in transit, so chances are you'll hear someone singing Dylan next door. The manager is so friendly he'll willingly sacrifice a few moments from his precious *telenovela* (soap opera) to make sure you have all you need. Singles are $6, doubles $8. *Juan Delgado 10, tel. 452/2-09-12. 2 blocks north of Jardín Morelos. 20 rooms, all with bath. Wheelchair access.*

Hotel Villa de Flores. As the name would suggest, flowers fill the halls here, accenting the whitewashed walls and black wrought iron. Rooms are large and clean and have balconies, phones, and TVs, making this hotel worth the extra expense. Singles and doubles are a bargain at $12 and $16 respectively. There's also a great restaurant in the hotel, open 7 AM–10 PM. *Carranza 15, tel. 452/4-28-00. 2 blocks west of Jardín Morelos. 28 rooms, all with bath. Wheelchair access. MC, V.*

FOOD

Uruapan is famous for *aguacates* (avocados), but, strangely enough, there's not a single avocado to be found in town. There is, however, plenty of good food to go around. A picnic lunch from the stands around the Jardín Morelos and behind the Templo de San Francisco (*see* Worth Seeing, *below*) won't set you back more than $2. Produce stands in this area sell wonderful fruits and vegetables, and tamales and fresh cheese can also be found here. Grilled meats are a local specialty.

Boca del Río. A tiny joint facing the Plaza La Ranita, this restaurant serves a *sopa de mariscos* (seafood soup; $4) that is famous throughout the city. You can also get *tostadas de ceviche* (crisp tortilla covered with lemon-marinated fish) for 50¢. *Juan Delgado 2, 1 block north of Jardín Morelos, tel. 452/3-02-03. Open daily 10-5. Wheelchair access.*

Comedor Vegetariano. Although not much to look at, this is the only vegetarian restaurant near the center that serves comidas corridas ($2.50). The 50¢ tortas are delicious, too. *Cnr of Morelos and Aldama, no phone. 2 blocks south and 1 block east of Jardín Morelos. Open daily 1:30 PM–4 PM. Wheelchair access.*

Lonchería La Uno. This tiny kitchen has seating for only about eight people, which makes conversations with your neighbors inevitable. Down-to-earth plates of homemade tacos, gorditas, and tortas are 50¢ each, and *licuados* (smoothies) are 75¢..You can also get a filling *bistec* (steak) for $2. *Independencia 21, tel. 452/3-34-17. Open daily 7-7.*

CAFES **Café La Lucha.** A popular afternoon hangout with a folk-art atmosphere, this comfortable café invites you to do some serious lounging. Musicians often stop by to croon a few pesos out of you. *Café de olla* (coffee flavored with chocolate and cinnamon), espresso, and hot chocolate are a few of the choices (all $1). Pies and pastries are also $1. *García Ortiz 22, tel. 452/4–03–75. ½ block north of Jardín Morelos. Open daily 9–2 and 4–9.*

Café Tradicional de Uruapan. This place has a menu of more than 20 coffees and teas. You can also get just about anything in your coffee, including ice cream ($2) or a stiff shot of brandy ($3). A plain old *café con leche* (coffee with milk) is 60¢. The menu also includes egg breakfasts ($3), and tamales of all types (50¢ each) are served after 6 PM. *Carranza 5-B, no phone. ½ block west of Jardín Morelos. Open daily 8:30–2 and 4–10.*

WORTH SEEING

A good place to get a sense of Uruapan's bustling activity is the **Jardín Morelos.** Though aesthetically uninspiring, the ice-cream vendors and children infuse the garden with liveliness. The **Mercado de Artesanías** is a testament to the fact that there is no city in Michoacán without a crafts market.

DESTILADORA EL TARASCO This distillery gives free tours in Spanish for those who want to know more about *charanda,* the local firewater. Here you can see the whole process, from the fermentation of sugar-cane juice to the distilling and bottling. Tours end with samples of the charanda concoction of your choice. Call before you go. *Km. 26, Carretera, Tazitán, tel. 452/4–00–75. Catch a CALZONZIN pesero on cnr of Obregón and Miguel Silva. Open weekdays 9–2 and 4–7, Sat. 9–2.*

LA HAUPATERA This large colonial structure, established by Fray Juan de San Miguel as a hospital for indigenous people, is now mainly a hangout for families and couples who toss coins into the wishing well or sit and chat on the moss-covered steps. A small museum shows traditional Michoacán handicrafts, and the shop next door has a knowledgeable staff and good bargains on quality crafts. Half a block west is the **Templo de San Francisco,** which has a gorgeous *cantera* (pinkish stone) plateresco exterior but a fairly dull modern interior. *North side of Jardín Morelos. Admission free. Museum open Tues.–Sun. 9:30–1:30 and 3:30–6. Store open daily 9–9.*

PARQUE NACIONAL EDUARDO RUIZ This property, which was a private garden in the 16th century, is now a public park. Here you can see the semitropical flora of Michoacán without stepping outside the city limits. Rich vegetation encroaches upon the stone paths that wind their way among streams, fountains, and waterfalls, and the air is heavy with the moist smell of earth, plants, and wet stone. The west side of the park offers the best scenery. Guides will tell you about the legends of the various fountains for about $1.50, but you might rather buy the book ($1.50) at the ticket window and read silently by a creek. If you're able to shake off that hangover on a Sunday morning, come to the *domingo saludable* (healthy Sunday) held in the park, consisting of free martial arts, yoga, aerobics, and ecology classes. The fun starts at 8 AM. *Calzada La Quinta, 7 blocks west of Jardín Morelos. Admission: 20¢. Open daily 8–6.*

GALLERIES Both **Catharsis** (Américas 48, no phone) and **Temetsi** (Independencia 15-A, tel. 452/4–06–29) display works by local artists. Exhibits change monthly, and if you hang around long enough, you might luck out and get invited to an opening reception, where you can drink white wine and schmooze with Uruapan's cool and friendly artistic community. Flyers announcing upcoming events are posted throughout Jardín Morelos and at the galleries' doors. Both are open daily 11 AM–2 PM.

Tons of good bargains can be found on everything from juice presses and fresh herbs to camouflage uniforms and wacky jewelry in the open-air market held daily under the portales across from the Jardín Morelos. The market winds around the Templo de San Francisco, ending in the Mercado de los Antojitos, where you can sample regional food for $2 a plate.

The Parque Nacional Eduardo Ruíz is the source of the Río Cupatitzio, which has given Uruapan its nickname "Perla del Cupatitzio," meaning Pearl of the Cupatitzio.

AFTER DARK

For a small town, Uruapan has a fairly progressive nightlife. Information on cultural activities such as film and theater is provided by the **Casa de la Cultura.** *García Ortiz 1, tel. 452/4-76-13. Open Mon.-Sat. 8-3 and 4-9.*

There's live blues, jazz, and Latin American folk music at the lesbian-owned **Temetsi** (*see* Galleries Worth Seeing, *above*) on Friday and Saturday nights after 9 PM. Cover is $2-$5 depending on who's playing, and drinks run $1-$2. The bar usually closes down after the show, around midnight. Other joints draw younger crowds who want to dance and scam (though not necessarily in that order). **Euforia's** (Madrid 10, off Lázaro Cárdenas, tel. 452/3-93-32) is a video bar with all-you-can-swill nights on Thursdays (free for women, $8 for men) and a $2 cover on the weekend. **La Scala** (Madrid 12, tel. 452/3-02-74) has a $3 cover for men, $2 for women, and $2-$3 drinks, but an unfortunate tendency to attract high-school students. Before deciding which of the two to hit (they're half a block apart), warm up for the evening at **Frente Café** (Madrid 11-A, tel. 452/3-37-58), open daily 11 AM-1 AM.

Near Uruapan

SAN JUAN PARANGARICUTIRO

A jolting hour-long bus ride will bring you to the small village of **Angahuan,** situated in the midst of a green, mountainous area. The small town sees dozens of tourists daily (in high season), but with its small wooden houses, dirt roads, and shy, reticent women, it's far from being a tourist trap. The **Paradero Turístico de Angahuan** (on edge of town, tel. 452/5-03-83) rents horses ($5) for the 5-kilometer trek to **San Juan Parangaricutiro,** a town buried by lava when Volcán Paricutín erupted in 1943. To reach the paradero (wayside station), you'll have to traverse the village, since it's located at the foot of the trail to San Juan. If you're feeling particularly active or adventurous, you can also hike the trail, but it's safest to follow some kind of group, as the trails tend to be confusing.

In 1943 the Paricutín volcano burst from the middle of an unlucky farmer's cornfield. Lava spouted for 11 years straight until the volcano suddenly fell dormant. The mysterious beast has been quiet ever since—though you never know.

Once you arrive, you'll have to clamber over twisted moss- and plant-speckled lava to see the top of a church that is the only visible part of the buried town. From the church you'll get a great view of the Volcán Paricutín. If you're interested in a longer trip, you can also rent horses to take you to the source of the destruction: Paricutín itself. Horses come with a guide, and the 6-hour round-trip trek should cost about $10 a head. Start out

Paracho

A small indigenous town, Paracho is renowned for its handcrafted guitars; those hanging in Michoacán shops all come from here. The town itself is of no particular interest—the "downtown" area basically consists of shops selling wooden crafts—but if you're in a shopping mood, Paracho merits a visit. If you're in the area in August, however, be sure not to miss the Feria Artesanal de la Guitarra, which attracts folkloric dance groups, luthiers, and the most talented guitarists from around Mexico. The festival lasts one week and is usually held in late August. The tourist office in Uruapan (see above) should have the exact date. Buses to Paracho ($1.50, 45 min) leave from the Central de Autobuses in Uruapan almost every half-hour.

early from Uruapan, pack food and water, and don't worry about finding a guide—he'll find you. From Uruapan's bus station, **Autotransportes Galeana** buses leave for Angahuan (1 hr, 50¢) about every half-hour. The last bus back to Uruapan leaves around 6 PM, but the Paradero Turístico de Angahuan also rents cabins for about $5 per person and provides free campsites. Local families also rent rooms in their homes; any guide should be able to point you in the right direction.

TZARARACUA

Ten kilometers south of Uruapan is the trailhead for a 2½-kilometer trek through a ravine to Tzararacua, a torrential 43-meter blanket of water that emerges from the dense, tropical vegetation, creating a swimming hole below. You can rent horses ($4) for the trip to the waterfall if you don't want to hike; you'll see them when you get off the bus. This is definitely one of the best day trips to be taken from Uruapan, though its popularity has taken a toll on the site in the form of litter and other icky human residue on the edges of the trail. **La Tzararacuita**, about 1 kilometer away from the main waterfall, is smaller and cleaner. To reach the trailhead for the waterfalls, catch a TZARARACUA bus (60¢) from the south side of the Jardín Morelos. Buses generally run on the hour, and the ride takes about 30 minutes.

Pátzcuaro

Bordered by a huge lake and green hills, the cool, rainy city of Pátzcuaro is a welcome sight for any traveler. Monuments, churches, and cobblestone streets give this small town a decidedly colonial feel, but the local Purépecha presence is also very strong. Purépecha women hurry to market early in the morning, while men stand around in circles, deep in conversation. Pátzcuaro's suburbs are expanding rapidly, but the city itself is tranquil, having managed to avoid becoming an overpopulated tourist resort, and 20th-century intrusions mar the colonial setting only slightly. This 19th-century ambience prevails at night, as well: Most hotels have evening curfews, but there's little point in going out, anyway, because the town pretty much shuts down after 10 PM.

A primary reason to visit Pátzcuaro is the surrounding lake region. About 3 kilometers from the town center, **Lake Pátzcuaro** has islands, such as the accessible **Janitzio** (*see* Near Pátzcuaro, *below*), where people of Purépecha descent still live. Not just a great place to relax and enjoy the beauty of the nearby countryside, Pátzcuaro is also home to countless *artesanía* (crafts) shops, and is especially famous for its wooden furniture. If you find yourself in Pátzcuaro on the **Día de los Muertos** (Day of the Dead, November 2), you'll see the town come alive with all-night fiestas. **Semana Santa** (Holy Week) in this city and in the nearby town of Tzintzuntzan (*see* Near Pátzcuaro, *below*) is also special. On Good Friday, locals reenact the Stations of the Cross, and on Holy Saturday they mourn Jesus's death with a silent candlelight procession. **The Día de Nuestra Señora de la Salud** (Day of Our Lady of Health) on December 8 honors the Virgin Mary with traditional Purépecha dances including the dance of Los Viejitos (the old men). A crafts festival, **Tianguis Artesanal**, draws artisans from around Michoacán in the first week of November.

BASICS

CASAS DE CAMBIO **Banamex** (Portal Juárez 32, tel. 434/2–10–31) on the Plaza Bocanegra changes cash and traveler's checks weekday mornings; rates are good, and the lines fairly short. There is also an ATM that accepts Cirrus, Plus, Visa, and MasterCard at Avenida Mendoza 16, half a block away from the bank. **Casa de Cambio Multidivisas** changes cash and traveler's checks and has longer hours. *Padre Lloreda, at Buena Vista, tel. 434/2–3–83. Open weekdays 9–2 and 4–6, Sat. 9–1:30.*

EMERGENCIES For emergency assistance, call the **police** (Ibarra, 3 blocks from center, tel. 434/2–00–04).

LAUNDRY **Lavandería Automática** will wash, dry, and fold your clothes ($2 for 3 kilos). Get here as soon as the place opens if you want same-day service. *Ponce de León 14, tel. 434/2–39–39. ½ block west of Plaza San Francisco. Open Mon.–Sat. 9–2 and 4–8.*

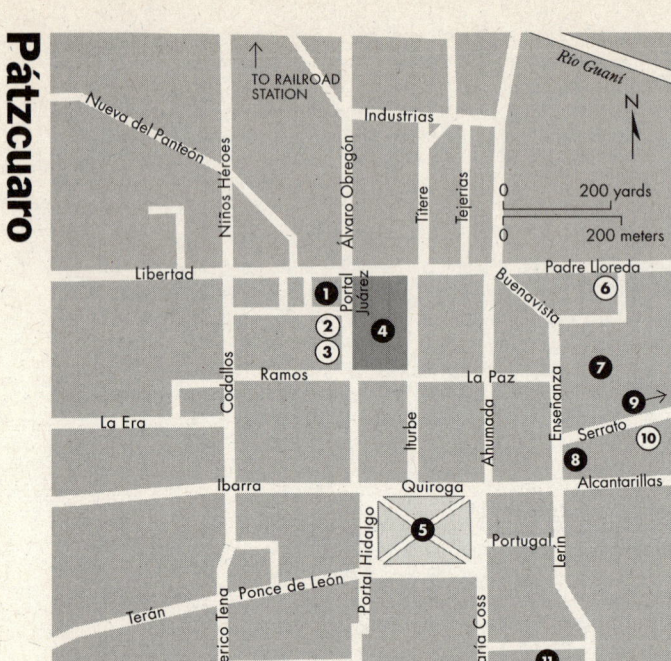

Pátzcuaro

Sights ●
Basílica de
Nuestra Señora, **7**
Casa de los
Once Patios, **11**
El Humilladero, **9**
Mercado, **1**
Museo de Artes
Populares, **8**
Plaza Bocanegra, **4**
Plaza Vasco de
Quiroga, **5**

Lodging ○
Posada de
la Rosa, **3**
Posada de
la Salud, **10**
Hotel
San Agustín, **2**
Hotel Valmen, **6**

MAIL The full-service post office will hold mail sent to you at the following address for up to 10 days: Lista de Correos, Administración de Correos, Pátzcuaro, Michoacán, CP 61600, México. *Obregón 13, tel. 434/2-01-28. 1 block north of Plaza Bocanegra. Open weekdays 9-2 and 4-7, Sat. 9-2.*

MEDICAL AID The **ISSSTE hospital** (Quiroga, tel. 434/2-12-27), a half block west of Plaza Vasco de Quiroga, has 24-hour service. **Farmacia Guadalupana** (Ibarra 34, no phone) is open around the clock. Other pharmacies take turns doing the night shift: Check the billboard under Portal Hidalgo 1, on the west side of the Plaza Vasco de Quiroga, for current information.

PHONES The two main plazas are surrounded by several casetas de larga distancia, but the best rates are at the **Hotel San Agustín**, where they charge a $1 fee for international collect calls. You can ask your party to call you back at no additional charge. *Portal Juárez 19, tel. 434/2-00-41. West side of Plaza Bocanegra. Open daily 8:30 AM-10 PM.*

VISITOR INFORMATION The staff at the **Delegación Regional de Turismo** will try (usually in vain) to answer your questions—maps are pretty much the only useful thing they can provide. *Ibarra 2, tel. 434/2-12-14. A few doors west of Plaza Vasco de Quiroga. Open Mon.-Sat. 9-2 and 4-7, Sun. 9-2.*

COMING AND GOING

BY BUS The **Central de Autobuses Pátzcuaro** (Libramiento Ignacio Zaragoza 2600) is about 1½ kilometers south of the town center. City buses and vans labeled CENTRO leave the station every five minutes or so for the town center and budget lodging areas. **Autobuses del Occidente** (tel. 434/2-00-52) goes to Guadalajara daily at noon (5 hrs, $9); Mexico City (5 hrs, $13) at

9:45 AM and 11:30 AM; and Morelia (1 hr, $1.75) on the hour. **Autotransportes Galeana** (tel. 434/2–08–08) has buses to Morelia (1 hr, $1.75) and Uruapan (1 hr, $1.75) every 15 minutes 6 AM–9 PM. The station also has luggage storage 6 AM–10 PM ($1) and a caseta de larga distancia, open daily 7 AM–8:45 PM.

BY TRAIN The train station is about 3 kilometers from the town center, near the Janitzio boating docks. Trains to Lázaro Cárdenas (9 hrs; $8 1st class, $2.50 2nd class), leave Pátzcuaro at 7 AM and stop in Uruapan (3 hrs; $1.50 1st class, 50¢ 2nd class). The train to Mexico City leaves at 9:30 PM and has first-class seats for $10, second-class assigned seats for $6, and you'll-get-one-if-you're-lucky seats for $2.50. The trip takes about 12 hours. Only second-class service is available to Morelia (1 hr, 50¢); that train leaves at 9:05 AM. There's a 24-hour restaurant across the street from the station where you can fortify yourself for a long ride. *Paseo Lázaro Cárdenas, tel. 434/2–08–03. Ticket window opens ½ hr before every departure.*

GETTING AROUND

You might have trouble finding street signs in Pátzcuaro—they're either high up on buildings or otherwise in the most improbable places—but the central area is small. Most points of interest are within walking distance of the two main plazas, the small and busy **Plaza Bocanegra** (also called Plaza Chica) and the **Plaza Vasco de Quiroga,** one block to the south. Streets change names at both plazas, and around the Plaza Quiroga most businesses use *portal* (walkway) names instead of street names. Several blocks north of Plaza Bocanegra you'll find the train station, a few bars, the dock for boats to Janitzio, and good seafood restaurants.

WHERE TO SLEEP

Prices for clean rooms here are reasonable, and hot water is usually available. Ritzier hotels are on the Plaza Vasco de Quiroga, while the slightly noisier Plaza Bocanegra hosts the budget places. Campsites are available on nearby **Yunuen** island (*see* Janitzio, *below*), and you can also rent cabins there for the solid sum of $30 for two people. Free camping can also be found in the wilderness surrounding Pátzcuaro—just drive off the main road or ask to be dropped wherever you fancy from a second-class bus. Roughing it is not recommended during the rainy season.

➢ **UNDER $10** • **Hotel San Agustín.** This establishment lacks charm but offers tidy, spartan rooms and bathrooms. Advantages of staying here include the great location, the lack of a curfew, and low prices; the bright courtyard is icing on the cake. Singles are $4, doubles with two beds $8. *Portal Juárez 27, on Plaza Bocanegra, tel. 434/2–04–42. 20 rooms, all with bath.*

Hotel Valmen. An extremely friendly owner and a courtyard filled with plants and chirping birds are the main attractions of this modest hotel. Rooms are large, and you have your choice of green or pink walls. It's the best of the bargain hotels but has a silly 10 PM curfew. Admittedly, there's not much nightlife to keep you out any later. Singles cost around $5, doubles $10. *Padre Lloreda 34, at Ahumada, tel. 434/2–11–61. 1 block east of Plaza Bocanegra. 16 rooms, all with bath. Luggage storage.*

Posada de la Rosa. Squeezed between the shops and hotels of Portal Juárez, this clean and reputable establishment overlooks the Plaza Bocanegra. The rooms, some with amazingly mismatched bedcovers, aren't great, but they'll do. The only drawbacks are the 11 PM curfew and the walk to the communal bathrooms. Bring your own toilet paper and towel. Both singles and doubles cost $5 without bath, $6.75 with. *Portal Juárez 29, tel. 434/2–08–11. 12 rooms, 3 with bath.*

➢ **UNDER $15** • **Posada de la Salud.** This cheerful establishment is priced a notch higher than the other budget hotels, and it's as sweet, quiet, and proper as the lady who owns it. Built in traditional Mexican style with a tiled patio and a well-tended garden, it has pleasant rooms with carved wooden furniture and large, clean bathrooms. Singles cost about $10, doubles $13.50. *Serrato 9, tel. 434/2–00–58. 12 rooms, all with bath. Luggage storage.*

FOOD

Among local specialties worth trying are *pescado blanco* (whitefish), freshly caught in the lake; *charales,* tiny fried fish served (of course) with lemon and chile; and *sopa tarasca* (a tomato and bean soup with tortillas, cheese, cream, and dried peppers). The best of the many fish restaurants are found near the lakefront; **Restaurant Cholita** (Embarcadero 2 No. 17, no phone), near the ticket booth for the boats, is one of the most popular, with a highly recommended pescado blanco ($5). A huge open-air **market** operates daily on the west side of the Plaza Bocanegra. Stop by **Chocolate Joaquinita** (Enseñanza 38, tel. 434/2-11-04) to buy a huge pack of gritty but delicious homemade chocolate for $3. Sweet tooths will delight in the *helado de pasta*, ice cream made from pasta but reminiscent of custard, sold in the stands lining the Plaza Vasco de Quiroga.

➢ **UNDER $5** • **Los Equipales.** This tiny, down-home taquería is always full in the evenings. Tacos with beef, sausage, or tripe, and quesadillas are ridiculously cheap at 15¢. *Portal Allende 57, no phone. North side of Plaza Vasco de Quiroga. Open daily 6 PM–10:30 PM.*

Hamburguesas y Tortas el Viejo Sam. If you can't handle tiny fish with eyeballs staring up blankly from your plate, you'll be glad to know there's a humble hamburger joint in town. Get 'em topped with cheese or ham for under $1. French fries are 50¢. *Mendoza 15, no phone. ½ block south of Plaza Bocanegra. Open daily 10 AM–11PM.*

Restaurant Doña Paca. The wrought-iron and dark wood interior of this restaurant provide an elegant setting, to which the *trucha al ajo* (trout in garlic) and other fish dishes (about $3.50) do justice. You can also simply enjoy a cappuccino Doña Paca for $1.50 at one of the tables set out on the plaza. Another good choice is the *churipo de la sierra* (beef with vegetables and herbs), served with corundas (triangular tamales), coffee, and dessert for $3. *Portal Morelos 59, in Hotel Mansión Iturbide, tel. 434/2-03-68. North side of Plaza Vasco de Quiroga. Open daily 8 AM–6 PM. Wheelchair access. MC, V.*

Restaurante Hotel Posada La Basílica. The enormous windows here open onto an incredible view of Pátzcuaro and the lake. The *menú del día* ($3) includes soup, rice, blue-corn tortillas, and breaded trout or beef prepared with tomatoes and onions. *Caldo de pescado,* a tomato-based fish consommé, is a lighter choice for $2.50. Be prepared for a leisurely meal—service is slow even when there are few customers, but at least you'll have more time to enjoy your meal. *Arciga 6, tel. 434/2-11-08. From Plaza Bocanegra, east on Padre Lloreda, then up Buena Vista. Open Wed.–Mon. 8–4.*

Restaurant Mery. Set in the front of a private home, this is a cheerful place for an excellent, cheap meal. The rich and filling sopa tarasca is 75¢; other dishes include corundas and *tortas* (sandwiches) of every combination for about the same price. Egg breakfasts are also available here for $1. For lunch, try the *mole* ($2), which comes with soup. The owner is very gracious and makes sure you have everything you need. *Enseñanza, next to Café de Flore, no phone. ½ block west of basilica. Open daily 8 AM–9:30 PM. Wheelchair access.*

CAFES **Café de Flore.** Named after its renowned Parisian counterpart and especially popular with American and European tourists, this charming Franco-Mexican enterprise serves warm pizzas ($1) and quiches (70¢). The amiable owner slaves over her pastries—and gets great results. *Portal Rayón 26, tel. 434/2-19-46. Open Tues.–Sun. 9:30 AM–10 PM. Wheelchair access.*

Cafetería Bota Fumeiro. This small café on Plaza Quiroga serves a killer cappuccino ($1.25) and amazingly sweet hot chocolate for 60¢. *Portal Aldama 12, tel. 434/2-13-13. Open daily 8–8.*

WORTH SEEING

The bustling *tianguis* (open-air market) is a good place to get a sense of Pátzcuaro's character. It begins on the west side of the Plaza Bocanegra and continues for several blocks. Here you'll find all kinds of fresh food, as well as vendors hawking local handicrafts and cheap plastic watches and toys. You can get some good deals on handmade woolens, including sweaters, blankets, and serapes. The area is a mass of humanity, so don't expect to go anywhere fast.

LA CASA DE LOS ONCE PATIOS This "House of 11 Patios" is a former convent, built in the 18th and 19th centuries by Dominican monks. Now it houses several craft shops. The convent was broken up to make way for streets, leaving only five of the original 11 garden patios, but a hexagonal bath remains in one of them. Prices here aren't too bad, but you can probably find better deals at the markets. The Casa's main appeal lies in watching artisans in action and learning about their work. *Madrigal de las Altas Torres, 2 blocks from Plaza Vasco de Quiroga. Open daily 9–5.*

MUSEO DE ARTES POPULARES This dilapidated edifice, which housed the Colegio de San Nicolás in the 16th century, now houses Pátzcuaro's crafts museum. On display is a wide variety of local wares including ceramic dishes, intricately painted masks, and lacquered goods. In the back garden is a traditional Tarascan hut set on a 12th-century stone platform, the heart of the indigenous ceremonial center over which the basilica was erected. *Enseñanza, at Alcantarillas, tel. 434/2-10-29. 1 block east of Plaza Vasco de Quiroga. Admission: $1, free Sun. Open Tues.–Sat. 9–8, Sun. 9–3.*

CHURCHES Pátzcuaro was the episcopal seat of Michoacán until that honor was moved to Morelia in 1508, and its impressive colonial churches reflect the city's historical importance. Two blocks east of the Plaza Vasco de Quiroga is the **Basílica de Nuestra Señora de la Salud**, built atop a sacred Purépecha site by order of Quiroga, the first bishop of Michoacán. The most interesting piece here is the **Virgen de la Salud** (Virgin of Health), made from cornhusk paste and orchid nectar, which Quiroga commissioned from the local Purépechas. At that time, dressing holy images in cloth was prohibited—a plan ostensibly to keep the *indígenas* (Indians) from hiding their own idols within the Catholic vestments and continuing to worship as before. The basilica is open daily until dusk, and the mass schedule is posted at the main entrance.

El Humilladero (The Place of Humiliation), about 3 kilometers east of downtown on the Antiguo Camino a Morelia (Old Road to Morelia), is so named because it is where the Purépecha surrendered peacefully to the Spanish. Inside this plateresque (an ornate Spanish style mixing Gothic and Renaissance elements) church is a stone cross with a 1553 carving of Christ. To get here, catch a bus or van marked CRISTO from the Plaza Bocanegra; they run 6 AM–9 PM and cost 50¢.

AFTER DARK

Strolling the plaza until about 9 PM or cruising the streets with bored 17-year-olds are about your only nightlife options. For those who absolutely must find some action, **El Rincón** (Vasco de Quiroga, 1 block from Plaza de Quiroga) is *the* bar in town (not the hip bar, just the bar). The under-18 clientele picks up on each other to the accompaniment of Bon Jovi and a loud TV. Beers are $1, other drinks $2. For those who don't mind a bit of seediness, there's always the cantina next to Hotel San Agustín (*see* Where to Sleep, *above*), on the Plaza Bocanegra. It's the choice spot among local men seeking a rowdy game of pool, but women aren't too welcome, if they're allowed in at all.

OUTDOOR ACTIVITIES

The **Volcán del Estribo Grande**, about 4 kilometers west of the town center, makes a great short (1-hour) hike, with a phenomenal view of both Pátzcuaro and the nearby lake and islands at the end. The walk takes you along cobblestone streets lined with centuries-old homes and towering trees. To reach the lookout, head west on Ponce de León from the southwest corner of the Plaza Vasco de Quiroga. Ponce de León turns into Terán, then Terán turns into Calle Paseo, which finally becomes Cerro del Estribo.

In colonial times, young men gathered in the Plaza Vasco de Quiroga for friendly games of "correr cañas" (running of the sugar cane), in which they conducted mock battles while dressed in full armor and carrying lances made of sugarcane.

You can also rent **bikes** from the hotel-restaurant Mansión Iturbide (*see* Food, *above*) for $3 an hour, $8 a day. Pátzcuaro's cobblestone streets make for a bumpy ride, but it's a great way to explore the town's quieter residential areas. Ignore the sign that says the bikes are for hotel guests only, since the management does.

Near Pátzcuaro

JANITZIO

The local Purépecha people, who are almost the only inhabitants of the largest of Lake Pátzcuaro's five islands, call their isle Xanichu. This name's meaning is disputed. Some say it means "ear of corn," others say "where it rains," and still others "cornflower," but during the summer rainy season there's no doubt which interpretation is most probable. Most of the islanders' income derives from fishing and from handicrafts produced for the tourist industry. Fishermen here use butterfly nets to catch the whitefish they sell to Pátzcuaro restaurants, but this occupation is neither easy nor particularly lucrative. The primary reason to come here, admittedly, is to shop, as dozens of *artesanía* stores line the main street. Crowning the top of the island is a huge, if grotesque statue of José María Morelos. You can climb inside it to the *mirador* (viewpoint) for an amazing view of the lake and countryside. The Purépecha here still speak, write, and study in their native tongue. **Tecuena**, **Pacanda**, and **Yunuen** are other islands on the lake that make worthwhile excursions. They're much less popular with tourists than Janitzio, lending them a completely different atmosphere. **Yunuen** is the only one with overnight accommodations and camping.

If you're near Janitzio on the first of November, don't miss the Día de los Muertos (Day of the Dead) celebration held here. It is renowned in Mexico for its fantastic dances and candlelight processions to the graveyards.

COMING AND GOING Boats to and from Janitzio run daily 8–5:30. Tickets can be purchased at Pátzcuaro's lakeside dock; the *taquilla* (ticket window) is among the shops. Round-trip tickets are $2 for Janitzio, $3 for the other islands. Boats leave whenever they're full, so plan to take your time. To reach the lakefront from downtown Pátzcuaro, go to Portal Juárez (which borders the Plaza Bocanegra), across from the market, and catch a northbound bus or van marked LAGO. The last boat leaves the island around 5:30. Don't miss it: There are no hotels on the island.

TZINTZUNTZAN

This small village, called "Place of Hummingbirds" in Purépechan, lies about 18 kilometers northeast of Pátzcuaro. Shops selling straw and ceramic handicrafts line the main street. Beside the crafts market is the 17th-century **Templo de San Francisco,** another of Vasco de Quiroga's legacies, which has a newly redone (and consequently somewhat sterile) interior. The olive trees in the front courtyard, planted by Quiroga himself, still bear fruit. The **Templo de la Soledad** next door is somewhat damp, but its original facade and elaborately clothed statues give it more character than the Templo de San Francisco.

The Purépecha deities were mostly female; important ones included Xaratanga, the goddess of fertility, and Cueraraperi, the goddess of the sky and mother of all gods and goddesses.

Roughly a kilometer outside Tzintzuntzan are the remains of the Purépecha kingdom's religious and administrative capital, where Vasco de Quiroga based his evangelical mission. The huge ceremonial platform is topped with circular stone structures known as *yácatas*, and the original altar used for decapitation and other sacrificial acts still stands behind them. There are no guides, but a small museum offers information in Spanish about the Purépecha people. To reach the ruins, walk back on the road to Pátzcuaro and turn left on a side road. You can't miss them—they look alarmingly like larger-than-life mud pies. If in doubt, ask for directions to the Yácatas. *Museum admission: $1.50, free Sun. Open daily 10–5.*

COMING AND GOING **Autotransportes Galeana** buses marked QUIROGA (½ hr, 50¢) leave every 15 minutes 6 AM–8:30 PM from Pátzcuaro's main bus terminal. Tell the driver to let you off at Tzintzuntzan's plaza. To get back, catch a bus at the same plaza; they go back every 15 minutes.

Morelia

Morelia's visual appeal is a product of its colonial past. From the gracefully arching walkways to the blocks and blocks of beige stone buildings with shady, foliage-studded courtyards, this expanding city manages to maintain dignity despite the crowds, traffic, and multitudes of street vendors hawking jeans and fake flowers on every sidewalk. Although much of Morelia's architecture evokes the past, the city lives jubilantly in the present. The capital of Michoacán, Morelia rivals Guanajuato in liveliness, making it one of the Heartland's most interesting destinations. Plaza-side cafés and a progressive arts scene supporting such activities as foreign-film screenings and poetry readings lend it a cultured air. On the streets, longhaired youths wearing their requisite Metallica T-shirts mingle with *campesinos* (peasants) from surrounding villages, creating a humorous contrast. You'll also see relatively few foreign tourists: While it's a popular vacation spot for Mexicans, the city remains largely unknown to the rest of the world.

Every year during Carnaval (February or early March), a group of Morelian musicians and dancers perform a bullfight reenactment called the "toritos de petate," with a fake bull and a man in drag.

Founded in 1541 by the Spanish, who named it Valladolid, the city became the provincial capital in 1580. The city's name was changed to Morelia in 1828, in honor of José María Morelos. Monuments, streets, and the usual hoopla commemorate the city's independence-minded namesake and make for a good crash course in early 19th-century Mexican history. Special events include Morelos's birthday on September 30 and the Aniversario de Morelia on May 18, both of which entail parades and fireworks. The Feria Regional de Morelia during the first two weeks in May has little directly to do with Morelos, but it's a great time to check out a bullfight or any of the many regional dances performed at this time.

BASICS

AMERICAN EXPRESS **Gran Turismo Viajes** provides all services for cardholders, including holding mail, emergency check cashing, and changing traveler's checks. *Carmelinas 3233, Las Américas, Morelia, Michoacán, CP 58270, México, tel. 43/24–04–84. 1st floor of Bancomer building, across from Gigante shopping center; take* RUTA ROJA *1 combi (VW bus) west from downtown. Open Mon.–Sat. 9–2 and 4–6.*

BOOKSTORES **Bazar Ocampo** is a dusty used-book store with a decent collection of English books. Don't despair: somewhere between *The Sensual Woman* and *The Sensual Man* are hidden a few intellectually stimulating paperbacks. Paperbacks run about a buck, or you can exchange yours on two-for-one terms. *Ocampo 242, no phone. From Plaza de Armas, 1 block north on Juárez, left on Ocampo. Open daily 9–8; sometimes closed 2–4 on weekends.*

En Bolsita, Por Favor

Once upon a time, Mexicans were forced to take time out whenever they wanted a soda or mineral water. Instead of paying a hefty deposit on the glass bottle containing the beverage of their choice, most people spent a few minutes inside the corner store, chatting with neighbors and relaxing while they drank. Nowadays, most folks ask for a bolsita (little bag). The drink is poured into a plastic bag, a straw is inserted, and the thirsty person goes on his or her way with the space-age contraption tightly in hand. Few bother to throw their empty bolsitas into a trash can. One look at the littered streets and it's obvious that the bolsitas are more detrimental to the environment, and less sociable, than glass bottles.

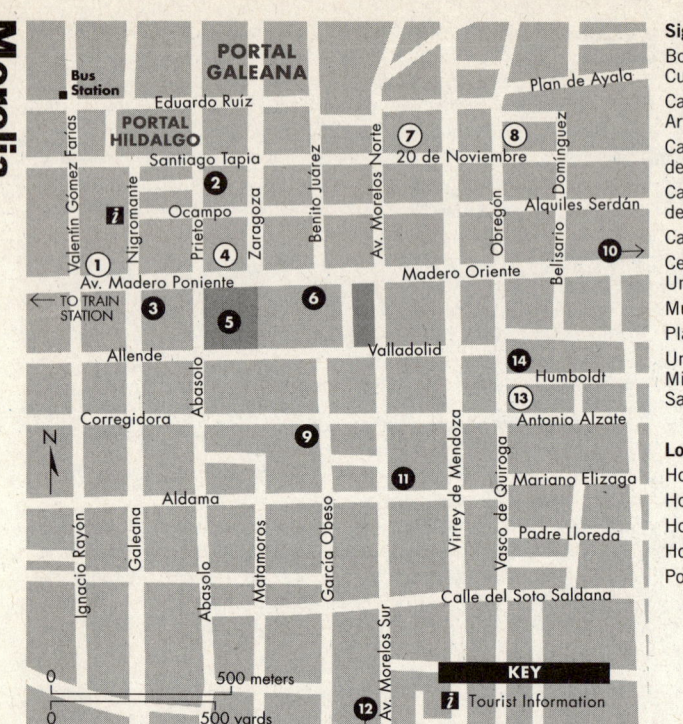

CASAS DE CAMBIO Banamex (Madero Ote. 63, tel. 43/12–27–70) changes cash and traveler's checks 9–11:30 weekday mornings and has an ATM that accepts Cirrus and Plus cards. If you're looking for a better exchange rate, go to **Casa de Cambio Majapara** (20 de Noviembre, at Pino Suárez, tel. 43/13–23–46), open weekdays 8:30–6:30.

EMERGENCIES If the need arises, call the **police** (Revolución, at 20 de Noviembre, tel. 43/12–22–22) or the **Cruz Roja** (Ventura Puente 270, tel. 43/14–51–51) for an ambulance.

MAIL Morelia's full-service main post office will hold mail sent to you at the following address for up to 10 days: Lista de Correos, Morelia, Michoacán, CP 58000, México. *Madero Ote. 369, tel. 43/12–05–17. 3 blocks east of Plaza de Armas. Open weekdays 8–7, weekends 9–1.*

MEDICAL AID The **Hospital Civil** (Isidro Huarte, at Fray de Margil, tel. 43/12–22–16), near the Bosque Cuauhtémoc, is open 24 hours a day. **Farmacia Gems** (Blvd. García de León 1711, tel. 43/15–35–76), far from the center but also open around the clock, has some English-speakers on its staff.

PHONES Long-distance phone service is available at the *caseta de larga distancia* (long-distance telephone office) in the bus station (*see* Coming and Going, *below*), but it doesn't allow collect calls. **Ladatel** phones are hard to come by, but there are a few in working order at the **Mercado de Dulces** (cnr of Vasco de Quiroga and Humboldt). You can make collect calls at the phone in **Hotel Valladolid** (*see* Where to Sleep, *below*).

SCHOOLS You must be affiliated with a U.S. university to take Spanish-language courses at the **Departamento de Idiomas** of the Universidad Michoacana de San Nicolás de Hidalgo, but if you are, make the effort to study here. Subjects available include language, literature, history, and philosophy. The department can arrange for homestays. Semester-long courses in Purépechan, the indigenous regional language, are also offered. For more details, contact Dr. Miguel García

Silva at the Departamento de Idiomas, UMSANH, Santiago Tapia 403, Col. Centro, Morelia, Michoacán, CP 58000, México, or call 43/16–71–01 between 10 and 4, local time.

VISITOR INFORMATION The **Secretaría Estatal del Turismo** is on the south side of the Palacio Clavijero. Here you'll find a friendly English-speaking staff ready to answer questions and give out maps and information about upcoming cultural events. *Nigromante 79, tel. 43/13–26–54. 1½ blocks from Plaza de Armas. Open weekdays 9–2 and 4–8, weekends 9–8.*

COMING AND GOING

BY BUS The busy **Central de Autobuses** (Eduardo Ruíz 526, 4 blocks NW of the Plaza de Armas, tel. 43/12–56–64) is home to Morelia's bus lines. **Flecha Amarilla** (tel. 43/12–32–13) takes the prize for most frequent departures and cheapest fares. Their buses go to Guadalajara (6 hrs, $11), Guanajuato (3½ hrs, $4.50), Mexico City (6 hrs, $8), Pátzcuaro (1 hr, $1.75), and Uruapan (2 hrs, $3.25). For a cushier traveling experience, try **ETN** (tel. 43/13–41–37), which has hourly service to Mexico City (4½ hrs, $16) as well as frequent departures for Guadalajara (5 hrs, $16) and a daily 10:30 PM bus to Manzanillo (8½ hrs, $21). The station also boasts a small post office, a 24-hour long-distance telephone service (no collect calls), several food stands, and a restaurant. Twenty-four-hour luggage storage is available for $1 to $1.50 a day. To get to the Plaza de Armas from the station, go left on Ruíz, then two blocks south (right) on Gómez Farías, and finally left on Madero. A taxi downtown costs about $1.75.

BY TRAIN Morelia's train station is about 2 kilometers west of town. The most comfortable way to get to or from the station is by taxi ($2), but a RUTA AZUL pesero (20¢) is also convenient. Two trains go to Mexico City (11 hrs, $8 1st class, $3.50 2nd class); one at 10:30 AM (2nd class only) and another at 10:55 PM (1st and 2nd classes). The train to Uruapan (3½ hrs, $3 1st class, $1.75 2nd class) leaves daily at 5:30 AM and 5:30 PM (2nd class only). *Av. del Periodismo, tel. 43/16–39–12. Ticket office open daily 5–6 AM, 10–11 AM, and 10–11 PM.*

GETTING AROUND

Most of the city's points of interest lie within a six-block radius of the **Plaza de Armas**. The plaza is bordered on the north by the main avenue, **Madero**, which runs east–west through most of the city. The only difficulty is that street names change north and south of Madero, and occasionally elsewhere without warning. Of the three or four nameplates posted on every street corner, the dark blue one usually corresponds to the name on your map. Asking directions might not help much, since most people will tell you the restaurant you seek, for instance, is next to the record store, rather than pinpointing a specific street.

Combis are VW buses marked with colored stripes denoting the routes they follow. It's easy to master the colors; the hard part is getting one of the combis to slow down for you. Even at designated blue-and-white *parada* (bus stop) signs, you have to wave a hand to let the driver know you're interested. They'll also stop for you on unmarked corners if you wave frantically. Always ask the driver if he's going to your destination, just in case. A ride costs about 20¢.

WHERE TO SLEEP

Hotels here are fairly inexpensive and easy to find. They surround the bus station, and this area is cheap and convenient, but the surrounding streets are constantly busy and it's not the most attractive part of town. The best places to stay are in the center, on or near the Plaza de Armas. The tourist office has a list of inexpensive hotels, but many of those are *hoteles de paso* (hotels that rent rooms by the hour). You're better off at any of the lodgings listed below. If the need arises, you'll be safe crashing at the bus station or on one of the quiet but uncomfortable benches on Portal Hidalgo (cnr of Guillermo Prieto and Santiago Tapia, 2 blocks from the station).

➢ **UNDER $10** • **Hotel Fénix.** This hotel is popular with older Mexicans, which at least means it's relatively quiet. Rooms are not exactly loaded with amenities, but they're clean, and the location is a plus. However, the street traffic can be annoying if your room is near the front.

The hot water runs all day. Singles without bath are a steal at $4, doubles without bath almost as cheap at $6. One or two people can share a room with private bath for about $8. Cheap breakfasts ($1) and lunches are served as well. *Madero Pte. 537, tel. 43/12–05–12. 3 blocks from Plaza de Armas. 24 rooms, 20 with bath. Wheelchair access.*

Posada San José. A light, airy courtyard, friendly management, and huge rooms filled with Brady-era furniture characterize this hotel, whose plant-filled courtyard is ideal for ditching the sights and spending a day with your favorite novel. You'll need to ring the bell to get in, as the door is kept locked all day. Negotiable prices are $4 for a single without bath ($5 with bath) and $5 for a double ($7.50 with bath). *Obregón 226, tel. 43/12–09–79. 5 blocks from Plaza de Armas. 20 rooms, 5 with bath.*

➤ **UNDER $15** • **Hotel Colonial.** Basic rooms with TVs are made more pleasant by their cleanliness and by this hotel's friendly, young staff. Ask for a room away from the street; cars and buses go by at all hours. Singles are $7.50, doubles $12. *20 de Noviembre 15, tel. 43/12–18–97. 2 blocks north of cathedral. 25 rooms, all with bath. Luggage storage. Reservations advised. MC, V.*

Hotel Mintzicuri. The two main attractions here are spectacular murals (in the lobby) and sauna baths. Rooms are smallish but clean and have TVs, phones, carpeting, and private baths. Singles go for $9, doubles $12. This is the most luxury you'll get in Morelia for this price. The restaurant next door offers cheap and hearty breakfasts for $2. *Vasco de Quiroga 227, tel. 43/12–05–90. 4 blocks from cathedral. 36 rooms, all with bath. Laundry, luggage storage. Reservations advised.*

Hotel Valladolid. On the Plaza de Armas, the Valladolid is immaculate, and most rooms have stone walls and curtained balconies. Hot water comes slowly, but the hotel is surprisingly quiet despite its location, and the staff is so friendly you might not want to leave. Singles are $10, doubles $12. *Portal Hidalgo 245, tel. 43/12–00–27. 21 rooms, all with bath. Luggage storage.*

HOSTELS **Villa Juvenil.** Unless you're a serious bargain hunter, you might rather pay another $2–$5 to lodge at a more central hotel. Here, you'll have to sleep four to a single-sex room, be in by 11 PM, and walk about 2 kilometers or catch two combis to reach most of the attractions in town. On the plus side, the place is clean, the managers are young and hip, and there's a pool out front. The cost is roughly $3 per person. Breakfast is dished up for about $2; lunches and dinners are about $2.75 each. Sheets and towels are provided, and you get a 10% discount with a hostel card. *Chiapas 180, near Oaxaca, tel. 43/13–31–77. Behind Instituto Michoacano de la Juventud y el Deporte. Take Madero west to Cuautla, turn left, then right on Oaxaca to Chiapas. Or catch* RUTA ROJA *combi to Cuautla, then* RUTA AMARILLA *to Oaxaca. 72 beds. Wheelchair access.*

FOOD

Morelia teems with hole-in-the-wall restaurants offering decent fare; most are within several blocks of the Plaza de Armas. The farther you go from the plaza, though, the cheaper the food—as low as $2 a meal. Stands on Gómez Farías, just outside the bus station, serve up the cheapest eats in town, with *comidas corridas* (premade lunch specials) for just over a buck. Several restaurants serve rich *sopa tarasca* (a tomato and bean soup with tortillas, cheese, cream, and dried peppers) as well as other regional specialties. Sweet-toothed travelers might try *cocada* (coconut candy); the popular *morelianas,* condensed milk paste between two *obleas* (wafers); or *ate,* a thick candy made of guava, fig, or pear paste.

➤ **UNDER $5** • **Los Comensales.** Tables are arranged around an open-air, interior courtyard filled with plants, flowers, and caged chirping birds. Two tasty specialties are *pollo con mole* (chicken in chile and chocolate sauce) for $3, and *paella* (saffron-flavored rice with seafood, sausage, and chicken) for $4.50. The $4.25 comida corrida includes fruit, soup, pasta or rice, an entrée, coffee or tea, and dessert. *Zaragoza 148, tel. 43/12–93–61. 2 blocks north of Plaza de Armas. Open daily 8 AM–10 PM.*

Restaurant Las Palmas. The TV dictates the atmosphere here, but service is friendly, and the typical Mexican fare is as good as it gets for the price. The excellent spicy egg *chilaquiles* (tortilla strips doused with salsa and sour cream) accompanied by juice, coffee, and refried beans make a filling breakfast for $2.50. Afternoon comidas corridas are $2. *Melchor Ocampo 215, btw Zaragoza and Prieto, no phone. 1 block north of Plaza de Armas. Open daily 9 AM–9:30 PM.*

Restaurant Vegetariano. The food is as original as the name, and the slow indifferent service is the same that seems to plague every single vegetarian restaurant in town. However, the interior courtyard setting is fresh and airy, the food is good, and the price is right—*comidas corridas* go for $2 and an *energético* (fruit, yogurt, and granola) is $1. *Hidalgo 75, at La Concordia, tel. 43/12–31–81. Open daily 8:30–5:30. Wheelchair access.*

El Rey Tacamba. This small, pleasant restaurant on the *portales* (arcades) surrounding the cathedral serves only specialties of Michoacán. The *pollo moreliano* (roasted chicken with red chile and cheese) comes with three enchiladas and costs $5. Also good are the *medallones en salsa chipotle* (beef filet in chile sauce, not spicy). Enchiladas are $2 à la carte. *Portal Galeana 157, tel. 43/12–20–44. Open daily 8:30 AM–11:45 PM. Wheelchair access.*

CAFES **Café Catedral.** This is the place where families and hipsters converge and converse. Coffee is $1.25; a variety of teas ($1.25), from hibiscus to chamomile, are also served. Come here for a pleasant breakfast ($1.75). *Portal Hidalgo, next to Hotel Casino, tel. 43/12–32–89. Open daily 8 AM–10 PM.*

Café del Olmo. This café has brick arches, and soft music plays in the background, making it a pleasant place for cappuccino ($1.25) and conversation. The young, amiable staff also serves up a variety of snacks, from cakes and pies ($1) to french fries or tacos (75¢). *Juárez 95, north of plaza. Open daily 9 AM–9:30 PM.*

Café del Teatro. On the second floor of the Teatro Ocampo, this café is the best spot in town for a cup of coffee and the most popular among the twenty- and thirtysomething crowd. Wood-beamed ceilings and red velvet curtains make you feel like you forgot your opera glasses. Grab a seat near the balcony overlooking the street and sip a cappuccino ($1.50) accompanied by a dessert ($2). *Ocampo, at Prieto, no phone. Open weekdays 8–3 and 5–10, Sat. 10–3 and 5–10, Sun. 5–10.*

WORTH SEEING

You don't have to look hard to find Morelia's center of activity—it jumps out at you as soon as you reach the downtown area. The **Catedral**, a 17th-century architectural marvel, took more than 100 years to build. Its bell towers are taller at some 61 meters than those of any other church in Mexico. By day the surrounding streets turn into markets whose vendors sell everything, from underwear to popcorn. The cathedral's baroque exterior, however, gives way to a somewhat disappointing neoclassical interior, brightened only by warm rose- and gold-colored ornamentation. Works of particular interest include a sculpture of Christ made from cane paste and a fantastic *churrigueresco* (ultra-baroque) organ. *Open daily dawn to dusk.*

"Dying is nothing when you die for the Fatherland."—José María Morelos (who did).

BOSQUE CUAUHTEMOC The first of the 18th-century aqueduct's 253 arches frames Morelia's largest park, the Bosque Cuauhtémoc, a 10- to 15-minute walk from the Plaza de Armas. At the edge of the park is the **Museo de Arte Contemporáneo**, with rotating exhibits of contemporary art from all over Latin America, including works by Chilean painters and female graphic artists. *Museum: Acueducto 342. 11 blocks east of Plaza de Armas, down Madero. Admission free. Open Tues.–Sun. 10–2 and 4–8.*

CASA DE LAS ARTESANIAS This former Franciscan monastery houses a wide variety of handicrafts from all over the state of Michoacán. The collection—from carved wood to guitars to copper dishes—is as varied and well-explained as that in the Museo del Estado (*see below*). The difference is that everything here is for sale. The Casa de las Artesanías also has workshops where you can see artisans practicing their crafts. *Vasco de Quiroga, at Humboldt, behind marketplace, tel. 43/12–17–48. Admission free. Open weekdays 10–8, weekends 10–6.*

CENTRO CULTURAL UNIVERSITARIO This is one of the best examples of colonial architecture in Morelia—only it was completed in the 20th century. The cultural center stages temporary exhibits of contemporary art from Mexico's up-and-coming artists, and also offers film festivals, poetry competitions, and concerts. Come to admire the murals and chat with the staff about upcoming events. *Madero Pte., at Galeana, tel. 43/12–19–09. Admission free. Open Mon.–Sat. 9–8.*

MUSEO CASA DE MORELOS City namesake José María Morelos once owned this home, and abandoned it to join the fight for independence. His life story is interesting, but unless you can read Spanish the displays featuring his reading glasses and family tree won't do much for you. One look at the beautiful yet butt-flattening 19th-century carriages in the courtyard will make you vow never to complain about buses again. *Morelos Sur 323, tel. 43/13–26–51. Admission: $3.50, free Sun. Open Mon.–Sat. 9–7, Sun. 9–6.*

MUSEO DEL ESTADO The Purépechas once dominated almost all of Michoacán, as this museum chronicles via pre-Columbian artifacts. Purépechan people still populate the area, producing a wide range of handicrafts, some of which you can see here along with rotating regional contemporary art exhibitions and artifacts from the independence movement in which you-know-who played such a big part. Especially worth a look is the section on Lake Pátzcuaro's fishing tradition. Explanations are in Spanish. *Prieto 176, tel. 43/13–06–29. 2 blocks north of Plaza de Armas. Admission free. Open weekdays 9–2 and 4–8, weekends 9–2 and 4–7.*

CHEAP THRILLS

Pay your homage to Morelos at his birthplace, **Casa Natal de Morelos,** where you can ooh and aah over his signature on documents. The real reason to come here, however, is to meet the students studying and hanging out in the sunny garden. The Cine Club sponsors free foreign films here several times a week, as well as cultural events such as poetry readings. Check the bulletin board. *Corregidora 113, tel. 43/12–27–93. 1 block south of cathedral on García Obeso. Admission free. Open weekdays 9–2 and 4–8, Sat. 10–2 and 4–7, Sun. 10–2.*

Universidad Michoacana de San Nicolás de Hidalgo is a series of simple white buildings plopped down in the middle of a field. Though architecturally uninspiring, it is, obviously, a great place to meet students. Hang out in the building that houses the Departamento de Idiomas (A-1, at the end of the campus; *see* School, *above*) and you will inevitably be approached by students wanting to practice their English or discuss their city with you. *Santiago Tapia 403. Take* SANTIAGUITO *bus from east side of Plaza de Armas and ask to be let off at Universidad.*

AFTER DARK

Morelia is at its best by night when the streets and the main plaza are illuminated by soft lights that cast a romantic glow over promenading couples. The Plaza de Armas is a constant hub of activity, with mimes, musicians, dancers, and cotton-candy vendors all vying for attention. Thursdays, Fridays, and Saturdays are the most active throughout the city, but most bars are open seven days a week.

BARS AND DANCING Morelia will not disappoint those who prefer mindless drinking and shaking. Highly recommended is **Siglo XVIII** (García de León, at Turismo 20, tel. 43/24–07–47), a bar decorated in the baroque style, complete with a water-spitting angel fountain. This is *the* place in Morelia, so arrive before 10 to avoid a wait. There's a $3.50 cover Friday and Saturday. **Antigua's** (Camelinas 514, tel. 43/15–90–47), a bar versatile enough to let you cavort comfortably on the dance floor or have a quiet conversation on the terrace, has a $3.50 cover on Saturdays, (the same fee includes drinks Thursdays and Fridays). Penny-pinchers should seek out **Carlos 'n Charlie's** (Camelinas 3340, tel. 43/24–37–42), which is usually packed with and energized by Morelia's preppy youth. Beers are $1.

MUSIC AND THEATER The Orquesta Sinfónica performs in the **Teatro Ocampo** Fridays and Saturdays at 8:30 PM. Schedules are seasonal and prices range from $5 to $10; contact the **Instituto Michoacano de Cultura** (tel. 43/13–13–20 or 43/13–12–15) for info.

The **Cantera Jardín** restaurant puts on theater shows Thursday–Saturday at 9 PM so that you can enjoy your meal while watching a play. Programs and cover charges vary. *Aldama 343, tel. 43/12–15–78.*

If you understand enough Spanish to get the jokes, check out the **Corral de la Comedia** (Ocampo 239, tel. 43/12–13–74), which stages comedies Thursday–Saturday at 8:30 PM and Sunday at 7 PM. Cover is usually about $5.

THE PACIFIC COAST

9

By Anna Gorman

Journeying along the Pacific Coast, you'll never stray far from the region's essence: the ocean. Its aquamarine swells provide a scenic backdrop to beachside *palapas* (thatched-roof huts) and stands of palm trees; the rolling waves provide a playground for boogie boarders, Jet Skiers, and surfers alike; and the salty waters offer up a smorgasbord of fresh seafood that is spiced, diced, and sliced into tasty regional dishes. It's not surprising that the Pacific Coast seems to have been created specifically as a tourist paradise: The region was targeted by the Mexican department of tourism as a means of luring foreign currency with which to boost the flagging economy. Today, the thousands of tourist dollars that turned small fishing ports like Mazatlán into coastal resorts keep the coasts' fishermen and restaurant owners in business. Many cities regularly celebrate the ocean as their source of livelihood: San Blas blesses the sea in a joyous festival, Manzanillo holds world-renowned sailfish tournaments, and Mexcaltitán honors the opening of its shrimping season with fireworks and a fiesta.

Each of the beaches along the "Mexican Riviera" is distinct: El Paraiso has pristine sand and sparkling waters, Manzanillo is dotted with black volcanic ash, and Puerto Vallarta is caked with litter, vendors, and tourists. Cities such as Ixtapa/Zihuatanejo and Acapulco continue to woo sun-worshippers and resort lovers to their beaches, while the less developed shores of Melaque, Barra de Navidad, and the mosquito-infested jungles of San Blas are havens for budget travelers and surfers.

Mexcaltitán, a small island in a saltwater lagoon in Nayarit, is reputed to be the site of Aztlán, the original home of the Aztecs.

If you can't possibly stand to hear the waves crash one more time, you'll find that the Pacific Coast states of Sinaloa, Nayarit, Jalisco, Colima, and Guerrero offer much more than the lively shore. Farmland, volcanoes, and mountains extend the natural setting of the Pacific Coast past the water, and behind the beaches, *pueblos* (towns), and jungles, the towering Sierra Madre Occidental and Sierra Madre Sur mountain ranges serve as hiking venues for adventurers and a refuge for native peoples. Booming westernized metropolises are only a bus ride away from the quiet, inland towns that are home to indigenous Indians. You'll see Huichols and Coras in their colorful handmade apparel in Tepic and Santiago Ixcuintla, selling embroidered paintings to ensure their cultural (and financial) survival. But whether you choose to hit the powerful surf, maneuver through a tropical jungle, or hike an active volcano, do it during summer—the off-season for tourists—when the crowded cities empty out and prices drop significantly.

The Pacific Coast

Map labels (north to south):

Durango state: Lázaro Cárdenas, Santiago Papasquiaro, Canatlán, El-Salto, Durango

Sinaloa state: Navolato, Culiacán, El Dorado, La Cruz, Estación Dimas, Concordia, Copala, Mazatlán, Villa Unión, El Caimanero, Rosario, Escuinapa de Hidalgo

To La Paz (ferry)

Sierra Madre Occidental

Rivers: Presidio, Mezquital, Río Grande de Santiago, Armería

Nayarit state: Teacapán, Tecuala, Agua Brava, Mexcaltitán, Tuxpán, Santiago Ixcuintla, San Blas, Bahía Matachén, Tepic, Chacala, Punta de Mita

Islas Marías

Jalisco state: Bahía de Banderas, Cabo Corrientes, Puerto Vallarta, Tequila, Ameca, Guadalajara, Jocotepec, Ajijic, Lake Chapala, Tomatlán, Bahía Chamela, Chamela, Ayotlán, Suchitlán, Tapalpa, Agua Caliente, Bahía Tenacatita, Ciudad Guzmán

Colima state: San Patricio–Melaque, Barra de Navidad, Manzanillo, Armería, Cuyutlán, Tecomán, Comala, Colima

Golfo de California

Pacific Ocean

KEY
- ┼┼┼ Rail Lines
- - - - Ferry Lines

0 — 100 miles
0 — 150 km

266

Mazatlán

Mazatlán has something of a split personality. While the new **Zona Dorada** (Golden Zone) bursts with trendy time-shares, perpetually expanding resorts, and over one million tourists a year, the old Mazatlán, **Mazatlán Viejo,** continues its role as a flourishing seaport, a shrimp-packing city, and a sport-fishing haven. Between the two, Mazatlán has something for everyone: While party-crazed travelers check out the city's happening discos, a resort-weary soul can wander the nearby streets of Mazatlán Viejo and see historical folk dance, music, and art, or colorful colonial-style buildings. Mazatlán has always satisfied the needs of a variety of people—from the pre-Spanish conquest pirates who rested at their "Island of Mazatlán," to the gold-driven miners in search of riches, to today's tourists, who come only for the warm-weather waves.

The changing seasons also bring different kinds of visitors to this popular resort town. During summer, Mazatlán becomes the humid playground of American students and Mexican tourists. When the mercury drops from the scorching 90s to the comfortable 70s, Mazatlán hits its winter high season, and older visitors from the United States and Canada flock to expensive hotels. And Mazatlán's party atmosphere really kicks in during **Carnaval,** the city's biggest fiesta, celebrated just before Lent (usually February). Thousands of tourists, both domestic and foreign, descend on the town for six days and nights to enjoy music, dancing, fireworks, parades, drinking, and hormonal revelry. If you can stomach the sweltering crowds and unabashed tourism, join the fun; if not, make a hasty getaway to the more secluded towns down the coast.

BASICS

AMERICAN EXPRESS The office changes traveler's checks at a decent rate, but charges a 1% commission. The staff also delivers MoneyGrams, and cardholders can cash a personal check or have mail sent here. *Camarón Sábalo, tel. 69/13–06–00. 1 block north of Dairy Queen. Open weekdays 9–5, Sat. 9–noon. Mailing address: T. Diagonal H, Av. Camarón Sábalo, Centro Comercial Balboa, Local 4, Mazatlán, Sinaloa, CP 82000, México.*

CASAS DE CAMBIO The Zona Dorada teems with *casas de cambio* (money-changing houses). **Banamex** (Flores, at Juárez, tel. 69/82–77–33) exchanges cash and traveler's checks weekdays 8:30–4:30 at the best rates in town, charges no commission, and has ATMs that accept Cirrus and Plus cards. Downtown, places to change money are scarcer. Try the **Casa de Cambio Camiga** in Plaza Concordia—the rates aren't great, but there's no commission on traveler's checks. *Belisario Domínguez 2, at Flores, tel. 69/85–00–03. Open Mon.–Sat. 9–1:30 and 3:30–7.*

CONSULATES Mazatlán doesn't have an actual **United States** consulate, but you can visit Geri Nelson (Loaiza 202, in Zona Dorada, tel. 69/16–58–89), the consular representative here. Geri's office, open weekdays 9–1, can be found in front of Hotel Playa Mazatlán. In an after-hours emergency, call 62/17–23–75 for the consulate in Hermosillo. **Canada's** representative can be found right next to Geri's office, at Loaiza 203 (tel. 69/13–73–20), with the same open hours. Citizens from other countries should try the tourist office at Olas Altas 1300 for information on consulates in Mexico City.

EMERGENCIES The number for the **police** is 69/83–45–10, and they will call an ambulance.

LAUNDRY For about $2.50 a load, **Lavandería Romy** will wash, dry, and fold your duds. *120 Hidalgo, near 5 de Mayo, tel. 69/82–80–42. Open daily 7 AM–8 PM.*

MAIL The post office will hold mail sent to you at the following address for up to 10 days: Lista de Correos, Administración Postal No. 1, Centro, Benito Juárez y 21 de Marzo, Mazatlán, Sinaloa, CP 82000, México. You can send or receive telegrams at the office next door. *Juárez, at 21 de Marzo, tel. 69/81–21–21. Open weekdays 8–6.*

MEDICAL AID Miguel Ángel Guzmán Elizondo (Nelson 1808, tel. 69/81–25–87) is a locally respected, English-speaking doctor. He sees patients weekdays 10–2 and 5–8, Saturday 10–2; consultations cost $20. If you need to see him after hours, call his home (tel. 69/81–51–17). For dental problems, call **Jorge Morelos** (Camarón Sábalo 204–30, tel. 69/13–

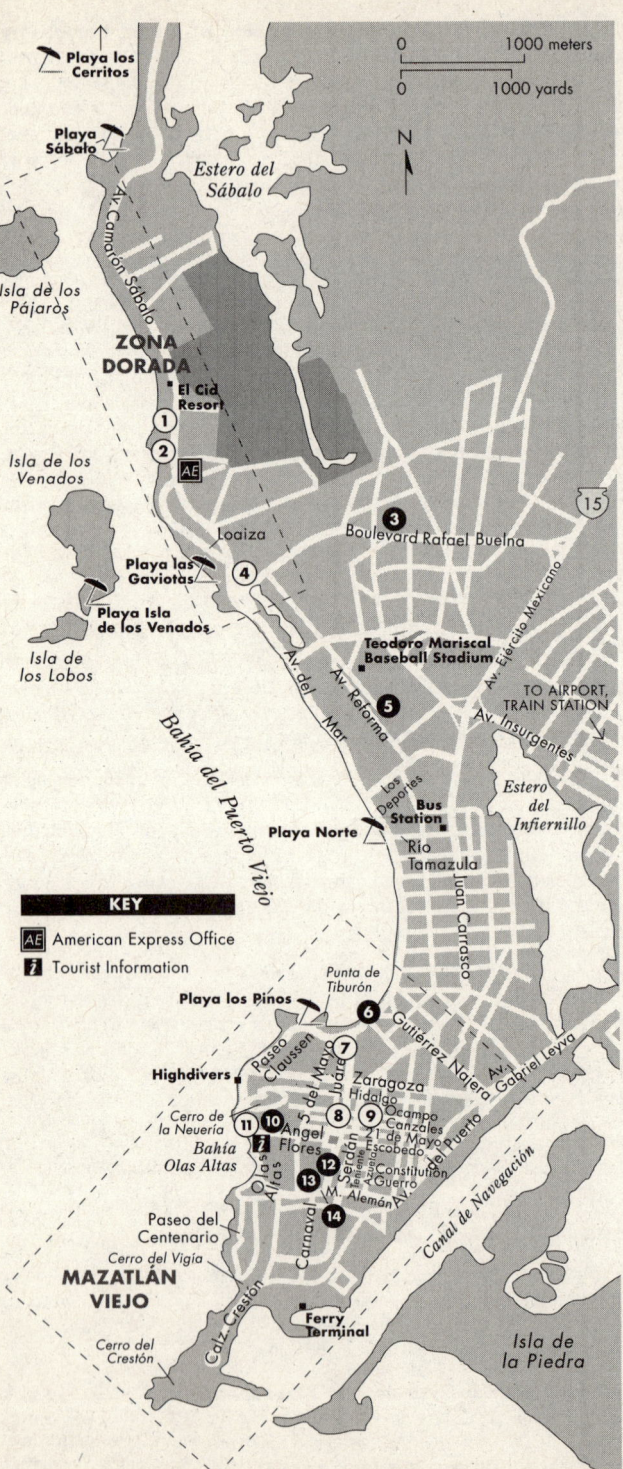

60–68). For minor problems or prescriptions, **Farmacia Cruz Verde** (Gutiérrez Najera 901, at Obregón, tel. 69/81–22–25) is open 24 hours.

PHONES You'll find pay phones on almost every other block throughout the Zona Dorada and Mazatlán Viejo. To place cash calls or send faxes, **Computel** (Serdán 1512, near Belisario Domínguez) stays open 24 hours a day.

VISITOR INFORMATION The huge federal tourist office has a helpful English-speaking staff. *Olas Altas 1300, at Escobedo, tel. 69/85–12–20. Open weekdays 8:30–3, Sat. 9–1.*

COMING AND GOING

BY BUS The bus station, **La Central Camionera** (Calle Río Tamazula, near Av. Ejército Mexicano, tel. 69/81–76–25) is in a large, semicircular building divided into sections: One is devoted to first-class buses, and the other to second-class buses with service to nearby towns. First class resemble chartered buses and are expensive; second-class buses are cheap, roomy, and air-conditioned. **Transportes Norte de Sonora** (tel. 69/81–38–46) buses stop here hourly on their way to Guadalajara (9 hrs, $13.50), Mexico City (18 hrs, $27), Tijuana (25 hrs, $37), and Nogales (18 hrs, $28). **Transportes Pacífico** (tel. 69/82–05–77) also has service to Mexico City, Guadalajara, and Tijuana. **Estrella Blanca** (tel. 69/81–53–81) runs six times a day to Durango (13 hrs, $14) and once a day to Monterrey (18 hrs, $23) and Zacatecas (13 hrs, $14). **Tres Estrellas de Oro** (tel. 69/81–36–80) serves the coast as well as most of Mexico. One daily first-class bus to Acapulco (25 hrs, $40) with stops in Puerto Vallarta (8 hrs, $14) and Manzanillo (12 hrs, $21) leaves at 9:45 PM, and buses to Tepic (4½ hrs, $7) leave every hour. To get downtown or to the market from the bus station, catch any bus marked INSURGENTES on Avenida Ejército Mexicano, or walk to the *malecón* (jetty) and take a southbound CAMARON SABALO bus. The same bus going in the opposite direction goes to the Zona Dorada. Luggage storage is available at the station ($1 per 4 hrs).

BY TRAIN The train station (tel. 69/84–67–10) is northeast of Mazatlán Viejo, on Avenida Ferrocarril in the Colonia Esperanza. It's a bit far from town, so hail a bus labeled ESPERANZA from Olas Altas. Mazatlán lies on the Pacific line, which runs from Mexicali (24 hrs, $28 1st class; 26 hrs, $5.50 2nd class) to Guadalajara (12 hrs, $16 1st class; 14 hrs, $6 2nd class). Major stops to the north are Culiacán (4 hrs, $6 1st class; 5 hrs, $2 2nd class), Sufragio (6 hrs, $13 1st class; 8 hrs, $4 2nd class), and Nogales (20 hrs, $33 1st class; 26 hrs, $12 2nd class). The Guadalajara-bound train stops in Tepic (6 hrs, $9 1st class; 7 hrs, $3 2nd class). The first-class northbound train leaves daily at 7 PM and fills up quickly, so reserve seats the morning of departure. The second-class train for the same route leaves at 12:30 AM. The southbound trains leave daily at 8 AM (1st class) and 4 AM (2nd class).

BY PLANE Mazatlán's airport is a 40-minute drive from town. Taxis make the trip for around $18, and *pulmonías* (literally, pneumonias; in this case, golf carts) charge $10. Cheaper still are Volkswagen *colectivos* (communal taxis), which charge roughly $4 between the airport and Mazatlán's major hotels. At the airport, numerous booths provide information on hotels and transportation. There are a few international phones if you want to call home, but no luggage storage area is available. Carriers that serve Mazatlán from Los Angeles, San Francisco, or Denver include **Aeroméxico** (Camarón Sábalo 310, tel. 69/14–11–11), **Alaska Airlines** (in airport, tel. 69/85–27–30), and **Mexicana** (Paseo Claussen 101-B, tel. 69/82–77–22). Domestic carriers include **Aerocalifornia** (tel. 69/13–20–42) and **Aviación del Noroeste** (tel. 69/14–38–55), both with offices in the El Cid Hotel on Camarón Sábalo.

BY FERRY **Sematur** makes the 18-hour ferry crossing to La Paz, Baja, at 3 PM every day except Thursday and Saturday. An uncomfortable reclining seat costs $15, and a berth in a four-person cabin is $30. A two-person cabin with a bathroom is $40 a head. Vehicles can be ferried as well, but price varies according to size. You can reserve and buy ferry tickets in the office at the ferry landing on Playa Sur (Prolongación Carnaval, tel. 69/81–70–21), which is open daily 8–3:30. For the same price, use the travel agency **Turismo Coral** (5 de Mayo 1705, tel. 69/81–32–90), open weekdays 8–2 and 3–7, Saturday 8–2. Make reservations a few days in advance, even earlier during Easter holidays, and arrive an hour before the boat departs. To reach the ferry terminal, take the PLAYA SUR bus from the market. The terminal has luggage storage, but no nearby markets, so stock up on edibles and water before you arrive. The boat has a high-priced restaurant and a snack bar on board.

GETTING AROUND

Mazatlán has two primary neighborhoods: Mazatlán Viejo, including the malecón and Playa Norte; and the Zona Dorada. Mazatlán Viejo, the southern end of the city, is the civic and commercial center. This easily walkable area centers around **Plaza Revolución** (the *zócalo*, or main square) and the **Basílica de la Inmaculada Concepción**, Mazatlán's main church, on Avenida Benito Juárez. **Olas Altas**, a relatively quiet strip of beach, lies along the waterfront in Mazatlán Viejo, about seven blocks east of the basilica along Avenida Ángel Flores. Avenida del Mar, which connects Old and New Mazatlán, runs north along Playa Norte to Valentino's disco, where its name changes to Camarón Sábalo. The Zona Dorada, with its resort hotels, overpopulated beaches, and time-share condos, begins here.

New Mazatlán is so stretched out that walking can be pretty time-consuming. Fortunately, buses run from the central market to just about anywhere in town; purchase the 25¢ ticket on board. Bus stops are rare, so wave your hands to flag a bus down. The SABALO-BASILICA bus travels from the downtown market to the Zona Dorada and runs 5 AM–10 PM. Golf carts driven by maniacs cruise the streets of Mazatlán, and charge less than taxis. Arrange the fare (and say your prayers) before boarding. If you're feeling adventurous, rent a scooter (and helmet) for $6.50 an hour or $25 a day at one of the rental shacks at the south end of the Zona Dorada. Try **Hot Wheels Moto Rent** (Camarón Sábalo 35, no phone) near McDonald's.

WHERE TO SLEEP

For a popular resort town, Mazatlán has a surprising number of decent, cheap hotels. You'll find budget lodgings downtown, behind the Monumento al Pescador, or in the area east of the Basílica; there are even a few pockets of sanity within the Zona Dorada. Prices listed below are for the low season—if you're in town around Semana Santa or the Christmas and New Year holidays, expect to pay more. If you're only in town for a night, the best of the hotels near the bus station is the **Hotel Emperador** (Río Panuco, tel. 69/82–67–24), where each room has a color TV and one or two people can pay $10 for a single with air-conditioning ($7 without).

MAZATLAN VIEJO **Casa de Huéspedes El Castillo.** The brightly colored brick entrance gives way to nine well-maintained, comfortable rooms. With only two shared baths, however, there may be a problem if the place is full. Singles are $3, doubles $5. *Teniente José Azueta 1612 Nte., btw Canizales and 21 de Marzo, tel. 69/81–58–97. Luggage storage.*

Hotel del Centro. What this hotel lacks in atmosphere, it makes up for with 19 large, clean, air-conditioned rooms—all with private bath. Each floor has a small lobby with potted plants and rocking chairs; singles cost $7, doubles $9. *Canizales 705 Pte., ½ block from Basílica, tel. 69/81–26–73. Luggage storage.*

Hotel Santa Bárbara. Only a block from the beach, this hotel is run by a hip sister-brother team. All 21 rooms have tidy bathrooms, and each floor has a bright, breezy patio. Singles cost $7, doubles $11. *Benito Juárez 2612, at 16 de Septiembre, tel. 69/82–21–20. Luggage storage.*

Hotel La Siesta. Directly overlooking the waves, this is the best—though not the cheapest—lodging on the aging-tourist strip of Olas Altas. All 56 clean, air-conditioned rooms come with a bath and some of them open onto a lush but noisy courtyard. Ask for a room with a sea view. Generally, singles are $11, doubles $15; about $2 more will get you a TV. *Olas Altas 11 Sur, tel. 69/81–26–40. Luggage storage. Wheelchair access. AE, MC, V.*

ZONA DORADA **Apartamentos Ibis.** This family-run place has 40 rooms with kitchenettes and clean bathrooms for $13. One or two people can stay in a room, although some are small—ask to see several. *Camarón Sábalo 1666, at Río Ibis, tel. 69/13–59–38. Luggage storage. Wheelchair access.*

Hotel Bugambilias. Hidden in the heart of Zona Dorada, this charming hotel has 10 medium-size, clean rooms for $17 (singles) and $20 (doubles)—all with bath. There are also 11 apartments with kitchenettes, which cost $33 for two people and an extra $7 for each additional person. *Camarón Sábalo, at Costa Azul, tel. 69/14–00–29. AE, MC, V.*

Hotel San Diego. The rooms here are decent but dark—stay here if being near the Zona Dorada is important to you. Bring an alarm clock, though, as no morning sun will shine on your face. The most basic singles are $10; doubles cost $20. *Rafael Buelna, at Av. del Mar, tel. 69/83–57–03. 63 rooms. Luggage storage. Wheelchair access.*

CAMPING The Zona Dorada has a few expensive trailer parks ($10–$14 per night for a tent space). The best is **Mar Rosa** (Camarón Sábalo, near Holiday Inn, tel. 69/13–61–87), right on the waterfront. The park has showers and a decent cafeteria, and 24-hour guards ensure an uninterrupted night's sleep. Prices vary according to the desirability of the spot. You can also camp on the **Isla de la Piedra** beach, across the old marina from Mazatlán Viejo. Catch the ferry ($1 round-trip) on Avenida del Puerto, near Gutiérrez Najera. Ferries depart every 15 minutes, 24 hours a day. If you try to camp on any other beach, the local police will not-so-politely ask you to relocate.

FOOD

Like cheap hotels, inexpensive eateries are scattered throughout town. The **mercado municipal** (city market; open daily 5 AM–6 PM), at Avenidas Serdán and Melchor Ocampo, is your cheapest option. For an afternoon meal of delicious, relatively cheap seafood, head for one of the palapas on Playa Norte. Mazatlán is known for its shellfish, or *marisco,* and shrimp, *camarón*; shrimp soup and shrimp with bacon and cheese are both popular dishes.

Restaurants in the tourist zone aren't cheap, but the food is good and the drinks are creatively concocted. **Club Natural** (Loaiza 315-B, tel. 69/16–51–09) serves fresh-squeezed versions of everything from pineapple to papaya juice 24 hours a day. They also have tasty sandwiches ($3) and a salad bar.

➤ **UNDER $5** • **La Casa de Ana.** Sit on the patio overlooking the plaza and feast on the $3 vegetarian *comida corrida* (pre-prepared lunch special), which usually includes soyburgers and salads. *Constitución 515, at Plaza Machado, no phone. Open Sun.–Fri. 8–4:30.*

Cenaduría El Velorio Feliz. This tiny sidewalk eatery on the Plaza Machado is usually packed with local actors, drama teachers, and directors eating great food and hanging out with the owner, Mirla, and her sisters. You can get everything from tacos or quesadillas to *aguas frescas* (juice drinks) for 50¢, and there are often specials such as steamed almond fish or beef in *mole* (chile and chocolate sauce) for $2. If Mirla remembers, there'll be desserts too. *Constitución 507, no phone. Open daily 7 PM–midnight.*

Royal Dutch. Started as an in-home bakery, this is now also a café, with intimate courtyard dining and an expansive menu. Two eggs, hash browns, and toast will cost you $2, soups are $2, and sandwiches are $2–$4. Breads and desserts are still made on the premises. *Juárez 1307, at Constitución, tel. 69/81–20–07. Open Mon.–Sat. 8 AM–9 PM.*

➤ **UNDER $10** • **Jungle Juice Restaurant and Bar.** The cheesy name says it all: This joint has a great selection of juice drinks ($2). They also serve a $4 soyburger platter with fries, beans, and rice, and a hearty $3 egg, potato, and toast breakfast. If you're tired of Mexican cuisine, try the shrimp-stuffed avocado or fresh fruit salad with yogurt ($6 each). *Calle de Las Garzas 101, btw Loaiza and Camarón Sábalo, tel. 69/13–35–15. Open daily 5 PM–1 AM; bar open until 2 AM.*

Karnes en su Jugo. "Meat In Its Juice" is the name of this restaurant, and the cook is very serious about living up to it. A hefty order of beef comes with onions, beans, bacon, and homemade tortillas for $6. For $3, you can try one of the many types of pasta. *Camarón Sábalo, across from American Express, tel. 69/82–13–22. Open daily noon–midnight.*

WORTH SEEING

The best way to see Mazatlán Viejo, with its mix of crumbling old mansions and smaller homes, is on foot. The center of town is the **Plaza Revolución,** from which the blue-and-gold spires of the adjacent **Basílica** rise above the downtown buildings. A few blocks away, **Plaza Machado** (Constitución and Carnaval) the former heart of the city, is surrounded by elegant colonial-style buildings that have been turned into cafés and restaurants with outdoor seating. On Sunday evenings the plaza fills with everyone from gray-haired grannies to giggly children, who come to sit on the park benches beside amorous teenagers. As Avenida del Mar meanders north toward the Zona Dorada, you'll pass the unusual **Monumento al Pescador** (Fisherman's Monument): an enormous statue of a voluptuous nude woman reclining on an anchor, her hand extended toward a fisherman, also naked, hauling his nets. The malécon ends where the Zona Dorada begins (marked, appropriately enough, by the monstrous disco, **Valentino's**). Join the locals in a visit to **Isla de la Piedra** (Stone Island), where unpaved streets surround a pueblo, and uncharted beaches are encased by palm trees (*see* Outdoor Activities, *below*).

ACUARIO MAZATLAN Halfway between Zona Dorada and Old Mazatlán is this aquarium/zoo offering an aviary swarming with chirping birds, and close-up views of tropical fish, turtles, and crocodiles. Visitors can observe fish in a feeding frenzy four times daily, the sea lion show (half an hour later), or watch the shark film (following the sea lions). Although the film is in Spanish, Anglophones won't have a hard time understanding what the sharks are doing to the smaller fish. *Av. de los Deportes 111, 2 blocks off Av. del Mar, tel. 69/81–78–17. Admission: $3.50. Open daily 9:30–6:30.*

MUSEO ARQUEOLOGICO One of the few nods to pre-Columbian Mexico you'll encounter here, this museum features a permanent display of local artifacts, including simple jewelry, cooking tools, and burial ornaments. Also featured are temporary exhibits by local painters, sculptors, and ceramicists. *Sixto Osuna, 76, 1 block east of beach. Admission: $1. Open Tues.–Sun. 10–1 and 4–7.*

PLAZA DE TOROS Bullfights are held here most Sundays between Christmas and Easter. You can buy tickets in advance at Valentino's disco or most big hotels on the strip, as well as at the bullring the day of the fight. The cheapest seats are about $10 and fights start at 4 PM. *Rafael Buelna, near Zona Dorada, tel. 69/84–16–66.*

TEATRO ANGEL PERALTA This striking theater, built in 1860, was declared a historic monument in 1990. After a two-year restoration, it now hosts the music and dance performances of Mazatlán's active arts community. Details on what's playing can be found at the office, to the right of the entrance. It's 50¢ to tour the theater, $7–$10 for a ticket to see a

---

¡Olé!

Is bullfighting a bloodthirsty sport in which an unsuspecting animal ends up dead, or a fair challenge between an artist dressed in his "suit of light" and a thoroughbred bull? Mexicans consider "La Corrida de los Toros" more of an art than a sport, but you can decide for yourself at a number of bullfighting arenas along the Pacific Coast. The dramatic fight was brought to Mexico by the Spaniards, and now visitors regularly cheer the proud matador and his assistants through the three-act event. After an opening parade, each corrida consists of three matadors and six bulls, and the matador has 16 minutes to triumph over each bull. A quick death brings applause and roses; a slow process results in a sea of boos. Audience members cheering for the bull will also attract an unpopular response.

choral group, opera, or play (all in Spanish). *Sixto Osuna, at Carnaval, tel. 69/82–44–47. Box office open daily 8:30–2 and 4–7.*

CHEAP THRILLS

Locals of all ages gather in front of the mermaid statue on **Olas Altas at Ángel Flores** to hear folk and rock bands on weekend afternoons. The tourist office offers calendars of these and other cultural events. If you've had enough of the party scene, take a moonlight swim in the small saltwater pool built into the rocks at the base of the **Cerro de la Nevería** (Icebox Hill). It's located off the malecón, along Paseo Claussen. For something more strenuous, try climbing *up* the hill, or take one of the short hikes listed below—you'll be rewarded with awesome views.

CERRO DEL VIGIA Just south of Olas Altas, about halfway down the peninsula, is Lookout Hill. It was originally used by the Spanish to keep watch for pirates—hence the rusty cannon here today. It's a steep climb up the Paseo del Centenario to the top, but there are vista points along the way where you can catch your breath while pretending to take in the stunning views.

EL FARO Farther down the peninsula from Olas Altas is the **Cerro del Crestón**. It's a 30-minute hike to the *faro* (lighthouse) at the top, which offers views of the sea and the city.

OUTDOOR ACTIVITIES

Playa Sábalo and **Playa Las Gaviotas** are worked by vendors that offer boogie boards, Jet Skis, or five-minute parasail rides. **Playa Norte,** populated by palapa restaurants, is more popular among locals, and **Olas Altas,** farther south in Mazatlán Viejo, is the place to be at sunset. To avoid the crowds, take a 15-minute boat ride to the three empty islands facing the Zona Dorada—**Isla de los Venados** (Deer Island), **Isla de los Pájaros** (Bird Island), **Isla de los Lobos** (Wolf Island), and **Isla de la Piedra** (Stone Island). Boats run from **El Cid Resort** (Camarón Sábalo, tel. 69/13–33–33) and cost about $5 round-trip. There are no facilities on the islands, but if you want to swim or snorkel with your own equipment, the tiny slices of sand that skirt each one are pleasant. North of the Zona Dorada are some quieter beaches, such as **Playa Bruja** and **Playa Cerritos.** To reach these, take a CERRITOS bus from the Zona Dorada and hop off when you see the signs.

As you might imagine, you can rent almost any kind of watersport equipment in Mazatlán, provided you're willing to pay through the nose for it. Surf- and boogie boards are often rented by vendors on the beach near Valentino's disco, and cost about $5 an hour. At the **Aqua Sports Center** (tel. 69/13–33–33), next to El Cid, you can rent a Waverunner (like a Jet Ski) for $40 per half hour, a Hobie Cat ($25 per hour), a boogie board ($3 per hour), or snorkeling gear ($8 for 2 hours). One-tank scuba dives for certified divers include equipment and transportation to the Isla de los Venados for $50. Uncertified divers can participate if they first take a $10 resort course. You can parasail for $20 or snorkel for $17 (both include transport there). The hotel also offers eight-hour sportfishing trips for five or six people that include boat, guide, and all equipment for $200. In the fall and winter months, people come here to fish for mahimahi and marlin.

AFTER DARK

Most of Mazatlán's many nightclubs and discos are in the Zona Dorada and are frequented by rowdy twentysomething gringos and done-up Mexican tourists. Most also have a cover charge, but it's often possible to take advantage of the mayhem at beach clubs and slip in through a back entrance. The best of the tacky clubs on Avenida del Mar are **Señor Frog's** (Av. del Mar, tel. 69/85–11–10) and **Valentino's** (Punta del Malecón, tel. 69/14–77–77). Señor Frog's doesn't charge a cover, opens daily around noon, and stays open until 2 AM. Valentino's gets started at 10 PM, rocks on until 4 AM, and charges $10 at the door. For a local happenin' spot, check out **Café Pacífico** (Constitución 501, tel. 69/81–39–72). Gay nightlife centers around **Pepe El Toro** (Av. de las Garzas 18, tel. 69/84–41–76).

Near Mazatlán

CONCORDIA AND COPALA

Concordia, located in the foothills east of Mazatlán, makes a good getaway from Mazatlán's commercialism. This small pueblo was founded in 1565 and is known for colonial furniture and brown clay pottery, which can be found in shops along the highway. Churchgoers, smooching couples, and rambunctious kids gather at the zócalo, which is the heart of this mining village. Overlooking the zócalo, the 18th-century **Iglesia de San Sebastián** is considered the only truly baroque church in Sinaloa. Second-class buses to Concordia leave from Mazatlán's main bus station every hour on the hour (45 min, $1.25). If you want to stay the night with crowing roosters and festive locals, spend $10–$12 at the **Hotel Rancho Viejo** (El Vado Carretera Mazatlán–Durango, tel. 69/68–02–90).

About 24 kilometers past Concordia is the mining-cum-tourist center of **Copala,** whose cobblestone streets, steep hills, and recently renovated **Iglesia de San José** attract an annoying number of tour groups from Mazatlán, especially in summer. However, during the rainy season (July–September), Copala offers peaceful streets, cool mountain air, and views of the lush surrounding hills. On the main square is the antique-furnished **Hotel San José** (tel. 69/85–42–25). Buses leave Concordia's main thoroughfare (1 block north of the Red Cross) every hour, and cost $1. If you're coming from Mazatlán, the bus will drop you off 1½ kilometers from the mining village.

San Blas

San Blas is a budget traveler's resort in the shell of a small seaside town. Between Mazatlán and Manzanillo, this friendly, bucolic spot on the Nayarit coast is a place of rustic houses and intense sun rays, and flourishing wildlife and tropical jungles make it a perfect stop for the semirugged traveler or the dabbling naturalist. After overcoming the endemic and relentlessly biting jejene insects, either type of wayfarer will be rewarded by iridescent waterfalls, river canals, and tangled vegetation. Egrets, ibises, and woodpeckers are among the 300 different bird species native to this region, and even if you don't see them, you will certainly hear their calls.

San Blas is the place to ponder the chemical reaction between suntan lotion and insect repellant: "Will they neutralize each other, leaving me unprotected, or will I simply burst into flame?"

San Blas wasn't always the epitome of tropical lethargy. From the 1500s to the 1800s it was an important Pacific port with a peak population of over 30,000. It was soon eclipsed by Mazatlán and Manzanillo, but the ruins of an old stone cathedral, fort, and accounting house still remain. One plausible reason for San Blas's decline is the vicious biting insects that plague it during the rainy season, from mid-June through October. The logs kept by Spanish explorers remark on the number of mosquitoes, and describe how local people took cover at dusk. The bugs' persistence still keeps San Blas unpopulated, and other than a handful of surfers and hippies, you will probably have the beach to yourself.

BASICS

AUTO PARTS/SERVICE The three brothers who run **Servicio Mecánico Sandoval** don't speak English but will deal with your car troubles at any time of day or night—just call if the office is closed. *Juárez 188, near gas station, tel. 321/5–04–05. Open Mon.–Sat. 7–7.*

BANK Banamex (Juárez 26, off zócalo) changes cash and traveler's checks weekdays 8:30 AM–11 AM, but lines are often long and they sometimes charge unwarranted commissions or run out of cash altogether. Fortunately, the adjoining ATM accepts Cirrus and Plus cards.

EMERGENCIES The **police station** (cnr of Sinaloa and Canalizo, tel. 321/3–31–27) is open 24 hours a day.

MAIL The post office is on Sonora, at Echevarría, one block up and one block left from the bus station. They'll hold mail sent to you at the following address for up to 10 days: Lista de Correos, San Blas, Nayarit, CP 63740, México. The office is open weekdays 9–1 and 3–6, Saturday 9–1. **Casa de María** (*see* Where to Sleep, *below*) also sells stamps.

MEDICAL AID **Farmacia Botica Mexicana** (Juaréz and Batallón, tel. 321/5–01–22), open daily 8:30–1:30 and 5–9, has an English-speaking owner and lots of mosquito repellant.

PHONES There is a public Ladatel phone in the Palacio Municipal on the zócalo. From the *caseta de larga distancia* (long-distance telephone office) on the zócalo, you can place cash calls or pay a $2 commission for long-distance collect or credit-card calls.

VISITOR INFORMATION Rosa, who greets visitors at the bus station, is extremely knowledgeable about the area, and Federico at **Posada Portola** (*see* Where to Sleep, *below*) can help too. Although open hours fluctuate at the **Delegación de Turismo Municipal**, across from McDonald's restaurant (*see* Food, *below*), Manuela Córdova Delgado or a member of her staff will direct you if they're around. *Juárez 60, tel. 321/5–02–67. Open daily 9–noon and 7–9.*

COMING AND GOING

The bus station (tel. 321/5–00–43) is on the corner of Sinaloa and Canalizo, just off the zócalo. One bus leaves for Guadalajara (7 hrs, $8) at 8:30 AM, and there are four daily buses to Santiago Ixcuintla (1½ hrs, $1.50) and Las Varas (1½ hrs, $2.50). Buses to Santa Cruz (30 min, 75¢) leave at 8:20 AM, 10:30 AM, 12:30 PM, and 2:30 PM from the corner of Sinaloa and Paredes, stopping in the tiny beach towns en route. The 3½-hour trip to Puerto Vallarta costs $4.50, and buses leave at 7 AM and 10:30 AM. Buses to Tepic (1½ hrs, $2) leave almost every hour between 6:30 AM and 7 PM.

WHERE TO SLEEP

If you arrive in San Blas by bus, you will invariably be greeted by Rosa, who offers to guide road-weary travelers to a hotel. Take advantage of her services; they won't cost you anything—she receives a commission from practically every hotel in town. Wherever you stay, if you're here between June and October, inspect the windows, screens, and door for any possible entryways, lest you get sucked dry by voracious mosquitoes. Hotel prices vary depending on the season; the prices listed below apply during summer and fall, but expect to pay a few more dollars in winter and around Easter.

➢ **UNDER $15** • **Casa de María.** You'll be greeted by Pinocchio the pelican when you arrive at these two casas, each run by half of a mother-daughter team (both named María). The casas are similar, so pick one and knock—you'll find kitchen facilities and a kind owner who will wash your clothes for free. Basic, clean doubles are $8.50 with bath, $6.50 without. *Batallón 52 and 108, tel. 321/5–06–32. 2 blocks south of zócalo, at Michoacán. 11 rooms, 8 with bath. Laundry, luggage storage. Wheelchair access.*

Hotel Bucanero. Right across from the tourist office, this place is a hotel and entertainment center all in one. You can take a dip in the swimming pool, poke the stuffed alligator, inspect retired cannons, or shoot a game of pool. Singles cost $11, doubles $13. *Juárez 75, tel. 321/5–01–01. 2 blocks west of zócalo. 30 rooms, all with bath. Laundry, luggage storage. Wheelchair access.*

El Tesoro de San Blas. These large, quiet bungalows, complete with a well-equipped kitchen and dining room, are run by a native Californian woman who is full of useful information. Each bungalow runs $15 a night, with cheaper weekly rates. *Campeche, at Hidalgo, tel. 321/5–05–37. 3 bungalows, all with bath. Luggage storage. Wheelchair access.*

➢ **UNDER $25** • **Posada Portola.** Each of the bungalows here has a large kitchen and living/dining room separated from a good-size bedroom. The gregarious owner, Federico, will gladly rent you a bike or car, wash a load of laundry for $2.50, or even make your plane reservations. A single costs about $17, a double $24. Peso pinchers should ask for the cheap apartment above the office. *Paredes 118, just past Yucatán, tel. 321/5–03–86. From church, 1 block west, then a few blocks north. 8 bungalows, all with bath. Laundry, luggage storage. Wheelchair access. AE, MC, V.*

CAMPING The palapa restaurants on the beach will often let you use their facilities to string up a hammock after closing. Prices range from free to $4, depending on how much money you spent at the restaurant and the proprietor's mood. On Playa Borrego, **Restaurante de Federico y Lucia** is a good bet, as the owners live there and will keep an eye on you. You can pitch a tent or borrow one of their two hammocks for the night. For tent camping with all the facilities, try the reasonably priced **Trailer Park Coco Loco** (Teniente Azueta, down Batallón toward the beach, tel. 321/5–00–55), conveniently near the beach and inconveniently near the mosquitoes. Facilities include decent bathrooms with hot water and an overpriced bar. Whether you're in an RV or a tent, the fee is $5 for one person and $6.50 for two. There are 100 sites, and the park is wheelchair accessible.

FOOD

San Blas is a fishing town, so the seafood is fresh and not too expensive; during the day, fried fish at a beach restaurant costs about $4. San Blas is also proud of its *pan de plátano* (banana bread). A group of local surfers called Team Banana supports its competitive surfing by selling some of the best in town. You can buy the sweet-smelling loaves for $2 at **Tumba de Yaco** on Batallón, or from the surfers themselves on **Playa Las Islitas** (*see* Near San Blas, *below*). If you're in the mood to whip up your own meal, swing by the market on the corner of Batallón and Sinaloa between 6 AM and 4 PM.

Sailing paraphernalia decorates **La Familia** (Batallón 16, tel. 321/5–02–58), which sells seafood daily noon–10 PM. Try the $4 octopus salad, or one of the many varieties of shrimp. La Familia has wheelchair access, as does **McDonald's** (Juárez 75, ½ block west of zócalo, tel. 321/5–01–27), open daily 7 AM–10 PM. No, gringo fast food has not infiltrated this sleepy town: As they say in San Blas, this is the *Mexican* Micky D's, without a golden arch in sight. A fruit platter is $2.50, as is a standard plate of *huevos rancheros*. The dinner specials (such as grilled chicken with enchiladas, french fries, beans, chips, salad, and tortillas) will immobilize you for $6. With an atmosphere approaching elegant, **La Hacienda** (Juárez 41, tel. 321/5–07–72) is the talk of the town. The food at this traditional restaurant is delicious; try their $5 specialty, *pescado gaviota* (shrimp-stuffed fillet of sea bass in a cheese sauce). La Hacienda is wheelchair accessible and is open Wednesday–Monday, 2 PM–10 PM (bar open until midnight).

CHEAP THRILLS

Just off the coast, the dusty **Isla del Rey** (Island of the King) sports a lighthouse and an empty beach, and is the place to go if you're suddenly seized by a severe case of misanthropy. Supposedly the indigenous Huichol Indians still gather here to make offerings; you probably won't witness any rituals, but you may spot a few of the burros and horses that roam the island. To reach Isla del Rey, take a 50¢ boat from the dock next to the customs house.

For a historical look at San Blas and a fantastic view of the area, make the 15-minute hike from town up to La Contadoría. Here you'll find the ruins of **Nuestra Señora del Rosario,** a fort built in 1769, now garrisoned only by sun-loving iguanas. The adjoining structure was built in 1770 to house Spanish bureaucrats. After San Blas's decline as a port town, the hill itself was used by pirates to hide the riches they seized. To get here, follow the main road out of town; before the bridge, veer right past the restaurants and follow the stone road up the hill on your right.

FESTIVALS The residents of San Blas are a jovial group known to look for any reason to throw a party. On January 31, the anniversary of the death of revolutionary Father José María Mercado is celebrated with *cerveza* (beer), food, and fireworks. Mercado, who resided in San Blas in the early 1800s, leapt to his death to escape capture by the Spaniards. The hero was said to have covertly helped Miguel Hidalgo accumulate war supplies. Three days later, on February 3rd, San Blas enters a state of festive upheaval on the feast day of the city's saint, San Blas. Mariachi bands and inebriated locals sing and dance in the center square, and the celebration migrates down to the beach as the day progresses.

AFTER DARK

Compared to the heady high season (December–May), the summer months see only very mellow nightlife. **Mike's Bar,** above McDonald's (*see* Food, *above*), plays contemporary music, along with dubbed American movies. From Thursday to Sunday, Mike tunes up the piano and couples come from all directions for a few slow dances. If you're here during *Semana Santa* (the week leading up to Easter), you might catch the annual transvestite show. On Saturdays people head to **Disco La Fitte,** a block down from McDonald's, which charges a $3 cover and attracts the young and old for a pool-playing, kick-up-your-heels kind of night. Keep an eye out for Los Bucaneros, a local band that plays salsa, merengue, and other tropical sounds at local events and at the bar **El Herradero** (Battallón, towards the beach).

OUTDOOR ACTIVITIES

At **Playa Borrego** (one kilometer from the town center), San Blas's main beach, you'll find tangled vegetation, pelicans, and carnivorous summer insects. Quieter beaches lie to the south, at the **Bahía de Matanchén.** Bike rentals are available at **Posada Portola** (*see* Where to Sleep, *above*) for $5 a day, even if you're not a paying guest. You can also ask here for Toño Palma, who will be happy to take you out on a boat to watch whales or to fish for tuna and red snapper. His fees vary according to the season, and perhaps how much he likes the look of you. For $10, Lucio of the tourist office will lead you on a four-hour nature trip/hike through waterfalls, streams, and canyons—a great way to count the 300 bird sounds known to San Blas. Trips leave as soon as a group forms at the office on Juárez.

LA TOVARA San Blas's famous jungle boat ride takes you through a labyrinth of thick mangrove swamps to this freshwater spring. Keep your eyes open for camera-shy crocodiles, exotic birds, and schools of turtles—you'll even pass by the fake huts used in the film *Cabeza de Vaca*. Boats embark on the three-hour tour (*sans* Gilligan) down the Río San Cristóbal from the bridge just outside of San Blas; the trek costs $25 for up to four people. For a shorter and cheaper trip ($20 for 4), take the SANTA CRUZ bus to Matanchén (10 min, $1) and leave from the embarcadero where the bus drops you off. This boat fits more people, but the price increases with additional passengers. Boats run until sundown, with no set schedule; if you take the first tour at 8 AM you'll have an hour to swim in the spring before the bulk of tourists arrives. For an extra $15, visit the new crocodile research center, **El Centro Reproductor de Cocodrilos,** where, if you're lucky, you can watch the birth of baby crocs. If you don't want to pay for a boat trip, or are feeling masochistic, you can hike to La Tovara during the dry season (November–early June), but it takes two hours and the rocks are slippery. Two kids will competently guide any size group for half of what the boats charge. Ask for them at Posada Portola (*see* Where to Sleep, *above*). Be sure to follow them out of the jungle again, though—camping here is dangerous and off-limits.

Near San Blas

Besides the nearby towns of Santiago Ixcuintla and Mexcaltitán, there also are a number of beaches along the **Bahía Matanchén,** just south of San Blas. The first and best is **Playa Las Islitas** (also called Stoner's Beach), which is famous for the kilometer-long wave that occasionally appears in summer or fall, depending on some fortuitous conjunction of equinoctial and lunar forces. Team Banana rents surfboards and boogie boards for $3 an hour and $6 a day at a hut at the entrance to the beach. Farther south along the bay, the beaches are rockier but less infested with mosquitoes in summer. The oyster-harvesting town of **Aticama** has a small beach that runs into **Playa los Cocos,** a beautiful spot with lots of coconut trees. Here you can find a few seafood stands that serve Aticama oysters. The trailer park here is difficult to miss, and although it isn't attractive, it does offer cheap, secure tent camping for about $5. The teeny town of **Santa Cruz,** at the extreme south end of the bay, is almost totally untouristed and has one hotel and one bungalow complex. From the corner of Sinaloa and Paredes in San Blas, buses run along the bay to Las Islitas (10 min, 35¢), Los Cocos (20 min, 50¢), Aticama (25 min, 45¢), and Santa Cruz (30 min, 75¢) at 8:20 AM, 10:30 AM, 12:30 PM, and 2:30 PM. The last returning bus sets out from Santa Cruz at 4 PM, so be sure to keep an eye on the time.

SANTIAGO IXCUINTLA

This midsize city is in the center of Nayarit's tobacco fields, 40 kilometers northeast of San Blas. Far off the tourist track, it's a good place to soak up the atmosphere of rural Mexico. The city's main attraction is the **Centro Cultural Huichol** (*see box, below*), located 10 blocks east of the plaza down Calle Zaragoza; one of the center's founders, Susana, is a great resource for information about the region. On a hot afternoon, wander down Calle Hidalgo Sur to the **Río Lerma,** a great place to count camouflaged lizards and iguanas. Cheap hotels surround Santiago's plaza and the central market. Try the reasonably priced **Hotel Santiago** (Ocampo y Arteaga, tel. 323/5-06-37), where most of the rooms have TVs; singles are $10, doubles $12. Buses leave from the **bus station** (Primera Correjidora 12, north side of pueblo, tel. 323/5-12-12) for Tepic (hourly, 1 hr, $2) and Acaponeta (1 per day at 9 AM, 2 hrs, $2.50). Buses to San Blas leave at 8:30 AM and 2:30 PM (1½ hrs, $2). Buses to Santiago Ixcuintla leave regularly from Tepic (1 hr) and Tuxpán (1 hr), and thrice daily from San Blas.

MEXCALTITAN

The village of Mexcaltitán, believed to be Aztlán, the mythical first city of the Aztecs, sits on an island in the middle of a saltwater lagoon. The island is laid out like a wheel; numerous spokes radiate out from a central hub, and a street runs around the circumference. The name Mexcaltitán means "the place of the temple of the moon" in Nahuatl, and legend describes how an eagle with a serpent in its beak landed here before descending on the site of Tenochtitlán (present-day Mexico City), indicating where the Aztec capital should lie. You can learn more about Mexcaltitán's myths at the **Museo del Origen,** on the main plaza. Opened in 1989, the museum houses indigenous art, maps, and costumes that tell the story of ancient Aztec culture. The museum is open Tuesday–Sunday 9–1 and 3–5. From June 20 to 29, the villagers (plus a few thousand visitors) celebrate the opening of the shrimping season and honor the patron saints of the city, Pedro and Pablo. The annual fiesta features all-night dancing, lively bands, and lots of home-cooked seafood.

It's not surprising Mexcaltitán's 1,300 inhabitants are a tight-knit group: From September through January, heavy rains raise the water level around the island over 3 meters. Helicopters must fly in food, and those with intact homes house those who were not so lucky.

You can reach Mexcaltitán from either Tuxpán or Santiago Ixcuintla—take the 2:30 PM bus from Tuxpán or a bus from Santiago Ixcuintla (times vary) to Embarcadero Batango, then jump on a boat to the village. Boats return to the embarcadero in time to catch the 3 PM bus back to Tuxpán ($2) or the $2 Santiago Ixcuintla bus, which leaves at 10:30 AM, 1 PM, 4 PM, and 6 PM. If you miss the boat, the simply named **Hotel** (Venecias 5, south of the plaza, tel. 20/21-11-28) is seldom full and offers $9 singles and $11 doubles. For fresh shrimp or shellfish try either **Restaurante El Camarón** on the plaza, or **Restaurante Camichina,** on the east edge of the island.

Tepic

The capital of the agricultural state of Nayarit, Tepic is not a city to linger in if you're short on time or have the beach and an ice-cold coconut drink on your mind. There are, however, a few reasons to visit this city. The bus station is a hub for transportation throughout western Mexico, so your travels between Puerto Vallarta and San Blas or Los Mochis might make Tepic a required stop. Tepic is also a good place to meet indigenous Huichols and Aztecs, who come down from the hills to buy supplies. The town is also populated by old men in cowboy hats, their faces darkened and wrinkled from labor in the sun, chatting on street corners and shopping in the small stores that sell leather goods, tools, ammunition, and chemical fertilizers.

The gray buildings of Tepic stand in marked contrast to the colorful Huichol embroidery and yarn paintings sold in the town's many markets.

If you're going to be in the city for more than a few hours, head for the free **Museo Regional de Nayarit** (México 91, at Zapata, tel. 321/2–19–00), near the zócalo, where you'll find a fine collection of pre-Columbian clay figurines. The museum is open weekdays 9–7, and Saturday 9–3. Farther south down Avenida México, the **Ex-Convento de la Cruz de Zacate** (México, at Calzada del Ejército) was built to guard a grass cross that, legend has it, miraculously appeared nearby in 1540. The building now houses the offices of the state tourism department, a ballet academy, an art store, and a progressive theater group, which offers acting and musical instrument lessons. To escape Tepic's noise and general drabness, take a stroll through **Paseo La Loma** (Insurgentes and Colegio Militar), a large park with pine and eucalyptus trees and a miniature train—hop aboard for a ride reminiscent of "The Little Engine That Could."

BASICS

AUTO PARTS/SERVICE Taller Mecánico Mana is near the main bus station and can help with most mechanical problems. *Insurgentes 328, no phone. Open weekdays 9–7, Sat. 9–2.*

CASAS DE CAMBIO Tepic's casas de cambio and banks are downtown along Avenida México. **Banamex** (Avenida México, at Zapata) has an ATM that accepts Cirrus and Plus cards. For traveler's checks and dollars, casas de cambio give slightly better rates, but banks don't charge a commission, so it's a toss-up between the two. Hours may be the deciding factor: Banks change money only 9 AM–noon, while the **Casa de Cambio Libra** (México 128, at Zapata, tel. 321/2–73–88) is open Monday–Saturday 8:30–2 and 4–7:30.

EMERGENCIES The number for the **police** is 321/2–01–63; they can also get you an ambulance.

MAIL A joint post and telegram office in the bus station is open weekdays 8–1. The main post office (Durango 33 Nte.) is open weekdays 8–7, Saturday 8–11:30 AM. The latter will hold mail sent to you at the following address for up to 10 days: Administración de Correos, Durango 33 Nte., Tepic, Nayarit, CP 63000, México.

Centro Cultural Huichol

Susana and Mariano Valadez, an American anthropologist and a Huichol artisan (respectively), founded this nonprofit center in Santiago Ixcuintla to provide local Huichol people with an alternative to working in chemical-ridden tobacco fields. The center provides medical care, shelter, legal aid, and training in art and farming techniques, as well as a place where Huichols can stay while working on the coast. The center helps indigenous people become economically self-sufficient through practicing sustainable agriculture and traditional art forms. Huichol artisans supposedly tap into the metaphysical world and then translate the acquired knowledge into meticulous beadwork, embroidery, yarn paintings, and weaving. Although the prices for the artesanía (crafts) aren't always lower here than in Tepic's stores, the work is often of higher quality, and proceeds go back into the project and community. There is also a small, free, on-site museum. People who are committed to learning about and participating in this social venture, especially those with valuable skills to share (such as medicine or carpentry) are welcome to stay for a while in exchange for labor. If you're interested, call 323/5–11–71, or fax 323/5–10–06 for more information, or try the U.S. office in Seattle (tel. 260/622–4067, fax 206/622–0646). Avenida 20 de Noviembre 452, at Constitución. Open daily 9 AM–8 PM.

MEDICAL AID You can get advice about minor medical problems as well as basic first aid at the **Farmacia de Descuento** near the zócalo. *México 65, tel. 321/2–17–17. Open Mon.–Sat. 9–7:30, Sun. 9–2.*

PHONES The best place to make long-distance calls in Tepic is the bus station, where you can place collect or credit-card calls. There's also a 24-hour telephone office on the first-class side of the bus station, but they won't let you make collect calls.

VISITOR INFORMATION The Nayarit regional **tourist office** can provide maps of Tepic and the state as well as handfuls of tourist brochures, most of which are in Spanish. *Av. de la Cultura 74, tel. 321/4–80–71. Open weekdays 9–9.*

COMING AND GOING

Central Tepic is walkable. The bus station and park are on Avenida Insurgentes, which crosses Avenida México, the main commercial street. Near the intersection of Avenidas Insurgentes and México you'll find casas de cambio, restaurants, hotels, most of Tepic's points of interest, and the zócalo. About 10 blocks north on México, you'll hit another main square, where the basilica and several cheap hotels and restaurants are located. Both main avenidas can be traversed by Volkswagen bus for about 15¢.

BY BUS Tepic's bus terminal is on Avenida Insurgentes, about six blocks east of Avenida México. If you're flat broke, store your luggage ($1 for 6 hours) and throw your sleeping bag down here. **Transportes del Pacífico** (tel. 321/3–23–20) has buses to Mazatlán (4 hrs, $7), Guadalajara (4 hrs, $7), Los Mochis (12 hrs, $20), Mexicali (30 hrs, $45), and Tijuana (32 hrs, $45). Service to Puerto Vallarta (3 hrs, $6) leaves on the half hour, 24 hours a day. If you ask the driver, the Puerto Vallarta bus will also let you off at Rincón de Guayabitos or other beaches on the way. **Transportes Norte de Sonora** (tel. 321/3–23–15) serves Acaponeta (2 hrs, $3.50), and **Omnibus de México** (tel. 321/3–13–23) has one bus leaving at 4:30 PM daily to Cuidad Juárez (28 hrs, $70), as well as hourly service to Guadalajara (3½ hrs, $8) and evening service to Mexico City (11 hrs, $26). To get downtown from the station, take an ESTACION FRESNOS bus.

BY TRAIN To reach the train station, hop an ESTACION FRESNOS bus, which passes the train station on its way to the bus station. Trains travel north from Tepic to Mexicali (32 hrs, $50 1st class; 38 hrs, $19 2nd class), with stops in Culiacán (8 hrs, $10 1st class; 10 hrs, $4 2nd class), Sufragio (10 hrs, $16 1st class; 12 hrs, $7 2nd class), and Nogales (23 hrs, $40 1st class; 28 hrs, $15 2nd class). The southbound train goes as far as Guadalajara (5 hrs, $6 1st class; 6 hrs, $1.50 2nd class). The northbound train leaves daily at 2 PM (1st class) and 5 PM (2nd class). The southbound train leaves at noon (2nd class) and 4 PM (1st class). Times may vary from season to season—call ahead to check. *Tel. 321/3–48–13 or 321/3–48–61. Ticket office open 10 AM–about midnight.*

WHERE TO SLEEP

Tepic has a few inexpensive hotels right by the bus station—convenient for weary travelers but also noisy. Turn left out of the bus station, make another immediate left, and walk one block to **Hotel Nayar** (Martínez 430, tel. 321/3–23–22). The bathrooms are clean and have hot water, and it's not a bad choice considering the price: Singles are $6.50, doubles $9. **Hotel Sarita** (Bravo 112 Pte., tel. 321/2–13–33) is close to the Basilica and has colonial-style furniture and clean, fan-cooled rooms. Rooms with one bed cost $8, $11.50 with two beds. A few rooms are wheelchair accessible. **Hotel Altamirano** (Mina 19, tel. 321/2–10–31), just off the zócalo and behind the Palacio Municipal, is quiet and wheelchair accessible. Singles cost $10 and doubles are $11.50. There is no campground in town, so those with a tent should head for the Laguna de Santa María del Oro (*see* Near Tepic, *below*).

FOOD

Food is generally cheaper in Tepic than in the seaside resorts, and better than you might expect. Fresh seafood comes straight from San Blas, and vegetarian restaurants pop up with surprising frequency. Grill joints stretch along Avenida Insurgentes below the park. Super-cheap grub is also sold near the bus station on Avenida Victoria, close to México. If you're in the mood for fruit and snacks, you'll find a market on the corner of Puebla and Zaragoza.

After 1 PM, **Antropós** (México 73 Nte., near Zapata, no phone) serves tacos with all the trimmings—cilantro, tomatoes, guacamole, salsa, and grilled onions—for less than $1. For tasty vegetarian food in a great location, try **Girasol** in Paseo La Loma park, where soyburgers are $1 and veggie *pozole* (corn soup) overflowing with mushrooms is about $2. The owner's brother runs the similar **Restaurant Vegetariano Quetzalcoatl** (León 220, at Lerdo, no phone) on the northern fringe of downtown. Carnivores in the mood for a real meal can head for **Restaurant Altamirano** (México 109 Sur, near Palacio Municipal, tel. 321/2-13-77), where high ceilings, stone walls, and the sound of frying tortillas create an "authentic" atmosphere. L*engua en salsa* (beef tongue) or *pollo en mole* (chicken in chile and chocolate sauce) will cost you $3.

Near Tepic

LAGUNA DE SANTA MARIA DEL ORO

About an hour's drive on a curvy mountain road will bring you to the **Laguna de Santa María del Oro**, a stunning turquoise lake. Situated in the crater of an extinct volcano, the laguna is frequented by families from Tepic who come for the lake's ideal swimming spots, shaded lakeshore food huts, and hidden campsites. Locals claim the 1985 quake killed off all the lake's catfish, but the aquatic life now seems to be replenished, and the lake is popular for fishing. Sample the local specialty, *pescado dorado* (grilled "golden fish"), at **Restaurante El Viejo Aztlán** or **Restaurante Los Tules,** both on the south side of the lake. **Bungalows Koala** (tel. 321/4-05-09) has the only lodgings in the area: Five bungalows ($17 a night) around a swimming pool and grassy field. You can also rent tents for $1.50 a night at **El Viejo Aztlán** and camp right on the warm sand. To reach the laguna, take a 10:30 AM or 2 PM bus ($1.25) from the Terminal Centro (Avs. Victoria and México) in Tepic. Keep your eyes on your watch if you don't want to stay—the last bus returns to Tepic at 4:30 PM.

Puerto Vallarta

Puerto Vallarta is famous for beaches, cobblestone streets, and the whitewashed, red-roofed buildings stacked along its precipitous hillsides. Unfortunately, many of the latter are condos and timeshares. Like most of the resorts on the Pacific Coast, the city has a gringo-ized hotel zone (the *zona hotelera*) separate from the "Mexican" part of town—staying here would be like living at your local shopping mall. The downtown area around the Río Cuale is more residential, with pleasant cafés, good restaurants, and places to rent snorkel gear. The biggest draw, however, is Puerto Vallarta's natural setting. Nestled between lush tropical hills and spectacular coastline, the resort gives way to a tropical jungle full of birds and natural caves.

Some credit for making Puerto Vallarta a popular destination belongs to *The Love Boat* and John Huston's *The Night of the Iguana* (or more specifically, the romance between Richard Burton and Liz Taylor that blossomed here during the filming of the latter). Mexicana also had a hand in its promotion—the airline "discovered," developed, and marketed the resort town in the early 1950s to combat Aeroméxico's monopoly on flights to Acapulco. Although the result is a big, often ugly resort, the rustic architecture of old Vallarta, the green waves of the Pacific, and palm-fringed beaches frequented by strolling mariachis may make a visit here worthwhile.

BASICS

AMERICAN EXPRESS The office sells traveler's checks and changes them at a good rate. Cardholders can cash personal checks and have their mail held here. *Calle Morelos 660, at Abasolo, Col. Centro Puerto Vallarta, Jalisco, CP 48300, México, tel. 322/3-29-55. Open weekdays 9–6, Sat. 9–1.*

CASAS DE CAMBIO Puerto Vallarta has many casas de cambio, usually in tiny storefront booths with caged-in employees. All of them change cash and traveler's checks at rates neither better nor worse than in other cities. **Casa de Cambio** (Díaz Ordaz 866, tel. 322/2–57–08), at the north end of the malecón, is open Monday–Saturday 9–9. The **Asociación Cambiaria** (Morelos 480, tel. 322/2–37–12), at the south end of the malecón, changes all sorts of currency Monday–Saturday 9–9.

CONSULATES Canada's **consulate** (Hidalgo 226, tel. 322/2–53–98) is open weekdays 10–2. The **U.S.** consulate (Parian del Puente 12-A, behind Restaurant Fuente del Puente, tel. 322/2–00–69) is open weekdays 9–1, but you can call at any time.

EMERGENCIES The number for the **police** is 322/2–01–23. To get an **ambulance**, call 322/5–03–86.

LAUNDRY The amiable staff at **Lavandería Blanquita** will wash, dry, and fold 3 kilos of clothes for $2. *Madero 407-A, no phone. Open Mon.–Sat. 8–8.*

MAIL The **post office** is a half block from the malecón, at Juárez. They offer the usual services and will hold mail sent to you at the following address for up to 10 days: Lista de Correos, Calle Mina 188, Puerto Vallarta, Jalisco, CP 48300, México. *Mina 188, tel. 322/2–18–88. Open weekdays 8–7:30, Sat. 9–1.*

MEDICAL AID The **CMQ** clinic (Badillo 365, ½ block east of Insurgentes, tel. 322/3–19–19) has English-speaking doctors with all kinds of specialties, and attends patients 24 hours a day. Prices start at $17 for an appointment, and walk-in emergency care is also available. Next door, **Farmacia CMQ** (Badillo 367, tel. 322/2–29–41) is also open 24 hours.

PHONES Both **Transportes del Pacífico** (Insurgentes 282, tel. 322/2–10–15) and **Tres Estrellas de Oro** (Carranza 322, tel. 322/3–11–17) stations have casetas de larga distancia, open 6:30 AM–midnight. Both charge a flat $2 for collect calls. Save your precious pesos by calling from a pay phone—the Plaza Principal and the malecón are lined with them.

VISITOR INFORMATION The only real tourist office is the **Delegación Federal de Turismo**—the rest are out to sell you something. They have a number of brochures and free copies of a decent English-language tourist newspaper. *In Palacio Municipal, tel. 322/2–02–42. Open weekdays 9–9.*

COMING AND GOING

BY BUS Puerto Vallarta does not have a central bus station. Instead, each bus line operates out of individual buildings, all of which are south of the Río Cuale, on or near Avenida Insurgentes. **Tres Estrellas de Oro** (Badillo 11, at Insurgentes, tel. 322/3–11–17), which also operates **Élite** buses, leaves for Hermosillo (24 hrs, $43) at 5 PM with stops in Tepic (3 hrs, $6) and Mazatlán (8 hrs, $13). Buses leave for Manzanillo (5 hrs, $8) at 7 AM and 1 PM. The 1 PM bus continues on to Acapulco (19 hrs, $23). They also send five buses every afternoon to Mexico City (14 hrs, $31). **Transportes del Pacífico** (Insurgentes 282, tel. 322/2–10–15) sends buses to Guadalajara (6 hrs, $11) every hour between 7 AM and 1 AM. Tepic-bound buses leave every half hour from 4:15 AM to 8:15 PM. A slightly more expensive *plus* service (nicer, cleaner buses with air-conditioning) is also available to these destinations. **Transportes Norte de Sonora** (Carranza 322, btw Insurgentes and Constitución, tel. 322/2–66–66) goes to San Blas (3 hrs, $4.50), as well as Mazatlán and Tepic. Luggage storage is available at this depot. **Transportes Cihuatlán** (Madero 296, at Constitución, tel. 332/2–34–36) has frequent service to Manzanillo (6½ hrs, $7.50) and to intermediate points such as Bahía Chamela (3½ hrs, $4) and Barra de Navidad (5 hrs, $7).

BY PLANE Puerto Vallarta's international airport is 6 kilometers north of town, near the major resorts. **Aeroméxico** (Plaza Genovesa, tel. 322/4–27–77) and **Mexicana** (Centro Comercial Villas Vallarta, in the zona hotelera, tel. 322/4–89–00) have daily flights to Guadalajara ($50 one-way) and Mexico City ($70 one-way). Both carriers also have service from Dallas, Houston, Los Angeles, New York, and San Diego. Check **Alaska, American, Continental,** or **Delta** for other flights to Puerto Vallarta. City buses marked AEROPUERTO, IXTAPA, or JUNTA drop you off on the highway a hop, skip, and jump from the terminals. You can also take an airport taxi from the town center for $6.

GETTING AROUND

Puerto Vallarta is divided into three parts: the northern zona hotelera (a long stretch of hotels, shopping centers, and overpriced restaurants); the pedestrian-friendly downtown (*Viejo Vallarta,* or "Old Vallarta"), which runs along the banks of the Río Cuale; and, to the south, **Playa de los Muertos, the** most popular beach in Puerto Vallarta proper. The **malecón** begins at Díaz Ordaz and runs south along the bay past the **Plaza Principal** (also called Plaza de Armas). Near the plaza is the **Iglesia de Nuestra Señora de Guadalupe,** which has a large crown atop its bell tower—a copy of the crown worn by the empress of Mexico in the late 1860s.

To reach the zona hotelera from the downtown area, hop a HOTELES, AEROPUERTO, or MARINAS VALLARTA bus on Insurgentes or Juárez. Buses return along Morelos and, south of the Río Cuale, along Insurgentes. Buses run from 5 AM until midnight and each trip costs about 30¢. You can also take one of the many taxis roaming Vallarta—the aggressive drivers will flag *you* down for a ride. Due to inattentive bus drivers and numerous one-way unpaved streets, renting bikes or scooters may be hazardous. If you decide to take the risk, **Sun Bike** (Badillo 381, tel. 322/2-00-80) rents mountain bikes ($10 for 4 hrs), and **Moto Gallo** (Badillo 324, tel. 322/2-16-72) rents Honda scooters ($6.50 an hr, $35 for the whole day).

WHERE TO SLEEP

Almost all budget hotels are just south of the Río Cuale along Madero. The good news is that they are close to the bus stations and a short 4–7 blocks from the beach. The bad news is that most have cramped hallways and rooms overlooking noisy interior courtyards. Remember that hotel prices jump as much as 30% between October and March.

➤ **UNDER $10** • **Hotel Azteca.** With special rates for families, this cheap hotel fills with loud children and working locals. The good news is that there's an airy courtyard. Singles cost $5, doubles $6.50. Rooms with kitchenettes are $10. *Madero 473, tel. 322/2–27–50. 47 rooms, all with bath. Luggage storage. Wheelchair access.*

Hotel Villa del Mar. This hotel, decorated with maps from all over Europe and America, is a steal during summer, when the clean exterior rooms with balconies and fancy beds cost $7.50 for a single ($6.50 for an interior room), $9 for a double ($8 interior). For $12 you can have an apartment-style room for two with a kitchenette. *Madero 440, 3 blocks east of Insurgentes, tel. 322/2–07–85. 49 rooms, all with bath. Luggage storage. Wheelchair access. MC, V.*

➤ **UNDER $15** • **Hotel Belmar.** Easily the nicest of the cheaper hotels, the Belmar has freshly painted walls, tile floors, creative artwork, and brightly striped bedcovers. The bathrooms are clean, and rooms ($10 singles, $12 doubles) open either onto a balcony over the street or onto the courtyard hallway. Ask for a room with TV—it's the same price. *Insurgentes 161, at Serdán, tel. 322/2–05–72. 29 rooms, all with bath. Luggage storage.*

Hotel Yazmin. A lush courtyard, clean rooms, and a fine location one block from Playa de los Muertos make this place well worth the few extra dollars. It's right in old Puerto Vallarta, upstairs from the fabulous Café de Olla (*see* Food, *below*). In summer, singles cost about $12.50, doubles $14.50, but again, prices hike up for the winter season. *Badillo 168, tel. 322/2–00–87. 27 rooms, all with bath. Luggage storage. Wheelchair access.*

➤ **UNDER $25** • **Hotel Rosita.** You'll pay a bit more here, but you'll be where the action is (near the beach and malecón), with a balcony overlooking the beach and access to a pool. Downstairs you'll find a restaurant with local specialties. In low season, a small single costs $12, a larger one $17; double occupancy costs $21 regardless of the size of the room. If Puerto Vallarta has put you in the mood to splurge, go for a "suite"—a high-ceilinged room with brick walls, air-conditioning, a beautiful tiled bathroom, and a comfy, new king-size bed ($24.50 for 2–4 people). Prices here jump a bit earlier than in other hotels, generally in August. *Díaz Ordaz 901 (north end of malecón), tel. 322/2–10–33. 112 rooms, all with bath. Luggage storage. AE, MC, V.*

CAMPING There is no real campground here, and the hotels and the police don't look favorably upon (and sometimes even hassle) people sleeping on hotel beaches. If you're set on beach camping, it's better to crash at the south end of **Playa de los Muertos,** where campers are safe and not bothered as frequently. During Semana Santa, temporary campgrounds are set up here to accommodate the crowds.

FOOD

There's a huge variety of food here, including many French and Italian restaurants, but prices are often exorbitant. You can even try Aztec fare, complete with *maguey* (century plant) worms, for $8 a plate at **Mogambo** (Díaz Ordaz, tel. 322/2–34–76). Good $3 comidas corridas can be found at Puerto Vallarta's **market,** just north of the Río Cuale. Cheap eats are also available along Insurgentes, on the other side of the Río Cuale. Fresh juice ($1.50) or a quick espresso (75¢) can be had at **Jugos y Café Malibu** (Morelos, at Guerrero, no phone).

➢ **UNDER $5** • **Café de Olla** has delicious $1.50 tamales, and $4 chiles rellenos (with rice, beans, tortillas, and tons of cheese). The coffee—café de olla—is good, too. *Badillo 168, btw Olas Altas and Pino Suárez, tel. 322/2–00–87. Open Wed.–Mon. 8 AM–midnight.*

Cenaduría el Campanario. This family-run restaurant is usually packed with locals and travel-smart tourists, sampling the excellent $2 pozole, 50¢ tamales, or a corn soup made with meat, chicken, or pork. *Hidalgo 339, at Independencia, tel. 322/3–15–09. Open Mon.–Sat. 7 PM–11 PM. Closed first 2 weeks of Aug. Wheelchair access.*

➢ **UNDER $10** • **Archie's Wok.** Founded by Archie Alpenia, once John Huston's private chef, this restaurant dishes out the best, most varied Asian food around. Choose from Hoisin ribs ($5.50) and Thai coconut fish ($6.50), or get your fix of stir-fried vegetables ($4). *Rodríguez 130, tel. 322/2–04–11. Near pier at Playa de los Muertos. Open Mon.–Sat. 2–11.*

La Dolce Vita. If you've been craving pizza, indulge yourself with one of the oven-baked pies ($6) here. They are nothing like the pale imitations served in most Italian restaurants in Mexico, and one feeds two hungry people. The $5 pasta is great too. *Díaz Ordaz 674, north end of malecón. tel. 322/2–38–52. Open Mon.–Sat. noon–2 AM, Sun. 6 PM–midnight.*

CAFES **Café San Cristobal.** This European-style coffee shop roasts its own beans, and supplies them to restaurants and other cafés around the city. They also have a small menu (a cheese, bread, and fruit plate is $2) to accompany the coffees and desserts. Espressos run 60¢, mochas $1.15, and hot chocolate is $1. *Corona 172, btw Juárez and Morelos, tel. 322/3–25–51. Open Mon.–Sat. 8 AM–10 PM.*

Café Twin Dolphin. This outdoor café specializes in crêpes—chocolate crepes ($1.50), crepes with fruit ($2.50), or any old type of crêpe you want. Sit under a pink umbrella and sip cappuccino while you eat. *Badillo 206, at Suárez, tel. 322/2–23–79. Open Mon.–Sat. 8 AM–10 PM.*

OUTDOOR ACTIVITIES

Most of the things to do in Puerto Vallarta involve getting wet; but if you've had enough of that, walk along the malecón and check out the dolphin, seahorse, and mermaid statues. For something a little more strenuous, **Bike Mex** (Guerrero 361, 1 block north of market, tel. 322/3–16–80) organizes mountain-biking trips. Trips are divided into beginner, intermediate, and advanced levels, and range from four-hour trips costing $30 to $800 week-long adventure tours. All equipment and food is included. Stop by Monday–Saturday 9–2 and 4–7 to enquire or make reservations.

Playa de los Muertos is the most popular beach in Puerto Vallarta, frequented by surfers, tourists, and vendors. The gloomy name (Beach of the Dead) was derived from a battle with the Spanish that took place here. At sunset, people congregate to watch the horizon turn persimmon red against the outline of distant mountains. Parasailing at the beach costs $30 and banana boat rides are $6. Snorkel gear can be rented ($9 for 24 hrs) or you may arrange guided snorkel or dive trips ($23 and $42 respectively) through **Chico's Dive Shop** (Díaz Ordaz 770–

5, tel. 322/2-18-95). They also offer more advanced (and more expensive) trips, as well as a $200 certification course.

Los Arcos (the Arches) are a set of large rocks under which caves have been formed by wave erosion. Chico's and other dive shops will take you scuba diving in these protected, tropical fish-filled waters. To save big bucks, however, rent your own snorkel gear, take a RUTA 2 combi (25¢) from Plaza Lázaro Cárdenas (corner of Vallarta and Badillo) to **Playa Mismaloya**. Get off at the Arcos Hotel, walk down to the rocky beach, and swim out yourself. Playa Mismaloya is also a good sunning/swimming beach. John Huston's classic film *Night of the Iguana* was shot here, but you might not recognize the spot due to the massive Arcos Hotel, now looming over everything. If you walk inland from Playa Mismaloya along the dirt road, you'll find **El Edén**, where the movie *Predator* was filmed. You'll be rewarded for your 90-minute uphill walk by a user-friendly waterfall where you can swim, slide down rocks, or swing on ropes into the water. To refuel, stop at either of the two restaurants along the way.

The more isolated beaches of **Las Animas** and **Yelapa** are on the southern side of the **Bahía de Banderas**, past Playa Mismaloya, and are accessible only by boat. Las Animas is less developed than Yelapa, which has a small colony of expatriate gringos who pretend they never left home. Yelapa has pricey and often full cabañas, but you can camp for free on the beach in either place. There's a small waterfall 15 minutes from the beach in Yelapa. When the tide is low enough, you can walk along the shore from Boca de Tomatlán to Las Animas, though you might get wet negotiating some pretty daunting rocks. The cheapest way to reach these beaches is by water shuttle, which leaves daily at 11 AM from the pier at Playa de los Muertos and returns at 4 PM. Fare is $10 round-trip.

AFTER DARK

There are a million discos in Puerto Vallarta, but most either extort an outrageous cover or charge scandalous prices for drinks. Fortunately, you can sometimes get free or discounted passes by playing up to the oh-so-friendly timeshare people, and once you're inside a club, you can often get free passes to return. Most of the Americanized bars/dance spots are on the north end of the malecón; south of the river on Juaréz and Vallarta is a collection of chic clubs. The zona hotelera is more expensive still.

The **Zoo** (Díaz Ordaz 630, tel. 322/2-49-45) and **Carlos O'Brien's** (Díaz Ordaz 786, tel. 322/2-14-44) are considered the hip malecón strip hangouts, and anything from a bathing suit to an evening gown is considered suitable attire. The Zoo, complete with bouncers dressed like gorillas and whistling waitresses offering tequila poppers, gets going at about 9 PM, and attracts American high school groups. Friday through Sunday, bring $6.50 for the cover. Carlos O'Brien's, which plays American dance music, also functions as a restaurant—crowds of shiny-faced, over-zealous teenagers shift from the dining side to the dancing side at about 10 PM. The candlelit **DIVA** (Vallarta 266, btw Carranza and Ardenas, no phone) attracts a mixed Mexican/American crowd that adheres to the "no shorts or sandals" dress code. DIVA charges $8.50 for men, $3.50 for women on Tuesday and Friday, which includes an open bar. Other nights bring other gimmicks—free tequila on Thursday, $1 drinks on Monday and two-for-one specials on Wednesday and Sunday. **Los Balcones Bar** (Juárez 182, 1 block south of Plaza Principal, tel. 322/2-46-71), open 9:30 PM-4 AM, is a popular gay hangout with quiet balcony tables that overlook the street. If you prefer live salsa and *música tropical* and want to mingle with some Mexicans, jump on a bus to the zona hotelera and get off at **Cielito Lindo**. To avoid the dance scene altogether, walk over the bridge from Insurgentes to the middle of the island **Le Bistro** (Río Cuale island 16, tel. 322/2-02-83), one of the sleekest restaurant/bars in town. Sit at the classy black-and-white bar or in the dinner lounge, and listen to the gurgling of the Río Cuale while a DJ spins your favorite jazz tunes. Another option is to shoot a game of pool with some local pool sharks at the **Pool Hall** (Madero 279). However, unaccompanied women are certain to get hassled here.

Sunday nights around sundown, there's usually a free dance or theater performance on the malecón.

Near Puerto Vallarta

North of Puerto Vallarta, off Highway 200, are a number of golden, sandy beaches not frequented by tourists, at least in summer. **Rincón de Guayabitos,** a family resort dotted with bungalows and restaurants, is the most developed beach in these parts. **San Francisco, Lo de Marco,** and **Chacala** are some of the cleaner and more deserted ones. All the beaches except Chacala (where you can camp on the beach relatively undisturbed) have small hotels and/or bungalows in a range of prices. With the exception of Chacala, all are also within fairly easy walking distance from the highway, and can be reached on any Tepic-bound bus (see Coming and Going, above). To reach the more isolated Chacala, get off the Tepic bus at Las Varas and catch a colectivo from the side of the highway road. The colectivos make the 8-kilometer trip infrequently (and only from dawn till dusk), and the road is unbelievably bumpy.

PUNTA DE MITA

On the northern tip of the Bahía de Banderas, Punta de Mita offers glassy water and high-breaking waves perfect for swimming and surfing (respectively), although the rocky ocean floor demands some caution. The landscape here is drier than what you find along most of the Pacific coastline, but the view of the bay and mountains is fantastic. The beach is often crowded, especially around the restaurants and **Playa El Anclote,** but a short walk along the coast in either direction brings you to solitary stretches of sand. You can sunbathe on the beach or hire a five-person boat ($20) to visit **Isla Marietas,** home to many seabirds; if you want to camp on the island, arrange a pickup time with the boat captain. Along the north shore of the bay are isolated beaches, such as **Cruz de Huanacaxtle, Arena Blanca,** and **Destiladeras,** all served by buses that run every 20 minutes. Catch them from the bus station in Puerto Vallarta or in front of the restaurants in Punta de Mita. If you want to spend the night, you can camp anywhere along Playa El Anclote, or head uphill to the brand-new **Hotel La Quinta del Sol,** run by a retired couple from Indiana. Apartment-style rooms with balconies and kitchens cost $30 in summer, $40 in winter. Head back down to the beach for **Restaurante Rocio,** which serves oysters for $5 or fish for $4. They'll even whip up a vegetarian dish or two.

Transportes Medina (Nicaragua 349, at Brasil, tel. 322/3–27–08) in Puerto Vallarta has service to Punta de Mita every half hour 6:30–6:30. The trip takes one hour and costs $1.50. When thinking about bus schedules, keep in mind that the time zone changes at the airport—2 PM in Punta de Mita is 3 PM in Puerto Vallarta.

Surfin' on the Pacific Coast

Once one of the Pacific Coast's surfing hot spots, Punta de Mita may soon see the last of its wave-riding beach bums. With the construction of a Four Seasons resort hotel, the road out to the point—the best spot for swells—is totally blocked off. Avid surfers still endure the one-hour bus trip from Puerto Vallarta and the 30-minute trek along the sand, board in hand, to the point. Others venture to up-and-coming surfin' spots like La Bahía, Punta Purra, or La Lancha—all possible sites for the August Punta de Mita competition. All of these can be reached by catching one of the buses that leaves every 20 minutes from the road. If you're itching to catch a wave, Sol y Arena, at Playa El Anclote, rents boards for $6.50 a day; during the high surfing season (January to March), you can try to hitch a ride with anyone who has a board on his or her roof.

Bahía de Navidad

Two towns have sprouted around the Bahía de Navidad, in the southern corner of the state of Jalisco: San Patricio-Melaque and Barra de Navidad, 6 kilometers apart. If simple living and soft, sandy beaches entice you, then look no further. Many who knew these towns 10 years ago lament that increasing tourism has marred their natural beauty, but both still offer something of a beach-bum paradise, as the sandy beaches are clean, the prices reasonable, and the pace decidedly laid-back. Besides, after a few too many bug bites and stomachaches, a visit to the *Costalegre* (Happy Coast) may be just what you need.

Melaque is popular with vacationers from Guadalajara, many of whom own beach homes that sit idle most of the year. People from the States and Canada roost here during winter months, but in general, Melaque has fewer tourists than Barra does, making it more accessible to the budget traveler. Melaque also feels more like a real town, especially in the evening, when people gather in the square under the neon glow of the church cross. When the sun shines, the most popular pastime is lounging on the golden beach that gently curves around the bay, or washing off the sand in the rolling waves.

Supposedly discovered by Spaniards on December 25, this relaxing coastal region was named Bahía de Navidad, the Bay of Christmas.

In **Barra de Navidad,** about 6 kilometers down the beach, the unfinished Church of Christ is separated from the square, leaving the town somewhat centerless. In the church, notice that Christ's hands have been released from the cross and are by his side. Local myth describes how Christ's hands fell during the 1973 hurricane to push away the water and save the village. Since then, however, most action happens at the hotels and restaurants along the bay side of the sand spit that stretches toward Isla de Navidad. Avenida Veracruz, where locals and tourists mingle, is a pleasant place for a stroll at any time of day.

The annual fiesta in Barra, celebrated June 5–13, honors the town's patron saint, San Antonio de Padua. Don't count on sleeping a wink through unremitting fireworks and resonating tuba tunes. San Patricio-Melaque's patron saint is, of course, San Patricio, and the merrymaking in his honor begins on March 10, ending on his feast day, March 17. During this time, there is a week-long party at **Los Pelícanos** (*see* Food, *below*), including a solemn mass and blessing of the fleet, folk dancing, and cake-eating contests.

BASICS

CASAS DE CAMBIO There's just one casa de cambio in Melaque (Gómez Farías 27-A, behind Farmacia Nueva, tel. 335/5–53–42), and its open Monday–Saturday 9–2 and 4–7, Sunday 9–2. They exchange traveler's checks and cash at no commission. In Barra, you can change money at the casa de cambio on the main strip. *Veracruz 212-C, tel. 335/5–61–77. Open Monday–Saturday 9–2 and 4–7.*

EMERGENCIES The number for the **police** in Melaque is 335/5–50–80; in Barra, the number is 335/5–55–99.

MAIL In Melaque, the post office will hold mail sent to you at the following address for up to 10 days: Lista de Correos, Melaque, Jalisco, CP 48980, México. *Orozco 13, at Gómez Farías, tel. 335/5–52–30. Open weekdays 8–3, Sat. 8–noon.*

For the same service in Barra, the address is Lista de Correos, Barra de Navidad, Jalisco, CP 48987, México. *Guanajuato 100, 1 block from zócalo, no phone. Open weekdays 9–6, Sat. 9–1.*

MEDICAL AID If you need a doctor while you're in the Bahía, Melaque's **hospital** is at the corner of Corona and Gómez Farías. For minor problems, stop by the **Farmacia Nuevo** (Gómez Farías 27, near bus station, tel. 335/5–51–01). The pharmacy is open daily 8 AM–10 PM.

PHONES Pay phones line Gómez Farías in Melaque and Avenida Veracruz in Barra. There's a caseta de larga distancia in Melaque (Corona 65, tel. 335/5–52–30) where you can place collect calls (about $1) and send faxes. Collect and cash calls can be placed in Barra at the caseta de larga distancia (Miguel López de Legazpi 117).

VISITOR INFORMATION Barra de Navidad is home to the sole tourist office in the Bahía, and it's a fairly ignorant one at that. *Veracruz 174, tel. 335/5–55–00. Open weekdays 9–7.*

COMING AND GOING

The bus station in Melaque (tel. 335/5–50–03) is on the corner of Gómez Farías and Carranza. From here, hourly second-class buses leave for Guadalajara (7½ hrs, $8), Puerto Vallarta (5 hrs, $6), and Manzanillo (1½ hrs, $2). For the longer trips to Guadalajara or Puerto Vallarta, it's definitely worth laying out an extra couple of bucks to take a faster *plus* bus, with videos and chilling air-conditioning. All buses above also stop at the bus station in Barra de Navidad (Av. Veracruz 228, 1 block south of zócalo, tel. 335/5–52–65). Green-and-white minibuses connect the two towns with each other and with nearby Cihuatlán. The fare is 25¢. In Barra, you can flag down buses to Melaque and Cihuatlán on Veracruz. From Melaque, buses run south along Juárez.

WHERE TO SLEEP

It's possible to crash almost anywhere on the beach, but the tourist office suggests camping in front of a hotel where the beaches are illuminated, so you won't be hassled by drunks tripping over the sand (or you) at night. However, some hoteliers claim this is prohibited. In Melaque, join the RV folk on a vacant-lot-turned-makeshift-campsite, on the beach north of the palapas. You can pay for a shower a few blocks south of here, but if you're nice to Phil at Los Pelícanos (*see* Food, *below*), she might let you use hers. For the cheapest spot in the Bahía, try **Hotel Hidalgo** (Hidalgo 7, tel. 335/5–50–45), a quiet and well-maintained hotel facing the beach. Singles run $6 and doubles $8, but expect prices to rise at all hotels by $5–$10 in summer, and around the Christmas and Easter holidays.

MELAQUE Bungalows El Márquez. This is a great deal for a group (up to six people can stay in one of them), especially if you like to cook. A large railroad car-style apartment with a kitchenette, dining room, two sleeping areas, and a large bath costs about $25 in low season, $60 in high season. Oh, and no itching and scratching here—the place is fumigated monthly. *Gómez Farías 78, btw Guzmán and Orozco, tel. 335/5–52–13. 4 bungalows, all with bath. Luggage storage.*

Bungalows Villa Mar. For the price of a standard hotel room, two people can stay here in a bungalow that fits up to eight people. A double with kitchenette and bathroom is $12; singles are $10, but watch out for water-loving ants. *Hidalgo 1, at Gómez Farías, tel. 335/5–50–05. Laundry ($2 a load), luggage storage. Wheelchair access.*

Posada Clemens. The 14 teal-and-yellow rooms here are all equipped with clean but run-down bathrooms. Singles cost $6.50, doubles $8.50. Speak loudly if you want any response from the elderly woman who works the desk. *Gómez Farías 70, at Guzmán, tel. 335/5–51–79. Wheelchair access.*

BARRA DE NAVIDAD Casa de Huéspedes Caribe. The Caribe is half garage, half living room, with old bicycles and sleeping family members everywhere. The 16 spartan rooms (singles $6, doubles $8.50) are generally clean, with new mattresses and recently redone bathrooms. Rest assured that the friendly owner sweeps the pigeon poop out of the hallway at every opportunity. *Sonora 15, btw Legazpi and Veracruz, tel. 335/5–52–37. Luggage storage. Wheelchair access.*

Hotel Delfín. You get immaculate rooms, managerial efficiency, and prices to match. Large rooms open onto a shared balcony, and guests (many of them German) have access to a pool, makeshift fitness room, and breakfast buffet. Life-size dolphin-shaped keys remind you which hotel is yours, lest you forget. Singles are $12 and doubles $15, and the 24 rooms all have bathrooms. Reservations are advised in winter. *Morelos 23, tel. 335/5–50–68. Luggage storage. MC, V.*

Posada Pacífico. Veteran travelers consider this the best budget hotel in town. Each room is different, reflecting the owner's intent to treat every guest like a member of the family. His son, Ernesto, is into ecology, and if you ask, he'll show you pictures of an untouched Barra de Navidad from 10 years ago. Singles cost $6.50, doubles $8.50, and all 22 rooms come with a bathroom. *Mazatlán 136, at Michoacán, tel. 335/5-53-59. 1 block from both beach and bus station. Laundry ($2 a load), luggage storage.*

CAMPING If you prefer not to take your chances on the beach, try **Trailer Park La Playa.** This well-maintained parking lot/campground in Melaque is crowded with RVs in winter. Tent spaces cost $7.50, and a trip to the bathroom is 15¢. A well-equipped store is good for snacks. *Gómez Farías 250, tel. 335/5-53-65. 1 block from bus station. 45 sites. Wheelchair access.*

FOOD

For cheap eats in Melaque, the **market** on López Mateos, near the zócalo, is a good place to start. The beach is also sprinkled with ubiquitous palapas that serve seafood at moderate prices. In Barra, Avenida Veracruz is lined with inexpensive food stands and restaurants. Only some of these amiable restaurants are open during the day, but those that are serve full breakfasts for about $2. The more expensive seafood restaurants along the bay provide orchestra seats for the setting sun.

If you like coconut, try an "atole de coco," a sweet, corn-based drink with coconut water. It's sold at stalls on Avenida Veracruz in Barra.

MELAQUE **César and Charly.** This seafood place has a patio that spills out onto the beach, and although it's a little more expensive than Los Pelícanos and has less character, you can get a delicious meal here without having to walk as far. Grilled fish costs about $6. *Gómez Farías 27-A, tel. 335/5-56-99. Past casa de cambio towards water. Open daily 7 AM–10 PM.*

Los Pelícanos. The best of Melaque's palapas is run with motherly care by Italian-born ex-New Yorker Philomena "Phil" García. Her ham and eggs would make Dr. Seuss green with envy, and rumor has it that Robert Redford flies in for breaded octopus ($6). Sit at one of the customer-decorated booths, if you can get one. *5th palapa from end of beach. Open daily 9 AM–10 PM.*

BARRA DE NAVIDAD **Memo's Restaurant.** Memo's friends and relatives are constantly stopping by, lending this place a fun but hectic atmosphere. The restaurant is known for its local specialties: you can get a $2.50 fish breakfast, or eggs any style with tortillas, beans, and coffee or juice for $2. A few tacos and a drink run $2–$3. *Veracruz 146, tel. 333/7-05-51. Open daily 7-2 and 6-11.*

Restaurant y Café Crêpes Ámbar. Run by a French-Mexican couple, this romantic second-story restaurant serves savory French wine and a large variety of delicious seafood, veggie, and dessert crêpes ($2.50–$6.50). Flamenco music plays throughout the night. *Veracruz 101-A, no phone. Open daily 2 PM–11 PM.*

OUTDOOR ACTIVITIES

The main diversions here (apart from bayside margarita-sipping) are swimming, surfing, splashing, or just plain gawking at the sunset. Melaque's beaches are a little rougher than Barra's few waves, and you can sit peacefully and gaze at the rocky peninsula, local lagoon, distant mountains, and **Gran Bahía,** the internationally financed castle-like hotel on the **Isla de Navidad.** Sometimes called "Colimilla," the Isla de Navidad is another peninsula that begins near the Manzanillo airport. For $5, somebody from Barra's **tourist-boat cooperative** (Veracruz 40, no phone) will ferry you to Isla de Navidad and its first-rate beachfront restaurants. They'll also take you on a two-hour bus ride ($26 round-trip) to the rougher but less touristed **Playa de Oro,** on the Pacific side of Colimilla. You can also reach Playa de Oro by taking a bus from Melaque or Barra to Naranjo and walking 15 minutes to the beach. Another option is fishing: The Barra cooperative charges $13 per hour for up to eight people, equipment included, to fish the coastal waters for marlin, tuna, and sailfish. Unlike most outfits, they don't set a minimum number of hours for a trip, so you can give it a shot without breaking the bank.

Near Bahía de Navidad

South of Puerto Vallarta, Highway 200 turns inland and doesn't meet the coast again for 150 kilometers, until it touches the **Bahía Chamela**. The coast between Bahías Navidad and Chamela is developed in isolated patches, some of which are self-contained deluxe resorts such as Careyes, El Tecuan, and Club Med's Playa Blanca. Bahía Chamela itself, however, is no more inhabited or built-up than Anaheim, California was before Disney hit town. Some say tourism has yet to discover the steep shore and neighboring offshore islands, but the army markers reading "No entrance" hint that Mexican military forces may be what's keeping some people away. An older RV crowd travels here from the States in winter, however, and Mexican holidays (August, Christmas, and Easter) signal the arrival of Guadalajaran families to the empty beaches. For the rest of the year, you can expect relative seclusion (along with fewer open hotels and restaurants) in this dry, breezy coastal area.

BAHIA CHAMELA

From the rocky point at **Punta Perula,** a sweeping crescent of sand curves 10 kilometers south to such beaches as **Playa Fortuna** and **Playa Chamela**. This area, visited annually by migrating seabirds, is popular for camping; supplies are available in Chamela, at the south end of the bay. About 5 kilometers outside Chamela, **Villas Polinesia Camping Club** (Carretera 200 Km 72, tel. 36/22–39–40) is not easily reached (it's a 1½-kilometer trek from the highway), so make a reservation before schlepping out here. Once you arrive you'll find tent spots for $5 per person and thatched, Polynesian-style, two-story huts with bathrooms for $15 per double, $32 for 3–4 people. The club provides barbecue pits where guests can cook their own food, but the camp is poorly kept during the off-season. The only restaurant is a 15-minute walk back up to the highway, and in winter, the staff of the Villas Polinesia Camping Club will cook for you if given advance notice.

South of Chamela is **Bahía Tenacatita,** a 9-kilometer stretch of narrow beach backed by small dunes, coconut plantations, a few palapa restaurants, and a hotel. On the far northern side of Chamela is **Boca de Iguanas**—a wider beach, with a few campgrounds and palapas. There are also a hotel and a few restaurants at Punta Perula, and from here you can take a short boat trip to **La Pajerera,** an island off the coast that has been designated an ecological sanctuary.

COMING AND GOING To reach Bahía Chamela, take one of the hourly second-class buses traveling from Barra de Navidad (2 hrs) and Melaque (1½ hrs) toward Puerto Vallarta; they'll drop you off at Chamela ($2) or any of the other beaches.

CIHUATLAN

Although Cihuatlán is the largest and most important commercial center in southern coastal Jalisco, there isn't much reason to visit—unless you count the $1 ride here through fields of banana and coconut trees. Cheaper than adjacent Barra de Navidad and San Patricio-Melaque, Cihuatlán catches the overflow of tourism during winter months and Semana Santa. If you've time to spare, walk down the commercial street, Alvaro Obregón, where you'll find farm-supply stores, restaurants with tortilla-makers, and a movie theater that features American films with English subtitles. Stop by the swallow-populated **Iglesia de Santa Cruz,** which provides a great view of the unexpected number of satellite dishes. Not many services can be found in this city, but the bank here is the only one in the region. **Banamex** (Obregón 58, on the zócalo, tel. 335/5–20–47) has an ATM that accepts Plus, Cirrus, Visa, and MasterCard, and will change cash and traveler's checks weekdays 9–1:30. Across from the bus station is **Farmacia San José** (Ocampo 50, no phone), where you can get any medicine or snack food you desire. If you decide to stay in this extremely quiet town, **Hotel Castrejón** (Torres 13, no phone) offers singles for $6 and doubles for $8. Across the street, locals gather in the evening for seafood at **Restaurante Mariscos El Che.** To reach Cihuatlán, take a green-and-white bus from the bus station in Barra de Navidad. Buses leave every 15 minutes, and the trip takes 20–30 minutes.

Manzanillo

Manzanillo, as the area encompassing the Bahías de Manzanillo and Santiago is known, seems to be trying for a happy medium between larger Pacific resorts such as Acapulco and relaxed beach towns like Barra de Navidad. Unfortunately, it doesn't succeed at either very well—perhaps because it's also the busiest seaport in Mexico. Foreigners are enough of a novelty here that they get a genuine, hospitable welcome, and if you strike up a conversation with the guy sweeping the street, he might invite you home for dinner. If you can't raise the nerve to chat with strangers and still need a place to crash, there are ritzy hotels clumped around the beaches of Península de Santiago and Bahía de Santiago, and more modest lodgings line the highway.

The town is spread out, so transport is neccessary to get anywhere, and one of the few places to relax quietly is the **Jardín Alvaro Obregón**—a good distance from any decent beach. Although all the beaches here are unexceptional, Manzanillo's one claim to fame is **Las Hadas**, an ultra-deluxe resort complex on the peninsula that separates the bays, notorious as the setting for the Bo Derek flesh fantasy *10*. However, most tourists go to beaches along the two bays—those on the Laguna San Pedrito and near the neighborhoods of Santiago, Salahua, Las Brisas, and Burocrática. Skip the beaches in Manzanillo proper altogether—"heinous" is the only word to describe the water lapping at the docks. In spite of this, the fish in the area somehow flourish: Manzanillo claims to be the "sailfish (*pez vela*) capital of the world," and marlin and red snapper can be regularly reeled in as well. Manzanillo is known for its annual national and international sailfishing tournaments in February and November; supposedly, tournament participants caught over 300 sailfish within three days in 1957, setting a world record. Visitors are invited to try their hand at deep-sea fishing here; ask at the tourist office about trips led by an English-speaking guide.

BASICS

AMERICAN EXPRESS The office is in the travel agency **Bahías Gemelas** in Salahua. They cash personal checks and hold mail for cardholders. You can also receive MoneyGrams here. *Blvd. Costero Miguel de la Madrid 1556, Manzanillo, Colima, CP 28200, México, tel. 333/3–10–00. Near IMSS building. Open weekdays 9–2 and 4–7, Sat. 9–2.*

CASAS DE CAMBIO **Banamex** (México 136, in Manzanillo, tel. 333/2–01–15) changes money weekdays 9–1:30, and has ATMs that accept Plus and Cirrus cards as well as MasterCard and Visa. There is another branch in Plaza Manzanillo on the Boulevard Costero in Salahua. The **Farmacia Americana** (México 218, tel. 333/2–37–55) also changes money and is open daily 9–9.

EMERGENCIES The number for the **police** is 333/2–10–04. For any kind of emergency assistance, dial 06.

MAIL The post office in Manzanillo proper will hold mail sent to you at the following address for up to 10 days: Lista de Correos, Manzanillo, Colima, CP 28200, México. *Juárez, at 5 de Mayo, tel. 333/2–00–22. Open weekdays 9–7, Sat. 9–1.*

MEDICAL AID **Hospital General** (tel. 333/2–19–03), off the Carretera a Santiago as you leave Manzanillo proper, charges on a sliding scale. **Hospital Naval** (on naval base Col. San Pedrito, tel. 333/3–27–40) seems to have better facilities, but is more expensive. You can get all the drugs you need at **Farmacia Americana** (*see* Casas de Cambio, *above*).

PHONES Phone and fax service are available daily 7 AM–10 PM on Morelos 144, just off Manzanillo's Jardín Obregón.

VISITOR INFORMATION The **tourist office** has lots of brochures on both Manzanillo and the state of Colima. The staff is friendly and helpful, but their English is limited. Other information is available from the hotels and the local AmEx agent (*see above*). *Blvd. Costero Miguel de la Madrid 4960, 2 blocks north of Hotel Fiesta Mexicana, tel. 333/3–22–77. Open weekdays 9–2 and 4–8, Sat. 9–1.*

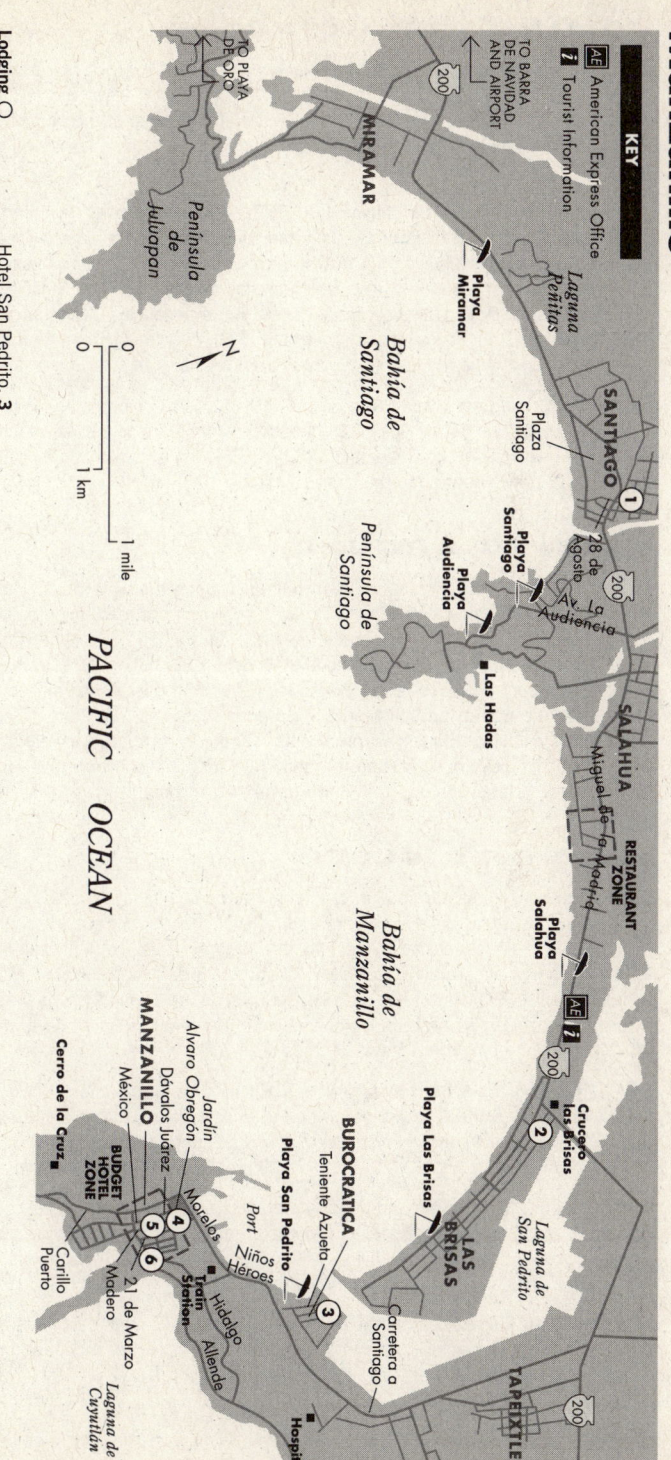

COMING AND GOING

BY BUS The **Central Camionera** is a long walk east of town. A taxi to the city center costs $1, or cross the street and hop on any ROCIO bus. This will leave you at the corner of México and Cuauhtémoc, a four-block walk from the Jardín and most of the budget hotels. Buses leave frequently for San Pedrito, Las Brisas, and Santiago from the back of the station, all the way to the left.

Autotransportes del Sur de Jalisco (tel. 333/2-10-03) serves Tecomán and Armería, the jumping-off points for El Paraíso, Cuyutlán, and Boca de Pascuales (*see* Near Manzanillo, *below*); buses leave every 15 minutes (30 min, 50¢). They also send buses to Colima (1½ hrs, $1) every half hour 2 AM-9:30 PM. **Tres Estrellas de Oro** (tel. 333/2-01-35) leaves for Acapulco (12 hrs, $20) at 12:30 PM and 6:30 PM. **Autotransportes Cihuatlán** (tel. 333/2-05-15) has second-class buses to Guadalajara (8 hrs, $10) every hour from 4 AM to 10 PM and Puerto Vallarta (6 hrs, $7) hourly between 3 AM and midnight.

BY TRAIN The train station (tel. 333/2-19-92) is on Avenida Niños Héroes, three blocks from the zócalo. Same-day tickets are sold here from 9 PM to 11 PM; help is hard to come by during the day. Train 91 to Guadalajara (8 hrs, $3.50) leaves Manzanillo at 11:10 PM, stopping in Colima ($1) two hours into the trip.

GETTING AROUND

Manzanillo winds its way around steep hills and along the waterfront. The main commercial street is Calle México, which hits the Jardín. The waterfront road, Avenida Morelos, goes out to Playa San Pedrito, about 1 kilometer from the Jardín. The Boulevard Costero Miguel de la Madrid runs through the neighborhoods of Salahua, Santiago, and Miramar; **Playa Las Brisas** is the first decent beach you'll hit. Fortunately, frequent bus service makes it easy to reach the beaches of the Bahías de Manzanillo and Santiago. Buses to Miramar, Santiago, Las Brisas, and Las Hadas leave frequently from the train and bus stations. They are slow but cheap (25¢ for a quick trip, 50¢ for most) and run from 7 AM to 9:30 PM. If you find yourself in Salahua or Santiago in the late evening, you'll have to take a taxi (about $4) back to Manzanillo.

WHERE TO SLEEP

Cheap hotels are concentrated in Manzanillo proper, near the train station and around the Jardín, but only a few rise above the sweatbox level. Most hotels outside central Manzanillo and near the water are expensive, especially in Santiago. If you're feeling wealthy, stay at Santiago's wheelchair-accessible **Hotel María Cristina** (28 de Agosto 36, btw Morelos and Hidalgo, tel. 333/3-09-66), which has $16 singles, $20 doubles, and a fish-shaped pool. As a last resort in Manzanillo itself, try the frenzied Hotel Emperador (Balbino Dávalos 69, tel. 333/2-23-74), where a single is $5 and doubles are $7 for one bed, $9 for two.

MANZANILLO **Casa de Huéspedes Petrita.** The small rooms here—basically wooden boxes with floor fans—overlook a courtyard filled with washing machines and clothes hanging out to dry. If you can bear the mugginess, these rooms are incredibly cheap ($5 per bed). *Allende 24, 5 blocks from Jardín, tel. 333/2-01-87. 19 rooms, 3 with bath. Wheelchair access.*

Hotel Colonial. Situated around a spiral staircase and pleasant restaurant, this hotel is reminiscent of an 18th-century mansion. Rooms for one or two (with fan) cost $12, and $15 gets you air-conditioning. Each room has a TV with English-speaking stations. *Bocanegra 28, at México, tel. 333/2-10-80. 36 rooms, all with bath.*

Hotel Miramar. The odd staircases here will lure you onto huge balconies with tiles and doors straight out of *Alice in Wonderland*. Snag a top-floor room for a cooling breeze. Singles cost $6.50, doubles $10. *Juárez 122, ½ block from Jardín, tel. 333/2-10-08. Look for FANTA sign. 38 rooms, all with bath.*

SAN PEDRITO **Hotel San Pedrito.** Although being near the port might not be appealing, a pool (with a mini-slide), tennis courts, and a picnic area may convince you to stay in this dumpy part of town. Being right next to the beach helps too. It's $11.50 for a single, $13 for a double. *Teniente Azueta 3, tel. 333/2–05–35. Laundry (25¢ per piece), luggage storage. Wheelchair access. MC, V.*

LAS BRISAS **Hotel Suites Nancy.** Adjacent to a string of condos, this hotel is in a secure spot right by the beach. Rooms with equipped kitchens open onto a pool, and cost $11.50 for one, two, or three people in low season. Prices jump $20 during high season. *Fraccionamiento Playa Sur, at Crucero Las Brisas, tel. 333/3–23–61. 9 rooms, all with bath. Laundry (50¢ per piece), luggage storage. Wheelchair access.*

CAMPING You can safely set up camp on the beach in San Pedrito, Las Brisas, or Playa Miramar. In San Pedrito, you can sack out right on the sand, but down by Miramar, there's a camping spot across the road from the beach.

FOOD

Manzanillo has restaurants for all budgets. The cheapest place to eat in town is the **market** (Cuauhtémoc, at Madero), preferably at lunchtime, when the food is fresh. Budget restaurants in town are located around the Jardín, and there are a few seafood restaurants and pizza joints on Boulevard Costero, near the American Express office in Salahua.

MANZANILLO **Chantilly.** Of the restaurants that surround the Jardín, this is the cheapest and most popular. The food at this cafeteria-style spot is typical Mexican —tacos, enchiladas, quesadillas, etc. You'll have to hit your waitress over the head with a menu to get her to take your order, but once she does, there's hardly a wait for your food. Chicken costs about $3, fish or shrimp about $5. *Juárez 60, at Madero, tel. 333/2–01–94. Open Sun.–Fri. 7 AM–10 PM. Wheelchair access.*

Plaza La Perlita. Located in front of the train station, this restaurant has outdoor seating around wrought-iron tables, and features live music Thursday through Sunday. The rest of the week you'll have to make do with the sound of chirping birds and passing trains. A regular shrimp cocktail costs $2, a huge one $3. A fish fillet, cooked to your liking, is $4. *Morelos, tel. 333/2–27–70. Open daily 10 AM–midnight. Wheelchair access.*

Restaurant Roca del Mar. This restaurant, decorated with Indian art, serves a filling, satisfying $3 comida corrida consisting of soup, rice, an entrée, and tortillas. Vegetarian soups are $1, and an order of meat or vegetarian quesadillas with guacamole is $2. Try an outdoor table, and watch the Jardín activities as you eat. *21 de Marzo 204, tel. 333/2–03–02. Open daily 7 AM–10:30 PM.*

SAN PEDRITO **El Último Tren.** When you order a drink here you get *free* snacks—tacos, ceviche, guacamole—all salty and often hot. The theory is, the more you eat, the more you'll drink: Most people leave here smashed. Clanging beer-bottle toasts, live mariachi music, and the drunken singing create what an ad calls "Real Macho Atmosphere." If you're careful, you can eat for cheap; if not, you probably won't be in a state of mind to care. *In Centro Botaneros, Blvd. Costero 22680, tel. 333/2–31–44. Take SANTIAGO or MIRAMAR bus or walk 15 min past San Pedrito. Open Mon.–Sat. 1 PM–9 PM.*

SANTIAGO **Restaurante Savoy 2.** Young locals, travel agents, and tourists fill the tables here for the $3 comida corrida and the wide choice of desserts (food selection dwindles towards the end of the day.). They've always got a movie on the VCR (usually in English with Spanish subtitles), and if that fails to entertain you, you can browse through the odd lamps sold in the back corner. *Plaza Santiago, across from zócalo, tel. 333/3–07–90. Open daily 7 AM–midnight. Wheelchair access.*

OUTDOOR ACTIVITIES

Manzanillo's biggest (and only) attraction is its beaches. Those along the highway in the twin bays of Santiago and Manzanillo are contiguous, noisy, and contaminated—although the moderately peaceful **Playa Audencia** on the Santiago Peninsula is a slight exception. **Playa San**

Pedrito, the beach nearest downtown, is heavily frequented by locals, especially on Sundays, when people kick sandy soccer balls between cases of beer. Woe the person who actually swims in the water, however; their feet would probably disintegrate before their knees got wet. To reach the beach, walk 1 kilometer down Niños Héroes, or take a SANTIAGO or MIRAMAR bus from the train station.

Playa Las Brisas is Manzanillo's most popular beach, though it may be too close to the port for comfort. Centered around the Las Brisas crossroads, this dirty-gold beach is lined with hotels, houses, and restaurants, shielding it from highway traffic. To get here, take a SANTIAGO or MIRAMAR bus to the *crucero* (crossroads) for Las Brisas, or a LAS BRISAS bus all the way into town.

Playa Audiencia, on the peninsula dominated by the Las Hadas resort, is the best beach in Manzanillo. It's small and can get crowded, but green hills on both sides create a feeling of seclusion absent from other beaches here. Take one of the minibuses provided by Las Hadas (they have dolphins on them) from Niños Héroes or from the Las Brisas crossroads and ask the driver to stop at the turnoff for Playa Audiencia. While you're here, take a self-guided tour of the fantastical **Las Hadas** hotel, which looks like something out of *Arabian Nights*. To avoid an entrance charge, say you just want to look around, not swim or eat.

Playa Miramar's sand is marbled with black and gold, but it appears more dirty than pretty, and the entire beach is smack against the freeway. You can rent horses ($6.50 an hour) and boogie boards ($1 an hour) from a very friendly guy named Abraham, who hangs out in front of the Hotel Maeva. He also offers banana boat rides for $3.50 per person. To get here from the train or bus station, take a bus marked MIRAMAR and get off wherever the beach looks appealing.

AFTER DARK

Manzanillo's nightlife centers around one area, Salahua, which can be reached by taking a MIRAMAR or SANTIAGO bus. The one happening disco, **Vog** (tel. 333/3-08-75), is on the Boulevard Costero—cover is about $6. There's no cover at the adjacent **Bar de Félix** (tel. 333/3-08-75), where the atmosphere is a little more mellow, but the music and movies play almost all night long. And it wouldn't be a Mexican resort without **Carlos 'n Charlie's** (Blvd. Costero Km. 6.5, tel. 333/3-11-50), a beachside restaurant/bar.

Near Manzanillo

South of Manzanillo is a stretch of coast dotted with black-sand beaches: a testament to the activity of Colima's volcanoes. Although life is cheaper and more tranquil here than in Manzanillo, the beaches still couldn't be described as tropical paradises. The sand is more gray than black, and the water sometimes turns an unappealing brown, especially during the summer rainy season. The isolated beaches do face the open sea, so surfers or anyone mesmerized by crashing waves will enjoy the isolated beaches of Cuyutlán, El Paraíso, and Boca de Pascuales (*see below*). Although there are hotels in the area, beach camping is free and encouraged. If you've got a hammock, most beachfront restaurants will let you string it up for a couple of bucks. To reach **Cuyutlán** or **El Paraíso**, you'll have to catch a local bus in the town of **Armería.** Buses leave Manzanillo for Armería (40 min, 75¢) every 15 minutes (there is also frequent service to Armería from Colima). **Tecomán** is the transfer point for Boca de Pascuales; the transfer depot is one block to the right as you leave Tecomán's main bus terminal. The bus to Tecomán from either Manzanillo or Colima takes one hour and costs 75¢.

Colima's Volcán de Fuego erupted in July of 1994, filling the mountain pueblos with lava and smoke, and the coastal towns with ash and seismic waves.

CUYUTLAN

The most developed of the three beach resorts, Cuyutlán fills up with Mexican vacationers during August, Christmas, and Easter. You'll see them strolling the malecón, lining the scalding beach sand, and sipping coconut milk straight out of the furry brown fruit. The rest of the year, the town is almost deserted; the rainbow of umbrellas folds up, and the beach takes on the lonely, run-down feel of Coney Island in winter. Cuyutlán is a real town, however, with a real center, and, on the square, a really big statue of Benito Juaréz's head. This town also has more hotels, restaurants, and services than other nearby beach resorts. But Cuyutlán is best known as the home of the *ola verde* (green wave). No one quite agrees on what ola verde is, but they certainly do talk about it a lot. Rosario at the Manzanillo bus station swears it was a tidal wave that wiped out the entire town of Cuyutlán in 1942. A tourist brochure claims that the ola verde happens every April and May, when the sun shines on the waves at a certain angle, making them look green. Still others believe it's just a local name for the phosphorescent algae that glows sparkly green in the water. Buses leave Armería for Cuyutlán (½ hr, 25¢) every 40 minutes between 6 AM and 8 PM.

WHERE TO SLEEP AND EAT You can pitch a tent for free on Cuyutlán's sandy beaches anytime except Easter week, but first you must obtain a permit from the daunting staff at the **Junta Municipal** (Hidalgo 144), which is open 24 hours. Cuyutlán also has a good selection of beachfront hotels, many of which are affordable. Located at the northern end of the boardwalk, **Hotel Tlaquepaque** has plain rooms and a long hall cooled by sea breezes. Singles are $5 and doubles are $9, but you can negotiate with the owner if you plan to stay a while. Five of the rooms at **Hotel Morelos** (2 blocks off zócalo toward water, tel. 332/4–18–10 ext. 107) have a kitchen/dining room for no extra cost. Prices are exactly the same as at the Tlaquepaque; although, during the high season, $16 per person gets you a room and dinner.

The hotels are also the best place to look for food. The Hotel Morelos serves a decent, filling breakfast for $3, lunch for $3, and dinner for $4; otherwise, try the adjacent **Hotel Fénix** (tel. 332/4–18–10 ext. 147), which specializes in seafood and has a happy hour with two-for-one drinks. From 6 PM on, **Cenaduría Juanito**, on the zócalo, offers cheap snacks like pozole or tacos for $1.

EL PARAISO

Smaller and less developed than Cuyutlán, El Paraíso has one short road that runs the length of the town, passing hotels and restaurants overlooking the ocean. The surf here isn't too strong, making it a better place to take a dip than neighboring Boca de Pascuales and Cuyutlán. The town is wondrously small, and the beaches are more often than not yours and yours alone, but don't expect to find diversions apart from the waves. Buses to El Paraíso leave from Armería approximately every 45 minutes between 6 AM and 7 PM. The fare is about 25¢.

WHERE TO SLEEP AND EAT Camping here is a breeze. No permit, no set sites—just plop your stuff on the beach and head to **Hotel Paraíso** for 25¢ showers. For less rugged lodgings, the Paraíso ($15 for one or two people) has the nicest rooms around, and also has a restaurant and pool. **Hotel Equipales** (5 minutes walk from the bus stop along the road) has clean but dark rooms ($8.50) with lumpy beds and tiny showers. Pick a restaurant, any restaurant, in El Paraíso—they all serve fresh fish for around $3.

BOCA DE PASCUALES

The smallest of the beach resorts isn't really a town, but a collection of palapa restaurants clustered on the beach where the Río Armería empties into the sea. Originating at the Volcanes de Colima (the Volcanoes of Colima), the river goes through several name changes before it dumps its less-than-clean water here. Boca de Pascuales is famous for its huge, aggressive waves, and swimming is a potentially perilous activity (look out for the red "do not swim" flags). Nevertheless, it's also a year-round hot spot for kamikaze surfers called *surfos*. They're known to survive here on only a few dollars a day, which means that you can, too. Indeed, the only people who will really want to visit Boca de Pascuales are surfers, admirers of surfers, or those looking for an inexpensive, isolated beach upon which to do nothing.

Boca de Pascuales is protected from the sea by a figure of the Virgin of Guadalupe, which was found wet, with sand on its feet, after the town was almost destroyed by waves in 1992. The locals decided that the Virgin came to the beach to save them. Each February, a procession now carries the statue high overhead from Tecomán to Boca de Pascuales.

WHERE TO SLEEP AND EAT You can camp anywhere along the beach in Boca de Pascuales, but a shower will be hard to find. If you're not in the mood to rough it, **Lupe's Place**, right next to the water tower, is slightly more comfortable—basic rooms with no bathroom cost $4, and rooms with a bathroom and a view of the waves are $10. **Restaurant Hamacas del Mayor** (tel. 332/4–21–36) is more expensive than the other palapas, but it's something of an institution here: They've been serving delicious seafood on white-draped tables under a huge palapa since the 1950s. People come from Manzanillo and Colima for the crayfish ($6), but if you're pinching pesos try the octopus or fish ($4). Other palapa restaurants serve fresh seafood for a few dollars less.

Colima

The easygoing capital of Colima state, Colima is a gleamingly clean city of well-maintained colonial buildings and safe, tidy streets. Its downtown, down-to-earth metropolis is graced by many tranquil parks—in fact, this city boasts more parks per capita than any other in western Mexico. Although the towering volcanic peaks that surround Colima are impressive, however, a visit here is really about history and culture. Colima was the third city founded by the Spaniards in Mexico, but its history reaches much further back. Archaeologists have discovered tombs filled with ceramic figurines that point to the existence of a complex indigenous culture here, rich in tradition, magic, and folklore. Many of the animal figurines are on display in Colima's museums, except for some titillating phallic ones that were whisked away to museums in Mexico City. In addition to the numerous museums, events such as poetry readings and performance-art pieces are frequent. The University of Colima put outs 10 local newspapers and is constantly publishing new books of poetry and prose. There's even a table of philosophers—the **Mesa de Despelleje**—at Los Naranjos Restaurant (Gabino Barreda 34, tel. 331/2–00–29) every night at 9 PM. Despite the potential for highbrow snobbery, Colima's friendly, politically progressive residents will make you feel welcome.

At almost any time of day, students of the University of Colima can be found ditching their classes to play a game of fútbol (soccer). Stop by the field (near the entrance to the "Uni") to meet the players, or at least their fans.

BASICS

AUTO PARTS/SERVICE If the English-speaking mechanics at **Tecno Mecánica** can't help you, they'll refer you to someone who can. *Independencia 131, tel. 331/3–30–00. 5 blocks SW of Jardín Principal. Open weekdays 9–2 and 5–7, Sat. 9–noon.*

BOOKSTORES Galería Universitaria (Torres Quintero 62, tel. 331/2–44–00), just off the Jardín Principal, carries books in Spanish, including those published by the university. It's open Monday–Saturday 9–3 and 4–9. **Las Palmeras** (Portal Medellín 14, tel. 331/4–35–06; open daily 8 AM–11 PM) is a small magazine store next to Hotel Ceballos on the Jardín Principal. They carry *Time*, *Newsweek*, and *National Geographic*, as well as many Mexican magazines.

CASAS DE CAMBIO Several banks on Madero have ATMs, but most only accept Visa and MasterCard. The ATM at **Banamex** (Hidalgo 90, tel. 331/2–01–03), right off Jardín Núñez, accepts Plus and Cirrus cards, and the bank itself changes cash and traveler's checks weekdays 9–noon. **Casa de Cambio Majaparas** offers better rates than banks for cash, but not for traveler's checks, which they change into U.S. dollars only. *Morelos 200, at Juárez, tel. 331/4–89–98. Open weekdays 9–2 and 4:30–7, Sat. 9–2.*

EMERGENCIES For assistance, call the **police** (tel. 331/2–18–01) or **fire** department (tel. 331/2–58–58).

LAUNDRY Lava-tec washes and dries 3 kilos of clothing for $2. Service is same-day. *Rey Colimán 4, tel. 331/2–58–72. Open daily 8:30–8:30.*

MAIL The full-service **post office** will hold mail sent to you at the following address for up to 10 days: Lista de Correos, Colima, Colima, CP 28001, México. *Madero, at Núñez, tel. 331/2–00–33. Open weekdays 8–7, Sat. 8–2.*

MEDICAL AID The **Hospital Civil** (San Fernando, tel. 331/2-02-27) is open 24 hours. For minor problems, try the **Farmacia Colima**, which also has a telephone caseta. *Madero 1, at Constitución, on Jardín Principal, tel. 331/2-00-31. Open Mon.–Sat. 8:30 AM–9 PM, Sun. 9–2.*

PHONES There are public phones on all four corners of the Jardín Principal. You can place cash calls at **Computel**, on Parque Núnez. The connection fee for collect calls here is $2. *Morelos 234, tel. 331/4-59-05. Open daily 7 AM–10 PM.*

VISITOR INFORMATION If you speak Spanish, ask about upcoming events at **Livornos Pizza** (*see* Food, *below*). For official information about Colima, city or state, talk to the immensely helpful staff at the air-conditioned **tourist office**. *Portal Hidalgo 20, west side of Jardín Principal, tel. 331/2-83-60. Open weekdays 8:30–3 and 5–9, weekends 9–1.*

COMING AND GOING

BY BUS The **Central de Autobuses de Colima** (tel. 331/2-58-99) is at the northeastern edge of town. To get downtown, catch any 4 CENTRO bus, or take a taxi (about $1). The major bus lines are **Tres Estrellas de Oro** (tel. 331/2-84-99) and **Omnibús de México** (tel. 331/4-71-90). Buses leave for Guadalajara (3 hrs, $12) and Manzanillo (½ hr, $4) every two hours from 7:30 AM to 7:30 PM. There is service to Mexico City (10 hrs, $26) that leaves at 9 PM, as well as to other cities both in and out of state. Luggage storage is available.

The **Central de Autobuses Sub-Urbana** (Carretera Colima-Coquimatlán), serves smaller, in-state destinations. Buses bound for Armería ($1), Manzanillo ($1.50), and Tecomán (75¢) depart every 20 minutes between 4:30 AM and 10 PM. Buses for nearby towns and villages such as Comala (50¢), Suchitlán (50¢), and San Antonio/Laguna La María leave frequently during the day. The bus station is a 20-minute walk southwest on Cuautéhmoc from the Jardín Principal. Taxi rides to the station cost $1.

BY TRAIN The train station (Colón, tel. 331/2-00-25) is 10 blocks south of the Jardín Principal near Parque Hidalgo, and is open daily 7:30–11:30 and 2:30–5. The one bus that passes by the station goes to the center of town. A taxi ride to or from the station costs about $1. Colima is a stop on the Manzanillo–Guadalajara route, with trains to Guadalajara (6 hrs, $2.50) leaving at 1:10 AM. The Manzanillo train (2 hrs, $1) leaves at 2:30 AM.

GETTING AROUND

On a clear day, you can orient yourself by the volcanoes to the north of Colima. When it's cloudy, the parks along Avenida Madero are landmarks that make downtown Colima easy to navigate. The **Jardín Libertad** (also known as the zócalo or the Jardín Principal) is at the corner of Avenidas Madero and Reforma. This is the center of town, where families and friends gather in the evening. One block east is the **Jardín Quintero**, with a fountain and more benches. Three blocks further east is the massive **Parque Núñez**.

In keeping with its clean and efficient image, Colima has a modern fleet of microbuses, which cost about 35¢ to ride. Most buses stop at the corner of Reforma and Díaz, on Medellín along the Jardín Quintero, or on Avenida Rey Colimán, near the southwest corner of Parque Núñez. A taxi ride anywhere in the city shouldn't be more than $2–$3.

WHERE TO SLEEP

Colima doesn't have a huge selection of hotels, but it's not exactly a tourist mecca, so finding a room isn't a problem. All budget hotels are near the center of town. If the hotels below are full, try the **Gran Hotel Flamingos** (Rey Colimán 18, tel. 331/2-25-25), which has quite a few singles ($10) and doubles ($12.50) right near the Jardín Núñez.

➤ **UNDER $10** • **Hotel Impala.** The best bargain in town, this hotel has 21 rooms, some with fans, but all with windows, clean bathrooms, and hot water. The downside is that it's the farthest hotel from the center. Singles are $6.50, doubles $9. *Moctezuma 93, 3 blocks west of Jardín Principal, tel. 331/4-30-97. Luggage storage.*

Hotel Núñez. Rooms surround a courtyard (often used as a parking lot) in this converted colonial house, sitting right on the park of the same name. The rooms are small and lack personality, but the communal baths are spic and span. Singles or doubles without bath are $5, $6.50 with private bath. *Juárez 88, tel. 331/2–70–30. 32 rooms, 16 with bath. Luggage storage. Wheelchair access.*

➢ **UNDER $20** • **Casa de Huéspedes Familiar.** Slightly worn but clean rooms are above the house of the friendly manager, Señora Saucedo, and her lush and overflowing garden. Singles cost $6 and doubles $12, but you may be able to talk her into giving you a better deal. *Morelos 265, near Pemex, tel. 331/2–34–67. 10 rooms, all with bath. Luggage storage.*

Hotel Ceballos. This grand hotel is cheaper than you'd think—$15 for a basic one- or two-person room with a fan; $25 for air-conditioning, TV, or a window opening to the patio. The stone-column flanked halls and courtyards are impressive, but the view of the volcanoes from the roof is even more stunning. Reservations are advised in summer. *Portal Medellín 12, tel. 331/2–44–44. 63 rooms, all with bath. Laundry (50¢ per piece), luggage storage.*

FOOD

Colima prides itself on its *antojitos* (appetizers) such as enchiladas with sweet sauce, *ceviche* (ground fish, tomato, and onion), and pozole. Restaurants are scattered throughout the city, but there are tons of cheap ones near the Jardín Principal.

Ah Qué Nanishe. For a change of pace, try the Oaxacan specialties at this downtown eatery (the name means "Oh, how delicious!" in Zapoteco). Chicken tamales with Oaxacan mole (chile and chocolate sauce) are $3 each, and a *huarache* (corn-fungus turnover) is $1.50. They also have an assortment of soup specialties ranging from 75¢ to $1.50. Sweet tamales are 50¢. *5 de Mayo 267, 4 blocks west of Jardín Principal, tel. 331/4–21–97. Open daily 1:30–midnight.*

Café de la Plaza. Surrounded by plants, a waterfall, and caged doves, the inner courtyard of this restaurant is a quiet retreat. A standard egg or pancake breakfast with juice and coffee costs $2.50, the daily special is $3.50, and *tortas* (sandwiches) are $1.50. *Portal Medellín 12, in Hotel Ceballos, tel. 331/2–44–44. Open Mon.–Sat. 7 AM–10:30 PM, Sun. 3:30 PM–10:30 PM.*

Livornos Pizza. At this pub-like pizzeria, $4 gets you a small meat or veggie pizza plus a drink. Have a beer and strike up a conversation with the manager for information about cultural events and the causes of *la ilusión óptica* (*see* Cheap Thrills, *below*). You can also catch CNN on their TV. *Constitución, near cathedral, tel. 331/4–50–30. Open daily 9 AM–11 PM.*

Restaurante Samadhi. Sit at a table overlooking the bright courtyard, and try the tasty soy-burger ($1.50) or the $2.50 breakfast of yogurt, fruit, eggs, and coffee. *Medina 129, 3 blocks north of Parque Núñez, tel. 331/3–24–98. Open Fri.–Wed. 8–8, Thurs. 8–5.*

WORTH SEEING

The **Jardín Principal** has been the center of Colima city since its founding, and is a good place to begin exploring. On the south side of the Jardín is the free **Museo Regional de Historia de Colima** (Morelos 1, at Reforma, tel. 331/2–92–28), where you'll find a few exhibits of pre-Columbian pottery and local crafts, as well as an occasional university art exposition. On the east side of the Jardín is the 19th-century, neoclassical **Santa Iglesia Cathedral** (Reforma 21, tel. 331/2–02–00), which is unlike many of Mexico's churches in that all the ornamentation is saved for the lavish interior. Next door is the beautiful **Palacio de Gobierno** (tel. 331/2–04–31), built at the turn of the century. Its mural portraying the history of Mexico was painted by Coliman artist Jorge Chávez Carrillo in honor of Independence leader Padre Miguel Hidalgo.

CASA DE LA CULTURA The Casa de la Cultura shows a permanent collection of works by Coliman artists, as well as rotating exhibitions. They give free classes in arts and crafts, music, and regional dance, and show foreign and national art films in the cinema club on Thursdays or Fridays. The gallery is open Tuesday–Sunday 9 AM–8:30 PM and admission is free. Within the complex, Café Dalí is a good place to stop for a drink and to listen to live music, featured daily 8 PM–11 PM. *Galván Norte, at Ejército Nacional, tel. 331/2-31-55.*

MUSEO DE LAS CULTURAS DEL OCCIDENTE Next to the Casa de la Cultura, this excellent museum is dedicated exclusively to pre-Hispanic ceramicware from the Colima area. On display are a collection of figurines, among them the famous Coliman dogs, supposedly the product of a culture in which dogs were believed to mirror human personalities (and were a source of food, as well). *Galván Norte., at Ejército Nacional, tel. 331/2-31-55. From Rey Colimán, take a bus toward the university. Admission free. Open Tues.–Sat. 8–8.*

The Parque de la Piedra Lisa (Park of the Smooth Stone) is near the university. Legend has it that if you slide down this big rock, you will soon be wed.

MUSEO UNIVERSITARIO DE CULTURAS POPULARES This university crafts museum is not particularly impressive, but it has a wonderful gift shop. Outside the museum, under a giant banyan tree, an artisan makes reproductions of pre-Columbian ceramics Monday–Saturday 9–3. Go to Room 30 in the museum building to find out about cultural events at the university. *Gallardo, at 27 de Septiembre, tel. 331/2-68-69. Admission free. Open Tues.–Sat. 9–2 and 4–7.*

CHEAP THRILLS

If you've got a car or access to one, you can experience a truly strange phenomenon on the road from Suchitlán to Comala (*see* Near Colima, *below*), just past Restaurante Los Pinos. Some say it's caused by an optical illusion (they call it *la ilusión óptica*), others say it's a magnetic field. Whatever the cause, bring the car to a dead stop where the road is level, just before the hill. Keep your foot off the gas and, somehow, your car will climb all the way to the top. If a car is not in the picture but you're ready for a break from museums and art exhibits, revert to childhood at the **Parque Regional Metropolitano** on Degollado. A fun water slide, mini-zoo, and man-made lake will keep you entertained for hours.

AFTER DARK

Café Colima (Jardín Corregidora, tel. 331/2-80-93) is Colima's version of a *peña,* in which local spectators participate in performances by folk musicians, and the music often takes on a political tone (nightly 6 PM). The seats are outdoors in the Jardín Corregidora, under an awning where patrons eat pricey food and sip beer, wine, and a variety of coffees. To get here, take a RUTA 9 bus from Medellín, at Jardín Quintero. On Avenida Felipe Sevilla del Río, a few blocks from the university, students hang out at any one of a sprinkling of party bars and restaurants, including the **Atrium, Grillos,** and **Cora,** none of which charge a cover. If you're in the mood for technopop, **Cheer's** (Zaragoza 521, tel. 331/4-47-00; $3 cover) is a disco that gets going around 10:30 PM and stays open until 3 AM.

Near Colima

VOLCANES DE COLIMA

Just north of Colima are two volcanoes, known as the Volcanes de Colima—despite the fact that one of them is actually just across the Jalisco state line. The taller, at 4,335 meters, is the **Volcán de Fuego** (Fire Volcano). The **Volcán Nevado de Colima** (also called the Volcán de Nieve, or Snow Volcano) rises 3,900 meters. The former has been living up to its name of late, with an eruption of smoke and a small amount of lava in July of 1994. It can, obviously, be dangerous to visit, and there are no buses to the trails or facilities for hikers. If you're determined to set out on your own, you'll need to catch a bus from the Central de Autobuses de Colima to the town of Atenquique, and get permission from the military there to embark on the 17-kilometer hike. Ask at the tourist office in Colima about hiking trails and current safety conditions.

The Volcán Nevado, on the other hand, is a hiker's paradise. About two-thirds of the way up the volcano is a shelter called **La Joya,** where you can stay for free in a cabaña—a no-frills hostel that fits at least 20 people. The cabaña has a fireplace and nothing else, so bring food, drink, and gear. From La Joya, it's a three- or four-hour hike to the snowy peak of the volcano. Bring layers of clothes to keep you warm at night and cool during the day. Buses going to Guadalajara from the Central de Autobuses de Colima stop in Ciudad Guzmán, where you can catch another bus to the the town of Fresnito, at the base of the volcano. From here, you'll need to either find someone willing to drive you to La Joya (it's about 37 kilometers) for a fee, or hitch a ride—because of the number of hikers who make this trip, this shouldn't be too difficult. Plan on a three-day trip, at least: It will probably take you the better part of a day to reach La Joya, another to climb and descend, and a third to return to Colima. If this sounds too ambitious for you, there are a number of small towns nearby, including **Laguna La María** (*see below*) and **San Antonio,** both at the base of the **Parque Nacional Nevado de Colima,** where you can see the volcanoes (albeit from the bottom) without having to expend much energy or time. Both of these can be reached by hopping a bus from the Sub-Urbana bus station in Colima.

COMALA

A 30-minute bus ride north of Colima, this village is called the "white town of America," not because of American tourists, but for the collection of white adobe houses with red-tile roofs. The town is also known for its creative artisans. Ten minutes walk south of the main plaza is **Escuela de Artesanías Comala** (Carretera Colima Km. 6, tel. 331/5–56–00), where artists and craftsmen handcarve elaborate wood furniture, and carefully paint it with intricate designs of birds and flowers. Small dressers or chairs range from $50 to $100, and can be shipped to the United States. After exploring the town and the surrounding farmland, enjoy a cheap meal in one of the *botaneros* (bars serving appetizers) on the zócalo. **Restaurante Bar Comala** (Progreso 7, on zócalo, tel. 331/5–51–11) offers $2 beer and alcoholic *ponche* (mezcal with assorted fruits), which comes with guacamole, ceviche, tacos, and other snacks. Each drink brings forth another round of food. **Farmacia Comala** (Progreso 47, tel. 331/5–51–43), a few doors down, sells everything from medicine to snacks to souvenirs.

LAGUNA LA MARIA

Laguna La María is a vacation retreat for Colimans at the edge of the Parque Nacional Nevado de Colima. The verdant, isolated lakeshore is not an easy trek from Colima, but once you're here, the lake offers great camping, swimming, and fishing—although frequent afternoon rains

In Case of an Eruption . . .

1) Stay calm. 2) Click your heel together three times and say, "There's no place like Colima." 3) Sacrifice your annoying travel companion to appease the irate volcano god. Then maybe, just maybe, the Volcán de Fuego, towering 4,335 meters above sea level, will return to its fitful slumber for another couple of years. Mexican and American geologists continue to predict when the impressive and constantly active volcano will explode into clouds of fire and lava. They say that such an eruption would not only destroy the vegetation of pines and evergreens in the fertile valley below, but the burning rocks and sulfur vapors would reach Colima's inland and coastal towns, causing destructive earthquakes and seismic waves. For Colimans, fear of the Volcán de Fuego, which has erupted five times this century, is a way of life. Some think the volcano's activity is simply a natural phenomenon. But others believe in a more spiritual reason— Colima's name in Nahuatl means, "the place where the elder God is dominated."

force visitors to take refuge under the *casitas* (picnic tables shaded by roofs). Pay 25¢ at the park entrance to enter, or $1.50 to camp anywhere along the shore. Public bathrooms (without showers) are accessible to campers, but the lack of restaurants means packing in your food. You can also stay at **Cabaña La María** (right by the lake), which has clean $20 singles and $30 doubles with small kitchens and bathrooms. It's wise to make reservations—get in touch with the tourist office in Colima and they'll do it for you. To get here, take the SAN ANTONIO bus from the Central de Autobuses Sub-Urbana in Colima at 7 AM, 1:20 PM, 2:30 PM, or 5 PM. From the bus stop it's a 15-minute walk to the lake. Buses return only at 9 AM, 3 PM, and 3:50 PM. If you miss the bus back to Colima, you can try to hitchhike from the main road, although cars going to Colima are not frequent.

Ixtapa/ Zihuatanejo

If only one resort on the Pacific Coast is worth visiting, it's Ixtapa/Zihuatanejo. A four-hour drive up the coast from Acapulco, this twin-town resort is less expensive and less frenetic than its big brother to the south. Only four miles apart, **Zihuatanejo** and **Ixtapa** have distinct personalities—the former is a sleepy fishing village and the latter is a happening resort. Yet a common natural setting of lush green hills freckled with houses, and stretches of beautiful, clear beaches bond the cities together as if they were siblings.

If you hear "Zee-wah" being murmured around the city you aren't hearing a native mating call. Locals shorten Zihuatanejo to an informal "Zee-wah."

Zihuatanejo is the base for budget travelers, with affordable hotels and guest homes right on the waterfront. Some rooms even have ocean views, and most are surrounded by local craft shops and inexpensive seafood restaurants. Playas **La Ropa** and **Las Gatas** on Zihuatanejo Bay are two of the most serene beaches in the area, attracting scuba divers and snorkelers alike.

Ixtapa is now one long strip of hot pavement, perfectly manicured lawns, and clunky buildings lining the white beach. As is par for the course in areas targeted for development by Fonatur (the federal tourism department), you'll find plenty of luxury hotels, pricey shops, and air-conditioned mini-malls. You'll also find rough surf and a nightlife that is quickly adopting a party-till-you-drop attitude. With these two cities you get the best of both worlds—dip into Ixtapa's liveliness, then beat a retreat to peaceful Zihuatanejo.

BASICS

AMERICAN EXPRESS The office, which caters to the upper-class traveler, leads numerous tours around the region. Card members can receive mail and cash personal checks here. *Area Comercial, Blvd. Ixtapa, Ixtapa/Zihuatanejo, Guerrero, México, CP 40880, tel. 755/3–08–53. Next to Hotel Kristal. Open Mon.–Sat. 9–6, Sun. 9–2.*

CASAS DE CAMBIO Banks seem to be on every street corner in Zihuatanejo. **Banco Mexicano Somex** (Juárez, near Mangos, tel. 755/4–24–16) is open weekdays 9–1:30, and there are ATMs at **Banamex** (Cuauhtémoc 4, near Nicolás Bravo, tel. 755/4–21–96) and **Serfín** (Juárez, at Nicolás Bravo, tel. 755/4–32–70). Casas de cambio don't have the greatest exchange rates, but they have better hours than the banks. The one by the waterfront (Galeana, near Nicolás Bravo, tel. 755/4–35–22) exchanges cash and traveler's checks daily 8 AM–9 PM.

EMERGENCIES Fire department (tel. 755/3–25–51); **police** (tel. 755/4–20–40).

LAUNDRY **Lavandería Super Clean** in central Zihuatanejo charges $1 per kilo, with a 3-kilo minimum. *González 11, at Galeana, tel. 755/4–23–47. Open Mon.–Sat. 8–8.*

MAIL The post office in Zihuatanejo is hard to find, but you can find boxes all over town. Walk up Guerrero away from the water and turn right onto Morelos. Turn right two blocks past the Pollo Feliz restaurant onto a dirt road—the white TELECOM building will be in front of you. They'll hold mail sent to you at the following address for up to 10 days: Lista de Correos, Domi-

Zihuatanejo

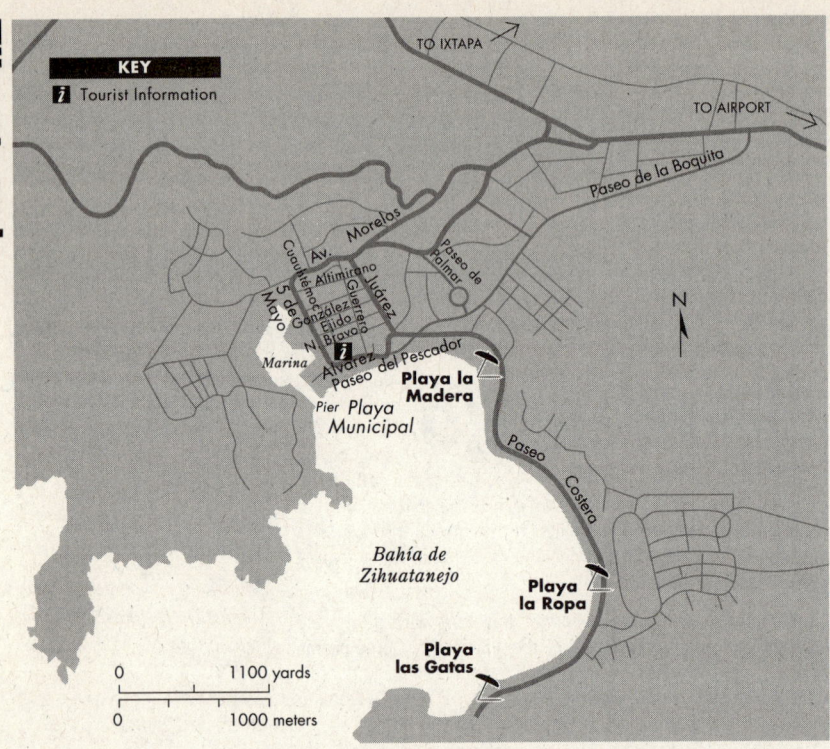

cilio Centro SCT, Zihuatanejo, Guerrero, CP 40880, México. (There is no post office in Ixtapa). Tel. 755/4-21-92. Open weekdays 8-7, Sat. 9-1.

MEDICAL AID The **Centro de Salud,** or **Hospital General** (Paseo de la Boquita, at Paseo del Palmar, tel. 755/4-20-88) in Zihuatanejo charges $2 for a consultation. There are no 24-hour pharmacies in town, but **Farmacia del Centro** (Cuauhtémoc 20, at Nicolás Bravo, tel. 755/4-20-77) is open daily 7 AM-10 PM.

PHONES There are two pay phones in front of Zihuatanejo's Palacio Municipal on Álvarez, or you can try the caseta de larga distancia, which will charge a $2 connection fee for a collect call. You can also pay cash for long-distance calls. Altamirano 6, at Guerrero, tel. 755/4-34-70. Open daily 8 AM-9:30 PM.

VISITOR INFORMATION Don't be misled by the booths advertising tourist information—they are really fronts for time-shares and offer next to no information. The real tourist office is next door to Zihuatanejo's Palacio Municipal. Álvarez, near Cuauhtémoc, tel. 755/4-20-01. Open weekdays 9-3 and 6-8, Sat. 9-2.

COMING AND GOING

BY BUS The new bus station is on the highway on the outskirts of Zihuatanejo. To reach downtown Zihuatanejo from here, take any bus or VW combi marked ZIHUATANEJO or CENTRO. You'll be let off on either Juárez or Morelos, both just a few blocks from most of the cheaper hotels in town. To return to the station, head to the corner of Juárez and Ejido and board a combi marked CORREO. The not-so-comfy 10-minute ride only costs 15¢.

Estrella Blanca (tel. 755/4-34-77) is the main bus line that operates out of the Zihuatanejo station. Direct buses to Acapulco ($7, 4 hrs) run on the hour from 6 AM to 6 PM. The bus to Huatulco (13 hrs, $23) leaves at 7:45 PM and 9:30 PM and stops in Puerto Escondido along the way. Three buses a day (2 AM, 10 AM, and noon) also head for Mazatlán (20 hrs, $34), stopping in Manzanillo (9 hrs, $12) and Puerto Vallarta (12 hrs, $21). A first-class bus to Mexico City (10 hrs, $26) leaves daily at 6 AM.

BY PLANE The international airport (tel. 755/4–22–37 or 755/4–26–34) is 11 kilometers east of Zihuatanejo on the Carretera Costera (Hwy. 200). **Aeroméxico** (tel. 755/4–20–18), **Mexicana** (tel. 755/4–22–27), and some U.S. carriers serve the airport, which is accessible only by taxi. A ride to or from Zihuatanejo costs $6 ($7.50 to or from Ixtapa).

GETTING AROUND

Zihuatanejo is easily walkable; you'll find budget hotels, restaurants, shops, and the beach all near the center. This area is marked by Álvarez along the beach to the south, Juárez to the east, 5 de Mayo to the west, and Morelos to the north. Ixtapa has one main thoroughfare, the Paseo de Ixtapa—essentially a 3-kilometer strip of hotels and malls. To get to Ixtapa from Zihuatanejo (a 15-minute trip), catch one of the blue-and-white buses on Morelos at Juárez and pay 15¢. Catch the bus back to Zihuatanejo anywhere along Ixtapa's Paseo de Ixtapa. If you feel like walking, head east on Morelos and follow the signs to Ixtapa—the 7-kilometer walk should take about an hour (unless the heat knocks you out).

WHERE TO SLEEP

Downtown Zihuatanejo is packed with fairly inexpensive hotels, many of which are near the waterfront. Unfortunately, budget hotels in Zihuatanejo are generally reluctant to let lots of people pack into a room for low rates, so groups may have a harder time getting a break. Staying in Ixtapa is pretty much out of the question—there are no nonresort hotels in sight, and the cheapest single will set you back $70. The prices listed below apply in Zihuatanejo's low season. Expect to pay a bit more from November to February.

➤ **UNDER $10** • **Casa Elvira.** The cheapest acceptable indoor sleep in town (except for the youth hostel) can be found here, two steps from the beach. The sweet, elderly proprietress keeps the rooms clean, and the mirrors, calendars, and flowered curtains make you feel right at home (until you step into the run-down bathroom). She charges $5 for a single and $8 for a double. *Álvarez 52, near 5 de Mayo, no phone. 6 rooms, 4 with bath. Luggage storage. Wheelchair access.*

Hotel Casa Aurora. The narrow entryway of this hotel is hidden by souvenir shops and grocery stores, but wade through them and you'll find a tiled interior patio with sprawling plants. Most of the clean rooms have stone walls and floors, and second-floor rooms have huge, shaded decks with comfortable lounge chairs. Rooms are $6.50 per person, or pay about $5 extra for air-conditioning. *Nicolás Bravo 27, near Juárez, tel. 755/4–30–46. 15 rooms, all with bath.*

➤ **UNDER $15** • **Hotel Raúl Tres Marías.** This hotel overlooks Zihuatanejo Bay and is the best in its price range. Each floor has a communal deck with tables, chairs, and a great view. The cement rooms (singles $10, doubles $13) are ample, clean, and have ceiling fans. The same management runs a slightly cheaper ($8.50 single, $11.50 double) hotel by the same name on La Noria, but there's no hot water there. *Álvarez, tel. 755/4–29–77. 1 block from beach. 25 rooms, all with bath. Luggage storage.*

Hotel Rosimar. This clean, breezy hotel has sitting areas on every floor, each overlooking the street. The downstairs lobby looks like a bus station waiting room, but the TV lures guests down. Singles cost $8.50, doubles $11.50. *Ejido 12, btw Galeana and Guerrero, tel. 755/4–21–39. 13 rooms, all with bath. Luggage storage. Wheelchair access.*

➤ **UNDER $30** • **Bungalows Pacífico.** Walk over to Playa La Madera (*see* Outdoor Activities, *below*) and treat yourself to one of these first-rate bungalows. You can lounge in a hammock, cook yourself a fish dinner and eat it on the deck outside your back door, or descend the vine-draped stairway for a walk on the beach. Each bungalow has four beds, a kitchen, a view, and a breeze. Doubles are $30 in low season, $50 in high season, and there's a $10 charge for each additional person. *Cerro de la Madera, tel. 755/4–21–12. 6 bungalows, all with bath. Luggage storage.*

HOSTELS **Villa Juvenil.** This friendly, crowded place is just outside town, less than a mile from the waterfront. Facilities are rudimentary but clean, and it's a good place to meet other travelers. A bed in one of the single-sex dorms costs $2.50. Breakfast costs about $1.50, and lunch and dinner are each $2. Be careful if you're going out at night—the doors lock at 10:30 PM. *Paseo de las Salinas, tel. 755/4-46-62. West on Morelos until it becomes Paseo de las Salinas, left at fork. 60 beds. Open 7 AM-10:30 PM. Luggage storage.*

CAMPING You can pitch a tent at the hostel (*see above*) and use their bathrooms and showers for $2.50 a night. Camping on the beach is also allowed at **Playa La Ropa,** south of Playa La Madera in Zihuatanejo, but at any other spot you'll have to ask the hotel behind the beach for permission.

FOOD

The restaurants in Ixtapa tend to be fancy and overpriced, but there are a few reasonably priced Italian places: **Cactus** (Paseo Ixtapa, no phone) gives you the choice of an Italian, Mexican, or seafood meal $5-$7. Zihuatanejo, however, has a good selection of serene seafood eateries, many of which are right on the beach. For quick snacks, try **Panadería Francesa** (González 15, tel. 755/4-27-42), a warehouse-size bakery with a wide selection of *pan dulce* (sweet rolls) and breads.

Cafetería Nueva Zelandia. Shiny wooden tables and hanging plants make this restaurant look like a health-food store, but it's really more of a breakfast place and café. Hotcakes cost $1, the large cappuccinos are $1, fruit salad is $1.50, and eggs any style go for $2. *Cuauhtémoc 23, tel. 755/4-23-40. Open daily 7 AM-10 PM.*

Restaurant Bar Tata's. This is a happening spot with great food and lots of atmosphere. Super-hip waiters bop to your beachside tables to the beat of the Top 40 pumping from loudspeakers. Breaded red snapper with rice and tortillas costs about $5, as does the *filete a la tampiqueña,* a steak served with enchiladas, beans, and rice. They run a two-for-one special during happy hour (5 PM-7 PM). *Paseo del Pescador, tel. 755/4-20-10. Open Mon.-Sat. 7 AM-11 PM.*

La Sirena Gorda. Seafood tacos are the specialty at this waterfront restaurant. The name means "the fat mermaid," and ceramic mermaids and other knickknacks adorn the tables and the busy wooden bar. The tasty smoked-fish tacos are $3 for an order of two; octopus tacos cost $4. *Paseo del Pescador 20-A, near pier, tel. 755/4-26-87. Open Thur.-Tues. 7 AM-10 PM. Wheelchair access.*

Tamales Atoles Any. This fun and lively place specializes in tamales of all varieties, including sweet ones. They also have soups, *queso fundido* (melted cheese), and vegetarian selections. A meal will run you $2-$3. *Ejido, at Guerrero, tel. 755/4-73-73. Open Wed.-Mon. 8 AM-midnight. Wheelchair access.*

OUTDOOR ACTIVITIES

The beaches at Las Gatas and Isla Ixtapa are well-known scuba-diving spots, and shops along the waterfront in Zihuatanejo, Playa Las Gatas, and Isla Ixtapa rent diving equipment. The NAUI-certified **Zihuatanejo Scuba Center** (Cuauhtémoc 3, near Álvarez, tel. 755/4-21-47) offers beginners pool lessons and one dive for $70, as well as all-day trips for certified divers for the same price. Also available are plastic kayaks ($5 an hour; $20 a day), which can be used to visit **Playa La Ropa** or **Playa Las Gatas.** A half-day snorkeling excursion with equipment (Thursdays only) costs $25, and includes a lesson on how to avoid killing coral. A cheaper option is to rent fins, snorkels, and other equipment ($5 a day) at almost any beach. Deepsea fishing is also popular, but it will cost you an arm and a leg: The **Cooperativa de Pescadores** (Paseo del Pescador, at 5 de Mayo, tel. 755/4-20-56) rents charter boats ($120-$200 a day). Parasailing is more affordable, at $10 for a 10-minute ride. To get away from the sand and surf, rent a bike ($3.50 an hour, $20 a day) at **BiciRent** (Paseo Ixtapa, tel. 755/3-04-57).

ZIHUATANEJO The **Playa Municipal** in Zihuatanejo, with its many restaurants and surf shops, is the easiest to reach from the budget hotels, but is not as impressive as others around the bay. **Playa La Madera,** a pretty stretch of sand with inviting water, is the next beach over. To get here, follow Álvarez east for half a mile until you reach a set of stairs leading over a canal; cross over and continue following the water. When you hear surf, cut to the right, past one of the big hotels. Past Playa La Madera is **Playa La Ropa,** with clean, calm waters perfect for swimming or waterskiing. Make the sweltering trek from Zihuatanejo's downtown on foot, or take a taxi ($1–$2). If you're walking, follow the route to Playa La Madera; keep to the right on the main road (the Paseo Costera), always heading up. As the road descends and the ocean comes into view, cut through the nearest hotel, or follow the road until it winds to the beach. You can also get here by walking 15 minutes north from Playa Las Gatas (*see below*).

The last beach off the Paseo Costera is the protected **Playa Las Gatas.** Unfortunately, the inviting waters here hide a rocky bottom that is hard on bare toes. Las Gatas is, however, perfect for snorkeling, as flippers will protect your feet. Colloquially named for the sharks that used to frequent the waters, Las Gatas now only attracts a few marlin and yellowfin sailfish. To get here from Playa La Ropa, walk south along the beach for 15 minutes; from the *muelle* (pier) in Zihuatanejo, take a pleasant 10-minute boat ride ($2 round-trip per person). Boats run 8:30–5.

Legend says an ancient Tarascan king ensured calm waters for his maidens by building a barrier of rocks at Playa Las Gatas.

IXTAPA Playa del Palmar is a long, sandy stretch bordering the Ixtapa hotels where rough surf pounds the shore. To the northwest are several more pristine beaches, including **Playa Quieta, Playa Linda,** and Ixtapa's **Club Med.** To reach Playa del Palmar, take the minibus to Ixtapa from the intersection of Morelos and Juárez in Zihuatanejo. Get off at any of the towering hotels and cut through to the beach. **Isla Ixtapa,** off the shore of Playa Quieta, has two good swimming and sunbathing beaches, and one that is better for divers. Snorkeling is popular too, and allowed on all three beaches. There are a few restaurants on the island, but no place to stay. The best thing about Isla Ixtapa is the hour-long boat trip from the pier in Zihuatanejo ($5 per person round-trip). Boats leave at 11:30 AM and return at 4 PM. They also leave every 15 minutes 8–5 from Playa Quieta ($2 per person round-trip).

AFTER DARK

You won't party as hard in Ixtapa/Zihuatanejo as in hedonistic Acapulco, but don't get ready for bed yet. Most of the action is where the dollars are: Ixtapa. If you crave a pulsating beat, try the local representative of the ubiquitous **Carlos 'n Charlie's** (Paseo del Palmar, tel. 753/3–00–85), which sits at the northwest end of the hotel strip. Cover is $5 for guys, $2.50 for girls. **Señor Frog's** (Centro Comercial Ixtapa, tel. 755/3–02–72) is the place if dancing on the table is your thing, or if you want to have a few icy tropical drinks. Next to the Hotel Kristal in Ixtapa is **Christine's,** which caters to the rich and sophisticated. Cover is $7, except for Wednesday, when you can boogie for free. Over in Zihuatanejo, the only night club/disco is **Roca Rock** (5 de Mayo, at Nicolás Bravo, tel. 755/4–33–24), which pulls in the city's gays and lesbians, and features a nightly drag show. It's open Thursday nights and weekends 10 PM–6 AM. The happy hour at **Restaurant Bar Tata's** (*see* Food, *above*) is also pretty happenin' among locals. For a more sedate evening, catch a flick at **Cinema Paraíso** (Cuauhtémoc, near Nicolás Bravo) in Zihuatanejo, which usually shows movies in English with Spanish subtitles.

Sunday nights around 9 PM, the basketball court on Playa Principal fills up with locals who've come to watch their friends and family perform traditional dances and music.

Near Ixtapa/Zihuatanejo

BARRA DE POTOSI

If even mellow Zihuatanejo is too touristy for you, make a midweek trip to the slow-paced seaside village of Barra de Potosí, where the main activity consists of hanging out between swims in one of several rustic beachfront restaurants. Here, red snapper with rice and tortillas will set you back about $3 (much less than in Ixtapa/Zihuatanejo). Try **Palapa Bacanona** (two palapas in from the end of the beach), where you will be served $1 quesadillas and any *refresco* (soft drink) you want. At night, visitors are welcome to sleep free of charge in the hammocks slung beneath the restaurant's eaves. If a bright-pink, unfinished hotel sounds better, try **Hotel Barra de Potosí** (tel. 755/4-82-90). Charming rooms (singles $12.50, doubles $16.50) overlook a pool, restaurant, and, of course, the beach. During the week, there's absolutely nothing to do in Barra de Potosí but relax, enjoy the fine weather and food, and chat with the locals. Weekends, however, are a different story: The beaches fill up with teenagers whose boomboxes pound as the kids hit volleyballs around the sand courts.

COMING AND GOING Catch a VW combi or one of the white minibuses that run along Juárez (heading away from the water), first checking that the driver is stopping at **Los Achotes** (30 min, 25¢). Here *camionetas* (small flatbed trucks) run to Barra de Potosí every half hour. The trip through tropical countryside and a small pueblo takes 10 minutes.

Acapulco

Acapulco is, to steal a phrase from Dorothy Parker, not a city to be tossed aside lightly. It should be thrown aside with great force. The air hangs thick with grime, and the water is not as pristine as it used to be. Once the crowning star of the Pacific Coast, this city is now in many ways a fortyish bachelor, still partying the night away but desperately pushing his thinning hair back to conceal an ever-growing bald spot. In the luxury-hotel zone, which has existed in all its tacky brilliance for only 40 years, tourists cruise the strip, shopping, dining, and spending. Acapulco Viejo, at the other end of the bay, is a maze of run-down streets swarming with buses and handicraft vendors. But Acapulco's main draw continues to be its discos, which are expensive, crowded, and rock through the night with special effects to rival Jurassic Park's. If you need to get away from this "Mexico City with a beach" (as one Mexican woman put it), less sensory overload can be found in the quieter town of Pie de la Cuesta, a 45-minute bus ride from the center of town.

People have inhabited the area around Acapulco Bay for over 2,000 years. In the 1530s, the Spanish settled where the downtown area (Acapulco Viejo) and the zócalo are now located. Today, both Acapulco Viejo and the newer luxury hotel strip are amazingly alive with people, stores, street vendors, and entertainment. The smells of the ocean and the freshly grilled fish and sweet fruit in the marketplace compete with heavy exhaust fumes, open sewers, and piles of garbage, which you'll sometimes see in the middle of the street. All of this coexists with the incredible natural beauty of the coastal setting, and the highly contrived beauty of the rich and tanned who come to the fancy hotels and clubs to strut their stuff.

BASICS

AMERICAN EXPRESS The main office is in the heart of the luxury-hotel strip, but the rates are comparable to those in any of the banks in Acapulco Viejo. They change traveler's checks, deliver MoneyGrams, and replace lost or stolen AmEx cards and checks. Cardholders can cash personal checks or receive mail here as well. *Costera Miguel Alemán 1628-4, Acapulco, Guerrero, CP 39300, México, tel. 74/69-11-00. Open Mon.–Sat. 10-7.*

AUTO PARTS/SERVICE **Taller Mecánico Ramiro Vargas Solís** in Acapulco Viejo is run by Señor Vargas himself. His English-speaking sons work with him daily. *18 de Marzo 135, tel. 74/85-01-04, or 74/85-23-84. From Costera, 4 blocks up Niños Héroes, right on 18 de Marzo. Open weekdays 9–7, Sat. 9–2.*

CASAS DE CAMBIO There are tons of casas de cambio on the luxury-hotel strip. Near the zócalo in Acapulco Viejo, **Ventanilla de Cambio** (Costera Miguel Alemán 207, no phone) changes cash and traveler's checks weekdays 9–5 and Saturdays 9–2. Also in this area is **Banamex** (Costera Miguel Alemán 211, tel. 74/82-57-50), where money is changed weekdays 9–3 and the ATM accepts Plus and Cirrus cards.

CONSULATES In the Club del Sol Hotel (Costera Miguel Alemán, tel. 74/85-66-00), you'll find the **United States** consulate (tel. 74/85-72-07), open weekdays 10–2, and the **Canadian**

consulate (tel. 74/85-66-21), open weekdays 9-1. The **United Kingdom** consulate is at Las Brisas Hotel (Carretera Escénica, tel. 74/84-66-05) and is open weekdays 10-2 and 5-6:30.

DISCOUNT TRAVEL AGENCIES Dozens of travel agencies along the Costera offer local tours and travel packages as well as international flight services. **Las Hamacas,** in the hotel of the same name, is an easy-to-locate, established agency. Costera Miguel Alemán 239, tel. 74/82-00-34. Near Comercial Mexicana, btw Acapulco Viejo and the strip. Open weekdays 9-2 and 3-6, Sat. 9-2.

EMERGENCIES The number for the **police** is 74/85-06-50; they can get you an **ambulance**. **The fire department** can be reached at 74/84-41-22.

LAUNDRY At **Ghost Cleaners Lavandería Automática,** $5 will get you 4 kilos washed, dried, and folded on the same day. José Marí Iglesias 9, tel. 74/82-70-22. 1 block west of zócalo. Open weekdays 8-8, weekends 8:30-2.

MAIL The huge main **post office** is on the Costera, a few blocks east of the zócalo. They will hold mail sent to you at the following address for up to 10 days: Lista de Correos, Costera Miguel Alemán 215, Acapulco, Guerrero, CP 39300, México. Tel. 74/82-20-83. Open Mon.-Sat. 8-8, Sun. 9-noon.

MEDICAL AID For an English-speaking doctor, call **Servicio Médico Especialista** (in Hotel Club del Sol, opposite Plaza Bahía, tel. 74/85-80-66) 24 hours a day; Dr. Luís Roberto García Ruiz charges $30 for a consultation and makes hotel calls anywhere in Acapulco for the same price. In an emergency, try the **Cruz Roja** on Ruíz Cortines (tel. 74/85-41-00) or the adjacent **Hospital General** (tel. 74/85-17-83). To reach either from the zócalo, follow Constituyentes north until it becomes Ruíz Cortines—the hospital and clinic are on the 600 block. For less urgent medical attention, try the 24-hour **Farmacia Super Flash** (Costera Miguel Alemán 86, no phone), a few blocks east of the post office.

PHONES There are pay phones on the zócalo, and calls can be placed from the convenient **Caseta TelPlus** (hidden in an alleyway off the west side of the zócalo). A $1.50 fee is charged for collect calls. Hidalgo 6, tel. 74/82-86-01. Open Mon.-Sat. 8-8, Sun. noon-8.

VISITOR INFORMATION The streets here are patrolled by tourist police dressed all in white—they'll answer any questions and come to the rescue if you have a problem. The main **tourist office** (Costera Miguel Alemán 187, a few blocks west of the Ritz, tel. 74/84-49-73) has an extremely helpful staff that is trained to send you away with an armful of reading material, much of it in English. The tourist office is open weekdays 9-2 and 4-7. If difficulties arise, the **tourist assistance bureau** (Costera Miguel Alemán 4455, tel. 74/84-45-83; open daily 8 AM-10 PM) in the luxury hotel area can help you. Limited tourist information is also available at the **Sendatur** booth in the bus station.

COMING AND GOING

BY BUS The **Central de Autobuses Líneas Unidas del Sur** (Ejido, btw Calles 6 and 7, tel. 74/86-80-29), commonly called Estrella Blanca, is in Colonia La Fábrica and can be reached from the zócalo area on any bus marked EJIDO or CENTRAL. Buses labeled CALETA or CENTRO make the trip in the opposite direction. The **Estrella Blanca** taxi company (tel. 74/83-30-70) will also take you to the zócalo for $2; you can call them from anywhere in the city between 7 AM and 10 PM. A number of companies serve the **Sendatur** booth in the bus station, but **Estrella Blanca** (tel. 74/69-20-30) has both first-class and ejecutivo (deluxe) service to most destinations. First-class buses to Mexico City (7 hrs, $15) leave every hour between 6 AM and 2 AM, usually stopping in Chilpancingo (2 hrs, $5), Taxco (4 hrs, $9), and Cuernavaca (5 hrs, $11.50). Direct, luxury buses to Mexico City (5 hrs, $23) leave on the same schedule. First-class buses also run to Zihuatanejo (4 hrs, $7.50) and Huatulco (9 hrs, $16), with a stop in Puerto Escondido (7 hrs, $12). You can catch buses from a number of other companies to far-flung destinations like Guadalajara, Monterrey, and Tampico. Luggage storage costs 25¢ per hour, and you can sleep, albeit uncomfortably, at the station.

The **Central de Autobuses Estrella de Oro** (Cuauhtémoc 751, Fracc. Las Anclas, tel. 74/85-93-60) is served only by **Estrella de Oro.** To reach the zócalo from here, cross Cuauhtémoc

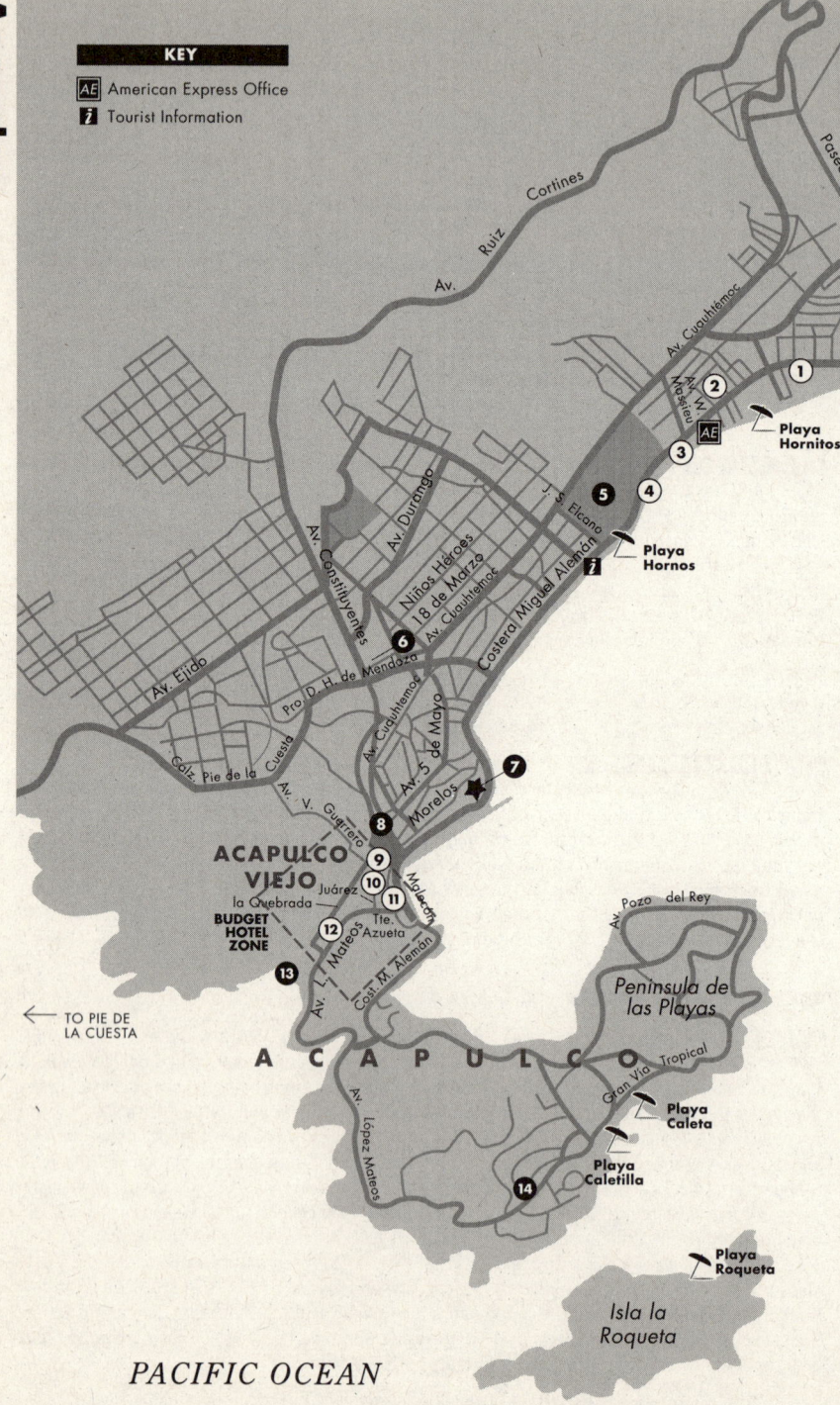

and catch any westbound bus. To get from the zócalo to the station, catch a bus labeled CINE RIO on the corner of 5 de Mayo and Constituyentes. Estrella de Oro has only two routes: north to Mexico City with stops in Chilpancingo, Taxco, and Cuernavaca, and west to Zihuatanejo with a stop in Lázaro Cárdenas. Service is comparable to Estrella Blanca's, and prices are a few pesos higher. Luggage storage is available at the station for 15¢ each hour, and you can sack out here too.

BY PLANE Acapulco's airport is 30 kilometers east of the city on Highway 200. There's no public transportation to the airport, and taxis cost $12–$15. If you're alone, a cheaper alternative is **Shuttle Aeropuerto Acapulco** (Blvd. de las Naciones Unidas, at Barra Vieja, tel. 74/62-10-95). The shuttle costs $5 per person, and if you call 24 hours in advance, they'll pick you up at your hotel. Phone hours are daily 7 AM–10 PM.

GETTING AROUND

Acapulco can be divided roughly into two sections: the city itself, known as Acapulco Viejo (Old Acapulco), and the strip, where all the fancy hotels are. Most of the budget hotels in Acapulco are in Acapulco Viejo, around the zócalo (also called **Plaza Álvarez**). On the zócalo you'll also find the city's cathedral, which is built over an unfinished movie theater. Bordering the zócalo to the south is the Costera Miguel Alemán, an 8-kilometer thoroughfare that runs along the bay. As you move east along the Costera, away from the zócalo, you'll encounter the **Fuerte de San Diego, Papagayo Park,** several beaches, the **Fuente Diana** traffic circle, and finally the tourist zone. The tourist zone stretches from the tunnel on the Costera to the naval base, and includes the decadent **CiCi** water park. The walk from the zócalo to CiCi takes just over an hour.

BY BUS Buses are by far the cheapest way to get around, with fares averaging 15¢. Buses marked LA BASE and HORNOS run in both directions along the Costera 6 AM–10 PM. The yellow aluminum structures are bus stops.

Tourism 101: A Crash Course in Resort-Town Economics

In the 1960s, the Mexican government decided that tourism was the ticket out of Debt City. Tourism means an influx of foreign currency, and for Mexico, that was supposed to translate into a painless way of repaying foreign debt. A department of tourism, Fonatur, was formed, and after careful consideration, five sites were singled out to become megaresorts: Acapulco, Cancún, Ixtapa, Los Cabos, and the Bahías de Huatulco. These billion-dollar babies have enjoyed varying success: Cancún, a paradise carved out of the Yucatecan landscape, reigns supreme, while Huatulco, in Oaxaca, is still in the development stages.

No one can argue with the fact that increased tourism has ushered in a flood of foreign dollars, but just how much of this remains in the country? Construction money stays, since the law states Mexican labor must be used to build megaresorts. Fees for water and electricity remain, as does money spent by tourists in Mexican-owned businesses—and, of course, there are always taxes. The cost of these resorts includes radical environmental degradation, however, and Hyatt and Sheraton—conspicuously foreign corporations—are now flowering along the coast. There's also this unpleasant statistic to deal with: More than half of all the profit made on tourism in developing countries manages to find its way back to the rich north.

BY TAXI Taxis are more expensive—you'll be charged $1 as soon as you take a seat. Even if you see a meter, set a price before getting in, and don't be afraid to haggle—remember that if the first *taxista* (cabbie) won't lower his price, another VW bug will be along in 30 seconds.

WHERE TO SLEEP

Don't even think about staying on the strip unless someone just died and left you a sizeable inheritance. You needn't lose heart, however: Budget lodging is easy to find nearby, and competition keeps prices down—although couples may be frustrated by the common policy of charging by the person, rather than by room or bed. The best lodgings are clustered around the zócalo in Acapulco Viejo. This area is generally safe, but, as always, you should be alert walking at night. There are even a few budget options further towards the strip, several blocks past the Fuerte de San Diego and within binocular-view of the ritzy part of town. Wherever you stay, expect prices to jump substantially in the high season (Semana Santa and around the Christmas and New Year holidays).

NEAR THE ZOCALO The best deals are on the west side of the zócalo. If everything listed below is full, try the super-cheap **Hotel Sacramento** (Carranza 4, tel. 74/82–08–21), where singles are $5 and doubles $8.50.

Casa Mama Helene. This slightly worn hotel is truly Mama Helene's house. The Ping-Pong table, bookshelves, aquarium, plants, and Mama Helene sitting around with her friends all testify to it. Rooms run $6.50 per person. *Juárez 12, 3 blocks west of zócalo, tel. 74/82–23–96. 20 rooms, all with bath. Laundry, luggage storage.*

Hotel Asturias. The Asturias has a pool and yard where it's easy to socialize and cool off. The environment is generally friendly and laid-back, and the small rooms all have working fans, comfortable beds, and clean bathrooms. A plus is that La Quebrada, of cliff-diving and sunset-watching fame, is only a five-minute walk away. Singles cost $8.50 and doubles are $11.50. *La Quebrada 45, 4½ blocks west of zócalo, tel. 74/83–65–48. 15 rooms. Luggage storage.*

Hotel Misión. This place has the most charm of any budget hotel in Acapulco. The atrium is filled with philodendrons, mango trees, and wicker rocking chairs, and the rooms are decorated with assorted artwork and classy wood furniture. Powerful fans keep the rooms cool, and each has a dimly lit bathroom. Singles cost $7.50 and doubles are $15. *Felipe Valle 12, 3 blocks west of zócalo, tel. 74/82–36–43. 28 rooms. Wheelchair access. Luggage storage.*

NEAR THE STRIP Acapulco never sleeps, and you might not either if you choose to stay in this noisy area, near the western beaches and within walking distance of the strip. Traffic pours past at all hours, and prices tend to be a bit higher for the same sort of rooms that you'll find near the zócalo.

Hotel Lupita. Statues of naked babies and mermaids surround the hotel's entrance and small pool. Narrow hallways open to spacious rooms, some of which can hold larger groups. Singles are $11.50 and doubles are $15 (except during high season, when all rooms are $23). *Gómez Espinoza, right off the Costera, tel. 74/85–94–12. 16 rooms, all with bath. Luggage storage.*

Hotel Playa Suave. This is a reasonable place to stay if you want to be as close to the beach as possible. The 25 rooms are dark but clean, and each has a bathroom. A breezy but noisy hallway leads to a restaurant, a swimming pool, and parking. Singles are $10, doubles $13.50, and a single or double with air-conditioning costs $16.50. *Costera Miguel Alemán 253, just west of Hotel de Brasil, tel. 74/85–12–56. Luggage storage.*

CAMPING Pitching a tent or even walking on the beach late at night is not a good idea—Acapulco has a high crime rate. Women especially should stay off the beaches and out of sparsely populated areas past dark. During high season, camping is allowed on the patrolled beach at Puerto Marqués (*see* Outdoor Activities, *below*). The **Playa Suave Trailer Park** (Costera Miguel Alemán 276, tel. 74/85–14–64) is right between Acapulco Viejo and the strip, a block away from the beach. For $9.50, one or two persons can comfortably and safely pitch a tent here.

FOOD

The deals are around the west side of the zócalo in Acapulco Viejo, especially on Juárez, where you'll find literally hundreds of small, clean establishments frequented by locals. **Restaurante Ricardos** (Juárez 9, tel. 74/82–11–40) and **Restaurante San Carlos** (Juárez 5, tel. 74/82–64–59) may lack atmosphere, but they're two of the best and cheapest in the area. For about $2 you can eat at one of the *fondas* (covered food stands) in the mercado—try **Fonda Christie** or **Fonda Doña Lupe.** To reach the market, take a HOSPITAL bus going inland from the zócalo. If you want to stock up on snacks for the beach, three warehouse-size grocery stores on the Costera between Acapulco Viejo and the strip sell cheap yogurt, fruit, deli meats, and freshly baked bread. Near the strip, expensive American restaurants and fast-food joints abound—there's even a Hard Rock Café.

NEAR THE ZOCALO Tucked in a secluded, shaded corner of the zócalo, **the** outdoor **Cafetería Astoria** (Plaza Álvarez, tel. 74/82–29–44; open daily 8 AM–11 PM) is the spot to sit and relax for hours with a cappuccino ($1) and some pan dulce. Also served are *chilaquiles rojos* (tortilla strips and chicken in red sauce; $1.50), meat enchiladas ($2), and club sandwiches ($1.50). A few blocks west of the zócalo you'll find about four seafood restaurants that all look the same: airy and comfortable, with starched tablecloths, stuffed fish on the walls, and solicitous waiters. **El Amigo Miguel** (Juárez 31, at José Azueta, tel. 74/83–69–81) has the freshest seafood, and a second-floor balcony overlooking Acapulco Bay. Fish soups are $2, and a fillet of sole comes with vegetables, rice, and warm bread for $4.50. Paella is only $3, while lobster costs $9. El Amigo is open daily 10–9.

ON THE STRIP Don't come to the strip to find a budget meal—come to see what's happening. In the afternoons, large crowds of young people flock to **El Zorrito.** The food is good and not too expensive—hearty eaters should try the $7 *filete a la tampiqueña,* steak served with a chicken taco, chicken enchilada, guacamole, and beans. The menu also includes hamburgers ($3.50), onion rings ($1.50), and fried chicken ($4). *Costera Miguel Alemán, just east of Ritz, tel. 74/85–37–35. Open Wed.–Mon. 24 hrs, Tues. 2 PM–6 AM. Wheelchair access.*

Acapulco's biggest health-food chain, **100% Natural** (Costera Miguel Alemán 4864, 1 block past CiCi, tel. 74/81–08–44) has several outlets that serve green salads, steamed vegetable dishes, and soyburgers. Main dishes range $3–$4, and the restaurant is wheelchair accessible. Some of the chain's restaurants are open 24 hours, so, if you're in overdrive, come here for a bit of sanity and lettuce. (Warning: The branch on the zócalo is an imitation and not worth your time.) **Suntory** (Costera Miguel Alemán 36, tel. 74/4–80–88; open daily 2–midnight) is a spotless, elegant, air-conditioned Japanese restaurant that serves an assortment of sushi for $10. Lighter fare includes miso soup ($1) and fried rice with vegetables ($2). It's located a few blocks east of CiCi.

DESSERT/COFFEEHOUSES **Cafetería Astoria** (*see above*), on the northeast corner of the zócalo, is where most coffee-sippers relax for the afternoon, reading the newspaper or playing dominoes. **Café Los Amigos** (La Paz 10, no phone), on the west side, serves ice cream, fresh juice drinks, and a mean cappuccino (75¢). Around the corner at the **Fat Farm** (Juárez 10, tel. 74/83–53–39), coffee goes well with a $1.50 banana split or cheesecake. These last two establishments also serve good breakfasts (about $1.50) and comidas corridas (about $3.50).

WORTH SEEING

Most points of interest lie within a Frisbee's throw of the Costera. Check out the **mercado municipal** (near Cuauhtémoc and Mendoza), where you'll find food, but also painted ceramic statues, shell earrings, and Guatemalan vests and backpacks. Head to the zócalo, or Parque Papagayo on Sundays—local bands play at both places around sunset.

FUERTE DE SAN DIEGO This fort, so well restored it imparts absolutely no sense of history, sits on a waterfront hill just east of the zócalo. The original fort, built in 1616, was destroyed by an earthquake; the present structure dates from the late 18th century when it was used to protect Acapulco from pirates. Today its huge beige stone walls encircle manicured lawns and exhibition rooms. *Costera Miguel Alemán, near Palacio Federal, tel. 74/83–97–30. Admission: $2.50, free Sun. Open Tues.–Sun. 10:30–4:40.*

PARQUE PAPAGAYO This huge park on the Costera—complete with kid-thrillers like a roller rink, an aviary, and bumper boats in a scum-covered lagoon—is a five-minute walk west of the Ritz Hotel. It's primarily a hangout for local youth and, on weekends, for families, but it also makes a nice break from the beach scene for tourists. Entrance is free, but the amusements cost up to $1 each. *Costera Miguel Alemán, at Manuel Morin, tel. 74/85–62–09. Open weekdays 3:30–10:30, weekends 3–11.*

PLAZA DE TOROS CALETILLA Bullfights take place almost every Sunday between Christmas and Easter at this bullring, just a few minutes' walk northwest of Playa Caletilla (*see* Outdoor Activities, *below*). Fights start at 5:30 PM and the cheapest tickets, available at the bullring, are $5. *López Mateos, Península de las Playas, tel. 74/82–11–82.*

LA QUEBRADA A 10-minute walk northwest of the zócalo, these beautiful cliffs offer breathtaking views of the ocean and surrounding landscape. Acapulco's famous divers, the **Clavadistas,** risk their lives daily, plummeting 60 meters into the rock-filled waters below. This being Acapulco, you have to pay a $1 admission charge to join the crowds of tourists vying for the best viewing spots. The divers also accept (expect?) small gratuities. Dives take place daily at 1 PM and once an hour 7:30 PM–10:30 PM; the last two feature divers flinging themselves into the water bearing flaming torches. You can also get a spectacular view of the divers from the classy **La Perla** restaurant (Plaza Las Glorias, tel. 74/82–26–49). The $10 cover includes a couple of drinks. To reach the cliffs, walk straight up La Quebrada, the street that begins directly behind the zócalo's main church.

The tradition of La Quebrada's celebrated and meticulously staged dives began in 1934, when talented youths first boasted their skills off Acapulco's most striking cliffs.

AFTER DARK

The legendary disco scene of Acapulco is mind-boggling in its excess of mirrored walls, strobe lights, disco music, and laser beams; however, it does slow down during low season (spring—except Semana Santa—and fall). Covers average $10–$15 year-round, and in many cases drinks are as high as $5. The deal to look for, assuming you lack a company expense account, is a *barra libre* (free bar). This means there's a hefty cover, but all drinks are included in the price. There are even discos on ships that cruise Acapulco Bay—**Bonanza Cruise** (Costera Miguel Alemán, a few blocks west of the zócalo, tel. 74/83–18–03) leaves at 11 AM, 4:30 PM, and 10:30 PM daily from the pier at Caleta Beach; $15 tickets include the three-hour trip, snacks, and an open bar. As at any beach resort, the gay bars in Acapulco are as active and seedy as the rest of the clubs. **Relax** (Lomas del Mar 4, tel. 74/84–04–21) is right behind Denny's on the Costera, and charges $5 to enter. **Open House Bar** (Plaza Condesa, tel. 74/84–72–55) is also popular among gays, and stays open 10 PM to 4 AM. Unfortunately, their cover (up to $25 some nights) may discourage the budget traveler.

BARS There are almost as many bars along the strip as there are fast-food places. **Carlos 'n Charlie's** (Costera Miguel Alemán 999, tel. 74/84–00–39), open 6 PM–midnight, is usually a guaranteed rockin' good time; get there early or you'll wait in line. Another fun place is the restaurant **El Zorrito** (*see* Food, *above*), which stays open all night. The **Hard Rock Café** (Costera Miguel Alemán 37, tel. 74/84–00–47) has live music and its regular funky music paraphernalia, but is only open till 2 AM.

DISCOS WITH NO COVER CHARGE You gotta love these places. **Disco Beach** (Costera Miguel Alemán, tel. 74/84–70–64) is an outdoor disco in the middle of the strip, overlooking the ocean. Expect lots of young muscle men, bleach blonds, and occasional $1-drink nights. Equally rowdy is **Iguanas Ranas** (Costera Miguel Alemán, tel. 74/85–27–03), on the beach near the tunnel, where music runs the gamut from Top 40 to world beat.

DISCOS The latest hot spot for young locals and Americans is **Atrium** (Costera Miguel Alemán 30, tel. 74/84–19–00), which gets going at 10:30 PM. The cover—$10 for women and $15 for men—includes drinks. **Baby O** (Costera Miguel Alemán, near Nelson, tel. 74/84–74–74) is probably the most popular spot with the 18–30 age group, and is packed almost every night of the week during high season. The jungle decor seems to bring out the animals, and there's little chance of going home alone unless you're determined. There's no cover for women, but men pay $16. The bar inside is free, and the doors open at 10:30 PM. At **B&B** (Gran Vía Tropical 5, tel. 74/83-04-41) you'll hear American music from the '60s and '70s on the first floor, and romantic Mexican pop on the second. B&B opens at 7 PM, the cover is $5, and drinks are $2-$3. This club is a distance from the zócalo, so you're better off taking a cab. The huge **D' Paradisse** (Costera Miguel Alemán, near Yucatán, tel. 74/84-88-15) has just finished renovations after a June '95 fire, and is now decorated entirely in black, with tables set in tiers around a circular dance floor. The bar opens at 10:30 PM, and the laser-light show starts at midnight. Women enter for free, men pay $15, and no one will be well received in sandals, shorts, or T-shirts.

LIVE MUSIC AND DANCING Nina's (Costera Miguel Alemán 41, tel. 74/84-24-00), a dance place with live tropical and salsa music, is one of the few alternatives to disco hell. They're open from 10 PM every night, and the $13.50 cover includes drinks. **Cats** (Juan de la Cosa 32, tel. 74/84-72-35) is a similar salsa saloon that also charges a $13.50 cover that includes all the (domestic-only) alcohol you can drink. Cats opens nightly at 10 PM, there's a drag show at 1 AM, and the bar closes at 4 AM. **Faces**, open 4 AM-8 AM, picks up where Cats left off (and it's right next door).

OUTDOOR ACTIVITIES

The beaches lining Acapulco Bay, in clockwise order, are: **Hornitos** and **Hornos**, frequented primarily by Mexican tourists; **La Condesa**, on the most densely populated part of the strip; and **Icacos**, a quieter stretch of sand that runs from the El Presidente Hotel to the naval base. Before diving into the deceptively beautiful water, remember that the bay is quite polluted—mostly with sewage. An alternative is to sneak into a hotel pool: **Club del Sol** (Costera Miguel Alemán, tel. 74/85-66-00) might not notice if you take a dip.

Lots of watersports are popular here, though you might want to choose one that requires the least amount of contact between you and the less-than-pristine water. Deep-sea fishing is a good bet: **Divers de Mexico/Fishing Factory** (Costera Miguel Alemán 100, a few blocks west of the zócalo, tel. 74/82-13-98) charges $55 per person (plus $8 for a fishing permit) for seven hours of marlin-, sailfish-, and tuna-fishing. All equipment and an English-speaking captain are included. Sailing ($13.50 per hour) and waterskiing ($40 an hour) are also available at Puerto Marqués. Scuba diving is expensive, although **Mantarraya** dive shop (Gran Vía Tropical 2, tel. 74/82-41-76), near Playas Caleta and Caletilla, has reasonable deals. Beginning and certified dive trips, including gear and transportation, are both $40, and snorkel trips are $20. On any of Acapulco's beaches, $3.50 will get you a 15-minute banana boat ride, and $35 will buy an hour of Jet-Skiing. Don't worry about finding these services—the salespeople roaming the beach will find *you*.

BEACHES The main draw of the beaches closest to the center of Acapulco Viejo, **Caleta** and **Caletilla,** are the big waves that crash in, tossing banana-hauling speedboats, paddling tourists, boogie-boarders, and swimmers like a big, wet, dirty salad. Formerly the hot spots of Acapulco, Caleta and Caletilla were left in the dust by the strip, and now cater to Mexican tourists more than to foreigners. While here, you can take a trip in a glass-bottom boat ($4) to see **La Virgen Sumergida**, a one-ton statue of the Virgin of Guadalupe placed at the bottom of the sea by a group of scuba divers some 35 years ago. Unfortunately, cloudy water means that visibility through the bottom of the boat is limited. The ticket hawkers for both the gawdy **Mágico Mundo Marino** aquarium ($3.50 and only worth it if you're with small children) and the various rides are very aggressive. Across the bay you can see **Isla Roqueta**, which is accessible from either beach by boat. The island itself has little to offer besides scrub brush, roaming tourists, a small beach, and a view from the lighthouse, although the boat ride there (10 min, $2.50 round-trip) is pleasant. Buy a ticket from the offices marked ISLA ROQUETA near the wharf (tel. 74/83-00-66), or from a roaming ticket seller on the beach. To reach the dock, board a bus marked CALETA heading west along Costera.

Acapulco's cleanest beaches lie on the **Bahía de Puerto Marqués,** east of the city near the airport freeway. The water here is less polluted than in Acapulco Bay, making the spot popular with water-skiers and skin-divers. On weekends the more developed **Playa de Puerto Marqués** usually fills up with Mexican tourists. Buses marked PUERTO MARQUES (30 min, 15¢) leave from the Costera across the street from Sanborn's. Farther along is the pristine **Princess Beach,** named for the hotel that looms over it. The waves are big, and swimmers should be very careful. To get here, take a cab ($1) or hitch a ride from the street beside Playa de Puerto Marqués.

Near Acapulco

PIE DE LA CUESTA

This stretch of sand is only 15 kilometers northwest of Acapulco. Residents don't swim here at all, though, due to the incredibly forceful current and riptide: Two or three people, usually foreigners, are killed each year. Locals advise visitors to stay out, especially "*si estás borracho*" (if you're drunk). However, **Laguna de Coyuca**, just on the other side of the street, is a lake of *agua dulce*—sweet, fresh water. Although the area around the lagoon is not safe at night, during the day locals and tourists take advantage of its calm waters to swim, waterski, and escape Acapulco. At **Club de Ski Chuy,** waterskiing for an hour costs $25. For a less exhausting excursion on the laguna, take a boat tour (3 hrs, $25). Boats take you through a swamp of thick mangrove trees and past Isla Presidio—a bird sanctuary inhabited by pelicans, flamingos, and storks. They also dock at Isla Montosa, supposedly inhabited by one large family (the man of the house is said to have had 7 wives.) Boats leave from the dock daily at 11:30 AM, 12:30 PM, and 1:30 PM. Look for the QUINTA ROSITA sign. To reach Pie de la Cuesta from Acapulco, catch a PIE DE LA CUESTA bus (1 hr, 15¢) headed east on 5 de Mayo, in front of Cine Tropical.

WHERE TO SLEEP **Bungalows María Cristina.** The best thing about these homey bungalows is their location: directly on the beach, and across the street from the tranquil lagoon and its towering palm trees. The wooden rocking chairs and hammocks on the small central porch invite you to enjoy the cool breeze and the sound of the rushing surf. The roomy bungalows fit up to five people, and have stocked kitchens. Rates are $10 for one person, $13.50 for two, and $40 for the whole bungalow. *Playa Pie de la Cuesta 607, tel. 74/60–02–62. 3 bungalows, all with bath. Luggage storage.*

Villa Nirvana. The Nirvana villas surround a small, shaded plaza and are right on the ocean. The airy rooms are simply furnished and clean, with fans, terraces, and no bugs. Although only one room has a kitchen, you can keep some perishables in the owner's fridge. Singles cost $16, doubles $25. *Playa Pie de la Cuesta 302, tel. 74/60–16–31. 7 rooms, all with bath. Laundry (free), luggage storage. Wheelchair access.*

➤ **CAMPING** • Pitching tents on the beach is not safe—your stuff will get stolen, and women should be cautious around the beach and the laguna. The **Acapulco Trailer Park** (Playa Pie de la Cuesta, tel. 74/60–00–10) charges $5 for one or two people. Bring your own tent, and they'll provide water, bathrooms, showers, and security.

FOOD **El Zanate.** During low season at this small storefront restaurant, the standard fare is the $1.50 comida corrida, which includes rice, beans, salad, tortillas, and your choice of anything from fish to steak to *chiles rellenos* (stuffed chiles). In the high season, referred to by owner Berta as "the time of the gringos," they have a wide selection of fresh fish and "whatever else the gringos want." For a big group, they will even prepare a feast, such as roasted pig. *Playa Pie de la Cuesta, tel. 74/60–17–09. Open daily 6 AM–11 PM. Wheelchair access.*

CENTRAL CITIES   10

By Viviana Mahieux and Lynette Ubois with Lourdes Haro

Many travelers pass through the region south of Mexico City on their way to somewhere else, but it is a destination in its own right for anyone interested in Mesoamerican or Spanish-American history, colonial architecture, or even volcano climbing. The early inhabitants of this region came from a number of distinct civilizations and left behind evidence of their greatness, such as the pyramids of Xochicalco, the murals of Cacaxtla, and the Great Pyramid of Cholula. This region was also important in postsettlement history, and many of the events that took place here formed the foundations of present-day Mexico: Cuautla (in Morelos state) was the site of one of the most dramatic battles in the War of Independence, and Emiliano Zapata issued his 1910 call for land reform in Ayala. In 1862 Puebla withstood a decisive battle in the war against French invaders led by Napoleon III, a battle commemorated annually by the city's residents on May 5 (Cinco de Mayo). The War of Independence and the Revolution of 1910 are memorialized throughout the area, and a visitor to this region will encounter constant reminders of this turbulent past in its imposing stone fortress, bullet-ridden palace, and in ubiquitous street names such as 5 de Mayo, Plan de Ayala, and Héroes de Independencia.

But what attracts people to the central cities is more than an uncontrollable urge to find out how Mexican city planners came up with such unoriginal road titles. Each city has so much variety that you're bound to find something that suits your style. The student atmosphere in both colonial Cuernavaca and historical Puebla make them favorites among travelers who want to brush up on their Spanish verb tenses. If you'd rather soak up a different brand of student life, go for the less international (but more activist) atmosphere of Chilpancingo, the capital of the state of Guerrero. Once you've learned the language, practice it with the jewelry vendors of Taxco—a breezy city with a Mediterranean feel and Mexico's silver artisan capital. If you simply need a break from the arduous task of being a tourist, the relaxed pace in Tlaxcala attracts urban Mexicans and international travelers to its sepia-colored hills.

Cuernavaca

Watched over by the great volcano Popocatépetl, the city of Cuernavaca spreads down onto the rich agricultural plateau of Morelos. Despite growing problems with poverty and pollution, Morelos's prosperous state capital attracts a steady stream of visitors, who regularly pour into the city's restaurants, bars, and hotels. Travelers come from all over the world to study in the city's language schools, visit historical sites, or simply hang out in large plazas amidst flowering trees and fountains. Mexicans also enjoy vacations here, and many wealthy *chilagos* (residents of Mexico City) buy second homes in Cuernavaca.

Central Cities

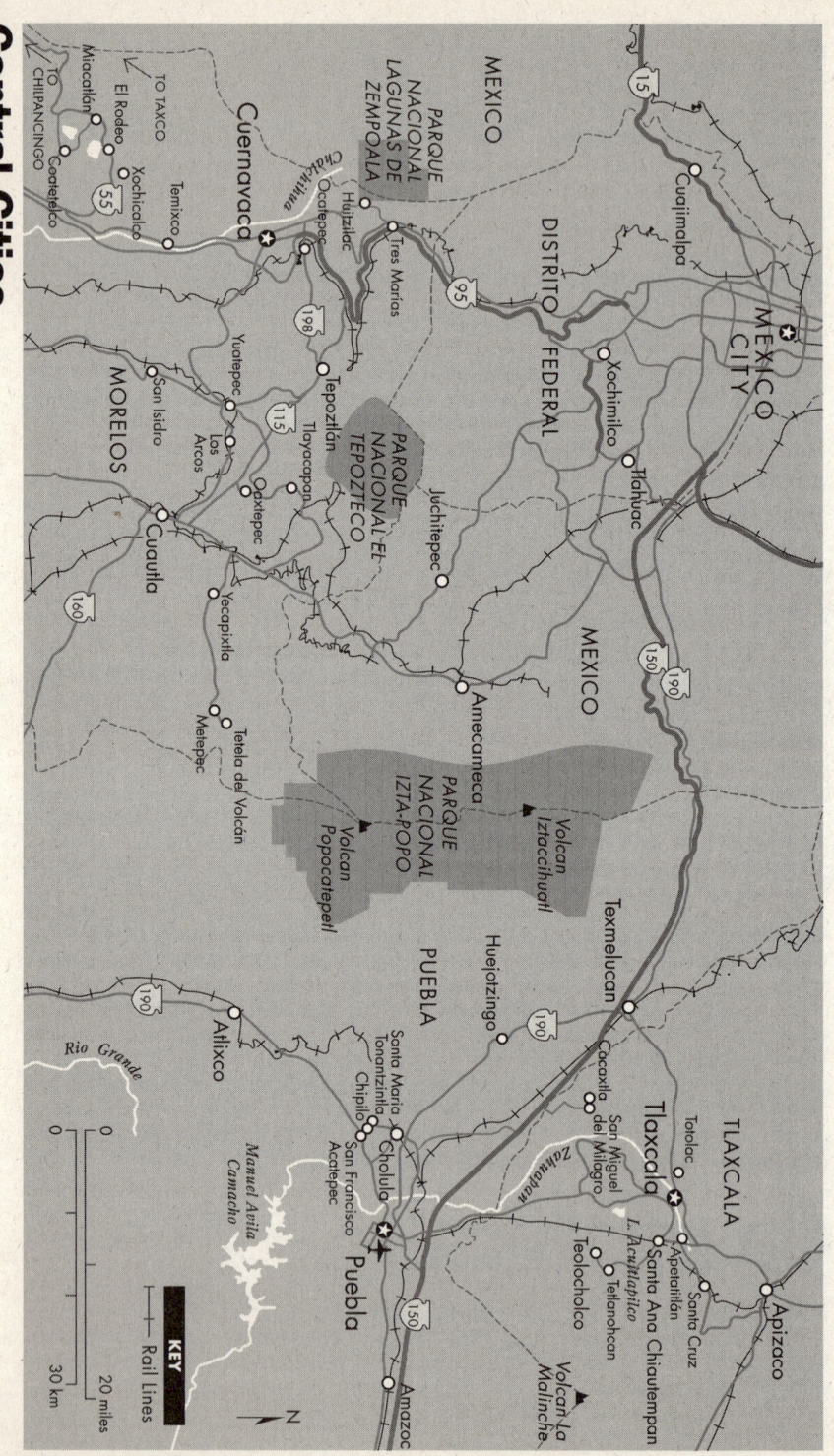

Vacationers are only the most recent invaders of Cuernavaca. At the ancient ruins of nearby Xochicalo, bas-relief sculptures suggest that this once-powerful religious center was influenced or even controlled by the Maya. In the 1300s, the indigenous Tlahuica Indians fell under Aztec domination, and the Aztecs demonstrated their supremacy by building new structures around existing Tlahuican pyramids. Pyramid ruins can still be found in Cuernavaca and neighboring Tepoztlán, despite Cortés's brutal devastation of most native structures a century later. Cortés ordered that the central Cuernavacan pyramid be destroyed, and an enormous cathedral and intimidating fortress be built from the remains.

The original name for Cuernavaca was Cuauhnáhuac, Nahuatl for "place near the woods," but after the Spaniards burned the city to the ground in the 1520s, the name was changed to a word they could pronounce more easily—"Cuernavaca."

Despite this history of foreign domination, *Cuernavaquenses* (Cuernavacan citizens) aren't easily pushed around. The state of Morelos, where revolutionary leader Emiliano Zapata and his movement for agrarian reform were born, led the southern front of the Mexican Revolution in the early 1900s. Today, however, the plaza overflows with street vendors hawking everything from beaded necklaces to Disney balloons, and the flowering bougainvillea and twilight chorus of birds may reveal how Cuernavaca earned its nickname "City of Eternal Spring."

BASICS

AMERICAN EXPRESS The AmEx office is in the **Marin** travel agency, in the Las Plazas shopping center, across Guerrero from the zócalo. They sell and exchange traveler's checks, and cardholders can cash personal checks or have their mail held for them here. *Edificio Las Plazas, Local 13, Cuernavaca, Morelos, CP 62000, México, tel. 73/14–22–66. AmEx services available weekdays 9–2 and 4–6, Sat. 10–1.*

CASAS DE CAMBIO Several casas de cambio cluster along Dwight Morrow, near the budget lodging area. The most reputable is **Gesta** (Dwight Morrow 9, tel. 73/14–01–95), which is open weekdays 9–5, Saturday 9–2. If you need money later than this, **Master Dollar** (Dwight Morrow 8-B, tel. 73/12–93–71) is open weekdays until 6, and Saturdays 9–2. **Banamex** (Arteaga, at Matamoros, tel. 73/14–04–03) has ATMs, and will change money weekdays 9–5.

EMERGENCIES Dial 06 for police, fire, or ambulance service.

LAUNDRY Only two blocks from the budget hotel area, **Tintorería Morelos** charges $3 to clean 3½ kilos of laundry and will return it the same day if you drop it off before 10 AM. Bring your questions about Cuernavaca with your dirty clothes—the staff is friendly and helpful. *Matamoros 406, tel. 73/10–05–18. Open Mon.–Sat. 9–8.*

MAIL The **post office** will hold your mail at the following address for up to 10 days: Lista de Correos, Administración 1, Cuernavaca, Morelos, CP 62001, México. Faxes, telexes, and telegrams can be sent and received at the **telecommunications office** (tel. 73/18–58–62), in the same building. *SW cnr of Plaza de Armas, tel. 73/12–43–79. Open weekdays 8–7, Sat. 9–1.*

PHONES Cuernavaca's zócalo is graced with several Ladatel phones. Cash calls can be made from **Caseta Morelos,** which charges about $2 per minute to the States. Collect calls are allowed everyday 2–3 PM. *Pasaje Galeana 4, tel. 73/18–30–31. In a minimall across from Plaza de Armas. Open daily 8 AM–9 PM.*

SCHOOLS **Cuauhnáhuac Escuela Cuernavaca** is recommended by students, and travelers are welcome to stop by and check it out. There are no more than four students to a class, and the campus has a swimming pool and volleyball court. The registration fee is $70, and classes cost $180 for a week-long course, $600 for a month. *Morelos Sur 1414, Col. Chipitlán, tel. 73/12–36–73 or 73/18–92–75. Mailing address: Aptdo. Postal 5-26, Cuernavaca, Morelos, CP 62051, México. U.S. contact: Marcia Snell, tel. 800/245–9335.*

VISITOR INFORMATION Although friendly and eager to help, the staff at the **state tourist office** is coping with severe budget cuts. Spanish information on language schools and various sights will be photocopied for you, but the free map is less than useful—significant streets are

Cuernavaca

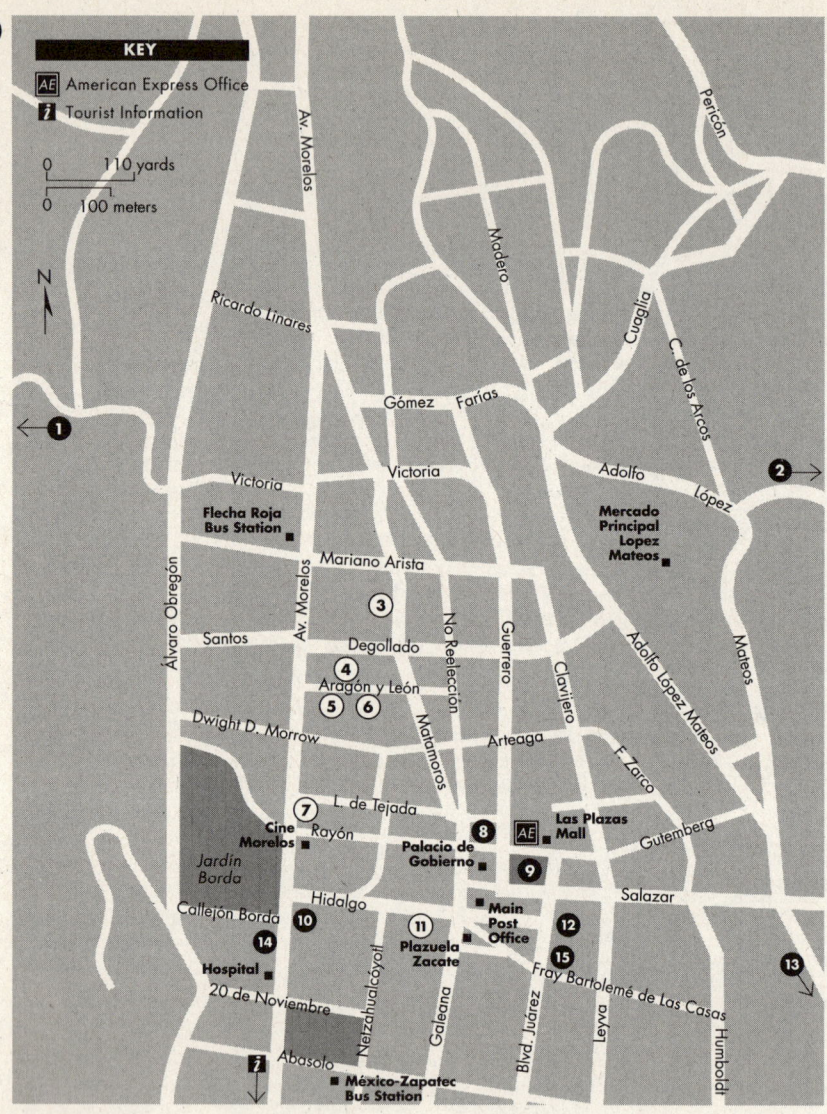

Sights ●
Ayuntamiento de Cuernavaca, **14**
Casa del Olvido, **13**
Catedral de la Asunción, **10**
Jardín de Arte Luis Betanzos, **15**
Jardín Juárez, **8**
Palacio de Cortés, **12**
Pirámide de Teopanzolco, **2**
Plaza de Armas, **9**
San Antón Falls, **1**

Lodging ○
Casa de Huéspedes la China Poblana, **6**
Hotel América, **4**
Hotel Colonial, **5**
Hotel España, **7**
Hotel Las Hortensias, **11**
Hotel Roma, **3**

covered by advertising logos. Better maps can be found in most *papelerías* (stationery stores) for $5. For tourist information in English, your best bet is to chat with Joel at Tintorería Morelos (*see* Laundry, *above*). Although he isn't always around, Joel is an authority on local day trips and nightspots. Morelos Sur 802, tel. 73/14-39-20. Take RUTA 4 combi down Galeana to Himno Nacional, then walk 1 block west. Open weekdays 9-3 and 5-8.

COMING AND GOING

BY BUS Those traveling by bus will find themselves at one of Cuernavaca's four bus stations. The largest is **Flecha Roja** (Morelos 503, at Arista, tel. 73/12-57-97), two blocks from the budget lodging area. The **Estrella Blanca** line (tel. 73/12-81-90) sends buses to Mexico City (1 hr, $5) every 15 minutes. First-class *directo* (direct) buses to Acapulco (3½ hrs, $17) leave every two hours; air-conditioning and a TV bump the price up to $21 or $23. Hourly *ordinario* (indirect) buses to Acapulco (5 hrs, $16.50) stop in Chilpancingo (3 hrs, $10). Buses to Taxco (2½ hrs, $3.50) depart every 30 minutes until 10 PM. One bus leaves at 4:15 PM for Nuevo Laredo (20 hrs, $57). You can stash your luggage at the luggage check (75¢ for 5 hrs, 20¢ each hr after that) or in lockers ($1.25-$2.50). The station is clean and well lit, but the plastic benches are uncomfortable, and the place gets a little too empty at night.

The **Estrella Roja** station (Galeana 401, at Cuauhtemoczin, tel. 73/18-59-34) has buses to Cuautla (1 hr, $2) every 30 minutes 6:15 AM-10:15 PM; transfer in Cuautla for Oaxaca. Buses to Puebla (3½ hrs, $7) leave every hour 5 AM-7 PM. The budget hotels are 7 blocks from the station—any CENTRO combi on Morelos to Aragón y Léon will take you there.

The remaining two bus stations are less significant. **México-Zacatepec Autos Pullman de Morelos** (Abasolo 106, at Netzahualcoyotl, tel. 73/14-36-50) is a few blocks from the zócalo and serves Mexico City, Zacatepec, Xoxocotla, Jojutla, and a few other towns near Puebla. Probably the only reason you'd use this station would be to get to Xochicalco (*see* Near Cuernavaca, *below*); buses to Coatlán or Miocatlán will drop you off at the Xochicalco crossroads. **Estrella de Oro** (Morelos Sur 900, tel. 73/12-30-55) is a *de paso* station, which means buses only stop here en route to somewhere else. As a result, departure times are sketchy. To reach the center of town from here, take any CENTRO combi up Morelos.

BY PLANE Cuernevaca doesn't have it's own airport, but Mexico City's International Airport is only an hour's drive away. **Aeorotransporte Terrestre** (tel. 73/22-04-45) van service makes the trip eight times a day (1 hr, $13). If you're arriving in Mexico City, look for the ticket kiosk in the main concourse, beneath the giant "A."

GETTING AROUND

Exploring Cuernavaca is not difficult; the budget hotel zone, major sights, and most of the bus stations are within walking distance of each other. The zócalo, at the center of town, is actually made up of two plazas: the Jardín Juárez and the Plaza de Armas. The main streets in Cuernavaca are Morelos, with northbound traffic, and Obregón and Matamoros/Galeana, on either side of Morelos, both of which allow only southbound traffic.

BY BUS Colectivos, also called *rutas* or *combis,* are the major means of daytime travel within Cuernavaca. Drivers of these white, squared-off minibuses cram in as many passengers as possible, but the 25¢ fare will get you almost anywhere. The name of the final destination is scrawled in whitewash on the front window of the combi, but routes vary, so double-check before boarding. Colectivos run from 6 AM to about 9 PM.

BY TAXI You'll have to travel by taxi if you plan to sample Cuernavaca's nightlife, as combis stop running after 9 PM. White Datsuns, VWs, and other small cars can usually be hailed on busy streets, major crossroads, and near tourist attractions. Taxis don't have meters, so fares should be negotiated *before* you get in. Generally the fare within the *centro* (downtown)

When you hear the piercing strains of "Für Elise" or "La Cucaracha," jump out of the way—a taxi or truck is honking its horn at you.

is $1.25, and about $1 more for outlying neighborhoods. Fares can shoot up to $5 late at night. A reliable cab service is **Radiotaxi Ejecutivo** (tel. 73/15-47-84 or 73/22-12-00).

WHERE TO SLEEP

Cuernavaca is popular on Fridays and weekends, so be sure to make a reservation. You may want to shop around during the high season (June–Aug. and Dec.–Feb.), when prices at some of the larger hotels rise above the ones listed here. The budget lodging area lies along and around Aragón y León, a few blocks south of the Flecha Roja bus station and north of the zócalo. If the places below are booked, try **Hotel Las Hortensias** (Hidalgo 22, tel. 73/18-52-65), which has a pleasant courtyard and lumpy beds. A single here is $13 and a double is $14-$16. If you're planning an extended stay, many of the city's language schools (see Schools, above) give students the option of living with a family, and you may be able to set up a similar arrangement.

➤ **UNDER $10** • **Casa de Huéspedes la China Poblana.** Hidden behind the restaurant of the same name, this hotel is clean, spacious, and a bargain at $5 for a single, $8 for a double, both with private bath. The architecture is unspectacular, but that's not what you're here for. There are only nine rooms, so reservations are essential. *Aragón y León 110, btw Morelos and Matamoros, tel. 73/12-37-12. 3 blocks north of zócalo and 3 blocks south of Flecha Roja station. Luggage storage.*

Hotel América. This hotel wins no awards for the small, dark, musty rooms, but the communal bathrooms aren't too bad. The big draw is the price: Singles cost $5, doubles are $6.75. The clientele consists mostly of young men. *Aragón y León 111, tel. 73/18-61-27. About 3 blocks north of zócalo. 40 rooms, none with bath. Luggage storage.*

Hotel Roma. The sunny courtyard with palm trees is more inviting than the clean and basic rooms, which have tiny bathrooms. Singles and doubles cost $8-$9, and quads are only $11.50. *Matamoros 405, tel. 73/18-87-78. 1 block east of Flecha Roja station and 4 blocks north of zócalo. 40 rooms, all with bath.*

➤ **UNDER $20** • **Hotel Colonial.** Smack in the middle of the budget lodging area, this hotel is a step above the competition. The large, clean rooms have high ceilings, and some boast wrought-iron terraces. Others don't even have windows, so ask to see a few before paying. This hotel is popular with Mexican and foreign travelers alike; the young female staff is friendly and helpful, and there is a rule of silence after 10 PM. Singles cost $10-$11.50, depending on the size of the room. Doubles go for $14-$16, and triples are $17.50. *Aragón y León 104, tel. 73/18-64-14. 3 blocks south of Flecha Roja station and 3 blocks north of zócalo. 14 rooms, all with bath. Luggage storage. Wheelchair access.*

➤ **UNDER $25** • **Hotel España.** This hotel lives up to its name, with Spanish arches, patterned tiles, and palm trees. On the first floor are a Spanish restaurant, the reception area, and a small lounge; second- and third-floor rooms cluster around a courtyard with potted flowers. The rooms are clean, but the furniture is worn and the noise level can be bothersome in the rooms facing the street. Singles cost about $16, doubles $22.50. The guests here are mostly Mexican businesspeople. *Morelos 200, at Rayón, tel. 73/18-67-44. 3 blocks west of zócalo and 5 blocks south of Flecha Roja station. 24 rooms, all with bath. Reservations advised.*

FOOD

Small, cheap restaurants abound in the budget lodging area and on the streets surrounding the zócalo. Most serve a mix of *antojitos* (appetizers) and tourist grub such as burgers and fries. Try the clean and cheap **Pollo y Más** (Galeana 4, tel. 73/12-18-15), on the west side of the zócalo, for enchiladas, tacos, or roasted chicken—each comes with beans and rice, and costs $1.20 a plate. A popular patio restaurant with a sparkling fountain and shady plants, **Los Arcos** (Jardin de los Heroés 4, tel. 73/12-44-86) serves a generous *comida corrida* (fixed-price lunch special) for $2.75. **La Universal** (Guerrero 1, tel. 73/18-67-32) serves stingier portions to a crowd of gringos, but the $2 daiquiris may prompt you to forget its faults. Early risers can breakfast at **Cuernavaca Jardin** (Matamoros 100, tel. 73/18–68–19), which starts serving at 7:30, before most other places open. The **Mercado Principal** (central market) is filled with cheap eats, but this one has a reputation for being particularly unhygienic.

➢ **UNDER $5** • **Naturiza.** Health-conscious locals of all ages—grandmothers, working men, and young teenagers—gather here to fill up on generous portions of creative vegetarian cooking or to buy vitamins from the small counter in the back. The menu changes daily, but look for such delights as creamed carrot soup and cauliflower dumplings. The fixed-price breakfast is $1.80, and lunch is $2.50. *Alvaro Obregón 327-1, btw Victoria and Ricardo Linares, tel. 73/12–46–26. Open Mon.–Sat. 8:30–6:30. Food available 8:30– 11:30 and 1–4:30.*

Restaurante Las Casuelas. This vegetarian-friendly restaurant specializes in delicious antojitos. Try the fabulous chiles rellenos and *jugo de guayaba* (guava juice), or order the $2 *menú del día* (daily special). *Galeana, at Abasolo, tel. 73/14–17–79. Open Tues.–Sun. 10–7.*

La Tarterie. This restaurant serves a $2 comida corrida, espresso, and a large variety of desserts under outdoor umbrellas. A breakfast of fried eggs or not-too-tender steak with beans, tortillas, fresh-squeezed orange juice, and coffee is $3.50. Vegetarians can enjoy the $2 soups and salads. *Fray Bartolomé de las Casas 103, tel. 73/12–41–52. In Plazuela Zacate (a.k.a. Plaza 2 de Mayo de 1812). Open daily 9–8.*

➢ **UNDER $10** • **Restaurant El Salto.** In the village of San Antón near the waterfall for which it's named, this off-the-beaten-track restaurant is filled with *cuernavaquenses* (residents of Cuernavaca) noisily eating and drinking. The menu includes a selection of fish, chicken, and game dishes, served in pottery made in the village. The most expensive dish is pigeon for two ($8); recommended are garlic soup ($3), the cactus tamale ($2), and the bowl-sized rum-and-tequila "Convento," which will set you back $4 and most of your faculties. *Bajada del Salto 31, San Antón, tel. 73/18–12–19. Take* RUTA *4 combi from anywhere on Morelos to El Salto de San Antón. Open daily 10–8.*

➢ **UNDER $15** • **Los Pasteles de Vienes.** Continental cuisine and European-style pastries are served here, while lace curtains and jazz music float on the breeze. The restaurant is a meeting place for couples and students, and its location—around the corner from the Teatro Ocampo—makes it a great spot to grab a cappuccino after the show. Recommended dishes include the veal cutlet in wine and mushroom sauce ($8), asparagus stuffed with ham in béarnaise sauce ($5), and spinach crêpes ($4). *Lerdo de Tejada 302, at I. Comonfort, tel. 73/12– 41–52. Open daily 8 AM–10 PM.*

WORTH SEEING

The zócalo is the heart of Cuernavaca; it's made up of the **Plaza de Armas,** where you can unwind beside the fountain, and the more lively **Jardín Juárez,** the oldest park in the city. The zócalo is also near a number of attractions that are easily visited in a day. Other sites, particularly the Casa del Olvido, San Antón Falls, and the Pirámide de Teopanzolco, are in outlying *colonias* (neighborhoods), so plan on taking some combis. Keep in mind that many museums and historical sites are closed on Monday.

The scrolled ironwork on the bandstand in the center of Jardín Juárez may look strangely familiar—it was designed by Gustave Eiffel, of Eiffel Tower fame.

AYUNTAMIENTO DE CUERNAVACA Also known as the Palacio Municipal, the Ayuntamiento displays murals by Salvador Tarazona that depict Cuernavaca's history and scenes of the Tlahuica civilization. *Morelos 199, at Callejón Borda. Admission free. Open weekdays 8–8.*

BALNEARIO TEMIXCO This aquatic park has 15 swimming pools, ten wading pools, water slides, sports fields, gardens, a full bar, and a history. Originally a 16th-century sugar plantation, it was used as a fort in the Mexican Revolution and as a prisoner-of-war camp during World War II. Ruins of a rice mill, chapel, and storage bins are still recognizable, and now a live orchestra plays dance music on weekends. The 8 kilometer bus trip from downtown (60¢)

takes half an hour. Ask the driver to let you off at the gate. *Emiliano Zapata 11, Col. Temixco, tel. 73/25–03–55. Take* TEMIXCO *combi from Galeana. Admission: $4.50. Open daily 9–6.*

CASA DEL OLVIDO This adobe house (also called Casa Maximiliano) was built for Emperor Maximilian, and is known as the "House of Forgetfulness." One reason given for this name is that Maximilian came here to escape political and domestic troubles. Another is that he "forgot" to build a room for his wife Carlota—but made sure to include a small house in the garden for his lover, La India Bonita. Today the casa houses the **Museo de Medicina Tradicional,** which features exhibits about the medicinal and religious uses of Mexican plants and herbs since pre-Columbian times. Many of the plants described in the museum can be found in the adjoining botanical garden. *Matamoros 200, Col. Acapantzinga, tel. 73/12–59–55. Take* RUTA *6 combi from Degollado and No Reelección. Admission free. Open Tues.–Sun. 9–5.*

CATEDRAL DE LA ASUNCION In use between the early 16th and late 19th centuries, the cathedral encloses a convent and three *capillas* (chapels) within its high walls. The oldest structure in the complex, the **Capilla Abierta de San José,** was built by Hernán Cortés in 1523. Its design, which leaves the priest covered by a roof and the faithful exposed to the open air, is said to have been chosen so the indigenous people, used to worshipping outside, would feel more at home. The **Templo de la Asunción Gloriosa de la Virgen María,** the largest structure, was completed in 1552. Newly uncovered remnants of early 17th-century frescoes, supposedly painted here by a Japanese immigrant, depict the crucifixion of Christian missionaries in Japan. The **Templo de la Tercera Orden de San Francisco** took 13 years to build, due to the elaborate ornamentation of its carved surfaces. The newest structure is the **Capilla de Carmen,** which dates from the late 19th century. Look for the *retablos* (altarpieces) on the walls. Sundays at 11 AM and 8 PM, you can see a "mariachi mass" (*see box* Liberation Theology, *below*). *Hidalgo, at Morelos. 3 blocks west of zócalo. Admission free. Open daily 7–2 and 4–8.*

JARDIN BORDA The mansion, landscaped grounds, and botanical gardens here were first built by Taxco silver millionaire Manuel de la Borda as a retreat for his father. In 1865 it became a symbol of imperial Mexico when the estate was turned into a summer retreat for Emperor Maximilian and his wife, Carlota. The original fruit trees and ornamental plants still flourish in 100 varieties, and the refurbished front rooms of the mansion now house the **Centro de Arte Jardín Borda,** where you can view the work of local artists. *Morelos 103, at Hidalgo, tel. 73/12–92–37. Admission: $1. Open Tues.–Sun. 10–5:30.*

MERCADO PRINCIPAL LOPEZ MATEOS The dirty, crowded, and noisy maze of bartering and haggling that is Cuernavaca's central market offers a glimpse of local life. Mounds of chiles tower over women selling *huitlacoche* (a corn-fungus delicacy), and eloquent *herbolarios* (herb vendors) will guarantee a cure for whatever ails you. *López Mateos. From zócalo, head north 4 blocks on Guerrero, right into the covered mall of vendors just before Degollado, and across pedestrian bridge to market below. Open daily about 6–4:30.*

PALACIO DE CORTES Built by the conquered Tlahuica people, this imposing building has been a potent symbol of power throughout Cuernavaca's history. When construction began in 1522, it followed a simple plan, but as Cortés gained wealth, influence, titles—and a wife—the palace grew. It later passed into the hands of the crown and, during the war for independence, was used as a prison for revolutionaries José María Morelos, Ignacio López Rayón, and Nicolás Bravo. During the Revolution of 1910, the palace was abandoned and became the office of the municipal government.

Today the palace houses a **Diego Rivera mural** and the **Museo Cuauhnáhuac,** which traces the history of Morelos from the time of the first pre-Hispanic settlers to today.

To the right of the palace is the **Jardín de Arte Luis Betanzos,** where indigenous artists sell anything from brightly painted wooden toys to beautiful silver work fairly cheaply. *Juárez, at Hidalgo, across from SE cnr of zócalo. Admission: $2; free Sun. Open Tues.–Sun. 10–5.*

PIRAMIDE DE TEOPANZOLCO This small, Tlahuican ceremonial center predates the Aztec presence in Cuernavaca, as its name suggests (Teopan = temple; zol = old; co = place: Place of the Old Temple). When the Aztecs conquered the Tlahuica, they began building a new temple around the old one to prove their domination, but were interrupted by the Spanish conquest. The unfinished remains were rediscovered in 1910, and today you can scramble up the stairs of the 30-foot central pyramid. It's a 15-minute ride out here, so you'll probably have the place to yourself. *From the east side of Mercado Principal take* RUTA *19 combis, which leave every 10–15 min. Admission: $1.50. Open daily 10–4:30.*

SAN ANTON FALLS Although this 40-meter waterfall cascades into a brown pool, it's still beautiful. The waterfall is located in the barrio of San Antón, which is also noted for a tradition of Virgin Mary figurines and terra-cotta pots. While you're here, stop for a meal at Restaurant El Salto (*see* Food, *above*), a half block away from the waterfall. *Bajada del Salto, Barrio de San Antón. Take* RUTA *4 combi (15 min) from anywhere on Morelos. Combis run every 20 minutes. Admission: $1; free Sun. and holidays. Open daily 8–6.*

FESTIVALS

The two-week **Feria de la Primavera,** which begins around the second week of April, is traditionally the biggest party in Cuernavaca. Horticulturists established this annual festival in

Liberation Theology

Liberation theology is an interpretation of the gospels emphasizing Christ's involvement in social justice; since the early 1960s it has been the point of intersection between religion and Latin American politics. Cuernavaca's bishop, Sergio Mendez Arceo, acted as the cornerstone of this movement, and played a prominent role in the Second Vatican Council (1962–65), which made a historic revision of Catholic doctrine. Arceo had a growing following among Latin America's Catholic leadership, and Cuernavaca became an international center for the reform-minded during the '60s and '70s. Ideas that Arceo had implemented nearly a decade earlier were adopted by the church, including administering mass in the vernacular (Spanish instead of Latin), and moving the figure of Jesus Christ so the priest no longer had to turn his back to the congregation to face it when leading prayer. Arceo also began using the music of the people to accompany religious services, and the "Mariachi Mass" is still held every Sunday in the cathedral.

Members of the church still uphold the ideals of liberation theology and continue to play a role in Latin American politics. Recently, Bishop Samuel Ruiz of Chiapas came into political prominence with his public support of indigenous people's demands for land and democracy in Chiapas. He has also worked as a facilitator in the negotiations between the Zapatista rebels and the Mexican government. Ray Plankey, a Catholic lay minister who had worked with Arceo, founded the Cuernavaca Center for International Dialogue on Development—a non-profit educational organization. The CCIDD runs programs that give groups of North Americans an opportunity to experience first-hand the harsh economic reality of many Mexicans, and to challenge their religious and social visions. For more information, write to CCIDD at 9297 Siempre Viva Rd., Suite MX, 921-063, San Diego, CA 92173. You may also call (73/12–65–64) or fax (73/12–93–92) the center directly.

1865 to promote the local flower industry, but due to recent economic hardship, music and dance concerts have been curtailed, and even the number of flower displays have diminished. In the nearby town of Acapancingo, the **Fiesta of San Isidro Labrador** is celebrated every May 15 to bring rain. Oxen wreathed in flowers are paraded through the streets, and lots of dancing, drinking, and eating follows. In Ocotepec, also near Cuernavaca, **Semana Santa** (Holy Week—the week preceding Easter Sunday) is celebrated with traditional dances, passion plays, and the presentation of altars to the dead.

SHOPPING

Cuernavaca is popular with tourists, and prices are jacked up accordingly. Still, the area is known for the quality of its *huaraches* (woven leather sandals), and you'll find good deals on custom-made pairs in the Mercado Principal. Several sandal stores crowd the corner of Hildalgo at Morelos; **Sandalias "Ayelet"** (Hidalgo 26, tel. 73/14–28–38) offers high-quality huaraches at correspondingly high prices. Ceramic chinelo masks make an unusual souvenir, but they're hard to find; try looking in the artisan's market next to Palacio de Cortes or in the zócalo. If the masks prove too elusive, the colorful $10 marionettes are hard to miss.

AFTER DARK

Cuernavaca is sedate during the week, but the scene livens up on weekends. Visitors ooze into the clubs, and almost every night is "Ladies Night," when women pay half the costly admission. Travelers interested in cultural events should check the bulletin board of the **University Cultural Center** (Morelos Sur 136), as well as the booth on the corner of Morelos and Rayón.

BARS The cafés on the zócalo are the most pleasant places to drink beer. **Harry's Bar** (Gutenberg 3, tel. 73/14–19–13), where yuppie chilangos and Cuernavaquenses hang out, is the first place any young resident will send you. Be advised that it's a meat market on weekends. Another trendy hangout, complete with blaring music, continuous videos, and obnoxious "Americana" decor, is the chain restaurant **Freeday** (Plan de Ayala Sur, tel. 73/15–67–62), where you can hear your favorite R.E.M. songs remixed beyond all recognition, and see drunken revelers dance on the tables in happy oblivion.

CINEMAS/THEATERS **Teatro Ocampo** (Galeana, across from Jardín Juárez, no phone) is the home of Cuernavaca's repertory company. Tickets for live performances are $1.50 (75¢ students). **Cine Morelos** (Morelos, at Rayón, tel. 73/18–84–18) screens a variety of international films (with Spanish subtitles) and regularly hosts national and international music and dance performances. **Cinematográfica Las Plazas** (Gutenberg 101, tel. 73/14–07–93), in the Las Plazas shopping center across from the north side of the Plaza de Armas, shows mostly Hollywood films with Spanish subtitles.

DANCING Cuernavaca has a number of flashy clubs with high cover charges. North of the centro, **Barba-Zul** (Prado 10, Col. San Jeronimo, tel. 73/13–19–76) charges a $10 cover, but women are admitted free on Wednesdays. From Morelos, you can take a RUTA 3 bus here; cabbing it home will cost about $2.50. There's no cover at **Kaova** (Morelos Sur 302, tel. 73/15–43–88), a private club frequented by *juniors* (sons and daughters of the wealthy elite). Thursday nights feature an open bar. It's also the closest popular disco to the zócalo and the budget hotel zone. **Zumbale** (Bajada de Chapultepec, tel. 73/22–53–43) plays live tropical music all night, and RUTA 17 and RUTA 20 buses from Degollado pass right by it. There's also a huge gay disco called **Shadé** (López Mateos, east side of Mercado Principal). The bus ride here is long and meandering, so catch a $1 cab from the zócalo.

LIVE MUSIC Live music plays on Sundays and Thursdays in the Jardín Juárez, and just about every weekend at the Jardin Borda (*see* Worth Seeing, *above*). For your own private concert, hire one of the mariachi bands that hang out on the northeast corner of the **Plaza de Armas**. The Catedral de la Asunción occasionally sponsors choral performances, but if you'd prefer a club atmosphere, **Flamingo's Teatro Bar** (Herradura de Plata 102, tel. 73/17–15–54) has jazz on weekends.

Near Cuernavaca

TEPOZTLAN

Barren, rocky hills tower over this small valley town, which boasts a mythology as dramatic as its landscape. The nearby village of Amatlán is the legendary birthplace of the feathered serpent god Quetzalcoatl—a place of supernatural powers and both positive and negative energy. The good vibes emanate from the site of the **Tlahuica ruins,** high above the town, while in the caves of the **Cerro del Tepozteco,** *brujos* (witches) supposedly perform their rituals. Unfortunately, entrance to the caves is restricted.

Perhaps because of the site's reputation, Spaniards in the 16th century ordered the construction of the grim Dominican **Convento de la Natividad.** Its imposing weathered walls are more than 2 meters thick—all the better to defy any natural or supernatural storms. Situated next to the **Iglesia de la Asunción,** the convent is known for its syncretic *tequitqui* style, in which Christian and indigenous symbols mingle in faded frescoes. Notice the subtle image of Quetzalcoatl painted into the intricate black and white border design running high along the antechamber walls. In the cloister is the **Museo Arqueológico Colección Carlos Pellicer,** which exhibits pre-Hispanic artifacts and photos of the archaeological sites where these relics were recovered. *Museum admission: $1. Open Tues.–Sun. 9–5.*

The path leading to the Tlahuica ruins begins at the end of Avenida Tepozteco, a 15-minute walk past the plaza. Look for the formation said to look like a flying saucer amongst the scarred cliffs of the looming *cerro* (hill) as you make the rocky, 45-minute climb. At the top is the **Pirámide Tepozteco,** dedicated to Tepoztécatl, the Tlahuica god of *pulque* (an alcoholic drink made from maguey). Carved images of figures relating to the sky and heavens lead many to believe the pyramid was an observatory. Although the structure itself isn't too spectacular, the view of the valley below is amazing. A small stand at the top sells water and soft drinks for about 75¢ each. *Admission: $1.50; free Sun. Open daily 10–4:30.*

On September 8th and 9th, a festival dedicated to Tepoztécatl, the god of pulque, features a procession to the Tepoztlán pyramid. In a time-honored attempt to erase "pagan" practices, the convent holds its own festival at the same time.

COMING AND GOING Buses (1 hr, 75¢) leave every half hour until 6 PM from the Mercado Principal in Cuernavaca. On the way back to Cuernavaca consider stopping in the town of **Ocotepec,** known for the beauty of its cemetery and its troubador traditions.

WHERE TO SLEEP This town doesn't really cater to itinerant students; **Hotel Tepoztlán** (Calle de las Industrias 6, tel. 739/5–05–03) and **Posada del Tepozteco** (Paraíso 3, tel.

Café la Arábica

Follow the smell of freshly ground coffee to the cooperative Café la Arábica and adjoining natural food store, Proyecto Milenio. The Proyecto offers several services to travelers and Tepoztecos alike, and the café is the place to relax after exploring your options. A sunny room off the café houses a varied collection of books in English, Spanish, and French, and a bulletin board lists tons of local events and activities, including yoga classes, courses in nutrition, and meditation practice. In back, a small garden adjoins a quiet room set aside for massage. In addition, you can use the Proyecto's long-distance telephone and fax services, and soon (they hope), their internet link. Avenida del Tepozteco 19, tel. 739/5–17–15, fax 739/5–00–46. Open daily 8 AM–9 PM.

739/5-00-10) are both pricey, with double rooms going for about $50. If you must stay here, a cheaper option is **Las Cabañas** (Cinco de Mayo 54), a tiny hostel on the edge of town. You can camp at the YMCA-run **Campamento Camohmila** (Ruta 115, on the Carretera Autopista a Oaxtepec, tel. 739/5-01-10). They prefer that you make advance arrangements through their Mexico City office (tel. 2/03-24-68), but unannounced arrivals may be able to talk their way into a campsite. Take a SANTIAGO combi from the zócalo in front of Farmacia Villamar, and ask the driver to let you off at the campground. You can also try **Campamento Meztitla** (Rte. 2, tel. 739/5-00-68) on the Tepoztlán-Yautepec highway, but it takes a taxi to get here. The local Boy Scouts office here offers tips on hiking, backpacking, and rappelling in the **Parque Nacional El Tepozteco,** nearby. You can't camp at the ruins anymore—the uncompromising entrance gate is locked by guards every night. But you're free to scour surrounding hillsides for a comfy spot—they're rumored to be safe, although crowded with school kids during holidays.

FOOD There are several good restaurants along Avenida de Tepozteco. You might try **Tlacualoyan** (Tepozteco 9), which has a delicious mole poblano ($5); or **Los Colorines**, a little farther down the street. On Sundays, market vendors sell enchiladas and tortas—look for the **Tepoznieves** stand selling tequila ice cream, a Tepoztlán specialty.

XOCHICALCO

The ancient city of Xochicalco, which translates as "Place of the House of the Flowers," sits atop terraced hills overlooking a valley. These partially excavated ruins are the most fascinating in Morelos, displaying elements of Olmec and Maya architecture; Toltecs, Mixtecs, or Zapotecs may also have inhabited this site at different points in time. Some believe that Xochicalco was a ceremonial center, where scholars met to correct their calendars.

Much of the site has been uncovered, but excavation work is ongoing. It is believed that when the Spaniards arrived in the early 16th century, the people of the valley came from miles around to protect the ancient city by covering it with rocks and earth. The pre-Columbian ruins of both Xochicalco and Teopanzolco weren't rediscovered until the Mexican Revolution. During one battle in the early 1900s, Emiliano Zapata and his troops found that bullets ricochetted off the hill they were holding; they later discovered their cannon fire had been bouncing off grass-covered walls.

The center of Xochicalco is the **Plaza Ceremonial** (Plaza 1), located at the city's highest base elevation. Only priests were allowed here, in what is believed to be the main ceremonial enclosure, with people of the valley congregating to trade goods in a local bazaar on the surrounding grounds. The intricately carved **Pirámide de Quetzalcoatl** depicts the alignment of the calendars of several Indian tribes. These are presided over by Quetzalcoatl, shown as a headdressed serpent with two mouths, two tongues, and a fan of feathers for a tail. Here, his left hand discards an erroneous date (represented by a hieroglyph) while his right hand pulls in a correct one. The correct date has been identified as 13 Monkey, of the 260-day Mesoamerican calendar. You can climb the steep staircase of the **Temple of the Stelae,** also on the Plaza Ceremonial, to get a commanding view of the surrounding hills and the valley below.

Down the hill in the **main plaza** (Plaza 2) is the **Two Glyph Stelae Square,** arranged to chart the sun's path through the day. Below this is a ball court—one of many found in ruins throughout Mexico. It is believed that the game played here involved two teams of five men, each attempting to get a small, hard ball through the circular stone hoops on either end of the court.

The underground **observatory,** one of 32 interconnected tunnels below the pyramids, was used to trace the sun's path throughout the year; its movement is traced by the small circle of light on the cavern floor. At noon on the annual summer solstice (usually June 21), the sun's rays enter to completely illuminate the chamber's interior. The event held great religious significance—for one moment each year the celestial, the terrestrial, and the subterranean were united.

The small snack bar at the ruins offers nothing substantial; take a picnic lunch or hitchhike toward the village of El Rodeo, about a kilometer east past the Crucero de Xochicalco (the intersection of Ruta 166 and the road to the ruins). The guards seem pretty vigilant about keeping campers away, so make sure you're on the last bus. *Admission: $2.50; free Sun. and with student ID. Ruins open daily 9–5. Observatory open daily 11–2.*

COMING AND GOING From the México-Zacatepec bus station in Cuernavaca, catch a bus bound for Coatlán del Río or Miacatlán and ask the driver to let you off at the Crucero de Xochicalco. The ride costs $1 and takes less than an hour. From the crucero it's a 4-kilometer walk uphill to the ruins; taxis charge about $1 on the way up, less on the way down.

CUAUTLA

Warmer, drier, and less built-up than Cuernavaca, Cuautla is the second-largest city in Morelos. Its dusty provinciality belies the fact that this is a favorite vacation spot for many Mexicans, drawn here by Cuautla's famed mineral baths. The tradition of the wealthy elite soaking in sulphur water reportedly dates back to *Moctezuma* (Montezuma), who apparently enjoyed the restorative powers of these springs. The city was built into a prosperous colonial spa by the Spanish in the 17th century, but today the palm-lined streets roar with traffic, the natural hot springs are now more like unkempt public pools than therapeutic spas, and the wide plazas retain only traces of their colonial legacy.

The few remaining historical attractions are clustered in the town center and are a source of local pride. Cuautla was a revolutionary stronghold during the war for independence and the Mexican Revolution, and both rebel leader Emiliano Zapata and revolutionary priest José María Morelos are honored here. In 1812 Morelos and his 3,000 men held the city for 72 days against the attacking Royalist force of 20,000. It was only when starvation set in that they surrendered. The Battle of Cuautla is commemorated by a dominating statue of Morelos, who now waves a machete over the Plaza Galeana.

Across from this statue is the church that served as Morelos's headquarters, the **Iglesia de San Diego** and the adjacent **Convento de San Diego.** This graceful convent was later converted into a railway station, and today houses the Casa de la Cultura. The convent also contains Cuautla's helpful **tourist office** (Galeana, tel. 735/2-52-21; open daily 9–6) and the tiny **Museo José María Morelos** (open Tues.–Sun. 10–5).

It's a five-minute walk south on Galeana to the zócalo and the **Palacio Municipal** (tel. 735/2-00-27). On the west side of the zócalo is the **Iglesia de Santo Domingo** (tel. 735/2-00-06), which served as a hospital during the War of Independence and was defended with four cannons, one in each corner. At the southwest corner of the zócalo sits the **Casa de Morelos** (Callejon del Castigo, tel. 735/2-83-31), Morelos's home while defending the Cuautla. This small building, with peeling red paint and a white doorway, now houses the **Museo de la Independencia,** open weekends 10–2.

A 15 minute walk south of the zócalo on Guerrero brings you to **Jardín Revolución del Sur** (Calle Laredos), where Emiliano Zapata is buried. Zapata was assassinated at Chinameca, 31 kilometers away, and his image has recently assumed renewed political meaning with the armed uprising of the Zapatista Army in Chiapas. Facing the Jardín is the **Iglesia Señor del Pueblo,** named in his honor.

COMING AND GOING Although the second-largest city in Morelos, Cuautla is fairly manageable on foot—but be prepared for frequent street-name changes and a scarcity of street signs. The city is shaped roughly like an L, with the centro at the crook and the Alameda a few blocks north of the zócalo, on Galeana. Most colectivos run on Zavala/Reforma and Alvaro Obregón, and cost about 15¢.

There are two bus stations in Cuautla. **México/Zacatepec/Cristóbal Colón** (2 de Mayo, at Reforma), serves Mexico City, Oaxaca, and Puebla; **Estrella Roja** (Costeño, at Vásquez), serves Cuernavaca, Oaxaca, and Mexico City. From the Estrella Roja station in Cuernavaca, buses to Cuautla (1 hr, $1.50) leave every 30 minutes between 6 AM and 10 PM.

WHERE TO SLEEP Cuautla's hotels aren't the cheapest in the region, but prices aren't ridiculous. **Hotel Central** (Fin del Rul 21, off Plaza Galeana, no phone) has very basic rooms grouped around a grassy courtyard. Some of the bathrooms here are very small and dark, so ask to see a few rooms before paying; singles are $8.50, doubles $11.50. The **Villa Juvenil Cuautla** (Unidad Deportiva Morelos, tel. 735/2–02–18) is the best deal in town. The friendly, English-speaking administrator, James A. Garcia, keeps the park-like grounds well groomed, and will let you in after hours (11 PM) if you're "discreet." It's only $1.50 for a dorm bed and use of the sparklingly clean communal bathrooms. The hotel is 10 minutes from the Cristóbal Colón bus station: Head toward the IMSS building, turn right on Niños Héroes, go over a bridge, and enter the parking lot to your right. For camping information, *see* Outdoor Activities, *below*.

FOOD There's no lack of cheap dining establishments in Cuautla. Around the zócalo, the cafeterias **El Cid** and **Colón** sell cheap comidas corridas until fairly late and have a good view of the square. Restaurants can be found on Galeana, between the zócalo and the Alameda, and just off Galeana on Ingeniero Ramírez. Try **Mario, Pirandello,** or **Cafetería y Jugos Alameda.** Popular hangouts at the Alameda include **La Terraza Bar** (a soda fountain) and a burger joint called **Las Tortugas,** located in the same building as the movie theater. For a more formal dinner, try the restaurant in the **Hotel Colonial** (José Perdiz 18, tel. 735/2–21–64), known for its *cabrito colonial* (specially prepared kid; $7) and paella.

OUTDOOR ACTIVITIES Splashing around in one of Cuautla's many *balnearios* (spa and swimming areas) isn't all it's cracked up to be. The baths are more like pleasant municipal pools, but if you're dying to get wet, these are your best options. **Oaxtepec** (Carretera México–La Pera–Oaxtepec, tel. 735/6–12–02) is the showpiece of the resorts, with 25 pools, a cable car, lodging, and water slides. Catch a blue OAXTEPEC combi (½ hr) and have $6 ready for admission. **Las Estacas** (Carretera México–La Pera–Tlaltizapan, tel. 734/2–14–44), about 24 kilometers outside town, features a spring-fed river that floats guests through a patch of jungle. The resort also has a restaurant and camping facilities; admission is about $4. If resort prices are too steep, there are four other pool areas in Cuautla. **Los Limones** (tel. 735/2–70–02) is the smallest and best, with two clean pools and grassy campsites for $2.50. **Agua Linda** (next to Villa Juvenil Cuautla) and **El Almeal** (two blocks east of Los Limones, tel. 735/2–17–51) each have a few pools and lots of aqua-blue cement. Admission to either balneario is $2, and you can camp at El Almeal for $6. You can't say you weren't warned about **Agua Hedionda** (tel. 735/2–00–44), a sulphur spring whose name means "stinking water." If you can stand the rotten-egg stench, the water circulating in the pools is fresh. To reach the spring, catch the AGUAS HEDIONDAS combi either across from Plaza Galeana or just past the Niños Héroes bridge, in front of the Unidad Deportiva.

Tlaxcala

Tlaxcala, meaning "the land of corn," is a tiny state, only 2½ times the size of Mexico City. Although it's only two hours away from the hectic capital of the country, the state capital, Tlaxcala, has remained relatively unaffected by such urban chaos. Somewhat bypassed by many of the economic and political changes affecting most of the central cities, Tlaxcala has a uniquely tranquil atmosphere and laid-back residents. Still, Tlaxcala is one of Mexico's poorest states, and most of its inhabitants rely on their *milpas* (small plots of land on which corn is grown) for subsistence. The country's recent economic crisis has taken its toll on Tlaxcala by radically reducing national tourism—during most times of the year you may be the only nonresident wandering the streets.

Apart from the absence of wandering tourists, Tlaxcala's attributes include the requisite churches and colonial buildings. The city is also often livened by cultural festivals and fairs, which fill the streets with music, dancing, colorful costumes, and crafts from around the region. Tlaxcalans are proud of both their indigenous heritage and the fact that the city was the first Catholic diocese in Mexico, and are not without a sense of irony about the fusion of their cultures: Today, the official name of the city is "Tlaxcala de Xicohténcatl," in honor of the only Tlaxcalteca chieftain who opposed an alliance with the conquistador Cortés.

BASICS

AUTO PARTS/SERVICE **Merchant Zamora Lilia** (1 de Mayo, at Abasolo, tel. 246/2–19–99) sells car parts, and **Reconstrucción y Mantenimiento Automotriz Josué** (Blvd. Revolución

Tlaxcala

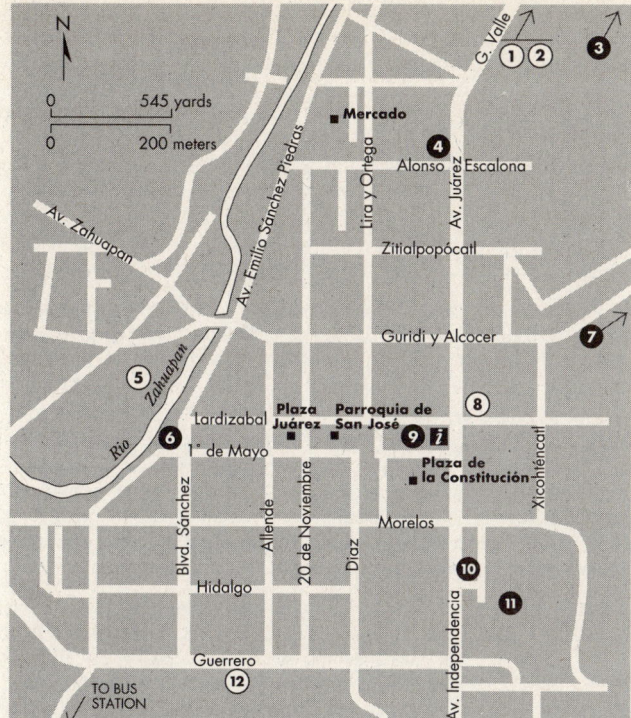

Sights ●
Basílica de Ocotlán, **7**
Ex-Convento de San Francisco, **11**
Jardín Botánico, **3**
Museo de Artes y Tradiciones de Tlaxcala, **6**
Palacio de Gobierno, **9**
Palacio de la Cultura, **4**
Plaza Xicohténcatl, **10**

Lodging ○
Albergue de la Loma, **12**
Hotel Frontera, **1**
Hotel Mansión de Xichtencatl, **8**
Hotel Plaza-Tlaxcala, **2**
Hotel Zahuapan, **5**

52, tel. 246/2-09-98) handles most mechanical problems. Neither speak English, but they are the most reliable mechanics around.

CASAS DE CAMBIO Change dollars or traveler's checks weekdays 9-noon at **Banamex** (Plaza Xicohténcatl 1, tel. 246/2-25-36). Banamex also has ATMs that accept Plus and Cirrus system cards.

EMERGENCIES In an emergency call the **police** (tel. 246/2-07-35, Av. Tlahuicole, Col. López Mateos); for the **Cruz Roja** (ambulance service) call 246/2-09-20.

LAUNDRY Lavandería San Felipe charges $3 to wash 3 kilos of laundry. *Guiridi y Alcocer 30, btw Juárez and Lira y Ortega, no phone. Open weekdays 8-7, Sat. 8-3.*

MAIL The full-service post office on the zócalo will hold mail sent to you at the following address for up to 10 days: Lista de Correos, Tlaxcala, Tlaxcala, CP 90000, México. *Plaza de la Constitución 20, tel. 246/2-00-04. Open weekdays 9-6, Sat. 9-1.*

MEDICAL AID The **IMSS clinic** (G. Valle 64, tel. 246/2-23-44) provides medical services 24 hours a day and has some English-speaking staff. For less serious medical problems, **Farmacia Zahuapan** (20 de Noviembre 1, tel. 246/2-21-56) is open 24 hours.

PHONES To make a collect call, you'll have to use a pay phone—several are located in front of the Parroquia de San José and Plaza Xicohténcatl—because none of the casetas lets you make them. For cash calls, try the *caseta de larga distancia* (long-distance telephone office) on Independencia across from the Plaza Xicohténcatl (open Mon.-Sat. 8 AM-9:30 PM). There are a number of *Ladetel* phones on the main plaza, but you'll have to go to the **telephone office** (Guiridi y Alcocer 7; open weekdays 9-4) to buy a card.

VISITOR INFORMATION The Secretary of Tourism has an information desk staffed by eager young people who distribute numerous flyers and can arrange for guides with a week's notice. *Juárez, at Lardizábal, tel. 246/2-00-27. Open weekdays 9-7, weekends 10-6.*

COMING AND GOING

BY BUS The **Central Camionera** (tel. 246/2-03-62) is eight blocks west of the zócalo. Buses to Mexico City (2 hrs, $4) and Puebla (1 hr, $1.75) leave every 15 minutes 6 AM–10 PM. Buses also depart daily at 10:30 AM and 3:30 PM for Veracruz (6 hrs, $7). To reach the zócalo from the bus station, take any CENTRO or SANTA ANA colectivo (5 min, 20¢). Colectivos marked CENTRAL head to the bus station from the corner of Lira y Ortega and Lardizábal.

BY TRAIN There's no train station in Tlaxcala, but trains to Puebla and Apizaco (the state's rail center) leave at noon, 2 PM, and 7:30 PM from Santa Ana Chiautempan, 10 minutes away. *Blvd. Emilio Sánchez Piedras 107, tel. 246/2-13-86. From zócalo, take a SANTA ANA colectivo (30¢) along Juárez.*

GETTING AROUND

Tlaxcala is a walkable city. The main street running roughly north–south is called Independencia on the south side of Plaza Constitución (the zócalo), becoming Juárez to the north. Past downtown, Juárez changes into Guillermo Valle, which becomes Boulevard Revolución farther on. Most anything of interest lies near or along Independencia/Juárez in the downtown area.

Colectivos (both combis and small buses) travel up and down the main drag, as well as to neighboring towns and the Central Camionera. Those heading north leave from the stop in front of Plaza Xicohténcatl on Independencia; those heading south, west, and to the Central Camionera depart from the northwest corner of the intersection of Lira y Ortega and Lardizábal. Colectivos stop running at about 10 PM. Taxi stands are in front of the southern porch of the zócalo and the Parroquia de San José. Within Tlaxcala, fares should stay under $2, and a ride to the nearby town of Santa Ana is $3.50. Unless you have heavy luggage, you probably won't need a taxi, though; the streets are pretty safe at night as long as you stick to the beaten path.

WHERE TO SLEEP

The hotels in Tlaxcala, which are nothing to rave about, reflect the fact that Tlaxcala's visitors are often few and far between. With no business to compete for, many hotel owners tend to veg out in front of the TV and forget they have a place to run. Reservations are only required during the fairs in October and May, and in the first week of July, when summer sessions start at the university. If the places below are full, your only alternative is a luxury hotel. The most affordable of these is **Hotel Jeroc's** (Revolución 4, tel. 246/2-15-77), which charges $25 for a single and $38 for a double.

➢ **UNDER $10** • **Hotel Frontera.** This is the cheapest hotel in town. The problem is, it's not really *in* town (12 long blocks north of the zócalo), and it's hard to find—look for the red door facing the pharmacy. On the plus side, the rooms are clean, and there's a *tiendita* (convenience store) next door that sells everything from toilet paper to chips. Singles are $5, doubles $7, but bargaining isn't out of the question. *G. Valle 82, tel. 246/2-12-26. Take SANTA ANA combi from bus station. 18 rooms, all with bath. Luggage storage.*

Hotel Zahuapan. This hotel, across the river from the Museo de Artes y Tradiciones, is a little tricky to find (especially at night). Once you find it, you'll be rewarded with exuberant bubblegum-pink bedrooms, bathrooms with hot water, and tiny TVs firmly chained to the wall (lest you decide they look better in your backpack). Singles are $7, doubles $9. *Priv. Río Zahuapan 1, tel. 246/2-59-86. From center, take Guiridi y Alcocer until it becomes J. Carillo, cross bridge, and take first left. 24 rooms, all with bath. Reservations advised in summer.*

➢ **UNDER $15** • **Hotel Mansión de Xicohténcatl.** This hotel is smack-dab in the middle of town, almost across the street from the tourist office. It doesn't, however, live up to its name.

Rooms are clean but drab, though some have small balconies. If you're a woman traveling alone, you might get some unwanted attention, but if you can ignore it, you'll find the hot showers and great location worth your while. Knock on the front door if you arrive after midnight. Singles cost $7.50, doubles $11. *Juárez 15, 1 block north of zócalo, tel. 246/2-19-00. 18 rooms, all with bath.*

Hotel Plaza-Tlaxcala. Next door to Hotel Jeroc's sits this quiet hotel, complete with a garden courtyard, a restaurant, and cold beer at the front desk. Rooms have TVs and a painful pastel decor. It's pretty far from the center of town, but a bargain at $10 for a single, $12 for a double. *Revolución 6, tel. 246/2-78-52. Take a* SANTA ANA *combi from center or bus station; you'll see Hotel Jeroc's sign on left. 12 rooms, all with bath. Laundry, luggage storage. MC, V.*

➤ **UNDER $25** • **Alberque de La Loma.** Perched atop a hill overlooking Tlaxcala, this hotel is nonetheless only four blocks from the center. Come here if you want to pamper yourself—the clean rooms are large and airy, and come with phones, TVs, a great view, and access to the restaurant upstairs. Singles run $17–$20; doubles are $20–$24. *Guerrero 58, tel. 246/2-04-24. 40 rooms, all with bath. Laundry (50¢-$1 per piece). AE, MC, V.*

FOOD

Most of Tlaxcala's restaurants cluster around the zócalo and Plaza Xicohténcatl. People here seem to favor anything that isn't Mexican, but you'll also find plenty of regional specialties. One of these is *pollo tocotlán,* chicken in maguey salsa, cooked in a thin paper bag. For the cheapest food in town, try the taco stands off 20 de Noviembre, near Plaza Juárez, which stay open late: Drinks are at room temperature, the salsa is searing, and you'll probably have to eat standing up, but tacos are 20¢ each. Another option is the *rosticerías* (restaurants specializing in roasted chicken), where a whole chicken with a side of tortillas, beans, *rajas* (chile strips), and salsa costs $1.50. There are several near the market on Emilio Sánchez Piedras, between Escalona and Lira y Ortega—try **El Pollo Rey,** open daily until 8:30. The market itself offers prepared food daily, as will be apparent by the swarming crowds around lunchtime.

➤ **UNDER $5** • **Café Avenida.** This relatively informal place offers a wide variety of Mexican and American food. *Filete al chipotle* ($5), steak covered with a smoked-pepper tomato sauce and cheese on a bed of refried beans, is especially good. The comida corrida includes soup, an entrée, and dessert, and runs $2.50–$3.50. If you're eating alone, you can amuse yourself by perusing the coffee menu: There are five different kinds of cappuccino, including Cappuccino Sexi ($2) with plum liqueur and honey. *Juárez 6, tel. 246/2-63-53. ½ block north of zócalo. Open daily 7* AM*–10* PM.

La Fonda del Convento. On the cobblestone pedestrian path that runs between the Ex-Convento de San Francisco and Plaza Xicohténcatl, this popular restaurant is small, quiet, and the place to go if you're tired of having lunch on the plaza with everybody staring at you as you eat. For a little more than $4, you can try the *carne fonda del convento* (steak served with an enchilada, rice, fries, beans, and guacamole). Vegetarians should try the quesadillas ($2) seasoned with *epazote,* an herb particular to Mexico rojas. *Calzada de San Francisco 1, tel. 246/2-07-65. Open Mon.–Sat. 10–8.*

Los Portales. Squeezed between the multitudes of restaurants that line the zócalo, this restaurant serves up traditional food such as $3 *pollo en pipian* (chicken in chile and pumpkin-seed sauce). You can also choose from a variety of steaks ($4) and exotic hamburgers—try the Hawaiian version with pineapple, cheese, bacon, and lettuce ($2.50). There's al fresco dining on the porch, but inside or outside, the restaurant is packed with locals of every age. *Independencia 8, tel. 246/2-54-19. Open daily 7* AM*–10* PM. *Wheelchair access.*

El Quinto Sol. Most vegetarian restaurants in the country cater to dieting Mexican women, and this one is no exception. Vegans will rejoice at the presence of soy milk on the breakfast menu—it's served hot and tastes suspiciously like *atole* (a sweet, corn-based drink). Add bread, fruit, yogurt, and some excellent granola, and you have breakfast for $1.75. The lunch menu varies, offering creative dishes such as soy steak. *Juárez, at Lardizábal, tel. 246/2-49-28. Next to Hotel Mansión de Xicohténcatl. Open Mon.–Sat. 7:30–7.*

➤ **UNDER $10** • **El Mesón Taurino.** This place is next to the Plaza de Toros, and its ambience is marred only by the severed heads of bulls staring down at you as you eat—try dining outdoors in the garden. Although open for breakfast, this restaurant's forte is dinner, when pasta dishes cost $3–$4. For just a bit more you can have filet mignon in mushroom sauce ($6.50) or *filete Cacaxtla* ($7), steak topped with *huitlacoche* (a fungus grown on corn) and chile strips. Adding a salad and wine to your meal brings the price to about $12. It's an ideal place to celebrate a special occasion, like having enough cash to eat here. *Independencia 12, at Guerrero, tel. 246/2–43–66. Open daily 8–8.*

WORTH SEEING

Tlaxcala's main points of interest are all within walking distance of the zócalo and can be seen in less than a day. **Plaza de la Constitución** is quieter than most Mexican zócalos; goods are only sold there during fairs or the Saturday market. Along the western edge is the **Casa de Piedra,** a colonial-era house with a distinctive stone facade. Legend has it that the doctor who lived here asked his poor patients to pay with a stone of a certain size. In this manner, he went about building his house, stone by stone. Dominating **Plaza Xicohténcatl** is a monument to the *cacique* (chieftain) of that name, who was hanged by the Spaniards after the successful assault on Tenochtitlán, for refusing to participate in the slaughter of the Aztecs. The plaza is bordered by a number of restaurants and is basically part of the zócalo.

BASILICA DE OCOTLAN This hillside shrine is one of Mexico's national treasures, and is considered the region's best example of the ornate churrigueresque style. The visitor is greeted by a gleaming white plaster facade, which is carved with intricate figures and flanked by two 33-meter-high towers. These are tiled in red and sky blue; red and white are the colors of the flag of the ancient kingdom of Tlaxcallan, and blue symbolizes the Virgin Mary, in whose honor the shrine was built in 1640. According to church history, the Virgin appeared to a pious Indian in answer to his prayers for water during a drought.

The **Chamber of the Virgin,** where a statue of Our Lady of Ocotlán is housed, took the sculptor Francisco Miguel Tlayoltehuamintzin 25 years to complete, and every single inch is gold plated. Facing the basilica, turn left down a small alley for the **Capilla del Pocito de Agua Milagrosa,** a tiny, round chapel housing a well of curative water. The chapel walls are brightly decorated with a series of murals on biblical themes related to water, designed by Desiderio Hernández Xochitiotzin *(see* Palacio de Gobierno, *below). From zócalo, north on Juárez, right at Guridi y Alcocer, left at Calzada de los Misterios, and uphill about 2 km. Admission free. Open daily until dusk; closed to visitors during church services (hourly on Sunday 7 AM–2 PM).*

EX-CONVENTO DE SAN FRANCISCO Services were held here before Cortés marched on to Tenochtitlán (present-day Mexico City). The **Capilla Abierta** (Open Chapel) is thought to be the earliest 16th-century construction of its type in New Spain.

Up the stairs and across the courtyard is the **Catedral de Nuestra Señora de la Asunción.** Built in 1526 after Tlaxcala was declared the first diocese in New Spain, it is known for its cedar ceiling, which is carved in the geometric *mosarabe* style. The four *caciques* (chieftains) of Tlaxcala were converted at the baptismal font, with Cortés and Alvarado acting as godfathers. The small museum next to the convent specializes in Tlaxcalan archeology and also traces the history of the conquest. Admission is $1, free for students with ID. *From zócalo, south 1 block past Plaza Xicohténcatl, left at Calzada de Capilla Abierta. Admission free. Open daily 8–7. Mass daily at 6 PM.*

The atrium of the Ex-Convento is known to locals as "el jardín del pulpo" (octopus garden) because of all the groping that goes on here in the late evening.

JARDIN BOTANICO TIZATLAN One of the newer attractions of Tlaxcala, this garden sprouts flora characteristic of the *altiplano* (highland) region. Plants are labeled with their scientific and common names, and some have descriptions of their medicinal and practical uses. The Jardín is also a good place for picnics or trysts. The **Sala Miguel Lira** theater (in the garden, tel. 246/2–46–85) shows recent American and Mexican films Tuesday–Sunday. Call to ask what's showing and to get specific times. *Take SANTA ANA combi from zócalo, get off just before aquaduct at Camino Real. Admission free. Open daily 9–5.*

MUSEO DE ARTES Y TRADICIONES DE TLAXCALA This living history museum celebrates the traditional Tlaxcalan way of life. In one room, a typical *campesino* (peasant) house is re-created, with Sunday clothes carefully stored in a cardboard box at the foot of the bed. Wednesday through Sunday, local artisans occupy the museum, and painstakingly demonstrate the step-by-step process of weaving and the making of pulque. Guides are available Wednesday–Sunday for tours in Spanish. Ask permission before taking photographs. *Emilio Sánchez Piedras 1, at Lardizábal, tel. 246/2–23–37. 3 blocks west of zócalo. Admission: $1, 75¢ students; free Sun. Open Tues.–Sun. 10–6.*

PALACIO DE GOBIERNO Now the municipal headquarters, this palace was built for Hernán Cortés around 1550. The interior walls are covered with spectacular, colorful murals painted by Desiderio Hernández Xochitiotzin (who had close ties to Diego Rivera). The murals are filled with symbolic and prophetic figures; the stairwell, for example, pictures the heavens overrun by fantastic creatures, as gods plunge headfirst to the earth. In the background an inferno swallows the city, while off in the corner a Spaniard mounted on a white horse strikes down the feathered serpent Quetzalcoatl, god of fertility. You can wander around for as long as you like, as long as you steer clear of the government offices. Guides will willingly explain the murals in detail. They charge about $5, but bargaining isn't out of the question. *North side of zócalo, tel. 246/2–00–06. Admission free. Open daily 6 AM–8 PM.*

PALACIO DE LA CULTURA This sprawling building, surrounded by an immaculate garden, houses Tlaxcala's cultural center. Music classes are held in the basement, don't be surprised to hear an unmelodic piano or erratic drumming. The first floor has a *Sala de Cultura*, with temporary exhibits by Tlaxcalan and national artists. *Juárez, at Escalona, tel. 246/2–39–79. Admission free. Open Mon.–Sat. 9–7.*

> Music lovers should check out Avenida Muñoz Camargo between Díaz and Allende. Several mariachi bands have small shops here, and in the afternoon they suit up and practice before hitting the lunch and dinner crowds in the zócalo restaurants. The interested should not be shy— the musicians are generally more than happy to answer questions about their art.

CHEAP THRILLS

Whether you live in constant fear of Moctezuma's revenge, or just want to guarantee your good health, head to the **Capilla del Pocito** (see Basílica de Ocotlán, *above*) for a sip of the miraculous curative water. People wander in frequently and take off with bucketfuls; a few plastic glasses are kept here for your convenience. The water itself is remarkably sweet and fresh, especially after the long hike up to the basilica.

There are many other places around town where locals enjoy Tlaxcala's charm free of charge. Across the street from the **Jardín Botánico** is a park where neighborhood soccer games are played on Sundays; watch or, if you're able, join in. The pedestrian walkway along the bank of the Río Zahuapan (which flows through the northwest corner of Tlaxcala) is known as the **Paseo de la Amistad** (Friendship Walkway). Take a stroll with the amorous couples, kids on bikes, and elderly folks enjoying the sunshine. You can also wander farther along the paseo to **Parque de la Juventud** (Park of Youth), a good spot for a picnic or jog. For a panoramic view of the city as the sun slips behind the hills, join the couples and families gathered on the steep stairway of the **Iglesia del Vecino** (above and behind the cathedral).

FESTIVALS

Late February: The best festival in Tlaxcala is **Carnaval**, celebrated the week prior to Ash Wednesday. The festival is characterized by street parades, where people dance around wearing masks and costumes. Each village uses a specific color or design for its masks.

July 6: In 1591 a group of 400 Christianized Tlaxcaltecan families left Tlaxcala under orders from King Philip II of Spain and Pope Gregory XIV to colonize the north of "New Spain." An impressive reenactment of their departure takes place at the ruins of the Convento de Nuestra Señora de las Nieves in the town of Totolac (half a kilometer from Tlaxcala, on the road to San

Martín Tlexmelucan) during the **Celebración de las Cuatrocientas Familias** (Celebration of the 400 Families). The highlight is a candlelight procession down from the hills.

Mid-July: The **Feria del Pan** in Totolac is a typical Tlaxcalan festival with dancing and fireworks. The bread baked for the festival is famous throughout Mexico, and can be purchased year-round.

August 15: The **Fiesta de la Asunción** in Huamantla, about a half hour east of Tlaxcala, is a two-week festival celebrating the Assumption and the Virgin of Charity. The highlight is when a figure of the Virgin is paraded through the streets, which are carpeted with flowers arranged in symbolic designs. The procession ends when the sun rises, and the running of the bulls, à la Pamplona, begins. To reach Huamantla, catch a bus ($1) from the station in Tlaxcala.

Late October: The **Tlaxcala Fair** features bullfights, *charreadas* (rodeos), cockfights, indigenous dances, carnival rides, and exhibitions of local handicrafts. The fair lasts about two weeks, usually until early November. Ask for more info at the tourist office.

AFTER DARK

Though the cafés are crowded in the early evenings, Tlaxcalans generally go to bed early. During festivals and in July and August, when students from Mexico City descend on Tlaxcala for summer classes, things pick up a bit. As for the rest of the year, if you go out after 10 PM, you've missed whatever action there was. If you just can't stay in, hook up with someone with a car to *dar una vuelta* (drive around aimlessly to see who else is also driving around), the activity of choice among local teenagers.

BARS/MUSIC Although Tlaxcala state is home to the Plains of Apam, where pulque is made, traditional pulquerías are nowhere to be found. A few bars play music; most of the others are seedy cantinas where women are unwelcome. **Bar Tendido 7** (Plaza San Ignacio, next to Cine Tlaxcala, tel. 246/2–86–87) is open daily until midnight, and has live music Tuesday–Sunday. **Valentina's** (1 de Mayo No. 9, at Allende, no phone) is open Thursday–Sunday 9 PM–2 AM, and occasionally hosts a fashionable band from Puebla. For a more laid-back and cultural atmosphere, head to **Mitlan** (Juárez 54, no phone). The bar doubles as a gallery, and occasionally hosts poetry readings and theater shows. There is usually live music on Fridays and Saturdays. Beers go for about $1 at these three places, and they rarely charge a cover.

CINEMAS Both **Cinema Tlaxcala** (tel. 246/2–19–62), on the south side of the zócalo, and **Cinemas 1 y 2** (G. Valle 113, tel. 246/2–35–44), 6½ blocks north of the center, show fairly recent Hollywood films with Spanish subtitles, as well as Mexican films. Shows cost $1.50.

DANCING Most dancing is at weddings, *quinceañeras* (girls' 15th-birthday parties), and festivals. If you haven't been invited to any of these, you don't have much else to choose from. **Century** (20 de Novembre, at Hidalgo, no phone) is close to the center of town, and draws a young student crowd. You can also go shake it at **Armando's** (Independencia 60-B, tel. 246/2–89–88), the most fashionable disco at present. Night owls (generally tourists) party until 2 or 3 AM at **Royal Adler's** (Revolución 4, tel. 246/2–15–77) in Hotel Jeroc's. Mexican and American pop and disco are played here, and drinks cost $2. All of the above discos charge a $4 cover.

Near Tlaxcala

About 6 kilometers north of Tlaxcala is **Tizatlán**, once the center of the kingdom of Tlaxcallan. It's now known for its hand-carved walking sticks and a Franciscan chapel with a Moorish roof, built on top of the ruins of a pre-Hispanic pyramid. Amidst the ruins you can detect the vestiges of an indigenous religious sanctuary, as well as representations of the deities Tezcatlipoca and Tlahuizcalpan Tecutli. This is also the birthplace of Xicohténcatl, the chieftain who opposed Cortés. *Take combi from cnr of 1 de Mayo and Blvd. Sánchez in Tlaxcala. Admission: $2; free Sun. and for students with ID. Open daily 10–5.*

Huamantla, about 45 kilometers west of Tlaxcala, houses the baroque **Iglesia y Convento de San Luis Obispo,** and the free **Museo Taurino** (Allende Nte. 203, 3 blocks from center; open Wed.–Sun. 9–4). The museum features posters, costumes, swords, and photographs of bullfighting, and is located next to La Taurina bullring. The occasional bullfights here are well publicized. To reach Huamantla, take an ATAH bus from the Central Camionera in Tlaxcala.

If you've seen enough churches and museums, take a break at the **Centro Vacacional La Trinidad**, 15 kilometers northwest of Tlaxcala, in Santa Cruz. This resort is on the banks of the Río Tequixquiatl, and you can swim and ride horses here. Rooms in the **Hotel Balneario** (tel. 246/1–03–33) are $22 for a double, and you can camp in the hotel grounds for $2. Colectivos (70¢) run between 20 de Noviembre in Tlaxcala and Santa Cruz, and once you reach the zócalo, you'll see La Trinidad. Another place for water sports is **Atlangatepec**, a dammed lake 1½ hours north of Tlaxcala. To get here, take a bus from Tlaxcala's Central Camionera to Apizaco and transfer to Atlangatepec. **Villa Quinta Olivares** (tel. 246/1–08–69 or 246/7–27–36) has bungalows here for $7 a night, or you can camp free of charge around the lake.

LA MALINCHE

A 4,462-meter volcano, **La Malinche** is covered and surrounded by many forests, making it the most beautiful volcano near Tlaxcala. During the rainy season (July–September) it's almost impossible to get to the top, but the rest of the year, this is a great place to hike. La Malinche is about 43 kilometers east of Tlaxcala, and can be reached by bus in 1½ hours. From the Central Camionera or the market in Tlaxcala, take a bus to Huamantla, and from there catch another bus to **Centro Vacacional La Malintzi** (tel. 246/2–40–98)—a government-run resort. It takes three hours to hike to the summit of the volcano from the Centro Vacacional, and one hour to get back. A guide isn't necessary, but they are usually available on weekends and charge $5–$7 per person. At the Centro Vacacional, you can camp for $3 per person, or rent one of the six-person cabins for $35 a night. There is a restaurant here, too, but it's pricey, so bring food and water for the hike.

La Malinche was named after the woman who was the translator and mistress of Hernán Cortés.

CACAXTLA

Cacaxtla, 16 kilometers southeast of Tlaxcala, consists of a group of pyramids, each with an amazing view of the endless cornfields—a sure sign of the strategic importance of these temples in pre-Columbian times. In 1975 a series of vivid polychrome murals was discovered here—one of the most important Mesoamerican archaeological finds in the past 50 years. Today you can still see these astonishingly well-preserved works, which are unique in their realistic style and detail. The current theory holds that the murals were painted by the Xicalancas, a group of warrior merchants who arrived in the Tlaxcala Valley in AD 600. The Xicalancas were descendants of the Maya, which explains why their murals contain elements more commonly found in southern Mexico. The figures adorned with blue body paint represent sacrificial victims, and the five-pointed stars are symbols of the goddess of fertility. Cacaxtla means "place where the water dies in the earth," and you'll see repeated representations of water and of Tlaloc, a rain god to whom human sacrifices were offered.

The Xicalancas, like the Maya, believed that human beings were made of corn.

The first set of murals, painted on columns flanking the entrance to a small room, depicts barefoot blue dancers. Archaeologists refer to this room as the **Star Chamber**, because the dancers are surrounded by five-pointed stars. It may have been here that captives were prepared for sacrifice. The next mural on the right represents water, fertility, and trade. Note that the ears of corn are actually human faces. The **Red Temple** is identifiable by the bands of red paint that run along the bottom of the walls, like a sea of blood. Unfortunately, the general public is not allowed inside the Red Temple: Murals depicting prisoners are painted on the floor of the temple and cannot be walked on.

The **battle mural** for which Cacaxtla is most renowned is found just beyond the Red Temple. The victors wear jaguar pelts, and the vanquished wear bird headdresses. One interpretation is that the mural depicts the aftermath of a real-life battle. It is also speculated that it does not represent a battle that actually took place, but rather symbolizes a confrontation between the two ethnic groups, whose union eventually gave rise to the Olmec-Xicalanca people. A final set of murals is located in **Building A,** to the right of the battle mural. The date on the **north mural** (denoted by the eye of a reptile in indigenous glyphs) corresponds with the supposed birthdate of Quetzalcoatl. Bordering these murals are pictures of various sea creatures, reminders of the Olmec-Xicalancas' origins on the Gulf of Mexico.

Although the ruins of Cacaxtla are no longer undergoing excavation, another temple, built around AD 200, lies below the visible structures, and it's possible that yet another is buried further down. In January of 1993 excavation began at **Xochitecal** (known as Pyramid of the Flowers, and named after the goddess Xochitecal) on the hill opposite Cacaxtla. The site consists of three temples, although human remains and close to 5,000 clay figures, mostly representing women, have also been discovered. Although female images dominate this site, archaeologists have yet to confirm whether this indicates a matriarchy, or what the link is between this temple and the nearby Cacaxtla. Xochitecal is half an hour's walk through the fields from the pyramid of Cacaxtla. Once you reach the top of the temple, you'll be rewarded by a incredible view of the surrounding plains. *Admission for both sites: $2.50, free Sun. Open daily 10–4:30.*

If you make the trek out to Cacaxtla, you might as well visit **San Miguel del Milagro,** 1 kilometer northeast of Cacaxtla. The archangel Michael is said to have appeared here in 1630 to Diego Lázaro de San Francisco. As in Ocotlán, a fountain of healing water bubbled forth, and to this day the **Santuario de San Miguel** is a destination for pilgrims. The **Pocito de Santa Agua** (Well of Holy Water) is in the courtyard outside the church, behind a locked gate. The church itself is filled with 17th- and 18th-century paintings depicting angels and biblical stories—the lacquered **Chinese Pulpit** and the **Cuarto de Exvotos** are of particular interest. Here, pilgrims who have been healed leave offerings—photographs, pairs of crutches, and handwritten notes.

COMING AND GOING From Tlaxcala, take a NATIVITAS combi from the market or a SAN MARTIN bus from the Central Camionera, and ask to be let off at the *calzada* (40 min, 70¢). You'll be dropped off at a crossroads, where combis wait to take people to San Miguel and Cacaxtla (about five minutes away). If you've taken the combi, chances are the driver can be convinced to drop you off all the way at the top. You can also take a SAN MARTIN bus (1 hr, 90¢) from Puebla's CAPU terminal.

FOOD The small cafeteria next to the museum in Cacaxtla has a *menú del día* (daily special) for $3, or you can pick up quesadillas (40¢) at the taco stands in San Miguel, a short walk away. Also try the *alegrías,* a honey and millet-grain candy native to Tlaxcala.

Puebla

Puebla, Mexico's fourth-largest city, is overwhelming at first. Music stores blast the latest Mexican hits onto crowded sidewalks and taxis and buses weave crazily down narrow cobblestoned streets while traffic cops calmly eat ice cream from a safe distance. Although your first instinct may be to run and hide, this cosmopolitan city will soon seem less chaotic, and its wealth of religious artifacts and carefully preserved architecture eventually provides a sense of continuity.

Founded in 1531, Puebla is first and foremost a colonial city, but the ruins in nearby Cholula (*see* Near Puebla, *below*) also reveal the rich indigenous culture that existed long before the arrival of the conquistadors. Puebla has also been important in the military history of Mexico. In 1862 the city was the site of a major battle, where 2,000 Mexicans defeated 6,000 French troops. In 1910 the massacre of activists by the army gave impetus to the uprising against dictator Porfirio Díaz. Recently, the state university has seen numerous student strikes and protests. Puebla has 14 universities, and students are always busy hanging out in cafés and organizing cultural events.

This is a city best explored on foot; as you walk past each building, a peek through the doors reveals exhibitions of folk art and antiques, extravagant church interiors laden with gilt, or steaming platters of *mole poblano* (*see box* Holy Mole, *below*). Food is special in Puebla, and almost anything you eat here, whether it was prepared on a makeshift brazier on the street or in a fancy restaurant, is wonderful. In fact, this is the only Mexican city where a kitchen—La Cocina de Santa Rosa—is considered a tourist attraction. Whether you're into spicy cuisine, or historic artifacts, there's something in Puebla for you. Although the city is becoming increasingly popular among both foreign and Mexican tourists, the sheer quantity of things to do means you won't feel like you're in a tourist trap.

BASICS

AMERICAN EXPRESS The AmEx office is in the Plaza Dorada shopping center, a five-minute bus ride from downtown. They exchange and sell traveler's checks, replace lost ones, deliver MoneyGrams, and exchange dollars. Cardholders can also cash personal checks, replace lost cards, and have their mail held. *Mailing address: Plaza Dorada 2, Local 21–22, Puebla, Puebla, CP 72530, tel. 22/37–55–58. Take* PLAZA DORADA *bus from 13 Ote., at Av. 2 Sur. Open weekdays 9–6, Sat. 9–1.*

AUTO PARTS/SERVICE Sears auto shop sells parts and does most mechanical repairs. They *say* some employees speak English, but don't count on it. *3 Pte. 138, tel. 22/42–45–55. Open Mon.–Sat. 8–7. AE, MC, V.*

BOOKSTORES **Librerías de Cristal** (Reforma 511, tel. 22/42–44–20) has an enormous selection of books, magazines, videos, and compact discs, and a small selection of English books. *Two blocks west of zócalo, btw 5 Nte. and 7 Nte. Open Mon.–Sat. 9:30–8.*

CASAS DE CAMBIO Exchange cash or traveler's checks at **Bancomer** (Reforma 116, tel. 22/32–00–22) or **Banco Internacional** (2 Pte. 107, tel. 22/46–40–44 ext. 2128), both open weekdays 9–noon. Many of the banks along Reforma have ATMs that accept Plus and Cirrus system cards, but those at **Banamex** (Reforma 135, tel. 22/32–47–60) are the most reliable. If you're set on changing cash later in the day, you'll have to go a bit out of the way: **Casa de Cambio Puebla** (Blvd. 5 de Mayo, tel. 22/37–74–73; open Mon.–Sat. 9–1:30 and 4:30–6) is 4 blocks from the Plaza Dorada shopping center.

EMERGENCIES Dial 06 from any public phone in Puebla for **police, fire,** or **ambulance.**

LAUNDRY **Lavandería Roly** has both self- and drop-off service. Someone will wash and dry your clothes for $3 per 3 kilos; it costs $1 to do it yourself. *7 Nte. 404, at 4 Pte., tel. 22/32–93–07. Open Mon.–Sat. 8 AM–9 PM, Sun. 8–3.*

MAIL The main post office is 2 blocks south of the zócalo. They'll hold mail for you at the following address for up to 10 days: Lista de Correos, 5 Ote. y 16 de Septiembre, Sur C, Puebla, Puebla, CP 72000, México. *5 Ote., at 16 de Septiembre, tel. 22/42–64–48. Open weekdays 8–8, Sat. 9–1. Other location: 2 Ote. 411, btw 6 Nte and 4 Nte.*

MEDICAL AID The **Hospital Universitario** (13 Sur, at 25 Pte., tel. 22/40–50–32) has 24-hour emergency service (some English spoken). **Farmacia Carmen** (16 de Septiembre 2107, tel. 22/43–11–88) is the only pharmacy in the city open 24 hours. Several other pharmacies around the zócalo offer 15%–30% discounts on prescriptions; try **Farmacia Portales** (2 Nte 5, tel. 22/42–52–71; open daily 9–9), which will deliver the medicine to your hotel.

PHONES Puebla probably has the highest percentage of functioning pay phones in Mexico. You can also make calls from any caseta de larga distancia, found in various stores around Puebla. Just look for a blue picture of a telephone and the initials L.A.D.A. on the side. **Printaform** (2 Sur 104, tel. 22/46–68–14) is right on the zócalo and offers cash calls and free collect calls. **Helados Holanda** (16 de Septiembre 103) has both long-distance service and a fax machine and is open on Sunday, but you can't make collect calls. Most casetas are open 9–8.

VISITOR INFORMATION Oddly enough, there are two tourist offices in Puebla. The **Oficina de Información Turística,** across from the cathedral and next to the **Casa de Cultura** is the state office. It is staffed by a helpful crew who provide good maps of the city and the state. The municipal office (Portal Hidalgo 14, tel. 22/46–10–93; open weekdays 9–8) can also give you tons of info. *5 Ote. 3, tel. 22/46–12–85. Open Mon.–Sat. 8–8, Sun. 9–2.*

COMING AND GOING

BY BUS Puebla's main bus terminal, **CAPU** (Blvd. Atlixco Nte.), is served by a number of bus lines. **Autobuses Unidos (AU)** (tel. 22/49-74-05) sends frequent buses to Mexico City (2 hrs, $3.75) and Veracruz (5 hrs, $8.50), and sends two buses to Oaxaca (8 hrs, $9) at 8:30 PM and 11:30 PM. **Estrella Blanca** (tel. 22/49-74-33) serves Acapulco (7 hrs, $23); buses leave every two hours until 11:30 PM. **Cristóbal Colón** (tel. 22/49-73-27) buses depart for Salina Cruz (10 hrs, $22) at 9 PM daily. Besides serving many of the destinations listed above, **Autobuses del Oriente (ADO)** (tel. 22/49-70-42) has buses daily at 9 PM for Mérida (21 hrs, $41) and Cancún (24 hrs, $49). Several local companies such as **Flecha Azúl** go to nearby towns such as Tehuacán and Tlaxcala for about $1. The terminal has luggage storage (open 7 AM-11:30 PM), a tourist information booth, a police station, and a bank that changes money 9 AM-noon. Several cafeterias, a pharmacy, and shops nearby ensure that you'll be occupied as you wait for your bus. The terminal is big and always bustling, so if you want to crash here, go ahead—you'll be uncomfortable but safe.

Unfortunately the bus terminal is nowhere near downtown Puebla. To get here you have to either take a combi or a cab. Authorized taxis (prepay the fare at the booth inside the terminal) charge $1.75 to the zócalo, where most of the budget hotels are. Take a cab if you can afford it; the combi ride is long (20 min, 30¢) and won't take you all the way to the zócalo. The RUTA 48 bus gets as close as 11 Norte and Reforma, 5 blocks from the zocálo.

BY TRAIN Trains pass through Puebla twice a day on their way to Oaxaca from Mexico City, and vice versa. They're slower than the buses, but if you're dying to take that midnight train, this is your chance. Pay the $11 for a first-class ticket; it's much more comfortable than second class ($6), and you'll be guaranteed some cushioning on your seat. The train for Oaxaca leaves at midnight; the train for Mexico City swings through at 7:20 AM. *9 Nte., at 80 Pte., tel. 22/20-16-64.*

GETTING AROUND

Puebla's streets are confusing at first, but they can be mastered. Use the zócalo as your compass. Streets are organized around the cardinal directions: norte (north), sur (south), oriente (east), and poniente (west). The main street, 5 de Mayo, becomes 16 de Septiembre south of the zócalo. Avenida Reforma becomes Avenida Ávila Camacho after passing the zócalo east-west. Otherwise, all streets are numbered. Even-numbered sur and norte streets (calles) are east of the zócalo, odd-numbered streets are west of it. Even-numbered oriente and poniente avenidas are north of the zócalo, odd-numbered ones south.

BY BUS Puebla has an extensive system of colectivos that run from 6 AM until 11 PM. However, colectivos and combis don't travel the streets right around the zócalo; the closest they come is 11 Pte., about 5 blocks away. A one-way trip costs about 20¢, and it's usually a bumpy, crowded ride.

BY TAXI Taxi fares within the city range from 50¢ to $2. As usual, determine the fare before you get in the cab. A ride to the bus station should cost about $2.

WHERE TO SLEEP

All of the hotels described below are within a few blocks of the zócalo, in the colonial Centro Historico (historical center) of the city. The only hotel anywhere near the CAPU bus station is **Hotel Terminal de Puebla** (Carmen Serdán 5101, tel. 22/32-79-80), where a room for one or two people costs $12.

➤ **UNDER $5** • **Hotel Avenida.** This is the best deal in town: For $3 you get a single or a double room ($5 with bath) and friendly service that borders on motherly. Of course it's best you bring your own towel, soap, and toilet paper. Hot water runs 6-11 AM and 7-11 PM. *5 Pte. 336, tel. 22/32-22-04. 1½ blocks west of cathedral. 52 rooms, 20 with bath. Wheelchair access.*

➤ **UNDER $10** • **Hotel Teresita.** The claustrophobic rooms, resplendent in a strange shade of orange, might send you running, but the price is right—$5 for a single ($7.50 with bath) and $8–$10 for a double with bath. The manager swears there is hot water all the time. 3 Pte. 309, tel. 22/32–70–72. 1½ blocks west of cathedral. 58 rooms, 40 with bath. Laundry, luggage storage. Wheelchair access.

Hotel Venecia. Established in 1897, Hotel Venecia isn't much to look at, but it's clean, and the clientele consists of friendly Mexican families. None of the rooms have baths, but there's hot water all the time. Singles are $5, doubles $7.50. 4 Pte. 716, tel. 22/32–24–69. 2 blocks north and 3 blocks west of zócalo. 24 rooms, none with bath. Luggage storage. Wheelchair access.

➤ **UNDER $15** • **Hotel Imperial.** Go out of your way to stay at this hotel. The owner gives anyone carrying this book a 40% discount, putting the ordinarily pricey rooms in the budget traveler's range. From the busy pool table and restaurant on the first floor to the remodeled split-level rooms complete with TVs, phones, and filtered tap water, you'll feel like you've gone to backpackers' heaven. The owner, Juan José Bretón Avalos (*el Licenciado*), is an expert on Puebla and Oaxaca and has his whole family working at the hotel: Put together, they're the most helpful guides of all Puebla. Discounted prices are $9 for a single, $11.50 for a double, and a complimentary breakfast (7:30–10:30) is thrown in, too. 4 Ote. 212, btw 2 Nte. and 4 Nte., tel. 22/42–49–81. 65 rooms, all with bath. Free laundry (bring your own soap) and luggage storage. Wheelchair access. MC, V.

➤ **UNDER $20** • **Hotel Victoria.** The hallways here are dim, but the colorful tile, quirky furniture, and homey comforters make up for it. Hot water is available only 6 AM–10 AM and 6 PM–10 PM. Singles are $15, doubles $16–$20. 3 Pte. 306, tel. 22/32–89–92. 1½ blocks west of cathedral. 35 rooms, all with bath. Wheelchair access.

Solo travelers may not want to look for lodging west of 7 Nte. The numerous brothels here make for a seedy atmosphere, and even a brief walk in the area can be uncomfortable.

➤ **UNDER $30** • **Hotel Colonial.** This is a favorite of American and European students taking courses at the university across the street. Fittingly, the entire place is done up in colonial style, with the requisite statues, dark wood, and arches. Rooms are spacious, tiled, clean, and fairly quiet. There's also cable TV, room service, a library, money exchange, and a popular restaurant. Many exchange students come in groups and stay for the whole summer, so hang out here if you're thirsting for some non-Spanish-speaking company. To stay here, though, you'll have to cough up $21.50 for a single, $28 for a double. 4 Sur 105, tel. 22/46–46–12. 1 block east of zócalo, across from university. 70 rooms, all with bath. Laundry ($2.50), luggage storage. Reservations advised. AE.

FOOD

Puebla's nuns had a special gift for culinary creation; *mole poblano* (see box Holy Mole, *below*) and *chiles en nogada* (chiles stuffed with beef and covered in a walnut sauce and pomegranate seeds) were both invented in convent kitchens here. For a particularly filling and original lunch, try the *tacos Arabes* (Arabian tacos, with meat and a yogurty sauce, rolled in pita bread); **Taquería La Oriental** (Portal Juárez 107) on the zócalo has some especially good ones for 50¢ each. Oddly enough, these tacos can only be found in Puebla. Several restaurants also serve huge "economical" breakfasts for about $3. If you prefer to eat a little lighter in the morning, bakeries such as **Pan de la Fe** (2 Ote. 208, tel. 22/32–21–37) have *pan dulce* (sweet rolls) and other pastries for 1 peso each. Another sweet experience is a stroll down the **Calle de los Dulces** (6 Ote., btw 5 de Mayo and 4 Nte.), past numerous shops selling Puebla's famous fruit candies. Specialties include *camote* (candied yam) and a meringue concoction called Beso del Ángel (angel's kiss). **Super Churrería** (2 Sur, at 5 Oriente) serves traditional

La Pasita (5 Pte., at 6 Sur) is the only place in the world where they make the drink of the same name, a liqueur made from raisins. They serve $1 shots of La Pasita and other regional liqueurs daily 12:30–5:30.

churros (1 peso) and chocolate (50¢). The twisted, sugary pastries dipped into hot chocolate will send you floating away into ecstasy.

➤ **UNDER $5** • **La Concordia.** Though the TV and the stereo compete for attention in this small, colorful café, the volume is low enough for a relaxed atmosphere. Come for the $2 breakfast, which includes juice or milk, coffee, eggs, and *chilaquiles* (tortilla strips doused with salsa and sour cream). At lunch they serve two types of comida corrida—regular ($2) and *ejecutivo* (executive; $2.50). *2 Ote. 205-A, at 2 Nte., tel 22/46–68–27. 1 block north of zócalo. Open daily 8 AM–10 PM. Wheelchair access.*

Fonda Carolina. This unassuming place, with great service, plastic tablecloths, bullfight paintings on the walls, and pop music in the air, is very popular with students. Their *chilaquiles*, a big, messy plate of tortillas, avocado, shredded chicken, green salsa, and cream, comes with a fruit cocktail and Nescafé or hot chocolate, all for $2. For lunch try the Puebla specialty, *chalupas poblanas* (fried tortillas with sauce and cheese; $2), which includes soup, an entrée, and dessert. *4 Nte. 5, tel. 22/32–23–39. 1 block east of zócalo. Open daily 8 AM–9 PM.*

San Francisco el Alto Mercado (Garibaldi). What used to be a market has now been turned into this enclosed setting for about 15 fondas. In this lively atmosphere, you'll find traditional poblano food, such as a $3.50 plate of chicken mole, rice, beans, and *chiles en nogada* (in season July–Sept.). On weekend nights mariachis play for the working-class crowd (upper-crust poblanos snub the place), and the market ends up resembling a rowdy bar. *14 Ote., at 14 Nte., no phone. 5 blocks north and 6 blocks east of zócalo. Open 24 hrs.*

El Vegetariano. This bare, vegetarian, downtown restaurant just happens to serve great food—they make a popular mole poblano with soy chicken ($2). Other dishes, such as *enchiladas suizas* (cheese enchiladas; $2) or *tacos de champiñones* (cheese and mushroom tacos; $2.50), are also recommended. The menú del día includes soup, salad, an entrée, and a fruit drink for $4. *3 Pte. 525, tel. 22/46–54–62. 3 blocks west of zócalo. Open daily 7:30 AM–10 PM.*

Villa del Mar. People wait in line to lunch at this terrace seafood restaurant. Try the shrimp, octopus, and oyster cocktails ($5), seasoned with cilantro, onion, avocado, chili, and sugar. Another good bet is the shrimp brochette with onion, bacon, and tomatoes ($5). *Juárez 1920,*

Holy Mole

Rumor has it mole was invented by the Aztecs as a topping for that tastiest of meats, human flesh, but the more plausible explanation is as follows: Sor Andrea de la Asunción, an 18th-century nun in the Santa Rosa convent, was given the task of creating a special dish for the Archbishop of Puebla. Wanting to combine the best of Mexican and Spanish cuisine, she began with four types of chiles—mulato, ancho, pasilla, and chipotle—for the Mexican element, and almonds as a symbol of Spain. Believing the sauce was too spicy, Sor Andrea added raisins, plantains, and chocolate to sweeten the kick. Sesame seeds and peanuts were thrown in to thicken the sauce, clove and cinnamon for flavor, and anise to make it all go down easily. The finished product had 18 ingredients, and quickly became a standard of Mexican cuisine.

The word mole may be a garbled version of muele ("grind"), which was what Sor Andrea did with all those ingredients), or the Nahuatl word mollí, which means "hot chile." Today there are as many different moles as there are cooks, but Pueblan restaurants keep a tight hold on what they claim is the original recipe. The Puebla mole festival, when poblanos compete to create the best recipe, is held every weekend of June.

in Zona Esmeralda, tel. 22/42-31-04. Take RUTA 7 combi from 11 Ote. and 16 de Septiembre, or walk 8 blocks west from zócalo, then 3 blocks south to Juárez. Open daily 10-5:30.

➢ **UNDER $10** • **Chesa Veglia/Casa Vieja.** This Swiss-style restaurant with an alpine theme serves up treats such as scallops "cordon bleu" ($5), and *pollo suizo* (chicken in a mushroom, cream, and paprika sauce; $6). Pastas, soups, and salads are also on the menu. Cheaper options include *consome poblano* (vegetable broth with melted cheese; $2). This is one of the few Pueblan restaurants open late, and live music starts at 10 PM Thursday-Sunday. *2 Ote. 208, tel. 22/32-16-41. 1 block north and ½ block east of zócalo. Open daily 7 AM-1 AM.*

Fonda de Santa Clara. Typical comida poblana is served in this famous restaurant, decorated with *papel picado* (traditional Mexican cut paper) and *lupe muñecas* (papier-mâché dolls). Although it caters to tourists and the food isn't cheap, you'd be hard pressed to find their seasonal specials anywhere else. The menu features *gusanos de maguey con salsa borracha* (maguey worms in tequila sauce; $10) in April and May, and *chapulines* (grasshoppers; $6) during October and November. The *café de olla* (coffee flavored wth cinnamon and chocolate; $1) will wake you from your post-meal coma. *3 Pte. 307, 2 blocks west of zócalo, tel. 22/42-26-59. Open Tues.-Sun. noon-11 PM. Wheelchair access. Also at 3 Pte. 920. Open Wed.-Mon. 8:30 AM-11 PM. AE, MC, V.*

Restaurant Hotel Colonial. This place is packed for lunch, and the clientele includes regulars who come for the food, and exchange students who come to socialize. The menú del día ($6), served 1:30-5, is enough food to immobilize you for several days. It includes soup, rice with fried plantains, a vegetable dish, an entrée with black beans on the side, dessert, and coffee. *4 Sur 105, tel. 22/46-46-12. 1 block east of zócalo. Open daily 7 AM-10 PM.*

CAFES Cafés fill up at night with students and artists. Coffee drinks include a shot of alcohol as often as not, and many cafés feature a guitarist or other entertainment.

Café Aroma. The Aroma is a romantic little place with brass lanterns and intimate tables. A cup of coffee here is less than $1 ($1.50 with alcohol), and appetizers such as *chalupas* (fried tortillas) are available. They also sell coffee beans from the nearby town of Villa Juárez ($3 per kilo). *3 Pte. 520-A, no phone.*

Café del Artista. Perched atop the *Plazuela del Torno,* this café offers a laid-back atmosphere and live music (Thursday-Sunday at 6 PM), accompanied by a killer cappuccino for $1.20. *8 Nte. 410, at 6 Ote, tel. 22/42-15-27. Open Mon.-Wed. 4 PM-midnight, Thurs.-Sat. 4 PM-2 AM.*

Teorema. This dimly lit café/bookstore has the feel of a literary salon: If clients aren't discussing the latest literary trend, they sure put up a good front. Daily live music and occasional poetry readings take place on the small stage from about 8:30 PM on. The menu, complete with a poem, includes coffees (try the *Ira bien,* with five liquors and cream, for $2.50), desserts ($2), and beer and wine ($1.50). *Reforma, at 7 Nte., tel. 22/42-10-14. $1-$2 cover, depending on show. Bookstore open 9:30-2:30 and 4:30-9. Café open until 1 AM.*

WORTH SEEING

Most sights are free, and the ones that aren't reduce admission with any student ID. Almost all museums are free on Sundays and closed Mondays, with the exception of the **Museo Amparo,** which is free Mondays and closed Tuesdays. **La China Poblana** restaurant (6 Nte. 1, no phone) is a must-see for a dose of folkloric overload. Everywhere you look there are *papel picado,* tiles, painted wood, and other assorted kitsch, topped off by the life-size mannequin dressed in a flashy China Poblana (*see box* La China Poblana, *below*) costume in the front room.

AFRICAN SAFARI This zoo on the outskirts of Puebla is considered by many the best zoo in the country. Founded in 1972, this wild animal reserve lets animals wander around free— but don't worry, you get to visit from the safety of a car or bus. The zoo has more than 3,000 animals and approximately 250 species, and is well worth your while. African Safari Buses leave Puebla's CAPU daily 10-4. The bus ride costs $1.75, and the zoo $4. For more information, call 22/35-87-13 or 22/35-87-00.

CASA DE ALFENIQUE Known as the wedding-cake house, perhaps because it looks like something straight out of "Hansel and Gretel," this 17th-century mansion is now the state museum. First-floor exhibits focus on Puebla's history and archaeology. The second floor is a re-creation of a colonial-era residence. A highlight of the museum's collection is the original dress of the legendary China Poblana (see box La China Poblana, below). *4 Ote. 416, tel. 22/41–42–96. 2 blocks north and 1 block east of zócalo. Museum admission: $1, 50¢ with student ID. Open Tues.–Sun. 10–5.*

CASA DE LOS HERMANOS SERDAN Known as the **Museo de la Revolución,** the house of Aquiles Serdán and his sister Carmen now honors a group of revolutionaries who perished here during a 14-hour gunfight with the policemen and 500 federal army soldiers sent to arrest them on conspiracy charges. The building's facade was left intact, and still bears the violent marks of the fight. In the parlor, pierced mirrors still hang on bullet-riddled walls, and broadsheets calling for revolution, published by the Serdán family, are on display. The assassination of Aquiles Serdán and his followers is believed by many to be the event that launched the Revolution of 1910. *6 Ote. 206, tel. 22/42–10–76. 3 blocks north of zócalo. Admission: $1. Open Tues.–Sun. 10–4:30.*

The city of Puebla has been famous since colonial times for its richly decorated and glazed ceramic work; brightly colored tiles decorate many of the city's historic buildings.

CATEDRAL DE LA CONCEPCION INMACULADA Construction on the cathedral began in 1575, and it's clear why it took almost two centuries to complete: This is one of the largest cathedrals in Mexico, with 14 chapels and the highest bell towers in the country. One tower is bell-less; according to one legend, the extra weight would have caused the tower to sink into an underground stream below. Another version claims that the builders simply ran out of money. The massive, gray-blue stone building is an example of the *mudéjar* (Moorish-influenced) style and boasts marble floors and a beautiful altar carved from gray onyx, as well as 300-year-old paintings. The altar at the center also functions as a crypt: The bishops of Puebla are buried here, and every November 2 (Day of the Dead) the crypt is opened to the public. Tours in Spanish take place in the afternoon. *On zócalo. Admission free. Open daily 10:30–noon and 4–7.*

CONVENTO SECRETO DE SANTA MONICA It is said that this convent went underground after the constitutional reform of 1857, which provided for the confiscation of church lands and the abolishment of ecclesiastical privileges. In the 1920s, during the persecution of the clergy by the Calles government, its nuns completely withdrew from the outside world. Sympathizers brought them food through secret traps; today guides show visitors the peep holes through which the nuns watched mass next door, and the underground crypt where they were buried. The heart of the convent's founder, some 130 years old, is kept on gruesome display here, and religious art fills the twisting and turning hallways. The velvet paintings from the

La China Poblana

Pueblans still speak of Mirra, the China Poblana (Chinese Woman of Puebla). One version of her legend claims that she was kidnapped as a child from Delhi and later sold to the viceroy of Mexico. Another version insists she was a Mongol princess, captured by pirates from Acapulco. Either way, she was sold to a Puebla merchant and his wife, who adopted and raised her. La China adapted her native dress to that of Mexico, and, according to the legend, the resulting costume was so beautiful and unusual that local women began to imitate her. A modern version of that dress, elaborately embroidered and sequined, is worn by dancers performing the jarabe tapatío (hat dance). As for Mirra herself, she is said to be buried underneath the altar of one of Puebla's churches.

1850s are startling; as you move from one side of the painting to the other, the faces and feet of the subjects seem to change position, and landscapes shift to the other side of the canvas.

Around the corner, on 5 de Mayo, is the **Señor de las Maravillas.** Crowds of Mexicans visit this statue of Christ, which is believed to perform miracles. The figure is said to be made from corn paste, but it looks remarkably similar to plaster. According to legend, the statue was fashioned by a fugitive carpenter hiding out in the convent. He and the Mother Superior both dreamed of the Señor on the same night, after which she ordered him to create this figure or be turned over to the police. *18 Pte., at 5 de Mayo, 103, tel. 22/32–01–78. 9 blocks north of zócalo. Admission to convent: $1. Open Tues.–Sun. 10–5. Mass twice on weeknights, 4 times on Sun.*

EX-CONVENTO DE SANTA ROSA Abandoned during the early 1860s, the convent today is almost completely restored. The centerpiece is a huge, tiled kitchen, the birthplace of mole poblano. Guides (who give tours only in Spanish) are well versed in its legends. The convent is now also the home of the **Museo de Artesanías,** featuring folk art from Puebla state's seven regions: Huochinango, Teziutlán, Ciudad Serdán, Cholula, Puebla, Izucar de Matamoros, and Tehuacán. There's also a gift shop, which sells expensive ceramics. For tours in English, call ahead to see if guides are available. *3 Nte. 1203, tel. 22/46–22–71. 1 block west and 6 blocks north of zócalo. Admission: 50¢. Open Tues.–Sun. 10–4:30.*

FUERTES DE LORETO Y GUADALUPE A popular destination for both poblanos and tourists, the forts are the main attraction of a hilltop park complex. **Fuerte Loreto** is dedicated to the Battle of Puebla (May 5, 1862), celebrated every Cinco de Mayo, and the original cannons used to defeat the French army now guard the victorious General Zaragoza's grave. Other aspects of the battle are exhibited in the **Museo de Historia** within the fort, but don't make a special trip just to see the museum. Across the plaza is the **Fuerte de Guadalupe,** which is not as well preserved. The complex features a cluster of museums: the **Museo de Antropología Regional,** which has artifacts from the early Puebla Valley cultures; the **Museo de Historia Natural,** with realistic wildlife scenes; and the excellent **planetario** (planetarium), which has shows for stargazers every hour between noon and 6 PM. Admission prices are separate for each museum, and range from $1 for the Museo de Historia Natural to $2 for the planetarium. *Take FUERTES combi from 8 Nte., at 10 Ote., or RUTA 72 combi from anywhere on 5 de Mayo after 8 Pte. Ride costs 30¢. Get off at Monumento Zaragoza; museums are to the east.*

IGLESIA DE SAN FRANCISCO Built in the 18th century, this church houses the preserved body of Franciscan Friar Sebastián de Aparicio, who is credited with convincing the Indians to stop carrying heavy loads on their backs and let oxen do the work instead. His skeleton is covered with a monk's robe, and there's a mask on his face because so many people have picked pieces from it. As a result, you can only tell he's a mummy by looking at his feet: His decomposed toes peek out from below his robe. Above the friar's body hangs the famous Conquistadora—Hernán Cortés's personal statue of the Virgin Mary. Her bloodstained gown is enough to make you shudder. Both the Franciscan and the Conquistadora are at the front of the church, to the left of the altar. *8 Nte., at Blvd. 5 de Mayo. 3 blocks east and 5 blocks north of zócalo. Admission free. Open daily 9–7:30.*

MUSEO AMPARO The building housing this airy, terra-cotta-colored museum used to be a hospital—today it's used for more leisurely purposes. The museo specializes in both Virreinal and Mesoamerican art, and beautiful examples of Maya, Olmec, and other artifacts are on display. Signs in English and Spanish guide you through the exhibits, and you can also listen to a recorded audio tour ($1 plus $1 deposit). Interactive computers inform visitors about selected pieces in the museum. The museum also houses a library with tons of information on Puebla's colonial past. You can sit and read here for as long as you like, but you can't check out books. *2 Sur 708, at 9 Pte., tel. 22/46–42–00. 2½ blocks south of zócalo. Admission: $2, $1 with student ID; free Mon. Museum open Wed.–Mon. 10–5. Library open 10–6. Free tour Sun. at noon. Wheelchair access.*

PALACIO DEL ARZOBISPO This grand, two-story building was once the residence of Juan de Palafox y Mendoza, the Archbishop of Puebla. It now houses the **Casa de la Cultura,** with a concert and lecture hall on the first floor and art exhibits on the second. Also on the second floor is the luxurious **Biblioteca Palafoxiana,** a library that dates back to 1646. Monks used to study on the uncomfortable-looking pull-out benches on the walls. Next door to the library is the newly opened **Sala del Tesoro Bibliográfico,** with rotating displays of antique books. The oldest book in the collection is a 1493 history of the world from the beginning of time to the date of publication. Miguel Ramírez Meya, the guy in charge, is hard of hearing and very protective of *his* library and books, but he's more than willing to lecture you on anything to do with the library and knows a lot of interesting tidbits. *5 Ote. 5, tel. 22/46–56–13. Across from cathedral. Admission free; $1 for the library. Open Tues.–Sun. 10–5.*

TEMPLO DE SANTO DOMINGO This church dates from 1659 and acquired its fame because of the **Capilla del Rosario** (Chapel of the Rosary), a baroque chapel with a surfeit of gold leaf and glitter. The figure of the Virgin is bedecked with precious and semiprecious jewels. Next door is the **Museo Bello Zetina** (tel. 22/32–47–20), which has an interesting display of religious art and antiques. *5 de Mayo 407, 1 block north of zócalo. Admission free. Open daily 10–4 (museum closed Mon.)*

CHEAP THRILLS

Those interested in Catholic paraphernalia will find plenty in Puebla's stores, including a wide variety of incense, rosaries, and electric "candles" with lights that flicker (for those opposed to the shameless consumption of wax). At **Librería Mariana** (Calles 2 Sur and 3 Ote., across from zócalo) you can buy prayer cards (20¢ each) identifying all those saints you've seen in churches around the city.

FESTIVALS **Cinco de Mayo.** On May 5 the city commemorates the 1862 Battle of Puebla, in which the Mexican army defeated French invaders. It is a day of celebration and special events, and the city center is transformed for a day as fireworks, a military parade, sporting events, and performances of traditional music take over.

Festival de San Agustín. Pueblans celebrate with music, dancing, and fireworks during most of August. On the 26th (St. Augustine's feast day) it is customary to prepare chiles en nogada (*see* Food, *above*), invented by the nuns of the Santa Monica convent.

Fiesta de San Francisco de Asis-Cuetzalán. The feast day of St. Francis on the 4th of October is the annual occasion for two weeks of indigenous dances, a *tianguis* (open-air market), and general merrymaking in the tiny town of Cuetzalán (*see* Near Puebla, *below*). Dancers wear traditional white robes and *tocas de lana* (large, turban-like hats almost 40 centimeters high).

Carnaval de Huejotzingo. Every year before Lent the residents of Huejotzingo (*see* Near Puebla, *below*) reenact the kidnapping of the daughter of a *corregidor* (magistrate) against the backdrop of the Mexican triumph against the French. The costumes and masks are elaborate, and the festival is noisy and sometimes dangerous—the tradition of shooting colored gun-powder at celebrants often results in injuries.

SHOPPING

The *majolica* techniques developed in Talavera de la Reina, Spain, are used for making tiles and other ceramicware in Puebla. You can learn about the process at **Uriarte** (4 Pte. 911, tel. 22/32–15–98), a factory and shop devoted exclusively to beautiful Talavera ceramics. Free tours in English and Spanish take place daily from 9 to 6. If the workers aren't too busy, they may even let you sit at the potter's wheel and make your own version. You'll find more Talavera pieces, including dishes and vases, at **El Parian** (6 Nte., btw 4 Ote. and 2 Ote.), a market that's been around since 1796. Nowadays the more artistic pieces are mixed in with a lot of cheap souvenirs, but it's a fun place to poke around and haggle. Across the street is the **Barrio del Artista** (8 Nte., at Av. 6 Ote.), where painters and sculptors open their studios to visitors. On 5 Ote. and 6 Nte. you'll find an antiques market known as the **Mercado de Los Sapos.**

AFTER DARK

Unless watching couples in various stages of passionate embrace is your idea of fun, the zócalo is not the happening place to be at night. Less voyeuristic fun can be had in the **Zona Esmer-**

alda, 10 blocks east of the zócalo on Avenida Juárez, where Puebla's youth come to party. Among the restaurants and bars that line the avenue, **Señor Frog's** (Juárez, past Blvd. Atlixo) will swallow you up for a few hours and spit you out, staggering, to the nearest taxi. Other popular options include **Freeday's** (Circuito, at 29 Sur, tel. 22/37-74-06), which has live rock Wednesday–Sunday and no cover. Diehards can also try **La Mulada** (Recta a Cholula 3500, Local 60, tel. 22/84-65-80), open Monday–Saturday until 3 AM. Getting to these last two places is sort of tricky, so it's best to take a taxi ($2-$3 from downtown).

For a quieter scene, **Las Buhardillas** (Juárez 2915, tel. 22/30-54-35) has live jazz or chamber music every night. **Antillanos** (Juárez 2109, tel. 22/46-58-47) is a must for Caribbean music lovers, with live salsa bands and an enthusiastic chain-smoking crowd that loves to dance. Cover is a mere $1. If you just want to drink, **María Bonita** (Av. 31 Pte., at 2 Sur), not far from the Plaza Dorada, is filled with college students on Friday and Saturday nights. Weekday nights, everyone heads to coffee bars such as **Teorema** (see Cafés, above) and **La Bóveda** (Plaza Los Sapos), open Tuesday–Saturday 3 PM–2 AM.

CINEMAS/THEATERS **Cinemática Luis Buñuel,** in the Casa de la Cultura (Av. 5 Ote. 5, tel. 22/46-36-32), has a tiny movie theater that shows international films Thursday–Sunday at 5 PM and 7 PM. New releases from the U.S. are shown at **Cinemas Doradas 1 y 2** (tel. 22/46-83-52) in the Plaza Dorada shopping center. **Multicinemas** (5 de Mayo 907, tel. 22/46-02-74) also has a good repertoire of Hollywood flicks. Both **Teatro Espacio 1900** (2 Ote. 412, tel. 22/46-83-53) and **Teatro Hermanos Soler** (5 Pte. 318, tel. 22/46-98-15) put on live theater and concerts. Teatro Hermanos Soler also has a post-show peña, at which people are invited to play music, sing, recite poetry, and generally make public spectacles of themselves from about 8:30 PM until the last vociferous poet has gone home. The second drink is always on the house. Call ahead to find out if there will be a cover.

OUTDOOR ACTIVITIES

Many people travel to Puebla with the sole purpose of attacking **Volcán Popocatépetl.** Officially you need to be a registered hiker to climb Popocatépetl. Moreover, it's a hassle to reach without a car. But if you're determined, take a bus from CAPU to Chalco, where you can transfer to Amecameca, and take another bus to Tlamacas; the whole trip takes about 3½ hours and costs less than $4. In Tlamacas there's a hostel serving mostly climbers that charges $3 a night for a dorm bed. It's best to reach the hostel in the early evening the day before you plan to climb. Bring food for a couple of days. The easiest route to the summit of the volcano, **La Ruta de las Cruces,** takes you to the top in about seven hours. The climb down should take three hours. Most people climb on the weekends, when there are guides available. For more information call the **Legión Alpina de Puebla** (tel. 22/32-39-00).

Near Puebla

CHOLULA

Only 20 minutes by bus from Puebla, the town of Cholula is gringo friendly, with signs and menus in English, and has plenty of restaurants that accept credit cards. Best of all, Cholulans are extremely helpful and much less harried than their Pueblan neighbors. The women of this town are much more open to conversation than in many other places, an aspect of life here that will put female travelers at ease.

Pueblans say that Cholulans counter the excessive religious devotion of their town by having the same number of bars as churches. That way they can strike the perfect balance between faith and sin.

Before the Conquest, Cholula reportedly had hundreds of temples and was a sacred city that rivaled Teotihuacán as a cultural center. It is often referred to as the City of Churches, because, according to legend, conquering Spaniards built a church for each day of the year atop the ruins of Cholulan temples. Although that number is exaggerated, there are approximately 130 churches in Cholula and the surrounding areas today. The view from atop the **Great**

Pyramid of Cholula reveals a panorama of steeples and spires. Crowning the pyramid is a blue and white church called **Nuestra Señora de los Remedios**.

COMING AND GOING In Puebla, catch a PUEBLA/CHOLULA combi at the bus stop on 11 Nte., at 12 Pte. (80¢), or catch an **Estrella de Oro** or **Estrella Roja** bus from CAPU (*see* Coming and Going, Puebla, *above*). These buses leave about every 10 minutes and cost 50¢. The bus stop in Cholula is 3 blocks north of the zócalo.

WHERE TO SLEEP Perhaps because of its proximity to Puebla, Cholula is short on affordable hotels. **Hotel Reforma** (4 Sur 101, tel. 22/47–01–49) is run by a friendly, talkative señora who will urge you to check out her husband's photographic collage of all the churches in the Cholula area. Rooms run $6–$11 for a single or double with bath. **Hotel Las Américas** (14 Ote. 5, tel. 22/47–22–75) charges $8 for a single, $13 for a double. It's close to the nightclub zone, but a 10-minute hike from the zócalo and most bus stops. A pricier option, but well worth the splurge, is **Hotel Calli Quetzalcoatl** (tel. 22/4–15–55), right on the zócalo under the portal. They charge $21 for singles, $25 for doubles. All three hotels are wheelchair accessible.

Campsites are available at the invitingly named **Trailer Park Las Américas** (tel. 22/47–01–34), a five minute bus ride outside Cholula on the road to Puebla; they charge $4 for two people to pitch a tent. There are hot showers and swimming facilities, but it's not the most scenic spot.

FOOD Restaurants are scattered around the city. Right on the zócalo under the portal are several serving Italian food: At **Los Jarrones** (tel. 22/47–02–92) you can get good pizza, served with salad, spaghetti, and a drink for $2, or huge burgers for under $2. **El Portal,** two restaurants down, offers substantial comidas corridas for $3. Two traditional restaurants near the pyramid, **La Lunita** and **La Pirámide**, are popular with locals and serve mole, pipian, and *filete milanesa* (breaded steak) for $3. Slightly more expensive is **Chialingo** (7 Pte. 113, 4 blocks south of zócalo, tel. 22/47–28–31), where you can sit under a big tree amid the bougainvillea and eat pasta, crepes ($2.50), or steak ($6). Chialingo is open 1–10 daily.

WORTH SEEING

➤ **CHIPILO** • Smack between the villages of Santa María Tonantzintla and Acetepec (*see below*), this town of blond, blue-eyed Italian immigrants was founded in 1882 when Porfirio Díaz imported a group of white, Catholic Venetians in an attempt to "save the nation." In addition to Spanish, the inhabitants also speak an Italian dialect. Chipilo's excellent cheese and other dairy products and Italian restaurants are famous throughout the region. **El Correo Español**, on the road to Chipilo serves excellent food for less than $10. From Cholula, take a CHIPILO bus from 5 de Mayo and 6 Poniente.

➤ **GREAT PYRAMID** • Cholula's Great Pyramid actually consists of three pyramids built on top of one another. The final pyramid would have been the largest in the world if it had been finished; its base is 4,500 square meters. The construction was started by the Cholultecas, a mix of people from several regions of Mexico, but was ended around AD 650 when they were attacked and conquered by warriors from nearby Cacaxtla (*see* Near Tlaxcala, *above*). For a $4.50 admission fee, visitors can explore nearly 8 kilometers of underground tunnels daily 10–4. To reach the pyramid from the zócalo, walk east (away from the volcanoes) along Avenida Morelos for 3 blocks. A museum across the road from the pyramid explains what you'll see in the caverns. Guides, available at the tunnel entrance, charge $9 for an interesting one-hour tour (it's $10 for the English version). Unfortunately, owing to the many flash-toting tourists, the murals depicting a Cholulan drinking party are off-limits to the public.

➤ **SANTA MARIA TONANTZINTLA/SAN FRANCISCO ACATEPEC** • These villages, 3 kilometers south of Cholula, are home to a pair of unique churches. Santa María Tonantzintla's **Iglesia de Tonantzintla** took almost 300 years to build, and is the only church in the area designed and built exclusively by Indians. The interior is a curious mix of baroque and indigenous aesthetics—an explosion of bright colors and gilt. Note that the angels and cherubs have Indian features, as does the Jesus on the cross to the left of the altar, and that the statue of the Virgin is framed in neon—wow. The graves of children taken by an early death are marked by the stones in the path leading up to the church.

The village of **Acatepec** boasts a 16th-century church, decorated on the outside with blue, yellow, and green Talavera tiles and twisting columns on the bell towers. Inside, the newly remodeled interior (the original was destroyed in a fire) rivals that of Santa María Tonantzintla's church in amount of gilt per square inch. You can visit the churches daily 10–6, unless there's a mass. Red and white CHIPILO buses leave from the corner of 5 de Mayo and 6 Poniente in Cholula. Ask the driver to let you off at the churches.

➤ **ZOCALO** • Down the hill, 7 blocks east of the Great Pyramid, is Cholula's zócalo, which supposedly has the longest *portal* (porch) in Latin America. Along the portal are several shops, boutiques, and restaurants. Try to visit the zócalo on Sunday (market day), or a saint's day celebration; considering the number of churches in the area, each celebrating at least 10 feast days annually, finding one isn't difficult. Facing the zócalo is the mustard-yellow **Convento Franciscano**, built in 1549 on the site of a temple dedicated to Quetzalcoatl; Cortés's troops and their Tlaxcaltecan allies massacred thousands of Cholulans here. The **Capilla Real** (Royal Chapel) inside the church is unique in that it has 49 domes, inspired by the Great Mosque of Córdoba, Spain.

AFTER DARK With the **Universidad de las Américas** on the east side of town, Cholula is a happening place where even Pueblans go for a change of scene. **Keops** (14 Ote., at 5 de Mayo) is a bright purple building that houses the area's only gay disco. Thursday and Friday nights see the best barhopping; the place to go is **Wilo** (tel. 22/47–21–06), with no cover charge and beers for $1. The place is jammed around 11 PM Thursday–Saturday, and the owner, best known as *el chofo,* says he'll give 30% discount on drinks if you come with this guide. For those drunken hunger pangs, **Cielito Lindo** next door offers free *botanas* (snacks: tacos, quesadillas) for as long as you consume their beer.

TEHUACAN

At one time people from all over Mexico traveled to Tehuacán to "take the waters" and enjoy the warm climate. While still famous for its bubbling waters, Tehuacán is now more of a stop on the way to Oaxaca than a destination in itself. Visitors are rarely seen here, so each new arrival is an object of interest for townspeople.

Northwest of the city are the bottling plants of **Peñafiel** and **Garci-Crespo**: Large industrial sites where water is bottled from a spring past the plant. These, however, can only be visited during Semana Santa (the week preceding Easter). Farther north is the town of San Lorenzo, where **Balneario San Lorenzo** park (admission: $1.50; open weekdays 6–6) features several large, natural spring-water pools. Locals visit this park to swim "where the water is born," picnic, and fill up on sparkling mineral water at the drinking fountain across the street. If you bring your own padlock, the park also has a place to store your stuff while you swim. To get here, catch a SAN LORENZO bus (25¢) heading north from any bus stop along Calle 3. Other sights within the city include the **Ex-Convento del Carmen** (Reforma, at 2 Ote., tel. 238/2–40–45; open Tues.–Sun. 10–5), which houses the **Museo del Valle de Tehuacán**. Though there are some interesting pre-Columbian artifacts, the museum consists mostly of stones, husks, and pods, and isn't worth the $1.25 admission.

The **Iglesia del Carmen** and the massive baroque cathedral, both across the street from the zócalo, testify to the symbolic significance of the feminine in Mexican Catholicism. Altars and walls feature paintings and statues of the Virgin Mary and several female saints. Mass is held at the cathedral hourly 6 AM–1 PM on Sundays. Diagonally across from the cathedral is the **Casa del Gobierno** (open weekdays 9 AM–3 PM), a baroque building covered with Talavera tiles. The Casa contains murals that were the collaborative efforts of several artists, including Desiderio Xochitiotzín of Tlaxcala, who studied with Diego Rivera.

COMING AND GOING Autobuses del Oriente (ADO) buses leave for Tehuacán (2 hrs, $5) from Puebla's CAPU every 20 minutes 6 AM–9 PM. From Tehuacán, buses run to Mexico City (4 hrs, $10.50), Oaxaca (6 hrs, $13), and Veracruz (4 hrs, $9). The bus station in Tehuacán (Independencia Nte. 119, tel. 238/2–19–36) is two blocks from the zócalo, and everything except the bottling plants is within walking distance. The main streets are Independencia and Reforma.

WHERE TO SLEEP Hotels are numerous in Tehuacán, and several bargains are available. **Hotel Madrid** (Calle 3 Sur 105, tel. 238/3-15-24) has a beautiful courtyard, and although the singles are very small and the communal bathrooms have seen better days, they're still a steal at $4; doubles are $10. The restaurant/hotel **Casa de Huéspedes** (Reforma Nte. 213, tel. 238/2-02-20) is hard to notice under the large Corona sign, but it has a friendlier staff and is only slightly more expensive; singles without bath are $7, doubles $17. Both hotels are wheelchair accessible.

FOOD The regional specialty is *mole de cadera,* a goat-meat stew only available in November (the goats have to be fed a special diet for six months beforehand). Around the 15th a woman nicknamed La Negrita serves the dish in the patio of the apartment complex next to Mercería el Botón (2 Pte. 221, at Carmen Serdán). Here, the meal costs $10—not bad when you compare it to the $17 most restaurants in the area charge. Cheaper food is available year-round at the family-owned **Restaurant Mary** (Independencia Nte. 130, no phone). It's across the street from the bus station, and sells filling breakfasts for $2, or comida corrida (including soup, rice, an entrée, and dessert) for $3.50. At **Hotel Iberia** (Independencia Nte. 217, tel. 238/3-15-00; open daily 8 AM–9:30 PM) the comida corrida ($7) includes paella every Thursday and Sunday.

ELSEWHERE NEAR PUEBLA

AMOZOC This town, 16 kilometers east of Puebla, is famous for the intricate silver work created for *charrería* (tack for rodeos). As a result, an abundance of spur-theme souvenirs is available. The second-class bus marked AMOZOC leaves from the corner of 14 Oriente and 18 Norte in Puebla ($1). The last returning bus for Puebla leaves at about 6 PM from the main plaza in Amozoc.

TEPEACA AND TECALI DE HERRERA The main plaza of Tepeaca was an important stagecoach stop during the colonial era, and there is a huge traditional market here every Friday. Architecture buffs will note that the Moorish clock tower is one of only two octagonal structures in Mexico.

Nearby onyx quarries give **Tecali,** 10 kilometers from Tepeaca, its name (Nahautl for "onyx"). The town is home to numerous onyx craftsmen and their workshops. Catch a TECALI or CUAWITAN-CHAN bus from Calle 11 Sur, on the west side of the Paseo Bravo in Tehuacán (30¢), and make sure the driver knows where you're going. From Puebla's CAPU, you can also catch Autobuses Unidos to Tepeaca. The ride costs $4.50, and buses leave every 12 minutes 4 AM–10 PM.

HUEJOTZINGO The main attraction of this little village is the imposing **Ex-monasterio Franciscano** on the zócalo. The church was one of the first built by the Spaniards and doubled as a fort. Today it houses a museum (open Tues.–Sun. 10–5), and admission is less than $1. Visit Huejotzingo early on Saturday, when the market is held. If you're in the area before Lent, come for the famous *Carnaval* (*see* Festivals, Puebla, *above*). From Puebla's CAPU, take an **Estrella de Oro** bus (60¢), which runs daily 6 AM–7 PM.

CUETZALAN Although this town is four hours from Puebla, it's worth visiting if you have time, as the indigenous population has preserved many of its traditional customs. The best day to visit is Sunday, market day, when the Totonacas and Nahoas come down from the *cerro* (hill)—the men dressed in striking *huipiles* (embroidered tunics), and the women in elaborate, towering headdresses. Most people attend a Catholic mass given in Totonac, the local language, after which there's a traditional dance in the zócalo. On October 4, the feast day of St. Francis is celebrated (*see* Festivals, *above*). A fairly obscure archaeological site, **Yohualichán,** is also in the area. The place to stay here is **Hotel Posada Viky** (Guadalupe Victoria 16, tel. 233/1-02-72), which charges $4 per person. Take a **VIA** bus from Puebla's CAPU terminal to Cuetzalán ($1). Buses depart daily 6:20 AM–7:15 PM.

Taxco

Taxco is a city of twisting, cobblestoned streets, red-tile colonial houses, silversmiths' shops, and, of course, busload upon busload of tourists, most of them hell-bent on bringing half of the town's silver supply home in their carry-on luggage. The town, so picturesque it hardly seems real, was built in a small cleft in the Sierra Madre mountains. As the city grows, it creeps higher into the mountains, and now many streets sport steep grades and sharp right-angle turns—unique and inviting, but unnavigable in a wheelchair. Anyone else will find this large town manageable, however, and may be surprised by its small-town atmosphere. Discover this for yourself any evening in the **Plaza Borda**, the peaceful zócalo, where local families mingle and gossip among the wrought-iron benches and well-kept walkways.

Overlooking this square is the **Catedral de Santa Prisca**, Taxco's incredibly ornate, pink-stone cathedral—a testament to the silver industry that sustains this town. Cortés's men set up the first mine in the Americas here in 1531, but it was only briefly profitable, and the aquaducts arching over the city's western entrance are the sole architectural remains of their stay. Following a 200-year lull, however, a more lucrative silver vein was found—this time by José de la Borda. According to local legend, the Frenchman accidentally discovered this vein when his horse stumbled on a rocky pathway. On this very spot stands Santa Prisca Cathedral, Borda's ostentatious gift to the city, and the source of the local aphorism: "If God gives to Borda, Borda gives to God." The Borda family also built a few of the mansions that surround the zócalo, but the restaurants and shops that now inhabit these buildings indirectly owe their existence to yet another foreign fortune hunter, U.S. college professor William Spratling. Spratling settled here in the 1930s, and his innovations in handwrought silver design inspired the tourist industry that thrives here today.

BASICS

CASAS DE CAMBIO Silver shops usually accept U.S. dollars, but you can change money at the banks along Cuauhtémoc, the street that connects Plaza Borda with the smaller Plazuela San Juan. **Banco Confia** (Plaza Borda 2, tel. 762/2–01–92) exchanges money weekdays 8:30–3. **Monedas Continentales** (Plazuela de San Juan 5, tel. 762/2–12–42), open weekdays 9–3 and 4–7, Saturdays 9–2, also changes traveler's checks and dollars. The ATM at **Banamex** (Plazuela del Convento 2, down Juárez from zócalo) accepts Plus, Cirrus, Visa, and MasterCard.

EMERGENCIES The number for **police** is 762/2–00–07; for the **Cruz Roja** (ambulance), call 762/2–32–32.

MAIL The post office is next to the Estrella de Oro bus station. They will hold mail sent to you at the following address for up to 10 days: Lista de Correos, Taxco, Guerrero, CP 40200, México. *Av. de Los Plateros 124, no phone. Open weekdays 8–7, Sat. 9–1.*

MEDICAL AID There are lots of pharmacies near the zócalo and the Plazuela de San Juan. A particularly well-stocked option is **Farmacia Guadalupana** (Hidalgo 8, tel. 762/2–03–95; open daily 8:30 AM–10 PM), just past the Plazuela de San Juan. For more urgent medical attention, the **Clínica de Especialidades** offers 24-hour emergency care. *Av. de Los Plateros, near Hotel Posada de la Misión, tel. 762/2–11–11.*

PHONES There are working pay phones on the zócalo and all over Taxco, where you can make collect or credit card calls. A more expensive option is to place your call from **Farmacia de Cristo**, down the street from Plazuela de San Juan. Collect calls cost $3–$5. *Hidalgo 18, tel. 762/2–11–19. Open daily 9–8:30.*

VISITOR INFORMATION Taxco's tourist office is run by a helpful, English-speaking staff. *Av. de Los Plateros 1, tel. 762/2–07–98. From Plaza Borda, ZOCALO combi to gas station. Open daily 9–6.*

COMING AND GOING

BY BUS Taxco has two bus stations, both on Avenida de Los Plateros. **Lineas Unidas del Sur** station (also called Flecha Roja), a few blocks downhill from Plaza Borda, offers first- and sec-

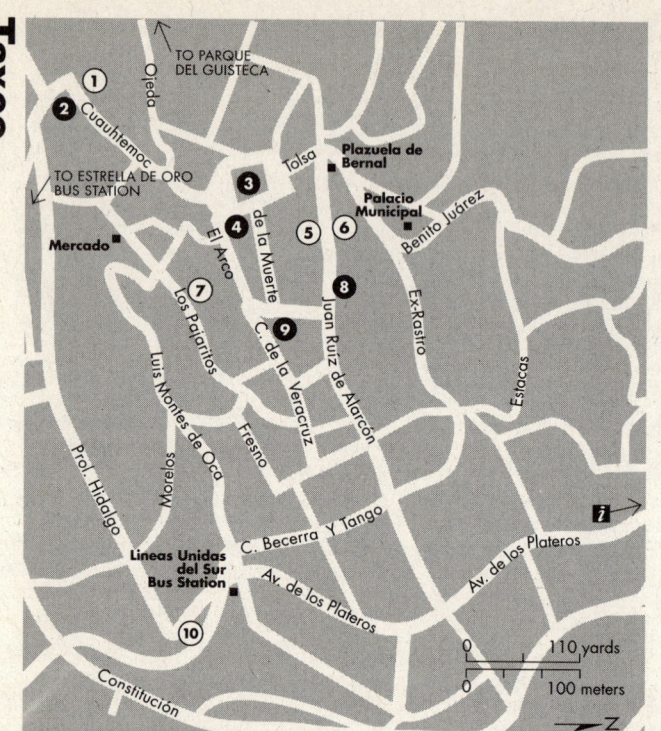

ond-class service (both with air-conditioning). *De lujo* (first-class) buses go to Mexico City (2½ hrs, $7) and Cuernavaca (2 hrs, $5). *Ordinario* (second-class) service to Mexico City is $5; to Cuernavaca, $3. Only ordinario buses go to Acapulco (5 hrs, $12) and Chilpancingo (3 hrs, $7). *Av. de Los Plateros 104, tel. 762/2–01–31.*

The first-class **Estrella de Oro** bus depot (Av. de Los Plateros 126, tel. 762/2–06–48) is 1 kilometer south of the Lineas Unidas station; the LOS ARCOS combi runs between the two. Five buses a day leave for Mexico City: two *plus* (2½ hrs, $6) and three *primera* (2½ hrs, $5). To reach Plaza Borda from either station, catch a ZOCALO combi (10 min, 20¢), or walk uphill 10–15 minutes, keeping the spires of Santa Prisca Cathedral in sight. A taxi to the zócalo will cost 75¢.

GETTING AROUND

Taxco is fairly accessible by foot, and most sights and budget hotels are clustered around the **Plaza Borda** (zócalo). As you move outward, the twisted, steep streets become increasingly difficult to navigate. If you need to be rescued, hop on one of the many combis roaming the area—that is, if you haven't already been run over by one. The main thoroughfare traverses the lower part of the city from south to north. It used to be named Avenida John F. Kennedy, but is now called Avenida de Los Plateros; people will often use these names interchangeably when giving directions. Plaza Borda is up the hill from Avenida de Los Plateros. On the east side of the plaza is **Santa Prisca Cathedral**, whose pink spires are visible from just about anywhere in the city. Taxco's other hub is **Plazuela de San Juan**, 1½ blocks southwest of Plaza Borda, up Cuauhtémoc.

BY BUS The bus system consists mainly of a fleet of white combis, the ubiquitous Volkswagen buses you'll see careening up and down the hills. Combis labeled LOS ARCOS travel the length of Avenida de Los Plateros; those marked ZOCALO run between Avenida de Los Plateros and the zócalo. Rides anywhere in the city cost 20¢.

WHERE TO SLEEP

Your pack may feel heavy, but your wallet will certainly feel lighter after a night here—hotels aren't cheap. The less expensive ones are around Plaza Borda and on the hill between the plaza and the Lineas Unidas bus station. You won't find any real bargains, but the picturesque setting and great views may compensate for the cash drain. Reservations are a good idea on holidays and weekends, especially Semana Santa (Holy Week—the week before Easter) and during July, August, and December. If the places below are full, try **Hotel Posada Santa Anita** (Av. de Los Plateros 106, tel. 762/2-07-52), a half block south of the Lineas Unidas station; singles $10, doubles $15. For somewhere quiet, try **Posada San Javier** (Two entrances: Ex-Rastro 4 or Estacas 1, tel. 762/2-31-77), which features courtyards, bougainvillea, and a large pool. The spacious, clean rooms are $17 for a single, $25 for a double.

➤ **UNDER $10** • **Casa de Huéspedes Arellano.** Only the most determined budget travelers will be able to find this well-hidden hotel, although every Taxco resident knows where it is—just keep asking and you'll get there. The hotel's decor and standard of cleanliness leave a bit to be desired, and the señora who runs the place isn't too pleasant, but it's the cheapest hotel in town. Singles and doubles with communal bath go for $7 and $10 respectively. *Pajaritos 23, tel. 762/2-02-15. Down alley to right of cathedral, right through market, and 3 levels down. 15 rooms, 8 with bath. Laundry, luggage storage.*

➤ **UNDER $15** • **Hotel Casa Grande.** Probably the best deal for the price, this large, old, stone building is clean and well-kept. Rooms vary from plain with small grungy bathrooms, to nicely decorated with elaborately tiled bathrooms. They're all the same price, so ask to see several. Singles and doubles go for about $12. *Plazuela de San Juan 7, tel. 762/2-01-23. From Plaza Borda, 1 block down Cuauhtémoc. 12 rooms, all with bath. Luggage storage.*

➤ **UNDER $20** • **Hotel Los Arcos.** This hotel was originally a gift for a viceroy of "New Spain," as Mexico was known during the colonial era. Some rooms have lofts, with beds overlooking the sitting area, and all open up to a cool patio of brick, stone, and tile. Singles are $14, and a double will set you back $20. Laundry costs $2.50 a kilo. *Juan Ruíz de Alarcón 2, 1½ blocks from Plaza Borda, tel. 762/2-18-36. 24 rooms, all with bath. Laundry, luggage storage. Reservations advised.*

Posada de Los Castillo. This striking mansion, just across the street from Hotel Los Arcos, has a fountain in its arched, stone lobby. Rooms are arranged around the interior patio and have simple, dark-wood furnishings, while the bathrooms are outfitted with tubs and hanging plants. The owner speaks English and is delighted to answer questions. Singles cost about $14, doubles $18. *Juan Ruíz de Alarcón 7, tel. 762/2-13-96 or 762/2-34-71. 14 rooms, all with bath. Luggage storage.*

CAMPING You can camp for free in the **Parque del Guisteco** at the top of the city. Locals tend to only camp in groups here, and discourage individual camping. *Parque del Guisteco, Zona Norte. From zócalo, north on Ojeda.*

FOOD

Food prices in Taxco reflect the city's popularity with tourists. Cheap meals can be had in the taquerías near the Lineas Unidas bus station and in restaurants on the side streets surrounding the zócalo. *Perros calientes* (hot dogs; 50¢) are sold by vendors that appear magically on the zócalo each evening. Cheap eats can also be found in the **market** (see Shopping, below), which is down the alley to the right of the cathedral. Purchase fresh fruits and vegetables here, as well as baked bread from one of the many panaderías. The specialty of the region is iguana; locals say it's an aphrodisiac, and that it tastes like chicken (surprise). Find out for yourself at **Casa Borda** (Plazuela de Bernal, ½ block from zócalo), where $4.50 buys a plate of fried iguana and rice.

➤ **UNDER $5** • **Jugos y Tortas Restaurante Cruz.** White-washed walls adorned with folk art and guitars add charm to this family-run restaurant, a favorite with locals wanting a quick lunch. Tacos are 75¢, and a burger, fries, and soda go for $2. *Calle del Arco 11, tel. 762/2-70-79. 2 blocks from zócalo. Open daily 9-6:30. Wheelchair access.*

El Rincón del Abuelo. This funky café serves a full breakfast of juice, fruit cocktail, coffee, toast, beans, and a choice of egg dishes or pancakes—all for $2.50. It's run by friendly young people who will happily share local information with you. They even have a selection of goofy postcards. A hamburger, fries, salad, and a drink will set you back $2.50. *Cuauhtémoc 1, btw Plazuela de San Juan and zócalo, no phone. Open daily 8 AM–11 PM.*

➤ **UNDER $10** • **Pizza Pazza.** The pungent aroma of pizza and garlic bread wafts over the zócalo from this pleasant place. The view is awesome and so is the pizza. A large cheese pie for 2–3 people is only $5, $10 with everything on it. If you're not in the mood for pizza, try the spaghetti ($3.50), *queso fundido* (cheese fondue; $2.50), or *pozole* (corn soup; $2). *Plaza Borda, next to cathedral, tel. 762/2–55–00. Open daily noon–midnight.*

Restaurant Sante Fé. Ask anyone in Taxco where they spend their precious pesos when taking the family to dinner, and they'll point you toward this colorful restaurant, around the corner from Plazuela de San Juan. The comida corrida features an entrée such as chile relleno or chicken in garlic sauce, with soup, beans, rice, tortillas, and dessert, all for $3.50. If you're not that hungry, try the $1 sandwiches or $2.50 enchiladas. *Hidalgo 2, tel. 762/2–11–70. 1 block east of Plazuela de San Juan. Open daily 7:30 AM–11 PM.*

WORTH SEEING

The city itself is the major attraction—which is why the Mexican government declared it a national monument in 1928—but there aren't many individual sights aside from the endless procession of silver shops. If you're in good shape, simply wandering through Taxco's many cramped alleyways and stairs makes for a strenuous but pleasant urban hike.

CASA HUMBOLDT This 18th-century mansion is named after Alexander von Humboldt, a German explorer who stayed here in 1803 and later traveled throughout South America, making maps and conducting scientific surveys. The interior was recently reconstructed, and there's a small, well-kept museum and several small shops selling local handicrafts. *Juan Ruíz de Alarcón 6. Admission: $2, $1 students. Open Mon.–Sat. 10–5, Sun. 9–3.*

MONTE TAXCO RESORT A 10-minute ride on the *teleferico* (cable car) takes you from Los Arcos to the luxurious resort at Monte Taxco, with its swimming pools, gardens, golf course, and spa. It costs $4 to use the pool and $2 to take a 20-minute horseback ride around the grounds. The incredible view costs only the price of a drink at the bar. The cable car runs daily 8 AM–7 PM, and the fare is $2.50 round-trip. *Monte Taxco, tel. 762/2–13–01 or 762/2–56–09. Combis (20¢) leave from Los Arcos; taxis cost about $2.*

The Catedral de Santa Prisca on Taxco's zócalo is considered one of the best examples of baroque architecture in Mexico.

MUSEO DE ARQUEOLOGIA GUILLERMO SPRATLING A short walk from the Catedral de Santa Prisca, this museum houses a collection of pre-Columbian artifacts that once belonged to writer William Spratling. The museum used to be Spratling's house, and now consists of three galleries: two dedicated to indigenous artwork and artifacts, the third to rotating exhibits of contemporary art. The museum is fairly small, its collection isn't extraordinary, and the $2.50 admission is hefty, so it's only worth seeing on Sunday or if you have a student ID (in both cases it's free). *Humboldt 1, tel. 762/2–16–60. Right behind Catedral de Santa Prisca. Open Tues.–Sat. 10–5, Sun. 9–3.*

CHEAP THRILLS

Cheap thrills in Taxco are more or less limited to Sunday nights on the zócalo, and the eternal search for the most incredible views of town—said to be from the **Monte Taxco Resort** (*see above*) and from **El Mirador,** a lookout high above the city. Think twice about visiting El Mirador alone; there have been several robberies here. If you can't stand the thought of what you might be missing, though, catch a PANORAMICA combi at Plazuela de San Juan and ask the driver to drop you at the top (20¢). Combis run 8 AM–9 PM.

FESTIVALS Aside from the usual festivals (Semana Santa, Las Posadas, Día de los Muertos), Taxco celebrates two special events: **La Feria Nacional de La Plata** (silver festival), held during the first week of December, and **El Día del Jumil** (Day of the Jumil Bug), held the first weekend in November. The week-long silver festival features the crowning of a Silver Queen and silver exhibitions. El Día del Jumil is held in honor of an insect said to be found nowhere else in the world but the Cerro de Huizteco, near Taxco. Traditional healers use the bugs for medicine, while others crush them into a tasty salsa. Families and groups of friends camp here, and there's a lot of singing and drinking in between bug-hunting expeditions. You'll have to make friends with some locals or hire a taxi to get out here—the Cerro de Huizteco is 6 kilometers outside Taxco. You can head up to Parque del Guisteco, where similar festivities take place. Special combis run from the zócalo to the park during the festival.

SHOPPING

Prices at the shops around Plaza Borda are outrageously high—the shopkeepers have figured out that many foreigners are rich and gullible. To see the prettiest silver work in Taxco, peek into **Los Castillos** (Plaza Bernal 10, tel. 762/2–06–52). If you want to actually buy some, stick to the vendors and small, crowded shops located below street level. To reach these stores, head down Cuauhtémoc from Plaza Borda and turn down the small alley at Banco Mexicano Somex. Also try the stores in the **El Pueblito** complex, down Hidalgo from Plazuela de San Juan and across from the park. Most shopkeepers have two price tiers: *Mayoreo* is the wholesale price given to those who buy at least $100 worth of silver, and *menudeo* is the price per gram for people buying less.

You're likely to see three types of merchandise in Taxco's silver shops: alpaca, a silver-colored metal also known as fool's silver; silver-coated alpaca; and solid sterling silver, identifiable by the .925 imprint. Real silver is priced by weight and intricacy of workmanship.

Taxco's extensive **mercado**, extending from the cathedral to **Avenida de Los Plateros**, is another good place to find less-expensive silver, as well as just about anything else. Haggling is common—two-thirds of the initial price is usually about the best you'll do. The market is held daily, but really heats up on weekends when merchants from nearby towns come to hawk their wares.

AFTER DARK

Most nights the zócalo is the hottest spot around—the place where Taxco youth flirt and local families gather for nightly gossip. Buy yourself a bag of popcorn from one of the street vendors and settle onto a park bench to watch the nighttime spectacle unfold. If you're lucky, you may see a small parade of adolescents dressed like wedding-cake decorations: This is a party for a girl's *quinceañera*, celebrating her 15th birthday and passage into womanhood.

The town's few drinking-and-dancing establishments close fairly early, and you can forget serious partying during the week. **Taxco Olé** (La Palma 1, facing Catedral de Santa Prisca, no phone), a bar popular with locals, is only open Friday, Saturday, and Sunday nights. Your best bet is the bars and restaurants next to the zócalo. **Restaurant/Bar Paco** (Plaza Borda 12, tel. 762/2–00–64) has the best view around and $2 beer. At **Señor Costilla's** the same beer costs $1.50, but the imitation-Hard Rock Cafe atmosphere is somewhat obnoxious. At the other end of the ambience spectrum is **Bar Berta** (Plaza Borda 9, tel. 762/2–01–72), a tiny place with a men's-club atmosphere. For dancing anywhere close to the town center, **EsCaparArtes Disco** (Plaza Borda 1, no phone) is your only choice. This Top-40 place is crammed on weekends with gyrating, under-18 youth, and the cover is $7. There's also a hopping disco (especially during summer) with a $4 cover at the **Monte Taxco Resort** (*see* Worth Seeing, *above*).

Near Taxco

LAS GRUTAS DE CACAHUAMILPA

The Cacahuamilpa caves, 30 kilometers outside Taxco, are an amazing expanse of subterranean chambers and crusty rock formations that extends 2 kilometers into the earth. The downward trek into this dimly lit world is occasionally steep and slippery, but otherwise fairly tame: The way is lit and marked by a smooth cement walkway. Guides conduct hourly tours in Spanish, but an English-speaking guide can be hunted up on request. The two-hour group tour is large, slow, and not particularly fascinating—you're better off starting with the tour and then moving on alone through the caves at your own pace. Bring a flashlight if you plan to wander, though, as there are blackouts. To reach the caves, take a bus from the Lineas Unidas station bound for Ixtapán and Toluca ($1.50). If you tell the driver where you're going, he'll drop you off at the crossroads, 1 kilometer from the caves. Large highway signs point you in the right direction, so follow the road downhill to the entrance. Buses for the return trip pass every half hour or so. You can also catch a LAS GRUTAS combi across the street from the bus station, which will take you all the way to the caves. It costs the same as the bus, but can be a lot more crowded. Combis run from 8–5. *Admission: $3. Open daily 10–5.*

Chilpancingo

If you've partied a little too heartily in Acapulco's world-famous discos, or if you simply refuse to go somewhere where showcase winners from *The Price is Right* are sent, then spend a day or two in Chilpancingo. Neither as glamorous as nearby Acapulco, nor as "charming" as its northern neighbor Taxco, Guerrero's state capital is an agricultural center and university town that may give you that needed break from the well-trodden tourist circuit. Site of the 1813 drafting of Mexico's Declaration of Independence, little of historical importance has happened here since the Spanish were sent packing. The result is a place where you can enjoy a few *cervezas*, gaze out at the green hills, and shoot the breeze with regular folks.

Chilpancingo is untouristed, and students of the Universidad de Guerrero fill the city's zócalo. The student center, **Casino del Estudiante** (Guerrero, at Madero, no phone) is a great place to hang out, full of people, ping-pong tables, and bulletin boards advertising upcoming dances, concerts, and movies. Although the university itself is a concrete atrocity, it's worth exploring to check out the event notices in the hallways. If you can't kick your museum habit, the **Instituto Guerrerense de la Cultura** is right on the zócalo, and contains some impressive murals depicting local and national historical events. The **Museo Regional de Guerrero** (tel. 747/2–70–5; open Tues.–Sun. 11–6) is housed within the Instituto, and has a small but interesting collection of pre-Columbian artifacts, as well as relics from the colonial period. Admission is free. If consumer culture is more your trend, there are plenty of shops near the zócalo, including a brand-new mall. Local crafts are sold at **La Casa de Artesanías** (open weekdays 9–9). To get here, take the URBANOS or JACARANDA combi from Avenida Insurgentes in front of the market.

At the 1813 Congress of Chilpancingo, Morelos and liberal delegates from all over Mexico drafted a Mexican Declaration of Independence, affirming universal male suffrage and the abolition of slavery, caste systems, and judicial torture.

BASICS

CASAS DE CAMBIO Around the zócalo are several banks that change cash and traveler's checks on weekday mornings, but the **Divisas de Guerrero** (Zapata 10, on zócalo, tel. 747/2–03–83) takes no commission and has better hours (weekdays 9–3:30). **Banamex**'s ATM (Zapata, on NW cnr of zócalo, tel. 747/2–20–20) accepts Cirrus and Plus cards, as does the ATM at **Banco Serfin** (Guerrero 5, just north of zócalo, tel. 747/1–04–87).

MAIL Chilpancingo's tiny **post office** is two blocks west of the zócalo. They'll hold mail sent to you at the following address for up to 10 days: Lista de Correos, Chilpancingo, Guerrero, CP 39000, México. *Hidalgo 9, tel. 747/2–22–75. Open weekdays 8–7, Sat. 9–1.*

PHONES You can make collect calls from the public phones on the zócalo. For other long-distance calls, go to **Caseta Auxiliar** (Ignacio Ramirez 9, 1 block east of zócalo), open Monday–Saturday 9–3 and 4–9. **Multiservicios de Oficina** has a fax and local and long-distance phone service. *Zapata 10, on zócalo, tel. 747/2-54-56. Open Mon.–Sat. 7 AM–10 PM.*

COMING AND GOING

Chilpancingo has two bus stations: the first-class **Estrella de Oro** (Juárez 53, tel. 747/2-21-30) and **Estrella Blanca** (21 de Marzo, tel. 747/2-76-45), which has first- and second-class service. First-class buses are nicer, generally faster, and only a little bit more expensive than second-class ones. From Estrella de Oro, buses run to Mexico City (5 hrs, $11), Cuernavaca (3 hrs, $6), Acapulco (1 hr, $6), Taxco (1½ hrs, $5), Puebla (5 per day, 6 hrs, $13) and Morelia (4 per day, 6 hrs, $16.50). To reach the zócalo from Estrella de Oro, hang an immediate left as you exit the station's front entrance and walk straight for about 7 blocks; or catch any bus or combi running up one-way Juárez. Buses to the station run along the parallel street, Guerrero. The Estrella Blanca station is 4 blocks farther up Juárez at 21 de Marzo; turn left down 21 de Marzo before the main market and walk 1 block. A **Sendatur** information office in the Estrella Blanca station (tel. 747/2-06-34) can direct you through this vast, shiny complex. Second-class buses leave frequently to Mexico City (5 hrs, $10), Acapulco (2½ hrs, $3), Taxco (2 hrs, $5), Cuernavaca (3½ hrs, $6), and Zihuatanejo (6½ hrs, $15).

WHERE TO SLEEP

While part of Chilpancingo's charm is its unaffected atmosphere, when it comes to lodgings, you'll wish it was equipped to deal with tourists. **Hotel Chilpancingo** (Alemán 8, tel. 747/2-24-46) is super cheap (singles $7, doubles $10), but rather depressing. The rooms resemble prison cells, and the bathrooms are on the far side of clean. **Hotel Cardeña** (Madero 13, no phone), in a former mansion 1 block off the zócalo, has rooms that open onto a courtyard. A smaller courtyard has a few stone washbasins in which you're welcome to scrub your clothes. Rooms are plain, and the bathrooms are only as frightening as the occasional cockroach. Singles cost $7.50 with bath or $5 without; doubles are $10.50 with bath, $7 without. The wheelchair-accessible **Hotel Roble** (Cuauhtémoc 5, tel. 747/2-53-23) is a slightly better choice. Although you won't see big bugs scuttling about, the rooms are small and the paint has begun to peel. Doubles with bath cost $11.50, singles with bath are $8, and rooms without bath cost $6.50; the communal bathrooms are a bit run-down.

FOOD

Cheap restaurants and cafés crammed with students are common on the zócalo and the streets surrounding it. Here, competition and student budgets keep the quality high and the prices low. For inexpensive fruits, vegetables, bread, meat, and cheese, head to the huge market on Guerrero near the second-class bus station. For something more upscale, try **Restaurant La Parroquia** (Nicolás Bravo 2, tel. 747/2-29-28), a sidewalk café just off the zócalo. Try the popular fish fillet in mole sauce ($6), or the daily comida corrida ($2.50). **El Portal** (zócalo, near Madero and Guerrero, tel. 747/2-46-68) is an open-air café that serves big $2 breakfasts, with coffee, fruit, and your choice of eggs or pancakes. They also have delicious $1 *aguas preparadas* (juice drinks). In the student center on the zócalo, **Fuente de Soda Casino del Estudiante** (Guerrero, at Madero, no phone), serves up hearty food at rock-bottom prices. The comida corrida includes soup, an entrée, and beans, all for about $1.70.

AFTER DARK

Partying is usually limited to the weekends, when students attend both *tardeadas* (afternoon dances) and *veladas* (parties from about 9 PM to 3 AM). The most popular spot for these is a club called **Sortilegio** (tel. 747/2-83-77), but it only hosts planned events—look for postings at the Fuente de Soda Casino del Estudiante (*see* Food, *above*), or ask a student. Sortilegio is on a winding street behind the mercado, so take a taxi—the driver will know where it is.

Chilpancingo also has its share of video bars, featuring blaring music and lots of intoxicated young people. Try **Ton's Que** (Portales Alto Centro, tel. 747/2-12-32), on the zócalo near Guerrero and Madero. For **Taco Rock** (Colón 5, tel. 747/2-34-91) take Abasolo south from the zócalo and turn right on Colón. The gay scene in Chilpancingo is almost nonexistent—the west side of the plaza is occasionally a meeting place for men at night, but lesbians seem to be out of luck. Anyone looking for a happening gay bar should head to Acapulco.

VERACRUZ   11

By Lynette Ubois

Veracruz—a narrow, verdant crescent of land—is warmed and watered by the humid tropical breezes that blow across the Gulf of Mexico. Home to a sizeable indigenous population as well as a large number of Mexicans of African descent, much of Veracruz's unique ambience derives from the diversity of its population. The prolonged interaction of African, Spanish, and indigenous peoples has produced a rich array of cultural traditions here, especially prominent in the vibrant festivals that occur all over the state.

Ever since that fateful Good Friday in 1519 when Hernán Cortés dropped anchor along this lush green coast, Veracruz has acted as a gateway between Mexico and the rest of the world. But even before the Spanish appeared, this region was at the center of Mexican cultural formations. The most ancient of all Mesoamerican cultures—the enigmatic Olmec—raised the first centers of civilization here; the monumental basalt heads they carved provide mute testimony to their mighty culture, which ruled the coast as early as 1200 BC. Originators of the ball game, and of the calendrical system adopted by the Maya, the Olmec are considered to be the "mother culture" of Mesoamerica. Little is known about the later city-states that flourished here, but the ruins at El Tajín, near Papantla, indicate that a highly complex culture—perhaps the early Totonac—governed the northern area of the state between AD 600 and 900. By the time Cortés came along, the Aztecs had conquered this region, and their oppressive tactics left the area ripe for rebellion. At Zempoala, the Totonac became the first indigenous allies of Cortés's conquering army—and were thanked with devastating diseases, forced labor, and war. Soon after the conquest, the Spaniards brought in boatloads of African slaves to fulfill their labor needs; by 1640, nearly 150,000 people of African descent were living here.

Huastec has linguistic ties to the Mayan language group, while Nahuatl is a remnant of the Aztec conquest.

Today the state is relatively wealthy, due to tourism and a thriving oil industry. It's a favorite region for Mexican vacationers, who come to enjoy the freshness of its seafood, the Caribbean rhythms of its music, and the relaxed, open attitude of its people. Along the coast, the calm beaches of Tuxpán offer a quiet place to relax, while the many marimba bands in Veracruz can keep you dancing all night long. The hilly, tobacco-growing region of Los Tuxtlas lures visitors to its many lakes and waterfalls. Finally, the state capital, Jalapa, sits nestled in the foothills of the colossal 5,610-meter peak, Pico de Orizaba. Still relatively undiscovered by travelers, Jalapa's progressive university population, colorful markets, and many lively *peñas* (musical gatherings) make it an excellent place to beat the coastal heat.

East Central Mexico

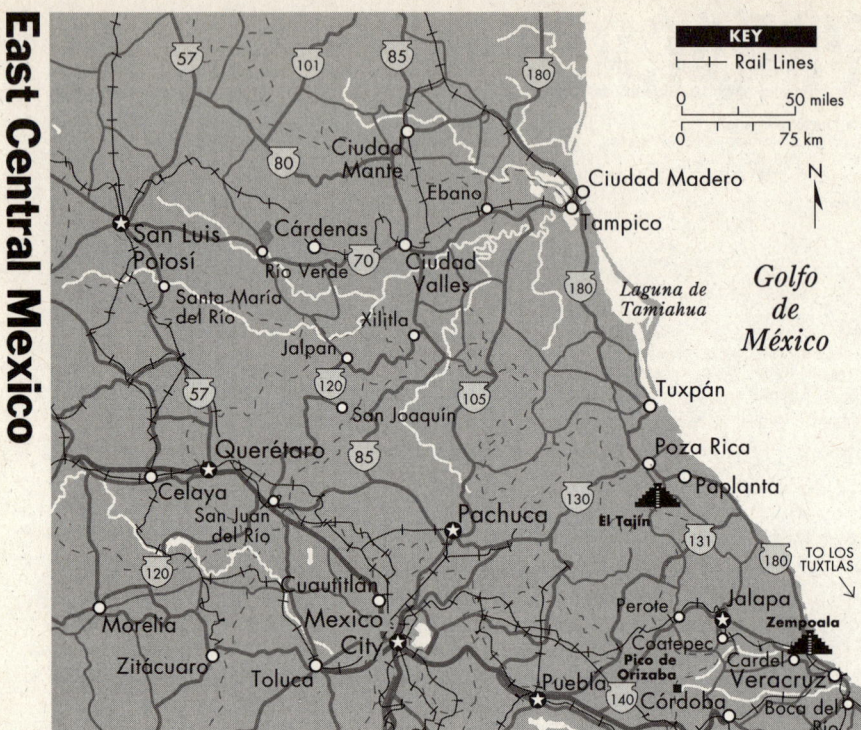

Veracruz

Veracruz is a hot, raucous port town. With its Caribbean flavor, lively music, and diverse population, the city holds a special place in the hearts of many Mexican tourists, who admire the welcoming, ready-to-celebrate attitude of the *jarochos*, as the city's residents are known. People come here for the seafood, the marimba music, and the breezes off the Caribbean—most tend not to frolic in the ocean, however. Since the day in 1519 when Cortés and his men landed here, Veracruz has been one of Mexico's most important ports, and more than five centuries of heavy traffic has taken its toll on the area's beaches.

Veracruz is the birth place of the song "La Bamba," and of Yuri, Mexico's answer to Madonna. More popular on the streets, though, is marimba music, played in the plazas and cafes by countless itinerant musicians.

The principal entry point for both people and goods headed to Mexico City, Veracruz has been a bitterly contested prize in many of this country's conflicts. An array of forts and walls, originally built as protection against pirates, failed to save the city from a succession of foreign attacks. Pirates sacked the city a number of times, most viciously in 1683, when a Frenchman known as Lorenzillo held the town hostage for three days and carried off enormous quantities of loot. The French invaded again in 1838, and the United States seized the town twice, first in 1847 and again in 1914. The most dramatic of the fortifications—the castle at San Juan de Ulúa—is one of the city's most popular attractions.

BASICS

AMERICAN EXPRESS The AmEx office is in **Viajes Olymar**. The agency provides the usual services for cardholders, including personal check cashing and mail holding. They also deliver

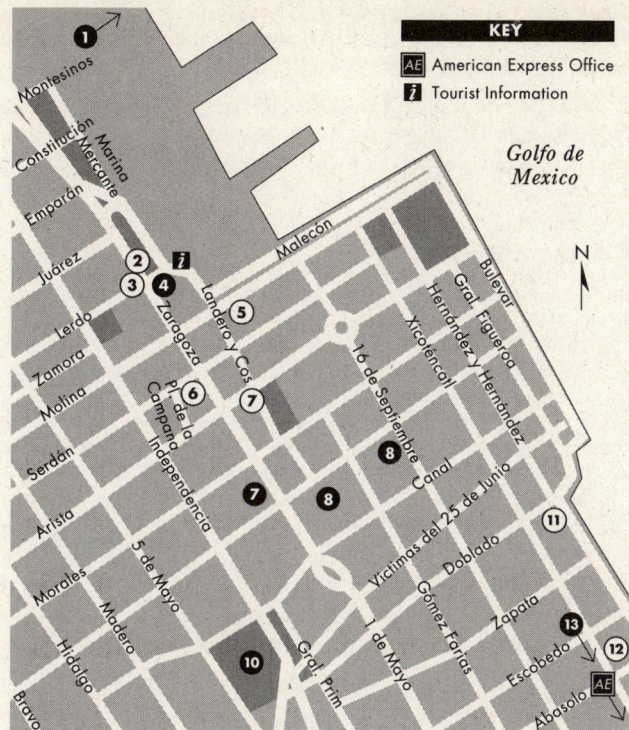

KEY
AE American Express Office
i Tourist Information

Golfo de Mexico

Sights ●
Acuario, **13**
Baluarte de Santiago, **9**
Fuerte de San Juan de Ulúa, **1**
Instituto Veracruzano de la Cultura, **8**
Museo de la Ciudad, **7**
Parque Zamora, **10**
Plaza de Armas, **4**

Lodging ○
La Concha Dorada, **3**
Gran Hotel Balneario Royalty, **12**
Hotel Amparo, **6**
Hotel Santander, **5**
Hotel Sevilla, **2**
Hotel Villa Rica, **11**

MoneyGrams and sell traveler's checks, but do not change money. *Ávila Camacho 2221, Veracruz, Veracruz, CP 91700, México, tel. 29/31–34–06. Open weekdays 9–8, Sat. 9–2.*

CASAS DE CAMBIO Rates in town are similar wherever you go. **Bancomer** (Juárez, at Independencia, tel. 29/32–74–34), only changes money weekdays 9–2, and you'll have to arrive early to make it through the lines. For later hours, try **Casa de Cambio Puebla** (Juárez 112, tel. 29/31–24–50), open weekdays 9–6, or use the 24-hour ATM at **Banamex** (Independencia 1027, near Juárez, tel. 29/32–47–00).

CONSULATES **United States.** *Víctimas del 25 del Julio 384, btw Gómez Farías and 16 de Septiembre, tel. 29/31–58–21. Open weekdays 9–1.*

EMERGENCIES **Police** (tel. 29/38–06–64); **ambulance** (tel. 29/37–55–00). **Oficinas Para La Seguridad del Turista** (tel. 91/800–90–392) operates a 24-hour toll-free hotline to provide legal and medical help for tourists in Veracruz.

LAUNDRY **Lavandería Automática del Parque** has self-service machines that wash a kilo of your dirtiest for $1; if you want someone else to wash them, it'll cost $1 more per kilo. *Collado 23, btw Juan de Dios and Begrete, tel. 29/31–06–75. Open weekdays 8–2 and 3–7, Sat. 8–7.*

MAIL The central **post office,** a magnificent building dating from the Porfirio Díaz era, offers the usual services. They will hold mail sent to you at the following address for up to 10 days: Lista de Correos, Administración No. 1, Veracruz, Veracruz, CP 91700, México. *María Mercante 210, tel. 29/32–20–38. Open weekdays 8–8, Sat. 9–1.*

MEDICAL AID **Benavides** (Independencia 1291, at Serdán, tel. 29/31–89–29) is a big, convenient drug store downtown, but it closes at 10 PM every day. For daily 24-hour service, try **Farmacia de la Sociedad Española Beneficencia** (16 de Septiembre, btw Escobedo and Abasolo, tel. 29/32–05–59).

PHONES The pay phones on the *zócalo* (main square) accept Ladatel phone cards. If you don't mind shelling out big bucks, you can also make long-distance phone calls at **Teléfonos Mirna** (Molina 127, tel. 29/31–40–07), behind the cathedral. They don't do collect calls and charge nearly $4 per minute for long distance.

VISITOR INFORMATION The bilingual staff at the **Subdelegación Federal de Turismo** has few helpful pamphlets but a lot of enthusiasm. *Palacio Municipal, on the zócalo, tel. 29/32–19–99. Open daily 9–9.*

COMING AND GOING

BY BUS The main bus terminal (Díaz Mirón 1698, tel. 29/37–57–44) is 4 kilometers south of the zócalo. The main bus company is **Autobuses del Oriente (ADO)** (tel. 29/37–57–88); it has daily service to Jalapa (3 hrs, $3) every 15–30 minutes between 5:30 AM and 11 PM, and buses for Mexico City (9 hrs, $14) depart very frequently, 24 hours daily. ADO also offers first- and second-class service to Reynosa (17 hrs, $36–$46), on the Texas border. First-class buses also regularly serve San Andrés Tuxtla, Santiago Tuxtla, and Catemaco between 6:30 AM and 11 PM for about $4. For those headed south, **Cristóbal Colón** (tel. 29/35–03–17) and **Cuenca** (tel. 29/35–54–05) run to Oaxaca and Chiapas. Luggage storage costs $2.50 a day, and public phones and a *caseta de larga distancia* (long-distance phone office) are in the station. **Autobuses Unidos** (tel. 29/37–57–32) and **Transportes Los Tuxtlas** (tel. 29/37–28–78) operate from the second-class station on the same block and offer frequent service to Jalapa (3½ hrs, $2) and San Andrés Tuxtla (3 hrs, $2).

Any city bus marked DIAZ MIRÓN on Avenida Zaragoza near the zócalo will stop right by both terminals (50¢). A taxi from the zócalo to the terminal should cost no more than $2.

BY TRAIN The train station (tel. 29/32–32–72) inhabits a romantic 19th-century building, five long blocks from the zócalo. The **Jarocho** train departs nightly at 10 PM for Mexico City (10 hrs). Classes of service include: first class (assigned seats; $8.50), first class *especial* (assigned seats and air-conditioning; $8.50), sleeper car (bed, sink, chair, and air-conditioning; $16), and second class (no guaranteed seating; $4.50). All tickets are sold at the same window. If you're traveling first class during peak tourist seasons (July, August, and holidays), buy your tickets in advance—they are available as much as a month before the departure date. Second-class only trains also run to Mexico City at 7:20 AM and 8:20 AM daily. They are somewhat slower (12 hrs), but tickets are $4.50. Tickets can be purchased Monday–Saturday 6–11 AM and 2–9 PM. To reach the station, follow María Mercante until it ends, then turn right.

BY PLANE Mexicana (tel. 29/32–22–42) has three direct flights a day to Mexico City for $70 one-way. The airline also has flights to other major cities, including Cancún and Monterrey. No city bus serves the airport, and a cab costs $7. Alternately, you can ride the minivan ($6 per person) that runs between the office of **Transportación Terrestre Aeropuerto** (Hidalgo 826, btw Canal and Morales, tel. 29/32–32–50) and the airport.

GETTING AROUND

Downtown Veracruz centers around two plazas: the **Plaza de Armas**, also known as the zócalo, and **Parque Zamora**, with its decorative old trolley car. The two are connected by Avenida Independencia, the city's busiest shopping street. While this downtown area is compact and walkable, you'll need to take buses to the outlying beaches and some of the further sights (such as Uluá). Buses cost 50¢, and most of the useful ones run along Molina and on Zamora, just behind the cathedral. The *malecón* (boardwalk) runs along the seashore. Called Molina in the downtown area, the malecón makes a 90-degree turn and becomes Boulevard Ávila Camacho, referred to by everyone as *el bulevard*. This winding street follows the southern coast of Veracruz, passing Playa de Hornos and Playa Mocambo before arriving in Boca del Río. Fortunately, most other streets adhere to a grid system.

WHERE TO SLEEP

There are more than 60 hotels scattered throughout this relatively small city, so finding a place to stay should be simple. Because Veracruz is a popular Mexican vacation spot, prices tend to be high for what you get, especially during July, August, and Carnaval (February/March). Lodging in the the older, more urban center of town is plentiful and cheap, but the room quality is low, and the area is unsafe at night.

NEAR THE ZOCALO Hotels near the zócalo tend to be cheaper than those near the beach, although luxuries like air-conditioning will bump up the price in either location. Staying in a hotel downtown is the way to keep yourself in the middle of the action, but the all-night noise might make some wish they'd taken a room in a less busy area.

➤ **UNDER $10** • **Hotel Amparo.** Big rooms, plenty of hot water, and enough little soaps to open a store make this hotel one of the best deals in town. The blaring TV in the lobby is *always* on, and the same old crowd of *cuates* (buddies) are slouched on the uncomfortable chairs in front of it day in and day out. The rooms on the main courtyard tend to be cleaner and cooler than interior rooms. Singles are a steal at $7, and doubles are only $10. *Serdán 478, btw Zaragoza and Independencia, tel. 29/32–27–38. 64 rooms, all with bath. Luggage storage.*

Hotel Sevilla. Everything in this small, otherwise nondescript hotel is light blue—the walls, the tiles, the sheets—everything. The rooms tend to be noisy, especially those that open onto Zaragoza, but all have ceiling fans, TVs, and clean bathrooms with plenty of hot water. The hotel itself is a two-second walk from the zócalo. Singles here are $8, doubles $10. *Morelos 359, btw Lerdo and Juárez, tel. 29/32–42–46. 30 rooms. Luggage storage.*

➤ **UNDER $20** • **Hotel Santander.** Once called the Hotel Vigo, this place is perhaps the only hotel in town with any character. Colored tiles, high ceilings, breezy balconies, and bamboo bed frames make it interesting. Singles with narrow beds are a manageable $8, and doubles run $12. *Lerdo y Cos 123, at Molina, tel. 29/32–45–29. 2 blocks from zócalo. 42 rooms, all with bath. Luggage storage.*

NEAR THE BEACH Hotels by the water may have breezier, slightly cooler rooms than those near the center of town, but don't count on it. If you're a lighter sleeper you may want to keep distance between you and the beach boardwalk, as the social scene here, although more mellow than in the city itself, often continues until 10 PM.

➤ **UNDER $15** • **Hotel Villa Rica.** This small hotel is one block south of the massive, turquoise Mar y Tierra hotel. The green-and-yellow lobby is welcoming, but the robust señora in charge is all business. The worn rooms are decent, if bare, but the bathrooms are slightly moldy. Still, it's a cheapie for the waterfront—$11 for singles and $12 for doubles. Some oceanside rooms have balconies, which cost $5 more in the high season. *Ávila Camacho 165, tel. 29/32–48—54. 33 rooms, all with bath. Luggage storage.*

➤ **UNDER $20** • **Gran Hotel Balneario Royalty.** Known to locals as "El Royalty," this gigantic building is one of the largest budget hotels in the city. Many rooms have breezy balconies with nice views of the bay, and all have phones and TVs. Singles and doubles with ceiling fans are $12 and $17 respectively. Air-conditioning bumps up the prices to $14 for a single, $22 for a double. *Abasolo 34, at Ávila Camacho, tel. 29/32–39–88. 270 rooms, all with bath. Garage, restaurant. MC, V.*

HOSTELS Except for a few food stands, Veracruz's **Villa Juvenil** stands alone on the beach, 30 kilometers north of the city. Plan to stay for a few days, because getting here through cane fields, villages, and flooded roads can take hours. The good news is that beds ($3 a night) are almost always available; the beach is among the cleanest in the area; there's great fishing off a nearby reef; and a 45-minute walk in either direction will bring you to isolated, virgin dunes bordered by jungle. The bad news is that after a major hassle to get here, you may find the place temporarily closed. They have no phone, so the only way to find out for sure if they're open (barring going yourself) is to call the main Villas Juveniles office in Mexico City (tel. 5/525–29–16). When the hostel is in operation, the friendly family that runs it also cooks up cheap and filling meals. To get here, catch an Autobuses Teziutecos bus to the town of Villa Cardel from Veracruz's second-class bus terminal (it's behind the main station). From the station in Villa Cardel, walk toward town and to the left, where you'll find dilapidated blue buses running to Paso Doña Juana, where the hostel is located (just tell the driver to let you off at the Villa Juvenil, or CREA, as it used to be known). *Paso Dona Juana, Municipio de Úrsulo Galván, Villa Cardel. 50 beds.*

FOOD

Veracruz offers a mind-boggling array of culinary choices, from tempura to lasagna, but seafood is the star attraction. People drive great distances to Boca del Río for the *robalo al mojo de ajo* (sea bass in garlic sauce; $8) at **Pardiño's** (Zamora 40, on zócalo, tel. 29/86–01–35). There's no real need to leave the city, though: The **municipal fish market**, one block south of the zócalo, has scores of stands where vendors cook up all kinds of seafood until late into the night. The stretch of Calle Serdán between Zaragoza and Madero also offers plenty of good, cheap eats. Picnic supplies, such as fresh vegetables, fruits, nuts, and cheeses are available at the **outdoor market** on Guerrero between Juan Soto and Serdán.

Café La Catedral. This sizeable café is usually crowded with locals intent on their coffee and animated conversations. Try the house specialty, *pescado relleno con camarones* (fish stuffed with shrimp), for $5. The *comida corrida* (pre-prepared lunch special) is a steal at $1.50. *Ocampo 202, near Parque Zamora, tel. 29/32–52–06. Open daily 8 AM–10 PM. Wheelchair access.*

Gran Café La Parroquia. Veracruz's busiest and most venerable café is best known for its coffee, sandwiches, and eggs. When you want some *café con leche* (coffee with milk), bang your glass with your spoon and a waiter armed with pitchers of hot milk and coffee will scurry over. The *tortilla parroquín* (chile-and-onion omelet cooked in chicken broth; $2) makes a filling meal, as do the other egg dishes or crêpes on the menu. *Gómez Farías 34, facing the malecón, tel. 29/82–25–84. Open daily 6 AM–1 AM.*

Pizza Palace. The afternoon buffet here is an extravagant, all-you-can-eat deal that runs from noon to 5 every day. Gorge yourself on pizza (which goes fast, so jump when it comes out) and an array of vegetables and other goodies, including fresh fruit for dessert, all for $2. Don't come for the atmosphere, though—it's pretty sterile. *Arista 686, tel. 29/31–77–06. Open Mon.–Sat. 9 AM–1 AM. Buffet served noon–5.*

The Nevería Amparito on Landero y Cos and Serdán, makes its own ice cream, with different flavors served every day. On Wednesdays, try the cacahuete (peanut) flavor.

Tacoyote. Away from the street, on a little fountain-filled plaza near the zócalo, this taquería serves a filling plate of beef tacos with *horchata* (a cool drink made with milk, rice, water, and cinnamon) for $2. Vegetarians can order quesadillas (5 for $3) or cheese *empanadas* (turnovers; $2.50). *Plazuela de la Campana 55-A, at Arista, no phone. Open Sun.–Wed. 2 PM–1 AM, Thurs.–Sat. 2 PM–3 AM. Wheelchair access.*

WORTH SEEING

Most main attractions are either near the zócalo and easily accessible on foot or are served by convenient public transporatation. The malecón is lively day and night, with men hawking boat rides, kids driving tiny toy cars, and scores of tacky souvenir shops. If you plan on cruising here at night (a popular weekend activity among young jarochos in the throes of puppy love), watch out for the street brawls that break out all too frequently.

ACUARIO The aquarium, located in a shopping plaza on Playa de Hornos (a quick bus ride from the center), is extremely popular with locals, who flock here on weekends. It contains a round tank with 3,000 different species of marine life native to the Gulf of Mexico, including nurse sharks, manta rays, barracudas, and sea turtles. Shark movies of the make-you-never-want-to-set-foot-in-the-ocean-again variety are shown near the exit. If that doesn't do the trick, check out the enormous shark-shaped outline on the far wall, above the caption: "This is the actual size of a great white shark caught off the coast of Tuxpán, Veracruz." *Plaza Acuario, tel. 29/34—79–84. Take* VILLA DEL MAR *or* BOCA DEL RIO *bus from cnr of Molina and Zaragoza to huge VIP's plaza on Ávila Camacho. Admission: $3. Open Mon.–Thurs. 10–7, Fri.–Sun. 10–7:30.*

BALUARTE DE SANTIAGO The Baluarte de Santiago is all that remains of the ramparts that once stood sentinel over the port of Veracruz. The colonial bulwark is impressively solid from the outside and inside is a small museum displays temporary art exhibits. None of it is worth the $3 admission fee, so come on Sunday when it's free. *Canal, at 16 de Septiembre. Open Tues.–Sun. 10–4:30.*

Veracruz's port-city swagger has earned its inhabitants the nickname "jarochos"—rude ones. Traditional jarocho apparel includes the ubiquitous men's guayabera shirt— pleated and pocketed—and the beautiful, but less commonly worn, women's embroidered white cotton dresses.

FUERTE DE SAN JUAN DE ULUA A miniature city in itself, the island fort of San Juan de Úlua is a maze of moats, ramparts, and drawbridges smack in the middle of the busy port area. Now connected to the mainland by a causeway, this island was witness to some of the most momentous events in Mexican history. Cortés landed here in 1519, establishing Veracruz as a major gateway for Spanish settlement of Mexico. Fortification of the island began in 1535 under the direction of Antonio de Mendoza, the first viceroy of New Spain. Ground coral, sand, and oyster shells were used for the original walls. A few centuries later, the fort was used as a prison, housing such figures as Benito Juárez, who did time here thanks to conservative dicatator Santa Anna before being exiled to Louisiana in 1853. *Tel. 29/38–51–51. Take* SAN JUAN DE ULUA *bus from zócalo to fort. Admission: $4.50, free Sun. and holidays. Open Tues.–Sun. 9–5.*

INSTITUTO VERACRUZANO DE LA CULTURA The bright blue Veracruz Cultural Institute building was a hospital until atrocious conditions caused health authorities to close it down in 1975. The massive 18th-century structure, with its long, arched hallways and green, tree-filled garden, now hosts cultural events and rotating art exhibits. *Canal, at Zaragoza, tel. 29/31–66–45. Admission free. Open Mon.–Sat. 9–9, Sun. 10–2.*

MUSEO DE LA CIUDAD If you've just arrived in Veracruz, the city museum is a good place to start exploring. The region's history is narrated via artifacts and displays, and scale models of the city give you a sense of the lay of the land. Also exhibited are copies of pre-Columbian statues and contemporary indigenous art. A $1 donation pays for a guided tour by a bilingual student. *Zaragoza 397, near Morelos. Admission: $1.50. Open Mon.–Sat. 9–4.*

CHEAP THRILLS

Boat tours of the bay leave from the malecón daily 7–7. Boats leave whenever they're full, and the $2, half-hour ride includes a talk (in Spanish) on Veracruz history.

Longer trips to nearby **Isla Verde** (Green Island), **Isla de Enmedio** (Middle Island), and **Isla de los Sacrificios** (Island of Sacrifices) leave daily from the small dock near the Instituto Oceanografico, on Ávila Camacho, and from the beach next to the Plaza Acuario. Boats leave whenever they're full, so it's best to come in a big group. The cost should be $5–$7 per person, but feel free to bargain; the old men near the Instituto tend to give better deals. Make sure your guide will give you at least an hour to enjoy the island beaches—some guides may try to hasten your trip by claiming the beaches are restricted, but don't believe it.

Land lubbers can stop by **Bicicentros Lezama** (Juan de Dios Peza 180, near Parque Zamora, tel. 29/31–04–32) and rent a bicycle ($1.50 per hr) for a breezy ride along the broad sidewalks of the malecón. Motor scooters ($4 per hr) are also available. Open 9–9.

AFTER DARK

To get away from the zócalo and soak in some of the grittier port atmosphere, try one of the traditional bars just south of the plaza, such as **Bella Época** on Lagunilla, an alley cordoned off

Every Tuesday and Friday night after 8 PM, the Plaza de Armas is the scene of open-air dances, with a dressed-up crowd and live marimba music. Sunday nights the dancing moves to Parque Zamora.

for pedestrians. The bar serves seafood, and drink prices are lower than what you'll find on the square. Bella Época's clientele is mostly male, so unaccompanied women can count on getting lots of attention here.

Discos and video bars are plentiful along the malecón, especially as you move south toward the beaches of Villa del Mar. Buses run down here until about 10:30, but you'll have to catch a cab ($2) to get back. The hippest places are **Boca del Ocean** (Ruíz Cortínez 8, at Ávila Camacho, tel. 29/37–63–27), a flashy, modern discotheque, and **Blue Ocean** (Ávila Camacho 9, tel. 29/22–03–66), a video bar with a light show. Both play a wide variety of music, and are open Thursday–Saturday only, so on Friday and Saturday nights are packed with a young, largely local crowd. Boca del Ocean charges a cover ($8) on Saturdays only. The more relaxed Blue Ocean charges $5 at the door and has a small dance floor and some pool tables.

OUTDOOR ACTIVITIES

Veracruz's beaches are much less inviting than you might expect: Although some locals aren't deterred from swimming, most beaches are dirty, and the water is fairly polluted. The beaches at Isla Verde, Isla de Enmedio, and Isla los Sacrificios are more isolated, but you're still swimming in the same water, so don't expect a noticeable improvement. If you're determined to get a glimpse of marine life anyway, rent snorkel or scuba gear from **Tridente** (Ávila Camacho 165-A, tel. 29/31–79–24) and venture into the murky depths. **Villa del Mar** is the beach closest to downtown, 2 kilometers south along the malecón, but most people don't dunk their heads underwater (except the most avid fans of hepatitis). A little better, though quite built-up and still a bit dirty and shallow, is **Playa Mocambo**, 8 kilometers farther south. The **Hotel Playa Mocambo** (Ruiz Cortines 4000, tel. 29/22–00–11) charges $4 to use their pools until 6 PM.

Better beaches are farther from town. About 4 kilometers south of Playa Mocambo is **Boca del Río**, a small fishing community at the mouth of the Río Jamapa that is getting quickly sucked into greater Veracruz. While Boca's beach gets dirtier as you move closer to the center, it's uncrowded, and the water is relatively unpolluted. Boca del Río also has a number of open-air restaurants that sell fantastic seafood at high prices. Don't expect a charming little seaside village, though: Boca is basically a suburb that happens to be by the water. Its beaches can be reached via any of the BOCA DEL RÍO buses that run along the malecón, leaving from Calle Serdán, a block east of the zócalo.

If you have more time to kill and are determined to find really nice beaches, you can head to **Villa Cardel**, where a youth hostel operates sporadically (*see* Where to Sleep, *above*), or 20 kilometers south of town to the village of **Antón Lizardo**, where a number of small islands and coral reefs just offshore offer some of the best scuba diving in the area. You can rent snorkel gear ($3 per hr) or scuba equipment ($18 per hr) at the local branch of **Tridente** (Pino Suárez, at Av. de la Playa, tel. 29/34–08–44); here you can also arrange boat rides to the islands. Three-hour boat trips are $10 per person (with a six-person minimum), and it's a good idea to call ahead and reserve at least a day in advance. **Autobuses Unidos** buses serve the town frequently from the main station in Veracruz (20 min, $2). The last bus back to Veracruz leaves the station at Antón Lizardo around 8:30 PM.

Near Veracruz

ZEMPOALA

Thick cane fields press against the perimeter of these small ruins, while in the distance, the irregular peaks of the Sierra Madre Oriental rise dramatically. Located just outside the small town of **José Cardel** (an hour north of Veracruz), Zempoala's pyramids are not particularly exciting architecturally, but they do have a distinguished past. Once a sizeable Totonac town, Zempoala was the first settlement to rebel against Moctezuma's empire by supporting Cortés's army. Originally plastered with white stucco and topped with small square shrines, the pyramids here gleamed so brightly that Cortés's first scouts reported that the city was made of silver (and we know what was on their minds). Time has now worn away the plaster, revealing surprisingly regular, rounded riverbed stones beneath.

As you enter the site, the **Templo Mayor** lies directly in front of you, its steep staircase ascending 13 levels to the faint remains of a three-room temple on top. When the governor of Cuba finally sent an expedition to arrest Cortés, this building, with its commanding view of the countryside, was probably their headquarters (with characteristic subtlety, Cortés later set fire to the thatched roofs of the temple, foiling his arrest and converting most of the expedition to his side). To the right of the Templo Mayor sits a smaller pyramid, **Las Chimeneas** (The Chimneys), named for the remains of two round towers in front of it. Cortés may have lodged at the top of this temple; before this, the chimneys were probably used for storage. Behind Las Chimeneas, out in the cane fields, lies another small structure. It's called **Las Caritas** (Little Faces) for the many pottery heads that once decorated its walls—unfortunately today you'll find only graffiti, scratched into the remaining traces of original paint.

Despite Zempoala's hospitality, Cortés broke his promise of friendship and ransacked the temples here, smashing sacred statues and replacing them with Christian icons. The **Gran Piramide** and the **Temple of the Wind God**, resting under the jacaranda trees at the western edge of the site, do little to invoke any long lost Totonac gods—but you may run into guides trying to sell you on their still-lingering powers. Back at the entrance you'll find friendly guards happy to discuss the region (but only in Spanish) or sell you colorful, informative pamphlets (some in English) for 50¢. The site is open daily 9–6; admission is $2 ($1 for students).

COMING AND GOING To reach Zempoala from Veracruz, take a **TRV** bus (tel. 29/37–57–32) from the second-class bus station to Cardel (45 min, $1). Buses leave every 10 minutes between 8 AM and 7 PM. In Cardel, turn left out of the **bus station** (tel. 296/2–01–69) and walk one block to the corner of Zapata and Avenida Cardel, on the zócalo. White *micros* (minibuses) marked Zempoala will take you to the ruins (10 min, 50¢) 6 AM–8 PM. The *colectivos* (collective taxis) that run by the ruins charge the same price. The last bus returns to Veracruz from Cardel at 10:30 PM. To reach Zempoala from Jalapa, catch a TRV bus from the central bus station in Jalapa (1½ hrs, $2).

WHERE TO SLEEP You can't camp at the ruins, but if you want to stay overnight, there are cheap lodgings in Cardel. **Hotel Garelli** (Flores Magnón, at Juárez, tel. 296/2–05–69) is basic and clean, and its jovial owner charges $4 per person. If you're dying for air-conditioning, try the frilly pink rooms at **Hotel Cardel** (Zapata, at Martinez, tel. 296/2–00–14); singles here are $13, doubles $17.

Los Tuxtlas

The small volcanic mountain range of Sierra de Los Tuxtlas meets the sea 140 kilometers south of Veracruz. Simply known as Los Tuxtlas, the area has lakes, waterfalls, rivers, mineral springs, and access to beaches, making it a popular stopover for travelers heading east from Mexico City to the Yucatán. The region's three principal towns—Santiago Tuxtla, San Andrés Tuxtla, and Catemaco—rest in mountains more than 200 meters above sea level, lending them a coolness even in summer that's the envy of the perspiring masses on the coast.

While much of Los Tuxtlas architecture is of the 1960s school (looming cement), all three towns are laid out in the colonial style, around a main plaza and a church, and retain a certain charm. The region was also a center of Olmec culture, and Olmec artifacts and small ruins abound, especially around

The Tuxtlas gain an air of mystery not only from the cool, gray fog that slips over the mountains and lakes but also from the whisperings among townspeople about the brujos (witches), also called curanderos (healers), who read tarot cards, prescribe herbal remedies, and cast spells here.

Santiago Tuxtla. Today, the economic life of Los Tuxtlas depends on cattle raising, cigar manufacturing, and tourism. The largest of the three towns is San Andrés, which is also the local transport hub. With plenty of hotels, it is a good base from which to explore the entire region. From Santiago, you can visit the ruins at Tres Zapotes; the town also has an informative museum where you can learn about the region's indigenous heritage. Lake Catemaco is popular among Mexicans as a summer and Christmas resort; it's also the place to go for a *consulta* (consulation) with a brujo or curandero, should you have any questions that require spiritual clarity or supernatural intervention.

BASICS

CASAS DE CAMBIO The only place in the Tuxtlas to change money is San Andrés, where **Bancomer** (Madero 20, tel. 294/2–00–41) changes cash and traveler's checks weekdays 9–1. **Banamex** (Madero 4, tel. 294/2–13–50) only changes traveler's checks on weekdays from 9 to 2:30, but it has a 24-hour ATM that accepts Plus, Cirrus, MasterCard, and Visa.

EMERGENCIES The **Cruz Roja** (González Boca Negra 242, tel. 294/2–05–00) in San Andrés provides emergency care for all three towns. You can reach the **police** in San Andrés at 294/2–02–34, in Santiago at 294/7–00–92, and in Catemaco at 294/3–00–55.

PHONES AND MAIL The largest **post office** (tel. 294/2–01–89) in the region is in San Andrés on 20 de Noviembre and La Frauga, a block down the hill from the main square. They will hold mail sent to you at the following address for up to 10 days: Lista de Correos, San Andrés Tuxtla, Veracruz, CP 95701, México. There are no Ladatel international phones in the Tuxtlas, but there are a few small **phone offices** in all three towns—just look for the blue-and-white signs marked LARGA DISTANCIA. One of the most convenient is in San Andrés at **Casetea "Pipisoles"** (Madero 6-B, tel. 294/2–25–88), just past the Banamex. It's open daily 8 AM–9 PM.

COMING AND GOING

The transport hub for Los Tuxtlas is San Andrés's **Autobuses del Oriente (ADO)** terminal (Juárez 762, tel. 294/2–04–46), about six blocks from the zócalo. Buses for Veracruz city (2½ hrs, $4) leave hourly between 5 AM and 8 PM. Several night buses leave in the hours around midnight for Mexico City (9 hrs, $18), and there are also frequent departures for Villahermosa (5 hrs, $9) and Jalapa (8 hrs, $7).

Second-class buses based in San Andrés connect the three towns—it's a 15-minute drive to both Catemaco and Santiago from here (50¢). Buses for Santiago leave the **Terminal de los Rojos** station (Juárez, 1 block past ADO) in San Andrés every 10 minutes. You don't have to go to the station to get the bus for Catemaco, however—just wait on the highway near the ADO terminal for one of the Rojos CATEMACO buses that pass every 10–15 minutes. In Catemaco, the second-class company operates a small station two blocks from the main square. In Santiago, the bus stop is at the corner of Morelos and Ayuntamiento, three blocks from the plaza.

San Andrés Tuxtla

Spotless San Andrés Tuxtla is the largest and most modern town in Los Tuxtlas. A graceful, red-domed cathedral presides over the central plaza, which is surrounded by relaxed, open-air cafés. The pleasant atmosphere combined with the town's central location and cool evenings make it an ideal stopover for travelers feeling abused by too many hours on buses. Those in need of more than just relaxation can try some of the curative teas and medicinal herbs at the **Farmacia Homeopática La Esperanza** (Juárez 264, at Hidalgo, tel. 294/2–08–79), two blocks from the zócalo. If you're more interested in polluting your body than purifying it, there's always the **Fábrica de Puros Santa Clara** (5 de Febrero 10, tel. 294/2–12–00), a huge cigar factory where you can see experts making fine cigars that cost $60 for a box of 24. If you buy a box, they'll print your name or slogan on each cigar at no extra charge. Also for sale are cartons of five for $13 and super-deluxe cigars that come in lovely, handmade wooden boxes and cost more than you can afford.

WHERE TO SLEEP On a quiet side street near the cathedral is the spotless **Hotel Catedral** (Pino Suárez 3, tel. 294/2-02-37). A night here costs $4 for one person, $5 for two; most rooms have large comfortable beds, and all have clean bathrooms with decent plumbing. If the Catedral is full, try **Hotel San Andrés** (Madero 6, tel. 294/2-06-04), where all have private bathrooms and exterior rooms have balconies that overlook the lively street. Singles are $12, doubles $15. **Hotel de Los Pérez** (Rascón 2, tel. 294/2-07-77) is your best bet at the high end. Carpeted rooms on the third floor cost $15 for a single and $21 for a double, but they tend to be mustier than their uncarpeted counterparts ($13 and $19, respectively) on the first and second floors. All rooms have phones, TVs, blissfully quiet air-conditioners, and spotless bathrooms. The hotel also has a decent restaurant.

The pre-Conquest name for San Andrés—Zacoalcos—means "locked up place." Some say it referred to the confusing landscape of rugged hills and narrow valleys, which made it difficult for people to find a way to the town.

FOOD The cafés by the zócalo on Madero serve cappuccino and fixed-price breakfasts. In the afternoons, the restaurant at **Hotel del Parque**, also on the zócalo, serves a filling comida corrida for $3. Otherwise, stop off at **Caperucita Roja** (Juárez 108, tel. 294/2-05-11) for a sandwich or a taco at rock-bottom prices. A favorite of local teenagers on dates, this small restaurant is outside under a bamboo roof, and meat for the tacos slowly turns over an open flame in one corner. Folks trying to beat the heat head to **Restaurante Tortacos** (tel. 294/2-31-00) in the cool, quiet La Fuente shopping center (cnr of Juárez and Argudín). The daily comida corrida is $2, and they serve excellent *mole poblano* (chicken in mole sauce). This is also the place to satisfy late-night cravings—it's open daily 7:30 AM–3 AM. For picnic supplies, head to **El Fénix** (Constitución 125), a big supermarket open daily 8:30 AM–9 PM.

OUTDOOR ACTIVITIES In the wet, tropical hills of Los Tuxtlas, opportunites abound for day trips to local swimming holes, rivers, and beaches. Just 3 kilometers outside San Andrés, the **Laguna Encantada** (Enchanted Lagoon) fills a small volcanic crater; the lake gets its name from its strange propensity to rise in the dry season and fall during the rains. Some taxis might brave the rutted road to the lake (for a $5 fee). You can also walk, although locals warn travelers not to go alone—thieves occasionally assault the unwary. Walk along Highway 180 until you see the sign for the lake, then follow the trail and bear left when the trail forks. The lake is uphill from here. More easily reached and more impressive is **Salto de Eyipantla**, a roaring 40-meter-wide waterfall that crashes 50 meters down into shallow, churning pools. A popular picnic spot, the falls are served by greenish micros marked SALTO that run every 5–10 minutes from the zócalo in San Andrés.

Catemaco

On the western shore of huge Lake Catemaco, the town of Catemaco is now almost entirely devoted to tourism, but has lost little of its bizarre personality. Populated by people of Spanish, African, and Indian descent, Catemaco is dotted with *consultorios* (consulting rooms) where brujos ply their trade. If you'd like to sample their services, the best way to avoid being scammed is to ask the locals to recommend someone—outward skepticism notwithstanding, most residents have snuck off for a *limpieza* (spiritual cleansing) once or twice themselves.

Catemaco is the local center for brujería (witchcraft). Practitioners of traditional medicine and magic come here from all over Mexico during the first eight days of March for a yearly convention.

Just two blocks downhill from the bus station and the zócalo, Catemaco's lakeside walkway or malecón is the town's center of activity. It bustles with seafood vendors, souvenir stands, small restaurants, and men hawking boat rides—all set against a gorgeous backdrop of lake and mountain. The fauna, too, is spectacular: You can see *changos* (monkeys), parakeets, and white herons without leaving the shore. For a better look at the local wildlife, take a ride in a *lancha* (motor boat) to **Isla de los Changos**, which is populated by peaceful monkeys with bright red behinds. Brought from Thailand by the University of Veracruz for research purposes, a recent sickness (perhaps due to their consumption of rotten food) has halved their population; the university asks that you do not feed them. On the way to visit the monkeys, you can also pass by **Isla de Garzas,** a resting spot for herons, and **El Tegal,** a grotto where the Virgin made a local appearance. It's now a shrine lit with countless votive candles. Tours are $6 per person, but you can probably bargain the price down to a couple of dollars, especially if you're in a big group. Back on shore, cavorting on the lakeside beaches is free, but they're pretty unspectacular. **Playa Hermosa** is more mud than sand, but buses (20¢) go there frequently; you can catch them in the zócalo.

The town's other attractions include the gaudy church on the zócalo dedicated to Catemaco's patron saint, the Virgen del Carmen, who appeared in 1714 to Juan Catemaxca—a local fisherman for whom the town is named. Every year on May 30, locals descend upon the malecón, where lanchas await to take them out to the **Monumento a Juan Catemaxca** (a tall statue of Catemaxca planted right off the coast) to leave offerings of fish, flowers, and fruit.

WHERE TO SLEEP You're allowed to camp by the lake, but it's not very safe, and nice campsites are hard to find. If you really want to plop down in the sand, you're better off taking a bus to the Gulf Coast (*see* Near Catemaco, *below*), although it's no longer perfectly safe there either. **Hotel Los Arcos** (Madero 7, at Mantilla, tel. 294/3–00–03) is the place to go if you find a few forgotten pesos stuffed deep in your pocket. The rooms are pricey ($20 singles, $25 doubles) but are as comfy as they come, and have phones, TVs, air-conditioning, private bathrooms, and balconies that overlook the lake. For $5 less you can stay in a room with a fan instead of air-conditioning, and there's even a small pool in the courtyard. The tiny **Hotel y Restaurant La Julita** (Playa 10, 2 blocks from plaza, tel. 294/3–00–08) has the cheapest rooms on the waterfront. Clean and well-furnished, they're only $5 per person, and the manager is unusually easygoing. At **Posada Koniapan** (Revolución, at malecón, tel. 294/3–00–63), air-conditioned rooms on the ground floor cost $15 for one or two people; upstairs rooms with ceiling fans cost $13 for one or two people. The hotel sits at a quiet end of the malecón, all its rooms have balconies facing the lake, and a good-sized pool sits in the grassy front yard.

FOOD The malecón is lined with small restaurants overlooking the lake. Most serve a variety of seafood—*mojarra,* a local fresh-water fish, is always a good choice; cooked with lime and chiles, oranges, or garlic, it usually costs about $2 a plate. The two-story **Las 7 Brujas** (tel. 294/3–01–57) has a great view of the lake, but **La Julita** (*see* Where to Sleep, *above*) offers a wider range of choices. For a cheaper meal or seafood appetizers, go to the **mercado** (market) just off the malecón, where *comedores* (sit-down food stands) sell hearty meals for less than $2, and a cocktail of shrimp, oysters, or octopus won't cost more than $2.50.

OUTDOOR ACTIVITIES For guided tours of the rainforest, as well as mud and mineral water baths, massages, and sweatlodge rituals, head to the self-proclaimed ecotourist paradise at **Nanciyaga.** A simple resort on the edge of Lake Catemaco, Nanciyaga is open daily 8:30–6 and charges a $1 admission fee. You can also rent cabañas here for $10 a night, single or double occupancy. Nanciyaga can be reached by bus (15 min, 50¢) from the zócalo in Catemaco, or by lancha from the malecón (10 min, $4–$6). About a 15 minute drive past Nanciyaga is **Río Cuetzalapan,** a cold-water mountain stream popular for swimming and fishing.

NEAR CATEMACO

The Gulf Coast beaches, 1½ bumpy hours by bus out of Catemaco, are one of Los Tuxtlas's great secrets. Foreign tourists rarely venture down this far, unless they're staying at one of the few isolated hotels dotted among the tiny fishing villages. The bus ride itself takes you through some beautiful ranching country before it stops at **Sontecomopan,** a small town on the shore of a quiet lagoon, which is formed by warm Gulf waters. From here, lanchas will take you out to sea for $3 to the small, pleasant beach called **La Barra.** Near the lagoon lies **Poza Enano,** a fresh-water swimming hole frequented by locals. They say the reflections in the water make you look like an *enano* (dwarf). From Sontecomopan you can catch pickups ($1) that take the dirt road down towards the Gulf Coast beaches. About 10 kilometers along this road is the stop for **Playas Jicacal** and **Escondida,** two of the best beaches in the region. When you get off the bus, follow the marked trail downhill for about a kilometer to the sandy expanse of Playa Jicacal. Playa Escondida lies on the other side of the promontory at the far end of the beach. (Keep your eyes open in the water here: Locals claim the area is frequented by sharks.) Pickups leave the Playas Jicacal and Escondida for the return trip to Catemaco as late as 8 PM, but you'd be crazy to try hiking back up the hill after nightfall. On top of the promontory, the basic **Hotel Playa Escondida,** where double rooms rent for $13 a night, is your best overnight option. You're allowed to camp, but the beach is narrow and locals warn that it's unsafe.

The farthest beach, at the spot along the sand most resembling a town, is **Montepío.** For rides along the beach here, you can usually find someone around town who will rent you a horse (about $2 an hour). Some say it's perfectly safe to camp here; others disagree. If you'd rather be safe, the **Hotel San José** (tel. 294/2–10–10) charges $12 for a single or double.

Santiago Tuxtla and Tres Zapotes

With its winding streets, red-tile roofs, and small market, Santiago Tuxtla, founded in 1525, has managed to retain more of its colonial character than the other two Tuxtla towns. Most visitors come to see the older traces of Olmec civilization here, centered at the nearby ruins of **Tres Zapotes.** A huge stone Olmec head dominates the town's zócalo, and the **Museo Tuxteco** (open Mon.–Sat. 9–6, Sun. 9–3; admission $1.50), also on the plaza, displays a collection of Olmec and early Huastec pieces, including detailed clay sculptures, black obsidian blades, and a skull showing evidence of ritual deformation. Dr. Fernando Bustamante, the museum's director, is an expert on local indigenous cultures and more than willing to answer (in Spanish) any question you may have. He is usually at the museum weekday mornings.

The ruins themselves are 21 kilometers west of town. Tres Zapotes, now decidedly unspectacular, was once an important Olmec ceremonial center; it is believed to have been occupied as early as AD 100. Little remains of the original site, except for **La Camila,** a burial mound that rises from the corn fields outside town. More than 15 meters tall, this large mound is rumored to be an important nexus of spiritualism and cosmic energy. More edifying is the **museum** to the left of the taxi stand in the village of Tres Zapotes, 1 kilometer from the ruins. Here you can see Stela C, a slab of bas-relief carving, with the date 7.16.6.16.18 (the 3rd of September 32 BC) inscribed upon it in the bar-and-dot calendrical system. This stela is one of the earliest examples of the "Long Count" calender, suggesting that the Olmec were the originators of a system the Maya would later adopt and perfect. The only way to make the bumpy, 25-minute trip from town to the ruins is by colectivo (about 50¢ per person). Taxis leave from **Los Pozitos** bar (just over the bridge from Hidalgo) whenever they're *very* full.

WHERE TO SLEEP Casa de Huéspedes Morelos (Obregón 15, at Morelos, tel. 294/7–04–74) is the cheaper of the town's two lodging options and feels like what it is: someone's cramped but comfy home. There's no air-conditioning, but each room has a fan, and the owner doesn't mind if you use her washboard and clothesline. Rooms cost $5 for a single and $8 for a double. The wheelchair-accessible **Hotel Castellanos** (5 de Mayo, at Comonfort, tel. 294/7–03–00), right off the main square, is the only real hotel in town. It's a small glass-and-iron tower with balconies off every room, which means you can choose to view whichever part of the city you prefer. The comfortable, even fancy, rooms have TVs, rugs, air-conditioning, and spotless bathrooms. The price is $15–$20 a night, $3 less if you forgo the air-conditioning.

FOOD Santiago is not noted for its restaurants. If you decide to stay here, head for the area near the bus terminal, which has several inexpensive *fondas* (covered food stands), and the market near the zócalo, which sells fruit and bread. For a little more atmosphere (and better-tasting food) try **Parrilla la Ribera** (Castellanos Quinto 43, tel. 294/7–06–73). The chicken tacos are a steal at $1 for an order of five, and the owner, Señor Gutierrez, is super-friendly. To get here, walk down Morelos to Victoria and go left over the bridge.

Jalapa

Jalapa is perched on the side of a mountain, between the coastal lowlands of Veracruz and the high central plateau. A little more than 1,400 meters above sea level, the city has an enviable climate that will come as a pleasant surprise to perspiration-soaked escapees from Veracruz city, which swelters on the coast some 100 kilometers to the southeast. The capital of the state of Veracruz and a university town, Jalapa boasts the finest anthropology museum outside Mexico City, as well as hills that pose intriguing engineering problems—in some places you'll find the twisting, cobblestone streets bordered by six-foot-high sidewalks built to compensate for sudden, sharp inclines. The presence of the university makes for a diverse population as well, and you are as likely to see long-haired young people sitting around in cafés as you are wizened campesinos walking to work. The town is also home to a symphony orchestra and a state theater that attract big-name performers.

BASICS

AMERICAN EXPRESS The travel agency **Viajes Xalapa** functions as the local AmEx representative from its office about a block from Parque Juárez. They exchange traveler's checks and provide all other AmEx services, including emergency check-cashing and mail-holding for cardholders, MoneyGram delivery, and replacement of lost or stolen AmEx cards or traveler's checks. *Carillo Puerto 24, Jalapa, Veracruz, CP 91000, México, tel. 28/17–87–44. Open weekdays 9–1:30 and 4–7, Sat. 9–1.*

CASAS DE CAMBIO Five blocks west of Parque Juárez, **Casa de Cambio Jalapa** (Zamora 36, tel. 28/18–68–60) offers excellent rates. It's open weekdays 9–1:30 and 4:30–6. You can also change money on weekday mornings at several banks near Parque Juárez. **Bancomer** (Lucío 1, next to the cathedral, tel. 28/14–43–22) only changes traveler's checks—no cash. **Banamex** (Xalapeños Ilustres 3, tel. 28/18–03–74) has similar rates, changes both cash and traveler's checks, and has an ATM that accepts Cirrus, Plus, Visa, and MasterCard.

EMERGENCIES To contact the **police** call 28/17–63–10, or call the **Cruz Roja** at tel. 28/17–34–31. In an emergency dial 06.

MAIL Seven blocks west of Parque Juárez, the full-service **post office** (Diego Lenyo, at Zamora, tel. 28/17–71–21) is open weekdays 8–8, Saturday 9–1. They will hold mail sent to you at the following address for up to 10 days: Lista de Correos, Administración No. 1, Jalapa, Veracruz, CP 91000, México. Next door, the **Centro de Servicios Integrados de Telecomunicaciones** (Zamora 70, tel. 28/17–71–60) offers fax, telegram, and telex services; it's open weekdays 8–6 and Saturday 9–1.

MEDICAL AID Calle Enríquez is lined with pharmacies. For 24-hour service, the pharmacy in **Super Tiendas Ramón** (Revolución 171, at Sagayo, tel. 28/18–09–35) is your best option.

PHONES There are Ladatel phones in front of the Palacio del Gobierno. Alternately, the long-distance service inside the **Restaurant Mariscos** charges $1.50 per minute for international calls. *Zaragoza 70, tel. 28/17–84–36. Open daily 7 AM–11 PM.*

SCHOOLS The **Escuela Para Estudiantes Extranjeros** of the Universidad Veracruzana offers language programs for foreign students. They offer six-week summer programs as well as four-month (one semester) programs. They can also tailor courses to your needs. Family stays can be arranged by the department. The director is Maestra Berta Cecilia Murrieta Cervantes, and she's more than willing to answer questions (in English) over the phone. You can also write to: Escuela Para Estudiantes Extranjeros, Apartado Postal 440, Jalapa, Veracruz, CP 91000, México. *Sebastián Camacho 5, at Zaragoza, tel. 28/17–86–87, fax 28/17–64–13. In center of town, near Cine Variedades.*

VISITOR INFORMATION The friendly but not terribly well-informed **tourist office** (Ávila Camacho 191, tel. 28/18–70–75) hands out unreadable maps and lots of pamphlets. The staff does not speak English. It's open weekdays 9–3 and 6–9, Saturday 9–1. The restaurant **La Sopa** (*see* Food, *below*) hands out a trilingual brochure (Spanish, English, French) with much better info.

COMING AND GOING

BY BUS Jalapa's modern **Central de Autobuses de Xalapa** (20 de Noviembre Ote. 571, tel. 28/18-92-29), commonly called CAXA, lies 2 kilometers east of the city center. It's served by the first-class **Autobuses del Oriente (ADO)** line (tel. 28/18-99-22), as well as the second-class **Autobuses Unidos (AU)** (tel. 28/18-70-77). ADO has frequent departures to Veracruz city (2 hrs, $3), Mexico City (5 hrs, $10), Catemaco ($7, 4 hrs), Papantla (4 hrs, $7.50), and Puebla (3½ hrs, $5). AU has equally frequent service and slightly lower prices. The terminal has a 24-hour pharmacy, a long-distance phone office, and luggage storage. To catch an *urbano* (large city bus) or colectivo (small VW van) to the center, walk down the wide stone stairs to the bus stop and take anything marked CENTRO. Both urbanos and colectivos charge 25¢. Taxis charge about 75¢.

BY TRAIN The small **Estación Nueva Miguel Alemán** (tel. 28/15-17-64) is in the northern part of Jalapa. Two painfully slow second-class trains creep to Mexico City (6 hrs, $4) and Veracruz (5 hrs, $2.50) daily; be advised that trains are also often slower than official estimates. A cab from downtown to the train station will cost less than $2.

GETTING AROUND

Jalapa is an easily walkable city, but the frequent name changes of its central streets can get confusing. Orient yourself around **Parque Juárez,** the city's emotional, if not geographic, heart. Enríquez runs along the north border of the park, becoming Zamora as it heads east past the purple Banamex building. Heading west, Enríquez turns into Ávila Camacho and passes the **Teatro del Estado** (state theater). At the southern border of Parque Juárez, Zaragoza turns into Allende as it passes the western edge of the park. Revolución begins at Enríquez and runs north past Juárez and the markets on Altamirano.

The most important city buses originate in front of the **3 Hermanos** shoe store on Enríquez, two blocks east of Parque Juárez. They cost 25¢; colectivos working the same routes cost 30¢. Taxis, which can be found on Enríquez (by the park) and on most of the main streets, are also relatively cheap and extremely convenient. They don't have meters—just get in, name your destination, and don't pay more than $1.

WHERE TO SLEEP

Because of its triple function as the seat of state government, a university town, and the only big city in a poor, thickly settled rural area, Jalapa offers plenty of lodging choices. You'll find several clean, comfortable, and surprisingly cheap hotels right in the center of town.

➢ **UNDER $10** • **Hotel Continental.** The Continental as a whole is beautiful, with gloriously high ceilings and a pretty, covered courtyard, but its rooms ($5 singles and $6 doubles) are anticlimactic: They're big and roomy with fairly clean bathrooms, but the musty odor is overwhelming and the hot water only works between 6 AM and noon. Still, it's just three blocks from the zócalo, and the courtyard restaurant serves satisfying $1 lunches. *Zamora 4, tel. 28/17-35-30. 22 rooms, all with bath. Luggage storage. Wheelchair access. MC, V.*

Hotel Plaza. Smack in the middle of the bustle on Enríquez, the rooms here are tidy, and fan-cooled, and the bathrooms have hot water, soap, and clean towels. Some rooms are a bit gloomy, but all feature a shiny, white spittoon for your expectorating pleasure. A single here costs $6, and doubles are $7. The reception desk is hidden at the top of a flight of stairs at the end of a long, yellow-tiled hallway next to Enrico's restaurant. *Enríquez 4, tel. 28/17-33-10. 36 rooms, all with bath. Luggage storage.*

Hotel Limón. Just one block north of the cathedral and set back from the busy traffic of Revolución under a pretty, tiled archway, the Limón is a great bargain. It features hand-painted tiles, brightly colored floors, and small, clean bathrooms with strong, hot showers. Ask to see a few rooms before you choose: The management charges solo travelers $5 and couples $6 regardless of room size, so you might as well take the biggest one available. *Revolución 8, tel. 28/17-22-04. 45 rooms, all with bath. Laundry, luggage storage.*

VERACRUZ

➢ **UNDER $15** • **Hotel Principal.** This aging but immaculate hotel is a short walk from Parque Juárez. Get an interior room or the traffic will set your teeth rattling. The rooms (singles $8, doubles $12) are big and comfy, with phones and ceilings high enough to accommodate a small herd of giraffes. The clean bathrooms are, oddly enough, configured to allow you to use the toilet and sink while showering. *Zaragoza 28, tel. 28/17-64-00. 40 rooms, all with bath. Laundry, luggage storage. Wheelchair access.*

FOOD

Like everything else in Jalapa, good restaurants are cheap and plentiful. If you eat all your meals at the markets on Altamirano, you'll spend less than $5 for breakfast, lunch, and dinner combined. You might even develop a taste for *hormigas chichantanas* (dried ants), a local delicacy. More familiar food can be found down the hill from the markets in the grocery section of the super-store **Chedraui Centro** (Lucío 28, tel. 28/18-71-77), open daily 8 AM-9 PM. Restaurants here don't cost much more than the markets, especially if you hang out around **Callejón Diamante,** a skinny, cobblestone alleyway off Enriquez whose brightly painted restaurants serve flavorsome, cheap meals to crowds of hungry students. You've found the Callejon when you've spotted the canary-yellow second-story restaurant **La Fonda** (Callejón Diamante 1, tel. 28/17-80-69); it's open Monday–Saturday 8-6. Pop inside for a taste of *tepache* (fermented pineapple juice).

Jalapa is home to the jalapeño pepper. With almost every bite of this city's spicy food, you'll be reminded of where you are.

El Balcón de la Ágora. This excellent café is set on the edge of a cliff in Parque Juárez overlooking the city and the mountain peaks beyond. It's a favorite hangout among both local students and the foreigners who visit Jalapa for the summer language program. Consequently, the management is accustomed to having young people with very little money linger over a soda or small sandwich for hours. *Bajos del Parque Juárez, tel. 28/18-57-30. Down stairs at south end of park. Open daily 8:30 AM-10 PM.*

Café La Parroquia. At this bustling cafe—*the* place for breakfast—anxious patrons tap their glasses with spoons to signal for another coffee. Tables are always filled with white-haired professor types, slouching school kids, and university students who all linger over baskets of sweetbreads. Breakfast or lunch here will only set you back $3. *Zaragoza 18, 2 blocks east of Parque Juárez, tel. 28/17-44-36. Open daily 7:30 AM-10 PM.*

La Sopa. You won't find better food at cheaper prices anywhere in town. Homemade tortillas, refreshing *agua de fruta* (fruit juice), and terrific garbanzo-bean soup come with the $2 comida corrida, which is served daily 1 PM-5 PM. The place is usually packed, but once you get a table the service is prompt and polite. La Sopa has live music Thursday–Saturday nights after 9 (*see* After Dark, *below*). *Antonio M. de Rivera (a.k.a. Callejón Diamante) 3-A, tel. 28/17-80-69. Open Mon.-Sat. 1 PM-11 PM. Wheelchair access.*

WORTH SEEING

The terraced gardens of **Parque Juárez** should be your starting point for exploring Jalapa. Aside from offering gorgeous views of Mexico's highest peak, the 5,610-meter Pico de Orizaba (or Citlaltépetl, as it was originally known), the park is within walking distance of almost everything. Next to the park sits the massive **Palacio del Gobierno** (Enríquez, at Revolución); the machine gun-toting guards will let you wander inside any time between 6 AM and 9 PM. Directly across the street, the **catedral** opens its doors daily 8-1 and 4-8.

CASA DE ARTESANIAS Jalapa's state-run handicrafts center is housed in a beautifully renovated colonial mansion that sits on a hill overlooking the lakes of the **Parque Paseo de los Lagos.** Inside the center is a studio with rotating exhibits and an enormous shop selling locally produced crafts and typical clothing. Fruit wines ($3 a bottle) are also sold. *Paseo de los Lagos, tel. 28/17-08-04. From Parque Juárez, straight down Herrera, right on Domínguez, left on Dique. Open weekdays 9-8, Sat. 10-1.*

CENTRO DEL ARTE This small cultural center hosts exhibitions of everything from photography and sculpture to finger painting. A billboard on the wall by the entryway provides the scoop on current cultural events. *Xalapeños Ilustres,* at Insurgentes, no phone. Admission free. Open Mon.–Sat. 11–8, Sun. 11–6.

GALERIA UNIVERSITARIA RAMON ALVA DE LA CANAL This two-story university gallery, with its polished wood floors and clean, white walls, houses rotating exhibits of art and photography, almost all of which is produced by university students. *Zamora 27, tel. 28/17–75–79. Admission free. Open weekdays 9–2 and 5–8, Sat. 10–noon.*

JARDIN BOTANICO FRANCISCO JAVIER CLAVIJERO These well-kept botanical gardens about 2 kilometers outside town contain more than 1,500 varieties of flora from throughout the state of Veracruz. A small arboretum houses a slew of palm species, and a large pond showcases a vast array of aquatic plants. Hilly stone walkways and narrow steps guide you into the woods, where most plants sport placards that bear their Spanish and scientific names and explain any useful properties the plants possess. Buses marked COATEPEC BRIONES will bring you here from the stop in front of the Teatro del Estado (at the corner of Ignacio de la Llave and Ávila Camacho) for 25¢. *Carretera Antigua a Coatepec Km. 2.5, tel. 28/18–60–09 ext. 253. Open Tues.–Sun. 10–5.*

MUSEO DE ANTROPOLOGIA DE JALAPA With more than 29,000 pieces on display, Jalapa's anthropology museum is second only to Mexico City's (*see* Worth Seeing, in Chapter 2). The building's long central corridor opens out onto extensive gardens and displays stunning artifacts from the three primary indigenous cultures of Veracruz: the Olmec, the Totonac, and the Huastec. Highlights include massive stone Olmec heads; lively, grinning Remojadas figurines, graceful jade masks; and a burial mound complete with bones, ritually deformed skulls, and ceremonial statuettes. There is also an exhibit on the clothing and customs of contemporary Totonac and Huastec cultures. Guided tours by English-speaking students are available weekdays, but you have to call in advance and make an appointment. *Av. Jalapa, tel. 28/15–07–08. Take* ALVARIO PANTEON *or* MERCADO TESORARIA *bus from Revolución, just beside market, to museum entrance. Admission: $2, $1 students. Open daily 9–5.*

AFTER DARK

Jalapa sleeps Sunday through Wednesday nights and parties—usually to live music—Thursday through Saturday. While lots of clubs still think black lights and billowing clouds of dry ice are imperative for a good time, most local bands (especially those at salsa clubs) are worth the damage to your senses. **La Sopa** (*see* Food, *above*) is a popular student hangout, mostly due to the free folklore and jazz offered Thursday–Saturday nights from 9 to 11. Two doors away, the popular salsa club, **El Callejón** (Callejón Diamante 7, tel. 28/18–77–46) draws an enthusiastic crowd with live shows that run 10 PM–2 AM. More laid-back is the live samba/jazz at the resturant and bar **La Casona del Beaterio** (Zaragoza 20, tel. 28/18–21–19); there's no cover, and you can linger over coffee and dessert as long as you like. If you want to rock, head to the other side of Parque Juárez; about four blocks along Ávila Camacho you'll find **B42** (Ávila Camacho 42, tel. 28/12–08–93), a video bar and rock club packed with well-dressed students and young professionals. Local groups play here Fridays and Saturdays 11 PM–2 AM; the cover is $3. Even more upscale is **La 7a Estación** (20 de Noviembre, near CAXA), the biggest, fanciest disco in Jalapa. They feature pop music, and let you in free before 10 PM—after that, it's $5.

The **Ágora** (SW cnr of Parque Juárez, downstairs, tel. 28/18–57–30) is a cultural center that stages art exhibits and the occasional folk-music performance, and shows classic and avant-garde films in its cinema club. Stop by during the day to see what's planned; it's open daily 9–9 and admission is free. The **Teatro del Estado** (Ignacio de la Llave, tel. 28/17–41–77 ext. 38) is the big, modern, state theater of Veracruz. The Orquesta Sinfónica de Jalapa performs here, often giving free concerts during its off-season (early June to mid-August). Check *El Diario de Jalapa* (the Jalapa city newspaper, available at newsstands) for dates and times of performances, or stop by the Ágora (*see above*) in Parque Juárez.

The arts department of the university frequently opens dress rehearsals of upcoming presentations. Performances run the gamut from modern dance to Shakespeare, and take place on campus and in the Teatro del Estado. Check El Diario de Jalapa for details.

Near Jalapa

COATEPEC

Just 8 kilometers along the highway from Jalapa, the colonial city of Coatepec is a center for coffee and orchid cultivation. You can see perpetually flowering orchids at the **Invernadero María Cristina** (Miguel Rebolledo 4, tel 28/16-03-79), right by the main square. Fruit wines are sold (and free samples offered) at **Licores Finos Bautista Gálvez** (Hernández y Hernández 5, tel. 28/16-01-35). And if you ever wanted to see a 13-hectare ecotourism wonderland, now's your chance. At **Agualegre** (Río La Marina, 5 blocks NW of plaza, tel. 28/17-07-21), you can enjoy the four swimming pools, water slide, restaurant, or trails for horseback riding or hiking, and then camp among the jagged green hills. Admission is $1.50, campsites are an additional $2, and an hour of horseback riding through the reserve costs $5. Longer trips to sites as far off as Xico (*see below*) can be arranged with advance notice.

In a small park north of the plaza on Hernández y Hernández sits a big cement structure called el hongo (the mushroom). Walk silently to the center, then speak softly, and see what happens.

COMING AND GOING To reach Coatepec from Jalapa (20 min, 50¢), first catch a bus marked TERMINAL from the stop in front of the **3 Hermanos** shoe store on Enríquez; it'll deposit you at a collection of bus stands, near the rusty, white TERMINAL EXCELSIOR sign. From here, blue buses marked COATEPEC leave every 5-10 minutes.

XICO

About 19 kilometers from Jalapa, Xico (pronounced He-koe) is a tiny town at the base of the steep, coffee-growing Perote foothills; it's also one of the few places left on Earth where donkeys are the major mode of transportation. Influenced by the heavy Spanish presence in the 16th century (Cortés passed through Xico on his way to the Aztec capital of Tenochtitlán), this very traditional town holds bullfights and *pamplonadas* (running of the bulls) each year as part of the **Feria de Santa María Magdalena** (July 22). However, Xico's year-round selling point is the roaring, 40-meter **Cascada de Texolo**, 3 kilometers outside town. A cobblestone path leads through banana plantations to the falls, but it's not easy to find. From the entrance to town on the main street (the sign marked ENTRADA), go up the hill. When the path forks, bear left and follow the CASCADA TEXOLO sign down the unpaved road. At the next fork, take the high road. Near the waterfall, there's also a restaurant that serves a $2 comida corrida; the owner moonlights as a taxi driver and will take you back to Xico ($3) if you're too beat to walk.

Be sure to leave Xico for Jalapa before nightfall, as there are no hotels here. The food is great, though, and almost all the restaurants near the plaza serve excellent dishes with *mole* (chile and chocolate sauce). Another local specialty is *verde*, a liqueur made with herbs.

COMING AND GOING To reach Xico from Jalapa (40 min, $1), first catch a bus marked TERMINAL from the stop in front of the **3 Hermanos** shoe store on Enríquez; it'll deposit you at a collection of bus stands, near the rusty, white TERMINAL EXCELSIOR sign. From here, blue buses marked XICO leave every 5-10 minutes.

Papantla de Olarte

Papantla de Olarte sits amid tropical hills, 250 kilometers northwest of Veracruz. The town's character is distinctive, largely due to the mix of Spanish and indigenous traditions here. Totonac men in flowing white pants lead their donkeys through crowded streets; palm trees shade the traditional, tiled zócalo; and a 25-meter pole next to the ornate cathedral is set up for a Totonac ritual in which four *voladores* (fliers) dive off (*see box*, Voladores of Papantla, *below*). Papantla is also the town nearest to the ruins of El Tajín (*see* Near Papantla, *below*). The town is also famous for the festival of Corpus Christi; held 9 weeks after Easter, it's a week-long event that celebrates both the Catholic sacrament of the Eucharist and ancient Totonac harvest rituals. Festooned with enormous wreaths of flowers, vanilla leaves, and ears of corn, the cathedral is the focal point, and Totonac dances are performed outside daily. Special night-time ceremonies occur at El Tajín itself, against the backdrop of dramatically lit pyramids.

BASICS

CASAS DE CAMBIO Papantla lacks a casa de cambio, but the **Banamex** (Enríquez 102, tel. 784/2–01–89), two blocks east of the zócalo, changes both cash and traveler's checks weekdays 9–1:30. It also has a 24-hour ATM that accepts Cirrus, Plus, Visa, and MasterCard.

EMERGENCIES **Police** (tel. 784/2–27–84); **Cruz Roja** (784/2–01–26).

MAIL The **post office** is down the hill from the zócalo; walk one block south on 20 de Noviembre, turn left on Serdán, right on Azueta, and then look for the CONSUTORIO MEDICO sign. The post office is in the same building. They will hold mail sent to you at the following address for up to 10 days: Lista de Correos, Azueta 198 Altos, Papantla, Veracruz, CP 93400, México. Azueta 198, tel. 784/2–00–73. Open weekdays 9–1 and 3–6, Sat. 9–noon.

MEDICAL AID **Farmacia Médico** is the biggest pharmacy in Papantla and it's right on the zócalo. The staff doesn't speak English but is good at charades. Gutiérrez Zamora 3, tel. 784/2–06–40. Open daily 7:30 AM–10 PM.

PHONES The three Ladatel phones in town are down the hill from the **Teléfonos de México** caseta (5 de Mayo 201, tel. 784/2–05–35). **Farmacia Médico** (see above) also has a caseta de larga distancia, but they only do collect calls.

VISITOR INFORMATION The **tourist office** has an attentive staff who hand out free maps and loads of good advice. Lourdes Bolaños is especially helpful, and she speaks perfect English. Palacio Municipal, on the zócalo, tel. 784/2–01–77. Open weekdays 9–3, Sat. 9–1.

COMING AND GOING

The first-class **Autobuses del Oriente (ADO)** station (Juárez 207, tel. 784/2–02–18) is a five-minute walk downhill from the zócalo. Eight buses leave daily for Jalapa (4 hrs, $7.50), and five leave for both Veracruz city (4 hrs, $7.50) and Mexico City (5 hrs, $8.50). One bus also leaves at 7:30 PM daily for Villahermosa (12 hrs, $22). Taxis between the zócalo and the station will cost $1, and local buses marked CENTRO cost 25¢. The ADO station in the nearby town of Poza Rica, which can be reached via a Transportes Papantla bus (see below), has a much more extensive schedule, so if you want a direct ride to some far-flung destination, you can try your luck there.

Second-class **Transportes Papantla** (20 de Noviembre, tel. 784/2–00–15) buses serve the surrounding villages and a few major cities in Veracruz, such as Jalapa (6½ hrs, $6), Veracruz city (7½ hrs, $5), and Zempoala (3½ hrs, $4). Buses to Poza Rica (20 min, $1) run every 20 minutes between 4 AM and 11:30 PM. The station is two blocks downhill from the zócalo, right behind the 15-10-15 superstore.

WHERE TO SLEEP

Hotels in Papantla are either cheap and lousy or expensive and passable, but almost all are within a block or two of the zócalo. If you have cash to burn, the pretentious and overpriced **Hotel Premier** (Enríquez 103, tel. 784/2–00–80) has tiny balconies overlooking the square and charges $23 for a single, $27 for a double. Penny pinchers will prefer one of the places listed below.

Hotel Pulido. If the rickety fans at this hotel don't fall from the ceiling and decapitate you, the carbon monoxide fumes from the parking lot are sure to finish you off. The rooms, however, are decent, though they do vary in size, so ask to see a few before you commit yourself. They cost

$7 for rooms with one bed, and $11 for rooms with two; those on the second floor offer more peace and somewhat fresher air. *Enríquez 205, tel. 784/2–00–38. 23 rooms, all with bath. Luggage storage.*

Hotel Tajín. Given your other options in Papantla, this place is worth the price. Its hilltop perch makes for beautiful views of the city, and the hotel itself features an upscale restaurant and clean rooms with big bathrooms. Singles and doubles with air conditioning cost $15 and $17, respectively; *económico* (budget) rooms have a fan instead of an air-conditioner (singles $12, doubles $14). *Núñez y Domínguez 104, 1½ blocks west of cathedral, tel. 784/2–06–44. 60 rooms, all with bath. Laundry, luggage storage.*

Hotel Trujillo. This is the cheapest hotel in town, and it feels like it. There's no hot water, the bathrooms are less than pristine, and each sparsely furnished room is illuminated by a single, naked light bulb. Rooms with one bed are $5; with two beds they jump to $7. *5 de Mayo 401, tel. 784/2–08–63. 30 rooms, all with bath.*

FOOD

Papantla doesn't offer many culinary options, but you'll be hard-pressed to blow more than $5 on a meal anywhere here. As usual, the fondas in the market (btw Azueta and 20 de Noviembre) are your cheapest option. The restaurant at **Hotel Tajín** (*see* Where to Sleep, *above*) is one of the better places in town, serving generous breakfasts and $2–$3 comida corridas. You can stock up on tacky souvenirs while you wait for your meal at **Restaurante Plaza Pardo** (Enríquez 105, tel. 784/2–00–59), which doubles as a gift shop but specializes in delicious chicken tacos ($2) and sweet aguas de fruta ($1). **Restaurant Enríquez** (Reforma 100, no phone) on the northeast corner of the zócalo, serves tasty seafood dishes ($3) and bite-size tacos (20¢).

Near Papantla de Olarte

EL TAJIN

Just 15 minutes outside Papantla is El Tajín, the ruins of an extensive city that dates back to AD 100. Although the central structures have been excavated and restored, many more remain hidden under thick jungle growth. Archaeologists speculate that the entire city covered about 146 acres, and that smaller, related structures could be spread over several thousand acres.

Little is known about the people who built El Tajín. Early theories attributed the complex to either the Totonacs or Huastecs, the two most important cultures of the Veracruz area. Today,

> ## *Voladores of Papantla*
>
> **The ritual of the voladores was originally performed as a tribute to the gods of the sun and rain—the fliers, dressed in bright red trousers, black boots, and tassled red caps dive backwards off a small platform at the top of the pole. Tied at the ankle, they swing upside down in the air, each one twisting 13 full rotations (to mark the months of the lunar calendar). Between them, the four fliers circle the pole 52 times, once for each year of the cycle of the Totonac calendar. A fifth man, the prayer giver, sits atop the pole and plays a small flute while keeping rhythm on a drum as the fliers descend. Originally, the ceremony was held on the spring equinox, but Catholicism and tourism have changed all that. Now the voladores fly for the crowds every Saturday and Sunday at noon, and give special performances during Corpus Christi.**

local Totonacs claim it as part of their heritage—"Tajín" is a Totonac word meaning "thunder"—although archaeologists remain unconvinced. Various clues reveal that whoever built El Tajín also had important relations to other Mesoamerican cultures. Archaelogical motifs that adorn the pyramids here, such as the repeated scroll pattern (symbolizing sea shells) and the step-and-fret design (symbolizing lightning), also show up at Teotihuacán and Xochicalco in the central highlands.

Guided tours of the site are not available, but the blue-shirted guards that wander the complex often know a great deal about the site. Near the entrance, the unremarkable **Plaza del Arroyo** is likely to have been the city's commercial center; pass by the four large pyramids of the plaza to get to El Tajín's ceremonial heart. Here, a squat statue of Mictlantecuhtli, a death god, guards the central stairway to a steep, blackened pyramid (structure 5). This pyramid is attached to the central **ball court** (shaped like a wide H), which is famous for the series of bas-relief carvings that adorn its walls (*see box, below*). At the north corners of the court, two panels depict pre- and post-game rituals; the death god watches both these scenes, floating eerily out of a jar. The ball game itself—common throughout Mesoamerica—was a team sport now thought to resemble basketball. The object of the game was to shoot a solid rubber ball through vertical stone hoops set high in the walls of the court using only hips, elbows, and knees. The consequences of the game were grim, as a carving in the northern wall attests. Three ball-players (identified by their characteristic belts and knee-pads) surround a fourth, who waits on his knees. The kneeling figure, arms bound and head thrown back, waits for the knife at his throat to plunge into his chest. Whether the sacrificial victim was the winner or loser of the match is still a subject of debate.

Behind structure 5 stands the ornate **Pyramid of the Niches**. Also called the *edificio calandario* (calendar building), its seven levels are punctuated by 365 framed, square cubby holes—one for each day of the solar year. Now bleached white, this pyramid, like all buildings at El Tajín, was once painted in vivid reds and blues—surely an impressive contrast to the surrounding intense green hills. Past the steep rise to the north lies **El Tajín Chico**, which is thought to have been the secular part of the city. The most important structure here is the **Building of the Columns**. Carved with complex narrative scenes, three of these columns are now housed in the museum near the entrance. Several carved human figures on the column, such as 13 Rabbit, bear names taken from the 260-day Mayan ceremonial calendar—but the relationship between El Tajín and the Mayan empire remains unknown.

Admission to the ruins is $2, except on Sunday, when it's free. Don't worry about finding food—the entrance is lined with fondas that sell cheap eats and mountains of tacky souvenirs, and there's even a big cafeteria-style restaurant at the site. El Tajín is a good place to see the voladores (*see box, above*); their pole is right outside the entrance. Performances take place on weekends, usually around noon, and during the week if enough people show up. Donations are the only wages the fliers receive.

Ritual Piercing

The major cultural groups of Mesoamerica shared several central rituals, including the ball game and human sacrifice. Archaeologists now believe that the ritualized piercing of tongues and genitals was also an important sacred practice among the rulers and priests of various civilzations. There's an excellent depiction of penis piercing at El Tajín in an intricate bas-relief carving on the southern wall of the central ball court (see above). A squatting Tlaloc (the rain god) carefully lances his own penis, pouring blood into a vat of pulque, an alcoholic brew made from the maguey plant. A figure in a fish headdress stands sternly in the stream of blood, while the laughing face of a two-bodied god presides over all.

COMING AND GOING The EL TAJIN/CHOTE buses that run along 16 de Septiembre in Papantla will get you to the ruins. Catch them at the bus stop behind the church ($1 round-trip). The last bus back to Papantla leaves at 5:45 PM.

Tuxpán

Tuxpán is a peaceful riverside town an hour or two north of Papantla. The city's main attraction is the stretch of Gulf Coast beaches that begins 7 kilometers to the east, although few foreign tourists ever enjoy them, perhaps due to the town's lack of impressive sights and development. So much the better for you: The white sandy beaches, beautiful green river, and tranquil setting make Tuxpán a prime destination for anyone seeking relative solitude among the palm trees. **Playa Tuxpán** is the place where the **Río Tuxpán**—the river that passes through town—meets the sea. The surf isn't huge here, but there's enough action to warrant shelling out $2 to rent a surfboard for the day. You'll find them for hire at the seafood and beer stands in the pine grove behind the beach.

Tuxpán itself is a pleasant town, with winding streets lined with two-story buildings. Juárez, the main street, runs parallel to the river and is home to numerous diners, hotels, and shops. The **Parque Reforma** is the center of social activity in town, with more than a hundred tables set around a hub of cafés and fruit stands. Lanchas shuttle passengers across the river to the **Casa de Fidel Castro** (Obregón, no phone), where Castro lived for a time while planning the overthrow of dictator Fulgencio Bautista. Now a museum of sorts, it's open daily 9–5, and you can wander in at no charge. A replica of the *Granma,* the ship that carried Fidel's freedom fighters from Tuxpán to battle in Cuba, rots outside. Inside, the casa is bare save some black-and-white photos of Fidel and Mexican president Lázaro Cárdenas.

BASICS

CASAS DE CAMBIO **Bancomer** (Juárez, at Escuela Médico Militar, tel. 783/4–00–09) changes cash and traveler's checks weekdays 9:30–noon. **Banamex** (Juárez, at Corregidora, tel. 783/4–08–40) has a 24-hour ATM that takes Cirrus, Plus, Visa, and MasterCard.

EMERGENCIES **Police** (tel. 783/4–02–52); **Cruz Roja** (tel. 783/4–01–58).

PHONES AND MAIL The full-service **post office** (Claviejro 28, tel. 783/4–00–88) is open weekdays 8–8 and Saturday 9–1. From Parque Reforma, walk one block east, turn left on Mina, and walk three blocks. They'll hold mail sent to you at the following address for up to 10 days: Lista de Correos, Administración 1, Tuxpán, Veracruz, CP 92801, México. You can make both long-distance and local calls at the ADO station (*see* Coming and Going, *below*).

VISITOR INFORMATION The small **tourist office** is in the red municipal building across the street from the cathedral. The friendly staff only speaks Spanish, and maps are in chronic short supply. *Juárez 23, tel. 783/4–03–22. Open daily 8–8.*

Bus tickets are a prized commodity in Tuxpán during such holidays as Christmas, Semana Santa, and the entire month of July. To avoid getting stuck here, it's best to buy your ticket at least two days before you want to leave.

COMING AND GOING

Tuxpán doesn't have a central first-class bus terminal; instead, each line has its own depot. The **Autobuses del Oriente (ADO)** station (Rodríguez 1, tel. 783/4–01–02), half a block off the river at the foot of Juárez, is the most convenient, with 10 buses a day to Mexico City (6 hrs, $10) and four buses a day to Papantla (1½ hrs, $2). If you can't get a ticket at the ADO terminal, try **Omnibus de México** (Independencia 50, tel. 783/4–11–47), which has a depot 1 kilometer farther down the river, near the bridge. Their service is similar to ADO's.

Second-class buses operate from the outdoor **Terminal ABC** (tel. 783/4–20–40) on Cuauhtémoc. Service is available to destinations such as Tampico (6 hrs, $6), Nuevo Laredo (16 hrs, $30), Monterrey (12 hrs, $25), and Reynosa (12 hrs, $25).

GETTING AROUND

Central Tuxpán is small and easily covered on foot. Juárez, the main street, runs parallel to the river, one block inland. You can walk down Juárez from the ADO station to Parque Reforma in about five minutes. Boat rides across the river cost only pennies. Buses marked PLAYA run frequently along the river's edge to and from the beach (15 min, 50¢); service starts at 7 AM and ends around 9 PM. The easiest place to flag them down is at the corner of Rodríguez and Reforma.

The last bus back to town leaves Playa Tuxpán at about 8:30 PM. Hitch back to town if you miss it—hammocks can be rented for a night on the beach, but a number of assaults have recently taken place.

WHERE TO SLEEP

Hotels tend to be expensive, but you'll find a few moderately priced establishments near the center. If the places below are full, try the bare but passable **Hotel del Parque** (Humboldt 11, on the zócalo, tel. 783/4–08–12), where both singles and doubles cost $8.

Hotel El Huasteco. Just a block east of Parque Juárez, the Huasteco tends to fill up fast. The rooms are basic but clean and air-conditioned. Singles go for $9, doubles for $11. *Morelos 41, tel. 783/4–18–59. 40 rooms, all with bath. Laundry, luggage storage.*

Hotel Posada San Ignacio. Potted plants fill the small central courtyard of this pretty hotel, and the rooms, which all have fans, are spotless. Sparkling-clean tile bathrooms have plenty of hot water. Rooms are $7 for one bed, $10 for two. *Melchor Ocampo 29, 1 block north of the zócalo, tel. 783/4–29–05. 17 rooms, all with bath. Laundry, luggage storage. Wheelchair access.*

Hotel Tuxpán. Also near Parque Juárez, this hotel is a bit overpriced considering the mediocre accommodations it offers: Rooms are relatively clean but small and stuffy, and bathrooms are long, skinny, awkward affairs, though they do have hot water. Singles cost $8, doubles $9. *Mina 2, at Juárez, tel. 783/4–41–10. 43 rooms, all with bath. Luggage storage.*

CAMPING Although it's free and legal to pitch a tent on **Playa Tuxpán,** word is that it's become increasingly less safe. If you want to risk it, hammocks are $1 per day, though you have to sweet-talk an overnight rental. It's also possible to camp on **Isla Lobos** (*see* Outdoor Activities, *below*), but you must first obtain a permit from the Coast Guard office (tel. 783/4–03–43), about 3 kilometers from the center, on the way to Playa Tuxpán. Permits can take up to four days to process, so plan ahead. More safe might be the **Unidad Deportiva** (Colonia Jardines, tel. 783/4–42–09). It's not close to the beach, but it has a pool and camping is free. Take the UV (Universidad Veracruzana) bus and get off at the Coca-Cola factory.

FOOD

Restaurants congregate on Juárez in the center of town. There are also several good, cheap taco stands up the street from the ADO depot.

Antonio's. This elegant, air-conditioned restaurant has a menu that runs the gamut from prohibitively expensive to happily budget-friendly. The *desayuno americano* (American breakfast) includes eggs, toast, jam, juice, and tea for $3.50, and a plate of chicken or cheese enchiladas is $2. There's also a full bar here. Friday and Saturday nights see live music beginning at 9 PM. *Juárez 25, at Garizurieta, tel. 783/4–16–02. Open daily 7 AM–midnight.*

Cafetería el Mante. This place is almost always packed with hungry locals and is especially popular for breakfast. The most popular dish is *bocoles con huevo* (fried dough filled with egg; $2). *Pipila 8, at Juárez, tel. 783/4–57–36. Open daily 6 AM–midnight.*

Del Puerto. There are always a few locals here, leisurely dining on seafood and watching the action in the Parque Juárez across the street. The excellent $3 seafood soup is a meal in itself, and you can get your fish cooked almost any way you want (try it *al mojo,* in garlic butter). Juárez y Humbolt, tel. 783/4-46-01. Open daily 7 AM-11 PM.

OUTDOOR ACTIVITIES

Playa Tuxpán is the most accessible beach in the area, about 7 kilometers from downtown. Pick up a PLAYA bus near the dock where the lanchas leave to cross the river, near Rodríguez and Reforma. The beaches in Tuxpán are lined with cheap *palapa* (thatched-hut) restaurants selling everything from crab burritos to ice-cold coconuts. For scuba diving or snorkeling, head to **Tamiaula,** a small village just north of Tuxpán, where you can hire a fishing boat for the 45-minute journey to the prime diving around **Isla Lobos** (Island of Wolves). You'll find a military outpost and a lighthouse on the island. In the shallow water offshore there are a few shipwrecks and colorful reefs that are home to a large variety of sealife, including pufferfish, parrotfish, damselfish, and barracuda. Buses to Tamiaula (30 min, $1) leave from the **Terminal ABC** (*see* Coming and Going, *above*).

If you didn't bring your own equipment you can rent gear from **Aquasport** (tel. 783/7-02-59), just before Playa Tuxpán, where they also arrange group trips to Isla Lobos ($75 per day) that include all permits, scuba gear, food, and transportation. No scuba classes are offered, so non-experts are stuck with snorkeling.

OAXACA   12
By Lourdes Haro

Oaxaca comes closer to the Mexico of dreams than perhaps any other destination in Mexico—here, 10,000 years of tradition passed down by artisans, farmers, fisherman, and storytellers has not been relegated to museums. In smaller villages, Maya rites and ceremonies—complete with traditional dress and musical instruments—still mark the passage of girls and boys into adulthood. The agricultural techniques used in mountainside fields are the same as they were centuries ago: Corn fields are plowed by ox-driven carts, and wooden-wheeled carriages still tote produce from village to village. The Sierra Madre del Sur mountains have somewhat protected the traditional lifestyles of indigenous peoples such as the Zapotec, Mixtec, Mixe, Huave, and Triqui. Today more than 17 distinct Indian languages are spoken in Oaxaca and cultures within this mountainous southern state vary as greatly as the landscape, which encompasses sunset-colored canyons, cacti-carpeted deserts, tropical jungles, scrubby coastland, and thriving cities.

At the confluence of three river valleys sits Oaxaca de Juárez, or Oaxaca city. This state capital is a laid-back city, and its shady, café-filled zócalo is a place where mestizo Indians and expatriates meet. Pre-Columbian sites such as Monte Albán and Mitla are easily accessible from here, as are many small towns filled with artisans and craftspeople. Farther from the city, the landscape changes more drastically. To the south, the Sierra Madre del Sur drops sharply to the sea, forming a long stretch of Pacific Coast beaches. Puerto Escondido is *the* surfer mecca, while Puerto Ángel, a cliffside fishing village, is a good place to snorkel. Nearby, Zipolite beach is favored by international hippies in the know, and Huatulco, although ear-marked by the Mexican government as the next Cancún, still has untouched coves and good places to camp. Although the Isthmus of Tehuantepec is usually viewed as a dull gateway to Chiapas and Tabasco, this is partly because the region reacts to the modern world by gripping to its old traditions and customs, instead of attracting tourists with fancy hotels. Largely Zapotec in population, pleasures here are simple: You can eat boiled iguana eggs, whiz around in a moped-propelled chariot, or simply watch the world go by. Regions such as this might not be for everyone, though—those interested in Zapotec culture will find plenty; otherwise the isthmus is just hot, flat, and dusty.

Oaxaca

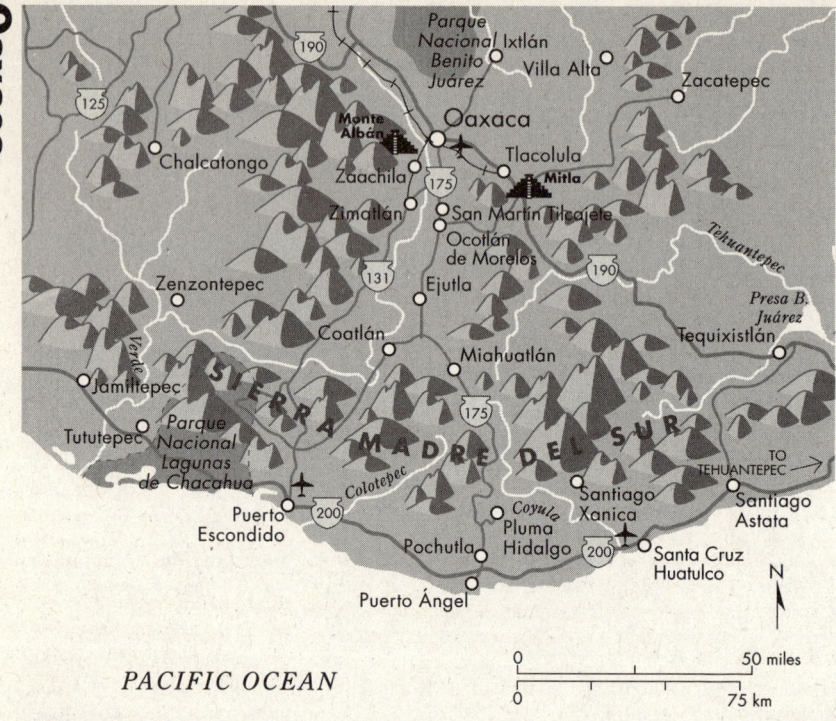

Oaxaca de Juárez

Oaxaca city is a microcosm of the diversity and cultural richness of this region—qualities that are most evident in the zócalo. Here, Triquis selling weavings made in high mountain villages sit alongside Tehuana women from the Isthmus, whose children cling to their long, colorful skirts. Demonstrations are common, whether they be for students' and Indians' rights, or better pay for school teachers. On quieter days, the fluid sounds of Spanish mingle with Zapotec and English, as shoe-shine boys chat to university students, but tacky commercialism is also present, so don't be surprised if giant helium-filled Teenage Mutant Ninja Turtles float over the whole scene. It is this meeting of worlds that energizes the city and fuels its people, who continue to innovate while respecting their traditions. Evidence of an even earlier, more violent meeting of cultures lies only an hour bus-ride away: Five important archaeological sites—Oaxaca city, Monte Albán, Mitla, Zaachila, Dainzú, and Yagul—lie crumbling alongside decaying Jesuit structures.

Despite its increasing popularity with tourists, Oaxaca de Juárez has managed to maintain a certain grace, dignity, and timelessness.

BASICS

AMERICAN EXPRESS The AmEx office, inside the travel agency **Viajes Micsa** (NE cnr of zócalo), exchanges all traveler's checks with no commission, replaces lost checks, and delivers MoneyGrams. They also cash personal checks, hold mail, and replace AmEx cards. *Valdivieso 2, Oaxaca, Oaxaca, CP 68000, México, tel. 951/6-27-00, fax 951/6-74-75. Open weekdays 9–2 and 4–6, Sat. 9–2.*

CASAS DE CAMBIO Although exchange places stay open longer, the banks in the zócalo give slightly better rates for dollars and traveler's checks. **Banamex** (Hidalgo 821, tel. 951/6–59–00, 1 block east of zócalo), open for exchange weekdays 9–noon, changes AmEx traveler's checks. **Bancomer** (Garcia Vigil 202, tel. 951/6–76–43) exchanges AmEx, Thomas Cook, and Visa checks, and has an ATM that accepts Plus, Cirrus, Visa and MasterCard.

CONSULATES **Canada and United Kingdom:** Hidalgo 817-5, Oaxaca, Oaxaca, CP 68000, tel. 951/6–56–00; open weekdays 9–1.

United States: Alcalá 201, Rooms 204 and 206, Oaxaca, Oaxaca, CP 68000, tel. 951/4–30–54; open weekdays 9–1.

EMERGENCIES In an emergency, dial 06 (no coins necessary) from any phone. Oaxaca also has a tourist-specific **police unit** (tel. 951/6–38–10).

LAUNDRY **Azteca Lavandería** will wash and deliver your clothes in under two hours, but they charge $5 for the first 3½ kilos. *Hidalgo, at Díaz Ordaz, tel. 951/4–79–51. Open Mon.–Sat. 8–8, Sun. 10–2.*

MAIL The **post office** (off zócalo, facing the cathedral, tel. 951/6–26–61; open weekdays 8–7; Sat. 9–1) will hold mail sent to you at the following address for up to 10 days: Lista de Correos, Administración 1, Oaxaca, Oaxaca, CP 68001, México. Next door, **Telecomunicaciones de México** provides telegram, money order, and fax service. *Tel. 951/6–42–55. Open weekdays 8–8, Sat. 9–2.*

MEDICAL AID The **Cruz Roja** (Armenta y López 700, tel. 951/6–44–55) offers 24-hour free medical service and emergency care. **Hospital San Antonio del Carmen** (Abasolo 215, tel. 951/6–26–12) has English-speaking doctors on call 24 hours a day. If you need a dentist or specialist, the tourist office at 5 de Mayo and Morelos can refer you to someone who speaks English. **La Farmacia Guadalupana** (Hidalgo 340, tel. 951/6–53–82) is open 24 hours daily.

PHONES You can make local and international collect calls from the orange phones scattered across town. The blue phones on the zócalo accept major credit cards, but not international calling cards. The public phones in front of **Telmex** (Matamoros, at Valdivieso), however, do accept calling cards. **Computel** provides the fastest and most expensive international calls as well as a fax machine. *Trujano 204, tel. 951/4–73–19. Off zócalo, btw Cabrera and 20 de Noviembre. Open daily 7 AM–10 PM.*

SCHOOLS Oaxaca has a number of reputable language schools, most of which will arrange homestays for you. The **Instituto Cultural de Oaxaca** (Juárez 503, tel. 951/5–34–04) offers intensive Spanish courses, as well as classes in Mexican cooking, ceramics, textiles, history, and archaeology, some of which are conducted in English. The **Instituto de Comunicación y Cultura** (Alcalá 307 No. 12, tel. 951/6–34–43) offers classes in Zapotec, as well as all levels of Spanish. The **Centro de Idiomas de la Universidad Autónoma "Benito Juárez"** (Burgoa, btw Armenta y López and Bustamante, tel. 951/6–59–22) offers college credit for intensive courses in Spanish, Mixtec, and Zapotec.

VISITOR INFORMATION Stop by the **Oficina de Turismo** (5 de Mayo, at Morelos, tel. 951/6–48–28; open daily 9–8), where the bilingual staff is more than happy to assist you and let you leave notes for fellow travelers here (for up to a month). To find out what's going on in town, pick up a copy of *Oaxaca Times* or *Oaxaca*. The Spanish *Guía Cultural*, which lists free films, art exhibits, and music and theater performances, is available here or at magazine stands on the zócalo. A second **Oficina de Turismo** (Independencia, at García Vigil; open Mon.–Sat. 9–3 and 6–8, Sun. 9–3) in the Palacio Municipal also provides free maps and bus schedules.

COMING AND GOING

BY BUS Oaxaca's crowded and noisy first-class bus terminal (Calzada Niños Héroes 1306) is 11 long blocks north of the zócalo—a 20-minute walk from downtown or about $2 by cab.

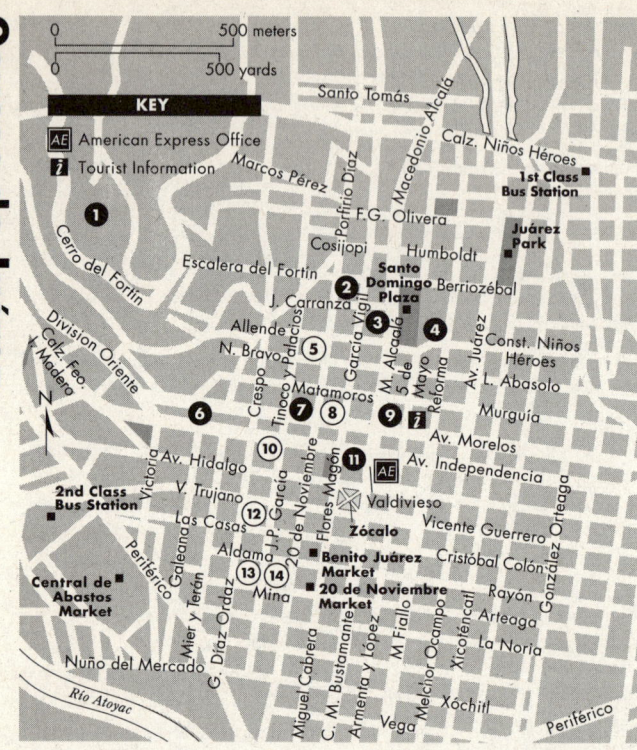

Cristóbal Colón (tel. 951/5-12-14) offers daily service to Mexico City's TAPO terminal (5 per day, 7 hrs, $18) and San Cristóbal (2 per day, 12 hrs, $21). **Autobuses del Oriente (ADO)** (tel. 951/5-17-03) serves Puebla (7 per day, 4 hrs, $13), Veracruz (2 per day, 9 hrs, $21), and Salina Cruz (5 hrs, $8.50).

The second-class station is south of the railroad tracks across from the Central de Abastos market, on the corner of Trujano and the Periférico expressway. The many bus companies based here serve outlying towns, as well as Mexico City (9 hrs, $15), Tapachula (12 hrs, $19), and other major cities. **Estrella del Valle** (tel. 951/4-57-00) runs to Puerto Escondido (7½ hrs, $8.50), Santa Cruz Huatulco (6½ hrs, $8), and Pochutla (6 hrs, $8). For about the same price, you can take a bus from **Hotel Mesón del Ángel** (Mina 518, tel. 951/6-53-27) to Puerto Escondido. The station isn't the safest place to crash overnight.

BY TRAIN The Oaxaqueño train goes (slowly) to Mexico City from the station on Madero (tel. 951/6-22-53) once a day at 7 PM. Tickets cost $25 first-class, $12 regular, and $8 second-class.

BY PLANE The **Aeropuerto Nacional de Oaxaca-Zozocatlán** (tel. 951/6-23-32) is 8 kilometers south of town. Two daily flights go to Mexico City (1 hr, $80 one-way). Tickets can be purchased at the airport or from agencies downtown—try **AVIACSA** (Porfirio Díaz 102 No. 2, tel. 951/3-18-01). For $3 **Transportación Aeropuerto** (in front of cathedral, tel. 951/4-43-50) will shuttle you between the airport and downtown Monday–Saturday 9–8. For tourist information at the airport, head for the desk inside the main terminal.

HITCHING While hitching is always risky, people who wouldn't hitchhike elsewhere in Mexico will do so in these parts, and it's fairly easy to get rides from here to the rest of the state and beyond. The best places to stand are on the main roads leading in and out of the city—try Calzada Niños Héroes and the Periférico.

GETTING AROUND

Oaxaca city is walker-friendly; you can cross it in 45 minutes. At its heart is the **zócalo**, bordered by the mammoth cathedral and the **Parque Alameda de León**. North of the zócalo is the posh part of town, where you can find (or avoid) luxury hotels with tourist-oriented discos. The southern rim of the city proper is edged by the **Periférico**. Here you'll find the second-class bus station, the huge **Central de Abastos** market, and the red-light district. The hill that overlooks Oaxaca, **Cerro del Fortín** (Fort Hill), is a 20-minute walk northwest from the zócalo. Keep in mind that most streets change names as they cross Avenida Independencia going north–south and Bustamante/Alcalá going east–west.

Buses are hardly used—or necessary—in the downtown area. Taxis are best for getting to and from the bus stations after dark, when the southwest corner of town gets a bit dicey. Standard fares within downtown are $2–$5, but agree on a price before getting in. **Bicicletas Martínez** (J. P. García 509, tel. 951/4–31–44) rents bikes for $8 a day, but downtown Oaxaca isn't particularly bicycle-friendly.

WHERE TO SLEEP

There are two main areas to crash in Oaxaca, one north and one south of the zócalo. You'll pay more to stay on the north side, a quiet, residential, colonial district. The south side, near the markets and second-class bus station, caters to working-class Mexicans and shoestring travelers. If you plan to stay a while, consider the beautifully maintained ex-convent, **Posada San Pablo** (Fiallo 102, tel. 951/6–49–14), which has furnished apartments with kitchens and private baths for $300 per month for two people. Be sure to make reservations if you'll be in town during La Guelaguetza (see box, below).

The **tourist office** on 5 de Mayo, at Morelos, provides lists of local families with rooms to let; the rates ($5–$15 per night) often include laundry service and meals. Oaxaca's Spanish-language schools (see Schools, above) can also arrange family stays for their students.

SOUTH OF THE ZOCALO Amongst the family-owned jewelry shops, street vendors, and working-class Oaxqueños, you'll find the cheapest lodging in town.

➢ **UNDER $10** • **Hotel El Palmar.** The simple, clean rooms here are $6 per person, $8 with private bath. Rooms facing the street are brighter but noisier than those in the interior. Be sure to shower in the morning, because the hot water is shut off in the afternoons. *J. P. García 507, btw Aldama and Mina, tel. 951/6–43–35. 30 rooms, 8 with bath. Luggage storage. Wheelchair access.*

➢ **UNDER $15** • **Hotel Pasaje.** A courtyard with blooming tropical foliage, festive tiles, and a gregarious green parrot make the Pasaje a favorite among budget travelers. The clean, comfy rooms have desks and private baths with hot showers. Ask to see the beds in your room first—some are more uncomfortable than others. Singles are $9, doubles $12. *Mina 302, tel. 951/6–42–13. ½ block west of 20 de Noviembre market, btw J. P. García and 20 de Noviembre. 18 rooms, all with bath. No check-in 2 AM–6 AM. Luggage storage.*

Hotel Vallarta. The clean, freshly painted rooms here are plain but blessed with amenities: private bathrooms, purified water, towels, soap, and desks. Doubles with one bed cost $14, with two beds $18. Singles fetch $10. *Díaz Ordaz 309, tel. 951/6–49–67. 3 blocks SE of zócalo, btw Trujano and Las Casas. 30 rooms, all with bath. Luggage storage.*

NORTH OF THE ZOCALO Even though this more upscale side of town tends to be more of a tourist magnet with its galleries and expensive restaurants, there are still plenty of lodging deals around.

➢ **UNDER $15** • **Hostal del Centro.** The large, carpeted rooms and a super-clean communal bathroom with 24-hour hot water make this place a bargain at $8 a single, $11 a double. The friendly management lets you use the small kitchen to fix yourself a cup of hot tea, which you can sip in the quiet, plant-filled courtyard. *Matamoros 206, btw Porfirio Díaz and García Vigil, tel. 951/6–84–16. 7 rooms, none with bath. Luggage storage. AE, V.*

➢ **UNDER $20** • **Las Golondrinas.** "The Swallows" offers quiet, clean, tastefully decorated rooms, and a number of patios overflowing with roses and tropical flowers. Sun-worshippers are welcome on the roof. Doubles cost $16, singles $12.70. A triple with a tiny living room is a great deal at $21. *Tinoco y Palacios 411, 5 blocks north of zócalo, tel. 951/4-21-26. 27 rooms, all with bath. Laundry, luggage storage.*

Hotel Francia. The Francia is where writer D.H. Lawrence stayed during his 1925 visit to Oaxaca. Mexico's colonial past is recalled in the dramatic rooms of the old wing, with high ceilings and tiled floors. The past is lost in the new wing, where rooms have modern furniture and bigger bathrooms. Ask to see a few before you choose. Doubles $16, singles $14. *20 de Noviembre 212, tel. 951/6-48-11. 1 block west of zócalo, btw Hidalgo and Trujano. 45 rooms, all with bath. Luggage storage. Wheelchair access. MC, V.*

FOOD

Oaxacan cuisine is spicy, delicious, and famed throughout Mexico (*see box,* Eat This! *below*). If you have a tolerant palate, the markets at Central de Abastos, 20 de Noviembre, and Benito Juárez offer a gastronomical extravaganza where you can sample the many local specialties without breaking the bank—go in the morning while the pots are still full. Restaurants on the south side of the zócalo are generally cheap and cater to a mostly Mexican crowd. More gringo-oriented fare can be had on Avenidas Morelos and Independencia, just north of the zócalo.

SOUTH OF THE ZOCALO

➢ **UNDER $5** • **Café Alex.** This popular restaurant near the second-class bus station offers a variety of Oaxacan specialties. Share the back patio with cages full of chattering parrots and parakeets as you sample the hearty chicken mole ($4). Breakfast specials are also a good deal, with juice and granola for less than $2. *Díaz Ordaz 218, at Trujano, tel. 951/4-07-15. Open Mon.-Sat. 7 AM-9 PM, Sun. 7-noon.*

Cafetería Tayu. The tranquil green patio of this restaurant is just steps away from the action on 20 de Noviembre. The simple but filling comida corrida includes a meat entrée, soup, *agua*

Eat This!

Modern Oaxacan food continues to be based on local ingredients and traditional recipes, elements of which predate the Spaniards' arrival. Oaxaca's three markets are the best places to sample any of the following regional specialties without paying tourist prices.

- **CHAPULINES:** tangy fried grasshoppers prepared with chile and lime. They go down a bit easier if you pull off the legs first. According to local folklore, one taste will charm you into never leaving Oaxaca.

- **JICUATOTE:** a wiggly, sweet, white gelatin made with milk, cloves, cinnamon, and cornmeal. It's served in tubs and usually colored red on top.

- **TEJATE:** a beverage made from the flowers and roasted seeds of the cacao tree, corn, coconut milk, sugar, water, and spices. Look for huge bowls of white paste and watery, brown liquid.

- **TLAYUDAS:** huge, flat tortillas spread with refried beans and topped with salsa, fresh vegetables, and guacamole.

fresca, and a dessert for only $2. Be prepared to share your table with Oaxacans who know a good value when they see it. *20 de Noviembre 416, tel. 951/6–53–63. Open Mon.–Sat. 7–7.*

El Sol de Oro. Although this vegetarian restaurant is a bit far from the zócolo, it's well worth the trip to sample the "fish" dish, consisting, strangely enough, of sautéed potatoes, onions, garlic, soy hamburger, and tofu. A full vegetarian lunch with soup, bread, rice, an entrée, and agua fresca costs $2.50. *Lázaro Cárdenas 114 (formerly Camino Nacional), tel. 951/3–38–63, 3 blocks east of Periférico. From cnr of Xicotencatl and Independencia, catch* SANTA LUCIA *bus and get off at Santas Perpetua y Felicitas church. Open Mon.–Sat. 10 AM–6 PM.*

NORTH OF THE ZOCALO

➢ **UNDER $5 • El Mesón.** The buffet-style lunches at this joint are a great way to sample the region's famed dishes, such as mole oaxqueño. The all-you-can-eat lunch buffet is $4. *Hidalgo 805, at Valdivieso, no phone. Open daily 8 AM–10 PM.*

Nutritortas Gigantes. This hole-in-the-wall has a variety of sandwiches priced $2–$3. The ones with tangy chapulines (*see box, above*) are crunchy, yummy, and perfect for late-night munchies. *Nicolás Bravo 216, tel. 951/6–64–69. 4 blocks NW of zócalo. Open daily 9 AM–10 PM.*

Quickly. This is probably how you'll attack the $3 *chilaquiles* (tortilla strips doused with salsa and sour cream). Also worthwhile is the dubiously named but tasty "gringa" hamburger ($3.50), loaded with ham, bacon, cheese, and tomato. Tlayudas (*see box, above*), at $4 apiece, are popular with locals. *Alcalá 100-B, ½ block NW of zócalo, tel. 951/4–70–76. Open weekdays 8 AM–11 PM, weekends 2–11.*

Señor de la Salud. The "Lord of Health" lives up to its name, offering nutritious vegetarian and meat dishes in an open, clean setting. Try the veggie chilaquiles with beans, tortillas, juice, and coffee for $3.50. Fresh carrot juice goes for $1. *Juárez 201-D, btw Morelos and Murgia, no phone. Open Mon.–Sat. 8–8.*

➢ **UNDER $10 • Flor de Loto-Plaza Gourmet.** Not to be mistaken for the adjoining vegetarian Flor de Loto-Sureste (whose owner "borrowed" the original's name and reputation), this eatery offers a tantalizing array of vegetarian and meat dishes. The owner personally shops for the fresh fruit, vegetables, fish, and meats every day. Breakfast specials cost $4, the comida corrida $5. *Morelos 509, tel. 951/6–91–46. Next to Museo Rufino Tamayo. Open Wed.–Mon. 8 AM–10 PM, Tues. 8–6.*

CAFES The tourist scene in Oaxaca revolves around the cafés on the zócalo, but those wrought-iron tables crowded with gringos are far from the last word on the city's café culture. The following are a couple of out-of-the-way spots recommended by Oaxacans.

Antojitos de los Olmos. It's easy to miss their tiny black sign on touristy Alcalá, but pass through the small doorway and you're welcomed into the patio of the private home of Antonia Olmos Guebarra. She serves the best *atole* (a sweet, corn-based drink, similar to hot chocolate) in town to her festive crowd of loyal customers for only 60¢. Delicious tamales, tacos, and tostadas are cooked up before your eyes for $1. *Alcalá 301, tel. 951/6–44–10. Open Mon.–Sat. 7:30 PM–11:30 PM.*

Café Hipótesis. The Hypothesis features shelves and shelves of eclectic literature and, occasionally, live guitar music. Pick an interesting title, sit back, and work on a *yarda* (a tall glass, literally a yard) of beer or sangría for less than $3. They also offer quesadillas, tostadas, and excellent sandwiches. *Morelos 511, no phone. Open Mon.–Sat. 1 PM–2 AM.*

Cafetería Morgan. Their bulletin board claims they serve "the best coffee for 4,000 miles," and it may well be true. Morgan's breakfasts ($2–$3) include a cup of their famous cappuccino. *Morelos 601-B, no phone. Open Mon.–Sat. 7:30–1 and 5:30–10.*

WORTH SEEING

Oaxaca city has a wealth of Roman Catholic churches, convents, and monasteries dating from the colonial period, only a few of which are mentioned below. Some have been converted into government offices and museums, but many remain active places of worship, where rituals have changed little in the past century. The life of the city is in the zócalo, markets, and busy southside streets, where old men gossip on street corners, and Zapotec vendors hawk their handmade crafts.

BASILICA DE LA SOLEDAD This 17th-century baroque church is breathtaking at dusk, when it reflects a golden glow, and local boys play soccer on the church's antique concrete plaza. The church holds a black-draped figure of the Virgen de la Soledad (Our Lady of Solitude) to which believers ascribe healing powers. On December 18, the **Danza de la Pluma** (Feather Dance; see Festivals, below), a dramatization of the Conquest, is performed here as part of the festival in her honor. Behind the church is the **Museo Religioso de la Soledad** (tel. 951/6-75-66), which displays a fascinating collection of trinkets dedicated to the Virgin. *Independencia 107, at Galeana. Museum admission: 35¢. Open Mon.–Sat. 9–2 and 4–6, Sun. 9–2.*

CATEDRAL DE OAXACA Construction of the cathedral began in 1553, but was interrupted by earthquakes, leaving the church unfinished for another 200 years. The beautifully carved baroque facade depicts the ascension of the Virgin, and the centerpiece of the cathedral is a bronze altar imported from Italy. The cathedral also houses the Señor del Rayo, a giant gold and silver crucifix which, legend has it, miraculously survived a fire begun by a bolt of lightning. *On the zócalo, facing the Alameda. Masses held daily and in English Sun. at 10 AM.*

CERRO DEL FORTIN The hill dominating the city has been a site of festivals and celebrations since pre-Columbian times. A long flight of stairs leads up to the Cerro from Avenida Crespo, about 2 kilometers northwest of the zócalo. Crowning the Cerro is an open-air auditorium used for the festivities of **La Guelaguetza** (*see box, below*), as well as a planetarium and observatory, both of which are unfortunately accessible only for large groups by special appointment. The lookout point has an awesome view of the city and a huge bronze statue of Benito Juárez, captioned by his famous phrase: "El respecto al derecho ajeno es la paz" (Respect for the rights of others is peace). *From zócalo, walk north 7 blocks along Díaz Ordaz.*

IGLESIA Y EX-CONVENTO DE SANTO DOMINGO Santo Domingo, built in the 16th century, is one of Oaxaca city's most ornate houses of worship. The rose-colored exterior is striking but pales in comparison to what is found inside. The ceiling of the entryway is decorated with an amazing tree sprouting depictions of church benefactors, and busts of saints and martyrs observe you from every corner and archway. The adjacent monastery, built in 1619, now houses the **Museo Regional de Oaxaca**, where exquisite Mixtec artifacts from the tombs of Monte Albán are artfully displayed, including skulls encrusted with jade and turquoise, gold earrings and ornaments, and elaborately carved jaguar bones. *Alcalá, at Gurrión, 5 blocks NW of zócalo. Admission: $4.50, free Sun. Open Tues.–Fri. 10–5:30, weekends 10–5.*

INSTITUTO DE ARTES GRAFICAS This often overlooked but splendid museum, library, and art gallery features a collection of books on contemporary and classic art, with an emphasis on graphic art prints. *Alcalá 507, near Santo Domingo, tel. 951/6-69-80. Donations encouraged. Open Wed.–Mon. 10:30–8.*

MUSEO CASA DE BENITO JUAREZ Benito Juárez (1806–1872), born in the town of Guelatao, remains the only Mexican president of pure indigenous (Zapotec) descent. Skip the three-hour bus ride to Guelatao and pay homage to him at the house where, for two years, Juárez worked for a Franciscan friar who taught him Spanish. The study, dining room, kitchen, and bedroom are open for viewing. Also on display are some personal letters, documents, and Juárez's death mask. *García Vigil 609, tel. 951/6-18-60. Admission: $2.50, free Sun. Open Tues.–Sun. 10–7.*

MUSEO DE ARTE CONTEMPORANEO DE OAXACA This excellent museum is dedicated to contemporary Oaxacan artists, both mestizo and indigenous, but occasionally features big-name European exhibits as well. Free films are shown on Friday, Saturday, and Sunday nights. *Alcalá 202, tel. 951/6-84-99. Donations encouraged. Open Wed.–Mon. 10:30–8.*

MUSEO RUFINO TAMAYO Pre-Columbian artifacts from all over Mexico are displayed in this beautifully restored colonial mansion. The collection, which belonged to Rufino Tamayo, one of Mexico's premier artists, is arranged chronologically to give an idea of the artistic development that preceded the Conquest. *Morelos 503, tel. 951/6-47-50. Admission: $3. Open Mon. and Wed.-Sat. 10-2 and 4-7, Sun. 10-3.*

CHEAP THRILLS

The **Casa de la Cultura Oaxaqueña** (González Ortega 403, tel. 951/6-18-29) features free films, dance, theater, art, and musical events. You can stop by weekdays 9-9 or early Saturday to find out what's going on. The theater at **Centro Cultural Juan Rulfo** (Independencia, at Mier y Terán) has nightly musical performances as well as frequent cultural events, most of which are free. Wednesdays there is live music, usually nueva canción, and Fridays are devoted to issues affecting women. Another freebie is the beautiful murals by Arturo García Bustos depicting Oaxaca's pre-Columbian and revolutionary history in the **Palacio del Gobierno** (south side of zócalo). In case you get homesick for English reading material, the **Biblioteca Circulante de Oaxaca** (Alcalá 205, no phone) has an extensive selection of books in English and over 50 different magazines—everything from *The Economist* to *Spin*.

SHOPPING

Oaxacan artisans are famous for the quality and inventiveness of their work. If you only want to browse, explore the expensive boutiques along the Andador Turístico and the shops north of the zócalo. Pesos are better spent in nearby villages (*see* Near Oaxaca, *below*).

MARKETS With their colorful mix of handicrafts, unfamiliar fruits and vegetables, and thick air filled with sweet, ripe, rank, stomach-churning, and tantalizing smells, the markets of Oaxaca present an adventure for all the senses. The **Central de Abastos** market, across from the second-class bus station, is a labyrinth of hanging bags, shoes, hammocks, fruit, witchcraft stores, and gory meat stands. On Saturdays, you'll find regional crafts: black and green ceramics, gold filigree jewelry, *alebrijes* (brightly painted wooden animals), *rebozos* (shawls), engraved knives, and *huipiles* (intricately embroidered tunics). The **Benito Juárez** market, hemmed by 20 de Noviembre, Las Casas, Cabrera, and Aldama, offers a smaller selection of the same just one block from the zócalo, and is ringed by *artesanía* (crafts) vendors. The **20 de Noviembre** market, directly across Aldama from the Mercado Benito Juárez, contains mostly food and cheap *comedores* (sit-down food stands).

La Guelaguetza

The most famous Oaxacan festival—and one of the most amazing floral festivities in all of Latin America—is also called "Lunes del Cerro" (Monday of the Hill). Celebrated on the two Mondays following the Fiesta de la Virgen del Carmen (July 16), thousands of people from all over Mexico gather to perform folk dances and exchange gifts. A pineapple dance giving thanks for the year's harvest is performed by Papaloapan women, while the Feather Dance is enacted by Zapotec men. Dances take place in the amphitheater atop the Cerro del Fortín, and good seats (sold at tourist agencies throughout the city) cost about $30. The preceding week is filled with music, parades, and cultural events. A high point is the dramatic portrayal of the martyrdom of the Zapotec princess Donaji, who was decapitated by the Mixtecs for spurning her Mixtec lover in favor of her people. Legend has it that when her corpse was found, lilies of the valley were growing from her severed head. Donaji remains an important symbol of regional pride, and the image of her head now graces the Oaxacan state seal.

AFTER DARK

At the heart of Oaxaca's nightlife is the zócalo, which bustles with action long into the night. At dusk you can check out the passersby, look for love, or just sip an icy Corona with lime.

BARS If you're not content simply having a beer on the zócalo, **La Casa del Mezcal** (Flores Magón 209, no phone) offers many different flavors and concentrations of tequila's sister drink in a Mexican saloon setting; get here before 10 PM, when the house closes its swinging wooden doors. **El Sol y La Luna** (M. Bravo 109, tel. 951/4–81–05), with its candlelit atmosphere and antique decor, is a tranquil place to bring your significant other. Their international menu includes small but succulent crêpes for $3. It's open daily 8 AM–11 AM and 7 PM–11 PM, and live music fills the front room weekends after 9 PM.

CINEMA A number of movie theaters often show subtitled or dubbed American movies. Right off the zócalo is **Plaza Alameda** (Independencia, at 20 de Noviembre, tel. 951/6–11–99), where admission is $2. The **Museo de Arte Contemporáneo** (see Worth Seeing, above) offers free films, usually with political or cultural themes, on Friday, Saturday, and Sunday nights.

DANCING **Candela** (Ignacio Allende 211, tel. 951/6–79–3) heats up with live salsa and Caribbean rhythms Monday–Saturday 9:30 PM–1:30 AM. A shot of mezcal is less than $2, and gay couples, rhythmically impaired gringos, and even lone women feel at ease jumping about on the dance floor. Depending on the band, the cover charge runs $3.50–$5. If you prefer to swim through smoke and flashing disco lights to the sound of technopop, go to **Eclipse** (Porfirio Díaz 219, tel. 951/6–42–36). It's as packed with young people as it is with attitude, and is open Thursday–Saturday 10 PM–2:30 AM and Sunday 7 PM–midnight. There's a hefty cover charge for men (about $8 Thurs.–Sat.); women pay the same on weekends but get a break Thursday nights. Sundays, everybody pays $3.

How do you tell a good mezcal? Shake it. If bubbles form, it's good; if not, it's been watered down.

MUSIC Tuesday, Thursday, and Sunday nights at 8 PM, the town bands play mariachi, marimba, and salsa in the zócalo's central gazebo. On Fridays and Saturdays, mariachi bands roam the zócalo serenading anyone who'll buy a song. **Los Tres Patios** is the place to chill out and sip a mixed drink while listening to live jazz. The cover is usually about $3.50. *Cosijopi 208, btw Porfirio Díaz and García Vigil, no phone. Open Mon.–Sat. 8 PM–2 AM.*

Near Oaxaca

Within 50 kilometers of Oaxaca are a number of important pre-Columbian ruins, most notably Monte Albán and Mitla, and indigenous communities that maintain distinct languages, customs, and folklore, as well as ties to the sacred ruins. When archaeologists discovered the tombs in Zaachila, townspeople insisted on being involved in the excavations because, after all, it was the burial site of their ancestors. Visiting the ruins and the indigenous communities on their market days is an unobtrusive way to gain an appreciation of the culture of this region.

The Valles de Oaxaca are dotted with small towns whose inhabitants have lived for generations largely from a single craft, such as pottery, carving, or weaving. Oaxacan artisans have earned a national and, in some cases, international reputation.

MONTE ALBAN

High on an artificially leveled plateau overlooking Oaxaca city lie the ruins of the greatest ceremonial center in the Valles de Oaxaca, Monte Albán. The Zapotecs began building Monte Albán as early as 500 BC, which at the height of its power had a population of over 40,000—more than the largest city in Europe at the time. The evidence of Zapotec, Mixtec, and even Olmec and Aztec civilizations have baffled archaeologists in their attempts to piece together Monte Albán's history. Even the

Monte Albán

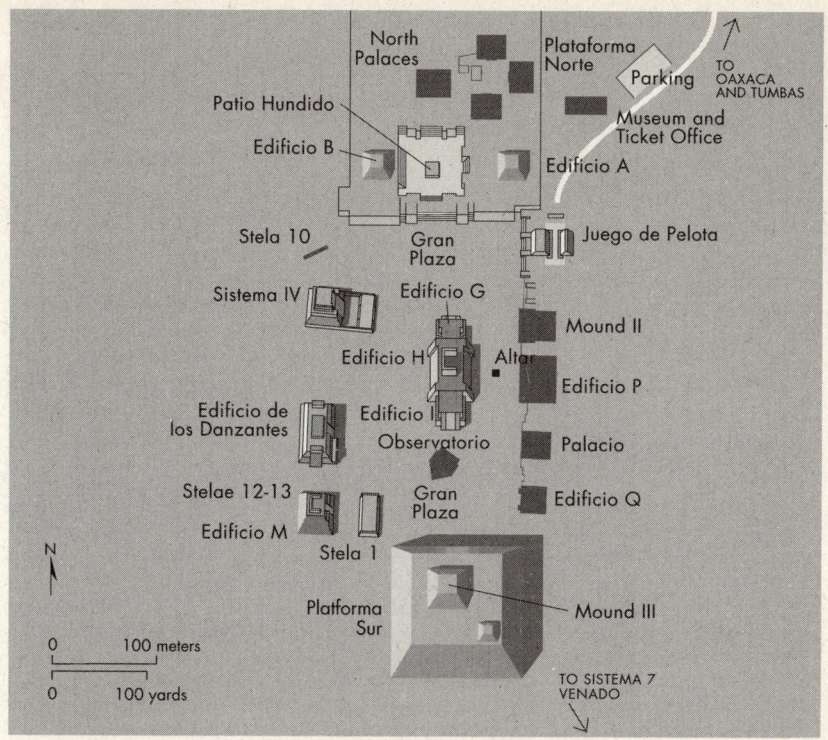

indigenous name for the city remains a mystery—it had been abandoned more than 500 years before the Spanish arrived. Monte Albán (White Mountain) is the name they gave it.

The site covers an area of more than 40 square kilometers, but the most impressive structures are in the **Gran Plaza**. At each end of the plaza are ceremonial platforms aligned along a north–south axis. The acoustics here are such that sound carries clearly from one platform to the other. Clockwise from the monument to Dr. Alfonso Caso, the Mexican archaeologist who began excavations in 1930, you find first the **Juego de Pelota** (ball court). Its capital "I" shape and sloping side walls are distinctive to the region. In contrast to the contests played in the ball courts of the Yucatán, those in Monte Albán didn't sacrifice the leader of the losing team.

Next is an open-air structure known as **Edificio P**, where a tunnel runs from the inner stairway in one corner to the central altar. Zapotec priests may have used the tunnel to appear, as if magically, during ceremonies. Next door is **El Palacio**, apparently the residence of a high-status Zapotec. A tomb was found in the middle of the patio, which is circled by 13 chambers, some with sleeping ledges. Not much of the **Plataforma Sur** (South Platform), which looms above the palace, has been excavated, so little is known about its construction.

Edificio L, the oldest building at the site and more commonly known as the **Edificio de los Danzantes** (Building of the Dancers), is covered with carvings of human figures. Originally the figures were thought to represent swimmers, acrobats, or dancers (hence the name); the current theory is that the building once served as a medical school and the carvings show various medical conditions. Others say that the figures represent tortured captives—though the figure of a woman in childbirth seems to rebuff this claim. In **Sistema IV**, the next building over, archaeologists constructed a tunnel that lets you view an enormous *talud* (altar) of large stones. Some are carved with *danzante*-style figures, indicating that later inhabitants may have stripped older buildings and recycled the stones.

The massive **Plataforma Norte** (North Platform) completes the circle. A path behind the platform leads to the entrances of a number of tombs: **Tomb 104** contains some of the site's best-preserved carvings and murals, which are said to depict the day the deceased passed away and their most notable lifetime achievements. Others suggest that the paintings could be written formulas soliciting the benevolence of the gods. The murals are closed off Sundays.

The **Observatorio** and **Edificios I, H,** and **G** are in the middle of the plaza. The arrowhead-shaped structure close to Plataforma Sur is the observatory. Unlike the other buildings, it's aligned with the pathway of the sun, not along the cardinal points. Its danzante figures are often upside down or placed on an incline, suggesting that they may have been recycled from older buildings.

On the descent from the ruins to the visitor center are various paths leading to the remains of **Tumbas** (tombs) **7, 72,** and **105**. These tombs were not built by the Zapotecs, who originally inhabited Monte Albán, but by their conquerors, the Mixtecs, who used the city as a necropolis. Tomb 7 contained one of the richest art finds in the world, now on display in the **Museo Regional de Oaxaca** (*see* Worth Seeing, *above*).

COMING AND GOING Buses from **Hotel Mesón del Ángel** (Mina 518, tel. 951/6-53-27) in Oaxaca city run to Monte Albán (20 min, $2). Departure times vary, but are typically every hour beginning at 8:30 AM. If you don't mind walking, catch a bus to Colonia Monte Albán (the town) from the second-class bus station for 30¢. From the colonia, it's a 15- to 20-minute painfully steep but beautiful walk to the ruins. The ruins are open daily 8–5 daily, and admission is $3 (except Sundays and holidays, when it's free). Bring a flashlight.

MITLA AND THE EASTERN VALLEY

While most visitors head in this direction just to see the ruins of Mitla, there are a number of worthwhile stops on the way, including less well-known archaeological sites, and little towns where traditional crafts are still produced. If you're planning to visit several towns, consider staying in one of the newly built **YU'U** (House of the Tourist) cabañas set up by the tourist office in Teotitlán del Valle, Tlacolula, Santa Ana del Valle, or Hierve el Agua. They offer comfortable dorm-style beds, kitchens, and super-clean bathrooms for around $8. Ask at the tourist office for details before you head out.

Buses leave Oaxaca for Mitla (25¢) every 20 minutes from the second-class bus station and drop you off less than a mile away from the ruins. If you want to be dropped off at the doorsteps, a bus leaves every hour from **Hotel Mesón del Ángel** (Mina 518, tel. 951/6-53-27) and costs about $2.

THE ROAD TO MITLA All buses for Mitla (*see above*) pass the places listed below—just let the driver know where you'd like to get off, and sit close to him so he doesn't forget you. The first stop out of Oaxaca city on your way east is the 2,000-year-old **El Tule** tree in tiny Santa

Hierve el Agua

After you've seen Mitla, consider trekking out to Hierve el Agua ("the water boils"), a group of spectacular, bubbling, turquoise mineral springs. You can clamber around the cliffs, swim, and camp out or stay in the newly built YU'U cabañas (see above). If you're driving, follow the road to San Lorenzo and keep your eyes peeled for signs, but be advised that it's a rough road and it's easy to get lost. The best bet for those without vehicles is to catch the 4:30 PM bus from the second-class bus station ($1.50 one-way). Otherwise, get a group together and hire a taxi from Mitla—be sure to set a round-trip fare (about $35) before leaving.

María del Tule, supposedly the largest cypress in the world. Farther on, you'll come to the crossroads for the partially unearthed Zapotec ruins of **Dainzú**. From here, walk about 20 minutes to the site, whose main attraction is its many carved bas-reliefs, some depicting ball players in full costume. Admission is $2.50 (free Sun. and holidays).

After Dainzú, you can hop off the bus at the crossroads for **Teotitlán del Valle**, or, shortly thereafter, the town of **Tlacolula**, which is also the crossroads for **Santa Ana del Valle**. Teotitlán is a small village whose inhabitants specialize in woven serapes, some still colored with homemade dyes from the dried carcasses of insects such as the *cochinilla,* the parasite of a native cactus, and the ink of sea snails. Monday is market day. Tlacolula provides yet another incentive to take this trip on a Sunday (when admission to all the ruins is free), in the form of its lively Sunday market. From Tlacolula it's a 20-minute walk up the road to Santa Ana (also called "Shandany," Zapotec for "at the foot of the mountains"), known for its Tuesday market as well as the locally funded **Zapotec Museum** (open weekdays 10–2 and 3–6). The museum holds a modest collection of historical and archaeological pieces, including a uniform that supposedly belonged to Hernán Cortés.

Somewhat more spectacular than Dainzú are the ruins at **Yagul**, about halfway between Tlacolula and Mitla. Yagul is believed to have been a residential area for high-status Zapotecs, such as priests and aristocrats. It features a grand **Palacio de 6 Patios** (Palace of 6 Patios) and a completely restored **Juego de Pelota**. A scramble up the path to the right of the entrance will give you a panoramic view of the ruins, tomb, and fortifications. Admission to Yagul is $2 (free Sun. and holidays).

MITLA The name Mitla (Mictlán) is Nahuatl for "place of the dead" or "place of rest." Mitla's Zapotec name is *Leobaa.* Here, 34 kilometers southeast of Oaxaca, the Zapotecs established a massive burial ground in 100 BC. The Mixtecs conquered the site in 1250 and it remained important up to the time of the Spanish invasion. According to popular myths, Quetzalcoatl would come here in search of bones that would aid in the formation of man.

Mexico's fascination with death dates back to pre-Columbian times, when many indigenous civilizations revered it. Today, during Día de los Muertos (Day of the Dead), all of Mexico laughs, toasts, and feasts to death.

Of the five groups of square structures at Mitla, only two have been fully excavated and restored. The **Conjunto de Columnas** (Group of Columns) was part of an official's private home. Inside the north structure is a room covered from stone floor to wooden ceiling with three distinct patterns of *greca* (mosaic), unique to Mitla, composed of thousands of bits of well-cut stone set in clay to form geometric patterns. These particular grecas represent air, earth, and water and at one time were coated with stucco and painted red. Some believe that this room was a library, and that the patterned greca hold coded knowledge. Also in this group you'll see what is popularly referred to as the **Columna de la Vida**. According to legend, you can tell how many years you've got left by embracing the column and calculating the space left between your outstretched hands. Presumably, the longer your arms, the sooner you can expect to die. The site, open daily, is directly in front of the Iglesia San Pablo, about a mile from where the second-class bus lets you off.

Downhill from the ruins, beyond the mezcal stands and shawl vendors, close to the center of the modern village of Mitla, the **Frissell Museum** exhibits beautiful pottery and other pieces recovered in Mitla and nearby sites. It's open Sunday–Friday 8–5 and donations are encouraged.

SOUTH OF OAXACA

In the valley to the south of Oaxaca city you can meet the personalities behind the green-and-black pottery, embroidered blouses, and painted wooden beasties that fill the city's open markets. All the villages listed below are within a 20-minute to half-day second-class bus ride from Oaxaca city. Arrazola and Zaachila both lie on one road, and together make an enjoyable day trip. San Martín Tilcajete and Ocotlán de Morelos together can also be visited in a day. Special markets are held on Thursday in Zaachila and on Friday in Ocotlán de Morelos.

ARRAZOLA Five kilometers off the main road between Oaxaca city and Zaachila is the small village of Arrazola, internationally famous for its wood carvers who create fantastic animals, called alebrijes, out of copal wood (also valued for its resin). These small wooden coyotes, elephants, and hybrid figurines fetch a pretty penny, especially if they bear the name of Don Manuel Jiménez, one of the town's best-known artisans and original creator of the brightly colored pieces. To get here, take a bus bound for Zaachila, get off at the Zaachila crossroads, and wait patiently for a colectivo to take you the two miles into town. Infrequent but direct colectivos to Arrazola also leave from the corner of the Periférico and Parque del Amor. The whole trip takes about 30 minutes.

Many place names in Southern Mexico and Guatemala are Nahua, some because they were once part of the expanding Aztec empire, others because the conquistadors traveled with Aztec guides who gave place names in their own language.

ZAACHILA Eighteen kilometers south of Oaxaca, Zaachila was once the Zapotec capital, long before the arrival of the Mixtecas. It's also the site of an archaeological find that was never looted, thanks to the townspeople's devotion to their ancestors' graves. One tomb is empty, but all the artifacts it once held are now in museums. The other tomb has tiny grecas similar to those found in Mitla (*see above*), and depictions of two figures. One figure, wearing a long alligator mask, represents the god of death. The other carries a bag of *copal* (resin used for ceremonial incense), suggesting that it represents a priest. The ruins are open daily 8–5. Admission is $2 (free Sun. and holidays).

More exciting than the ruins is Zaachila's Thursday market, which feels a bit like a country fair, with dozens of bulls, rabbits, chickens, sheep, and goats being hauled from one prospective buyer to another. The bus ride to Zaachila from the second-class bus station in Oaxaca city takes about half an hour and costs 25¢.

SAN MARTIN TILCAJETE In this tiny town, you'll be invited into private homes to see fantastically painted animals, the sale of which supports entire families. It's well worth the half-hour bus ride and 20-minute walk. It's best to buy here, where you can be sure the money goes straight to the artist. To reach this hospitable town, ask the driver of any bus headed to Ejutla de Crespo to drop you off at the road leading to San Martín Tilcajete, and walk or hitch the rest of the way.

OCOTLAN DE MORELOS This wonderful little town is home to the famous Aguilar Sisters: Guillermina, Josefina, Irene, and Concepción, all of whom are skilled pottery painters. You can visit their adjoining homes and workshops on Continuación de Morelos, near the entrance of town. The best day to come is Friday, when Ocotlán holds its small market. It takes about an hour on the Ejutla del Crespo bus to get here, and the ride costs $1.

Oaxaca Coast

The Sierra Madre del Sur mountain range looms over almost 400 kilometers of scorching hot Oaxacan coastline, including many, many deserted beaches. Because much of this region is undeveloped, most visitors do their frolicking around three main tourist destinations: Puerto Escondido, Puerto Ángel, and the Bahías de Huatulco. Within the last decade, all three places have seen a lot more *extranjeros* (foreigners) and construction, but the recent devaluation of the peso has brought much of the construction to a temporary halt.

Sporting opportunities abound here. In Puerto Escondido, surfers from around the world congregate to ride the Mexican Pipeline at Playa Zicatela. Snorkelers head out to the calmer waters nearby at Puerto Angelito and Carrizalillo, or to Estacahuite near Puerto Ángel. Scuba enthusiasts make their way to Roca Blanca off the shores of Cacoletepec. Most travelers, however, come here to kick back and enjoy the sun and ocean breeze. Zipolite beach, near Puerto Ángel, is famous for the hippies who come to commune with nature and each other, and get sunburned (and otherwise baked) on the beach. Santa Cruz Huatulco is the Mexican government's latest target for development; fortunately, the planned megaresort is still in its infancy, and nearby beaches remain undisturbed campers' paradises.

Puerto Escondido

The touristy part of Puerto Escondido actually consists of two separate but coexisting resorts: one for the surfers drawn to the area by the famous Mexican Pipeline, the other for Mexican families on vacation. High seasons for tourism are the summer and Christmas holidays. Puerto Escondido also plays host to two championship surfing contests—a local one in August, and an international one in November. If you decide to visit during these months, be prepared for the *pachanga* (party) that ensues. Still, Puerto Escondido is much less flashy and pretentious than most of Mexico's other coastal hot spots. Out-of-towners come here to hang out, relax, surf, or play in the waves and do little else. The same cannot be said of the inhabitants of the "other" Escondido, which lies to the north away from the resort areas, on the other side of the Carretera Costera (the Coast Highway). This is where the locals live, and where you'll find the post and telegraph offices, the bus stations, and a typical Mexican town atmosphere with cheap food, busy streets, and friendly people.

BASICS

➢ **CASAS DE CAMBIO** • The only casa de cambio in town is on Pérez Gasga, near the hotel Rincón del Pacífico; it's open weekdays 9–2 and 5–8. **Bancomer** (Pérez Gasga, across from Rincón del Pacífico, tel. 958/2–04–11) changes cash and traveler's checks and is open weekdays 9 AM–1:30 PM.

➢ **MEDICAL AID** • Emergency medical care is available 24 hours a day at the **Comisión Nacional de Emergencia** (Tlacochahuaya, at Fracc. Bacocho) and the **Centro de Salud** (Pérez Gasga 409), where the English-speaking Dr. Luis Flores is on staff. The free **Cruz Roja** (Marina Nacional, at Pérez Gazga, tel. 958/2–01–46) is open 24 hours.

➢ **PHONES AND MAIL** • You can make collect and cash calls at the **caseta de larga distancia** (long-distance telephone office) on Pérez Gasga by the Andador Revolución, a stairway connecting Pérez Gasga to the Carretera Costera. There are also public phones that accept credit cards in front of the pharmacy at the west end of Pérez Gasga. The **post office** (Calle 7 Nte., at Oaxaca, tel. 958/2–09–59) is a long, hard uphill walk on the inland side of the highway. They'll hold mail for you at the following address for up to 10 days: Oficina de Correos, Puerto Escondido, Oaxaca, CP 71980, México. You can send or receive telegrams, money orders, and faxes at the **telegraph office** (tel. 958/2–09–57) next door.

➢ **VISITOR INFORMATION** • The main **tourist office** (Calle 5 Pte., at the highway, tel. 958/2–01–75; open weekdays 9–2 and 5–8, Sat. 9–1) is at least a half-hour walk west from town, but they do provide maps, semi-useful hotel info, and an earful of warnings about theft. The minuscule *caseta* (booth) on Pérez Gasga, across from the Hotel Roca Mar, provides information on hotels, guided tours, and general directions until 1 PM.

COMING AND GOING

The town is split in two by the Carretera Costera. Uphill to the north is the untouristed, residential part of town. The street that snakes south down the hill from the highway and then east along the coast is Pérez Gasga, popularly known as the **Andador Turístico** (tourist walkway). Running parallel to the main beach, Playa Principal, the Andador is where many of the town's hotels and restaurants are. **Zicatela**, the town's most famous surfing spot, lies directly to the east.

➢ **BY BUS** • The **Estrella del Valle-Oaxaca Pacífico** bus station (cnr of Hidalgo and 16 de Septiembre) is uphill from the beach, a good 15-minute walk from the beachfront. Destinations include Oaxaca city (7 hrs, $9.50) at 8:30 AM and 8 PM; Pochutla (1½ hrs, $2.50) every hour 5:30 AM–7:30 PM; and Acapulco (7 hrs, $9.50) at 6 AM, 8 AM, 8 PM, and 11 PM. **Transportes Oaxaca-Istmo** and **Transportes Galeca/Lineas Unidas Del Sur** (both on Hidalgo, at 5 de Mayo) offer frequent service to Pochutla, Oaxaca city, Salina Cruz, and Acapulco. You can also flag down a bus for Pochutla along the highway—there's one every 15–20 minutes.

➢ **BY PLANE** • The national airport is at Kilometer 3 of the Carretera Costera. **Mexicana** (tel. 958/2–04–22) flies daily to Mexico City ($100 one-way), while **Aeromorelos** and **Aerovías Oaxaqueñas** fly small planes to Oaxaca city ($85 one-way). **Transportes Aeropuerto y Turístico** (tel. 958/2–01–23) will take you into and out of town for about $2 in a VW van; look for their signs at the airport. You can also make arrangements with your hotel to be picked up by a *combi*. For general airport information, call 958/2–04–92.

WHERE TO SLEEP Puerto Escondido's hotels and cabaña villages charge up to three times their normal prices (listed here) during the summer, surfing championships, and around the Christmas and New Year holidays. Make reservations during these months whenever possible. The cabañas on Zicatela are clean, fairly simple, and cater to a surfcat's lifestyle, with an emphasis on convenience (i.e., proximity to the water).

➢ **UNDER $10** • **Cabañas Aldea Marinero.** Not to be confused with Cabañas Marinero across the way, this small cluster of huts just off Playa Marinero surrounds a small garden. A wall of graffiti attests to the satisfaction of former guests. The brick-floored cabañas have cots, electric lights and outlets, and mosquito netting and rent for $5 per person. The semi-clean *sanitarios* (bathrooms) are communal. Hammocks and fans can both be rented for $2. *Calle del Morro, Playa Principal, no phone.*

➢ **UNDER $15** • **Hotel San Juan.** The clean rooms here have fans and private baths with hot water for $8 a single, $10 a double. Ask for an interior room; those facing the outside catch lots of highway noise. *Felipe Merklin 503, tel. 958/2–03–36, fax 958/2–06–12. 26 rooms, all with bath. Luggage storage. MC, V.*

Rockaway Surfer Village. A wall encloses this well-kept, inexpensive, beachfront cabaña village, where guests lounge and drink beer on the porch of the surf shop. They also have a clean freshwater pool. All cabañas have ceiling fans, mosquito netting, and private bathrooms, and cost $12 during high season. *Playa Zicatela, just past Bruno's, tel. 958/2–06–68. 12 cabañas, all with bath.*

➢ **UNDER $20** • **Bungalows/Cabañas Acuario.** The cabañas here have refrigerators and simple furnishings; some of the larger ones (called bungalows) have full kitchens. The friendly, laid-back management can provide info on excursions and scuba lessons, and arrange for airport pickup and medical services. A two-person cabaña is $18, a two-person bungalow (with kitchen) about $35. *Calle del Morro, Zicatela, tel. 958/2–03–57. 14 cabañas, all with bath.*

➢ **UNDER $25** • **Flor de María.** Half a block from Playa Marinero, this hotel is meticulously decorated inside and out. It has comfortably furnished rooms with private baths and hot water, as well as a pool and restaurant. More to the point, there's an out-of-this-world bakery across the street. Singles cost $15, doubles $22. *Playa Marinero, next to Cabañas Aldea Marinero, tel. 958/2–05–36. 24 rooms, all with bath. Luggage storage. MC, V.*

➢ **CAMPING** • It's illegal to plop your tent down on the beach, but you can pitch a tent at **Neptuno** (Pérez Gasga, tel. 958/2–03–27) or pay too much (about $12 per spot) to stay at the **Puerto Escondido Trailer Park,** both on the cliff overlooking Playa Carrizalillo on the Carretera Costera near Fraccionamiento Bacocho.

FOOD The selection of lobster, fish, shrimp, squid, and cuttle fish makes seafood your best bet. There are also a number of Italian restaurants in town. Pasta is usually safe, but you'll likely be disappointed with the local version of pizza. Apart from Bruno's (*see below*), the restaurants on Playa Zicatela serve little besides hamburgers, fries, and *cerveza* (beer) because—according to the cooks—their clientele will accept nothing else.

➢ **UNDER $5** • **Las 7 Regiones.** Tables on the second floor overlook the action on the Andador Turístico, and the fondue, pastas, salads, and soups are all excellent. Particularly good are the shrimp with chile and bacon ($4.50) and the daily fresh fish special ($4) cooked in cream and garlic. *Pérez Gasga, tel. 958/2–05–51. Open daily 7 AM–11 PM.*

Bruno's. Zicatela surfers who appreciate good food, good music, and each other's company fill this place regularly. They've got a happening bar and a message board advertising everything from massages to long-term rentals. A killer vegetarian stir-fry costs $4. *Playa Zicatela, no phone. Open daily 7 AM–11 PM.*

Restaurant Alicia. Simple, but filling entrées are served here pronto. A spaghetti dish with shrimp goes for $2. *Pérez Gasga, next door to Casa de Cambio, tel. 958/2-06-90. Open 8 AM-11 PM.*

➤ **UNDER $10** • **Cucina Italiana.** Where else can you watch classic Mexican flicks while chowing down on a pizza topped with—what else—seafood. Try the *menú turístico* ($4), consisting of Margherita Pizza, salad, dessert, and coffee. Stop by for happy hour (6-8 PM) for two-for-one drinks overlooking Playa Principal. *Azucena, at Pérez Gasga. Open 8 AM-midnight.*

BEACHES The beaches around Puerto Escondido offer a variety of sporting opportunities. If you want to snorkel (best at Puerto Angelito and Carrizalillo), boogieboard (best at Playa Principal and Carrizalillo), or surf (best at Zicatela), you're better off renting your equipment in town for the entire day, rather than hourly on the beach. You can get surfing equipment, lessons, and scuba gear at **Bungalows/Cabañas Acuario** (*see above*). **Mango Club** (Pérez Gasga 605-A, tel. 958/2-00-05) rents snorkel gear ($7 a day), inflatable rafts ($10 a day) and boogieboards ($10 a day). If you'd like to explore further afield, they also rent motorcycles ($50 a day) and bicycles ($17 a day), but only with a deposit or a credit card. They're supposed to be open daily 9-8, but often close down for a while in the afternoon.

➤ **PLAYA PRINCIPAL** • This beach, which runs parallel to the Andador Turístico, is a favorite spot for Mexicans on vacation, and for everyone to stroll and take in the sun. You can also go sailing ($10 per hr), rent horses ($8.50 per hr), hire any one of the numerous *lanchas* (motorboats) to Puerto Angelito or Carrizalillo, or head out to sea to frolic with the sea turtles ($10 per hr). Mario López, with his boat *Venus-125,* gives a good deal on lancha tours and sport fishing. The eastern section of the beach, called **Playa Marinero,** is separated from the rest by a lagoon. It's ideal for learning to surf, clambering on the rocks, swimming, and exploring tidepools.

It's too expensive to rent a room at the Santa Fe Hotel between Playas Principal and Zicatela, but come at sunset to have a drink on the balcony.

➤ **ZICATELA** • East of Playa Marinero lies this famed and perilous surfing spot. Considered one of the top surf beaches in the world, Zicatela's waves roll in with impressive force. If you're not a surfer, you can also rent horses or dune buggies, as well as the ubiquitous boogie boards and snorkel gear, from vendors who set up tents on the sand. When you do venture into the water, be careful of the currents—they're notoriously deadly.

➤ **PUERTO ANGELITO** • It's about a 20-minute walk or a $3 taxi ride to this small inlet and the neighboring beach of **Manzanillo.** The calm water attracts families with young children. It's a great area for swimming and snorkeling, and, sure enough, young boys rent out the necessary gear for about $4 an hour. If you'd prefer something sedentary, rent a hammock and take a nap or have a meal or drinks at one of the many palapa (thatched hut) restaurants. To get here, walk west along Pérez Gasga until it curves uphill toward the highway. Here you'll see the Camino a Puerto Angelito, which leads to a set of cement stairs down to the beach.

➤ **CARRIZALILLO** • This isolated beach is relatively free of the hordes of families that crowd Puerto Angelito, its neighbor to the east. The U-shaped cove does draw snorkelers and strong swimmers (the currents can be tricky). You can make the long, dusty trek on land by walking west along the Carretera Costera toward Bacocho; the sign pointing to Carrizalillo is visible from the Carretera. Or, take a boat ride from Puerto Angelito or Playa Principal (see above), and have them pick you up two hours later. **Bacocho,** the most westerly beach, is good for swimming, but has a resort development.

AFTER DARK During the summer, the November surfing championships, and around Christmas time, the Andador Turístico itself is the party, with locals checking out the tourists, surfers mingling with sightseers, and everybody out to have a good time. It's also lined with quite a few bars and clubs, which range from absolutely dead in the low season to hopping and jammed when everyone's in town. At the western end of the Andador, **Bananas** (Pérez Gasga, tel. 958/2-00-05; open 8 AM-12:30 AM) offers canned pop music along with Ping-Pong and table football. **Tío Mac,** a video bar across the street, has juicy burgers and pounding rock music. A more out-of-the-way spot for American music is **El Tubo,** down a flight of stairs on the beach side of Pérez Gasga (look for the sign with a surfer riding a tube), which rocks 11 PM-3 AM.

Open nightly 9:30 PM–2 AM, **Barfly** (Pérez Gasga, no phone) has an extensive drink menu and a rickety upstairs overlooking the Andador. Downstairs, surfers down beer after beer while watching re-runs of old surfing championships. **El Son y La Rumba** (Andador Mar y Sol, above Pérez Gasga, no phone) features dancing to live salsa, jazz, or reggae on a small dance floor after 10 PM. They often charge a cover during the high season.

NEAR PUERTO ESCONDIDO

Trying to organize the following trips on your own can be frustrating, because once you get where you're going, you still need to negotiate horse or boat rentals (boat trips are the best way to see these places). This is one time when working with a guide will save you time, money, and hassles. Contact Ana Marquez at the Hotel Flor de María (Playa Marinero, next to Cabañas Aldea Marinero, tel. 958/2-05-36), a native Mixteca who can arrange or at least provide further information on all of the following excursions.

MANIALTEPEC This briny lagoon 18 kilometers northwest of Puerto Escondido is home to a remarkable variety of wildlife, including wild geese and herons. You can rent a boat (about $16 an hr) from the bar/restaurant **Isla del Gallo** to explore the lagoon. There aren't any hotels out here, just the beach and a lot of mosquitos, so plan your transportation carefully. To get here from Puerto Escondido, take a bus heading toward Acapulco and get off at the signs for Manialtepec. If you take a taxi, don't let the driver charge you more than $3. A guided tour with Ana Marquez takes half a day and runs about $14.

CACALOTEPEC About 1 kilometer offshore from the picturesque village of Cacalotepec is **Roca Blanca** (White Rock), a little-known diving area with extraordinary coral. Contact Maurizio Mendici at the Hotel Aldea del Bazar (Benito Juárez L7, tel. 958/2-05-08) in Puerto Escondido to rent diving equipment. On the walk back to the highway, you're likely to see the *árboles amorosos,* parasitic vines that grow around palm trees and choke them. In a similar fashion, missionaries have recently invaded Cacalotepec, and are busy building large-scale bible buildings and making the locals suspicious of foreigners. To reach Cacalotepec from Puerto Escondido, take a bus toward Acapulco and get off at Cacalotepec. Arrangements for a tour can be made through Ana Marquez (*see above*) or another locally based guide.

ZAPOTALITO AND PARQUE NACIONAL LAGUNAS DE CHACAHUA About 74 kilometers west of Puerto Escondido is a tropical park encompassing two lagoons—**Chacahua** and **Pastoría**—deserted beaches, and much wildlife. The town of Zapotalito, many of whose inhabitants are descended from African slaves, sits close to the entrance of the park. Due to the size of the park, you might want to rent a boat or hire a guide here.

You can enjoy the pristine beaches, lunch on grilled fish and bananas sold by local women at **Playa Chacahua,** or visit the alligator hatchery in the village for which the beach is named. The hatchery workers can show you small bathtubs full of tiny, squirming alligators, their eyes still shut but their jaws already snapping. It takes about an hour to cross the lagoon to Chacahua in a boat, and you need a guide. Slightly closer to Zapotalito (about a 45-minute boat ride down the river) is **Playa Cerro Hermoso,** an isolated lagoon beach, ringed with mango trees. You can hunt for rare black orchids on this lagoon, which is separated from the sea by only a narrow ridge of sand.

If you go with a guide from Puerto Escondido (about $20 for a full day with Ana Marquez) your transportation to and within the park is arranged. If you prefer to hire a guide in Zapotalito, catch an early bus heading toward Acapulco and ask to get off at the road leading to the park. It's about a 10-kilometer hike to the town. Park admission is free, but boat rentals run $50–$75. Go with a group and allow a full day for the excursion to make it worth your while.

Puerto Ángel

Puerto Ángel, 11 kilometers off the main highway, is touted as an unspoiled beach paradise. Although the village *has* managed to stave off much of the development and commercialization that has plagued Puerto Escondido and Santa Cruz Huatulco, Puerto Ángel is showing signs that it may not be far behind its coastal neighbors. A laid-back atmosphere still prevails, though, and you can join the locals for a swim in the blue-green bay off the main beach, or arrange for a day of snorkeling or sightseeing by boat from one of the coves on either side of town. There's no direct bus service to Puerto Ángel—to get here you need to take a bus to the nearby town of **Pochutla** and catch a colectivo or a cab. In addition to the places listed below in Puerto Ángel, you can change money, send a letter, or make a long-distance call in Pochutla.

Puerto Ángel is a cliffside fishing village where the nightlife consists of hiking up to the lighthouse to catch the sunset and then strolling down to the main street with a paleta (popsicle).

Playa Panteón, in a sheltered cove just west of town (walk along the Andador just west of Puerto Ángel's *muelle*, or dock), is where local families splash around in gentle waves, and where, among other things, you can rent snorkel equipment or arrange a boat trip. In the opposite direction (about a 20-minute walk from town), you'll find **Estacahuite,** where you can rent snorkel gear on the beach and explore the offshore coral reef. After Estacahuite, the next beach is **La Mina,** an undeveloped, palm-shaded lounger's paradise. Puerto Ángel also serves as a comfortable base for trips up into the sparsely visited towns of the green Sierra Madre del Sur mountains that loom to the north.

BASICS Hotel Soraya, at the entrance to Puerto Ángel, will change your dollars at a lousy rate; it's better to exchange at one of the two banks in nearby Pochutla. There aren't any pay phones in Puerto Ángel—**Ferretería Velasco** (in front of the naval base; open 9–9) charges $1 to make an international collect call. The **post office** (open 9–2) lies at the entrance to town along the main road. For medical care, both the **Centro de Salud** (take the stairway up to Rincón Sabroso, past the church, no phone) and the naval base's emergency center (down the street from Restaurante Beto, *see* Food, *below*) are open 24 hours. The conspicuous **Visitor Information** booth (main road, in front of dock, no phone; open weekdays 9–2 and 5–7) can provide you with maps, hotel phone numbers, and directions.

COMING AND GOING The bus to and from Pochutla runs 6 AM–8 PM and costs about 35¢ each way. Frequent colectivos run the same route frequently for about 70¢; a private taxi shouldn't cost you more than $3.50.

GETTING AROUND Puerto Ángel is a tiny town, but finding places can be somewhat complicated because very few have street addresses. Just consider the faded signs pointing down twisting alleyways part of the town's charm, and you won't get frustrated. The highway from Pochutla turns into Avenida Principal at the entrance to town, and later turns into Boulevard Virgilio Uribe (though few make this distinction). The bus will drop you off or pick you up at *el árbol* (the tree), on the main street (officially Virgilio Uribe at this point) just before the naval base. Farther on, the road crosses a dry creek bed and then forks just after the navy store—the high road leads to Zipolite, the low road to Playa Panteón.

WHERE TO SLEEP Most of Puerto Ángel's hotels are planted high atop rocky cliffs, and reaching them often requires climbing a healthy number of stairs. The rewards for your efforts will be unobstructed ocean breezes and a tremendous view of the cove. Regular room prices (listed below) jump about $5 when the gringos roll in during the summer and around Christmas vacation. Cheaper accommodations, usually along the lines of a hammock and maybe some mosquito netting, are to be had at nearby Zipolite (*see below*).

➢ **UNDER $15** • **Pensión Puesto del Sol.** This multilevel, red-roofed pension is perched amid a profusion of hibiscus flowers and lemon and pomegranate trees. The rooms are simple and clean; the spotless bathrooms, both private and communal, have cold water 24 hours a day. Harold, the proprietor, will share his maps and bus schedules (and perhaps a beer) with you in the open-air lounge. Doubles are $8, $15 with bath. *Tel. 958/4–30–96. From el árbol, follow the road toward Zipolite; it's to the right just beyond the navy store. 13 rooms, 8 with bath.*

Posada Cañon de Vata. This posada is spread out over a tranquil valley just behind Playa Panteón. Rooms run $10–$23 a single, $13–$27 a double, depending on whether or not you want a private bath or a stunning view. The owners, a transplanted Californian named Suzanne and her artist husband Mateo, offer day-long snorkeling trips ($6.50) and fishing expeditions ($5). They also rent snorkel equipment ($5 a day) and give advice on all Puerto Ángel has to offer. Their small restaurant offers vegetarian fare. *Playa Panteón. 20 rooms, 17 with bath. Luggage storage. Closed May–June.*

➢ **UNDER $25** • **La Buena Vista.** This hotel allows you to appreciate the tranquility of this small fishing town without being too far from the "action" on the main drag. Singles $16, doubles $22. *Take main road across bridge; it's to the left. 12 rooms, all with bath. Luggage storage.*

FOOD Everything except seafood must be trucked into Puerto Ángel, so plan on spending a bit more than usual. Even so, prices are not unreasonable, and you'll find a handful of simple restaurants and, in the evenings, a few taco stands along the main road. If you manage to catch something at sea, somebody at your guest house will likely prepare it for a nominal charge.

La Buena Vista. This hotel restaurant is more Tex-Mex than Mexican, but the food is great. Try the delicious barbecued chicken ($5) with a piña colada ($2.75). *Take main road across bridge; it's to the left. Open Mon.–Sat. 7–11 and 6–10.*

Gundi y Tomás. The restaurant at this guest house offers a limited selection of basic fare. They serve a good fruit salad for $2.50. *Up the stairs just west of el árbol. Open daily 7 AM–9 PM.*

Restaurante Beto. Obscured by heavy foliage, this patio-style restaurant is the place to sip a soda and enjoy their specialty lobster dishes ($8). *Take main road just past naval base and Super de Puerto Ángel; it's on the right at end of town. Open Mon.–Sat. 4–11.*

El Tiburón Dormido. This open-air palapa on the main beach dishes up grilled fresh fish and shrimp for less than $6.75. Fish tacos ($1.75) and garlic-and-onion soup ($2) make satisfying light meals, and the margaritas are $2.50. *Open daily 7 AM–10 PM.*

NEAR PUERTO ANGEL

The green mountains of the Sierra Madre del Sur hide villages that seem worlds away from the beach towns on the coast. San José del Pacífico and Chacalapa are both in the foothills north of Pochutla and can be reached from any Oaxaca city-bound bus from there. You can make a day trip of it, but if you decide to spend the night, both towns have small, well-furnished *hospedajes* (guest houses) that charge about $17 double occupancy. A local family may very well ask you to stay or invite you to hang a hammock on their front porch—you might be the most exciting thing that's happened in a long time.

CHACALAPA This quiet town, set in a green valley, is just 12 kilometers from Pochutla. Here you'll find Tom Bachmaier, an artist who etches Oaxacan landscapes on small bamboo beads. Even if you're not interested in buying, stop by his meticulous home to admire his beautiful work and garden. Across the path is **Alberca El Paraíso** (closed Tues.), a swimming pool filled with turquoise mineral water from a nearby natural spring. Octavio Ramos, who owns the pool and surrounding ranch, will happily guide you through the forest and show you how those unfamiliar tropical fruits you see in the markets grow. There's a $1 charge to use the pool for a day, or, if you're drawn in by the warmth of the Ramos family, you can enjoy free use of the pool and stay in one of the brand-spanking-new cabañas with hot water, private baths, and ceiling fans ($10). To get here, take a microbus or Oaxaca city-bound bus (25¢) north to the entrance of Chacalapa. Ask for the *callejón* (alley) that leads to *La Alberca* and walk for about 2 kilometers.

SAN JOSE DEL PACIFICO This small village is off Route 175, about an hour from Pochutla. It is the jumping-off place for the trails of the nearby cloud forest. It's also a favorite destination of foreigners who, after being transformed into beach bums in Zipolite, come in search of the hallucinogenic mushrooms rumored to be found here. As with anything that might get you in trouble with the Mexican police, caution is the watchword.

Zipolite

A sweaty 30-minute walk from Puerto Ángel brings you to Zipolite (Beach of the Dead), and another world. The feeling here is 1970s—Led Zep, Marley, scruffy gringos, and lots of dope.

Nudity is the rule on the beach, and the southern section, known as **Playa del Amor,** has a pretty active gay scene. Be *extremely* cautious about swimming here: Zipolite's name refers not, as some seem to think, to the Grateful Dead, but to the many lost to its currents every year.

Just past Zipolite are the less populated beaches of **San Agustinillo** and **Mazunte.** Just before the first you'll find a hammock-making co-op (*see box, below*); the second is home to an abandoned turtle slaughterhouse and the El Mazunte Sea Turtle Protection Program (*see* Near Zipolite, *below*) that replaced it.

COMING AND GOING It's about a 30-minute walk from Puerto Ángel to Zipolite. Buses (35¢) run between Zipolite and Puerto Ángel and Pochutla every half hour 6 AM–8 PM along the roads connecting the three towns. You can also catch a colectivo to or from Pochutla for $1. If you arrive in Pochutla at night, you'll need to take a private taxi here (about $3.50). Boats from Puerto Ángel also run irregularly to Zipolite; the going rate is $3–$7.

WHERE TO SLEEP You can rent a hammock in a communal palapa for about a dollar; double that amount if you want a little privacy. Don't expect much as far as the communal bathrooms are concerned—they're usually an upgraded version of an outhouse. Showers or *regaderas* are abundant, but in some places there's no water 10 AM–6 PM, so ask before you go in. Also keep in mind that theft is common, so you might do well to ask a hotel in Puerto Ángel to store the bulk of your gear while you're here. Some people never stray from the beach, but the *posadas* (inns) up in the hills merit the diversion. The coolest one is **Shambala,** also known as Gloria's, up on the hill at the northern end of the beach. Sprawling over half the hillside, it has meditation altars and a patio restaurant with a spectacular view of a hidden bay. Drugs are a no-no here. Gloria, the transplanted Californian who owns the place, offers a variety of lodging options: Run-down cabañas on the beach with a bed and private bath run $10; huts with locking doors are $5 (ask for a room farther up on the hill—you might not like the "rooms"/caves next to the restaurant); rooms with a hammock or "bed" (a straw mat on a raised plat-

Hammocks That Won't Let You Down

In San Agustinillo, just beyond Shambala, you'll find the workshop of a cooperative association of highly skilled hammock makers. The following are some of their tips on how to tell a good hammock from what could become a tangled, uncomfortable ball of string:

First, stretch out a section and look at the cross weave. Most Oaxacan hammocks are made of heavy cotton or thick nylon thread (the latter lasts longer but is a little less comfortable), and good ones have a double weave. Next, grip the material near the loop where the rope is attached to get an idea of the amount of material in the hammock. An average-size gringo needs at least a fistful of threads. You'll probably want a matrimonial (double) or familiar (family size). Single-size hammocks may look big, but try to sleep in one and you'll decide to take it home for your baby sister.

Now look at the number of threads attaching the loop to the cross weave. In the best hammocks, each thread coming out of the loop anchors only one cross weave. (Two or three are also okay.) This allows better flexibility and weight distribution. Finally, check the edges to be sure there are a large number of straight threads before the cross weave begins. These will keep the hammock from breaking if you sit on the edges (and ensure that it's strong enough to support a moment or two of passion).

form) cost $3, as do the palapas with hammocks; a simple campsite costs $1. Luggage storage and a safe-deposit box are provided. **Lo Cósmico**, right next to Shambala, offers clean, cool palapas complete with two hammocks for $5.

FOOD Zipolite has no market, so you're stuck with the posadas and beachfront palapas, which serve mostly seafood and tortilla dishes. There are a handful of restaurants that serve pizzas, including **Gemini's** on the eastern end of the beach, **Pizzería Panadería**, and **El 3 de Diciembre** (Roca Blanca, in front of La Puesta; open daily 7 PM–3 AM), which serves an exquisite slice of pie ($1). **Lo Cósmico**, with board games and rock music, is a groovy place to nurse a beer and sample the specialty crepes ($2–$4). You can get a California-style granola breakfast in Shambala's hilltop restaurant, or try their tasty chicken mole or vegetarian turnovers (each about $2.50) over candlelight for dinner.

AFTER DARK Zipolite's commercial development has been marked by the construction of two new discotheque/bars. **La Puesta** is up the beach from Shambala and plays salsa music on its open dance floor. A bit more varied in music and crowd is **Zipolitas**, where they won't close up shop until you decide to go back to your cabaña. Always an option is relaxing at one of the bonfires along the beach.

NEAR ZIPOLITE

MAZUNTE AND PUNTA COMETA As you ride past San Agustinillo, you'll notice a cluster of dilapidated, rusty buildings on the far end of the beach, once centers for processing turtle meat and shells. Today, just past them in Mazunte, is a center for the turtles' protection. The **Centro Mexicano de la Tortuga** (tel. 958/4–00–58) offers educational tours in Spanish and English Tuesday–Saturday 10:30–5 and Sundays 11–3. You can watch all the species of sea turtles that inhabit Mexico's coastal waters swim in huge tanks. Individual turtles are only kept on display a short time, after which they're released or used in conservation research. The $3.50 entrance fee goes toward conservation and education projects. Buses come here from Zipolite (10 min, 25¢), Puerto Ángel (15 min, 50¢), and Pochutla (40 min, 70¢). West of Mazunte is **Punta Cometa**, a cactus-ridden set of cliffs with a fantastic view of the coast. It's a great place from which to appreciate the force of Oaxaca's coastal currents without being a casualty. Ask someone in Mazunte to point out the path to Punta Cometa.

Bahías de Huatulco

The area often simply referred to as Huatulco in fact consists of nine bays spread out over 20 miles of coast. The heart of it all is Santa Cruz Huatulco, which just 10 years ago was a small fishing village of simple adobe huts on a pristine bay. That was before the Mexican government chose it as the site of a luxury tourist development meant to duplicate Cancún's success in attracting foreign sun-seekers and their money. Now, wide, palm-lined boulevards with new electric lights and grassy dividers, rolling golf courses, and huge hotel complexes like the Sheraton and Club Med make it seem closer to Santa Barbara or Palm Beach than to Oaxaca city. But while this area is certainly set up to cater to a five-star clientele, it actually still has a lot to offer the traveler of more limited means. Due to the government's policy of "responsible ecodevelopment," the outlying bays and the forests that ring them remain relatively unspoiled. And it's even more convenient to visit these places now that the brand-new Ladatel phones and air-conditioned banks of Santa Cruz are within easy reach.

Huatulco's bays, from west (closest to Puerto Ángel) to east, are: San Agustín, Chachacual, Cacaluta, Maguey, Órgano, Santa Cruz, Chahué, Tangolunda, and Conejos. Along with Santa Cruz, Chahué and Tangolunda are the most developed, while Órgano, which can usually only be reached by foot or water, is the most pristine. The town of **La Crucecita** (about 5 minutes inland from Santa Cruz) is where most of the people who work in Santa Cruz's boutiques and hotels live, shop, and eat, and is the budget traveler's base for the area.

BASICS **Bancomer, Banamex**, and **Comermex**, next to each other on the main road in Santa Cruz, all have ATMs and change traveler's checks 9 AM–1:30 PM. The **post office** is in La

Crucecita, just off Benito Juárez where it turns toward Chahué. You can find maps and helpful English speakers in Santa Cruz at the **Asociación de Hoteles y Moteles** (Monte Albán, at Santa Cruz, tel. 958/7–08–48; open Mon.–Sat. 9–2 and 4–7) and the **Tourist Information Center** in Tangolunda (Benito Juárez, across from Hotel Fa-sol, no phone). For medical aid contact **IMSS** (next door to Telmex, tel. 958/7–11–82), **Cruz Roja** (tel. 958/7–11–88), or the **Centro de Salud** (tel. 958/7–04–03). In La Crucecita, **Dr. Ricardo Carrillo** (Sabali 403, at Gardenia, tel. 958/7–06–00 or 958/7–06–87) makes house calls, speaks English, and accepts American Express.

COMING AND GOING Direct buses to Oaxaca city ($9.50, 7 hrs) leave Santa Cruz Huatulco (cnr of Yuca and Gardenia) at 5:30 PM and 10 PM; arrive a half hour before departure. Buses also run between Pochutla and La Crucecita every 15 minutes (1 hr, $1). There are daily flights to Oaxaca city and Mexico City from the Santa María de Huatulco airport (tel. 958/1–04–44). To get here, take the main highway (Carretera 200) from La Crucecita north, or take a taxi ($7). Tickets and airport transportation can be arranged at any of the travel agencies in Santa Cruz or La Crucecita.

GETTING AROUND The bays are extremely spread out, and though they're now accessible by paved roads, it's a bit of a haul to get from one to the other. The rich tourists overcome this obstacle by touring by boat. The rest of us, however, can reach the three central bays—Tangolunda, Chahué, and Santa Cruz—by *urbanos* (city buses; 25¢), which leave from La Crucecita along the road that leads toward Chahué. They run from about 6 AM to 11 PM, but there are about half as many on the weekends as on the weekdays.

Colectivos ($2) leave early in the morning along the road from Santa Cruz to Chahué and at the crossroads for Santa María Huatulco to take workers out to Conejos, Maguey, and Cacaluta. A cab costs $5. To reach Órgano, you'll have to walk over the hill on the east end of Maguey; it should take about half an hour. To reach San Agustín and Chachacual, catch any bus toward Pochutla and get off at the crossroads for Santa María Huatulco. From here it's a $5 taxi ride or $2 colectivo (if you're lucky enough to get one) to the bay of your choice. Another option for all the bays is to show up at the Santa Cruz marina bright and early and try to hitch a ride with someone boating out to one of the beaches to work. If you luck out and someone's willing, expect to pay between $2 and $7.

WHERE TO SLEEP AND EAT Camping is the way to go in Huatulco. It's officially allowed only on Chahué, but you'll find deserted beaches and forest galore if you venture farther afield, and slinging a hammock or pitching a tent is no problem. Órgano is the most deserted bay; it has no palapas or tourist facilities, so you'll have to bring food, fresh water, and plenty of insect repellant if you're going to stay the night. Most of the other beaches have some palapas, but these close by late afternoon, and the beaches are deserted in the evenings. If you prefer not to camp, **Posada Primavera** (Palo Verde, behind Gardenia, tel. 958/7–11–67), in the nearby town of La Crucecita, rents the cleanest, cheapest rooms around with fans and private baths for $9 a single, $20 a double. If there's no room there, try **Posada Michelle** (cnr of Calle Gardenia and Palma Real, tel. 958/7–05–35).

In La Crucecita, comidas corridas and 35¢ tacos abound. Avoid the touristy restaurants on the zócalo (you'll know 'em when you see 'em), and you'll find no shortage of cheap eats. **Antojitos Oaxaqueños** (Palo Verde, at Bugambilia) offers hearty Oaxacan specialties for less than $4. A few steps farther from the zócalo, **La Cascada de Huatulco** (Chacah 213, 1 block NE of zócalo, no phone) serves up cheap homemade Oaxaqueño eats. Their filling *quesillo* and bean *huaraches,* a delicious version of the tostada, are less than $1.

AFTER DARK A weekend night out in the Bahías will cost you more than your hotel in La Crucecita. Both **Magic Circus** (Av. Santa Cruz in Hotel Marlín) and **Savage** (Benito Juárez, in front of the Sheraton, Tangolunda) charge a cover of $8–$12, which includes an open bar of *nacional* (Mexican) drinks. **Magic Circus** (Av. Santa Cruz, tel. 958/700–17) has no cover on Wednesdays, but who wants to feel obligated to wear a tie or sequins to have a drink? Instead, do what locals advise—check out the nightlife in nearby Chahué.

OUTDOOR ACTIVITIES Budget travelers aren't what the Mexican government had in mind when they built up Huatalco, but you can still have some fun without draining your pockets.

Snorkeling is best at Cacaluta and Chachacual. **Soc. Cooperativa Turístico** (tel. 958/7-00-81) rents snorkeling gear ($6 a day) on the Tangolunda dock and offers a full-day boat excursion to the nine bays with free drinks (about $17) leaving daily at 10:45 AM. There are also on- and offroad bike paths to several of the bays. To rent bikes, inquire at one of the travel agencies next to Hotel Castillo on Avenida Santa Cruz in Bahía Santa Cruz. One option is to bike to Cacaluta and paddle back by boat from Playa Entrega to Santa Cruz; the whole package costs $18. You can also rent jet skis on the beach in Santa Cruz. A 15-minute thrill is an exorbitant $7.

The Isthmus of Tehuantepec

The Isthmus of Tehuantepec stretches a mere 215 kilometers from the Caribbean to the Pacific, and encompasses parts of both Oaxaca and Tabasco. Most tourists do not consider it a destination in itself, but a stop along the gringo trail between Oaxaca and Chiapas to switch buses or refuel. From that vantage point the isthmus can seem particularly unattractive—dusty, hot, provincial, and boring, especially after the Oaxacan coast or the Chiapan highlands. If, however, you're interested in Zapotec culture you'll find the region fascinating. The large Zapotec population here has resisted being "Mexicanized" and instead identifies with the isthmus itself. You'll see this in the teaching of Zapotec poetry in the cultural centers, and in the distinctive local costumes and foods.

Calls in Zapotec announcing "geta tzuki" (small, dense breads) and "geta bingi" (shrimp-filled tortillas) for sale resound in the zócalos and marketplaces of the isthmus towns.

The three main cities on the Oaxacan part of the isthmus are Salina Cruz, Tehuantepec, and Juchitán. Despite the fact that they are all within 32 kilometers of one another, they have developed in very different ways. Salina Cruz has the most modern conveniences (such as ATMs). Tehuantepec, the area's namesake, is the smallest and prettiest of the three, while Juchitán, recognized as the cultural center of the isthmus, is where the Zapotec presence can be most strongly felt.

Salina Cruz

There's not much in Salina Cruz to distinguish it from other industrial port cities. Despite having the highest concentration of services such as banks, phones, and clinics in the area, there is hardly a tourist in sight. Those desperate for a beach should take a VENTOSA bus from the corner of 5 de Mayo and Acapulco to **La Ventosa**, a clean, windswept stretch of coast just before you hit the city. When the bus drops you off, head northwest (left) toward the sandy strip of beach. On the rocky end of the beach, at the edge of a windy cliff, stands a lighthouse Cortés utilized as he was conquering the Pacific. The northwestern end of the bay is home to a fairly secluded indigenous Huave community, whose last names include the likes of Davidson and Stevenson. People in the town of La Ventosa, who are very intrigued and curious about their neighbors, will tell you that the Huave bought these last names to replace their own.

BASICS **Bancomer** on Camacho exchanges currency weekdays 10–noon. For medical aid, both **IMSS** (on the Carretera Transístmica on the outskirts of town, tel. 971/4-15-72) and the **Centro de Salud** (cnr of Camacho and Frontera, near the post office) are open 24 hours. For the best rates on international and domestic calls and a private booth in an air-conditioned facility, head to **Servicio Telefónico y Fax SONEX** (cnr of Camacho and Mazatlán, tel. 971/4-56-21, fax 971/4-56-51, open daily 8 AM–midnight). The **post office** (cnr of Camacho and Frontera, no phone) is open weekdays 8–7, Saturday 9–1.

COMING AND GOING If you don't want to flag down a second-class bus on the highway, first-class **Cristóbal Colón** (tel. 971/4-02-59) buses leave from the station at 5 de Mayo 412, two blocks from the zócalo. Destinations include Tapachula (8 hrs, $12), Tuxtla Gutiérrez (6 hrs, $9), and San Cristóbal (8 hrs, $12) in Chiapas, as well as Huatulco (2½ hrs, $4) and Puerto Escondido (5 hrs, $7) on the Oaxacan coast. There are several buses to Oaxaca (5 hrs,

$8) and three evening buses to Mexico City (12 hrs, $28). Micros and second-class buses also depart daily from the railroad tracks for Puerto Escondido and Santa Cruz Huatulco, as well as other villages on the isthmus.

WHERE TO SLEEP AND EAT Hotels in Salina Cruz cater to businessmen and tend to be expensive. **Hotel Fuentes** (Camacho 114, tel. 971/4–02–43) has clean rooms with color TVs; a double is $12, $18 with air-conditioning. A few doors down and a bit cheaper is **Hotel Posada del Jardín** (Camacho 108, tel. 971/4–01–62), where doubles cost $10. You'll find taco stands and women selling dried fish and seafood around the market on 5 de Mayo, and stands near the zócalo offer hot tacos and terrific fresh seafood cocktails. If you want to enjoy your seafood sitting down, **La Pasadita** (Camacho 613-A, no phone; open 7 AM–11:30 PM) serves the best shrimp cocktail around for $4. **Café Istmeño** (5 de Mayo 305-A, across from zócalo, tel. 971/4–17–40) serves great coffee and $1.50 *tortas* (sandwiches) 24 hours a day. **Jugos Hawaii** (Camacho, 1 block from zócalo) offers a good selection of tropical fruit *licuados* (smoothies).

Tehuantepec

Sixteen kilometers north of Salina Cruz, Tehuantepec, on the river of the same name, feels the least modern of the main isthmus towns. You can start exploring at the **Casa de la Cultura,** housed in a crumbling former convent on an alley off Calle Guerrero, which has a small garden and fountain and often sponsors cultural events. If you're going to be in town for a few days, check out **Guiengola,** the site of a Zapotec fortress that was the locus of battles between the Zapotecs and Aztecs. Although the site is prime for camping, it's a good 15 kilometers out of town. To get here, make arrangements with Victor Velasco at the Palacio Municipal in the zócalo or get the Boy Scouts, who tend to congregate at the Palacio Municipal on Saturdays 10–noon, to guide you up the mountain.

Tehuanas still wear their unique costume—a brightly patterned cotton skirt, a hand-embroidered huipil, and, on special occasions, a headdress of starched lace called a bidainiró or olan.

BASICS Both the **Centro de Salud** (Guerrero, 3 blocks north of zócalo) and the **Cruz Roja** (cnr of Roberto E. Salazar and Calle Soto, near Carretera Transístmica) offer emergency care. **El Paraíso** (5 de Mayo 1, tel. 971/5–02–12) provides long-distance and collect service 8 AM–10 PM. The **post office** (cnr of Hidalgo and 22 de Marzo) is open 8–6.

COMING AND GOING First- and second-class buses operate out of the station (tel. 971/8–57–52) on the Carretera Transístmica, two blocks from the zócalo. From here, first- and second-class buses, including the Istmeños (urbanos), will take you to and from the three main towns on the isthmus.

WHERE TO SLEEP One block past the zócalo is **Hotel Oasis** (Ocampo 8, tel. 971/5–00–08). Doubles with private baths and ceiling fans are $10; singles are $8. The three-story **Hotel Donaji** (Juárez 10, tel. 971/5–00–64) is built around a peaceful, ivy-covered courtyard, though rooms that face the street can be a bit noisy. A double with private bath costs about $12; a few dollars more gets you air-conditioning. For the simplest and cheapest sleeping arrangements, head down the street from the Oasis toward the railroad tracks to **Posada Hasdar** (Ocampo 10, tel. 971/5–02–07), where slightly rumpled rooms with private baths and ceiling fans are $6.

FOOD **El Portón** (Juana C. Romero 54, off zócalo; open Mon.–Sat. 8–6 and Sun. 8–1) sells simple, fresh regional food. Soups are 50¢ a bowl, and big plates of enchiladas, chiles rellenos, or tacos are all a steal at $2. The beer ($1) is kept cold and they'll turn on the fan and stereo on request. Two blocks from the zócalo is **Café Colonial** (Juana C. Romero 66, tel. 971/5–01–15; open daily 8–7), where *huevos motuleños,* a messy but yummy concoction of sunny-side up eggs, tortillas, ham, cheese, and salsa, goes for about $3.

Juchitán

Juchitán's dusty, potholed streets give the town a grubby feel, but it buzzes with activity and culture, making it well worth a visit. The **Mercado 5 de Septiembre** (Efraín Gómez), an excellent place to find cheap food, is also the place to observe Juchitán's matriarchal society, where women peddle everything from clothing and accessories to produce. The **Casa de la Cultura** (Colón, at Juárez, tel. 971/1-13-51; open daily 9-2 and 4-7) is a free regional art center with a focus on artists from Juchitán, housed in the 16th-century **Iglesia San Vicente Ferrer**. Come in the early afternoons, when Juchitán children attend catechism and sing church hymns. About 10 kilometers outside of town you'll find an estuary called **Mar Muerto** (Dead Sea), ideal for fishing and boating; you can try to get one of the fisherman to take you out on his boat for a couple of dollars. To get here, take a bus labeled 7TH SEC. (50¢) from behind the market in Juchitán.

BASICS **Banamex** (5 de Septiembre, at Efraín Gómez) exchanges currency weekdays 10-noon. For medical attention, **IMSS** (eastern end of Efraín Gómez, past Constitución) is open 24 hours but there isn't always a doctor in the house. The **Centro de Salud** (Libertad, near Efraín Gómez) offers emergency service 8-3. You'll find two **Ladatel** phones across from the telephone office at 16 de Septiembre. For a surcharge, you can also make long distance collect calls at the caseta at the corner of 5 de Septiembre and Juárez, near the Casa de la Cultura. The **post office** (cnr of 16 de Septiembre and Efraín Gómez, no phone) is open 8-5.

COMING AND GOING There is a sprawling bus station next to the Pemex station off the main Carretera to Salina Cruz. **Fletes y Pasajeros** (tel. 971/1-04-19), **Alas de Oro** (tel. 971/1-04-69), and **Cristóbal Colón** (tel. 971/1-10-22) bus lines operate out of this station. If your headed for Guatemala, Colón's bus for Tapachula leaves at 10:15 PM. Locals advise against hitching.

WHERE TO SLEEP Your best choice on the zócalo is **Hospedaje Echazarreta** (Juárez 23, tel. 971/1-12-05), run by a friendly family who stocks the clean rooms with fresh towels daily. A double is $7, $10 with private bath. For the same price, **Hotel Juchitán** (16 de Septiembre 51, tel. 971/1-10-65) offers decently clean rooms with private baths in their sky-blue hotel. Farther down the road, **Hotel Gonzanelly** (16 de Septiembre 70, tel. 971/1-13-89) charges $14 for large air-conditioned doubles with private baths.

In Juchitán's market, women sell iguana eggs as well as live iguanas with their mouths sewn shut and legs tied behind their backs. The little leathery eggs are eaten by biting off the top of the shell and sucking out the yolky, slightly salty contents. The iguanas are also tasty, especially entomado (cooked in tomato sauce).

FOOD Juchitán is regionally famous for its seafood. The popular **Mariscos Sylvia Juchitán** (2 de Abril, btw Aldama and Hidalgo, tel. 971/1-22-35; open 8-7) serves an enormous *vuelva a la vida* (back to life) cocktail ($5.50), crammed with chunks of octopus, shrimp, conch, oysters, avocado, onion, and cilantro. **Restaurant Casa Grande** (Juárez 12, on zócalo, tel. 971/1-34-60; open 8 AM-10 PM), has linen tablecloths and a cool courtyard; their pungent garlic soup is well worth $2.

CHIAPAS AND TABASCO

13

By Lourdes Haro

The states of Chiapas and Tabasco share a narrow strip of land between the Gulf of Mexico, the Pacific Ocean, and Guatemala, encompassing mountains, swampy lowland, desert, volcanoes, cloud forests, and thick jungle. This region, at the heart of the great Olmec and Classic Maya empires, was hotly contested by many Mesoamerican civilizations. Despite the close geographical proximity and shared history of these two states, however, the contrast today between them couldn't be more striking. The oil boom of the 1970s left Tabasco—a relatively prosperous, largely mestizo state—with many modern, air-conditioned buildings, massive cement expressways, and modern, flashy hotels. Today, indigenous peoples are a rare sight in Tabasco. The larger and more mountainous Chiapas, on the other hand, is rich in colonial history and indigenous culture—Spanish is the *second* language of much of the population—but little else. Although Chiapas provides Mexico with abundant agricultural goods and enough electricity to light up Mexico City, it remains the poorest state in the country, and Chiapans sometimes feel they are not part of the "prospering" México they see on TV or in the newspapers ads.

It was partially in response to this type of regional inequity that, in January 1994, the Zapatista National Liberation Army invaded the historic Chiapan city of San Cristóbal de las Casas, and effectively put some of Chiapas's chronic problems into the political limelight. While those who lost businesses during the uprising and the ensuing economic crisis bear some ill will, many extend their thanks toward the Zapatistas. Since 1994, Chiapas has seen the construction of new roads and public services where there were none before. And although peaceful talks between the government and the Zapatistas have progressed, locals say that should a new uprising occur, the Zapatista-led fight for indigenous rights and land reform will gather even stronger support.

Even before the uprising, relatively few tourists had explored these two states. The dense jungles of Tabasco, dotted with impressive Mayan ruins and intriguing caves, are rarely explored, and some of the state's beaches are hidden paradises where you can dine on seafood and cool off with tropical fruit concoctions for less than most places in Mexico. Tabasco is by no means an untouched Eden though: While Tabasco's oil boom was used to encourage new business and fund the arts in the capital, parts of the gulf coastline were contaminated. While Tabascans now enjoy a relatively high standard of living, the cost to the environment (not yet known) could be high. But most residents point proudly to the cultural vitality of Villahermosa and to the fact that oil money paid for projects like the draining of the basin containing La Venta, the largest Olmec archaeological find in Mesoamerica.

The wonders of Chiapas have received less fanfare but are mind-blowing to even the most worldly of travelers. The state contains a large tract of endangered rain forest and is home to vital indigenous cultures unlike any others in the country. The hilly terrain near San Cristóbal is the living fabric of Maya culture, with over a score of indigenous groups speaking several Mayan languages. San Cristóbal itself, just two hours from the hot and humid state capital of Tuxtla Gutiérrez, offers a cool climate, pine forests, and some of the country's best-preserved colonial architecture. Although the Zapatistas occupied the city for just a few days, their presence can still be felt in the form of army checkpoints dotting the countryside, and hotels and cafés are now just beginning to see a steady flow of travelers again.

The coffee- and cacao-growing region of southern coastal Chiapas is almost never visited by the package-tour crowd. The town of Tapachula is a gateway to Guatemala for backpack-toting adventure seekers, and a lively city in its own right. From here, you can hit a few undeveloped beaches or head for the cool mountain air in the beautiful town of Unión Juárez, with access to great hiking in the wilderness around the volcano and among the foothills dotted with coffee plantations. Farther inland are Comitán and the Parque Nacional Lagos de Montebello, which is home to more blue-green lakes than one person could ever swim in; surrounding the park are a number of major Maya archaeological sites.

The eastern region of Chiapas is mostly rain forest, though more and more acreage is being lost to cattle ranching as Mexico pushes to colonize the untouched land and relocate people from the overpopulated highlands. The famous ruins of Palenque and Toniná are here, and rivers and waterfalls coarse through the land, offering luxurious escapes from the heat. In the southeast corner of Chiapas, the Lacandón rain forest hides the remote ruins of Yaxchilán and Bonampak. This ever-shrinking paradise is home to the Lacandón Indians, whose Maya culture and religious rites are considered by many to be more closely related to the ancient Maya than those of any other living group.

Tuxtla Gutiérrez

"The new ugly capital of Chiapas," declared Graham Greene in 1939, "is like an unnecessary postscript to Chiapas, which should be all wild mountain and old churches and swallowed ruins and Indians plodding by." You may not agree with him, but he has a point. Tuxtla can't match the beauty of Chiapas's most stellar spots; it's popular with travelers mainly because it offers bus connections to surrounding states and nearly everywhere within Chiapas. This busy administrative and university city with a long, well-lit strip evokes Las Vegas at night. But in the midst of all the cement islands and superexpressways, however, you'll find a great zoo, botanical gardens, and cultural museums worth at least one day of exploration. A short trip outside the city takes you to the colonial town of Chiapa de Corzo, the departure point for a boat ride through the deep, narrow Sumidero Canyon.

This part of Chiapas gets a lot of rain from the end of May until as late as October. The rest of the year it hardly rains at all.

Tuxtla became the capital of Chiapas in 1892 after a bloody battle with liberal forces at the old capital of San Cristóbal de las Casas. Tensions arose because of Tuxtla's support of dictator Porfirio Díaz's land policy that favored a few *ladino* (Spanish-descended) families over the indigenous *campesinos* (peasants). To this day, Chiapas's fertile land is concentrated in the hands of a tiny, powerful fraction of the population. Although land reform is still a hot issue in southern Chiapas, you won't see the EZLN (Zapatista National Liberation Army) graffiti here that's so evident on the walls of country corner stores as far north as Oaxaca and all over Tuxtla's sister city, San Cristóbal.

BASICS

AMERICAN EXPRESS AmEx operates through **Agencia de Viajes Marabusco.** Cardholders can cash personal checks, receive advances on AmEx cards, or have their mail held here; anyone can change money, receive a MoneyGram, or have their lost traveler's checks replaced. *Av. Central, at 15a Pte., across from federal tourist office, tel. 961/2–69–98 or 961/2–84–49. Mailing address: Pl. Bonampak, Local 14, Sedetur, Tuxtla Gutiérrez, Chiapas, CP 29030, México. Open weekdays 9–2 and 4–7, Sat. 9–2.*

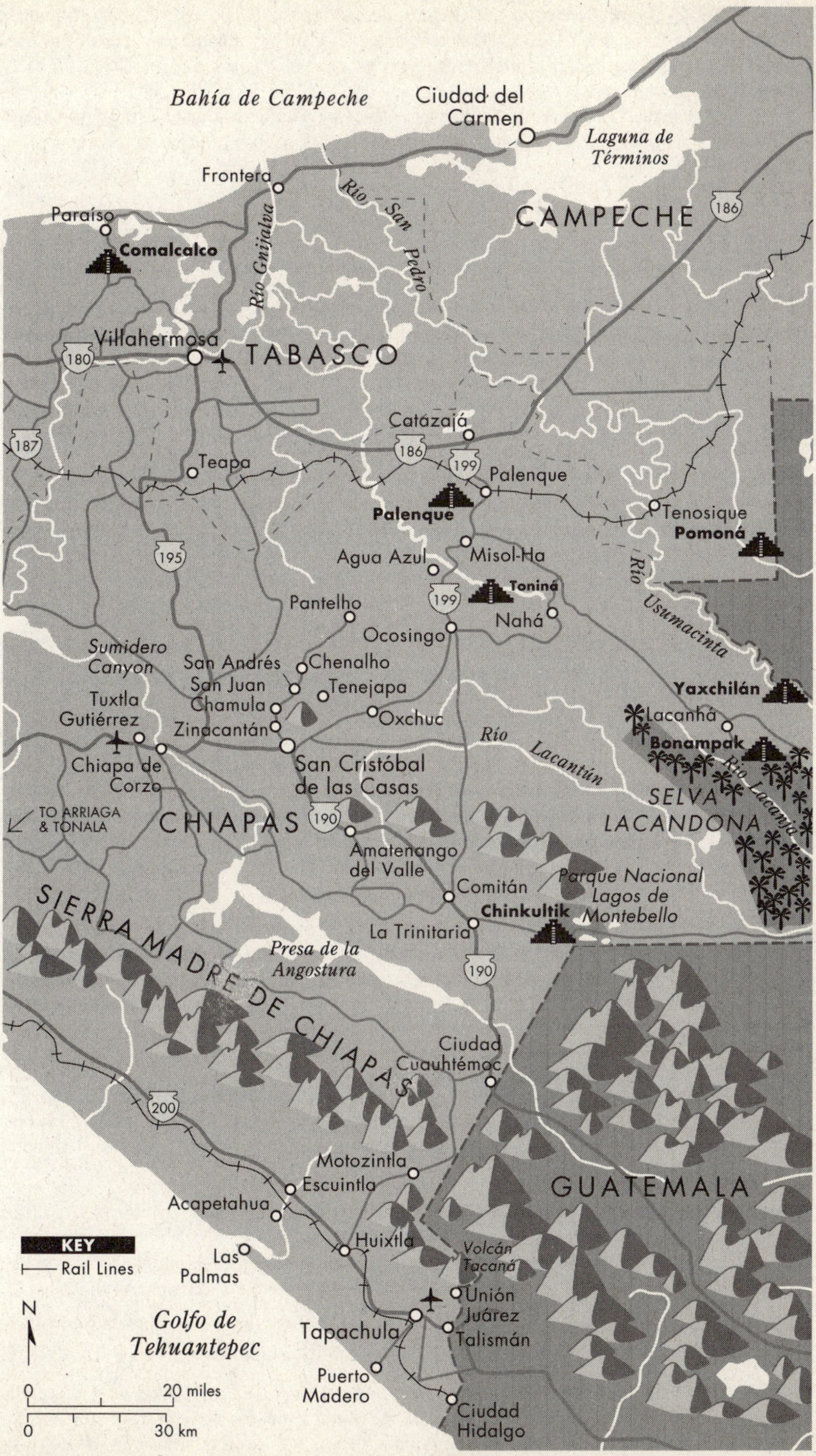

CASAS DE CAMBIO **Bancomer** (Av. Central, at 2a Pte., tel. 961/2-82-51) and **Banamex** (1a Sur Pte. 141, tel. 961/2-87-44) both change traveler's checks on weekdays 10-noon. Bancomer changes cash and offers cash advances on credit cards until it closes at 3. At **Cafetería Bonampak** (Blvd. Belisario Domínguez 180, tel. 961/3-20-50, ext. 127), you can change cash or traveler's checks or get a cash advance on your Visa, MasterCard, or AmEx card after hours or on weekends; it's open daily 7 AM–midnight.

EMERGENCIES For an ambulance, call the **Cruz Roja** at 961/2-00-96 or 961/2-95-14. For any other emergency, call the **police** (961/2-05-30).

LAUNDRY **Lavandería La Burbuja** will wash and dry 3 kilos for $5. *1a Nte. Pte., at 3a Pte. Nte., tel. 961/2-52-34. Open weekdays 9-2 and 4-8, Sat. 9-4.*

MAIL The **post office** (NE cnr of Parque Central, tel. 961/2-04-16) will hold mail sent to you at the following address for up to 10 days: Lista de Correos, Tuxtla Gutiérrez, Chiapas, CP 29002, México. Next door, the **telegram office** (tel. 961/2-02-81) sends packages and faxes. Both are open weekdays 8-7 and Saturday 9-1.

MEDICAL AID The **Centro de Salud** (9a Sur Ote., at 2a Ote. Sur, tel. 961/2-03-15) is open Monday–Saturday 7:30–noon for walk-in appointments. Free, round-the-clock medical attention is available at the **Cruz Roja** (5a Nte. Pte. 1480, tel. 961/2-00-96).

PHONES Blue Ladatel phones (dial 09 for collect calls) can be found in front of the movie theaters near the zócalo. Cash calls can be made from *casetas de larga distancia* (long-distance telephone offices), as can collect calls, which generally cost $3. There's a convenient caseta on 5a Oriente Sur 122 that's open 9 AM–10 PM, but be aware that hours at casetas, especially smaller ones, are erratic.

VISITOR INFORMATION Here, you can pick up maps, restaurant and hotel guides, and information on everything from taxi fares to boat rides up the Sumidero Canyon. *2a Nte., at Central beneath Parque Central, tel. 961/3-76-90. Open weekdays 9-3 and 6-9, Sat. 9-1.*

The **federal tourist office** is staffed by helpful young people fresh out of college who speak decent English. While you're here, try to get your hands on *La Cartelera*, a monthly publication that lists cultural events taking place in Tuxtla and other Chiapan cities. Photocopied brochures with maps and practical information about other towns in Chiapas are also available. The tourist police unit, the Green Angels, has an office in the same building upstairs; travel-related thefts or other criminal activity can be reported to these green-banded guys through the tourist office. *Blvd. Belisario Domínguez 950, tel. 961/2-45-35. Open weekdays 8 AM–9 PM.*

COMING AND GOING

BY BUS The first-class **ADO/Cristóbal Colón** station (2a Nte. Pte. 268, tel. 961/2-51-22) is two blocks northwest of the zócalo. Buses to San Cristóbal (1½ hrs, $2.50) leave every hour 5 AM–9 PM. After 1 PM daily several regular first-class and two plush, bathroom-equipped "Servi-Plus" buses leave for Mexico City (12 hrs, $34; $38 for Servi-Plus). You must hop on a Mexico City bus to get to Puebla (10 hrs, $30) or Córdoba (9 hrs, $23). The *juguería* (juice bar) across from station will hold luggage all day until midnight for 50¢. Lock your bags and don't leave any money or valuables in them.

Near the market, **Autotransportes Tuxtla Gutiérrez** station (3a Sur Ote. 712, tel. 961/2-02-30 or 961/2-02-88) offers both first- and second-class service. Second-class buses go to Ocosingo (3½ hrs, $3.25), Palenque (6 hrs, $6), Tapachula (8 hrs, $9), and Villahermosa (8½ hrs, $9). Inquire at the window about service to less-frequented destinations in Chiapas.

Small **regional buses** leave the dusty terminal at the corner of 2a Oriente Sur and 2a Sur Oriente for Chiapa de Corzo every 15 minutes 4 AM–10:30 PM. The ride takes 20 minutes and costs 35¢.

BY PLANE **Aeropuerto Francisco Sarabia** (Carretera Panamericana, 10 km west of Tuxtla, tel. 961/5-10-11) is commonly known as "Terán." **Aerocaribe** (tel. 961/2-20-53 or 961/5-15-30 at airport) serves Mérida, Cancún, Villahermosa, and Oaxaca; a one-way Mexico City flight costs about $90 during the summer. **AVIACSA** (tel. 961/2-06-01) flies to the Yucatán, Oaxaca, Monterrey, and Mexico City. There is no money exchange or luggage storage, but there is a rundown tourist information booth. Colectivos de Terán (tel. 961/3-50-29), run by AVI-ASCA, will take you to the airport from the corner of 3a Pte. and 6a Sur for 35¢ if you aren't overflowing with luggage. Taxis ($5) are the second-best means of transport to Terán.

GETTING AROUND

Although Tuxtla is a large, sprawling city, it's fairly easy to navigate. Two main thoroughfares (the east–west Calle Central and north–south Avenida Central, aka Avenida 14 de Septiembre) intersect at the zócalo and divide the city into four quadrants. All the other streets are named and numbered according to their position relative to the center. To reach the American Express office, main tourist office, and discos from the center you'll need to take an AV. CENTRAL colectivo down Avenida Central until it turns to Boulevard Belisario Domínguez toward the western outskirts of town.

Learning the Spanish names for the cardinal directions will help you find your way around Tuxtla Gutiérrez: Norte (Nte.) = North; Sur = South; Oriente (Ote.) = East; and Poniente (Pte.) = West.

BY BUS Colectivos run throughout the city between 6 AM and 9 PM. Destinations are plainly marked on the front windshields, and stops are indicated on the street by blue signs. Unlike those in many Mexican cities, the colectivos here pick up passengers only at marked stops. Microbuses are bigger and run to Tuxtla's outlying sights, such as the zoo and botanical gardens. They can be hailed on most main streets and their destinations are also clearly marked on the front windows.

BY TAXI Taxis, necessary if you want to return from one of the discos late at night, run 24 hours. Don't let them rip you off—the most you should pay within city limits is $2. Agree on the price before getting in.

BY CAR Budget (Blvd. Domínguez 2510, tel. 961/5-06-83), **Dollar** (5a Av. Nte. Pte. 2260, tel. 961/2-89-32), and **Hertz** (Blvd. Domínguez 180, tel. 961/1-39-50) are the best budget rental agencies. The going day rate for a sedan is $45, which includes insurance, 200 free kilometers, and a full tank.

WHERE TO SLEEP

Most hotels in Tuxtla are modern and bland, but relatively clean and cheap rooms are easy to come by. Rather than ambience, look for a working fan and clean sheets. If you're too lazy to lug that backpack, **Hotel Santo Domingo,** across from the Cristóbal Colón bus station, is the cheapest dive you'll find at $5 a night per person. The rooms have private baths but no hot water.

Casa de Huéspedes Muñiz. The dusty upper rooms of this guest house have a view of the surrounding urban squalor, but for $5 a single and $6 a double ($2 each additional person) with communal bath, one shouldn't expect to be insulated from reality. The water's not hot, but there are fans and a nice family runs the place. *2a Sur Ote. 733, no phone. 32 rooms, 13 with bath. Laundry, luggage storage.*

Hotel Casablanca. The Casablanca features a pleasant courtyard filled with plants, and all its rooms have ceiling fans. The bathrooms even have blue tiling, towels, soap, and toilet paper. With communal bath, singles are $6, doubles $8. Rooms with private bath are $8 for a single and $12 for a double. The showers in both the communal and private bathrooms have hot water 24 hours a day. *2a Nte. Ote. 251, 1 block NE of zócalo, tel. 961/1-03-05. 52 rooms, 37 with bath. Luggage storage.*

Hotel La Catedral. A maze of stairways and corridors lead to sparkling clean, quiet guest rooms. All rooms have ceiling fans and private bathrooms with hot showers. A single goes for $6, a double for $8. *1a Nte. Ote. 367, at 2a Ote. Nte., tel. 961/3-08-24. 30 rooms, all with bath.*

Hotel Plaza Chiapas. Clean, new rooms come complete with fans and color-coordinated bathrooms with hot water and towels. Singles are $8.50, doubles $10.50, and triples $15. *2a Nte. Ote. 299, 2 blocks NE of zócalo, tel. 961/3-83-65. 34 rooms, all with bath.*

Hotel San Antonio. With only 15 exceptionally clean rooms—all with fans and private bathrooms—this place is usually full, but it's worth a try. Singles cost $8, doubles $10, and triples $12. *2a Sur Ote. 540, tel. 961/2-27-13. Around cnr from 2nd-class bus station.*

HOSTELS **INDEJECH Villa Juvenil/Chiapas.** Located in a youth-sports center, this clean hostel provides single-sex dorm-style accommodations complete with clean sheets, pillowcases, and towels for $3 a night. When there are groups of people, meals are available at the cafeteria ($2). You're even allowed use of the backyard basketball courts and soccer fields. It's an excellent deal, even with the cold showers and 11 PM curfew. *Av. Central, at 18a Ote., tel. 961/3-34-05. Take a colectivo from centro along Av. Central for about 10 min.*

FOOD

Because people from all over the state come here on business, Tuxtla offers a chance to sample cuisine from almost anywhere in Chiapas. The center swarms with eateries and cafés; look for the striped umbrellas off the zócalo. Most restaurants serve local favorites, including crumbly Chiapan cheese, tamales, and spicy tacos top-heavy with chiles. The city's prosperity has also bred a substantial middle class, which, like its counterparts worldwide, has time to worry about things like whether meat is good for them. The result: Gyms and health-food stores are scattered about town, and most restaurants have a selection of vegetarian dishes.

In the morning or early afternoon, look for people sitting around stands drinking out of gourd bowls. These are filled with pozol, a cold, corn-based drink flavored with sugar and/or cacao, with chewy cornmeal at the bottom.

➢ **UNDER $5** • **Las Pichanchas.** The menu here includes *tamales chiapanecos* (with mole sauce, olives, raisins, and meat wrapped in banana leaves, $2.50) and *milanesas de ternera* (breaded cuts of veal) for the same price. In an attempt to make you feel like you're in Chiapas, a danza folklórica is put on around 9 PM every evening. *Central Ote. 838, tel. 961/2-53-51. Open daily 8 AM-midnight.*

Restaurante Imperial. This central restaurant serves tasty and inexpensive local fare such as *entomatadas de pollo* (chicken in tomato sauce). The ample menu includes soup, a meat entrée, tortillas, a drink, and dessert for $3. *2 Nte. Pte. 106, at Calle Central, no phone. Open daily 7 AM-6:30 PM.*

Restaurante Vegetariano Nah-Yaxal. Vegetarians are in for a treat here. Tasty *tortas* (sandwiches) made with soy beef on whole wheat, or chilaquiles with gluten are both $2, and the mammoth Energética Nah-Yaxal (fruit salad smothered in yogurt and granola) is $2.50. Cookbooks for sale include *The Power of Respiration* and *Sprouts: The Most Perfect and Complete Natural Food. 6a Nte. Pte. 124, tel. 961/3-33-16. Open Mon.-Sat. 7:30 AM-9 PM.*

Trattoria San Marco. Of the tourist traps on the zócalo, this place wins for variety. Specialties include spaghetti bolognese ($4) and crepes ($5). Come and enjoy a $1 cappuccino or $2 beer alongside businesspeople, teenagers, and a cadre of chess players. *Behind cathedral, tel. 961/2-69-74. Open daily 7 AM-midnight.*

WORTH SEEING

Tuxtla's main attractions lie in three distinct areas of the city: **Parque Madero**, in the northeast; **Parque Zoológico**, to the southeast; and the city center, which contains **Parque Central**, the **zócalo**, and the **cathedral**, which houses one of the world's first musical clocks. To reach the zoo from the center, you'll need public transportation, but the other two areas can be easily reached on foot. The **market**, just 2 blocks south of the zócalo, is a dimly lit maze of giant papayas and other fruits, local cheeses, costume jewelry, and crisped *chicharrón* (pork rind).

PARQUE MADERO Just a few years old, the Parque Madero complex brings together a variety of indoor and outdoor Chiapan wonders, all within easy walking distance. The park begins at the intersection of 5a Norte Oriente and 5a Oriente Norte, about 9 blocks northeast of the zócalo. Immediately outside Parque Madero is **Teatro Bonampak**, an open-air theater for cultural events. Consult *La Cartelera* (*see* Visitor Information, *above*) for a list of special performances.

➢ **CENTRO DE CONVIVENCIA INFANTIL** • You don't have to be a kid to enjoy this kiddie park on the east esplanade, which features giant renditions of a demented Mickey Mouse. There are also pony rides ($1), a miniature train, and piped-in music. *Admission free. Open Tues.–Sun. 9–6.*

➢ **MUSEO REGIONAL DE ANTROPOLOGIA E HISTORIA** • This sleek museum provides a look at the Chiapan past and present. Permanent exhibits—packed with Olmec, Maya, and Aztec artifacts—trace the growth of early indigenous civilizations. Look for oddly shaped Olmec skulls: Cosmetic cranial deformation was performed on noble Olmec children. Across the courtyard and upstairs is an exhibition on the Spanish invasion—contrasting with huge colonial paintings of the Virgin Mary and numerous Spanish artifacts are historical narratives and images of the enslavement and displacement of indigenous people. *Admission free. Open Tues.–Sun. 9–4.*

> *The Chiapan rain forest is home to representatives of 40% of all species found in Mexico, yet it's rapidly disappearing as a result of the government's eagerness to sell the highly marketable wood.*

➢ **MUSEO Y JARDIN BOTANICO** • Farther down the esplanade is a botanical museum run by the Chiapan Botanical Institute. Displays include native trees, flowers, and medicinal plants and provide a sense of the scope of preservation efforts being undertaken across the state. Across the esplanade from the museum is the botanical garden. Winding paths that crisscross the garden are filled with kissing teenagers walking through canopies of bamboo, mango trees, and twisting vines. *Admission free. Museum open Tues.–Sun. 9–3; garden open Tues.–Sun. 9–6.*

➢ **TEATRO EMILIO RABASA** • This huge modern theater that hosts frequent cultural events is the park's central landmark. *La Cartelera* (*see* Visitor Information, *above*) provides information on performances. Two tree-lined walkways extend from the theater: The western path, lined with bronze busts of famous Mexican leaders, winds its way to the museums and botanical garden; the eastern path cuts through the children's recreational park.

PARQUE ZOOLOGICO The Parque Zoológico, one of the best in Latin America, features a selection of the spectacular and diverse flora and fauna of Chiapas. Concrete paths climb through cool, lush tropical canopies ringing with the songs of birds and insects. More than 100 species of native Chiapan creatures, many of them endangered, wander here in an approximation of their natural surroundings. There's an environmental education center, aviary, and even an insect zoo filled with giant roaches and huge, hairy spiders. The zoo affords rare glimpses of tapirs, black panthers, *guacamayas* (macaws), and the spectacularly plumed quetzal. *SE of town, off Libramiento Sur. Take* CERRO HUECO *bus, which leaves every half hour from 1a Ote. Sur, btw 6a and 7a Sur Ote. Donations encouraged. Open Tues.–Sun. 9–5.*

AFTER DARK

For a reputedly humdrum town, Tuxtla has a number of late-night surprises. In addition to the movie theaters near the zócalo, you'll find a wide variety of nightlife options that range from Budweiser monster-truck rowdiness to candle-lit melancholy. The music of street performers—which could be anything from a marimba ensemble or romantic balladeer to a military band—is common in the Parque Central, especially on Sundays. For authentic and free marimba, stroll by the *kiosko* in the appropriately named **Parque de la Marimba** (Av. Central, 7 blocks west of Parque Central btw 9a Pte. and 8a Pte.) weekdays 7 PM–10 PM, rain or shine. *La Cartelera* (*see* Visitor Information, *above*) provides the rundown on more folkloric cultural events, and rock concerts are advertised in record stores.

BARS The clientele at the bars and cafés tends to change as the evening passes. Early on, a college-age crowd congregates to find out where the real action will be taking place later that night. Next, middle-aged regulars come around to listen to live bands and/or watch *fútbol* (soccer) on TV. Check out **Obsession** (3a Ote. Nte. 142) and **Bar El Nucu** (Hotel María Eugenia, Av. Central Ote. No. 507) for throaty Mexican ballads from about 9 PM until 3 AM.

DANCING Tuxtla's discos attract a young crowd and tend to host events like bikini and "best legs" contests. The cover is generally about $3.50–$6 (usually a little less for women for some odd reason), and music ranges from Mexican pop to tropical to American Top 40. Some weekend boogeying options are **Sheik** (Hotel Flamboyant, Blvd. Belisario Domínguez Km. 1081, tel. 961/5–08–88), **Colors** (Hotel Arecas, Blvd. Belisario Domínguez Km. 1080, tel. 961/5–11–21), and **Freeday** (Blvd. Los Laureles, at Blvd. Belisario Domínguez). All are too far from the zócalo to walk. You can take a colectivo down Avenida Central until 9 PM, but after that you'll need to take a taxi ($2). Closer to the center is **Úngalo** (Av. Central Ote., 3 blocks east of zócalo), which is packed with teeny-boppers rockin' to reggae and American pop on weekend nights. The cover here is $3.50.

Near Tuxtla Gutiérrez

CHIAPA DE CORZO

You might not guess that a quiet, friendly riverside town awaits you only 20 minutes by bus from Tuxtla. In the early morning you'll hear crowing roosters and the early bells of mass intertwined with the putt-putt of cars. Nearly every Tuxtlan you meet will ask if you've taken the boat ride through the **Cañon del Sumidero** from Chiapa de Corzo. The locals' opinion of the place is exalted but justified: Gliding between the kilometer-high canyon walls is an experience not to be missed.

Chiapa de Corzo was an important pre-Columbian and colonial center because of its strategic location on the Río Grijalva. Today, its main sights are clustered around the **zócalo**, with its colonial clock tower and 16th-century fountain representing Queen Isabella's crown (the latter in the Moorish-influenced mudéjar architectural style). The **Palacio Municipal**—just off the zócalo in the arched **Plaza de Ángel Albino Corzo**—has murals depicting scenes from local and national history, including portrayals of the Chiapa Indians, who threw themselves into the Sumidero Canyon to escape enslavement by the Spanish. Handicraft shops around the plaza sell lacquerware, leather goods, and regional clothing. The free **Museo de la Laca** (Lacquerware Museum), on the top floor of the 16th-century **Ex-convento de Santo Domingo** (behind the cathedral), has an extensive collection of bowls, chests, masks, and crosses from all over Mexico and Guatemala. Behind the museum lacquer artisans teach young apprentices their craft. If you're lucky, you can catch a weekend class and learn the basics of this complex art.

The fountain in the zócalo is connected to an abundant underground water source that helped townspeople to survive the epidemics that swept through much of Mexico in colonial times.

You Get What You Pay For

Lacquerware is made in Chiapa de Corzo by a labor-intensive process in which a gourd is rubbed with fat, then with a natural colorant (such as charcoal or earth), and buffed. This process is repeated at least four times before the gourd is ready to be painted. Most of the so-called lacquerware sold in the shops is in fact simply coated with oil paint and decorated. How do you tell the difference?

- Oil paint is slick and shiny and has a distinguishable odor, even when dry.

- Because lacquerware is repeatedly buffed, the surface is relatively blemish-free, resembling smooth pottery. Imitations will have a less uniform surface.

- If it's really cheap, it's not real.

If you opt not to take the 2-hour boat ride through the canyon, you can take a taxi from Tuxtla or Chiapa to any of four *miradores* (lookouts), which afford a bird's eye view of Sumidero. But the best way to enjoy it is to take the cruise along the Río Grijalva. The canyon is full of birds, crocodiles, and iguana, and your pilot will be more than eager to maneuver into caves and close to shore to point them out. In July and August, heavy rains create four waterfalls, the largest of which is the **Árbol de Navidad,** a conical plume of water that cascades down the green canyon wall in the shape of a giant Christmas tree.

Expeditions originate from Chiapa's embarcadero and from Cahuaré (about 5 minutes up the road toward Tuxtla). To get to Chiapa's embarcadero from the zócalo, head past the cathedral and down the hill on Calle 5 de Febrero for 2 blocks. The fare is $5–$12, depending on the number of people. Trips run daily, from early morning until around 4 PM. Come in the morning if you're alone and want to get in on a group deal.

Cascada El Chorreadero is a waterfall and swimming hole 7 kilometers east of Chiapa, toward San Cristóbal. The site is most beautiful in the rainy season (June–August), when the waterfall is strongest. Go on a weekday if you want some solitude. Take a bus from Chiapa toward San Cristóbal or pay $3 for a taxi.

COMING AND GOING Microbuses leave from 3a Oriente Sur between 2a and 3a Sur Poniente in Tuxtla every five to 10 minutes and go directly to Chiapa for 35¢. The buses run 6 AM–8 PM, and the ride takes about 20 minutes. Chiapa's bus station is 1 block east of the zócalo on 21 de Octubre, but you can always jump on a bus as it passes the Parque Central. Taxis between Tuxtla and Chiapa are also readily available and cost about $5.

WHERE TO SLEEP Chiapa is an easy day trip from Tuxtla and even from San Cristóbal, so few visitors stay the night. **Hotel Los Ángeles** (Julián Grajales 2, on southern end of zócalo near fountain, tel. 961/6–00–48) is the only budget lodging in town. The colonial-style building has somewhat grimy but spacious rooms with desks, fans, and French doors that look out onto the town and mountains. In high season (December and January, Semana Santa, late summer), it's best to call ahead and make reservations. Singles are about $8.50, doubles $10.50.

FOOD Central Chiapa has a number of food stands and small restaurants. For a little extra money and a lot more ambience, head down the hill to one of the restaurants at the embarcadero and try the local fare. You'll also get a view of the river and perhaps some live marimba music. On a corner just outside the Museo de la Laca, a local family sells some of the best *pozol* (a tasty cold, local beverage made of finely ground corn, available in different flavors) in Chiapas—especially good is the chocolatey cacao pozol. Weekdays, it's only served before noon, so come early.

El Ausente (Embarcadero, no phone; open daily 8–6), a favorite of locals, serves a whopping plate of prawns fried in garlic with tortillas and condiments for $5.50. Although it costs more than most local places and caters to tourists, **Jardines de Chiapa** (Francisco I. Madero 395, tel. 968/6–01–98, 1 block from zócalo toward pier; open daily 9 AM–8 PM) serves tasty and unusual local specialties unavailable elsewhere. *Sopa fiestera,* the hearty soup typically served on religious holidays, will fill an empty stomach with shredded chicken, avocado, hard-boiled eggs, tomatoes, onions, cheese, and noodles for $2.50. Also try *chipilín con bolita* (balls of corn paste, tomato sauce, and cheese cooked with a local tarragon-like herb). Average prices for a complete meal are $6–$10. Don't confuse this restaurant with another one of the same name on the zócalo.

FESTIVALS Every January, Chiapa de Corzo plays host to the **Fiesta de Enero.** The festival is kicked off on January 9 with a series of dances including the **Las Chuntá** dance, in which men dress as women, and the **Parachico,** in which street dancers mimic Spanish conquistadores. The **Combate Naval,** a reenacted Naval Combat on the river complete with fireworks, takes place on January 21, and is followed by a day or two of concluding festivities.

San Cristóbal de las Casas

The capital of Chiapas until the 1890s, San Cristóbal today still maintains an unmistakably colonial feel. Crisp mornings see Chiapan highlanders in traditional dress flood the city's markets, main plazas, and church steps to sell homegrown produce and woven clothing. It was in this usually tranquil town, long a favorite of the international backpacking set, that made front-page headlines abroad when the EZLN (Zapatista National Liberation Army), made up mostly of Tzeltal and Tzotzil speakers, took over the main square, demanding national agrarian reform. The occupation left the municipal palace in shambles, leaving the ruling elite's moral commitment to the poor, indigenous, and exploited in question. The rebels' stated objective was to focus international attention on their demands for democratic reform, land redistribution, and improved education and health care for the region's desperately poor Indian population.

The masked, green-eyed EZLN Spokesman Subcomandante Marcos has emerged as a cult figure—the first postmodern guerrilla for some. Shortly after Mexican and U.S. intelligence identified Marcos as the intellectual Rafael Sebastián Guillén, he responded in a witty communiqué, "Ah, come now, I'm not that unattractive—you'll be ruining my fan mail."

Contrary to the impression created by the international press, however, the real action of the uprising in Chiapas took place around Ocosingo and the Lacandón jungle, not in San Cristóbal. Nevertheless, the impact of the Zapatistas on the city (not to mention the country) has been profound, and you'll see masked dolls bearing sticks inscribed "EZLN," being sold on the zócalo. As of late 1995, the tension had died down to a level hospitable to European expatriates and backpackers, who have started to come back to hang out and sip cappuccino in the cafés and bookshops downtown. However, given the volatile nature of politics in this region, unrest could resurface again at any time.

BASICS

BOOKSTORES **Librería La Quimera** (Real de Guadalupe 24-B, tel. 967/8–59–70; open Mon.–Sat. 9–2 and 4–8), run by a friendly Frenchman named Lucas, carries a wide selection of Spanish, English, French, and German literature. Books on Maya culture and history are featured. **Soluna** (Real de Guadalupe 13-B, no phone) has an equally impressive selection and is open weekdays 9:30–8:30.

CASAS DE CAMBIO **Bancomer, Banamex,** and **Serfín,** all clustered around the zócalo, exchange currency 10–noon. Banamex offers advances on both Visa and MasterCard during these hours. For after-hours or weekend currency exchange go to **Casa de Cambio Lacantún** (Real de Guadalupe 12-A, tel. 967/8–30–63), half a block from the zócalo. It's open for exchanging cash and traveler's checks Monday–Saturday 8:30–2 and 4–8, Sunday 9–1.

EMERGENCIES These days, San Cristóbal's **police** are scattered around town guarding government offices against insurgents, but they can be reached at 967/8–05–54. For an ambulance, call the **Cruz Roja** at 967/8–07–72.

LAUNDRY **Lavorama** (Guadalupe Victoria 20-A, tel. 967/8–35–99; open Mon.–Sat. 9–7, Sun. 9–2) washes and irons your clothes in a couple of hours for about $1.50 per kilo.

MAIL The post office will hold mail sent to you at the following address for up to 10 days: Lista de Correos, San Cristóbal de las Casas, Chiapas, CP 29200, México. Cuauhtémoc, at Crescencio Rosas, tel. 967/8–07–65. Open weekdays 8–7, Sat. 9–1.

MEDICAL AID The **Hospital Regional** (Insurgentes, at Santa Lucía, tel. 967/8–07–70) offers 24-hour emergency care. **Cruz Roja** (Prolongación Ignacio Allende 57, tel. 967/8–07–72) does the same, and it's free. **Farmacia Regina** (Diego de Mazariegos, at Crescencio Rosas, tel. 967/8–02–41) is open day and night; after 10 PM, knock on the metal door for service.

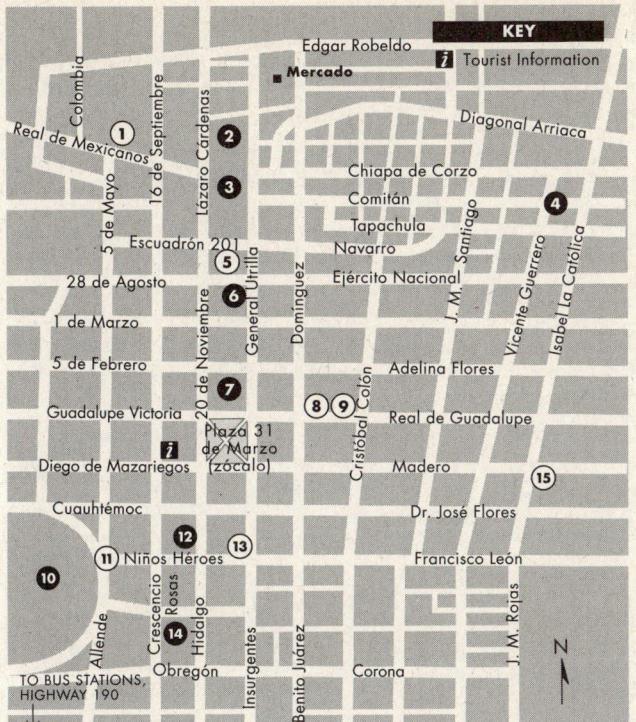

San Cristóbal de las Casas

PHONES To use public phones in front of the Palacio Municipal, buy your **Ladatel Plus** cards at the telephone office (cnr Niños Heroes and Miguel Hidalgo) before 1:30 PM weekdays, or at **Casa de Cambio Lacantún** (see above). **Los Péricos** (16 de Septiembre 22, near 1 de Marzo, no phone; open Mon.–Sat. 9–8:30) offers collect and cash long-distance service, but they'll make you pay for the first minute if your call isn't accepted.

SCHOOLS The cultural center **El Puente** (Real de Guadalupe 55, tel. 967/8-22-50) offers one-on-one or group Spanish instruction at negotiable rates and can arrange homestays.

TOURS AND GUIDES Privately run tours to ruins and the surrounding indigenous communities are cheaper than those arranged by travel agencies. See Moisés at **Casa Margarita** (Real de Guadalupe 34, tel. 967/8-09-57) for information about trips to Toniná, the Sumidero canyon, Palenque, Agua Azul, and the Lacandón jungle. Prices may seem steep to budget travelers ($100 for a minimum of four people to see the Lacandón jungle, Yaxchilán, and Bonampak; about $20 for tours to other sites), but keep in mind that the cost includes a bilingual guide, transportation, and several meals. For a guided visit to nearby villages, meet Mercedes Hernández Gómez on the zócalo at 9 AM (see Near San Cristóbal, below).

VISITOR INFORMATION The newly established **SEDETUR** tourist office can answer questions in English and French. Got any obscure questions about history or local festivities? Licenciada Gabriela Gudiño is attentive and a buff on local trivia. Miguel Hidalgo 2, west of Palacio Municipal, tel. 967/8-06-70. Open weekdays 9–9, Sat. 9–8, and Sun. 9–2.

COMING AND GOING

BY BUS From the first-class **Cristóbal Colón** bus terminal (Insurgentes, about 8 blocks south of zócalo, tel. 967/8-02-91), buses depart daily for Mexico City (21 hrs, 4 per day, $35), with luxury service ($45) at 4:30 PM. Buses leave for Oaxaca city (12 hrs, $16) at 1:30 PM and

5:30 PM; Ocosingo (3 hrs, 4 per day, $2.50); Palenque (7½ hrs, $5), with two buses at 9 AM, and frequently in the evening; Tapachula (9 hrs, 4 per day, $10); Tuxtla Gutiérrez (2 hrs, $2.50) and Comitán (1½ hrs, $1.50), hourly from 6:30 AM to about 10 PM; Mérida (15 hrs, $20–$25) at 5:30 PM and 7:30 PM; and even Cancún (21 hrs, $35) at 4:35 PM. It's wise to book ahead since buses fill up quickly.

Several second-class bus stations along the Carretera Internacional can get you almost anywhere in Chiapas cheaper than Colón. At **Transportes Tuxtla Gutiérrez** (Allende, ½ block up from Carretera Internacional, tel. 967/8–48–69), 10 buses per day serve Palenque (8 hrs, $5), with a stop in Ocosingo (3½ hrs, $2.25). There's hourly service to Tuxtla Gutiérrez (2 hrs, $2.25) and Comitán (2 hrs, $2) during the day.

School buses and microbuses run by **Transportes Lacandonia** (Pino Suárez, at Carretera Internacional, tel. 967/8–14–55) leave for Ocosingo (3½ hrs, $1.75) and Palenque (8 hrs, $6) almost every hour from 7 AM to 6 PM; Villahermosa (9 hrs, $7) at 7 AM; and Mérida (18 hrs, $15) at 6 PM. To reach the station from the zócalo, walk 8 blocks down Insurgentes to the Carretera Internacional, then head right 2 blocks.

HITCHING Hitching to the villages surrounding San Cristóbal is fairly easy, but once out of town you may have to wait a while before a vehicle passes by. If you're going to a remote locale, don't wait until evening to come back—you may not get a ride. Drivers will let you ride for free, but it's acceptable and appropriate to offer some money.

GETTING AROUND

Most sights are within easy walking distance from the center, and the farthest are only a 20- or 30-minute walk away. The hub of the town is the zócalo, otherwise called the **Plaza 31 de Marzo,** bordered on the north by the cathedral. The streets off the square are loaded with budget eateries and hotels. Although they're clearly labeled, remember that all streets change names as they come level with the zócalo. (For example, Insurgentes becomes Utrilla as it passes through the center going north.)

BY BUS Crowded colectivos and combis run frequently. Major routes are north to south along Insurgentes/Utrilla from the Carretera Internacional to the market, and east to west along Real de Guadalupe/Guadalupe Victoria. The fare is about 25¢. To get a ride, flag down one of the always attentive drivers at any point on the road and pay him directly. To get off, shout "se baja!" ("someone's getting off").

BY TAXI Taxis await passengers in front of the cathedral on the north side of the zócalo. Rates within the city are standardized; without baggage the cost is about $2, with baggage $2.50. Rates to surrounding sites and villages are negotiable. Coming from the Cristóbal Colón station, hail a taxi to the centro ($2) or take an INSURGENTES/UTRILLA colectivo headed north into town.

BY CAR Budget Rent A Car (Diego de Mazariegos 36, tel. 967/8–18–71) will rent you a VW bug for a hefty $40 a day (more for a truck or four-wheel drive), including insurance and 100 free kilometers. In the rainy season (summer), watch the dangerously slippery roads where the pavement ends, and think twice about driving on the winding roads at night.

WHERE TO SLEEP

Loads of hotels—many with colonial flourishes—have sprung up here in the last two decades. Competition keeps prices low and cleanliness standards high. For the most part, posadas (not hotel posadas) are cheaper than hotels. Anywhere you stay, make sure the hot water is in working order; the morning air in San Cristóbal can be chilly. Be especially wary of people advertising their "pensiones" at bus stations—travelers have been known to get robbed at these pensiones. If all the places listed below are full, try **Posada El Candil** (Real de Mexicanos 7, tel. 967/8–27–55).

➢ **UNDER $10** • **Casa Margarita.** At this former private mansion, rooms have high ceilings and triple-blanketed beds. Singles are $6, doubles $9, and dormitory beds $4. Everyone shares the clean communal bathrooms, and the showers are hot all day. Here, you can make contact with lost companions via the bulletin board, and arrange horseback riding and excursions (*see* Tours and Guides, *above*). *Real de Guadalupe 34, 3 blocks east of zócalo, tel. 967/8–09–57. 26 rooms, none with bath. Luggage storage. Reservations advised. Wheelchair access.*

Hospedaje Bed and Breakfast. The prices at this guest house make up for the walk it takes to get here from the center of town. Doubles without private bathrooms are $9.50. Singles and doubles with private bath are $5 and $12.50 respectively, and a bed in one of the dorm rooms is $3.50; the prices include a generous breakfast. Weekly and monthly rates are also available. Rooms aren't luxurious, but the proprietor is kind and hot water is available early in the mornings. *Madero 83, 8 blocks east of zócalo, tel. 967/8–04–40. 25 rooms, 9 with bath; 9 dorm beds. Luggage storage.*

Posada Caridad. Though a bit drab, this inn is in a great location. Rooms are $6 without bath or $8 with private bath for both single and double occupancy. The tap spouts hot water all day. *Escuadrón 201 No. 6, 4 blocks north of zócalo, no phone. 14 rooms, 7 with bath. Luggage storage.*

Posada Santiago. Although Santiago gets Casa Margarita's overflow clientele, its small rooms are nonetheless comfortable. The dark, heavy red drapes shut out unwanted light and there's hot water. They accept Visa. Singles are $6.75, doubles $7.50. *Real de Guadalupe 32, tel. 967/8–00–24. 9 rooms all with bath. Luggage storage.*

➢ **UNDER $20** • **Hotel Posada San Cristóbal.** The huge rooms in this grand old building have high ceilings, white walls, dark plank floors, antique furniture, and tall, heavy French doors that block all light and sound. Newly remodeled bathrooms and balconies off every room are a plus. Singles are $15, doubles $19, triples $23, and quadruples $25. *Insurgentes 2, 2 blocks south of zócalo, tel. 967/8–38–42. 10 rooms, all with bath. Luggage storage.*

➢ **UNDER $30** • **Na-Bolóm.** This colonial home (*see* Worth Seeing, *below*) once belonged to Gertrude and Frans Blom, who turned it into a cultural center devoted to the study and preservation of the Lacandón Maya and the rain forest in which they live. It also features 12 luxurious guest rooms, each decorated in the style of a different indigenous village. Singles are $25, doubles $30, and the price of the room includes meals eaten with the center's staff and other guests. Fireplaces, books, bathtubs, art, and access to the garden and educational events are extra perks. *Vicente Guerrero 33, tel. 967/8–14–18. From Santo Domingo, walk 8 blocks east on Comitán. 12 rooms, all with bath. Luggage storage. Reservations advised. MC, V.*

CAMPING Rancho San Nicolás Camping and Trailer Park (tel. 967/8–00–57), less than a kilometer east of town at the end of Francisco León, has tent spaces and cabins. Facilities include kitchens, electricity, and hot water for showers. Camping for two people costs $2.50; a room for two is about $5. If you don't mind going without the amenities, you can bypass the park and camp for free a short ways downriver. To get here, take a RANCHO SAN NICOLÁS combi.

FOOD

The large expatriate presence has had a decisive influence on San Cristóbal's cuisine. In addition to Chiapan fare, many restaurants and cafés serve yogurt, whole-wheat bread, green salads, and pizza. Budget eateries abound on the streets around the center, ranging from 50¢ taco stands to sit-down restaurants that serve five-course meals for $3.50. If you're broke, try some corn on the cob at the zócalo, or shop at the market just north of Santo Domingo. If you have $6 to spend, **Na-Bolom** (*see* Where to Sleep, *above*) serves lunch at 1:30 and dinner at 7 PM at a communal table where you can eat with the staff and other travelers; reservations must be made at least two hours in advance.

➢ **UNDER $5** • **Casa de Pan.** This bakery/restaurant is run by baker extraordinaire Kippy Nigh. Fresh bread, the best bagels in Mexico, organic salads, and veggie empanadas with curry ($2.50) are served on the comfortable patio. There's live music on Thursdays and weekend nights. *Navarro 10, at Domínguez, tel. 967/8–04–68. Open daily 7 AM–9 PM (Thur.–Sun. until midnight).*

Comedor Familiar Normita II. Norma herself presides benevolently over this comfortable spot, where the enchiladas in red mole ($3.50) are especially tasty. A fireplace takes the bite out of the cold mountain air. *Benito Juárez 6, at José Flores, no phone. Open daily 8 AM–10 PM.*

Madre Tierra. "Mother Earth" sells fresh yogurt with fruit and granola, big bowls of lentil soup, and vegetarian or chicken entrées ($4 and $5, respectively). Homemade whole-wheat bread comes free with your meal. The white iron chairs on the patio make for a good place to enjoy a casual beer when it's not raining. *Insurgentes 19, 3 blocks south of zócalo, tel. 967/8–42–97. Open daily 8 AM–9:45 PM.*

Restaurant Las Estrellas. Tangy brown rice with veggies and salad sets you back $2 at this unpretentious but tourist-filled eatery. A heaping plate of spaghetti with meat sauce ($3) and the filling quiche ($2), followed by a goblet of creamy hot chocolate (less than $1), primes you for a deep sleep. The pies ($1), especially the lemon chiffon, are also wonderful. *Escuadrón 201 No. 6-B, in front of Santo Domingo, no phone. Open daily 9 AM–10 PM.*

Restaurant Tuluc. The daily offering here changes regularly, but it's always a bargain. Dinner might include an aperitif of milk, rum, and nuts; spicy vegetable potato soup; pasta; chicken bathed in olive oil, garlic, onions, and mushrooms; and flan with coffee—all for $4. Breakfast begins as early as 6 AM, but lunch and dinner are the best reasons to come. *Insurgentes 5, 1 block south of zócalo, tel. 967/8–20–90. Open daily 6 AM–10 PM.*

➤ **UNDER $10** • **El Teatro.** Jazz plays in the background as you dine on French and Italian food in this elegant restaurant. The daily special ($5) includes a filling plate of spaghetti. The crepes with chicken and mushrooms ($3) are so good that even the competition raves about them. *1 de Marzo 8, 2 blocks north of cathedral, tel. 967/8–31–49. Open daily 11–11; closed Tues. off-season.*

DESSERT/COFFEEHOUSES Espresso, cappuccino, tea, and pastries are always at hand in San Cristóbal. Near the Colón bus station, **Cafetería/Restaurante Palenque** (Insurgentes 40, no phone) is a friendly place that serves specialty coffee drinks; try their fried plantains ($1). Locals spend hours playing chess and reading newspapers at **Cafetería San Cristóbal** (Cuauhtémoc 2, at Insurgentes, tel. 967/8–38–61). "American" coffee and espresso are 50¢; the excellent cappuccino is $1. The sun-lit spacious parlor above the popular café/art gallery/handicrafts shop **La Galería** (Hidalgo 3, south of zócalo, tel. 967/8–15–47) lures locals and foreigners alike. Try the excellent pies and cakes (less than $2) and stay for live music after 8:30 PM.

WORTH SEEING

San Cristóbal is a conglomeration of many neighborhoods, each with its own church and patron saint, but the center of town is the **Plaza 31 de Marzo**, the zócalo. The **Hotel Santa Clara** on the south side of the zócalo was supposedly conquistador Diego de Mazariegos's house and is adorned with stone sirens and the royal lions of Castille, Spain. On the north side of the zócalo is the **Catedral**. It was first constructed in 1528 as a run-of-the-mill church, but 10 years later the pontiff declared it a cathedral, and paintings, altars, and an ornate facade were added. San Cristóbal's **market** (8 blocks north of zócalo on Utrilla) is a huge conglomeration of vegetables, tropical fruits, medicinal herbs, poultry, and cassette stands blaring reproduced regional music and American pop. The produce comes from the small plots of land farmed by local Tzotzil and Tzeltal people, who carry it into town each day.

Sunday mass at the Cathedral, usually filled with political and human rights overtones, is given by Bishop Samuel Ruíz when he's not busy mobilizing in Mexico and abroad on behalf of the EZLN (Zapatista National Liberation Army).

For a good view of the city, take a walk east of the zócalo and up the stairs to the yellow-and-white **Iglesia de Guadalupe**. You can see even farther from the the top of the stairs at **Iglesia de San Cristóbal de las Casas**, which lead up the Cerro de San Cristóbal. Although you'll have to hike up the steep Cerro de Santa Cruz to get to the city's third vista point, **Iglesia de Santa Cruz**, you'll be rewarded with a magnificent view.

ARCO DEL CARMEN This tower (said to be the only one of its kind in Latin America) is an example of the Moorish-influenced *mudéjar* architectural style, which incorporates elements of Islamic art. Built in 1597, the tower was nearly destroyed in 1652 in one of the city's worst floods and was rebuilt by 1680. Bad luck struck again in 1993 when a fire raged through the tower and church, destroying many early 18th-century religious paintings. But it's still worth a look from the outside. *Hidalgo, 3 blocks south of zócalo.*

CASA DE LAS ARTESANIAS DE CHIAPAS This store/museum is run by a government program meant to encourage handicraft production while improving the quality of life in indigenous villages. The handicrafts for sale are quality-controlled, and the excellent ethnographic museum is free. *Hidalgo, at Niños Héroes, tel. 967/8–11–80. Open Mon.–Sat. 9–2 and 5–8.*

CENTRO DE ESTUDIOS CIENTIFICOS NA-BOLOM This cultural center, museum, library, garden, home, and guest house is devoted to the study and preservation of the culture and rain forest environment of the Lacandón Indians, whose way of life is considered closer to the pre-contact Maya than any other contemporary indigenous community. It was established by the late Frans and Gertrude Blom, a Danish/Swiss couple who dedicated much of their lives to the study of and advocacy for the Lacandón people.

The house has a comfortable library with 2,500 books on Chiapan culture, not to mention travel guides, the Bloms' writings, and other books on Mexico. Frans's collection of religious art is on display in the chapel; an exhibit of Lacandón artifacts fills the museum; and Gertrude's black-and-white photos of Chiapan Indians decorate the halls of the house. The bookstore carries volumes of Gertrude's photography and Frans' map of the Lacandón jungle, supposedly the best available. Hour-long tours take place twice a day and are followed by a film about the Lacandón Maya and the rain forest they inhabit. You can stay the night here (*see* Where to Sleep, *above*), or come for a meal featuring fresh produce from the garden (*see* Food, *above*). *Vicente Guerrero 33, at Comitán, tel. 967/8–14–18. Admission for non-guests (including tour): $3.50. Tours Tues.–Sun., in English at 4:30, Spanish at 4:40.*

EX-CONVENTO DE SANTO DOMINGO The 16th-century former monastery of Santo Domingo houses **Sna Jolobil** (tel. 967/8–26–46), or "Weaver's House" in Tzotzil. It is the outlet store of a weaver's cooperative made up of about 800 Tzotzil and Tzeltal women. The cooperative's aim is to preserve Mayan techniques of weaving on the back-strap loom, and to ensure that the artisans receive a fair price for their work. Local *huipiles* (embroidered tunics), wool vests, brocade shirts, and ribboned hats are displayed and sold here. If you haven't yet heard Tzotzil or Tzeltal spoken, listen discreetly. Depending on the tourist flow, the store is open Monday–Saturday 9–2 and 4–7, Sunday 9–2. The adjacent **Templo de Santo Domingo** (above Escuadrón 201, btw Lázaro Cárdenas and Utrilla), with an interior of Chiapan cedarwood plated with gold, is open 6 AM–10 PM. **J'pas Joloviletik** (Utrilla 43, tel. 967/8–28–48), another weaver's cooperative store across the street, is open Monday–Saturday 9–1 and 4–7, Sunday 9–1.

MUSEO CULTURAL DE LOS ALTOS DE CHIAPAS At this small museum focusing on local history and culture, all posted explanations are in Spanish, but you'll get the gist even if you can't read them. There are exhibits on the *encomienda* system by which the conquistadores were awarded the right to exact tribute from certain groups of Indians, and on the quantities of booty the Spanish sent back to Europe. Textiles from surrounding indigenous communities are displayed upstairs. *Next to Santo Domingo. Admission free. Open Tues.–Sun. 10–5.*

MUSEO DEL AMBAR DE LOS ALTOS DE CHIAPAS Amber, a yellow-brown fossil tree resin, is on display and sold at this tiny museum. Most of it comes from the Simojovel valley and Totolapa, two of only a few of the areas in Mexico where amber is still mined. After excavation, it's tediously polished and set in earrings, necklaces, and other ornaments and sold at a moderate price—especially when you consider that some sediment and bugs trapped in amber have been carbon-dated to the Jurassic Age. Be sure to check out the display of ants, beetles, butterflies, and mosquitos trapped in amber, as well as the carvings of Maya figures. *Utrilla 10, 2 blocks north of zócalo, tel. 967/8–35–07. Admission free. Open weekdays 10–8.*

CHEAP THRILLS

A relaxing treat, particularly if your hotel doesn't have hot water, are the **Baños Mercedarios,** where you can choose between a steam or dry-heat sauna followed by a shower. The whole ritual comes to less than $3. Soap, towels, razors, and refreshments cost about 50¢ each. *1 de Marzo 55, tel. 967/8–10–06. Open Mon.–Sat. 6 AM–7 PM, Sun. 6 AM–2 PM.*

FESTIVALS

With its many neighborhoods and their patron saints, San Cristóbal celebrates something almost every week. The five-day **spring fair,** following Easter Sunday, is the biggest festival of the year, with street artists, music, and food. On July 25 it's the **Fiesta de San Cristóbal.** On November 22, the **Fiesta de Santa Cecilia,** honoring the patron saint of musicians, is held. December 12–14 is the **Fiesta de la Virgen de Guadalupe.** For a comprehensive list of smaller festivals, ask at the tourist office (*see* Visitor Information, *above*).

SHOPPING

Once upon a time, San Cristóbal was divided into sectors, each dedicated to one trade or skill. Those in the sector of La Merced, for example, were known for their candle work, and would sell or trade candles to the merchants in the central sector, who were skilled in making candy and *embutidos* (jam-filled candies). The tradition still continues: The sector of San Antonio is well-known for its fireworks, La Cerrería for its carpentry, and San Ramón for its baked goods. Shops crowd Real de Guadalupe and Utrilla, selling quality woven and leather goods and amber jewelry. You can also buy Guatemalan goods in many of these shops, but they cost a lot more than they would across the border. The finest weaving is to be found in the cooperatives Sna Jolobil and J'pas Joloviletik, and the government-run Casa de Las Artesanías de Chiapas (*see* Worth Seeing, *above*). Don't buy amber off the street—it could easily be plastic or glass.

AFTER DARK

San Cristóbal holds tightly to Mexican colonial traditions: In the evenings, especially on Sundays, everyone congregates on the zócalo. Locals stroll with cotton candy or popcorn from the numerous stands and soak in the scene. The cathedral's stone steps are a great place to sit and watch the crowds and the storm clouds climb over the surrounding mountains. Many restaurants feature live music around dinnertime (about 8), usually without a cover charge. Whatever you do, do it early, because the town shuts down (Cinderella fashion) at midnight sharp.

San Cristóbal's one real movie house is **Cinemas Santa Clara** (16 de Septiembre 30, tel. 967/8–23–45), showing mostly films of the sex-and-violence variety. Cultural center **La Puente** (*see* Schools, *above*), run by California expatriate Bill English, shows free, smart international

Sergio Castro's Private Museum

A longtime resident of Chiapas, Sergio Castro has dedicated most of his life to preserving local indigenous cultures, working particularly with the Tzotzil community of Chamula. He has a one-of-a-kind collection of indigenous textiles and a detailed photographic record of local community development projects. Sergio works 7–5 every day in local indigenous communities and entertains small groups at his house after 6 PM. You need to get some friends together and call in advance for an appointment (be persistent, there's often nobody home). Sergio speaks French, English, and Italian as well as Spanish. The tour is free, but donations are encouraged. Guadalupe Victoria 47, tel. 967/8–42–89.

films Tuesday–Saturday at 8 PM. "The Bridge" also offers an extensive (often free) array of services including a language school, art workshops, a message board, and a new and used book collection. Call or stop by to see what's up.

For the best salsa and nueva canción, try **La Galería** or **Casa de Pan** (see Food, above), where the music starts around 9 PM. **Restaurante Pizzería La Taberna** (Real de Guadalupe 73, tel. 967/8–16–28) features a variety of bands from about 7:30 PM to midnight. For a candle-lit ambience decorated with your favorite icons, Marilyn Monroe and Jim Morrison, try **Las Velas Bar** (Madero 14, no phone). Live music (salsa, rock, reggae) starts at around 11 PM; crowds suck down $1 beers until 3 AM.

OUTDOOR ACTIVITIES

Trails for hiking and mountain biking abound in the mountains surrounding San Cristóbal. Bikes are available from **Pinguinos** (5 de Mayo 10-B, no phone; open daily 9–2 and 3:30–6:30) for $1 an hour or $10 a day. You can also take horseback-riding excursions to Chamula or **Las Grutas de San Cristóbal,** a dank, stalactite- and stalagmite-filled cave about 11 kilometers southeast of town. Two-hour horseback trips from Casa Margarita (see Where to Sleep, above) cost $20–$25 per person. Others leave from Hotel Real del Valle (Real de Guadalupe 14, tel. 967/8–06–80) and cost $25–$30 per person. Alternately, head out to the Grutas by hopping on any Comitán-bound bus and telling the driver where to let you off.

The **Huitepec Ecological Reserve,** just 3 kilometers out of town, is alive with hundreds of birds, bright flowers, and 600 plant species. There's a 4-kilometer loop trail that affords a quiet, 1½-hour hike up through the cloud forest on the side of the Muktevitz volcano. The reserve is run by Pronatura, a conservation group that buys land and establishes parks to preserve wildlife for educational purposes and to promote sustainable farming alternatives. To get to the reserve, take a colectivo bound for Chamula or Zinacantán from the market and ask to be let off at Huitepec. Guided tours are offered on Tuesdays, Thursdays, and Saturdays 9:30 AM–11 AM; sign up in advance at the Pronatura office (Adelina Flores 21, tel. 967/8–40–69). Admission to the park is free, and it's open Tuesday–Sunday 9–5.

Near San Cristóbal

Several indigenous communities, each 30 minutes to two hours from San Cristóbal, can easily be visited on day trips. You'll know you're in a distinctly different indigenous community because the village dress changes. Sundays—when local Tzotzil and Tzeltal people congregate in the markets to sell livestock, fruits, vegetables, and textiles—are the best days to go. Wonderful tours to Chamula and Zinacantán are led by Mercedes Hernández Gómez, who grew up in Zinacantán. The tour group meets daily (except for major holidays) at 9 AM at the kiosko in San Cristóbal's zócalo; look for Mercedes' umbrella. The tour is well worth it at $14, transportation included.

All villages listed below are accessible by infrequent bus service or colectivo, with the exception of Zinacantán and Chamula, which are served frequently. If you do choose to go on your own, dress conservatively, don't take pictures without permission (if you do, it's appropriate to pay your model), and stick to the main public areas—injudicious wandering will not be appreciated.

SAN JUAN CHAMULA Chamula's wood-and-mud houses and cornfields spread out into a small valley. Residents are recognizable by their dark-blue shawls and shirts, with ribboned braids for women and wool serapes and leather belts for men. The religion of the Chamula people is unique in that it's a hybrid of Maya rituals and Catholicism. In their church you'll see patron "saints" not found in the Bible, and the cross they've erected is not the Catholic cross, but a broader Mayan style that you'll find in archeological stelae around the region.

If you look closely, you'll notice mirrors behind the saints in the church and tiny mirrors sewn into some of the women's blouses. Chamulans believe the soul is reflected by mirrors—which is probably why people feel you've snatched their soul when you take a picture of them.

The best time to visit is during the Sunday morning market, when vendors expect visitors as well as locals. One of the most impressive Chiapan festivals is San Juan Chamula's Carnaval, one week before Ash Wednesday, when Chamulans dance atop fire to purify their souls.

Whenever you visit, however, don't expect an overly friendly welcome here—outsiders are treated with detached suspicion. Photography is an especially sensitive issue. You can enter Chamula's church for 50¢, but keep your distance from worshippers and put your camera away. The floor of the church is covered with pine needles, and Chamulans pray in their native tongue, while shamans heal sick villagers. Colectivos to Chamula (20 min, 50¢) leave from the San Cristóbal market.

The Father, Sun, and Holy Ghost

While pre-Hispanic religions are still practiced in various forms throughout Mexico, the beliefs of many indigenous people today combine the symbols and deities of their ancestors with the Catholicism brought by the Spaniards and the Protestantism of more recent missionaries. The conventional exteriors of Catholic churches in Indian pueblos of southern Mexico often give way to pine-strewn, candle-lit interiors redolent with the fumes of copal, an incense sacred to the Maya. The sun god of the Maya pantheon has been recast in the figure of Jesus Christ—who has taken on many of his attributes—and San Juan Bautista is worshipped with many of the ritual elements once reserved for Chaac, god of rain and lightning. The most famous example of this sort of syncretism is the cult of the Virgin of Guadalupe, the brown-skinned Mary who first appeared in 1531 in a vision to a converted Indian, Juan Diego, on the hill of Tepeyacac (where local people had traditionally worshipped her).

Other uniquely Mexican "Christian" traditions include Día de los Muertos, or the Day of the Dead. This ritual honoring dead friends and relatives is celebrated on November 2 throughout Mexico. The beginning of November was an important Aztec festival in honor of the glorious deaths of warriors and children; it was merged with All Souls Day, a Catholic holiday for remembering the dead. Families sprinkle the graves of loved ones with marigolds, then eat an honorary meal in a candle-lit cemetery at midnight. Children eat candy skulls painted with their names in bright icing, a reminder that death is not something to fear.

Even before the Spanish arrived in Mexico, however, the groundwork was laid for a union of Christian and native religions. The symbol of the cross, for example, was a potent one for ancient Mexico: It is said that just before he disappeared from the Earth, the feathered serpent god Quetzalcoatl planted a giant wooden cross on the beach at Huatulco that resisted all efforts to pull it down. The cross symbolized the ceiba tree that held up the Mesoamerican world, and life itself. Also, the stone covering the sarcophagus of Lord Escudo Pakal, 7th-century ruler of Palenque, depicts his descent into the underworld with a giant cross, representing life, emerging from his body. And the underground tombs of Mitla beneath the Columnas de Vida also form a cross. Today, pine branches (another symbol of life) are tied to crosses overlooking highland towns, a testament to the blending of Mesoamerican and European beliefs.

ZINACANTAN The men of Zinacantán wear elaborate, hot-pink serapes; the women wear beautifully embroidered huipiles and colorful shawls with red borders. The quiet town's main industry is the cultivation and sale of chrysanthemums and gladiolas. Sunday morning brings a small market (come early for the freshest flowers) and religious services; if you're lucky you may also catch the town's elders—wearing ceremonial white shorts with high-backed Mayan sandals—as they exit the church playing handmade guitars, harps, and drums. To get here, take a colectivo (20 min, 50¢) from the San Cristóbal market. There is also a path between Zinacantán and Chamula, but it has been the site of several assaults and should be avoided.

SAN ANDRES LARRAINZAR The Tzotzil village of San Andrés is about half an hour north of Chamula by bus. The people are friendly, and the Sunday market is interesting mainly for the brocade shirts sold here. Lately, San Andrés made national headlines when it was selected by the Zapatistas for panel discussions with the Mexican government.

Be sure to make the 15-minute trek to the **Iglesia de Guadalupe** from the center of town for a stunning view of the surrounding highlands. The major festivals are the Fiesta de Santiago Apóstol (July 24–26), the Fiesta de la Virgen de Guadalupe de Santa Lucía (December 12–13), and the Fiesta de San Andrés (November 30). There are no hotels, so leave early to catch a colectivo (45 min, 75¢) from the church back to San Cristóbal; they leave San Cristóbal from the market.

CHENALHO Chenalhó lies about an hour's bus ride north of San Cristóbal, through tiny settlements and dramatic mountain scenery. The Sunday market fans out from the Iglesia de San Pedro in the center of town. Enter the church on Sunday and you'll find yourself in the midst of candles and thick, pine-fragrant incense. If you're lucky, you may catch a ceremony in which carbonated drinks, such as Coca-Cola, are used (as in other highland villages) to cause burping, which clears the body of evil spirits. Chickens and eggs are also passed over the body to absorb evil spirits and sickness, then are killed or broken.

The major festival here (June 27–30) honors San Pedro, and the entire town seems to fall into a drunken stupor. A terrific procession of horses, children, women, and men in their traditional garb chant in Tzeltal as they carry a statue of their patron saint into the incense-fogged church. The town has a hotel, **Posada Anabel,** in front of the Iglesia de San Pedro; if the none-too-receptive management feels like letting you stay, it's $3 per night for a scary room and tolerable communal bath. If you don't plan to stay over, plan a morning visit, since colectivos become scarce in late afternoon. Buses depart from San Cristóbal's market.

AMATENANGO DEL VALLE This Tzeltal town, about 39 kilometers south of San Cristóbal on the road to Comitán, is known for its pottery. Local red clay is mixed with black or white sand, and a ground rock called *bash* is added to help the pottery harden. The work is done entirely by hand, without the aid of a pottery wheel (incredible, given the uniformity of the pieces). The town will seem deserted at first, but soon a child may approach and ask you to look at her clay animals. People work out of their houses and are likely to invite you in to look at their wares if you show an interest. The major festivals are celebrations of the village's patron saint, San Francisco, from April 28 to 30; of San Pedro Mártir, on October 4; and of Santa Lucía, on December 13. Any Comitán-bound bus (40 min, $1) will get you here.

Ocosingo and Toniná Ruins

Ocosingo is a medium-size, low-profile Tzeltal town in the green foothills of the Sierra Madre. It's at a confluence of valleys that run from the Chiapan highlands to the Lacandón jungle, making it a prime gateway to the jungle. It was here, in January 1994, that the Zapatista rebels confronted the Mexican army in one of the biggest battles of the uprising. Peasants suspected of rebel activity were executed by the army in Ocosingo's central plaza—the images of the bloodied bodies made worldwide front pages. From Ocosingo on, you can expect a lot of army checkpoints—after all, this is Zapatista territory. If you keep your eyes on the news, you shouldn't get stuck in the middle of a war. This may be your best chance to get a glimpse of the reality behind the biggest Chiapas news story of the last two years.

The Zapatistas weren't the first to appreciate Ocosingo's strategic location. Just over 10 kilometers from town are the impressive but little known ruins of Toniná, a Maya city that was at its height from AD 500 to 1000. The ruins are tough to get to, but well worth the effort. Passageways wind through the imposing seven-tiered pyramid and descend into tombs complete with stone sarcophagi and still-discernible depictions of jaguars, skeletons, and the god of the underworld clutching the heads of decapitated ball players. A small museum displays a fair selection of Toniná statuary; many of these pieces were also decapitated, supposedly by the invading forces of a rival city. The site and museum are open daily 9–4. Admission to pyramid and museum is $2 (free Sundays).

COMING AND GOING Frequent buses connect Ocosingo with San Cristóbal and Palenque. First-class buses depart from the **Cristóbal Colón** station (Carretera Ocosingo–Palenque Km. 2, tel. 967/3–04–31). The station is about a 20-minute walk from the zócalo along 1a Oriente Norte. Buses leave for Palenque (3 hrs, 2 per day, $3.50), Puebla (13 hrs, 4:45 PM, $31), Mexico City (16 hrs, 4:30 PM, $36), Tuxtla Gutiérrez (5 hrs, 3 per day, $4.50), and Villahermosa (5½ hrs, 4:30 PM, $8.50).

From the zócalo in Ocosingo, walk 3½ blocks up the gentle hill on Avenida 1a Norte Poniente for the departure point of the second-class lines. **Autotransportes Ocosingo** has second-class service to Tuxtla Gutiérrez (4 hrs, $3) and San Cristóbal (2½ hrs, $1) frequently between 5 AM and 3:30 PM daily. The most reliable second-class bus service is offered by **Transportes Tuxtla Gutiérrez** (Carretera Ocosingo–Palenque, across from Las Casas), which goes to Tuxtla (4 hrs, $3), San Cristóbal (2 hrs, $2), and Palenque (3 hrs, $3). **Transportes Lacandonia** passes through and parks near the Tuxtla station; they run second-class buses into the Lacandón jungle, including the village of Nahá (see *Near Palenque, below*). Also, at a tiny little bus stop north of the market, **Unión de Transportes y Cargos** leaves for Nahá (6 hrs, $6) between 7 and 10 AM. If you want to leave your luggage for the day (50¢) near the bus stations, drop it at the nameless boutique/fax shop on 1a Oriente Norte (1½ blocks from the bus stations on the Carretera Ocosingo–Palenque, no phone).

There is no public transportation to Toniná, so unless you have a car or want to hire a taxi ($8–$10 for the trip), you'll need to go to the market painfully early—around 6 or 7—and ask around until you get on a truck that passes the road leading to the ruins. A reasonable cost is 50¢. Your best bet is someone headed to Guadalupe, a town just past the ruins, but make it clear where you're headed. Don't be fooled by the signs for Toniná—the first, which is about 2 kilometers from Ocosingo, is a good three-hour walk from the site. With luck, you'll be let off at the last crossroads, a 20-minute walk from the ruins. Be sure to head out early to hitch a ride for the return trip, as traffic is light and you may be in for a 3½-hour walk back to town. If it's late, you might be able to scam a ride home with the people who work at the site and museum. You'll be expected to pay 50¢–$1 for the ride.

WHERE TO SLEEP Ocosingo's few hotels are nothing to write home about, so consider making a day trip here from San Cristóbal or Palenque. If you do decide to brave the cockroaches and other friendly little critters, your options begin with **Hospedaje San José** (1 Ote. Nte. 9, tel. 967/3–00–39), whose beds are simple and dark but fairly clean. Most rooms on the second floor have been redone—they're brighter, more airy, and 10 times cleaner. A double with bath on the bottom floor costs $9; the newer doubles on the second floor are $12. They claim there's hot water, but don't count on it. For rooms with a cabaña-in-the-jungle feel, head to **Hotel Agua Azul** (1a Av. Ote. Sur 127, tel. 967/3–03–02). Rooms (with bath) are surprisingly cheap, clean, and come with hot water. Singles are $7, doubles $9, triples $12, and quadruples $14. The market's around the corner, but the management serves simple breakfasts. Fans in every room of **Hotel Bodas de Plata** (1a Sur, at 1a Pte. just south of Palacio Municipal, tel. 967/3–00–16) cool things off during the midday heat, and there is piping hot water for chilly Ocosingo mornings. Singles are $7, doubles $9, and triples $11. **Hotel Central** (Calle Central 5, tel. 967/3–00–24) provides small, quiet, comfortable rooms. All have tiny black-and-white TVs with cable and bathrooms with plenty of hot water. The restaurant/café downstairs offers a vantage point above the action on the zócalo. Singles are $10, doubles $13, and triples $16.

FOOD Ocosingo's morning market offers cheap fruit, bread, fresh tortillas, and locally made cheese; to find it, walk downhill on 2a Avenida Sur Oriente and turn left just before the dusty lot. Good, cheap tacos are cooked up in front of you at **El Buen Taquito** (tel. 967/3–02–51) on Avenida Central near the zócalo. There are also a few tiny, reasonably priced food stores here. At **La Michoacana** (Av. Central Ote. 3, in front of zócalo, tel. 967/3–02–51; open daily 6 AM–9 PM), fill up on quesadillas made with local cheese (three for $1) or order *sincronizadas* (tortilla sandwiches) with cheese, ham, onions, chiles, and avocados for only $1.50. With a wide selection of *licuados* (smoothies) for $1, you can afford to indulge in banana, *guanábana* (custard-apple), and oatmeal. The patio at **Restaurante La Montura** (off zócalo beneath Hotel Central, tel. 967/3–05–50; open daily 7 AM–11 PM) is a great place to enjoy a platter of spicy chicken *chilaquiles* (with tortilla strips, salsa, and sour cream, $5), or filling fried plátanos with cream ($1.50). Order a foamy cappuccino ($1), or head for the full bar and watch the sun melt into a hazy orange behind the church.

Palenque

The ruined Classic Maya city of Palenque is truly magical. As you watch the morning mist rise over the temples and listen to the unmistakable pitch of the howler monkeys reverberate through the jungle, it's hard not to be awestruck. The nearby town of Palenque doesn't have quite the same effect. It's dusty, small, and relatively expensive. Although most of the town's main shops, hotels, and restaurants make their livelihood off the overflowing tourism drawn by the ruins, the ever-growing town of Palenque maintains a life of its own—look to its market on Calle Suárez, behind the Palacio Municipal.

According to Mayan legend, fools were turned into monkeys by the deities because they had neither heart nor an understanding of life.

The conflict in Chiapas shut down a number of businesses, but tourism appears to be picking up again, which means you'll have to enjoy the ruins with the hoardes of other tourists descending on Palenque's archaeological sites. Because the site was previously flooded with package-type tourists, restaurant and hotel owners are accustomed to charging top dollar for meager services. But don't let this sour your dreams; the dense and exotic jungle vistas from atop Palenque's temples shouldn't be missed. Plan to spend long days exploring the ruins and rain forests.

BASICS

CASAS DE CAMBIO At either **Bancomer** (Juárez 25, tel. 934/5–01–98) or **Banamex** (Juárez 28, tel. 934/5–01–30), both several blocks west of the zócalo, expect to wait up to two hours to exchange traveler's checks and receive Visa advances (open weekdays 10–noon). Both have ATMs. The **Casa de Cambio** in front of Banamex has longer hours but exchanges at a slightly lower rate. **Viajes Yax-ha** (Juárez, at Aldama; open daily 9–2 and 5–9.), along with most other travel agencies, will change cash and traveler's checks, although the exchange rate drops after the banks close.

LAUNDRY If you leave your clothes early in the morning, **Lavandería Mundo Maya** will wash and dry a 3-kilo load for $2.50 by the end of the day. *Jiménez, 1 block south of Parque Central, no phone. Open Mon.–Sat. 7–7.*

MAIL The post office has the usual services and will hold mail sent to you at the following address for up to 10 days: Lista de Correos, Palenque, Chiapas, CP 29640, México. *Independencia, at Nicolás Bravo in Palacio Municipal, tel. 934/5–01–43. Open weekdays 9–1 and 3–6, Sat. 9–1.*

MEDICAL AID The **Centro de Salud** (Juárez, tel. 934/5–00–25) at the west end of town, is open weekdays 7 AM–8 PM and charges $2 for a general consultation. The **Hospital Regional** (Prolongación Juárez, tel. 934/5–07–33) has expensive 24-hour emergency service. **Farmacia 24 Horas** (Juárez, at Allende) is the place for late-night self-medication.

PHONES The blue Ladatel phones around the zócalo are plagued by vandalism. If they're in working order, they're your best bet (dial 09 for an international collect call). You'll have to pay a service charge of about $2 for international collect calls at a long-distance *caseta,* which are often unreceptive to your wanting to make a collect call. **Caseta Levis** (Juárez 13, tel. 943/5-08-56; open daily 7 AM-11 PM) is the best in town.

TRAVEL AGENCIES A number of travel agencies offer charter flights and other package deals to Bonampak, Yaxchilán, and the Lacandón jungle that will make your wallet go limp. Two-day trips to Yaxchilán and Bonampak include transportation, meals, lodging, and guides for $100 per person. Day trips to Yaxchilán (van and boat) and Bonampak (van and a two-hour hike) cost about $75 and $65 per person, respectively. Most require a minimum of four people. The one-day plane trip to both places costs $600 for one to four people. Other options include jungle tours, horseback riding, and fishing trips. Travel agencies are clustered around Avenida Juárez and Aldama and coordinate with each other in putting together tour groups (usually four to six people are needed). Travelers who have taken the trips advise you to establish a big group and haggle like mad. Agencies known to wheel-and-deal on prices include **Viajes Misol-Ha** (Juárez 48, tel. 934/5-04-88), **Viajes Toniná** (Juárez 105, tel. 934/5-02-09), and **Viajes Yax-Ha** (Juárez 123, tel. 934/5-07-57). To see the Chiapan countryside, ruins, and sites on your own, these agencies will rent you a VW bug for about $40 per day with 300 free kilometers and insurance.

VISITOR INFORMATION There are two tourist information sites around the Parque Central. The smaller office (Juárez, ½ block west of park; open Mon.-Fri. 8 AM-9 PM, Sat. 8-7) has English-speaking staff, but tends to be short on maps. The main office (Jiménez, at 5 de Mayo, tel. 934/5-08-28; open Mon.-Fri. 9-3 and 6-9), on the southeast end of the park, is somewhat disorganized but friendly. They hand out travel agencies' business cards, distribute maps of the city with a brief explanation of the Palenque ruins in Spanish, and have a message board to reconnect lost friends and traveling companions.

COMING AND GOING

BY TRAIN Pick some other way to travel to and from Palenque unless you've got lots of time and/or very little money; the train that passes through Palenque offers ridiculously cheap and ridiculously slow third-class service only. The train station is several kilometers north of town, so you'll have to take a taxi (about $1.50) to get there.

BY BUS First-class, air-conditioned **ADO** buses (5 de Mayo, at Juárez, tel. 934/5-00-00) serve Mexico City (14 hrs, $32) at 6 PM and Villahermosa (2 hrs, 6 per day, $6). The bus bound for Mérida (8 hrs, 4 per day, $17) stops in Campeche (6 hrs, $11). **Cristóbal Colón** (past Maya statue on main road to Palenque, tel. 934/5-01-40) has buses to Villahermosa (2 hrs, 8 per day, $5); and San Cristóbal (5½ hrs, 2 per day, $6.50) and Tuxtla Gutiérrez (7½ hrs, 2 per day, $8), stopping in Ocosingo on the way.

Roomy second-class **Transportes Tuxtla Gutiérrez** (tel. 934/5-10-12) has six daily buses leaving from the end of Avenida Juárez for Tuxtla Gutiérrez (8 hrs, $7) and San Cristóbal (6 hrs, $6). The station has day-long storage with purchase of a ticket. If you want to try your luck getting to the Lacandón jungle without paying exorbitant package prices, inquire about bus schedules at least a day in advance at **Transportes Lagos de Montebello** (Av. Velasco Suárez, near market). They can probably get you to the Bonampak entrance in 6½ hours for $4.

GETTING AROUND

Palenque is easy to cover on foot. The town centers around the zócalo, which is 3 to 5 blocks from most hotels, restaurants, and bus stations. In typical Chiapan fashion, calles run north-south and avenidas run east-west. Most of the town's hotels, restaurants, pharmacies, travel agencies, juice bars, and other shops are on the main drag, Avenida Juárez. Taxis congregate on the east side of the zócalo. They're good for getting to the train station and to the Mayabell campground (*see below*) after the combis stop running, but they're a rip-off to the ruins or Agua Azul.

Microbuses and colectivos run by **Transportes Palenque** (20 de Noviembre, at Allende, 3 blocks SE of zócalo) and **Transportes Chambalu** (Allende, at Juárez, 3 blocks NE of zócalo) go to the ruins, Misol-Ha, and Agua Azul. Both offer service to the ruins every 10 minutes from 8 to 5 daily for about 50¢. Package plans to Misol-Ha and Agua Azul leave at 10:30 AM and noon, spending half an hour at Misol-Ha, then moving on to a three-hour visit at Agua Azul. The whole deal lasts about six hours and costs about $6.50, which is a bargain since it costs almost $5 to get to these places on your own, and you can't count on front-porch delivery to the sites on local buses.

WHERE TO SLEEP

You can find fairly cheap dives as well as the purest air-conditioned luxury, although most places fall in the middle to upper price range. If you want to sleep surrounded by jungle, camp out at Mayabell (*see below*) or rent a hammock in Agua Azul (*see* Near Palenque, *below*) for about $2. In town, various posadas—simple fan-equipped rooms with toilet paper, clean towels, and luggage storage—are the cheapest accommodations. At **Posada Santo Domingo** (20 de Noviembre, at Allende, no phone), singles are $5 and doubles $6. For similar rooms in the same price range (albeit, with lumpier beds), try **Posada Charito** (20 de Noviembre 15-B). One final consideration is the time of year you're in town: The months of April, July, August, November, and December bring about a 15% price increase for rooms.

➤ **UNDER $10** • **Hotel Misol-Ha.** Straightforward lodging in the heart of the city, Misol-Ha is surprisingly quiet and neat. During low season, singles are $7, doubles $9—but they tend to jump 15% during high season. *Juárez 14, tel. 934/5–00–92. 28 rooms, all with bath. Luggage storage.*

Hotel Posada San Juan. On a dirt road off the tourist track, San Juan feels like it's in a cooler climate than the rest of Palenque. It's a deal for its pleasant, airy singles ($7), doubles ($9), and triples ($11). *Off Allende, near cnr of 3a Av. Sur, tel. 934/5–06–16. From zócalo, walk up Juárez to Allende, then left 4 blocks. 18 rooms, all with bath. Luggage storage.*

➤ **UNDER $15** • **Hotel Lacroix.** This unusual place has been an institution since 1956, when archaeologists began to frequent the ruins. Painted on the lobby walls are replicas of letters written by colleagues of late French archaeologist Señor Lacroix, who owned Palenque. The better-kept rooms tend to fill quickly. Singles are $9, doubles $11, and triples $12. *Hidalgo 10, tel. 934/5–00–14. To left of zócalo when heading from bus stations. 8 rooms, all with bath. Luggage storage. Wheelchair access.*

HOSTELS **Youth Hostel Posada Canek.** Because they're the cheapest in town at $3.50 per person, beds in these comfortable, clean rooms fill up fast. Aside from the excellent price, this is the place to meet fellow travelers. If you want a bed for the night, come in around the 10 AM checkout. *20 de Noviembre, across from Posada Charito, tel. 934/5–01–50. 8 rooms, all with bath; 5 dorm beds. Luggage storage.*

CAMPING **Mayabell** (tel. 934/5–05–67 for reservations) is known worldwide to the hip, burned-out, and curious who come to camp in overgrown surroundings and get the score on the 'shrooms. Avoid loose drug talk; locals have turned traveling *jipis* (hippies) over to the police. Stringing your own hammock costs about $2 per night; pitching a tent runs $3 per person. They'll rent you a hammock for another $2 (plus a $9 deposit). Cabañas for two with private bath are $11 (plus $9 deposit). The communal bathrooms lack hot water but are super clean, and there's a full-service restaurant on the premises. The campground is on the road to the ruins, several kilometers out of town. Take a colectivo headed for the ruins for about 10 minutes; simply tell the driver to let you off at Mayabell.

FOOD

Though Palenque is expensive and touristy in general, the prices at the many restaurants along Avenida Juárez and around the zócalo are moderate and cater to gringo tourists. For a simple, cheap meal, try the snack stands on the upper side of the square, where you can find tacos, tortas, licuados, and corn on the cob. Buy cheap bread and cheeses of every color at the small market 4 blocks south of the zócalo.

➤ **UNDER $5** • **Restaurante "El Rodeo."** The Rodeo serves a decent, ample *comida corrida* (pre-prepared lunch special) for $3.50. The "rodeo burger," with ham, cheese, bacon, and all the trimmings, is $2.50, and soups are $2. Run by the same management, **El Patio**'s upstairs terrace is perfect for sipping coffee or a beer. *Juárez 10, tel. 934/5-02-03. Open daily 7 AM–11 PM.*

Restaurante Girasoles. Of the cheap restaurants in town, "sunflowers" is one of the best and cleanest. An added bonus is its proximity to the ADO and Tuxtla bus stations, and the fact that it's a good place to meet fellow travelers. Breakfast begins at 7 AM and runs about $1–$4. Although it doesn't appear on the menu, the gargantuan strawberry yogurt and granola-topped fruit salad won't leave you hungry. A hamburger piled high with bacon, cheese, and avocado comes with fries for just $2.50. *Juárez 189, tel. 934/5-03-83. Open daily 7 AM–11 PM.*

Restaurante Maya. Popular with Mexican and foreign tourists, this place serves quality local food. The best deals are the sandwiches ($2.50–$4) and breakfast specials ($2.50–$4.50). Breakfasts include fruit, bread and jam, eggs, black beans, a stack of tortillas, and coffee. The pleasant atmosphere and view of the zócalo invite you to sip cappuccino ($1) and write postcards after dinner. There's also a full bar. *Independencia, at Hidalgo, tel. 934/5-00-42. Open daily 7 AM–11 PM.*

Restaurante Mero-Lec. Live music and starlight seating are extra perks here, but the real attraction is good food at good prices. A shrimp cocktail or a hearty order of tacos are just $3. After dinner you can have a drink or play a game of Ping-Pong. *Merle Green, in Centro Turístico La Cañada, no phone. Follow dirt road near Maya statue and turn right at Hotel Maya Tulipanes. Open daily 4 PM–midnight. Live music Wed.–Sat. 9:30–midnight.*

Restaurante Yunyuén. This restaurant in Hotel Vaca Vieja serves generous appetizers for $3 or less and light meals of yogurt and fruit for just $2. A monstrous goblet of chocolate milk is $1.50. The entertaining bilingual menu advertises tantalizing "sparrow gas" (asparagus) and the ancient Mayan delicacy, "pouches" (peaches). *5 de Mayo, at Chiapas, tel. 934/5-03-77. 3 blocks east of zócalo.*

WORTH SEEING

One of the greatest Classic Maya cities, Palenque enjoys its fame for good reason—its ruins are not only spectacular, but truly beautiful. No one should miss scaling these ancient ruins for the view of the surrounding jungle. It's hard to imagine that what you see is only a fraction of the ancient city—the rest lies buried in dense jungle. The city—probably founded in the 3rd century AD and abandoned for unknown reasons in the 9th—was at the height of its glory in the 7th century AD under the rule of the clubfooted Lord, Escudo Pakal. He is represented in numerous bas-reliefs and is most remembered for his tomb, one of the most important archaeological finds of the century.

Palenque's rulers did not often marry outside the dynasty, and the physical deformations that resulted were considered marks of divinity. Zak-Kuk, mother of Pakal, had a massive head and jaw. Pakal, who was clubfooted, may have married both his mother and his sister. His son, Chan-Bahlum, had six toes on each foot and six fingers on one hand.

You should allow a couple of hours to see everything. Guidebooks to the ruins are not sold on the premises, but you can buy a pamphlet with a map and description of each major structure. The English version is $2, the Spanish 75¢. For more in-depth explanations, a private tour, arranged by a local travel agency or at the entrance to the ruins, costs about $20 per group. A cheaper and more flexible alternative is to simply blend in with another tour group. The ruins are open daily 8–5, and the entrance fee is $3, free on Sunday. Be prepared to slap down an additional $5 if you're toting a video camera. Colectivos shuttle frequently between the town and ruins (*see* Getting Around, *above*).

MAYAN MUSEUM The brand-new museum features bits and pieces from the site's digs as well as a general overview of the religious, social, and political structures of the Maya. Most notable are the stone slabs covered with hieroglyphics and the carved sculptures of Maya faces, which illustrate the custom of cranial deformation for aesthetic ends. There's a snazzy map/electronic switchboard of the site's main ruins. It's perfect for orienting yourself; just push the button of the ruin or temple you're curious about, and a picture and trail indicating how to get there lights up. Take a colectivo (35¢) from the ruins to get here. *1 km down hill from ruins on main highway. Admission: $4. Open Tues.–Sun. 10–5.*

TEMPLE OF THE INSCRIPTIONS This wins the building-you're-most-likely-to-see-on-a-postcard contest. For the vertigo-free, the spectacular view from the top of the 26-meter pyramid provides a sense of the vast lands once under Palenque's domain. It is the vantage point from which to see the surrounding buildings' roof combs, vertical extensions that are characteristic of southern Maya architecture.

From the top of the pyramid you can descend to Pakal's tomb, a chamber 1½ meters below ground. The six-toed Chan-Bahlum, Pakal's son, buried his father here in AD 683 and then had the entire 38-meter space above the tomb filled with debris. Mexican archaeologist Alberto Ruz uncovered the tomb in 1952 after spending four years plowing through the rubble, thwarting Chan-Bahlum's efforts to deter grave-robbers and nosy academics. Ruz found Pakal's body wrapped in red cloth and decorated with jade jewelry, an obsidian death mask, and other items to ensure his comfort in the next world. These are now exhibited in Mexico City's Museo Nacional de Antropología. At the site, you can see the tomb's 5-ton lid, intricately carved with a likeness of Pakal as a young man, descending through the gateway to the afterworld. The enormous crypt is comparable to the huge tombs found in Egypt. The tomb, open daily 10:30–4, is definitely worth the slimy, narrow, downward trek.

PALACE Next to the Temple of the Inscriptions, in the center of the site, is a cluster of buildings including steam baths, latrines, dwellings supposedly inhabited by priests, and rooms for religious ceremonies. From the center tower you can see walls of stucco friezes and masks in relief, many depicting Pakal and his dynasty.

THE THREE TEMPLES To the east of the Temple of the Inscriptions, these three pyramids were constructed by Chan-Bahlum. The **Temple of the Cross** holds an image of a cross, representing the ceiba tree; the **Temple of the Foliated Cross,** which looks like a gingerbread house with giant keyholes for windows, has a stone slab whose hieroglyphs recount the Maya's stuggles for survival in the tropical jungle. In the **Temple of the Sun** is a depiction of a shield, a sign of the sun god. Present-day Maya culture is certainly far removed from the Classic period, but such symbols retain their significance. In contemporary indigenous villages, for example, crosses decorated with pine branches still mark sacred places of worship.

TEMPLE OF THE JAGUAR This tiny temple is hidden up a short trail to the left of the Temple of the Inscriptions—follow the dirt path into the jungle alongside the Otolum River. The temple features a slippery stairwell leading to an exposed chamber. The trail continues on to some other smaller ruins amid dense jungle.

QUEEN'S BATHS Pakal's wife reportedly dipped her queenly body into the various small waterfalls and swimming holes that dot a 3-kilometer trail leading to the ruins from the museum. You can refresh your aching bones in these pools set against the rain forest, but good luck trying to sneak into the ruins along this path—the guards are wise to that trick. If you just want to cool off before entering the ruins legally, the guard will let you splash around the first bathing pool for free. *Take a colectivo to museum (1 km after ruins) and walk across street to tiny path leading through dense vegetation; it's about 100 m to first swimming hole.*

AFTER DARK

A growing town, Palenque has two spots to get down and rowdy to some disco music, modern tech, and even Tex-Mex songs. **Chablís Bar** is a little dank with a small dance floor, but their beers are only a $1.25 and their margaritas $2. Down the road, **Fulano's Bar** charges a minimal cover of $1 but locals fill up the dance floor on weekends as early as 9 PM. Both are on Merle Green in the Centro Turístico La Cañada, down the road from Mero-Lec (*see above*). They're both open daily and claim not to close until people start going home.

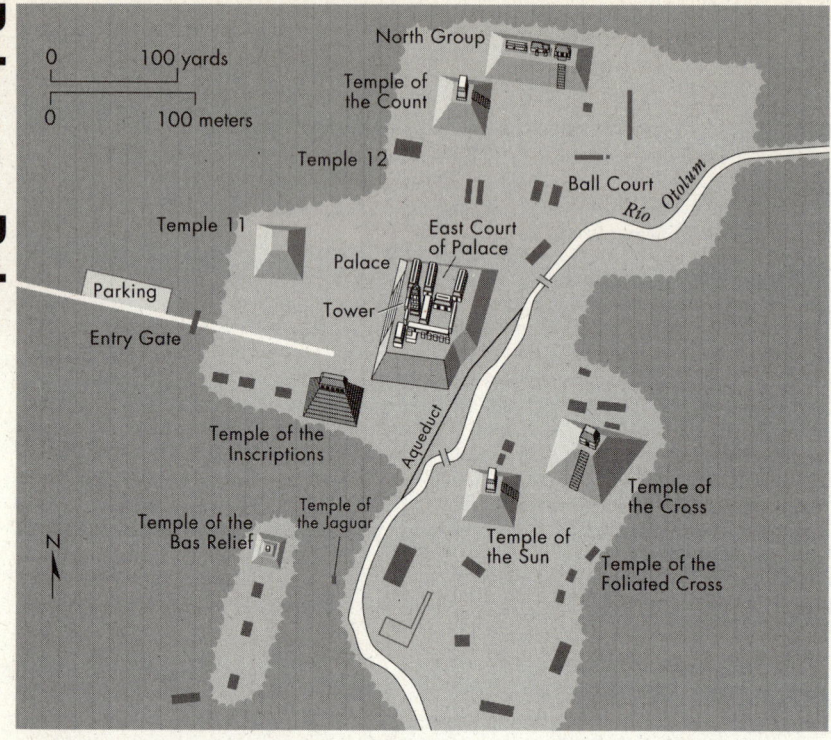

Palenque Ruins

Near Palenque

MISOL-HA AND AGUA AZUL

Rivers snake through the Chiapan rain forest, forming crashing waterfalls and deep swimming holes. Misol-Ha and Agua Azul are two such places, both popular tourist stops which have yet to become completely overrun. Eighteen kilometers down Route 199 from Palenque, the single towering cascade at Misol-Ha thunders into a deep, cold, green pool. You can swim, sun on the rocks, and scramble and slide on the slippery boulders in the misty regions behind the falls.

> *Crosses by the river mark the spots where people have perished. The marker for a German traveler named Franz reads: "He always loved the water."*

Twenty-three kilometers farther south toward Ocosingo is Agua Azul, which, during the rainy months (July–Sept.) isn't quite the vibrant blue depicted in postcard photos. Nevertheless, it's still a treat to float down the river or play on the rope swing. To get away from the families and aggressive souvenir vendors, walk up the trail along the cascades from the main swimming area for just under 2 kilometers to the calm, colorful pools; they alternate with waterfalls in a steplike pattern. You can continue up the trail or climb from one level to the next in the water. It's safe to climb in this spot but watch for areas clearly marked with skulls and crossbones and multilingual warnings.

COMING AND GOING Microbuses from **Transportes Chambalu** and **Transportes Palenque** (*see* Getting Around, in Palenque, *above*) run directly to both spots from Palenque, and the journey takes about two hours one way. If you prefer to go at your own pace, all buses bound for Ocosingo or Yajalón from Palenque pass the *cruceros* (crossroads) for Misol-Ha and Agua Azul. The Misol-Ha crossroads is about 3 kilometers from the falls, and the ride will cost you $1. The 1½-hour ride to the crossroads for Agua Azul costs about $2, and the bus lets you off about 5 kilometers from the river. The downhill walk is on a narrow, hot, paved road; watch out for microbuses swerving around corners. When you enter Agua Azul, you may be asked to pay an entrance fee of $1 ($2 if you come by car), depending on how attentive the guards are.

WHERE TO SLEEP At the base of the Misol-Ha waterfall are several family-style cabañas with all the modern amenities—refrigerators, stoves, ovens, cooking utensils—as well as giant beds, hot water, and fans. Best of all is the private access to the spectacular falls and surrounding rain forest. The tourist industry hasn't discovered Misol-Ha yet, so you're in for a tranquil respite in these cabañas, which—considering the surrounding lush paradise—are a better deal than accommodations in Palenque. Even the simple double cabañas have private baths with hot water, mosquito screens, and color TVs. Get a group of four friends and rent the *familiar* (family-size) for about $25 during low season, $45 during high season (early July to mid-August). Cabañas for one to two people cost $13 during low season and $20 during high season. Ask permission to pitch a tent at the reception desk; they'll probably let you do it for free.

You can hang your own hammock at Agua Azul for $2, or rent one for $2 more. Tent spots are also $2. Another alternative is to head toward the upper falls, where the people who run the *comedores* (food stands) may let you hang your hammock for free and offer you shelter if the rain sets in. Camping is also an option, but be prepared to fork out about a dollar for the space. Wherever you sleep, you'll need to bring some food, because lunch is the only meal sold here.

THE LACANDON RAIN FOREST

The Lacandón rain forest is not as untouched as one might imagine, especially where humans have encroached, stripping it of its precious wood and razing the land for cattle ranches and farms. A road built smack-dab through the center of the forest—connecting Palenque with Nahá—has effectively done away with the natural and cultural isolation of the region. It is still home, however, to the Lacandón Indians, considered to be the living indigenous group most similar to their Maya ancestors, and it contains two important Maya archaeological sites, Bonampak and Yaxchilán.

NAHA AND LACANHA Most Lacandón people now live in or around the two main towns of Nahá and Lacanhá. Neither town offers hotel lodging, but local families will often let visitors sling hammocks in their homes. Be polite and bring your own provisions plus delicacies such as sugar and salt as gifts. If you go to northern Nahá, mayonnaise is a favorite of patriarch Chan K'in Viejo (*see box, below*). Most of the southern Lacandón live in Lacanhá, and until very recently, most of them worshipped at Yaxchilán (the northerners worshipped at Palenque). Nahá is more isolated than Lacanhá, and these days northerners worship at Yaxchilán, while most of the southerners have converted to Christianity. While some speak only Mayan languages, many—especially those living in Lacanhá—now speak Spanish. Crafts, including bows and arrows and seed jewelry, are for sale in both places.

The best road into the Lacandón jungle runs straight to Lacanhá, a six-hour trip from Palenque. Nahá is farther, on a worse road, and takes about nine hours to reach from Palenque, or six from Ocosingo on public transportation; you may also check travel agencies in San Cristóbal and Palenque. You should bring a tent or hammock, and locals will tell you where you can spend the night. Before venturing off into the jungle, it's a good idea to pick up a map, available in bookshops and at Na-Bolom (*see* Worth Seeing, in San Cristóbal, *above*), because many of the towns don't appear on most maps of Chiapas.

BONAMPAK In the grand scheme of things, this small ceremonial center played only a minor role during the Late Classic Maya period. What's notable about Bonampak, built between AD 400 and 700, are the colorful frescoes in three distinct rooms complete with altars that seem to depict an epic. According to guides at the site, Room 1 illustrates preparation for a war; Room 2, the battle in action (Yaxchilán under the reign of Governor Chaan Muan is the supposed foe); and Room 3, the various bloodletting rituals associated with victory, and the passing of Bonampak to a young heir. The first white explorers to the region were on a 1946 National Fruit Company expedition looking to build a road through the rain forest. They stumbled upon this tiny palace, its murals strangely preserved in living color by a thin coating of limestone. Excavations took place soon after (National Fruit footed much of the bill), and several partially destroyed buildings and a plaza were uncovered. The colors in rooms 2 and 3 are rather faded, and some claim that seeing the reproductions in Mexico City's anthropology museum will save you a lot of time and unnecessary effort. But don't believe it: Seeing the remnants of a great civilization in its original context, plus the adventure of getting to the site, is worth the trip. Just don't expect comic-strip clarity on the walls. Admission to the site is $4, free on Sundays.

> **COMING AND GOING** • Transportation to the ruins is most easily set up through a travel agency (*see* Travel Agencies, in Palenque or in San Cristóbal, *above*); many can get you there in about four hours. If you're coming by car, drive past Lacanhá until the road ends and then hike 9 kilometers to the ruins on a gravel path through the most beautiful, humid jungle—you won't notice the two-hour walk, just watch out for the *nahauyacas*, highly poisonous, black-striped snakes. You can also get here by bus. From Palenque, take the six-hour trip on a **Transportes Lagos de Montebello** second-class bus down the winding road to Lacanhá and walk 13 kilometers to the ruins.

YAXCHILAN The Yaxchilán ruins lie on the shores of the Usumacinta River, 32 kilometers north of Bonampak, at the Guatemalan border. This ceremonial center, built between AD 500 and 800, was considerably more important than Bonampak and is still considered sacred by the present-day descendents of the Maya. For several years, the Lacandón people were prevented from worshipping at Yaxchilán and Palenque by INAH (National Institute for Anthropology and History), because it was feared they would damage the temples. Access has been restored, and inhabitants of the northern Lacandón once again perform their ceremonies

Most health workers at archaeological sites carry injections to counteract snakebites—the most venomous of them all comes from a slithery serpent known as the nahauyaca. Locals say that if you encounter one of these fanged, striped vipers more than a mere 15 minutes away from a life-saving injection, you might as well kiss your butt goodbye.

The Lacandón Maya

The arrival of the Spanish in Chiapas induced many diverse Maya groups to band together and flee into the jungle. The Spaniards (wisely) didn't follow them into the treacherously unfamiliar territory. These Maya called themselves Hachack-Winick (the True People) and lived in isolation—scattered throughout the rain forest—until they were first contacted by anthropologists this century.

Currently, the physical existence of the Lacandón people is not in jeopardy, but they are becoming assimilated in greater numbers. Phillip Bayer, a Baptist missionary, spent 12 years trying to convert the people of Nahá with meager results. When he heard the last two elders of Lacanhá had died, he rushed in and successfully converted virtually all of southern Lacandón to Christianity in just a couple of years. The 104-year-old (or older—he never kept count) patriarch of Nahá, Chan K'in Viejo, has taken upon himself the task of preserving Lacandón social and cultural traditions.

To the many who have turned away from tradition, Chan K'in warns that to "cut the umbilical cord connected to one's traditions" means to "be denied the key to the heavens." Some predict that traditional Lacandón culture will fall apart when Chan K'in Viejo dies. Chan K'in has had three wives, one of whom has passed away; two still live with him. Together, their children (the youngest of which is said to have been conceived when Chan K'in was 102) are estimated to comprise 35% of the population of Nahá.

here. They used to worship at Palenque, but according to Lacandón elder Chan K'in Viejo, "the spirits have left there now," to retreat to their last home in Yaxchilán.

The site was ingeniously landscaped around the twisting Usumacinta River; the ruins remain accessible only by boat. The highlight is the series of high temples, many with stelae and glyphs. Carvings depict the two most important rulers: Jaguar Escudo (Shield Jaguar), in power in the 7th century, and Jaguar Pájaro (Bird Jaguar), who ruled a century later. You'll probably have to fork out a tidy sum for a visit here, so try to see everything you can—don't miss the series of temples set high on a hill, deeper in the jungle behind the eastern structure dedicated to Jaguar Pájaro. Transportation is arranged by travel agencies, or you can try to arrange boat transportation with a local resident in Lacanhá for about $15. Boat trips also leave the border town of Frontera Echeverría, called Corozal on the Guatemalan side, for $120 each way (up to eight people).

There's a large palapa for sleeping in Yaxchilán, but no facilities. You can bathe and fish in the river, and have your catch or any other food prepared by the woman who cooks for the guards. Any gifts of cigarettes, liquor, or fresh food are well appreciated. You'll pay a $3 fee to enter the ruins, except on Sundays. Spanish-language guided tours are free and mandatory.

Comitán and Lagos de Montebello

Though usually only used as a stopover for those traveling to and from Guatemala, Comitán has a pleasantly cool climate, some unusual little museums, and a pretty zócalo complete with ceiba trees, bougainvillea, flowers, and white benches. The real draw to this area, however, is the Parque Nacional Lagos de Montebello, comprised of over 2,000 acres of pine-forested hills dotted with lakes in brilliant shades of blue, green, and gray.

Comitán was originally a Tzeltal-speaking Maya community called Balún-Canán, meaning "Place of the Nine Stars." Its current name is derived from the name given by the Aztecs, Comitlán, which translates from Nahuatl as "Place of the Potters." You can see remnants of Maya civilization dating back as far as AD 900 near the Lagos de Montebello at the Chincultic (see Near Comitán, below) and Tenam Puente ruins (see Cheap Thrills, below), and in the archaeology museum (see below) in the library adjoining the Casa de la Cultura.

The Maya ruins of Tenam Puente are 8 kilometers from Comitán, off the road to the Lagos de Montebello. The ruins, comprised of a number of buildings and stelae, are set on a hill affording a view of the green valley below.

BASICS

CASA DE CAMBIO Bancomer (Av. 1 Ote. Sur 10, tel. 963/2-02-10), near the zócalo, has an ATM and is open weekdays 9:30 AM–11:30 AM for exchange on cash and traveler's checks and advances on Visa cards.

CONSULATES The **Guatemalan Consulate** (1a Calle Sur Pte. 26, at 2a Av. Pte. Sur, tel. 963/2-26-69) is open weekdays 8–4:30. For specific information on visas and border crossings, see box Going to Guatemala, below.

LAUNDRY **Lavandería Takana** (1a Calle Sur Pte., at 2a Av. Pte. Sur, next to the Guatemalan Consulate; open Mon.–Sat. 9–2 and 4–8) washes and dries your clothes for $1 a kilo. If you can't get next-day service there, try **Lavandería Chulul** (2a Av. Pte. Nte., around cnr from Restaurant Alis), which has identical hours.

MAIL The post office provides the usual services and will hold mail sent to you at the following address for up to 10 days: Lista de Correos, Comitán, Chiapas, CP 30000, México. Av. Central Belisario Domínguez Sur 45, tel. 963/2-04-27. Open weekdays 8–7, Sat. 9–1.

MEDICAL AID For emergencies, go to the **Hospital General** (9a Calle Sur Ote., tel. 963/2-01-35) 24 hours a day. The **Centro de Salud** (7a Calle Sur Ote. 3, tel. 963/2-36-49 or 963/2-01-64; open weekdays 8 AM–3 PM) is well-prepared to treat visitors with cholera or *turista*.

PHONES There are Ladatel phones on the zócalo in front of the Palacio Municipal. **Caseta Maguis** charges a 35¢ per minute commission on international collect calls, and a $2.75 service charge if the party doesn't accept your call. *2a Calle Sur Pte. 6, at Av. Central Belisario Domínguez. Open Mon.–Sat. 8 AM–9 PM, Sun. 9–2 and 5–8.*

VISITOR INFORMATION The tourist office in the Palacio Municipal is stocked with an excellent selection of brochures, as well as good maps of the city and region. The staff is well-versed in local history, geography, and transportation options, but doesn't speak English. *On the zócalo, tel. 963/2-40-47. Open Mon.–Sat. 9–2 and 4–8, Sun. 9–2.*

COMING AND GOING

BY BUS The first-class **Cristóbal Colón** station (Av. Central Belisario Domínguez Sur 43, tel. 963/2-09-80) is on the highway about 12 blocks southwest of the center. Buses for Tuxtla Gutiérrez (3½ hrs, $5) with stops in San Cristóbal (1½ hrs, $2) leave frequently every day between 5:30 AM and 8 PM. Buses leave for Ciudad Cuauhtémoc on the Guatemalan border (1½ hrs, 6 per day, $3), and for Villahermosa (8½ hrs, $15) at 6:30 PM. Three buses leave daily for the 22-hour trek to Mexico City; it's $32 for regular-first class (10 AM departure), and $41 for a more luxurious version with extra-comfortable seats, TV, and beverage service.

Second-class **Transportes Tuxtla Gutiérrez** (tel. 963/2-10-44) and **La Angostura** (same phone) buses leave from the station at Boulevard Belisario Domínguez Sur 27. To get here, walk 6 blocks west of the zócalo on Calle Central Benito Juárez, then left 1½ blocks down the highway. They serve Tuxtla Gutiérrez (3½ hrs, $4) and San Cristóbal (2 hrs, $3) from 5 AM to 7:30 PM. Buses for Ciudad Cuauhtémoc (2½ hrs, $3) also leave several times daily. Buses to Tzimol (30 min, 75¢) and La Mesilla (45 min, $1) leave about every half-hour between 8 and 5.

GETTING AROUND

Comitán is hilly, and the walk from the bus terminals with a loaded pack seems endless—it's better to take a CENTRO colectivo (25¢) to the center. The town itself, however, is easy to navigate once you master the grid system. Calle Central Benito Juárez runs east–west, Avenida Central Belisario Domínguez (otherwise known as "el boulevard") north–south. The two divide the city into four quadrants. All calles run east–west, all avenidas north–south. The two cardinal directions (Ote. for east, Pte. for west, Nte. for north, and Sur for south) in each street name indicate which of the four quadrants the street is in. The number in each street name indicates how far it is from either Avenida Central Belisario Domínguez or Calle Central Benito Juárez. For example, 2a Calle Sur Pte. runs east–west two blocks south of Calle Benito Juárez in the southwestern quadrant of the city. As the street crosses Avenida Central Belisario Domínguez into the southeastern quadrant of the city, it's called Calle 2a Sur Ote. Got it?

The bus terminals are on the highway (called Boulevard Belisario Domínguez or Carretera Internacional), west of the center, and can be reached via the colectivos marked CARRETERA INTERNACIONAL that leave from the east side of the zócalo.

WHERE TO SLEEP

Many of Comitán's budget hotels are near the center of town. The climate here is cooler than in most other areas of Chiapas, so when it comes to choosing a room hot water should be more of a consideration than fans or air-conditioning. If there's no room at the places listed below, try **Posada Las Flores** (1 Av. Pte. Nte. 17, tel. 963/2-33-24) or **Posada San Miguel** (1 Av. Pte. Nte. 19, tel. 963/2-11-26) next door; double rooms at both are $5. Head to Lagos de Montebello (*see* Near Comitán, *below*) to camp.

➢ **UNDER $10** • **Hospedaje Montebello.** An amiable young couple runs this rather noisy but clean and traveler-friendly place, which is always full. The hot water is erratic in some of the private bathrooms, but the communal showers are reliable. Singles with communal bath are $4, $6 with private bath; doubles are $7 with communal bath, $10 with private bath. *1a Calle Pte. Nte. 10, tel. 963/2–35–72. 14 rooms, 8 with bath. Luggage storage.*

Pensión Delfín. With clean, plain rooms and a dingy courtyard facing all the commotion on the zócalo, this inn is unspectacular—but the hot-water supply is dependable. Singles cost $8, doubles $9.50, triples $11, and quadruples $13. *Av. Central Belisario Domínguez Sur 21, tel. 963/2–00–13. 21 rooms, all with bath. Luggage storage.*

Posada Continental. Very clean singles with communal bathrooms (stocked with soap, towels, and toilet paper) go for a cheap $3. Doubles without bath are $5, and a double or single room with bath goes for $8. *1a Av. Pte. Sur 12, tel. 963/2–37–52. 13 rooms, 8 with bath. Luggage storage.*

➢ **UNDER $20** • **Hotel Internacional.** Just 1 block south of the center, this spacious hotel with perfumed, spotless rooms and plentiful hot water is a luxurious bargain for two or more. For better or worse, it's crawling with jovial Mexican businessmen in suits. Singles are $14, doubles $17, and triples $20. *Av. Central Belisario Domínguez Sur 16, tel. 963/2–01–12. 28 rooms, all with bath. Luggage storage. MC, V.*

FOOD

The affordable restaurants lining Comitán's zócalo serve international dishes and regional specialties, particularly soups and coffee made from locally grown beans; try **Restaurant Nevelandia** (tel. 963/2–00–95) for tacos and quesadillas (under $3) or breakfast specials of eggs, tortillas, beans, fruit, and coffee for $2.50. **El Rico Jugo** (cnr of Central Benito Juárez Sur Ote. and Av. Rosario Castellanos, no phone; open 7 AM–9 PM) serves up healthy fruit juices, smoothies, and granola-topped fruit salads. The **market,** in a huge yellow building 1 block east of the zócalo, is the place to find the cheapest food, including Chiapan specialties and fruits and veggies. It is open until late afternoon.

Café Gloria. In this family-owned restaurant you can find both regional and non-regional treats, including locally grown coffee and tasty *sopes* (fried tortillas topped with beans, salsa, and meat or cheese) at two for $1. Other dishes are similarly priced, and all come with four kinds of homemade salsa. Little boys sometimes serve as waiters here, and they'll introduce each dish to you as if it's a person. *Av. Central Belisario Domínguez Nte. 22, tel. 963/2–16–22. Open daily 6 PM–11 PM.*

Restaurant Alis. This is the place to go for excellent typical Comitecan food. Their *platón chiapaneco* (Chiapan platter, $7) includes *butifarras* (beef sausage) and *cecina* (dry, salted beef), and is enough for two. Their lunch specials are a tasty bargain for $3. *Calle Central Benito Juárez Pte. 21, tel. 963/2–12–62. Open daily 8:30 AM–9 PM.*

WORTH SEEING

Comitán has some fine examples of colonial architecture and well-curated museums. The 16th-century **Templo de Santo Domingo** on the zócalo displays elements of the Moorish-influenced *mudéjar* style. Just off the northeast corner of the zócalo stands the **Iglesia del Calvario,** whose columns and gables are probably Islamic-influenced via Andalucía, Spain.

IGLESIA DE SAN CARALAMPIO The festival honoring San Caralampio (*see* Festivals, *below*) is one of the biggest religious events of the year. Caralampio was a pious Christian who was burned to death by nonbelievers in his native Greece. Years later, a rancher named Raymundo Solís, inspired by a book about Caralampio, commissioned a statue of him for his ranch. At the time, a cholera epidemic was devastating Comitán. When no one on Don Solís's ranch was affected, townspeople attributed this to Caralampio's protection. The statue was then brought to town and installed in the 17th-century church. *1a Calle Nte. Ote., at 4a Av. Ote. Nte. Open 6–6.*

MUSEO ARQUEOLOGICO DE COMITAN This new museum and library displays Maya artifacts from the sites near Comitán. Especially notable is the display of bones and ornately decorated pottery found in the caves of Cam-Cum and Los Andasolos. Also displayed are artifacts and area photos from present excavations at Tenam Puente. *1a Calle Sur Ote., behind Casa de la Cultura. Admission free. Open Tues.–Sun. 10–5.*

MUSEO DE ARTE HERMILA DOMINGUEZ This museum 2 blocks south of the center features modern works by Mexican artists, including Rufino Tamayo. Many of the pieces deal with mystical themes, depicting mestizo and indigenous people and their connections to the earth, sky, and water. *Av. Central Belisario Domínguez Sur 53. Admission: 35¢. Open weekdays 10–1:45 and 4–6:45, Sat. 10–1:45.*

MUSEO DR. BELISARIO DOMINGUEZ Dr. Domínguez was a statesman and proponent of preventive medicine who represented Chiapas in the Senate under President Francisco Madero just after the Mexican Revolution. After Madero was assassinated by U.S.-backed General Victoriano Huerta in 1913, Dr. Domínguez publicly denounced Huerta as a brutal tyrant. Predictably, Domínguez was then murdered. This museum, once his home, displays his pharmaceuticals, ominous-looking medical instruments, photographs, letters, and other personal effects. *Av. Central Belisario Domínguez Sur 35, tel. 963/2–13–00. Admission: 35¢. Open Tues.–Sat. 10–6:45, Sun. 10–12:45.*

CHEAP THRILLS

For over two years, archaeologists have been excavating nearby **Tenam Puente,** and some feel that once it's fully unearthed, it may prove to encompass an area larger than that of Palenque. So far, archaeologists and INAH workers have dug up several good-size pyramids and three ball courts. The site is officially closed, but visitors can visit (Mon.–Fri. 8–5 is best) and chat with the archaeologists as they excavate. To get here, catch the 8 AM Transportes La Trinitaria bus (50¢) that leaves from the corner of 1a Calle Sur Poniente and Eje Vial Oriente. To get back, take the same bus at 6 PM or hitch a ride with the site workers who leave around 5 PM. Licenciada María Trinidad Pulido, who is in charge of the Museo Arqueológico de Comitán (*see above*), is very knowledgeable and can answer all your queries.

FESTIVALS

Comitán has many festivals, some barrio-specific and others citywide. The most important citywide events are the **Festival de San Caralampio,** featuring floats, flowers, music, and processions February 8–22; **Semana Santa** (Easter); and the **Feria de Agosto,** a 10-day festival of Comitecan agriculture, theater, and cuisine in honor of Santo Domingo that takes place in early August.

AFTER DARK

Since the Zapatista uprising in 1994, there has ceased to be a band on every block, but there are still plenty of places to relax and hear live music at no charge. **Helen's Enrique** (Av. Central Belisario Domínguez Sur 19, across from zócalo, tel. 963/2–17–30) is the prime hangout. They have live music Thursday–Saturday after 8 PM; cappuccino is $1.50. The bar in **Restaurant Nevelandia** (*see* Food, *above*), with live music nightly, is an equally mellow scene. More alcohol-driven, smoky, and male-dominated is **El Rincón de la Guitarra** (1 Calle Sur Ote. 13, no phone), which has live music every night 7 PM–3 AM. They offer some funky drinks, like the Muppet (tequila with Squirt) or the Cucaracha (tequila, anise, and Kahlua) for $4 each. A more sedate and casual spot is **Casa del Recuerdo** (1a Av. Ote. Nte. 6, tel. 963/2–05–44; open 11 AM–2 AM), housed within the elegant confines of Plaza Margarita.

Near Comitán

The main draw to the area surrounding Comitán is the lake country, but there are some other nice swimming spots and interesting towns to see if you have time. In a green valley 8 kilometers west of Comitán is the town of **Tzimol,** where sugar is grown with the same farming methods that have been used for hundreds of years. The town is known for its *panela* (cakes of hardened sugar-cane juice used in Chiapan pastries). A 15-minute bus ride past Tzimol brings you to the town of **La Mesilla,** from which a 5-kilometer path leads to great swimming at an isolated waterfall called **El Chiflón.** Transportes La Angostura buses serve both towns (*see* Coming and Going, *above*).

Twenty-five minutes northwest of Comitán is the pretty town of **Villa Las Rosas.** It's served by buses from Comitán's **Transportes Cuxtepeques** station (Blvd. Belisario Domínguez Sur 12, at 1a Calle Nte. Pte., tel. 963/2–17–28). Take a direct microbus (they leave every half-hour) to the center of Las Rosas. If you decide to go to freshwater spring **Manantial el Vertedor,** just outside of town, take another micro ($1) from the center—ask the driver if he's going to "el puente al manantial." From here it's a 1-kilometer hike down a dirt road. Follow the muddy path behind the dam and you can take a cool dip in the clear pool. In May and June, you'll see tiny shrines dedicated to the rain god.

LAGOS DE MONTEBELLO

Set among a forest of pine trees, blackberry bushes, and maples, the 60-odd blue, gray, and green lakes of the Parque Nacional Lagos de Montebello provide a spectacular setting for wonderful hikes and swimming. The most popular lakes are those close to the road: Esmeralda, Ensueño, Agua Tinta, La Encantada, and Bosque Azul. A 45-minute walk on the unpaved road from the park gates leads to **Lago Montebello,** the larger **Laguna Tziscao,** and a dozen tiny lakes. A bus continues past this junction and parks at **Lago Bosque Azul.** Two dirt paths lead into the forest from here. The one to the left takes you to a riverside picnic spot called **El Paso del Soldado.** The other takes you to **San José El Arco,** a natural limestone arch and cave. Bring a flashlight to explore the cave. Little boys will offer to be your guide; tip them a few pesos if you accept. At Bosque Azul, older boys will offer to take you to more isolated lakes on foot or horseback. Be sure to agree on a price before setting out ($3 an hour is reasonable, but bargain if you can), and wear a watch, since most guides aren't too concerned about getting you back in time for the last bus. The lakes **Peinita** and **Bartolo,** surrounded by white cliffs that offer spectacular views of the surrounding farmland and mountains, are best reached accompanied by a guide. You can pick up a useful map of the lakes at the tourist office in Comitán (*see* Visitor Information, *above*).

Just at the edges of the park are the Maya ruins of **Chincultic.** This site has a number of stelae, a ball court, and pyramids from which you can admire the surrounding lakes and the deep *cenote* (spring-fed water hole) from which Chincultic gets its name (it means "terraced well"). The ruins are a half-hour hike from the main road that leads to the lakes, and buses between Comitán and the park pass the turnoff; ask the driver to let you off at Chincultic. The ruins are open every day 8:30–4 ($2 Mon.–Sat.).

COMING AND GOING Colectivos and combis from **Transportes Comitán-Montebello** (2a Av. Pte. Sur 17, at 2a Calle Sur Pte., tel. 963/2–08–75) let you off at Lago Bosque Azul; they leave every half-hour from 5:45 AM until 4:45 PM daily. The trip takes about an hour and costs $2. The last bus back to Comitán leaves Bosque Azul around 4 PM.

WHERE TO SLEEP You can easily stay in Comitán and make day trips to the lakes, but if you want to stay overnight, bring warm gear and expect a chilly evening. The restaurant at Lago Bosque Azul offers simple cabañas for about $3 a night—but out here, camping is the way to go. It's officially permitted at Bosque Azul, La Encantada, and Tziscao, all of which are outfitted with palapas, fire pits, and rest rooms.

Tapachula

The southernmost city of any size in Mexico, Tapachula is the center of the Soconusco region, extending from the Chiapan mountains to the coast and down into southwestern Guatemala. Modern-day Tapachula is home to a diverse population. Significant numbers of European and Asian immigrants—many fleeing World War II and the Communist Revolution in China—were attracted to the area by its coffee- and cacao-driven prosperity. Guatemalans come here to shop, do business, find work on the plantations, or escape political persecution, and budget travelers are attracted by its amenities and proximity to the Guatemalan border. All this activity has rendered Tapachula a relaxed, cosmopolitan town with better-than-average budget hotels and good cappuccino (in the Parque Central). The area also has much to offer outdoorsy types: The nearby beach towns of Puerto Madero and Las Palmas are pleasant places to cool off in the gentle ocean waves; and the Izapa archaeological zone, where easy hikes through cacao fields lead you to infrequently visited ruins, lies close to the city. A bit farther away, at the foot of the Tacaná volcano, the cool mountain town of Unión Juárez offers limitless camping, hiking, and swimming. During the summer months, June–August, it really rains in Tapachula.

Tapachula, which means "Place of Sour Prickly Pears" in Nahuatl, was originally designated an administrative, tribute-paying region of the Aztec empire. The Aztecs demanded colored feathers, jade, jaguar pelts, and cacao as tribute from their southern subjects.

BASICS

CASAS DE CAMBIO Banco Internacional (2a Av. Nte., at 1a Calle Pte., tel. 962/5–05–01) changes traveler's checks and cash weekdays 10–noon. Your best bet for good exchange rates for not only American traveler's checks—but also Guatemalan quetzales, Honduran lempiras, and Salvadoran colones—is the **Casa de Cambio** (4a Av. Nte., at 3a Calle Pte., tel. 962/6–51–22). It's open Monday–Saturday 7:30–7:30, Sunday 7–1.

CONSULATES Get a visa for travel into Guatemala (*see box* Going to Guatemala, *below*) at the Guatemalan Consulate. *2a Calle Ote. 33, tel. 962/6–12–52. Open weekdays 8–4:30.*

LAUNDRY Lava Ropa will wash and dry 3 kilos of clothing for $2.50. *Av. Central Nte. 33, tel. 962/6–35–25. Open Mon.–Sat. 8–8.*

MAIL The post office is a 7-block trek from the center. They offer all the usual services and will hold mail sent to you at the following address for up to 10 days: Lista de Correos, Tapachula, Chiapas, CP 30700, México. *1a Calle Ote. 32, at 7a Av. Nte., tel. 962/6–39–22. Open weekdays 8–7, Sat. 9–1.*

MEDICAL AID Farmacia 24 Horas (8a Av. Nte. 25, tel. 962/6–24–80) offers chips and Coke as well as medication round the clock.

PHONES There are two blue Ladatel phones on the southwest corner of the zócalo and some in a quieter area just a block north of the zócalo on 1a Calle Poniente, at 6a Avenida Norte. The public phones scattered around downtown are your best bet for an international collect call (dial 09 for an operator).

VISITOR INFORMATION Housed in the Casa de la Cultura, the tourist office has three wonderful employees, Enrique, Magui, and Amelinda, who are very proud of their region and will help you arrange treks into the countryside or provide information on crossing into Guatemala. *Cnr 8a Av. Nte. and 3a Poniente, tel. 962/5–54–09. Open weekdays 9–3 and variable evening hours.*

COMING AND GOING

BY BUS The first-class bus terminal (17a Calle Ote., at 3a Av. Nte., tel. 962/6–28–81) is a good 12 blocks from the center. To get here, either take a taxi ($1) or a CRISTOBAL COLON or LOMA DE SAYULA combi (25¢) down Avenida Central Norte. **Cristóbal Colón** and **UNO** offer first-class direct service to San Cristóbal (10 hrs, $9) with six departures a day. Four buses a day go to Salina Cruz (8 hrs, $12) and Mexico City (24 hrs, $40), and two leave daily for Oaxaca city (14 hrs, $23).

If your next destination is San Cristóbal or Comitán, second-class **Transportes Casa Lombargo** (9a Calle Pte. 63, at 11a Av. Nte.) offers the most frequent service, with about 10 departures per day to each city. It's $7 for the 10-hour trip to San Cristóbal, and $4 for the six-hour trip to Comitán.

Autobuses General Paulino Navarro (7a Calle Pte., at Av. Central Nte., tel. 962/6–31–02) offers two second-class buses a day to Tuxtla Gutiérrez (7 hrs, $10) and frequent service to nearby towns and border crossings. **Unión y Progreso** (5a Calle Pte., tel. 962/6–33–79) buses serve Talismán and Unión Juárez infrequently between 5:30 AM and 8 PM for about $1. Colectivos also depart for Cuidad Hidalgo and Talismán from the bus stations and near the market along 10a Avenida Norte.

BY TRAIN The train station (Calle Central Sur, at 18a Calle Pte., tel. 962/5–21–76) is far from the center but accessible by colectivo or taxi. Trains depart for Juchitán, Mexico City, and Veracruz. Service in this area is slow and uncomfortable—opt for the bus. If you do decide to take the train, head to the station early in the morning and buy your tickets in advance, since the office often closes capriciously.

BY PLANE Aeroméxico (tel. 962/6–20–50), **AVIACSA** (tel. 962/6–31–47), and **Taesa** (tel. 962/6–37–32) serve the airport (tel. 962/6–22–91), at Kilometer 22 on the Carretera Puerto Madero. All three companies fly directly to Mexico City, but fares vary dramatically, from $70 during low season (February, April, May, and October) to as much as $219. The airport is about 18 kilometers from the city and is accessible by taxi (a rip-off at $10), or by airport bus for $4. Call or stop by the airport bus office (2 Av. Sur 40, tel. 962/5–12–87) in advance to make arrangements for a hotel pickup.

GETTING AROUND

The city's main sights and many budget establishments are clustered around the zócalo, at the intersections of 3a and 5a Calles Poniente and 4a and 6a Avenidas Norte. Most of the city is easily walkable, but colectivos and taxis crowd the streets and can take you around cheaply. Two long boulevards—Avenida Central Norte/Sur and Avenida Central Poniente/Oriente—divide the city into four parts. Calles run east–west and avenidas run north–south. Even-numbered calles are south of Avenida Central Poniente/Oriente, and odd-numbered calles are north of it. Even-numbered avenidas are west of Avenida Central Norte/Sur, and odd-numbered avenidas are east of it.

WHERE TO SLEEP

Many better-than-average budget hotels are concentrated around the center. If you lack the means for anything more than the bare minimum, **Casa de Huéspedes Yuli** and **Hospedaje La Mexicana** (both at 8a Av. Nte. 60, near 2nd-class bus stations) offer fairly clean, padlock-secured double rooms for $5 a night.

➢ **UNDER $10** • **Hospedaje Las Américas.** This hotel is just steps away from the market and second-class bus stations. The quiet, clean rooms open onto a tree-filled central courtyard and are a terrific deal at $5 a single or $7.50 a double. *10a Av. Nte. 47, tel. 962/6–27–57. 20 rooms, all with bath. Luggage storage.*

Hotel Cervantino. Four blocks from the center, this is an exceptionally clean hotel, and all rooms have fans and tables. The management is friendly and extremely helpful. Singles are $7, doubles $10, and a room for four (two beds) is $12. *1a Calle Ote. 6, tel. 962/6–16–58. 21 rooms, all with bath. Luggage storage, wheelchair access. MC, V.*

➢ **UNDER $15** • **Hospedaje Colonial.** This downtown hotel is overflowing with plants and character. "Hanging herbs keep the bats away," according to the kind owners—and the beautiful gardens keep the guests happy. It looks like a hole-in-the-wall from the street, but it's actually a pleasant, tranquil spot to spend the night. Come in past 11:30 PM, though, and the owners get kind of irritated. Singles are $6, doubles $12. *4a Nte. 31, tel. 962/6-20-52. 10 rooms, all with bath. Luggage storage.*

Hotel Puebla. This four-story hotel right next to the Palacio Municipal offers spacious rooms overlooking the action on the zócalo. All rooms have fans and hot water. Singles are $11, doubles $13. *3a Pte. 40, tel. 962/6-14-36. 40 rooms, all with bath. Luggage storage. Wheelchair access.*

FOOD

Perhaps because of the many Guatemalan migrant workers who work on the coffee and cacao plantations here and have no place to go for the night, Tapachula has a number of restaurants open around the clock. Most of them are around the zócalo. **La Parrilla** (on the zócalo, tel. 962/6-51-98; open 7 AM-midnight) offers cheap sandwiches and breakfasts, as well as filet mignon with a baked potato for $7.50. **La Michoacana** (6a Av. Nte., at 7a Calle Pte., no phone), is filled with Guatemalan workers watching TV and slowly sipping $1 licuados into the wee hours. If you're looking for something more exotic, you won't be disappointed, either. Thanks to Tapachula's large Chinese and European immigrant populations—as well as its proximity to both the mountains and coast—the city offers a surprising variety of great food.

El Mandarín. Ascend a narrow flight of stairs and you'll emerge into an elegant dining room decked with red tablecloths and *the* most comfortable matching red chairs. Try the *cha siu agridulce* (sweet-and-sour pork) for $4 or broccoli in oyster sauce for less than $2. The vegetables are crunchy and not drowned in the salt and grease you'll encounter in most Chinese restaurants in Mexico. *8a Av. Nte., at 7a Calle Pte, tel. 962/6-20-12. Open Mon.–Sat. 1-10, Sun. 1-7.*

Ostionería El Pulpo Jarocho. After you get past the name (it translates as the "Veracruzan Octopus Oyster Bar"), the small patio of this busy and unassuming seafood restaurant is a fun place to eat. Seafood cocktails with conch, oysters, octopus, squid, and shrimp are only $4–$6 and come with crackers and crunchy fried tortillas. *5a Privada Sur, tel. 962/6-73-03. In alley just south of Calle Central Ote., about 6 blocks from zócalo, near post office. Open Mon.–Sat. 11-5.*

WORTH SEEING

The labyrinthine **Mercado Sebastián Escobar,** on the side of a steep hill next to the zócalo, is a 2-block indoor/outdoor market where tropical fruits, vegetables, live birds, and every trinket you can imagine are sold. The indoor part is open in the morning only, and the fruit selection is best before midday.

Also worth a visit is the **Museo Regional del Soconusco,** inside the splendid art deco **Palacio Municipal** (tel. 962/6-35-43) just off the zócalo. The museum displays bits of stelae and other artifacts from nearby ruins, as well as photos of excavation sites. Admission to the museum is $2 (free Sundays), and it's open Tuesday–Sunday 10-5. Next door is the **Casa de la Cultura** which offers music, art, and dance classes. Upstairs, the Casa often holds a display of regional arts and crafts. It's free and open daily 9-9.

FESTIVALS

About 7 kilometers out of the city on the road to Puerto Madero is the site of the **Feria Internacional,** Tapachula's big yearly bash in celebration of the agricultural, artistic, and commercial richness of the area. Another big event is the **Feria de San Agustín,** which takes place August 20-28.

Near Tapachula

While Tapachula is attractive enough to tempt you to stay put for a while, there are a number of towns easily visited on day trips from here. The seaside town of **Puerto Madero,** 27 kilometers southwest of Tapachula, is the closest place to breathe some sea air, although its little beach, **Playa San Benito,** is a bit dirty. The water is pleasant and warm, and iguanas bake themselves on the boulders that line the beach. If you decide to stay the night, the village has easy beach camping and one hotel of dubious quality. Microbuses from Tapachula's **General Paulino Navarro** bus station (*see* Coming and Going, *above*) leave about every half-hour until 5:30 PM and charge about $1 for the 20-minute ride. A better beach a bit farther away (45 minutes north up the coast) is the gloriously quiet, palm-fringed **Las Palmas.** To get here from Tapachula you need to take a General Paulino Navarro bus (*see* Coming and Going, *above*) to Acapetahua or Escuinala where you can catch a colectivo to Las Palmas. If you're not camping, plan on catching a bus back by afternoon.

Also easily accessible is the impressive **Izapa** archaeological zone, only 15 minutes away on the road to Talismán. Closest to Tapachula are ruin groups A and B, about 20 minutes down a jungle path marked by a sign at the highway. Group A is sadly uncared for. Continue farther

Going to Guatemala

Mexico has three official border crossings into Guatemala: Talismán and Ciudad Hidalgo (both near Tapachula) and Ciudad Cuauhtémoc (near Comitán). Boats also navigate the Río Usumacinta from the town of Tenosique in Tabasco to Guatemala's Petén region, but there are no immigration offices on this route, so you'll need to obtain a visa before setting out or risk being arrested as an illegal alien once you arrive in Guatemala. Because of occasional flare-ups between rebel forces and the Guatemalan government in the Petén region, such considerations may end up being the least of your worries. Safer and more convenient is Talismán, where all the customs offices are near one another and the border itself; military types keep a low profile to avoid scaring the tourists, and frequent buses make the four-hour trek to Guatemala City.

When you reach the border you'll be shuffled from office to office and charged a number of small processing fees. Cash can easily be changed at the border, but change just what you need because rates are generally poor. It's also a good idea to bring some U.S. currency in small bills to help you through any "formalities." To enter Guatemala you must have a valid passport and either a visa (obtainable at the Guatemalan consulates in Tapachula and Comitán) or a tourist card (available at the border). U.S. citizens are eligible for free, 30-day, multiple-entry visas. Canadian, British, Irish, and Australian citizens are given 30-day single-entry visas. These are free for Canadians but cost $10 for everyone else. Tourist cards ($5 regardless of nationality, payable in cash only) are available at all three border crossings and allow for a stay of 30–90 days, depending on the mood of the immigration officer or your brown-nosing skill. You'll want to keep your passport and tourist card handy at all times—buses traveling along border routes routinely stop at immigration checkpoints, where officers sometimes mysteriously single out passengers and demand to inspect their papers and/or baggage.

along the path and through the cacao fields to Group B, where you'll find a huge pyramid and some better-preserved stelae. The largest and most impressive ruins (Group F) are visible from the highway, and are less than a kilometer farther along to the left. This fully restored ceremonial center—complete with pyramids, a ball court, altars, and stelae—enjoyed its heyday around BC 300–200. To reach the sites, take one of the frequent colectivos from either of Tapachula's second-class stations—General Paulina Navarro or Unión y Progreso—toward Talismán and ask the driver to let you off at Izapa. Buses ($1) run 5:30 AM–8 PM. The sites are officially free, but you might want to give a donation to one of the three families who maintain the ruins.

UNION JUAREZ

If you're going to be in the area for any length of time, do not fail to visit Unión Juárez. This coffee-growing town clinging to the base of **Volcán Tacaná**, 30 kilometers northeast of Tapachula, offers great swimming and hiking, plus good food and places to stay. Its steep cobblestone roads wind through coffee plantations and cool, lushly forested valleys crisscrossed by rivers. The **Cascadas de Muxbal** (Muxbal Waterfalls) have a deep pool for swimming and are situated in a narrow canyon hung with gargantuan ferns. There are also pools for bathing on the **Río Mala**. Two sublime vantage points are each about an hour's hike out of town: **Pico de Loro** (Parrot's Beak) is an outcropping of rock overlooking the jungle that resembles (what else?) a parrot's beak, and affords a beautiful view of Guatemala and the ocean. **La Ventana** (The Window), the other vista point, is on a hill overlooking a forested valley. Ask for directions and maps at the Palacio Municipal in Unión Juárez. The climb to the top of Tacaná is a day-long enterprise; if you brave it, you'll have to spend the night on the summit. Don Humberto Ríos at **Restaurante La Montaña** or Roberto Moody at **Posada Aljoad** (*see* Where to Sleep and Eat, *below*) provide guide service for Tacaná and elsewhere. Whatever you choose to do, head out early in the morning, since the fog and rain arrive like clockwork in the afternoon.

COMING AND GOING   Direct buses between Tapachula and Unión Juárez are hard to come by. The simplest way to get here is to catch a minibus or combi from Avenida 12 Norte in Tapachula to the town of Cacahuatán (40 min, $1.50), where you can squeeze into one of the always crowded VW buses that frequently make the hour-long trip to Unión Juárez.

WHERE TO SLEEP AND EAT   Pay about $16 a night for a double room or $30 for a private chalet at the A-frame **Hotel Colonial Campestre** (Hidalgo 1) and enjoy hot water, TVs, telephones, and even a disco. The other option is to join nature enthusiasts and groups of young hikers at the **Hotel Posada Aljoad** (Mariano Escobedo, right off zócalo). The hot water here is temperamental. Neither hotel has a private line but you can call 962/2–02–25 for lodging information.

For such a remote town, Unión Juárez has remarkably good food. **La Montaña** and **Restaurante Carmelita**, both on Avenida Juárez in the zócalo, offer tasty regional entrées at shoestring prices. Don't leave without trying La Montaña's *plátanos fritos* (fried plantains) for less than $2.

Villahermosa

Villahermosa is largely the product of the 1970s, when the region's rich oil reserves brought prosperity and expansion to the city. Huge luxury hotels, the massive Tabasco 2000 complex—with its modern apartments, shopping mall, fairgrounds, municipal palace, and tourist office—and active cultural centers and museums were among the additions. The city that resulted lacks the natural beauty of the verdant highlands and forests outside its boundaries, but it does have a certain human-made appeal—there are lots of parks and pedestrian-only streets.

The city was originally established farther north, but was relocated after British, French, and Dutch pirates repeatedly looted the area for cacao and *palo de tinta* (a tree used for making dyes) during the 16th and 17th centuries. The city moved south, away from the river connecting it to the pirates' sea route, and was renamed San Juan Bautista. In the late 1700s, King Felipe II of Spain gave it its final name: Villahermosa. The area disappeared from the world market until the Mexican Revolution in the early 1900s, when exports of bananas and cacao began to flourish.

At its worst, Villa is an excessive jumble of streamlined '70s cement architecture, expressways reminiscent of Southern California, and huge multipurpose stores filled with imported modern amenities. At its best, Villahermosa is an oasis of culture, with museums, a beautiful archaeological park, an ecological reserve that puts Sea World to shame. Many affordable hotels to serve as a base for exploring the nearby coast, as well as Comalcalco, Teapa, and even Palenque. At any rate, do be prepared for a brief bit of culture shock, especially if you've been tramping around the remote Chiapan highlands.

BASICS

AMERICAN EXPRESS Turismo Nieves runs a full-service American Express desk that will hold mail, replace lost cards, and cash personal checks for cardholders, as well as deliver MoneyGrams and exchange or replace traveler's checks for anyone. *Sarlat Incidencia 202, tel. 93/14–18–88. From Zona Luz walk down Carranza 1 block past Parque Juárez and turn left. Mailing address: American Express, Turismo Nieves, Sarlat Incidencia 202, Villahermosa, Tabasco, CP 86000, México. Open weekdays 9–1:30 and 4–6, Sat. 9–noon.*

BOOKSTORES Books in English are hard to come by, but if you read Spanish, **Librería Fondo de Cultura** (27 de Febrero 603, Plazuela la Aguila, tel. 93/12–24–24) has a large selection of novels and books on Tabasco's natural and cultural heritage. **Librería El Alba** (Madero 616, tel. 93/12–22–24) also has Spanish novels, textbooks, and crafts.

CASAS DE CAMBIO At last count, there were nine banks squeezed in among the shops and budget hotels of the Zona Luz area. All major banks (**Banamex, Bancomer,** and **Banco Internacional**) will change U.S. dollars and traveler's checks weekdays 10–5.

For longer hours, head to **Blahberl** (27 de Febrero 1537, tel. 93/13–34–19), open weekdays 8:30–6:30 and Saturday 8:30–4. Take a cathedral-bound bus down 27 de Febrero and ask to be let off at *el reloj con tres caras* ("the clock with three faces"). They change Canadian dollars as well as cash from most major European countries. For a commission, you can also cash personal checks written in U.S. dollars.

EMERGENCIES The police can be reached at 93/13–21–10 or 93/3–37–32. For help in an emergency, dial 06.

LAUNDRY **Lavandería Automática** (Reforma 502, tel. 93/14–37–65), just out of the Zona Luz toward the river, will wash 1 kilo for about $1. Same-day service is 25¢ more.

MAIL The most convenient post office is in the Zona Luz. They'll hold mail sent to you at the following address for up to 10 days: Lista de Correos, Villahermosa, Tabasco, CP 86000, México. *Sáenz 131, tel. 93/12–10–40. Open weekdays 8–7, Sat. 9–noon.*

MEDICAL AID Two of several places to get 24-hour emergency service are the **Cruz Roja** (Cesar Saudino, Col. Primera de Mayo, tel. 93/13–35–93) and **Rescate Civil** (cnr Periférico and 16 de Septiembre, tel. 93/13–19–00). Pharmacies abound in the Zona Luz, but all close at 9 PM. **Farmacia Mariana** (27 de Febrero 626, tel. 93/14–23–66), a few blocks up from the Zona Luz, is open 24 hours a day.

PHONES You can't walk 10 paces in the Zona Luz without running into a blue Ladatel phone, from which you can make international calls with a Ladatel Plus card sold at various *papelerías* (stationery stores) in the Zona Luz. If you want to make a cash call or phone anywhere besides the United States collect, you can use the caseta in **Café Barra** (Lerdo de Tejada 608). It's open Monday–Saturday 7–1 and 3:30–10, and charges a fee for unaccepted collect calls. There is also a 24-hour caseta across from the ADO station (*see below*).

VISITOR INFORMATION The federal tourist office (Paseo Tabasco 1504, Tabasco 2000 Complex, tel. 93/16–36–33), open weekdays 9–3 and 6–9, offers glossy brochures on various local sights, as well as a map of the city and information on Tabasco. Some members of the well-informed staff speak English. To get here, take the TABASCO 2000 or PALACIO MUNICIPAL bus from the *malecón* (boardwalk).

COMING AND GOING

BY BUS The first-class bus station (Francisco Javier Mina 297, at Lino Merino) is big and efficient, with computers at the ticket windows. It's served by many of the major first-class bus companies, including **ADO** (tel. 93/12–76–92), **Cristóbal Colón** (tel. 93/14–56–80), and **UNO** (tel. 93/14–20–54). Be sure to buy your ticket in advance, as lines are always long and seats sell out. Service is frequent to destinations like Chetumal (9 hrs, $16), Mérida (10 hrs, $18), Mexico City (16 hrs, $30), Oaxaca city (16 hrs, $21), Palenque (2 hrs, $5), Tapachula (16 hrs, $22), Teapa (1½ hrs, $1.50), and Tuxtla Gutiérrez (6½ hrs, $8). Luggage storage ($1–$2) is available at the station 24 hours. To get to the city center, walk a good 12 blocks southeast, or take a bus marked PARQUE JUÁREZ. Buses marked CENTRO will take you to the Palacio Municipal; those marked CENTRAL will take you to the Central Camionera.

The huge **Central Camionera** (Ruíz Cortínez, east of intersection with Javier Mina) is the city's second-class bus station. Here, ticket sellers from a zillion different bus companies sit in tiny cages. Buses range from clean and plush to sticky and grimy, but serve a dizzying array of destinations more frequently and cheaply than the first-class buses. You can get to Mexico City for $24, to Puebla for $20, Jalapa for $17, Veracruz for about $11, Palenque for $2, and Teapa for $1. To get here from the the Zona Luz take any bus marked CENTRAL along the malecón.

Buses to the coast and Comalcalco leave from the **Transportes Somellera** terminal (Ruíz Cortínez, at Llergo, tel. 93/14–41–18). There is service to Comalcalco (1½ hrs, $1.50) every half-hour and to Paraíso (2 hrs, $2) every hour. The easiest way to get here is to take a bus to the Central Camionera, cross the bridge over the highway, and walk down Ruíz Cortínez 3 long blocks towards the Hotel Maya Tabasco. You'll see the station a block or so past the hotel on your left.

BY PLANE The airport (tel. 93/12–11–64) is served by **Aeroméxico** (tel. 93/14–16–75), **AVIACSA** (tel. 93/14–47–55), **Mexicana** (tel. 93/12–11–64), and **Aerolitoral** (tel. 93/14–36–14). No public transportation goes to the airport. Taxis charge about $8, but you might be able to bargain. Luggage storage is available at the airport.

GETTING AROUND

Villahermosa can be difficult to navigate, even with the blurry map given out at the tourist office. But a few prominent landmarks, abundant city buses, and cheap taxis will help you visit all the sights.

The center of town is bordered by three avenues, along which lie many of the major points of interest. The main highway is **Ruíz Cortínez,** a huge expressway with fast and deadly traffic. The Central Camionera (2nd-class bus terminal), Transportes Somellera, and the biggest food **market** are all here. Cortínez turns south at the **Parque Museo La Venta**—you'll see the rectangular *mirador* (viewing tower) jutting out where it intersects with another main avenue, **Paseo Tabasco.** This street runs from the **Tabasco 2000 complex**—with its huge, black mushroom of a water tower—to the **malecón** (boardwalk), which runs along the bank of the Río Grijalva. CICOM (*see* Worth Seeing, *below*) is on **Carlos Pellicer,** which is the name the malecón takes on just past the roundabout where it hits Paseo Tabasco.

The bus system in Villahermosa can be confusing—so confusing, in fact, that you'll probably see more than one local anxiously asking the bus driver for reassurance about the route. You would be wise to follow suit.

Within this ring, the streets that will be most important to you are Francisco Javier Mina, which heads up to Cortínez and the first-class bus station; Méndez, which runs from Llergo to the malecón, crossing Mina, parallel to Mina. Follow the one-way flow of traffic north on Madero and you'll pass the **Parque Benito Juárez,** at the northeast corner of the **Zona Luz.** The Zona Luz is a largely pedestrian-only area bordered by Madero on the east, Zaragoza on the north, Castillo to the west, and 27 de Febrero to the south. This is where you'll find the best budget lodging and restaurants.

BY BUS Destinations are usually marked on windshields, but routes are often very roundabout. To reach the tourist office or La Venta, take either the TABASCO 2000 or PALACIO MUNICIPAL bus from Madero, 1 block north of Parque Juárez. From the same stop, you can catch buses for CICOM (see Worth Seeing, below). For buses to the second-class bus station or market, take either the CENTRAL or MERCADO bus from the malecón.

BY TAXI Because drivers pack their tiny Nissans with passengers, taxi rides are cheap ($1–$2 within the city). Wait in line at a taxi stand and an attendant will shuffle you into the proper taxi. There are taxi stands in front of the first-class bus station and on Madero near Reforma.

WHERE TO SLEEP

Villahermosa has a number of large (some residential) hotels with standard rooms and competitive prices. Since many hotels have permanent residents, you may have to check a few before you find space, but most hotels will store your luggage for you while you look. The best time to search is noon–1, the usual checkout time. Budget hotels are clustered in the Zona Luz on Madero and side streets such as Lerdo de Tejada, where the quietest hotels overlook pedestrian walkways.

➢ **UNDER $10** • **Hotel Madero.** The conscientious proprietor has seen to it that this is one of the cleanest, most comfortable inexpensive hotels in the city. The rooms are decorated in various tranquil shades of blue, the bathrooms have hot water, and the staff is more than eager to help you find your way around town. Singles are $8, doubles $9.50, and triples $11. Madero 301, tel. 93/12–05–16. 28 rooms, all with bath. Luggage storage.

Hotel Oriente. On a busy section of Madero under the arched awning, this modest, fairly clean (although somewhat dark) hotel is a decent value. Request the "penthouse" rooms (nos. 43 and 44), with cross-ventilation from three sets of windows. Simple singles are $7, doubles $9.50. Madero 425, tel. 93/12–11–01. 22 rooms, all with bath. Luggage storage.

Hotel Tabasco (Lerdo de Tejada 317, tel. 93/12–00–77) and the adjacent **Hotel Oviedo** are the cheapest places in town that still maintain reasonable standards (despite cracked windows that let mosquitos in at night). You'll have to scramble for a room, but if you're lucky enough to secure one, you'll save enough for three tacos around the corner. At both hotels, basic rooms with fans vary dramatically in quality and noise level. Hotel Tabasco's rooms and doorless bathrooms are more spacious, and neither place has hot water, but with the Tabascan heat, who cares? If possible, check a few rooms before paying. At Oviedo, singles are $6.50, doubles $8 (Hotel Tabasco's rooms are a dollar cheaper), and triples $10. Both hotels have laundry and luggage storage.

➢ **UNDER $15** • **Hotel San Miguel.** The clean, orange-toned rooms have phones and the floors are decorated with orange-and-white circus stripes. This is one of the more popular budget places and is consistently full. Singles are $8, doubles $12, and triples $14.50, a few dollars more for air-conditioning. Lerdo de Tejada 315, tel. 93/12–12–85. 45 rooms, all with bath. Luggage storage.

➢ **UNDER $20** • **Hotel Palma de Mallorca.** All the rooms here are sunny and clean. With fans, singles are $10, doubles $13, triples $16; with the luxury of air-conditioning, singles and doubles run about $17. Madero 510, tel. 93/12–01–45. 36 rooms, all with bath. Luggage storage.

ROUGHING IT The absolutely broke and the fearless could try crashing at the **Parque de la Choca,** the city fairgrounds, where (unless some event is taking place) you'll find lots of empty palapas, large lawns, and abandoned, creepy-looking amusement park rides. Drivers have also been known to park their cars in the lot here to crash for the night.

FOOD

Variety is not a problem here. The large, enclosed **Mercado Pino Suárez** (Bastar Zozaya, 2 blocks west of Río Grijalva) is open mornings and has a good selection of fruit and bread and a bunch of dirt-cheap taco stands, some of which look much cleaner than others. You can also cool off with a *paleta* (popsicle), a ladle of juice from the many *agua fresca* (juice drink) shops, or with icy vats of tamarind, lime, pineapple, horchata, and other flavored drinks. Try *jamaica*, a hibiscus-flower drink that quenches your thirst like a soda never could. **Mini-Leo** (Juárez 504) is a citywide chain with burgers, fries, tacos, quesadillas, and the like. Frozen-yogurt shops, bakeries, and supermarkets fill the Zona Luz. **Las 2 Naciones** (Juárez 533, tel. 93/12-12-22) has temptingly fresh baked goods from 7 AM to 9 PM every day except Sunday.

➢ **UNDER $5** • **Aquarius.** You'll find vegetarian sandwiches, soups, and yogurt, as well as medicinal herb teas and vitamins at both Aquarius locations. A filling, hot sandwich with beans, cheese, avocado, alfalfa sprouts, and more is about $2. For 75¢, serious health food nuts can detoxify their systems with a beet, carrot, and celery juice concoction called *vampiro* that leaves the mouth bright red. Wheat breads are also sold in the adjacent health-food store. Two locations: Zaragoza 513, in Zona Luz, tel. 93/12–05–79, open Mon.–Sat. 8 AM–9 PM; and Javier Mina 309, 2 blocks from ADO bus station, tel. 93/14–25–37, open daily 8 AM–10 PM.

El Torito Valenzuela. Tender beef tacos on fresh, handmade tortillas with lots of cilantro and onion (four for $2) are the specialty here, but the *queso fundido* (cheese fondue) and quesadillas ($1) are excellent as well. Their comida corrida ($3) is more than one person should ever eat in one sitting: soup, tortillas, entrée, french fries, beans, rice, fried plantains, a drink, and dessert. Also good are the hearty breakfast specials ($2.50). 27 de Febrero, at Madero, tel. 93/14–18–89. Open daily 8 AM–midnight.

Tortillería Chetumalito. In addition to fabulously cheap 75¢ quesadillas (with meat, $1), this place serves up plenty of comfortable neighborhood cheer. Chat with the jovial owner while you eat. Madero 804, tel. 93/12–04–87. Open Mon.–Sat. 8 AM–9 PM.

➢ **UNDER $10** • **Birbiri's.** This teal-and-pink restaurant is a bit pricey and out of the way, but locals swear by the seafood. Have the shrimp in garlic ($7) and linger after dinner, sipping a drink from their full bar and listening to the singer who performs in the evenings. Madero 1032, tel. 93/12–61–45. Open Mon.–Sat. 10–8.

WORTH SEEING

Villahermosa is rich with places to stroll—along the river's malecón, through Benito Juárez Park, above the river at the end of Aldama, and around the Zona Luz. Sunday is the big day for families, who often head for nearby beaches. **La Feria del Desarrollo** (Development Fair) during late April and early May celebrates the diversity of culture in Tabasco, and each municipality showcases its typical dances, arts, and music. There's also a parade of decorated boats down the Grijalva, with fireworks and general revelry. The main action takes place in **Parque de la Choca,** past Tabasco 2000. In February, **Carnaval** is especially big here, with music, dance contests, and processions.

MUSEUMS Most of Villa's museums offer free guided tours in Spanish. Olmec art and artifacts are on display at La Venta and the Museo Regional de Antropología. The museums in the Zona Luz are cheap (or free) hole-in-the-wall operations only a short walk from the budget lodgings, and they hold worthwhile evening events. All museum close on Mondays.

➢ **PARQUE-MUSEO LA VENTA** • Perhaps Villahermosa's biggest attraction, this sprawling park displays all the major finds from the La Venta archaeological site (on the border with Veracruz), which was threatened by oil drilling in the '70s. The jungly park has dirt paths that wind past 20 or so Olmec carvings, mosaics, and stelae. Exaggerated sculptures of ancient Maya folk and half-jaguar/half-human creatures predominate. Provided there's a group of four or more, free guided tours in Spanish leave every half-hour from the entrance; tours in English can be arranged. Warning: Bring bug repellent for the 30- to 40-minute walk through the steamy jungle. Before you enter La Venta, you'll pass through a dismal zoo, the **Centro de Convivencia,** with small cages housing lonely animals. The yawning jaguars are as excited about being there as you are. When you buy your ticket, you'll also have the option of getting a ticket to the nearby **Museo de Historia Natural**; don't bother. Ruíz Cortínez, tel. 93/15–22–28. Take a TABASCO 2000 bus from Parque Juárez, get off at cnr of Paseo Tabasco and Ruíz Cortínez, and walk along lakeshore to entrance. Admission to zoo, La Venta, and museum: 75¢; buy tickets before 4 PM. Open Tues.–Sun. 9–5. Wheelchair access.

➤ **MUSEO REGIONAL DE ANTROPOLOGIA CARLOS PELLICER CAMARA** • This museum in the CICOM cultural center (*see below*) emphasizes Olmec influence on the cultures that succeeded them, particularly the Maya to the south and the Huasteca to the north. There are a few well-worn Olmec heads, altars, and stelae, and a number of pieces from as far away as Nayarit, Chihuahua, and the Yucatán. CICOM, Carlos Pellicer 511, tel. 93/12–18–03. Take any CICOM bus along Madero. Admission: $1. Open Tues.–Sun. 10–4.

➤ **MUSEUMS IN THE ZONA LUZ** • Near the budget lodgings are three museums, each worth a quick peek. The small, free **Casa-Museo Carlos Pellicer** (Saenz 203, tel. 93/12–01–57) has miscellanea that once belonged to this famous Tabascan poet who funded the excavation of La Venta and helped save its pieces from destruction. Be sure to check out the gruesome metal cast of his face taken at his death. The **Museo de Cultura Popular** (Zaragoza 810, tel. 93/12–11–17) has mannequins dressed in local costumes, as well as a collection of Tabasco's famous carved gourds. In the back is a dusty "typical" hut and a small pond with *pejelargarto* (alligator gar), large, toothy freshwater fish popular in regional dishes around Nacajuca. Admission is free here, too. The largest of these museums is the **Museo de Historia de Tabasco** (Juárez, at 27 de Febrero, tel. 93/12–49–96), whose displays chronicle the history of Tabasco from pre-Hispanic times through the modern industrial age. It houses mostly posters and illustrations, but there are also a few old books, colonial uniforms, and even an antique X-ray machine that once belonged to a Villahermosan doctor. The interior is covered with many beautiful tiles, hence its nickname *La Casa de Azulejos* (House of Tiles). Admission is 50¢. Sprinkled among the museums are art galleries and cultural centers (*see below*). All three museums are open Tuesday–Sunday 10–4.

CULTURAL CENTERS The numerous free cultural centers are a testimony to the fact that Tabasco's oil revenues were put to good use. Tabascans are quite proud about their region's devotion to the arts.

CICOM, The Center for the Investigation of Olmec and Maya Cultures, lies along the malecón, above the Río Grijalva. Of main interest is the Museo Regional de Antropología Carlos Pellicer Cámara (*see above*). Near the museum is the **Teatro Esperanza Iris**, a modern, plush, red-curtained center for national and regional events. Major events, such as performances by the National Ballet, tend to be jam-packed and cost $3–$7, although frequent lesser-known attractions—such as local dance and folk-music performances—are often free and usually only half full. The **CEIBA** arts center offers classes in music, dance, theater, and graphic arts. They also have a small gallery and poetry readings.

CICOM also houses the mammoth **public library** (open Mon.–Sat. 9–9), where you'll find an impressive collection of books in Spanish and English (look in the shelves upstairs and to the right for English). University students punch away at calculators downstairs, where there is also a cafeteria. On Sundays, free movies are shown three times a day in the auditorium to the left of the main library entrance. On weekdays, videos are shown at 7 PM. The bookshop here is also worth checking out. *Av. Carlos Pellicer, south of Paseo Tabasco. From Parque Juárez, take a* CICOM *bus. Open Tues.–Sun. 10–4.*

➤ **CENTRO CULTURAL DE LA UNIVERSIDAD AUTONOMA DE TABASCO** • Just steps away from the Zona Luz, this cultural center has two galleries showcasing local artists and sponsors a wide variety of events. There are free films Wednesday nights, and "cultural Thursdays" feature music, dance, or performing arts. Every couple of Saturdays they hold *paseos culturales* (cultural outings) to nearby towns and archaeological sites. Sign up in advance to be sure you'll get a spot. It usually costs $5–$7 for an all-day outing that includes transportation and a knowledgeable guide. *27 de Febrero 640, tel. 93/12–45–57. Open weekdays 8 AM–9 PM.*

➤ **CENTRO CULTURAL DE VILLAHERMOSA** • Across from the Zona Luz, this brand-new center has wonderful art exhibits from all over Mexico, foreign films, concerts, a shop dedicated to Tabasco's crafts, and a good café. All performances and exhibits are free. *Madero, at Zaragoza, tel. 93/14–55–52. Open Mon.–Sat. 10–9.*

ART GALLERIES

Calle Sáenz in the Zona Luz features two small art galleries. In an old house in the Zona Luz, the **Galería Tabasco** (Saenz 122, tel. 93/121–43–66; open Tues.–Sat. 3–8) features exhibits by local artists. Styles range from your basic still-life oil paintings to surreal dreamscapes. Just up the street (and open until 10 PM) is **Galería El Jaguar Despertado** (Saenz 117, tel. 93/14–12–44), a combination café, art gallery, and bookshop. Admission to both galleries is free.

YUMKA: CENTRO DE INTERPRETACION Y CONVIVENCIA CON LA NATURALEZA

The recently opened Yumká, the Mayan name for a magical dwarf who looks after the jungles, is a 250-acre ecological park featuring tropical rain forest, savanna, and a lagoon, each with all the corresponding flora and fauna. The two-hour guided quest ventures through rain forest by foot, savanna by open-air tram, and lagoon by raft—all, of course, in the most environmentally friendly manner. Yumká was set aside as a nature reserve in 1984, but not developed until 1992. The guides are professional biologists, gifted at instilling in visitors a deeper appreciation of (and hopefully a desire to preserve) the natural beauty and diversity of Tabasco. Dr. Luis Palazuelos, who oversees the operation, can provide further details for those interested. *Take a YUMKÁ bus from Las Blancas Mariposas restaurant, next to La Venta ($1.50). Admission: $5. Open daily 9–5.*

Yumká's brochures highlight the imported African animals that draw Tabascans into the park. But don't be fooled—this is no packaged wild-animal safari. The main focus of the park is actually the Tabascan rain forest and lagoon ecosystems, and the African animals act mainly to draw in local visitors, who might not otherwise come to see the amazing things living in their own backyard.

AFTER DARK

For a modern and apparently cosmopolitan city, Villahermosa goes to bed early. Around dinner (7-ish) is the prime time to be out and about, as this is when street bands entertain crowds, dancers fill the plazas, and old men gossip over heated games of dominoes. **Café Casino** (Juárez 531) and **Café Barra** (Lerdo de Tejada 608) both offer cappuccino, espresso, and the buzz of heated conversation. Come 9 PM, however, all grinds to a sudden halt. By 10, the Zona Luz is a virtual ghost town, with used napkins and empty cups rolling in the soft breeze. The cultural centers (*see above*) put on the occasional event, but if you're determined to party, you'll have to content yourself with one of the not-too-hopping bars or head to a ritzy disco elsewhere in town.

BARS For live Latin music, hit the bar in **Hotel Don Carlos** (Madero 518, tel. 93/12–24–99), just across from the Zona Luz. Bands start about 9:30 PM and keep swingin' until 1:30 in the morning. There's no cover, no minimum, and drink prices aren't too outrageous ($2 for a beer, $2.50 for a margarita). **Baccarat "Ladies Bar"** (Sánchez Marmol 410, across from Parque Juárez, tel. 93/14–17–50) is a small, upstairs place with soft lights, wood paneling, and velvet seats. Live, mellow jazz plays from 8 to 11 on weekend nights. Contrary to the name, most of the clientele seems to be single and male, but the atmosphere is relatively relaxing.

DANCING The young and trendy spend their weekend evenings at **Tequila Rock**, a modern, neon-lit extension of the Holiday Inn in Tabasco 2000 (tel. 93/16–44–00). **Ku Rock House** (Prolongación de Saudino 548, tel. 93/15–94–31) and **Snob** at the Hyatt Hotel (Juárez 106, tel. 93/13–44–44) are also popular. As of late, Snob has been putting on risqué shows, drawing a more red-blooded male clientele. Cover charges are stiff (usually $5–$10), but the action starts about 10 and lasts until 1 or 2 AM.

Near Villahermosa

COMALCALCO

One of the easternmost Maya sites, Comalcalco is best known for the fired brick with which all of its lasting edifices were constructed. Because the jungle in these whereabouts had no rock, the Chontal Maya who lived here made a mixture of clay, sand, and ground conch shell to form thin reddish bricks that were fired and used for 282 buildings covering an area of 10 square kilometers. The city was built in the 7th century, and its sloping roofs (suited to heavy rains) and stucco figures show evidence of the influence of Palenque.

Comalcalco has two major groups of buildings and many unexcavated grassy mounds. **Temple I**, the main pyramid, is on the large plaza. A flight of red-painted steps leads you up to the **Great Acropolis** and **Temples IV–VII**. Temple VI features a huge stucco mask representing the sun god. From the hill of the Acropolis, you can enjoy the cooling winds and a view of the emerald-green mounds and thick jungle canopy interrupted by cacao plantations. Since the temples at the site lack description, visit the **museum** first for a chronological breakdown of the site. The ticket window closes at 4 PM. Don't forget the insect repellent. *Admission to site and museum: $2.50, free on Sundays. Open daily 10–5.*

COMING AND GOING Buses to Comalcalco leave every half hour from **Transportes Somellera** in Villahermosa (*see* Coming and Going, *above*). The last buses for Villahermosa leave Comalcalco's main bus station, known as La Central/Comalcalco (Méndez 411, tel. 931/4–00–27), around 6 PM. From the Comalcalco station you can take a microbus (25¢) directly to the ruins or to the highway drop-off point for the ruins, a 1-kilometer walk away. Microbuses leave from the highway and Avenida Gregorio Méndez, across from the roundabout with the small brick pyramid in the center. Comalcalco has modest hotel and food offerings, but it's easier to commute from Villahermosa. Tabasco's coast is only 21 kilometers from the Comalcalco ruins; you can catch a bus marked PARAISO at the intersection of the highway and the road from the ruins.

THE TABASCAN COAST

Although once pristine, the '70s oil boom brought black death to some of the coastline. But whatever ecological destruction ultimately results from the drilling, right now the effects aren't readily apparent in certain places; the most visible uncleanliness stems from humans too lazy to pick up their trash. Few foreign travelers pass through, and—other than on weekends and during Semana Santa (Holy Week)—the beaches are often empty. There's generally not lodging here apart from palapas with hammock hooks, but most beaches are within day-trip distance of towns with hotels and restaurants, such as Villahermosa, Comalcalco, and Paraíso.

The beaches with the most facilities (showers, lockers, shaded restaurants and palapas) are **Limón** and **Laguna de Mecoacán/El Bellote**, both within a short bus ride of the medium-size city of **Paraíso**. Both have long stretches of white sand and pleasant shallow water with little waves. Palm tree-lined **Limón** has family-size cabañas that go for $20 (price doubles in April), lots of palapas, and a few restaurants offering grilled chicken. A better place to eat is in **El Bellote** at **Restaurante/Bar Viña del Mar,** which offers a never-ending list of tasty Atlantic-coast seafood dishes for under $6. Sometimes, a local Mexican jazz ensemble will accompany your dinner. Nearby, the staff at **La Posta** gives out information on boat rentals to beach spots along the Laguna Mecoacán (about $7 for a boat ride) and places to hang your hammock for $3 a night. Limón has endless stands of coconut trees, giving you a better chance to hang your hammock for free. Be sure to hit the beaches on a weekday or be prepared to share your retreat with the entire state of Tabasco.

Colectivos leave for the beaches fairly frequently from Paraíso's central bus station, about six blocks from the market. Colectivos also run between Paraíso and the beach near **Puerto Ceiba**, which is more deserted and a bit farther away. Second-class **Transportes La Somellera** buses run between Paraíso and Villahermosa (1½ hrs, $2.50), and microbuses make the trip from Comalcalco (15 min, 25¢).

TEAPA

Tabasco is not all oil fields and muggy wetlands. The air feels remarkably clean and fresh in the city of Teapa, just one hour's worth of banana fields from Villahermosa. The pretty **zócalo** is forested with enormous trees and houses a community library at one end, and the Río Teapa runs right through town. You can swim in the river here (the best spot is just off the main street as it approaches the zócalo on the way into town) or take excursions out of town for a cooling swim, a healing sulfur bath, or some subterranean exploration.

The Puyacatengo river in **Tacotalpa**, a short bus ride away, has rapids and is a popular place to play among locals. You can also camp here; there are no real facilities, but you're safe if you're not alone. A 6-kilometer bus ride toward the town of Pichucalco and a $2 entrance fee will buy you almost unlimited hedonism at **El Azufre Spa**, where the clean pool and bubbling sulfur spring are known for their healing properties. Once you've paid the entrance fee, you're free to store your stuff in the administration office and camp on the soft green lawns of the gorgeous valley for free as long as you like, enjoying use of the pools, palapas, and picnic tables. If you'd rather have a room, the adjoining **Hotel Azufre** rents huge ones with fans and bathrooms for $10 (double) and $21 (triple). The kicker is that the hammock hooks in the double cabañas mean they sleep up to eight people for the same price.

If you prefer something a bit less lazy, you can tromp around inside the **Grutas de Coconá**, a set of spectacular caves out in the country. A bus marked MULTIGRUTAS leaves for the caves every half-hour or so from the side of the church in Teapa. To walk here, go down Méndez to the Pemex station and turn right onto Avenida Carlos Madrazo—a green sign alerts you—and follow the road about 2 kilometers until it turns to countryside; you'll find the grutas shortly thereafter. Once here, pay the 50¢ fee and enter the still darkness, where you'll hear only the squeaking of tiny bats and the dripping of water. The caves may not be lighted, so bring a flashlight and see if you can make out the figures of King Kong and his family, a giant peanut, a cow's tongue, a headless chicken, and, of course, Jesus Christ in the rocks. Be careful about going late in the afternoon, as robberies have been known to occur. The caves are open daily 10–4.

COMING AND GOING Autotransportes Villahermosa Teapa (Méndez 218, tel. 932/2–00–07) has hourly buses to Villahermosa ($2 1st class, $1 2nd class) between 5 AM and 5:30 PM. The station can be hard to find—look for a small square with a giant tree in the middle, and lots of maroon taxis parked outside; it's about 5 blocks from the zócalo where the island in the middle of the main road begins. Arrive early, as buses fill quickly.

Those headed farther afield can take advantage of the Córdoba–Mérida **train** that passes through town. The station (Ignacio Zaragoza, end of the main drag, tel. 932/2–01–65) is a 20-minute walk from the zócalo. If you're headed for Veracruz (18 hrs, $5.50) or Mexico City, you'll have to take the train to Córdoba (16 hrs, $7), which generally leaves between 6 AM and 8 AM, and transfer there. The train leaves for Mérida (14 hrs, $8) every day between 7 PM and 11 PM, passing Palenque (2 hrs, $1.50), Tenosique (4 hrs, $2), and Campeche (10 hrs, $5) on the way. In this direction, however, the trains are infamously dangerous and slow.

GETTING AROUND Teapa has one main street that stretches from the train station (about a km from center) to the zócalo. It begins as 21 de Marzo, changes to Carlos Ramos at the Pemex station, and changes again to Gregorio Méndez as it approaches the zócalo. Many of the city's side streets are pedestrian walkways, and the town is definitely manageable on foot. Buses and colectivos to the grutas and other attractions leave from the zócalo and from the lime-green clock on the outskirts of town.

WHERE TO SLEEP In addition to the places listed below, you can camp around Teapa if you keep a low profile. No formal camping facilities exist, but the area along the river is rife with opportunity. Plus, there's always **El Azufre Spa** (*see above*) just a few kilometers away. The worst hazard you're likely to face is mosquitoes. Plant-strewn hallways make up for small rooms at **Casa de Huéspedes Miye** (Méndez 211, 2 blocks from the zócalo, tel. 932/2–04–20). Singles with communal baths are $5, doubles $6; rooms with private baths for one or two are $12. There's no hot water, but you probably won't need it anyway. Pastel rooms and a lobby filled with porcelain animals make the wheelchair-accessible **Hotel Jardín** (Plaza Independencia 123, tel. 932/2–00–27) unique. The airy rooms with bath (cold water) overlooking the patio are $5 for singles, $8.50 for doubles.

FOOD Food establishments in Teapa tend to be either greasy or expensive. It's better to stick to the 60¢ sandwiches from any of the many hole-in-the-wall restaurants like **Café y Antojitos Queta** (across from Casa de Huéspedes Miye), rather than test your digestive system exploring more ambitious fare. **Restaurant El Jacalito** and **El Mirador** are both rather expensive for mediocre food. Another safe option is the market, right across from the lime-green clock.

THE YUCATÁN PENINSULA   14

By Lean Sweeney

At the heart of the ancient Maya city of Chichén Itzá stands El Castillo, a soaring 27-meter pyramid honoring the god Kukulcan. Every year at the spring and autumn equinoxes, the sun casts a shadow on the temple that makes it appear as if the serpent god is slithering down the pyramid to the city's sacred well. In its way, this monument of astrological precision embodies everything that attracts visitors to the Yucatán today: the ingenuity of the ancient Maya, whose ruined cities dot the peninsula, and an emphasis on the sun that manifests itself today in the form of pale gringos immolating themselves on the beaches of Cozumel, Cancún, Playa del Carmen, and Isla Mujeres.

Kukulcan is the Mayan name for Quetzalcoatl, the feathered serpent god of the Toltec (and Aztec) pantheons. Evidence that Kukulcan took on added importance after Toltec incursions into the Yucatán is found in architecture of the post-classic period, most prominently at Chichén Itzá.

Encompassing the states of Yucatán, Campeche, Quintana Roo, Belize, and part of Guatemala, the Yucatán Peninsula covers 113,000 square kilometers. Much of the peninsula is vast, scrubby desert covering porous limestone ("one living rock," as an early Spanish priest put it) with a smattering of *cenotes* (spring-fed water holes), jungles, and telltale mounds hiding unexcavated ruins. Many Mayan families still live in the surrounding jungle, though the ruins themselves are excavated and their history most often told by outsiders from Mérida or Mexico City. The Yucatán's eastern coastline has everything you could ask for—clear Caribbean waters, a tropical climate, unbroken stretches of beach, and stunning coral reefs. Although much of this land is being sold to foreign resort developers or government-owned tourism agencies (causing nearby families to rely more heavily on the tourist trade for their survival), so far only Cancún has been transformed into an obscene tourist complex. Isla Mujeres, Playa del Carmen, and Tulum remain laid-back havens for budget travelers, and some of the most beautiful beaches along the coast are still undeveloped.

Often overlooked in the sprint for the beaches, though, are the towns of the Yucatán. The peninsula was one of the first areas of the New World to be settled by the Spanish, and the legacy of the colonists lives on in towns such as Mérida and Campeche. Huge baroque churches, old mansions, and winding cobbled streets give these towns a distinctly European look, albeit softened by age and tropical heat.

But most visitors to the Yucatán are attracted by the Maya ruins, ancient cities dating back as much as 4,000 years. Hundreds of Maya sites dot the Yucatán, only a handful of which have been excavated. Chichén Itzá is the best known; other major ruin sites are Uxmal, near Mérida, and Cobá, within easy reach of Caribbean beaches. If you're prepared to forgo the most famous

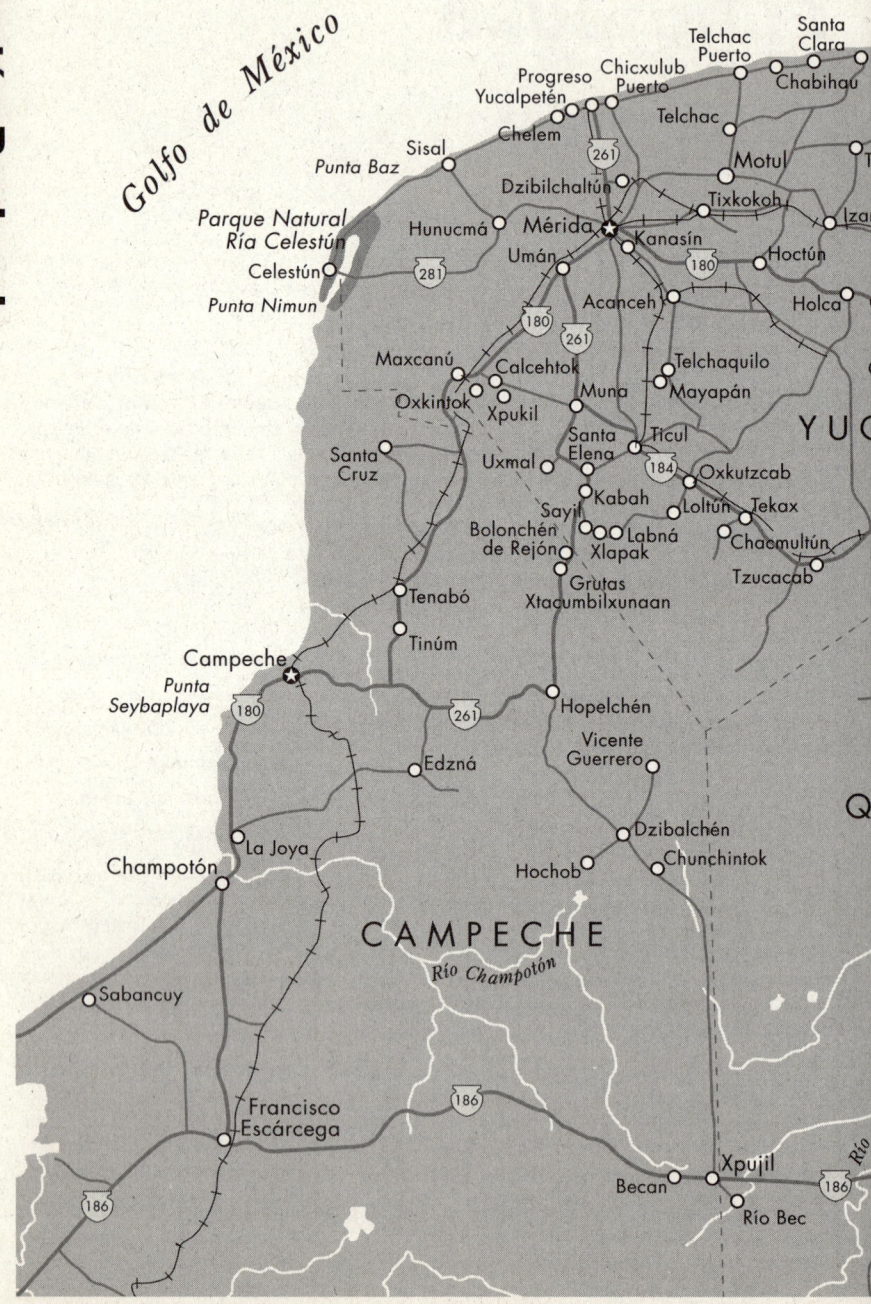

The Yucatán Peninsula

Maya ruins in favor of less spectacular or unexcavated sites, you can wander through entire cities with no company but the jungle and the iguanas.

The Maya cities now lie in ruins, but the Maya people and their culture are very much alive, despite the best efforts of the early Spanish colonists. Indeed, traveling into the Yucatán from elsewhere in Mexico is like entering another country. The people are visibly different. Most of the population is mestizo (mixed Maya and Spanish blood), and a fair amount are pure Maya, identifiable by their broad faces, dark skin, and short stature. Mayan, not Spanish, is the predominant language in many country towns and villages.

Christianity for many *Yucatecos* (Yucatecans) is a mix of Catholicism and traditional animism, a belief that the sun, the earth, the plants, the animals, and the rain are gods. This melding of the ancient and the new is actually the result of a particularly bloody and cruel period of colonization. Since Hernan Cortés's landing on the shores of the Yucatán in 1519, the Maya have battled for their land and their freedom. The Spanish burned religious texts, including astronomical works, and destroyed stone idols. Disease and forced labor decimated the Maya population, but the Spanish never really succeeded in breaking their resistance. In the 1840s, after losing much of their lands, the Maya captured much of the peninsula during the War of the Castes, but they failed to follow through and take the principal city, Mérida. The inevitable retaliation of the *hacendados* (landowners) resulted in the extermination of nearly half the Maya. Not until 1935, when the Chan Santa Cruz people signed an accord with the government, did the fighting cease.

Here, as in much of Mexico, poverty is the enemy, aggravated by the peninsula's thin, parched topsoil. Increasingly, Yucatecos are turning away from agriculture to more lucrative jobs in the oil industry, tourism, and at fish-processing plants. After oil, tourism is now the second-biggest industry here. Development continues apace, particularly along the Caribbean coast—a boon to the local economy and a scourge for those travelers who jealously protect their quiet tropical retreats.

Campeche

Surrounded by jungle, caves, and small Mayan towns such as Becal, Kobén, Edzná and Holpechén, Campeche's lofty Catholic churches and cannon-laden forts stand like slowly disintegrating monuments to its long-forgotten past. It was through Campeche that Mexico's gold and silver were shipped to Spain during the 16th and 17th centuries, making it the target of raids by Dutch and English pirates, who preyed continually on the city and its ships. A brutal pirate attack in 1663 resulted in the massacre of almost the entire population of Campeche, spurring the construction of the forts that make Campeche one of the few walled cities in the Americas. Today, Campeche is all business, holding fast to the 9–5 workday and the daily transport of goods from nearby towns to be sold in the main market. Still, Campeche's fortified churches, Moorish arches, and narrow streets, along with its refusal to succumb to blatant tourism, makes the city a pleasant respite from the commercialism of Mérida, Cancún, and the Caribbean resorts.

To become a policeman in Campeche, candidates need only show proof of a high school education and fill out an application; there is no training involved. Locals complain that officers aren't even given driving tests.

BASICS

AMERICAN EXPRESS Cardholders can pick up mail and everyone can replace lost traveler's checks at the AmEx office run by the travel agency **Viajes Programados**. Unfortunately, you can't change money or cash personal checks here. *Prolongación Calle 59, Edificio Belmar, Apartado Postal 82, Campeche, Campeche, CP 24000, México, tel. 981/1–10–10. Open weekdays 9–1:30, Sat. 9–2.*

CASAS DE CAMBIO Bancomer (16 de Septiembre 120, tel. 981/6–66–22) changes money weekdays 8–2. On weekends, your only exchange option is the **Ramada Inn** (Ruíz Cortínez 51, tel. 981/6–22–33). The ATMs at **Banamex** (cnr of Calles 10 and 53, tel. 981/6–06–29) accept Visa, MaterCard, and Plus.

EMERGENCIES The **police** station is open 24 hours a day. *Calle 12, btw Calles 57 and 59, tel. 981/6-21-11.*

MEDICAL AID You can walk into the **IMSS** (López Mateos, at Baluartes, tel. 981/6-52-02 or 981/6-18-55) for 24-hour emergency service. For minor medical needs, try **Farmacia Canto** (Calle 10, at Calle 55, tel. 981/6-52-48), open Monday–Saturday 8–2 and 5–9, Sunday 9–1.

PHONES AND MAIL There are very few coin-operated phones in Campeche; try the main bus terminal on Gobernadores or the public library (Calle 12, btw Calles 61 and 63). Buy Latadel cards at **Tel Mex** (Calle 10, btw Calles 61 and 63; open weekdays 8–1:30). **Computel** (Calle 8 No. 255, fax 981/1-01-29; open daily 7 AM–10 PM) lets you place international collect calls. The **Oficina de Correos** is the joint post/telephone office, offering fax, long-distance phone, telex, and mail services. They'll hold mail sent to you at the following address for up to 10 days: Lista de Correos, Oficina Urbana 1, Campeche, Campeche, CP 24000, México. *16 de Septiembre, 2 blocks east of Parque Principal, tel. 981/6-21-34. Open weekdays 8–8, Sat. 8–1.*

VISITOR INFORMATION For information about the city's churches, museums, and upcoming public events, ask the ticket man at the **Puerta de Tierra** (*see* Worth Seeing, *below*). The friendly and enthusiastic staff at the **state tourist office** does little more than hand you a couple of free but illegible city maps and grin. *Calle 14, at Circuito Baluartes Sur, tel. 981/6-67-67. Open weekdays 8–3.*

COMING AND GOING

BY BUS The main terminal is on Gobernadores, about a kilometer north from Parque Principal, just outside the city walls. It's composed of two adjoining stations, one offering second-class service, the other supplying only first-class buses. **Autobuses del Oriente (ADO)** (tel. 981/6-28-02), the principal first-class carrier, offers daily trips to Mérida (2½ hrs, $5), Mexico City (18 hrs, $44), and Veracruz (14 hrs, $26). You can store luggage here for 50¢ a day, and the station is open 24 hours. The dusty and dilapidated second-class bus station (tel. 981/6-23-32) is open only until 7 PM; from here you can catch frequent buses to Hopelchén (1½ hrs, $1.50), Bolonchén (2 hrs, $2.25), and Dzibalchén (2 hrs, $2.25). Five daily buses also leave for Iturbide (3 hrs, $2.50), Escárcega (3 hrs, $2.75), Uxmal (2½ hrs, $3), Santa Elena (3 hrs, $3.25), and Mérida (4 hrs, $4.50). To reach town from the ADO terminal, turn left onto Gobernadores; the first fort you reach marks the beginning of the old town. Otherwise, catch a bus across the street and ask to be left near the Parque Principal.

BY TRAIN Train travel in the Yucatán is fairly grim. Even though theft has diminished since trains were installed with lighting, second-class service is notoriously unsafe. There is service to Mexico City (2 days, $15) at 11 PM, and Mérida (6 hrs, $3) at 5 PM. *Héroes de Nacozari, 3 km from downtown, tel. 981/6-51-48. Take CHINA bus, which runs frequently between train station and market.*

BY PLANE **Aeroméxico** (tel. 981/6-66-56) has flights from Campeche's small airport to cities all over the country, most with a stopover in Mexico City (about $108). The airport, about 10 kilometers southeast of downtown, is accessible only by taxi ($5).

GETTING AROUND

Virtually everything of interest lies inside the walls of the *villa vieja* (old city) and is easily accessible by foot. Even-numbered streets run parallel to the waterfront, and odd-numbered streets run perpendicular. All buses stop at the **mercado** and at the **Palacio de Gobierno** (Malecón, at Calle 61) and run from 5 AM to 11 PM. The fare is about 35¢.

BY CAR The only car rental place around is **Hertz**, where you have to be 21 and hold a credit card. They charge $50 per day including unlimited mileage and insurance, or $19 per day and about 15¢ per kilometer without insurance. Be prepared to show your license and passport. *Hotel Baluartes, Ruíz Cortínez, at Calle 61, tel. 981/6-39-11. Open Mon.–Sat. 8–1 and 4–7.*

WHERE TO SLEEP

Hotels in Campeche tend to be packed with businesspeople rather than tourists. If you arrive at the bus station in the wee hours, you're better off paying the cab fare (about $1.75) to any of the following hotels (all located in the old city) rather than staying in one of the noisy, overpriced holes near the station.

➤ **UNDER $10** • **Hotel Campeche.** This rambling colonial mansion was a single-family home during the colonial era, and the wide stairways and shoulder-height doorways are a holdover from this time. Slightly dilapidated rooms are equipped with sturdy beds, some with windows overlooking the park. Singles $6.75, doubles $8.25. *Calle 59 No. 2, tel. 981/24–92–55. 42 rooms, all with bath. Luggage storage.*

Hotel Castelmar. A friendly family keeps the gigantic rooms in this airy, colonial-style hotel fairly clean. Some have balconies with sea views, while others face onto a noisy street. The beds must have made good trampolines once, because they're uncomfortable now. Slightly dingy bathrooms are separated from the rooms by curtains and don't afford much privacy. Singles and doubles cost $7.50. *Calle 61 No. 2, btw Calles 8 and 10, tel. 981/6–28–86. 18 rooms, all with bath. Luggage storage. Reservations advised July–Sept.*

➤ **UNDER $15** • **Hotel Colonial.** This beautifully tiled, chandelier-adorned hotel has a shady, rocking-chair equipped rooftop patio, as well as a pleasant, palm-fringed inner courtyard. At $10.25 a single, $11.50 for a double, the sparkling-clean rooms get snatched up pretty quickly, especially during July and August. Reservations are accepted until 7 PM. *Calle 14 No. 122, btw Calles 55 and 57, tel. 981/6–22–22. 30 rooms, all with bath. Luggage storage.*

Hotel López. This hotel's designers must have been obsessed with cruise ships. It's built around a rectangular courtyard, above which rise two stories of portholes and wildly curving balconies. The rooms (singles and doubles $13.25, $17 with air-conditioning) are not so exciting. Not all bathrooms are entirely functional, but you can enjoy your bedside TV at all hours. *Calle 12, btw Calles 61 and 63, tel. 981/6–33–44. 39 rooms, all with bath. Luggage storage, restaurant. Wheelchair access.*

HOSTELS **Villa Deportiva de Campeche.** Like most hostels, this place is dirt cheap ($1.75 a night, plus $1 deposit). At first glance it appears to be perfectly clean and functional, but—surprise!—the only rooms with fans belong to the administrators, water subsides to a trickle during prime shower hours, and bug spray is a must. Don't bother with the meals here—you'll get much better food for the same price downtown. *Agustín Melgar, tel. 981/6–18–02. From ADO station take* DIRECTO/UNIVERSIDAD *bus (25¢); ask driver to let you off close to hostel. 76 beds. Curfew 11 PM. Meal service. Wheelchair access.*

FOOD

Campeche's seafood has a well-deserved reputation throughout Mexico. Local specialties include *pan de cazón* (finely shredded baby shark layered with tortillas, beans, fresh tomato purée, and avocado) and *camarón chiquito* (an ultra-small shrimp). Many of the city's better restaurants, as well as a handful of small sandwich shops, line Calle 8 across from the Parque Principal. If you're pinching pennies, go to the huge, frenzied market on Gobernadores just outside the city wall, open daily 5 AM–3 PM. Here you can buy luscious regional fruits such as pitaya and mamey (a red kiwi-like fruit), as well as *panuchos* (fried tortilla filled with beans and topped with chicken), tacos, and tamales for less than 25¢.

➤ **UNDER $5** • **Lonchería Miau.** This corner restaurant is about as hip as Campeche gets. Popular rock tunes from the kitchen's battered radio blend with the sizzle of beef and eggs on the hot iron grill. Fifty cents will buy you a taco, quesadilla, or tostada, and you can wash it all down with a cool glass of horchata (20¢). Their extensive array of sandwiches includes a thick mushroom *torta* oozing with melted cheese ($1). *Cnr of Calle 16 and 59, no phone. Open daily 9 AM–10 PM.*

Restaurant La Parroquia. A great place to hang out and listen to old men gossip, La Parroquia features a huge menu, daily specials, and low prices. The truly penniless sate themselves with a rice and fried plantain combo for only 75¢, or indulge in a generously stuffed *torta de camarón* (french bread sandwiches stuffed with chunky shrimp salad) for $3. A fluffy pile of pancakes with hot honey and syrup ($1) can be ordered round the clock. For refreshment, try *Jamaica*, a juice made from the iced pulp of a boiled hibiscus flower (50¢). *Calle 5 No. 8, 1 block west of Parque Principal, tel. 981/6–80–86.*

La Perla. Whirring fans and the constant buzz of the TV keep locals pinned to their tables after a filling meal of shrimp or conch with rice ($1.50). Also good is the fish *filete* (filet) stuffed with shrimp and shellfish ($2.75). You can get any number of alcoholic beverages, including beer (75¢) and tequila (65¢). *Calle 10, btw Calles 57 and 59, in same building as Lonchería Colón, tel. 981/6–40–92. Open Mon.–Sat. 7 AM–11 PM, Sun 10–6.*

La Uva. This salt-soaked seaside eatery is a great place to relax with an ice-cold *chelada* (beer mixed with lemon juice and salt) while enjoying pan de cazón ($3) and filete ($4). Guitarists belting not-so-soothing ballads make for difficult conversation, but nobody here minds if you shout. *Calle 20, no phone. Take* LERMA *bus from in front of Hotel Baluartes on 16 de Septiembre; get off just after turnoff for Puerta de San Miguel (20 min). Open daily 10–6.*

➤ **UNDER $10** • **Marganzo.** For occasional live music and truly fabulous regional dishes served by suave waiters in festive costumes, count your pesos and head for Marganzo. Seafood specialties range from $4.25 to $6.50, but the delicious shrimp or crab salads are only $3.75. Pan de cazón ($3.25), the regional specialty, is outstanding. *Calle 8 No. 268, tel. 981/1–38–99. Open daily 7 AM–10 PM.*

WORTH SEEING

A walk through Campeche is like a trip through the military and commercial history of the Spanish colonies. Forts that protected the city from marauding pirates still stand, as do centuries-old churches and homes. Newly restored museums have attracted newly found artifacts from the nearby ruins of Edzná and Calaknul. Most of the interesting colonial buildings in Campeche are within the old city, and all are easily accessible on foot.

On weekends, locals head south to **Playa Bonita,** just past the Campeche/Lerma border. The water here may be dark with seaweed, but after a few games of volleyball in the hot sand, most people jump in without a thought. To get here, take the bus (25 min, 75¢) from in front of Hotel Baluartes.

CIRCUITO DE BALUARTES Five years after much of the city was wiped out by pirates in 1663, the first stones of a new defense system were laid. The fortifications consisted of a 10-foot-thick wall running around the city, protected by seven *baluartes* (forts). Even ships had to pass through the four gates that controlled access to the city. The construction took more than 35 years, but effectively ended Campeche's role as the Yucatán's 98-pound weakling. Today, it's possible to follow the Circuito de Baluartes around the various forts, many of which are government buildings.

The best place to start a tour of the city's forts is at the **Puerta de Tierra,** the arched entrance to the city about 2 blocks south of the market. Just north of here stands the **Baluarte de San Francisco** (Calle 18, at Calle 57), an excellently restored blockhouse now containing a small cobwebbed library (open weekdays 8–2 and 4–6, Sun. 8–noon; admission free) whose caretaker is often asleep or unwilling to answer the door (if you peek in the west window you can usually get his attention). Continuing northwest toward the market, you'll find the **Baluarte de San Pedro** (Calle 51, at Gobernadores), an impressive stone tower crammed onto a little island of pavement surrounded by city traffic. The fort's tiny eastside park has become a choice site for political protests. Official hours are weekdays 9–1 and 5–8, Saturday 9–1, but they fluctuate during restoration. Across the street from San Pedro is **Iglesia de San Juan.** Built in 1675, the church still has its original stone exterior. White flowers adorn the altar, and birds fly freely through the church. Probably the most interesting of the surrounding forts is the **Baluarte de Santiago,** in the northern corner of the city (Calle 8, at Calle 49), demolished at the end of the last century and reconstructed in the 1950s. Today it houses the beautiful **Jardín**

Botánico (botanical garden), where you can check out the region's lush flora. *Calle 8, at Calle 49. Admission: $1. Open Tues.–Fri. 8–2, Sat. 9–1 and 4–8, Sun. 9–1.*

The other relic of the old city wall is the **Baluarte de San Carlos** (Calle 8, at Calle 65), on Campeche's east side. The city's first fort, completed in 1676, the baluarte is now the site of the **Museo de la Ciudad,** a collection of photos, maps, and models illustrating Campeche's history. The real attraction however is the fort itself: Standing in the turrets, you can imagine yourself fending off pirates and other vermin. Admission is free, and the museum is open Tuesday–Saturday 8–8, Sunday 8–1. Farther along Calle 8 stands the **Baluarte de la Soledad,** now a three-room museum featuring some 30 Maya stelae (carved stone slabs), mostly from the ruins of Cayal, Acannuíl, and Xcalumkin.

Most impressive of all the forts is the **Fuerte de San Miguel.** Located at the city's highest point, San Miguel is surrounded by a moat, and the cannon-ringed rooftop offers an extensive view of Campeche's shoreline ports. Several galleries on the fort's ground level display artifacts from the ever-growing number of archaeological sites being discovered. *Take LERMA bus from in front of Hotel Baluartes or the market (about 10 min). Fort admission: $2.25, 50¢ Sun. Open Tues.–Sun. 8–8.*

CHURCHES Facing the **zócalo** (main plaza), the beautiful **Catedral de la Concepción** dates from the 18th century. Inside, note the illustrations of the Stations of the Cross, and the small but brilliant stained-glass windows under the cupola at the front of the church. Other beautiful churches in the old city include the **Iglesia de San Franciscuito** (Calle 12, btw Calles 59 and 61), which dates from the 18th century. The **Iglesia de Jesús El Nazareno** (Calle 55, at Calle 12) features dramatic, elaborate icons on ostentatious altars. The churches are open weekdays 9–noon, Saturday 5–7, and all day Sunday.

MUSEO REGIONAL DE CAMPECHE Campeche has consolidated its most important historical pieces in the former mansion of the royal governor. Pre-Conquest artifacts on the first floor include the skull of a child whose head had been flattened with boards, thought to be a mark of beauty. Some of the small statues from the classical period are quite detailed and marvelously preserved. Low-relief stelae and jade-work complete the collection. Spanish artifacts include a full-size cabriolet and the usual assortment of swords, guns, and armor. *Calle 59, btw Calles 14 and 16, tel. 981/6–91–11. Admission: $2.50, 50¢ Sun. Open Tues.–Sun. 8–8.*

AFTER DARK

Like most cities on the peninsula, Campeche goes to sleep early. On weekends the **malecón** (boardwalk) is the happening place to be—it's perfectly safe to cruise the well-lit walk until around midnight, when people head indoors. Commonly acknowledged as the hippest disco in town, **Atlantis** (Ruíz Cortínez 51, in the Ramada Inn) is frequented by well-off locals and tourists staying at the expensive waterfront hotels. Usually just men get slapped with the $3 cover. **Mazehual** (Av. Gobernadores), a vast, palapa-covered beer hall, features live funked-out '50s tunes sung by satin-bedecked soloists striding around in sparkling 10-inch heels. The

Boats for Bail

Among some of Campeche's most famous handicrafts are the intricate model boats designed by inmates of the nearby prison of Kobén. Government-supplied lathes and saws enable prisoners to produce beautifully detailed models, which they sell to individual buyers from Campeche or Kobén. Visitors aren't allowed in the prison, but those eager to get first dibs can take a Kobén-bound bus from Campeche's main market to the highway alongside the prison. Here individual vendors display the carefully varnished wares for about ¾ of the price found in Campeche's downtown.

singing ends abruptly at 8, when the transvestite cabaret show begins. There's no cover and beers are only $1, but the place empties out by 10. It's a 20-minute taxi ride ($3) to **La Ceiba** (Resurgimiento 393, 10 km from Parque Principal, tel. 981/1-38-09), which has live music 6 PM–2 AM and hosts Cuban dance shows at 7 and 10 for a $2.50 fee. Beers are only $1, and you're welcome to join in the dancing. The light show at **Puerta de Tierra** (Gobernadores, toward old city from main bus station) rehashes Campeche's history of pirate invasions. The spectacle is performed by local musicians and dancers at 8 PM on Fridays. The performance, offered in Spanish and shaky English and French, costs $2 ($1 students). Or if you're penniless, there's free *música romántica* in the Parque Principal on Thursday and Sunday nights, usually starting around 8 PM.

Near Campeche

EDZNA

Slightly less accessible than the more popular archaeological sites, Edzná is a virtual junglegym of hills, tunnels, and tumbling stairways. Evidence suggests that this large site 60 kilometers southeast of Campeche may have been settled as early as 600 BC, but the city thrived during the late Classic Period, from AD 600 to 900. The beauty here lies in the overall building scheme rather than in ornamentation. Later styles of architecture (as seen at Uxmal, for example) may be more elaborate, but according to some they signal the decline of the Mayan unity and autonomy that produced grand achievements in science and art. The classic style is also characterized by the superb stelae found all over Edzná. Many of these are still on the premises, although they have been moved to a roped-in, palapa-covered gallery outside the ruins.

Edzná's main attraction is the **Temple of Five Stories**, an example of early Puuc architecture situated on the Plaza Central. The temple on the top story is capped with a 7-meter roof comb, once decorated with a mask of Chaac that seemed to change expression as the sun rose and fell. The mask is believed to be the origin of the name Edzná, meaning House of the Expressions. Edzná can also be translated as House of Echoes, probably referring to the amazing acoustics among the principal buildings—standing in the doorway at the top of the pyramid, you can hear the voice of someone at the far end of the **Gran Acrópolis**. Several other excellently restored buildings cluster around the Gran Acrópolis, including the **House of the Moon**, the **Temazcal** (sweat house), and three additional structures. On the first day of the Maya year, the sun reaches its zenith over Edzná, leading to speculation that the amazingly accurate Maya calendar was devised here. Vicious mosquitoes breed in surrounding swamps and stagnant water holes, so bring repellent. Don't worry about the skittering iguanas—they may be the size of small cats, but they're harmless. *Admission: $2.25, free Sun. and holidays. Open daily 8–5.*

COMING AND GOING Servicios Turísticos Picazh (Calle 16 No. 348, tel. 981/6-44-26) in Campeche has organized tours departing from the Puerta de Tierra (Calle 59, at Gobernadores) at 9 AM and 2 PM. Cost is about $10 per person, or $17 including lunch, guided tour, and admission. A cheaper way to get here is to take the **Camioneros de Campeche** bus, which runs about every hour from behind the ADO station, to Hopelchén and ask to be let off at Cayal (40 min, $1). From the crossroads at Cayal, you can try hitching the 19 kilometers to the ruins—this isn't impossible, but 20 minutes of waiting can seem like an eon on a hot day. An excellent alternative is the direct bus to Edzná, which leaves daily from Gobernadores in Campeche (1 block up from Pemex station) between 7 and 7:30 AM and between 11:30 AM and noon. The old white-and-blue bus is marked PICH, and fare is about $2. On the return trip, only one bus passes the ruins (at about 3 PM); if you go on a Sunday, it will probably be packed with Jehovah's Witnesses on their way to church. Otherwise, it's easy to hitch or flag down a Camioneros de Campeche bus at the crossroads; the last bus bound for Campeche passes Cayal around 5 PM.

CHENES RUINS/XTACUMBILXUNAAN

Any comprehensive tour of Maya archaeology in the region should include the Chenes ruins. The sites aren't included in most package itineraries, which is a bonus if you're tired of dodging tour buses. The remote ruins at Hochob and El Tabasqueño are rarely visited, in part because reaching them is tough, even if you have a car. Those who persevere will discover that their solitude is interrupted only by the occasional animal. Hochob displays one of the purest styles of Chenes architecture, which is characterized by elaborate decoration. Naturally ornate and more accessible than the ruins are the Xtacumbilxunaan caves, lying just off Highway 261. **Servicios Turísticos Picazh** (Calle 16 No. 348, Campeche, tel. 981/6-44-26) arranges pricey trips there.

COMING AND GOING It's virtually impossible to make the bus odyssey to any of the Chenes ruins and return to Campeche in one day. It's best to stay the night in Hopelchén, and leave early in the morning for the ruins. Starting at 8 AM, six buses leave Campeche daily for Hopelchén ($1.50), 53 kilometers east of Campeche, before continuing on to Mérida. From the south side of the park in Hopelchén, catch a bus 41 kilometers south to Dzibalchén, which serves as the crossroads to the ruins. Buses to Dzibalchén run every 2 hours from 9 to 9, and cost $1. A pickup truck also carries passengers from the park in Hopelchén to Dzibalchén and Iturbide ($1), about 15 kilometers farther south, three times a day. The last bus back to Hopelchén ($1) leaves Iturbide at 5 PM, passing through Dzibalchén at about 5:30 PM. To reach Mérida from Hopelchén, wait for the bus (3 hrs, $3.25) on the park's south side (in front of the pharmacy), a half block from the town's sole hotel, where you can inquire about bus schedules. Campeche-bound buses leave from the west side of the park, opposite the hotel.

WHERE TO SLEEP AND EAT The only hotel in the area is **Los Arcos** (Calle 20, at Calle 23, tel. 981/2-00-37) in Hopelchén, which offers huge, sunny rooms and clean bathrooms with hot water ($6 singles, $6.75 doubles, $8.75 triples). Several open-air loncherías (snack bars) line the avenue between the church and Los Arcos (next to the taxi stand), where you can eat like a king (two fat tamales and a Coke) for less than $1. If you're left high and dry at any of the sites, you can pitch a tent or string a hammock, but the mosquitoes will drive you stark raving mad.

WORTH SEEING

➤ **DZIBILNOCAC** • Among the scattered dirt mounds hidden in the thick vegetation are two buildings which, until a few years ago, were unrecognizable. Recently, however, the western pyramid has been excavated and reconstructed and now stands in almost perfect condition. Masks of Chaac cover the uppermost temple, and the curled pattern of his nose is repeated in relief on all sides. A neighboring structure, as yet unrestored, houses the remains of beautiful red-and-green frescoes. Don't mistake the primitive-looking black graffiti in one of the chambers for ancient cave painting—it's more contemporary. Admission to the ruins is about $1.75, and the place closes by 4:30. To reach Dzibilnocac, walk 1 kilometer west of Iturbide on the dirt road leading out of town.

➤ **HOCHOB** • Reaching this site deep within the rain forest is not easy, but Hochob's appeal lies in its splendid isolation. There is little to suggest that you aren't the true discoverer of a long-lost civilization, a sensation that is heightened if you camp overnight. Only the central plaza has been excavated, but countless other buildings lie unexplored under the thick vegetation. The main building is the **Temple of Chaac,** a rectangular building 40 meters long and 7 meters high. Look carefully at the facade to see a giant image of Chaac: The motifs on the lintel above the entrance to the temple are his eyes, and the open door represents his mouth.

Getting to Hochob is difficult, even if you have your own car. There is no public transport, so your only option is to walk or bike the 13 kilometers from Dzibalchén. Take the Campeche road

The Mennonites of Hopelchén

Hopelchén is home to a community of tall, blue-eyed people who look like they just stepped off the set of Little House on the Prairie. As their overalls, boots, and utility shirts might suggest, they're farmers—very good ones, as townspeople will tell you. Weekdays, a metallic-sounding bell signals the arrival of vendors selling the Mennonites' delicious skimmed milk cheese in both Campeche and the outskirts of Kobén.

north for 1 kilometer, then turn left onto a dirt road leading to the tiny village of Chencoh. The 8 or so kilometers to Chencoh are clay, sand and rock—not ideal for traversing on a bike. They trek is even worse if it's raining—bicycles (and cars) will slowly grind to a stop after 25 pounds of instant pottery has glommed onto the tires.

When you reach Chencoh, turn left again and head another 4 kilometers into the rain forest. José William Chan (tel. 981/2-01–06), the self-appointed guide and bushwhacker in Dzibalchén, rents bikes for $3.25, and he is more than happy to show you the way as well; his services cost $8–$10, depending on the number of people and your means. If you miss the last bus out of Dzibalchén at 5:30 PM, José and his family sometimes allow visitors to spend the night in hammocks in their back room. Bring your mosquito repellent and anticipate a pre-dawn wake-up call from roosters, insects, and birds. To find José, walk straight out of town on the road to Iturbide. You can't miss his large signs reading TOURIST INFORMATION.

Avoid visiting Hochob on a bicycle during the rainy season (June–August); gallons of water pour down, and rattlesnakes come out of their holes to avoid drowning. Also don't go alone—if you fall down one of the many hidden chultunes (underground cisterns), you'll be food for the birds.

➤ **EL TABASQUEÑO** • If your Indiana Jones ambitions have not been satisfied by Hochob, El Tabasqueño, a.k.a. Xtabas, may be just the place for you. Seven kilometers from Dzibalchén and 2 kilometers off the road, El Tabasqueño is completely hidden in the forest. The trek through the jungle to reach it is probably the most interesting part of the trip. The site has only one building, a temple featuring masks of Chaac and the face of Itzamná. Decorations include the double-headed serpent, the symbol of Kukulcan. The only way to get to El Tabasqueño is through the paid services of José William Chan (*see* Hochob, *above*); there is no sign indicating where to begin your hike and no discernible path leading to the ruins. In the rainy season, you may be especially glad to have José trailblazing through the jungle with his machete. He charges $8–$10 to accompany you on this trip.

➤ **XTACUMBILXUNAAN CAVES** • Two kilometers from the town of Bolonchén and 34 kilometers north of Hopelchén, are the Grutas Xtacumbilxunaan (Caves of the Hidden Girl). Legend has it that the Maya lost a young girl here when they arrived searching for water. The colorful caves are unbelievable, especially if you see them before heading on to the Loltún Caves, which spoil you for anything else. Seven underground wells, each of a different color, lie deep beneath the main caverns and are accessible only to those with climbing equipment, lanterns, and a sense of adventure. The surreal two-day excursion is rarely attempted. You'll need to negotiate the price for a guide with the necessary equipment—you can find them hanging around during open hours. You may also camp for free at the sight, but be prepared to share your flesh with thirsty mosquitoes. An attendant charges $1 to visit the site daily from 8 to 5. Xtacumbilxunaan lies on Highway 261 between Hopelchén and Bolonchén. Take the Mérida-bound bus from Hopelchén and ask the driver to drop you at the "grutas" (caves). On the way back, catch the same bus; the last one passes the caves at about 7:30.

The Puuc Region

The Puuc Hills, a low-lying mountain range covering about 156 square kilometers, contain six major archaeological sites and some of the most distinctive Maya architecture on the peninsula. You'll want to dedicate at least three days to the region: one to see the main site at Uxmal; another for the surrounding Maya ruins of Kabah, Sayil, Labná, and Xlapac; and a third to explore the spectacular caves at Loltún and the surrounding towns, where many of the residents speak only Mayan.

Considered the most beautiful of all Maya building styles, Puuc architecture is characterized by finely shaped limestone veneers applied to lime-base concrete. The lower facades of Puuc buildings are typically smooth and plain, contrasting with elaborate upper facades decorated with intricate mosaics. Among the most common motifs are X-shape lattices, geometric designs, serpents, and masks. It is a highly complex architectural style that nonetheless draws on a simple idea: that of the *choza,* or one-room thatched hut, common in the region. Stylized representations of the choza appear on the greatest works, such as the archway at Labná. Later Puuc architecture, with its profusion of mosaics, serpents, and masks, displays a Toltec influence that is somewhat top-heavy with decoration.

BASICS

COMING AND GOING The Puuc route snakes its way from Campeche to Mérida, and many travelers take in the sights on their way between the two towns. The main attractions, Uxmal and Kabah, are about 25 kilometers apart along Highway 261. Buses from Campeche run along Route 261 to Uxmal (5 per day, 2½ hrs, $3.25), leaving from the second-class station at Gobernadores. From Mérida, take Highway 180 south to Umán and Highway 261—the journey is only about 97 kilometers. Six second-class buses make the 1½-hour trip to Uxmal daily from Mérida's main second-class station (Calle 70, btw Calles 69 and 71) for about $2; or, take the daily direct bus ($6 round-trip) that leaves Mérida at 8 AM and returns from Uxmal at 2 PM. To return to Mérida or continue on to Kabah from Uxmal, flag down a bus along Highway 261—north to Mérida or south to Kabah. The problem is getting them to stop when you want to come back. Some of the bus drivers consider passengers an unnecessary nuisance and won't stop even if you wave your arms madly.

Exploring the other sites on the Puuc Route, such as Labná, Xlapak, Sayil, and the Loltún Caves, is not so easy. The **Ruta Puuc ADO** bus ($5) leaves Mérida's **ADO** station (Calle 69, at Calle 70) daily at 8 AM, and deposits you unceremoniously for about 25 minutes at each site, giving you just enough time to scan the plaques, climb a few rubbled steps, and poke your nose into a crevice or two. You get an added hour and a half at Uxmal before returning to Mérida between 4 or 5 PM. The bus stops at the plaza in Santa Elena both coming and going. If you have the money, a much better idea is to spend the extra $20 on a rental car and spend as much time as you want at each site. Try to leave by mid-morning though—the ruins close by 5 PM.

A less reliable option is to hitch to the sites—a foolish undertaking in the dark. During the day, the road is not regularly traveled, but you can usually get a ride. Just be patient and bring lots of water; it could take a couple hours. The best places to pick up rides with tourists are in Kabah or Loltún (*see* Oxkutzcab and the Loltún Caves, *below*).

WHERE TO SLEEP Many people visit as a day trip from Mérida, since lodging options in the Puuc region are severely limited. But if you want to explore the area in depth, it doesn't make sense to keep commuting back and forth. Staying in the small towns of **Santa Elena, Ticul,** or **Oxkutzcab** (*see below*) is a more convenient option. You can also camp for $4 a night at Loltún (*see,* Oxkutzcab and the Loltún Caves, *below*) as long as you have no problems sleeping next to a gaping black hole in the ground. In any of these cases, you'll still have to take a bus or hitch to get anywhere, but it's no more than 56 kilometers to any of the sites.

Of the Puuc sites, only Uxmal has accommodations, most of which are expensive hotels. If you insist on staying in the area, head for **Rancho Uxmal,** a hotel 4 kilometers north of the Uxmal ruins. Singles are $16.75; each additional person is $3. However, you can pitch a tent or hang a hammock on the palapa-covered cement platforms (and still have use of bathrooms, hot showers, and an enticing swimming pool) for only $2.50 per person, $1.75 extra per rented hammock. *Hwy. 261, no phone. Walk, hitch, or flag down a Mérida-bound bus and ask to be let off at Rancho Uxmal. 20 rooms, all with bath. Laundry, luggage storage, restaurant.*

It makes more sense to stay at the **Sacbé Campgrounds,** just outside of Santa Elena along Highway 261. It's halfway between Uxmal (to the north) and four other major archaeological sites (to the south). The campground is clean and pleasant, and you can sling a hammock or pitch a tent for $2.50. They have three bungalows as well for less than $10 for a single or a double. The cheerful owners also cook a reasonably priced breakfast or dinner for guests. They know the local bus schedules and offer insider info about free activities, shortcuts to sites, and local wildlife. *¼ km south of road to Santa Elena. Take any bus from Mérida or Campeche that travels down 261 and ask driver to let you off at campo deportivo. From Ticul, take a combi (tarp-covered truck) to Santa Elena and walk north ¼ km on highway.*

VISITOR INFORMATION Admission fees to the archaeological sites can quickly destroy your budget, but there are ways to get around them. Your best bet is to schedule your visit to Loltún and the Puuc towns for a Sunday or holiday, when admission is free. If you want to buy a guidebook to the Puuc Hills, get it before you leave Mérida or Campeche, or you'll pay through the nose. Otherwise, Uxmal has a large tourist center, which runs half-hour documentaries on the archaeological, cultural, and environmental riches of the Yucatán. A small museum also displays a few archaeological remains with descriptions printed in Spanish. But apart from small tourist shops selling crafts and soft drinks, smaller sites have no amenities, not even bathrooms.

UXMAL AND THE PUUC ROUTE

Although the carefully kept lawns and hordes of plaid-clad tourists at Uxmal (pronounced oosh-MAHL) provide an unfortunate reality check, the beauty and scale of the buildings are such that you will soon forget the manicured surroundings. The *Chilam Balam*, a chronicle of the Maya of this region, says that Uxmal was founded in the mid-6th century. Uxmal means "built three times," but the structures were apparently reconstructed at least five times. No one knows exactly who used these buildings, but one theory suggests that the Xives, a people from the central Mexican plain, occupied Uxmal briefly in the 10th century. Some evidence of this remains in inscriptions, but their paucity suggests that the Xives's stay was relatively short. Whatever the case, the city was abandoned soon afterward.

Beauty contests are annually filmed in Uxmal's Nun's Quadrangle, where a backdrop of glowing white stucco can do much for a scantily clad figure on her way to preeminence in the world of high fashion.

The satellite Puuc towns of Kabah, Sayil, Labná, and Xlapak (pronounced shla-PAK) are not as large or as historically impressive as Uxmal. However, their remote setting in the Puuc Hills adds to their appeal. Many of the temples and pyramids remain hidden by the low vegetation, and tropical birds flit among the ruins. Apart from Kabah, the towns lie along the 48-kilometer back road that runs from Highway 261 to the town of Oxkutzcab and Highway 184. If you do travel this road, plan to visit the Loltún Caves along the way (*see* Oxkutzcab and the Loltún Caves, *below*).

UXMAL The archaeological ruins are open daily 8–5. Admission is $3.75, except on Sunday, when it's free. Mayan history and culture is the focus of the nightly light-and-sound shows (Spanish $1, English $1.50).

The magnificent **Pyramid of the Magician** is the first thing you'll see when you enter the archaeological site. The pyramid has an unusual oval base and stands 39 meters tall. The first stage of its construction dates to the 6th century, and five temples were added during the next 400 years. To reach the fifth temple, you'll have to climb 150 narrow steps at a 60° angle. If vertigo hasn't done you in, climb down the west side to the temple just below it. The entrance is framed by the mouth of a huge mask of Chaac. Most impressive is the careful stone-by-stone construction and the way the shape of the pyramid seems to change when viewed from different perspectives.

Behind the pyramid is the Nun's Quadrangle, an imposing complex of four long, narrow buildings around a central courtyard. The complex received its name from the Spanish, who thought the layout and the 74 small rooms inside resembled a European convent. Its real purpose remains unclear: Red handprints covering one wall have led to speculation that the building was associated with Itzamná, the god of sun and sky. However, images of Chaac, the rain god with the distinctive hooked nose, are also prevalent. Many walls are decorated with geometric patterns and animal carvings, including images of a two-headed serpent. Facing the Nun's Quadrangle is a four-building complex called the **Cemetery Group.** Now badly decayed, the structures were once decorated with carved skulls and bones.

Head southwest from the Nun's Quadrangle to reach the **juego de pelota** (ball court). The badly deteriorated complex used to have stone bleachers from which spectators watched players put balls through stone rings (*see box, below*). Close to the ball court is the **House of the Turtles,** a simple structure typical of Puuc architecture. The upper half of the building, which consists of

Uxmal

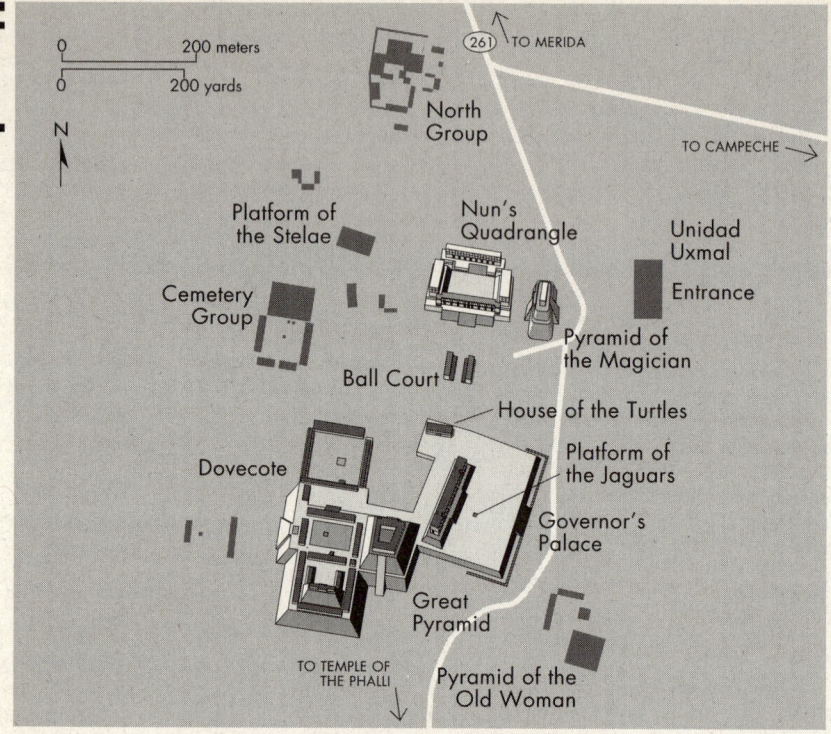

a series of rooms, is most interesting: A series of columns supports a cornice sculpted with small turtles. The Maya believed that turtles would appeal to Chaac on behalf of drought-stricken humans.

Set on a large raised platform, the **Governor's Palace** is one of the finest examples of pre-Hispanic architecture in Mesoamerica. Its 107-meter length is divided by three corbeled arches, creating narrow passageways or sanctuaries. The friezes along the uppermost section of the palace are as intricate as any in Maya architecture, with carvings of geometric patterns overlaid with plumed serpents and Chaac masks. These mosaics supposedly required over 20,000 individually cut stones.

Southeast of the Governor's Palace is a badly deteriorated pyramid with a rectangular base and the remains of a temple on its top. Now covered by vegetation, the whole complex is known as the **Pyramid of the Old Woman,** referring to the witch who hatched the dwarf magician. The latter is said to have imprisoned her here. Continuing south from the Pyramid of the Old Woman, you reach the small **Temple of the Phalli.** Suspended from the cornices, the phalli were used to channel rain into storage containers. Most phalli have been destroyed or stolen, but you can see one in the museum at the tourist center.

Southwest of the Governor's Palace are the remains of the Great Pyramid. The structure is in poor condition and cannot compare with the Pyramid of the Magician, but the view from the 33-meter mound is rewarding and the climb up the reconstructed stairway is relatively easy. Inside the temple at the top is a shrine to Chaac. Small bowls are carved into parts of the mask, presumably to hold water or a small offering.

Behind the Great Pyramid is the **Dovecote,** a long building topped by eight triangular belfries perforated with what appear to be pigeonholes, hence the name of the building. No one has a clue as to what the place was actually used for. About half a kilometer south from the Dovecote is a small building half-covered by dirt and vegetation. The geometric carvings on its facade look like a centipede, giving the building the name *chimez* (centipede in Mayan).

KABAH About 25 kilometers south of Uxmal, Kabah is among the most impressive sites in the Puuc region and dates from AD 850–900. Highway 261 from Mérida to Campeche splits Kabah in two: The most interesting structures uncovered so far lie on the eastern side of the road, while the ruins on the western side remain partly hidden beneath dense vegetation.

The **Codz Pop** is the principal structure at Kabah. The fantastic western facade is decorated with nearly 300 masks of Chaac, the god of rain, to whom the building was dedicated. The name Codz-Pop means "coiled mat," possibly a reference to the noses, which curl like rolled-up mats. The noses may have been used as supports for lanterns, in which case the wall would have been brilliantly lit and visible for miles. Some archaeologists have suggested that the building had a legal or military function.

Behind the Codz Pop are two structures built in the plainer, more traditional Puuc style: **El Palacio**, a palace that featured over 30 chambers, half of which still remain; and the **Temple of the Columns**, which boasts well-preserved columns at the back of the building.

On the other side of the road are several more magnificent structures, still largely unexcavated. Over hundreds of years, the roots of jungle vines and trees have transformed the **Great Pyramid**, once the most important temple in Kabah, into a mound of rubble. Traces of a stairway appear on its southern side. The **Arch of Triumph** marks the end of a *sacbé*, a raised road leading from Kabah to Uxmal. Southwest of the arch is the newly excavated **Templo de las Manos Rojas** (Temple of the Red Hands), which features small red hands imprinted in the northern wall of the first chamber. The handprints have been variously interpreted as the signatures of the ancient architects and the marks of Itzamná, the spiritual guide of the Maya. Admission: $1.75, free Sun. and holidays. Open daily 8–5.

SAYIL Meaning "the place of the ants" in Maya, Sayil, 10 kilometers south of Kabah, is best known for its magnificent **palace**. Built in AD 730, the palace is 65 meters long, with more than 50 rooms sprawling over three levels. The second level is decorated with columns similar to those found in Greek temples. The sculpted frieze above these columns features masks of the rain god, as well as images of the Descending God, an upside-down figure, and the Blue Lizard, a

On the southeasternmost edge of Sayil's ancient city center stands a lone stela representing the importance of fertility to Maya culture. The carved male figure appears, at first glance, to have three legs—this, however, is not the case.

Ball Courts

Ball courts, found in virtually all Maya ceremonial centers, were laid out in the shape of a wide H. The object of the game was for players on two opposing teams to knock a rubber ball through a stone ring mounted on the wall using only their hips, elbows, and knees. The game resembled present-day soccer, albeit with greatly reduced salaries.

The games celebrated the creation of the cosmos and mankind by the great Progenitors. The movements of the players and the ball reenacted the tests that ancient heroes faced, as well as the movements of the stars and planets. The walls of the courts were often elaborately decorated with mosaics depicting beheadings and other bloody rituals, presumably performed upon the defeated team. Though subject to debate, some archaeologists believe the losing team's captain was sacrificed, and the defeated players turned into the victors' slaves.

snakelike figure. South of the palace is the badly decayed **El Mirador,** which features a roostercomb roof and a **juego de pelota** (ball court). Don't leave Sayil without getting a good look at the city from a distance—the best view is from the hill across the road from the entrance. *Admission: $1.75, free Sun. and holidays. Open daily 8–5.*

XLAPAK About 6 kilometers east of Sayil is Xlapak, the smallest and least important site on the Puuc Route, with only one partially restored palace. The smooth-wall structure is typical of Puuc style, featuring geometric designs and masks of Chaac. *Admission: $1.25, free Sun. and holidays. Open daily 7–6.*

LABNA Probably the oldest of the Puuc cities, Labná (4 kilometers from Xlapak) is thought to have been built during the early Classic Period (about AD 500). Labná means "The House of Old Women" in Mayan, but it probably received this name after the city was abandoned. Only a few structures have been uncovered at Labná, but they are exquisite. The best-preserved site is the arch; once part of a larger building, it now stands alone except for two surviving rooms leading off the corbeled passageway—richly decorated with geometric patterns, mosaics, and small columns. The **palace,** probably built some time in the 9th century, is the other major ruin at Labná. The largest complex in the Puuc Hills, it sits on a huge platform more than 150 yards long. Despite its size, the palace isn't nearly as inspiring as the palace at Sayil. However, the decoration of its facade is noteworthy. Another impressive structure at Labná is **El Mirador,** a pyramid with a temple on top. The pyramid is little more than rubble today, but the temple has survived better. *Admission: $1.75, free Sun. and holidays. Open daily 8–5.*

OXKUTZCAB AND THE LOLTUN CAVES

Sixteen kilometers southeast of Ticul, the small town of Oxkutzcab (pronounced osh-kootz-KAAB) is seldom explored by tourists—most of whom come only to get a bus or taxi to the nearby caves at Loltún. During the morning, however, Oxkutzcab is in a state of pandemonium, filled with people and trucks. The huge **market** (Calle 51, btw Calles 48 and 50) draws people from throughout the region who come to buy produce at some of the lowest prices in Mexico. If you decide to spend the night, try **Hospedaje Trujeque** (Calle 48 No. 102-A, btw Calles 51 and 53, tel. 997/5–05–68), which has pleasant rooms with private bathrooms and hot water for $5 (singles) and $6 (doubles).

The Grutas de Loltún are the largest and most spectacular caves on the peninsula, and definitely deserve your time. About 19 kilometers east of Labná and 10 kilometers west of Oxkutzcab, Loltún consists of a maze of underground labyrinths filled with enormous stalagmites and stalactites. Archaeologists have had a field day here, unearthing evidence about the Maya and their ancestors, who inhabited these caves for more than two millennia. Religious ceremonies were held in the **Catedral,** a vast chamber crowded with stalagmites and stalactites. Some formations in the center of the chamber resemble an altar. In another cavern you can see the soot from cooking fires and the remains of *metates* (stones used for grinding corn). The caves also contain several carvings of figures and hieroglyphs, some of which date back to 2000 BC, as well as black ink paintings. Over thousands of years, dripping water has carved the rocks into bizarre shapes, and tour guides find no end of amusing resemblances, including the Virgin of Guadalupe, a dolphin's head, a camel, a jaguar, and an eagle. Especially interesting are two semi-hollow rock formations extending from the ceiling to the floor. If you tap them the right way, they produce musical tones. According to legend, only virgins can produce this sound, so think twice before you strike. The floor of the dark caves is slippery and uneven, so bring a sturdy pair of shoes. Guided tours are led daily every 1½ hours 9:30–3. Guides expect a tip—a dollar or two each is about right. *Admission: $3; $1 Sun.*

COMING AND GOING Combis (tarp-covered trucks) leave from the Parque San Juan in Mérida (Calle 62, btw Calles 69 and 67) for Oxkutzcab whenever they're full; ADO buses leave from Mérida's bus terminal (Calle 71, btw Calles 68 and 70) about every 3 hours, 9 AM–8:30 PM. Combis and buses both take 1½ hrs and cost $3. From anywhere besides Mérida, you'll have to go to Ticul first and catch a combi (20 min, 50¢) from Calle 25 (btw Calles 26 and 28) to Oxkutzcab. The last bus leaves at 7 PM from Ticul.

To reach Loltún from Oxkutzcab, you'll have to wait until one of the trucks carrying workers to the fields fills up—wait in front of the market. The 11-kilometer trip costs only about 50¢ and takes about 20 minutes. If you don't want to wait around, you can hire one of the many taxis or combis to take you to the grutas for about $1.50. There are three ways to return from Loltún: Wait (and hope) for the truck to come back; wait for a combi outside the entrance of the main parking lot; or hitch. Hitching is pretty easy (especially if you've made friends during the cave tour) and isn't dangerous during the day. From Oxkutzcab, combis leave for Ticul from Calle 52 (btw Calles 51 and 53), or from the northwest corner of the park (the last leaves at 7 PM). Buses leave for Mérida from Oxkutzcab every half hour until 9 PM.

TICUL

The small town of Ticul, 86 kilometers south of Mérida, is a convenient base from which to explore the region. The town itself has little to offer, but those with a shoe fetish will have a fine old time in this shoe manufacturing center: Piles of high heels can be seen poking out of plastic milk crates strapped to the bicycles of local shoemakers on their way to the market. To see the cobblers in action, pay a visit to **Abigail and Aurora** (Calle 30, btw Calles 17 and 19) where an extensive two-level factory supplies everything from patent-leather party shoes to fat-buckled leather sandals. The main market (Calle 23, btw Calles 28 and 30) is the least expensive (prices run about $5–$10, depending on size), but you'll have to sniff around for quality. Though expensive (upwards of $75), the hand-embroidered shoes are at least worth a look. **Camita España** makes her own and is hired out on special occasions by women around town. You can visit her at her home (Calle 32, btw Calles 25 and 27, Colonia San Roman) or you can drop by her store, **La Camita** (cnr of Calles 28 and 23, near the market).

Probably the most interesting feature of Ticul is the extent to which Mayan is spoken—you are likely to hear it as often as Spanish.

BASICS Banco Atlántico (Calle 23, tel. 997/2–02–48), diagonally across from the plaza, changes money 9–1:30. Medical aid is available 24 hours at the **clínica** (Calle 23, at Calle 30, tel. 997/2–09–44).

COMING AND GOING From Campeche and Hopelchén, you'll have to take the Mérida bus via Highway 261 and change at Santa Elena (2 hrs, $3)—combis await incoming buses to take passengers on to Ticul 5:30 AM–6 PM. Combis leave Mérida for Ticul ($1.75) from the Parque San Juan whenever they are full. Buses also make the 80-minute trip from the main bus station for about the same price.

To reach Uxmal and Kabah, take a combi for Santa Elena from the plaza or from the combi station (Calle 30 No. 214, at Calle 25). In Santa Elena, catch the Campeche-bound bus to Kabah (50¢) or the Mérida-bound bus to Uxmal ($1). To reach Loltún, your best bet is to take a combi (20 min, 50¢) to Oxkutzcab. They hang out near the plaza at Calle 25, between Calles 26 and 28.

Some Helpful Phrases in Mayan

B'ish ka' ba?	What is your name?
Im ka' ba . . .	My name is . . .
Baax a kajal?	What is your town?
In kajale' (Berkeley).	I live in (Berkeley).
Bis a wool?	How are you?
Jach kimac in wool, tin o'k'ot.	I'm content./I'm dancing.

WHERE TO SLEEP AND EAT The little old man who runs **Hotel San Miguel** (Calle 28 No. 213, btw Calles 21 and 23, tel. 997/2–03–82) speaks Mayan, but his Spanish is rough. At least the clean rooms have hot water and fans. Singles are $4.25, doubles $6. The woman who works at **Hotel Sierra Sosa** (Calle 26 No. 199, tel. 997/2–00–08) in the afternoons speaks excellent English. The simple rooms have comfortable beds, fans, and hot water. Street noise can be annoying in the front rooms, so request a room in the back. Singles are $6.75, doubles $7.50 ($12.50 with air-conditioning). They have laundry facilities and will hold your luggage.

Unlike the Puuc sites, Ticul has plenty of cheap eateries. For breakfast, head to the **market** (Calle 23, btw Calles 28 and 30) for fruit or food from one of the many *fondas* (covered food stands). For lunch or a snack, **Lonchería Mary** (Calle 23, btw Calles 26 and 28) serves licuados for 60¢ and tamales for 15¢. If you need a break from Mexican food, head for **Cafetería y Pizzería La Góndola** (cnr of Calles 23 and 26, tel. 997/2–01–12), open daily 7–1 and 6–midnight. They serve spaghetti for $3 and even deliver pizzas with all the toppings for $3–$4. **Restaurant Los Almendros** (Calle 23, btw Calles 26 and 28, tel. 997/2–00–21), open daily 9–7, has excellent Yucatecan dishes ($4–$6).

Mérida

Mérida is the largest and hippest city on the Yucatán Peninsula. From aging, elegant neighborhoods to frenzied commercial districts, each sector of the city has a distinct ambience. The Paseo de Montejo is a broad street with restored mansions, sidewalk cafés, and ritzy hotels. In the Parque Central, students, tourists, and locals hang out near the cathedral and the Palacio de Gobierno, monuments to the 500-year struggle between European and Maya culture. With all this going for it, Mérida is a wonderful place to dawdle and a good base from which to explore the Gulf Coast and the ruins of the Puuc Hills. If you only have one day to spend in Mérida, try to make it a Sunday, when the central streets are closed off and the whole city turns out for festivities like Yucatecan folk dancing and an especially grand market. The best time to visit is generally during the dry season, November–April.

Founded in 1542, Mérida has long enjoyed prosperous trade with Europe, much of it based on henequen, a hemp used to make twine. The city is built on the site of the Maya settlement of T'hó, where temples and columns reminded the Spanish of the Roman ruins at Mérida in Spain, hence the name. The colonists forced the Maya to dismantle their temples and used the masonry to create new buildings, churches, and mansions. Like its buildings, Mérida's residents are the result of a merger of indigenous and European cultures: Maya aesthetics and tradition flavor the opulence and formality of Spanish colonial culture.

BASICS

AMERICAN EXPRESS AmEx sells traveler's checks and offers emergency check cashing as well as lost-card and lost-check service. They hold clients' mail for a month. *Paseo de Montejo 494, Mérida, Yucatán, CP 97000, México, tel. 99/28–42–22. Btw Calles 43 and 45. Open weekdays 9–2 and 4–5, Sat. 9–1.*

AUTO PARTS/SERVICE The **Ángeles Verdes** (Green Angels), a government-funded road service agency with a small office in Mérida, answers questions about service, tolls, and other car-related matters. *Calle 14 No. 102, btw Calles 73 and 75, tel. 99/83–11–84. Open 7 AM–8 PM.*

BOOKSTORES **Librería Dante** (Calle 59 No. 540, at Calle 68, tel. 99/24–72–18), open Monday–Saturday 8 AM–10 PM, and **Teatro Peón Contreras** (Calles 60 and 57) have a limited selection of English titles.

CASAS DE CAMBIO Most banks are on Calle 65, between Calles 60 and 64, and change money weekdays 9–12:30. A **Banamex** ATM (cnr of Calles 56 and 59) accepts Visa, MasterCard, Cirrus, and Plus cards. **Agencia de Cambio Money Exchange** (Calle 56 No. 491, btw Calles 57 and 59, tel. 99/28–21–52) is open weekdays 9–5, Saturday 9–2. On Sunday, its branch moves to the Palacio de Gobierno on Calle 61, and is open 9–5.

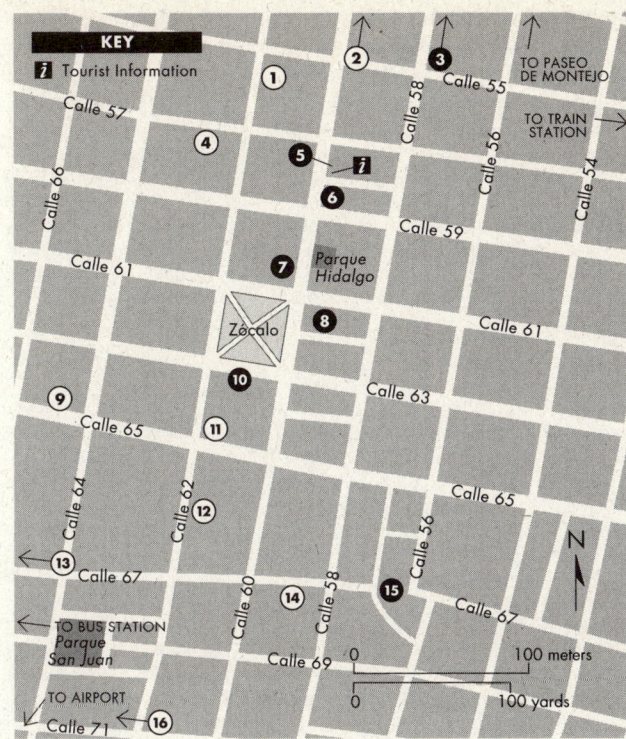

Mérida

Sights ●
Casa de Montejo, **10**
Catedral, **8**
Iglesia de la Tercera Orden, **6**
Mercado Municipal, **15**
Museo de Antropología e Historia, **3**
Palacio de Gobierno, **7**
Teatro Peón Contreras, **5**

Lodging ○
Hotel Alamo, **16**
Hotel América, **14**
Hotel Casa Becil, **13**
Hotel Galería Trinidad, **2**
Hotel La Gran Posada, **9**
Hotel Montejo, **4**
Hotel Sevilla, **11**
Hotel Trinidad, **1**
Hotel La Paz, **12**

CONSULATES United Kingdom, Belize Vice-Consulate. *Calle 58 No. 450, tel. 99/28-61-52. Open weekdays 9-noon.*

United States. *Paseo de Montejo 453, at Colón, tel. 99/25-50-11. Open weekdays 7:30-4.*

EMERGENCIES The **police** station (tel. 99/25-25-55) is on Calle 72, between Calles 39 and 41.

LAUNDRY **La Lavamática Lafe** charges $2.50 to wash and dry 3 kilos of clothing. *Calle 61 No. 518, btw Calles 62 and 64, tel. 99/24-45-31. Open weekdays 8-7, Sat. 8-4.*

MEDICAL AID **Farmacia Yza** (Calle 71, at Aviación, tel. 99/23-81-16) is open round the clock. The **Cruz Roja** offers 24-hour ambulance service. *Calle 68, btw Calles 65 and 67, tel. 99/28-53-91 or 99/83-02-32.*

Hospital O'Horan's Medicina Preventativa division gives out free condoms Monday–Saturday 9–5. *Av. de Los Itzaes 59, tel. 99/24-41-11. Take CENTENARIO bus from north side of zócalo.*

PHONES AND MAIL The **post office** will hold mail sent to you at the following address for up to 10 days: Lista de Correos, Administración Urbana 1, Mérida, Yucatán, CP 97000, México. *Calle 65, at 56, tel. 99/28-54-04. Open weekdays 7-7, Sat. 9-1.*

You can find **public telephones** on the zócalo, at the Palacio Municipal, and in parks around the city. Dial 09 for international collect calls. You can only call direct from *casetas* (booths)—**Computel** (Calle 59, at Calle 58; open 7 AM–10 PM) charges $3.50 a minute for calls to the United States.

SCHOOLS The **Academia de Cultura e Idiomas** offers beginning through advanced Spanish classes, including classes geared toward scientists and businesspeople. Four-week courses entail 4 hours of class per day and cost about $100 a week. The school arranges affordable homestays for students. *Calle 13 No. 23, tel. and fax 99/44-31-48. Take* SAN ANTONIO *bus from cnr of Calles 56 and 59. Mailing address: Aptdo. Postal 78-4, Mérida, Yucatán, CP 97100, México.*

TRAVEL AGENCIES Shop around for tours to the Maya ruins near Mérida—prices of day trips fluctuate widely. Trips to Uxmal and Chichén Itzá should cost about $25. Reliable agencies include **Ceiba Tours** (Calle 60 No. 495, tel. 99/24-44-77; open weekdays 8-7, Sat. 8-2) and **Eco-Turismo Yucatán** (Calle 3 No. 235, btw Calles 32 and 34, tel. 99/20-27-72).

VISITOR INFORMATION The **tourist information center** at Teatro Peón Contreras has a knowledgeable staff that speaks English fairly well. They also have copies of *Yucatán Today*, with general info and some maps. Information booths at the airport and the bus station stock similar material. *Calle 60, at Calle 57, tel. 99/24-92-90. Open daily 8-8.*

COMING AND GOING

BY BUS Mérida is home to several exhaust-filled transport hubs, the biggest and most confusing of which is **Unión de Camioneros del Yucatán** (Calle 71, btw Calles 70 and 72). From here, **ADO** (Calle 70, btw Calles 69 and 71, tel. 99/24-86-10) has first-class service to Cancún (4 hrs, $10) and Villahermosa (9 hrs, $18) as well as frequent first-class service to Campeche (2½ hrs, $5). Other destinations include Chetumal (3 per day, 6 hrs, $10), Palenque (daily, 9 hrs, $16.50), and San Cristóbal de las Casas (daily, 10 hrs, $20). **ATF** (Calle 69, btw Calles 68 and 70, tel. 99/23-22-87) sends second-class buses every 3 hours until 7 PM to Uxmal (1½ hrs, $1.50), Hopelchén (3 hrs, $3), and Maxcanú (1 hr, $1).

Buses to smaller regional towns leave from various points around the city. Buses to Dzibilchatún (6 per day, 1 hr, 65¢) or Umán (every ½ hr, 1 hr, 75¢) leave from the corner of **Parque San Juan** (Calle 64, btw 69 and 71). To reach Hunucmá (1½ hrs, $1), Sisal (2 hrs, $1), or Celestún (2 hrs, $2), go to the station on Calle 71 (btw Calles 64 and 66), around the corner from Parque San Juan. Frequent buses to Mayapan (2½ hrs, $1), Progreso (1½ hrs, $1), and Dzilam de Bravo (2½ hrs, $1) leave from the station at Calle 50, between Calles 65 and 67.

BY CAR Avoid the evil toll road ($12 to Valladolid, another $12 to Cancún) by veering to the right at Kilometer 67 of Highway 180 out of Mérida. The *carretera de cuota* (toll road) and the *carretera libre* (free road) go through the same places, but you can't get off the toll road (which, admittedly, is a hell of a lot faster) until Valladolid.

BY TRAIN **Estación Central de Ferrocarriles** (Calle 48, at Calle 55, tel. 99/23-59-44) serves Córdoba (30 hrs, $16) at 6:15 PM every day. The train makes many stops, including Campeche (5 hrs, $1.75) and Palenque (4 hrs, $5.75), but you're much better off taking the bus. Robberies on trains are common; strap all important papers onto your body, and never let your baggage out of sight. The station is 6 blocks east and 3 blocks north of the zócalo, where most budget accommodations are located. It's open 24 hours, but the ticket office is open only from 5 PM until the daily train departs; buy tickets the day you intend to travel.

BY PLANE Mérida's airport is 7 kilometers west of the city's central square. **Aeroméxico** (Paseo Montejo 460, tel. 99/27-90-00) has flights to Cancún ($47) and Mexico City ($161). **Aerocaribe** (Paseo Montejo 500-B, at Calle 47, tel. 99/28-67-90) flies to Oaxaca ($140) and Villahermosa ($63). The airport has a tourist office (open weekdays 8-8) but no currency exchange office; taxi drivers outside will change small amounts of U.S. dollars at lousy rates. It's fairly easy and cheap to get to town: Just take Autobus 79 (AVIACION) to the corner of Calles 67 and 60 downtown. The half-hour trip costs about 25¢. An airport taxi (usually a VW combi) to your hotel costs $5 for up to four people.

GETTING AROUND

Despite its size, Mérida is easy to figure out; most of the interesting buildings and budget hotels are around the zócalo. Streets are numbered, not named, with odd-numbered streets running east-west and even-numbered streets running north-south. The zócalo is bordered by Calles 60, 61, 62, and 63.

BY CAR Most rental agencies are on Calle 60, between Calles 57 and 59. **Hertz** (Calle 60, btw Calles 55 and 57, tel. 99/24–28–34) rents VW Bugs for $24 a day, which includes 400 free kilometers and insurance. **National Inter Rent** (Calle 60, just north of Hertz, tel. 99/28–63–08; open daily 7 AM–10 PM) charges $27.50 a day with unlimited mileage and insurance, and you must be 21 or older with a credit card. Most companies will bargain if you tell them someone else offered you a better price. At $18.50 a day, the cheapest place is **Rentadora México** (Calle 60 No. 495, tel. 99/23–36–37; open Mon.–Sat. 8–1 and 6–8).

BY BUS You won't need to use the bus to see the sights in the center of Mérida. If you want to go beyond the area around the zócalo, however, bus travel is a cheap option; city buses (25¢) run daily 5 AM to midnight. Some buses stop earlier, so be sure to ask the driver. Buses leave from Calle 59 between Calles 56 and 58, and from Calle 56 between Calles 59 and 67, around the market area. Destinations are marked on the windshields.

BY TAXI Avoid the regular taxis, which are very expensive. Instead, look for *colectivos,* or shared taxis (50¢), which have fixed routes throughout the city. Tell the driver where you want to go before you get in, and he'll tell you if it's on his way. Colectivos leave from the zócalo, the market area, and Parque San Juan at Calles 67 and 62.

WHERE TO SLEEP

Mérida's best budget hotels are conveniently located near the zócalo. If you must stay near the bus station, try **Hotel Alamo** (Calle 68 No. 549, at Calle 71, tel. 99/28–62–90), which rents boxes with breathing-holes and private bath for $5 (nicer doubles $6); or the more comfortable **Hotel Casa Becil** (*see below*). Real penny pinchers can hang a hammock in giant, bare rooms for $2.50 at **La Gran Posada** (Calle 65, btw Calles 64 and 66). For $3.50 you can sleep in a single bed with a shoebox-size shared bathroom—but bring the mosquito netting.

➤ **UNDER $10** • **Hotel América.** The simple rooms here have private bathrooms (most with hot water), but the beds are a bit uncomfortable. A couple of blocks from the zócalo, the hotel is popular with families but the owner is not used to chatting it up with solo backpackers. Singles cost $7, doubles $7.50. *Calle 67 No. 500, btw Calles 58 and 60, tel. 99/28–58–79. 43 rooms, all with bath (30 with hot water). Luggage storage, meal service. Wheelchair access.*

Hotel Trinidad. Oddly carved wood columns, tons of plants, and a hodgepodge of paintings give this place a homey, attic-like feel. (Their communal bathrooms, however, are not the cleanest.) Guests can enjoy coffee and toast with eggs or cereal (not included with lodging) on the hotel's central patio. Singles are $6.75, $8.25 buys one bed with a private bath, and doubles with private bath are $9.25. *Calle 62 btw Calles 65 and 67, tel. 99/21–30–29. Laundry (75¢ per piece), luggage storage, meal service.*

La Paz. This plaster-dusted, sunlit hotel has a large patio, pastel-colored rooms, and a narrow, whitewashed balcony. Airy, fan-cooled rooms with private bathrooms are about as cheap as they come ($6.75 singles, $7.50 doubles). Inquire about prices for hanging hammocks. *Calle 62, btw 65 and 67, tel. 99/23–94–46. Look for* HOTEL MILO *sign at entranceway. 15 rooms, all with bath. Wheelchair access.*

➤ **UNDER $15** • **Hotel Casa Becil.** Close to the zócalo and the bus station, this place attracts an over-30 American crowd and features a sun deck with oh-so-tasteful plastic flamingos and a garden with white iron chairs. The bathrooms are clean, but the rooms' deluxe dark-wood furniture doesn't make up for a lack of air-conditioning. Singles and doubles are $10, and they accept American dollars. *Calle 67 No. 550-C, btw Calles 66 and 68, tel. 99/24–67–64. 12 rooms, all with bath. Kitchen, laundry ($2.50 for 12 pieces), luggage storage. Reservations advised July and Aug. Wheelchair access.*

Hotel Galería Trinidad. This funky hotel is decorated with everything from weathered sculptures, to avant-garde Mexican paintings, to blow-up plastic Mickey Mouses. Every room has its own unique character and some even have waterbeds. The swimming pool is the icing on the cake. Rooms start at $10 for doubles with a shared bath, $12.50 for a single with a private bath. *Calle 51, at Calle 60, tel. 99/23–24–63. 30 rooms, 27 with bath. Laundry (75¢ per piece), luggage storage, meal service. Wheelchair access.*

Hotel Montejo. A gorgeous courtyard, stout columns, and colonial-style arches are what you'd expect in a hotel of this caliber in Mérida. Elegant singles cost $11.75, doubles $13.25. Air-conditioned rooms are $1.75 more. *Calle 57 No. 507, btw Calles 62 and 64, tel. 99/28–02–77. 22 rooms, all with bath. Laundry, luggage storage, restaurant.*

Hotel Sevilla. Vast archways, a beautiful patio, and small but airy rooms give this well-kept hotel a cozy atmosphere. All rooms have ceiling fans and hot water, but those facing the street tend to be a bit noisy. Singles are $9.75, doubles $11.25, and triples $17. *Calle 65 No. 511, at Calle 62, tel. 99/28–24–81. 32 rooms, all with bath. Luggage storage. Wheelchair access.*

FOOD

Eating is one of the highlights of a trip to Mérida. Yucatecan food is delicious, and nowhere is it better prepared than here. Unfortunately, eating out can be downright expensive. However, many small loncherías and street stands around town sell *antojitos* (appetizers), tortas, and *panuchos* and *salbutes* (both variations on the taco)—all for under $1. The second floor of the **mercado municipal** (Calles 65 and 67, btw Calles 54 and 56) has more than 20 simple loncherías offering full lunches for under $3; on the north side of the market are dozens of cheap *cocktelerías*, selling amazingly fresh ceviches and full-sized shrimp and conch cocktail cups for $2–$3. The municipal market is also a wonderful place to buy fresh fruits and vegetables brought daily from the villages.

Tasty Yucatecan fare doesn't have to be expensive or elaborate. For free veggie or fish appetizers, chilly 50¢ beers, and lively conversation, head to Le Montparnasse (Calle 58, btw Calles 65 and 67; open daily 11–10).

➤ **UNDER $5** • **Amaro.** Lilting music and flickering candles make this shaded courtyard kitchen almost embarrassingly romantic. Specialties include vegetarian delights like cream of zucchini soup ($1.75) and eggplant curry with cheese (or soy) and rice ($3.25). For something more filling, try the delicious grilled green peppers stuffed with a savory mixture of tofu, onion, and cheese ($4). Finish it all off with a rice and almond or *chaya* (Mayan spinach) shake ($1). *Calle 59 No. 507, btw Calles 60 and 62, tel. 99/28–24–51. Open daily 8:30 AM–10 PM.*

Café y Restaurante El Louvre. There's nothing French about Mérida's answer to the American coffee shop. Stout waiters with little black bow ties and white shirts patrol the brown-tiled restaurant yelling orders to the cook, who stands behind a glass counter hacking at a pot roast. If you're still up before sunrise try the pancakes ($1) or eggs ($1–$2). The hot lime soup (with bits of chicken and fried tortilla; 75¢) is amazing. Huge daily specials are only $2.25. *Calle 61, at Calle 62, on the zócalo, tel. 99/24–50–73. Open 24 hrs.*

Cafetería Pop. This "concept" café is brilliantly decorated with orange and lavender pop art designs. Vigorously air-conditioned and often crowded, Pop is always a good place for conversation. A standard breakfast (eggs, beans, fruit, coffee, and meat) is $2. Chicken mole is $2.50, and the club sandwich $2. Iced coffee goes for 75¢. *Calle 57 No. 501, btw Calles 60 and 63, tel. 99/28–61–63. Open daily 7 AM–11 PM.*

Restaurante Nicte-Há. Raucous groups of men wearing guayaberas (big-collared, button-down cotton blouses) flock here to enjoy delicious Yucatecan specialties at amazingly cheap prices. The *combinación yucateca* is a must—for only $3.25 you get a panucho, *papadzule* (hard-boiled eggs wrapped in a tortilla with pumpkin sauce), *pollo pibil* (marinated chicken baked in a banana peel), a tamale, and a Yucatecan sausage. Vegetarians can feast on rice and banana soup ($1) or *frijoles kabax* (savory whole-bean soup, 75¢). *Calle 61, btw 60 and 62, tel. 99/23–07–84. Open daily 7 AM–midnight.*

El Trapiche Restaurant y Juguería. Papayas, watermelon, and glistening mameys are piled along the back wall of the bar, within easy reach of deft smoothie makers. Sandwiches are tasty and cheap—try the veggie sub with mushrooms, onion, peppers, and tomatoes ($1.25). Garlic lovers won't be able to get enough of the 50¢ *pan con ajo* (toasted french bread smothered with grilled garlic and melted cheese). Elaborate egg-and-tortilla breakfasts are about $2.25. *Calle 62 No. 13, btw Calles 59 and 61, tel. 99/28–12–31. Open daily 7:30 AM–10:30 PM.*

➤ **UNDER $10** • **Pizza Bella.** This wanna-be Italian restaurant with its checkered tablecloths and waiters in red berets has tables out on the patio facing the park, making it a great place to kick back, meet people, and savor the tantalizing aroma of exhaust from passing cars and buses. The menu features spaghetti ($2.50) and good pizzas $5–$7. Espresso and cappuccino go for $1. *Calle 61 No. 500, btw Calles 60 and 62, tel. 99/23–64–01. Open daily 8 AM–midnight.*

Restaurant Express. The food here is quite good and servings are abundant, but plan to spend $4–$5 for typical Yucatecan dishes. The specialty is *pollo pibil* ($4.25), or try *chilaquiles* (tortilla strips and chicken doused with salsa and sour cream) for $1.50. Save room for dessert: *pasta de guayaba* ($1), a square of luscious guayaba wrapped in a cool blanket of creamy cheese. *Calle 60, at Calle 59, tel. 99/28–16–91. Open daily 7 AM–11 PM.*

WORTH SEEING

Since Mérida was founded, wealthy residents have invested an enormous amount of money and pride in their city, and the government continues to dole out the dough to keep the city's colonial heritage in good shape. Museums, galleries, and stores are stocked with antiques and artwork from ancient, colonial, and contemporary times, and every week new listings of dance, theatrical, and music performances appear. For info on upcoming events, ask at the tourist office or check the local newspaper, *Por Esto* (25¢). The tourist office also has a list of weekly events in *Yucatán Today,* a free tourist magazine.

The sites listed below are only part of what makes Mérida interesting. Take the time to walk around the zócalo area and you will find old mansions, churches, and theaters. Some restoration jobs are better than others, but even if you walk into a run-down hotel, you're likely to see beautiful stained glass, decaying hardwood furniture, oil paintings dating back one or two hundred years, columns, marble and ceramic tiles, and beautiful courtyards.

CASA DE MONTEJO On the south side of the zócalo stands the old Montejo family palace, built between 1543 and 1549 by Francisco de Montejo, the destroyer of the Maya city T'hó and founder of Mérida. The bas-relief on the facade depicts Montejo The Younger, his wife and daughter, and a number of Spanish soldiers standing on the heads of the vanquished Maya. The house has been converted into a Banamex branch and is open to the public weekdays 9–1. *Calle 63, btw Calles 60 and 62. Admission free.*

CHURCHES The splendid twin-spire **catedral** stands austerely at the front of the zócalo. It looks more like a fort than anything else and is a subtle reminder of how difficult the Spanish found it to convert the Maya to Christianity. Built in 1561 entirely of stone (much of which came from razed Maya buildings), the cathedral was indeed designed for defense—gunnery slits, not windows, stare out onto the square. The interior is rather bleak, having been ransacked during the Mexican Revolution and never restored. However, the pillagers did not touch **El Cristo de las Ampollas** (Calle 60, at Calle 61; open daily 7–noon and 5–8), which translates as "Christ of the Blisters." Legend has it that a local peasant once claimed he saw a tree burning all night, but that the tree was not consumed by the flames. A statue of Christ was carved from the tree and placed in a church in a nearby town. Later, the church burned down, but the statue survived, albeit covered in blisters. The **Iglesia de la Tercera Orden** (Church of the Third Order), across from Parque Hidalgo at Calles 60 and 59, was built by Jesuit monks in the 17th century. The stones of the facade come from the great pyramid of T'hó; if you look carefully, especially on the Calle 59 side, you can still distinguish Maya designs on them. *Open daily 7–11 and 5–8.*

MERCADO MUNICIPAL Mérida's gargantuan municipal market, occupying the area between Calles 65 and 67 and Calles 54 and 56, is considered by many travelers to be the best on the peninsula. If you're hunting for a hammock, hold out for the fine ones sold here (*see* Shopping, *below*). There's even a saint-repair shop, in case your traveling icon has been damaged. *Market open daily 6–5.*

MUSEO DE ANTROPOLOGIA E HISTORIA The museum, about a kilometer from the zócalo, is worth visiting despite the $5 admission fee. Exhibits are mostly Maya artifacts, including figurines of the Maya messenger between the gods and man, Chac Mool, and artifacts retrieved from the sacred cenote at Dzibilchaltún. There's a reconstruction of a burial chamber, as well as deformed skulls: The Maya flattened their children's skulls with boards for cosmetic reasons. *Paseo de Montejo, at Calle 43. Admission: $5, free Sun. and holidays. Open Tues.–Sat. 8–8, Sun. 9–2.*

PALACIO DE GOBIERNO Built in 1892 on the northern side of the zócalo, the Governor's Palace is a beautiful example of neoclassical architecture, with Doric columns topped by arches. Inside, murals by Fernando Castro Pacheco, a Yucatecan painter, depict the tumultuous history of the Yucatán, including the Caste War (*see box, below*), in which Maya fought against Mexicans of European extraction. *Calle 61, btw Calles 60 and 62. Admission free. Open 8 AM–9:30 PM.*

PASEO DE MONTEJO The Champs-Elysées in Paris was the inspiration for this avenue (Calle 47, btw Calles 56 and 58), built when Mérida enjoyed extensive trade links with Europe and was home to many French merchants. Sidewalk restaurants (open for dinner only) and expensive hotels and discos line the wide avenue, and stately old homes, many of which were built with profits from the henequen trade, line the side streets. *From the zócalo, walk north on Calle 60 and left on Calle 47 (about 8 blocks); or, take a bus up Calle 60 to Calle 47.*

TEATRO PEON CONTRERAS In front of the Iglesia de la Tercera Orden is the Teatro Peón Contreras (Calles 60 and 57), another city landmark. The current building dates from 1877 but has undergone several transformations, the most drastic in 1905, when Italian artists gave it a neoclassical design. Ballet tickets usually run $9, and same-night seats go on sale at 9 AM. The theater hosts classical music recitals and ballets on Tuesdays at 9 PM; check out *Por Esto* for current shows. *Ticket office open Mon.–Sat. 9–9, Sun. 9–1:30.*

The Caste War

When Mexico earned its independence from Spain in 1821, the Maya had no reason to celebrate. They had lost much land under Spanish rule, including access to precious water sources, and still suffered the condemnation of their religion. In 1847, a Maya rebellion began in Valladolid. Not only did the Maya win control of the town, but within a year, they conquered all of the Yucatán except Mérida and Campeche. Europeans in the capital appealed for help from Spain, France, and the United States, but none was forthcoming. The outnumbered Europeans made plans to evacuate. Just as the Maya prepared for a final, decisive assault, the winged ant (symbolic of coming rains) made an early appearance. The Maya took the insects' arrival as an omen, packed up their weapons, and returned to the fields to plant the sacred corn, without which they could not survive.

Help for the Spanish settlers then arrived with a vengeance from Mexico City, Cuba, and the United States. The Maya were mercilessly slaughtered until their population dropped from 500,000 to 300,000. Survivors escaped into the jungles of Quintana Roo, and held out against the Mexican government until 1974, when the region officially accepted statehood with Mexico.

SHOPPING

Mérida is the best place on the Yucatán Peninsula to buy a hammock, but the experience can be like looking for a used car. Salesmen are aggressive and will tell you anything, so visit at least two shops and don't be afraid to bargain. Street vendors near the zócalo and the bus station offer the best bargains, but it's wiser to cruise the shops along Calle 58 near the market (btw Calles 63 and 69) to see what's out there. The best places to go are **El Hamaguero** (Calle 58, btw Calles 69 and 71), which makes and sells their own hammocks, and **Artesanías Uxmal** (Calle 58, btw Calles 63 and 65). In both of these places, be ready to bargain and have some prices in mind before walking in.

Hammocks come in several sizes—single, double, matrimonial, large matrimonial, and family. Judge the size for yourself by comparing the weights of different hammocks—don't trust a salesman's claims. Light cotton and nylon weigh about the same, while stronger cotton hammocks weigh much more. You'll probably have to ask in the stores to see the stronger hammocks, since merchants make less profit from them and don't display them prominently. Cotton-nylon hammocks are the most comfortable, but more expensive nylon ones last twice as long and the colors don't fade. Yucatecans like to sleep in big hammocks; they allow you to sleep diagonally, which is better for your back. Prices vary, but the smallest ones should be no more than $9 for the cotton-nylon, $11 for the nylon. Matrimonial hammocks cost about $15 for cotton-nylon, $20 for nylon. Whether you buy a cotton or a nylon hammock, the end-strings should be nylon for greater strength. Also, several long, straight strings should run along each side of the hammock for stability. Ask the salesman to hang the hammock for you, and see how closely it's woven.

AFTER DARK

The bar and disco scene in Mérida could be more exciting, and residents seem to prefer strolling around the zócalo, where mariachis dressed in white eagerly serenade the strollers for tips. Things liven up a bit on the weekends, when the city goes all out, staging huge cultural events and folkloric shows that are often free.

BARS Located in an open-patioed colonial mansion, **Kabukis** (Calle 60, at Calle 53, tel. 99/24-65-65) is frequented by a predominantly gay crowd. A mellow bar during the early evening, Kabukis turns into a sizzling disco after about 10 PM, featuring transvestite shows Thursday and Friday nights (show cover $6.50). Waiters in giant sombreros carry drinks (beers $1.50, piña coladas, $2) to patrons at intimate wrought-iron patio tables at **Panchos** (Calle 59 No. 509, btw Calles 60 and 62, tel. 99/23-09-42; open daily 6 PM–2 AM). It's hardly a secret, but the lack of cover and the lively bands that take the stage keep it a favorite among locals. Come to the dimly lit **El Trovador Bohemio** (Calle 55 No. 504, btw Calles 60 and 62, tel. 99/23-03-85; open daily 9 PM–2:30 AM) to watch wealthy Meridense couples get serenaded with romantic ballads. Drinks are expensive (beers $2, margaritas $3) and there's a $3 cover.

DANCING The really slick discos popular among the upper-class youth are on Prolongación Montejo. The bus situation is sketchy at night though, and a taxi from Mérida costs about $4. Serious dancers should go to **Kalia** (Calle 22 No. 282, tel. 99/44-42-35; open Thurs.–Sat. until 2 AM), where a varied crowd—from 18 to 40 years old—works up a healthy sweat on a multi-platformed stage lit by a huge video screen. They charge a $4 cover every night, but women get in free Wednesdays. Downtown, a somewhat older crowd dances to salsa at **Estelares** (Calle 60 No. 484, btw Calles 55 and 57, tel. 99/28-28-58; open Thurs.–Sat. 9–3). Cuban dance groups put on two excellent shows a night here, each lasting an hour but not interrupting the dancing; cover is $2.50. The **Sala de Fiesta Montejo** (Calle 62, at Calle 65, in front of bus station, tel. 99/24-90-36) is a parking lot during the week, but on weekend nights between 8 and 3, it's where working-class Mexicans come to dance to live tropical music and drink $1 beers. Admission is $5 for men and free for women, who should think twice about coming here alone.

Near Mérida

Yucatán state is home to some of the most exciting sites in Mexico, from beautiful caves and impressive ruins to deserted fishing villages. Mérida is a convenient base from which to explore the surrounding area, but in your rush to visit places, don't overlook the inhabitants. Scattered around Mérida are numerous *pueblos* (villages) that provide a window on the real Yucatán. Most Yucatecan towns have historic churches that will interest fans of colonial architecture; the largest and most elaborate examples can be seem at **Umán**, 18 kilometers southwest of Mérida, and **Hunucmá**, 29 kilometers west of Mérida. To reach Umán from Mérida, take a bus (every 2 hrs, 1 hr, 75¢) from Parque San Juan. To reach Hunucmá (1½ hrs, $1), take a Sisal- or Celestún-bound bus from the station (Calle 71, btw Calles 70 and 72).

CALCEHTOK AND OXKINTOK

The spectacular caves at Calcehtok (Mayan for "Bleeding of the Deer's Throat") are unknown to all but the most ambitious travelers because they aren't easily accessible. Although they are only 70 kilometers southwest of Mérida and about 15 kilometers from Maxcanú, you have to wait an eternity for transport to the village of Calcehtok and then hike 3 kilometers on a dirt road to the caves. Just when you think the heat and the monochromatic vegetation will drive you mad, you reach the caves. After the first immense chamber, where sunlight illuminates tropical plants and singing, swooping birds, it's pure obscurity and silence, except for the sound of water dripping from stalactites and the occasional chirping of a bat or two. A lantern reveals formations in the multi-colored rock and the remnants of ancient visitors. Don't explore these endless, narrow caves on your own unless you're an expert. At the adobe house adjacent to the bus stop you'll find Roger and his sons, who have been leading tours of the caves for three generations. Tours last about 2 hours, at about $7 an hour. Ropes and ladders, mud, bees, and lots of bat guano are involved in a cave trip—it's not for the weak of heart or the less than agile. A flashlight of your own is also helpful.

On the road back to the village of Calcehtok is the turnoff for the badly preserved and seldom visited ruins of **Oxkintok**, a few kilometers away. The enormous site, about 2 kilometers square, was probably the largest of all Puuc cities and was populated during the late Classic Period. The central area features three large pyramids, as well as the pitiful remains of small pyramid temples, palace-like buildings, a ball court, and a variety of houses. Of particular interest are the three carved anthropomorphs (stylized human figures) that stand in their original places in front of a slightly better preserved temple. Ringing the central area like suburbs are three other sets of ruins, each connected by a system of *sacbés* (roads connecting important cities). Despite the relative isolation of the site, once you reach the ruins an informally dressed state official emerges from his VW to charge you the $2 admission.

COMING AND GOING Getting to Calcehtok and Oxkintok by public transport is tiring and time-consuming. Take a Maxcanú-bound bus from the main bus station in Mérida—they make the 1-hour trip every hour or so. The detour for Calcehtok is a few hundred yards before Maxcanú—just tell the driver you want to get off at the "grutas" (caves) or "ruinas" (ruins). From here, either hitchhike or catch a minitruck taxi to the village. From Calcehtok, it's 5 kilometers to Oxkintok and 3 kilometers to the caves. You may be able to arrange transport in the village; otherwise you'll have to walk or hitch. To try both on foot would be an exhausting endeavor. If you can't make a good deal in advance with the only taxi driver in town, then forget the ruins and go to the caves. The closest hotels are in Ticul and Mérida.

MAYA RUINS

MAYAPAN A day trip to Mayapán, about 52 kilometers southeast of Mérida, is a must for every amateur archaeologist. The ruins, dismissed by many as cheap imitations of Chichén Itzá, are nevertheless impressive. Even more impressive is the fact that so few tourists come this way. Mayapán was built during the Post-Classic Period and inhabited by the Cocam, a tribe of Mexican origin. The Cocam, along with the Xiú of Uxmal and the Itzá of Chichén Itzá, formed a powerful alliance which lasted from about 1000 to 1200, when Mayapán broke the alliance and established its hegemony over the already weakened Mayan empire. The city's dominance lasted only a couple of centuries, however—a coup d'état by a noble family ousted the rulers, leading to the city's demise some time before 1450.

The buildings of Mayapán have not fared as well as those of Chichén Itzá, partly due to the poorer quality of the construction. The most interesting building is the **Great Pyramid,** similar to El Castillo at Chichén but without the temple chamber at the summit. The **Temple of Chaac,** next to the pyramid, is a long, low building decorated with carved masks of the rain god. This is also an excellent place to check out colorful birds like the chachalaca, which can be heard from its perch in the surrounding flora. The site's rock-rimmed cenote sustains a bonanza of

Maya Civilizations: Time Periods

The Maya first settled in the lowland areas of Guatemala, Mexico, and Belize and then moved north onto the Yucatán Peninsula. Hence, the height of the Classic Period in the northern settlements occurred at about the same time the southern centers were being abandoned. The history of Maya civilization is traditionally broken down into the following eras. These divisions are not absolute, and archaeologists often differ on the criteria used to designate them.

Pre-Classic Period (1500 BC–AD 300, also called the Formative Period): During this time, agriculture replaced the hunter/gatherer, nomadic lifestyle. Toward the end of this era, monumental buildings with corbeled arches and roof combs appeared, as did the first hieroglyphics and early calendric notation.

Classic Period (AD 300–900): During this period, the Maya developed a strong self-identity, and their architecture shows few traces of outside influence. Inspiration for the Maya's art, language, science, and architecture came from a unified way of thinking about the world. Temples and pyramids built with precise relation to one another illustrate the close tie between religion and aesthetics. Buildings were placed on superstructures atop stepped platforms and were often decorated with bas-reliefs and ornate frescoes. The population's growing dependence on agriculture inspired the creation of the highly accurate Maya calendar, which is based on planting cycles. Economy and trade flourished, and the Maya began to observe class distinctions and live extremely lavish lifestyles around great ceremonial centers. Toward the end of this period, more palaces were constructed on top of or in place of temples, evidence of the growth of secular authority and centralized political rule.

Post-Classic Period (900–1520): Maya civilization declined during this period, which is marked by increased military activity and the growth of conquest states. The Toltecs of Mexico invaded the Yucatán during this time, greatly influencing the Maya architecture and lifestyle. The invasion ultimately led to a more warlike society, more elaborate temples and palaces, and a greater number of human sacrifices. Architectural techniques involved less detailed and careful craftsmanship. For example, carved-stone building facades were replaced at this time by carved stucco.

floral life, including banana trees and a dark-leafed avocado tree. *Admission: $1.25, free Sun. and holidays. Open daily 8–4:30.*

➤ **COMING AND GOING** • Hourly buses (1¼ hrs, $1.75 round-trip) from Mérida travel down Road 18 to Telchaquillo and the Mayapán turnoff every hour from the station at Calles 50 and 67. Ask the driver to drop you off at "las ruinas." Buses from Mayapán back to Mérida are pretty frequent until 5:30 PM; after that it's a long wait for the last bus (8 PM) back. There are no hotels anywhere in the area, so you'll probably have to return to Mérida for the night.

In Mayapán you're likely to be the only living thing in sight, apart from the giant iguanas admiring the ruins.

DZIBILCHALTÚN Dzibilchaltún (pronounced TSEE-bill-chal-toon) is one of the most visited archaeological sites in the region, perhaps because of its proximity to Mérida. As popular as it is, Dzibilchaltún will not impress most visitors. Most of its archaeological riches lie underground, and the two remaining buildings cannot compare with the grandeur of the ruins of Uxmal and the Puuc Hills or even Mayapán. Still, Dzibilchaltún's location, within a natural park just 20 kilometers north of Mérida, makes it an accessible half-day trip. The site was first inhabited in about 2000 BC, reaching its apogee during the Classic Period, from AD 600 to 900, when it became a major ceremonial and residential center. In the late 1500s it was turned into an open chapel and, about 200 years later, a cattle ranch. Remains of all three epochs litter the city "center," giving one the strange feeling of being plopped into a cemetery of forgotten artifacts. At the southern end of a well-maintained 20-meter-wide sacbé is the **Temple of the Seven Dolls**, noteworthy for its structural elegance and for the fact that it is the only known Maya temple with windows. The temple received its name from the seven clay dolls found under the floor.

Near the ruins is the **Cenote Xlacah**, a natural, fresh-water pool that supplied the population of Dzibilchaltún with drinking water; it now provides visitors with a refreshing dip. It was also used for religious ceremonies, judging from the bones of sacrificial victims found inside. The small **museum** at the entrance to the ruins displays pottery samples found in the cenote, as well as the original seven dolls from the temple. Outside the museum is a modest stela garden with artifacts from several Maya sites—especially interesting are the *jugadores de pelota*, with their heavily ornamented sumo-wrestler-like belts. *Admission to ruins and museum: $2.25, free Sun. and holidays. Open daily 8–5; museum closes at 4.*

➤ **COMING AND GOING** • Buses to Dzibilchaltún (45 min, 65¢) leave Mérida from the station at Parque San Juan every couple of hours. Otherwise, you can catch a bus or combi heading north along Highway 261 to Progreso. These drop you at the turnoff to the ruins, which lie about 6 kilometers down a side road. Hitching is fairly easy, especially during late morning. To return to Mérida or Progreso, flag down a passing bus at the end of the driveway to the ruins (five-minute walk); they run every 1–2 hours, cost 65¢, and the last one leaves for Mérida at 7 PM. Otherwise, flag down a bus to either Mérida or Progreso from the highway.

THE GULF COAST

The Gulf Coast has a look all its own, quite different from the azure perfection of the Caribbean coast. The coast road between Progreso and Dzilam de Bravo passes by savannas and *aguadas* (shallow silted puddles) to one side, and grassy dunes, palm trees, and the dark sea on the other. Birds fly in patterns overhead or float in the waters, seemingly oblivious to the awesome summer storms that occasionally fill the moody skies with dramatic clouds and flashes of lightning. Modern beach houses belong to wealthy residents of Mérida, who use them only in July and August. During the rest of the year, you can share miles of white beaches and the sea with a few fishermen. In most of these villages accommodations are limited or nonexistent, but don't despair. If you look respectable enough, it's easy to convince a local family to rent you hammock hooks.

PROGRESO The largest town on the Gulf Coast is one of those curious hybrids that is increasingly common in Mexico. On the one hand, Progreso is a growing tourist resort, catering mainly to residents of Mérida who make the 32-kilometer pilgrimage to its beaches during the latter half of summer. On the other hand, Progreso maintains a small-town atmosphere, and locals live their lives independently of the tourists. During the low season (September–June),

Progreso is the ideal destination for those looking to enjoy mostly deserted beaches but not yet ready to abandon the comforts of city life. During July and August everything is crowded, so be prepared to have difficulty finding a room (at higher prices), to wait for tables, and to share the beach with countless others. Progreso's beaches are nice enough, although you can walk for hundreds of meters before the water becomes deep enough to cover your belly button, and seaweed can be a nuisance.

➢ **COMING AND GOING** • In Mérida, Progreso buses (hourly, 1 hr, $1) leave from the station on Calle 62 between Calles 65 and 67. Buses back to Mérida leave the Progreso bus station (Calle 29, btw Calles 80 and 82) every 15 minutes between 5 AM and 9:30 PM; combis labeled COSTERA (75¢) leave for Mérida every 10 minutes until 9:30 PM from Calle 31, between Calles 78 and 80. Buses for Telchac Puerto (75¢) leave Progreso (cnr of Calle 31 and 80) at 7 AM and 2 PM.

➢ **WHERE TO SLEEP** • During the low season, you should have no problem getting a room in one of Progreso's several hotels. Prices fluctuate, but never get dirt cheap. Each of the large, sandy rooms at **Playa Linda** (Av. Malecón, near Calle 26, tel. 993/5–06–67) has a small pseudo-kitchen with a table, chairs, and a burner; rooms on the second floor have balconies. Both singles and doubles cost $10. **Hotel Progreso** (Calle 78, at Calle 29, tel. 993/5–00–39) offers immaculate rooms and the nicest bathrooms in the Yucatán. It's sort of far from the beach, but the added comfort is worth the walk. Singles are $9, doubles $14.25 ($11 and $16 with air-conditioning). If you're eager to camp, you're not alone; during July and August, the beach in front of the *malecón* (boardwalk) is covered with noisy, beer-toting "campers" doing everything but sleeping. Unfortunately, the less crowded parts of the beach (east or west of the malecón) are not policed and can be dangerous—nighttime robberies are not uncommon.

➢ **FOOD** • Progreso is a port town surrounded by fishing villages, so it's no surprise that seafood is a staple at the town's restaurants. If cheap food is what you're looking for, head for the **market** (cnr of Calles 27 and 80), where you can buy fresh fruits and vegetables or eat in one of the many fondas or loncherías. For fresh bread and drinks, try the supermarkets and bakeries on Calle 27. **Sol y Mar** (Av. Malecón, at Calle 80) is a great place to hang out with a beer and nachos or some fish *botanas* (snacks).

TELCHAC PUERTO Few tourists ever get to Telchac Puerto, yet the town is lovely. Several tire-track "roads" lead through grassy dunes, past a few small restaurants, and down to an unspectacular but peaceful beach. Four buses make the trip daily from Progreso (1 hr) and Mérida (1½ hrs), dropping you off on the side of the road, about 400 meters south of the beach. If you miss the 5 PM bus back to Progreso, you may be able to arrange lodgings with a local family—ask at **city hall** (Calle 19, btw Calles 20 and 22) at the park in front of the basketball court.

SISAL A quiet fishing village on the western Gulf Coast, Sisal remains almost undiscovered by tourists. Some Americans come here during hunting season (November–March) to shoot game, but the hunters generally stick to the Club de Patos (Duck Club). The beaches are deserted during most of the year, and they are much broader and whiter than those on the northern Gulf Coast. From here, you can visit **Puerto de Abrigo**, a fishing *refugio* (refuge) 2 kilometers west of the pier; just walk along the beach. The small, red-and-white lighthouse, reconstructed in 1909, is still in use and occupied by a family. For a tip, a girl named Wendy will lead you up the stairs for a terrific view of the town. From the main street, head toward the water and take the last right before the beach for **Balneario Las Felicidades** (Av. 6 No. 104), which has small rooms on the beach with clean private baths. If you're a light sleeper, ask the owner if they'll be playing music at the disco that night. Singles with private bath are $6.75, doubles $10 (he'll let two sleep in a single). **Hotel Marea Roja** (Av. 6 No. 72, 300 meters east of main street, no phone) has fairly clean rooms with no hot water. A room with a double bed and hammock hooks costs $6.75. Several good, cheap restaurants line Sisal's main street.

➢ **COMING AND GOING** • Buses leave Mérida (Calle 71, btw Calles 70 and 72) hourly during the day for Sisal via Hunucmá. The last bus back to Mérida ($1, 2 hrs) leaves Sisal at 6 PM. To go from Sisal to Celestún, change buses in Hunucmá (½ hr, 50¢). From Hunucmá, buses to Celestún leave hourly (1 hr, $1; last bus 6 PM).

CELESTÚN On the tip of a narrow strip of land that separates the estuaries of Río Esperanza from the Gulf of Mexico, Celestún is one of the most-visited places around Mérida, and with good reason. Set in the middle of the Parque Natural Ría Celestún, the town has beaches and large colonies of exotic birds. Star billing goes to the flamingos, thousands of whom stand quietly in the waters of the estuary in pink formations. Although it's illegal to approach them closely enough to make them fly, they might give you a show anyway if you wait long enough. You can rent a boat ($50) from the dock under the bridge that spans the river (about a kilometer out of town) or get a cheaper deal right off the beach at the center of town. Before reaching the flamingos, you must navigate around Celestún's mangrove-lined peninsula. Boat rentals run $30–$40 (negotiable), so it's wise to share the cost with other tourists, of which there are plenty in high season and on weekends. The beaches at Celestún are speckled with glittering white shells, and the warm, clear waters make for beautiful swimming, but afternoon winds can kick up clouds of sand. If you can arrange to stay here for the night, be sure not to miss the magnificent sunset over Celestún's calm, misty blue waters. Buses for Celestún leave Mérida every 2 hours from the bus station (Calle 71 btw Calles 65 and 67) and cost about $2.

> *There's free flamingo-watching from Celestún's dock in the afternoon. The birds take to the sky all at once, creating a bright pink cloud.*

➤ **WHERE TO SLEEP AND EAT** • There are plenty of restaurants on the main street between the zócalo and the beach, and on the beach itself. Most serve only seafood, but **Restaurant La Playita** on the beach always has one non-seafood dish for about $2. The few budget accommodations on the beach fill up during July and August and on weekends. **Hotel María del Carmen** (Calle 12, at Calle 15, tel. 993/28–69–78) offers clean new rooms (singles $11.75, doubles $16.75), some with great sundecks. **Hotel San Julio** (Calle 12 No. 93-A, no phone), also on the beach, has comparable rooms at $6.75 singles, $8.25 doubles, or $10 for two beds (up to three people). Camping is free along the beach, but stay within the town limits or you may have trouble with homeless locals. Free camping on the beach in front of Hotel María del Carmen is allowed.

DZILAM DE BRAVO Seventy-five kilometers northeast of Mérida is Dzilám de Bravo, a birdwatcher's paradise. Unfortunately, sand flies make the beach a sunbather's nightmare. A thin strip of land just offshore serves as a resting place for birds nesting in the nearby savannas. This "island" is just a five-minute boat ride from shore, and you can get a fisherman to bring you out here for a few dollars. If you're feeling rich or traveling with a fairly large group, consider a day trip to the **Bocas de Dzilám,** a group of freshwater springs flowing from the sea floor about 40 kilometers away. The whole region is an avian extravaganza, with colonies of pelicans, albatross, and seagulls. The one-day excursion, including stops at various beaches and islets, costs about $60–$70 for up to six people. To arrange a trip, ask around for Javier "Chacate" Nadal, who calls El Pescador restaurant (2 blocks north of bus stop) home. Dzilám's sole decent hotel is **Hotel y Restaurant Los Flamencos** (Calle 11 No. 120, btw Calles 22 and 24, no phone), which offers clean, basic rooms, some with great sea views. You can fit up to four people in one room for $6.75, but unfortunately the bathrooms are tiny and lack hot water. The other option is to stay at **Cabañas Totolandia,** on the beach 2 kilometers west of town (toward Progreso). A cabaña with private bath costs $6.75 a night (up to four people). The palapa-cum-restaurant here is only open July and August.

➤ **COMING AND GOING** • From Mérida, take one of the nine daily buses (2 hrs, $1.75) from the Autobuses del Noroeste station (Calle 50, btw Calles 65 and 67). To return to Mérida, catch the bus outside the store at the southern end of the park (last bus around 6 PM). Two buses also leave from Progreso (2 hrs, $2) at 7 AM and 2 PM, traveling along the gorgeous coastal road to Dzilám. From the park, you can catch a COSTERA bus back to Progreso and Telchac at 9 AM and 4 PM.

IZAMAL

Tourism boosters often point to Izamal, 70 kilometers east of Mérida, as *the* colonial city in the Yucatán. The well-kept buildings around the main plaza do indeed recall the peninsula's colonial past, but most actually weren't built until the 19th century. There isn't really any reason to spend a great deal of time in Izamal, but it breaks up the long bus trip between Mérida and Valladolid or Cancún. Particularly impressive is the **Convento de San Antonio de Padua**, a magnificent example of colonial architecture. Built in 1549 by Franciscan monks, the convent is the largest of its kind in the Yucatán and looms above the surrounding buildings. The bright yellow convent complex is built on the ancient ruins of the Maya temple Popol-Chac and contains a church, a chapel, a sacristy, and an 80-square-meter grassy atrium surrounded by arched galleries. Admission free. Open daily 6 AM–8 PM. Mass held daily at 6:30 AM and 7:30 PM.

Two blocks north of the main plaza are the remains of the **Pyramid of Kinichkakmo**, whose summit is the highest point for miles around. The large pyramid and six other scarcely discernible structures are all that remain of the ancient Maya city of Itzamal, founded in AD 500 and named after the great Maya sun god Itzamná. The site has deteriorated but remains interesting both for its proximity to the colonial city and the fact that it is of pure Maya design, free of Toltec or Aztec influence. Follow Calle 28 north past the park to where it runs into Calle 27. Admission free. Open daily 8–5.

COMING AND GOING   Buses for Izamal (15 per day, 2 hrs, $1.25) leave Mérida from the station on Calle 62 (btw Calles 65 and 67). You can also catch a bus here from Valladolid (4 per day, 2½ hrs, $2.25). The best way to see Izamal is en route from one city to another. Take an early bus to Izamal and store your luggage for free at the station. You can see everything in an hour or two and be on the next bus out of town. To reach Chichén Itzá, take a bus from in front of Restaurant Wayné Né (Calle 30, at Calle 33) to Kantunil (45 min, $1). Wait here for the next bus to Valladolid, and tell the driver to let you off in Chichén Itzá (1½ hrs, 75¢).

WHERE TO SLEEP AND EAT   Izamal is ill-prepared for visitors. Rooms in the two hotels here are small, dark and bug-infested. **Hotel Kabul** (Calle 31 No. 301, tel. 995/4–00–08) has rooms with bathrooms (no hot water) that cost $4.25 for a single, $5 for a double. Next door, **Hotel Canto** (no phone) has a nice courtyard and rooms ($6.75) that look like jail cells. If you're determined to enjoy the luxuries of hot water and spotless bedcovers, try finding Naifa, who rents spanking new *apartamentos* (two-room flats) for $13.25 each. Naifa can be reached at her liquor store (Calle 28, across from movie theater) until 7 PM; afterward, try her at home (Calle 29 No. 300, btw Calles 28 and 30). Restaurants and *loncherías* are plentiful around the zócalo, and the market in front of the convent is also a cheap source of nourishment. **Restaurant Wayné Né** (Calle 30, at Calle 33, tel. 995/4–01–67; closed Tues.) has *pollo pibil* ($2.25) and *enchiladas de mole* for $2. Fresh juices are 25¢–40¢.

Chichén Itzá

Chichén Itzá is probably the most complex and interesting archaeological site on the peninsula. It is also the most crowded. People come from all over the world to admire the remains of this great city, and then are grossly misinformed by overly creative tourist guides who try to titillate rather than inform. Chichén is only 120 kilometers east of Mérida and 157 kilometers southwest of Cancún, and can be hurriedly explored on a day trip from either town. A better idea, though, is to stay in the nearby village of Pisté or even in Valladolid, and save yourself the 2- or 3-hour bus ride to the ruins. Another advantage of staying nearby is that you can avoid the crowds. Around midday literally scores of tour buses arrive, and the mass of humanity completely changes the feel of the place. It's much better to arrive early in the morning, when relatively few people are around and the sun isn't as intense.

Chichén Itzá is Mayan for "opening of the wells," a reference to the area's cenotes, around which the Maya first settled. Humans built this site into a major metropolis around AD 520, centuries before Mayan tribes emigrated from northern Guatemala. The new occupants modified many of the existing buildings, creating an eclectic architecture. For this reason, visiting Chichén is like being at several sites at one time, and trying to make "sense" of everything can be exhausting. Those who have been to Uxmal (and other Puuc and Chenes ruins) will notice similarities between the buildings there and the ones clustered around the observatory—characteristic of both are choza motifs, Chaac masks, and elaborate latticework on the upper facades. Added features such as columns and carvings of serpents, jaguars, and eagles are typical of a later Toltec-Maya style. The buildings surrounding El Castillo, the great pyramid of

Chichén Itzá

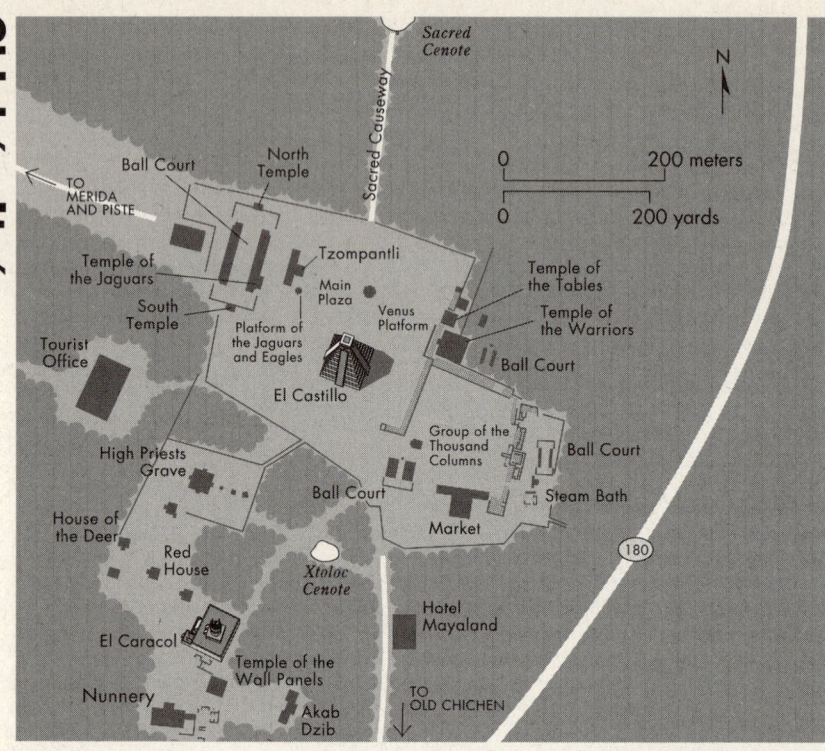

Kukulcan, were constructed from scratch by the Toltec-Maya, and have a more definitive style, with exquisite stone carvings glorifying human sacrifice, and images of Chac Mool, whose semi-recumbent figure waits everywhere, ready to receive offerings from the high priests.

COMING AND GOING

First- and second-class buses leave Mérida (2½ hrs, $3), Cancún (3 hrs, $3.50), and Valladolid (40 min, $1.50) on the hour for Chichén Itzá; there are also three daily buses from Playa del Carmen (5½ hrs, $6). Hourly second-class service returning to Valladolid and Cancún ends at 8 PM, to Mérida at 9 PM. Most buses stop at the ruins, the bus station in the nearby village of Pisté (about 700 meters from the zócalo), and downtown Pisté. If you have luggage in the storage compartment, you'll have to get off at the bus station. Most restaurants, hotels, and handicraft stores line Calle 15, the road leading from Pisté's zócalo to the ruins. You can walk between the two easily (it's only 2½ kilometers), or take a taxi for about $1.

WHERE TO SLEEP

Accommodations and food near Chichén Itzá are geared toward wealthy tourists; budget travelers will do much better in the small village of Pisté, 3 kilometers to the west. Pisté is a characterless town, but it's cheap. Campers can pitch a tent at the **Pirámide Inn Hotel and Trailer Park** (Calle 15, next to bus station, no phone) for $2.50. If you're feeling resourceful, string a hammock on a tree in the park for $2.50; if you don't have a hammock, the owner often lends them free of charge. Either way, you get access to the hotel pool. During the fall and spring equinoxes (Sept. 20, 21 and Mar. 20, 21) be prepared to settle for any amount of square footage you can get; even the most rundown fleabags are packed, and sleeping next to a stranger on the floor of a private kitchen is not a rarity.

Posada Chac Mool. These are clean, stereotypical budget hotel rooms with beds, hammock hooks, hot water, and very clean bathrooms. Singles are $10, doubles $11.50 ($11.50 and $13.25 with air-conditioning). *Calle 15, no phone. A short walk toward town from Pisté bus station. 6 rooms, all with bath, 2 with air-conditioning. Kitchen, laundry, luggage storage. Wheelchair access.*

Posada Olalde. Located down a side street about 150 meters from Pisté's main strip, this family-owned hotel offers large, clean rooms—cozy despite their size. The bathrooms are spacious and tidy but only supply tepid to cold water. You can wash your clothes in the tubs behind the house. Singles $8.50, doubles $12, triples $15. *Calle 6 No. 49, no phone. From bus station, walk toward town, left at Carrousel restaurant, continue down dirt road 150 meters. 4 rooms, all with bath. Kitchen, laundry, luggage storage. Wheelchair access.*

FOOD

Eating in Pisté is affordable as long as you avoid tourist-oriented restaurants. For drinks and snacks, head to the small stores along Calle 15, just east of Pisté's zócalo. **El Alba** and **La Lidia** are convenience stores where you can buy fresh bread. The **market,** open each morning, is just east of downtown Pisté. In front of the plaza are three **loncherías,** where you can get tortas for $1, salbutes and panuchos for 65¢, and main dishes for $3.25.

Restaurant El Parador Maya. Mama serves up daily specials, while neighbors drop in for cervezas (75¢). *Pac chuc* (grilled pork) marinated in orange and *pollo pibil* cost $3.25; an order of salbutes or a quesadilla is only $1.25. This is also a good place for breakfast—try the veggie-packed huevos rancheros ($1.75). El Parador is only open when there are customers—just knock if the door isn't open between 8 AM and 11 PM, or inquire across the street at Posada Maya. *Calle 15, 2 blocks east of zócalo. No phone.*

Restaurant Los Pájaros. This restaurant seems to be popular among baby lizards waiting out the rain under the festive thatch roof. Sandwiches and veggie soup are both $1.25. If you're up for something more substantial, try the pac chuc for $3.75. Beers are 75¢. *Calle 15, 2 doors west and across street from El Carrousel, no phone. Open daily until 10 PM.*

Restaurant Sayil. This tiny restaurant is about as close as you'll get to sitting in someone's kitchen. Flowered tablecloths cover three long tables overlooked by a small ceramic Virgin Mary. A dejected-looking chalkboard displays a limited menu, but they'll usually make a vegetarian dish to order. Main dishes (poc chuc, pollo pibil, beef filete) go for $1.75; for the same price you get an endless pile of rice, beans, and tortillas. *Calle 15 No. 57, west of bus station, no phone. Open daily 7 AM–10 PM.*

WORTH SEEING

Exploring Chichén Itzá can take a whole day—two if you're moving at a leisurely pace. It's a large site so bring plenty of water. There are bathrooms, as well as an expensive refreshment stand serving cold drinks and snacks. During the rainy season the vegetation and muddy paths reaching some of the ruins get sloppy. Guided tours in Spanish, French, or English are available; they last 2–2½ hours and cost $5 per person ($28 for 4–6 people). Make sure your guide is certified. Around noon, it's not too hard to tag along with one of the many tour groups. Every night an overwrought sound and light show is put on between the ball court and the Castillo, offering an entertaining, easy-to-swallow overview of the ancient city's history as well as the fall of the Mayan empire. The show in Spanish at 7 PM costs $2; the English one at 9 PM costs $3. *Admission: $6.50, free Sun. and holidays. Parking $3.50. Open daily 8–5.*

At night, Chichén's mountainous stone facades and gaping serpent mouths take on an eerie, vigilant glow under the moonlit jungle sky. As is always the case around the ruins, keep your eyes out for snakes.

EL CASTILLO The first building you see when you enter the site is this awe-inspiring steppyramid. Ninety-one steps up is a temple to Kukulcan, the feathered serpent deity. Symbolism abounds in El Castillo—the four stairways face the cardinal directions and the steps total 365, the number of days in the year. Fifty-two panels on the sides stand for the 52 years in the secular Maya calendar, and the 18 terraces symbolize the 18 months in the Maya year. By the base of one balustrade is the carved head of a giant serpent. At the spring and fall equinox (March 20/21 and September 20/21), the afternoon light hitting the balustrade forms a shadow that resembles the slithering form of Kukulcan descending the pyramid toward the Sacred Cenote. Northeast of El Castillo is the **Group of a Thousand Columns,** a large plaza surrounded by intricately carved columns that probably supported arches and a roof. Some archaeologists speculate that this plaza was the town market.

TEMPLE OF THE JAGUARS This temple, appended to the eastern side of the ball court, faces El Castillo. The columns that support the lower enclosure are thought to depict the cosmogony, or creation of the world and all of its beings—from plants, fish, and fowl to serpents and men—springing from the head of a god. Inside the enclosure, a detailed mural of a village scene depicts soldiers and townspeople.

BALL COURT The court is similar to others found at ancient centers in Mexico, but this one is bigger and more elaborate. The long, rectangular stadium featured two stone circles embedded high in the walls, into which players tried to shoot a large, rubbery ball using every bodily appendage except their hands (*see box* Ball Courts, *above*). On either side of the ball court are two small temples decorated with images of warriors and Kukulcan. From the north temple you can clearly hear the voice of anyone in the south temple—the sound travels along the walls of the court.

THE TZOMPANTLI Tzompantli means "place of the skulls" in Toltec, and the T-shape platform is indeed decorated with the carved images of hundreds of human skulls. Tribes from the west used to display the heads of defeated captains on stakes, and some think that the Maya-Toltecs used this platform for similar purposes.

THE PLATFORM OF JAGUARS AND EAGLES Immediately southeast of the Tzompantli is a small rectangular structure with a staircase on each side. Supposedly both the eagles and jaguars carved here represent the kings or captains of certain tribes. Scroll-like designs coming out of their mouths suggest that they may be discussing the plight of the sacrificial victims whose hearts they clutch.

SACRED CENOTE Many sacrifices took place at the Sacred Cenote, a well about 1 kilometer from the main ceremonial area. It was once believed that virgins were hurled into these waters to appease the rain gods, but diving archaeologists have since discovered skeletons belonging to individuals of all ages. The slippery walls were impossible to climb, and most sacrificial victims could not swim well enough to survive until noon, when the survivors were fished out to relate the stories of what they had learned from the spirits in the water. Thousands of gold and jade artifacts, highly precious to the Maya, have also been found in the murky depths of the cenote, which undoubtedly holds more treasures. First explored by Edward Thompson in 1903, the Sacred Cenote was excavated twice in the course of the next 60 years, both times resulting in the salvaging of scores of valuable pieces of jewelry and artifacts. During the second diving, a special chemical was used to make the water clearer, enabling divers to dredge up more than twice what had been previously found, but in the process the chemical also killed off most of the cenote's marine life.

The Reptilian Bogeyman

Superstition and magic still have a tenacious hold on the hearts of modern Yucatecos. One story common in the villages to the south and east of Mérida tells of a venomous snake whose hiss sounds just like a crying child. At night, the snake visits the houses of newborns. It sits by the cradle and cries in the dark, until the mother comes to comfort the child. What she encounters, of course—to her horror—is a deadly snake bite.

TEMPLE OF THE WARRIORS Carved warriors adorning the rectangular columns in front of this temple stand in perfect file guarding the staircase. The upper facade of the temple features gruesome masks of Chaac, as well as an eagle with a serpent head projecting itself fearsomely out of the stone surface. A closer look reveals the head of a human being emerging from the serpent's mouth.

STEAM BATH Steam baths were popular for hygiene and therapy all over pre-Columbian Mesoamerica. In Chichén's steam bath, you can still see the stone benches on which bathers waited their turn. A narrow doorway leads to a room containing two benches and a hearth where stones were heated, then sprinkled with water to produce steam.

MARKET There is no evidence to suggest that this building was used as a market—the decorations on the altar are human figures, not avocados—but some have speculated that the columns supported a palapa-style roof under which vendors sold their merchandise.

HIGH PRIEST'S GRAVE Following the road southwest of El Castillo you'll reach the High Priest's Grave, with its succession of underground chambers. The last of the seven humans buried here appeared to be the most important, possibly a priest.

RED HOUSE AND HOUSE OF THE DEER Farther along the road past the High Priest's Grave is the small House of the Deer, a Puuc-style building from the late Classic Period. The house owes its name to the mural of a deer that once decorated a wall. Next door is a similar building known as the Red House, after the red border painted around the doorway. The building is pure Puuc style, and hieroglyphs on its frieze date to 870 AD.

EL CARACOL El Caracol is the second most famous building in Chichén Itzá, after El Castillo. It was enlarged and renovated several times, making it a truly weird hybrid of shape and style. Astronomers used this building to observe the motion of the sun and stars in order to plan festivals, ceremonies, planting cycles, and other important events. A spiral staircase (hence the Spanish name, referring to the shape of a snail or a conch) leads to a small observation chamber. Square windows or slits are oriented toward key astronomical points. Southeast of the Caracol is **Akab-Dzib**, a 9th-century building. Akab-Dzib means "obscure writing" in Mayan, and if you look at the lintel of the southern doorway you'll notice a carving of a priest sitting on a throne surrounded by hieroglyphics.

LA IGLESIA This building stands behind the less interesting **Temple of the Wall Panels**, just southeast of El Caracol. It is a beautiful example of Puuc architecture, adorned with masks of Chaac and other geometrical motifs. In between the masks are animal gods—a bee, snail, turtle, and armadillo—which represent the four Bacabes, the beings that hold up the heavens.

NUNNERY COMPLEX Next door to La Iglesia is the Nunnery Complex, a strange cluster of buildings named by Spaniards who thought it resembled a European convent (it was probably a palace). Chenes designs adorn the east building, whose doorway is the gaping mouth of Chaac. The form of the central building, with its classic corbeled arches, seems to suffer a bit from several additions.

OLD CHICHEN Two kilometers down a path from the Nunnery Complex is group of poorly preserved ruins known as the **date group**. Here, two Atlantes (god-like figures who supposedly balance the weight of the world above their large, long-haired heads) stand atop a black block carved with Maya dates and hieroglyphs dating back to AD 879. If you're tired of dodging video cameras and potbellied tourists in order to get a glimpse of the ruins, try heading down the path to Chichén Viejo, a barely excavated group of ruins 2 kilometers from Chichén's more popular sites. Among the rubble lies what is thought to be a ceremonial center. The **Temple of the Phallic Symbols**, displaying early Maya triangular arches and the only examples of Toltec-influenced columns, was supposedly the place where virgins came to "know" a man's body. Indeed, numerous phallic reliefs jut out from the temple's walls. About 20 minutes farther into the jungle is another group of ruins, most badly decayed, with the exception of the **Temple of the Three Lintels**, a beautiful Puuc-style building similar to the buildings at Uxmal. The three-roomed building was supposedly used by healers, who brought the ailing here to be cured. Unless you're a real bushwhacker, it is *not* recommended that you visit these ruins on your own.

Instead, strike up a deal with an official guide. Groups of four or five may end up paying $10–$15 each for the excursion. Bring lots of water.

Near Chichén Itzá

BALANKANCHE CAVES

A mere 6 kilometers from Chichén Itzá are the immense Balankanché caves, thought to have been a Maya ceremonial center in the 10th and 11th centuries. In 1959 a local tour guide stumbled upon the stalactite-filled caves and discovered a number of ceramic and carved artifacts inside. The images engraved on some of the artifacts are thought to be that of Tlaloc, the Toltec god of rain. Unfortunately, you have to join a tour group to see the caves, and this usually means shuffling along behind a large, cigar-smoking tour guide from the nearby Mayaland Hotel. Although the cave's length and size are impressive, and bulbous, petrified knobs of stalactites are fascinating to observe at eye-level, a visit to the caves is only recommended if you're not heading on to the more impressive caves of Loltún. The caves are open daily 9–5; tours in English ($3, $1.25 on Sunday) are supposed to leave at 11, 1, and 3, but they're canceled unless there are at least two participants. To reach Balankanché, take any second-class bus between Chichén Itzá and Valladolid, and ask the driver to drop you "en las grutas." From the road it's a couple hundred yards to the caves. On the way back, flag down a bus on the road.

Valladolid

Much slower-paced than Mérida or Cancún, Valladolid (which lies smack-dab between the two) is also less frequented by crowds of picture-snapping tourists. The city's colonial past provides a slightly dilapidated architectural framework for what is today a well-traversed commercial center, with people coming from miles around to sell their wares at the local market (Calles 37 and 34). Shiny new mountain bikes and rusty 3-speeds lean up against well-washed store fronts, and at night, riders zip around the always-shady zócalo.

Valladolid was originally the Maya ceremonial site of Zací. The Spanish conquistador Francisco de Montejo was driven off by the indomitable Maya in 1543, but his son, Montejo the Younger, succeeded where his father failed. He laid out Valladolid in the classic Spanish colonial style and built six churches. The Maya, who had been banned from the city, constantly raided Valladolid, sending many a Mexican fleeing back to Mérida.

Every July 7, Valladolid celebrates the Fiesta del Barrio Sisal, a two-week-long fiesta featuring vaquerías (a succession of mestiza dances), local music, and afternoon corridas (bullfights). After the corrida, the freshly killed bull is split open and hung by its haunches alongside the bullring.

BASICS

CASAS DE CAMBIO **Bancomer** (Calle 40, facing the zócalo, tel. 985/6-32-95) is open for currency exchange weekdays 9–1. The ATM accepts Visa.

EMERGENCIES You can call the **police** (Calle 41 No. 156-A, btw Calles 20 and 22, tel. 985/6-21-00) or an **ambulance** (tel. 985/6-24-13) round the clock.

MEDICAL AID Half a block from the zócalo, **Farmacia Canto** (Calle 39, btw Calles 42 and 44, tel. 985/6-32-17) is open 8 AM–10 PM. For 24-hour medical service, try **Clínica Santa Anita** (Calle 40 No. 221, at Calle 47, tel. 985/6-28-11).

PHONES AND MAIL The **post office** (Calle 40, facing the zócalo) is open weekdays 8–2, Saturdays 8–noon. They'll hold mail sent to you at the following address for up to 10 days: Lista de Correos, Valladolid, Yucatán, CP 97780, México. Card-and coin-operated **phones** are located just outside the bus terminal and near the zócalo. For privacy and air-conditioning try the **Computel,** either in the bus terminal or next door to Hotel San Clemente (Calle 42, at Calle 41). Both are open daily 7 AM–10 PM.

VISITOR INFORMATION A sporadically attended *modulo de turismo* (tourist info booth) is located just inside the doors of the *ayuntamiento* (city hall, SE cnr of zócalo; open daily 9–2). The English spoken here is shaky, but you can get free maps and copies of *Yucatán Today*. For more info on local fiestas, tours, and historical sites, you can call Emma Montes at **Hotel Mesón del Margués** (tel. 985/6-38-74).

COMING AND GOING

Valladolid is a major crossroads for buses headed almost anywhere on the peninsula. Small and clean, the terminal is open 24 hours but is located about 6 blocks from downtown, and can get fairly lonely at night. **Autobuses del Norte** and **Autobuses del Centro del Estado de Yucatán** share the same terminal (Calle 37, at Calle 54, tel. 985/6-34-49). All buses listed below are second class. Buses run to Cancún (3 hrs, $3.25), hourly 5 AM–10 PM, and to Mérida (3 hrs, $3.25), hourly 5 AM–11 PM. There is also service to Cobá (2 hrs, $2.75), Tulum (3 hrs, $3.75), Playa del Carmen (4 hrs, $5), and Tizimín (5 per day, 1 hr, $1.25). Three buses leave for Izamal (1½ hrs, $3.25), and all of the Mérida-bound buses stop there, too. To reach Isla Holbox, take the 3 AM bus to the ferry port at Chiquilá (2½ hrs, $3.75).

WHERE TO SLEEP

The few budget hotels in Valladolid are conveniently located between the bus station and the zócalo. Nearest to the bus station, **Hotel Maya** (Calle 41 No. 231, btw Calles 48 and 50, tel. 985/6-20-69) is clean and quiet and has an inner patio blossoming with exotic flowers and palms. Singles and doubles go for $7.50, $13.25 with air-conditioning. **Hotel Lily** (Calle 44 No. 190, btw Calles 37 and 39, tel. 985/6-21-63) has singles with rather grimy shared baths for a mere $4.25, doubles $5 (private baths are $1). Hot water here is sporadic and cockroaches are frequent, but the vigorous fan will send your clothes flying. **Hotel San Clemente** (Calle 42 No. 206, btw Calles 39 and 41, tel. 985/6-22-08) borders on deluxe. To get the most for your pesos, avoid the rooms with noisy pigeons nesting outside. Singles are $11.25, doubles $14. Rooms with air-conditioning are $3 more, and all have TVs.

FOOD

Valladolid's restaurants don't offer the variety that Mérida does, but you can still sample Yucatecan food at reasonable prices. The local hangout is **El Bazar** (Calle 39, at Calle 40, NE cnr of zócalo), a plaza shared by several small *comedores* (sit-down food stands). Great comidas corridas with soup, a meat dish, tortillas, and a drink will run you about $3.25. Tacos and panuchos are readily available for about 65¢ each. **Restaurant del Parque** (Calle 42, at Calle 41, tel. 985/6-23-65) has daily specials ($2.50) and an excellent shrimp cocktail ($3.25), both served daily 7 AM–10 PM. At **El Jacal de los Dzeles** (Calle 40 No. 211, btw Calles 41 and 43; open daily 9–9), small groups of tired-looking men sit around drinking beer (50¢) and eating large plates of beef *filetes* ($2.50). A generously stuffed cheese, onion, tomato, and avocado sandwich is only 75¢, and a heaping pile of beans, rice, and tortillas goes for $1. If you're just looking to soothe your sweet tooth, try the corn ice cream at **Paletería La Flor de Michoacán** (Calle 40, btw Calles 37 and 39, tel. 985/6-20-52).

WORTH SEEING

Valladolid's churches are more impressive from the exterior, since interiors were looted during the Caste War. Nonetheless, for anyone interested in colonial architecture or exploring old buildings, the **Iglesia de San Bernardino de Siena** and the **Convento de Sisal** (both at end of Calle 41-A, at Calle 49) are definitely worth a visit. Currently the local priest's residence, the buildings are flanked on one side by an overgrown garden containing a grill-covered cenote. Admission free. Church open Tues.–Sun. 8–noon and 5–8; garden open 8–noon.

CENOTES Within walking distance of anywhere in town, the **Cenote Zací** (Calle 36, btw Calles 37 and 39; open for swimming daily 8–6) is well worth a visit on a hot afternoon. Though it glows an eerie green, the water is cool and fresh. Admission (75¢) includes access to the cenote and a museum (complete with family photographs and a henequen exhibit), and a peek at a few cooped-up animals in a haphazardly organized zoo. Though not as convenient as Cenote Zací, **Cenote Dzitnup** will enlighten you as to why the Maya regarded these pools as sacred. If you haven't been paralyzed by awe, have a swim with the blind fish in the brilliant blue water. If you arrive early, enjoy the magic of having the place to yourself. Don't let the rain dissuade you from coming—it's underground. Admission is 85¢, and it's open daily 7–5 (there are also changing rooms and a shower). To reach Cenote Dzitnup from Valladolid, take a westbound bus on the highway, ask to be let off at the crossroads, and walk 2 kilometers along the pleasant country road. Otherwise, you can rent a bicycle for 50¢ an hour from Antonio "Negro" Águilar, whose shop (Calle 44, btw Calles 39 and 41) is open 24 hours.

Near Valladolid

RÍO LAGARTOS

The creatures that gave "Alligator River" its name have long since been sacrificed to fashion—flamingos steal the show here now. The people of this small fishing village 103 kilometers north of Valladolid are especially friendly and appreciate the peace and tranquility of their home. You won't find much in the way of nightlife here, but Río Lagartos outdoes itself during the **festival of Apostle Santiago** (July 20–26), with folk dances, bullfights, and processions. On the first of June, all the boats get decked out and parade in the lagoon in celebration of **Día de Marina**.

Río Lagartos is a bird-watcher's heaven. Pelicans stand by the side of the road like old men, looking as if they'd strike up a conversation at any moment. Flamingos supposedly inhabit the area throughout the year, but August and September are the time to catch them en masse. June and July, they're busy laying eggs, and nesting sites are a 3- to 4-hour boat ride away. Laws prohibit approaching the nesting areas too closely, for fear the birds will suddenly take flight and disturb the eggs. You're also likely to see snowy egrets, red egrets, snowy white ibis, and great white herons, among other winged creatures. Arrangements for a boat trip to the flamingos' favorite hangout can be made with any of the motor boat owners along the malecón (usually about $20 for the 3-hour trip). You can also take a shortened ride to see the flamingos (which doesn't include the mangroves, salt flats, or their nesting sites) with an added stop at the beach for about $8 (this can be split among a group). If you're only interested in swimming, paddle around in the gulf off the Río Lagartos Peninsula, or get a boat to take you across to the beach for about $2.50 per person. **Chiquilá**, a natural *ojo de agua dulce* (freshwater pool) is 1 kilometer east of town (walk along the eastern shore from the malecón).

COMING AND GOING The 2½-hour excursion from Valladolid could be staged as a day trip if you live by a rigid itinerary. Otherwise, plan to spend at least one night. Buses leave Valladolid hourly for Tizimín (1 hr, $1.25); combis to Tizimín ($1.25) leave Valladolid from in front of the liquor store (Calle 40, at Calle 37). From Tizimín, you'll have to transfer to a second-class bus to Río Lagartos (12 per day, $1.25, 1 hr), which leaves roughly every hour between 5:15 AM and 7 PM. The last bus back to Tizimín from Río Lagartos leaves at 5:30 PM.

WHERE TO SLEEP AND EAT **Hotel Nefertiti** (Calle 14 No. 123, tel. 985/3-26-68 ext. 61) is the sole hotel in town, and its bare, blockish appearance isn't exactly inviting. The extra-large rooms have big bathrooms with clean towels. Singles are $8.25, doubles $11.75. **Cabañas Los Dos Hermanos** (Calle 19, 50 meters from bus station, no phone) rents two excellently equipped cabañas, complete with private baths and mosquito netting, for $8.25. (They're currently adding two cement-floor apartments, which will cost about $13.25 each.) If you're a beach lover, don't bother with the hotels—camp on the vast and unpeopled beaches along the gulf and hike the 14 kilometers to see the flamingos. Bring all the supplies you'll need, including anti-mosquito paraphernalia. Bargain with a fisherman to take you across the lagoon—you should be able to get him down to $3 for two people.

Food here is amazingly fresh and cheap, especially the seafood. **Restaurant Los Negritos** (2 blocks from bus station, no phone) serves fried manta ray in tomato sauce for $3.75, as well as a tasty fish soup for $2. They also serve egg breakfasts ($1.75). The kitchen is open daily 8–7; at 10 Los Negritos becomes a disco. **Restaurant Isla Contoy** (next to Hotel Nefertiti, no phone; open 7:30 AM–9 PM) is owned by a friendly family. Generous ceviches go for $2.50, and their fish fillets ($3.50) make a plentiful meal. Otherwise, try **La Cueva de Macumba** (Calle 14, at Calle 11, just west of gazebo on malecón) for enchiladas de mole and excellent flautas ($2.50) in a festive jungle-colored palapa.

Cancún

The only reason for budget travelers to go to Cancún is to catch a plane out. Paradise it may be for unadventurous vacationers, but it has little to offer the rest of us. The story of how this 22-kilometer, elbow-shape sand bar became a tourist mecca is fairly well known. Looking for a new location for a money-making resort, the Mexican government asked a computer to come up with the site, and a computer knows a good stretch of silicon when it sees one. Cancún's setting on the northern coast of Quintana Roo is ideal, with white-sand beaches, warm Caribbean waters, and coral reefs. Construction in Cancún began in 1972 and hasn't stopped since. The result is a mass of five-star hotels, shopping malls, and overpriced restaurants without coherence or personality—it is a city without a soul. Sure, it still has beautiful beaches—but so do Playa del Carmen, Isla Mujeres, and Cozumel. If you're not ready to spend those hard-earned pennies sharing a man-made wonderland with a bunch of sun-baked tourists, your best bet is to leave Cancún where it looks best—in the glossy brochures.

BASICS

AMERICAN EXPRESS The office has a travel agency, replaces lost cards and checks, cashes personal and traveler's checks, changes cash, and holds customers' mail for up to 30 days. *Tulum 208, at Brisas A, near Hotel América, tel. 988/4–19–99. Open weekdays 9–6, Sat. 9–1.*

CASAS DE CAMBIO Cancún's many casas de cambio are open until around 9 or 10 PM. Rates at banks are better, but the lines are long. **Banamex** (Tulum 19, 988/4–54–11) and **Bancomer** (tel. 988/4–54–00) change money weekdays 9:30–1:30. Banamex has an ATM that accepts Plus and Cirrus cards, and you can also get cash advances with a Visa or MasterCard.

CONSULATES Canada. *Plaza México 312, 2nd floor, tel. 988/4–37–16. Open weekdays 10–2.*

United States. This is not an official consulate, but an impotent representative office. For any real help you'll have to go to Mérida. *Edificio Marruecos 31, Av. Náder 40, tel. 988/4–24–11. Open weekdays 9–2 and 3–5:30.*

EMERGENCIES The **police** station (tel. 988/4–12–02) is downtown, on Avenida Tulum next to the banks. **Cruz Roja** (Labná 2, at Yaxchilán, tel. 988/4–16–16) has 24-hour ambulance service.

LAUNDRY Lavandería Las Palapas does up to three kilos of your laundry for $2. *Alcatraz, at Orquidea, on Plaza Las Palapas. Open Mon.–Sat. 7 AM–9 PM, Sun. 8–2.*

MEDICAL AID The **Hospital Americano** (Viento 15, at Tulum, tel. 988/4–61–33) is open 24 hours. **Farmacia París** (Yaxchilán 32, in Edificio Marruecos, tel. 988/4–01–64) is open 24 hours. The tourist information booklet *Cancún Tips* also has a list of English-speaking doctors.

PHONES AND MAIL The **post office** will hold mail sent to you at the following address for up to 10 days: Lista de Correos, Cancún, Quintana Roo, CP 77500, México. *Av. Sunyaxchen, Supermanzana 28, tel. 988/4–14–18. Open weekdays 8–7, Sat. 9–noon.*

You can place collect calls from **Computel** (Av. Tulum, near bus terminal, tel. and fax 998/7–42–24) between 7 AM and 10 PM; the service charge for five minutes is $2, and rates for domestic calls are 50% off on the weekends.

Cancún

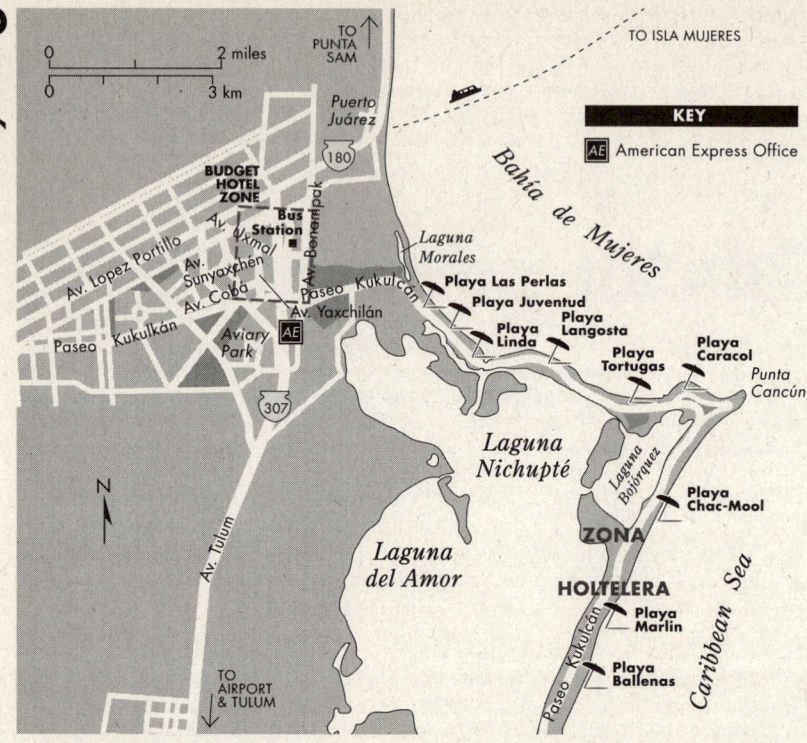

VISITOR INFORMATION The main office of the **Secretaría Estatal de Turismo** (Tulum 26, tel. 988/4-80-73) has a knowledgeable, English-speaking staff ready to shower you with brochures. During peak season (Nov.–Apr., July, and Aug.) the office is open daily 9–9; other months, the staff runs the main office 9–2 and then heads to the central booth (Av. Tulum, across from Palacio Municipal) to work 3–9. Your best printed resource is the ubiquitous *Cancún Tips*. The publication's frank and helpful staff (Tulum 29, near bus station, tel. 988/4-04-44), on duty weekdays 8–7, is a valuable resource for the most up-to-date discounts offered by local sport and tour companies.

COMING AND GOING

BY BUS The bus station is downtown, on Uxmal near Avenida Tulum. Two major bus companies, the first-class **Autotransportes del Oriente (ADO)** and the second class **Autotransportes del Caribe,** serve most points in Quintana Roo and the Yucatán, as well as other major cities in Mexico. Buses leave frequently for Mérida (4 hrs, $10), Valladolid (3 hrs, $4 2nd class), Chichén Itzá (4 hrs, $5 2nd class; 3 hrs, $6 1st class), Chetumal (6 hrs, $8 2nd class), and points in between. Buses for Playa del Carmen and Puerto Morelos ($2) depart every 15 minutes from the southeast side of the station. The bus stop for Puerto Juárez is on the east side of Avenida Tulum near the Monumento a la Historia. To reach the Zona Hotelera, cross Avenida Tulum and catch a HOTELES bus. The budget hotels are within walking distance of the station, and if you're desperate, you can store luggage here for a ridiculous 75¢ per hour.

BY CAR If you've got the money to rent a car, the drive to Tulum is a pleasant one: There are no tolls, and Highway 307 is well maintained. The road to the ruins via Valladolid and Mérida, however, is another story. Many an unsuspecting driver has paid through the nose after taking the *carretera de cuota* (toll road) to Mérida, which costs $24 ($12 at X-Can and $12 at Pisté). The toll is charged in both directions. You can really cruise on the toll road, but you can't get off it until Valladolid, meaning you won't see much more than painted lines. Highway 180, which is a *carretera libre* (free road), follows the same route as the toll road but passes through small towns. To avoid the toll road, take the highway out of Cancún and keep going straight—a CUOTA sign on your right will try to lure you in, but don't bite.

➤ **RENTAL CARS** • You can rent cars at the airport, in hotels, and all along Avenida Tulum. VW bugs typically cost $35 a day, but look around for discounts. Try **Avis** (in the airport, 988/3–08–03) or **Auto-Rent** (Av. Tulum, west of turn around in front of bus station, tel. 988/7–07–09). Coupons often appear in *Cancún Tips*.

BY BOAT Boats leave Puerto Juárez and Punta Sam (both north of Cancún) for Isla Mujeres every hour. The fare is about $1 for the 40-minute trip, and $2 for the 30-minute "express" trip. To reach the ports from Avenida Tulum, take a PUERTO JUAREZ bus for 50¢. Unless you're using the Punta Sam ferry to bring a car across to Isla Mujeres, you're better off leaving from Puerto Juárez.

BY PLANE Cancún's airport is the largest and busiest on the peninsula and is a frequent destination for many U.S. airlines (*see* Coming and Going in Chapter 1, Basics). Domestic airlines include **Aeroméxico** (tel. 988/4–10–97) and **Mexicana** (tel. 988/7–44–44). The casa de cambio at the airport, humorously named $EXCHANGE, is open during the day, but rates are better in town. It's also possible to crash in the airport; tourists clear out by nighttime and comfortable chairs can be found in the upstairs restaurant.

➤ **AIRPORT TRANSIT** • Unfortunately, no public buses serve the airport. A taxi into Cancún costs about $16 and a combi costs $7; you'll see the station wagons lined up outside as you leave the terminal. The alternative is a long, 1½-kilometer trek. Walk down the road all the taxis take out of the airport, and when you get to the highway, cross the street and flag down a CANCUN bus from below the overpass. The $1, 20-minute ride takes you right to the bus station in the center of town.

GETTING AROUND

Cancún is divided into two sections: the **Zona Hotelera** (Hotel Zone), home to monstrous resorts, and the **centro**. Only one street, Paseo Kukulcan, runs through the Zona Hotelera. The centro is on the mainland at the base of the elbow-shape sand bar that is the Zona Hotelera. It's divided into dozens of numbered zones—some only 1 block long—called *supermanzanas*, and addresses are often designated as "S.M." followed by a number. Avenida Tulum is the main drag, lined with restaurants and shopping centers selling expensive Mexican crafts. Buses marked HOTELES, CENTRO, and HOTELES/DOWNTOWN run west from the centro down Avenida Tulum, then toward the Zona Hotelera via Cobá, returning along the same route. Buses run every few minutes 5 AM–1 AM and cost 50¢.

BY TAXI Taxis are as expensive as you'd expect in Cancún. Fare within downtown should be around $1.50, from downtown to the youth hostel $2.50, $3.50 to Puerto Juárez, and an outrageous $6 to the Zona Hotelera. Still, you'll probably have to bargain for these prices.

WHERE TO SLEEP

Unless you happen to be a well-to-do foreigner, your hotel room will be downtown, away from the water. If you want to stay near the beach, your only option is the youth hostel (*see below*). Sleeping on the beach is out of the question.

➤ **UNDER $15** • **Hotel Alux.** This painstakingly sterilized place has air-conditioning and hot showers. Singles are $11, doubles $12.50. *Uxmal 21, tel. 988/4–05–56. ½ block north of bus station. 32 rooms, all with bath. Laundry, luggage storage.*

Hotel Canto. This hotel offers clean, air-conditioned rooms with large bathrooms and all the *agua purificada* you can swallow. If you get lonely, hang out in the lobby and watch cartoons with the kids. Singles and doubles are $13.50, triples $16. *Yaxchilán 22, at Sunyaxchen, tel. 988/4–12–67. 23 rooms, all with bath. Luggage storage. MC, V.*

Hotel Villa Rossana Cancún. This conveniently located hotel is cheap, and you're bound to meet some pretty interesting neighbors. The singles are huge, and some rooms have decks that look out above the city. Singles are $8.50, doubles $10, and triples $15. *Yaxchilán 68, just north of Sunyaxchen, tel. 988/4–19–43. 10 rooms, all with bath. Luggage storage.*

➢ **UNDER $30** • **Hotel El Rey del Caribe.** If atmosphere is more important than proximity to the beach, this is the place: It's set in a jungle-like garden with tropical plants, a pool, and Jacuzzi. Rooms are spacious and comfortable, with kitchens and clean bathrooms. Singles and doubles cost $27 plus $3 for each additional person. *Uxmal, at Náder, tel. 988/4–20–28. 23 rooms, all with bath. Luggage storage, reservations advised. Wheelchair access.*

HOSTELS **Villa Deportiva Juvenil Cancún.** Still known to bus drivers as the **CREA** hostel, this is the cheapest place in town and the only budget lodging on the beach. The sand isn't great, but Ping-Pong tables, a volleyball net, and a swimming pool provide great recreation. There are separate wings for men and women, and dorm rooms are equipped with bunks and lockers—some even have views of the sea. The place stays fairly clean, though bathrooms lack toilet paper and hot water; during rainy season, leaks cause ants and mice to seek refuge here. Beds cost $5 plus a $5 deposit for sheets and towels. *Paseo Kukulcan Km. 3.2, tel. 988/3–13–37. 300 beds. Meal service, luggage storage. Wheelchair access.*

CAMPING **Villa Deportiva Juvenil Cancún** (*see above*) lets travelers camp on its grassy lawns and use the hostel facilities for $4 per person.

FOOD

Food isn't cheap in Cancún, but if you're willing to stick to typical Mexican fare, it's affordable. In the Zona Hotelera, the pickings are extremely slim—guests at the youth hostel can choose between the meager fare offered there and **Superdeli,** a 24-hour minimarket 250 meters east of the hostel. Downtown, look for cheaper options on Avenidas Uxmal and Cobá and nearby streets. **Comercial Mexicana** (Av. Tulum, at Uxmal) serves ready-made food by weight, from spaghetti dishes ($2) to black beans and rice ($1 a pound). **Mercado 28** (Av. Xelha, across from the post office), a fake-colonial shopping mall, has an array of *loncherías* serving cheap, homemade meals and *antojitos*. Fruit vendors also swamp the morning market behind the post office; to get here take a RUTA 5 bus and get off at the post office.

➢ **UNDER $5** • **Restaurant Tlaquepaque.** Candy-colored tablecloths and high-backed bamboo chairs make you feel like you're sitting in a dollhouse. The owner is great company and a true connoisseur of Mexican cuisine—his delicious *ceviche* (steamed shrimp and raw fish with lemon juice, cilantro, and onion) is $4.25, and four tacos cost $3.25. *Yaxchilán 59, tel. 988/4–44–41. Next to Hotel Villa Rossana. Open Thurs.–Tues. 6 AM–9 PM.*

Rincón Yucateco. This place lacks in ambience, but low prices and a pleasant outdoor patio make it a great place to grab some soup ($1.75) or *parmuchas* (crisp, bean-filled tortillas topped with sliced chicken; $1.75) before a long bus ride. *Uxmal 24, next to Hotel Alux, no phone. Open daily 7:30 AM–9 PM.*

➢ **UNDER $10** • **La Parrilla.** This colorful labyrinth of tables entices even the most timid passerby. Unfortunately it's not a secret; you'll find the dining room dotted with yuppie tourists sharing the *Parrillada Mexicana*, a combination of grilled beef, pork, chicken, and vegetables, served with tortillas, salad, beans, and rice ($11). Vegetarians will delight in the *lopalitos* ($1.75), cactus- and onion-filled tacos topped with cheese and salsa. *Yaxchilán 51, tel. 988/7–61–41. Open daily noon–4 AM.*

La Peña Taurino. If you're willing to walk a bit out of your way, hang here with a crowd of locals on the industrial end of town. Mariachi bands and pictures of famous Hollywood couples provide the ambience while you drown your sorrows at the fully stocked bar. *Carne asada* is $6, and seafood (when they have it) is $7. *Chichén Itzá 48, btw Uxmal and Ceibo, no phone. Open Mon.–Sat. noon–midnight.*

AFTER DARK

The great advantage Cancún has over other Caribbean coastal towns is the abundance of nightlife, but it's generally what you'd expect: Huge discos bedecked with pseudo-Mayan motifs illuminated by flashing lights, and bars offering every drink imaginable blanket the Zona Hotelera and downtown. Cover charges are a high $8, but many set aside one day a week (usually Monday) for free admission; also check *Cancún Tips* for special offers. Discos in Cancún are known for their discriminatory policies. In many places (especially the Zona Hotelera), Mexicans are prohibited from entering, lest they offend gringos by their presence or behavior. The places listed below do not follow this policy.

If you are in downtown Cancún on a Friday night, head to the park behind Tulipanes. At around 8 PM, a special show called **Noche Caribeña** (Caribbean Night) features songs, dances, poetry readings, and raffles. Best of all, it's for locals, giving you a chance to escape the tourist crowd.

BARS The majority of bars in Cancún feature "shows," usually female strip acts. If this doesn't appeal to you, ask about the nightly show before you enter. One of the less touristy bars without a striptease is **El Manicero** (Sunyaxchen 69, at Yaxchitlan), featuring soloists singing *musica tropical,* a kind of spritzed-up tropical elevator music that makes you feel like you should be dancing with a pineapple balanced on your head. A few brave couples get up and dance, but most come for the tropical drinks (about $2) or to take in the night breeze. Right next door, locals pack the much more lively **Katakumbas** (Yaxchitlan 69). It's the one bar in town that serves beer on tap; a mere $1.25 gets you a frothy mug.

CINEMAS If you're craving some reel fun, try one of the many downtown cinemas that show recently released American movies. **Cine Royal,** on Avenida Tulum, and **Cine Cancún,** on Avenida Cobá, show English-language and Mexican films.

DANCING There are plenty of places to shake your bod in Cancún as long as you're willing to pay the price. Always packed is **La Boom** (short distance from hostel, tel. 988/3–14–58), a block-like edifice with a tiny door and smoky interior where singles mingle and sip $4 margaritas. The biggest salsa hub, **Barachá** (Hotel Miramar, in the Zona Hotelera) starts up at around 11 PM. Although the decor makes it look like the set of *Fiddler on the Roof,* **Margarita and Marijuana's** (Tulum 53) is surprisingly hip. It gets crowded after 11, when people amble in to sway to salsa and mariachi music.

OUTDOOR ACTIVITIES

BEACHES Most travelers come to Cancún expecting a flawless turquoise sea, tropical palms, and immaculate white-sand beaches. For the most part, Cancún delivers. Beaches in Cancún usually face the Caribbean Sea or the calmer Bahía de Mujeres, and the ones on the Caribbean side have become very narrow since Hurricane Gilbert swept through. Many of the best beaches are backed by luxury hotels but all are public. If you're discreet, you can make easy use of hotel facilities such as hammocks, lounges, huge pools, bars (watch out—a Coke could set you back $3.50), and showers. Warning flags indicate the water's danger lever: Green or blue means calm, yellow means caution, and red or black signifies danger.

The best Caribbean beaches are those in front of the **Hyatt Cancún** and **Sheraton** hotels, and **Playa Chac Mool,** all all of which are near **Punta Cancún,** the northeast point of the Zona Hotelera. Calm **Playa Linda,** near the youth hostel, is just 10 minutes from town by bus, and **Playa Tortugas,** another mile farther along Paseo Kukulcan, has some of Cancún's clearest water. If you're bent on avoiding the crowds, head to **Playa Ballenas** (Km. 14, just north of Cancún Place Hotel), where bigger waves and rocky outcroppings make for slightly hazardous swimming but beautiful views. If you want to take it all off, head for the **nude beaches** near Club Med, at the southern end of the Zona Hotelera. Buses don't make it all the way out here, so you'll need to take a taxi or hitchhike. To reach the beaches along the Zona Hotelera, hop one of the HOTELES buses (50¢) that run all day and tell the driver where you're going.

WATER SPORTS • Most water activities in Cancún are expensive and short-lived, and you'll have to contend with crowds of people doing the same thing. Street vendors and hotels offer fairly consistent prices for parasailing ($35 for a 15-minute ride), sailwaving ($25 for 20 minutes strapped to the sail of a catamaran) and waverunners ($40 for a half-hour ride on a Jet-Ski-like machine). If you plan on windsurfing (about $15 per hour) be aware that the current can get pretty strong beyond the shoreline. Lifeguards keep a good watch, but you might want to get their attention before heading out just to be sure. Windsurfer rentals and lessons can be arranged at **Marina Aqua World** (Paseo Kukulcan Km. 15, tel. 988/3–30–07).

➣ **DEEP SEA FISHING** • Cancún is known as one of the best game-fishing spots in the world, with barracuda, red snapper, bluefin, grouper, and mackerel running year-round. **Marina Aqua Tours** (Av. Tulum, tel. 988/3–04–00) arranges 4- to 6-hour tours ranging in price from $40 to $99. Beer, bait, and gear are all supplied.

➣ **SCUBA DIVING** • Don't come to Cancún to scuba dive: The underwater scene at Cozumel is far superior. Unfortunately, in Cancún you can only rent diving equipment if you're certified, and most of the three-day certification courses will set you back as much as $350. Some marinas, such as **Marina Aqua Ray** (in front of Villas Plaza Hotel, tel. 988/3–30–07), offer short resort courses and easy dives for about $80. Diving trips to the reefs in Bahía de Mujeres cost about $50 for one-tank dives and $70 for two-tank dives. There is also excellent diving at Punta Nizuc (*see below*).

The removal of coral from reefs causes thousands of species to lose their habitat. Although stores all over Mexico's Caribbean coast sell black coral jewelry, buying it contributes to the destruction of this fragile ecosystem.

➣ **SNORKELING** • Despite the incredible clarity of the water, snorkeling off the beaches around Cancún is not as rewarding or affordable as at some other Caribbean resorts—it's usually cheaper to snorkel from Isla Mujeres. Many marinas in town offer tours to **Los Chitales** (2 km north of Cancún) or **Punta Nizuc,** a jungle-like underwater grove at the island's southernmost tip. Snorkeling tours usually run $40 for 3½ hours (including lunch and beer), or you can rent your own gear (about $25 a day) and head to Punta Nizuc by bus—take the HOTELES bus to the Westin Regina resort, 2 kilometers from the best snorkeling spots. Longer offshore snorkeling, diving, or fishing trips require one-day advance reservations. **Marina Aqua Tours** (Av. Tulum, tel. 988/3–04–00) and **Marina del Rey** (tel. 988/3–03–00) offer a large selection of trips at decent prices, but a better idea is to take the ferry to Isla Mujeres, where rentals are less expensive and good reefs and fishing sites are in close proximity.

Near Cancún

ISLA HOLBOX

Secluded at the end of a long and arduous series of bus rides and an equally painstaking ferry ride, Isla Holbox sits like a glittering patch of heaven amidst mosquitoes and pungent fishnets. The island is long and skinny (about 4 by 2 kilometers) with a curved western tip, framing Laguna Yalahua to the west and bordered by Cabo Catoche to the east. The town is small, sleepy, and excruciatingly hot—most people stay in the shade of their homes with the doors and curtains open. At the end of the town's main drag, you'll find the deep-sanded north coast beach, a glistening strip of rockless grains stretching eastward to a lighthouse. If you aren't up for the 7-kilometer trek down the coast, it's worth renting a moped ($10 per half day, but negotiable) and heading along the beachside path to the lighthouse's edge to watch the flamingos cluster around their nests.

COMING AND GOING • To reach Isla Holbox, you must first take a bus to Kantunilkin (50 km south of Isla Holbox) from Valladolid (6 hrs, $8) or Cancún (5 per day, 2½ hrs, $3). From Kantunilkin, wait for a bus to Chiquilá (1 per hour, ½ hr, 75¢). From Chiquilá the ferry leaves for Holbox (1 hr, $1) 8 AM and 2 PM, and returns at 6 AM and noon. An alternative is the *barquito,* which departs Chiquilá for Holbox at 8 AM and Holbox for Chiquilá at 5 AM.

WHERE TO SLEEP AND EAT **Posada Amapola** (on the zócalo) rents nice rooms with clean baths for $7 (singles) and $8 (doubles). Also on the zócalo is **Posada Los Arcos,** where doubles go for $10. The owner also has five cabañas on the beach near town, each one with a private bathroom. Units with a kitchen are $13; without are $10. Inquire at the Tienda Dinora on the zócalo. Other *posadas* (inns) in town are **Hotel Flamingo's** ($10 for a double) and **Posada Playa Bonita** ($12.50 for a double). The island also offers unlimited camping possibilities; the ocean side is the best place to look for a camping spot, but bring your mosquito net or some strong repellent.

Lonchería El Parque (on the zócalo) serves whopping portions of local fish for $2–$3, and beers for 65¢. Otherwise, the supermarket sells fruit and cookies, and you can buy fresh bread at the bakery.

PUERTO MORELOS

South of Cancún is the tranquil fishing town of Puerto Morelos, a welcome change from the resort frenzy to the north. It's fairly upscale, benefiting from the overflow of tourists on country drives in rented 4x4s. There isn't much to do in town, and the beaches aren't great—if you want to bake in the sand, walk a couple of kilometers south to more secluded, attractive areas. Puerto Morelos's main draw is an offshore reef where you can snorkel or dive. **Sub Aqua Explorers** (SW cnr of zócalo, tel. 987/1–00–78) rents snorkel equipment ($15 per day), offers diving trips ($55 for 2 tanks, $45 for 1 tank, $50 cavern dive), and fishing trips ($80 for 2 hrs). If you're staying overnight, consider **Posada Amor** (Javier Rojo Gómez, tel. 987/71–00–33), a great little hotel just south of the zócalo that offers singles for $22 and doubles for $25; a private bath costs about $5 extra. **Restaurant Las Palmeras** and **Restaurant Los Pelícanos,** both on Avenida Rafael Melgar, serve typical seafood dishes for about $7.50.

COMING AND GOING Minibuses (5 per day, ½hr, $1.50) run from Cancún's bus station to Puerto Morelos every 2 hours 6–10 and 2–8, with the last bus leaving Cancún at 8:30 PM. Seven buses return to Cancún; return tickets are sold at the pharmacy on the northwest side of the plaza 8–1 and 4–9. Another way to reach Puerto Morelos is to take one of the three daily ferries from Cozumel. The 2½-hour ride costs $7 per person and $45 per car. At these rates, you're much better off ditching your car and taking one of the frequent ferries from Playa del Carmen.

Isla Mujeres

At first sight, Isla Mujeres, just 10 kilometers east of Cancún, is a stereotypical resort. The carefully arranged souvenir and *artesanía* (handicraft) shops jostle for space with a handful of expensive restaurants and charmless hotels. But Isla Mujeres has retained its sweet and simple essence, drawing budget travelers from all over the world. They come for quiet and peaceful white beaches perfect for reading, walking, and playing ball, and snorkeling and diving opportunities that include trips to the Cave of Sleeping Sharks, a natural phenomenon straight out of *National Geographic*. Still, the main reason to come to the island is to relax, read a couple books, make new friends, and avoid doing much of anything.

How the island got its alluring name is open to debate. One fanciful story says pirates stashed their women here while they went off for a good plunder. A more plausible explanation is that the island is named after Maya female figurines found here by Francisco Hernández de Córdoba, the commander of a Spanish expedition, who "discovered" the island in 1517. The subsequent history of the island is common to the Caribbean: It was a hideaway for pirates and later became a fishing village. During the late '60s and '70s, the island became a hammock haven for hippie castaways, but that's pretty much faded with the movement.

Apart from Carnaval, Isla Mujeres's most important event is the Regata del Sol al Sol, celebrated yearly in late April, when boats leave St. Petersburg, Florida, and arrive here amid much partying. The event is concluded by a basketball game between Mexican and American teams, which the Mexicans always win.

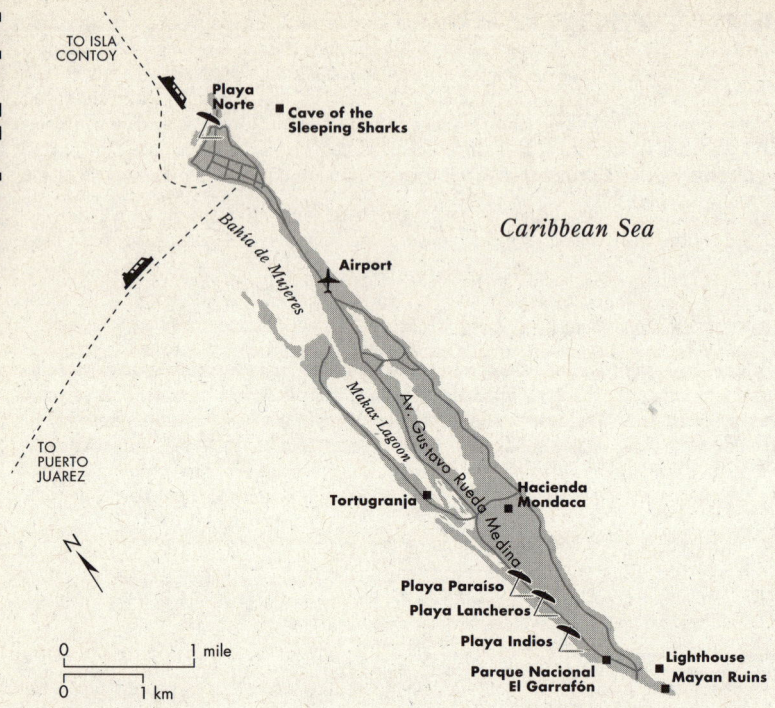

BASICS

CASAS DE CAMBIO **Banco del Atlántico,** on your right as you come off the ferry from Puerto Juárez, offers good exchange rates. *Rueda Medina 3, btw Morelos and Bravo, tel. 987/7–00–05. Money exchange weekdays 9–5.*

LAUNDRY **Tim Phó** does your laundry for $2. *Juárez, at Abasolo, tel. 987/7–05–29. 2 blocks from zócalo. Open Mon.–Sat. 7 AM–9 PM.*

MEDICAL AID The **Centro de Salud** (Guerrero 5, tel. 987/7–01–17) offers 24-hour emergency service. The English-speaking doctor, **Antonio Salas** (Hidalgo, next to Farmacia Lily, tel. 987/7–04–77) makes house calls round the clock. **Farmacia Lily** (Madero, at Hidalgo, tel. 987/7–01–64) is open daily 9 AM–9:30 PM.

PHONES AND MAIL The **post office** will hold mail sent to you at the following address for up to 10 days: Lista de Correos, Isla Mujeres, Quintana Roo, CP 77400, México. *Guerrero, at Mateos, tel. 987/7–00–85. Open weekdays 8–7, Sat. 9–1.*

The long-distance **telephone office** (Rueda Medina 9b, near ferry terminal) is open daily 9–9. You can also find coin- and card-operated phones scattered about the town. Buy phone cards at **Tienda de Artesanías Yamili** (Hidalgo 4, tel. 987/7–05–20), open Monday–Saturday 9–9, Sunday 9–3.

VISITOR INFORMATION The staff at the **tourist office** (Hidalgo 6, near zócalo, tel. 987/2–03–16) is knowledgeable but speaks little English. Make sure to pick up a copy of *Islander,* a monthly publication with good maps of the island and general tourist information; the office is open weekdays 8–2 and 5–8. For a free map and some friendly advice, you can also try the **tourist information booth** at the Puerto Juárez ferry dock in downtown Isla Mujeres.

COMING AND GOING

You can reach Isla Mujeres from either Puerto Juárez or Punta Sam. Hourly ferries and water taxis make the 40-minute trip from Puerto Juárez for 75¢, or take the smaller, quicker ferry (5 min, $2). Puerto Juárez is 15 minutes from Cancún by bus (50¢)—catch one from any of the bus stops on Avenida Tulum. A taxi will cost about $2.50.

Although it's farther from Isla Mujeres than Puerto Juárez, Punta Sam is the best departure point if you're bringing a car over. **Ferries** (45 min, $1) leave every 2 to 3 hours. The cost of transporting a car starts at about $6, depending on the car's size. **Water taxis** make the crossing in 10–15 minutes for about $3 per person (if you have four or more people, you should be able to bargain). The taxis run at amazing speeds, and the ride is bumpy but exhilarating—if you're prone to seasickness, take the ferry. To reach Punta Sam from Cancún, take a PUERTO JUÁREZ bus from Avenida Tulum, and ask the driver if he continues to Punta Sam. **Boats** also leave Isla Mujeres for Isla Contoy from the Cooperativa dock just north of the Puerto Juárez/Isla Mujeres pier. Trips to Isla Contoy can be arranged through various hotels and vendors throughout town, or you can contact **La Isleña** (see *Isla Contoy, below*).

GETTING AROUND

The island of Isla Mujeres is only about 8 kilometers long and 810 meters wide, and most travelers stay in the town at the northern tip of the island. The majority of shops and restaurants are on the west side of town, and the zócalo is at the town's southernmost end, at Morelos and Benito Juárez. Consider renting a bicycle or moped to see the "other" Isla Mujeres, consisting of locals' houses and unspoiled coastal views.

BY BUS The only bus in town (85¢) runs down the main street at the ferry docks, passing the designated bus stop just north of the taxi stands every hour, and heads south to Playa Cancheros, where it turns around and makes its way through the residential areas on the island's edge before heading back into town.

BY MOPED AND BIKE Isla Mujeres's flat terrain makes for beautiful rides. Several places around town rent mopeds for about $3.25 an hour, $10 for the whole day (gas included); you'll usually need to leave a deposit or your ID. You can rent bicycles for only $3.50 a day at **Micha's Motorent** (Abasolo 13). **Sport Bike** (Juárez and Morelos, just below zócalo, tel. 987/2–00–36) rents bikes with locks overnight for $4.50; they're open daily 8–5.

WHERE TO SLEEP

Most hotels on Isla Mujeres are in town. Prices, which have skyrocketed over the last few years, rise even more during high season (Nov.–Apr. and July–Aug.); prices listed below reflect the low-season range. Those craving romance should consider staying in the dreamy **Nic Te Ha**, (Zazil-Ha 1, at Playa Norte), near the abandoned Na-Balaam Hotel. Cozy, enclosed *palapas* (huts) sit beside a small stony inlet, providing the perfect setting for a private midnight skinny-dip or a late-afternoon read. Each palapa shares a small but clean living room and has two double beds, access to kitchen facilities, and a conch-littered terrace complete with beach chairs and hammocks. A double palapa goes for $20 a night ($5 for each extra person). Reservations are recommended during high season: From Cancún call 988/3–06–08; from Mérida call 99/25–31–71; from Isla Mujeres call 987/7–00–45.

➢ **UNDER $10** • **Hotel Caribe Maya.** This hotel near the main ferry terminal is comfortable, clean, and bugless, and the water gets so hot you can actually steam your clothes in it. The $8 fan-only rooms (singles and doubles) stay pretty cool, but air-conditioning is also available for a mere $3 extra. They also rent mopeds for $10 a day and offer trips to Isla Contoy for $21. Credit cards are accepted, but there's a 6% usage fee. *Madero 9, tel. 987/1–05–23. From Rueda Medina, head east on Madero about 2 blocks. 25 rooms, all with bath. Luggage storage. Reservations advised Dec.–Apr. MC, V.*

Hotel Osorio. Osorio's neatly painted one- and two-story balconies are hard to miss from the street. Beds are small, and ants seem to amble in and out of every crevice, but rooms are about as cheap as they get—$6.50 for a single or double. The hotel also offers daily trips to Isla Contoy for $25. *Madero 10, at Juárez, tel. 987/7–02–56. 40 rooms, all with bath. Luggage storage. Reservations advised Dec. and Jan. Wheelchair access.*

Hotel Xul-Ha. The constant construction work here is slightly unnerving, but the clean, spartan rooms are in a fairly stable wing. Bathrooms are pleasantly grunge-free, and large shower stalls with hot water provide a welcome end to a long day at the beach. Singles $7, doubles $8.50. *Hidalgo 23, tel. 987/7–00–75. From Rueda Medina, head east on Lopez Mateos 1 block, take left on Hidalgo. 11 rooms, all with bath. Luggage storage. Wheelchair access. MC, V.*

Poc-Na. Budget travelers and adventure seekers from all over the world converge here for good company and comfy hammocks. Hang out on the rooftop under the stars, or listen to the jukebox under the large palapa that doubles as a dining room and living area. The coed dorm rooms ($3 per person) have bunks and hammock hooks, and you can use towels, sheets, and pillows for a $3 deposit. *Matamoros, tel. 987/7–00–90. From main ferry docks, north on Rueda Medina, east 4½ blocks on Matamoros toward east coast beach. Laundry, luggage storage, meal service. Wheelchair access.*

➢ **UNDER $15** • **Hotel Carmelina.** Despite the occasional cucaracha, rooms are large and sunny and have fans and clean bathrooms. Ask for a top-floor room; they're bright, cheery, and overlook the rest of town. Singles cost $7, and doubles are $10 ($12.50 with air-conditioning). Each extra person costs $1.75. They also rent bicycles for $3.50 a day. *Guerrero 4, tel. 987/7–00–06. From ferry, up Morelos and left on Guerrero. 18 rooms, all with bath. Laundry, luggage storage. Wheelchair access.*

➢ **UNDER $25** • **Hotel Francis Arlene.** This hotel offers a little bit of luxury for a reasonable price. The rooms, all with terraces, are individually decorated, and there's even art on the walls. If you're tired of the beach, you can grab a chaise lounge and sunbathe on the beautifully tiled roof. Singles start at $18.50, doubles at $22, and triples at $26. *Guerrero 7, tel. 987/7–03–10. 12 rooms, all with bath.*

CAMPING Camping is not allowed here and police do patrol the beaches. However, if you're in a secluded enough spot, they aren't likely to notice. You can also camp at the beach by Poc-Na, but they'll charge you the regular $3 room fee.

FOOD

Inexpensive loncherías are scattered throughout town, including four on Avenida Guerrero between Matamoros and Mateos. Small sandwiches cost about $1, a plate of tacos is $1.50, and main dishes, such as fish, cost about $3. Especially good is the tiny nameless lonchería on Guerrero between Matamoros and Abasolo. If you have your own stove or are staying at a hotel with cooking facilities, buy your food at the **market** on Guerrero at Mateos. **Panadería La Reina** (Madero, at Juárez) sells fresh pastries and great banana bread.

➢ **UNDER $5** • **Cafecito.** Sitting beside a stained-glass wave at a table decorated with seashells, you may think you've fallen into a tourist trap, but as you sip a cappuccino ($1.50) or hover over a huge banana split ($4), you probably won't care. Breakfast lovers take note: Belgian waffles smothered with whipped cream and strawberries fetch $2.25, and a variety of egg dishes go for $1.75. *Matamoros 42, at Juárez, no phone. Open daily 8–noon and 6–10.*

Chen Huaye. With Silvio Rodríguez tapes in the stereo and pink flamingos on the wall, this is the path to enlightened eating. The name of the place means "always here," which describes where you might be after you discover *chaya* ($1), a green drink made from a tropical plant resembling spinach. Popeye never had it so good. The chicken tortas, at $1.25 a pop, make the wallet as happy as the soul. *Hidalgo 17, no phone. Near zócalo, behind basketball courts. Open daily 9 AM–11 PM.*

La Peña. Perched atop a rock outcropping on the island's western shore, this restaurant serves smaller portions than most other places in town, but romantics can't resist sipping a margarita ($1.75; half-price 4–8) as the salty breeze drifts in through the open windows. The tomato-based fish soup ($1.50) is incredibly fresh. For something more filling, try the *chicken mole* (chicken in red chile and chocolate sauce; $3). *Guerrero 5, in front of Palacio Municipal, tel. 987/7-03-09. Open 10 AM-11 PM.*

Restaurant Las Flores. This small place has whitewashed walls, an outdoor grill, and live music. If you want to ignore mom's perennial advice, plunge into their pool after taking advantage of the $8–$15 all-you-can-eat lunch buffet. *Juárez 32, btw Mateos and Matamoros, tel. 987/7-05-06. Open daily 12:30–3:30.*

WORTH SEEING

HACIENDA MONDACA Not much is left of this mansion once owned by the reputed pirate Fermín Mondaca de Marechaja. In the 1860s, Mondaca moved to Isla Mujeres, where he supposedly fell in love with a local woman. She married another man and Mondaca went mad. In the local cemetery you can still see his tombstone, inscribed with the epitaph, "As you are, I was. As I am, you will be." *From taxi stand on Rueda Medina, take bus (25¢) to the end of the line (Playa Lancheros); backtrack on main road to park entrance. Admission free. Open 8–7.*

MAYA RUINS The island's Maya ruins are just that—ruins—and visitors today see little. A small sandstone building at the southern tip of the island was once a temple to Ixchel, the Maya goddess of fertility. Female figurines, believed to be votive offerings, were found here by Hernández de Córdoba and provide the most plausible explanation of the island's name. Despite the temple's disrepair, the striking effect of the waves breaking on the steep cliffs below is spectacular. Ask the lighthouse keeper if you can climb to the top floor for the beautiful view; if you're lucky, he may also have some ice-cold Cokes for sale. *From town, follow road as far south as possible and walk up dirt path. Or, take bus to Playa Lancheros and walk 2 km.*

TORTUGRANJA Among many ardent save-the-sea-turtle enterprises dotting the Quintana Roo coastline, this is probably the most elaborate. The best time to come is near the end of the egg-laying season (May–October), when newly hatched baby turtles can be found darting around the central building's shallow, raised tanks. It gets hot here, so bring water. Otherwise, you can opt to take a dip off the dock out front—just make sure you jump in the non turtle-inhabited side. *Take the (only) bus and get dropped off at Mondaca and walk north for 20 min. Admission: $1. Open daily 9–5.*

AFTER DARK

For weekend shebangs, check the postings at Poc-Na (*see* Where to Sleep, *above*). For the best in techno/house, head for **La Peña** (*see* Food, *above*), which transforms into a steamy (and touristy) disco after 11. There's no cover, and beers are under $2. A sand-dusted crowd of younger Mexicans goes to **Las Palapas** (Hidalgo, at Playa Cocos), for salsa and disco dancing in a huge palapa complex right on the beach. There's no cover, and drinks are two-for-one between 9 PM and midnight. Mellow ex-hippies-turned-yuppies spill out onto Hidalgo in front of **Mexico Lindo,** where a Canadian guitarist has a regular gig playing classic rock tunes. If you're looking for some company, a *mojito* (rum with mint, lime, and soda water; $2) can lead to a long, adventure-filled night at **Cuba Ron** (Guerrero, at Morelos), which supposedly closes at 10, but regulars drift in and out until midnight. The *zócalo* is also a fun place to hang out at night, with music, games, fried plantain stands, and basketball under the lights.

OUTDOOR ACTIVITIES

BEACHES Northwest of town is **Playa Norte,** a wide, white-sand beach. It's the traditional topless beach, but until the Europeans arrive in July and August, mammary toasting is not all that common. A plethora of water sports are available at Playa Norte, including snorkeling, water cycling, sailing, and water skiing (*see* Snorkeling, *below*). You can use the bathrooms and showers on the beach near Hidalgo for $1.

The three modest beaches on the west coast of the island—**Playa Paraíso, Playa Lancheros,** and **Playa Indios**—don't have the fine white sand you'd expect from a Caribbean island. The shallow sea is rocky and full of seaweed, making it a less than ideal place to swim and snorkel.

Playa Paraíso still sees its share of visitors, as it's a popular harbor for tourist boats from Cancún, which deliver tired guests for an expensive lunch or dinner after a day of snorkeling at El Garrafón. The beach has quite a few restaurants, a number of small stands selling souvenirs, and clean bathrooms. Someone may ask you to pay an entrance fee, but the beaches are government-owned and the fee is a scam. From town, take a bus, bicycle, or moped south down the main road about 4 kilometers.

ISLA CONTOY Isla Contoy, 45 minutes north of Isla Mujeres by boat, is a lush bird sanctuary where you can see brown pelicans, cormorants, frigate birds, herons, and flamingos. The quality of snorkeling off the thin strip of white-sand beach depends on the weather—if it's windy, sand can make visibility close to zero. Most travel agencies in town offer day trips to the island. **Poc-Na** (*see Where to Sleep, above*) arranges day-long sailboat trips to the island for $18 a person ($20 for fewer than 10 people), including snorkeling and fishing equipment as well as food and drink. **La Isleña** (Morelos, at Juárez, tel. 987/7–05–78) arranges 4-hour tours for $25 per person that include food, drink, and snorkeling equipment. They usually require a six-person minimum, but you may be able to talk them down to four. The tours consist of a boat ride, a stop on the beach to snorkel and eat lunch, and bird-watching on the island.

SCUBA DIVING Isla Mujeres offers one of the world's most exciting and unusual diving trips. Aside from the obvious attraction of the coral reefs, divers have a chance to explore the **Sleeping Shark Caves** (*see* box, *below*). Diving trips to the coral reefs around the island (such as Chitales, Banderas, and Manchones reefs) cost between $20 and $65, depending on the amount of gear and tanks you use, and where you go—trips to the Sleeping Shark Caves are usually about $15 more than other dives. If you're not certified, you must take the $80, 3-hour introductory course before diving with an instructor. **Bahía Dive Shop** (Rueda Medina, near ferry dock, tel. 987/7–03–40) offers trips to Manchones, Banderas, Chitales, and the Sleeping Shark Caves. Carlos Gutiérrez at **Mexico Divers** (Rueda Medina, near ferry dock, tel. 987/7–02–74) is helpful and has reasonable prices.

Sleeping Shark Caves

It may sound like something from "Ripley's Believe It Or Not", but a series of underwater caverns off Isla Mujeres are a crash pad for a dangerous species of shark. The sharks are not actually sleeping but are in a state of relaxed nonaggression seen nowhere else. There are two explanations for why the sharks come to the caves. One theory is that the water inside the caves has a different makeup than the water outside. It contains more oxygen, more carbon dioxide, and less salt. The decrease in salinity causes the parasites that plague sharks to loosen their grip and allows the remora fish (the sharks' personal vacuum cleaner) to eat the parasites more easily.

Because of the deep state of relaxation of these sharks, another theory (our personal favorite) is that the sharks come to the caves to get high. Fresh water seeps up into the caves from the ground, and the combination of fresh and salt water may produce an effect akin to that of humans' smoking marijuana. Whatever they experience while "sleeping" in the caves must be well worth the extra effort: The sharks inside the caves must continuously pump water over their gills to breathe, which requires more energy than does swimming. If you dive in this area, be cautious: Most of the sharks are reef sharks, a species normally responsible for the largest number of attacks on humans. The sharks may appear to sleep, but they're still a potential nightmare.

If you're really serious about getting into diving, consider taking a PADI certification course. The course usually lasts 4–5 days, and with it you get four tanks worth of diving: two in shallower waters and two deep-water dives. With a certificate, you can dive anywhere you want at cheaper rates; if you've only taken an introductory course, you'll have to retake the course every time you dive with a different company or in a different place. Carlos Gutiérrez at Mexico Divers (*see above*) is a good to talk to if you're considering taking the plunge.

SNORKELING The island is fringed by coral reefs, and in many places you can just wade in and start snorkeling. Remember that coral is a living organism—walking on or just touching the coral can easily damage or kill it. **Marina Amigos del Mar** (Playa Norte, near Hidalgo, tel. 987/7–03–92) rents almost every type of water equipment. Snorkeling equipment is $5 a day, and hourly rates for aqua cycles ($8.50), sailboats ($7.50), Windsurfers ($7.50), and kayaks ($5) are reasonable. If you want to snorkel close to town, the best spot is on the northern corner of the island, across from the bridge connecting the town to a small peninsula and a luxury hotel.

A few years ago the **Parque Nacional El Garrafón**, at the southern tip of the island, was a paradise for snorkelers. There's still a lot to see here, but unfortunately much of the coral has died, and many of the fish have found new homes. What remains are hundreds of day-trippers from Cancún, floating on the surface of the water like a fat, white, algae bloom. The tourist-geared park complex includes a diving center, gallery of shops, restaurant, snack bar, bathrooms, showers, and lockers (too small for a backpack; $1.50). The dive shop rents snorkels, masks, and fins for about $4, but the snorkeling is better at Playa Norte. You can easily bike to El Garrafón, or take the bus to Playa Lancheros and walk the rest of the way. *Admission: $1.75. Open daily 8–4.*

You can take a 1½- to 3-hour snorkeling trip to the huge coral reef of **Manchones**. You could also try **El Farrito Reef**, which is supposed to be the best snorkeling experience off Isla Mujeres. All agencies in town, as well as the one at El Garrafón, offer almost identical versions of this trip for $20 per person. Both trips usually include a visit to a couple of small coral reefs, and all trips should include use of snorkeling gear. Poc-Na (*see* Where to Sleep, *above*) offers a particularly good trip; try asking them for a discount. If you want to rent snorkeling gear and hit the beach by yourself, La Isleña, on Morelos at Juárez (*see* Isla Contoy, *above*), rents the snorkel, mask, and fins for $4 per day.

Playa del Carmen

Don't kid yourself into believing that Playa del Carmen is a quaint little seaside fishing village—tourism is the main industry here. Increasingly, herds of tourists are lured by the empty white-sand beaches stretching for miles in each direction. Nonetheless, it's affordable, with many hotels and restaurants geared toward the budget travelers that come here from all corners of the world. The warm, clear waters are all you've dreamt about and are free of the seaweed common to other Caribbean resorts. And if cavorting on the beautiful beaches has lost its thrill, the Maya ruins of Tulum and Cobá are both an easy day trip away.

Depending on when you go, you'll find two different types of visitors here. The Playa of July, August, and December through April is a destination for package tourists, as travelers spill over from Cancún and Cozumel. Hotel prices skyrocket, and even the roach motels are full. The beaches are packed and gasoline from the boats pollutes the water in the harbor. The rest of the year, Playa is relatively peaceful, with a group of hip, young travelers taking advantage of empty hotels offering great deals.

BASICS

CASAS DE CAMBIO The **money exchange center** (cnr of 5a Av. and Juárez) offers lousy rates, but it's open Monday–Saturday 8–8. **Banco del Atlántico** (Juárez, 1 block from bus station) changes cash and traveler's checks weekdays 8 AM–9 PM. Bring your empty wallet and your Visa to the ATM at **Bancomer** (Juárez, 4 blocks from 5a Av.), where they keep the cash flowing and they don't take American Express. Visa—it's everywhere you want to be.

LAUNDRY Maya Laundry washes clothes for $2 per kilo and underwear and socks for 15¢ each. *Calle 2, at 5a Av., tel. 987/2–12–11, ext. 165. Open Mon.–Sat. 8–8.*

MEDICAL AID Both the **clinic** (tel. 987/3–03–14) on Avenida Juárez, 3 blocks up from 5a Avenida, and **Farmacia Vero's** (15 Av., btw Calles Z and Y Nte., tel. 987/3–06–55) are open 24 hours.

PHONES AND MAIL The **post office** (Juárez, btw Calles 15 and 20) is open weekdays 9–1 and 3–6, Saturdays 9–1. They will hold mail sent to you at the following address for up to 10 days: Lista de Correos, Playa del Carmen, Quintana Roo, CP 77710, México. Public, card-operated **phones** are located near the post office on Juárez and across from the bus station on 5a Avenida and Juárez. The **Computel** long-distance phone office (Juárez, ½ block NW of bus station, tel. 987/3–04–69) is open daily 7 AM–10 PM.

VISITOR INFORMATION The information booth supplies free maps and copies of *Destination*, Playa del Carmen's monthly tourist magazine, which has useful tips, phone numbers, a map, and snippets of Quintana Roo history. They also sell Latadel cards. *Juárez, at 5a Av., tel. 987/7–77–10. Btw bus station and zócalo. Open daily 8–1 and 5–8.*

COMING AND GOING

The avenues run parallel to the beach and are numbered in multiples of five. Quinta (5a) Avenida, 1 block from the beach, is the *malecón* (boardwalk) and the social center of town. Playa del Carmen's main street is Avenida Juárez, also known as Avenida Principal, which runs perpendicular to the beach. Calles are numbered in multiples of 2 and also run perpendicular to the beach.

BY BUS Three bus lines serve Playa del Carmen. **ADO** and **Autotransportes del Caribe**, with first- and second-class service, operate out of the same building (cnr 5a Av. and Juárez). One second-class bus travels from Playa del Carmen to Tulum ($1.25), stopping in Xcaret (50¢), Punta Aventuras (50¢), Chemuyil ($1), Akumal ($1), and Xel-Ha ($1.25) along the way. Both companies also have 5 daily buses to Chetumal (4 hrs, $8.25 1st class; 5 hrs, $6.50 2nd class), Mérida (4 hrs, $11.50 1st class; 7 hrs, $8.25 2nd class), and 3 daily trips to Cancún (1 hr, $2 with air-conditioning; 1 hr, $1.50 2nd class). There is also direct service to Cancún every 2 hours, and to Tulum (1 hr, $1.75 with air-conditioning, $1.50 2nd class) every 1–2 hours. **Playa Express,** a slightly cheaper second-class line, operates out of a parking lot just 50 yards up Juárez from the 5a Avenida station and provides service up and down the highway between Playa del Carmen and Tulum.

BY FERRY The second-class **Cozumeleño** (tel. 987/2–18–02) ferry departs for Cozumel every 2–3 hours from 9:30 AM–7:30 PM (45 min, $3.25 one-way, $6.50 round-trip). There are 12 first-class ferries per day to Cozumel (25 min, $4.25 one-way). The ferry leaves from the pier just in front of Plaza Marina Playacar.

BY PLANE Aero Saab will fly you from Playa del Carmen's airport (Calle 15a, ½ block south of Calle 1, tel. 987/2–05–01) to Cozumel for $13.50 ($20 round-trip).

WHERE TO SLEEP

Playa del Carmen is affordable during the off-season, but in July, August, and December, rates tend to run $5–$10 higher than those listed here. Most budget hotels are on 5a Avenida close to the beach, or on Juárez near the bus station.

➢ **UNDER $10** • **La Ruina.** More like an international hippie commune than a hotel, this spot on the beach is the cheapest and by far the most fun place to stay in Playa, as long as you don't mind a little grit in your backpack. Hang your hammock in a huge, open-air palapa-cum-dormitory and stash your stuff in a locker (palapa rental $4; locker and hammock rental $1), or rent a cabaña for two ($9, $2 each extra person). You can also pitch a tent in the grass for $3. The shared bathrooms are passable, and the women's shower farthest east usually has hot water—no one will hassle guys if they use it. *Calle 2, on beach, 987/3–04–05. From bus station, 1 block left on 5a Av. and first right. 21 huts, 32 palapa spaces. Luggage storage.*

Posada Mayeli. Rooms here aren't anything spectacular, but it's a great place to be—the neighbors are friendly and you'll soon feel like one of the family. Step out the front gate, and you're right on 5a Avenida. Bare, fan-equipped singles and doubles with erratic toilets cost $9. *Calle 2a Nte, at 5a Av., no phone. Behind Pez Vela restaurant. 6 rooms, all with bath. Luggage storage.*

➤ **UNDER $15** • **Hotel Playa del Carmen.** The walls and floors here gleam with fresh paint, and dark-wood dressers and doorways have a nice, cooling effect. It's $12.50 for a single or double only 3 blocks from the beach. *Juárez, at 10a Av., 1½ blocks from bus station, tel. 987/3–02–92. 17 rooms, all with bath. Laundry, luggage storage. Wheelchair access.*

Posada Marinelly. Lonely travelers appreciate the incredibly friendly family that owns this place. The large rooms are bare, but the floors sparkle and the fan somehow manages to keep things pretty cool. The owners are happy to help you with the temperamental plumbing. Singles are $9.50, doubles $11. *Juárez, at 10a Av., tel. 987/3–01–40. Next to Hotel Playa del Carmen. 10 rooms, all with bath. Wheelchair access.*

➤ **UNDER $20** • **Casa Tucán.** Surrounded by lush trees, this quiet, clean building has dark-wood beams, whitewashed walls, and a rooftop dining room. Cabaña rooms ($14.50) are bare but cozy; rooms with balconies and kitchenettes start at $18. *Calle 4, btw Avs. 10a and 15a, tel. 987/3–02–83. 2 cabañas and 10 rooms, all with bath. Laundry. Wheelchair access.*

➤ **UNDER $25** • **Hotel Posada Sian-Ka'an.** Large iguanas crawl around this place, supposedly to entertain guests. Clean rooms with shared bath cost $20 for a double. Singles with private bath run $25, doubles $27. Two rooms have a kitchen, and the upper-floor deck overlooks the sea. The hotel accepts Visa but charges a 6% usage fee. *5a Av., tel. 987/3–02–02. 1 block north of bus station. 17 rooms. V.*

HOSTELS **Villa Deportiva Juvenil Playa del Carmen.** This hostel is way out in the boonies, about a kilometer from civilization and (more importantly) far from the beach. The pink sex-segregated dorm rooms are low-ceilinged and unattractive, but homey in a shabby sort of way. For $2.50 you get a bunk and a locker without a lock. The bathrooms are clean but lack toilet paper, hot water, and shower walls. If dorm life doesn't appeal to you, depressingly dank rooms with large double beds and private baths go for $7.50, but at these rates you might as well get something closer to the beach. A $4.50 deposit is required, and guests receive a 10% discount with an HI card. *Calle 8, at 30a Av., no phone. From bus station, walk up Av. Juárez 5 blocks, right on Av. 30a and continue 4 blocks NE to Muscle Beach Gym; hostel is just beyond gym, down a short dirt road heading NW. 198 beds, 18 people per room. Luggage storage. Wheelchair access.*

CAMPING You can pitch your tent in the yard of La Ruina (*see above*) and have access to their facilities for $3 per tent. Otherwise, pick a spot and crash on the beach. To the northeast of town you'll have a little more privacy, but with that comes greater risk of theft. If you're inconspicuous, try the beach right in front of La Ruina.

FOOD

An array of restaurants and loncherías makes it easy to eat cheaply in Playa del Carmen. **El Huerto de Chapo** (5a Av., btw Calles 4 and 6) sells fruits and vegetables daily 7:30–1 and 5–9:30, and 5a Avenida is lined with supermarkets and stores. Most restaurants are also on 5a Avenida, and a few cheap taco stands dot Juárez and 10a Avenida. **El Tortón** (Juárez, btw 10a and 15a Avs.) serves yummy veggie sandwiches for about $1.25.

Jarro Café. Along with egg combinations ($1.50) and hotcakes (50¢), this dark little café serves one of the most exotic food items around—the *sope*. Somewhere between a Swedish pancake and a generously topped pizza, the crust of the sope is made with a milk-and-butter-based dough, which is piled high with your choice of cabbage, beans, chicken, or beef. The sope is then topped with thinly sliced tomatoes and chiles, and dusted with mozzarella-like cheese (75¢). *Calle 1, at 5a Av. 2 doors NW of the malecón. Open Mon.–Sat. 8–8.*

Media Luna. This little vegetarian brunch spot is only discernible from the street by a black rusting sign with a white half-moon. Tropical combinations like crepes stuffed with banana, mango, granola, and fresh sweet cream ($2.75) will have you licking your fingers. Or try hot cheese-and-veggie sandwiches stuffed with juicy tomatoes on wheat bread. Finish off the meal with a *café frío* (iced coffee with milk, cream, vanilla, cinnamon, and sugar; $1.25). *5a Av., 4 ½ blocks from Juárez, no phone. Open Mon.–Sat. 8–2.*

Pez Vela. This lively restaurant serves elaborate fish and meat dishes at reasonable prices, and the waiters will supply you with all the chips and salsa you can handle. Try the Veracruz-style squid, in a fresh tomato sauce flavored with onions, olives, and capers ($3.25), or the *ceviche* (chunks of raw fish marinated in lemon, onions, and herbs; $3). They also serve gargantuan-size nachos ($1.75) and cheap quesadillas ($2.25). *5a Av. at Calle 2. Open daily 7 AM–midnight.*

Sabor. A mellow, newspaper-reading crowd comes here to pick at the tasty pastries ($1) and indulge in a vast array of tropical fruit drinks ($1). Tofu enthusiasts shouldn't leave here without trying the odd-looking soy tacos. *5a Av., no phone. Open daily 8 AM–10 PM.*

OUTDOOR ACTIVITIES

Playa del Carmen is a beach town and little else. If you don't like sand and swimming, keep on going. The beaches here are spectacular—seaweed-free surf slides up the shore, and the long stretches of white sand are perfect for barefoot walks or lounging with a book. The best section of beach in town is near La Ruina (*see* Where to Sleep, *above*), though during peak season (June–Nov.) litter and the lack of trees turn some people off. Walking south along the beach a couple of kilometers brings you to narrow, deserted beaches backed by thick vegetation. More than 1 kilometer north of Playa del Carmen is a series of protected lagoons with cleaner water and few visitors beyond the occasional fisherman.

Playa del Carmen isn't known for its archaeological sites, but locals take pride in the ruins of Xaman-Ha, in the woods behind the Continental Plaza Hotel. If you arrive just before sunset, you can catch orange rays as they enter the building's small stone windows.

Hotel Maya Bric (5a Av. Nte., btw Calle 8 and 10, tel. 987/3–00–11) rents snorkeling equipment for $3.50 a day from 7 to 7. To snorkel off the beach, head around the point north of the Blue Parrot Inn to a small coral reef. It's also possible to organize snorkeling, diving, and fishing trips on charter boats; a small-boat fishing trip should cost about $55 for four people. Jaime at **Price Tours** (5a Av., ½ block from Juárez, tel. 987/3–09–25) can arrange big- and small-boat fishing. For snorkeling, try **Seafari Adventures Dive Shop** (5a Av., at Juárez, tel. 987/3–09–01), open 8–1 and 5–10; it's $100 for six people, including lunch and drinks. Scuba diving tours go to a number of reefs lying just offshore; **Playacar Divers** (in front of Plaza Marina Playacar, south of ferry dock, tel. 987/3–04–49) and **Tank-Ha Dive Center** (5a Av. Nte., btw Calles 8 and 10, tel. 987/3–03–02), next to Hotel Maya Bric, offer comparable prices and a professional dive staff. A two-tank dive is $55, and a snorkeling trip to the shallower reefs is $25 per person, with a minimum of two people.

AFTER DARK

Playa del Carmen at night is much like it is in the day—lots of long-haired tourists in cut off jeans lounging around the beach drinking tropical drinks and listening to music emanating from the surrounding bars and restaurants. A favorite spot among the European budget-hunters is the **Blue Parrot** (6 blocks north of Juárez, on the beach) where couples nurse banana daiquiris ($2.50) and a live rock band plays Tuesday–Sunday. A slightly more energetic crowd of Mexicans and tourists hangs out at **Caribe Swing** (Calle 4, on the beach) where a local reggae band keeps hard-core dancers dancing and mellow beach-goers mellow. The bartender at **Pez Vela** doubles as a disc jockey (he's a big Lou Reed fan). Try any number of drinks from their extensive bar menu (beers are about $1, mixed drinks $2.50); happy hour is the first 10 minutes of every hour from 6 to 10.

Near Playa del Carmen

PUNTA BETE Punta Bete, at least the southern end of it, is idyllic—kilometers of pristine white sand, coconut palms, and gentle waves curling in from the sea. The only thing missing is naked dancers singing "Bali Hai." If you can't arrange that, try the snorkeling, which is excellent just 20 or 40 meters offshore. Schools of fantastically colored fish, octopus, and stingrays are within wading distance. Palapas **Los Pinos** and palapas **Playa Xcalacoco** both rent snorkeling gear (about $5 a day) and offer snorkeling and fishing trips (about $20 per person per day). Although upscale hotels are beginning to appear along the 4-kilometer stretch of beach, you can hang your hammock under a palapa roof for about $4; at Xcalacoco (a little farther north on the beach) you can rent a cabaña big enough for four people for $20. Tent camping at Playa Xcalacoco, where there is also a restaurant, is $3 per person and includes use of clean showers. Fix a price and pay in advance to avoid being surprised by overnight rate changes.

➤ **COMING AND GOING** • If you've got the energy, the 1½-hour, 12-kilometer walk from Playa del Carmen to Punta Bete takes you along a gorgeous stretch of beach. Start early in the morning before the sun gets too high. You can lock your things up at La Ruina if you're just going for the day. Otherwise take an **ADO** or **Autotransportes del Caribe** bus (75¢) heading towards Cancún, tell the bus driver to let you off at Punta Bete, and walk 20 minutes down the bug-ridden, pot-holed, dirt road. To get back, wave down the same bus heading the opposite direction.

XCARET No more than 10 kilometers south of Playa lies Xcaret, where the Maya used to come for bathing rituals before setting sail for Cozumel. Although the site is still surrounded by lagoons, cenotes, and voluptuous jungle brush, it's about as authentically Maya as Disneyland. The main attraction is a 530-meter underground river which would make for beautiful snorkeling if it didn't get so packed. You can rent snorkeling equipment for $6; lockers are 75¢. The biggest drawback is the price—the entrance fee is an astounding $25, most of which goes toward the park's upkeep and the preservation of endangered animal species.

➤ **COMING AND GOING** • Your best bet is to get here early and make a day of it. Take the Tulum bus from Playa del Carmen (or anywhere along the highway—it passes about every ½ hour) and ask to be dropped off at Xcaret. From there, walk 20 minutes to the park's entrance, or wait for the free tourist-toting buggy. *Open Oct.–Mar., daily 8:30–5; Apr.–Sept., daily 8:30–6.*

PAAMUL About 15 kilometers south of Xcaret is Paamul, the famous nesting site of giant turtles weighing upward of 200 pounds. Now an endangered species, the turtles emerge from the ocean on June and July nights to lay as many as 200 eggs each. They may like Paamul's beach, but you probably won't—it doesn't have the white sandy expanses found in tourist brochures. It is a great spot for beachcombing, though, since shells and dead coral wash ashore in abundance. Snorkeling over the reef, about 375 meters offshore, is excellent. **Scuba Mex** (next to Restaurant Arrecifes, tel. 987/4–17–29) rents snorkeling equipment for $6 a day; they'll also motor you out to the reef for about $5 (open to haggling). To reach Paamul, take any bus going to Tulum and asked to be dropped off at Paamul; to return, flag down the bus on the opposite side of the highway.

Cozumel

If you want to dive, come to Cozumel—it's as simple as that. Even jaded Jacques Cousteau raved about the coral reefs that ring this island 19 kilometers from Playa del Carmen. While Cozumel is not the snorkeling paradise it once was (tourism has killed a lot of the coral), it's still the best site on the Yucatán Peninsula. Most famous of all the reefs is **Palancar Reef,** where underwater visibility extends more than 65 meters; divers can experience the whole gamut of underwater excitement at other reefs, too, including plunging walls, passages, caves, and even a phony airplane wreck left behind by a film crew. Most people also come to Cozumel prepared to drop a bundle on diving and accommodations, so it's not exactly a budget paradise. Consider staying in Playa del Carmen and taking the ferry to Cozumel, especially if you're more a beach bum than a dive enthusiast.

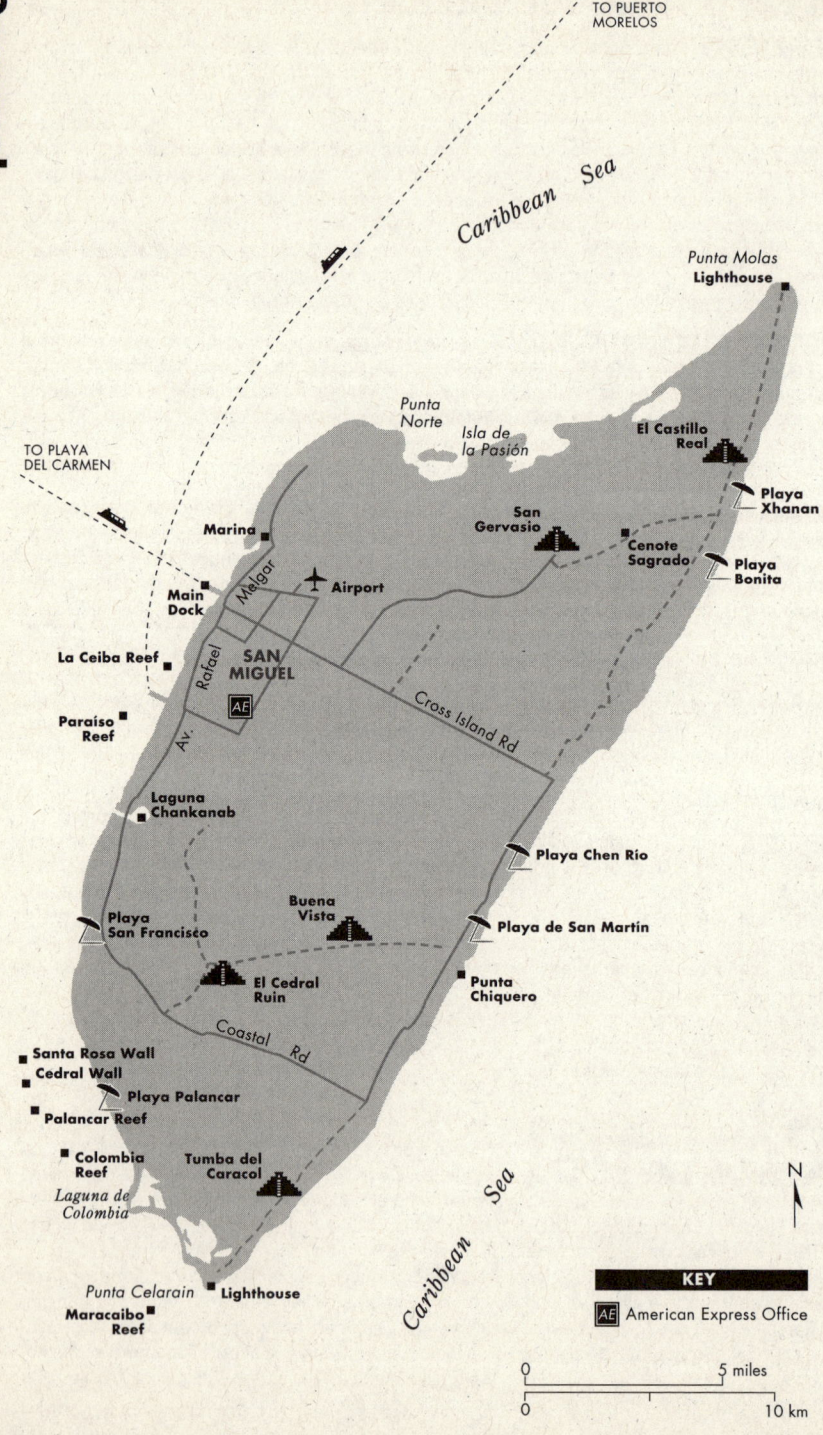

During Mayan times, Cozumel was a sacred island covered with temples and shrines to Ixchel, the goddess of fertility. Maya women from all over what is now Central America and southern Mexico were expected to make the pilgrimage here at least once in their lifetime, in order to pray and leave votive offerings. Unfortunately, many temples were ransacked by Cortés in 1519, and the U.S. military destroyed others while constructing an airstrip during World War II. What does remain are vast tracts of thick jungle, covering the entire northeast half of the island, as well as much of its interior. Even if you're only on Cozumel a couple of days, it's worth renting a scooter or bike and exploring the teeming jungles and swamplands, if only to escape the tourist scene.

Less advertised than its abundance of tropical fish is Cozumel's large reptile population. Crocodiles and sea snakes inhabit the various lagoons and boas lurk in the low-lying forests. Less ominous are the cat-sized armadillos whose shiny bodies dot the highway just outside of town at night.

BASICS

AMERICAN EXPRESS The AmEx representative here is **Fiesta Cozumel.** They cash and issue traveler's checks, but don't give cash advances. *Calle 11 Sur, btw Pedro Joaquín and 25a Av., tel. 987/2–07–25. Follow Rafael Melgar south to Calle 11, take a left, and walk 6½ blocks. Open weekdays 8–1 and 4–8.*

CASAS DE CAMBIO Most banks are in downtown San Miguel. You can change cash or traveler's checks 8 AM–9 PM at **Banco del Altántico** (Calle 1 Sur 11, southern cnr of zócalo, tel. 987/2–01–42) or **Banamex** (5a Av., btw Calle 1 and Rosado Salas) from 9 to 5. The ATM at Banamex accepts MasterCard, Cirrus, and Visa. American dollars are accepted all over the island.

CONSULATES Cozumel has no consulates, but citizens of all nations can get help from **Bryan Wilson** (Calle 13 Sur, at 15a Av. Sur, tel. 987/2–06–54), who works as an unofficial ombudsman and interpreter. On call 24 hours a day, he speaks perfect Spanish, is well acquainted with Mexican law, and can help you out of sticky situations. His services are free unless they result in considerable savings for you, in which case he'll take a commission.

EMERGENCIES Contact the **police** (Rafael Melgar, at Calle 13 Sur, tel. 987/2–00–92) or an **ambulance** (tel. 987/2–06–39).

LAUNDRY **Margarita Laundromat** charges $2.50 per load to wash, $2 per 10 minutes of drying, and sells detergent. *20a Av. Sur, at Calle 3 Sur, tel. 987/2–28–65. Open Mon.–Sat. 7 AM–9 PM, Sun. 9–5.*

MEDICAL AID For 24-hour medical assistance, contact **Dr. Gustavo Ambriz** or go to his clinic (Calle 5 Sur 21-B, 4 blocks south of ferry dock, tel. 987/2–16–71 or 987/2–14–30). He specializes in travel medicine and diving-related problems (he has a decompression tank). **Farmacia Kiosco** (zócalo, tel. 987/2–24–85) is open 8–1 and 2–10 Monday–Saturday, or you can hike all the way to the **Centro de Especialidades Medicas** 24-hour pharmacy (20a Av. Nte., at Calle 8 Nte., tel. 987/2–14–19 or 987/2–29–19).

PHONES AND MAIL The **post office** (Rafael Melgar, at Calle 7 Sur, tel. 987/2–01–06) is open weekdays 9–6, Saturdays 9–noon. They will hold mail sent to you at the following address for up to 10 days: Lista de Correos, Cozumel, Quintana Roo, CP 77600, México. **Computel** (Calle 1 Sur 165, btw 5a and 10a Avs., tel. 987/2–40–87, fax 987/2–41–54) lets you make local and long-distance calls. It's open daily 7 AM–10 PM. **Studio Blue** (Rosado Sales, btw 5a and 10a Avs., tel. 987/2–44–14) sells Ladatel phone cards.

VISITOR INFORMATION *The Blue Guide* is a pocket-sized publication with important phone numbers and a small map of the city, found at any hotel or the ferry dock. Cozumel's **Oficina Estatal de Turismo** is difficult to find and often closed, but they do have some interesting information on the island's wildlife and plants, and can supply you with free maps of the island as well as a self-guided tour of San Gervasio. *Edificio Plaza del Sol, tel. 987/2–09–72. From tall clock on east side of zócalo, head east behind Farmacia toward Centro de Conven-*

ciones, head north, and look for tower on the left. Office is on west side of upper level balcony. Open weekdays 8:30–3.

COMING AND GOING

BY FERRY Ferries between Cozumel and the mainland leave from **Playa del Carmen,** with about 10 departures in each direction daily (*see* Coming and Going, in Playa del Carmen, *above*).

BY PLANE Cozumel has a small international airport, with flights to and from the States on **Continental. Mexicana** (tel. 987/2-29-45) and **Aero Cozumel** (tel. 987/2-34-56) offer service to cities all over Mexico, including Cancún, Mérida, and Mexico City. **Aero Banana** (tel. 987/2-50-40) flies to nearby Isla Mujeres and Cancún. You can also fly to Cozumel from Playa del Carmen (*see* Coming and Going, in Playa del Carmen, *above*). To reach town from the airport, walk two minutes out of the terminal towards the *glorieta* (roundabout) with the big sparrow and catch a $3.50 taxi from there. The CIRCUMBACACION bus will take you right to the ferry terminal for a mere 25¢.

GETTING AROUND

Cozumel is the largest of Mexico's islands, 53 kilometers long and 14 kilometers wide. San Miguel de Cozumel, the small town on the western coast of the island, is the hub of activities. It's easy to get around San Miguel on foot, since the streets are laid out in a grid, and run either parallel or perpendicular to the coast. Apart from the main avenues, all streets have numerical designations. The avenue running along the malecón is Rafael Melgar; parallel avenues are numbered in multiples of five (5a Avenida is followed by 10a Avenida and 15a Avenida). Avenida Benito Juárez, the main drag, runs directly inland from the ferry dock and cuts the town in two. Streets and avenues north of Avenida Juárez receive the appellation Norte; those to the south, Sur. To further confuse the situation, streets north of Avenida Juárez have even numbers, and those to the south have odd numbers. If you have some sort of transportation, a road circles the rest of the island, making it easy to explore, and several other roads and trails cut through the flat jungle.

BY SCOOTER The most popular way to see the island is by scooter. The going rate is $20 for 24 hours, but bargaining is not out of the question. **Rentadora Leo** (5a Av. 199, at Rosado Salas) charges only $15 for same-day returns.

BY BIKE The island is a bit too large to explore thoroughly on bicycle, but if you ride, take plenty of water. Taxis constantly circle the island, so bring enough money to take one back if you get stranded—if the driver is feeling benevolent, he'll let your bike come along for the ride. **Rentadora Águila** (685 Rafael Melgar, btw Calles 3 and 5 Sur, tel. 987/2-07-29 or 987/2-25-09) rents bikes for $5 a day and is open Monday–Saturday 8–8, Sunday 8–7.

BY BUS There are three bus routes in Cozumel, connecting downtown to the *colonias* (residential areas). The CIRCUMBACACION bus is most useful for visitors; it runs up Calle 11 from Rafael Melgar and turns north on 65 Avenida; after passing through the eastern colonias, it returns ot town via Boulevard Aeropuerto. The bus is 25¢ and runs every 20 minutes until about 7:30 PM.

BY TAXI Taxi rates are regulated, so you have the right to report any excessive charges to the local **Sitio de Taxis** (Calle 2 Nte., btw 5a and 10a Avs, tel. 987/2-00-41), and you may even get your money back. Within town, you shouldn't be charged more than $1; if you're going as far as Chankanab, you'll have to pay about $1.50 (rates rise slightly after midnight). If you take a taxi from the ferry dock, hold out for a good price.

WHERE TO SLEEP

After Cancún, Cozumel is the most expensive place on the peninsula. Budget travelers should choose between camping and staying in the hotels in San Miguel, most of which are within a few blocks of the central plaza. If you plan to camp out, get permission in the morning at the

Palacio Municipal or the Sector Naval, both on Rafael Melgar near Calle 11 Sur. You can crash on **Playa del Sol** and **Playa Casita,** both a short walk south of town, or try the secluded places on the southern and eastern portions of the island. Try the 4-kilometer stretch of dirt road that follows the beach to **Punta Celarain.** Also, several spots along the paved road parallel to the eastern shore are sequestered by dunes or scrub. Authorities will warn you to be careful of thieves because the beaches are not patrolled, but there have been few incidents recently.

➤ **UNDER $15** • **Hotel Cozumel Inn.** The sunny balconies of this three-tiered hotel look out onto a plant-filled inner patio. Tiny but tidy bedrooms come equipped with shoebox-size bathrooms, and the patio rooms are perfectly positioned for the occasional afternoon breeze. Singles are $11.75, doubles $13.50, and triples $20 ($25 with air-conditioning). *Calle 4 Nte. 3, at Rafael Melgar, tel. 987/2–03–14. 30 rooms, all with bath. Luggage storage.*

Hotel Posada Edém. This is the cheapest downtown hotel, and it's conveniently located next to a taxi stand, bakery, and the central plaza. Flying red ants are a nuisance, but for the most part this place is clean and well-kept. Singles are $8.50, doubles $10, plus $2.50 for air-conditioning or an extra person. You can also rent mopeds for $20 a day. *Calle 2 Nte. 12, btw 5a and 10a Avs. Nte., tel. 987/2–11–66. 14 rooms, all with bath. Luggage storage. MC, V.*

Posada del Zorro. Down-and-out scuba-diving-junkies flock here when downtown prices rise. The walls are patched with blistering paint and the bathrooms are rust-tinted and bare, but at least there aren't any noticeable forms of animal life. Large rooms with two double beds are only $8 for a single and $10 for a double; squeeze in as many friends as you want for an extra $2.50 each. *Juárez, at 30a Av., 6 blocks east of ferry dock, tel. 987/2–07–90. 8 rooms, all with bath. Luggage storage.*

➤ **UNDER $20** • **Hotel Kary.** After trudging the 7 blocks from the ferry dock, you'll be overjoyed to see these impeccable rooms. The gorgeous pool and patio will make you feel pampered, especially after a couple of margaritas under the poolside palapa. Singles and doubles are $17 ($19 with air-conditioning) and suites with kitchenettes are about $19. *25a Av. Sur, at Rosado Salas, tel. 987/2–20–11. From ferry dock, 2 blocks south (right) and 5 blocks east. 17 rooms and 2 suites, all with bath. Luggage storage. MC, V.*

Hotel Marycarmen. Just when you think it can't get any better than wood furniture, air-conditioning, and great bathrooms, you get plush bedding with satin ruffles. The small atrium is ideal for sunbathing. Singles and doubles cost $18.50, triples $25. *5a Av. Sur 4, btw Calle 1 Sur and Rosado Salas, tel. 987/2–05–81. From ferry dock, 1 block inland and 1½ blocks right. 27 rooms, all with bath. Luggage storage. Wheelchair access. MC, V.*

➤ **UNDER $25** • **Hotel Pepita.** Located on a somewhat run-down street, the photo-filled office of this lovely hotel is a welcome surprise. Rooms are small but sunny and surprisingly quiet, with refrigerators and colorful bedspreads. Doubles are $20, triples $25. *15a Av. Sur, at Calle 1 Sur, 3 blocks from main pier, tel. 987/2–00–98. 30 rooms with bath. Wheelchair access.*

FOOD

If you're willing to walk a little, you can eat quite cheaply in Cozumel. The **mercado** (Rosado Salas, at 25a Av.) sells fresh fruits and vegetables daily 7–5. Several **loncherías** in the market also offer breakfast deals and main dishes for less than $2.

➤ **UNDER $5** • **La Casa del Waffle.** A bunch of surfers got together and formed this waffle joint to finance their aquatic habit. Delicacies include plain waffles ($3.50), waffles Benedict ($5), excellent pancakes ($1.75), and an obscenely sweet waffle with fruit, syrup, and whipped cream ($5.50). Bathing suit-clad tourists stop for a bite to eat and end up staying for the bottomless coffee. *Juárez, btw Avs. 20 and 25, no phone. Open daily 8–1 and 6–10.*

Casa Denis. The owner does a good job of hiding from the tourists—while they mill among the patio tables, he remains in a secluded pantry behind the dining area. If you can get ahold of a menu, you'll be overwhelmed by choices—they've got everything from fried chicken tacos ($2) to fresh fish kabobs ($3.50) to tasty avocado soup ($1.25). Beer is less than $1. *Calle 1 Sur, btw 5a and 10a Avs., ½ block east of zócalo, tel. 987/2–00–67. Open Mon.–Sat. 7 AM–11 PM.*

Restaurant Toñita. Strategically placed fans protrude from the walls and ceiling to keep flies off your food. The food is cheap and the menu changes daily. Great meals including soup, a meat dish, veggies, rice, and tortillas will run you about $3. *Rosado Salas, btw 10a and 15a Avs., 2½ blocks east of zócalo, tel. 987/2-04-01. Open Mon.-Sat. 8-6.*

➢ **UNDER $10** • **Costa Brava.** A roof of shellacked wood and a huge tree growing out of green astroturf carpet give this place an outdoorsy feel . . . sort of. Less aesthetically minded tourists come here after some hard-core diving to indulge in delicious seafood dishes or a margarita ($2). Fresh squid with squid-ink rice is $6.75, and chicken shish kebob with grilled tomato, pepper, and onion is only $3.50. *Rafael Melgar, across from Sector Naval, no phone. Open daily 6:30 AM-11:30 PM.*

DESSERT/COFFEEHOUSE **Café Caribe.** A welcome relief for travelers in a serious Nescafé rut, this place has more character than the sports bars and Texas-style grills that prevail in San Miguel. It's a Euro-coffeehouse where quiet jazz and classical music plays. The pastry selection isn't all that inviting, but the iced cappuccino ($1.50) is excellent. *10a Av. Sur, btw Rosado Salas and Calle 3 Sur, tel. 987/2-36-21. Open Mon.-Sat. 8-1 and 6-9:30.*

WORTH SEEING

The wild and rocky eastern coast of Cozumel is well worth exploring: It's still mostly deserted despite the paved road that runs along the shoreline. You can swim in some places, especially **Punta Chiquero, Chen Río,** and the beach at **Punta Morena Hotel.** At other points, however, the strong undertow makes a leisurely dip dangerous. You can get a great view of the island from the top of the lighthouse on **Punta Celarain** (southern tip of island, at end of 4-km dirt road), which looks out over pounding surf that hurls spray high over the rocks. If you clamber over the sand dunes, you'll find some empty, untouristed beaches where you can swim nude in relative privacy.

EL CASTILLO REAL AND SAN GERVASIO The most important of the island's ruins, El Castillo Real maintains an aura of serenity in the face of foreign intruders. The ruin is on the northeast side of the island and is almost impossible to reach without four-wheel drive. A practiced scooter driver could also make it here, but be prepared for a 2- to 3-hour ride. Take the eastern road about 17 kilometers past the point where it meets the cross-island road; a dirt track leads to the ruins. On the way back from El Castillo stop at the ancient *cenote sagrado* for an excellent rope swing, then continue south to the dilapidated ruins of San Gervasio, in the middle of Cozumel's jungle. To get here, go south on the eastern road and take the trail that originates at Playa Bonita inland. **Turismo Aviomar** (5a Av., btw Calles 4 and 6, tel. 987/2-04-77 or 987/2-05-88) offers a 2-hour tour of the San Gervasio ruins for $25. Tours leave Monday-Wednesday at 7 and 8 AM; call ahead to check availability. You can also take a taxi to the ruins, but it'll cost $30 round-trip. Admission to San Gervasio is $2, free Sunday and holidays.

On Sunday nights, local bands gather in the zócalo to play everything from mambo and salsa to jarane, *a fast-paced Yucatecan step dance that requires the tiptoeing dancer to sidestep an invisible bull to the rhythm of the yelping crowd.*

MUSEO DE LA ISLA DE COZUMEL This beautiful whitewashed museum is a necessary stop for anyone wanting to learn more about the island's spectacular array of exotic plants and animals. Clearly drawn, color-coded maps with English subtitles explain the island's geographic history and the development of the island's ecological riches. In addition to life-size nature scenes and an entire room dedicated to the origins and nature of coral, the museum also has a gallery delineating the history of the Maya, complete with replicas of important ruins and artifacts found on the island. The doorman is also a great source of information—if business is slow enough, he'll walk you through the museum himself. *Rafael Melger, btw Calles 4 and 6 Nte. Admission: $2; free Sun. Open daily 10-6.*

OUTDOOR ACTIVITIES

Come to Cozumel for the underwater sights and beaches, and leave the cultural stuff for another time and place. Although you can see some Mayan ruins here, activities are geared toward exploring the island's magnificent coral reefs. If you don't dive or snorkel, consider a tour in a glass-bottom boat. **Maya Glass Bottom Boat and Snorkel Tours** (tel. 987/2–46–37 or 987/2–14–49) has two trips a day ($30) departing Marine Sports Pier (in front of Hotel Fiesta Zun) at 9 AM and 1 PM.

SNORKELING Snorkeling is a cheap and relatively painless way to explore Cozumel's sea life. Particularly good is the snorkeling off the western coast beach, especially in the area between Hotel Sol Caribe and Playa Maya. Equipment rental costs about $6 at any of the dive shops in town; a snorkeling trip to the shallow reefs is about $20. **Bel Mar Aquatics** (Hotel La Ceiba, 1 km south of ferry dock on Rafael Melgar, tel. 987/2–16–65), **Blue Bubble Divers** (5a Av. Sur and Calle 3 Sur, tel. 987/2–18–65), and **Diving Adventures** (Calle 5 Sur, at Rafael Melgar, tel. 987/2–30–09) all offer snorkeling trips.

➢ **LAGUNA CHANKANAB** • This national park 9 kilometers south of San Miguel is the most popular snorkeling spot in Cozumel. At the center of the park is a lagoon separated from the beach, fed by an underwater cave; a large botanical garden with a replica of Maya housing surrounds the lagoon. Swimming is no longer allowed in the lagoon (paddling tourists were slowly killing it), but snorkeling in the clear waters of the adjacent bay is spectacular, as is diving at the offshore reef. Underwater you can see interesting coral heads, a myriad of tropical fish, and a large statue of Christ, sunk for the entertainment of divers. Chankanab is, unfortunately, a little too crowded: Head elsewhere if you want a solitary snorkel. Four dive shops on the premises rent snorkeling and diving equipment. To get here, take a taxi ($4) or rent a scooter or bike. *Admission: $4. Open daily 9–5:30.*

➢ **LA CEIBA REEF** • La Ceiba Reef, in front of La Ceiba Hotel, is another good place to snorkel or dive. A 120-meter trail has been marked out on the reef, starting at a fake airplane wreck (it was sunk during the filming of a movie) and continuing past several interesting coral formations. *4 km south of San Miguel; walk or take a scooter or taxi ($5). Admission free.*

SCUBA DIVING Diving is the raison d'être of tourism in Cozumel. Dozens of dive shops offer instruction, as well as a wide range of boat trips to shallow and deep reefs; anybody, from beginner to expert, can find a suitable dive. Beginners hone their skills over shallow **Yocab Reef**, close to shore and just south of Laguna Chankanab. Expert divers will want to head for the more challenging (and thrilling) reefs, such as **Maracaibo, San Juan, Santa Rosa Wall,** and

Coral Reefs

The Yucatán may offer some of the most beautiful reefs in the world, but some of these areas have paid a high price for their popularity. Coral reefs are the undersea equivalent of rain forests: They're one of the most complex ecosystems on earth. Like rain forests, they're severely threatened and underprotected. Once damaged, coral reefs repair themselves slowly, growing at a rate of just one centimeter every 10 years. They're endangered by divers, boat anchors, overfishing, severe storms and hurricanes, and pollution. The following are a few tips for environmentally aware travelers: When diving in reef areas, do not break off a piece of coral for a keepsake of your trip to Mexico—it may be beautiful, but it is also home to thousands of tropical fish, plants, and crustacea and is itself a living organism.

Coral is often used to create souvenirs and jewelry. Do not purchase these items. Like the trade in elephant ivory and tortoise shells, each purchase you make supports exploitation and is detrimental to the coral's survival. If you're mooring a boat, be careful where you drop anchor—a 30-pound weight can do a lot of damage.

Colombia. You must be certified to rent diving gear and take diving trips. At the more reputable agencies, the staff will test your diving ability before letting you attempt advanced dives. Good agencies are more expensive but safer: **Aqua Safari** (Rafael Melgar 429, btw Calles 5 and 7 Sur, tel. 987/2–01–01), **Cozumel Equalizers** (Rosado Salas 72, at 5a Av. Sur, tel. 987/2–35–11), and **Dive Paradise** (Rafael Melgar 601, tel. 987/2–10–07) are among the most reputable. Four-day certification courses cost about $300. Two-tank dives cost about $50 (usually with a six-diver minimum), and night dives are $30.

➤ **PALANCAR REEF** • The most famous of Cozumel's reefs, Palancar lies about 1½ kilometers from Playa Palancar on the island's southwestern shore. The reef stretches intermittently for about 5 kilometers and offers divers a range of underwater experiences. The best known formation is the **Horseshoe,** a collection of coral heads that form a horseshoe curve right at the drop off. The visibility—some 85 meters in places—is extraordinary.

➤ **PARAISO REEF** • Just north of the Stouffer Presidente Hotel, near San Miguel, this reef lies 12–22 meters deep and has excellent star and brain coral formations. The northern part of Paraíso is accessible from the beach; the southern part is farther offshore, but merits taking a boat to see the extensive marine life there. **Diving Adventures** (Calle 5 Sur, at Melgar, tel. 987/2–30–09) offers daily dive trips to Paraíso for $35.

HORSEBACK RIDING A handful of stables on the island offer tours on horseback—a great way to see the jungle and some of the inland ruins. The best package can be arranged at **Acuario Restaurant,** next to the Sector Naval. Come in person or contact Kelly or Aido at 987/2–10–97. The 4-hour, $60 tour includes transportation to and from the stables, a bilingual guide, and soft drinks or beer.

Tulum

The setting of the ancient Maya city of Tulum is breathtaking. A backdrop of talcum-powder beaches, rocky cliffs, and clear Caribbean waters gives the crumbling gray ruins a unique aura. Tourists generally come here on organized day trips from Cancún to admire the ruins, take a few pictures, buy some souvenirs, and get back to their air-conditioned hotel rooms. Budget travelers, on the other hand, have made Tulum one of their favorite hangouts. The beaches south of the ruins attract a friendly, low-budget crowd in various stages of undress—mostly young Europeans come here to let their hair grow, peel off their tie-dyed shirts, and make jewelry. The beaches at Tulum are secluded and relatively untouched compared with those at Playa del Carmen.

Tulum was built and rebuilt in various stages, beginning sometime between AD 700 and 1300 with the Putún-Maya, the same people associated with the Mayapán. Originally named "Zama" (Mayan for "sunrise"), Tulum was intended as an observatory and ceremonial center. Burial platforms surround the leftover buildings and the tiny, windowed observatory hovers above the old city. Tulum's most prestigious inhabitants (priests, astrologers, and carpenters) were separated from outlying peasant farmers by a 7-meter wall—a wise insurance policy considering Tulum was apparently involved in several wars with other Maya states. Juan de Grijalva, who sighted the city in 1518 when his Spanish expedition sailed past the coast, compared Tulum, with its red, white, and blue buildings, with Seville. The city was still occupied by Maya at the time of the Spanish conquest: One of the images in the Temple of the Frescoes depicts Chaac riding a horse, an animal introduced by the Spanish.

COMING AND GOING

The ancient city of Tulum is 63 kilometers south of Playa del Carmen and 127 kilometers south of Cancún. The first-class **Premier** bus station (serving Mérida and Valladolid) is downtown, across from the Maya Hotel; second-class buses can be caught opposite the first-class station. From Tulum there's frequent second-class service to Playa del Carmen (2 per hr, $1.50), Cancún (2 per hr, $3), Chetumal (via Bacalone; 5 per day, 3½ hrs, $6.50; last bus 6:30 PM), Cobá (4 per day, 45 min, $1), and Valladolid (1 per day, 2½ hrs, $4). One lone bus

Tulum

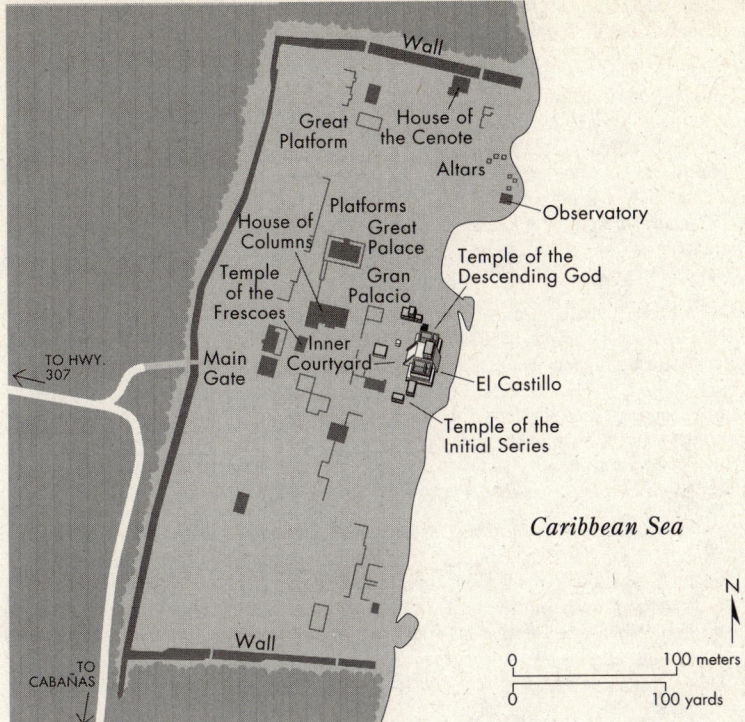

heads to Mérida at 1:30 PM (5 hrs, $8). If you're broke, hitchhiking along the main highway is common and relatively easy.

GETTING AROUND

The *crucero* (turnoff) for the ruins and budget lodging is about 4 kilometers north of the modern town of Tulum. Ask the driver to let you off at the crucero, then continue east down the paved road for five minutes, toward the coast. There's also a $1 trolley bus running from the parking lot just south of the crucero to the entrance to the ruins. As you enter the ruins, another paved road heads south along the coast to the cabañas and beaches. It's a five-minute taxi ride ($1.50) from the ruins and campgrounds to the modern town of Tulum, equipped with one hotel, a handful of restaurants, fruterías (fruit stands), a panadería (bakery), grocery store, pharmacy, post office, and telephone office.

WHERE TO SLEEP

The cabañas that lie along the beach south of the ruins are the best (but most primitive) lodging option. If you plan to stay here, arrive before 9 PM, when the managers head elsewhere. The only good reason to stay in town is to catch the 6 AM bus to Cobá—the next one leaves at 11 AM and only gives you about 3 hours in Cobá. In a pinch, **Hotel Maya** (Tulum 32) has singles and doubles for $8.50.

➤ **UNDER $10** • **Cabañas El Mirador.** These cabañas are quieter and more isolated than Santa Fe and Don Armando and attract fewer people. The two cabañas with beds ($8.50 each) go quickly. Cabañas with hammocks are $3.50, $4.50 for two people, and hammock rental is $1. The showerless bathrooms are primitive, but discrete guests use the bathing facilities at Santa Fe. The best part about the place are the friendly owners, who serve up a hearty plate of spaghetti at the restaurant overlooking the campsite. *On the beach, 1 km from ruins. 20 cabañas. Laundry, luggage storage, meals.*

Camping Santa Fe. This place is very popular with budget travelers, especially earthy types who get a primal thrill from sand floors, no electricity, and grungy huts. The repugnant bathrooms lack running water (the sinks are purely aesthetic), and open showers mean you may share the experience with plenty of naked campers. Cram as many people as you want into a small, bare hut for $3 or pay $6.50 for one with a bed. Camping on the grass costs $2.50 per person. Mosquito netting (recommended late May–early July) and hammocks can be rented for $1 each. You can store your belongings with the administration, though it's best to keep valuables at your side. *On beach, 1 km south of ruins. 15 cabañas. Key deposit ($3.50), laundry, meals.*

➤ **UNDER $15** • **Cabañas Don Armando.** These well-constructed cabañas are comfortable, but more expensive than the ones next door at Camping Santa Fe. The cabañas have beds on cement platforms, hammock hooks, sand floors, and windows. The bathrooms are clean and locked (you get a key). If you intend to turn in at twilight, rocking your hammock to the gentle sound of Caribbean surf, go elsewhere: The nearby disco plays the same loud, obnoxious music every night until about 2 AM. Cabañas cost $8.50 with one bed and one hammock, $10 with two beds, and $12 for a beachfront hut with one bed and one hammock. Camping costs $3 per person. *1 km south of ruins. 24 cabañas. Laundry, luggage storage, meals.*

Cabañas Los Gatos. After one night nestled in these palm-shaded cabañas, you may decide to stay indefinitely. A 20-minute walk south of the other campsites, Los Gatos sits atop a rocky, rain-whipped shelf overlooking the vigorous surf. Cozy cabañas have small double beds swinging from sturdy knotted ropes, but the best bet is hanging a hammock (ask Felix, the owner, to lend you one) in the abandoned restaurant at the site's entrance. Single cabañas cost $8, doubles $10; camping is $2.50 a night. *Take road leading south by ruins 2 km (wheelchair accessible). Or walk south along beach to rocky curve in the shore and climb around to your right. Wheelchair access.*

FOOD

The restaurants outside the ruins and at the crucero are nothing spectacular and ridiculously expensive. Instead, go downtown or eat at one of the cabaña sites. **Don Armando** and **Santa Fe** (*see* Where to Sleep, *above*) offer main dishes for $4–$5 and beer for $1. The food is particularly good at **Restaurant El Mirador**, where tuna, cheese, or ham sandwiches are $1.25, a huge plate of spaghetti with bread is $2.25, and a pile of hot cakes are less than $1. For the best fish, head to **Mar Caribe Cooperativo de Pescadores,** a cabaña just south of Don Armando, for $3 fish dishes, $5 shrimp platters, and 75¢ beers. If you come into town, you pick up supplies at the grocery store. Otherwise eat at **Restaurant El Paradero,** where *chuletas* (pork chops) and carne asada are each $3, or at the more expensive 24-hour **Restaurant Ambrosia,** which serves tasty salbutes for $2.50 and generously cheesed quesadillas for $3.

WORTH SEEING

The ruins of Tulum are open daily 8–5, and admission is $2.75, free Sunday and holidays. If you're determined not to pay, it's fairly easy to climb over the city wall where it runs along the road; tagging along with the guided tours is equally manageable. Bring a bathing suit and a book and come early—when the onslaught of tour buses arrives at 10:30, head to the grassy south end of the ruins where the the trees provide pleasant shady spots, or take a dip in the nearby surf.

Tulum is the product of a war-troubled, declining Mayan Empire. Thick walls enclose the city on three sides, and watchtowers enable the inhabitant to know about invasions in advance. The city's castle and the nobles' homes surrounding it are evidence of three different building phases, each using the previous structure as a base from which to erect the building's next level. There are some reliefs carved into the stucco walls of the buildings, but frescoes were the most prevalent form of decoration in Tulum.

➤ **TEMPLE OF THE FRESCOES** • This small yet well-preserved structure consists of two temples, one inside the other. Large stucco masks, probably representing the god Quetzalcoatl, stare from the corners of the outer facade. The mask on the southern corner with one eye open and one shut symbolizes the duality of the Maya belief system, which understood evil and darkness (the closed eye) not as the absence of good and light, but as equally important aspects of nature.

Inside the temple, the murals are divided into three sections, symbolizing the realms of the universe: the underworld, the mortal world, and the heavens. Unfortunately, the murals are hard to see from outside the roped-off entrance, but archaeologists point to the depiction of a figure riding a horse-like animal as an indication they were completed or reworked after the Spanish arrived.

➤ **EL CASTILLO** • The most impressive structure at Tulum, El Castillo is a small two-chamber temple built atop a tall pyramid. A staircase on the western side leads to the temple, from which you get an extensive view of the sea, jungle, and surrounding ruins. At some point, the columns supporting the doorway were modified to look like feathered serpents, the symbol of Kukulcan—further evidence of the strong Toltec influence in Tulum.

➤ **TEMPLE OF THE DESCENDING GOD** • Immediately north of El Castillo, this temple is a small, elevated structure that received its name from the beautiful relief above the doorway. The stucco carving depicts a deity diving headfirst from the sky. This deity is thought to represent Quetzalcoatl—it has wings and a strange pointed tail, and carries what seems to be a flower. Some say the figure is a honeybee, of central significance in Yucatecan Maya religion, medicine, and commerce.

OUTDOOR ACTIVITIES

Even if you're not a snorkeling fan, the many underground cenotes littered throughout the Tulum/Cobá area are worth a look, and many are sufficiently remote to enjoy the experience in the buff. One of the most beautiful cenotes near Tulum is the **Gran Cenote,** first discovered after hurricane Gilbert caved in its porous limestone roof, exposing the cenote's cavernous interior. To reach the Gran Cenote, take a taxi ($1.50) down the road opposite the crucero, 4 kilometers west to the ruins. Otherwise, make the half-hour walk or hitch a ride. The family that lives on the land surrounding the cenote usually charges about $1 at the cenote's entrance.

Near the ruins is a small beach that's clean and free of seaweed. The beach continues south, but a wall divides it in two at the ruins. To reach the rest of the beach, enter through the campground at El Mirador (*see* Where to Sleep, *above*). Nude bathing is allowed at the beaches in front of the cabañas, and you can snorkel over a reef about 500 yards offshore. The water is not as clear as Playa del Carmen's, but the sea life is just as abundant. Tulum's only dive shop is between Camping Santa Fe and Camp Don Armando, under a red-flagged palapa (if the owners aren't there, ask at the bar at Santa Fe). A snorkeling trip to the reef and a few inland cenotes costs $8.50, while scuba diving trips cost $7 for one tank and $9.25 for two.

Near Tulum

BEACHES AND LAGOONS

The coast road (Highway 307) running north to Playa del Carmen passes some of the most spectacular beaches in the Caribbean, as well as a variety of lagoons that support a vast array of fish and wildlife. Hop on the Tulum–Playa del Carmen bus (every 20 min until 9 PM) and tell the driver where you want to get off. Otherwise, it isn't too difficult to hitch a ride, particularly during the day. For information about towns and beaches north of Akumal, *see* Near Playa del Carmen, *above*.

XEL-HA LAGOON Now a national park, Xel-Ha ("clear water" in Mayan) is home to tropical fish, including parrotfish and angelfish. Underwater caverns filled with coral (and, in one case, a Maya altar) make for interesting snorkeling. Unfortunately, tourism and tanning oil have polluted this lagoon. Hordes of day-trippers from Cancún, Playa del Carmen, and Cozumel jostle for space in the water, dramatically reducing the lagoon's visibility. If you're determined, come early in the morning, before the rush starts. Admission is a whopping $10, and on the northeast side of the lake, you can rent snorkeling equipment ($6), lockers ($1, $2 deposit), and towels ($1). *15 km north of Tulum; take* TULUM–PLAYA DEL CARMEN *bus (10 min, 50¢) and ask driver to let you off at Xel-Ha, or hitch along the main road.*

XCACEL About 3 kilometers north of Xel-Ha, Xcacel provides an excellent refuge from the pricey tourist stops of Xel-Ha and Akumal. Most people come here to park their campers and hang out in the sand. To arrange diving and snorkeling trips in the nearby breathtaking underwater caves and cenotes, visit Buddy in the camper just west of the turtle farm, or call Tony and Nancy Derosa of **Aquatic Divers** (tel. 987/4–12–71) in Akumal. Walk through the swampy jungle at the beach's southern end to see the cenote, dark with salt- and fresh-water animal life and untouched by divers. Just south of the cenote is a giant coconut grove where some of the only remaining *palmeras reales* (royal palms) still stand. *Admission: $1.50, plus $1 to camp overnight.*

CHEMUYIL The sign at the intersection on Highway 307, 4 kilometers north of Xcacel, calls Chemuyil the most beautiful beach in the world, but it ain't what it used to be. Most of the palm trees have succumbed to disease, leaving gray stumps littering what might otherwise be a very attractive stretch of sand. It's a great place to camp (as long as you distance yourself from the pastel condominiums at the beach's northern end), and snorkeling in the nearby coves is said to be the best on the coast. You can rent snorkeling equipment ($3.50) just south of Chemuyil's entrance (behind the mediocre and overpriced restaurant). Camping costs $2.50 (including the $1.50 entrance fee), and you can rent a cabaña with a bed and hammock for $8.50. *Admission: $1.50.*

AKUMAL An upscale resort 7 kilometers north of Chemuyil, Akumal has riches everyone can afford—a coral reef, a long white crescent beach, and crystal-clear water. The name means "Place of the Turtle" in Mayan, and giant green turtles lurch ashore in October to lay their eggs before returning to the sea. Budget travelers probably can't afford to stay here (there is no camping), but it's worth coming just for the beach and the sea. You can rent snorkeling gear at the dive shops for about $5 a day.

SIAN KA'AN BIOSPHERE RESERVE Twenty-five kilometers south of Tulum are the ruins of **Muyil**. The six structures here are far from spectacular, but merit a stop if you've got a car. Otherwise, continue south into the Sian Ka'an Biosphere Reserve. This expanse of quiet bays, deserted beaches, mangrove swamps, and jungle is populated with birds, crocodiles, jaguars, and boars, as well as wild orchids. Within the reserve, the marshy area around **Laguna Chunyaxche** is an ideal spot for bird-watching. It's a popular rest stop and habitat for over 300 species of birds, including flamingos, herons, and egrets. **Isla Pájaros** is equally popular with our feathered friends, as well as crocodiles. Small canals believed to have been built by the Maya and used as ceremonial sites are also of interest—wade, swim, or haggle with a fisherman for a boat ride. Sian Ka'an is only affordable if you're going to camp out—cabañas at the northern entrance start at about $60, and lodging in the fly-fishing resort of **Boca Paila** are even steeper. You can camp along the beach; if there are people around, ask permission just to be polite. Restaurants are few and far between, and those that exist are expensive, so bring your own provisions. During the tourist season (December–April, July and August), pickup trucks sometimes depart from the intersection about 3 kilometers south of the Tulum ruins (just past Cabañas Los Gatos). From there, it's a 50-kilometer trek. Drivers should fill up at the gas station in Tulum before making the trip. **Amigos de Sian Ka'an** in Cancún (tel. 988/4–95–83) may also be able to get you aboard one of their tour buses.

COBA

This site, covering more than 70 square kilometers, has been largely ignored by archaeologists and the Mexican government. Dense jungle envelops much of it, and visitors will feel like pioneers stumbling onto something unknown and exotic. You can't help becoming excited at the sight of mounds and mounds of unexcavated ruins. Distances between the structures are all

1–2 kilometers, so be prepared to walk; bring water and *lots* of insect repellent. The jungle that surrounds the ruins is no less an attraction. If you're adventurous and not afraid of snakes, follow any of the paths into the undergrowth.

Cobá is one of the oldest sites on the peninsula. It was built around several shallow lakes and marshes, and was settled about 400 BC but didn't develop into a city until around AD 500. The city's inhabitants died out mysteriously 600 years before the arrival of the Spanish, and the ruins weren't discovered until the late 19th century. The remains of more than 30 roads, once paved with smoothed stones, indicate that Cobá was a large commercial center. The two huge pyramids that archaeologists have unearthed here bear more resemblance to the structures at Tikal, Guatemala, than to local architecture, suggesting royal ties with the wealthy Maya of the Petén jungle. More than 6,500 structures have yet to be excavated.

Closest to the entrance is a group of temples known as the **Cobá Group,** the first of which is the enormous pyramid called the **Iglesia,** the second-largest on the peninsula (26 meters high). The vigorous climb up the pyramid rewards you with a fantastic view of two lakes, the jungle surrounding the ruins, and Nohoch Mul (*see below*). In front of the pyramid is a small shrine where local Maya occasionally leave offerings to the gods.

Walk a short way back down the main trail to **Las Pinturas** (The Paintings). Unfortunately, the pyramidal temple bears only scant remnants of frescoes on its walls, but it's still worth climbing up the pyramid's clunky steps and poking around its topmost level for a peek into the surrounding jungle. At the foot of the pyramid lie 13 square stone wells, thought to be altars or sites for offerings to the gods. On the way back to the entrance is a 3-kilometer side trip to the **Stelae Group.** More than 30 deteriorating but intricately carved stelae have been found at Cobá, depicting tyrannical rulers standing imperiously on the backs of captives, subjects, and slaves.

Back on the main trail, follow the signs to **Nohoch Mul,** the Yucatán's tallest Maya structure. It's well worth the 2-kilometer trek to see this pyramid, which soars 41 meters from the jungle floor. The climb is not for the weak of heart, but the view from the top is superb. Chances are you'll have the summit to yourself, a rarity in this region. The temple on top of the pyramid is thought to have been constructed long after the pyramid itself was finished. Note the carvings of diving gods on the front wall.

Admission to Cobá is $2, but the adventurous can enter clandestinely. Remember, the admission price pays workers and goes toward the upkeep of the ruins, which may or may not matter to you. Here goes: Across from the Restaurant Isabel, a dirt road passes by a white-and-blue water tower. Take the road straight through the village and follow it past the small pharmacy and a square thatched home with a red roof. There the road turns into a trail and enters the jungle. Stay on the main trail for about 15 minutes and when you come to a wider, well-trod road, take a left. The hulking Nohoch Mul pyramid is 100 meters ahead. The ruins are open daily 8–5.

COMING AND GOING Getting to Cobá is not too difficult. Four daily buses make the 45-minute ride from Tulum ($1). Though buses rarely leave early, it's best to wait at the downtown Tulum bustop ahead of time—drivers won't wait if the stop is empty. If you catch the last bus (6 PM), you'll have to stay the night in Cobá (the last bus back to Tulum leaves at 3 PM). If you're desperate to get back to Tulum, take a taxi to the main highway (10 km, about $2) and flag down a Valladolid–Tulum bus.

WHERE TO SLEEP AND EAT Hotel El Bocadito (main road, no phone) has eight dusty rooms with beds on cement bases and private bathrooms; they charge $5 for a single, $6.50 for a double. If you have your own hammock, most people will let you hang it in their houses—look for SE RENTAN CUARTOS signs or ask in the stores. If you're desperate you can camp, but slather yourself with bug repellent beforehand. Try the lakeshore south of the ruins near the Club Med or the patch of grass near the entrance to the ruins.

Eating in Cobá doesn't have to be expensive: **Restaurant El Bocadito,** next to the hotel, serves main dishes for around $4 and will prepare a cooked vegetable dish for $2.50. Behind the basketball court, **Lonchería La Amistad** is a cheaper option, where you can get sandwiches for 75¢, salbutes for 50¢, and great licuados with fresh fruit for $1.

Cobá

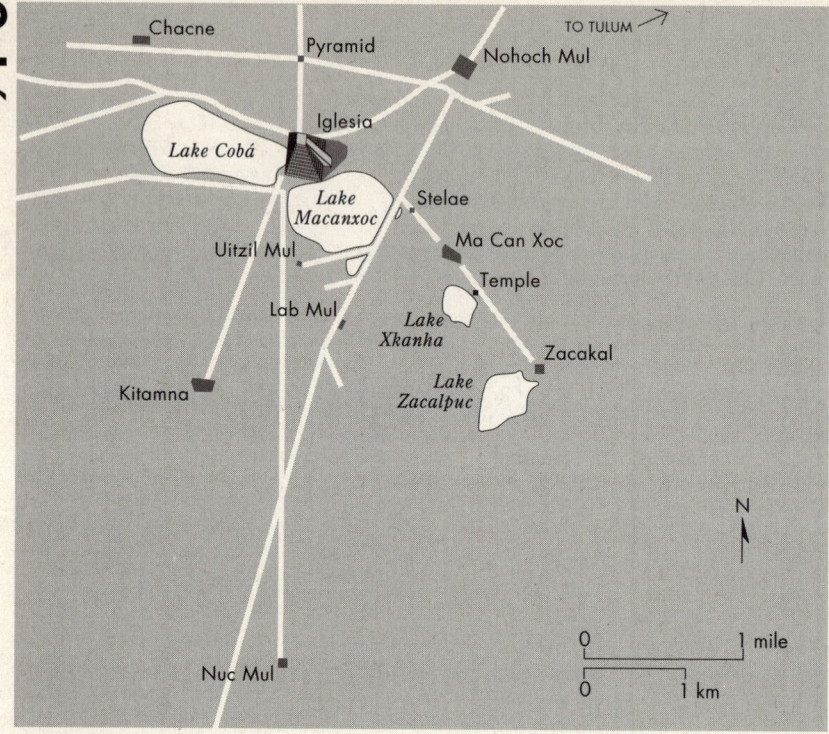

Chetumal

Travelers come to Chetumal, at the southern tip of Quintana Roo, for two reasons: to use the city as a springboard for trips to Belize and Guatemala, and to take advantage of duty-free bargains. Architecturally, this state capital has little to offer: Its modern block-style buildings are dull at best. Chetumal survives today only because its duty-free status attracts people in search of cheap stereos, refrigerators, and every other kind of electronic gadget. Still, Chetumal isn't a total letdown: The **Museo de la Cultura Maya** offers an excellent overview of Maya history and culture, and the beautiful lagoons on the city's outskirts make for worthwhile day trips. For a dose of mayhem, visit the **mercado nuevo** (Segundo Circuito at Calzada Veracruz), 10 blocks north of the city center, where regional fruit and vegetable vendors pour in to sell produce from their bikes and trucks at rock-bottom prices.

BASICS

CASAS DE CAMBIO Bancomer (tel. 983/2–52–53) and **Banamex** (tel. 983/2–10–44), both on Juárez at Obregón, change money weekdays 9–2 and have ATMs that accept Master-Card, Visa, and Cirrus cards.

CROSSING THE BORDER

➤ **TO BELIZE** • Travelers pay nothing to enter Belize. American and British Commonwealth citizens do not need visas to enter Belize, but they do need passports. To reach the México/Belize border, take a bus from the **Central de Autobuses** or from the mercado nuevo (see Coming and Going, below).

➤ **TO GUATEMALA** • For information on visas and tourist cards, see box Going to Guatemala, in Chapter 10. You can also contact the **Guatemalan Consulate**. Chapultepec 354, at Cecilio Chi, tel. 983/2–85–85. Open weekdays 9–5, but try knocking after hours.

MEDICAL AID There are a number of hospitals near the budget hotels. The cleanest is **Hospital Morelos** (cnr of Juárez and Águilar, tel. 983/2–45–99), with 24-hour emergency ambulance service. For minor medical needs, **Farmacia Canto** (Héroes, at Gandhi, tel. 983/2–04–83) is open 7 AM–11 PM.

PHONES AND MAIL The **post office** (Plutarco Elías and Calle 2a, 2 blocks east of Héroes, tel. 983/2–25–78) is open weekdays 9–5, Saturdays 9–noon. They will hold mail sent to you at the following address for up to 10 days: Lista de Correos, Chetumal, Quintana Roo, CP 77000, México. The Latadel phone cards used here are different from those used in Playa del Carmen and Cancún. If your card doesn't work, purchase a new one at **La Fuente** (Lázaro Cárdenas, at Juárez, just south of Teletono de Mocio) or **Hotel Tulum** (see Where To Sleep, below). There's also a **Computel** at the bus station, open daily 7 AM–10 PM.

VISITOR INFORMATION The **tourist booth** (Héroes, at Águilar, in front of mercado viejo, tel. 983/2–36–63) is open Monday–Saturday 8:30–1:30 and 6–9. The **Secretaría de Turismo** has a helpful English-speaking staff. *Palacio Municipal, on Bahía, 1 block west of Héroes, tel. 983/2–08–55. Open Mon.–Sat. 8–2.*

COMING AND GOING

BY BUS Chetumal's **Central de Autobuses** (Insurgentes, at Belice, about 15 blocks from downtown) is a 75¢ taxi ride from downtown. The 24-hour station has a **Computel** office, an upstairs restaurant, and luggage storage (20¢ per hour). Frequent first- and second-class buses leave daily for Cancún (5 hrs, $10 1st class; 5½ hrs, $8 2nd class) and Playa del Carmen (2½ hrs, $8 1st class; 3 hrs, $6.50 2nd class). There are four direct buses to Tulum (3½ hrs, $6.50) every 2 hours 12:30–6:30 PM. The first-class bus to Campeche leaves at noon (6 hrs, $12), and second-class buses leave at 4:30 AM and 3:30 PM. Four first-class buses head to Mérida (6 hrs, $10 1st class; 8 hrs, $9 2nd class). One bus makes a direct trip to Palenque at 10:15 PM (8 hrs, $13), and two daily buses leave for Escárcega at 12:30 PM and 3:30 PM (45 min, $7 2nd class), stopping at Villahermosa on the way. Three buses a day leave for México City (23 hrs, $43).

Batty's runs hourly buses to Belize 7 AM–10 PM (4 hrs, $5), which can be caught at the Central de Autobuses or at the mercado nuevo. If you're heading to Belize, pay the bus fare in Belizean dollars—you'll get a better exchange rate. Batty's also has service to Guatemala City at 3:30 PM (8 hrs, $30).

To reach Bacalar, Cenote Azul, or Laguna Milagros (*see* Near Chetumal, *below*), take one of the small buses that leave from the station at Hidalgo and Francisco Primo de Verdad. Buses for Xcalak ($5) leave at 7 AM from Avenida 16 de Septiembre, at Gandhi. To reach Calderitas, take a combi from the station on Belice, between Colón and Gandhi.

BY PLANE The small airport 2 kilometers outside of Chetumal only handles destinations in México, Guatemala, and Belize. Carriers serving the airport include **Aeroméxico** (tel. 983/2–15–76) and **Aerocaribe** (tel. 983/2–66–75). Take a taxi downtown ($2), or walk east on Revolución (the main street north of the airport), which becomes Águilar.

GETTING AROUND

It's easy to get around Chetumal on foot, and almost everything you need is in the downtown area. The most important street running north–south is Avenida Héroes, where the **mercado viejo** (old market), budget lodging, and tourist information booth are all located. The **mercado nuevo** (new market) and bus station are located about 15 blocks north. Taxis are cheap and abundant; within the downtown area, you shouldn't pay more than 50¢; north of Insurgentes, you'll have to pay 75¢.

WHERE TO SLEEP

There are plenty of budget hotels in Chetumal catering to shoppers who come for the city's cheap wares. The best place to start looking is the plaza around the intersection of Héroes and Águilar, where there are cheap loncherías and bookstores.

➤ **UNDER $10** • **Hotel Cristal.** This centrally located hotel has large, clean, and very bare rooms. The bathrooms feature reliable hot water and fluorescent soap. Windowless, airless singles go for a mere $4.50, doubles $7. Doubles with air-conditioning are $11, triples $13. *Cristobal Colón 207, btw Juárez and Belice, tel. 983/2–38–78. Wheelchair access.*

Hotel Tulum. Both singles and doubles in this downtown hotel go for $7, but the cleaning lady often forgets to sweep up the cockroach cadavers in the large, bare rooms. The breezy but often noisy hallway leads to clotheslines and patios—relief for the claustrophobic. *Héroes 164, btw Gandhi and Águilar, tel. 983/2–05–18. 17 rooms, all with bath. Luggage storage. Reservations advised in summer. Wheelchair access.*

Hotel Ucum. The bright-red tubes and barrel-shaped tanks on the roof make you feel like you're going to work in a boot-making factory, but the dark-wood furniture and freshly painted rooms make for a down-home feel. Beds are small and rickety, but adequate, and bathrooms supply a healthy jet of piping-hot water. Singles are a low $7 ($10 with air-conditioning) and doubles are $8.50 ($10 with air-conditioning). *Gandhi 167, btw Héroes and 16 de Septiembre, tel. 983/2–00–11. 58 rooms, all with bath. Luggage storage.*

➤ **UNDER $15** • **Hotel Real Azteca.** Shiny wooden carvings of Mayan gods and modern-looking hieroglyphics decorate this unabashedly tourist-friendly hotel. A circular stairway winds up to air-conditioned rooms equipped with TVs and black-and-white checkered bathrooms reeking of industrial-strength air-freshener. Bring your own agua purificada—they charge 50¢ a glass here. Singles are $10, doubles $12.50, and triples $14. *Belice 186, btw Águilar and Gandhi, tel. 983/2–06–66. 30 rooms, all with bath. Luggage storage.*

HOSTELS **Albergue Juvenil CND.** One of the best-run hostels on the peninsula, CND is clean and well-staffed. The free-flowing showers in the spacious bathrooms are positively blissful. Four-person, wood-shuttered rooms have a fan and lockers, and guests get a free chocolate bar with their sheets and towel (BYO soap). The 11 PM curfew is negotiable with the friendly manager. Beds are $2.25 (10% discount with HI card) or you can camp on the lawn for $2 a night. *Naval, at Veracruz, tel. 983/2–34–65. 1 block north of Obregón and about 5 blocks east of Héroes. 66 beds. Key deposit ($3.50), luggage storage, meal service.*

CAMPING You can tent-camp on the lawn of the youth hostel (*see above*) for $2 per person. A more scenic option is **Laguna Milagros** (*see* Near Chetumal, *below*), 12 kilometers west of town.

FOOD

In Chetumal you'll find Yucatecan food, sometimes with a Belizean influence, including lime soup and *tikinchic* (fried fish seasoned with sour orange). If you're trying to save money, pick up some fruit at **Frutería La Merced** (Héroes, at Cristóbal Colón). There's a convenient bakery, **Pan La Terminal,** at Héroes and Colón. If you're in Chetumal after the sun sets, **New Caribbean's** (Veracruz 451, at Insurgentes, tel. 983/2–91–45), open 7 AM–3 AM, has 50¢ beers and $2 cocktails after 6 PM. Local and Belizean bands play reggae and *musica caribe* (a mixture of Mexican and Belizean pop-rock and rhythm) daily from 4 PM–3 AM. There's a $2.50 cover Friday and Saturday nights.

Restaurant/Super Las Arcades. Open-air seating and clean wood tables make this a preferred spot among tourists, but 24-hour service and consistently good food also attracts a group of local regulars. Mean appetites can be sated with the *cubana*, a bulging sandwich stuffed with ham, beef, cheese and breaded chicken, slathered in salsa, and accompanied by hot chips ($2.75). Choose from an elaborate selection of egg, bean, and rice dishes ($2–$3) or try yogurt and granola for $1.25. *Heroes 74, at Zaragosa, tel. 983/2–08–84.*

Restaurant Ucum. This is probably the only color-coordinated place in Chetumal—too bad they chose mint green. Fortunately, there's more variety in terms of food. Hearty breakfast dishes ($1.75) include eggs, rice, beans, salad, and tortillas. Also good is the $2 comida corrida. *Gandhi 167, btw 16 de Septiembre and Héroes, tel. 983/2–21–88. Open Mon.–Sat. 7:30 AM–9 PM.*

El Vaticano. This place serves large dishes of fresh fish for much less than in Cancún or Playa del Carmen. Excellent dishes with fried, grilled, or marinated conch in lemon and garlic are

$3.75, and octopus goes for $3. Nestled in a corner across from the old market, it's a nice place to sit outside and sip a beer (50¢). *Belice, at Gandhi, no phone. Open Mon.–Sat. 10–5, Sun. 10–3. Wheelchair access.*

WORTH SEEING

If you plan to check out any of the peninsula's ruins or if you've already done so and are looking for a refresher on Mayan history and culture, it's worth your while to pay a visit to the recently opened **Museo de la Cultura Maya**. Gear-shaped wheels depict the passage of time according to the 18-month Mayan calendar, and easy-to-use computers offer a variety of information on Mayan history as well as regional plants and animals. You can also walk along glass-encased replicas of the peninsula's ancient temples and hieroglyph-covered stelae. Virtual realists will get a kick out of the subterranean models of Uxmal and Tulum, which you can peer down at through brightly lit glass floor panels. A central gallery exhibits contemporary photography, sculpture, and paintings. *Héroes and Colón, just north of mercado viejo. Open daily 10–6. Admission to permanent exhibit: $1.50; galleries free.*

Near Chetumal

Calderitas, a beach town 8 kilometers north of town, has excellent swimming. To get here, take a minibus (every ½ hr, 10 min, 20¢) from the bus stop in back of the mercado viejo (Belice, btw Colón and Gandhi). Divers head for **Xcalak**, a beautiful beach near **Banco Chinchorra**, a 42-kilometer coral atoll littered with shipwrecks, about 2 hours offshore. One daily bus leaves at 7 AM from the station at 16 de Septiembre and Gandhi (4½ hrs, $5). Snorkeling and diving gear can be rented right on the beach or at **Costa de Cocos**, 1 kilometer before the bus stops in Xcalak. Chetumal's major water attractions, however, are inland: Laguna Milagros, Cenote Azul, and Laguna de Bacalar (*see below*) are all easily reached by the combi ($1) from the corner of Hidalgo and Primo de Verdad in Chetumal. The last buses head back to Chetumal around 7 PM. Or consider renting a VW bug for $49 a day at **Rentadora Kohumlich** (Calzada Veracruz 121, tel. 983/2-38-75), open Monday–Saturday 8:30–2 and 5:30–8.

LAGUNA MILAGROS The area surrounding Laguna Milagros is unspectacular, but its warm water is inviting and peaceful. It's also a good place to pitch a tent: You can walk about 1 kilometer south around the lagoon without crashing into the heavy undergrowth, or just bed down on the southern shore (beware of falling coconuts). To avoid dogs and the occasional curious onlooker, ask permission to camp at **Las Brisas** restaurant, where a verdant lawn and constant breeze make for a more restful night. You can also hang your hammock for free in the open-air patio of **El Campesino** restaurant. Both restaurants close at 5 PM and open up again at 8 AM, so be ready to head out early. The 12-kilometer trip here by minibus takes 15 minutes, and the lake is about 110 meters from the main road. Catch a bus back to Chetumal at one of the stops on the main road.

CENOTE AZUL If you have time to visit only one place near Chetumal, it should be Cenote Azul. The largest cenote in the world, it's 89 meters deep and 220 meters across and surrounded by thick jungle. Its name derives from the intensity of its blue waters, home to an array of beautiful fish. Unfortunately, strong underwater currents make diving dangerous, but careful floaters can see plenty from the water's surface (bring your own gear—there aren't any shops here). Located 30 kilometers north of Chetumal, the cenote is a popular watering hole, so come early or late in the day to avoid crowds. From Chetumal, take any minibus to Bacalar and ask the driver to let you off at Cenote Azul. To get back, stand on the roadside and flag down a passing bus or minibus.

LAGUNA DE BACALAR About 40 kilometers north of Chetumal, this is a favorite destination for day-tripping locals. Also known as Laguna de Siete Colores (Lagoon of Seven Colors), the lagoon changes color according to the light and the depth of the water. The warm, shimmering waters are safe and attract families on holidays and weekends. The lagoon is surrounded by private property and the neighboring town of Bacalar, accessible by bus from Chetumal. The lagoon eventually feeds into the Río Hondo, which forms the México–Belize border. You can take a 1-hour boat ride around the lagoon and down the adjoining Río Depiratas for $3 per person or make the 3-hour boat trip to Belize ($10 per person, minimum of 7 people). For more information about both trips, talk to the bartender at Restaurant Ejidal. Camping at Ejidal costs $2, including use of the toilet and shower facilities. You'll have to move out at daybreak, though, because the restaurant/bar is open all day. To reach Ejidal, walk away from the central square toward the water, turn left on the road that runs along the water, and walk about 800 meters. While in Bacalar, take a look at the perfectly preserved **Fuerte San Felipe Bacalar,** just east of the park. The fort has an impressive view of the area, and the main room serves as the town museum. It's open Tuesday–Sunday 10–6; admission is 25¢.

Spanish Glossary

In Spanish, what you see is what you get: Every letter is pronounced and the accent usually falls on the second-to-last syllable, unless there is an accent mark. Of course, there are exceptions to both rules. And, to confound matters, you'd be hard pressed to find a Mexican who actually pronounces everything clearly. Still, if you learn a few rules, you should be able to pronounce almost any Spanish word; figuring out what it means may take a little more effort. The following letters are pronounced as follows:

a like the **a** in ah	**e** like the **e** in deck
i like the **ee** in beet	**o** like the **o** in cold
u like the **oo** in loot	**y** like the **ea** in eat
ñ like the **ni** in senior	**ll** like the **y** in kayak

The **h** is silent in Spanish, and the Spanish **j** is pronounced like the **h** in horse. **G** before **a**, **o**, **u**, or a consonant is hard (like in gate); when before **e** or **i**, it's soft, sounding just slightly harder than the **h** in hay. However, when **g** is paired with **u** (**gu**), the **u** sounds like the English **w**. For all practical purposes, **b** and **v** sound the same—roughly like a **b** in English. **C** before **a**, **o**, and **u** is hard like the English **k**; before **e** and **i** it's soft like the English **s**.

English	Spanish
Basics	
Yes/no	Sí/no
Hello/goodbye	Hola/adiós
Good morning	Buenos días
Good afternoon	Buenas tardes
Good night	Buenas noches
How are you?	¿Cómo está?
I'm fine, thanks	Estoy bien, gracias
Pardon me	Perdóneme
Excuse me	Con permiso
What's your name?	¿Cómo se llama?
My name is . . .	Me llamo . . .
I'm from the United States	Soy estadounidense
I'm Australian	Soy australiano(a)
I'm Canadian	Soy canadiense
I'm English	Soy inglés(a)
I'm Scottish	Soy escocés(a)
Kiss me, I'm Irish	Bésame, soy irlandés
Do you speak English?	¿Habla inglés?
I don't speak Spanish	No hablo español
I don't understand	No entiendo
How do you say . . .	¿Cómo se dice . . . ?
More slowly, please	Más despacio, por favor
Could you please repeat that?	¿Podría repetir, por favor?
I don't know	No sé
Please	Por favor
Thank you	Gracias
You're welcome	De nada
Where is (are) . . . ?	¿Dónde está(n) . . . ?

Are there . . .?	¿Hay . . .?
Bathroom	Baño, sanitario
Backpack	Mochila
Post office	Oficina de correos
Long-distance telephone office	Caseta de larga distancia
Collect call	Llamada al cobrar
Laundromat	Lavandería
Bank/money exchange place	Banco/casa de cambio
Open	Abierto(a)
Closed	Cerrado(a)
Yesterday	Ayer
Today	Hoy
Tomorrow	Mañana
This morning	Esta mañana
This evening	Esta tarde
Tonight	Esta noche
What time is it?	¿Qué hora es?
Entrance	Entrada
Exit	Salida
Floor/story	Piso
Neighborhood	Colonia/barrio
How much is this/it?	¿Cuánto es?
Cheap	Barato
Expensive	Caro

Emergencies and Medical Aid

Help!	¡Socorro!
Leave me alone!	¡Déjame en paz!
Call the police	Llame la policía
Call a doctor	Llame un médico
Hospital	Hospital
I'm sick	Estoy enfermo(a)
I need a doctor	Necesito un médico
I have a headache	Me duele la cabeza
I have a stomachache	Me duele el estómago
Fever	Fiebre
Prescription	Receta
Medicine	Remedio
Aspirin	Aspirina
Condom	Preservativo
AIDS	SIDA

Coming and Going

Right	Derecha
Left	Izquierda
Straight	Derecho/recto
On foot	A pie
Hitchhike	Hacer dedo
Ride	Aventón
Ticket window	Taquilla
A ticket for . . .	Un boleto para . . .
One-way	Ida
Round-trip	Ida y vuelta
First/second class	Primera/segunda clase
Where are you going?	¿A dónde va?
How many kilometers?	¿Cuántos kilometros?

How long is the trip?	¿Cuánto tiempo dura el viaje?
I'm going to . . .	Me voy a . . .
I want to get off at . . .	Quiero bajar en . . .
Map	Mapa
Arrival	Llegada
Departure	Salida
Airport	Aeropuerto
Train station	Estación de ferrocarril
Bus	Autobús, camión
Bus station	Terminal de autobuses
Bus stop	Parada
Car	Carro
I'd like to rent a car	Me gustaría alquilar un carro
Insurance	Seguros
Gas	Gasolina
Tire	Llanta
Stoplight	Semáforo
Motorcycle	Motocicleta
Highway	Carretera
The road to . . .	El camino a . . .
Bridge	Puente
Metro stop	Estación de Metro
Fare	Tarifa
To cross	Cruzar
Bicycle	Bicicleta

Where to Sleep

Guest house	Casa de huéspedes
Key	Llave
Manager	Gerente
Room	Habitación/cuarto
For two people	Para dos personas
With/without	Con/sin
Shower	Ducha
Hot/cold water	Agua caliente/fría
Fan	Ventilador
Air-conditioning	Aire acondicionado
Double bed	Cama matrimonial
Sheets	Sábanas
Toilet paper	Papel de baño/papel higiénico
Included	Incluido
Camping	Campground
Hammock	Hamaca
I would like to make a reservation	Me gustaría hacer una reservación
Is there a private bathroom?	¿Hay un baño privado?
Can I leave my bags here?	¿Puedo dejar mi equipaje aquí?

Food

Food	Comida
Bakery	Panadería
Supermarket	Supermercado
Groceries	Abarrotes
I'm hungry/thirsty	Tengo hambre/sed
I'm a vegetarian	Soy vegetariano(a)
I'm diabetic	Soy diabético(a)
Waiter/waitress	Mesero(a)

Breakfast	Desayuno
Lunch	Almuerzo
Dinner	Cena
Daily special	Menú del día
Pre-prepared lunch special	Comida corrida
Bill/check	Cuenta
(Wheat) bread	Pan (integral)
Toast	Pan tostado
(Purified) water	Agua (purificada)
Ice	Hielo
Cocktail	Trago
Tea/coffee	Té/café
Soda	Refresco
Milk	Leche
Juice	Jugo
Vegetables	Verduras
Fruit	Fruta
Apple	Manzana
Orange	Naranja
Pineapple	Piña
Lemon/Lime	Limón/Lima
Coconut	Coco
Strawberry	Fresa
Potato	Papa
French fries	Papas fritas
Rice	Arroz
Egg	Huevo
Salt/Pepper	Sal/Pimienta
Sugar	Azúcar
Meat	Carne
Steak	Bistec
Chicken	Pollo
Pork	Puerco
Fish	Pescado
Shellfish	Mariscos
Fork	Tenedor
Spoon	Cuchara
Knife	Cuchillo
Napkin	Servilleta
Ice cream	Helado

Numbers

One	Uno/una
Two	Dos
Three	Tres
Four	Cuatro
Five	Cinco
Six	Seis
Seven	Siete
Eight	Ocho
Nine	Nueve
Ten	Diez
Eleven	Once
Twelve	Doce
Thirteen	Trece
Fourteen	Catorce
Fifteen	Quince

Sixteen	Dieciséis/diez y seis
Seventeen	Diecisiete/diez y siete
Eighteen	Dieciocho
Nineteen	Diecinueve/diez y nueve
Twenty	Veinte
Thirty	Treinta
Forty	Cuarenta
Fifty	Cincuenta
Sixty	Sesenta
Seventy	Setenta
Eighty	Ochenta
Ninety	Noventa
One hundred	Cien
One thousand	Mil

Days and Months

day	día
month	mes
Sunday	Domingo
Monday	Lunes
Tuesday	Martes
Wednesday	Miércoles
Thursday	Jueves
Friday	Viernes
Saturday	Sábado
January	Enero
February	Febrero
March	Marzo
April	Abril
May	Mayo
June	Junio
July	Julio
August	Agosto
September	Septiembre
October	Octubre
November	Noviembre
December	Diciembre

Index

A

Acapulco, *308–317*
Acatepec, *351*
Acueducto del Cuba, *225*
African Safari (zoo), *345*
Agua Azul, *436–437*
Aguascalientes, *227–230*
Air travel, *24–25, 27*
Airfares, *7–9*
 APEX tickets, *8*
 charter flights, *8–9*
 consolidators, *8*
 courier flights, *9*
 standby fares, *8*
 student discounts, *9*
Akumal, *522*
Alamos, *139–140*
Allende, Ignacio, *189, 198, 206*
Alley of the Kiss, *216–217*
Amatenango del Valle, *429*
Amazoc, *352*
Angahuan, *250*
Arrazola, *398*
Arteaga, *184, 186*
Aticama, *277*
Avenue of the Dead, *80*
Ayuntamiento de Cuernavaca, *325*
Aztec ruins, *80–82*
 Tepoztlán and Xochicalco, *329–331*

B

Backpacks, *12*
Bahía Chamela, *291*
Bahía de Concepcion, *113*
Bahía de Matanchen, *277*
Bahía de Navidad, *288–290*
Bahía Kino, *135–136*
Bahuichivo, *161*
Baja California, *85–126*
Baja California Norte, *87–105*
Baja California Sur, *105–115*
Balankanché Caves, *492*
Ball courts, *205, 206, 381, 469, 471, 472, 490*
Balneario Temixco (aquatic park), *325–326*
Barra de Navidad, *288–290*
Barra de Potosí, *307–308*
Barranca de Cobre, *156–157*
Basaseachic Falls, *160*
Basketball, *186*
Batopilas, *160–161*
Beaches
 Acapulco, *316–317*
 Bahía de Navidad, *290*
 Boca de Pascuales, *297*
 Cabos region, *122, 125*
 Cancún, *498, 499*
 Catemaco, *372–373*
 Celestun, *486*
 Chemuyil, *522*
 Chetumal, *527*
 Cozumel, *516*
 Cuyutlán, *296–297*
 El Paraíso, *297*
 Ensenada, *101*
 Guerrero Negro, *108*
 Isla Mujeres, *505–506*
 Ixtapa/Zihuatanejo, *306–307*
 La Paz, *119*
 Las Palmas, *447*
 Los Tuxtlas, *371*
 Manzanillo, *295–296*
 Matamoros, *171*
 Mazatlán, *273*
 Mulegé, *113*
 Oaxaca Coast, *398*
 Playa del Carmen, *510*
 Playa Malarrimo, *108*
 Puerto Angel, *403*
 Puerto Escondido, *401*
 Puerto Madero, *447*
 Puerto Vallarta, *285–286, 287*
 Punta Bete, *511*
 Punta de Mita, *287*
 Rosarito, *93*
 San Blas, *277*
 San Quintin, *104*
 Santa Rosalía, *110*
 sleeping on, *30*
 Tabasco, *455*
 Tampico, *188*
 Topolobampo, *144*
 Tulum, *521–522*
 Tuxpán, *382, 384*
 Veracruz, *368*
 Xcaret, *511*
 Zipolite, *404–405*
Bedding, *13*
Belize, *524*
Bella Unión, *186*
Biblioteca de las Californias, *119*
Bicycles, *24, 27–28, 255, 367, 408*
Bird-watching, *486, 494, 506*
Boca de Pascuales, *297–298*
Bocatoma, *173*
Bolsitas, *257*
Bonampak, *437–438*
Boojum trees, *109*
Books on Mexico, *31*
Border crossings
 Chetumal, *524*
 Ciudad Juárez, *146*
 Guatemala, *447*
 Matamoros, *168*
 Mexicali, *95*
 Nogales, *129*
 Nuevo Laredo, *174*
 Reynosa, *172*
 Tiujuana, *88*
Bribery, *91*
Bucket shops, *8*
Budget travel organizations, *4*
Bullfighting
 Acapulco, *315*
 Ciudad Juárez, *150*
 Mazatlán, *272*
 Mexico City, *79*
 Tiujuana, *93*

534

Business hours, *29*
Bus travel, *26*

C

Cable-car rides, *226*
Cabo San Lucas, *123–125*
Cabos region, *120–125*
Cacalotepec, *402*
Cacaxtla, *339–340*
Calcehtok, *482*
Cameras, *14*
Campeche, *460–465*
Camping, *30*
Camping gear, *14*
Cancún, *495–500*
Car rentals, *25*
Car travel, *25–27*
Casa del Olvido, *326*
Cash machines, *12*
Castillo de Chapultepec, *65*
Catedral Basilica Menor, *225*
Catemaco, *371–372*
Caves
 Balankanché, *492*
 Cacahuamilpa, *357–358*
 Calcehtok, *482*
 Cave of the Sleeping Sharks, *506*
 Grutas de Coconá, *456*
 Grutas de Garcia, *183*
 Loltun, *472–473*
 Puerto Villarta, *286*
 San Cristóbal, *427*
 San Ignacio, *109–110*
 Teapa, *456*
 Tepoztlán, *329*
 Xiltla, *197*
 Xtacumbilxunaa, *467*
Celestún, *486*
Cemetery Group, *469*
Cenote Azul, *527*
Cenotes, *484, 490, 494, 521*
Center for Investigation of Olmec and Maya Cultures, *453*
Centro de Estudios Cientificos Na-Bolom, *425*
Centro Vacacional La Malintza, *339*
Cerocahui, *161–162*
Cerro de la Bufa, *225*
Cerro del Fortin, *392*
Cervantes, Miguel de, *213, 218*
Chacalapa, *404*
Chapultepec Park, *65, 67*

Chemuyil, *522*
Chenalho, *429*
Chenes ruins, *465–467*
Chetumal, *524–527*
Chiapa de Corzo, *418–419*
Chiapas, *411–412*
Chichén Itzá, *487–492*
Chihuahua, *145, 152–155*
Chilpancingo, *358–360*
China Poblana Legend, *346*
Chincultic, *443*
Chipilo, *350*
Cholula, *349–351*
Cihuatlán, *291*
Circuito de baluartes, *463–464*
Ciudad Juárez, *146, 148–150*
Ciudad Obregón, *139*
Ciudad Valles, *196–197*
Climate, *1, 2*
Clothing, *13*
Coatepec, *378*
Cobá, *522–523*
Cock fighting, *243*
Codz-Pop, *471*
Colima, *265, 298–301*
Comala, *302*
Comalcalco, *454–455*
Comitán, *439–442*
Concordia, *274*
Consulates
 Acapulco, *308–309*
 Cancún, *495*
 Ciudad Juárez, *146*
 Comitán, *439*
 Cozumel, *513*
 Guadalajara, *232*
 Hermosillo, *132*
 Matamoros, *168*
 Mazatlán, *267*
 Mérida, *475*
 Monterrey, *177*
 Oaxaca de Juarez, *387*
 Puerto Vallarta, *283*
 San Miguel de Allende, *207*
 Tapachula, *444*
 Tijuana, *88*
 Veracruz, *363*
Contraceptives, *17*
Copala, *274*
Copper Canyon, *156–157*
Coral reefs, *517*
Coronel, Pedro, *225–226*
Coronel, Raphael, *226*
Costs of travel, *9–10*
Cozumel, *511–518*

Craft centers
 Guadalajara, *240*
 Jalapa, *376*
 Oaxaca de Juarez, *393*
 San Cristóbal, *426*
Credit cards, *10, 11–12*
Creel, *156, 157–160*
Crime, *31*
Cuauhtémoc Brewery, *181*
Cuautla, *331–332*
Cuernavaca, *319, 321–328*
Cuetzalán, *352*
Currency exchange, *10–11*
Customs, *22–24*
Cuyutlán, *296–297*

D

Disabilities, resources for people with, *20–21*
Diseases, *17–19*
Diving
 Acapulco, *316*
 Cabo San Lucas, *125*
 Cancún, *500*
 Chetumal, *527*
 Cozumel, *517*
 Ensenada, *101*
 Isla Mujeres, *506–518*
 Ixtapa/Zihuatanejo, *306*
 La Paz, *119*
 Loreto, *115*
 Mazatlán, *273*
 Mulegé, *113*
 Oaxaca Coast, *398*
 Playa del Carmen, *510*
 San Carlos, *138–139*
 Tulum, *521*
 Tuxpán, *384*
 Veracruz, *368*
Divisadero, *161*
Dog racing, *93*
Dolores Hidalgo, *219*
Domínguez, Belisario, *442*
Dovecote, *470*
Durango, *163–166*
Duties, *22–24*
Dzibilchaltun, *484*
Dzibilnocac, *466*
Dzilam de Bravo, *486*

E

Edzná, *465*
El Caracol, *491*
El Castillo, *489–490*
El Fuerte, *144*
El Garrafón National Park, *507*

INDEX

El Paraíso, *297*
El Tabasqueño, *467*
El Tajín, *380–382*
Embassies, *35. See also* Consulates
Emergencies, *15–16*
Acapulco, *309*
Aguascalientes, *227*
Bahía de Navidad, *288*
Campeche, *461*
Cancún, *495*
Ciudad Chihuahua, *152*
Ciudad Juárez, *146*
Colima, *298*
Cozumel, *513*
Cuernavaca, *321*
Durango, *163*
Ensenada, *98*
Guanajuato, *213*
Guyamas, *136*
Hermosillo, *133*
Ixtapa/Zihuatanejo, *303*
Jalapa, *374*
La Paz, *116*
Los Mochis, *141*
Los Tuxtlas, *370*
Manzanillo, *292*
Matamoros, *168*
Mazatlán, *267*
Mérida, *475*
Mexicali, *95*
Mexico City, *35, 38*
Monterrey, *177*
Morelia, *258*
Nogales, *129*
Nuevo Laredo, *174*
Oaxaca, *387*
Papantla de Olarte, *379*
Patzcuaro, *251*
Puebla, *341*
Puerto Vallarta, *283*
Querétaro, *198*
Reynosa, *172*
Saltillo, *184*
San Blas, *274*
San Cristóbal de las Casas, *420*
San Luis Potosí, *190*
San Miguel de Allende, *207*
Tampico, *186*
Taxco, *353*
Tepic, *279*
Tijuana, *88*
Tlaxcala, *333*
Tuxpán, *382*
Tuxtla Gutierrez, *414*
Uruapan, *247*
Valladolid, *492*
Veracruz, *363*
Villahermosa, *449*
Zacatecas, *222*
Ensenada, *97–101*

F

Festivals
Chiapa de Corzo, *419*
Comitán, *442*
Cuernavaca, *327–328*
Durango, *163*
Guadalajara, *242–243*
Guanajuato, *218*
Janitzio, *256*
Mexico City, *72–73*
Oaxaca, *393*
Pátzcuaro, *251*
Puebla, *348*
Querétaro, *204*
San Blas, *276*
San Cristóbal, *426*
San Luis Potosí, *195*
San Miguel de Allende, *212*
Tapachula, *446*
Taxco, *356–357*
Tlaxcala, *337–338*
Uruapan, *246*
Film, *14*
First-aid kit, *16–17*
Fishing
Acapulco, *316*
Bahía de Navidad, *290*
Cancún, *500*
El Fuerte, *144*
Ensenada, *101*
Ixtapa/Zihuatanejo, *306*
Loreto, *115*
Playa del Carmen, *510*
Saltillo, *186*
San Felipe, *103–104*
Forts
Acapulco, *314*
Bacalar, *528*
Campeche, *463–464*
Puebla, *347*
San Blas, *276*
Veracruz, *367*

G

Gay and lesbian travelers, *20*
Guadalajara, *244*
Mexico City, *76–77*
Goitia, Francisco, *225*
Government tourist offices, *3–4*
Governor's Palace, *470*
Gran Piramide (Zempola), *369*
Grave of the High Priest, *491*
Great Pyramid, *471*
Great Pyramid of Cholula, *350*
Grutas de Cacahuamilpa, *357–358*
Grutas de Coconá, *456*
Grutas de García, *183*
Grutas de San Cristóbal, *427*
Guadalajara, *230–245*
Guanajuato, *189, 212–219*
Guatemala, *447, 524*
Guaymas, *136–138*
Guerrero Negro, *105, 107–108*

H

Hammocks, *405*
Health concerns, *14–19*. *See also* Emergencies
Hermosillo, *132–135*
Hidalgo y Costilla, Father Miguel, *189, 198, 219*
Hierve el Agua, *396*
Hiking. *See also* Mountaineering
Colima, *302*
Comitán, *443*
Copper Canyon, *157*
Creel, *160*
Mazatlán, *273*
Puebla, *349*
Saltillo, *186*
San Cristóbal, *427*
Union Juárez, *448*
Valle de Bravo, *83*
Hitchhiking, *28*
Copper Canyon, *157*
Oaxaca de Juárez, *388*
San Cristóbal de las Casas, *422*
San Felipe, *103*
Hochob, *466–467*
Holidays, *1–2*
Hopelchén, *466*
Horse racing, *79*
Horseback riding, *296, 401, 427, 518*
Hostels, *29*
Cabo San Lucas, *124*
Campeche, *462*
Cancún, *498*
Chetumal, *526*

Ciudad Juárez, *149*
Guadalajara, *236*
Ixtapa/Zihuatanejo, *306*
La Paz, *118*
Monterrey, *180*
Morelia, *260*
Palenque, *433*
Playa del Carmen, *509*
Querétaro, *201*
San Luis Potosí, *193*
San Miguel de Allende, *209–210*
Tijuana, *91*
Tuxtla Gutiérrez, *416*
Veracruz, *365–366*
House of the Turtles, *469–470*
Huamantla, *338–339*
Huatulco, *406–408*
Huejotzingo, *352*
Huichol Indians, *242, 279*
Huitepec Ecological Reserve, *427*

I
Immunizations, *15*
Instituto Allende, *211*
Instituto Cultural Cabanas, *238–239*
Instituto Tecnológico de Monterrey, *181*
Insurance, *15*
Isla Contoy, *506*
Isla Holbox, *500–501*
Isla Marietas, *287*
Isla Mujeres, *501–507*
Isthmus of Tehuantepec, *408–410*
Ixtapa, *303–307*
Izamal, *486–487*
Izapa, *447*

J
Jaguar Palace, *81*
Jai alai, *79, 93*
Jalapa, *374–377*
Jalisco, *265*
Janitzio, *256*
José Cardel, *368*
Juárez, Benito, *392*
Juárez. *See* Ciudad Juárez
Juchitán, *409–410*

K
Kabah, *471*
Kahlo, Frida, *70*
Kayaking, *120, 125*

L
La Bufadora, *101–102*
La Casa de los 11 Patios, *255*
La Cascada Cola de Caballo, *183*
La Ceiba Reef, *517*
La Paz, *116–120*
La Pintada, *136*
La Tovara, *277*
La Villa de Guadalupe/La Basilica, *72*
Labná, *472*
Lacandón Maya, *438*
Lacandón rain forest, *437–439*
Lacanhá, *437*
Lacquerware, *418*
Lagos de Montebello, *439, 443*
Laguna Chankanab, *517*
Laguna de Bacalar, *527–528*
Laguna de Coyuca, *317*
Laguna de San Ignacio, *105, 108, 109*
Laguna de Santa Maria del Oro, *281*
Laguna Encantada, *371*
Laguna La Maria, *302–303*
Laguna Milagros, *527*
Lagunas de Chacahua, *402*
Lakes
Chapala, *245–246*
Lagos de Montebello, *443*
Language, *31*
Las Palmas, *447*
Laundry, *13*
León, *219*
Liberation theology, *327*
Loltún Caves, *472–473*
Lonely Coast, The, *108*
Loreto, *113–115*
Los Arcos, *286*
Los Cabos, *120–126*
Los Mochis, *140–143*
Los Tuxtlas, *369–374*
Luggage, *24*

M
Mail service, *29*
Manialtepec, *402*
Manzanillo, *292–296*
Mariachi music, *245*
Matamoros, *167–171*
Mayan history, *480, 483*
Mayan Museum, *434–435*
Mayan phrases, *473*
Mayan ruins
Bonampak, *437–438*
Cacaxtla, *339–340*
Chenes ruins, *465–467*
Chichén Itzá, *489–492*
Chincultic, *443*
Cobá, *522–523*
Comalcalco, *454–455*
Cozumel, *516*
Dzibilchaltún, *484*
Edzná, *465*
Isla Mujeres, *505*
Izamal, *487*
Izapa, *447*
Mayapán, *482–484*
Muyil, *522*
Oxkintok, *482*
Oxkutzcab and Loltun, *472*
Palenque, *434–435*
Puuc hills, *467–474*
Toniná, *429–431*
Tulum, *520–521*
Yaxchilán, *438–439*
Yucatán peninsula, *457, 460*
Mayapan, *482–484*
Mazatlán, *267–273*
Mazunte, *406*
Medical services, *15–17*. *See also* Emergencies
Mennonites, *466*
Mérida, *474–481*
Mexcaltitán, *278*
Mexicali, *95–97*
Mexico City
Alameda Central, *52, 59, 61–63*
Bosque de Chapultepec, *65–67*
cheap thrills, *72*
Coyocán, *57–58, 68, 70–71*
festivals, *72–73*
food, *55–59*
lodging, *48–55*
Metro Pino Suarez, *54*
Metro Revolucion, *52–54*
nightlife, *75–79*
outdoor activities, *79*
San Angel, *58, 67–68*
shopping, *73–75*
sightseeing in, *59–72*
tourist services, *34–35, 38–39*
transportation, *39–47*

INDEX

Zócalo, *48–49, 55–56, 63–64*
Zona Rosa, *54–55, 56–57*
Mezcal, *131*
Mina el Eden, *225*
Misol-Ha, *436–437*
Mitla, *396–397*
Mixtec ruins, *396*
Mole cuisine, *344*
Mondaca de Marechaja, Fermín, *505*
Money, *9–12*
Monte Albán, *394–396*
Monterrey, *177–182*
Morelia, *257–263*
Morelos, *319*
Morelos, José María, *257, 331*
Motorcycles/motorbikes, *27*
Mountaineering, *349*
Mulegé, *111–113*
Mummy museum, *217*
Museo de Aguascalientes, *229–230*
Museo de Antropologia de Jalapa, *377*
Museo de Arqueologia del Occidente, *240*
Museo de Arte Moderno, *65*
Museo de Artes e Industrias Populares, *61*
Museo de Frida Kahlo, *70*
Museo de la Alhondiga de Granaditas, *217*
Museo de la Caricatura, *64*
Museo de la Independencia, *219*
Museo de la Pinacoteca, *182*
Museo de las Culturas de Occidente, *301*
Museo de las Momias, *213, 217*
Museo Franz Mayer, *61*
Museo Mural de Diego Rivera, *61*
Museo Nacional de Antropologia, *65*
Museo Nacional de Arte, *61*
Museo Nacional de Historia, *65*
Museo Nacional de la Revolucion, *61–62*
Museo Regional del Valle del Fuerte, *143*

N
Nahá, *437*
National Parks
El Garrafón National Park, *507*
Laguna Chankanab, *517*
Parque Nacional Constitución de 1857, *102*
Parque Nacional Eduardo Ruíz, *246, 249*
Parque Nacional Nevado de Colima, *302*
Parque Nacional Sierra San Pedro Mártir, *102*
Xel-Ha Lagoon, *521–522*
Nayarit, *265*
Nogales, *129–131*
Nuevo Casas Grandes, *150–151*
Nuevo Laredo, *174–176*
Nunnery Complex, *491*
Nun's Quadrangle, *469*

O
Oaxaca Coast, *398–410*
Oaxaca de Juárez, *386–394*
Oaxaca Isthmus, *408–410*
Ocosingo, *429–431*
Ocotlan de Morelos, *398*
Off-road vehicles, *101*
Olmec ruins
Cacaxtla, *339–340*
Los Tuxtlas, *369–370*
Santiago Tuxtla and Tres Zapotes, *373*
Veracruz, *361*
Villahermosa, *453*
Oxkintok, *482*
Oxkutzcab, *472–473*

P
Paamul, *511*
Packing, *12–14*
Palacio de Bellas Artes, *62*
Palacio de Cortes, *326*
Palacio de Gobierno (Aguascalientes), *229*
Palacio de Gobierno (Durango), *166*
Palacio de Gobierno (Guadalajara), *239*
Palacio de Gobierno (Tlaxcala), *337*
Palacio de la Cultura (Tlaxcala), *337*
Palacio de Quetzalpapalotl, *81*
Palacio del Gobierno (Zacatecas), *226*
Palacio del Gobierno Federal (Querétaro), *203*
Palacio Nacional, *64*
Palancar Reef, *518*
Palenque, *431–435*
Papantla de Olarte, *378–380*
Paquimé, *150–151*
Paracho, *250*
Paraíso el Oso, *162*
Paraíso reef, *518*
Parasailing, *285, 306, 500*
Parque Nacional Constitución de 1857, *102*
Parque Nacional Cumbres de Monterrey, *183*
Parque Nacional Eduardo Ruíz, *246, 249*
Parque Nacional Lagunas de Chacahua, *402*
Parque Nacional Nevado de Colima, *302*
Parque Nacional Sierra San Pedro Mártir, *102*
Parque Natural Nevado de Colima, *302*
Passports, *5–7*
Pátzcuaro, *251–255*
People of color, resources for, *20*
Pharmacies. *See* Emergencies
Photography, *14*
Pie de la Cuesta, *317*
Pisté, *487–489*
Platform of Jaguars and Eagles, *490*
Playa Bagdad, *171*
Playa del Carmen, *507–510*
Playa Las Islitas, *277*
Playa los Cocos, *277*
Plaza de las Tres Culturas/Tlatelolco, *62*
Police, *31, 91*
Pozos, *219*
Prescription drugs, *16*
Progreso, *484–485*
Puebla, *319, 340–349*
Puerto Angel, *402–404*
Puerto Escondido, *399–102*
Puerto Morelos, *501*
Puerto Peñasco, *131–132*
Puerto Vallarta, *281–286*
Punta Bete, *511*

INDEX

Punta Corneta, *406*
Punta de Mita, *287*
Puuc hills, *467–474*
Pyramid of Quetzalcoatl, *330*
Pyramid of the Magician, *469*
Pyramid of the Moon, *80*
Pyramid of the Niches, *381*
Pyramid of the Old Woman, *470*
Pyramid of the Sun, *80, 81*

Q

Querétaro, *197–204*
Querétaro Missions, *197*
Quetzalcoatl, *81*

R

Rain forests, *196, 372, 437–439*
Ranas ruins, *205–206*
Real de Catorce, *195*
Religious practices, *428*
Reynosa, *171–174*
Río Lagartos, *494–495*
Río Verde, *195–196*
Ritual piercing, *381*
Rivera, Diego, *61, 62, 213, 217*
Rosarito, *93–94*

S

Sacred Cenote, *490*
Sailing, *104, 125*
Salina Cruz, *408–409*
Saltillo, *183–186*
San Andrés Larrainzar, *429*
San Andrés Tuxtla, *370–371*
San Antón Falls, *327*
San Blas, *274–277*
San Carlos, *138–139*
San Cristóbal de las Casas, *420–427*
San Felipe, *102–104*
San Francisco Acatepec, *350–351*
San Ignacio, *108–109*
San Javier, *115*
San Joaquin, *205*
San José del Cabo, *120–122*
San José del Pacifico, *404*
San Juan Chamula, *427–428*
San Juan del Río, *204–205*
San Juan Parangaricutiro, *250–251*
San Luis Potosí, *190–195*
San Martin Tilcajeta, *398*
San Miguel de Allende, *189–190, 206–212*
San Patricio-Melaque, *288–290*
San Quintín, *104–105*
Santa Ana del Valle, *397*
Santa Cruz, *277*
Santa Maria del Rio, *195*
Santa Maria Tonantzintla, *350*
Santa Rosalía, *110–111*
Santiago Ixcuintla, *278*
Santiago Tuxtla, *373*
Sayil, *471–472*
Scuba diving. *See* Diving
Servas, *30*
Sharks, *506*
Sian Ka'an Biosphere Reserve, *522*
Sierra de Juarez, *102*
Silver jewelry, *353, 357*
Sinaloa, *265*
Sisal, *485*
Snorkeling
  Acapulco, *316*
  Cancún, *500*
  Chemuyil, *522*
  Cozumel, *517*
  Ensenada, *101*
  Huatalco, *408*
  Isla Mujeres, *507*
  La Paz, *119*
  Loreto, *115*
  Mazatlán, *273*
  Mulegé, *113*
  Oaxaca Coast, *398*
  Playa del Carmen, *510*
  Puerto Escondido, *401*
  Puerto Vallarta, *285–286*
  Punta Bete, *511*
  Tulum, *521*
  Tuxpán, *384*
  Xcarcet and Paamul, *511*
Soccer, *79*
So-tano de las Golondrinas, *197*
Spas and thermal springs
  Catemaco, *372*
  Cuautla, *331, 332*
  Hierve el Agua, *396*
  La Tovara, *277*
  Taxco, *356*
  Teapa, *456*
  Tehuacán, *351*
  Steam baths, *491*
Student ID cards, *4–5*
Studying in Mexico, *22*
Surfing
  Ensenada, *101*
  Los Cabos, *121*
  Oaxaca Coast, *398*
  Puerto Escondido, *401*
  Puerto Vallarta, *285, 287*
  San Blas, *277*
  Todos Santos, *125*

T

Tabasco, *411–412*
Tabasco coast, *455*
Tampico, *186–188*
Tapachula, *444–446*
Tarahumara, *158*
Taxco, *353–357*
Teapa, *455–456*
Tecali de Herrera, *352*
Tecate, *94–95*
Tehuacán, *351–352*
Tehuantepec, *409*
Telchac Puerto, *485*
Teleferico, *226*
Telephones, *28*
Temple of Chaac, *466*
Temple of Jaguars, *490*
Temple of Quetzalcoatl, *81*
Temple of the Columns, *471*
Temple of the Cross, *435*
Temple of the Foliated Cross, *435*
Temple of the Inscriptions, *435*
Temple of the Phalli, *470*
Temple of the Seven Dolls, *484*
Temple of the Sun, *435*
Temple of the Warriors, *491*
Temple of the Wind God, *369*
Templo de las Manos Rojas, *471*
Templo Mayor, *64*
Tennis, *186*
Teotihuacán, *80–82*
Teotitlán del Valle, *397*
Tepeaca, *352*
Tepic, *278–281*
Tepozteco Pyramid, *329*
Tepoztlán, *329–330*
Tequila, *246*
Ticul, *473–474*
Tijuana, *87–93*
Timing the visit, *1–2*
Tipping, *30*

Tizatlan, *338*
Tlaquepaque, *240*
Tlaxcala, *332–338*
Todos Santos, *125–126*
Toiletries, *13–14*
Toluquilla ruins, *206*
Tonalá, *240–241*
Toniná, *429–431*
Topolobampo, *144*
Tortugranja (turtle enterprise), *505*
Tourist cards, *5–6. See also* Visas
Train travel, *26*
Transportation
in Mexico, *26–28*
to Mexico, *24–26*
Traveler's checks, *11*
Traveling alone, *132*
Tres Zapotes, *373*
Trollies, *90*
Trotsky, Leon, *68, 70*
Tula, *82*
Tulum, *518–521*
Tuxpán, *382–384*
Tuxtla Gutiérrez, *412, 414–418*
Tzararacua, *251*
Tzeltal culture, *427–429*
Tzimol, *443*
Tzintzuntzán, *256*
Tzompantli, *490*
Tzotzil villages, *426, 427–429*

U
Unión Juárez, *448*
Universidad de Guadalajara, *239*
Universidad de Guanajuato, *218*
Universidad Nacional Autónoma de México (UNAM), *71–72*
Urique, *163*
Uruapan, *246–250*
Uxmal, *469–471*

V
Valladolid, *492–494*
Valle de Bravo, *82–83*
Veracruz, *361–367*
Villa Las Rosas, *443*
Villahermosa, *448–454*
Visas, *447*
Vizcaíno Desert, *108*
Voladores, *380*
Volcanoes
La Malinche, *339*
Paricutín, *246*
Volcán de Fuego, *301, 302*
Volcán del Estribo Grande, *255*
Volcán Nevado de Colima, *301–302*
Volcán Popocatépetl, *349*
Volcán Tacaná, *448*
Volunteer programs, *22*

W
Waterfalls
Agua Azul, *436*
Basaseachic Falls, *160*
Cascada de Muxbal, *448*
Cascada de Tamul, *197*
Cascada de Texolo, *378*
Cuernavaca, *327*
El Chifón, *443*
La Cascada Cola de Caballo, *183*
Las Pozas, *197*
Misol-ha, *436*
Queen's Baths, *435*
Tzararacua, *251*
Waterski, *83, 316, 317*
Whale-watching, *105, 108, 109, 119*
Women travelers, *19*
medical aid, *17*
Working in Mexico, *21–22*

X
Xcacel, *522*
Xcarcet, *511*
Xel-Ha Lagoon, *521–522*
Xicalanca culture, *339–340*
Xico, *378*
Xilitla, *197*
Xlapak, *472*
Xochicalco, *330–331*
Xochimilco, *80*
Xtacumbilxunaan caves, *467*

Y
Yagul, *397*
Yaxchilan, *438–439*
Yucatán peninsula. *See specific areas*
Yumká, *454*

Z
Zaachila, *398*
Zacatecas, *221–226*
Zapopan, *241*
Zapotalito, *402*
Zapotec culture, *408*
Zapotec ruins, *394–397, 409*
Zempoala, *368–369*
Zihuatanejo, *303–307*
Zinacantán, *429*
Zipolite, *404–406*
Zoos, *67, 166, 417*

TELL US WHAT YOU THINK

We're always trying to improve our books and would really appreciate any feedback on how to make them more useful. Thanks for taking a few minutes to fill out this survey. We'd also like to know about your latest find, a new scam, a budget deal, whatever . . . Please print your name and address clearly and send the completed survey to: The Berkeley Guides, 515 Eshelman Hall, U.C. Berkeley, CA 94720.

1. Your name _____
2. Your address _____
   _____ Zip _____
3. You are: Female   Male
4. Your age: under 17   17–22   23–30   31–40   41–55   over 55
5. If you're a student: Name of school _____ City & state _____
6. If you're employed: Occupation _____
7. Your yearly income: under $20,000 $21,000–$30,000 $31,000–$45,000
   $46,000–$60,000 $61,000–$100,000   over $100,000
8. Which of the following do you own? (Circle all that apply.)
   Computer   CD-ROM Drive   Modem
9. What speed (bps) is your modem?
   2400   4800   9600   14.4   19.2   28.8
10. Which on-line service(s) do you subscribe to apart from commercial services like AOL?
    _____
11. Do you have access to the World Wide Web? If so, is it through a university or a private service provider? _____
12. If you have a CD-ROM drive or plan to have one, would you purchase a Berkeley Guide CD-ROM? _____
13. Which Berkeley Guide(s) did you buy? _____
14. Where did you buy the book and when?   City _____ Month/Year _____
15. Why did you choose The Berkeley Guides? (Circle all that apply.)

    Budget focus   Design
    Outdoor emphasis   Attitude
    Off-the-beaten-track emphasis   Writing style
    Resources for gays and   Organization
       lesbians   More maps
    Resources for people with   Accuracy
       disabilities
    Resources for women   Price

    Other _____

16. How did you hear about The Berkeley Guides? (Circle all that apply.)

- Recommended by friend/acquaintance
- Bookstore display
- TV
- Article in magazine/newspaper (which one?) _____
- Ad in magazine/newspaper (which one?) _____
- Radio program (which one?) _____
- Other _____

17. Which other guides, if any, have you used before? (Circle all that apply.)

- Fodor's
- Let's Go
- Rough Guides
- Frommer's
- Birnbaum
- Lonely Planet
- Other _____

18. When did you travel with this book? Month/Year _____

19. Where did you travel? _____

20. What was the purpose of your trip?

- Vacation
- Business
- Volunteer
- Study abroad
- Work

21. About how much did you spend per day during your trip?

- $0–$20
- $31–$45
- $61–$75
- over $100
- $21–$30
- $46–$60
- $76–$100

22. After you arrived, how did you get around? (Circle all that apply.)

- Rental car
- Personal car
- Plane
- Bus
- Train
- Hiking
- Bike
- Hitching

23. Which features/sections did you use most? (Circle all that apply.)

- Book Basics
- City/region Basics
- Coming and Going
- Hitching
- Getting Around
- Where to Sleep
- Camping
- Roughing It
- Food
- Worth Seeing
- Cheap Thrills
- Festivals
- Shopping
- After Dark
- Outdoor Activities

24. The information was (circle one): V = very accurate U = usually accurate
S = sometimes accurate R = rarely accurate

Introductions	V U S R	Worth Seeing	V U S R
Basics	V U S R	After Dark	V U S R
Coming and Going	V U S R	Outdoor Activities	V U S R
Where to Sleep	V U S R	Maps	V U S R
Food	V U S R		

25. I would _____ would not _____ buy another Berkeley Guide.